Kalat Premium Website*
Featuring Try It Yourself Activities and Critical Thinking Video Exercises

Succeed in your course with these hands-on learning opportunities! The **Kalat Premium Website** features engaging and helpful learning tools that will help you interact with the very concepts you're learning about in your class! The **Online Try It Yourself activities** offer short animations illustrating concepts like motion aftereffects, universal emotions, false memories, and hemisphere control. Also available on the **Kalat Premium Website** are **Critical Thinking Video Exercises**.

Try It Yourself activities explore:

- Psychic Phenomenon
- Illustration of Binding
- Hemisphere Control
- Brightness Contrast
- Muller-Lyer Illusion
- Filling in the Blind Spot
- Blindness in Visual Periphery
- Motion Aftereffect
- Matching High School Photos

- Afterimage
- Sperling Effect
- Decay of Short-Term Memory
- False Memory
- Implicit Memories
- Word Superiority Effect
- Emotional Stroop Test
- Overconfidence
- Framing Questions
- Change Blindness
- McGurk Effect
- Universal Emotions
- Stop Signal Task
- Genetic Generations
- And more!

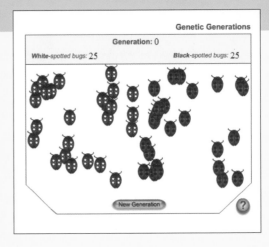

"These are excellent ways to help students gain a personal understanding of some of the processes and concepts presented."

Susan Anderson, University of South Alabama

Critical Thinking video exercises provide an opportunity for you to learn more about psychological research on different topics. You can watch each of the video clips and then answer accompanying questions that will help you refine your critical thinking skills—and help you prepare for your next exam.

Critical Thinking videos include:

- Psychic Phenomenon
- Addiction
- Neural Networks
- Weight Control
- Health & Stress
- Implicit Association
- Virtual Reality Therapy

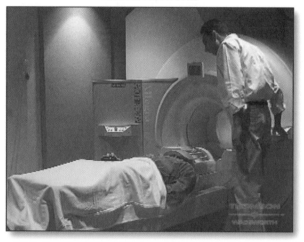

Neural Networks

Psychologist James McClelland discusses how and where information is stored in our brain.

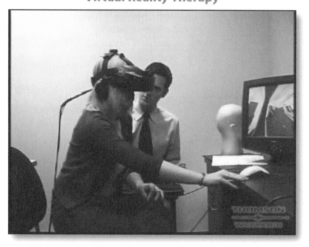

Virtual Reality Therapy

Psychologist David Barlow teaches how high-tech procedures—usually associated with the entertainment industry—are helping people overcome fears.

*Your instructor may have chosen to package the Access Code card to the **Kalat Premium Website** with your new text. In this case, you'll find the Access Card within this text. If your instructor did not order the free Access Code card to be inserted in your text—or if you have a used copy of the text—you can still obtain an access code for a nominal fee. Just visit **www.thomsonedu.com**, where easy-to-follow instructions help you purchase your access code.

INTRODUCTION TO
Psychology

EIGHTH EDITION

James W. Kalat
North Carolina State University

THOMSON ™
WADSWORTH

Australia • Brazil • Canada • Mexico • Singapore • Spain • United Kingdom • United States

THOMSON

WADSWORTH

Acquisitions Editor: *Erik Evans*
Development Editor: *Kirk Bomont*
Assistant Editor: *Gina Kessler*
Editorial Assistant: *Christina Ganim*
Technology Project Manager: *Lauren Keyes*
Marketing Manager: *Sara Swangard*
Marketing Assistant: *Melanie Cregger*
Senior Marketing Communications Manager: *Linda Yip*
Content Project Manager: *Jerilyn Emori*
Director of Design: *Rob Hugel*
Senior Art Director: *Vernon Boes*
Senior Print Buyer: *Judy Inouye*

Permissions Editor: *Roberta Broyer*
Production Service: *Nancy Shammas, New Leaf Publishing Services*
Text Designer: *tani hasegawa*
Photo Researcher: *Sabina Dowell*
Copy Editor: *Frank Hubert*
Illustrator: *Precision Graphics*
Cover Designer: *Patrick Devine*
Cover Image: *Burke/Triolo Productions*
Compositor: *Graphic World, Inc.*
Text and Cover Printer: *Courier Corporation/Kendallville*

Library of Congress Control Number: 2007923679

Student Edition:
ISBN-13: 978-0-495-10288-5
ISBN-10: 0-495-10288-1

Cloth Edition:
ISBN-13: 978-0-495-10289-2
ISBN-10: 0-495-10289-X

Loose-leaf Edition:
ISBN-13: 978-0-495-10290-8
ISBN-10: 0-495-10290-3

Thomson Higher Education
10 Davis Drive
Belmont, CA 94002-3098
USA

For more information about our products, contact us at:
Thomson Learning Academic Resource Center
1-800-423-0563
For permission to use material from this text or product, submit a request online at **http://www.thomsonrights.com**.
Any additional questions about permissions can be submitted by e-mail to **thomsonrights@thomson.com**.

To my family

About the Author

James W. Kalat (rhymes with ballot) is Professor of Psychology at North Carolina State University, where he teaches Introduction to Psychology and Biological Psychology. Born in 1946, he received an AB degree summa cum laude from Duke University in 1968 and a Ph.D. in psychology from the University of Pennsylvania, under the supervision of Paul Rozin. He is also the author of *Biological Psychology, Ninth Edition* (Belmont, CA: Wadsworth, 2007) and co-author with Michelle N. Shiota of *Emotion* (Belmont, CA: Wadsworth, 2007). In addition to textbooks, he has written journal articles on taste-aversion learning, the teaching of psychology, and other topics. A remarried widower, he has three children, two stepsons, and two grandchildren. When not working on something related to psychology, his hobby is bird-watching.

Brief Contents

Contents

3 Biological Psychology 65

4 Sensation and Perception 99

5   Nature, Nurture, and Human
         Development   151

8 Cognition and Language 285

11   Motivated Behaviors   397

12 Emotional Behaviors, Stress, and Health 435

13 Social Psychology 477

14 Personality 529

15 Abnormality, Therapy, and Social Issues 567

16 Specific Disorders and Treatments 599

Preface to the Instructor

A few years ago, I was on a plane that had to turn around shortly after takeoff because one of its two engines had failed. When we were told to get into crash position, the first thing I thought was, "I don't want to die yet! I was looking forward to writing the next edition of my textbook!" True story.

I remember taking my first course in psychology as a freshman at Duke University more than 40 years ago. Frequently, I would describe the fascinating facts I had just learned to my roommate, friends, relatives, or anyone else who would listen. I haven't changed much since then. When I read about new research or think of a new example to illustrate some point, I want to tell my wife, children, colleagues, and students. Through this textbook, I can tell even more people. I hope my readers will share this excitement and want to tell still others.

Ideally, a course or textbook in psychology should accomplish two goals. The first is to instill a love of learning so that our graduates will continue to update their education. Even if students remembered everything they learned in this text—and I know they won't—their understanding would gradually go out of date unless they continue to learn about new developments. I fantasize that some of my former students occasionally pick up copies of *Scientific American Mind* or similar publications and read about psychological research. The second goal is to teach people skills of evaluating evidence and questioning assertions, so that when they do read or hear about some newly reported discovery, they will ask the right questions and draw the appropriate conclusions (or lack of them). That skill can carry over to other fields besides psychology.

Throughout this text I have tried to model the habit of critical thinking or evaluating the evidence, particularly in the **What's the Evidence** features, which describe research studies in some detail. I have pointed out the limitations of the evidence and the possibilities for alternative interpretations. The goal is to help students ask their own questions, distinguish between good and weak evidence, and ultimately, appreciate the excitement of psychological inquiry.

Approaches, Features, and Student Aids

Many years ago I read in an educational psychology textbook that children with learning disabilities and attention problems learn best from specific, concrete examples. I remember thinking, "Wait a minute. Don't we *all* learn best from specific, concrete examples?" It is for this reason that science classes use laboratories: to let students try demonstrations and experiments. Few introductory psychology classes offer laboratories, but we can nevertheless encourage students to try certain procedures that require little or no equipment. At various points the text describes simple **Try It Yourself** exercises, such as negative afterimages, binocular rivalry, encoding specificity, and the Stroop effect. These activities are available as **Online Try It Yourself** activities on the companion website at www.thomsonedu.com/psychology/kalat. Students who try these activities will understand and remember the concepts far better than if they read about them only in abstract terms. A few of the online activities enable students to collect and report their own data.

Reading the material is good, but using it is better. Researchers find that we learn more if we alternate between reading and testing than if we spend the same amount of time reading. The **Concept Checks** pose questions that attentive readers should be able to answer, with a little thought. The answers are available at the end of each chapter's modules. Students who answer correctly can feel encouraged; those who miss a question should use the feedback to reread the relevant passages. Questions marked **A Step Further** are more challenging and a possible basis for class discussion or short extra-credit papers. Because these questions invite creativity, none has a single "correct" answer; nevertheless, the Instructor's Resource Guide provides the author's attempts to answer them.

Education was long a very traditional field in which the procedures hardly changed since the invention of chalk and desks. Recently, however, educators have been learning to use the power of new technologies, and this text offers several important technological enhancements. The website already mentioned includes the Online Try It Yourself exercises as well as flash cards, quizzes, an online glossary, and links to other interesting sites related to each chapter. The V-Mentor option enables students to obtain live tutoring from an experienced instructor.

A **Kalat Premium Website** with Critical Thinking Video Exercises accompanies this text and includes a series of short videos, with accompanying questions to encourage critical thinking. Video topics include neural networks, addiction, and weight loss. On the Kalat Premium Website, you will also find additional Online Try It Yourself exercises as well as a convenient portal to the website.

Each chapter of this text is divided into two to five modules, each with its own summary. Modules provide flexibility for the instructor who wishes to take sections in a different order—for example, operant conditioning before classical conditioning—or who wishes to omit some section altogether. Modular format also breaks up the reading assignments so that a student reads one or two modules for each class. Key terms are listed at the end of each chapter; a list with definitions can be downloaded from the website. At the end of the text, a combined Subject Index and Glossary provides definitions of key terms as well as page references for those terms and others.

What's New in the Eighth Edition

Does psychology really change fast enough to justify a new edition of an introductory text every 3 years? Some areas of psychology admittedly do not, but others do. This edition has almost 500 new references from 2003 or later. A few entirely new topics have been added, such as research on consciousness, synesthesia, overcoming procrastination, and the difference between maximizing and satisficing in decision making. Even in topics where the content has not changed much, an author always finds many small ways to clarify the discussion, and my publisher has improved or replaced many of the photographs and figures. Throughout the text you can find new Concept Checks, Try It Yourself exercises, and What's the Evidence sections.

This edition has been reorganized in several ways. The chapter on development has been moved earlier, becoming chapter 5. The main reason is that the topic of genetics, included in this chapter, is important background for other chapters, especially the one on intelligence, so we need to discuss development first. The chapter on consciousness has been revised in several ways and moved later, becoming chapter 10. The

module on drugs, formerly part of the consciousness chapter, is now part of the chapter on biological psychology, because the material illustrates the functioning of synapses and their importance for behavior better than it elucidates anything about consciousness. A new module, added to the consciousness chapter, relates new research on consciousness from biological and cognitive standpoints. Consciousness used to seem totally beyond the realm of scientific exploration. It is still difficult, but more accessible than it used to be.

The order has been reversed between chapters 13 and 14. Social psychology is now chapter 13 and personality 14 to put personality right before abnormal psychology. Social psychology has traditionally been the last chapter of introductory psychology texts, mainly because social psychologists wanted to do research on introductory psychology students before they read about social psychology. Logically, social psychology should be one of the first chapters because other topics build on social psychology more than it builds on them. Here I'm compromising, putting it just a little earlier than its traditional place. The social psychology chapter has been reorganized. Note in particular the new module about cooperation and competition. This includes research on the prisoner's dilemma, other research on prosocial behavior, and the development of moral reasoning (Kohlberg's work)—a topic more familiarly covered in the chapter on development. Any time an author breaks with tradition, many people feel uncomfortable, but I hope you will eventually agree that it makes sense to discuss various aspects of prosocial behavior together in one module. Besides, the developmental psychology chapter has plenty of other topics to consider.

Here is a chapter-by-chapter list of major changes.

Chapter 1 (What Is Psychology?)

- Illustrates the various approaches to psychology by contrasting how each would approach a single topic: how we choose which foods to eat.

Chapter 2 (Scientific Methods in Psychology)

- New illustration of why the mean is sometimes misleading: The vast majority of people have an "above average" number of legs because the mean is 1.99 . . .

Chapter 3 (Biological Psychology)

- Rearranged, putting the module about the nervous system first. The reason is to start with some interesting examples of what brain damage can do, before getting into the details of neurons and synapses.
- New examples of brain plasticity and a new Try It Yourself activity.

Chapter 4 (Sensation and Perception)

- A new section on synesthesia—the tendency of some people to have extra sensations, such as perceiving the letter A as red.
- Revision of the section on optical illusions.
- Binocular rivalry moved from this chapter to the module on consciousness.

Chapter 5 (Nature, Nurture, and Human Development)

- Substantially revised and reorganized the module on genetics.
- Moved most of the material about infancy from the first module (genetics) to the second one (cognitive development).
- Moved the discussion of Kohlberg and moral development to the module on social psychology that discusses cooperation, competition, and moral behavior.
- Interesting new studies on how infants react to distorted pictures of faces.
- New section, "How Grown Up Are We?" highlights ways in which adults sometimes revert to childlike thinking.
- Moved temperament from the fourth module to the first one, so that the fourth module can focus more exclusively on diversity issues.
- Revised and expanded discussions of gender and ethnic influences.

Chapter 6 (Learning)

- New example of how stimulus generalization explains one oddity of animal evolution: Harmless frogs in Ecuador evolved to resemble the less toxic of two toxic frogs, because the generalization gradient is sharper for the less dangerous and broader for the more dangerous frog.
- Expanded treatment of imitation, including mirror neurons.

Chapter 7 (Memory)

- Reorganized discussion of memory for items on a list, including new examples.
- Brief case history of a woman with exceptional autobiographical memory.
- Revised and expanded discussion of the timing of study sessions.
- New examples of hindsight bias.

Chapter 8 (Cognition and Language)

- New discussion of the relationship between expertise and brain changes.
- Added Dijksterhuis's research on unconscious heuristic decision making.
- New section on maximizing and satisficing in decision making.

- Moved attention deficit here, to be with other material on attention, instead of in the chapter on abnormal psychology.
- Revised description of attention, with new examples.
- New examples of the availability heuristic, including the false belief that "you should stick with your first impulse on multiple-choice tests."

Chapter 9 (Intelligence)

- Reversed order in first module to discuss theories of intelligence before IQ tests.
- Updated discussion of hierarchical models of intelligence.
- A new hypothesis about the Flynn effect: genetic heterosis from outbreeding.
- Updated discussion of test validity.
- Revised discussion of test bias. The bias of a test depends on the use to which it is put.
- Deleted the section on hereditary and environmental contributions to ethnic differences in IQ scores. I have become increasingly uncomfortable with this topic because the best studies are more than a quarter of a century old.
- A new "What's the Evidence" section dealing with stereotype threat.
- New research on environmental interventions that aid intellectual development.

Chapter 10 (Consciousness)

- Entirely new module on consciousness, featuring research on the brain mechanisms necessary for consciousness, sensory neglect, blindsight, déjà vu, and the role of consciousness in controlling movement.
- The module on drugs moved from here to chapter 3 to illustrate synapses.
- Reorganized section on the functions of sleep.
- New research on sleep specializations in animal species, including the fact that migratory birds and newborn whales and dolphins go weeks with little or no sleep, while showing no ill effects.

Chapter 11 (Motivated Behaviors)

- New mention of the possible role of high-fructose corn syrup in the obesity epidemic.
- Simplified and updated discussion of brain mechanisms in feeding.
- New section on differences between men and women in their likelihood of bisexual response.
- Rewritten and updated material on sexual orientation.
- New section on overcoming procrastination.
- New section on people's powerful tendency to underestimate how long a task will take.

Chapter 12 (Emotional Behaviors, Stress, and Health)

- Expanded and clarified the discussion of alternatives to the idea of "basic emotions."

- Broader discussion of the usefulness of emotions.
- Added Fredrickson's "broaden and build" hypothesis.
- Important study that links aggressive behavior to the interaction between one identified gene and childhood maltreatment.
- More information about events and activities that improve or impair happiness.
- Added McEwen's definition of stress to contrast with Selye's.
- New section on how stress affects health.

Chapter 13 (Social Psychology)

- Expanded discussion of evolutionary thinking in relation to social behavior.
- New first module on cooperation and competition includes prisoner's dilemma, bystander apathy, social loafing, Kohlberg's approach to the development of moral reasoning, and cultural transmission of morality.
- Milgram's obedience study moved to the module on influence.
- New research indicates that we form first impressions based on people's appearance in a split second.
- New material about stereotypes and prejudice.
- New section on how coercive persuasion can lead to false confessions.

Chapter 14 (Personality)

- New discussion of belief in a just world as an example of a personality trait.

Chapter 15 (Abnormality, Therapy, and Social Issues)

- Added the controversy about whether psychological disorders are categorical or dimensional.

Chapter 16 (Specific Disorders and Treatments)

- New material on gene–environment interactions in the onset of psychological disorders.
- "Kindling hypothesis": After a first episode of depression, the brain learns how to produce depression more easily, and later episodes occur with less provocation.
- New hypotheses and research on the causes of bipolar disorder and schizophrenia.

Teaching and Learning Supplements

You're familiar with those television advertisements that offer something, usually for $19.95, and then say, "But wait, there's more!" Same here. In addition to the text, the publisher offers many supplements:

Study Guide, revised by Mark Ludorf of Stephen F. Austin State University, provides learning objectives, chapter outlines, other study aids and practice test items, with an explanation of why each wrong answer is wrong. It also includes a guide for nonnative speakers of English by Theodore D. Joseph of Stephen F. Austin State University.

Test Bank, revised by Deana B. Davalos of Colorado State University, includes items from the previous edition, hundreds of new items contributed by James Kalat and tested in his classes, and many new ones by Deana B. Davalos. That bank is also available in ExamView® electronic format. Many of the items have already been tested with classes at North Carolina State University, and the Test Bank indicates the percentage correct and point biserial. Note also that the Test Bank includes a special file of items that cut across chapters, intended for a comprehensive final exam.

Instructor's Resource Manual, revised by Nancy Jo Melucci of Long Beach City College, is both thorough and creative. It includes suggestions for class demonstrations and lecture material. It also contains the author's suggested answers to the Step Further questions in this text.

Multimedia Manager Instructor's Resource CD-ROM is designed to facilitate an instructor's assembly of PowerPoint® or similar demonstrations and contains lecture slides by Nancy Jo Melucci, figures and tables from the text, the Instructor's Resource Manual and Test Bank, and Resource Integration Guide.

ThomsonNOW for Introduction to Psychology, 8th Edition, is an online self-study and assessment system that helps students study efficiently and effectively while allowing instructors to easily manage their courses. ThomsonNow analyzes student performance and discovers which areas students need the most help with. The students take a pretest, and based on their answers, the system creates a personalized learning plan unique to them. This learning plan is full of engaging media-driven pedagogy that aids student understanding of core concepts in psychology. After completing the personalized learning plan, the student follows up with a posttest to ensure mastery of the material. The self-study and assessment questions were revised for this edition by Alisha Janowsky of the University of Central Florida.

Available on ThomsonNOW or the Kalat Premium Website for *Introduction to Psychology,* 8th Edition, **Online Try It Yourself** exercises and **Critical Thinking Video Exercises** illustrate concepts and promote critical thinking about various topics in the text.

Acknowledgments

To begin the job of writing a textbook, a potential author needs self-confidence bordering on arrogance and, to complete it, the humility to accept criticism of favorite ideas and carefully written prose. A great many people provided helpful suggestions that made this a far better text than it would have been without them.

In preparing this edition, I began with Vicki Knight, who was my extraordinary acquisitions editor for many years until her retirement from the company. For a few months, I worked with Marcus Boggs as an interim editor, and then Erik Evans, a gifted young editor. I think the transition has proceeded as smoothly as I could hope, and I thank each of these people for their encouragement, friendship, support, and advice. Kate Barnes began as my developmental editor, providing early guidance about the direction of this revision. Kirk Bomont served as developmental editor through most of the work, offering detailed suggestions ranging from organization of a chapter to choice of words. I thank each of these people for their tireless help.

Gina Kessler did a tireless job of supervising all the supplements. Frank Hubert is one of the quickest and most cooperative copy editors I have dealt with in my two decades of textbook writing. Christina Ganim secured numerous quality peer reviews throughout the entire project. Karol Jurado did a marvelous job of supervising the production, a complicated task with a book such as this. Vernon Boes, who managed the design development, Lisa Torri, who managed the art development, and Tani Hasegawa, who designed the interior, had the patience and artistic judgment to counterbalance their very nonartistic author. Sara Swangard planned and executed the marketing strategies. Sabina Dowell, the photo researcher, found an amazing variety of wonderful photographs, and managed the permissions requests. To each of these, my thanks and congratulations.

My wife, Jo Ellen Kalat, not only provided support and encouragement, but also listened to my attempts to explain concepts and offered many helpful suggestions and questions. My son Samuel Kalat provided many insightful ideas and suggestions. I thank my department heads, David Martin and Douglas Gillan, and my N.C. State colleagues—especially Lynne Baker-Ward, Jeff Braden, Bob Pond, and Larry Upton—for their encouragement, ideas, and free advice.

I also thank the following for their helpful comments and suggestions: Dale Purves, Duke University, and Anne Tabor-Morris, Georgian Court University.

For this edition, reviewers provided unusually extensive and helpful comments, leading to a final version that is, I think, significantly improved over the versions they examined. I thank the following people, as well as those who wish to remain anonymous, for their helpful reviews of all or part of this new edition:

Jeffrey Adams, Trent University
Judi Addelston, Valencia Community College
Susan A. Anderson, University of South Alabama
Richard W. Bowen, Loyola University Chicago
Liz Coccia, Austin Community College
Deana Davalos, Colorado State University
Darlene Earley-Hereford, Southern Union State Community College
David J. Echevarria, University of Southern Mississippi
Vanessa Edkins, University of Kansas
Anna L. Ghee, Xavier University
Bill P. Godsil, Santa Monica College
Kerri Goodwin, Loyola College in Maryland
Troianne Grayson, Florida Community College at Jacksonville
Julie A. Gurner, Quinnipiac University; Community College of Philadelphia
Alexandria E. Guzmán, University of New Haven
Wendy Hart-Stravers, Arizona State University
Christopher Hayashi, Southwestern College
Bert Hayslip, University of North Texas
Manda Helzer, Southern Oregon University
W. Elaine Hogan, University of North Carolina Wilmington
Susan Horton, Mesa Community College
Linda A. Jackson, Michigan State University
Alisha Janowsky, University of Central Florida
Mark J. Kirschner, Quinnipiac University
Kristina T. Klassen, North Idaho College
Linda Lockwood, Metropolitan State College of Denver
Mark R. Ludorf, Stephen F. Austin State University
Pamelyn M. MacDonald, Washburn University
David G. McDonald, University of Missouri
Tracy A. McDonough, College of Mount St. Joseph
J. Mark McKellop, Juniata College
Nancy J. Melucci, Long Beach City College
Anne Moyer, Stony Brook University
Brady J. Phelps, South Dakota State University
Bridget Rivera, Loyola College in Maryland
Linda Ruehlman, Arizona State University
Troy Schiedenhelm, Rowan-Cabarrus Community College
Eileen Smith, Fairleigh Dickinson University
Jim Stringham, University of Georgia
Natasha Tokowicz, University of Pittsburgh
Warren W. Tryon, Fordham University
Katherine Urquhart, Lake Sumter Community College
Suzanne Valentine-French, College of Lake County
Ellen Weissblum, State University of New York Albany
John W. Wright, Washington State University

I would also like to thank the following reviewers who have contributed their insight to previous editions: Mark Affeltranger, University of Pittsburgh; Catherine Anderson, Amherst College; Susan Anderson, University of South Alabama; Bob Arkin, Ohio State University; Susan Baillet, University of Portland; Cynthia Bane, Denison University; Joe Bean, Shorter College; Mark Bodamer, John Carroll University; Michael Brislawn, Bellevue Community College; Delbert Brodie, St. Thomas University; John Broida, University of Southern Maine; Gordon Brow, Pasadena City College; Gregory Bushman, Beloit College; James Calhoun, University of Georgia; Bernardo Carducci, Indiana University Southeast; Mar Casteel, Pennsylvania State University, York Campus; Karen Couture, Keene State College; Patricia Deldin, Harvard University; Katherine Demitrakis, Albuquerque Technical Vocational Institute; Janet Dizinno, St. Mary University; Kimberly Duff, Cerritos College; Susan Field, Georgian Court College; Deborah Frisch, University of Oregon; Gabriel Frommer, Indiana University; Rick Fry, Youngstown State University; Robe Gehring, University of Southern Indiana; Judy Gentry, Columbus State Community College; Joel Grace, Mansfield University; Joe Grisham, Indiana River Community College; Richard Hanson, Fresno City College; Richard Harris, Kansas State University; W. Bruce Haslam, Weber State University; Debra Hollister, Valencia Community College; Charles Huffman, James Madison University; Linda Jackson, Michigan State University; Robert Jensen, California State University, Sacramento; James Johnson, Illinois State University; Craig Jones, Arkansas State University; Lisa Jordan, University of Maryland; Dale Jorgenson, California State University, Long Beach; Jon Kahane, Springfield College; Peter Kaplan, University of Colorado, Denver; Arthur Kemp, Central Missouri State University; Martha Kuehn, Central Lakes College; Cindy J. Lahar, University of Calgary; Chris Layne, University of Toledo; Cynthia Ann Lease, Virginia Polytechnic Institute and State University; Chantal Levesque, University of Rochester; John Lindsay, Georgia College and State University; Mary Livingston, Louisiana Technical University; Sanford Lopater, Christopher Newport University; Mark Ludorf, Stephen F. Austin State University; Steve Madigan, University of Southern California; Don Marzoff, Louisiana State University; Christopher Mayhorn, North Carolina State University; Michael McCall, Ithaca College; Mary Meiners, San Diego Miramar College; Dianne Mello-Goldner, Pine Manor College; Rowland Miller, Sam Houston State University; Gloria Mitchell, De Anza College; Paul Moore, Quinnipiac University; Jeffrey Nagelbush, Ferris State University; Bethany Neal-Beliveau, Indiana University Purdue University at Indianapolis; Jan Ochman, Inver Hills Community College; Wendy Palmquist, Plymouth State College; Elizabeth Parks, Kennesaw State University; Gerald Peterson, Saginaw Valley State University; Brady Phelps, South Dakota State University; Shane Pitts, Birmingham Southern College; Thomas Reig, Winona State University; David Reitman, Louisiana State University; Jeffrey Rudski, Muhlenberg College; Richard Russell, Santa Monica College; Mark Samuels, New Mexico Institute of Mining and Technology; Kim Sawrey, University of North Carolina at Wilmington; Michele N. Shiota, University of California, Berkeley; Noam Shpancer, Purdue University; James Spencer, West Virginia State College; Robert Stawski, Syracuse University; Whitney Sweeney, Beloit College; Alan Swinkels, St. Edward's University; Patricia Toney, Sandhills Community College; Stavros Valenti, Hofstra University; Douglas Wallen, Mankato State University; Michael Walraven, Jackson Community College; Donald Walter, University of Wisconsin–Parkside; Jeffrey Weatherly, University of North Dakota; Fred Whitford, Montana State University; Don Wilson, Lane Community College; David Woehr, Texas A&M University; Jay Wright, Washington State University.

Preface to the Student

Welcome to introductory psychology! I hope you will enjoy reading this text as much as I enjoyed writing it. When you finish, I hope you will write your comments on the Student Reply page, cut the page out, and mail it to the publisher, who will pass it along to me. If you are willing to receive a reply, please include a return address.

The first time I taught introductory psychology, several students complained that the book we were using was interesting to read but impossible to study. What they meant was that they had trouble finding and remembering the main points. I have tried to make this book interesting and as easy to study as possible.

Features of This Text

Modular Format

Each chapter is divided into two or more modules so that you can study a limited section at a time. Each chapter begins with a table of contents to orient you to the topics considered. At the end of each module is a summary of some important points, with page references. If a point is unfamiliar, you should reread the appropriate section. At the end of a chapter, you will find suggestions for further reading, a few Internet sites to visit, and a list of important terms.

Key Terms

When an important term first appears in the text, it is highlighted in blue type and defined in *italics*. All the blue terms reappear in alphabetical order at the end of the chapter and again in the combined Subject Index and Glossary at the end of the book. You might want to find the Subject Index and Glossary right now and familiarize yourself with it. You can also consult or download a list of key terms with their definitions from this Internet site: www.thomsonedu.com/psychology/kalat.

I sometimes meet students who think they have mastered the course because they have memorized all the definitions. You do need to understand the defined words, but don't memorize the definitions word for word. It would be better to try to use each word in a sentence or think of examples of each term. Better yet, when appropriate, think of evidence for or against the concept that the term represents.

Questions to Check Your Understanding and Go Further

People remember material better if they alternate between reading and testing than if they spend the whole time reading. At various points in this text are Concept Checks, questions that ask you to use or apply the information you just read. Try to answer each of them and then turn to the indicated page to check your answer. If your answer is correct, you can feel encouraged. If it is incorrect, you should reread the section.

You will also find an occasional item marked "A Step Further . . ." Here you are asked to go beyond the text discussion and think about possible answers to a more challenging or speculative question. I hope you will spend time with these questions, perhaps talk about them with fellow students, and maybe ask your instructor for his or her opinion. (Instructors can check for my own answers in the Instructor's Resource Guide. But to these items, there is no single right answer.)

Try It Yourself Activities

The text includes many items marked Try It Yourself. Most of these can be done with little or no equipment in a short time. You will understand and remember the text far better if you try these exercises. Also available are more than 20 Online Try It Yourself activities. These interactive exercises can be accessed at www.thomsonedu.com/psychology/kalat. The purpose of these is the same as the Try It Yourself activities in the text; the difference is that online activities can include sounds and motion. The description of a research study will be easier to understand and remember after you have experienced it yourself.

 ## What's the Evidence Sections

Every chapter except the first includes a section titled What's the Evidence? These sections highlight research studies in more than the usual amount of detail, specifying the hypothesis (idea being tested), research methods, results, and interpretation. In some cases the discussion also mentions the limitations of the study. The purpose of these sections is to provide examples of how to evaluate evidence.

 ## Internet Site

The text website is **www.thomsonedu.com/psychology/kalat.** This site offers flash cards, quizzes, interactive art, an online glossary, and links to other interesting websites related to each chapter. The site also includes Online Try It Yourself activities. In addition, it includes a new V-Mentor opportunity, in which you can ask questions and receive live tutoring from an experienced instructor during certain hours. To do so, go to your companion website and follow the links to the V-Mentor virtual classroom. All of these opportunities are highly recommended; please explore them.

Indexes and Reference List

A list of all the references cited in the text is at the back of the book in case you want to check something for more details. The combined Subject Index and Glossary defines key terms and indicates where in the book to find more information.

Optional Study Guide

Also available is a Study Guide to accompany this text, written by Mark Ludorf at Steven F. Austin State University. It provides detailed chapter outlines, learning objectives, study hints, and other helpful information. The most valuable part for most students is the sample test questions, with an answer key that explains not only which answer is right but also why each of the others is wrong. The website also offers sample questions, but not as many. The study guide also includes a language-building component by Theodore D. Joseph of Stephen F. Austin University. The Study Guide is recommended for students who have struggled with multiple-choice tests in the past, and who are willing to spend some time in addition to reading the book and studying lecture notes. If your bookstore does not stock the Study Guide, you can ask them to order a copy. The ISBN is 0495103632.

Answers to Some Frequently Asked Questions

Do you have any useful suggestions for improving study habits? Whenever students ask me why they did badly on the last test, I ask, "When did you read the assignment?" Some answer, "Well, I didn't exactly read *all* of the assignment," or "I read it the night before the test." If you want to learn the material well, read it before the lecture, review it again after the lecture, and quickly go over it again a few days later. Then reread the textbook assignments and your lecture notes before a test. Memory researchers have established that you will understand and remember something better by studying it several times spread out over days than by studying the same amount of time all at once. Also, of course, the more total time you spend studying, the better.

When you study, don't just read the text but stop and think about it. The more actively you use the material, the better you will remember it. One way to improve your studying is to read by the SPAR method: **S**urvey, **P**rocess meaningfully, **A**sk questions, **R**eview.

Survey: Know what to expect so that you can focus on the main points. When you start a chapter, first look over the outline to get a preview of the contents. When you start a new module, turn to the end and read the summary.

Process meaningfully: Read the chapter carefully, stopping to think from time to time. Tell your roommate something you learned. Think about how you might apply a concept to a real-life situation. Pause when you come to the Concept Checks and try to answer them. Do the Try It Yourself exercises. Try to monitor how well you understand the text and adjust your reading accordingly. Good readers read quickly through easy, familiar content but slowly through difficult material.

Ask questions: When you finish the chapter, try to anticipate what you might be asked later. You can use questions in the Study Guide, on the website, or compose your own. Write out the questions and think about them, but do not answer them yet.

Review: Pause for at least an hour, preferably a day or more. Now return to your questions and try to answer them. Check your answers against the text or the answers in the Study Guide. Reinforcing your memory a day or two after you first read the chapter will help you retain the material longer and deepen your understanding. If you study the same material several times at lengthy intervals, you increase your chance of remembering it long after the course is over.

What do those parentheses mean, as in "(Andreano & Cahill, 2006)"? Am I supposed to remember the names and dates? Psychologists generally cite references in the text in parentheses rather than in footnotes. "(**Andreano & Cahill, 2006**)" refers to an article written by Andreano and Cahill, published in 2006. All the references cited in the text are listed in alphabetical order (by the author's last name) in the References section at the back of the book.

You will also notice a few citations that include two dates separated by a slash, such as "(Wundt, 1862/1961)." This means that Wundt's document was originally published in 1862 and was republished in 1961.

No, you should not memorize the parenthetical source citations. They are provided so an interested reader can look up the source of a statement and check for further information. The names that *are* worth remembering, such as B. F. Skinner, Jean Piaget, and Sigmund Freud, are emphasized in the discussion itself.

Can you help me read and understand graphs? The graphs in this book are easy to follow. Just take a minute or so to study them carefully. You will encounter four kinds: pie graphs, bar graphs, line graphs, and scatter plots. Let's look at each kind.

Pie graphs show how a whole is divided into parts. Figure 1 shows the proportion of all people, and then of all recipients of a master's degree in psychology, who belong to several ethnic groups The total circle represents 100% of all people in the United States.

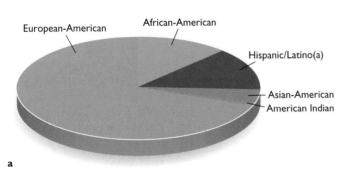

Total Population

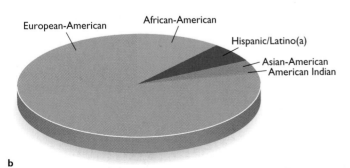

Master's Degrees

a

b

FIGURE 1

Bar graphs show the frequency of various possible events or types of people. Figure 2 shows how many adults in the United States have certain psychological disorders. The length of the bars indicates the frequency of particular disorders.

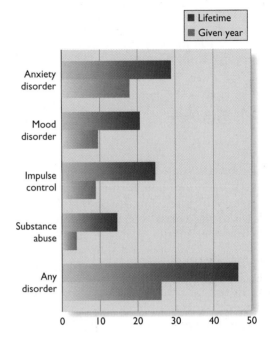

FIGURE 2

Line graphs show how one variable is related to another variable. In Figure 3 you see that the probability of depression increases for people who have experienced a greater number of highly stressful life events. It also shows that the effect of stressful events differs for three groups of people who have different genes.

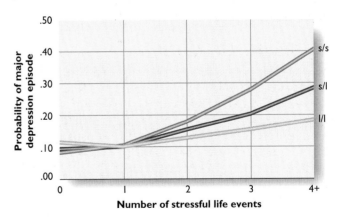

FIGURE 3

Scatter plots are similar to line graphs, with this difference: A line graph shows averages, whereas a scatter plot shows individual data points. By looking at a scatter plot, we can see how much variation occurs among individuals.

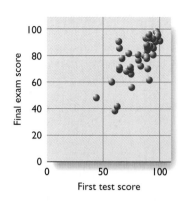

FIGURE 4

To prepare a scatter plot, we make two observations about each individual. In Figure 4 each student is represented by one point. If you take that point and scan down to the *x*-axis, you find that student's score on the first test of the semester. If you then scan across to the *y*-axis, you find that student's score on the final exam. A scatter plot shows whether two variables are closely or only loosely related.

We may have to take multiple-choice tests on this material. How can I do better on those tests?

1. Read each choice carefully. Do not choose the first answer that looks correct; first make sure that the other answers are wrong. If two answers seem reasonable, decide which of the two is better.
2. If you don't know the correct answer, make an educated guess. Eliminate answers that are clearly wrong. An answer that includes absolute words such as *always* or *never* is probably wrong; don't choose it unless you have a good reason to support it. Also eliminate any answer that includes unfamiliar terms. If you have never heard of something, it is probably not the right answer.

Last Words Before We Start . . .

Most of all, I hope you enjoy the text. I have tried to include the liveliest examples I can find. The goal is not just to teach you some facts but also to teach you a love of learning so that you will continue to read more and educate yourself about psychology long after your course is over.

What Is Psychology?

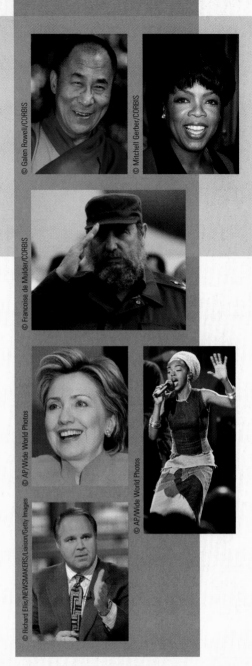

Who has the correct answers? None of us do, at least not always. Even when people we trust seem very confident of their opinions, we should ask for their evidence or reasoning.

If you are like most students, you start off assuming that just about everything you read in your textbooks and everything your professors tell you must be true.

But what if it isn't? Suppose a group of impostors has replaced the faculty of your college. They pretend to know what they are talking about and they all vouch for one another's competence, but in fact they are all unqualified. They have managed to find textbooks that support their prejudices, but the information in the textbooks is all wrong, too. If that happened, how would you know?

As long as we are entertaining such skeptical thoughts, why limit ourselves to colleges? When you read advice columns in the newspaper, read books about how to invest money, or listen to political commentators, how do you know who has the right answers?

The answer is that *no one* has the right answers all of the time. Professors, textbook authors, advice columnists, politicians, and others have strong reasons for some beliefs and weak reasons for others, and sometimes, they think they have strong reasons but discover to their embarrassment that they were wrong. I don't mean to imply that you should disregard everything you read or hear. But you should expect people to tell you the reasons for their conclusions so that you can draw your own conclusions. At least if you make a mistake, it will be your own and not someone else's.

You have just encountered the theme of this book: Evaluate the evidence. You have heard and you will continue to hear all sorts of claims concerning psychology. Some are valid, others are wrong, many are valid under certain conditions, and some are too vague to be either right or wrong. When you finish this book, you will be in a better position to examine evidence and to judge for yourself which claims to take seriously.

Psychologists' Goals

- *What is psychology?*
- *What philosophical questions motivate psychologists?*
- *What do various kinds of psychologists do?*
- *Should you consider majoring in psychology?*

The term *psychology* derives from the Greek roots *psyche,* meaning "soul" or "mind," and *logos,* meaning "word." Psychology is literally the study of the mind or soul. In the late 1800s and early 1900s, psychology was defined as the scientific study of the mind. Around 1920, psychologists became disenchanted with the idea of studying the mind. First, science deals with what we can observe, and no one can observe a mind. Second, talking about "the mind" seemed to imply that mind is a thing with an independent existence. Most researchers consider mind a process, more like a fire than like the piece of wood that is undergoing the fire. At any rate, through the mid-1900s, psychologists defined their field simply as the study of behavior.

However, people care about what they see, hear, and think, not just about what they do. When you look at this optical illusion and say that the horizontal part of the top line looks longer than that of the bottom line (although really they are the same length), we want to know why it *looks* longer to you, not just why you *said* it looks longer. So for a compromise, let's define **psychology** as *the systematic study of behavior and experience.* The word *experience* lets us discuss your perceptions without implying that a mind exists independently of your body.

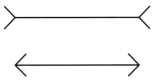

The kind of psychologist familiar to most people is clinical psychologists—those who try to help worried, depressed, or otherwise troubled people. That field is only part of psychology. Psychology also includes research on sensation and perception, learning and memory, hunger and thirst, sleep, attention, child development, and more. You might expect that a course in psychology will teach you to "analyze" people, to decipher hidden aspects of their personality, perhaps even to use psychology to control them. It will not. You will learn to understand certain aspects of behavior, but you will gain no dazzling powers. Ideally, you will become more skeptical of those who claim to analyze people's personality from small samples of their behavior.

General Points About Psychology

Let's start with six general themes that arise repeatedly in psychology. They may not be the most important things you learn about psychology; depending on your own interests, something that strikes other people as a minor detail might be extremely important for you. However, the following points apply so widely that we shall encounter them frequently.

"It Depends"

That is, few statements apply to all people's behavior at all times. For example, almost any statement depends on age. (Newborn infants differ drastically from older children, and children from adults.) Almost any behavior varies among individuals depending on their genetics, health, past experiences, and whether they are currently awake or asleep. Some aspects of behavior differ between males and females or between one culture and another. Some aspects depend on the time of day, the temperature of the room, or how recently someone ate. The way people answer a question depends on exactly how the question is worded, what other questions they have already answered, and who is asking the question.

When I describe "it depends" as a general truth of psychology, you may think I am making fun of psychology, suggesting that psychology has no real answers. On the contrary, I believe that "it depends" is a serious point. The key is to know *what* it depends on. The further you pursue your studies of psychology, the more you will become attuned to the wealth of influences on our behavior, some of which are so subtle that we might easily overlook them. For one example, decades ago, two psychology laboratories in different parts of the United States were conducting similar studies on human learning but consistently reporting contradictory results. Both researchers were experienced and highly respected, they thought they were following the same procedures, and they did not understand why their results differed. Eventually, one of them traveled to the other's university to watch the other in action. Almost immediately, he noticed a key difference in procedure: the chairs in which the participants sat! His colleague at the other university had obtained some chairs from a dentist who retired. So the research participants were sitting in these *dentist's* chairs, which reminded them of visits to the dentist. They were sitting there in a state of heightened anxiety, which altered their behavior (Kimble, 1967).

Another way of saying "it depends" is that no one reason explains your behavior fully. To illustrate, you might try listing the reasons you are reading this book right now, such as (a) I like to keep up to date on reading assignments, (b) I was curious what psychology is all about, (c) my roommate who is also taking this course read the chapter and said it was interesting, (d) I have about an hour before dinner with nothing else to do, (e) it's raining outside so I don't want to go anywhere, (f) I want to procrastinate working on a less pleasant assignment for some other course, and so on. In short, people seldom do anything for just one reason.

Research Progress Depends on Good Measurement

Nobel Prize–winning biologist Sidney Brenner was quoted as saying, "Progress in science depends on new techniques, new discoveries, and new ideas, probably in that order" (McElheny, 2004, p. 71). For example, brain scans and other new techniques enable researchers to measure brain activity in more detail and with greater accuracy than in the past, resulting in rapid increases in our knowledge. Similarly, psychologists' understanding has advanced fastest on topics such as sensory processes, learning, and memory because researchers can measure these aspects of behavior fairly accurately. On topics such as emotion and personality, research progress has been slower because of the difficulty of measurement. As you proceed through this text, especially in the second half, you will note that we occasionally have to interrupt some discussion to ask, "Wait . . . how well do those scores measure intelligence?" or "When people say they are happy, how do we know whether they really are happy?" Areas of psychology with less certain measurement have only tentative conclusions and slow progress.

Correlation Does Not Indicate Causation

This statement will make more sense to you after you read about correlation in chapter 2. Here, let's consider the idea briefly: A correlation indicates that two things tend to go together. For example, taller people tend to be heavier than shorter people, on the average. Better educated people tend to have better paying jobs than less educated people. And so forth. Sometimes, we are tempted to draw cause-and-effect conclusions after observing a correlation. For example, people with schizophrenia are more likely than other people to abuse alcohol, tobacco, and marijuana. Although we might be tempted to assume that these substances increase the risk of schizophrenia, we cannot draw that conclusion. It is equally plausible that having schizophrenia increases one's uses of alcohol, tobacco, and marijuana (Degenhardt, Hall, & Lynskey, 2003). That is, a correlation between two items does not tell us which one caused the other or, indeed, whether either of them caused the other. As long as you continue studying psychology or related fields, your instructors and texts will continue emphasizing this point.

Variations Among Individuals Reflect Both Heredity and Environment

Within any group people differ in their interests, preferences, abilities, and personalities. What accounts for these differences? Some relate to differences in experience. For example, suppose you enjoy using computers. You could not have nurtured that interest if you had lived in some part of the world without electricity. However, experiences and opportunities do not account for all of the differences among people. With regard to almost everything psychologists have measured, identical twins resemble each other more closely than fraternal twins do. The greater similarity between identical twins is taken as evidence of a genetic influence on behavior. Environment and heredity can also combine their influences in many ways (Moffitt, Caspi, & Rutter, 2006). For example, a gene that enhances fear produces a bigger effect after you have had frightening experiences.

The Best Predictor of Future Behavior Is Past Behavior in Similar Situations

People are fairly consistent in how they act. If in the past you have usually started on every schoolwork task as soon as it was assigned, you will probably do the same this semester. If you have almost always procrastinated your assignments until the last possible minute, you will probably do the same this semester, despite your good intentions to the contrary. (If this is you, I shall be delighted if you prove me wrong.)

Similarly, if you consider marrying someone and wonder how that person would treat you after marriage, ask how that person treats you now. If we want to predict how dangerous some prisoner will be after release, we should ask how dangerous this person has been in the past. If you wonder whether you can trust someone to fulfill a promise, ask how well that person has kept promises in the past.

Some Statements in Psychology Reflect Stronger Evidence Than Others

Authors revise psychology textbooks because of new research, and psychologists conduct new research because of the many things we don't know. Unfortunately, people sometimes express strong opinions even when the evidence is weak. Admittedly, we sometimes have to form opinions without complete evidence. For example, parents have to decide how to rear children without waiting for conclusive research about what works best. Still, it is important to know what evidence supports an opinion. For example, solid evidence indicates that a woman who drinks much alcohol during pregnancy risks damage to her infant's brain. Therefore, we take whatever steps we can to discourage pregnant women from drinking. On the other hand, what are the consequences of letting children watch television all day? Here, opinions run strong, but the evidence is weak. Anyone who expresses an opinion should state his or her evidence (or lack of it) so that others can overrule that opinion in the light of newer, better evidence.

Major Philosophical Issues in Psychology

Many psychological concerns date back to the philosophers of ancient Greece. Although psychology has moved away from philosophy in its methods, it continues to be motivated by some of the same questions. Three of the most profound are free will versus determinism, the mind–brain problem, and the nature–nurture issue.

Free Will Versus Determinism

The scientific approach seeks the *immediate* causes of an event (what led to what) instead of the *final* or *ultimate* causes (the purpose of the event in an overall plan). That is, scientists act on the basis of determinism, *the assumption that everything that happens has a cause, or determinant, in the observable world.*

Is the same true for human behavior? We are, after all, part of the physical world, and our brains are made of chemicals. According to the *determinist* assumption, everything we do has causes. This view seems to conflict with the impression all of us have that "*I* make the decisions about my actions. Sometimes, when I am making a decision, like

what to eat for lunch or which sweater to buy, I am in doubt right up to the last second. The decision could have gone either way. I wasn't controlled by anything, and no one could have predicted what I would do." The *belief that behavior is caused by a person's independent decisions is known as* free will.

Some psychologists maintain that free will is an illusion (Wegner, 2002): What you call a conscious intention is more a prediction than a cause of your behavior. When you have the conscious experience of "deciding" to move a finger, the behavior is already starting to happen. Other psychologists and philosophers reply that you do make decisions in the sense that something within you initiates the action. Nevertheless, your behavior still follows laws of cause and effect. When you order soup and salad for lunch, the decision was a product of forces within you, as well as the external situation. The kind of person you are also determines what career you will choose, how hard you will work at it, how kind you will be to others, and so forth. However, the "you" that makes all these decisions is itself a product of your heredity and the events of your life. (You did not create yourself.) In this sense, yes, you have a will, and you might even call it "free" will depending on what you mean by "free" (Dennett, 2003). If you mean uncaused, then your will is not free.

The test of determinism is ultimately empirical: If everything we do has a cause, our behavior should be predictable. In some cases it definitely is. For example, after a sudden, unexpected, loud noise, I can predict that, unless you are deaf, in a coma, or paralyzed, you will tense your muscles. I can even be more precise and predict you will tense your neck muscles in less than a quarter of a second.

Behavior is guided by external forces, such as waves, and by forces within the individual. According to the determinist view, even those internal forces follow physical laws.

In other cases psychologists' predictions are more like those of a meteorologist. A meteorologist who wants to predict tomorrow's weather for some city will want to know the location and terrain of that city, today's weather, and so forth. Even with all that information, the meteorologist will predict something such as, "High temperature around 30, low temperature around 20, with a 10% chance of precipitation." The imprecision and occasional errors do not mean that the weather is "free" but only that it is subject to so many influences that no one can predict it exactly.

Similarly, a psychologist trying to predict your behavior for the next few days will want to know as much as possible about your past behavior, that of your friends and family, your current health, your genetics, where you live, and a great deal more. Even with all that information, the psychologist cannot predict perfectly.

Determinists are unembarrassed by their inability to predict behavior precisely; after all, human behavior is subject to a great many influences. Still, the more knowledge we gain, the better predictions we can make. Anyone who rejects determinism must insist that predictions of behavior could *never* become accurate, even with *complete* information about the person and the situation. To that idea a determinist replies that the only way to find out is to try.

Let's note an important point here: The assumption that behaviors follow cause and effect seems to work, and anyone planning to do research on behavior is almost forced to start with this assumption. Still, to be honest, it is an assumption, not a certainty. We can test the assumption only by extensive research, and in a sense all research in psychology tests the assumption. The question of determinism arises explicitly in chapter 6 (learning) and module 10.1 (consciousness).

CRITICAL THINKING
A STEP FURTHER

Determinism

What kind of evidence, if any, would support the concept of free will? To support the concept of free will, one would need to demonstrate that no conceivable theory could make correct predictions about some aspect of behavior. Should a psychologist who believes in free will conduct the same kind of research that determinists conduct, a different kind, or no research at all?

The Mind–Brain Problem

Everything we experience or do depends on the physics and chemistry of the nervous system. Then what, if anything, is the mind? The *philosophical question of how experience relates to the brain* is the mind–brain problem (or mind–body problem). In a universe composed of matter and energy, why is there such a thing as a conscious mind? One view, called dualism, holds that *the mind is separate from the brain but somehow controls the brain and therefore the rest of the body.* However, dualism contradicts the law of conservation of matter and energy, one of the cornerstones of physics. According to that principle, the only way to influence any matter or energy, including the matter and energy that compose your body, is to act on it with other matter or energy. That is, if the mind isn't composed of matter or energy, it can't *do* anything. For that reason nearly all brain researchers and philosophers favor monism, *the view that conscious experience is inseparable from the physical brain.* That is, either the mind is something the brain produces, or mind and brain activity are just two terms for the same thing. As you can imagine, the mind–brain problem is a thorny philosophical issue, but it does lend itself to research, some of which we shall discuss in chapter 3 on the brain and chapter 9 on consciousness.

The photos in Figure 1.1 show brain activity while a person is engaged in nine different tasks, as measured by a technique called positron-emission tomography (PET). Red indicates the highest degree of brain activity, followed by yellow, green, and blue. As you can see, the various tasks increase activity in different brain areas, although all areas show some activity at all times (Phelps & Mazziotta, 1985). Data such as these show a close relationship between brain activity and psychological events. You might well ask: Did the brain activity cause the thoughts, or did the thoughts cause the brain activity? Most brain researchers reply that neither brain activity nor mental activity causes the other; rather, brain activity and mental activity are the same thing (see Dennett, 1991).

Even if we accept this position, we are still far from understanding the mind–brain relationship. Is mental activity associated with all brain activity or just certain types? Why does conscious experience exist at all? Could a brain get along without it? Research studies are not about to resolve these questions and put philosophers out of business. But research results do constrain the philosophical answers that we can seriously consider.

CRITICAL THINKING
A STEP FURTHER

Mind and Brain

One way to think about the mind–brain relationship is to ask whether something other than a brain—a computer, for example—could have a mind. How would we know? If we built a computer that could perform all the intellectual functions that humans perform, could we then decide that the computer is conscious, as human beings are?

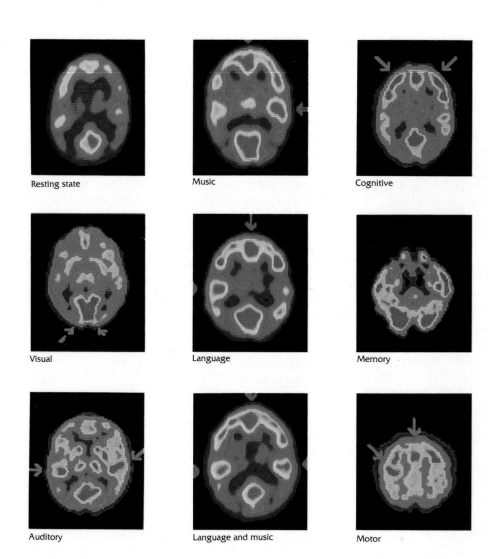

Resting state

Music

Cognitive

Visual

Language

Memory

Auditory

Language and music

Motor

FIGURE 1.1 PET scans show the brain activity of normal people engaged in different activities. Left column: Brain activity with no special stimulation, while passively watching something or listening to something. Center column: Brain activity while listening to music, language, or both. Right column: Brain activity during performance of a cognitive task, an auditory memory task, and the task of moving the fingers of the right hand. Red indicates the highest activity, followed by yellow, green, and blue. Arrows indicate the most active areas.

(Courtesy of Michael E. Phelps and John C. Mazziotta, University of California, Los Angeles, School of Medicine)

The Nature–Nurture Issue

Why do most little boys spend more time than little girls with toy guns and trucks and less time with dolls? Are such behavioral differences mostly the result of biological differences between boys and girls, or are they mainly the result of differences in how society treats boys and girls?

Alcohol abuse is a big problem in some cultures and a rare one in others. Are these differences entirely a matter of social custom, or do genes influence alcohol use also?

Certain psychological disorders are more common in large cities than in small towns and in the countryside. Does life in crowded cities somehow cause psychological disorders? Or do people develop such disorders because of a genetic predisposition and then move to big cities in search of jobs, housing, and welfare services?

Each of these questions is related to the **nature–nurture issue** (or heredity–environment is-

sue): *How do differences in behavior relate to differences in heredity and environment?* The nature–nurture issue shows up from time to time in practically all fields of psychology, and it seldom has a simple answer. It is the central issue of chapter 5 (development) and also important in chapters 9 (intelligence), 11 (motivation), and 16 (abnormal behavior).

CRITICAL THINKING

A STEP FURTHER

Nature and Nurture

Suppose researchers conclude that alcohol abuse is uncommon in Turkey because of Turkey's strict legal sanctions against alcohol use. Should we then assume that the differences in alcohol use among people in other countries is also due to nongenetic causes?

Why do different children develop different interests? They may have had different hereditary tendencies, but they have also experienced different environmental influences. Separating the roles of nature and nurture can be difficult.

 CONCEPT CHECK

1. In what way does all scientific research presuppose determinism?
2. What is one major objection to dualism? (Check your answers on page 16.)

What Psychologists Do

We have considered some major philosophical issues related to the entire field of psychology. However, psychologists usually deal with smaller, more answerable questions.

Psychology is an academic discipline with specialties that range from the helping professions to research on brain functions. The educational requirements for becoming a psychologist vary from one country to another. In the United States and Canada, a psychologist starts with a bachelor's degree (usually requiring 4 years of college) and then probably a PhD degree (at least another 4 or 5 years, often more). A growing number of clinical psychologists (those dealing directly with clients) have a PsyD (doctor of psychology) degree, which generally requires less research experience than a PhD but a similar period of training. Some work with a master's degree (intermediate between a bachelor's degree and a doctorate), but the opportunities are more limited.

Psychologists work in many occupational settings, as shown in Figure 1.2. The most common settings are colleges and universities, private practice, hospitals and mental health clinics, and government agencies.

Psychologists in Teaching and Research

Many psychologists, especially those who are not clinical psychologists, have positions in colleges and universities where they teach and do research that will ideally lead to a greater understanding of behavior and experience. Here, let's preview a few major categories of psychological research. To some extent different kinds of psychologists study different topics. For example, a developmental psychologist might observe children's attempts to control their emotions, while biological psychologists might examine the consequences of some kind of brain damage. However, different kinds of psychologists sometimes study the same questions but approach them in different ways. To illustrate, let's consider

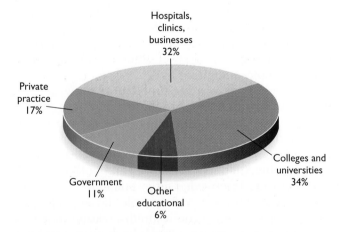

FIGURE 1.2 More than one third of psychologists work in academic institutions; the remainder find positions in a variety of settings. (Based on data of Chamberlin, 2000)

Infants and young children will try to eat almost anything. As they grow older, they learn to avoid foods for reasons other than just taste.

People associate what they eat, especially unfamiliar foods, with the way they feel afterward. If you ate corn dogs and cotton candy and then got sick on a wild ride, something in your brain would blame the food, regardless of what you think consciously. Ordinarily, however, this kind of learning teaches us to avoid harmful substances.

the example of how we select what to eat. How do you know what is edible and what isn't? We won't find just one answer; as usual, your behavior has many explanations. Different kinds of psychologists seek different kinds of explanations.

Developmental Psychology

Developmental psychologists *study how behavior changes with age,* "from womb to tomb." For example, they might examine language development from age 2 to 4 or memory from age 60 to 80. After describing the changes over age, they try to explain those changes, frequently dealing with the nature–nurture issue.

With regard to food selection, some taste preferences are present from birth. Newborns prefer sweet tastes and avoid bitter and sour substances. However, they appear indifferent to salty tastes, as if they could not yet taste salts (Beauchamp, Cowart, Mennella, & Marsh, 1994). Toddlers around the age of 1½ will try to eat almost anything they can fit into their mouths, unless it tastes sour or bitter. For that reason parents need to keep dangerous substances like furniture polish out of toddlers' reach. Later, they become increasingly selective, even "picky" about what foods they will accept. However, even up to age 7 or 8, about the only reason children give for refusing to eat something is that they think it would taste bad (Rozin, Fallon, & Augustoni-Ziskind, 1986). As they grow older, they cite more complex reasons for rejecting foods, such as health concerns.

Learning and Motivation

The research field of **learning and motivation** studies *how behavior depends on the outcomes of past behaviors and current motivations.* How often we engage in any particular behavior depends on the results of that behavior in the past.

We learn our food choices largely by learning what *not* to eat. For example, if you eat something and then feel sick, you form an aversion to the taste of that food, especially if it was unfamiliar. It doesn't matter whether you consciously think the food made you ill. If you eat something at an amusement park and then go on a wild ride and get sick, you may never again like that food. Even though you know the ride was at fault, your brain still associates the food with the sickness.

Cognitive Psychology

Cognition refers to *thought and knowledge.* A **cognitive psychologist** *studies those processes.* (The root *cogn-* also shows up in the word *recognize,* which literally means "to know again.") Consider the role of cognition in food selection: Most animals will eat anything they can find that tastes good and does not make them sick. Humans, however, often refuse an edible food just because of the very idea of it (Rozin & Fallon, 1987; Rozin, Millman, & Nemeroff, 1986). In the United States, most people refuse to eat meat from dogs, cats, or horses. Vegetarians reject all meat and some are distressed even to watch other people eat it. The longer people have been vegetarians, the more firmly they tend to regard meat eating as not only undesirable but also immoral (Rozin, Markwith, & Stoess, 1997).

How would you like to try the tasty morsels described in Figure 1.3? Most people find the idea of eating insects repulsive, even if the insects were sterilized to kill all the germs (Rozin & Fallon, 1987). Would you be willing to drink a glass of apple juice after a dead cockroach had been dipped into it? What if the cockroach had been carefully sterilized? Some people not only refuse to drink that glass of apple juice but say they have lost their taste for apple juice in general (Rozin et al., 1986). Would you drink pure water from a brand-new, never-used toilet bowl? Would you eat a piece of chocolate fudge shaped like dog feces? If not, you are guided by the idea of the food, not its taste or safety.

Biological Psychology

A **biopsychologist** (or **behavioral neuroscientist**) *tries to explain behavior in terms of biological factors, such as electrical and chemical activities in the nervous system, the effects of drugs and hormones, genetics, and evolutionary pressures.* How would a biological psychologist approach the question of how people (or animals) select foods?

A major contributor to food selection is taste, and we have some built-in taste preferences. From birth on, people (and nearly all other mammals) avidly consume sweets but spit out anything sour or bitter.

A small part of the difference among people in their taste preferences relates to the fact that some people have up to three times as many taste buds as others do, mostly for genetic reasons. The genes vary within each population, although the relative frequencies of strong tasters and weak tasters are fairly similar for Asia, Eu-

Different cultures have different taboos. Here is an assortment of insect and reptile dishes. (Yum, yum?)

rope, and Africa (Wooding et al., 2004). People with the most taste buds usually have the least tolerance for strong tastes, including black coffee, black breads, hot peppers, grapefruit, radishes, and Brussels sprouts (Bartoshuk, Duffy, Lucchina, Prutkin, & Fast, 1998; Drewnowski, Henderson, Short, & Barratt-Fornell, 1998). They also tend to be satisfied with small portions of desserts, as they don't need much sugar to satisfy their craving for sweet tastes.

Hormones also affect taste preferences in several ways. For example, many years ago, a young child showed a strong craving for salt. As an infant he licked the salt off crackers and bacon without eating the food itself. He put a thick layer of salt on everything he ate, and sometimes, he swallowed salt directly from the shaker. When deprived of salt, he stopped eating and began to waste away. At the age of 3½, he was taken to the hospital and fed the usual hospital fare. He soon died of salt deficiency (Wilkins & Richter, 1940).

The reason was that he had defective adrenal glands, which secrete the hormones that enable the body to retain salt (Verrey & Beron, 1996). He craved salt because he had to consume it fast enough to replace what he lost in his urine. (We are often told to limit our salt intake for health reasons, but too little salt can also be dangerous.) Later research confirmed that salt-deficient animals immediately show an increased preference for salty tastes (Rozin & Kalat, 1971). Apparently, becoming salt deficient causes salty foods to taste especially good (Jacobs, Mark, & Scott, 1988). People often report salt cravings after losing salt by bleeding or sweating.

Evolutionary Psychology

An **evolutionary psychologist** *tries to explain behavior in terms of the evolutionary history of the species, including reasons evolution might have favored a tendency to act in particular ways.* For ex-

---

Crispy Cajun Crickets

Adapted from a recipe in the *Food Insects Newsletter*, March 1990

Tired of the same old snack food? Perk up your next party with Crispy Cajun Crickets ("pampered" house crickets, *Acheta domestica,* available from Flucker's Cricket Farm, P.O. Box 378, Baton Rouge, LA 70821, 800-735-8537).

1 cup crickets
1 pinch oatmeal
4 ounces butter, melted
Salt
Garlic
Cayenne

1. Put crickets in a clean, airy container with oatmeal for food. After one day, discard sick crickets and freeze the rest.
2. Wash frozen crickets in warm water and spread on a cookie sheet. Roast in a 250-degree oven until crunchy.
3. Meanwhile heat butter with remaining ingredients and sprinkle this sauce on crickets before serving.

Yield: 1 serving

FIGURE 1.3 People avoid some potential foods because they are disgusted by the very idea of eating them. For example, most Westerners refuse to eat insects, despite assurances that most are nutritious and harmless. *("Recipe for fried crickets" from* The Food Insects Newsletter. *Reprinted by permission of Douglas Whitman, Illinois State University)*

ample, *why* do people and other animals crave sweets and avoid bitter tastes? Here, the answer is easy: Most sweets are nutritious and almost all bitter substances are poisonous (Scott & Verhagen, 2000). Ancient animals that ate fruits and other sweets survived to become our ancestors. Any animals that preferred bitter substances, or that chose foods without regard to taste, were likely to die before they had a chance to reproduce.

However, although some evolutionary explanations of behavior are persuasive, others are uncertain or debatable (de Waal, 2002). Yes, the brain is the product of evolution, just as any other organ is, but the question is whether evolution has micromanaged our behavior. The research challenge is to separate the evolutionary influences on our behavior from what we have learned during a lifetime. Chapter 13 on social psychology will explore this question in more detail.

Social Psychology and Cross-Cultural Psychology

Social psychologists *study how an individual influences other people and how the group influences an individual.* For example, people usually eat together, and on the average we eat about twice as much when we are in a large group than we do when eating alone (de Castro, 2000). If you invite guests to your house, you offer them something to eat or drink as an important way of strengthening a social relationship.

Cross-cultural psychology *compares the behavior of people from different cultures.* It often resembles social psychology, except that it compares one culture to another. Cuisine is one of the most stable and defining features of any culture. In one study researchers interviewed Japanese high school and college students who had spent a year in another country as part of an exchange program. The satisfaction reported by students with their year abroad had little relationship to the educational system, religion, family life, recreation, or dating customs of the host country. The main determinant of their satisfaction was the food: Students who could sometimes eat Japanese food had a good time. Those who could not became homesick (Furukawa, 1997).

The similarity between the words *culture* and *agriculture* is no coincidence, as cultivating crops was a major step toward civilization. We learn from our culture what to eat and how to prepare it (Rozin, 1996). Consider, for example, cassava, a root vegetable that is poisonous unless someone washes and pounds it for 3 days. Can you imagine discovering that fact? Someone had to say, "So far, everyone who ate this plant died, but I bet that if I wash and pound it for 3 days, then it will be okay." Our culture also teaches us good ways of combining foods. American corn (maize) has a deficit of certain nutrients and beans are deficient in other nutrients, but corn and beans

Cassava, a root vegetable native to South America, is now a staple food in much of Africa as well. It grows in climates not suitable for most other crops. However, people must pound and wash it for days to remove the cyanide.

together make a good combination—as the Native Americans discovered long ago.

 CONCEPT CHECK

3. **a.** Of the kinds of psychological research just described—developmental psychology, learning and motivation, cognitive psychology, biological psychology, evolutionary psychology, social psychology, and cross-cultural psychology—which field concentrates most on children?
   b. Which two are most concerned with how people behave in groups?
   c. Which concentrates most on thought and knowledge?
   d. Which is most interested in the effects of brain damage?
   e. Which is most concerned with studying the effect of a reward on future behavior?
4. Why do many menstruating women crave potato chips? (Check your answers on page 17.)

Service Providers to Individuals

When most people hear the term *psychologist,* they first think of *clinical psychologists,* who constitute one type of mental health professionals. Clinical psychologists deal with problems ranging from depression, anxiety, and substance abuse to marriage conflicts, difficulties making decisions, or even the feeling that "I should be getting more out of life." Some clinical psychologists are college professors and researchers, but most are full-time practitioners.

It is important to distinguish among several types of mental health professionals. The term *ther-*

apist itself has no precise meaning, and in many places even untrained, unlicensed people can hang out a shingle and call themselves therapists. Some of the main kinds of service providers for people with psychological troubles are clinical psychologists, psychiatrists, social workers, and counseling psychologists.

Clinical Psychology

Clinical psychologists *have an advanced degree in psychology, with a specialty in understanding and helping people with psychological problems.* Most have a PhD, which requires research training and the completion of a substantial research dissertation. As part of their training, clinical psychologists undergo at least a year of supervised clinical work called an *internship.* An alternative to the PhD is a PsyD (doctor of psychology) degree, which requires internship experience but little or no research experience. PsyD programs vary strikingly, including some that are academically strong and others that have low admissions standards (Norcross, Kohout, & Wicherski, 2005).

Clinical psychologists can base their work on any of various theoretical viewpoints, or they can use a pragmatic, trial-and-error approach. They try, in one way or another, to understand why a person is having problems and then help that person overcome the difficulties.

Psychiatry

Psychiatry is a *branch of medicine that deals with emotional disturbances.* To become a psychiatrist, someone first earns an MD degree and then takes an additional 4 years of residency training in psychiatry. Psychiatrists and clinical psychologists provide similar services for most clients: They listen, ask questions, and try to help. Psychiatrists, however, are medical doctors and can therefore prescribe drugs, such as tranquilizers and antidepressants, whereas in most places psychologists cannot. Some states now permit psychologists with additional specialized training to prescribe drugs. More psychiatrists than clinical psychologists work in mental hospitals, and psychiatrists more often treat clients with severe disorders.

Does psychiatrists' ability to prescribe drugs give them an advantage over psychologists in places where psychologists cannot prescribe them? Sometimes, but not always. Some psychiatrists habitually treat anxiety and depression with drugs, whereas psychologists treat problems by changing the person's way of living. Drugs can be useful, but relying on them too extensively can be a hazard.

Other Mental Health Professionals

Several other kinds of professionals also provide help and counsel. Psychoanalysts are *therapy providers who rely heavily on the theories and methods pio-*

neered by the early 20th-century Viennese physician Sigmund Freud and later modified by others. Freud and his followers attempted to infer the hidden, unconscious, symbolic meaning behind people's words and actions, and in various ways psychoanalysts today continue that effort.

There is some question about who may rightly call themselves psychoanalysts. Some people apply the term to anyone who attempts to uncover unconscious thoughts and feelings. Others apply the term only to graduates of a 6- to 8-year program at an institute of psychoanalysis. These institutes admit only people who are already either psychiatrists or clinical psychologists. Thus, people completing psychoanalytic training will be at least in their late 30s.

A clinical social worker *is similar to a clinical psychologist but with different training.* In most cases a clinical social worker has a master's degree in social work with a specialization in psychological problems. A master's degree takes less education than a doctorate and requires much less research experience. Many health maintenance organizations (HMOs) steer most of their clients with psychological problems toward clinical social workers instead of psychologists or psychiatrists because the social workers, with less formal education, charge less per hour. Some psychiatric nurses (nurses with additional training in psychiatry) provide similar services.

Counseling psychologists *help people with educational, vocational, marriage, health-related, and other decisions.* A counseling psychologist has a doctorate degree (PhD, PsyD, or EdD) with supervised experience in counseling. The activities of a counseling psychologist overlap those of a clinical psychologist, but the emphasis is different. Whereas a clinical psychologist deals mainly with anxiety, depression, and other emotional distress, a counseling psychologist deals mostly with important life decisions and family or career readjustments, which, admittedly, can cause anxiety or depression. Counseling psychologists work in educational institutions, mental health centers, rehabilitation agencies, businesses, and private practice.

You may also have heard of forensic psychologists, *those who provide advice and consultation to police, lawyers, courts, or other parts of the criminal justice system.* Forensic psychologists are, in nearly all cases, trained as clinical or counseling psychologists with additional training in legal issues. They help with such decisions as whether a defendant is mentally competent to stand trial and whether someone eligible for parole is dangerous (Otto & Heilbrun, 2002). Several popular films have depicted forensic psychologists helping police investigators develop a "psychological profile" of a serial killer. That may sound like an exciting, glamorous profession, but few psychologists engage in such activities (and the accuracy of their profiles is uncertain, as discussed in chapter 14). Most criminal profilers today have training and experience in law enforcement, not psychology.

Table 1.1 compares various types of mental health professionals.

TABLE 1.1 Several Types of Mental Health Professionals

Type of Therapist	Education
Clinical psychologist	PhD with clinical emphasis or PsyD plus internship. Ordinarily, 5+ years after undergraduate degree.
Psychiatrist	MD plus psychiatric residency. Total of 8 years after undergraduate degree.
Psychoanalyst	Psychiatry or clinical psychology plus 6–8 years in a psychoanalytic institute. Many others who rely on Freud's methods also call themselves psychoanalysts.
Psychiatric nurse	From 2-year (AA) degree to master's degree plus supervised experience.
Clinical social worker	Master's degree plus 2 years of supervised experience. Total of at least 4 years after undergraduate degree.
Counseling psychologist	PhD, PsyD, or EdD plus supervised experience in counseling.
Forensic psychologist	Doctorate, ordinarily in clinical psychology or counseling psychology, plus additional training in legal issues.

 CONCEPT CHECK

5. Can psychoanalysts prescribe drugs? (Check your answer on page 17.)

Service Providers to Organizations

Psychologists also work in business, industry, and school systems in some capacities that might be unfamiliar to you, doing things you might not think of as psychology. The job prospects in these fields have been good, however, and you might find these fields interesting.

Industrial/Organizational Psychology

The psychological study of people at work is known as **industrial/organizational (I/O) psychology**. It deals with issues you might not think of as psychology, such as matching the right person with the right job, training people for jobs, developing work teams, determining salaries and bonuses, providing feedback to workers about their performance, planning an organizational structure, and organizing the workplace so that workers will be both productive and satisfied. I/O psychologists study the behavior of both the individual and the organization, including the impact of economic conditions and government regulations. We shall consider work motivation in chapter 11.

Here's an example of a concern for industrial/organizational psychologists (Campion & Thayer, 1989): A company that manufactures complex electronic equipment needed to publish reference and repair manuals for its products. The engineers who designed the devices did not want to spend their time writing the manuals, and none of them were skilled writers anyway. So the company hired a technical writer to prepare the manuals. After a year she received an unsatisfactory performance rating because the manuals she wrote contained too many technical errors. She countered that, when she asked various engineers in the company to check her manuals or to explain technical details to her, they were always too busy. She found her job complicated and frustrating; her office was badly lit, noisy, and overheated; and her chair was uncomfortable. Whenever she mentioned any of these problems, however, she was told that she "complained too much."

In a situation such as this, an industrial/organizational psychologist can help the company evaluate the problem and develop possible solutions. Maybe the company hired the wrong person for this job. If so, they should fire her and hire some expert on electrical engineering who is also an outstanding writer and *likes* a badly lit, noisy, overheated, uncomfortable office. However, if the company cannot find or afford such a person, then it needs to improve the working conditions and provide the current employee with more training or more help with the technical aspects of the job.

When a company criticizes its workers, I/O psychologists try to discover whether the problem is poor workers or a difficult job. Depending on the answer, they then try to improve the hiring decisions or improve the working conditions.

 CRITICAL THINKING

A STEP FURTHER

I/O Psychology

Industrial/organizational psychologists usually consult with business and industry, but suppose they were called on to help a university where certain professors had complained that "the students are too lazy and stupid to understand the lectures." How might the I/O psychologists react?

Ergonomics

Many years ago, my son Sam, then about 16 years old, turned to me as he rushed out the door and asked me to turn off his stereo. I went to the stereo in his room and tried to find an on–off switch or a power switch. No such luck. I looked in vain for the manual. Finally, in desperation I had to unplug the stereo.

Learning to operate our increasingly complex machinery is one of the perennial struggles of modern life. Sometimes, the consequences can be serious. Imagine an airplane pilot who intends to lower the landing gear and instead raises the wing flaps. Or a worker in a nuclear power plant who fails to notice a warning signal. In one field of psychology, an **ergonomist, or human factors specialist,** *attempts to facilitate the operation of machinery so that ordinary people can use it efficiently and safely.* The term *ergonomics* is derived from Greek roots meaning "laws of work." Ergonomics was first used in military settings, where complex technologies sometimes required soldiers to spot nearly invisible targets, understand speech through deafening noise, track objects in three dimensions while using two hands, and make life-or-death decisions in a split second. The military turned to psychologists to determine what skills their personnel could master and to redesign the tasks to fit those skills.

Ergonomists soon applied their experience not only to business and industry but also to everyday devices. As Donald Norman (1988) pointed out, many intelligent and educated people find themselves unable to use all the features on a camera or a microwave oven; some even have trouble setting the time on a digital watch.

At various universities the ergonomics program is part of the psychology department, engineering, or both. Regardless of who administers the program, ergonomics necessarily combines features of psychology, engineering, and computer science. It is a growing field with many jobs available.

School Psychology

Many if not most children have academic problems at one time or another. Some children have trouble sitting still or paying attention. Others get into trouble for misbehavior. Some have specialized problems with reading, spelling, arithmetic, or other academic skills. Other children master their schoolwork quickly and become bored. They too need special attention.

School psychologists are *specialists in the psychological condition of students,* usually in kindergarten through the 12th grade. Broadly speaking, school psychologists identify the educational needs of children, devise a plan to meet those needs, and then either implement the plan themselves or advise teachers how to implement it.

School psychology can be taught in a psychology department, a branch of an education department, or a department of educational psychology. In some countries it is possible to practice school psychology with only a bachelor's degree. In the United States the minimum is usually a master's degree, but job opportunities are much greater for people with a doctorate degree, and a doctorate may become necessary in the future. Job opportunities in school psychology have been strong and continue to grow. Most school psychologists work for a school system; others work for mental health clinics, guidance centers, and other institutions.

Table 1.2 summarizes some of the major fields of psychology, including several that have not been discussed.

Should You Major in Psychology?

Can you get a job if you major in psychology? Psychology is one of the most popular majors in the United States, Canada, and Europe. So if psychology majors cannot get jobs, a huge number of people are going to be in trouble!

The bad news is that few jobs specifically advertise for college graduates with a bachelor's degree in psychology. The good news is that an enormous variety of jobs are available for graduates with a bachelor's degree, not specifying any major. Therefore, if you earn a degree in psychology, you will compete with history majors, English majors, astronomy majors, and everyone else for jobs in government, business, and industry. According to one survey, only 20 to 25% of people who graduated with a degree in psychology

Ergonomists help redesign machines to make them easier and safer to use. An ergonomist uses principles of both engineering and psychology.

© Firefly Productions/CORBIS

TABLE 1.2 Some Major Specializations in Psychology

Specialization	General Interest	Example of Interest or Research Topic
Biopsychologist	Relationship between brain and behavior	What body signals indicate hunger and satiety?
Clinical psychologist	Emotional difficulties	How can people be helped to overcome severe anxiety?
Cognitive psychologist	Memory, thinking	Do people have several kinds of memory?
Community psychologist	Organizations and social structures	Would improved job opportunities decrease psychological distress?
Counseling psychologist	Helping people make important decisions	Should this person consider changing careers?
Developmental psychologist	Changes in behavior over age	At what age can a child first distinguish between appearance and reality?
Educational psychologist	Improvement of learning in school	What is the best way to test a student's knowledge?
Environmental psychologist	How noise, heat, crowding, etc. affect behavior	What building design can maximize the productivity of the people who use it?
Ergonomist	Communication between person and machine	How can an airplane cockpit be redesigned to increase safety?
Evolutionary psychologist	Evolutionary history of behavior	Why do men generally show more sexual jealousy than women?
Industrial/organizational psychologist	People at work	Should jobs be made simple and foolproof or interesting and challenging?
Learning and motivation specialist	Learning in humans and other species	What are the effects of reinforcement and punishment?
Personality psychologist	Personality differences	Why are certain people shy and others gregarious?
Psychometrician	Measuring intelligence, personality, interests	How fair are current IQ tests? Can we devise better tests?
School psychologist	Problems that affect schoolchildren	How should the school handle a child who regularly disrupts the classroom?
Social psychologist	Group behavior, social influences	What methods of persuasion are most effective for changing attitudes?

took a job closely related to psychology, such as personnel work or social services (Borden & Rajecki, 2000). Still, many other jobs were good ones, even if they were not in psychology.

Even if you get a job that seems remote from psychology, your psychology courses will have taught you much about how to evaluate evidence, organize and write papers, handle statistics, listen carefully to what people say, understand and respect cultural differences, and so forth. You will, of course, also gain useful background in your other courses. Regardless of your major, you should develop your skills in communication, mathematics, and computers. (If you don't have those skills, you will work for someone who does.)

Psychology also provides a good background for people entering professional schools. Many students major in psychology and then apply to medical school, law school, divinity school, or other programs. Find out what coursework is expected for the professional program of your choice and then compare the coursework required for a psychology major. You will probably find that the psychology major is compatible with your professional preparation.

If you want a career as a psychologist, you should aspire to an advanced degree, preferably a doctorate. A doctorate will qualify you to apply for positions as a college professor or, depending on your area of specialization, jobs in hospitals, clinics, private practice, school systems, industry, or research. An increasing percentage of doctorate-level psychologists now work in business, industry, and the military doing research related to practical problems. If you are a first- or second-year college student now, it is hard to predict what the job market will be by the time you finish an advanced degree. If you are just looking for a safe, secure way to make a living, psychology offers no guarantees. A career in psychology is for those whose excitement about the field draws them irresistibly to it.

For more information about majoring in psychology, prospects for graduate school, and a great variety of jobs for psychology graduates, visit either of these websites:

www.drlynnfriedman.com/
www.apa.org/students/

IN CLOSING

Types of Psychologists

An experimental psychology researcher, a clinical psychologist, an ergonomist, and an industrial/organizational psychologist are all psychologists, even though their daily activities have little in common. What does unite psychologists is a dedication to progress through research.

I have oversimplified this discussion of the various psychological approaches in several ways. In particular, biological psychology, cognitive psychology, social psychology, and the other fields overlap significantly. Nearly all psychologists combine insights and information gained from a variety of approaches. To understand why one person differs from another, psychologists combine information about biology, learning experiences, social influences, and much more.

As we proceed through this book, we shall consider one type of behavior at a time and, generally, one approach at a time. That is simply a necessity; we cannot talk intelligently about many topics at once. But bear in mind that all these processes do ultimately fit together; what you do at any given moment depends on a great many influences. ∎

Summary

The page number after an item indicates where the topic is first discussed.

- *What is psychology?* Psychology is the systematic study of behavior and experience. Psychologists deal with both theoretical and practical questions. (page 3)
- *Six generalities.* Almost any statement in psychology depends on many factors, and few statements apply to everyone all the time. Research progress depends on good measurement. Correlation does not mean causation. People differ from one another because of heredity and environment. The best

predictor of future behavior is past behavior. Some conclusions in psychology are based on stronger evidence than others. (page 3)
- *Determinism–free will.* Determinism is the view that everything that occurs, including human behavior, has a physical cause. That view is difficult to reconcile with the conviction that humans have free will—that we deliberately, consciously decide what to do. (page 5)
- *Mind–brain.* The mind–brain problem is the question of how conscious experience is related to the activity of the brain. (page 6)
- *Nature–nurture.* Behavior depends on both nature (heredity) and nurture (environment). Psychologists try to determine the influence of these two factors on differences in behavior. The relative contributions of nature and nurture vary from one behavior to another. (page 7)
- *Research fields in psychology.* Psychology as an academic field has many subfields, including biological psychology, learning and motivation, cognitive psychology, developmental psychology, and social psychology. (page 8)
- *Psychology and psychiatry.* Clinical psychologists have either a PhD, PsyD, or master's degree; psychiatrists are medical doctors. Both clinical psychologists and psychiatrists treat people with emotional problems, but psychiatrists can prescribe drugs and other medical treatments, whereas in most states psychologists cannot. Counseling psychologists help people deal with difficult decisions; they sometimes but less often also deal with psychological disorders. (page 12)
- *Service providers to organizations.* Nonclinical fields of application include industrial/organizational psychology, ergonomics, and school psychology. (page 13)
- *Job prospects.* People with a bachelor's degree in psychology enter a wide variety of careers or continue their education in professional schools. Those with a doctorate in psychology have additional possibilities depending on their area of specialization. In psychology, as in any other field, job prospects can change between the start and finish of one's education. (page 14)

Answers to Concept Checks

1. Any attempt to make discoveries about nature presupposes that we live in a universe of cause and effect. (page 8)
2. Dualism conflicts with the principle of the conservation of matter and energy. A nonmaterial mind could not influence anything in the universe. (page 8)

3. a. Developmental psychology. **b.** Social psychology and cross-cultural psychology. **c.** Cognitive psychology. **d.** Biological psychology. **e.** Learning and motivation. (page 11)

4. By losing blood, they also lose salt, and a deficiency of salt triggers a craving for salty tastes. (page 11)

5. Most psychoanalysts can prescribe drugs because most are psychiatrists, and psychiatrists are medical doctors. However, in most states, those who are not medical doctors cannot prescribe drugs. (page 13)

Psychology Then and Now

- *How did psychology get started?*
- *What were the interests of early psychologists?*
- *How has psychology changed over the years?*

Imagine yourself as a young scholar in 1880. Enthusiastic about the new scientific approach in psychology, you have decided to become a psychologist yourself. Like other early psychologists, you have a background in either biology or philosophy. You are determined to apply the scientific methods of biology to the problems of philosophy.

So far, so good. But what questions will you address? A good research question is both interesting and answerable. (If it can't be both, it should at least be one or the other!) In 1880 how would you choose a research topic? You cannot get research ideas from a psychological journal because the first issue won't be published until next year. (And incidentally, it will be all in German.) You cannot follow in the tradition of previous researchers because there haven't *been* any previous researchers. You are on your own.

Furthermore, in the late 1800s, psychologists were not sure which questions were answerable. Sometimes, psychologists today are still unsure: Should we study interesting questions about consciousness, or should we concentrate on observable behavior? Many of the changes that have occurred during the history of psychology have reflected investigators' decisions about which questions are answerable.

In the next several pages, we shall explore some of these changes in psychological research, including projects that dominated psychology for a while and then faded from interest. We shall discuss additional historical developments in later chapters. Figure 1.4 outlines some major historical events inside and outside psychology. For additional information about the history of psychology, visit either of these websites:

www.cwu.edu/~warren/today.html
www.uakron.edu/ahap

The Early Era

At least since Aristotle (384–322 B.C.), philosophers and writers have debated why people act the way they do, why they have the experiences they do, and why one person is different from another. Without discounting the importance of these great thinkers, several 19th-century scholars wondered whether a scientific approach would be fruitful. Impressed by the great strides made in physics, chemistry, and biology, they hoped for similar progress in psychology by conducting research.

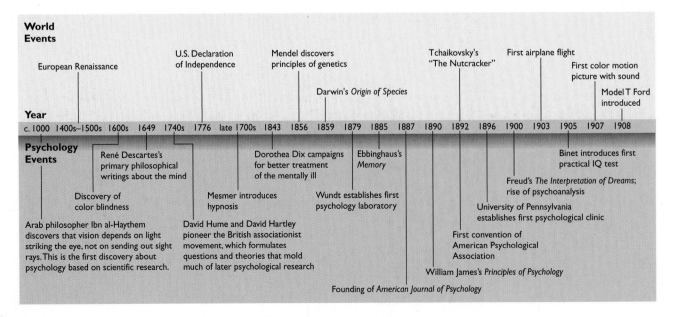

FIGURE 1.4 Dates of some important events in psychology and elsewhere. (Based partly on Dewsbury, 2000a)

Wilhelm Wundt and the First Psychological Laboratory

The origin of psychology as we now know it is generally dated to 1879, when medical doctor and sensory researcher Wilhelm Wundt (pronounced VOONT) set up the first psychology laboratory in Leipzig, Germany. Psychological research was not new, but this was the first laboratory intended exclusively for psychological research.

Wundt's broad interests ranged from the physiology of the sense organs to cultural differences in behavior, with emphases on motivation, voluntary control, and cognitive processes (Zehr, 2000). One of Wundt's fundamental questions was: What are the components of experience, or mind? He proposed that experience is composed of elements and compounds, like those of chemistry. Psychology's elements were, he maintained, sensations and feelings (Wundt, 1896/1902).[1] So at any particular moment, you might experience the taste of a fine meal, the sound of good music, and a certain degree of pleasure. These would merge into a single experience (a compound) based on the separate elements. Furthermore, Wundt maintained, your experience is partly under your voluntary control; you can shift your attention from one element to another and get a different experience.

Wundt tried to test his idea about the components of experience by collecting data. He presented various kinds of lights, textures, and sounds and asked sub-

jects to report the intensity and quality of their sensations. That is, he asked them to introspect—*to look within themselves.* He recorded the changes in people's reports as he changed the stimuli.

Wundt demonstrated the possibility of meaningful psychological research. For example, in one of his earliest studies, he set up a pendulum that struck metal balls and made a sound at two points on its swing (points b and d in Figure 1.5). People would watch the pendulum and indicate where it appeared to be when they heard the sound. Often, the pendulum appeared to be slightly in front of or behind the ball when people heard the strike. The apparent position of the pendulum at the time of the sound differed from its actual position by an average of ⅛ of a second (Wundt, 1862/1961). Apparently, the time we think we see or hear something is not the same as when the event occurred. Wundt's interpretation was that a person needs about ⅛ of a second to shift attention from one stimulus to another.

Wundt and his students were prolific investigators, and the brief treatment here cannot do him justice. He wrote more than 50,000 pages about his research, but his most lasting impact came from setting the precedent of studying psychological questions by collecting scientific data.

Edward Titchener and Structuralism

At first most of the world's psychologists received their education from Wilhelm Wundt himself. One of Wundt's students, Edward Titchener, came to the United States in 1892 as a psychology professor at Cornell University. Like Wundt, Titchener believed that the main question of psychology was the nature of mental experiences.

[1]A reference citation containing a slash between the years, such as this one, refers to a book originally published in the first year (1896) and reprinted in the second year (1902). All references are listed at the end of the book.

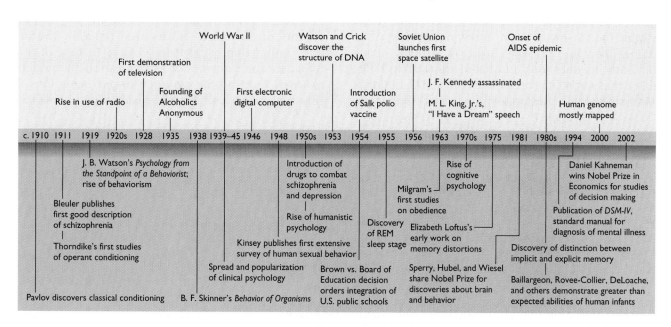

FIGURE 1.5 (Left) In one of Wilhelm Wundt's earliest studies, the pendulum struck the metal balls (b and d), making a sound each time. To an observer, however, the ball appeared to be somewhere else at the time of the sound, approximately the distance that it would travel in ⅛ of a second. Wundt inferred that a person needs that much time to shift attention from one stimulus to another. (Right) The Walt Disney studios rediscovered Wundt's observation decades later: The character's mouth movements seem to be in synchrony with the sounds if the movements precede the sounds by ⅛ to ⅙ of a second.

Titchener (1910) typically presented a stimulus and asked his subject to analyze it into its separate features—for example, to look at a lemon and describe its yellowness, brightness, shape, and other characteristics. He called his approach structuralism, *an attempt to describe the structures that compose the mind,* particularly sensations, feelings, and images. For example, imagine you are the psychologist: I look at a lemon and say my experience of its brightness is separate from my experience of its yellowness.

You see the problem with this approach. How do you know whether I am lying, telling you what I think you want me to say, or even deceiving myself? After Titchener died in 1927, psychologists virtually abandoned both his questions and his methods. Why? Remember that a good scientific question is both interesting and answerable. Regardless of whether Titchener's questions about the elements of the mind were interesting, they seemed unanswerable.

William James and Functionalism

In the same era as Wundt and Titchener, Harvard University's William James articulated some of the major issues of psychology and earned recognition as the founder of American psychology. James's book *The Principles of Psychology* (1890) defined many of the questions that dominated psychology long afterward and still do today.

James had little patience with searching for the elements of the mind. He focused on what the mind *does* rather than what it *is.* That is, instead of trying to isolate the elements of consciousness, he preferred *to learn how people produce useful behaviors.* For this reason we call his approach functionalism. He

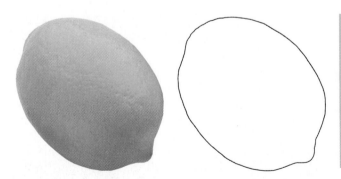

Edward Titchener asked subjects to describe their sensations. For example, they might describe their sensation of shape, their sensation of color, and their sensation of texture while looking at a lemon. Titchener had no way to check the accuracy of these reports, however, so later psychologists abandoned his methods.

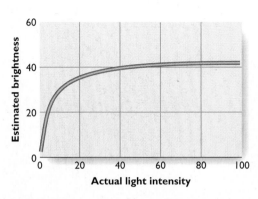
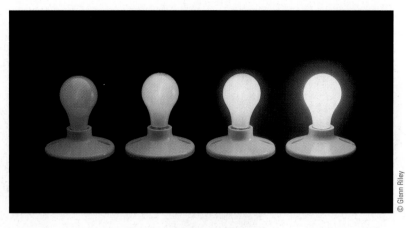

FIGURE 1.6 This graph of a psychophysical event shows the perceived intensity of light versus its physical intensity. When a light becomes twice as intense physically, it does not seem twice as bright. (Adapted from Stevens, 1961)

suggested the following examples of good psychological questions (James, 1890):

- How can people strengthen good habits?
- Can someone attend to more than one item at a time?
- How do people recognize that they have seen something before?
- How does an intention lead to action?

James proposed possible answers but did little research of his own. His main contribution was to inspire later researchers to address the questions that he posed.

Studying Sensation

One of early psychologists' main research topics was the relationship between physical stimuli and psychological sensations. To a large extent, the study of sensation *was* psychology. The first English-language textbook of the "new" scientifically based psychology devoted almost half of its pages to the senses and related topics (Scripture, 1907). By the 1930s standard psychology textbooks devoted less than 20% of their pages to these topics (Woodworth, 1934), and today, the proportion is down to about 5 to 10%. Why were early psychologists so interested in sensation?

One reason was philosophical: They wanted to understand mental experience, and experience consists of sensations. Another reason was strategic: A scientific psychology had to begin with answerable questions, and questions about sensation are more easily answerable than those about, say, personality.

Early psychologists discovered that what we see, hear, and otherwise experience is not the same as the physical stimulus. For example, a light that is twice as intense as another one does not look twice as bright. Figure 1.6 shows the relationship between the intensity of light and its perceived brightness. *The mathe-*

matical description of the relationship between the physical properties of a stimulus and its perceived properties is called the **psychophysical function** because it relates psychology to physics. Such research demonstrated that, at least in the study of sensation, scientific methods can provide nonobvious answers to psychological questions.

☑ CONCEPT CHECK

6. What topic was the main focus of research for the earliest psychologists and why?

7. What was the difference between structuralists and functionalists? (Check your answers on page 26.)

Darwin and the Study of Animal Intelligence

Charles Darwin's theory of evolution by natural selection (Darwin, 1859, 1871) had an enormous impact on psychology as well as biology. Darwin argued that humans and other species share a remote common ancestor. This idea implied that each species has specializations adapted to its own way of life but also that all vertebrate species have many basic features in common. It further implied that nonhuman animals should exhibit varying degrees of human characteristics, including intelligence.

Based on this last implication, early **comparative psychologists,** *specialists who compare different animal species,* did something that seemed more reasonable at first than it did later: They set out to measure animal intelligence. They apparently imagined that they could rank-order animals from the smartest to the dullest. Toward that goal they set various species to such tasks as the delayed-response problem and the detour problem. In the *delayed-response problem,* an animal was given a signal indi-

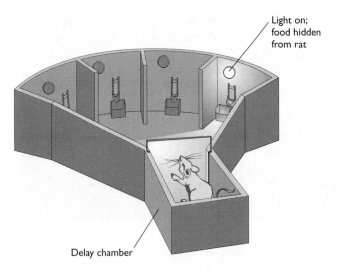

Light on;
food hidden
from rat

Delay chamber

FIGURE 1.7 Early comparative psychologists assessed animal intelligence with the delayed-response problem. A stimulus was presented and a delay ensued; then the animal was expected to respond to the remembered stimulus. Variations on this delayed-response task are still used today.

Food

FIGURE 1.8 Another task popular among early comparative psychologists was the detour problem. An animal needed to first go away from the food in order to move toward it.

cating where it could find food. Then the signal was removed, and the animal was restrained for a while (Figure 1.7) to see how long it could remember the signal. In the *detour problem,* an animal was separated from food by a barrier (Figure 1.8) to see whether it would take a detour away from the food in order to reach it.

However, measuring animal intelligence turned out to be more difficult than it sounded. Often, a species seemed dull-witted on one task but brilliant on another. For example, zebras are generally slow to learn to approach one pattern instead of another for food, unless the patterns happen to be narrow stripes versus wide stripes, in which case they suddenly excel (Giebel, 1958) (see Figure 1.9). Rats seem unable to find food hidden under the object that looks different from the others, but they easily learn to choose the object that *smells* different from the others (Langworthy & Jennings, 1972).

Eventually, psychologists realized that the relative intelligence of nonhuman animals was probably a meaningless question. The study of animal learning can illuminate general principles of learning and shed light on evolutionary questions (Papini, 2002), but no one measurement applies to all. A dolphin is neither more nor less intelligent than a chimpanzee; it is simply intelligent in different ways.

Psychologists today do study animal learning and intelligence, but the emphasis has changed. The question is no longer which animals are the smartest, but "What can we learn from animal studies about the mechanisms of intelligent behavior?" and "How did each species evolve the behavioral tendencies it shows?"

FIGURE 1.9 Zebras learn rapidly when they have to compare stripe patterns (Giebel, 1958). How "smart" a species is perceived to be depends in part on what ability or skill is being tested.

Measuring Human Intelligence

While some psychologists studied animal intelligence, others pursued human intelligence. Francis Galton, a cousin of Charles Darwin, was among the first to try to measure intelligence and to ask whether intellectual variations were based on heredity. Galton was fascinated with trying to measure almost everything (Hergenhahn, 1992). For example, he invented the weather map, measured degrees of boredom during lectures, suggested the use of fingerprints to identify individuals, and—in the name of science—attempted to measure the beauty of women in different countries.

In an effort to determine the role of heredity in human achievement, Galton (1869/1978) examined whether the sons of famous and accomplished men tended to become eminent themselves. (Women in 19th-century England had little opportunity for fame.) Galton found that the sons of judges, writers, politicians, and other noted men had a high probability of similar accomplishment themselves. He attributed this edge to heredity. (I'll leave this one for you to judge: Did he have adequate evidence for his conclusion? If the sons of famous men become famous themselves, is heredity the only explanation?)

Galton also tried to measure intelligence using simple sensory and motor tasks, but his measurements were unsatisfactory. In 1905 a French researcher, Alfred Binet, devised the first useful intelligence test, which we shall discuss further in chapter 9. At this point just note that the idea of testing intelligence became popular in the United States and other Western countries. Psychologists, inspired by the popularity of intelligence tests, later developed tests of personality, interests, and other psychological characteristics. Note that measuring human intelligence faces some of the same problems as animal intelligence: People have a great many intelligent abilities, and it is possible to be more adept at one than another. However, a great deal of research has been done to try to make tests of intelligence fair and accurate.

The Rise of Behaviorism

Earlier in this chapter, I casually defined psychology as "the systematic study of behavior and experience." For a substantial period of psychology's history, most experimental psychologists would have objected to the words "and experience." Some psychologists still object today, though less strenuously. From about 1920 to 1960 or 1970, most researchers described psychology as the study of behavior, period. These researchers had little to say about minds, experiences, or anything of the sort. (According to one quip, psychologists had "lost their minds.") What did psychologists have against "mind"?

Recall the failure of Titchener's effort to analyze experience into its components. Most psychologists concluded that questions about mind were unanswerable. Instead, they addressed questions about observable behaviors: What do people and other animals do and under what circumstances? How do changes in the environment alter what they do? What is learning and how does it occur? These questions were clearly meaningful and potentially answerable.

John B. Watson

Many regard John B. Watson as the founder of **behaviorism,** *a field of psychology that concentrates on observable, measurable behaviors and not on mental*

processes. Watson was not the first behaviorist, but he systematized the approach, popularized it, and stated its goals and assumptions (Watson, 1919, 1925). Here are two quotes from Watson:

> Psychology as the behaviorist views it is a purely objective experimental branch of natural science. Its theoretical goal is the prediction and control of behavior. (1913, p. 158)

> The goal of psychological study is the ascertaining of such data and laws that, given the stimulus, psychology can predict what the response will be; or, on the other hand, given the response, it can specify the nature of the effective stimulus. (1919, p. 10)

Studies of Learning

Inspired by Watson, many researchers set out to study animal behavior, especially animal learning. One advantage of studying nonhuman animals is that the researcher can control the animals' diet, waking–sleeping schedule, and so forth far more completely than with humans. The other supposed advantage was that nonhuman learning might be simpler to understand. Many psychologists optimistically expected to discover simple, basic laws of behavior, more or less the same from one species to another and from one situation to another. Just as physicists could study gravity by dropping any object in any location, many psychologists in the mid-1900s thought they could learn all about behavior by studying rats in mazes. One highly influential psychologist, Clark Hull, wrote, "One of the most persistently baffling problems which confronts modern psychologists is the finding of an adequate explanation of the phenomena of maze learning" (1932, p. 25). Another wrote, "I believe that everything important in psychology (except perhaps . . . such matters as involve society and words) can be investigated in essence through the continued experimental and theoretical analysis of the determiners of rat behavior at a choice-point in a maze" (Tolman, 1938, p. 34).

As research progressed, however, psychologists found that even the behavior of a rat in a maze was more complicated than they had expected, and such research declined in popularity. Just as psychologists of the 1920s abandoned the structuralist approach to the mind, later psychologists abandoned the hope that studying rats in mazes would uncover universal principles of behavior. Psychologists continue to study animal learning, but the methods have changed.

The behaviorist approach is still alive and well today, as we shall see in chapter 6, but it no longer dominates experimental psychology the way it once did. The rise of computer science showed that it was possible to talk about memory, knowledge, and information processing in machines, and if machines can have such processes, presumably humans can too. Psychologists demonstrated the possibility of mean-

© Dario Perla/International Stock

▌ Early behaviorists studied rats in mazes, hoping to find general laws of behavior. As they discovered that this apparently simple behavior was very complicated, their interest declined and they turned to other topics.

ingful research on cognition (thought and knowledge) and other topics that behaviorists had avoided.

From Freud to Modern Clinical Psychology

In the early 1900s, clinical psychology was a small field devoted largely to visual, auditory, movement, and memory disorders (Routh, 2000). The treatment of psychological disorders (or mental illness) was the province of psychiatry, a branch of medicine. The Austrian psychiatrist Sigmund Freud revolutionized and popularized psychotherapy with his methods of analyzing patients' dreams and memories. He tried to trace current behavior to early childhood experiences, including children's sexual fantasies. We shall examine Freud's theories in much more detail in chapter 14. Here, let me foreshadow that discussion by saying that Freud's influence has decreased sharply over the years. Freud was a persuasive speaker and writer, but the evidence he proposed for his theories was weak. Nevertheless, Freud's influence was enormous, and by the mid-1900s, most psychiatrists in the United States and Europe were following his methods.

During World War II, more people wanted help, especially soldiers traumatized by war experiences. Because psychiatrists could not keep up with the need, psychologists began providing ther-

FIGURE 1.10 Mary Calkins, one of the first prominent women in U.S. psychology.

Courtesy of Wellesley College Archives, © Notman

apy. Clinical psychology became a more popular field and more similar to psychiatry. Research began to compare the effectiveness of different methods, and new methods have taken the place of Freud's procedures, as we shall see in chapters 15 and 16.

Recent Trends in Psychology

The rest of this book will focus on the current era in psychology, with occasional flashbacks on the history of particular topics. Psychology today ranges from the study of simple sensory processes to interventions intended to change whole communities. Recall that some of the earliest psychological researchers wanted to study the conscious mind but became discouraged with Titchener's introspective methods. Since the mid-1960s, cognitive psychology (the study of thought and knowledge) has gained in prominence (Robins, Gosling, & Craik, 1999). Instead of asking people about their thoughts, today's cognitive psychologists carefully measure the accuracy and speed of responses under various circumstances to draw inferences about the underlying processes. They also use brain scans to determine what happens in the brain while people perform various tasks.

Another rapidly growing field is neuroscience. Research on the nervous system has advanced rapidly in recent decades, and psychologists in almost any field of specialization need to be aware of developments in neuroscience and their theoretical implications (Norcross et al., 2005).

New fields of application have also arisen. For example, health psychologists study how people's health is influenced by their behaviors, such as smoking, drinking, sexual activities, exercise, diet, and reactions to stress. They also try to help people change their behaviors to promote better health. Sports psychologists apply psychological principles to helping athletes set goals, train, concentrate their efforts during a contest, and so forth.

Psychologists today have also broadened their scope to include more of human diversity. In its early days, around 1900, psychology was more open to women than most other academic disciplines, but even so, the opportunities for women were limited (Milar, 2000). Mary Calkins (Figure 1.10), an early memory researcher, was regarded as the Harvard psychology department's best graduate student, but she was denied a PhD because Harvard insisted on its tradition of granting degrees only to men (Scarborough & Furomoto, 1987). She did, however, serve as president of the American Psychological Association, as did Margaret Washburn, another important woman in the early days of psychology.

Today, women receive about two thirds of the psychology PhDs in North America and most of those in Europe (Bailey, 2004; Newstead & Makinen, 1997). Women heavily dominate some fields, such as developmental psychology, and hold many leadership roles in the major psychological organizations. The number of African American and other minority students studying psychology has also increased, and today, minority students receive bachelor's and master's degrees almost in proportion to their numbers in the total population (Figure 1.11). However, the percentages continue to lag for minority students receiving PhD degrees or serving on college faculties (Maton, Kohout, Wicherski, Leary, & Vinokurov, 2006).

What will psychology be like in the future? We don't know, of course, but we assume it will reflect the changing needs of humanity. A few likely trends are foreseeable. Advances in medicine have enabled people to live longer, and advances in technology have enabled them to build where there used to be forests and wetlands, heat and cool their homes, travel by car or plane to distant locations, and buy and discard enormous numbers of products. In short, we are quickly destroying our environment, using up natural resources, and polluting the air and water. Sooner or later, it will become necessary either to decrease the population or to decrease the average person's use of resources (Howard, 2000). Convincing people to change their behavior is a task for both politics and psychology.

 CONCEPT CHECK

8. Why did behaviorists avoid the topics of thought and knowledge?
9. What event led to the rise of clinical psychology as we know it today? (Check your answers on page 26.)

We can learn much about what is or is not a stable feature of human nature by comparing people of different cultures.

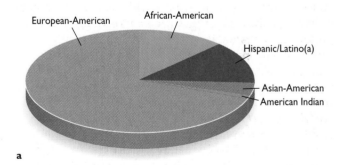

Total Population

European-American
African-American
Hispanic/Latino(a)
Asian-American
American Indian

a

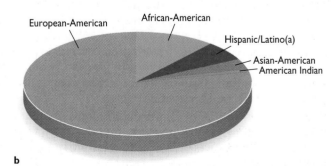

Master's Degrees

European-American
African-American
Hispanic/Latino(a)
Asian-American
American Indian

b

FIGURE 1.11 Ethnic groups as a percentage of the U.S. population and as a percentage of people receiving master's degrees in psychology during 2002. (Based on data of K. I. Maton et al., 2002)

Psychology Through the Years

Throughout the early years of psychology, many psychologists went down blind alleys, devoting enormous efforts to projects that produced disappointing results. Not all the efforts of early psychologists were fruitless, and in later chapters you will encounter many classic studies that have withstood the test of time. Still, if psychologists of the past spent much of their time on projects we now consider misguided, can we be sure that many of today's psychologists aren't on the wrong track?

We can't, of course. In later chapters you will read about careful, cautious psychological research that has amassed what seems in many cases to be strong evidence, but you are welcome to entertain doubts. Maybe some psychologists' questions are not as simple as they seem; perhaps some of their answers are not solid; perhaps you can think of a better way to approach certain topics. Psychologists have better data and firmer conclusions than they used to, but still, they do not have all the answers.

But that is not a reason for despair. Much like a rat in a maze, researchers make progress by trial and error. They pose a question, try a particular research method, and discover what happens. Sometimes, the results support fascinating and important conclusions; other times, they lead to rejections of old conclusions and a search for replacements. In either case the experience leads ultimately to better questions and better answers. ∎

Summary

- *Choice of research questions.* During the history of psychology, researchers have several times changed their opinions about what constitutes an interesting, important, answerable question. (page 18)
- *First research.* In 1879 Wilhelm Wundt established the first laboratory devoted to psychological research. He demonstrated the possibility of psychological experimentation. (page 19)
- *Limits of self-observation.* One of Wundt's students, Edward Titchener, attempted to analyze the elements of mental experience, relying on people's own observations. Other psychologists became discouraged with this approach. (page 19)
- *The founding of American psychology.* William James, generally considered the founder of American psychology, focused attention on how the mind guides useful behavior rather than on the contents of the mind. By doing so James paved the way for the rise of behaviorism. (page 20)
- *Early sensory research.* In the late 1800s and early 1900s, many researchers concentrated on studies

of the senses, partly because they were more likely to find definite answers on this topic than on other topics. (page 21)

- *Darwin's influence.* Charles Darwin's theory of evolution by natural selection influenced psychology in many ways. It prompted some prominent early psychologists to compare the intelligence of different species. That question turned out to be more complicated than anyone had expected. (page 21)
- *Intelligence testing.* The measurement of human intelligence was one concern of early psychologists that has persisted through the years. (page 22)
- *The era of behaviorist dominance.* As psychologists became discouraged with their attempts to analyze the mind, they turned to behaviorism. For many years psychological researchers studied behavior, especially animal learning, to the virtual exclusion of mental experience. (page 23)
- *Maze learning.* Clark Hull exerted a great influence on psychology for a number of years. Eventually, his approach became less popular because rats in mazes did not seem to generate simple or general answers to major questions. (page 23)
- *Freud.* Sigmund Freud's theories, which were historically very influential, have given way to other approaches to therapy, based on more careful use of evidence. (page 24)
- *Clinical psychology.* At one time psychiatrists provided nearly all the care for people with psychological disorders. After World War II, clinical psychology began to assume much of this role. (page 24)
- *Psychological research today.* Today, psychologists study a wide variety of topics. Cognitive psychology has replaced behaviorist approaches to learning as the dominant field of experimental psychology. However, we cannot be certain that we are not currently going down some blind alleys, just as many psychologists did before us. (page 24)

Answers to Concept Checks

6. Early psychological research focused mainly on sensation because sensation is central to experience and because the early researchers believed that sensation questions were answerable. (page 21)
7. Structuralists wanted to understand the components of the mind. They based their research mainly on introspection. Functionalists wanted to explore what the mind could *do*, and they focused mainly on behavior. (page 20)
8. Behaviorists concentrate on observable behaviors, whereas thought and knowledge are unobservable processes within the individual. (page 23)
9. During and after World War II, the need for services was greater than psychiatrists could provide. Clinical psychologists began providing treatment for psychological distress. (page 24)

CHAPTER ENDING

Key Terms and Activities

Key Terms

You can check the page listed for a complete description of a term. You can also check the glossary/index at the end of the text for a definition of a given term, or you can download a list of all the terms and their definitions for any chapter at this website:

www.thomsonedu.com/ psychology/kalat

behaviorism (page 23)
biopsychologist (or behavioral neuroscientist) (page 10)
clinical psychologist (page 12)
clinical social worker (page 12)

cognition (page 9)
cognitive psychologist (page 9)
comparative psychologist (page 21)
counseling psychologist (page 12)
cross-cultural psychology (page 11)
determinism (page 5)
developmental psychologist (page 9)
dualism (page 6)
ergonomist (or human factors specialist) (page 14)
evolutionary psychologist (page 10)
forensic psychologist (page 12)
free will (page 5)
functionalism (page 20)

industrial/organizational (I/O) psychology (page 13)
introspection (page 19)
learning and motivation (page 9)
mind–brain problem (page 6)
monism (page 6)
nature–nurture issue (page 7)
psychiatry (page 12)
psychoanalyst (page 12)
psychology (page 3)
psychophysical function (page 21)
school psychologist (page 14)
social psychologist (page 11)
structuralism (page 20)

 Suggestion for Further Reading

Sechenov, I. (1965). *Reflexes of the brain.* Cambridge, MA: MIT Press. (Original work published 1863). One of the first attempts to deal with behavior scientifically and still one of the clearest statements of the argument for determinism in human behavior.

 Web/Technology Resources

Student Companion Website

www.thomsonedu.com/psychology/kalat

Explore the Student Companion Website for Online Try-It-Yourself activities, practice quizzes, flashcards, and more! The companion site also has direct links to the following websites.

Careers in Psychology

www.drlynnfriedman.com/

Clinical psychologist Lynn Friedman offers advice on majoring in psychology, going to graduate school, and starting a career.

Nontraditional Careers in Psychology

www.apa.org/students

Advice and information for students from the American Psychological Association.

Podcasts

www.yorku.ca/christo/podcasts/

You can download weekly podcasts about the history of psychology.

Today in the History of Psychology

www.cwu.edu/~warren/today.html

Warren Street, at Central Washington University, offers a sample of events in the history of psychology for every day of the year. Pick a date, any date (as they say) from the History of Psychology Calendar and see what happened on that date. The APA sponsors this site, which is based on Street's book, *A Chronology of Noteworthy Events in American Psychology.*

More About the History of Psychology

www.uakron.edu/ahap

The University of Akron has assembled a museum of old psychology laboratory equipment and other mementos from psychology's past.

What Else Would You Like to Know?

psychclassics.yorku.ca

This online library offers many of the most famous books and articles ever written in psychology.

Annotated Links

www.psywww.com
www.psychology.org

Both of these sites provide annotated links to a vast array of information about psychology.

Scientific Methods in Psychology

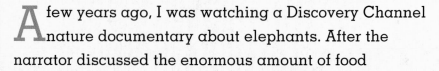

A few years ago, I was watching a Discovery Channel nature documentary about elephants. After the narrator discussed the enormous amount of food elephants eat, he started on their digestive system. He commented that the average elephant passes enough gas in a day to propel a car for 20 miles (32 km). I thought, "Wow, isn't that amazing!" and I told a couple of other people about it.

A while later I started to think, "Wait a minute. *Who measured that? And how?* Did someone really attach a balloon to an elephant's rear end and collect gas for 24 hours? And then put it into a car to see how far they could make it go? Was that a full-sized car or an economy car? City traffic or highway? How do they know they measured a typical elephant? Maybe they chose an extra gassy one. Did they determine the mean for a broad sample of elephants?" The more I thought about it, the more I doubted the claim about propelling a car on elephant gas.

"Oh, well," you might say. "Who cares?" You're right; how far you could propel a car on elephant gas doesn't matter. However, my point is not to ridicule the makers of this documentary but to ridicule *myself*. Remember, I said I told two people about this claim before I started to doubt it. For decades I have been teaching students to question assertions and evaluate the evidence, and here I was, uncritically accepting a silly statement and telling other people, who for all I know, may have gone on to tell other people who told still other people until someday it might become part of our folklore: "*They say* that you can propel a car 20 miles on a day's worth of elephant gas!" The point is that all of us yield to the temptation to accept unsupported claims, and we all need to discipline ourselves to question the evidence, especially for the interesting or exciting claims that we would most like to believe. This chapter concerns the evaluation of evidence in psychology.

Thinking Critically and Evaluating Evidence

- *How do scientists evaluate theories?*
- *Why are most scientists so skeptical of theories and claims that contradict our current understanding?*

The American comedian and politician Will Rogers once said that what worried him was not the things that people don't know but the things they *think* they know that really aren't so. You have heard people make countless claims about psychology, medicine, politics, religion, and so forth. But frequently, one confident claim contradicts another, so someone must believe something that isn't true. How can you know what is true?

One way is to rely on logical **deduction,** *the process of deriving a conclusion from premises already accepted.* Here is an example:

Premise 1. All human beings are mortal.
Premise 2. You are a human being.
Conclusion. Therefore, you are mortal.

Logical deduction gives us a definite conclusion but only if the premises are true. How do we know that you are a human being? Are we sure that all humans are mortal? Our knowledge about nature cannot come from deduction but only from **induction,** *the process of inferring a general principle from observations,* and nearly all scientific conclusions depend on induction. For example, we rely on induction to infer that you are a human because you resemble other humans, and we infer that all humans are mortal because so far we have not found an exception. But inductions are never completely certain (Pigliucci, 2003). The fact that something happened many times in the past does not guarantee that it will continue to happen. For that reason most scientists avoid the word *prove,* which sounds too final, except when they are talking about mathematical proofs. Neither deduction nor induction gives us complete certainty about the real world.

The lack of absolute certainty, however, does not mean that "you may as well believe anything you want" or that "anything has as much chance of being true as anything else." What it means is that people should state the evidence behind a conclusion and not just the conclusion itself. If you see the evidence, you can decide for yourself how confidently to hold the conclusion.

 CONCEPT CHECK

I. How does induction differ from deduction? (Check your answer on page 39.)

Evidence and Theory in Science

Scientists collect evidence to develop and test theories. People sometimes say "I have a theory . . ." when they mean they have a guess. A scientific **theory** is more than a guess; it is *an explanation that fits many observations and makes valid predictions.* A good theory helps us make sense of our experience. Fitting old observations into a theory is important, but predicting new observations is more important and more impressive (Lipton, 2005).

Can we ever be sure a theory is "true"? Philosopher Karl Popper argued that no observation can prove a theory to be correct. Consider the simple theory that every dropped object falls to the ground. We test by dropping an object, and sure enough, it falls. Did our observation prove the theory true? No, we showed only that this object fell at this time and place. So we try other objects at other times and places. As one object after another falls, we become more confident in the theory, but how many confirmations do we need before we are *certain?* Popper insisted that repeated confirmations never add up to certainty, and therefore, the purpose of research is to find which theories are *incorrect.* That is, research can *falsify* the incorrect theories, and a good theory is one that withstands all attempts to falsify it. It wins by a process of elimination.

A well-formed theory, therefore, is **falsifiable**—that is, *stated in such clear, precise terms that we can see what evidence would count against it* (if, of course, such evidence existed). For example, the law of gravity states that an object in a vacuum falls toward the earth with an acceleration of 981 cm/s^2. That is a precise prediction, and if the theory were incorrect, its falsity should be easy to demonstrate. This point is worth restating because "falsifiable" sounds like a bad thing. Falsifiable does not mean we actually have evidence against a theory. (If we did, it would be falsi*fied.*) Falsifiable means we can imagine what would be evidence against the theory.

A theory that is vague or badly stated is not falsifiable because we cannot imagine evidence that would count against it. For example, consider the claim that some people have psychic powers that enable them to get information that did not pass through their senses. What would count as evidence against that theory? Suppose you find that you are unable to read other people's minds or predict the future. Other people try, and they also fail. Do these failures disconfirm the theory? No. A theory that "some" people can do something under some (unstated) conditions is so vague that no result clearly contradicts it. If no conceivable evidence counts against a theory, it is too vague to be meaningful.

However, contrary to what Karl Popper wrote, some scientific statements can be verified but not falsified. It depends on how the statement is phrased. "All objects fall to the earth at an acceleration of 981 cm/s²" is falsifiable. "Some objects fall" is not falsifiable. If it *were* false, you could not *demonstrate* it to be false. Similarly, "all people demonstrate psychic powers in all circumstances" is falsifiable, but "some people have psychic powers sometimes" is not. "All people forget the events of early childhood" is a falsifiable statement; "some people forget the events of early childhood" is not.

So instead of insisting that all research is an effort to falsify some theory, a better idea is to use a phrase familiar to debaters and lawyers: Burden of proof *is the obligation to present evidence to support one's claim.* In a criminal trial, the burden of proof is on the prosecution. If the prosecution does not make a convincing case, the defendant goes free. The reason is that the state should be able to find good evidence of guilt, but in many cases innocent defendants cannot demonstrate their innocence.

Similarly, in science the burden of proof is on anyone who makes a claim that should be demonstrable if it is true. The obligation is to verify a claim that should be demonstrable if true (e.g., "some people have psychic powers") and to try to falsify any claim that one doubts (e.g., "all people forget the events of early childhood"). Scientists can accept either a statement that is verified by evidence or one that resists all attempts to falsify it.

CRITICAL THINKING

A STEP FURTHER

Burden of Proof

If one person claims that intelligent life exists in outer space and someone else doubts it, which side has the burden of proof? When finding evidence to support either view is difficult, what is a reasonable conclusion?

Steps for Gathering and Evaluating Evidence

The word *science* derives from a Latin word meaning "knowledge." Science is distinguished from most other human endeavors by the fact that scientists generally agree on how to evaluate theories. Whereas most people can hardly imagine evidence that would change their religious or political views, scientists can generally imagine evidence that would disconfirm their favorite theories. (Oh, not always, I admit. Some can be stubborn.)

In that sense psychologists—most of them, anyway—follow the scientific method. Obviously, our knowledge of psychology lacks the precision of physics or chemistry. But psychologists do generally agree on what constitutes good evidence.

Research ordinarily begins with careful observations. The sciences of astronomy and anatomy are based almost entirely on observation and description. In psychology, too, researchers observe what people do, under what circumstances, and how one person differs from another. For example, in a study on laughter, Robert Provine (2000) simply recorded who laughed and when and where.

Eventually, we want to go beyond observations to try to explain the patterns we see. To evaluate competing explanations for some set of observations, researchers collect new data, guided by a hypothesis, which is *a clear predictive statement* such as "people who watch violent television programs will act more violently." Researchers form a hypothesis, devise a method to test it, collect results, and then interpret the results (Figure 2.1). Most articles in scientific publications follow this sequence too. In each of the remaining chapters of this book, you will find at least one example of a psychological study described in a section entitled "What's the Evidence?" In this chapter the example concerns the question of how televised violence relates to aggressive behavior.

Hypothesis

A hypothesis—such as "watching violence leads to more violent behavior"—can be based on preliminary observations, such as noticing that some children who watch much violence on television are themselves aggressive. It can also be based on a larger theory, such as "children tend to imitate the behavior they see, so those who watch a great deal of violence on television will themselves become more violent." A hypothesis can also emerge from trends in society. It has been estimated that the average child, before graduating from elementary school, will have watched 8,000 murders and 100,000 other violent acts on television (Bushman & Anderson, 2001) in addition to countless violent acts in video games (Anderson & Bushman, 2001).

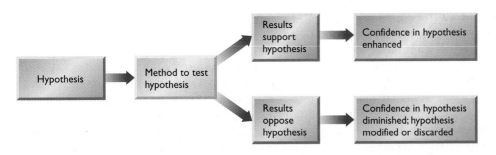

FIGURE 2.1 An experiment tests the predictions that follow from a hypothesis. Results either support the hypothesis or indicate a need to revise or abandon it.

Presumably, all those experiences must produce *some* effect.

Method

Any hypothesis could be tested in many ways, and almost any method has its strengths and weaknesses. The next module considers the main categories of methods in more detail. One way to test the effects of violent television shows would be to examine whether children who watch more violent programs engage in more violent behavior. The main limit of this approach is that we cannot conclude cause and effect: Watching violence may lead to violence, but it is also likely that people who are already violent like to watch violence. Another method is to see whether violent behavior increases in some geographical region after an increase in the availability of televised violence. However, other social, economic, and political events may occur at the same time, and we cannot separate the effects of televised violence from the other factors. A third method is to take a set of children, such as those attending a summer camp, let some watch violent programs while others watch nonviolent programs, and see whether the two groups differ in their violent behaviors. That kind of study can justify a cause-and-effect conclusion if indeed the groups differ (Parke, Berkowitz, Leyens, West, & Sebastian, 1977). The limitation is that the results concern only short-term exposure compared to what children watch over many years.

Because any method has strengths and weaknesses, researchers try to use a variety of methods. A conclusion based on several different kinds of studies is more certain than one based on a single method.

Results

Fundamental to any research is measuring the outcome. A phenomenon such as "violent behavior" can be especially tricky to measure. (How do we decide what is *real* violence and what is just playfulness? Do threats count? Does verbal abuse?) It is important for an investigator to follow clear rules for making measurements. After making the measurements, the investigator must determine whether the results are impressive enough to call for an explanation.

Interpretation

The final task is to determine what the results mean. If they clearly contradict the hypothesis, researchers should either abandon or modify the original hypothesis. (Maybe it applies only to certain kinds of people or only under certain circumstances.) If the results match the prediction, investigators gain confidence in their hypothesis, but they also need to consider other hypotheses that fit the results.

Replicability

Most scientific researchers are scrupulously honest in reporting their results. Distortions of data are rare and scandalous. However, despite their customary honesty, scientists do not accept the statement "trust me" or "take my word for it." Anyone who reports a result in a scientific article also reports the methods in enough detail that other people could repeat the study, and those who doubt the result are invited to do so. If they get the same results, they presumably will be convinced. But if they cannot, they should not trust the original finding. Indeed, one reason most scientists are so honest is that they know that they can get caught if someone tries to repeat their study and fails.

Replicable results are *those that anyone can obtain, at least approximately, by following the same procedures,* and scientists insist on replicable results. Consider an example of a nonreplicable result. In 1993 a team of researchers had several groups of young people listen to a Mozart sonata, a "relaxation tape," or silence and then take some psychological tests. They reported that the people who listened to Mozart performed better than the others on a test of spatial reasoning (Rauscher, Shaw, & Ky, 1993). The implication was that listening to music with a particular level of complexity might promote ideal brain functioning.

Wouldn't it be great if we could increase people's intelligence that easily? Unfortunately, the effect has not been replicable. Several other researchers found virtually no difference between the Mozart listeners and the other groups (Chabris, 1999; Steele, Bass, &

Crook, 1999). Two studies found mild improvements after any pleasant, relaxing experience but no evidence that Mozart's music was special (Nantais & Schellenberg, 1999; W. F. Thompson, Schellenberg, & Husain, 2001).

So, what conclusion should we draw? When the results are inconsistent, we draw no conclusions at all. Until or unless someone finds conditions under which the phenomenon is replicable (consistently repeatable), we do not take it seriously. This rule may seem harsh, but it is our best defense against error.

Sometimes, however, an effect is small but real. For example, one method of teaching might work better than another, but the effect is small and has to compete with many other influences, so we might not see it in every study. The same is true for research on how to run an organization, how to deliver psychotherapy, and many other complex human behaviors. When we are looking at small trends in the data, we can combine the results of many studies to get an approximate measure of the size of the effect. A **meta-analysis** *combines the results of many studies and analyzes them as though they were all one very large study.* In most cases a meta-analysis will also determine which variations in procedure increase or decrease the effects.

Criteria for Evaluating Scientific Hypotheses and Theories

After investigators collect mounds of evidence and identify the replicable findings, they compare the results to what their hypotheses or theories had predicted. One goal of scientific research is to establish theories. A good theory starts with as few assumptions as possible and leads to many correct predictions. In that way it reduces the amount of information we must remember. For example, in chapter 4 you will read about the trichromatic theory of color vision. This theory asked people to assume—more than a century before anyone could demonstrate it—that the eye has three kinds of receptors, sensitive to different wavelengths of light. That theory enabled scientists to explain and predict many aspects of color vision.

What do we do if we encounter several theories that fit the known facts? For example, suppose you did not wake up at your usual time, and three friends offer these competing explanations:

- Your alarm clock didn't work.
- You slept through the alarm.
- Space aliens kidnapped you and then returned you to your room after the alarm went off.

All three explanations fit the observation, but we don't consider them on an equal basis. *When given a choice among hypotheses or theories that all seem to fit the facts, scientists prefer the one whose assumptions are fewer, simpler, or more consistent with other well-established theories.* This is known as the principle of **parsimony** (literally "stinginess") or *Occam's razor* (after the philosopher William of Occam). The principle of parsimony is a conservative idea: We stick with ideas that work, and we don't introduce new assumptions (e.g., space aliens) unless we have strong evidence to support them.

Parsimony and Degrees of Open-Mindedness

The principle of parsimony tells us to adhere to what we already believe, to resist radically new hypotheses. You might protest: "Shouldn't we remain open-minded to new possibilities?" Yes, if open-mindedness means a willingness to consider proper evidence, but not if it means that "anything has as much chance of being true as anything else." The stronger the reasons behind our current opinion, the more evidence we should need before replacing it. Consider two examples.

Visitors from outer space. Many, probably most, physicists and astronomers doubt that visitors from other planets have ever landed on Earth or ever will. To get from one solar system to another in less than thousands of years, you need to travel at nearly the speed of light. At that speed a collision with a dust particle would be catastrophic. However, we could imagine alien life forms whose biology enables them to survive a journey of thousands of years or whose technology permits greater speed than seems possible for the kind of travel we know. So we remain open-minded to new evidence. If weird-looking beings stepped out of an odd-looking spacecraft, we should consider the possibility of a hoax by other people, but solid evidence could persuade us of visitors from outer space.

Perpetual motion machines. A "perpetual motion machine" is one that generates more energy than it uses. For centuries people have attempted and failed to develop such a machine. (Figure 2.2 shows one example.) The U.S. Patent Office is officially closed-minded on this issue, refusing even to consider patent applications for such machines, because a perpetual motion machine violates what physicists call *the second law of thermodynamics.*

According to that law, within a closed system, entropy (disorder) can never decrease. A more casual statement is that any work wastes energy, and therefore, we need to keep adding energy to keep any machine going. Could the second law of thermodynamics

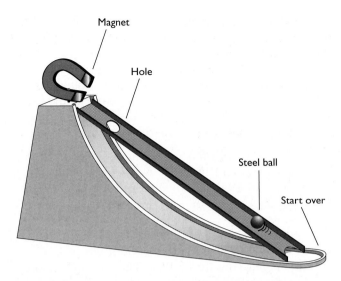

FIGURE 2.2 A proposed perpetual motion machine: After the magnet pulls the metal ball up the inclined plane, the ball falls through the hole and returns to its starting point, from which the magnet will again pull it up. Can you see why this device is sure to fail? (See answer A on page 39.)

be wrong? I recommend only the slightest amount of open-mindedness. It is supported by an enormous amount of data plus logical arguments about why it must be true. If someone shows you what appears to be a perpetual motion machine, look carefully for a hidden battery or other power source—that is, some simple, parsimonious explanation. Even if you don't find a hidden power source, it is more likely that you overlooked one than that the second law of thermodynamics is wrong. A claim as extraordinary as a perpetual motion machine requires extraordinary evidence.

What does this discussion have to do with psychology? Sometimes, people claim spectacular results that would seem impossible. Although it is only fair to examine the evidence behind such claims, it is also reasonable to maintain a skeptical attitude and to look as closely as possible for a simple, parsimonious explanation of the results. We shall consider two examples.

Applying Parsimony: Clever Hans, the Amazing Horse

Early in the 20th century, Mr. von Osten, a German mathematics teacher, set out to prove that his horse, Hans, had great intellectual abilities, particularly in arithmetic. To teach Hans arithmetic, he first showed him a single object, said "one," and lifted Hans's foot once. He raised Hans's foot twice for two objects and so on. Eventually, when von Osten presented a group of objects, Hans learned to tap his foot by himself, and with practice he managed to tap the correct number of times. With more practice it was no longer necessary for Hans to see the objects. Von Osten would just

call out a number, and Hans would tap the appropriate number of times.

Mr. von Osten moved on to addition and then to subtraction, multiplication, and division. Hans caught on quickly, soon responding with 90 to 95% accuracy. Then von Osten began touring Germany; he asked questions and Hans tapped out the answers. Hans's abilities grew until he could add fractions, convert fractions to decimals or vice versa, do simple algebra, tell time to the minute, and give the values of all German coins. Using a letter-to-number code, he could spell out the names of objects and even identify musical notes such as B-flat. (Evidently, Hans had perfect pitch.) He responded correctly even when questions were put to him by people other than von Osten, in unfamiliar places, with von Osten nowhere in sight.

Given this evidence, many people were ready to believe that Hans had great intellectual powers. But others sought a more parsimonious explanation. Enter Oskar Pfungst. Pfungst (1911) discovered that Hans could not answer a question correctly unless the questioner had calculated the answer first. Apparently, the horse was somehow getting the answers from the questioner. Next Pfungst found that Hans was highly accurate when the questioner stood in plain sight, but almost always wrong when he could not see the questioner.

Eventually, Pfungst observed that anyone who asked Hans a question would lean forward to watch Hans's foot. Hans had simply learned to start tapping whenever someone stood next to his right forefoot and leaned forward. As soon as Hans had given the correct number of taps, the questioner would give a slight upward jerk of the head and change facial expression in anticipation that this might be the last tap. (Even

After Pfungst, 1911, in Fernald, 1984

▌ Clever Hans and his owner, Mr. von Osten, demonstrated that the horse could answer complex mathematical questions with great accuracy. The question was, "How?"

skeptical scientists who tested Hans did this involuntarily. After all, they thought, wouldn't it be exciting if Hans got it right?) Hans simply continued tapping until he received that cue.

In short, Hans was indeed a clever horse, but we do not believe that he understood mathematics. Note that Pfungst did not demonstrate that Hans *didn't* understand mathematics. Pfungst merely demonstrated that he could explain Hans's behavior in the simple, parsimonious terms of responses to facial expressions, and therefore, no one needed to assume that Hans did anything more complex. The same principle applies in general: We prefer a simple explanation over one that requires new assumptions. We adopt new assumptions only when the simple and familiar ones clearly fail.

Applying Parsimony: Extrasensory Perception

The possibility of **extrasensory perception (ESP)** has long been controversial in psychology. Supporters of extrasensory perception claim that *at least some people, at least some of the time, can acquire information without using any sense organ and without receiving any form of physical energy.* For example, supporters of this view claim that people with ESP can identify someone else's thoughts (telepathy) just as accurately from a great distance as from an adjacent room, in apparent violation of the inverse-square law of physics, and that their accuracy is not diminished by a lead shield that would interrupt any known form of energy. Some ESP supporters also claim that certain people can perceive inanimate objects that are hidden from sight (clairvoyance), predict the future (precognition), and influence such physical events as a roll of dice by sheer mental concentration (psychokinesis).

Acceptance of any of these claims would require us not only to overhaul some major concepts in psychology but also to discard the most fundamental tenets of physics, even the idea that we live in a universe of matter and energy. What evidence is there for ESP?

Anecdotes

One kind of evidence consists of anecdotes—people's reports of isolated events, such as an amaz-

Master magician Lance Burton can make people and animals seem to suddenly appear, disappear, float in the air, or do other things that we know are impossible. Even if we don't know how he accomplishes these feats, we take it for granted that they are magic tricks, based on methods of misleading the audience. The same assumption should apply when someone claims to be using psychic powers.

© AP/Wide World Photos

ing coincidence or a dream or hunch that comes true. Such experiences may seem impressive, but they are not scientific evidence. Sooner or later, occasional bizarre coincidences are almost sure to occur, and people tend to remember them. For example, as you have probably heard, people have found many parallels between the lives of Presidents Abraham Lincoln and John Kennedy, including the following:

- Lincoln was elected to Congress in 1846 and elected president in 1860; Kennedy was elected to Congress in 1946 and elected president in 1960.
- The names Lincoln and Kennedy each contain seven letters.
- Both Lincoln and Kennedy were shot in the head on a Friday, while seated next to their wives.
- Lincoln was shot in the Ford Theater, and Kennedy was shot while in a Ford Lincoln.
- Both were succeeded in office by a southerner named Johnson.

The problem is, if you try hard enough, you can find parallels for many pairs of people. Consider Attila the Hun and former U.S. President Harry S. Truman:

- Attila the Hun was king of the Huns from 445 until 453; Harry S. Truman was president of the United States from 1945 until 1953.
- Both Attila and Truman took office upon the death of the previous leader; both were succeeded in office by a military general.
- The initials for "The Hun" are T. H. The initials for "Harry Truman" are H. T.
- Both the name Attila the Hun and Harry S. Truman consist of 12 letters and 2 spaces.
- Both had a middle name that is meaningless out of context ("The" and "S").

Pick two people in history, or two people you know, and see how many "uncanny" similarities you can find.

Try It Yourself

Furthermore, we remember and talk about the hunches and dreams that come true but forget the others. People hardly ever say, "Strangest thing! I had a dream, but then nothing like it actually happened!" People often exaggerate the coincidences that occur and some-

Photo © Palace of Versailles, France/ET Archive, London/SuperStock

1. The great man will be struck down in the day by a thunderbolt. An evil deed, foretold by the bearer of a petition. According to the prediction another falls at night time. Conflict at Reims, London, and pestilence in Tuscany.

2. When the fish that travels over both land and sea is cast up on to the shore by a great wave, its shape foreign, smooth, and frightful. From the sea the enemies soon reach the walls.

3. The bird of prey flying to the left, before battle is joined with the French, he makes preparations. Some will regard him as good, others bad or uncertain. The weaker party will regard him as a good omen.

4. Shortly afterwards, not a very long interval, a great tumult will be raised by land and sea. The naval battles will be greater than ever. Fires, creatures which will make more tumult.

FIGURE 2.3 According to the followers of Nostradamus, each of these statements is a specific prophecy of a 20th-century event (Cheetham, 1973). Can you figure out what the prophecies mean? Compare your answers to answer B on page 39.

times misremember them. We could evaluate anecdotal evidence only if people recorded their hunches and dreams *before* the predicted events and then determined how many unlikely predictions actually came to pass.

You might try keeping track of psychics' predictions in tabloid newspapers for the new year. By the end of the year, how many came true? How many would you expect to come true just by chance? (The latter number is, of course, difficult to estimate.)

You may have heard of the "prophet Nostradamus," a 16th-century French writer who allegedly predicted many events of later centuries. Figure 2.3 presents four samples of his writings. All of his "predictions" are at this level of vagueness. After something happens, people imaginatively reinterpret his writings to fit the event. (If we don't know what a prediction means until *after* it occurs, is it really a prediction?)

 CONCEPT CHECK

2. How could someone scientifically evaluate the accuracy of Nostradamus's predictions? (Check your answer on page 39.)

Professional Psychics

Various stage performers claim to read other people's minds and to perform other amazing feats. One is The Amazing Kreskin, who has consistently denied doing anything supernatural. He prefers to talk of his "extremely sensitive" rather than "extrasensory" perception (Kreskin, 1991). Still, part of his success as a performer comes from allowing people to believe

he has powers that defy explanation.

After carefully observing Kreskin and others, David Marks and Richard Kammann (1980) concluded that they used the same kinds of deception commonly employed in magic acts. For example, Kreskin sometimes begins his act by asking the audience to read his mind. Let's try to duplicate this trick right now: Try to read my mind. I am thinking of a number between 1 and 50. Both digits are odd numbers, but they are not the same. For example, it could be 15 but it could not be 11. (These are the instructions Kreskin gives.) Have you chosen a number? Please do.

All right, my number was 37. Did you think of 37? If not, how about 35? You see, I started to think 35 and then changed my mind, so you might have got 35.

If you successfully "read my mind," are you impressed? Don't be. At first, it seemed that you had a lot of numbers to choose from (1 to 50), but by the end of the instructions, you had only a few. The first digit had to be 1 or 3, and the second had to be 1, 3, 5, 7, or 9. You eliminated 11 and 33 because both digits are the same, and you probably eliminated 15 because I cited it as a possible example. That leaves only seven possibilities. Most people like to stay far away from the example given and tend to avoid the highest and lowest possible choices. That leaves 37 as the most likely choice and 35 as the second most likely.

Second act: Kreskin asks the audience to write down something they are thinking about while he walks along the aisles talking. Then, back on stage, he "reads people's minds." He might say something like, "Someone is thinking about his mother . . ." In any large crowd, someone is bound to shout, "Yes, that's me. You read my mind!" On occasion he describes something that someone has written out in great detail. That person generally turns out to be someone sitting along the aisle where Kreskin was walking.

After a variety of other tricks (see Marks & Kammann, 1980), Kreskin goes backstage while the local mayor or some other dignitary hides Kreskin's paycheck somewhere in the audience. Then Kreskin comes back, walks up and down the aisles and across the rows, and eventually shouts, "The check is here!" The rule is that if he guesses wrong, then he does not get paid. (He hardly ever misses.)

This is an impressive trick, and even more impressive if you're part of the audience. How does he do it? Very simply, it is a Clever Hans trick. Kreskin studies people's faces. Most people want him to find the check, so they get more excited as he gets close to it and more disappointed or distressed if he moves away. In effect they are saying, "Now you're getting closer" and "Now you're moving away." At last he closes in on the check.

Of course, someone always objects, "Well, maybe you've explained what some professional psychics do. But there's this other guy you haven't investigated yet. Maybe he really does possess psychic powers." Well, maybe. But until there is solid evidence to the contrary, it is simpler (more parsimonious) to assume that other performers are also using illusion and deception.

Experiments

Because stage performances and anecdotal events always take place under uncontrolled conditions, we cannot determine the probability of coincidence or the possibility of deception. Laboratory experiments provide the only evidence about ESP worth serious consideration.

For example, consider the *ganzfeld* procedure (from German words meaning "entire field"). A "sender" is given a photo or film selected at random from four possibilities, and a "receiver" in another room is asked to describe the sender's thoughts and images. Typically, the receiver wears half Ping-Pong balls over the eyes and listens to static noise through earphones to minimize normal stimuli that might overpower the presumably weaker extrasensory stimuli (Figure 2.4). Later, a judge examines a transcript of what the receiver said and compares it to the four photos or films, determining which one it matches most closely. On the average it should match the target about one in four times. If a receiver "hits" more often than one in four, we can calculate the probability of accidentally doing that well. (ESP researchers, or parapsychologists, use a variety of other experimental procedures, but in each case the goal is to determine whether someone can gain more information than could be explained by chance without using his or her senses.)

Over the decades ESP researchers reported many apparent examples of telepathy or clairvoyance, none of which were replicable under well-controlled conditions. In the case of the ganzfeld studies, one review reported that 6 of the 10 laboratories using this method found positive results (Bem & Honorton, 1994); the authors suggested that here was, at last, a replicable phenomenon.

However, 14 later studies from 7 laboratories failed to find evidence that the receiver chose the target stimulus any more often than one would expect by chance (Milton & Wiseman, 1999). In short, the

FIGURE 2.4 In the ganzfeld procedure, a "receiver," who is deprived of most normal sensory information, tries to describe the photo or film that a "sender" is examining.

ganzfeld phenomenon, like other previous claims of ESP, is nonreplicable.

The lack of replicability is one major reason to be skeptical of ESP, but it is not the only one. The other is parsimony. If someone claims that a horse does mathematics or a person reads the minds of other people far away, we should search thoroughly for a simpler explanation and adopt a radically new explanation only if the evidence compels us. Even then we cannot accept a new explanation until someone specifies it clearly. Saying that some result demonstrates "an amazing ability that science cannot explain" is not a testable theory.

Would you like to test your own ability to find a parsimonious explanation for apparent mind reading? Go to **www.thomsonedu.com/psychology/kalat**. Navigate to the student website, then to the Online Try It Yourself section, and click Psychic Phenomenon.

Online Try It Yourself

IN CLOSING

Scientific Thinking in Psychology

What have we learned about science in general? Science does not deal with proof or certainty. All scientific conclusions are tentative and subject to revision. The history of any scientific field contains examples of theories that were once widely accepted and later revised. Nevertheless, this tentativeness does not imply a willingness to abandon well-established theories without excellent reasons.

Scientists always prefer the most parsimonious theory. Before they will accept any claim that requires a major new assumption, they insist that it be supported by replicable experiments that rule out simpler explanations and by a new theory that is clearly superior to the theory it replaces. ∎

Summary

- *Uncertainty in science.* Neither deduction nor induction can give us completely certain information about the real world. Therefore, scientific conclusions are tentative, and one should always explain the reasons for a conclusion and not just the conclusion itself. (page 31)
- *Burden of proof.* In any dispute the side that should be capable of presenting clear evidence has the obligation to do so. (page 32)
- *Scientific approach to psychology.* Psychology shares with other scientific fields a commitment to scientific methods, including criteria for evaluating theories. (page 32)
- *Steps in a scientific study.* A scientific study goes through the following sequence of steps: hypothesis, method, results, and interpretation. Because almost any study is subject to more than one possible interpretation, we base our conclusions on a pattern of results from many studies. The results of a given study are taken seriously only if other investigators can replicate them. (page 32)
- *Criteria for evaluating theories.* A good theory agrees with observations and leads to correct predictions of new information. All else being equal, scientists prefer the theory that relies on simpler assumptions. (page 34)

- *Skepticism about extrasensory perception.* Psychologists carefully scrutinize claims of extrasensory perception because the evidence reported so far has been unreplicable and because the scientific approach includes a search for parsimonious explanations. (page 36)

Answers to Concept Checks

1. Induction is the process of inferring a general principle from a series of observations, such as "Every dropped object falls." Deduction is the process of deriving a conclusion from premises already given or assumed, such as "If A, then B. If B, then C. Therefore, if A, then C." (page 31)
2. To evaluate Nostradamus's predictions, we would need to ask someone to tell us precisely what his predictions mean before the events they supposedly predict had transpired. Then we would ask someone else to estimate the likelihood of those events. Eventually, we would compare the accuracy of the predictions to the advance estimates of their probability. (page 36)

Answers to Other Questions in the Module

A. Any magnet strong enough to pull the metal ball up the inclined plane would not release the ball when it reached the hole at the top. (page 35)
B. The prophecies of Nostradamus, as interpreted by Cheetham (1973), refer to the following: (1) the assassinations of John F. Kennedy and Robert F. Kennedy, (2) Polaris ballistic missiles shot from submarines, (3) Hitler's invasion of France, and (4) World War II. (page 37)

Conducting Psychological Research

- *How do psychological researchers study processes that are difficult to define?*
- *How do they design their research, and what special problems can arise?*
- *How do psychologists confront the ethical problems of conducting research?*

A radio talk show once featured two psychologists as guests. The first argued that day care was bad for children because she had seen in her clinical practice many sadly disturbed adults who had been left in day care as children. The second psychologist, researcher Sandra Scarr (1997), pointed out that the clinician had no way of knowing about the well-adjusted adults who had also been left in day care as children. Scarr then described eight well-designed research studies, concerning thousands of children in four countries, each of which found no evidence that day care produced any harmful consequences.

Which of these types of evidence strikes you as stronger? To Scarr's dismay, the people who called in to the program seemed just as convinced by the anecdotes of disturbed people as by the extensive research studies, and several callers described anecdotes of their own.

In the first module, we considered how to evaluate hypotheses and theories, presuming that we already had good research results. Here, we examine the methods of doing research and some of the special problems of applying scientific methods to psychological issues.

General Principles of Psychological Research

The primary goal of this module is not to prepare you to conduct psychological research but to help you be an intelligent interpreter of research. When you hear about some new study, you should be able to ask pertinent questions to decide how good the evidence is and what conclusion (if any) it justifies.

Although we shall review such basic procedures for how to do an experiment, many of the ideas are probably familiar to you from courses in other sciences. However, psychology faces some special problems that chemistry and physics do not. In chemistry one water molecule is about the same as another, but one person is not the same as another. Participants in psychological research know they are being watched, and often, the fact of being watched changes their behavior. Perhaps the biggest difference is measurement. Chemists and physicists long ago established highly accurate measurements, whereas psychologists are still struggling to improve their measurements of many important items.

Operational Definitions

Before we can start any research study, we need to specify what we are trying to measure. Suppose a physicist asks you to measure the effect of temperature on the length of an iron bar. You ask, "What do we *really mean* by temperature?" The physicist might reply, "Don't worry about it. Temperature *really is* the rate of motion of molecules, but for practical purposes what I mean by temperature is the reading on the thermometer."

We need the same strategy in psychology. If we want to measure the effect of hunger on students' ability to concentrate, we could spend hours attempting to define what hunger and concentration really are, or we could say, "Let's measure hunger by the hours since the last meal and concentration by the length of time that the student continues reading without stopping to do something else." By doing so we are using an **operational definition**, *a definition that specifies the operations (or procedures) used to produce or measure something, ordinarily a way to give it a numerical value.* An operational definition is not like a dictionary definition. You might object that "time since the last meal" is not what hunger really *is*. Of course not, but the reading on a thermometer is also not what temperature really is. An operational definition just tells you how to measure something. It enables us to get on with research.

Suppose someone wants to investigate whether children who watch violence on television are likely to behave aggressively themselves. In this case the investigator needs operational definitions for *televised violence* and *aggressive behavior*. For example, the investigator might define *televised violence* as "the number of acts shown in which one person physically injures or attempts to injure another person." According to this definition, a 20-minute stalking scene would count as much as a quick attack. Threatening a murder would not count. An unsuccessful attempt to injure someone would count, but verbal insults would not (because they would not inflict physical injury). This definition might not be the best, but at least it states how one investigator measures violence so that other people could try to replicate the results. If researchers using this definition cannot get consistent results, they can try some other operational definition.

Similarly, the investigator needs an operational definition of *aggressive behavior.* To define it as "the number of murders or criminal assaults committed within 24 hours after watching a particular television program" would be an operational definition but not a practical one because (we hope!) almost everyone would have a score of zero. A better operational definition of *aggressive behavior* specifies more likely acts. For example, the experimenter might place a large plastic doll in front of a young child and record how often the child punches it.

Consider another example: What is love? Never mind what it *really is.* If we want to study love, we need to measure it, and therefore, we need an operational definition. One possibility would be "how many hours you are willing to spend with another person who asked you to stay nearby."

 CONCEPT CHECK

3. Which of the following is an operational definition of intelligence?
   a. the ability to comprehend relationships,
   b. a score on an IQ test,
   c. the ability to survive in the real world, or
   d. the product of the cerebral cortex of the brain.
4. What would you propose as an operational definition of friendliness? (Check your answers on page 55.)

Population Samples

After defining the variables, the next step is to identify individuals to study. The **population** *is the group of individuals to whom we hope our conclusions will apply.* Researchers generally wish to draw conclusions that apply to a large population, such as all 3-year-olds or all people with depression or even all human beings. Because it is not practical to examine everyone in the population, researchers study a *sample* of people and assume that the results for the sample apply to the whole population. For example, pollsters ask 1,000 or so voters which candidate they support and then project the probable result for the entire city, state, or country.

In some cases almost any sample is satisfactory. For example, investigators interested in basic sensory processes do not worry much about sampling problems. The eyes, ears, and other sense organs operate similarly for all people, with obvious exceptions of those with visual or hearing impairments. Similarly, many of the principles of hunger, thirst, and so forth are similar enough among all people that an investigator can do research with almost any group—students in an introductory psychology class, for example. Indeed, for some purposes researchers could use laboratory animals. We refer to *a group chosen because of its ease of study* as a **convenience sample.**

However, college students are atypical in certain ways. Usually, the results obtained from college students resemble those for other populations, but occasionally, they do not (Peterson, 2001). For example, many of today's U.S. college students have spent most of their lives indoors and are far less familiar with common animals and plants than are the uneducated farmers and fishers of other countries (Medin & Altran, 2004). If you wanted to contrast men's behavior with women's, the similarities and differences you found on a college campus would not apply to the rest of the world (Wood & Eagly, 2002). To study any behavior that varies strikingly from one group to another, we need a broader sample of people.

A **representative sample** *closely resembles the population in its percentage of males and females, Blacks and Whites, young and old, city dwellers and farmers, or whatever other characteristics are likely to affect the results.* To get a representative sample of the people in a given region, an investigator would first determine what percentage of the residents belong to each category and then select people to match those percentages. Of course, a sample that is representative in some regards might not be representative in other ways, such as religion or education.

In a **random sample,** *every individual in the population has an equal chance of being selected.* For example, to produce a random sample of Toronto residents, an investigator might start with a map of Toronto and select a certain number of city blocks at random, randomly select one house from each of those blocks, and then randomly choose one person from each of those households. Truly random sampling is difficult. Even after the difficult process of choosing a random sample, not every chosen person will agree to participate. However, a random sample has one big advantage: The larger a random sample, the smaller the probability that its results differ substantially from the whole population.

A researcher who wants to compare one group to another should use the same kind of sample from both groups. Every year the newspapers report the average SAT scores for different American states. The problem

❚ A psychological researcher can test generalizations about human behavior by comparing people from different cultures.

cultures, it can be useful to study **cross-cultural samples,** *groups of people from at least two cultures.* For example, consider questions about human nature: Do people learn facial expressions of emotions, or are the expressions built-in? Is a financially prosperous society likely to be a happy society? Are people biologically predisposed to marriage? Cross-cultural data are critical for dealing with issues such as these. Table 2.1 reviews the major types of samples.

Cross-cultural sampling is difficult, however (Matsumoto, 1994). Obvious problems include the expense, language barriers, and convincing members of another culture to answer personal questions and cooperate with unfamiliar kinds of tests. Also, imagine trying to compare "typical" behaviors between two cultures. There may be so much diversity within each that the comparison between them becomes almost meaningless.

is that the samples are different. In some states, most high school students take the SAT. In states where the in-state schools require the ACT instead, students take the SAT only if they plan to apply to out-of-state schools such as MIT, the Ivy League universities, and so forth. We cannot meaningfully compare the results for different states if we have a narrow sample from some states and a wide sample from others.

What if we want to draw generalizations about all humans, everywhere? If you imagine trying to get a random sample of all the people on the planet, you will quickly realize the impracticality. Nevertheless, although we cannot expect to study people from all

 CONCEPT CHECK

5. Suppose I compare the interests and abilities of male and female students at my university. If I find a consistent difference, can I assume that it represents a difference between men and women in general? (Obviously, the answer is no, or else I would not have asked the question.) Why not? (Check your answer on page 55.)

TABLE 2.1 Types of Samples

Sample	Individuals Included	Advantages and Disadvantages
Convenience sample	Anyone who is available	Easiest to get, but results may not generalize to the whole population
Representative sample	Same percentage of male/female, White/Black, etc. as the whole population	Results probably similar to whole population, although sample may be representative in some ways and not others
Random sample	Everyone in population has same chance of being chosen	Difficult to get this kind of sample, but it is best suited for generalizing to the whole population
Cross-cultural sample	People from different cultures	Difficulties include language barriers, cooperation problems, etc., but essential for studying many issues

Eliminating the Influence of Expectations

Ethically, researchers cannot study people without first getting their permission, so human research participants know they are being studied. Their behavior is influenced by what they think the experimenters expect. The experimenters are human beings too, and how they record the data may reflect their own expectations. Good research requires finding ways to reduce the influence of all these expectations.

Experimenter Bias and Blind Studies

Experimenter bias is *the tendency of an experimenter (unintentionally, in most cases) to distort or misperceive the results of an experiment based on the expected outcome.* Imagine that you, as a psychological investigator, are testing the hypothesis that left-handed children are more creative than right-handed children. (I don't know why you would be testing this silly hypothesis, but suppose you are.) If the results support your hypothesis, you expect to be on your way to fame and success as a psychology researcher. Now you see a left-handed child do something, and you are trying to decide whether it counts as "creative." You want to be fair. You don't want your hypothesis to influence your decision about whether to consider the act creative. Just try to ignore your hypothesis.

To overcome the potential source of error in an investigator's bias, psychologists prefer to use a **blind observer**—that is, *an observer who can record data without knowing what the researcher has predicted.* For example, we might ask someone to record creative acts by a group of children without any hint that we are interested in the effects of handedness. Because blind observers do not know the hypothesis being tested, they can record their observations more fairly.

Ideally, the experimenter will conceal the procedure from the participants as well. For example, suppose experimenters gave one group of children a pill that was supposed to increase their creativity. If those children knew the prediction, maybe they would act differently just because of their expectation. Or maybe the children not receiving the pill would be disappointed and therefore not try hard.

The best solution, therefore, is to give the drug to one group and a **placebo** (*a pill with no known pharmacological effects*) to another group without telling the children which pill they are taking or what results the experimenter expects. The advantage of this kind of study is that any difference between the two groups cannot be due to their expectations.

In a **single-blind study,** *either the observer or the participants are unaware of which participants received which treatment* (Table 2.2). In a **double-blind study,** *both the observer and the participants are un-*

aware. Of course, the experimenter who organized the study would need to keep records of which participants received which procedure. (A study in which *everyone* loses track of the procedure is known jokingly as "triple blind.")

TABLE 2.2 Single-Blind and Double-Blind Studies

Who is aware of which participants are in which group?

	Experimenter Who Organized the Study	Observer	Participants
Single-blind	aware	unaware	aware
Single-blind	aware	aware	unaware
Double-blind	aware	unaware	unaware

Demand Characteristics

Many people who know they are part of an experiment figure out, or think they have figured out, the point of the experiment. Sometimes, those expectations produce big effects.

To illustrate, in some well-known studies on sensory deprivation that were popular in the 1950s, people were placed in an apparatus that minimized vision, hearing, touch, and other sensory stimulation (Figure 2.5). Many participants reported that this procedure led to hallucinations, anxiety, and difficulty

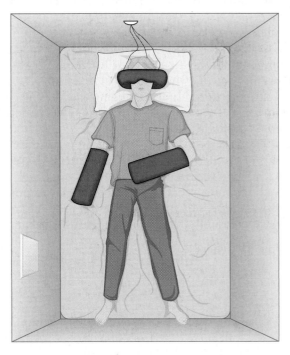

FIGURE 2.5 In experiments on sensory deprivation, someone who is deprived of most sensory stimulation reports disorientation and sometimes hallucinations. But might these results depend partly on people's expectations of distorted experience?

concentrating. Now suppose you have heard about these studies, and you agree to participate in an experiment described as a study of "meaning deprivation." The experimenter asks you about your medical history and then asks you to sign a form agreeing not to sue if you have a bad experience. You see an "emergency tray" containing medicines and instruments, which the experimenter assures you is there "just as a precaution." Now you enter an "isolation chamber," which is actually an ordinary room with two chairs, a desk, a window, a mirror, a sandwich, and a glass of water. You are shown a microphone you can use to report any hallucinations or other distorted experiences and a "panic button" you can press for escape if the discomfort becomes unbearable.

Staying in a room for a few hours should hardly be a traumatic experience. But all the preparations suggested that terrible things were about to happen, so when this study was conducted, several students reported that they were hallucinating "multicolored spots on the wall," that "the walls of the room are starting to waver," or that "the objects on the desk are becoming animated and moving about." Some complained of anxiety, restlessness, difficulty concentrating, and spatial disorientation. One pressed the panic button to demand release (Orne & Scheibe, 1964).

Students in another group were led to the same room, but they were not shown the "emergency tray," were not asked to sign a release form, and were given no other indication that anything unusual was likely to happen. They in fact reported no unusual experiences.

Sensory deprivation probably does influence behavior. But as this experiment illustrates, sometimes what appears to be the influence of sensory deprivation (or any other influence) might really be the result of people's expectations. Martin Orne (1969) defined **demand characteristics** as *cues that tell a participant what is expected of him or her and what the experimenter hopes to find.* To minimize demand characteristics, many experimenters take elaborate steps to conceal the purpose of the experiment. A double-blind study serves the purpose: If two groups share the same expectations but behave differently because of some treatment, then the differences in behavior are presumably not the result of their expectations.

Observational Research Designs

The general principles that we just discussed apply to many kinds of research. Psychologists use various methods of investigation, and each has its own advantages and disadvantages. Most research in any field starts with description: What happens and under what circumstances? Let's first examine several kinds of observational studies. Later, we shall consider experiments, which have a much greater ability to illuminate cause-and-effect relationships.

Naturalistic Observations

A **naturalistic observation** is *a careful examination of what happens under more or less natural conditions.* For example, biologist Jane Goodall (1971) spent years observing chimpanzees in the wild, recording their food habits, their social interactions, their gestures, and their whole way of life (Figure 2.6).

FIGURE 2.6 In a naturalistic study, observers record the behavior of people or other species in their natural settings. Here, noted biologist Jane Goodall records her observations on chimpanzees.

Similarly, psychologists sometimes try to observe human behavior "as an outsider." A psychologist might observe what happens when two unacquainted people get on an elevator together: Do they stand close or far apart? Do they speak? Do they look toward each other or away? Does it matter whether they are both men, both women, or a man and a woman? Does their ethnic background make a difference?

Case Histories

Some fascinating psychological conditions are rare. For example, some people have amazingly good or poor memories. People with Capgras syndrome believe that some of their relatives have been replaced with duplicates, who look, sound, and act like the real people, but aren't. A psychologist who encounters someone with a rare condition may report a **case history**, *a thorough description of the person, including the person's abilities and disabilities, medical condition, life history, unusual experiences, or whatever else seems relevant.* It is, of course, possible to report a case history of any person, not just the unusual, but the unusual cases attract more attention. A case history is a kind of naturalistic observation; we distinguish it because it focuses on a single individual.

A case history can be extremely valuable, but it runs the risk of being just an anecdote. Unless other observers can interview and examine this special person or someone else who is very similar, we are at the mercy of the original investigator. A good case history can be a guide for further research, but we should interpret a single report cautiously.

Surveys

A **survey** is *a study of the prevalence of certain beliefs, attitudes, or behaviors based on people's responses to specific questions.* Surveys are widespread in Western society. In fact no matter what your occupation, at some time you will probably conduct a survey of your employees, your customers, your students, your neighbors, or fellow members of an organization. You will also frequently read survey results in the newspaper or hear them reported on television. You should be aware of the ways in which survey results can be misleading.

Sampling

Getting a random or representative sample is important in research, particularly with surveys. In 1936 the *Literary Digest* mailed 10 million postcards, asking people their choice for president of the United States. Of the 2 million responses, 57% preferred the Republican candidate, Alfred Landon.

Landon later lost by a wide margin to the Democratic candidate, Franklin Roosevelt. The problem was that the *Literary Digest* had selected names from the telephone book and automobile registration lists. In 1936, at the end of the Great Depression, few poor people (who were mostly Democrats) owned telephones or cars.

The Seriousness of Those Being Interviewed

When you answer a survey, do you carefully think about your answer to every question, or do you answer some of them impulsively? In one 1997 survey, only 45% of the respondents said they believed in the existence of intelligent life on other planets. However, a few questions later on the survey, 82% said they believed the U.S. government was "hiding evidence of intelligent life in space" (Emery, 1997). Did 37% of the people *really* think that the U.S. government is hiding evidence of something that doesn't exist? More likely, they were answering without much thought.

Here's another example: Which of the following programs would you most like to see on television reruns? Rate your choices from highest (1) to lowest (10). (Please fill in your answers, either in the text or on a separate sheet of paper, before continuing to the next paragraph.)

Try It Yourself

____ South Park   ____ Xena, Warrior Princess
____ Lost   ____ The X-Files
____ Cheers   ____ Teletubbies
____ Seinfeld   ____ Space Doctor
____ I Love Lucy   ____ Homicide

When I conducted this survey with my own students at North Carolina State University, nearly all did exactly what I asked—they gave every program a rating, including *Space Doctor,* a program that never existed. More than two thirds rated it either seventh, eighth, or ninth—it usually beat *Teletubbies*—but more than 10% rated it in the top five, and a few ranked it as their top choice. (This survey was inspired by an old *Candid Camera* episode in which interviewers asked people their opinions of the nonexistent program *Space Doctor* and recorded confident, and therefore amusing, replies.)

Students who rated *Space Doctor* did nothing wrong, of course. I asked them to rank all of the pro-

Some odd survey results merely reflect the fact that people did not take the questions seriously.
(© ZITS PARTNERSHIP, King Features Syndicate. Reprinted by permission.)

grams and they did. The fault lies with anyone who interprets such survey results as if they represented informed opinions. People frequently express opinions based on little or no knowledge. The same is true of political surveys.

The Wording of the Questions

Let's start with a little demonstration. Please answer these three questions:

Try It Yourself

1. I oppose raising taxes. (Circle one.)
   1   2   3   4   5   6   7
   Strongly agree   Strongly disagree
2. I make it a practice to never lie. (Circle one.)
   1   2   3   4   5   6   7
   Strongly agree   Strongly disagree
3. Monogamy is important to me. (Circle one.)
   1   2   3   4   5   6   7
   Strongly agree   Strongly disagree

Now cover up those answers and reply to these similar questions:

4. I would be willing to pay a few extra dollars in taxes to provide high-quality education to all children. (Circle one.)
   1   2   3   4   5   6   7
   Strongly agree   Strongly disagree
5. Like all human beings, I occasionally tell a white lie. (Circle one.)
   1   2   3   4   5   6   7
   Strongly agree   Strongly disagree
6. Sexual freedom is important to me. (Circle one.)
   1   2   3   4   5   6   7
   Strongly agree   Strongly disagree

Most students at one college indicated agreement (1, 2, or 3) to all six items (Madson, 2005). Note that item 1 contradicts 4, 2 contradicts 5, and 3 contradicts 6. For example, you can't be opposed to raising taxes and in favor of raising taxes. However, a different wording of the question has a different connotation. Question 4 talks about raising taxes "a few dollars" for a worthy cause. Yes, that is different from raising taxes in general, by some unknown amount for an unknown reason. Similarly, depending on what you mean by a "white lie," you might tell one occasionally while still insisting that you "make it a practice to never lie"—at least not much. Still, the point is that someone could bias your answers one way or the other by rewording a question.

Another point about the wording of questions: Suppose a survey asks "how satisfied are you with your dating or marriage?" Much later in the survey, you find the question "how satisfied are you with your life in general?" Most people who give a high rating to the first question also give a high rating to the second one, as you might guess. However, if the survey asks

the two questions back to back, then many people don't give them the same answer; for example, they might rate their marriage high and their life just average (Schwarz, Strack, & Mai, 1991). Apparently, when the questions are back to back, people interpret the second one to mean, "How happy are you with aspects of your life *other than* your dating or marriage?"

In short, the next time you hear that "38% of the people surveyed replied . . . ," ask how the question was worded and what choices were offered. Even a slightly different wording could yield a different percentage.

Surveyor Biases

Sometimes, an organization words the questions of a survey to encourage the answers they hope to receive. Here is an example: According to a 1993 survey, 92% of high school boys and 98% of high school girls said they were victims of sexual harassment (Shogren, 1993). Shocking, isn't it? However, perhaps the designers of the survey *wanted* to show that sexual harassment is rampant. The survey defined sexual harassment by a long list of acts ranging from serious offenses (e.g., having someone rip your clothes off in public) to minor annoyances. For example, if you didn't like the sexual graffiti on the rest room wall, you could consider yourself sexually harassed. If you tried to make yourself look sexually attractive (as most teenagers do, right?) and then attracted a suggestive look from someone you *didn't* want to attract, that stare would count as sexual harassment. (Don't you wonder about those who said they *weren't* sexually harassed? They liked *all* the graffiti on the rest room walls? No one *ever* looked at them in a sexual way?) Sexual harassment is, of course, a serious problem, but a survey that combines major and minor offenses is likely to mislead.

Figure 2.7 shows the results for two surveys conducted on similar populations at about the same time. The issue is whether stem cells derived from aborted fetuses can be used in medical research. The question on the left was written by an organization opposed to abortion and stem cell research. The question on the right was worded by an organization that is either neutral or favorable to stem cell research (Public Agenda, 2001). As you can see, changes in the wording of the question led to very different distributions of answers.

Correlational Studies

Another type of research is a correlational study. I might ask students at the start of the semester how interested they are in psychology and then later determine whether those with the greatest interest usually get the highest grades. A **correlation** is *a measure of*

Stem cells are the basic cells from which all of a person's tissues and organs develop. Congress is considering whether to provide federal funding for experiments using stem cells from human embryos. The live embryos would be destroyed in their first week of development to obtain these cells. Do you support or oppose using your federal tax dollars for such experiments?

Sometimes fertility clinics produce extra fertilized eggs, also known as embryos, that are not implanted in a woman's womb. These extra embryos either are discarded, or couples can donate them for use in medical research called stem cell research. Some people support stem cell research, saying it's an important way to find treatments for many diseases. Other people oppose stem cell research, saying it's wrong to use any human embryos for research purposes. What about you — do you support or oppose stem cell research?

FIGURE 2.7 The question on the left, written by opponents of stem cell research, led most people to express opposition. The question on the right, worded differently, led most people to express support. *(From ICR/National Conference of Catholic Bishops, 2001 and ABC News/Bellnet, June 2001, © 2004 by Public Agenda Foundation. Reprinted by permission.)*

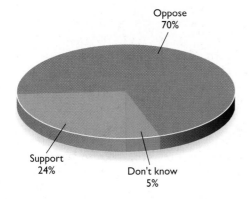

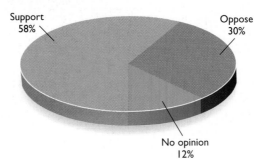

the relationship between two variables. (A variable is anything measurable that differs among individuals, such as years of education or reading speed.) A **correlational study** is *a procedure in which investigators measure the correlation between two variables without controlling either of them.* For example, investigators have observed correlations between people's height and weight simply by measuring and weighing them without attempting to influence anything. Similarly, one can find a correlation between scores on personality tests and how many friends someone has.

The Correlation Coefficient

Some correlations are stronger than others. For example, we would probably find a strong positive correlation between hours per week spent reading novels and scores on a vocabulary test. We would observe a lower correlation between hours spent reading novels and scores on a chemistry test.

The standard way to measure the strength of a correlation is known as a **correlation coefficient**, *a mathematical estimate of the relationship between two variables. The coefficient can range from +1 to −1.* A correlation coefficient indicates how accurately we can use a measurement of one variable to predict another. A correlation coefficient of +1, for example, means that as one variable increases, the other increases also. A correlation coefficient of −1 means that as one variable increases, the other decreases. A correlation of either +1 or −1 enables us to make perfect predictions of one variable from measurements of the other one. (In psychology you probably will never see a perfect +1 or −1 correlation coefficient.) A negative correlation is just as useful as a positive correlation and can indicate just as strong a relationship. For

example, the more often people practice golf, the lower their golf scores, so golf practice is negatively correlated with scores.

A 0 correlation indicates that measurements of one variable have no linear relationship to measurements of the other variable. As one variable goes up, the other does not consistently go up or down. A correlation near 0 can mean that two variables really are unrelated or that one or both of them were poorly measured. (If something is inaccurately measured, we can hardly expect it to predict anything else.)

Figure 2.8 shows scatter plots for three correlations (real data). In each graph each dot represents one student in an introductory psychology class. The value for that student along the *y*-axis (vertical) in each case represents percentage correct on the final exam. In the first graph, values along the *x*-axis (horizontal) represent scores on the first test in the course. Here the correlation is +.72, indicating a fairly strong relationship. That is, most of the students who did well on the first test also did well on the final, and most who did poorly on the first test also did poorly on the final. In the second graph, the *x*-axis represents times absent out of 38 class meetings. Here you see a correlation of −.44. This negative correlation indicates that, in general, those with more absences had lower exam scores. The third graph shows how the final exam scores related to the last three digits of each student's social security number. We would not expect any relationship, and we do not see one. The correlation is −.08, close to 0. The small negative correlation in the actual data represents a random fluctuation; if we examined the data for larger and larger populations of students, the correlation would no doubt come closer and closer to 0.

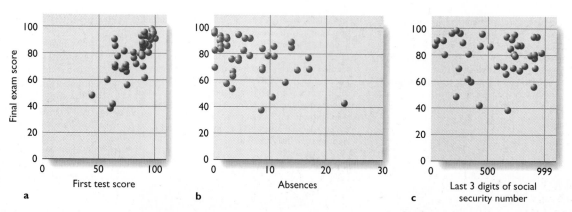

FIGURE 2.8 Scatter plots for three correlations. **(a)** Scores on first test and scores on final exam (correlation = +.72). **(b)** Times absent and scores on final exam (correlation = –.44). **(c)** Last three digits of social security number and scores on final exam (correlation = –.08). (This kind of graph is called a scatter plot. Each dot represents the measurements of two variables for one person.)

 CONCEPT CHECK

6. Identify each of these as a positive, zero, or negative correlation:
   a. The more crowded a neighborhood, the lower the income.
   b. People with high IQ scores are neither more nor less likely than other people to have high telephone numbers.
   c. People who awaken frequently during the night are more likely than other people to feel depressed.
7. Which indicates a stronger relationship between two variables, a +.50 correlation or a –.75 correlation?
8. The correlation between students' grades and their scores on a self-esteem questionnaire is very low, not much above 0. Give a possible reason. (Check your answers on pages 55–56.)

Illusory Correlations

Sometimes, with unsystematic observations we "see" a correlation that doesn't really exist. For example, many people believe that consuming sugar makes children hyperactive. However, extensive research has found little effect of sugar on activity levels, and some studies find that sugar *calms* behavior (Milich, Wolraich, & Lindgren, 1986; Wolraich et al., 1994). How, then, do we handle reports that sugar makes children hyperactive? Researchers watched two sets of mothers with their 5- to 7-year-old sons after telling one group that they had given the sons sugar and the other that they had given the sons a placebo. In fact they had given both a placebo. The mothers who *thought* their sons had been given sugar rated their sons as being hyperactive during the observation period, whereas the other mothers did not (Hoover &

Milich, 1994). That is, people see what they expect to see.

When people expect to see a connection between two events (e.g., sugar and activity levels), they remember the cases that support the connection and disregard the exceptions, thus perceiving an **illusory correlation,** *an apparent relationship based on casual observations of unrelated or weakly related events.*

As another example of an illusory correlation, consider the widely held belief that a full moon affects human behavior. For hundreds of years, many people have believed that crime and various kinds of mental disturbance are more common under a full moon than at other times. In fact the term *lunacy* (from the Latin word *luna,* meaning "moon") originally meant mental illness caused by the full moon. Some police officers claim that they receive more calls on nights with a full moon, and some hospital workers say they have more emergency cases on such nights.

These reports, however, are based on what people recall rather than on carefully analyzed data. Careful reviews of the data have found no relationship between the moon's phases and either crime or mental illness (Raison, Klein, & Steckler, 1999; Rotton & Kelly, 1985). Why, then, does this belief persist? People remember the occasions that fit the belief and disregard those that do not.

Correlation and Causation

A correlation tells us whether two variables are related to each other and, if so, how strongly. It does not tell us *why* they are related. If two variables—let's call them A and B—are positively correlated, it could be that A causes B, B causes A, or some third variable, C, causes both of them. Therefore, a correlational study does not justify a cause-and-effect conclusion.

For example, there is a strong positive correlation between the number of books people own about chess and how good they are at playing chess. Does owning chess books make someone a better chess player? Does being a good chess player cause someone to buy chess books? Both hypotheses are partly true. People who start to like chess usually buy chess books, which improve their game. As they get better, they become even more interested, buy more books, and play the game even better. But neither the chess books nor the skill exactly causes the other.

"Then what good is a correlation?" you might ask. The simplest answer is that correlations help us make useful predictions. For example, if your friend has just challenged you to a game of chess, you can quickly scan your friend's bookshelves and estimate your chances of winning.

Here are three more examples to illustrate why we cannot draw conclusions regarding cause and effect from correlational data (see also Figure 2.9):

• *Unmarried men are more likely than married men to spend time in a mental hospital or prison.* That is, for men marriage is negatively correlated with mental illness and criminal activity. Does the correlation mean that marriage leads to mental health and

People's expectations and faulty memories produce illusory correlations, such as between the full moon and abnormal behavior.

good social adjustment? Or does it mean that the men in mental hospitals and prisons are unlikely to marry? The second conclusion is certainly true; the first may be also.

• *According to one study, people who sleep about 7 hours a night are less likely to die within the next few years than those who sleep either more or less* (Kripke, Garfinkel, Wingard, Klauber, & Marler, 2002). It's easy to believe that sleep deprivation impairs your health, but should we conclude (as some people did) that sleeping too much also impairs your health? Here is an alternative explanation: People who already have life-threatening illnesses tend to sleep more than healthy people. So perhaps illness causes extra sleep rather than extra sleep causing illness. Or perhaps advancing age increases the probability of both illness and extra sleep. (The study included people ranging from young adulthood through age 101!)

• *On the average the more often parents spank their children, the worse their children misbehave.* Does this correlation indicate that spankings lead to misbehavior? Possibly, but an alternative explanation is that the parents resorted to spanking because their children were already misbehaving (Larzelere, Kuhn, & Johnson, 2004). Yet another possibility is that the parents had genes for "hostile" behavior that led them to spank; the children inherited those genes, which led to misbehaviors.

Now, let me tell you a dirty little secret: In rare circumstances, correlational results *do* imply cause and effect. It is a "dirty little secret" because professors want students to avoid cause-and-effect conclusions from correlations, and mentioning the exceptions seems risky. Still, consider the fact that people are generally in a better mood when the weather improves (Keller et al., 2005). A likely explanation is that the weather changes your mood. What other possibility is there? Your mood changes the weather? Hardly. Does something else control the weather and your mood independently? If so, what? In the absence of any other hypothesis, we conclude that the weather changes your mood. As another example, consider that how often a U.S. congressional representative votes a profeminist position (as de-

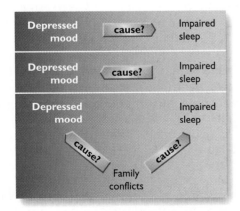

FIGURE 2.9 A strong correlation between depression and impaired sleep does not tell us whether depression interferes with sleep, poor sleep leads to depression, or whether another problem leads to both depression and sleep problems.

fined by the National Organization for Women) correlates with how many daughters the representative has (Washington, 2006). It is implausible that someone's voting record would influence the sex of children born many years previously; it is highly likely that having daughters could influence political views. Again, the results suggest cause and effect. Nevertheless, the point remains: We should almost always be skeptical of causal conclusions that anyone draws from a correlational study.

To determine causation an investigator needs to manipulate one of the variables directly through a research design known as an *experiment*. When an investigator manipulates one variable and then observes corresponding changes in another variable, a conclusion about causation can be justified, presuming, of course, that the experiment is well designed.

 CONCEPT CHECK

9. Suppose we find a .8 correlation between students' reported interest in psychology and their grades on a psychology test. What conclusion can we draw?

10. On the average the more medicine people take, the more likely they are to die young. Propose alternative explanations for this correlation.

11. On the average drug addicts who regularly attend counseling sessions are more likely to stay drug-free than those who drop out. Propose alternative explanations for this correlation. (Check your answers on page 56.)

Experiments

An **experiment** is *a study in which the investigator manipulates at least one variable while measuring at least one other variable.* Experimental research in psychology and biology faces problems that are not common in the physical sciences. Suppose, for example, physicists measure the length of a metal bar at one temperature, increase the temperature, and then find that the bar has lengthened. They conclude that a higher temperature caused the bar to expand. Now imagine a comparable procedure in psychology: Researchers measure the language skills of some 5-year-old children, provide them with a 6-month special training program, and then find that the children have increased their language skills. Can we conclude that the training program was effective? No, because the children probably would have improved their language during 6 months even without the training. Physicists don't have to worry that a metal bar might grow on its own.

A better design is to compare two groups: An investigator might assemble a group of 5-year-old children, randomly divide them into two groups, and provide the training for one group (the *experimental group*) but not the other (the *control group*). Someone, preferably a blind observer, evaluates the language skills of the two groups. If the two groups become different in some consistent way, then the difference is probably the result of the experimental procedure. Table 2.3 contrasts experiments with observational studies.

TABLE 2.3 Comparison of Five Methods of Research

Observational Studies
• *Case Study* Describes a single individual in detail.
• *Naturalistic Observation* Describes behavior under natural conditions.
• *Survey* Studies attitudes, beliefs, or behaviors based on answers to questions.
• *Correlation* Describes the relationship between two variables that the investigator measures but does not control.

Experiment
Determines how a variable controlled by the investigator affects some other variable that the investigator measures

To illustrate the use of experiments, let's use the example of experiments conducted to determine whether watching violent television programs leads to an increase in aggressive behavior.

Independent Variables and Dependent Variables

An experiment is an attempt to measure how changes in one variable affect one or more other variables. The **independent variable** is *the item that an experimenter changes or controls—for example, the amount of violent television that people are permitted to watch.* It might be measured in terms of hours of programs containing violence or number of violent acts. The **dependent variable** is *the item that an experimenter measures to determine how it was affected.* In our example the experimenter measures the amount of aggressive behavior that the participants exhibit. You can think of the independent variable as the cause and the dependent variable as the effect (Figure 2.10).

Experimental Group, Control Group, and Random Assignment

An **experimental group** *receives the treatment that an experiment is designed to test.* In a study of the effects of violence on aggressive behavior, the experi-

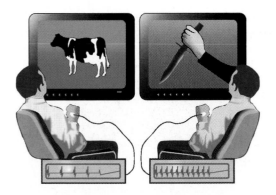

FIGURE 2.10 An experimenter manipulates the independent variable (in this case the programs people watch) so that two or more groups experience different treatments. Then the experimenter measures the dependent variable (in this case pulse rate) to see how the independent variable affected it.

mental group would watch televised violence. The **control group** is *a set of individuals treated in the same way as the experimental group except for the procedure that the experiment is designed to test.* People in the control group would watch only nonviolent television programs (Figure 2.11). (The type of television program is the independent variable; the resulting behavior is the dependent variable.)

In principle this procedure sounds easy, although difficulties arise in practice. For example, if we are studying a group of teenagers with a history of violent behavior, it may be difficult to find nonviolent programs that hold their attention. As their attention wanders, those who were watching the nonviolent programs start picking fights with one another, and suddenly, the results of the experiment look very odd indeed.

Suppose we conduct a study inviting young people to watch either violent or nonviolent programs, and then we discover that those who watched violent programs act more aggressively. What conclusion could we draw? None. Those who chose to watch violence were probably different from those who chose the nonviolent programs. Any good experiment has **random assignment** of participants to groups: *The experimenter uses a chance procedure, such as drawing names out of a hat, to make sure that every participant has the*

same probability as any other participant of being assigned to a given group.

 CONCEPT CHECK

12. Which of the following would an experimenter try to minimize or avoid?
    falsifiability, independent variables, dependent variables, blind observers, demand characteristics.
13. An instructor wants to find out whether the frequency of testing in an introductory psychology class has any effect on students' final exam performance. The instructor gives weekly tests in one class, just three tests in a second class, and only a single midterm exam in the third class. All three classes are given the same final exam, and the instructor then compares their performances. Identify the independent variable and the dependent variable. (Check your answers on page 56.)

 CRITICAL THINKING
WHAT'S THE EVIDENCE?

Effects of Watching Violence on Aggressive Behavior

We have talked in general terms about how to measure the effects of watching violent programs. The controversy is an old one. In the

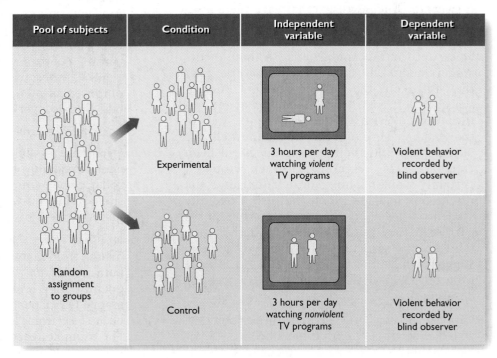

Pool of subjects	Condition	Independent variable	Dependent variable
Random assignment to groups	Experimental	3 hours per day watching *violent* TV programs	Violent behavior recorded by blind observer
	Control	3 hours per day watching *nonviolent* TV programs	Violent behavior recorded by blind observer

FIGURE 2.11 Once researchers decide on the hypothesis they want to test, they must design the experiment. These procedures test the effects of watching televised violence.

1930s and 1940s, people worried about whether listening to crime programs on the radio was harmful to young people (Dennis, 1998), and way back in the time of Plato and Aristotle, people worried whether it was dangerous for children to listen to certain kinds of storytellers (Murray, 1998). Let's consider some research in detail. The first is an experiment; the second is an analysis of correlations.

FIRST STUDY

Hypothesis. People who have watched violent films will engage in more hostile behaviors than people who watched nonviolent films (Zillman & Weaver, 1999).

Method. The study had two parts: (a) first watching violent or nonviolent films and (b) being "provoked" and then given an opportunity to retaliate in a hostile way.

Film watching: Ninety-three college students agreed to be randomly assigned to watch different kinds of films on Monday through Thursday evenings. One group was asked to watch four extremely violent films; the other group watched films that had been about equally popular at the theaters but which included nothing more violent than occasional shouting or shoving.

Provocation with opportunity to retaliate: On Friday evening the students all participated in what appeared to them an unrelated study: A graduate-student researcher gave them a series of face photographs and asked them to identify the emotions expressed in each. The faces were in fact ambiguous, so none of the students could be sure of their answers. After they filled out the answer booklets, the researcher left, marked the booklets, and returned them with written comments. Half of the students were told they had done well; the others were told their performance had been "terrible." The researcher further wrote, "I certainly wouldn't hire you." Later, after the researcher had left, someone else asked the students to evaluate this graduate student. In particular they were to indicate whether they thought this student should receive financial support while in graduate school on a scale from 0 (not at all deserving) to 10 (extremely deserving).

Results. To no one's great surprise, students who had been told their performance was "terrible" did not like the graduate student and gave at best a mediocre rating to how well he or she deserved financial support. The more interesting result is that students who had spent the previous four nights watching violent films gave lower ratings than those who watched nonviolent films:

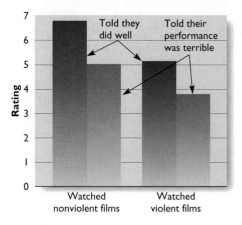

Interpretation. Watching violence made people more likely to behave in a hostile manner (giving someone a low rating for getting financial support). This is one of many experiments that have shown some increase in hostility after watching violent films. What makes this study particularly interesting is that the hostile act occurred a day after the last violent film. That is, the effect can last at least a day and presumably longer.

Any study has its limitations. One limitation of this study is that the "hostile" response was just giving someone a low rating on worthiness for financial support—hardly like a serious physical attack. A second limitation is that the study provided only four evenings of violent films, a small amount compared to a lifetime of watching television. Of course, no experimenter could control people's viewing habits for months or years. The best way to get around the limitations of this experiment is to try other research methods. Next is a very different kind of study.

SECOND STUDY

Hypothesis. Children who watch violent programs frequently, beginning when they are young, will become more violent over time, in contrast to similar children who watch less violence (Huesmann, Moise-Titus, Podolski, & Eron, 2003).

Method. In 1977 researchers collected information from more than 500 children, ages 6 to 9, both male and female, concerning how frequently they watched various television programs. Other people rated the various programs on a scale from "not violent" to "very violent." For example, certain police dramas were rated very violent, as were *Roadrunner* cartoons. Researchers also got ratings of these children's aggressive behaviors by interviewing other children in their class. Fifteen to eighteen years later, the researchers again interviewed more than 80% of these young people, asking about their current television watching and their current aggressive behaviors. They also checked police arrest records.

Results. The amount of violent television watching in childhood correlated about .2 with measures of adult aggressive behavior. That is not a very high correlation, but the correlation between child violent television watching and adult aggression was *higher* than the correlation between child violent television and child aggressive behavior, or adult violent television and adult aggressive behavior.

Interpretation. Apparently, watching violent television predicts future violence to a modest degree. Another study with a similar design obtained similar results: The amount of violence that people watched during adolescence predicted the amount of violent behavior in adulthood, 17 years later, independently of the adolescents' current aggressive behavior (J. G. Johnson, Cohen, Smailes, Kasen, & Brook, 2002).

The combined conclusion from the studies by Zillman and Weaver and by Huesmann et al. is firmer than we could draw from either study alone. Watching televised violence does not *cause* people to be violent; obviously, some people are more easily influenced than others. In particular other studies find that watching violence has little influence on friendly, "agreeable" people (Meier, Robinson, & Wilkowski, 2006). Still, it appears that extensive viewing of violence tends to increase the likelihood of aggressive behavior for some people. Similar results have been reported for playing violent video games (Carnagey & Anderson, 2005; Sheese & Graziano, 2005). Research also finds that adolescents who watch much television portrayal of sexuality are likely to become sexually active at a younger than average age (Collins, 2005). In short, what we watch influences what we do.

Ethical Considerations in Research

In any experiment psychologists manipulate a variable to determine how it affects behavior. Perhaps you object to the idea of someone trying to alter your behavior. If so, consider that every time you talk to people you are trying to alter their behavior at least slightly. Still, some experiments do raise difficult issues, and researchers are bound by both law and conscience to treat their participants ethically.

Ethical Concerns with Humans

In this chapter we considered research on the effects of televised violence. If psychologists believed that watching violent programs might really transform viewers into murderers, then it would be unethical to conduct experiments to find out for sure. It would also be unethical to perform procedures likely to cause significant pain, embarrassment, or other harm.

The central ethical principle is that experiments should include only procedures that people would agree to experience. Therefore, psychologists ask prospective participants to give their **informed consent** before proceeding, *a statement that they have been told what to expect and that they agree to continue.* When experimenters post a sign-up sheet asking for volunteers, they give at least a brief statement of what will occur. At the start of the experiment itself, they provide more detail. In most studies the procedures are innocuous, such as watching a computer screen and pressing a key when a certain pattern appears. Occasionally, however, the procedure includes something that people might not wish to do, such as examining disgusting photographs, drinking concentrated sugar water, or receiving mild electrical shocks. Participants are told they have the right to quit at any point if they find the procedure too disagreeable.

Special problems arise in research with children, people who are mentally retarded, or anyone else who does not understand the instructions enough to provide informed consent (Bonnie, 1997). Individuals with severe depression pose a special problem (Elliott, 1997) because some seem to have lost interest in protecting their own welfare. In such cases researchers either consult the person's guardian or nearest relative or simply decide not to proceed.

Experiments conducted at a college must first be approved by an institutional review board (IRB). An IRB judges whether the proposed studies include procedures for informed consent and whether they safeguard each participant's confidentiality. An IRB also tries to prevent risky procedures. For example, it probably would not approve a proposal to offer large doses of cocaine, even to people who were ready to give their informed consent. A committee would also ban procedures that they consider seriously embarrassing or degrading to participants. Many "reality television" shows would be banned if they needed approval from an IRB (Spellman, 2005).

The committee also judges procedures in which investigators want to deceive participants temporarily to hide the purpose of the study. For example, suppose researchers want to test whether it is harder to persuade people who know someone is trying to persuade them. The researchers want to use two groups of people—one group that is informed of the upcoming persuasion and one that is not. The second group might even be misinformed about the intent of the study. The researchers cannot fully inform everyone about the procedures without losing the whole point of the study. Most people see little objection to this temporary deception, but the institutional committee has to review the procedures before the study can proceed.

Finally, the American Psychological Association, or APA (1982), publishes a booklet detailing the proper ethical treatment of volunteers in experiments. The APA censures or expels any member who disregards these principles.

Ethical Concerns with Nonhumans

Some psychological research deals with nonhuman animals, especially in research on basic processes such as sensation, hunger, and learning (Figure 2.12). Researchers are especially likely to turn to nonhumans if they want to control aspects of life that people will not let them control (e.g., who mates with whom), if they want to study behavior continuously over months or years (longer than people are willing to participate), or if the research poses health risks. Animal research has long been essential for preliminary testing of most new drugs, surgical procedures, and methods of relieving pain. People with untreatable illnesses argue that they have the right to hope for cures that might result from animal research (Feeney, 1987). Much of our knowledge in psychology either began with animal research or made use of animal studies at some point.

FIGURE 2.12 One example of animal research: A mirror mounted on a young owl's head enables investigators to track the owl's head movements and thereby discover how it localizes sounds with one ear plugged. The findings may help researchers understand how blind people use their hearing to compensate for visual loss.

Nevertheless, some people oppose much or all animal research. Animals, after all, cannot give informed consent. Some animal rights supporters insist that animals should have the same rights as humans, that keeping animals (even pets) in cages is nothing short of slavery, and that killing any animal is murder. Others oppose some kinds of research but are willing to compromise about others.

Psychologists vary in their attitudes. Most support at least some kinds of animal research, but almost all would draw a line somewhere separating acceptable from unacceptable research (Plous, 1996). Naturally, different psychologists draw that line at different places.

In this debate, as in so many other political controversies, one common tactic is for each side to criticize the most extreme actions of its opponents. For example, animal rights advocates point to studies that exposed monkeys or puppies to painful procedures that seem difficult to justify.

On the other hand, researchers point to protesters who have distorted facts, vandalized laboratories, and even threatened to kill researchers and their children—and in one case, oddly enough, threatened to kill a researcher's pet dog. Some protesters have stated that they would oppose the use of any AIDS medication if its discovery came from research with animals. Unfortunately, when both sides concentrate on criticizing their most extreme opponents, they make points of agreement harder to find.

One careful study by a relatively unbiased outsider concluded that the truth is messy: Some research is painful to the animals *and* nevertheless valuable for scientific and medical progress (Blum, 1994). We must, most people conclude, seek a compromise.

Professional organizations such as the Neuroscience Society and the American Psychological Association publish guidelines for the proper use of animals in research. Colleges and other research institutions maintain laboratory animal care committees to ensure that laboratory animals are treated humanely, that their pain and discomfort are kept to a minimum, and that experimenters consider alternatives before they impose potentially painful procedures on animals. Because such committees must deal with competing values, their decisions are never beyond dispute.

How can we determine in advance whether the value of the expected experimental results (which is hard to predict) will outweigh the pain the animals will endure (which is hard to measure)? As is so often the case with ethical decisions, reasonable arguments can be raised on both sides of the question, and no compromise is fully satisfactory.

Psychological Research

As you read at the beginning of this chapter, most scientists avoid the word *prove*. Psychologists certainly do. (The joke is that psychology courses don't have true–false tests, just maybe–perhaps tests.) The most complex, and therefore most interesting, aspects of human behavior are products of genetics, a lifetime of experiences, and countless current influences. Given the practical and ethical limitations, it might seem that psychological researchers would become discouraged. However, because of these difficulties, researchers have been highly inventive in designing complex methods. A single study rarely answers a question decisively, but many studies can converge to increase our total understanding. ▊

Summary

- *Operational definitions.* For many purposes psychologists prefer operational definitions, which state how to measure a given phenomenon or how to produce it. (page 40)
- *Sampling.* Psychologists hope to draw conclusions that apply to a large population and not just to the small sample they have studied, so they try to select a sample that resembles the total population. They may select either a representative sample or a random sample. To apply the results to people worldwide, they need a cross-cultural sample. (page 41)
- *Experimenter bias and blind observers.* An experimenter's expectations can influence the interpretations of behavior and the recording of data. To ensure objectivity investigators use blind observers, who do not know what results are expected. In a double-blind study, neither the observer nor the participants know the researcher's predictions. Researchers try to minimize the effects of demand characteristics, which are cues that tell participants what the experimenter expects them to do. (page 43)
- *Naturalistic observations.* Naturalistic observations provide descriptions of humans or other species under natural conditions. (page 44)
- *Case histories.* A case history is a detailed research study of a single individual, generally someone with unusual characteristics. (page 45)
- *Surveys.* A survey is a report of people's answers on a questionnaire. It is easy to conduct a survey and, unfortunately, easy to conduct one badly. (page 45)
- *Correlations.* A correlational study examines the relationship between variables that are outside the investigator's control. The strength of this relationship is measured by a correlation coefficient, which ranges from 0 (no relationship) to plus or minus 1 (a perfect relationship). (page 46)
- *Illusory correlations.* Beware of illusory correlations—relationships that people think they observe between variables after mere casual observation. (page 48)
- *Inferring causation.* A correlational study ordinarily cannot uncover cause-and-effect relationships, but an experiment can. (page 48)
- *Experiments.* Experiments are studies in which the investigator manipulates one variable to determine its effect on another variable. The manipulated variable is the independent variable. Changes in the independent variable may lead to changes in the dependent variable, the one the experimenter measures. (page 50)
- *Random assignment.* An experimenter should randomly assign individuals to form experimental and control groups. That is, all individuals should have an equal probability of being chosen for the experimental group. (page 51)
- *Ethics of experimentation.* Experimentation on either humans or animals raises ethical questions. Psychologists try to minimize risk to their participants, but they often cannot avoid making difficult ethical decisions. (page 53)

Answers to Concept Checks

3. A score on an IQ test is an operational definition of intelligence. (Whether it is a particularly *good* operational definition is a different question.) None of the other definitions tells us how to measure or produce intelligence. (page 40)
4. Many operational definitions are possible for "friendliness," such as "the number of people that someone speaks to within 24 hours" or "the percentage of people one smiles at while walking down the street." You might think of a better operational definition. Remember that an operational definition specifies a clear method of measurement. (page 41)
5. Clearly not. It is unlikely that the men at a given college are typical of men in general or that the women are typical of women in general. Moreover, at some colleges the men are atypical in some respects and the women atypical in different ways. (page 42)
6. **a.** Negative correlation between crowdedness and income. **b.** Zero correlation between telephone numbers and IQ test scores. **c.** Positive correlation between awakenings and depression. (page 47)
7. The −.75 correlation indicates a stronger relationship—that is, a greater accuracy of predicting one variable based on measurements of the other. A negative correlation is just as useful as a positive one. (page 47)

8. One possibility is that grades are unrelated to self-esteem. Another possibility is that we have used an inaccurate measurement of either self-esteem or academic performance or both. If anything is measured poorly, it cannot correlate strongly with anything else. (page 47)

9. We can conclude only that if we know either someone's interest level or test score, we can predict the other with reasonably high accuracy. We *cannot* conclude that an interest in psychology will help someone learn the material or that doing well on psychology tests increases someone's interest in the material. Either conclusion might be true, of course, but neither conclusion follows from these results. (page 49)

10. Perhaps people get sick from complications caused by taking too many pills. Or maybe the people who take many medicines are those who already had serious illnesses. (page 49)

11. Perhaps the counseling sessions are helpful to people who want to quit drugs. Or perhaps the people with the most serious addictions are the ones most likely to quit. (page 49)

12. Of these, only demand characteristics are to be avoided. If you did not remember that falsifiability is a good feature of a theory, check page 31. Every experiment must have at least one independent variable (what the experimenter controls) and at least one dependent variable (what the experimenter measures). Blind observers provide an advantage. (page 43)

13. The independent variable is the frequency of tests during the semester. The dependent variable is the students' performance on the final exam. (page 50)

Measuring and Analyzing Results

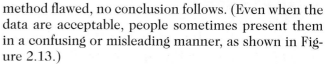

- *How can researchers state the "average" results in a study?*
- *How can we describe the variations among individuals?*
- *How can a researcher determine whether the results represent something more than just chance fluctuations?*

Some years ago a television program reported that 28 young people known to have played the game Dungeons and Dragons had committed suicide. Alarming, right?

Not necessarily. At that time at least 3 million young people played the game regularly. The reported suicide rate among D&D players—28 per 3 million—was considerably *less* than the suicide rate among teenagers in general.

So do these results mean that playing D&D *prevents* suicide? Hardly. The 28 reported cases are probably an incomplete count. Besides, no matter what the correlation between playing D&D and committing suicide, it could not tell us about cause and effect. Maybe the kinds of young people who play D&D are simply different from those who do not.

Then what conclusion should we draw from these data? *None.* When the data are incomplete or the method flawed, no conclusion follows. (Even when the data are acceptable, people sometimes present them in a confusing or misleading manner, as shown in Figure 2.13.)

Let's consider some proper ways of analyzing and interpreting results.

Descriptive Statistics

To explain the meaning of a study, an investigator must summarize the results in an orderly fashion. If a researcher observes 100 people, we do not want complete details about every person. We want the general trends or averages. We might also want to know whether most people were similar to the average or whether they varied a great deal. An investigator presents the answers to those questions through **descriptive statistics**, which are *mathematical summaries of results*, such as measures of the average and the amount of variation. The correlation coefficient, discussed earlier in this chapter, is an example of a descriptive statistic.

Measures of the Central Score

Three ways of representing the central score are the mean, median, and mode. The **mean** is *the sum of all the scores divided by the total number of scores.* Generally, when people say "average," they refer to the mean. For example, the mean of 2, 10, and 3 is 5 (15 ÷ 3). The mean is especially useful if the scores approximate the **normal distribution** (or normal curve), *a symmetrical frequency of scores clustered around the mean.* A normal distribution is often described as a bell-shaped curve. For example, if we measure how long it takes various students to memorize a poem, their times will probably follow a pattern similar to the normal distribution.

The mean can be misleading, however, in many cases. For example, *every* student in

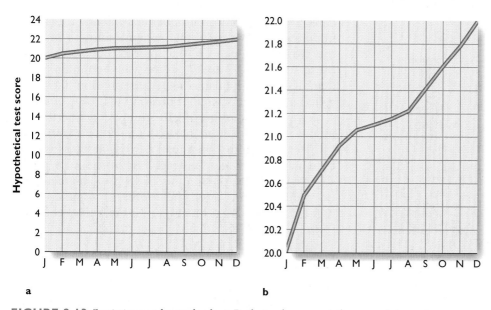

a   b

FIGURE 2.13 Statistics can be misleading: Both graphs present the same data, an increase from 20 to 22 over 1 year's time. But graph **(b)** makes that increase look more dramatic by ranging only from 20 to 22 (rather than from 0 to 22). (After Huff, 1954)

my class this semester has a greater than average number of arms and legs! It's true. Think about it. What is the average (mean) number of arms for a human being? It is not 2, but 1.99, because a few people have lost one or both arms. The same is true for legs. So if the "average" refers to the mean, it is possible for the vast majority to be above average. Here is another example: A survey asked people how many sex partners they hoped to have, ideally, over the next 30 years. The mean for women was 2.8 and the mean for men was 64.3 (L. C. Miller & Fishkin, 1997). But those means are extremely misleading. Almost two thirds of women and about half of men replied "1." That is, they wanted a loving relationship with just one partner. Most of the others said they hoped for a few partners during their lifetime, but a small number of men said they hoped for hundreds, thousands, or tens of thousands.

I repeated this survey with my own classes and found that some men had grandiose ambitions, such as 3.5×10^5. Others said, "as many as possible" or "all of them" (whatever that means). If most men reply "1" or "2," but a few reply with huge numbers, a mean such as "64.3" can be misleading.

When the population distribution is far from symmetrical, we can better represent the typical scores by the median instead of the mean. To determine the **median**, *we arrange all the scores in order from the highest score to the lowest score. The middle score is the median.* For example, for the set of scores 2, 10, and 3, the median is 3. For the set of scores 1, 1, 1, and 3.5×10^5, the median is 1. In short, extreme scores greatly affect the mean but not the median.

The third way to represent the central score is the **mode**, *the score that occurs most frequently.* For ex-

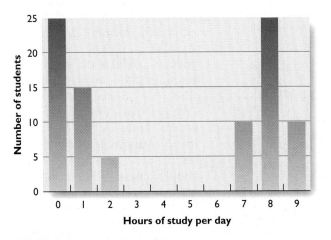

FIGURE 2.14 Results of an imaginary survey of study habits at one college. This college apparently has two groups of students—those who study much and those who study little. In this case both the mean and the median are misleading. This distribution is bimodal; its two modes are 0 and 8.

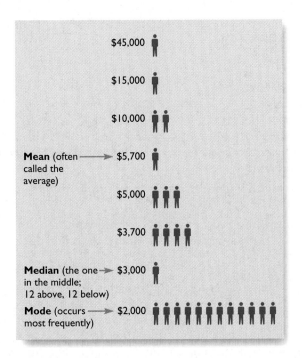

FIGURE 2.15 The monthly salaries of the 25 employees of company X, showing the mean, median, and mode. (After Huff, 1954)

ample, in the distribution of scores 2, 2, 3, 4, and 10, the mode is 2. The mode is seldom useful except under special circumstances. Suppose we asked college students how much they study and gathered the results shown in Figure 2.14. Half of the students at this college study a great deal, and half study very little. The mean for this distribution is 4.28 hours per day, a very misleading number because all the students study either much more or much less than that. The median is no better as a representation of these results: Because we have an even number of students, there is no middle score. We could take a figure midway between the two scores nearest the middle, but in this case those scores are 2 and 7, so we would compute a median of 4.5, again misleading. A distribution like this is called a *bimodal distribution* (one with two common scores); the researcher might simply describe the two modes and not even mention the mean or the median.

To summarize: The mean is what most people intend when they say "average." It is the sum of the scores divided by the number of scores. The median is the middle score after the scores are ranked from highest to lowest. The mode is the most common score (Figure 2.15).

 CONCEPT CHECK

14. a. For the following distribution of scores, determine the mean, the median, and the mode: 5, 2, 2, 2, 8, 3, 1, 6, 7.

b. Determine the mean, median, and mode for this distribution: 5, 2, 2, 2, 35, 3, 1, 6, 7. (Check your answers on page 61.)

Measures of Variation

Figure 2.16 shows two distributions of test scores. Suppose these represent scores on two introductory psychology tests. Both tests have the same mean, 70, but different distributions. If you had a score of 80, you would beat only 75% of the other students on the first test, but with the same score, you would beat 95% on the second test.

To describe the difference between Figure 2.16a and b, we need a measurement of the variation (or spread) around the mean. The simplest such measurement is the **range** of a distribution, *a statement of the highest and lowest scores.* The range in Figure 2.16a is 38 to 100, and in Figure 2.16b it is 56 to 94.

The range is a simple calculation, but it is not very useful because it reflects only the extremes. Statisticians need to know whether most of the scores are clustered close to the mean or scattered widely. The most useful measure is the **standard deviation (SD)**, *a measurement of the amount of variation among scores.* In the appendix to this chapter, you will find a formula for calculating the standard deviation. For present purposes you can simply remember that when the scores are closely clustered near the mean, the standard deviation is small; when the scores are more widely scattered, the standard deviation is large.

As Figure 2.17 shows, the SAT was designed to produce a mean of 500 and a standard deviation of 100. Of all people taking the test, 68% score within 1 standard deviation above or below the mean (400–600); 95% score within twice the standard deviation (300–700). Only 2.5% score above 700; another 2.5% score below 300.

Standard deviations provide a useful way of comparing scores on different tests. For example, if you scored 1 standard deviation above the mean on the SAT, you tested about as well as someone who scored 1 standard deviation above the mean on another test, such as the American College Test. We would say that both of you had a deviation score of +1.

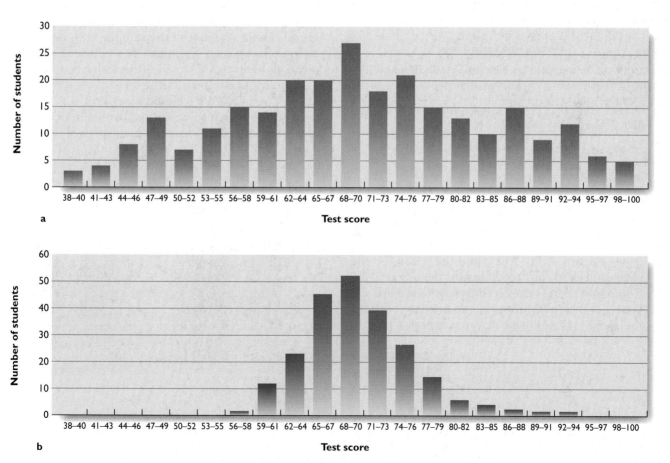

FIGURE 2.16 These two distributions of test scores have the same mean but different variances and different standard deviations.

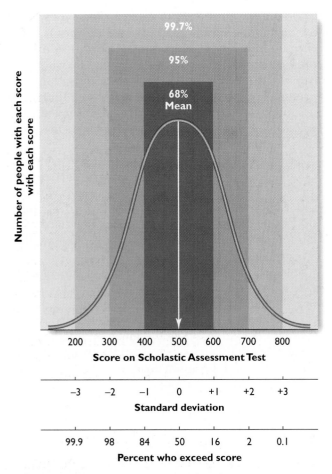

Number of people with each score with each score

99.7%

95%

68%
Mean

200   300   400   500   600   700   800
Score on Scholastic Assessment Test

−3   −2   −1   0   +1   +2   +3
Standard deviation

99.9   98   84   50   16   2   0.1
Percent who exceed score

FIGURE 2.17 In a normal distribution of scores, the amount of variation from the mean can be measured in standard deviations. In this example scores between 400 and 600 are said to be within 1 standard deviation from the mean; scores between 300 and 700 are within 2 standard deviations.

 CONCEPT CHECK

15. Suppose you score 80 on your first psychology test. The mean for the class is 70, and the standard deviation is 5. On the second test, you receive a score of 90. This time the mean for the class is also 70, but the standard deviation is 20. Compared to the other students in your class, did your performance improve, deteriorate, or stay the same? (Check your answer on page 61.)

Evaluating Results: Inferential Statistics

Suppose researchers conducted a study comparing two kinds of therapy to help people quit smoking cigarettes. At the end of 6 weeks of therapy, people who have been punished for smoking average 7.5 ciga-

rettes per day, whereas those who have been rewarded for not smoking average 6.5 cigarettes per day. Presuming that the smokers were randomly assigned to the two groups, is this the kind of difference that might easily arise by chance? Or should we take this difference seriously and recommend that therapists use rewards and not punishment?

To answer this question, we obviously need to know more than just the numbers 7.5 and 6.5. How many smokers were in the study? (10 in each group? 100? 1,000?) Also, how much variation occurred within each group? Are most people's behaviors close to the group means, or are there a few extreme scores that distort the averages?

One way to deal with these issues is to present the means along with an indication of how confident we are that the mean is close to where we say it is. We call that indication the **95% confidence interval,** *the range within which the true population mean lies, with 95% certainty.*

"Wait a minute," you protest. "We already know the means: 7.5 and 6.5. Aren't *those* the 'true' population means?" No, those are the means for particular samples of the population. Someone who studies another group of smokers may not get the same results. What we care about is the mean for all smokers. It is impractical to measure that mean, but if we know the sample mean, the size of the sample, and the standard deviation, we can estimate how close the sample mean is likely to be to the population mean. Figure 2.18 presents two possibilities.

In part a the 95% confidence intervals are small; that is, the standard deviations were small, the samples were large, and the sample means are almost cer-

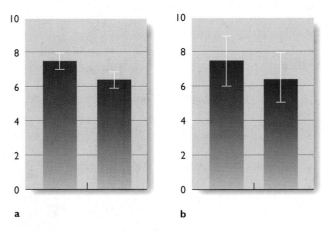

a   b

FIGURE 2.18 The vertical lines indicate 95% confidence intervals. The pair of graphs in part a indicate that the true mean has a 95% chance of falling within a very narrow range. The graphs in part b indicate a wider range and therefore suggest less certainty that reward is a more effective therapy than punishment.

tainly close to the true population means. In part b the confidence intervals are larger, so the numbers 7.5 and 6.5 are just rough approximations of the true population means. Presenting data with confidence intervals can enable readers to decide for themselves how large and impressive the difference is between two groups (Hunter, 1997; Loftus, 1996). A 95% confidence interval is one kind of **inferential statistic**, which is a *statement about a large population based on an inference from a small sample.*

 CONCEPT CHECK

16. Should we be more impressed with results when the 95% confidence intervals are large or small? (Check your answer on page 61.)

IN CLOSING

Statistics and Conclusions

Sometimes, psychological researchers get consistent, dependable effects, and they do not even have to consider statistics: Turn out the lights in a sealed room; people will no longer be able to see. Add sugar to your iced tea; it tastes sweet. The bigger the effect, the less we need to rely on complicated statistical tests. We pay more attention to statistics when we measure smaller effects: Does a change in wording alter people's responses to a survey? Does the use of an electronic study guide improve students' test scores? Does family therapy provide better results than individual therapy to treat alcohol and drug abuse? Many psychological researchers deal with small, fragile effects and therefore need a solid understanding of statistics.

Examining the statistics is only the first step toward drawing a conclusion. A statistical analysis might indicate that we would be unlikely to get such results merely by chance. If not by chance, then how? At that point psychologists use their knowledge to try to determine the most likely interpretation of the results. ∎

Summary

* *Mean, median, and mode.* One way of presenting the central score of a distribution is via the mean, determined by adding all the scores and dividing by the number of individuals. Another way is the median, which is the middle score after all the scores have been arranged from highest to lowest. The mode is the score that occurs most frequently. (page 57)
* *Standard deviation (SD).* To indicate whether most scores are clustered close to the mean or whether they are spread out, psychologists report a measure of the variation of scores, called the standard deviation. If we know that a given score is a certain number of standard deviations above or below the mean, then we can determine what percentage of other scores it exceeds. (page 59)
* *Inferential statistics.* Inferential statistics are attempts to deduce the properties of a large population based on the results from a small sample of that population. (page 60)

Answers to Concept Checks

14. **a.** Mean = 4; median = 3; mode = 2. **b.** Mean = 7; median = 3; mode = 2. Note that changing just one number in the distribution from 8 to 35 greatly altered the mean without affecting the median or the mode. (page 57)
15. Even though your score rose from 80 on the first test to 90 on the second, your performance actually deteriorated in comparison to other students' scores. A score of 80 on the first test was 2 standard deviations above the mean, better than 98% of all other students. A 90 on the second test was only 1 standard deviation above the mean, a score that beats only 84% of the other students. (page 59)
16. A small 95% confidence interval indicates high confidence in the results. (page 60)

CHAPTER ENDING

Key Terms and Activities

Key Terms

You can check the page listed for a complete description of a term. You can also check the glossary/index at the end of the text for a definition of a given term, or you can download a list of all the terms and their definitions for any chapter at this website:

www.thomsonedu.com/
psychology/kalat

95% confidence interval (page 60)
blind observer (page 43)
burden of proof (page 32)
case history (page 44)
control group (page 51)
convenience sample (page 41)
correlation (page 46)
correlation coefficient (page 47)
correlational study (page 47)

cross-cultural samples (page 42)
deduction (page 31)
demand characteristics (page 44)
dependent variable (page 50)
descriptive statistics (page 57)
double-blind study (page 43)
experiment (page 50)
experimental group (page 50)
experimenter bias (page 43)
extrasensory perception (ESP)
    (page 36)
falsifiable (page 31)
hypothesis (page 32)
illusory correlation (page 48)
independent variable (page 50)
induction (page 31)
inferential statistics (page 61)
informed consent (page 53)
mean (page 57)

median (page 58)
meta-analysis (page 34)
mode (page 58)
naturalistic observation (page 44)
normal distribution (or **normal**
    curve) (page 57)
operational definition (page 40)
parsimony (page 34)
placebo (page 43)
population (page 41)
random assignment (page 51)
random sample (page 41)
range (page 59)
replicable result (page 33)
representative sample (page 41)
single-blind study (page 43)
standard deviation (SD) (page 59)
survey (page 45)
theory (page 31)

 ## Suggestions for Further Reading

Martin, D. (2004). *Doing psychology experiments* (6th ed.). Pacific Grove, CA: Brooks/Cole. A discussion of all aspects of research, including methods of conducting research and statistical analyses of results.

Stanovich, K. E. (2004). *How to think straight about psychology* (7th ed.). Boston: Pearson, Allyn & Bacon. An excellent discussion of how to evaluate evidence and avoid pitfalls.

 ## Web/Technology Resources

Student Companion Website

www.thomsonedu.com/psychology/kalat

Explore the Student Companion Website for Online Try-It-Yourself activities, practice quizzes, flashcards, and more! The companion site also has direct links to the following websites.

Statistical Assessment Service (STATS)

www.stats.org/

Here you'll learn how statistical and quantitative information and research are represented (and misrepresented) by the media and how journalists can learn to convey such material more accurately and effectively.

Psychological Research Opportunities

http://psychexps.olemiss.edu/

The Psychology Department at the University of Mississippi invites you to participate in some of their research projects online.

 ## For Additional Study

Kalat Premium Website

http://www.thomsonedu.com

For Critical Thinking Videos and additional Online Try-It-Yourself activities, go to this site to enter or purchase your code for the Kalat Premium Website.

ThomsonNOW!

http://www.thomsonedu.com

Go to this site for the link to ThomsonNOW, your one-stop study shop. Take a Pretest for this chapter, and Thomson-NOW will generate a personalized Study Plan based on your test reults. The Study Plan will identify the topics you need to review and direct you to online resources to help you master those topics. You can then take a Posttest to help you determine the concepts you have mastered and what you still need to work on.

Statistical Calculations

This appendix shows you how to calculate two of the statistics mentioned in chapter 2. It is intended primarily to satisfy your curiosity. Ask your instructor whether you should use this appendix for any other purpose.

Standard Deviation

To determine the standard deviation (SD):

1. Determine the mean of the scores.
2. Subtract the mean from each of the individual scores.
3. Square each of those results, add the squares together, and divide by the total number of scores.

   The result is called the *variance*. The standard deviation is the square root of the variance. Here is an example:

Individual scores	Each score minus the mean	Difference squared
12.5	–2.5	6.25
17.0	+2.0	4.00
11.0	–4.0	16.00
14.5	–0.5	0.25
16.0	+1.0	1.00
16.5	+1.5	2.25
17.5	+2.5	6.25
105		36.00

The mean is 15.0 (the sum of the first column, divided by 7). The variance is 5.143 (the sum of the third column, divided by 7). The standard deviation is 2.268 (the square root of 5.143).

Correlation Coefficients

To determine the correlation coefficient, we designate one of the variables x and the other one y. We obtain pairs of measures, x_i and y_i. Then we use the following formula:

$$r = \frac{[(\Sigma x_i y_i) - n \cdot \bar{x} \cdot \bar{y}]}{n \cdot sx \cdot sy}$$

In this formula $(\Sigma x_i y_i)$ is the sum of the products of x and y. For each pair of observations (x, y), we multiply x by y and then add together all the products. The term $n \cdot \bar{x} \cdot \bar{y}$ means n (the number of pairs) times the mean of x times the mean of y. The denominator, $n \cdot sx \cdot sy$ means n times the standard deviation of x times the standard deviation of y.

Web/Technology Resource

Introductory Statistics: Concepts, Models, and Applications

http://www.psychstat.missouristate.edu/introbook/sbk00.htm

You can read an entire statistics textbook by David W. Stockburger, Missouri State University, on the Web or download it, free!

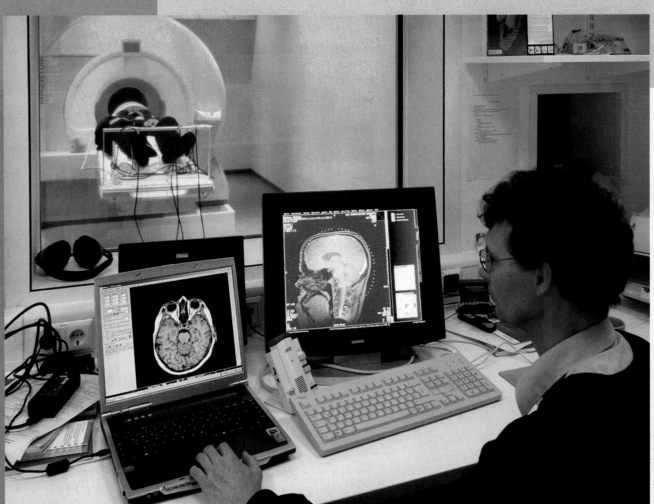

Biological Psychology

It is easy to marvel at the abilities of a human brain, which weighs only 1.2 to 1.4 kg (2.5 to 3 lb). A bee's brain, which weighs only a milligram, also produces complex behaviors. A bee locates food, evades predators, finds its way back to the hive, and then does a dance that directs other bees to the food. It also takes care of the queen bee, protects the hive against intruders, and so forth. Not bad for a microscopic brain.

Understanding brain processes is a daunting challenge. Researchers necessarily proceed piecemeal, first answering the easiest questions. We now know a great deal about how nerves work and how brains record sensory experiences. What we understand least is why and how brain activity produces conscious experience. (Philosopher David Chalmers calls this "the hard problem.") Will we someday understand nerves well enough to understand the origins of consciousness? Maybe, maybe not, but the fascination of the mind–brain question motivates many researchers to tireless efforts.

© T. Dickinson/The Image

▌ *A bee has amazingly complex behavior, but we have no way to get inside the bee's experience to know what (if anything) it feels like to be a bee.*

The Biological Approach to Behavior

- *If you lose part of your brain, do you also lose part of your mind?*

What constitutes an explanation? Consider the following quote, from a prestigious journal ("The Medals and the Damage Done," 2004):

> In 2002, [Michael] Brennan was a British national rowing champion . . . As the UK Olympic trials loomed, Brennan was feeling confident. But . . . for much of the past 12 months, Brennan's performance has been eroded by constant colds, aching joints and fatigue . . . When the trials rolled round this April, Brennan . . . finished at the bottom of the heap. "I couldn't believe it," he says. To an experienced sports doctor, the explanation is obvious: Brennan has "unexplained underperformance syndrome" (UPS).

What do you think? Is "unexplained underperformance syndrome" an *explanation?* Or is it just a name for our ignorance?

Consider another example: Young birds, born in the far north and now just months old, migrate south for the winter. In some species the parents migrate before the youngsters are ready, so the young birds cannot follow experienced leaders. How do the young birds know when to migrate, which direction, and how far? How do they know they should migrate at all? "It's an instinct," someone replies. Is that an explanation? Or is it no better than "unexplained underperformance syndrome"?

An explanation can take many forms, but it should be more than just a name. We explain a machine in terms of the workings of its parts and in terms of how and why it was assembled the way it was. Similarly, one way to explain behavior is in terms of biological mechanisms, and another is to describe how and why the organism evolved as it did (Tinbergen, 1951). Other explanations, such as developmental explanations, are also important.

A **physiological explanation** *describes the mechanism that produces a behavior.* For example, in the case of a migrating bird, researchers might identify which signals tell the bird to migrate—such as changes in the amount of sunlight per day. They would also identify whether the bird finds south by watching the sun, watching the stars, detecting the earth's magnetic field, or something else. The next step would be to discover how these signals alter the bird's hormones, stimulate various brain areas, and so forth.

An **evolutionary explanation** *relates behavior to the evolutionary history of the species.* At any point in time, various members of a species behave differently, partly because of their genetics. Some behaviors help individuals survive, find mates, take care of their young, and therefore pass on their genes to the next generation. Individuals with less successful behaviors are less likely to pass on their genes. Consequently, later generations come to resemble those who behaved most successfully. This process is what Charles Darwin called "descent with modification" and later biologists called *evolution.*

In the case of bird migration, we cannot actually observe how the behavior evolved because the evolution happened long ago, and behavior—unlike bones—leaves no fossils (with rare exceptions such as footprints, which identify the animal's gait). However, researchers can try to understand why some species evolved the ability to migrate whereas others did not. They also explore the various adaptations that make migration possible, such as a light, streamlined body to facilitate long-distance flight and the ability to tolerate sleep deprivation during the long journey (Rattenborg et al., 2004).

In this chapter and parts of the next, we concentrate on physiological explanations. To understand ourselves, one of the things we need to know is how the brain works. Evolutionary explanations will appear where relevant in several later chapters.

Measuring Brain Activity

How could anyone determine how different parts of the brain contribute to behavior? For many years nearly all of the conclusions came from studies of patients with brain damage, whose brains were examined after death. Researchers can now supplement such evidence with modern techniques that examine brain anatomy and activity in living people.

An **electroencephalograph (EEG)** *uses electrodes on the scalp to record rapid changes in brain electrical activity* (Figure 3.1). A similar method is a **magnetoencephalograph (MEG)**, *which records magnetic changes.* Both methods provide data on a millisecond-by-millisecond basis, so they can measure

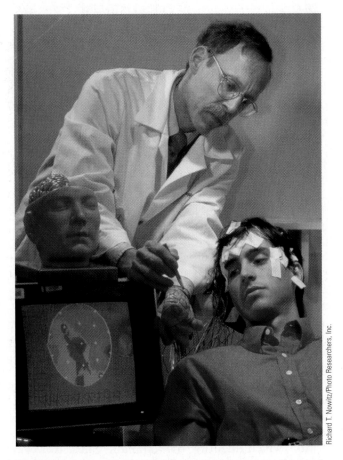

FIGURE 3.1 An EEG records momentary changes in electrical potential from the scalp, revealing an average of the activity of brain cells beneath each electrode.

the brain's reactions to lights, sounds, and other events. However, because they record from the surface of the scalp, they provide little precision about the location of the activity.

Another method offers much better anatomical localization but less information about timing: **Positron-emission tomography (PET)** *records radioactivity of various brain areas emitted from injected chemicals* (Phelps & Mazziotta, 1985). First, someone receives an injection of a radioactively labeled compound such as glucose. Glucose, a simple sugar that is the brain's main fuel (almost its only fuel), is absorbed mainly in the most active brain areas. Therefore, the labeled glucose emits radioactivity primarily from those areas. Detectors around the head record the radioactivity coming from each brain area and send the results to a computer, which generates an image such as the one in Figure 3.2. Red indicates areas of greatest activity, followed by yellow, green, and blue. Unfortunately, PET scans require exposing the brain to radioactivity.

Another technique, **functional magnetic resonance imaging (fMRI)**, *uses magnetic detectors outside the head to compare the amounts of hemoglobin with and*

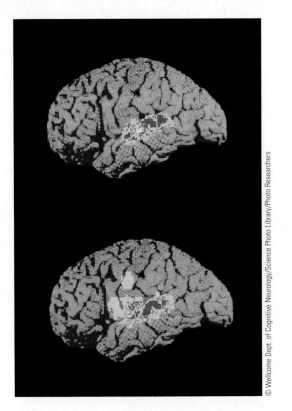

FIGURE 3.2 A PET scan of the human brain. Red shows areas of most-increased activity during some task; yellow shows areas of next most-increased activity.

without oxygen in different brain areas (J. D. Cohen, Noll, & Schneider, 1993). (Adding or removing oxygen changes the response of hemoglobin to a magnetic field.) The most active brain areas use the most oxygen and therefore decrease the oxygen bound to hemoglobin in the blood. The fMRI technique thus indicates which brain areas are currently the most active, as in Figure 3.3. For more detail about brain scan techniques, check this website: http://www.pbs.org/wnet/brain/scanning/index.html.

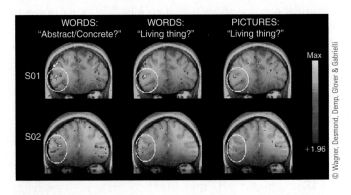

FIGURE 3.3 This brain scan was made with functional magnetic resonance imaging (fMRI). Participants looked at words or pictures and judged whether each item was abstract or concrete, living or nonliving. Yellow shows the areas most activated by this judgment; red shows areas less strongly activated. (*From Wagner, Desmond, Demb, Glover, & Gabrieli, 1997. Photo courtesy of Anthony D. Wagner*)

Brain scans are a potentially powerful research tool, but interpreting the results requires careful research. For example, suppose we want to determine which brain areas are important for recent memory. We record activity while someone is engaged in a memory task and compare that activity to times when the person is doing . . . what? Doing nothing? That comparison wouldn't work; the memory task presumably includes sensory stimuli, motor responses, attention, and other processes besides memory. Researchers must design a comparison task that requires attention to the same sensory stimuli, the same hand movements, and so forth as the memory task.

 CRITICAL THINKING

A STEP FURTHER

Testing Psychological Processes

Suppose you want to determine which brain areas are active during recent memory. Try to design some task that requires memory and a comparison task that is similar in every other way except for the memory requirement.

The Major Divisions of the Nervous System

Of all the insights that researchers have gained about the nervous system, one of the most fundamental is that different parts perform different functions. Your perception and thinking seem like a single integrated process, but it is possible for you to lose particular parts of that process after brain damage.

Biologists distinguish between the central nervous system and the peripheral nervous system. The **central nervous system** consists of *the brain and the spinal cord.* The central nervous system communicates with the rest of the body by the **peripheral nervous system,** which consists of *bundles of nerves between the spinal cord and the rest of the body.* Sensory nerves bring information from other body areas to the spinal cord; motor nerves take information from the spinal cord to the muscles, where they cause muscle contractions. The peripheral nerves that control the heart, stomach, and other organs are called the autonomic nervous system. Figure 3.4 summarizes these major divisions of the nervous system.

Early in its embryological development, the central nervous system of vertebrates, including humans,

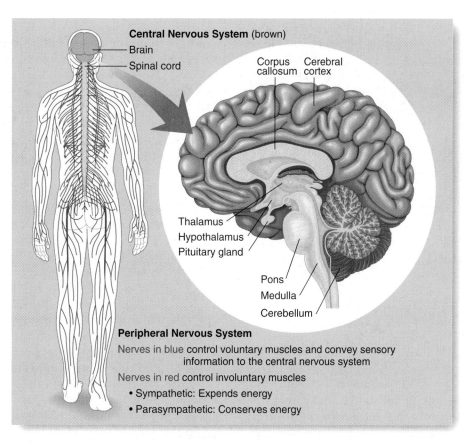

FIGURE 3.4 The major components of the nervous system are the central nervous system and the peripheral nervous system, which includes the autonomic nervous system.

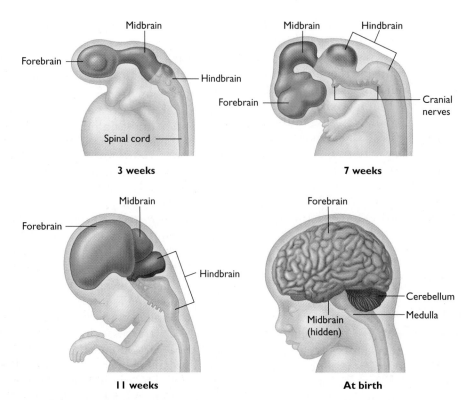

FIGURE 3.5 The human brain begins development as three lumps. By birth the forebrain has grown much larger than either the midbrain or the hindbrain, although all three structures perform essential functions.

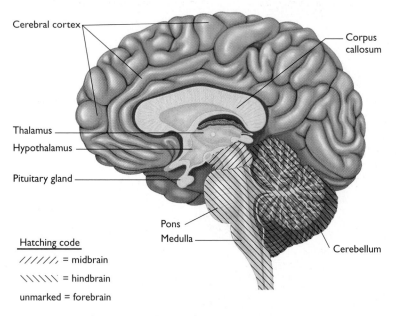

FIGURE 3.6 The major divisions of the human central nervous system, as seen from the midline.

is a tube with three lumps, as shown in Figure 3.5. These lumps develop into the *forebrain, midbrain,* and *hindbrain;* the rest of the tube develops into the spinal cord (Figure 3.6). The forebrain, which contains the cerebral cortex and other structures, is by far the dominant portion of the brain in mammals, especially in humans.

The Forebrain: Cerebral Cortex

The forebrain consists of two **hemispheres,** *left and right* (Figure 3.7). Each hemisphere is responsible for sensation and motor control on the opposite side of the body. (Why does each hemisphere control the opposite side instead of its own side? People have speculated, but no one knows.) We shall consider the differences between the left and right hemispheres in more detail later in this chapter.

The *outer covering of the forebrain,* known as the **cerebral cortex,** is especially prominent in humans. To compare the brain anatomy of humans and many other species, visit this website: **www.brainmuseum.org/sections/index.html.**

For the sake of convenience, we describe the forebrain in terms of four *lobes:* occipital, parietal, temporal, and frontal, as shown in Figure 3.8. The **occipital lobe,** *at the rear of the head, is specialized for vision.* People with damage in this area have *cortical blindness:* They have no conscious vision, no object recognition, and no visual imagery (not even in

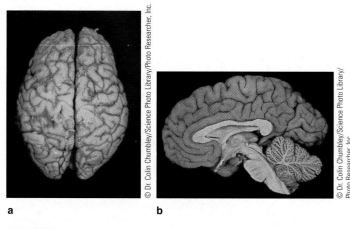

FIGURE 3.7 The human cerebral cortex: **(a)** left and right hemispheres; **(b)** inside view of a complete hemisphere. The folds greatly extend the brain's surface area.

dreams), although they still have visual reflexes, such as eye blinks, that do not depend on the cerebral cortex. Light can also set their wake–sleep cycles so they wake up in the day and get sleepy at night, because this aspect of behavior depends on areas outside the cerebral cortex.

The **temporal lobe** of each hemisphere, *located toward the left and right sides of the head, is the main area for hearing and some of the complex aspects of vision.* Damage to parts of the temporal lobe sometimes produces striking and specialized deficits. One area in the temporal lobe, found in monkeys as well as humans, responds only to the sight of faces (Tsao, Freiwald, Tootell, & Livingstone, 2006). People with damage in that area can no longer recognize faces, although they see well in other regards and recognize people by their voices (Tarr & Gauthier, 2000). People with damage to another part of the temporal lobe become motion blind: Although they can see the size, shape, and color of an object, they do not track its speed or direction of movement (Zihl, von Cramon, & Mai, 1983).

People with damage in the auditory parts of the temporal lobe do not become deaf, but they are impaired at recognizing sequences of sounds,

as in music or speech. Just as damage in one area makes people motion blind, damage in another area makes them motion deaf. The source of a sound never seems to be moving (Ducommun et al., 2004).

Part of the temporal lobe of the left hemisphere is important for language comprehension. People with damage in that area have trouble understanding speech and remembering the names of objects. Their own speech, largely lacking nouns and verbs, is hard to understand, and they resort to made-up expressions, as do normal people if they are pressured to talk faster than usual (Dick et al., 2001).

Other parts of the temporal lobe are critical for certain aspects of emotion. The *amygdala* (Figure 3.9), a subcortical structure deep within the temporal lobe, responds strongly to emotional situations. People with damage to the amygdala are capable of feeling emotions, but they are slow to process the emotional aspects of information, such as facial expressions and descriptions of emotional situations (Baxter & Murray, 2002). If you were driving down a steep, winding mountain road and suddenly discovered that your brakes weren't working, how frightened would you be? On a scale from 0 to 9, most people

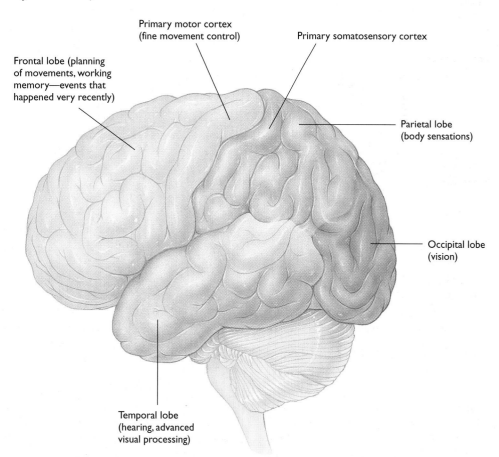

FIGURE 3.8 The four lobes of the human forebrain, with some of their major functions.

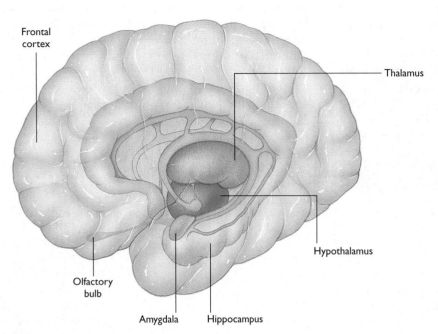

FIGURE 3.9 A view of the forebrain, showing internal structures as though the outer structures were transparent.

of the location of body parts in space. The **primary somatosensory** (so-ma-toh-SEN-so-ree, meaning body-sensory) **cortex,** *a strip in the anterior portion of the parietal lobe, has cells sensitive to touch in different body areas,* as shown in Figure 3.10. Note that in Figure 3.10a, larger areas are devoted to touch in the more sensitive areas, such as the lips and hands, than to less sensitive areas, such as the abdomen and back. Damage to any part of the somatosensory cortex impairs sensation from the corresponding part of the body. Extensive damage also interferes with spatial attention. After parietal damage, people see something but cannot decipher where it is relative to their body. Consequently, they have trouble reaching toward it, walking around it, or shifting attention from one object to another.

Although the somatosensory cortex is the primary site for touch sensations, touch also activates parts of the temporal lobe that are important for emotional responses. After loss of input to the somatosensory cortex, a person loses all conscious perception of touch but still reports a "pleasant" feeling after a gentle stroke along the skin (Olausson et al., 2002). That is, the person responds

rate this situation as 9, but someone with amygdala damage rates it about 6 (Adolphs, Russell, & Tranel, 1999).

The **parietal lobe,** *just anterior (forward) from the occipital lobe, is specialized for the body senses, including touch, pain, temperature, and awareness*

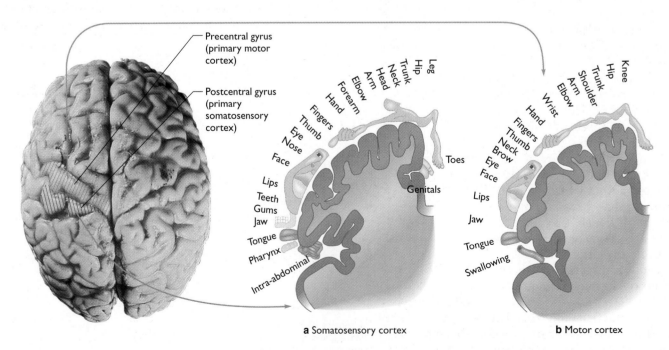

a Somatosensory cortex   **b** Motor cortex

FIGURE 3.10 **(a)** The primary somatosensory cortex and **(b)** the primary motor cortex, illustrating which part of the body each brain area controls. Larger areas of the cortex are devoted to body parts that need to be controlled with great precision, such as the face and hands. *(parts a and b after Penfield & Rasmussen, 1950)*

emotionally to the touch without knowing why! You see again that brain damage can produce surprisingly specialized changes in behavior and experience.

The **frontal lobe**, *at the anterior (forward) pole of the brain*, includes the **primary motor cortex**, *important for the planned control of fine movements*, such as moving one finger at a time. As with the primary somatosensory cortex, each area of the primary motor cortex controls a different part of the body, and larger areas are devoted to precise movements of the tongue and fingers than to, say, the shoulder and elbow muscles. The *anterior sections of the frontal lobe*, called the **prefrontal cortex**, contribute to certain aspects of memory and to the organization and planning of movements—that is, decision making. For example, certain areas of the prefrontal cortex are essential when you decide to pass up an immediate reward in favor of some later benefit (Frank & Claus, 2006). People with impairments of the prefrontal cortex often make impulsive decisions that hurt them. Some also seem to have trouble imagining how they will feel emotionally after various possible outcomes, and the results can include acts harmful to others, from which most people would feel guilt (Anderson, Bechara, Damasio, Tranel, & Damasio, 1999; Damasio, 1999). The left frontal lobe also includes areas essential for speaking, as we shall see in chapter 8. In short, the prefrontal cortex is important for many key aspects of human behavior.

 CONCEPT CHECK

1. The following five people have suffered damage to the forebrain. From their behavioral symptoms, state the probable location of each one's damage:
   a. impaired touch sensations and spatial localization
   b. impaired hearing and some changes in emotional experience
   c. inability to make fine movements with the right hand
   d. loss of vision in the left visual field
   e. difficulty planning movements and remembering what has just happened. (Check your answers on page 80.)

The Forebrain: Subcortical Areas

The interior of the forebrain includes additional important structures, some of which are shown in Figure 3.9. At the center is the thalamus, which is the last stop for almost all sensory information on the way to the cerebral cortex. Surrounding the thalamus are other areas called the *limbic system*. (A limbus is a margin or border.) One of these areas, the hippocam-

pus, is important for memory and will appear again in chapter 7, memory. The hypothalamus, located just below the thalamus, is important for hunger, thirst, temperature regulation, sex, and other motivated behaviors. The hypothalamus will appear again in chapter 11, motivation. The amygdala is a key area for emotion, chapter 12.

Motor Control

The cerebral cortex does not directly control the muscles. It sends some of its output to the **pons** and **medulla** (parts of the hindbrain), *which control the muscles of the head* (e.g., for chewing, swallowing, and breathing). The rest of its output passes through the pons and medulla to the **spinal cord**, *which controls the muscles from the neck down* (Figures 3.6 and 3.11). The spinal cord also controls some reflexes, such as the knee-jerk reflex, without relying on any input from the brain. A **reflex** is a *rapid, automatic response to a stimulus*, such as unconscious adjustments of your legs while you are walking or quickly jerking your hand away from something hot.

The **cerebellum** (Latin for "little brain"), *part of the hindbrain*, is important for any behavior that requires aim or timing, such as tapping out a rhythm, judging which of two visual stimuli is moving faster, and judging whether the delay between one pair of sounds is shorter or longer than the delay between another pair (Ivry & Diener, 1991; Keele & Ivry, 1990). It is also essential to learned responses that require precise timing (Krupa, Thompson, & Thompson, 1993). People with damage to the cerebellum show a variety of motor problems that resemble those of al-

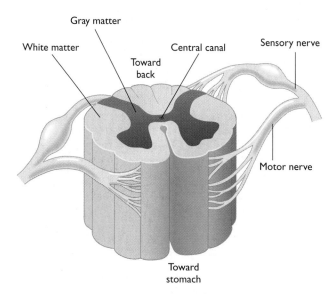

FIGURE 3.11 The spinal cord receives sensory information from all parts of the body except the head. Motor nerves in the spinal cord send messages to control the muscles and glands.

coholic intoxication, including slurred speech, staggering, and inaccurate eye movements.

 CONCEPT CHECK

2. Someone with a cut through the upper spinal cord still shows many reflexive movements but no voluntary movements of the arms or legs. Why not? (Check your answer on page 80.)

The Autonomic Nervous System and Endocrine System

The autonomic nervous system, closely associated with the spinal cord, *controls the internal organs such as the heart.* The term *autonomic* means involuntary, or automatic, in the sense that we have little voluntary control of it. A loud noise can suddenly increase your heart rate, but you can't just decide to increase your heart rate in the same way that you could decide to wave your hand. Your brain does, nevertheless, receive information from, and send information to, the autonomic nervous system. For example, if you are nervous about something, your autonomic nervous system will react more strongly than usual to a loud noise; if you are relaxed, it will respond less.

The autonomic nervous system has two parts: (a) The *sympathetic nervous system,* controlled by a chain of cells lying just outside the spinal cord, increases heart rate, breathing rate, sweating, and other processes important for vigorous fight-or-flight activities. It inhibits digestion, sexual arousal, and other activities not important to an emergency situation. (b) The *parasympathetic nervous system,* controlled by cells at the top and bottom levels of the spinal cord, decreases heart rate, increases digestive activities, and in general promotes activities of the body that take place during rest and relaxation (Figure 3.12).

Sympathetic system	Parasympathetic system
Uses much energy	**Conserves energy**
• Pupils open	• Pupils constrict
• Saliva decreases	• Saliva flows
• Pulse quickens	• Pulse slows
• Sweat increases	• Stomach churns
• Stomach less active	
• Epinephrine (adrenaline) secreted	

FIGURE 3.12 The sympathetic nervous system prepares the body for brief bouts of vigorous activity. The parasympathetic nervous system promotes digestion and other nonemergency functions. Although both systems are active at all times, one or the other can predominate at a given time.

We shall return to this topic in more detail in the discussion of emotions (chapter 12).

The autonomic nervous system influences the **endocrine system,** *a set of glands that produce hormones and release them into the blood.* Hormones controlled by the hypothalamus and pituitary gland also regulate the other endocrine organs. Figure 3.13 shows some of the major endocrine glands. **Hormones** are *chemicals released by glands and conveyed by the blood to alter activity in various organs.* Some hormonal effects last just minutes, such as a brief change in heart rate or blood pressure. In other cases hormones alter the activity of genes, preparing the body for pregnancy, migration, hibernation, or other activities that last months. A woman's menstrual cycle depends on hormones and so does the onset of puberty. Within the brain hormones can produce temporary changes in the excitability of cells, and they also influence in a more lasting way the survival, growth, and connections of cells. The sex hormones (*androgens* and *estrogens*) have particularly strong effects during early development, when they are responsible for many differences, on the average, between male and female brains as well as external anatomy (Woodson & Gorski, 2000). Module 11.3, sexual motivation, considers the role of sex hormones in more detail.

 CONCEPT CHECK

3. While someone is trying to escape danger, the heart rate and breathing rate increase. After the danger passes, heart rate and breathing rate fall below normal. Which part of the autonomic nervous system is more active during the danger, and which is more active after it? (Check your answer on page 80.)

The Two Hemispheres and Their Connections

Now that we have traced activity from the brain to the spinal cord and then out to the autonomic nervous system, let's return to the brain. As mentioned, each hemisphere of the brain gets sensory input mostly from the opposite side of the body and controls muscles on the opposite side. The hemispheres differ in some other ways too. For almost all right-handed people and more than 60% of left-handed people, parts of the left hemisphere control speech. For most other left-handers, both hemispheres control speech. Few people have complete right-hemisphere control of speech. The right hemisphere

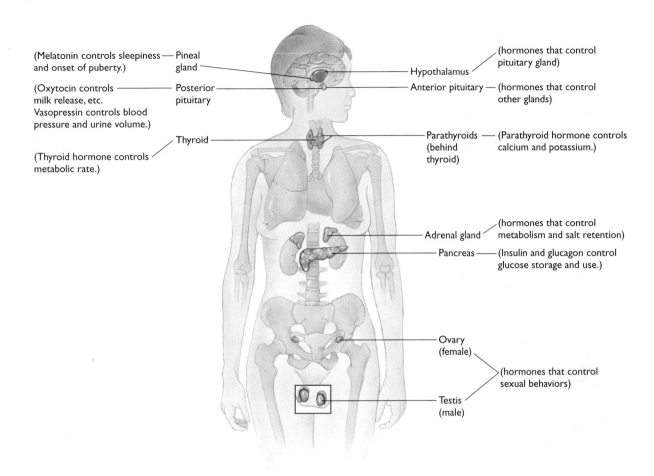

FIGURE 3.13 Glands in the endocrine system produce hormones and release them into the bloodstream. This figure shows only some of the glands and some abundant hormones.

is more important for certain other functions, including the ability to imagine what an object would look like after it has rotated and the ability to understand the emotional connotations of facial expressions or tone of voice (Stone, Nisenson, Eliassen, & Gazzaniga, 1996). People with right-hemisphere damage often can't tell when a speaker is being sarcastic, and they frequently don't understand jokes (Beeman & Chiarello, 1998).

In one study people watched videotapes of 10 people speaking twice. In one speech they described themselves honestly, and in the other case they told nothing but lies. Do you think you could tell when someone was telling the truth? The average for MIT undergraduates was 47% correct, slightly less than they should have done by random guessing. Other groups did about equally badly, except for one group that managed to get 60% correct. That's not great, but it's better than anyone else did. This group consisted of people with left-hemisphere brain damage! They could understand almost nothing of what people were saying, so they relied on gestures and facial

expressions—which the right hemisphere interprets quite well (Etcoff, Ekman, Magee, & Frank, 2000).

The two hemispheres constantly exchange information. If you feel something with the left hand and something else with the right hand, you can tell whether they are made of the same material because the hemispheres pass information back and forth through the **corpus callosum,** *a set of axons that connect the left and right hemispheres of the cerebral cortex* (Figure 3.14). What would happen if the corpus callosum were cut?

Occasionally, brain surgeons cut it to relieve **epilepsy,** *a condition in which cells somewhere in the brain emit abnormal rhythmic, spontaneous impulses*—usually as a result of inadequate inhibitory processes. Most people with epilepsy respond well to antiepileptic drugs and live normal lives. A few, however, continue having frequent major seizures. When all else fails, surgeons sometimes recommend cutting the corpus callosum. The original idea was that epileptic seizures would be limited to one hemisphere and therefore less incapacitating.

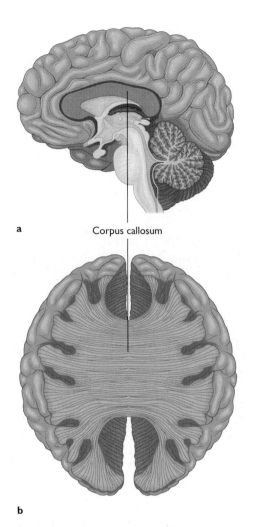

a — Corpus callosum

b

FIGURE 3.14 The corpus callosum is a large set of fibers that convey information between the two hemispheres of the cerebral cortex. **(a)** A midline view showing the location of the corpus callosum. **(b)** A horizontal section showing how each axon of the corpus callosum links one spot in the left hemisphere to a corresponding spot in the right hemisphere.

The operation was more successful than expected. Not only are the seizures limited to one side of the body, but they also become less frequent. Apparently, the operation interrupts a feedback loop that allows an epileptic seizure to echo back and forth between the two hemispheres. However, although these split-brain patients resume a normal life, they show some fascinating behavioral effects. First, we need to consider some anatomy.

Connections Between the Eyes and the Brain

Because each hemisphere of the brain controls the muscles on the opposite side of the body, each half of the brain needs to see the opposite side of the world. This does *not* mean that your left hemisphere sees with the right eye or that your right hemisphere sees with the left eye.

Convince yourself: Close one eye, then open it, and close the other. Note that you see almost the same view with both eyes.

Try It Yourself

Figure 3.15, which shows the human visual system, warrants careful study. Light from each half of the world strikes receptors on the opposite side of *each* retina. (The retina, containing visual receptors, is the lining in the back of each eye.) Information from each retina travels via the *optic nerves* to the optic chiasm, where half of the fibers cross to the opposite hemisphere of the brain, and half return to their own side. As a result each hemisphere sees the opposite side of the world, through half of each eye.

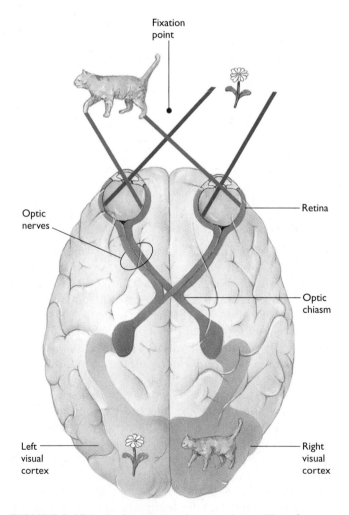

FIGURE 3.15 In the human visual system (viewed here from above), light from either half of the world crosses through the pupils to strike the opposite side of each retina. Information from the left half of each retina travels to the left hemisphere of the brain. Information from the right half of each retina travels to the right hemisphere of the brain.

Effects of Severing the Corpus Callosum

Assuming you have left-hemisphere control of speech, your talking hemisphere can easily describe what you feel on the right side or see in the right visual field. Can you talk about something you feel with the left hand or see in the left visual field? Yes, easily, if your brain is intact: The information that enters your right hemisphere passes quickly across the corpus callosum to your left hemisphere.

However, imagine someone with damage to the corpus callosum. A split-brain patient (someone whose corpus callosum has been cut) feels something with the left hand but cannot describe it because the information goes to the right (nonspeaking) hemisphere (Nebes, 1974; Sperry, 1967). If asked to point to it, the person points correctly with the left hand, but might say, "I have no idea what it was. I didn't feel anything." Evidently, the right hemisphere understands the instructions and answers with the hand it controls but cannot talk.

Now consider what happens when a split-brain patient sees something (Figure 3.16). The person in Figure 3.16 focuses the eyes on a point in the middle of the screen. The investigator flashes a word such as *hatband* on the screen for a split second, too briefly for an eye movement, and asks for the word. The person replies, "band," which is what the left hemisphere saw. (Information from the right side of the world goes to the left side of each retina and from there to the left hemisphere.) To the question of what *kind* of band, the reply is, "I don't know. Jazz band? Rubber band?" However, the left hand (controlled by the right hemisphere) points to a hat (which the right hemisphere saw).

Shortly after the surgery, some individuals report conflicts between the two sides, as if people with dif-ferent plans were occupying the same body. One person reported that his left hand sometimes changed the channel or turned off the television set while he (the talking side, the left hemisphere) was enjoying the program. Once he was going for a walk and the left leg refused to go any farther and would move only if he turned around to walk home (Joseph, 1988). In some ways it is as if the person has two "minds" occupying one skull.

CONCEPT CHECK

4. After damage to the corpus callosum, a person can describe some, but not all, of what he or she sees. Where must the person see something to describe it in words? That is, which visual field? (Check your answers on page 80.)

Split-brain surgery is rare. We study such patients not because you are likely to meet one but because they teach us something about brain organization: We see that our experience of a unified consciousness depends on communication across brain areas. If communication between the two hemispheres is lost, then each hemisphere becomes partly independent of the other.

The Binding Problem

Even if someone has a unified brain, with the corpus callosum intact, how do the different brain areas combine to produce the experience of a single self? One part of your brain is responsible for hearing, another for touch, others for various aspects of vision, and so forth, but those areas have few connections with one another. When you play a piano, how do you know

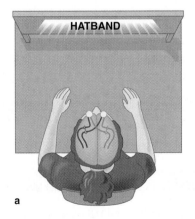

FIGURE 3.16 (a) When the word *hatband* is flashed on a screen, a split-brain patient reports only what the left hemisphere saw, *band*, and (b) writes *band* with the right hand. However, (c) the left hand (controlled by the right hemisphere) points to a hat, which is what the right hemisphere saw.

that the object you see is also what you hear and feel? *The question of how separate brain areas combine forces to produce a unified perception of a single object* is the **binding problem** (Treisman, 1999). The binding problem is at the heart of the mind–brain problem mentioned in chapter 1.

A naive explanation would be that all the various parts of the brain funnel their information to a "little person in the head" who puts it all together. However, research on the cerebral cortex has found no central processor that could serve that purpose. Few cells receive a combination of visual and auditory information or visual and touch information.

In fact the mystery deepens: When you see a brown rabbit hopping, one brain area is most sensitive to the shape, another most sensitive to the movement, and another most sensitive to the brownness. The division of labor is not complete, but it is enough to make researchers wonder how we bind the different aspects of vision into a single perception (Gegenfurtner, 2003).

Part of the answer lies with the parietal cortex, important for spatial perception. Consider the piano example: If you can identify the location of the hand that you feel, the piano you see, and the sound you hear, you link the sensations together. The parietal cortex is important for localizing all kinds of sensations. If, like someone with parietal cortex damage, you cannot locate anything in space, you probably won't bind sensations into a single experience. You might look at a yellow lemon and a red tomato and report seeing a yellow tomato and no lemon at all (L. C. Robertson, 2003).

We also know that binding occurs only for precisely simultaneous events. Have you ever watched a film or television show in which the soundtrack is noticeably ahead of or behind the picture? If so, you knew that the sound wasn't coming from the performers on screen. You get the same experience watching a poorly dubbed foreign-language film. However, when you watch a ventriloquist, the motion of the dummy's mouth simultaneous with the sound causes you to perceive the sound as coming from the dummy. Even young infants can figure out which person in the room is talking based on whose lip movements synchronize with the sounds (Lickliter & Bahrick, 2000).

You can experience a demonstration of binding with an Online Try It Yourself activity. Go to **www.thomsonedu.com/ psychology/kalat.** Navigate to the student website, then to the Online Try It Yourself section, and click Demonstration of Binding. You can also try the following (I. H. Robertson, 2005): Stand or sit by a large mirror as in Figure 3.17, watching both your right hand and its reflection in the mirror. Hold your left hand out of sight. Then repeatedly clench

We hear the sound as coming from the dummy's mouth only if sound and movements are synchronized. In general, binding depends on simultaneity of two kinds of stimuli.

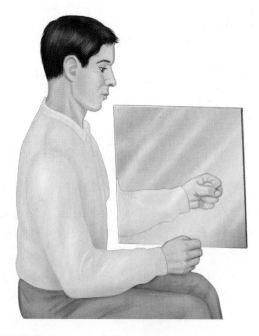

FIGURE 3.17 Move your left and right hands in synchrony while watching the image of one hand in a mirror. Within minutes you may experience the one in the mirror as being your own hand. This demonstration illustrates how binding occurs.

and unclench both hands, and touch each thumb to your fingers and palm in unison. You will feel your left hand doing the same thing that you see the hand in the mirror doing. After a couple of minutes, you may start to experience the hand in the mirror as your own left hand. You might even feel that you have three hands—the right hand, the real left hand, and the apparent left hand in the mirror. You are binding your touch and visual experiences because they occur at the same time, apparently in the same location.

Try It Yourself

People with parietal lobe damage have trouble binding aspects of a stimulus, such as color and shape, because they do not perceive visual locations accurately (Treisman, 1999; Wheeler & Treisman, 2002). People with intact brains experience the same problem if they see something very briefly while distracted (Holcombe & Cavanagh, 2001). What would it be like to see objects without binding them? You can get some feel for this experience with an Online Try It Yourself activity. Go to **www.thomsonedu.com/psychology/ kalat.** Navigate to the student website, then to the Online Try It Yourself section, and click Possible Failure of Binding.

Online Try It Yourself

IN CLOSING

Brain and Experience

The main point of this module is that mind and brain activity are tightly linked. Indeed, they appear to be synonymous. If you lose part of your brain, you lose part of your mind. If you activate some aspect of your mental experience, you simultaneously increase activity in some part of your brain. The study of brain activity helps us to understand the components that combine to form our behavior.

Another major point is that although different brain areas handle different functions without feeding into a central processor, they still manage to function as an organized whole. When we perceive two events simultaneously in the same location, we bind them together as a single object. Brain areas act separately and nevertheless produce a single experience.

Research on brain functioning is challenging because the brain itself is so complex. Just think about all that goes on within this 1.3 kg mass of tissue composed mostly of water. It is an amazing structure. ∎

Summary

- *Learning about brain functions.* Modern technology enables researchers to develop images showing the structure and activity of various brain areas in living, waking people. (page 67)
- *Central and peripheral nervous systems.* The central nervous system consists of the brain and the spinal cord. The peripheral nervous system consists of nerves that communicate between the central nervous system and the rest of the body. (page 69)
- *The cerebral cortex.* The four lobes of the cerebral cortex and their primary functions are: occipital lobe, vision; temporal lobe, hearing and some aspects of vision; parietal lobe, body sensations; frontal lobe, preparation for movement. Damage in the cerebral cortex can produce specialized deficits depending on the location of damage. (page 70)
- *Communication between the cerebral cortex and the rest of the body.* Information from the cerebral cortex passes to the medulla and then into the spinal cord. The medulla and spinal cord receive sensory input from the periphery and send output to the muscles and glands. (page 73)
- *Autonomic nervous system and endocrine system.* The autonomic nervous system controls the body's organs, preparing them for emergency activities or for vegetative activities. The endocrine system consists of organs that release hormones into the blood. (page 74)
- *Hemispheres of the brain.* Each hemisphere of the brain controls the opposite side of the body. In addition the left hemisphere of the human brain is specialized for most aspects of language in most people. The right hemisphere is important for understanding spatial relationships and the emotional aspects of communication. (page 74)
- *Corpus callosum.* The corpus callosum enables the left and right hemispheres of the cortex to communicate with each other. If the corpus callosum is damaged, information that reaches one hemisphere cannot be shared with the other. (page 75)
- *Split-brain patients.* The left hemisphere is specialized for language in most people, so split-brain people can describe information only if it enters the left hemisphere. Because of the lack of direct communication between the left and right hemispheres in split-brain patients, such people show signs of having separate fields of awareness. (page 77)
- *The binding problem.* We develop a unified experience of an object even though our registers of hearing, touch, vision, and so forth occur in different brain areas that do not connect directly to one another. Binding requires perception of the location of various aspects of a sensation. It also requires simultaneity of various sensory events. (page 77)

Answers to Concept Checks

1. **a.** parietal lobe; **b.** temporal lobe; **c.** primary motor cortex of the left frontal lobe; **d.** right occipital lobe; **e.** prefrontal cortex. (pages 70-73)
2. The spinal cord controls many reflexes by itself. However, voluntary control of muscles depends on messages from the brain to the spinal cord, and a cut through the upper spinal cord interrupts those messages. (page 73)
3. The sympathetic nervous system predominates during the danger, and the parasympathetic system predominates afterward. (page 74)
4. To describe something, a person must see it in the right visual field, because information from the right visual field goes to the left hemisphere. (page 77).

Neurons and Behavior

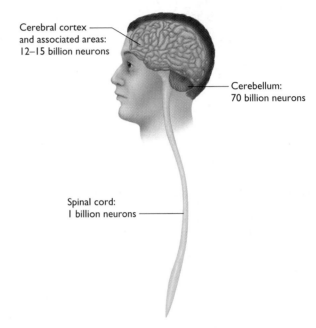

- *To what extent can we explain our experiences and behavior in terms of the actions of individual cells in the nervous system?*

A highly productive strategy in science is *reductionism*—explaining complex phenomena by reducing them to combinations of simpler components. Biologists explain breathing, blood circulation, and metabolism in terms of chemistry and physics. Chemists explain chemical reactions in terms of the properties of the elements and their atoms. Physicists explain the properties of the atom in terms of a few fundamental forces.

How well does reductionism apply to psychology? Can we explain human behavior and experience in terms of chemical and electrical events in the brain? The only way to find out is to try. Here, we explore efforts to explain behavior based on single cells of the nervous system.

Nervous System Cells

You experience your "self" as a single entity that senses, thinks, and remembers. And yet neuroscientists have found that your brain consists of an enormous number of separate cells. The brain processes information in **neurons** (NOO-rons), or *nerve cells.* Figure 3.18 shows estimates of the numbers of neurons in various parts of the human nervous system (R. W. Williams & Herrup, 1988). The nervous system also contains another kind of cells called **glia** (GLEE-uh), *which support the neurons in many ways such as by insulating them, synchronizing activity among neighboring neurons, and removing waste products.* The glia are smaller but more numerous than neurons.

How do so many separate neurons and glia combine forces to produce the single stream of experiences that is you? The answer is communication. Sensory neurons carry information from the sense organs to the central nervous system, where neurons process the information, compare it to past information, and exchange information with other neurons.

To understand our nervous system, we must first understand the properties of both the individual neurons and the connections among them. Neurons have a variety of shapes depending on whether they receive

FIGURE 3.18 Estimated distribution of the neurons in the adult human central nervous system. No one has attempted an exact count, and the number varies from one person to another. *(Based on data of R. W. Williams & Herrup, 1988)*

information from a few sources or many and whether they send impulses over a short or a long distance (Figure 3.19).

A neuron consists of three parts: a cell body, dendrites, and an axon (Figure 3.20). The **cell body** *contains the nucleus of the cell.* The **dendrites** (from a Greek word meaning "tree") are *widely branching structures that receive transmissions from other neurons.* The **axon** is a *single, long, thin, straight fiber with branches near its tip.* Some vertebrate axons are covered with *myelin,* an insulating sheath that speeds up the transmission of impulses along an axon. As a rule an axon transmits information to other cells, and the dendrites or cell body of each cell receives that information. That information can be either excitatory or inhibitory; that is, it can increase or decrease the probability that the next cell will send a message of its own. Inhibitory messages are important for many purposes. For example, during a period of painful stimulation, your brain has mechanisms to inhibit further sensation of pain.

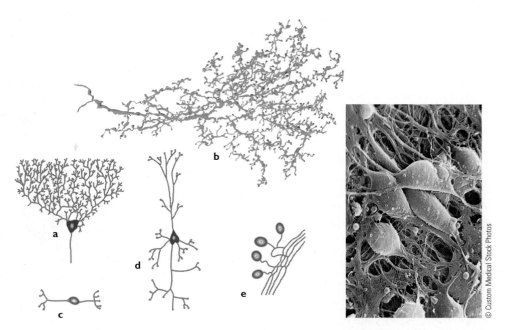

FIGURE 3.19 Neurons, which vary enormously in shape, consist of a cell body, branched attachments called axons (coded blue for easy identification), and dendrites. The neurons in **(a)** and **(b)** receive input from many sources, the neuron in **(c)** from only a few sources, and the neuron in **(d)** from an intermediate number of sources. The sensory neurons **(e)** carry messages from sensory receptors to the brain or spinal cord. Inset: Electron micrograph showing cell bodies in yellow and axons and dendrites in green. The color was added artificially; electron micrographs are made with electron beams, not light, and therefore, they show no color.

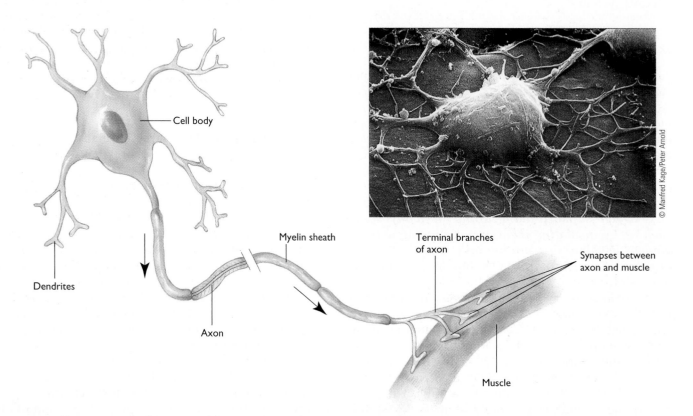

FIGURE 3.20 The generalized structure of a motor neuron shows the dendrites, the branching structures that receive transmissions from other neurons, and the axon, a single, long, thin, straight fiber with branches near its tip. Inset: A photomicrograph of a neuron.

☑ **CONCEPT CHECK**

5. Which part of a neuron receives input from other neurons? Which part sends messages to other cells? (Check your answers on page 89.)

The Action Potential

Axons are specialized to convey information over long distances. In large animals such as giraffes and whales, some axons extend several meters. Imagine what would happen if axons relied on electrical conduction: Electricity is extremely fast, but because animal bodies are poor conductors, electrical impulses would weaken noticeably during travel. Short people would feel a pinch on their toes more intensely than tall people would—if indeed either felt their toes at all.

Instead, axons convey information by a special combination of electrical and chemical processes called an **action potential,** *an excitation that travels along an axon at a constant strength, no matter how far it must travel.* An action potential is a yes–no or on–off message, like a standard light switch (without a dimmer). This principle is known as the *all-or-none law.*

The advantage of an action potential over simple electrical conduction is that action potentials from distant places like your toes reach your brain at full strength. The disadvantage is that action potentials are slower than electrical conduction. Your knowledge of what is happening to your toes is at least a twentieth of a second out of date. A twentieth of a second is seldom worth worrying about, but your information about different body parts is out of date by different delays. Consequently, if you are touched on two or more body parts at almost the same time, your brain cannot accurately gauge which touch came first.

Here is a quick description of how the action potential works:

1. When the axon is not stimulated, its membrane has a **resting potential,** *an electrical polarization across the membrane (or covering) of an axon.* Typically, the inside has a charge of about –70 millivolts relative to the outside. It gets this value from the negatively charged proteins inside the axon. In addition a mechanism called the sodium-potassium pump pushes sodium ions out of the axon while pulling potassium ions in. Consequently, sodium ions are more concentrated outside the axon, and potassium ions are more concentrated inside.

2. An action potential starts in either of two ways: First, many axons produce spontaneous activity.

Second, input from other neurons can excite a neuron's membrane. In either case sodium gates open and allow sodium ions to enter, bringing with them a positive charge (Figure 3.21). If that charge reaches the *threshold* of the axon (variable, but typically about –55 millivolts), the sodium gates open even wider. The resulting influx of positively charged sodium ions is the action potential.

3. After the sodium gates have been open for a few milliseconds, they snap shut. Then potassium gates open to allow potassium ions to leave the axon. The potassium ions carry a positive charge, so their exit drives the inside of the axon back to its resting potential (Figure 3.22b).

4. Eventually, the sodium-potassium pump removes the extra sodium ions and recaptures the escaped potassium ions.

A quick review: Sodium enters the cell (excitation). Then potassium leaves (return to the resting potential).

Conduction along an axon is analogous to a fire burning along a string: The fire at each point ignites the next point, which in turn ignites the next point. In an axon, after sodium ions enter the membrane, some of them diffuse to the neighboring portion of the axon, exciting it enough to open its own sodium gates. The action potential spreads to this next area and so on down the axon, as shown in Figure 3.22. In this manner the action potential remains equally strong all the way to the end of the axon.

Here is the relevance of this information to psychology: First, it explains why sensations from your

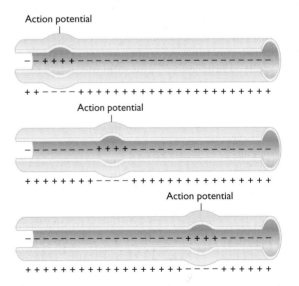

FIGURE 3.21 Ion movements conduct an action potential along an axon. At each point along the membrane, sodium ions enter the axon. As each point along the membrane returns to its original state, the action potential flows to the next point.

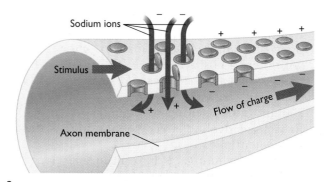

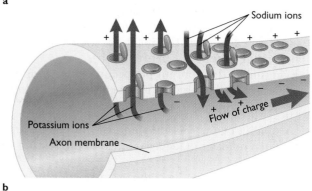

FIGURE 3.22 **(a)** During an action potential, sodium gates open, and sodium ions enter the axon, bearing a positive charge. **(b)** After an action potential occurs, the sodium gates close at that point and open at the next point along the axon. As the sodium gates close, potassium gates open, and potassium ions flow out of the axon, carrying a positive charge with them. *(Modified from Starr & Taggart, 1992)*

fingers and toes do not fade away by the time they reach your brain. Second, an understanding of action potentials is one step toward understanding the communication between neurons. Third, anesthetic drugs (e.g., Novocain) operate by clogging sodium gates and therefore silencing neurons. When your dentist drills a tooth, the receptors in your tooth send out the message "Pain! Pain! Pain!" But that message does not reach your brain because the sodium gates are blocked.

 CONCEPT CHECK

6. If a mouse and a giraffe both get pinched on the toes at the same time, which will respond faster? Why?

7. Fill in these blanks: When the axon membrane is at rest, the inside has a _____ charge relative to the outside. When the membrane reaches its threshold, ____ ions enter from outside to inside, bringing with them a _____ charge. That flow of ions constitutes the _____ _____ of the axon. (Check your answers on page 89.)

Synapses

Communication between one neuron and the next is not like transmission along an axon. At a **synapse** (SIN-aps), *the specialized junction between one neuron and another* (Figure 3.23), *a neuron releases a chemical that either excites or inhibits the next neuron.* That is, the chemical can make the next neuron either more or less likely to produce an action potential. By altering activity of various cells, synapses regulate everything your nervous system accomplishes.

A typical axon has several branches, each ending with a little bulge called a *presynaptic ending,* or **terminal bouton,** as shown in Figure 3.24. When an action potential reaches the terminal bouton, it releases a **neurotransmitter,** *a chemical that can activate receptors on other neurons* (Figure 3.24). Several dozen chemicals are used as neurotransmitters in various brain areas, although any given neuron releases only one or a few of them. The neurotransmitter molecules diffuse across a narrow gap to receptors on the **postsynaptic neuron,** *the neuron on the receiving end of the synapse.* A neurotransmitter fits into its receptor like a key fits into a lock. Its presence there produces either an excitatory or an inhibitory effect on the postsynaptic neuron. Depending on the receptor, the effect might last just milliseconds or many seconds or minutes. The neural communication process is summarized in Figure 3.25.

Depending on the neurotransmitter and the type of receptor, the attachment enables either positively charged or negatively charged ions to enter the postsynaptic cell. If the positive charges outweigh the negative charges enough for the cell to reach its threshold, it produces an action potential. The process resembles making a decision: When you are trying to

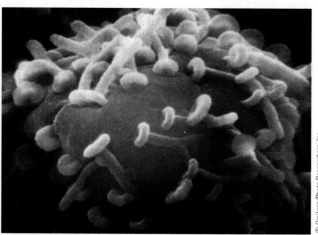

FIGURE 3.23 This synapse is magnified thousands of times in an electron micrograph. The tips of axons swell to form terminal boutons.

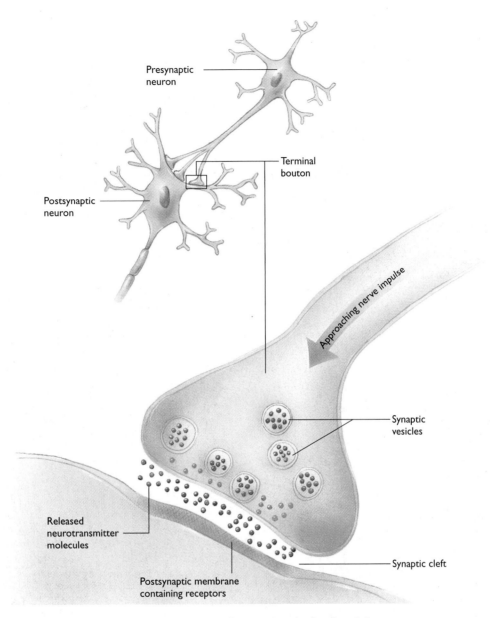

FIGURE 3.24 The synapse is the junction of the presynaptic (message-sending) cell and the postsynaptic (message-receiving) cell. At the end of the presynaptic axon is the terminal bouton, which contains many molecules of the neurotransmitter. The thick, dark area at the bottom of the cell is the synapse.

decide whether to do something, you weigh the pluses and minuses and act if the pluses are stronger.

Inhibition is not the absence of excitation; it is like stepping on the brakes. For example, when a pinch on your foot stimulates a reflex that contracts one set of muscles, inhibitory synapses in your spinal cord block activity in the muscles that would move your leg in the opposite direction.

After a neurotransmitter excites or inhibits a receptor, it separates from the receptor, ending the message. From that point on, the fate of the receptor molecule varies. It could become reabsorbed by the axon that released it (through a process called *reuptake);* it

could diffuse away from the synapse; enzymes could degrade it to an inactive chemical; or it could bounce around, return to the postsynaptic receptor, and reexcite it. Most antidepressant drugs act by blocking a transmitter's reuptake, thus prolonging its effects.

Different neurotransmitters are associated with different functions, although it is misleading to assign any complex behavior to a single transmitter. An alteration of a particular kind of synapse will affect some behaviors more than others. For that reason it is possible to develop drugs that decrease depression, anxiety, appetite, and so forth, as we shall see in later chapters. However, because each transmitter has sev-

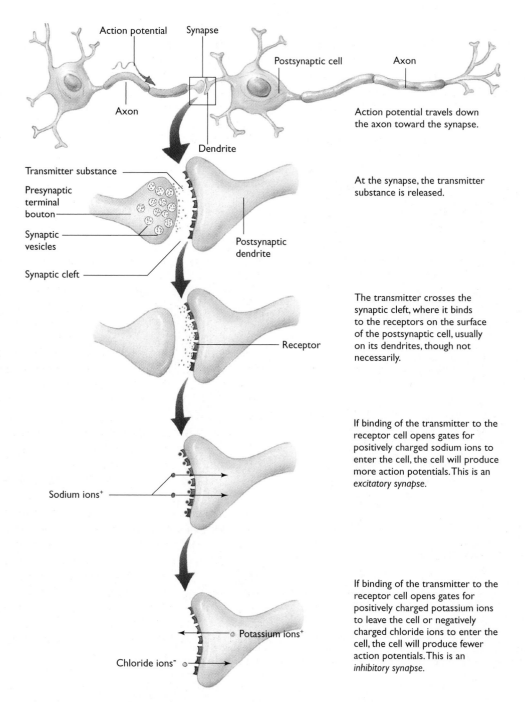

Action potential travels down the axon toward the synapse.

At the synapse, the transmitter substance is released.

The transmitter crosses the synaptic cleft, where it binds to the receptors on the surface of the postsynaptic cell, usually on its dendrites, though not necessarily.

If binding of the transmitter to the receptor cell opens gates for positively charged sodium ions to enter the cell, the cell will produce more action potentials. This is an *excitatory synapse*.

If binding of the transmitter to the receptor cell opens gates for positively charged potassium ions to leave the cell or negatively charged chloride ions to enter the cell, the cell will produce fewer action potentials. This is an *inhibitory synapse*.

FIGURE 3.25 The complex process of neural communication takes only 1–2 milliseconds.

eral functions, any drug intended for one purpose has other results too, referred to as *side effects*.

 CONCEPT CHECK

8. What is the difference between the presynaptic neuron and the postsynaptic neuron?
9. GABA is a neurotransmitter that inhibits postsynaptic neurons. If a drug were injected to prevent GABA from attaching to its receptors, what would

happen to the postsynaptic neuron? (Check your answers on page 89)

 CRITICAL THINKING

WHAT'S THE EVIDENCE?

Neurons Communicate Chemically

You have just learned that neurons communicate by releasing chemicals at synapses. What evidence led to this important conclusion?

Today, neuroscientists have a wealth of evidence that neurons release chemicals at synapses. They can radioactively trace where chemicals go and what happens when they get there; they also can inject purified chemicals at a synapse and use extremely fine electrodes to measure the response of the postsynaptic neuron. Scientists of the 1920s had no fancy equipment, yet they managed to establish that neurons communicate with chemicals. Otto Loewi conducted a simple, clever experiment, as he later described in his autobiography (Loewi, 1960).

Hypothesis. If a neuron releases chemicals, an investigator should be able to collect some of those chemicals, transfer them to another animal, and thereby get the second animal to do what the first animal had been doing. Loewi had no method of collecting chemicals released within the brain itself, so he worked with axons communicating with the heart muscle. (The communication between a neuron and a muscle at the nerve-muscle junction is like that of a synapse between neurons.)

Method. Loewi electrically stimulated certain axons that slowed a frog's heart. As he continued the stimulation, he collected fluid around that heart and transferred it to the heart of a second frog.

Results. When Loewi transferred the fluid from the first frog's heart, the second frog's heart rate also slowed (Figure 3.26).

Interpretation. Evidently, the stimulated axons had released a chemical that slows heart rate. At least in this case, neurons send messages by releasing chemicals.

Loewi eventually won a Nobel Prize in physiology for this and related research. Even outstanding experiments have limitations, however. In this case the results did not indicate whether axons release chemicals at all synapses, most, or only a few. Answering that question required technologies not available until several decades later. The answer is that most neuronal communication uses chemicals, but a few synapses communicate electrically.

Neurotransmitters and Behavior

The brain has dozens of neurotransmitters, each of which activates many kinds of receptors. For example, serotonin activates at least 15 kinds, probably more (Roth, Lopez, & Kroeze, 2000). Each receptor type controls somewhat different aspects of behavior. For example, because serotonin type 3 receptors are responsible for nausea, researchers have developed drugs to block nausea without much effect on other aspects of behavior (Perez, 1995).

Any disorder that increases or decreases a particular transmitter or receptor produces specific effects on behavior. One example is **Parkinson's disease,** *a condition that affects about 1% of people over the age of 50. The main symptoms are difficulty in initiating voluntary movement, slow movement, tremors, rigidity, and depressed mood.* All of these symptoms can be traced to a gradual decay of a pathway of axons that release *the neurotransmitter* dopamine (DOPE-uh-meen) (Figure 3.27). One common treatment is the drug L-dopa, which enters the brain, where neurons convert it into dopamine. The effectiveness of this treatment in most cases supports our beliefs about the link between dopamine and Parkinson's disease.

As we shall see in chapter 16, drugs that alleviate depression and schizophrenia also act on dopamine and serotonin synapses, although the relationship between the neurotransmitters and the behavior is complex. We still have much to learn about the relationship between synapses and their behavioral outcomes.

 CONCEPT CHECK

10. People suffering from certain disorders are given haloperidol, a drug that blocks activity at dopamine synapses. How would haloperidol affect someone with Parkinson's disease? (Check your answer page 89.)

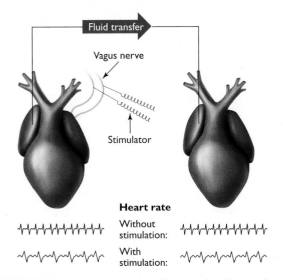

Heart rate

Without stimulation:

With stimulation:

FIGURE 3.26 Otto Loewi electrically stimulated axons known to decrease a frog's heart rate. He collected fluid from around the heart and transferred it to another frog's heart. When that heart slowed its beat, Loewi concluded that the axons in the first heart released a chemical that slows heart rate.

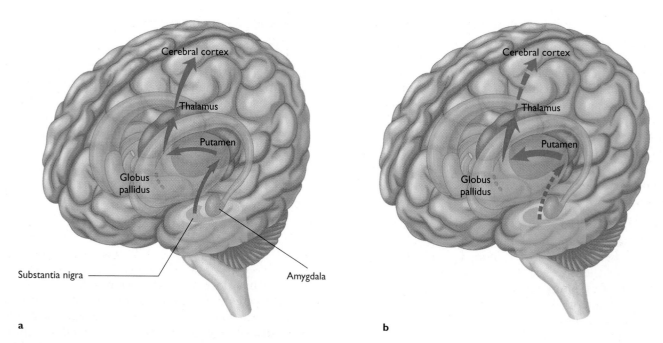

a

b

FIGURE 3.27 With Parkinson's disease axons from the substantia nigra gradually die. **(a)** Normal brain. **(b)** Brain of person with Parkinson's disease. Green = excitatory path; red = inhibitory.

▌ Former boxing champion Muhammad Ali developed symptoms of Parkinson's disease.

Experience and Brain Plasticity

When we talk about brain anatomy or synapses, it is easy to get the impression that the structures are fixed. They are not. The structure of a brain shows considerable *plasticity*—that is, change with experience. Changes are especially prominent at the microscopic level of axons, dendrites, and synapses, but sometimes, changes are visible to the unaided eye. For example, one part of the temporal cortex (devoted to hearing) is 30% larger in professional musicians than in other people (Schneider et al., 2002). We can't be sure whether that difference was a result of training, but other studies have reported that the brains of children who are starting musical training appear indistinguishable from those of children not in musical training (Norton et al., 2005). This result suggests that differences emerge during training instead of being present at the start.

For many decades researchers believed that the nervous system produced no new neurons after early infancy. Later researchers found that *undifferentiated cells called* **stem cells** can develop into additional neurons in a few brain areas (Gage, 2000; Graziadei & deHan, 1973; Song, Stevens, & Gage, 2002), at least in a few species, although we are not yet sure about humans (Eriksson et al., 1998; Rakic, 2002).

In contrast to the small effect on the number of neurons, new experiences produce huge effects on synapses, as the axons and dendrites expand and withdraw their branches. These changes, which are extensive in young individuals and slower in old age (Grutzendler, Kasthuri, & Gan, 2002), enable the brain to adapt to changing circumstances. Consider, for example, the changes that accompany blindness.

Ordinarily, the occipital cortex at the rear of the head is devoted to vision alone. However, in people born blind, the occipital cortex receives no visual input. Gradually, axons from other systems invade the occipital cortex and displace the inactive axons representing visual input. Within years the occipital cortex becomes responsive to touch information and language information that would not activate this area at all in sighted people. The behavioral effects include an enhanced ability to make fine distinctions by touch, as in reading Braille, for example, as well as enhanced language skills on the average (Amedi, Floel, Knecht, Zohary, & Cohen, 2004; Burton et al., 2001; Sadato et al., 1996, 1998). For someone who becomes blind later in life, the occipital cortex reorganizes less extensively (Gothe et al., 2002). In short, if you concentrate your efforts on one kind of task, your brain will reorganize to specialize more and more at that kind of task.

☑ CONCEPT CHECK

11. On the average blind people do better than sighted people at using their hands to recognize shapes, even though the touch receptors themselves do not change. What accounts for this advantage? (Check your answer on page 89.)

IN CLOSING

Neurons, Synapses, and Behavior

Behavior is complicated. You might describe some action with just a few words ("I ate a meal" or "I argued with my roommate"), but that short description corresponds to an immensely complicated sequence of coordinated and well-timed movements. Each complex behavior emerges from synapses, which in their basic outline are simple processes: A cell releases a chemical, which excites or inhibits a second cell for various periods of time. Then the chemical washes away or reenters the first cell to be used again.

Complex behavior emerges from those simple synapses because of the connections among huge numbers of neurons. No one neuron or synapse does much by itself; indeed, it is misleading to say that "dopamine does this" or "serotonin does that," as if a single type of neurotransmitter controlled anything by itself. Your experience results from dozens of types of neurotransmitters, billions of neurons, and trillions of synapses, each contributing in a small way. ∎

Summary

- *Neuron structure.* A neuron, or nerve cell, consists of a cell body, dendrites, and an axon. The axon conveys information to other neurons. (page 81)
- *The action potential.* Information is conveyed along an axon by an action potential, which is regenerated without loss of strength at each point along the axon. (page 83)
- *Mechanism of the action potential.* An action potential depends on the entry of sodium into the axon. Anything that blocks this flow will block the action potential. (page 83)
- *How neurons communicate.* A neuron communicates with another neuron by releasing a chemical called a neurotransmitter at a specialized junction called a synapse. A neurotransmitter can either excite or inhibit the next neuron. (page 84)
- *Neurotransmitters and behavioral disorders.* An excess or a deficit of a particular neurotransmitter can lead to abnormal behavior, such as that exhibited by people with Parkinson's disease. (page 87)
- *Experience and brain structure.* The anatomy of the nervous system is constantly in flux in small ways. New experiences can modify brain structure, especially for younger people. (page 88)

Answers to Concept Checks

5. Dendrites receive input from other neurons. Axons send messages. (page 82)
6. The mouse will react faster because the action potentials have a shorter distance to travel in the mouse's nervous system than in the giraffe's. (page 83)
7. negative . . . sodium . . . positive . . . action potential (page 83)
8. The presynaptic neuron releases a neurotransmitter that travels to the postsynaptic neuron, where it activates an excitatory or inhibitory receptor. (page 84)
9. Under the influence of a drug that prevents GABA from attaching to its receptors, the postsynaptic neuron will receive less inhibition than usual. If we presume that the neuron continues to receive a certain amount of excitation, it will then produce action potentials more frequently than usual. (page 84)
10. Haloperidol would increase the severity of Parkinson's disease. In fact large doses of haloperidol can induce symptoms of Parkinson's disease in anyone. (page 87)
11. If someone is blind from birth, touch sensation invades the occipital cortex as well as its normal site in the parietal cortex. The greater brain representation of touch enables the person to attend to fine details of touch that a sighted person would not notice. (page 89)

Drugs and Their Effects

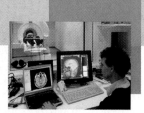

- *How do drugs affect synapses?*
- *How do they affect behavior?*

Imagine yourself typing a paper at your computer, except that you have extra fingers that do things you hadn't planned. Sometimes, they press the Caps Lock key AND EVERYTHING COMES OUT IN CAPITAL LETTERS. Sometimes, they press other keys and your words come out **boldface,** *italicized,* underlined, enlarged, or distorted in other ways. Sometimes, your extra fingers delete lettrs, add exxtras, or add a space in the mid dle of a word. Drugs have analogous effects on behavior. They enhance certain experiences or behaviors, weaken others, and garble thinking and speech.

In chapter 16 we shall consider drug abuse and addiction, including alcoholism. Here, the emphasis is on how the drugs act at synapses. A study of drugs illustrates many principles from the previous module.

Drugs affect synapses in many ways. They can attach to a receptor and activate it or fit imperfectly, like a key that almost fits a lock and jams it. They can increase or decrease the release of transmitters or decrease reuptake (the return of released transmitters to the neuron that released them). A drug that increases activity at a synapse is called an *agonist,* based on the Greek word for a contestant or fighter. A drug that decreases activity at a synapse is an *antagonist,* from the Greek word for an enemy.

Stimulants

Stimulants are *drugs that increase energy, alertness, and activity.* Amphetamine, methamphetamine, and cocaine prevent neurons from reabsorbing dopamine or serotonin after releasing them. The result is to prolong the effects of those transmitters at their receptors (Volkow, Wang, & Fowler, 1997; Volkow et al.,

1998). Amphetamine and methamphetamine not only block reuptake but also increase the release of the transmitters (Giros, Jaber, Jones, Wightman, & Caron, 1996; Paladini, Fiorillo, Morikawa, & Williams, 2001). Dopamine synapses are critical for almost anything that strongly motivates people, ranging from sex and food to gambling and video games (Koepp et al., 1998; Maldonado et al., 1997). By increasing the activity at dopamine synapses, amphetamine and methamphetamine hijack the brain's motivational system. They affect other brain systems as well, resulting in confusion, anxiety, and irritability. Physical effects include higher heart rate, blood pressure, and body temperature, and sometimes tremors, convulsions, heart attack, and death. Amphetamine and methamphetamine are similar, but methamphetamine produces stronger effects.

Cocaine has long been available in the powdery form of cocaine hydrochloride, which can be sniffed. Its stimulant effects increase gradually over a few minutes and then decline over about half an hour. It also anesthetizes the nostrils and sometimes damages the lungs. Before 1985 the only way to get a more intense effect from cocaine hydrochloride was to transform it into *freebase cocaine*—cocaine with the hydrochloride removed. Freebase cocaine enters the brain rapidly, and fast entry intensifies the experience.

The drug known as *crack cocaine* first became available in 1985. Crack is cocaine that has already been converted into freebase rocks, ready to be smoked (Brower & Anglin, 1987; Kozel & Adams, 1986). It is called "crack" because it makes popping noises when smoked. Within a few seconds, crack produces a rush of potent effects usually described as pleasant, although some people report intense anxiety instead and a few suffer heart attacks. Cocaine use can lead to mental confusion, lung diseases, and neglect of other life activities. A study of

© Roy Morsch/CORBIS

Crack cocaine reaches the brain much faster than other forms of cocaine. All else being equal, the faster a drug reaches the brain, the more intense the experience will be and the greater the probability of addiction.

twins, in which one abused cocaine or amphetamine and the other did not, found that the one who used the drugs had impairments of motor skills and attention, which lasted a year or more after quitting the drugs (Toomey et al., 2003).

Because amphetamine and cocaine inhibit the reuptake of dopamine and other transmitters, the transmitters eventually wash away from the synapse. Because they wash away faster than the presynaptic neuron can resynthesize them, the availability of these transmitters declines. A user experiences lethargy and mild depression for a few hours until the supply recovers.

Methylphenidate (Ritalin), a drug often prescribed for people with attention-deficit disorder, works the same way as cocaine, at the same synapses (Volkow et al., 1997, 1998). The difference is that methylphenidate, taken as pills, reaches the brain gradually over an hour or more and declines slowly over hours. Therefore, it does not produce the sudden "rush" that makes crack cocaine so addictive.

Tobacco delivers nicotine, which increases wakefulness and arousal by stimulating acetylcholine synapses. Although nicotine is classed as a stimulant, most smokers say it relaxes them. The research points to an explanation for this paradox. Smoking increases tension and stress levels, but abstaining from cigarettes leads to even greater tension and displeasure. Smoking another cigarette relieves the withdrawal symptoms and restores the usual mood, which is slightly tense but not as bad as the withdrawal state (Parrott, 1999). Nicotine also produces mixed effects on motivation: It decreases energy and motivation in low-reward situations while increasing activity in high-reward situations (Rice & Cragg, 2004). We shall consider nicotine addiction again in chapter 16.

Caffeine, another stimulant, blocks receptors for a chemical called adenosine. Because adenosine inhibits wakefulness and arousal, blocking it leads to increased arousal. Caffeine is the safest stimulant, although its use can lead to restlessness and poor sleep.

 CONCEPT CHECK

12. The drug AMPT (alpha-methyl-para-tyrosine) prevents the body from making dopamine. How would a large dose of AMPT affect someone's later responsiveness to cocaine, amphetamine, or methylphenidate?

13. Some people with attention-deficit disorder report that they experience benefits for the first few hours after taking the pills but begin to deteriorate in various ways in the late afternoon and evening. Why? (Check your answers on pages 95-96.)

Depressants

Depressants are *drugs that predominantly decrease arousal,* such as alcohol and *anxiolytics* (anxiety-reducing drugs). People have been using alcohol since prehistoric times. When archeologists unearthed a Neolithic village in Iran's Zagros Mountains, they found a jar that had been constructed about 5500–5400 B.C., one of the oldest human-made crafts ever found (Figure 3.28). Inside the jar, especially at the bottom, the archeologists found a yellowish residue. They were curious to know what the jar had held, so they sent some of the residue for chemical analysis. The unambiguous answer came back: The jar had been a wine vessel (McGovern, Glusker, Exner, & Voigt, 1996).

© University of Pennsylvania Museum

FIGURE 3.28 This jar, dated about 5500–5400 B.C., is one of the oldest human crafts ever found. It was used for storing wine.

Alcohol is a *class of molecules that includes methanol, ethanol, propyl alcohol (rubbing alcohol), and others. Ethanol is the type that people drink;* the others are toxic if consumed. Alcohol is a depressant that acts as a relaxant at moderate doses. In greater amounts it can increase aggressive and risk-taking behaviors, mainly by suppressing the fears and inhibitions that ordinarily limit such activities. In still greater amounts, as in binge drinking, alcohol leads to unconsciousness and death.

Excessive use can damage the liver and other organs, aggravate or prolong many medical conditions, and impair memory and motor control. A woman who drinks alcohol during pregnancy risks damage to her baby's brain, health, and appearance.

Another type of depressant drugs, **tranquilizers** or **anxiolytic drugs** *help people relax.* The most common drugs of this type are *benzodiazepines,* including diazepam (Valium) and alprazolam (Xanax). Benzodiazepines exert their calming effects by facilitating transmission at synapses that use GABA, the brain's main inhibitory transmitter. Alcohol facilitates transmission at the same synapses, though by a different mechanism (Sudzak et al., 1986). Taking alcohol and tranquilizers together can be dangerous because the combination suppresses the brain areas that control breathing and heartbeat.

One benzodiazepine drug, flunitrazepam (Rohypnol), has attracted attention as a "date rape drug." Flunitrazepam, which dissolves quickly in water, has no color, odor, or taste to warn the person who is consuming it. The effects of this drug, like those of other anxiolytics, include drowsiness, poor muscle coordination, and memory impairment (Anglin, Spears, & Hutson, 1997; Woods & Winger, 1997). That is, someone under the influence of the drug does not have the strength to fight off an attacker and may not remember the event clearly afterward. A hospital that suspects someone has been given this drug can run a urine test to determine its presence. Another "date rape drug" is GHB (gamma hydroxybutyrate), which has become more widespread because it can be made easily (though impurely) by mixing a degreasing solvent with drain cleaner. Like flunitrazepam, it relaxes the body and impairs muscle coordination. Large doses can induce vomiting, tremors, coma, and death.

Narcotics

Narcotics are *drugs that produce drowsiness, insensitivity to pain, and decreased responsiveness.* The classic examples, **opiates,** are *either natural drugs derived from the opium poppy or synthetic drugs with a chemical structure resembling natural opiates.* An opiate drug makes people feel happy, warm, and content, with little anxiety or pain. Unpleasant consequences include nausea and withdrawal from the real world. Once the drug has left the brain, the affected synapses become understimulated, and elation gives way to anxiety, pain, and hyperresponsiveness to sounds and other stimuli.

Morphine (named after Morpheus, the Greek god of dreams) has important medical use as a painkiller. Opiate drugs such as morphine, heroin, methadone, and codeine bind to specific receptors in the brain (Pert & Snyder, 1973). The discovery of neurotransmitter receptors demonstrated that opiates block pain in the brain, not in the skin. Neuroscientists then found that the brain produces several chemicals, called **endorphins,** that *bind to the opiate receptors*

(Hughes et al., 1975). Endorphins serve to inhibit chronic pain. They also inhibit neurons that inhibit the release of dopamine (North, 1992); by this double negative, they increase dopamine release and therefore produce reinforcing effects. The brain also releases endorphins during pleasant experiences, such as the "runner's high" or the chill you feel down your back when you hear especially thrilling music (Goldstein, 1980).

Marijuana

Marijuana (*cannabis*) is difficult to classify. It is certainly not a stimulant. It has a calming effect but not like that of alcohol or tranquilizers. It softens pain but not as powerfully as opiates. It produces some sensory distortions, especially an illusion that time is passing more slowly than usual, but not distortions like the hallucinations from LSD use. Because marijuana does not closely resemble any other drug, we discuss it separately.

The disadvantageous effects of marijuana include memory impairments and decreased drive. Most studies reporting memory problems in marijuana users are hard to interpret. Does marijuana impair memory or do people with memory problems like to use marijuana? As always, correlation does not indicate causation. However, one study found that a few months after people quit using marijuana, their memory improved (Pope, Gruber, Hudson, Huestis, & Yurgelun-Todd, 2001). This result strongly suggests that poor memory was a result of marijuana use, not a lifelong characteristic of those who chose to use marijuana.

Marijuana has several potential medical uses. It reduces nausea, suppresses tremors, reduces pressure in the eyes, and decreases cell loss in the brain just after a stroke (Glass, 2001; Panikashvili et al., 2001). Because of legal restrictions in the United States, research on these medical uses has been limited. On the negative side, marijuana increases the risk of Parkinson's disease (Glass, 2001), and long-term use probably increases the risk of lung cancer, as tobacco cigarettes do.

You may have heard that marijuana is dangerous as a "gateway drug"; that is, many heroin and cocaine users had used marijuana first. True, but they also tried cigarettes and alcohol first, as well as other risky experiences. It is unclear that marijuana leads to the use of more dangerous drugs any more than tobacco or alcohol does.

Although people are aware of marijuana's effects for no more than 2 or 3 hours after using it, it dissolves in the fats of the body, so traces of it can be found for weeks after the drug has been used (Dackis,

Pottash, Annitto, & Gold, 1982). Consequently, someone can "test positive" for marijuana use long after quitting it.

The active ingredient in marijuana is THC, or tetrahydrocannabinol. THC attaches to receptors that are abundant throughout the brain (Herkenham, Lynn, deCosta, & Richfield, 1991). The presence of those receptors implies that the brain produces THC-like chemicals of its own. Researchers discovered two chemicals named *anandamide* (from *ananda,* the Sanskrit word for "bliss") and 2-AG (short for *sn-2* arachidonylglycerol) that attach to the same receptors as THC (Devane et al., 1992; Stella, Schweitzer, & Piomelli, 1997). Receptors for these chemicals are abundant in brain areas that control memory and movement but not in the medulla, which controls heart rate and breathing (Herkenham et al., 1990). In contrast, the medulla has many opiate receptors. Consequently, heroin and morphine impair heart rate and breathing, whereas marijuana does not.

Unlike the more familiar kinds of neurotransmitter receptors, those for anandamide and 2-AG (and therefore marijuana) are located on the *presynaptic* neuron. When the presynaptic neuron releases a transmitter, such as glutamate or GABA, the postsynaptic (receiving) cell releases anandamide or 2-AG, which returns to the presynaptic cell to inhibit further release (Kreitzer & Regehr, 2001; R. I. Wilson & Nicoll, 2001, 2002). In effect it says, "I received your signal. You can slow down on sending any more of it." Marijuana, by resembling these natural reverse transmitters, has the same effect, except that it slows the signal even before it has been sent. It is as if the presynaptic cell "thinks" it has sent a signal, when in fact it has not.

Hallucinogens

Drugs that induce sensory distortions are called **hallucinogens** (Jacobs, 1987). Many of these drugs are derived from certain mushrooms or other plants; some are manufactured. Hallucinogenic drugs such as the synthetic drug LSD (lysergic acid diethylamide) distort

After California legalized marijuana for medical uses, many clubs and stores opened for the sale and distribution of the drug.

sensations and sometimes produce a dreamlike state or an intense mystical experience. Peyote, a hallucinogen derived from a cactus plant, has a long history of use in Native American religious ceremonies (Figure 3.29).

LSD attaches mainly to one kind of serotonin receptor (Jacobs, 1987). It stimulates those receptors at irregular times and prevents neurotransmitters from stimulating them at the normal times. We have an interesting gap in our knowledge at this point: We know *where* LSD exerts its effects, but we do not understand *how* altering those receptors leads to the experiences.

The drug MDMA (methylenedioxymethamphetamine), better known as "ecstasy," produces stimulant effects similar to amphetamine at low doses and hallucinogenic effects similar to LSD at higher doses. Of all abused drugs, this is the one for which the evidence of

FIGURE 3.29 The Huichol of Mexico use the hallucinogenic peyote cactus in traditional religious ceremonies. This yarn painting by Fabian Soarez depicts peyote upon a sacred altar.

brain damage is strongest. Use of MDMA stimulates dopamine and serotonin axons, thus producing the stimulant and hallucinogenic effects, but in the process damages those axons, at least in laboratory animals and presumably in humans also (McCann, Lowe, & Ricau-

rte, 1997). Perhaps for this reason, many users report that their first use was intense and pleasant, the next occasion less pleasant, and so forth.

Repeated users of MDMA show increased anxiety and depression, and impairments of attention, mem-

TABLE 3.1 Commonly Abused Drugs and Their Effects

Drug Category	Effects on the Nervous System	Short-term Effects	Risks (partial list)
Stimulants			
Amphetamine	Increases release of dopamine and decreases reuptake, prolonging effects	Increases energy and alertness	Psychotic reaction, agitation, heart problems, sleeplessness, stroke
Cocaine	Decreases reuptake of dopamine, prolonging effects	Increases energy and alertness	Psychotic reaction, heart problems, crime to pay for drugs, death
Methylphenidate (Ritalin)	Decreases reuptake of dopamine, but with slower onset and offset than cocaine	Increases alertness; much milder withdrawal effects than cocaine	Increased blood pressure
Caffeine	Blocks a chemical that inhibits arousal	Increases energy and alertness	Sleeplessness
Nicotine	Stimulates some acetylcholine synapses; stimulates some neurons that release dopamine	Increases arousal; abstention by a habitual smoker produces tension and depression	Lung cancer from the tars in cigarettes
Depressants			
Alcohol	Facilitates effects of GABA, an inhibitory neurotransmitter	Relaxation, reduced inhibitions, impaired memory and judgment	Automobile accidents, loss of job
Benzodiazepines	Facilitate effects of GABA, an inhibitory neurotransmitter	Relaxation, decreased anxiety, sleepiness	Dependence. Life-threatening if combined with alcohol or opiates
Narcotics			
Morphine, heroin, other opiates	Stimulate endorphin synapses	Decrease pain; withdrawal from interest in real world; unpleasant withdrawal effects during abstention	Heart stoppage; crime to pay for drugs
Marijuana			
Marijuana	Excites negative feedback receptors of both excitatory and inhibitory transmitters	Decreases pain and nausea; distorted sense of time	Impaired memory; lung diseases; impaired immune response
Hallucinogens			
LSD	Stimulates serotonin type 2 receptors at inappropriate times	Hallucinations, sensory distortions	Psychotic reaction, accidents, panic attacks, flashbacks
MDMA ("ecstasy")	Stimulates neurons that release dopamine; at higher doses also stimulates neurons that release serotonin	At low doses increases arousal; at higher doses hallucinations	Dehydration, fever, lasting damage to serotonin synapses
Rohypnol and GHB	Facilitate action at GABA synapses (which are inhibitory)	Relaxation, decreased inhibitions	Impaired muscle coordination and memory
Phencyclidine (PCP or "angel dust")	Inhibits one type of glutamate receptor	Intoxication, slurred speech; at higher doses hallucinations, thought disorder, impaired memory and emotions	Psychotic reaction

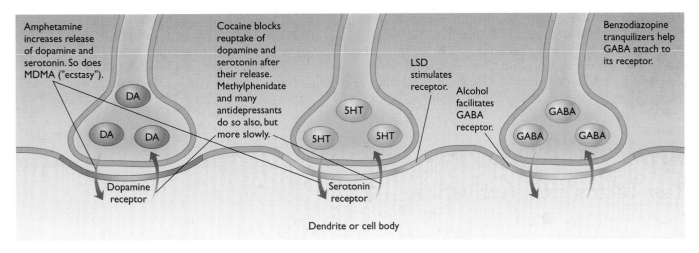

FIGURE 3.30 Both legal and illegal drugs operate at the synapses. Drugs can increase the release of neurotransmitters, block their reuptake, or directly stimulate or block their receptors.

ory, and sleep, which persist a year or two after they quit using the drug (Montoya, Sorrentino, Lucas, & Price, 2002; Reneman et al., 2001). Another study found that repeated users have apparent shrinkage of certain areas of the brain (P. M. Thompson et al., 2004). Conceivably, those people may have had such problems before they started using MDMA, but the pattern of results suggests danger. The drug also sometimes encourages prolonged dancing or other activity to the point of dehydration, a serious and sometimes fatal problem.

Yet another hallucinogen, phencyclidine (PCP, or "angel dust") acts by inhibiting receptors for the neurotransmitter glutamate. At low doses PCP's effects resemble those of alcohol. At higher doses it produces hallucinations, thought disorder, memory loss, and loss of emotions.

Table 3.1 summarizes the drugs we have been considering. Figure 3.30 diagrams the effects of several drugs. The list of risks is incomplete because of space. Large or repeated doses of any drug can be life-threatening.

IN CLOSING

Drugs and Synapses

If you were to change a few of a computer's connections at random, you could produce an "altered state," which would almost certainly not be an improvement. Giving drugs to a human brain is a little like changing the connections of a computer, and almost any drug at least temporarily impairs brain functioning in some way. By examining the effects of drugs on the brain, we can gain greater insight into the brain's normal processes and functions. ∎

Summary

- *Stimulants.* Stimulant drugs such as amphetamines and cocaine increase activity levels and pleasure. Compared to other forms of cocaine, crack produces more rapid effects on behavior, greater risk of addiction, and greater risk of damage to the heart and other organs. (page 90)
- *Alcohol.* Alcohol, the most widely abused drug in our society, relaxes people and relieves their inhibitions. It can also impair judgment and reasoning. (page 91)
- *Anxiolytics.* Benzodiazepines, widely used to relieve anxiety, can also relax muscles and promote sleep. (page 92)
- *Opiates.* Opiate drugs bind to endorphin receptors in the nervous system. The immediate effect of opiates is pleasure and relief from pain. (page 92)
- *Marijuana.* Marijuana's active compound, THC, acts on abundant receptors, found mostly in the hippocampus and certain brain areas important for the control of movement. Marijuana acts on receptors on the presynaptic neuron, putting the brakes on release of both excitatory and inhibitory transmitters. (page 92)
- *Hallucinogens.* Hallucinogens induce sensory distortions. LSD acts at one type of serotonin synapse. MDMA produces stimulant effects at low doses, hallucinogenic effects at higher doses, and a risk of brain damage. (page 93)

Answers to Concept Checks

12. Someone who took AMPT would become much less responsive than usual to amphetamine, cocaine, or methylphenidate. These drugs increase

the release of dopamine or prolong its effects, but if the neurons haven't been able to make dopamine, they cannot release it. (page 90)

13. Remember what happens after taking cocaine: Neurons release dopamine and other transmitters faster than they can resynthesize them. Because cocaine blocks reuptake, the supply of transmitters dwindles, and the result is an experience approximately the opposite of the stimulation and pleasure that cocaine initially provokes. The same process occurs with methylphenidate, except more slowly and to a smaller degree. (page 91)

CHAPTER ENDING

Key Terms and Activities

Key Terms

You can check the page listed for a complete description of a term. You can also check the glossary/index at the end of the text for a definition of a given term, or you can download a list of all the terms and their definitions for any chapter at this website:

www.thomsonedu.com/ psychology/kalat

action potential (page 83)
alcohol (page 91)
autonomic nervous system (page 74)
axon (page 81)
binding problem (page 78)
cell body (page 81)
central nervous system (page 69)
cerebellum (page 73)
cerebral cortex (page 70)
corpus callosum (page 75)
dendrite (page 81)

depressant (page 91)
dopamine (page 87)
electroencephalograph (EEG) (page 67)
endocrine system (page 74)
endorphins (page 92)
epilepsy (page 75)
evolutionary explanation (page 67)
frontal lobe (page 73)
functional magnetic resonance imaging (fMRI) (page 68)
glia (page 81)
hallucinogens (page 93)
hemisphere (page 70)
hormone (page 74)
magnetoencephalograph (MEG) (page 67)
medulla (page 73)
narcotics (page 92)
neuron (page 81)
neurotransmitter (page 84)
occipital lobe (page 70)
opiates (page 92)

parietal lobe (page 72)
Parkinson's disease (page 87)
peripheral nervous system (page 69)
physiological explanation (page 67)
pons (page 73)
positron-emission tomography (PET) (page 68)
postsynaptic neuron (page 84)
prefrontal cortex (page 73)
primary motor cortex (page 73)
primary somatosensory cortex (page 72)
reflex (page 73)
resting potential (page 83)
spinal cord (page 73)
stem cells (page 88)
stimulants (page 90)
synapse (page 84)
temporal lobe (page 71)
terminal bouton (page 84)
tranquilizers (or anxiolytic drugs) (page 92)

Suggestions for Further Reading

Kalat, J. W. (2007). *Biological psychology* (9th ed.). Belmont, CA: Wadsworth. Chapters 1 through 4 deal with the material discussed in this chapter in more detail.

Klawans, H. L. (1996). *Why Michael couldn't hit.* New York: Freeman. Informative and entertaining account of how the rise and fall of various sports heroes relates to what we know about the brain.

 Web/Technology Resources

Student Companion Website

www.thomsonedu.com/psychology/kalat

Explore the Student Companion Website for Online Try-It-Yourself activities, practice quizzes, flashcards, and more! The companion site also has direct links to the following websites.

The Whole Brain Atlas

www.med.harvard.edu/AANLIB/home.html

Stunning photographs of both normal and abnormal brains.

Brain Scans

www.biophysics.mcw.edu

Click various links to see images and movies of the three-dimensional structure of the brain.

Brain Anatomy of Various Species

www.brainmuseum.org/section/index.html

Compare the brains of humans, chimpanzees, dolphins, weasels, hyenas, polar bears, and a great many other mammals.

Web of Addictions

www.well.com/user/woa/

Andrew L. Homer and Dick Dillon provide factual information about alcohol and other abused drugs. Fact sheets and other material are arranged by drug, with links to Net resources related to addictions, in-depth information on special topics, and a list of places to get help with addictions.

National Clearinghouse for Alcohol and Drug Information

www.health.org/newsroom/

News reports about drug and alcohol abuse, with links to many other sites.

 *For Additional Study*

Kalat Premium Website

http://www.thomsonedu.com

For Critical Thinking Videos and additional Online Try-It-Yourself activities, go to this site to enter or purchase your code for the Kalat Premium Website.

ThomsonNOW!

http://www.thomsonedu.com

Go to this site for the link to ThomsonNOW, your one-stop study shop. Take a Pretest for this chapter, and Thomson-NOW will generate a personalized Study Plan based on your test reults. The Study Plan will identify the topics you need to review and direct you to online resources to help you master those topics. You can then take a Posttest to help you determine the concepts you have mastered and what you still need to work on.

Sensation and Perception

When my son Sam was 8 years old, he asked me, "If we went to some other planet, would we see different colors?" He did not mean a new mixture of familiar colors. He meant colors that were as different from familiar colors as yellow is from red or blue. I told him that would be impossible, and I tried to explain why.

No matter where we go in outer space, no matter what unfamiliar objects or atmospheres we might encounter, we could never experience a color or a sound or any other sensation that would be fundamentally different from what we experience on Earth. Different combinations, perhaps. But fundamentally different sensory experiences, no.

Three years later, Sam told me he wondered whether people who look at the same thing are all having the same experience: When different people look at something and call it "green," how can we know whether they are having the same experience? I agreed that there is no way of knowing.

Why am I certain that colors on a different planet would look the same as they do here on Earth and yet uncertain whether colors look the same to different people here? The answer may be obvious to you. If not, perhaps it will be after you read this chapter.

Sensation is *the conversion of energy from the environment into a pattern of response by the nervous system*. It is the registration of information. **Perception** is *the interpretation of that information*. For example, light rays striking your eyes give rise to sensation. Your experience of seeing and recognizing your roommate is a perception. (In practice the distinction between sensation and perception is often difficult to make.)

▌ *No matter how exotic some other planet might be, it could not have colors we do not have here. The reason is that our eyes can see only certain wavelengths of light, and color is the experience our brains create from those wavelengths.*

© A. Gragera/Latin Stock/Photo Researchers

Vision

- *How do our eyes convert light into something we can experience?*
- *How do we perceive colors?*

The comic book superhero Superman is said to have x-ray vision. Would that be possible? Never mind whether it would be possible for a biological organism to generate x-rays. If you *could* send out x-rays, would you improve your vision?

What is vision, anyway? It is the detection of light. Sensation in general is the detection of **stimuli**—*energies from the world around us that affect us in some way.* Our eyes, ears, and other sensory organs are packed with **receptors**—*specialized cells that convert environmental energies into signals for the nervous system.* You probably already learned this account in a high school or even elementary school science class. But did you believe it? Evidently, not everyone does. One survey posed the questions, "When we look at someone or something, does anything such as rays, waves, or energy go out of our eyes? Into our eyes?" Among first graders (about age 6), 49% answered (incorrectly) that energy went out of the eyes, and 54% answered (correctly) that energy came into the eyes. (It was possible to say *yes* to both.) Among college students, 33% said that energy went out of the eyes; 88% said that energy came in (Winer & Cottrell, 1996).

Follow-up studies revealed that the college students did not simply misunderstand the question. They really believed that their eyes sent out rays that were essential to vision. Even after reading a textbook chapter that explained vision, they did no better. After a psychologist patiently explained that the eyes do *not* send out sight rays, most answered correctly, but when asked again a few months later, almost half had gone back to believing their eyes sent out sight rays (Winer, Cottrell, Gregg, Fournier, & Bica, 2002).

So back to Superman: X-rays do not bounce off objects and come back; thus, even if he sent out x-rays, his brain would receive no sensation from the rays. The x-rays would ac-complish nothing. (Nothing good, anyway. They might cause cancer.)

Many people have other misconceptions about vision. We are often led astray because we imagine that what we see is a copy of the outside world. It is not. For example, color is not a property of objects; it is something your brain creates in response to light of different wavelengths. Brightness is not the same as the intensity of the light. (Light that is twice as intense does not appear twice as bright.) Our experiences *translate* the stimuli of the outside world into very different representations.

The Detection of Light

What we call *light* is part of the **electromagnetic spectrum**, *the continuum of all the frequencies of radiated energy*—from gamma rays and x-rays with very short wavelengths, through ultraviolet, visible light, and infrared, to radio and TV transmissions with very long wavelengths (Figure 4.1). What makes light visible? The answer is our receptors, which are equipped to respond to wavelengths from 400 to 700 nanometers (nm). With different receptors we might see a different range of wavelengths. Some species—many insects and birds, for example—respond to wavelengths shorter than 350 nm, which are invisible to humans.

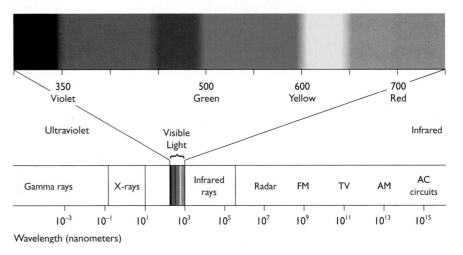

FIGURE 4.1 Visible light, what human eyes can see, is only a small part of the entire electromagnetic spectrum. While experimenting with prisms, Isaac Newton discovered that white light is a mixture of all colors, and color is a property of light. A carrot looks orange because it reflects orange light and absorbs all the other colors.

The Structure of the Eye

When we see an object, light reflected from that object passes through the **pupil**, *an adjustable opening in the eye through which light enters.* The **iris** is the *colored structure on the surface of the eye, surrounding the pupil.* It is the structure we describe when we say someone has brown, green, or blue eyes. The pupil can widen or narrow to control the amount of light entering the eye.

Light that passes through the pupil travels through the *vitreous humor* (a clear jellylike substance) to strike the retina at the back of the eyeball. The **retina** is a *layer of visual receptors covering the back surface of the eyeball* (Figure 4.2). The cornea and the lens focus the light on the retina as shown in the figure. The **cornea,** *a rigid transparent structure on the outer surface of the eyeball,* always focuses light in the same way. The **lens** is a *flexible structure that can vary in thickness,* enabling the eye to **accommodate,** that is, *to adjust its focus for objects at different distances.* When we look at a distant object, for example, our eye muscles relax and let the lens become thinner and flatter, as shown in Figure 4.3a. When we look at a close object, our eye muscles tighten and make the lens thicker and rounder (Figure 4.3b).

The **fovea** (FOE-vee-uh), *the central area of the human retina,* is adapted for highly detailed vision (see Figure 4.2). Of all retinal areas, the fovea has the greatest density of receptors. Also, more of the cerebral cortex is devoted to analyzing input from the fovea than input from other areas. When you want to see something in detail, you look at it directly so the light focuses on the fovea.

Hawks, owls, and other predatory birds have a greater density of receptors on the top of the retina (for looking down) than on the bottom of the retina (for looking up). When these birds are flying, this arrangement enables them to see the ground beneath them in detail. When they are on the ground, how-

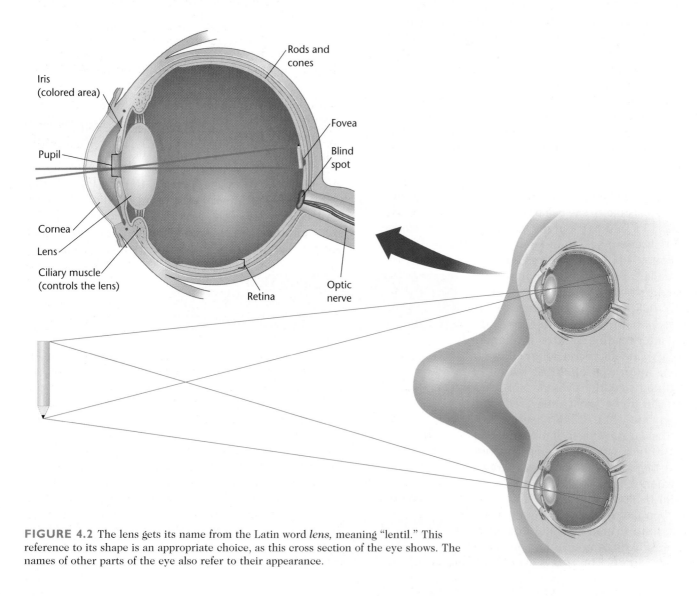

FIGURE 4.2 The lens gets its name from the Latin word *lens,* meaning "lentil." This reference to its shape is an appropriate choice, as this cross section of the eye shows. The names of other parts of the eye also refer to their appearance.

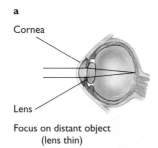

a

Cornea

Lens

Focus on distant object
(lens thin)

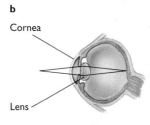

b

Cornea

Lens

Focus on close object
(lens thick)

FIGURE 4.3 The flexible, transparent lens changes shape so that objects **(a)** far and **(b)** near can come into focus. The lens bends entering light rays so that they fall on the retina. In old age the lens becomes rigid, and people find it harder to focus on nearby objects.

FIGURE 4.4 The consequence of having receptors mostly on the top of the retina: Birds of prey, such as these owlets, can see down much more clearly than they can see up. In flight that arrangement is helpful. On the ground they have to turn their heads almost upside down to see above them.

ever, they have trouble seeing above themselves (Figure 4.4).

Some Common Disorders of Vision

As people grow older, they gradually develop **presbyopia,** *impaired ability to focus on nearby objects because of decreased flexibility of the lens.* (The Greek root *presby* means "old." This root also shows up in the word *presbyterian,* which means "governed by the elders.") Many people's eyes are not quite spherical. Someone whose eyeballs are elongated, as shown in Figure 4.5a, can focus well on nearby objects but has difficulty focusing on distant objects. Such a person is said to be *nearsighted,* or to have **myopia** (mi-O-pee-ah). About half of all 20-year-olds are nearsighted and need glasses or contact lenses to focus at a distance. An older person with both myopia and presbyopia needs bifocal glasses to help with both near focus and distant focus. A person whose eyeballs are flattened, as shown in Figure 4.5b, has **hyperopia,** or *farsightedness.* Such a person can focus well on distant objects but has difficulty focusing on close objects.

Two other disorders are glaucoma and cataracts. **Glaucoma** is a *condition characterized by increased pressure within the eyeball;* the result can damage the optic nerve and therefore impair peripheral vision ("tunnel vision"). A **cataract** is a *disorder in which the lens becomes cloudy.* People with severe cataracts can have the lens surgically removed and replaced. Because the normal lens filters out more blue and ultraviolet light than other light, people with artificial lenses sometimes report seeing blue more clearly and

distinctly than ever before (Davenport & Foley, 1979). However, they suffer increased risk of damage to the retina from ultraviolet light.

 CONCEPT CHECK

1. Suppose you have normal vision and try on a pair of glasses made for someone with myopia. How will the glasses affect your vision? (Check your answer on page 113.)

The Visual Receptors

The visual receptors of the eye, specialized neurons in the retina at the back of the eyeball, are so sensitive to light that they can respond to a single photon, the smallest possible quantity of light. The two types of visual receptors, cones and rods, differ in function and appearance, as Figure 4.6 shows. The **cones** are *adapted for color vision, daytime vision, and detailed vision.* The **rods** are *adapted for vision in dim light.*

Of the visual receptors in the human retina, about 5% are cones. Most birds have the same or a higher proportion of cones and good color vision. Species that are active mostly at night—rats and mice, for example—have mostly rods, which facilitate detection of faint light.

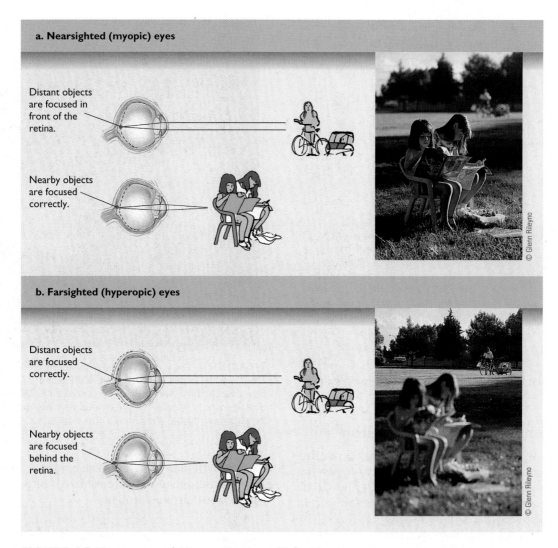

a. Nearsighted (myopic) eyes

Distant objects are focused in front of the retina.

Nearby objects are focused correctly.

b. Farsighted (hyperopic) eyes

Distant objects are focused correctly.

Nearby objects are focused behind the retina.

© Glenn Rileyno

© Glenn Rileyno

FIGURE 4.5 The structure of **(a)** nearsighted and **(b)** farsighted eyes distorts vision. Because the nearsighted eye is elongated, light from a distant object focuses in front of the retina. Because the farsighted eye is flattened, light from a nearby object focuses behind the retina. (The curved dashed line shows the position of the normal retina in each case.)

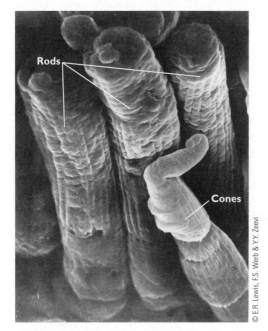

Rods

Cones

© E.R. Lewis, F.S. Werb & Y.Y. Zeevi

FIGURE 4.6 Rods and cones seen through a scanning electron micrograph. The rods, which number over 120 million in humans, provide vision in dim light. The 6 million cones in the retina distinguish gradations of color in bright light, enabling us to see that roses are red, magenta, ruby, carmine, cherry, vermilion, scarlet, and crimson—not to mention pink, yellow, orange, and white.

The proportion of cones is highest toward the center of the retina. The fovea consists solely of cones (see Figure 4.2). Away from the fovea, the proportion of cones drops sharply. For that reason you are color-blind in the periphery of your eye.

Try this experiment: Hold several pens or pencils of different colors behind your back. (Any objects will work as long as they have about the same size and shape and approximately the same brightness.) Pick one at random without looking at it. Hold it behind your head and bring it slowly into your field of vision. When you just barely begin to see it, you will probably not be able to see its color. (If glaucoma has impaired your peripheral vi-

Try It Yourself

sion, you will have to bring the object closer to your fovea before you can see it at all, and then you will see its color at once.) You can also try an Online Try It Yourself activity. Go to **www.thomsonedu.com/psychology/kalat.** Navigate to the student website, then to the Online Try It Yourself section, and click Color Blindness in Visual Periphery.

The rods are more effective than the cones for detecting dim light for two reasons: First, a rod is slightly more responsive to faint stimulation than a cone is. Second, the rods pool their resources. Only a few cones converge their messages onto the next cell, called a *bipolar cell,* whereas many rods converge their messages. In the far periphery of the retina, more than 100 rods send messages to a bipolar cell (Figure 4.7). Table 4.1 summarizes some of the key differences between rods and cones.

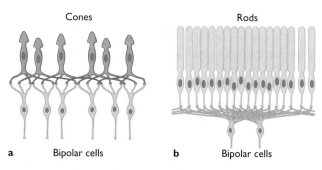

FIGURE 4.7 Because so many rods converge their input into the next layer of the visual system, known as bipolar cells, even a small amount of light falling on the rods stimulates the bipolar cells. Thus, the periphery of the retina, with many rods, readily detects faint light. However, because bipolars in the periphery get input from so many receptors, they have only imprecise information about the location and shape of objects.

TABLE 4.1 Differences Between Rods and Cones

	Rods	Cones
Shape	Nearly cylindrical	Tapered at one end
Prevalence in human retina	90–95%	5–10%
Abundant in	All vertebrate species	Species active during the day (birds, monkeys, apes, humans)
Area of the retina	Toward the periphery	Toward the fovea
Important for color vision?	No	Yes
Important for detail?	No	Yes
Important in dim light?	Yes	No
Number of types	Just one	Three

CONCEPT CHECK

2. Why is it easier to see a faint star in the sky if you look slightly to the side of the star instead of straight at it? (Check your answer on page 113.)

Dark Adaptation

Suppose you go into a basement at night trying to find your flashlight. The only light bulb in the basement is burned out. A little moonlight comes through the basement windows but not much. At first you hardly see anything. A minute or two later, you begin to see well enough to find your way around, and your vision continues improving as time passes. This *gradual improvement in the ability to see in dim light* is called **dark adaptation.**

Here is the mechanism behind dark adaptation: Exposure to light causes a chemical change in molecules called *retinaldehydes,* thereby stimulating the visual receptors. (Retinaldehydes are derived from vitamin A.) Under moderate light the receptors *regenerate* (rebuild) the molecules about as fast as the light alters them, and the person maintains a constant level of visual sensitivity. In darkness or very dim light, however, the receptors regenerate their molecules without interruption, so the ability to detect faint lights improves.

Cones and rods adapt to the dark at different rates. During the day our vision relies on cones. When we enter a dark place, our cones regenerate their retinaldehydes faster than the rods do, but by the time the rods finish their regeneration, they are far more sensitive to faint light than the cones are. At that point we see mostly with rods.

Here is how a psychologist demonstrates dark adaptation (E. B. Goldstein, 2007): You enter a room that is completely dark except for a tiny flashing light. You are told to use a knob to adjust the light so that you can barely see it. Over 3 or 4 minutes, you gradually decrease the intensity of the light, as shown in Figure 4.8a. Note that a decrease in the intensity of the light indicates an increase in the sensitivity of your eyes. If you stare straight at the point of light, your results demonstrate the adaptation of your cones to the dim light. (You are focusing the light on your fovea, which has no rods.)

Now the psychologist repeats the study with a change in procedure: You are told to stare at a faint light while another light flashes to the side of your field of vision, where it stimulates both rods and cones. You adjust a knob until the flashing light in the periphery is barely visible. (Figure 4.8b shows the results.) During the first 7 to 10 minutes, the results are the same as before. But then your rods become more

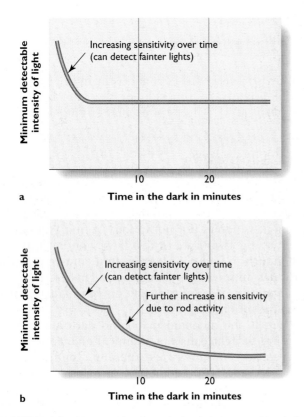

a   **Time in the dark in minutes**

b   **Time in the dark in minutes**

FIGURE 4.8 These graphs show dark adaptation to **(a)** a light you stare at directly, using only cones, and **(b)** a light in your peripheral vision, which you see with both cones and rods. *(Based on E. B. Goldstein, 1989)*

sensitive than your cones, and you begin to see even fainter lights. Your rods continue to adapt over the next 20 minutes or so.

To demonstrate dark adaptation for yourself without any apparatus, try this: At night turn on one light in your room. Close one eye and cover it tightly with your hand for at least a minute, preferably longer. Your covered eye will adapt to the dark while your open eye remains adapted to the light. Next turn off your light and open both eyes. You will see better with your dark-adapted eye than with the light-adapted eye. (This instruction assumes you still have some faint light coming through the window. In a *completely* dark room, of course, you will see nothing.)

Try It Yourself

☑ **CONCEPT CHECK**

3. You may have heard people say that cats can see in total darkness. Is that possible?

4. After you have thoroughly adapted to extremely dim light, will you see more objects in your fovea or in the periphery of your eye? (Check your answers on page 113.)

The Visual Pathway

If you or I were designing an eye, we would probably run some connections from the receptors directly back to the brain. But your eyes are built differently. The visual receptors send their impulses *away from* the brain, toward the center of the eye, where they make synaptic contacts with other neurons called bipolar cells. The bipolar cells in turn make contact with still other neurons, the **ganglion cells,** which are *neurons that receive their input from the bipolar cells.* The *axons from the ganglion cells join to form* the **optic nerve,** *which turns around and exits the eye,* as Figures 4.2 and 4.9 show. Half of each optic nerve crosses to the opposite side of the brain at the optic chiasm (KI-az-m). Axons from the optic nerve then separate and go to several locations in the brain. In humans most go to the thalamus, which then sends information to the primary visual cortex in the occipital lobe. People vary in the number of axons they have in the optic nerve; some have up to three times as many as others. Those with the thickest optic nerves can detect fainter or briefer lights and smaller amounts of movement (Andrews, Halpern, & Purves, 1997; Halpern, Andrews, & Purves, 1999).

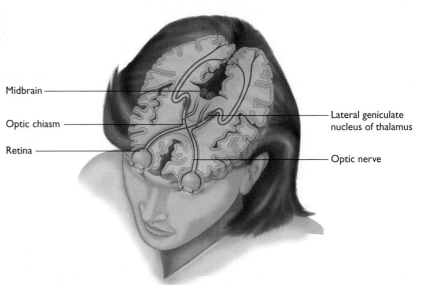

FIGURE 4.9 Axons from cells in the retina depart the eye at the blind spot and form the optic nerve. In humans about half the axons in the optic nerve cross to the opposite side of the brain at the optic chiasm.

The *retinal area where the optic nerve exits* is called the **blind spot.** That part of the retina has no room for receptors because the exiting axons take up all the space. Ordinarily, you are unaware of your blind spot.

To illustrate, cover your left eye and stare at the center of Figure 4.10; then slowly move the page forward and backward. When your eye is about 25 to 30 cm (10 to 12 inches) away from the page, the lion disappears because it falls into your blind spot. In its place you perceive a continuation of the circle. Also, go to **www.thomsonedu.com/ psychology/kalat.** Navigate to the student website, then to the Online Try It Yourself section, and click Filling in the Blind Spot.

Try It Yourself

Online Try It Yourself

In fact you have tiny "blind spots" throughout your retina. Many receptors lie in the shadow of the

retina's blood vessels. Your brain fills in the gaps with what "must" appear visually (Adams & Horton, 2002).

We become aware of visual information only after it reaches the cerebral cortex. Someone with a damaged visual cortex has no conscious visual perception, even in dreams, despite having normal eyes. However, someone with damaged eyes and an intact brain can at least imagine visual scenes. One laboratory developed a way to bypass damaged eyes and send visual information directly to the brain. As shown in Figure 4.11, a camera attached to a blind person's sunglasses sends messages to a computer, which then sends messages to electrodes that stimulate appropriate spots in the person's visual cortex (Dobelle, 2000). After hours of practice, such people see well enough to find their way around, identify simple shapes, and count objects. However, the vision has little detail because of the small number of electrodes. Further research is underway with monkeys, in hopes of developing a

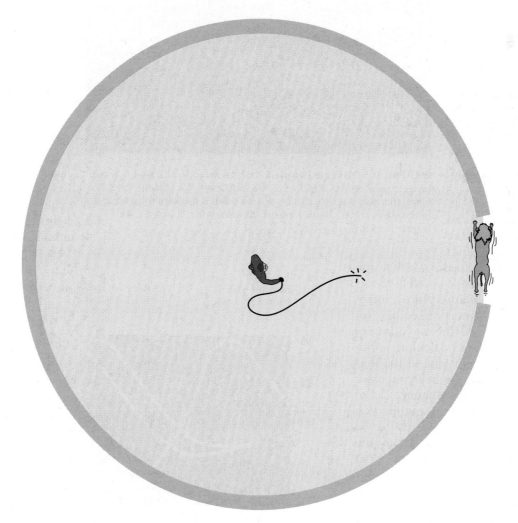

FIGURE 4.10 Close your left eye and focus your right eye on the animal trainer. Move the page toward your eyes and away from them until you find the point where the lion on the right disappears. At that point the lion is focused on the blind spot of your retina, where you have no receptors. What you see there is not a blank spot but a continuation of the circle.

practical aid for people who are blind (D. C. Bradley et al., 2005).

Color Vision

As Figure 4.1 shows, different colors of light correspond to different wavelengths of electromagnetic energy. How does the visual system convert these wavelengths into a perception of color? The process begins with three kinds of cones, which respond to different wavelengths of light. Later, cells in the visual path code this wavelength information in terms of pairs of opposites—roughly, red versus green, yellow versus blue, and white versus black. Finally, cells in the cerebral cortex compare the input from various parts of the visual field to synthesize a color experience for each object. Let's examine these three stages in turn.

The Trichromatic Theory

Thomas Young was an English physician of the 1700s who, among other accomplishments, helped to decode the Rosetta stone (making it possible to understand Egyptian hieroglyphics), introduced the modern concept of energy, revived and popularized the wave theory of light, showed how to calculate annuities for insurance, and offered the first theory about how people perceive color (Martindale, 2001). His theory, elaborated and modified by Hermann von Helmholtz in the 1800s, came to be known as the **trichromatic theory**, or the **Young-Helmholtz theory**. It is called *trichromatic* because it claims that our receptors respond to three primary colors. In modern terms we say that *color vision depends on the relative rate of response by three types of cones.* Each type of cone is most sensitive to a particular range of wavelengths (Figure

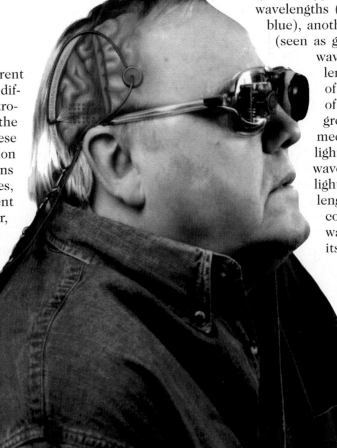

FIGURE 4.11 William Dobelle developed an apparatus that takes an image from a camera attached to the sunglasses of a person who is blind, transforms it by a computer, and sends a message to electrodes in the visual cortex. By this means someone with damaged eyes regains partial vision.

© Reuters New Media Inc./CORBIS

4.12). One type is most sensitive to short wavelengths (which we generally see as blue), another to medium wavelengths (seen as green), and another to long wavelengths (red). Each wavelength prompts varying levels of activity in the three types of cones. So, for example, green light excites mostly the medium-wavelength cones, red light excites mostly the long-wavelength cones, and yellow light excites the medium-wavelength and long-wavelength cones about equally. Every wavelength of light produces its own distinct ratio of responses by the three kinds of cones. White light excites all three kinds of cones equally.

Young and Helmholtz proposed their theory long before anatomists confirmed the existence of these three types of cones (Wald, 1968). Helmholtz relied on this behavioral observation: Observers can mix various amounts of three colors of light to match all other colors. (Mixing lights is different from mixing paints. Mixing yellow and blue *paints*

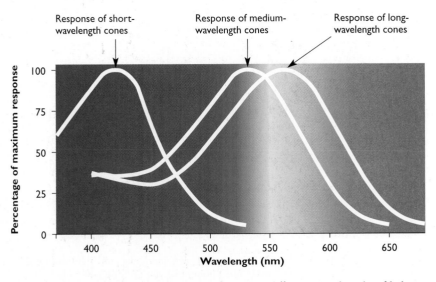

FIGURE 4.12 Sensitivity of three types of cones to different wavelengths of light. *(Based on data of Bowmaker & Dartnall, 1980)*

FIGURE 4.13 Blue dots look black unless they cover a sizable area. Count the red dots; then count the blue dots. Try again while standing farther from the page. You will probably see as many red dots as before but fewer blue dots.

produces green; mixing yellow and blue *lights* produces white.)

The short-wavelength cones, which respond most strongly to blue, are less numerous than the other types of cones. Consequently, a tiny blue point may look black. For the retina to detect blueness, the blue must extend over a moderately large area. Figure 4.13 illustrates this effect.

 CONCEPT CHECK

5. According to the trichromatic theory, how does our nervous system tell the difference between bright yellow-green and dim yellow-green light? (Check your answer on page 113.)

The Opponent-Process Theory

Young and Helmholtz were right about how many cones we have, but our perception of color has features that the trichromatic theory does not easily handle. For example, four colors, not three, *seem* primary or basic to most people: red, green, yellow, and blue. Yellow simply does not seem like a mixture of reddish and greenish experiences, nor is green a yellowish blue. More important, if you stare for a minute or so at something red and look away, you see a green afterimage. If you stare at something green, yellow, or blue, you see a red, blue, or yellow afterimage. The trichromatic theory provides no easy explanation for these afterimages.

Therefore, a 19th-century scientist, Ewald Hering, proposed the **opponent-process theory** of color vision: *We perceive color not in terms of independent colors but in terms of a system of paired opposites—red versus green, yellow versus blue, and white versus black.* This idea is best explained with the example in Figure 4.14. *Please do this now.*

AP/Wide World Photos

© USPS 1998

FIGURE 4.14 Stare at one of Daffy's pupils for a minute or more under a bright light without moving your eyes or head; then look at a plain white or gray background. You will see a negative afterimage.

When you looked away, you saw the cartoon in its normal coloration. After staring at something blue, you get a yellow afterimage. Similarly, after staring at yellow, you see blue; after red, you see green; after green, you see red; after white, black; and after black, white. These *experiences of one color after the removal of another* are called **negative afterimages.**

Presumably, the explanation depends on cells somewhere in the nervous system that maintain a spontaneous rate of activity when unstimulated, increase their activity in the presence of, say, green, and decrease it in the presence of red. After prolonged green stimulation fatigues them, they become less active than usual; that is, they respond as if in the presence of red. Similarly, other cells would be excited by red and inhibited by green, excited by yellow and inhibited by blue, and so forth. Patterns of this type have been found in many neurons at various locations in the visual parts of the nervous system (DeValois & Jacobs, 1968; Engel, 1999).

 CONCEPT CHECK

6. Which theory most easily explains negative color afterimages?
7. The negative afterimage that you created by staring at Figure 4.14 may seem to move against the background. Why doesn't it stay in one place? (Check your answers on page 113.)

Try It Yourself

The Retinex Theory

The opponent-process theory accounts for many phenomena of color vision but overlooks an important one. Suppose you look at a large white screen illuminated entirely with green light in an otherwise dark room. How would you know whether this is a white screen illuminated with green light or a green screen illuminated with white light? Or a blue screen illuminated with yellow light? (The possibilities go on and on.) The answer is that you wouldn't know. But now someone wearing a brown shirt and blue jeans stands in front of the screen. Suddenly, you see the shirt as brown, the jeans as blue, and the screen as white, even though all the objects are reflecting mostly green light. The point is that we do not perceive the color of an object in isolation. We perceive color by comparing the light an object reflects to the light that other objects reflect. As a result we can perceive blue jeans as blue and bananas as yellow regardless of the type of light. This *tendency of an object to appear nearly the same color under a variety of lighting conditions* is called **color constancy** (Figure 4.15).

In response to such observations, Edwin Land (the inventor of the Polaroid Land camera) proposed the **retinex theory**. According to this theory, *we perceive color through the cerebral cortex's comparison of various retinal patterns.* (*Retinex* is a combination of the words *retina* and *cortex*.) The cerebral cortex compares the patterns of light coming from different areas of the retina and synthesizes a color perception for each area (Land, Hubel, Livingstone, Perry, & Burns, 1983; Land & McCann, 1971).

As Figure 4.15 emphasizes, it is wrong to call short-wavelength light "blue" or long-wavelength light "red" as the text implied a few pages ago. In Figure 4.15 a gray pattern looks blue in one context and yellow in another (Lotto & Purves, 2002; Purves & Lotto, 2003). The "color" is a construction by our brain, not a property of the light itself, and which color our brain constructs depends on multiple circumstances.

In the 1800s the trichromatic theory and the opponent-process theory were considered rival theories. Today, vision researchers consider those two and the retinex theory correct with regard to different aspects of vision. The trichromatic theory is certainly correct in stating that human color vision starts with three kinds of cones. The opponent-process theory explains how later cells organize color information. The retinex theory adds the final touch, noting that the cerebral cortex compares color information from various parts of the visual field.

CRITICAL THINKING

A STEP FURTHER

Color Afterimages

If you stare for a minute at a small green object on a white background and then look away, you will see a red afterimage. But if you stare at a green wall nearby so that you see nothing but green in all directions, then when you look away, you do not see a red afterimage. Why not?

Color Vision Deficiency

For a long time, people apparently assumed that anyone who was not blind could see and recognize colors (Fletcher & Voke, 1985). Then during the 1600s, the phenomenon of color vision deficiency (or colorblindness) was unambiguously recognized. Here was the first clue that color vision is a function of our eyes and brains and not just of the light itself.

The older term color*blindness* is misleading because very few people are totally unable to distinguish colors. However, about 8% of men and less than 1% of women have difficulty distinguishing red from green and yellow (Bowmaker, 1998). The ultimate cause is a recessive gene on the X chromosome. Because men have only one X chromosome, they need just one gene to become red-green color deficient. Women need two such genes to develop the condition because they have two X chromosomes. Red-green color-deficient people

FIGURE 4.15 **(a)** When the block is under yellow light (left) or blue light (right), you can still recognize individual squares as blue, yellow, white, red, and so forth. However, the actual light reaching your eyes is different in the two cases. Parts **(b)** and **(c)** show the effects of removing more and more of the background: The squares that appear blue in the left half of part **(a)** are actually grayish; so are the squares that appear yellow in the right half. (Why We See What We Do, by D. Purves and R. B. Lotto, figure 6.10, p. 134. Copyright 2003 Sinauer Associates, Inc. Reprinted by permission.)

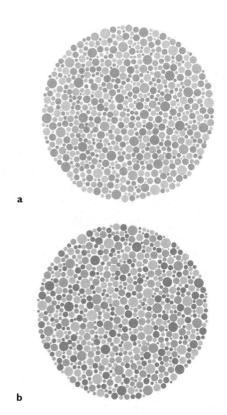

a

b

FIGURE 4.16 These items provide an informal test for red-green color vision deficiency, an inherited condition that mostly affects men. What do you see? Compare your answers to answer A on page 113. *(Reproduced from Ishihara's Test for Colour Blindness, Kanehara & Co., Ltd., Tokyo, Japan. A test for color blindness cannot be conducted with this material. For accurate testing, the original plate should be used.)*

have only two kinds of cones, the short-wavelength cone and either the long-wavelength or the medium-wavelength cone (Fletcher & Voke, 1985).

Figure 4.16 gives a crude but usually satisfactory test for red-green color vision deficiency. What do you see in each part of the figure?

Try It Yourself

How does the world look to people with color vision deficiency? They describe the world with all the usual color words: Roses are red, bananas are yellow, and grass is green. But their answers do not mean that they perceive colors the same as other people do. Can they tell us what a "red" rose actually looks like? In most cases no. Certain rare individuals, however, are red-green color deficient in one eye but have normal vision in the other eye. Because these people know what the color words really mean (from experience with their normal eye), they can tell

us what their deficient eye sees. They say that objects that look red or green to the normal eye look yellow or yellow-gray to the other eye (Marriott, 1976).

If you have normal color vision, Figure 4.17 will show you what it is like to be color deficient. First, cover part b, a typical item from a color deficiency test, and stare at part a, a red field, under a bright light for about a minute. (The brighter the light and the longer you stare, the greater the effect will be.) Then look at part b. Staring at the red field has fatigued your red cones, so you will now have only a weak sensation of red. As the red cones recover, you will see part b normally.

Try It Yourself

Now stare at part c, a green field, for about a minute and look at part b again. Because you have fatigued your green cones, the figure in b will stand out even more strongly than usual. In fact certain people with red-green color deficiency may be able to see the number in b only after staring at c.

Color Vision, Color Words, and Culture

Some languages have more color words than others. For example, English has many words for shades of red, including carnation, crimson, maroon, ruby, and scarlet. Some languages do not even have a word for blue. For example, Modern Irish and Scots Gaelic languages use the word *glas,* which applies to both green and blue (Lazar-Meyn, 2004). Several languages have a word that applies to both blue and dark.

In most cases psychologists and anthropologists simply report cultural differences without any attempt to explain why they arose. In this case researchers suggested a possible reason. Most cultures in temperate climates have a word for blue, whereas many cultures in the tropics do not, as shown in Figure 4.18. People in tropical climates generally have greater exposure to direct sunlight, and the sun's ultraviolet radiation accelerates aging of the lens of the eye. Prolonged exposure to ultraviolet radiation accel-

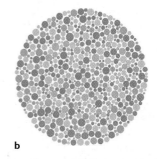

a   b   c

FIGURE 4.17 Adaptation to these stimuli temporarily alters sensitivity to reds and greens. First, stare at pattern **(a)** under bright light for about a minute and then look at **(b)**. What do you see? Next stare at **(c)** for a minute and look at **(b)** again. Now what do you see? See answer B on page 113. *(Reproduced from Ishihara's Test for Colour Blindness, Kanehara & Co., Ltd., Tokyo, Japan. A test for color blindness cannot be conducted with this material. For accurate testing, the original plate should be used.)*

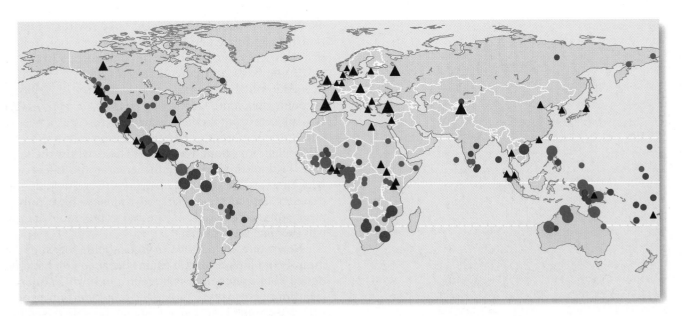

FIGURE 4.18 Each dot represents one culture. Those with a blue triangle have a separate word for blue. Those with a word meaning "either green or blue" are marked in red. Cultures marked with a green dot have only a word for "dark." Note that the cultures lacking a word for blue are concentrated mostly in or near the tropics. *(From Lindsey & Brown, 2002)*

erates the yellowing of the lens, thus impairing perception of short-wavelength (blue) light. As the lens ages, what used to appear blue becomes greenish or dark. One suggestion is that tropical cultures do not use a word for blue because many of them, especially their older people, have trouble seeing blue (Lindsey & Brown, 2002).

Could you imagine a way to test this interesting idea? Psychologists tested young and older adults in the United States. Even for people who spend their lives indoors, the lens gets yellower with age, though not as fast as in tropical societies. The researchers asked each person to examine and name the colors of chips varying in hue and brightness. The result was that the older people, despite their yellowed lenses, called the same chips "green" and "blue" as the younger people (Hardy, Frederick, Kay, & Werner, 2005). Given that changes in the lens do not prevent people from recognizing colors, exposure to ultraviolet light probably does not explain why some cultures lack a separate word for blue. Alas, an appealing hypothesis is disconfirmed.

CRITICAL THINKING
A STEP FURTHER

Color Experiences

The introduction to this chapter suggested that we would see no new colors on another planet and that we cannot be certain that different peo-

ple on Earth really have the same color experiences. Now try to explain the reasons behind those statements.

IN CLOSING

Vision as an Active Process

Before the existence of people or other color-sighted animals on Earth, was there any color? *No.* Light was present, to be sure, and different objects reflected different wavelengths of light, but color exists only in brains, not in the objects themselves or the light they reflect. Our vision is not just a copy of the outside world; it is a construction that enables us to interact with the world to our benefit.

If you take additional courses on sensation and perception, you will be struck by how complicated and how different from common sense notions the visual system is. You might imagine that you just see something and there it is. No, your brain has to do an enormous amount of processing to determine what you are seeing. If you doubt that, just imagine building a robot with vision. Light strikes the robot's visual sensors, and then . . . what? How will the robot know what objects it sees or what to do about them? All those processes—which we do not understand well enough to copy in a robot—happen in a fraction of a second in your brain. ∎

Summary

- *Common misconceptions.* The eyes do not send out "sight rays," nor does the brain build little copies of the stimuli it senses. It converts or translates sensory stimuli into an arbitrary code that represents the information. (page 101)

- *Focus.* The cornea and lens focus the light that enters through the pupil of the eye. If the eye is not spherical or if the lens is not flexible, corrective lenses may be needed. (page 102)

- *Cones and rods.* The retina contains two kinds of receptors: cones and rods. Cones are specialized for detailed vision and color perception. Rods detect dim light. (page 103)

- *Blind spot.* The blind spot is the area of the retina through which the optic nerve exits; this area has no visual receptors and is therefore blind. (page 107)

- *Color vision.* Color vision depends on three types of cones, each most sensitive to a particular range of light wavelengths. The cones transmit messages so that the bipolar and ganglion cells in the visual system are excited by light of one color and inhibited by light of the opposite color. Then the cerebral cortex compares the responses from different parts of the retina to determine the color of light coming from each area of the visual field. (page 108)

- *Color vision deficiency.* Complete colorblindness is rare. Certain people have difficulty distinguishing reds from greens; in rare cases some have difficulty distinguishing yellows from blues. (page 110)

Answers to Concept Checks

1. If your vision is normal, then wearing glasses intended for a myopic person will make your vision blurry. Such glasses alter the light as though they were bringing the object closer to the viewer. Unless the glasses are very strong, you may not notice much difference when you are looking at distant objects because you can adjust the lens of your eyes to compensate for what the glasses do. However, nearby objects will appear blurry in spite of the best compensations that the lenses of your eyes can make. (page 103)

2. The center of the retina consists entirely of cones. If you look slightly to the side, the light falls on an area of the retina that consists partly of rods, which are more sensitive to faint light. (page 105)

3. As do people, cats can adapt well to dim light. No animal, however, can see in complete darkness. Vision is the detection of light that strikes the eye. (page 106)

4. You will see more objects in the periphery of your eye. The fovea contains only cones, which cannot become as sensitive as the rods do in the periphery. (page 106)

5. Although bright yellow-green and dim yellow-green light would evoke the same ratio of activity by the three cone types, the total amount of activity would be greater for the bright yellow-green light. (page 108)

6. The opponent-process theory most easily explains negative color afterimages because it assumes that we perceive colors in terms of paired opposites, red vs. green and yellow vs. blue (as well as white vs. black). (page 109)

7. The afterimage is on your eye, not on the background. When you try to focus on a different part of the afterimage, you move your eyes and the afterimage moves with them. (page 109)

Answers to Other Questions in the Module

A. In Figure 4.16a a person with normal color vision sees the numeral 74; in Figure 4.16b the numeral 8.

B. In Figure 4.17b you should see the numeral 29. After you have stared at the red circle in part a, the 29 in part b may look less distinct than usual, as though you were red-green color deficient. After staring at the green circle, the 29 may be even *more* distinct than usual. If you do not see either of these effects at once, try again, but this time stare at part a or c a little longer *and* continue staring at part b a little longer. The effect does not appear immediately, only after a few seconds.

The Nonvisual Senses

- *How do hearing, the vestibular sense, skin senses, pain, taste, and smell work?*

Consider these common expressions:

- I *see* what you mean.
- I *feel* your pain.
- I am deeply *touched* by everyone's support and concern.
- The Senate will *hold* hearings on the budget proposal.
- She is a person of fine *taste*.
- He was *dizzy* with success.
- The policies of this company *stink*.
- That *sounds* like a good job offer.

Each sentence expresses an idea in terms of sensation, though we know that these terms are not meant to be taken literally. If you compliment people on their "fine taste," you are not referring to their tongues.

The broad metaphorical use of terms of sensation is not accidental. Our thinking and brain activity deal mostly, if not entirely, with sensory stimuli. Perhaps you doubt that assertion: "What about abstract concepts?" you might object. "Sometimes, I think about numbers, time, love, justice, and all sorts of other nonsensory concepts." Yes, but how did you learn those concepts? Didn't you learn numbers by counting objects you could see or touch? Didn't you learn about time by observing changes in sensory stimuli? Didn't you learn about love and justice from specific events that you saw, heard, and felt? Could you explain any abstract concept without referring to something you detect through your senses?

We have already considered how we detect light. Now let's discuss how we detect sounds, head tilt, skin stimulation, and chemicals.

Hearing

What we familiarly call the "ear" is a fleshy structure technically known as the *pinna*. It serves to funnel sounds to the inner ear, where the receptors lie. The mammalian ear converts sound waves into mechanical displacements that a row of receptor cells can detect. **Sound waves** are *vibrations of the air or of another medium*. They vary in both frequency and amplitude (Figure 4.19). The frequency of a sound wave is the number of *cycles (vibrations) that it goes through per second*, designated **hertz (Hz)**. **Pitch** is a *perception closely related to frequency*. We perceive a high-frequency sound wave as high pitched and a low-frequency sound as low pitched.

Loudness is a *perception that depends on the amplitude of sound waves*—that is, their intensity. Other things being equal, the greater the amplitude of a sound, the louder it sounds. Because pitch and loudness are psychological experiences, however, they are influenced by factors other than the amplitude of sound waves. For example, tones of different frequencies may not sound equally loud, even though they have the same amplitude.

The ear, a complicated organ, converts relatively weak sound waves into more intense waves of pressure in the *fluid-filled canals of the snail-shaped organ* called the **cochlea** (KOCK-lee-uh), *which contains the receptors for hearing* (Figure 4.20). When sound waves strike the eardrum, they cause it to vi-

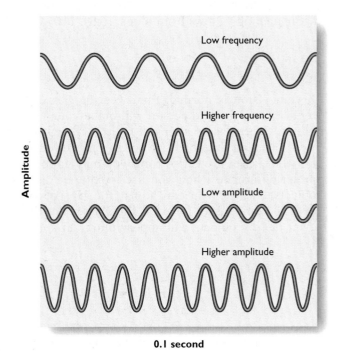

FIGURE 4.19 The period (time) between the peaks of a sound wave determines the frequency of the sound; we experience frequencies as different pitches. The vertical range, or amplitude, of a wave determines the sound's intensity and loudness.

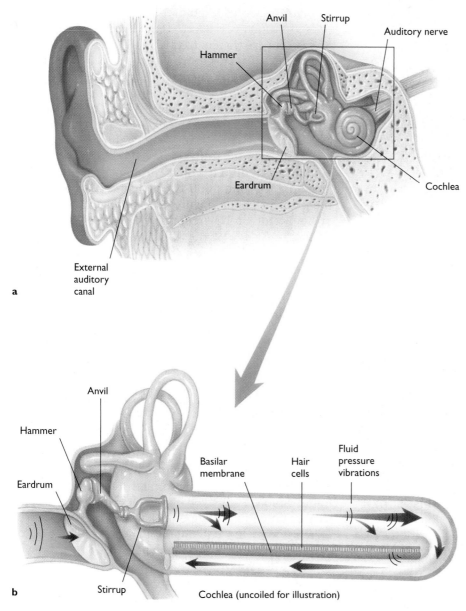

FIGURE 4.20 When sound waves strike the eardrum **(a)**, they make it vibrate. The eardrum is connected to three tiny bones—the hammer, anvil, and stirrup—that convert the sound wave into a series of strong vibrations in the fluid-filled cochlea **(b)**. These vibrations displace the hair cells along the basilar membrane in the cochlea, which is aptly named after the Greek word for *snail*. Here, the dimensions of the cochlea have been changed to make the general principles clear.

neurons whose axons form the auditory nerve. The auditory nerve transmits impulses to the brain areas responsible for hearing.

Understanding the mechanisms of hearing helps us explain hearing loss. One kind of hearing loss is **conduction deafness,** which *results when the bones connected to the eardrum fail to transmit sound waves properly to the cochlea.* Surgery can sometimes correct conduction deafness by removing whatever is obstructing the bones' movement. Someone with conduction deafness can still hear his or her own voice because it is conducted through the skull bones to the cochlea, bypassing the eardrum altogether. The other type of hearing loss is **nerve deafness,** which *results from damage to the cochlea, the hair cells, or the auditory nerve.* Nerve deafness can result from heredity, disease, or prolonged exposure to loud noises. Surgery cannot correct nerve deafness. Hearing aids can compensate for hearing loss in most people with either type of deafness (Moore, 1989). Hearing aids merely increase the intensity of the sound, however, so they are of little help in cases of severe nerve deafness.

Many people have hearing impairments for only certain frequencies. For example, people with damage to certain parts of the cochlea have trouble hearing high frequencies or medium-range frequencies. Modern hearing aids can be adjusted to intensify only the frequencies that a given person has trouble hearing.

brate. The eardrum connects to three tiny bones: the hammer, the anvil, and the stirrup (also known by their Latin names: malleus, incus, and stapes). As the weak vibrations of the large eardrum travel through these bones, they are transformed into stronger vibrations of the much smaller stirrup. The stirrup in turn transmits the vibrations to the fluid-filled cochlea, where the vibrations displace hair cells along the basilar membrane in the cochlea. These hair cells, which act much like touch receptors on the skin, connect to

Pitch Perception

Adult humans can hear sound waves from about 15–20 hertz to about 15,000–20,000 Hz (cycles per second). The low frequencies are perceived as low pitch; the high frequencies are perceived as high pitch, but frequency is not the same as pitch. For example, doubling the frequency doesn't make the pitch seem twice as high; it makes it one octave higher. The upper limit of hearing declines with age and also after

ICM Artists, NY

▌ Hearing is the sensing of vibrations. Evelyn Glennie, profoundly deaf since childhood, has become a famous percussionist. Although she cannot hear her music, she detects the vibrations through her stocking feet.

exposure to loud noises. Thus, children hear higher frequencies than adults do.

We hear pitch by different mechanisms at different frequencies. At low frequencies (up to about 100 Hz), *a sound wave through the fluid of the cochlea vibrates all the hair cells, which produce action potentials in synchrony with the sound waves.* This is the **frequency principle.** For example, a sound with a frequency of 50 Hz makes each hair cell send the brain 50 impulses per second.

Beyond about 100 Hz, hair cells cannot keep pace. Even so, each sound wave excites at least a few hair cells, and *"volleys" of them (groups) respond to each vibration by producing an action potential* (Rose, Brugge, Anderson, & Hind, 1967). This is known as the **volley principle.** Thus, a tone at 1000 Hz might send 1,000 impulses to the brain per second, even though no single neuron was firing that rapidly. Volleys can keep up with sounds up to about 4000 Hz, good enough for almost all speech and music. (The highest note on a piano is 4224 Hz.)

At still higher frequencies, we rely on a different mechanism. At each point along the cochlea, the hair cells are tuned resonators that vibrate only for sound waves of a particular frequency. That is, *the highest frequency sounds vibrate hair cells near the stirrup end and lower frequency sounds (down to about 100–200 Hz) vibrate hair cells at points farther along the membrane* (Warren, 1999). This is the **place principle.** Tones less than about 100 Hz excite all hair cells equally, and we hear them by the frequency principle. We identify tones from 100 to 4000 Hz by a combination of the volley principle and the place principle. Beyond 4000 Hz we identify tones only by the place principle. Figure 4.21 summarizes the three principles of pitch perception.

 CONCEPT CHECK

8. Suppose a mouse emits a soft high-frequency squeak in a room full of people. Which kinds of people are least likely to hear the squeak?
9. When hair cells at one point along the basilar membrane produce 50 impulses per second, we hear a tone at 5000 Hz. What do we hear when the same hair cells produce 100 impulses per second? (Check your answers on page 126.)

You have heard of people who can listen to a note and identify its pitch by name: "Oh, that's a C-sharp." This ability, called absolute pitch or perfect pitch, is found almost exclusively in people with extensive musical training in childhood (Takeuchi & Hulse, 1993). It is probably more common among people who grew up speaking tonal languages, such as Chinese or Vietnamese, in which the meaning of a sound depends on its pitch. Speakers of those languages say specific words on the same pitch, day after day (Deutsch, Henthorn, & Dolson, 2004).

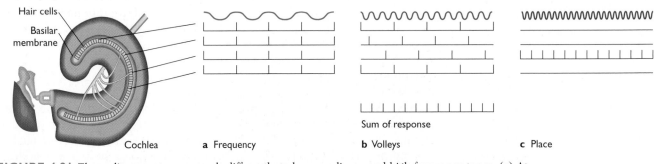

FIGURE 4.21 The auditory system responds differently to low-, medium-, and high-frequency tones. **(a)** At low frequencies hair cells at many points along the basilar membrane produce impulses in synchrony with the sound waves. **(b)** At medium frequencies different cells produce impulses in synchrony with different sound waves, but a volley (group) still produces one or more impulses for each wave. **(c)** At high frequencies only one point along the basilar membrane vibrates; hair cells at other locations remain still.

If you are amazed at absolute pitch, your own ability to recognize (though not name) a specific pitch might surprise you. In one study 48 college students with no special talent or training listened to 5-second segments from television theme songs, played either in their normal key or one-half or one note higher or lower. The students usually could choose which version was correct, but only if they had repeatedly watched the program (Schellenberg & Trehub, 2003). That is, they remembered the familiar pitches.

You probably also have heard of people who are "tone-deaf." Anyone who is *completely* tone-deaf could not understand speech, as slight pitch changes differentiate one speech sound from another. However, for unknown reasons some people are greatly impaired at detecting pitch changes, such as that between C and C-sharp. The result is that any melody sounds the same as any other, and music is no more pleasant than random noise (Hyde & Peretz, 2004).

Localization of Sounds

What you hear is a stimulus in your ear, but you experience the sound as "out there," and you can generally estimate its approximate place of origin. What cues do you use?

The auditory system determines the direction of a sound source by comparing the messages from the two ears. If a sound is coming from a source directly in front, the messages arrive at the two ears simultaneously with equal intensity. If it comes from the left, however, it will reach the left ear first and be more intense there (Figure 4.22). The timing is important for localizing low-frequency sounds; intensity helps us localize high-frequency sounds.

You can also detect the approximate distance of a sound source. If a sound grows louder, you interpret it as coming closer. If two sounds differ in pitch, you assume the one with more high-frequency tones is closer. (Low-frequency tones carry better over distance, so if you can hear a high-frequency tone, its source is probably close.) However, loudness and frequency tell you only the *rel-*

ative distances of sound sources, not the *absolute* distance. The only cue for absolute distance is the amount of reverberation (Mershon & King, 1975). In a closed room, you first hear the sound waves coming directly from the source and a little later the waves that reflected off the walls, floor, ceiling, or other objects. If you hear many echoes, you judge the source of the sound to be far away. People have trouble localizing sound sources in a noisy room where echoes are hard to hear (McMurtry & Mershon, 1985).

✓ CONCEPT CHECK

10. Why is it difficult to tell whether a sound is coming from directly in front of or directly behind you?
11. If someone who needs hearing aids in both ears wears one in only the left ear, what will be the effect on sound localization?
12. Suppose you are listening to a monaural (nonstereo) radio. Can the station play sounds that you will localize as coming from different directions, such as left, center, and right? Can it play sounds that you will localize as coming from different distances? Why or why not? (Check your answers on page 126.)

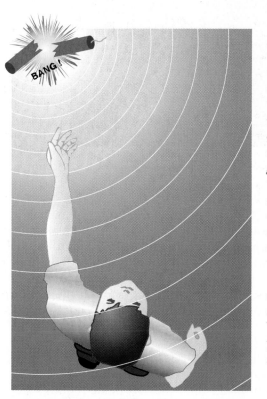

FIGURE 4.22 The ear located closest to the sound receives the sound waves first. That cue is important for localizing low-frequency sounds.

The Vestibular Sense

In the inner ear on each side of the head, adjacent to the structures responsible for hearing, is a structure called the *vestibule*. The **vestibular sense** that it controls *reports the tilt of the head, acceleration of the head, and orientation of the head with respect to gravity.* It plays a key role in posture and balance and provides the sensations of riding on a roller coaster or sitting in an airplane during takeoff. Intense vestibular sensations are responsible for motion sickness.

The vestibular sense also enables us to keep our eyes fixated on a target when the head is moving. When you walk down the street, you can keep your eyes fixated on a distant street sign, even though your head is bobbing up and down. The vestibular sense detects each head movement and controls the movement of your eyes to compensate for it.

To illustrate, try to read this page while you are jiggling the book up and down and from side to side, keeping your head steady. Then hold the book steady and move your head up and down and from side to side. You probably find it much easier to read when you are moving your head than when you are jiggling the book. The reason is that your vestibular sense keeps your eyes fixated on the print during head movements. After damage to the vestibular sense, people report blurry vision while they are walking. To read street signs, they must come to a stop.

Try It Yourself

© Julie Lemberger/CORBIS

The vestibular sense plays a key role in posture and balance as it reports the position of the head.

The vestibular system is composed of three semicircular canals, oriented in three separate directions, and two otolith organs (Figure 4.23b). The *semicircular canals* are lined with hair cells and filled with a jellylike substance. When the body accelerates in any direction, the jellylike substance in the corresponding semicircular canal pushes against the hair cells, which send messages to the brain. The *otolith organs* shown in Figure 4.23b also contain hair cells (Figure 4.23c), which lie next to the *otoliths* (calcium carbonate particles). Depending on which way the head tilts, the particles excite different sets of hair cells. The otolith organs report the direction of gravity and therefore which way is up.

If the otoliths provide unreliable information, we can use vision instead. For astronauts in the zero-gravity environment of outer space, the otoliths cannot distinguish up from down; indeed, the up–down dimension becomes meaningless. Instead, astronauts learn to rely on visual signals, such as the walls of the ship (Lackner, 1993).

The Cutaneous Senses

What we commonly think of as touch consists of several partly independent senses: pressure on the skin, warmth, cold, pain, itch, vibration, movement across the skin, and stretch of the skin. These sensations depend on several kinds of receptors, as Figure 4.24 shows (Iggo & Andres, 1982). A pinprick on the skin feels different from a light touch, and both feel different from a burn because each excites different receptors. Collectively, these sensations are known as the cutaneous senses, meaning the *skin senses*. Although they are most prominent in the skin, we also have them in our internal organs. Therefore, the cutaneous senses are also known as the *somatosensory system,* meaning *body-sensory system.*

Have you ever wondered about the sensation of itch? Is it a kind of touch, pain, or what? The receptors have not been identified, but we know they are stimulated by histamine, a chemical released by injured tissues. When a mosquito bites you or when you are recovering from a wound, released histamines cause an itching sensation. It is definitely not pain; in fact it is inhibited by pain (Andrew & Craig, 2001). When you scratch an itchy spot, your scratching has to produce some pain to relieve the itch. For example, if a dentist anesthetizes one side of your mouth for dental surgery, as the anesthesia wears off, the itch receptors may recover before the pain and touch receptors. At that point you can scratch the itchy spot, but you don't feel the scratch and it does not relieve the itch.

Tickle is another kind of cutaneous sensation. Have you ever wondered why you can't tickle yourself? Actually, you can, a little, but it's not the same as when someone else tickles you. The reason is that tickle requires surprise. When you are about to touch yourself, certain parts of your brain build up an anticipation response that is quite similar to the result of the actual stimulation (Carlsson, Petrovic, Skare,

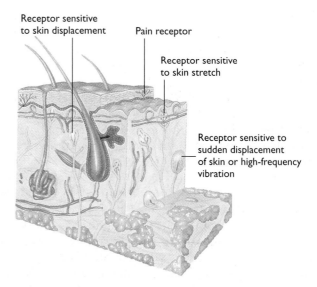

FIGURE 4.24 Cutaneous sensation is the product of many kinds of receptors, each sensitive to a particular kind of information.

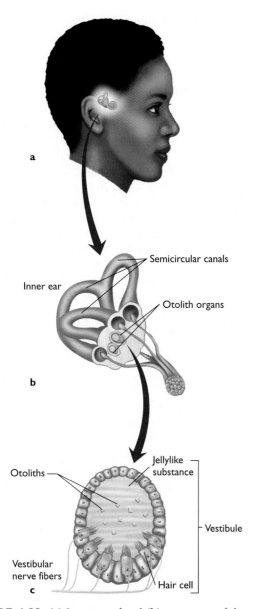

FIGURE 4.23 (a) Location of and (b) structures of the vestibule. (c) Moving your head or body displaces hair cells that report the tilt of your head and the direction and acceleration of movement.

Petersson, & Ingvar, 2000). That is, when you try to tickle yourself, the sensation is no surprise.

Pain

Pain is important both for its own sake and because of its relation to depression and anxiety. The experience of pain is a mixture of sensation (the information about tissue damage) and emotion (the unpleasant reaction). The sensory and emotional qualities depend on different brain areas (Craig, Bushnell, Zhang, & Blomqvist, 1994; Fernandez & Turk, 1992). The brain area responsive to the emotional aspect of pain—the *anterior cingulate cortex*—also responds

to the emotional pain of feeling rejected by other people (Eisenberger, Lieberman, & Williams, 2003) or of watching someone else get hurt (Singer et al., 2004). Telling people to expect pain or distracting them from the pain changes the emotional response, including the activity in the anterior cingulate cortex, but does not change the sensation itself (Ploghaus et al., 1999).

The Gate Theory of Pain

You visit a physician because of severe pain, but as soon as the physician tells you the problem is nothing to worry about, the pain starts to subside. Have you ever had such an experience? Pain can increase or decrease because of expectations.

Recall the term *placebo* from chapter 2: A placebo is a drug or other procedure that has no important effects other than those that result from people's expectations; researchers ordinarily give placebos to control groups in an experiment. Placebos have little effect on most medical conditions, but they sometimes relieve pain, or at least the emotional distress of pain, quite impressively (Hróbjartsson. & Gøtzsche, 2001). Even the effects of the drug itself depend partly on expectations. When people have a catheter in their arm and receive painkilling medicine without knowing it, the drug is less effective than when people know they are receiving it (Amanzio, Pollo, Maggi, & Benedetti, 2001).

In one experiment college students had a smelly brownish liquid rubbed onto one finger. It was in fact a placebo, but they were told it was a painkiller. Then they were given a painful pinch stimulus to that finger and a finger of the other hand. They consistently reported less pain on the finger with the placebo (Montgomery & Kirsch, 1996). How placebos work is far from clear, but these results eliminate mere relaxation, which would presumably affect both hands equally.

Because of observations such as these, Ronald Melzack and P. D. Wall (1965) proposed the **gate theory** of pain, the idea that *pain messages must pass through a gate, presumably in the spinal cord, that can block the messages.* That is, pain fibers send an excitatory message, but input from the brain or other receptors can inhibit the pain messages, in effect closing the gate. For example, if you injure yourself, rubbing the surrounding skin sends inhibitory messages to the spinal cord, closing the pain gates. Pleasant or distracting events also send inhibitory messages. The gate can also enhance the pain messages; for example, inflamed skin (e.g., after sunburn) increases sensitivity of the spinal cord neurons so that almost any stimulation becomes painful (Malmberg, Chen, Tonegawa, & Basbaum, 1997). In short, the activities of the rest of the nervous system can facilitate or inhibit pain messages (Figure 4.25).

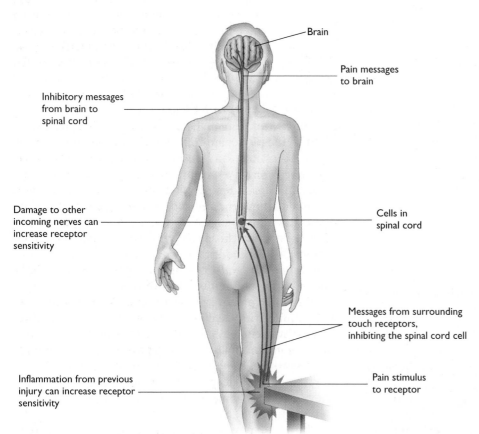

Inhibitory messages from brain to spinal cord

Damage to other incoming nerves can increase receptor sensitivity

Inflammation from previous injury can increase receptor sensitivity

Brain

Pain messages to brain

Cells in spinal cord

Messages from surrounding touch receptors, inhibiting the spinal cord cell

Pain stimulus to receptor

FIGURE 4.25 Pain messages from the skin are relayed from spinal cord cells to the brain. According to the gate theory of pain, those spinal cord cells serve as a gate that can block or enhance the signal. The proposed neural circuitry is simplified in this diagram. Green lines indicate axons with excitatory inputs; red lines indicate axons with inhibitory inputs.

Ways of Decreasing Pain

Some people are completely insensitive to pain. Before you start to envy them, consider: They often burn themselves by picking up hot objects, scald their tongues on hot coffee, cut themselves without realizing it, and sometimes bite off the tip of the tongue. They sit in a single position for hours without growing uncomfortable, thereby damaging their bones and tendons (Comings & Amromin, 1974).

Although it would be a mistake to rid ourselves of pain altogether, we would like to limit it. One way is to provide distraction. For example, postsurgery patients in a room with a pleasant view complain less about pain, take less painkilling medicine, and recover faster than do patients in a windowless room (Ulrich, 1984).

Several other methods depend on medications. *Pain stimuli cause the nervous system to release a neurotransmitter,* called **substance P,** for intense pains and another transmitter, glutamate, for all pains including mild ones. Mice that lack substance P receptors react to all painful stimuli as if they were mild (DeFelipe et al., 1998). Another set of neurons release **endorphins,** *neurotransmitters that inhibit the release of substance P and thereby weaken pain sensations* (Pert & Snyder, 1973) (see Figure 4.26). The term *endorphin* is a combination of the terms *endogenous* (self-produced) and *morphine*. The drug morphine, which stimulates endorphin synapses, has long been known for its ability to inhibit dull, lingering pains. Endorphins are also released by pleasant experiences, such as sexual activity or thrilling music (A. Goldstein, 1980). (That effect may help explain why a pleasant view helps to ease postsurgical pain.) In short, endorphins are a powerful method of closing pain gates.

Paradoxically, another method of decreasing pain begins by inducing it. The *chemical* **capsaicin** *stimulates receptors that respond to painful heat* (Caterina, Rosen, Tominaga, Brake, & Julius, 1999) and thereby *causes the release of substance P.* Capsaicin is the chemical that makes jalapeños and similar peppers taste hot. Injecting capsaicin or rubbing it on the skin produces a temporary burning sensation (Yarsh, Farb, Leeman, & Jessell, 1979). However, after that sensation subsides, the skin has less

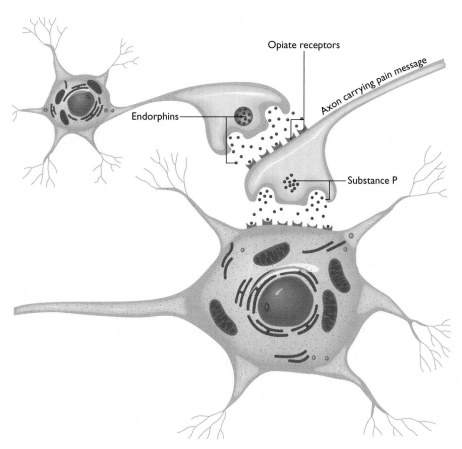

FIGURE 4.26 Substance P is the neurotransmitter responsible for intense pain sensations. Endorphins are neurotransmitters that block the release of substance P, thereby decreasing pain sensations. Opiates imitate the effects of endorphins.

pain sensitivity than usual. Several skin creams intended for the relief of aching muscles contain capsaicin. One reason capsaicin decreases pain is that it releases substance P faster than the neurons can resynthesize it. Also, high doses of capsaicin damage pain receptors.

 CONCEPT CHECK

13. Naloxone, a drug used as an antidote for an overdose of morphine, is known to block the endorphin synapses. How could we use naloxone to determine whether a pleasant stimulus releases endorphins?
14. Psychologist Linda Bartoshuk recommends candies containing moderate amounts of jalapeño peppers as a treatment for people with pain in the mouth. Why? (Check your answers on page 126.)

Phantom Limbs

A particularly fascinating phenomenon is the **phantom limb,** *a continuing sensation of an amputated*

body part. For example, someone might report occasional feelings of touch, tingling, or pain from an amputated hand, arm, leg, or foot. The phantom sensation might last only days or weeks after the amputation, but it sometimes lasts years or a lifetime (Ramachandran & Hirstein, 1998).

Physicians and psychologists have long wondered about the cause of phantom sensations. Some believed it was an emotional reaction, and others believed it began with irritation of nerves at the stump where the amputation occurred. Research in the 1990s established that the problem lies within the brain.

In the last chapter, Figure 3.10 shows how each part of the somatosensory cortex gets its input from a different body area. Figure 4.27a repeats part of that illustration. Part b shows what happens immediately after an amputation of the hand: The hand area of the cortex becomes inactive because the axons from the hand are inactive. (You might think of the neurons in the hand area of the cortex as "widows" that have lost their old partners and are signaling their eagerness for new ones.) As time passes, axons from the face, which ordinarily excite only the face area of the cortex, strengthen their connections to the hand area of the cortex, which is adjacent to the face area. So any stimulation of the face continues to excite the face area but now also excites the hand area. When it stimulates the hand area, it produces a hand experience—that is, a phantom limb (Flor et al., 1995; Ramachandran & Blakeslee, 1998).

One way is known to relieve phantom sensations: Individuals with amputations who learn to use an artificial limb gradually lose their phantoms (Lotze et al., 1999). Evidently, the hand and arm areas of their cortex start reacting to the artificial limb, and this sensation displaces the abnormal sensation coming from the face.

 CONCEPT CHECK

15. A phantom hand sensation is greater at some times than others. When should it be strongest? (Check your answer on page 126.)

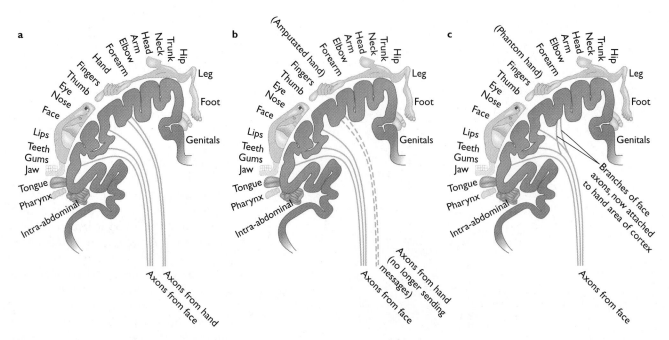

FIGURE 4.27 **(a)** Each area in the somatosensory cortex gets its input from a different part of the body. **(b)** If one body part, such as the hand, is amputated, its part of the cortex no longer gets its normal input. **(c)** However, the axons from a neighboring area, such as the face, can branch out to excite the vacated area or strengthen existing synapses. Now, any stimulation of the face will excite both the face area and the hand area. But when it stimulates the hand area, it feels like the hand, not the face.

The Chemical Senses

Most textbooks of sensation and perception concentrate mainly on vision and hearing. Taste and smell get brief treatment, if any. Humans, however, are unusual compared to most animal life. Most life on Earth consists of one-celled animals or small invertebrates with no more than a vague sense of light and dark. They can detect strong vibrations of the land or water, but you probably wouldn't call that "hearing." They rely mainly on taste and smell to find food and mates. We humans too often overlook the importance of taste and smell.

Taste

Vision and hearing provide information relevant to all kinds of actions and choices. The sense of taste, which *detects chemicals on the tongue,* serves just one function: It governs our eating and drinking.

The *taste receptors are* in the taste buds, *located in the folds on the surface of the tongue,* almost exclusively along the outside edge of the tongue in adults (Figure 4.28). (Children's taste buds are more widely scattered.)

Try this demonstration (based on Bartoshuk, 1991): Soak something small (a cotton swab will do) in sugar water, salt water, or vinegar. Then touch it to the center of your tongue, not too far back. You will feel it but taste nothing. Then slowly move the soaked substance toward the side or front of your tongue. Suddenly, you taste it.

Try It Yourself

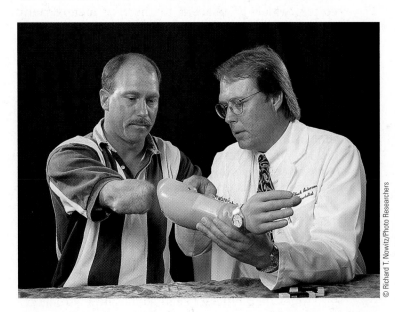

After a person with an amputation gains experience using an artificial limb, phantom limb sensations fade or completely disappear.

© Richard T. Nowitz/Photo Researchers

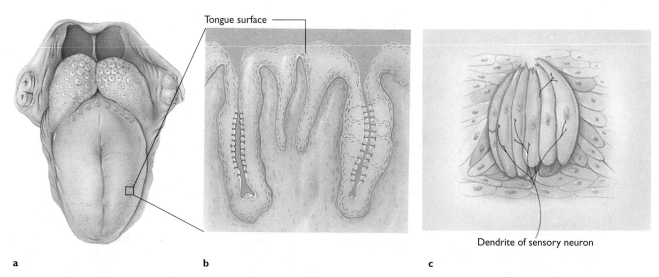

Tongue surface

Dendrite of sensory neuron

a   b   c

FIGURE 4.28 (a) Taste buds, which react to chemicals dissolved in saliva, are located along the edge of the tongue in adult humans but are more widely distributed in children. (b) A cross section through part of the surface of the tongue showing taste buds. (c) A cross section of one taste bud. Each taste bud has about 50 receptor cells within it.

If you go in the other direction (first touching the side of the tongue and then moving toward the center), you will continue to taste the substance even when it reaches the center of your tongue. The explanation is not that you suddenly grew new taste buds. Rather, your taste buds do not tell you *where* you taste something. When you stimulate touch receptors on your tongue, your brain interprets the taste perception as coming from the spot where it feels touch.

Different Types of Taste Receptors

Traditionally, Western cultures have talked about four primary tastes: sweet, sour, salty, and bitter. However, the taste of monosodium glutamate (MSG), common in many Asian cuisines, cannot be described in these terms (Kurihara & Kashiwayanagi, 1998; Schiffman & Erickson, 1971), and researchers found a taste receptor specific to MSG (Chaudhari, Landin, & Roper, 2000). English had no word for the taste of MSG (similar to the taste of unsalted chicken soup), so researchers adopted the Japanese word *umami*. Further research found that rodents at least, and possibly humans, also have a receptor for the taste of fats (Laugerette et al., 2005). So perhaps we have six primary tastes: sweet, sour, salty, bitter, umami, and fat.

Bitter taste is puzzling from a chemical standpoint because such diverse chemicals taste bitter. About the only thing they have in common is being poisonous or at least harmful in large amounts. How could such diverse chemicals all excite the same receptor? The answer is that they don't. We have a large number of different bitter receptors—40 or more—each sensitive to different types of chemicals (Adler et al., 2000;

Matsunami, Montmayeur, & Buck, 2000). Any chemical that excites any of these receptors produces the same bitter sensation. One consequence is that a wide variety of harmful chemicals taste bitter. Another consequence is that we do not detect low concentrations of bitter chemicals; with so many different kinds of bitter receptors, we do not have many of any one kind.

Smell

The *sense of smell* is known as **olfaction**. The olfactory receptors, located on the mucous membrane in the rear air passages of the nose (Figure 4.29), detect the presence of certain airborne molecules. Chemically, these receptors are much like synaptic receptors, but they are stimulated by chemicals from the environment instead of chemicals released by other neurons. The axons of the olfactory receptors form the olfactory tract, which extends to the olfactory bulbs at the base of the brain.

How many kinds of olfactory receptors do we have? Until 1991 researchers did not know. In contrast researchers in the 1800s established that people have three kinds of color receptors. They used behavioral methods, showing that people can mix three colors of light in various amounts to match any other color. Regarding olfaction, however, no one reported comparable studies. Can people match all possible odors by mixing appropriate amounts of three, four, seven, ten, or some other number of odors?

Perhaps it is just as well that no one spent a lifetime trying to find out. Linda Buck and Richard Axel

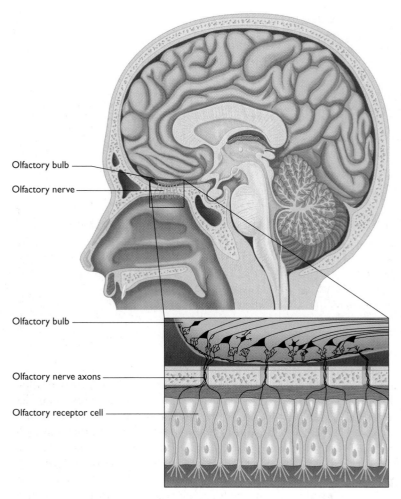

FIGURE 4.29 The olfactory receptor cells lining the nasal cavity send information to the olfactory bulb in the brain.

al., 2003). In one experiment researchers asked participants to report on weak odors, such as those of roses or lemons, while imagining the same odor, imagining a different odor, or not imagining any odor. Imagining the same odor as the one they were trying to detect did not help. Imagining a different odor impaired performance for some but not others (Djordjevic, Zatorre, Petrides, & Jones-Gotman, 2004). In short, olfactory imagery is a weak experience at best.

Olfaction also serves social functions, especially in nonhuman mammals that identify one another by means of **pheromones**, which are *chemicals they release into the environment.* Nearly all nonhuman mammals rely on pheromones for sexual communication. For example, a female dog in her fertile and sexually responsive time of year emits pheromones that attract every male dog in the neighborhood. Pheromones act on the vomeronasal organ, a set of receptors near, but separate from, the standard olfactory receptors (Monti-Bloch, Jennings-White, Dolberg, & Berliner, 1994). Each of those receptors responds to one and only one chemical, identifying it at extremely low concentrations (Leinders-Zufall et al., 2000).

Most humans prefer *not* to recognize one another by smell. The deodorant and perfume industries exist for the sole purpose of re-

(1991), using modern biochemical technology, demonstrated that the human nose has hundreds of types of olfactory receptors. Rats and mice have about a thousand (Zhang & Firestein, 2002). Each olfactory receptor detects only a few closely related chemicals (Araneda, Kini, & Firestein, 2000).

Much remains to be learned about how the brain processes olfactory information (Figure 4.30). Many neurons in the brain respond to combinations of two or more odorant chemicals and not to the individual chemicals alone (Zou & Buck, 2006). This result explains why a combination of two odors can smell so different from either one separately. For example, a mixture of clove and rose smells like carnation.

Olfaction differs from the other senses in an interesting way: You can imagine things that you might see or hear, but can you imagine the smell of, say, roses? Some people say yes and others say no, but most agree that the imagined sensation is weak. Curiously, when people try to imagine an odor, they sniff, especially when imagining pleasant odors (Bensafi et

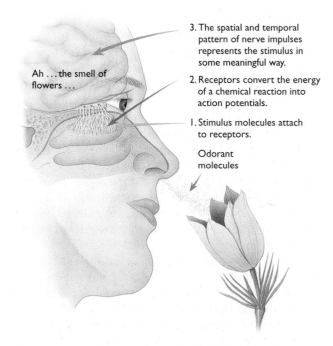

3. The spatial and temporal pattern of nerve impulses represents the stimulus in some meaningful way.

2. Receptors convert the energy of a chemical reaction into action potentials.

1. Stimulus molecules attach to receptors.

Ah ...the smell of flowers ...

Odorant molecules

FIGURE 4.30 Olfaction, like any other sensory system, converts physical energy into a complex pattern of brain activity.

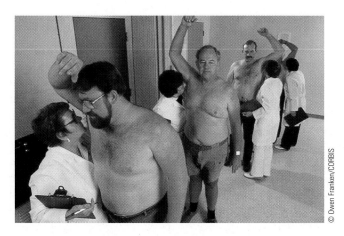

Professional deodorant tester: That's a career option you probably never considered. U.S. industries spend millions of dollars to eliminate the kinds of personal odors that are essential to other mammalian species.

```
555555555555 555555555555 555555555555 5555555525555
555555555555 555555555525 555555555555 555555555555
555555555555 555555555555 555255555555 555555555555
552555555555 555555555555 555555555555 555555555555
555555555555 555555555555 555555555555 555555555555


44444444444 44444444444 44444444444 444444444444
44444444444 44A444444444 44444444444 444444444444
44444A444444 44444444444 44444444444 444444A444444
44444444444 44444444444 44444444444 444444444444
44444444444 44444444444 44444444A44 444444444444
```

One person with synesthesia found it just as hard as anyone else to find the As among 4s, because both looked red to her. However, because 2s look violet and 5s look yellow to her, she was quicker than average to find the 2s, almost as if—but not quite as if—the displays had been printed like this (Laeng, Svartdal, & Oelmann, 2004):

```
555555555555 555555555555 555555555555 5555555525555
555555555555 555555555525 555555555555 555555555555
555555555555 555555555555 5552555555555 555555555555
5552555555555 555555555555 555555555555 555555555555
555555555555 555555555555 555555555555 555555555555
```

These results are surprising. The colors helped her find the 2s, but somehow she had to know the 2s from the 5s *before* she could produce the color experiences. Similarly, people with word-taste synesthesia sometimes experience the taste before thinking of the word. For example, someone might say, "It's on the tip of my tongue . . . I can't think of the word, but it tastes like tuna" (Simner & Ward, 2006).

At this point synesthesia remains a fascinating mystery. Researchers have a few hypotheses about possible causes and brain mechanisms, but so far none are supported strongly.

---

moving and covering up human odors. But perhaps we respond to pheromones anyway, unconsciously. For example, young women who are in frequent contact, such as roommates in a college dormitory, tend to synchronize their menstrual cycles, probably as a result of pheromones they secrete (McClintock, 1971).

One study examined women in Bedouin Arab families. The advantages of studying that culture are that an unmarried woman has extensive contact with her mother and sisters, almost none with men, and does not use oral contraceptives. Thus, pheromones have a maximum opportunity to show their effects. The results showed that the women within a family might not begin to menstruate on exactly the same day, but they were close (Weller & Weller, 1997).

Synesthesia

We end our tour of the senses with synesthesia, an unusual *condition in which a stimulus of one type, such as sound, also gives rise to another experience, such as color*. Researchers estimate that one person in 500 has synesthesia, but the actual number may be higher because some people try to hide an experience that others regard as a sign of mental illness (Day, 2005). (It is not.)

No two people with synesthesia have quite the same experience. In fact people with this condition sometimes argue vigorously with one another about the color of Tuesday or the taste of some melody. It is, however, a real phenomenon. For illustration, as quickly as possible find the 2s and As in the following displays.

Try It Yourself

IN CLOSING

Sensory Systems

The world as experienced by a bat (which can hear frequencies of 100,000 Hz) or a dog (which can discriminate odors that you and I would never notice) or a mouse (which depends on its whiskers to explore the world) is in many ways a different world from the one that people experience. The function of our senses is not to tell us about everything in the world, but to alert us to the information we are most likely to use, given our way of life. ∎

Summary

- *Pitch.* At low frequencies of sound, we identify pitch by the frequency of vibrations of hair cells. At intermediate frequencies we identify pitch by volleys of responses from many neurons. At high frequencies we identify pitch by the location where the hair cells vibrate. (page 115)

- *Localizing sounds.* We localize the source of a sound by detecting differences in the time and loudness of the sounds our two ears receive. We localize the distance of a sound source primarily by the amount of reverberation, or echoes, following the main sound. (page 117)
- *Vestibular system.* The vestibular system tells us about the movement of the head and its position with respect to gravity. It enables us to keep our eyes fixated on an object while the rest of the body is in motion. (page 117)
- *Cutaneous receptors.* We experience many types of sensation on the skin, each dependent on different receptors. Itch is a sensation based on tissue irritation, inhibited by pain. Tickle depends on the unpredictability of the stimulus. (page 118)
- *Pain.* The experience of pain can be greatly inhibited or enhanced by other simultaneous experiences, including touch to surrounding skin or the person's expectations. Pain depends largely on stimulation of neurons that are sensitive to the neurotransmitter substance P, which can be inhibited by endorphins. (page 119)
- *Phantom limbs.* After an amputation the corresponding portion of the somatosensory cortex stops receiving its normal input. Soon axons from neighboring cortical areas form branches that start exciting the silenced areas of cortex. When they receive the new input, they react in the old way, which produces a phantom sensation. (page 121)
- *Taste receptors.* People have receptors sensitive to sweet, sour, salty, bitter, and umami (MSG) tastes, and possibly fat. We have many kinds of bitter receptors, but not many of any one kind. (page 123)
- *Olfactory receptors.* The olfactory system—the sense of smell—depends on at least 100 types of receptors, each with its own special sensitivity. Olfaction is important for many behaviors, including food selection and (especially in nonhuman mammals) identification of potential mates. (page 123)
- *Synesthesia.* Some people have consistent experiences of one sensation evoked by another. For example, they might experience particular letters or numbers as having a color. (page 125)

Answers to Concept Checks

8. Obviously, the people farthest from the mouse are least likely to hear it. In addition older people would be less likely to hear the squeak because of declining ability to hear high frequencies. Another group unlikely to hear the squeak are those who had damaged their hearing by repeated exposure to loud noises, including loud music. (page 115)

9. We still hear a tone at 5000 Hz, but it is louder than before. For high-frequency tones, the pitch we hear depends on which hair cells are most active, not how many impulses per second they fire. (page 116)

10. We localize sounds by comparing the input into the left ear with the input into the right ear. If a sound comes from straight ahead or from directly behind us (or from straight above or below), the input into the left and right ears will be identical. (page 117)

11. Sounds will be louder in the left ear than in the right, and therefore, they may seem to be coming from the left side even when they aren't. (However, a sound from the right will still strike the right ear before the left, so time of arrival at the two ears will compete against the relative loudness.) (page 117)

12. Various sounds from the radio cannot seem to come from different directions because your localization of the direction of a sound depends on a comparison between the responses of the two ears. However, the radio can play sounds that seem to come from different distances because distance localization depends on the amount of reverberation, loudness, and high-frequency tones, all of which can vary with a single speaker. Consequently, the radio can easily give an impression of people walking toward you or away from you, but not of people walking left to right or right to left. (page 117)

13. First determine how much the pleasant stimulus decreases the experience of pain for several people. Then give half of them naloxone and half of them a placebo. Again measure how much the pleasant stimulus decreases the pain. If the pleasant stimulus decreases pain by releasing endorphins, then naloxone should impair its painkilling effects. (page 120)

14. The capsaicin in the jalapeño peppers will release substance P faster than it can be resynthesized, thus decreasing the later sensitivity to pain in the mouth. (page 120)

15. The phantom hand sensation should be strongest when something is rubbing against the face. (page 121)

The Interpretation of Sensory Information

- *What is the relationship between the real world and the way we perceive it?*
- *Why are we sometimes wrong about what we think we see?*

According to a popular expression, "a picture is worth a thousand words." If so, what is a thousandth of a picture worth? One word? Perhaps not even that.

Printed photographs, such as the one on page 125, are composed of a great many dots. Ordinarily, you will be aware of only the overall patterns, but if you magnify a photo, as in Figure 4.31, you see the individual dots. Although one dot by itself tells us nothing, the pattern of many dots becomes a meaningful picture.

Actually, our vision is like this all the time. Your retina includes about 126 million rods and cones, each of which sees one dot of the visual field. What you perceive is not dots but lines, curves, and complex objects. In a variety of ways, your nervous system starts with an array of details and extracts the meaningful information.

Perception of Minimal Stimuli

Some of the earliest psychological researchers tried to determine what were the weakest sounds, lights, and touches that people could detect. They also measured the smallest difference that people could detect between one stimulus and another—the *just noticeable difference* (JND). Researchers assumed they could answer these questions quickly and then proceed with further research. We considered a little of this research in chapter 1. As is often the case, however, the questions were more complicated than they seemed.

Sensory Thresholds and Signal Detection

Imagine a typical experiment to determine the threshold of hearing—that is, the minimum intensity that one can hear: Participants are presented with tones of varying intensity in random order and sometimes no tone at all. Each time, the participants are asked to say whether they heard anything. Figure 4.32 presents typical results. Notice that no sharp line separates sounds that people hear from sounds that they do not. Researchers therefore define an **absolute sensory threshold** as the *intensity at which a given individual can detect a stimulus 50% of the time.* Note, however, that people sometimes report stimuli below the threshold or fail to report stimuli above it. Also people sometimes report hearing a tone when none was present. We should not be surprised. Throughout the study they have been listening to faint tones and saying "yes" when they heard

FIGURE 4.31 Although this photograph is composed of dots, we see objects and patterns. The principles at work in our perception of this photograph are at work in all our perceptions.

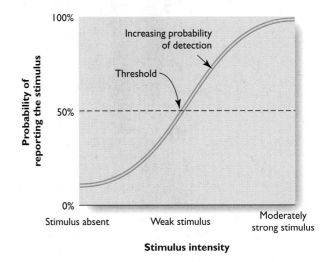

FIGURE 4.32 Typical results of an experiment to measure an absolute sensory threshold. No sharp boundary separates stimuli that you perceive from those that you do not.

almost nothing. The difference between nothing and almost nothing is slim.

When people try to detect weak stimuli, they can be correct in two ways: reporting the presence of a stimulus (a "hit") and reporting its absence (a "correct rejection"). They can also be wrong in two ways: failing to detect a stimulus when present (a "miss") and reporting a stimulus when none was present (a "false alarm"). Figure 4.33 outlines these possibilities.

Signal-detection theory is the *study of people's tendencies to make hits, correct rejections, misses, and false alarms* (D. M. Green & Swets, 1966). The theory originated in engineering, where it applies to such matters as detecting radio signals in the presence of noise. Suppose someone reports a stimulus present on 80% of the trials when it is actually present. That statistic is meaningless unless we also know how often the person said it was present when it was not. If the person also reported it present on 80% of trials when it was absent, we would conclude that the person can't tell the difference between stimulus-present and stimulus-absent.

In a signal-detection experiment, people's responses depend on their willingness to risk a miss or a false alarm. (When in doubt you have to risk one or the other.) Suppose you are the participant and I tell you that you will receive a 10-cent reward whenever you correctly report that a light is present, but you will be fined 1 cent if you say "yes" when it is absent.

When you are in doubt, you will probably guess "yes," with results like those in Figure 4.34a. Then I change the rules: You will receive a 1-cent reward for correctly reporting the presence of a light, but you will suffer a 10-cent penalty and an electrical shock if you report a light when none was present. Now you will say "yes" only when you are certain, and the results will look like those in Figure 4.34b. In short, people's answers depend on the instructions they receive and the strategies they use, not just what their senses tell them.

People become cautious about false alarms for other reasons too. In one experiment participants were asked to read words that flashed on a screen for a split second. They performed well with ordinary words such as *river* or *peach.* For emotionally loaded words such as *penis* or *bitch,* however, they generally said they were not sure what they saw. Several expla-

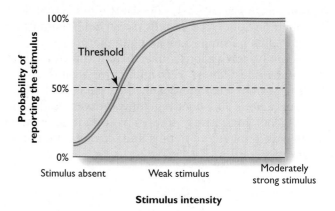

Instructions: You will receive a 10-cent reward for correctly reporting that a light is present. You will be penalized 1 cent for reporting that a light is present when it is not.

a

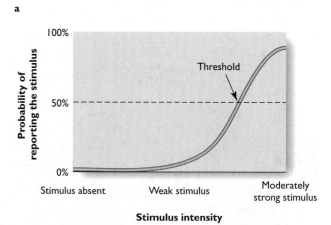

Instructions: You will receive a 1-cent reward for correctly reporting that a light is present. You will be penalized 10 cents *and* subjected to an electric shock for reporting that a light is present when it is not.

b

FIGURE 4.34 Results of measuring a sensory threshold with different instructions.

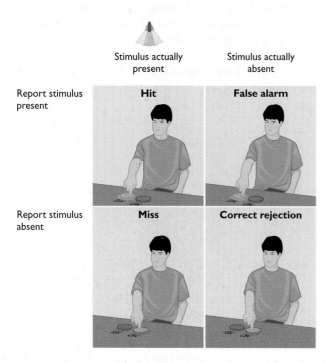

FIGURE 4.33 People can make two kinds of correct judgments (green backgrounds) and two kinds of errors (tan backgrounds). If you tend to say the stimulus is "present" whenever you are in doubt, you will get many hits but also many false alarms.

nations are possible (e.g., G. S. Blum & Barbour, 1979); one is that participants hesitate to blurt out an emotionally charged word unless they are certain they are right.

The signal-detection approach is useful in many settings remote from the laboratory. For example, the legal system is also a signal-detection situation. When we examine the evidence and try to decide whether someone is guilty or innocent, we can be right in two ways and wrong in two ways:

	Defendant is actually guilty	Defendant is actually innocent
Jury votes "guilty"	Hit	False alarm
Jury votes "not guilty"	Miss	Correct rejection

If you were on a jury and you were unsure, which mistake would you be more willing to risk? Most people agree that you should vote "not guilty," because a "miss" (setting a guilty person free) is less bad than a false alarm (convicting an innocent person).

Another example is screening baggage at an airport. The airport security people do not want to miss any weapons or other illegal substances, but they also do not want to inconvenience large numbers of travelers by making extensive checks without good reason. Because the x-ray images are often ambiguous, the screeners are sure to make mistakes of both kinds—missing dangerous items and issuing false alarms (Wolfe, Horowitz, & Kenner, 2005).

 CONCEPT CHECK

16. Suppose we find that nearly all alcoholics and drug abusers have a particular pattern of brain waves. Can we now use that pattern as a way to identify people with an alcohol or drug problem? Think about this problem in terms of signal detection. (Check your answer on page 146.)

Subliminal Perception

Subliminal perception is the idea that *a stimulus can influence our behavior even when it is presented so faintly or briefly that we do not perceive it consciously.* (*Limen* is Latin for "threshold"; thus, subliminal means "below the threshold.") Generally, the criterion for "not perceived consciously" is that the person reports not seeing it. Is subliminal perception powerful, impossible, or something in between?

What Subliminal Perception Cannot Do

Many years ago claims were made that subliminal messages could control people's buying habits. For ex-

ample, a theater owner might insert a single frame, "EAT POPCORN," in the middle of a film. Customers who were not consciously aware of the message could not resist it, so they would flock to the concession stand to buy popcorn. Despite many tests of this claim, no one found any support for it, and the advertiser who made the claim eventually admitted he had no evidence (Pratkanis, 1992).

Another claim is that certain rock-'n'-roll recordings contain "satanic" messages that were recorded backward and superimposed on the songs. Some people allege that listeners unconsciously perceive these messages and then follow the evil advice. Psychologists cannot say whether any rock band ever inserted such a message. (There are a lot of rock bands, after all.) The issue is whether a backward message has any influence. If people hear a backward message, can they understand it? Does it influence their behavior? Researchers have recorded various messages (nothing satanic) and asked people to listen to them backward. So far, no one listening to a backward message has been able to discern what it would sound like forward, and the messages have not influenced behavior in any detectable way (Vokey & Read, 1985). Thus, even if certain music does contain messages recorded backward, we have no evidence that the messages matter.

A third unsupported claim: "Subliminal audiotapes" with faint, inaudible messages can help you improve your memory, quit smoking, lose weight, raise your self-esteem, and so forth. In one study psychologists asked more than 200 volunteers to listen to a popular brand of audiotape. However, they intentionally mislabeled some of the self-esteem tapes as "memory tapes" and some of the memory tapes as "self-esteem tapes." After 1 month of listening, most people who *thought* they were listening to self-esteem tapes said they had improved their self-esteem, and those who *thought* they were listening to memory tapes said they had improved their memory. The actual content made no difference; the improvement depended on people's expectations, not the tapes (Greenwald, Spangenberg, Pratkanis, & Eskanazi, 1991).

What Subliminal Perception Can Do

Subliminal messages do produce effects, although they are in most cases brief and subtle. For example, people in one study viewed a happy, neutral, or angry face flashed on a screen for less than one thirtieth of a second, followed immediately by a neutral face. Under these conditions no one reports seeing a happy or angry face, and even if asked to guess, people do no better than chance. However, when they see a happy face, they slightly and briefly move their facial muscles in the direction of a smile; after seeing an angry face, they tense their muscles slightly and briefly in the direction of a frown (Dimberg, Thunberg, & Elmehed, 2000).

In other experiments people who saw or heard a word subliminally were better able than usual to detect the same word presented briefly or faintly (Kouider & Dupoux, 2005). In some studies seeing a word subliminally (e.g., FRIEND) facilitated the detection of a related word (HAPPY) a few milliseconds later (Abrams, Klinger, & Greenwald, 2002). However, in those cases other researchers question whether the first word was completely subliminal. For example, even if you did not consciously detect the word FRIEND, might you have seen at least some of the letters (FR***D)? Under conditions when we are sure the viewer could not see the first word, it does not help the person detect a later word of related meaning (Kouider & Duoux, 2004).

The fact that subliminal perception affects behavior at all shows that we can respond unconsciously, at least in a limited way (Greenwald & Draine, 1997). However, the effects emerge only as small changes in average performance over many individuals or many trials. Subliminal advertising has little practical effect, if any (Trappey, 1996).

 CONCEPT CHECK

17. Suppose someone claims that the subliminal words "Don't shoplift," intermixed with music at a store, will decrease shoplifting. What would be the best way to test that claim? (Check your answer on page 146.)

Perception and the Recognition of Patterns

How do you know what you're seeing? Let's start with an apparently simple example: When you look at a light, how does your brain decide how bright it is? We might guess that the more intense the light, the brighter the appearance.

However, perceived brightness depends on comparison to the surrounding objects. Brightness contrast *is the increase or decrease in an object's apparent brightness by comparison to objects around it.* Consider Figure 4.35. Compare the pink bars in the middle left section to those in the middle right. The ones on the right probably look darker, but in fact they are the same. Also go to **www.thomsonedu.com/psychology/kalat.** Navigate to the student website, then to the Online Try It Yourself section, and click Brightness Contrast.

Try It Yourself

Online Try It Yourself

FIGURE 4.35 The pink bars in the left center area are in fact the same as the pink bars in the right center area, but those on the left seem lighter.

If two spots on the page reflect light equally, why don't they look the same? When the brain sees something, it uses its past experience to calculate how that pattern of light probably was generated, taking into account all the contextual information (Purves, Williams, Nundy, & Lotto, 2004). In Figure 4.35 you see what appears to be a partly clear white bar covering the center of the left half of the grid, and the pink bars look light. The corresponding section to the right also has pink bars, but these appear to be under the red bars and on top of a white background; here the pink looks darker, because you contrast the pink against the white background above and below it.

If perceiving brightness is that complicated, you can imagine how hard it is to explain face recognition. People are amazingly good at recognizing faces, though inept at explaining how they do it. When you someday attend your 25th high school reunion, you will probably recognize many people despite major changes in their appearance. Can you match the high school photos in Figure 4.36 with the photos of the same people as they looked 25 years later? Probably not, but other people who had attended that high school succeeded with a respectable 49% accuracy (Bruck, Cavanagh, & Ceci, 1991). You can also go to **www.thomsonedu.com/psychology/kalat.** Navigate to the student website, then to the Online Try It Yourself section, and click Matching High School Photos.

Try It Yourself

Online Try It Yourself

We recognize faces by whole patterns, based on abilities that depend on early experiences and genetically determined specializations in certain brain areas (Farah, 1992; Kanwisher, 2000; La Grand, Mondloch, Maurer, & Brent, 2004). Changing even one feature can sometimes make a face hard to recognize. Perhaps you have had the experience of failing to recognize a friend who has changed his or her hairstyle. Can you identify the person in Figure 4.37?

High-school photos

a   b   c   d   e

25 years later

1   2   3   4   5

6   7   8   9   10

FIGURE 4.36 High school photos and the same people 25 years later. Can you match the photos in the two sets? (Check answer C on page 146.)

FIGURE 4.37 Who is this? We recognize people by hair as well as facial features. If you're not sure who it is, check answer D, page 146.

The Feature-Detector Approach

Even explaining how we recognize a simple letter of the alphabet is difficult enough. According to one explanation, we begin recognition by breaking a complex stimulus into its component parts. For example, when we look at a letter of the alphabet, *specialized neurons in the visual cortex,* called **feature detectors,** *respond to the presence of certain simple features, such as lines and angles.* One neuron might detect the feature "horizontal line," while another detects a vertical line, and so forth.

CRITICAL THINKING

WHAT'S THE EVIDENCE?

Feature Detectors

What evidence do we have for the existence of feature detectors in the brain? We have different kinds of evidence from laboratory animals and humans.

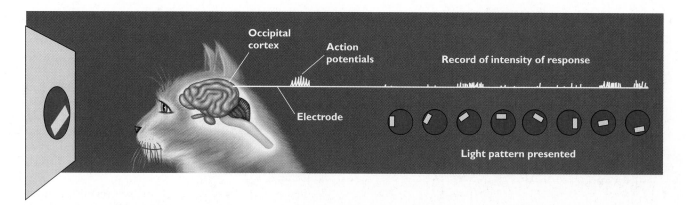

FIGURE 4.38 Hubel and Wiesel implanted electrodes to record the activity of neurons in the occipital cortex of a cat. Then they compared the responses evoked by various patterns of light and darkness on the retina. In most cases a neuron responded vigorously when a portion of the retina saw a bar of light oriented at a particular angle. When the angle of the bar changed, that cell became silent but another cell responded.

FIRST STUDY

Hypothesis.   Neurons in the visual cortex of cats and monkeys respond specifically when light strikes the retina in a particular pattern.

Method.   Two pioneers in the study of the visual cortex, David Hubel and Torsten Wiesel (1981 Nobel Prize winners in physiology and medicine), inserted thin electrodes into cells of the occipital cortex of cats and monkeys and then recorded the activity of those cells when various light patterns struck the animals' retinas. At first they used mere points of light; later they tried lines (Figure 4.38).

Results.   They found that each cell responds best in the presence of a particular stimulus (Hubel & Wiesel, 1968). Some cells become active only when a vertical bar of light strikes a given portion of the retina. Others become active only when a horizontal bar strikes the retina. In other words such cells appear to act as feature detectors. In later experiments Hubel and Wiesel and other investigators found cells that respond to other kinds of features, such as movement in a particular direction.

Interpretation.   Hubel and Wiesel reported feature-detector neurons in both cats and monkeys. If the organization of the occipital cortex is similar in species as distantly related as cats and monkeys, it is likely (though not certain) to be similar in humans as well.

A second line of evidence is based on the following reasoning: If the human cortex does contain feature-detector cells, one type of cell should become fatigued after we stare for a time at the features that excite it. When we look away, we should see an aftereffect created by the inactivity of that type of cell. (Recall the negative afterimage in color vision, as shown by Figure 4.14.) Try the Online Try It Yourself activity. Go to **www.thomsonedu.com/ psychology/kalat.** Navigate to the student website, then to the Online Try It Yourself section, and click Motion Aftereffect.

One example of this phenomenon is the waterfall illusion: *If you stare at a waterfall for a minute or more and then turn your eyes to some nearby cliffs, the cliffs will appear to flow upward.* By staring at the waterfall, you fatigue the neurons that respond to downward motion. When you look away, those neurons become inactive, but others that respond to upward motion continue their normal activity. Even though the motionless cliffs stimulate those neurons only weakly, the stimulation is enough to produce an illusion of upward motion

For another example here is a demonstration that you can perform yourself.

SECOND STUDY

Hypothesis.   After you stare at one set of vertical lines, you will fatigue the feature detectors that respond to lines of a particular width. If you then look at lines slightly wider or narrower than the original ones, they will appear to be even wider or narrower than they really are.

Method.   Cover the right half of Figure 4.39 and stare at the little rectangle in the middle of the left half for at least 1 minute. (Staring even longer will increase the effect.) Do not stare at one point, but move your focus around within the rectangle. Then look at the square in the center of the right part of the figure and compare the spacing between the lines of the top and bottom gratings (Blakemore & Sutton, 1969).

Online Try It Yourself

Try It Yourself

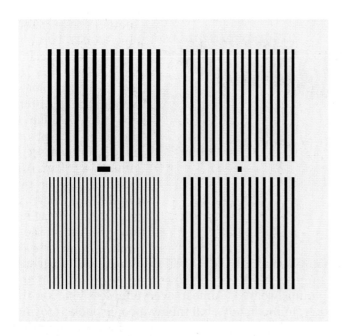

FIGURE 4.39 Use this display to fatigue your feature detectors and create an afterimage. Follow the directions in Experiment 2. *(From Blakemore & Sutton, 1969)*

Results. What did you perceive in the right half of the figure? People generally report that the top lines look narrower and the bottom lines look wider, even though they are the same.

Interpretation. Staring at the left part of the figure fatigues neurons sensitive to wide lines in the top part of the figure and neurons sensitive to narrow lines in the bottom part. Then, when you look at lines of medium width, the fatigued cells become inactive. Therefore, your perception is dominated by cells sensitive to narrower lines in the top part and to wider lines in the bottom part.

To summarize, we have two types of evidence for the existence of visual feature detectors: (a) The brains of other species contain cells with the properties of feature detectors, and (b) after staring at certain patterns, we see aftereffects that can be explained as fatigue of feature-detector cells in the brain.

The research just described was the start of an enormous amount of activity by laboratories throughout the world. Later results revised our views of what the earlier results mean. For example, even though certain neurons respond better to a single vertical line

than to points or lines of other orientations, the vertical line may not be the best stimulus for exciting

those neurons. Most respond even more strongly to a sine-wave grating of lines:

Thus, the feature that cells detect is probably more complex than just a line. Furthermore, because each cell responds to a range of stimuli, no one cell provides an unambiguous message about what you see at any moment.

One important point about scientific advances: A single line of evidence—even Nobel Prize-winning evidence—seldom provides the final answer to any question. We always look for multiple ways to test a hypothesis.

✓ **CONCEPT CHECK**

18. What is a feature detector, and what evidence supports the idea of feature detectors? (Check your answer on page 146.)

Do Feature Detectors Explain Perception?

The neurons just described are active during the early stages of visual processing. Do we simply add up the responses of a great many feature detectors so that the sum of enough feature detectors constitutes your perception of, say, your psychology professor's face?

No, feature detectors cannot provide a complete explanation even for how we perceive letters, much less faces. For example, we perceive the words in Figure 4.40a as CAT and HAT, even though the A in CAT is identical to the H in HAT, and therefore, both of them stimulate the same feature detectors. Likewise, the character in the center of Figure 4.40b can be read as

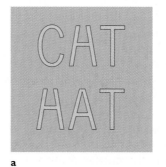

a   b

FIGURE 4.40 We perceive elements differently depending on their context. In **(a)** the A in CAT is the same as the H in HAT, but we perceive them differently. In **(b)** the central character can appear to be a B or the number 13 depending on whether we read horizontally or vertically. *(Part b from Kim, 1989)*

© Courtesy of McDonnell Douglas

FIGURE 4.41 According to Gestalt psychology, the whole is different from the sum of its parts. Here we perceive an assembly of several hundred people as an airplane.

either the letter B or the number 13. The early stages of visual perception use feature detectors, but the perception of a complex pattern requires further processing.

Gestalt Psychology

Figure 4.41, which we see as the overall shape of an airplane, is a photo of several hundred people. The plane is the overall pattern, not the sum of the parts. Recall also Figure 4.31 from earlier in this chapter: The photograph is composed of dots, but we perceive a face, not just dots.

Such observations derive from **Gestalt psychology,** *a field that focuses on our ability to perceive overall patterns. Gestalt* (geh-SHTALT) is a German word translated as "overall pattern or configuration." The founders of Gestalt psychology rejected the idea that a perception can be broken down into its component parts. A melody broken up into individual notes is no longer a melody. Their slogan was, "The whole is different from the sum of its parts." According to Gestalt psychologists, visual perception is an active creation, not just the adding up of pieces. We considered an example of this principle in Figure 4.41. Here are some further examples.

In Figure 4.42 you may see animals or you may see meaningless black and white patches. You might see only patches for a while, and then one or both animals suddenly emerge. To perceive the animals, you must separate **figure and ground**—that is, you must distinguish the *object from the background.* Ordinarily, you make that distinction almost instantly; you become aware of the process only when it is difficult (as it is here).

Figure 4.43 contains five **reversible figures,** *stimuli that can be perceived in more than one way.* In effect we test hypotheses: "Is this the front of the object or is that the front? Does the object face left or right? Is this section the foreground or the background?" The longer you look at a reversible figure, the more frequently you alternate between one perception and

another (Long & Toppine, 2004). Part a of Figure 4.43 is called the *Necker cube,* after the psychologist who first called attention to it. Which is the front face of the cube? You can see it either way. Part b is either a vase or two profiles. In part c, with a little imagination, you might see a woman's face or a man blowing a horn. (If you need help, check answer F on page 147.) Part d shows both an old woman and a young woman. Almost everyone sees one or the other immediately, but many people lock into one perception so tightly that they cannot see the other

a

b

FIGURE 4.42 Do you see an animal in each picture? If not, check answer E on page 147. *(From "A Puzzle Picture with a New Principle of Concealment," by K.M. Dallenbach,* American Journal of Psychology, *1951, 54, pp. 431–433. Copyright © by The Board of Trustees of the University of Illinois.)*

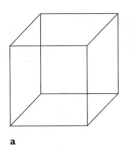    

a b c d e

FIGURE 4.43 Reversible figures: **(a)** The Necker cube. Which is the front face? **(b)** Faces or a vase. **(c)** A sax player or a woman's face ("Sara Nader"). **(d)** An old woman or a young woman. **(e)** A face or what? *("Sara Nader" and "Faces or Vase" from* Mind Sights, *© 1990 by Roger N. Shepard. Reprinted by permission of Henry Holt & Company, LLC.)*

one. The 8-year-old girl who drew part e intended it as the picture of a face. Can you find another possibility? (If you have trouble with parts d or e, check answers G and H on page 147.) Overall, the point of the reversible figures is that we perceive by imposing order, not just by adding up lines and points.

 CONCEPT CHECK

19. In what way does the phenomenon of reversible figures conflict with the idea that feature detectors explain vision? (Check your answer on page 146.)

The Gestalt psychologists described several principles of how we organize perceptions into meaningful wholes, as illustrated in Figure 4.44. **Proximity** is the *tendency to perceive objects that are close together as belonging to a group.* The objects in part a form two groups because of their proximity. The *tendency to perceive objects that resemble each other as forming a group* is called **similarity.** In part b we group the Xs together and the ●s together because of similarity. Even 3- and 4-month-old infants begin to show this tendency, after a little practice. Suppose an infant examines a series of displays suggesting vertical lines:

☐ ● ☐ ●   \\ // \\ //
☐ ● ☐ ●   \\ // \\ //
☐ ● ☐ ●   \\ // \\ //
☐ ● ☐ ●   \\ // \\ //
☐ ● ☐ ●   \\ // \\ //

After spending some time with these, the infant will spend more time looking at a set of horizontal lines ≡ than a set of vertical lines ⦀, suggesting that the horizontal lines are a novelty, whereas the vertical lines resemble what the child has been watching for the last few minutes (Quinn & Bhatt, 2005).

When lines are interrupted, as in part c, we may perceive **continuation,** *a filling in of the gaps.* You probably perceive this illustration as a rectangle covering the center of one very long hot dog.

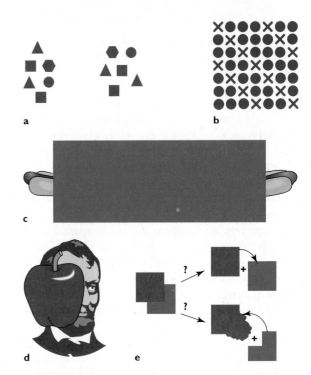

FIGURE 4.44 Gestalt principles of **(a)** proximity, **(b)** similarity, **(c)** continuation, **(d)** closure, and **(e)** good figure.

When a familiar figure is interrupted, as in part d, we perceive a **closure** of the figure; that is, *we imagine the rest of the figure.* The figure we imagine completes what we already see in a way that is simple, symmetrical, or consistent with our past experience (Shimaya, 1997). For example, you probably see the following as an orange rectangle overlapping a blue diamond, although you don't really know what, if anything, is behind the rectangle:

Of course, the principle of closure resembles that of continuation. With a complicated pattern, however, closure deals with more information. For example, in Figure 4.44c you fill in the gaps to perceive one long hot dog. With some additional context, you might perceive the same pattern as two shorter hot dogs:

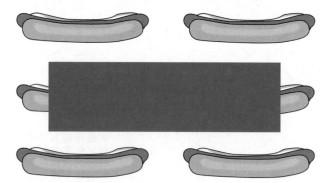

Yet another Gestalt principle is **common fate:** *We perceive objects as being part of the same group if they change or move in similar ways at the same time.* Suppose you see an array of miscellaneous objects differing in shape, size, and color. If some of them move in the same direction and speed, you see them as a related group. Also, if some grow brighter or darker at the same time, you see them as related (Sekuler & Bennett, 2001).

The principle of common fate is useful in everyday life. Imagine you see a snake's head sticking out of one hole in the ground and a tail sticking out of another. If the head starts moving forward and the tail moves down into the ground, you perceive it as all one snake. If the head moves and the tail doesn't, you see that you have two snakes.

Here is an example that pits similarity and common fate against each other: Suppose you see an array of green and red dots. In the center all the green dots are moving up, and the red dots are moving down. However, near the edges the green dots are moving down and the red ones up. Because of similarity, you tend to see all the green dots together and the red dots together, and therefore, it seems that all the dots of a given color are moving in the same direction. It is a fascinating phenomenon, but you will have to see it in motion to grasp the idea. Check **http://neuro .caltech.edu/~daw-an/** and click Steady-State Misbinding of Color and Motion.

Finally, when possible, we tend to perceive a **good figure**—*a simple, familiar, symmetrical figure.* Many important, familiar objects in the world are geometrically simple or close to it: The sun and moon are round, tree trunks meet the ground at almost a right angle, faces and animals are nearly symmetrical, and so forth. When we look at a complex pattern, we tend to focus on regular patterns. If we can interpret some-

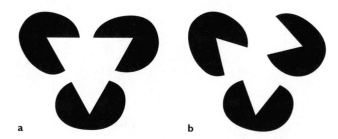

FIGURE 4.45 In **(a)** we see a triangle overlapping three irregular ovals. We see it because triangles are "good figures" and symmetrical. If we tilt the ovals, as in **(b)**, they appear as irregular objects, not as objects with something on top of them. *(From "Contour Completion and Relative Depth: Petter's Rule and Support Ratio," by M. Singh, D. D. Hoffman & M. K. Albert,* Psychological Science, *1999, 10, 423–428. Copyright © 1999 Blackwell Publishers Ltd. Reprinted by permission.)*

thing as a circle, square, or straight line, we do. In Figure 4.44e the part on the left could represent a red square overlapping a green one or a green backward L overlapping a red object of irregular shape. We are powerfully drawn to the first interpretation because it includes "good," regular, symmetrical objects.

In Figure 4.45a we perceive a white triangle overlapping three ovals (Singh, Hoffman, & Albert, 1999). That perception is so convincing that you may have to look carefully to persuade yourself that there is no line establishing a border for the triangle. However, if we tilt the blue objects slightly, as in Figure 4.45b, the illusion of something lying on top of them disappears. We "see" the overlapping object only if it is a symmetrical, good figure.

Similarities Between Vision and Hearing

The perceptual organization principles of Gestalt psychology apply to hearing as well as vision. Analogous to reversible figures, some sounds can be heard in more than one way. For instance, you can hear a clock going "tick, tock, tick, tock" or "tock, tick, tock, tick." You can hear your windshield wipers going "dunga, dunga" or "gadung, gadung."

The Gestalt principles of continuation and closure work best when we see something that has interrupted something else. For example, consider Figure 4.46. In parts c and d, the context suggests objects partly blocking our view of a three-dimensional cube. In parts a and b, we are much less likely to see a cube, as nothing suggests an object occluding the view. Similarly, in Figure 4.47a we see a series of meaningless patches. In Figure 4.47b the addition of some black glop helps us see these patches as the word *psychology* (Bregman, 1981). We get continuation or closure mainly when we see that something has blocked the presumed object in the background.

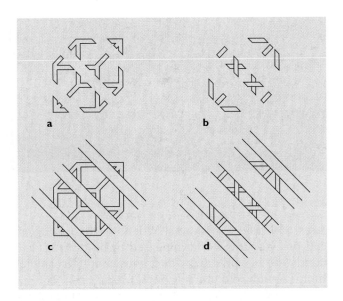

FIGURE 4.46 (a) and (b) appear to be arrays of flat objects. Introducing a context of overlapping lines causes a cube to emerge in (c) and (d). *(From* Organization in Vision: Essays on Gestalt Perception, *by Gaetano Kanizsa, pp. 7-9. Copyright © 1979 by Gaetano Kanizsa. Reproduced with permission of Greenwood Publishing Group, Westport, CT.)*

The same is true in hearing. If a speech or song is broken up by periods of silence, we do not fill in the gaps and find the utterance hard to understand. However, if the same gaps are filled by noise, we "hear" what probably occurred during those gaps. That is, we apply continuation and closure (C. T. Miller, Dibble, & Hauser, 2001; Warren, 1970).

Feature Detectors and Gestalt Psychology

The Gestalt approach to perception does not conflict with the feature-detector approach as much as it might seem. The feature-detector approach describes the first stages of perception—how the brain takes individual points of light and connects them into lines and forms. According to the feature-detector ap-

proach, the brain says, "I see these points here, here, and here, so there must be a line. I see a line here and another line connecting with it here, so there must be a letter L." The Gestalt approach describes how we combine visual input with our knowledge and expectations. According to the Gestalt interpretation, the brain says, "I see what looks like a circle, so the missing piece must be part of a circle too."

Which view is correct? Both are, of course. Our perception must assemble the individual points of light or bits of sound, but once it forms a tentative interpretation of the pattern, it uses that interpretation to organize the information.

Perception of Movement and Depth

As an automobile moves away from us, its image on the retina grows smaller, yet we perceive it as moving, not as shrinking. That perception illustrates **visual constancy**—our *tendency to perceive objects as keeping their shape, size, and color, despite certain distortions in the light pattern reaching our retinas.* Figure 4.48 shows examples of two visual constancies: shape constancy and size constancy. Constancies depend on our familiarity with objects and on our ability to estimate distances and angles of view. For example, we know that a door is still rectangular even when we view it from an odd angle. But to recognize that an object keeps its shape and size, we have to perceive movement or changes in distance. How do we do so?

Perception of Movement

Moving objects capture our attention for a good reason. A moving object could be a person or animal, something people have made (e.g., a car), something thrown, or something that has fallen. In any case it is more likely to require our immediate attention than something stationary.

People are particularly adept at perceiving biological motion—that is, a body in motion. Suppose we attach small lights to someone's shoulders, elbows, hands, hips, knees, and ankles. Then we turn out all other lights so that you see just the lights on this person. When the person is at rest, the lights form an apparently meaningless array. As soon as the person starts to walk, you see the lights as a person in motion. In fact you have a brain area special-

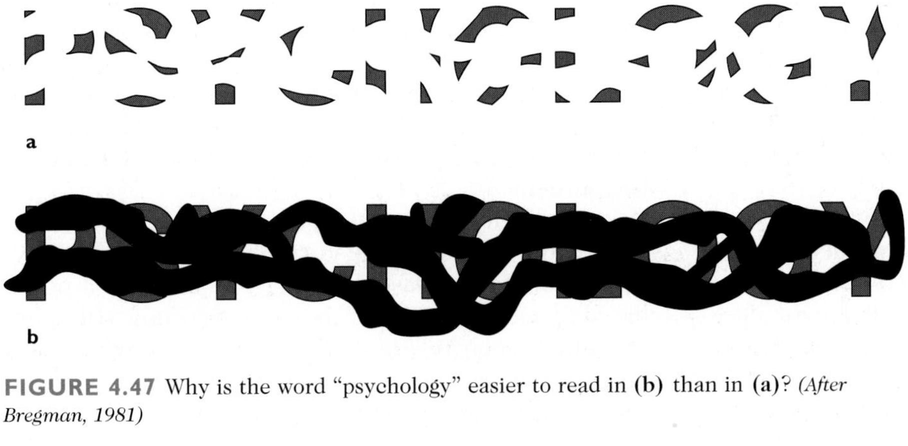

FIGURE 4.47 Why is the word "psychology" easier to read in (b) than in (a)? *(After Bregman, 1981)*

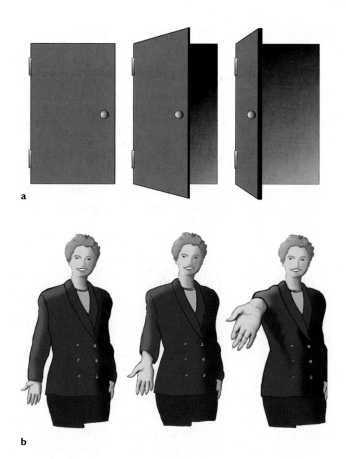

FIGURE 4.48 **(a)** Shape constancy: We perceive all three doors as rectangles. **(b)** Size constancy: We perceive all three hands as equal in size.

ized for just this task (Grossman & Blake, 2001). You can see this fascinating phenomenon for yourself at this Web site: **http://www.biomotionlab.ca/Demos/BMLwalker.html**

Try It Yourself

The detection of motion raises some interesting issues, including how we distinguish between our own movement and the movement of objects. Try this simple demonstration: Hold an object in front of your eyes and then move it to the right. Now hold the object in front of your eyes and move your eyes to the left. The image of the object moves across your retina in the same way when you move the object or move your eyes. Yet you perceive the object as moving in one case but not in the other. Why?

The object looks stationary when you move your eyes for two reasons. One is that the vestibular system informs the visual areas of the brain about your head movements. When your brain knows that your eyes have moved to the left, it interprets what you see as being a result of the movement. One man with a rare kind of brain damage could not connect his eye movements with his perceptions. Whenever he moved his head or eyes, the world appeared to be moving. Frequently, he became dizzy and nauseated (Haarmeier, Thier, Repnow, & Petersen, 1997).

The second reason that the object does not appear to move is that we perceive motion when an object moves *relative to the background* (Gibson, 1968). For example, when you walk forward, stationary objects in your environment move across your retina but do not move relative to the background. If something moves relative to the background but fails to move across your retina, you perceive it as moving in the same direction as you are.

What do we perceive when an object is stationary and the background moves? In that unusual case, we may *incorrectly perceive the object as moving against a stationary background,* a phenomenon called **induced movement**. For example, when you watch clouds moving slowly across the moon, you might perceive the clouds as stationary and the moon as moving. Induced movement is a form of *apparent movement,* as opposed to *real movement.*

You have already read about the waterfall illusion (page 132), another example of apparent movement. Yet another is **stroboscopic movement,** an *illusion of movement created by a rapid succession of stationary images.* When a scene is flashed on a screen and is followed a split second later by a second scene slightly different from the first, you perceive the objects as having moved smoothly from their location in the first scene to their location in the second scene (Figure 4.49). Motion pictures are actually a series of still photos flashed on the screen.

Our ability to detect visual movement played an interesting role in the history of astronomy. In 1930 Clyde Tombaugh was searching the skies for a possible undiscovered planet beyond Neptune. He photographed each region of the sky twice, several days apart. A planet, unlike a star, moves from one photo to the next. However, how would he find a small dot that

FIGURE 4.49 A movie consists of a series of still photographs flickering at 86,400 per hour. You perceive moving objects, however, not a series of stills. Here you see a series of stills spread out in space instead of time.

moved among all the countless unmoving dots in the sky? He put each pair of photos on a machine that would flip back and forth between one photo and the other. When he came to one pair of photos, he immediately noticed one dot moving as the machine flipped back and forth (Tombaugh, 1980). He identified that dot as Pluto, which astronomers now list as a dwarf planet (Figure 4.50).

Perception of Depth

Although we live in a world of three dimensions, our retinas are in effect two-dimensional surfaces. **Depth perception,** our *perception of distance,* enables us to experience the world in three dimensions. This perception depends on several factors.

One factor is **retinal disparity**—*the difference in the apparent position of an object as seen by the left and right retinas.* Try this: Hold a finger at arm's length. Focus on it with one eye and then the other. Note that the apparent position of your finger shifts

with respect to the background. Now hold your finger closer to your face and repeat the experiment. Notice that the apparent position of your finger shifts even more. The discrepancy between the slightly different views the two eyes see becomes greater as the object comes closer. We use the amount of discrepancy to gauge distance.

A second cue for depth perception is the **convergence** of the eyes—that is, the *degree to which they turn in to focus on a close object* (Figure 4.51). When you focus on a distant object, your eyes are looking in almost parallel directions. When you focus on something close, your eyes turn in, and you sense the tension of your eye muscles. The more the muscles pull, the closer the object must be.

Retinal disparity and convergence are called **binocular cues** because they *depend on both eyes.* **Monocular cues** enable a person to *judge depth and distance with just one eye* or when both eyes see the same image, as when you look at a picture, such as Figure 4.52. The ability to use monocular cues for depth depends on our experience, including experiences with photographs and drawings. For example, in Figure 4.53 does it appear to you that the hunter is aiming his spear at the antelope? When this drawing was shown to African people who had seldom seen drawings, many said the hunter was aiming at a baby elephant (Hudson, 1960). Clearly, people have to learn how to judge depth in drawings.

Let's consider some of the monocular cues we use to perceive depth:

Object size: Other things being equal, a nearby object produces a larger image than a distant one. How-

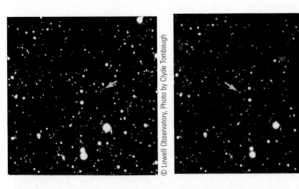

FIGURE 4.50 Clyde Tombaugh photographed each area of the sky twice, several days apart. Then he used a machine to flip back and forth between the two photos of each pair. When he came to one part of the sky, he immediately noticed one dot that moved between the two photos. That dot was Pluto.

FIGURE 4.51 Convergence of the eyes as a cue to distance. The more this viewer must converge her eyes toward each other to focus on an object, the closer the object must be.

FIGURE 4.52 We judge depth and distance in a photograph using monocular cues (those that would work even with just one eye): (a) Closer objects occupy more space on the retina (or in the photograph) than do distant objects of the same type. (b) Nearer objects show more detail. (c) Closer objects overlap certain distant objects. (d) Objects in the foreground look sharper than objects do on the horizon.

Linear perspective: As parallel lines stretch out toward the horizon, they come closer and closer together. Examine the road in Figure 4.52. At the bottom of the photo (close to the viewer), the edges of the road are far apart; at greater distances they come together.

Detail: We see nearby objects, such as the jogger, in more detail than distant objects.

Interposition: A nearby object interrupts our view of a more distant object. For example, the closest telephone pole (on the right) interrupts our view of the closest tree, so we see that the telephone pole is closer than the tree.

Texture gradient: Notice the distance between one telephone pole and the next. At greater distances the poles come closer and closer together. The "packed together" appearance of objects gives us another cue to their approximate distance.

Shadows: Shadows help us gauge sizes as well as locations of objects.

ever, this cue is useful only for objects of known sizes. For example, the jogger in Figure 4.52 produces a larger image than do any of the houses, which we know are actually larger. So we see the jogger as closer. However, the mountains in the background differ in actual as well as apparent size, so we cannot assume the ones that look bigger are closer.

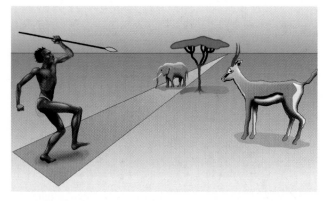

FIGURE 4.53 Which animal is the hunter attacking? Many people unfamiliar with drawings and photographs thought he was attacking a baby elephant. *(From Hudson, 1960)*

If you were a passenger on this train looking toward the horizon, the ground beside the tracks would appear to pass by more quickly than the more distant elements in the landscape. In this photo's version of motion parallax, the ground is blurred and more distant objects are crisp.

Accommodation: The lens of the eye accommodates—that is, it changes shape—to focus on nearby objects, and your brain detects that change and thereby infers the distance to an object. Accommodation could help tell you how far away the photograph itself is, although it provides no information about the relative distances of objects in the photograph.

Motion parallax: Another monocular cue helps us perceive depth while we are moving, although it does not help with a photograph. If you are walking or riding in a car and fixating at the horizon, nearby objects move rapidly across the retina, while those farther away move much less. The *difference in speed of movement of images across the retina as you travel* is the principle of **motion parallax.** Television and film crews use this principle. If the camera moves very slowly, you see closer objects move more than distant ones and get a good sense of depth.

 CONCEPT CHECK

20. Which monocular cues to depth are available in Figure 4.53?
21. With three-dimensional photography, cameras take two views of the same scene from different locations through lenses with different color filters or with different polarized-light filters. The two views are then superimposed. The viewer looks at the composite view through special glasses so that one eye sees the view taken with one camera and the other eye sees the view taken with the other camera. Which depth cue is at work here? (Check your answers on page 146.)

Optical Illusions

Our vision is well adapted to understanding what we see in the world around us. However, it is not perfect under all circumstances. An **optical illusion** is a *misinterpretation of a visual stimulus.* Figure 4.54 shows a few examples. For many more, visit either of these sites:

www.exploratorium.edu/exhibits

www.michaelbach.de/ot/index.html

Psychologists would like to explain the optical illusions using the same principles for as many illusions as possible. (Remember the principle of parsimony from chapter 2.) One approach, which applies to some of the illusions but not all, pertains to mistakes of depth perception.

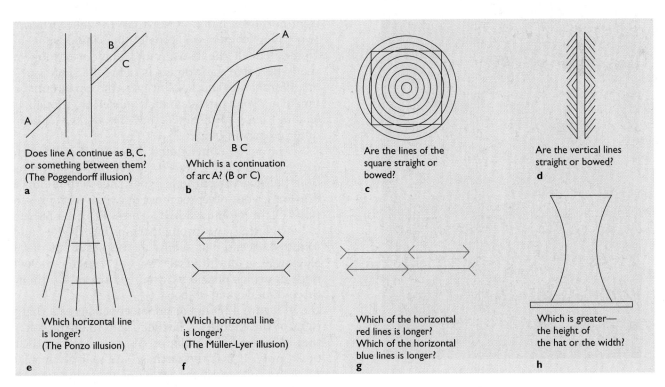

FIGURE 4.54 These geometric figures illustrate optical illusions. Answers (which you are invited to check with ruler and compass): **(a)** B, **(b)** B, **(c)** straight, **(d)** straight, **(e)** equal, **(f)** equal, **(g)** equal, **(h)** equal.

Depth Perception and Size Perception

As you see in Figure 4.55, a given image on the retina may represent either a small, close object or a large, distant object. If you know either the size or the distance, you can estimate the other one. However, if you misperceive either size or distance, you will be mistaken about the other also.

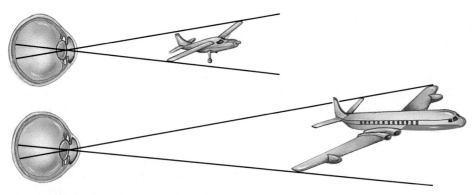

FIGURE 4.55 The trade-off between size and distance: A given image on the retina can indicate either a small, close object or a large, distant object.

FIGURE 4.56 Because fish come in many sizes, we can estimate the size of a fish only if we know how far away it is or if we can compare its size to other nearby objects. See what happens when you cover the man and then cover the hand.

Watch what happens when you take a single image and change its apparent distance: Stare at Figure 4.14 again to form a negative afterimage. Examine the afterimage while you are looking at a sheet of paper. As you move the paper backward and forward, you can make the apparent size change.

Try It Yourself

The real world provides many cues about the size and distance of objects. However, the cues are occasionally inadequate (Figure 4.56). I once was unsure whether I was watching a nearby toy airplane or a distant, full-size airplane. Airplanes come in many sizes, and the sky has few cues to distance.

A similar issue arises in reported sightings of UFOs. When people see an unfamiliar object in the sky, they can easily misjudge its distance. If they overestimate its distance, they also will overestimate its size and speed.

Certain optical illusions occur when we misjudge distance and therefore misjudge size. For example, Figure 4.57a shows people in the Ames room (named for its designer, Adelbert Ames). The room is designed to look like a normal rectangular room, though Figure 4.57b shows its true dimensions. The right corner is much closer than the left corner. The two young women are actually the same height. If we eliminated all the background cues, we would correctly perceive the women as being the same size but at different distances. However, the apparently rectangular room provides such powerful (though misleading) cues to distance that the women appear to differ greatly in height.

Even a two-dimensional drawing on a flat surface can offer cues that lead to erroneous depth perception. Because of your long experience with photos and drawings, you interpret most drawings as representations of three-dimensional scenes. Figure 4.58 shows a bewildering two-prong/three-prong device and a round staircase that seems to run uphill all the way clockwise or downhill all the way counterclockwise. Both drawings puzzle us when we try to see them as three-dimensional objects.

In Figure 4.59 linear perspective suggests that the right of the picture is farther away than the left. We therefore see the cylinder on the right as being the farthest away. If it is the farthest and still produces the same size image on the retina as the other two, then it would have to be the largest. In short, by perceiving two-dimensional representations as if they were three-dimensional, we misjudge distance and conse-

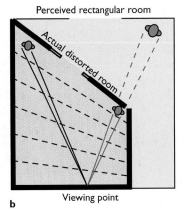
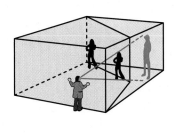

FIGURE 4.57 The Ames room is a study in deceptive perception, designed to be viewed through a peephole with one eye. **(a)** Both people are the same height, although they appear very different. **(b)** This diagram shows how the shape of the room distorts the viewer's perception of distance. *(Part b from J. R. Wilson et al., 1964)*

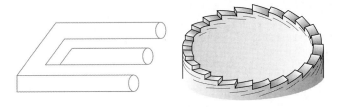

FIGURE 4.58 These two-dimensional drawings puzzle us because we try to interpret them as three-dimensional objects.

quently misjudge size. When we are somehow misled by the cues that ordinarily ensure constancy in size and shape, we experience an optical illusion (Day, 1972).

Figure 4.60 shows the tabletop illusion (Shepard, 1990). Here, almost unbelievably, the vertical dimension of the blue table equals the horizontal dimension of the yellow table, and the horizontal dimension of

the blue table equals the vertical dimension of the yellow table. (Take measurements at the center of each table. The shapes of the tables are not exactly the same.) The yellow table appears long and thin compared to the blue one because we interpret it in depth. In effect your brain constructs what each table would have to really *be* in order to look this way (Purves & Lotto, 2003).

We experience an *auditory illusion* by a similar principle: If you misestimate the distance to a sound source, you misestimate the intensity of the sound. That is, if you hear a sound that you think is coming from a distant source, you hear it as loud. (It would have to be loud for you to hear it so well from a distance.) If you hear the same sound but think it is coming from a source near you, it sounds softer (Kitigawa & Ichihara, 2002; Mershon, Desaulniers, Kiefer, Amerson, & Mills, 1981).

Purves's Empirical Approach to Optical Illusions

The tabletop illusion suggests another approach to optical illusions. You see the tables in depth, to be sure, but in more general terms, you call on all your experience to see what the object probably *is*. Anything you see, especially in two dimensions, is ambiguous.

For example, this object △ might be a flat triangle, a long rectangle trailing off toward the horizon, or a countless variety of other possibilities. When the context suggests one possibility or another, you perceive it that way, and in the case of the tabletops, you see a long thin yellow table and a square blue table. When the context is less helpful, you unconsciously calculate, "When I have seen something like this in the

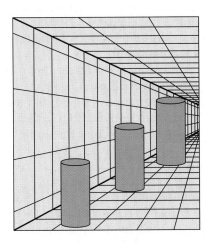

FIGURE 4.59 Several optical illusions depend on misjudging distances. The cylinder on the right seems larger because the context makes it appear farther away.

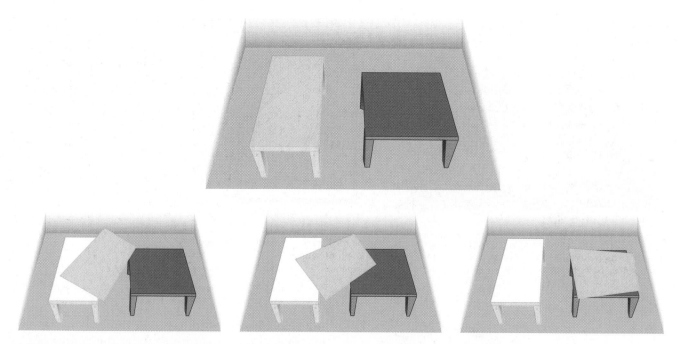

FIGURE 4.60 The tabletop illusion. The blue table is as wide as the yellow table is long, and as long as the yellow table is wide, if you measure in the middle of each table. The parts below show rotation of the blue table to overlap the yellow one.

past, what has it usually been?" According to Dale Purves and his colleagues, your perception is wholly empirical—that is, based entirely on the statistics of your experience (Howe & Purves, 2005b; Purves & Lotto, 2003).

For example, consider the Poggendorff illusion, first shown in Figure 4.54a, with two more versions in Figure 4.61. The diagonal lines are straight, but they do not appear to be. Researchers photographed about a hundred scenes of many types and then had a computer analyze all kinds of lines. They found that when a line slanting downward went behind a barrier, more often than not, when it emerged on the other side, it

was slightly higher than would happen with a truly straight line (Howe, Yang, & Purves, 2005). That is, in nature,

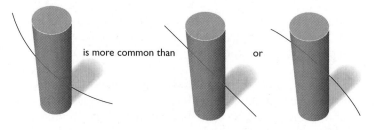

Therefore, when you see something like the diagrams in Figure 4.61, your visual system sees the slanted line on the right as "lower than expected."

Consider a similar approach to the Müller-Lyer illusion, one of the most robust illusions and one of the most difficult to explain convincingly. When people are asked to regard just the straight lines,

nearly all say that ⟩——⟨ looks longer than ⟨——⟩ .

Again, researchers used computers to analyze about 100 photographs of all kinds of scenes, both indoor and outdoor. On the average, lines connected to outward arrows (> and <) were slightly shorter than

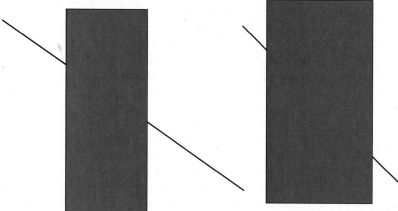

FIGURE 4.61 Two versions of the Poggendorff illusion.

lines connected to inward arrows (< and >). Therefore, because experience tells us that lines connected to inward arrows are usually a bit shorter than lines connected to outward arrows, when we see lines connected to inward and outward arrows, we tend to see the one connected to inward arrows as shorter (Howe & Purves, 2005a). Exactly why lines with inward arrows should be longer in nature than those with outward arrows is not obvious, but the researchers' approach is simply to go by the statistics of what they recorded. Application of the same approach accounted for each of the other illusions in Figure 4.54.

The Moon Illusion

To most people the *moon close to the horizon appears about 30% larger than it appears when it is higher in the sky.* This **moon illusion** is so convincing that many people have tried to explain it by referring to the bending of light rays by the atmosphere or other physical phenomena. However, if you photograph the moon and measure its image, you will find that it is the same size at the horizon as it is higher in the sky. For example, Figure 4.62 shows the moon at two positions in the sky; you can measure the two images to demonstrate that they are really the same size. (The atmosphere's bending of light rays makes the moon look orange near the horizon, but it does not increase the size of the image.) However, photographs do not capture the full strength of the moon illusion as we see it in real life. In Figure 4.62 (or any similar pair of photos), the moon looks almost the same at each position; in the actual night sky, the moon looks enormous at the horizon.

One explanation is that the vast terrain between the viewer and the horizon provides a basis for size comparison. When you see the moon at the horizon, you can compare it to other objects you see at the horizon, which look tiny. By contrast the moon looks large. When you see the moon high in the sky, however, it is surrounded only by the vast, featureless sky, so in contrast it appears smaller (Baird, 1982; Restle, 1970).

A second explanation is that the terrain between the viewer and the horizon gives an impression of great distance. When the moon is high in the sky, we have no basis to judge distance, and perhaps we unconsciously see the overhead moon as closer than when it is at the horizon. If we see the "horizon moon" as more distant, we will perceive it as larger (Kaufman & Rock, 1989; Rock & Kaufman, 1962). This explanation is appealing

FIGURE 4.62 Ordinarily, the moon looks much larger at the horizon than it does overhead. In photographs this illusion disappears almost completely, but the photographs do serve to demonstrate that the physical image of the moon is the same in both cases. The moon illusion requires a psychological explanation, not a physical one.

because it relates the moon illusion to our misperceptions of distance, a factor already accepted as important for many other illusions.

Many psychologists are not satisfied with this explanation, however, primarily because they are not convinced that the horizon moon looks farther away than the overhead moon. If we ask which looks farther away, many people say they are not sure. If we insist on an answer, most say the horizon moon looks *closer,* contradicting the theory. Some psychologists reply that the situation is complicated: We unconsciously perceive the horizon as farther away; consequently, we perceive the horizon moon as very large; then, because of the perceived large size of the horizon moon, we secondarily and consciously say it looks closer, while continuing to unconsciously perceive it as farther (Rock & Kaufman, 1962).

One major message arises from work on optical illusions and indeed from all the research on visual perception: What we perceive is not the same as what is "out there." Our visual system does an amazing job of providing us with useful information about the world around us, but under unusual circumstances we have distorted perceptions.

IN CLOSING

Making Sense Out of Sensory Information

You have probably heard the expression, "Seeing is believing." The saying is true in many ways, including that what you believe influences what you see.

Perception is not just a matter of adding up all the events striking the retina; we look for what we expect to see, we impose order on haphazard patterns, we see three dimensions in two-dimensional drawings, and we see optical illusions. The brain does not simply compute what light is striking the retina, but tries to learn what objects exist "out there" and what they are doing. ▮

Summary

- *Perception of minimal stimuli.* There is no sharp dividing line between sensory stimuli that can be perceived and sensory stimuli that cannot be perceived. (page 127)
- *Signal detection.* To determine how accurately someone can detect a signal or how accurately a test diagnoses a condition, we need to consider not only the ratio of hits to misses when the stimulus is present but also the ratio of false alarms to correct rejections when the stimulus is absent. (page 128)
- *Subliminal perception.* Under some circumstances a weak stimulus that we do not consciously identify can influence our behavior, at least weakly or briefly. However, the evidence does not support claims of powerful effects. (page 129)
- *Face recognition.* People are amazingly good at recognizing faces. (page 130)
- *Detection of simple visual features.* In the first stages of the process of perception, feature-detector cells identify lines, points, and simple movement. Visual afterimages can be interpreted in terms of fatiguing certain feature detectors. (page 131)
- *Perception of organized wholes.* According to Gestalt psychologists, we perceive an organized whole by identifying similarities and continuous patterns across a large area of the visual field. (page 134)
- *Visual constancies.* We ordinarily perceive the shape, size, and color of objects as constant, even though the pattern of light striking the retina varies from time to time. (page 137)
- *Motion perception.* We perceive an object as moving if it moves relative to its background. We can generally distinguish between an object that is actually moving and a similar pattern of retinal stimulation that results from our own movement. (page 137)
- *Depth perception.* To perceive depth, we use the accommodation of the eye muscles and retinal disparity between the views that our two eyes see. We also learn to use other cues that are just as effective with one eye as with two. (page 139)
- *Optical illusions.* Some optical illusions result from interpreting a two-dimensional display as three-dimensional or from other faulty estimates of depth. More generally, we perceive displays by comparing them to our previous experiences with similar objects. (page 141)

Answers to Concept Checks

16. We have been told the hit rate, but we cannot evaluate it unless we also know the false alarm rate. That is, how many people without any alcohol or drug problem have this same pattern of brain waves? If that percentage is large, the test is useless. The smaller that percentage is, the better. (page 128)
17. Play that message on half of all days, randomly chosen, for a period of weeks. On other days play no subliminal message or an irrelevant one. See whether the frequency of shoplifting is significantly less common on days with the message. (page 129)
18. A feature detector is a neuron that responds mostly in the presence of a particular visual feature, such as a straight horizontal line. One kind of evidence is that recordings from neurons in laboratory animals indicate increased response of different cells to different visual stimuli. Another line of evidence is that people who have stared at one kind of stimulus become temporarily less sensitive to that kind of stimulus, as if the feature detectors for that stimulus have become fatigued. (page 131)
19. Feature detectors cannot fully explain how we see a reversible figure in two or more ways. If vision were simply a matter of stimulating various line detectors and adding up their responses, then a given display would always produce the same perceptual experience. (page 134)
20. Object size and linear perspective are cues that the elephant must be far away. (page 140).
21. Retinal disparity. (page 139)

Answers to Other Questions in the Module

C. a. 7. b. 1. c. 5. d. 9. e. 4.
D.

E.

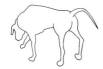

F.

G.

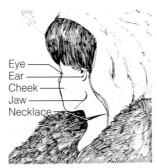

Eye
Ear
Cheek
Jaw
Necklace

Eye
Nose
Mouth
Chin

Young woman   Old woman

H.

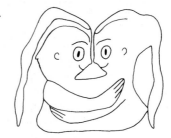

CHAPTER ENDING

Key Terms and Activities

Key Terms

You can check the page listed for a complete description of a term. You can also check the glossary/index at the end of the text for a definition of a given term, or you can download a list of all the terms and their definitions for any chapter at this website:

www.thomsonedu.com/ psychology/kalat

absolute sensory threshold (page 127)
accommodation of the lens (page 102)
binocular cues (page 139)
blind spot (page 107)
brightness contrast (page 130)
capsaicin (page 120)
cataract (page 103)
closure (page 135)
cochlea (page 114)
color constancy (page 110)
common fate (page 136)
conduction deafness (page 115)
cone (page 103)
continuation (page 135)
convergence (page 139)
cornea (page 102)
cutaneous senses (page 118)
dark adaptation (page 105)
depth perception (page 139)

electromagnetic spectrum (page 101)
endorphin (page 120)
feature detector (page 131)
figure and ground (page 134)
fovea (page 102)
frequency principle (page 116)
ganglion cells (page 106)
gate theory (page 120)
Gestalt psychology (page 134)
glaucoma (page 103)
good figure (page 136)
hertz (Hz) (page 114)
hyperopia (page 103)
induced movement (page 138)
iris (page 102)
lens (page 102)
loudness (page 114)
monocular cues (page 139)
moon illusion (page 145)
motion parallax (page 141)
myopia (page 103)
negative afterimage (page 109)
nerve deafness (page 115)
olfaction (page 123)
opponent-process theory (page 109)
optic nerve (page 106)
optical illusion (page 141)
perception (page 100)

phantom limb (page 121)
pheromone (page 124)
pitch (page 114)
place principle (page 116)
presbyopia (page 103)
proximity (page 135)
pupil (page 102)
receptor (page 101)
retina (page 102)
retinal disparity (page 139)
retinex theory (page 110)
reversible figure (page 134)
rod (page 103)
sensation (page 100)
signal-detection theory (page 128)
similarity (page 135)
sound waves (page 114)
stimuli (page 101)
stroboscopic movement (page 138)
subliminal perception (page 129)
substance P (page 120)
synesthesia (page 125)
taste (page 122)
taste bud (page 122)
trichromatic theory (or Young-Helmholtz theory) (page 108)
vestibular sense (page 117)
visual constancy (page 137)
volley principle the (page 116)
waterfall illusion (page 132)

Suggestions for Further Reading

Purves, D., & Lotto, R. B. (2003). *Why we see what we do.* Sunderland, MA: Sinauer Associates. Insightful and creative account of human perception.

Ramachandran, V. S., & Blakeslee, S. (1998). *Phantoms in the brain.* New York: Morrow. Fascinating explanation of phantom limbs and related phenomena.

Warren, R. M. (1999). *Auditory perception: A new analysis and synthesis.* Cambridge, England: Cambridge University Press. Superb treatment of hearing, with a CD-ROM disc that includes demonstrations of auditory phenomena.

Web/Technology Resources

Student Companion Website

www.thomsonedu.com/psychology/kalat

Explore the Student Companion Website for Online Try-It-Yourself activities, practice quizzes, flashcards, and more! The companion site also has direct links to the following websites.

Vision Science Demonstrations

http://www.visionscience.com/vsDemos.html

Links to many fascinating demonstrations, mostly visual but a few auditory. It's one amazing experience after another.

More Illusions

www.exploratorium.edu/exhibits

www.michaelbach.de/ot/index.html

Here are wonderful illusions, both visual and auditory. Enjoy.

Seeing, Hearing, and Smelling

www.hhmi.org/senses/

Elaborate psychological and medical information, courtesy of the Howard Hughes Medical Institute.

Smells and Flavors

http://www.leffingwell.com/

Rich source of information about olfaction, ranging from the chemistry of perfumes to the olfactory receptors and how our brains handle olfaction.

For Additional Study

Kalat Premium Website

http://www.thomsonedu.com

For Critical Thinking Videos and additional Online Try-It-Yourself activities, go to this site to enter or purchase your code for the Kalat Premium Website.

ThomsonNOW!

http://www.thomsonedu.com

Go to this site for the link to ThomsonNOW, your one-stop study shop. Take a Pretest for this chapter, and Thomson-NOW will generate a personalized Study Plan based on your test reults. The Study Plan will identify the topics you need to review and direct you to online resources to help you master those topics. You can then take a Posttest to help you determine the concepts you have mastered and what you still need to work on.

Nature, Nurture, and Human Development

Suppose you buy a robot. When you get home, you discover that it does nothing useful. It cannot even maintain its balance. It makes irritating, high-pitched noises, moves its limbs haphazardly, and leaks. The store you bought it from refuses to take it back. And you're not allowed to turn it off. So you are stuck with this useless machine.

A few years later, your robot walks and talks, reads and writes, draws pictures, and does arithmetic. It follows your directions (usually) and sometimes finds useful things to do without being told. It beats you at memory games.

How did all this happen? After all, you knew nothing about how to program a robot. Did your robot have some sort of built-in programming that simply took a long time to phase in? Or was it programmed to learn all these skills?

As we grow older, our behavior changes in many ways. Developmental psychologists seek to describe and understand these changes.

Children are much like that robot. Parents wonder, "How did my children get to be the way they are?" The goal of developmental psychology is to understand how nature and nurture combine to produce human behavior "from womb to tomb."

Genetics and Evolution of Behavior

• *How do genes influence behavior?*

Everyone has tens of thousands of genes that control development. If we could go back in time and change just one of the genes you were born with, how would your experience and personality be different?

Obviously, it depends on *which* gene. Hundreds of your genes control olfactory receptors. A mutation in one of them would decrease your sensitivity to a few smells, and you might not even notice your deficiency. At the other extreme, some genes lead to disorders that would change your life drastically or end it early.

The effect of changing a gene also depends on your environment. Suppose you had (or didn't have) a gene that magnifies your reactions to stressful experiences. How would that have changed your life? The answer depends on how many stressful experiences you have faced. The more stressful experiences, the greater the effect of that gene.

Psychologists widely agree that both heredity and environment are essential for everything you do. Nevertheless, in some cases the *differences* among people relate mainly to *differences* in their heredity or environment. For analogy we cannot meaningfully ask whether a computer's activity depends on its hardware or software because both are essential. However, two computers might differ because of differences in their hardware, their software, or both. Similarly, the difference between having color vision and being color vision deficient depends almost entirely on genetics, whereas the difference between speaking English and speaking some other language depends on the community in which you were reared. Most behavioral differences depend on differences in both heredity and environment, often in complicated ways.

The study of genetics has become increasingly important for citizens of the 21st century. Because biologists have mapped the human genome (the set of genes on our chromosomes), physicians who examine your chromosomes can predict your likelihood of getting various diseases and how well you will respond to various medications if you do get those diseases. Laboratories can use samples of blood or sperm to determine which suspect might have committed some crime. The possibilities for further applications are huge. Let's first review some basic points about genetics and then explore their application to human behavior.

Genetic Principles

Except for your red blood cells, all of your cells contain a nucleus, which includes *strands of hereditary material* called **chromosomes** (Figure 5.1). Each human nucleus has 23 pairs of chromosomes, except those in egg and sperm cells, which have 23 unpaired chromosomes. At fertilization the 23 chromosomes from an egg cell combine with the 23 of a sperm cell to form 23 pairs for the new person (Figure 5.2).

Sections along each chromosome, known as **genes,** *control the chemical reactions that direct development*—for example, controlling height or hair color. Genes are composed of the chemical DNA, which controls the production of another chemical called RNA, which among other functions controls the production of proteins. The proteins either become part of the body's structure or control the rates of chemical reactions in the body. The actual nature of genes is more complicated than we once thought. In some cases part of one gene overlaps part of another one, or parts of a single gene are located on different parts of a chromosome or even on different chromosomes. However, we can ignore those complications for most purposes in psychology.

To explain the concept of genes, educators often use an example such as eye color. If you have either one or two genes for brown eyes, you will have brown

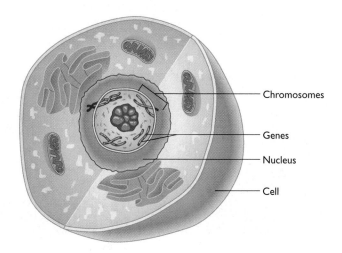

FIGURE 5.1 Genes are sections of chromosomes in the nuclei of cells. (Scale is exaggerated for illustration purposes.)

153

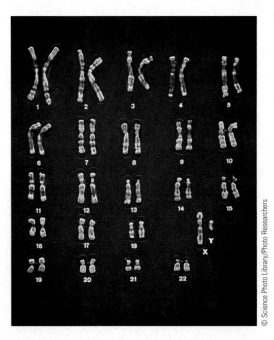

FIGURE 5.2 The nucleus of each human cell contains 46 chromosomes, 23 from the sperm and 23 from the ovum, united in pairs.

FIGURE 5.3 A single gene determines whether you can curl your tongue.

eyes because the brown-eye gene is **dominant**—*that is, a single copy of the gene is sufficient to produce its effect.* The gene for blue eyes is **recessive**—*its effects appear only if the dominant gene is absent.* You can have blue eyes only if you have two genes for blue eyes. A behavioral example is the ability to curl your tongue lengthwise (Figure 5.3). If you have either one or two copies of this dominant gene, you can curl your tongue. If you have two of the recessive gene, you can't. (You will be seldom inconvenienced.)

However, examples like this are misleading because they imply that each gene has only one effect, which it controls completely. Most genes influence many outcomes without completely controlling any of them.

☑ CONCEPT CHECK

1. If two parents cannot curl their tongues, what can you predict about their children? (Check your answer on page 162.)

Sex-Linked and Sex-Limited Genes

Because chromosomes come in pairs (one from the mother and one from the father), you have two of almost all genes. The exceptions are those on the **sex chromosomes,** which *determine whether an individual develops as a male or as a female.* Mammals' sex chromosomes are known as X and Y (Figure 5.4). *A female has two X chromosomes in each cell; a male has one X chromosome and one Y chromosome.* The mother contributes an X chromosome to each child, and the father contributes either an X or a Y. Because men have one X chromosome and one Y chromosome, they have unpaired genes on these chromosomes. Women have two X chromosomes, but in each cell one of the X chromosomes is activated and the other is silenced, apparently at random.

FIGURE 5.4 An electron micrograph shows that the X chromosome is longer than the Y chromosome. *(From Ruch, 1984)*

a

b

c

▌ Albinos occur in many species, always because of a recessive gene. **(a)** Striped skunk. **(b)** American alligator. **(c)** Mockingbird.

Genes located on the X chromosome are known as **sex-linked** *or* **X-linked genes.** Genes on the Y chromosome are also sex-linked, but the Y chromosome has fewer genes. An X-linked recessive gene shows its effects more in men than in women. For example, the most common type of color vision deficiency depends on an X-linked recessive gene. A man with that gene on his X chromosome will be colorblind because he has no other X chromosome. A woman with that gene probably has a gene for normal color vision on her other X chromosome. Consequently, far more men than women have color vision deficiency (Figure 5.5).

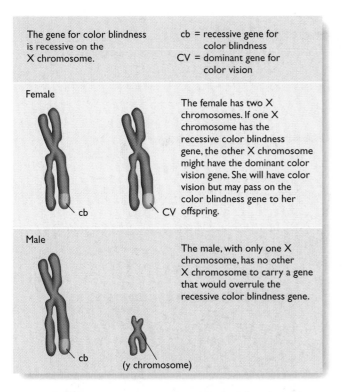

The gene for color blindness is recessive on the X chromosome.

cb = recessive gene for color blindness
CV = dominant gene for color vision

Female

The female has two X chromosomes. If one X chromosome has the recessive color blindness gene, the other X chromosome might have the dominant color vision gene. She will have color vision but may pass on the color blindness gene to her offspring.

cb   CV

Male

The male, with only one X chromosome, has no other X chromosome to carry a gene that would overrule the recessive color blindness gene.

cb

(y chromosome)

FIGURE 5.5 Why males are more likely than females to be colorblind.

A **sex-limited** gene *occurs equally in both sexes but exerts its effects mainly or entirely in one or the other.* For example, both men and women have the genes for facial hair, but men's hormones activate those genes. Similarly, both men and women have the genes for breast development, but women's hormones activate those genes.

 CONCEPT CHECK

2. Suppose a father has color vision deficiency and a mother has two genes for normal color vision. What sort of color vision will their children have? (Check your answer on page 162.)

Estimating Heritability in Humans

As discussed in the section on nature and nurture in chapter 1, all behavior depends on both heredity and environment, but variation in a given behavior might depend more on the variation in genes or variations in the environment. Suppose we want to estimate how much of the variation in some behavior depends on differences in genes. The answer is summarized by the term **heritability,** *an estimate of the variance within a population that is due to heredity.* Heritability ranges from 1, indicating that heredity controls all the variance, to 0, indicating that it controls none of it. For example, tongue curling has a heritability of almost 1. Note that the definition of heritability includes the phrase "within a population." For example, in a population with little genetic diversity, heritability is low, because whatever differences occur can't be due to differences in genes. In some other population with great genetic diversity, the genetic variations produce major differences among individuals, so heritability is likely to be higher. To estimate the heritability of a behavior, researchers rely on evidence from twins and adopted children.

However, estimates of heritability are sometimes misleading, because we cannot fully separate the effects of heredity and environment. For example, imagine you have a gene that makes you tall. If you live where people play basketball, probably you will spend more than the average amount of time playing basketball. As time goes on, because of your early success, you will be on basketball teams, you will receive coaching, and your skills will improve. Your success encourages more practice and therefore leads to more success and further encouragement. What started as a small genetic increase in height develops into a huge advantage in basketball skill, but that development reflects environmental influences as well as genetics. Researchers call this tendency a **multiplier effect:** *A small initial advantage in some behavior, possibly genetic in origin, alters the environment and magnifies that advantage* (Dickens & Flynn, 2001).

Genes ⟶ Initial tendencies ⟶ Learning and encouragement

Improvements in the behavior

 CONCEPT CHECK

3. If our society changed so that it provided an equally good environment for all children, would the heritability of behaviors increase or decrease? (Check your answer on page 162.)

Studies of Twins

One kind of evidence for heritability comes from studies of twins. **Monozygotic (mon-oh-zie-GOT-ik) twins** *develop from a single fertilized egg (zygote) and therefore have identical genes.* Most people call them "identical" twins, but that term is misleading. Sometimes, monozygotic twins are mirror images—one right-handed and the other left-handed and different in other regards also. It is also possible for a gene to be activated in one twin and suppressed in the other. You should therefore learn the somewhat awkward term *monozygotic.* **Dizygotic (DIE-zie-GOT-ik) twins** *develop from two eggs and share only half their genes, like brother and sister* (Figure 5.6). They are often called "fraternal" twins because they are only as closely related as brother and sister. If dizygotic twins resemble each other almost as much as monozygotic twins do in some trait, then we conclude that the heritability of that trait is low, because the amount of genetic similarity did not have much influence on the outcome. If monozygotic twins resemble each other much more strongly, then the heritability is high. This procedure is based on the assumption that both kinds of twins share their environment to the same extent. That assumption is approximately correct but not entirely, as other people tend to treat monozygotic twins more similarly than they do dizygotic twins.

Researchers also examine pairs of monozygotic twins who grew up in separate environments. In the United States and Europe today, adoption agencies place both twins in one family, but in previous times many twins were adopted separately. One pair of monozygotic twins were reunited in adulthood after being reared in different western Ohio cities (Figure 5.7). They quickly discovered that they had much in common: Both had been named Jim by their adoptive parents. Each liked carpentry and drafting, had built a bench around a tree in his yard, and worked as a deputy sheriff. Both chewed their fingernails, gained weight at the same age, smoked the same brand of cigarettes, drove Chevrolets, and took their vacations in western Florida. Each married a woman named Linda, divorced her, and married a woman named Betty. One

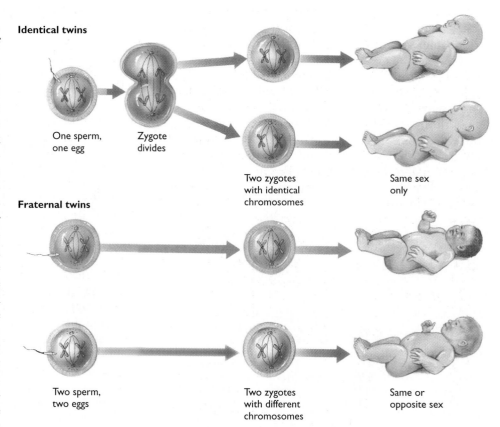

Identical twins

One sperm, one egg

Zygote divides

Two zygotes with identical chromosomes

Same sex only

Fraternal twins

Two sperm, two eggs

Two zygotes with different chromosomes

Same or opposite sex

FIGURE 5.6 Monozygotic twins develop from the same fertilized egg. Dizygotic twins grow from two eggs fertilized by different sperm.

FIGURE 5.7 Monozygotic twins Jim Lewis and Jim Springer were separated at birth, reared in separate cities of western Ohio, and reunited in adulthood.

had a son named James Alan and the other had a son named James Allen; both had a pet dog named Toy.

How many of these similarities are mere coincidences? Chevrolets are popular cars, for example, and many people from western Ohio vacation in western Florida. It's hard to believe these twins had genes causing them to marry a Linda and divorce her to marry a Betty. (If they had been adopted in Afghanistan, they would have had trouble finding either a Linda or a Betty.) And did these women have genes that attracted them to men named Jim?

All right, but consider other monozygotic twins separated at birth. One pair of women each wore rings on seven fingers. A pair of men discovered that they used the same brands of toothpaste, shaving lotion, hair tonic, and cigarettes. When they sent each other a birthday present, their presents crossed in the mail and each received the same present he had sent. Another pair reported that when they went to the beach, they waded into the water backward and only up to their knees (Lykken, McGue, Tellegen, & Bouchard, 1992).

Researchers examined about 100 pairs of twins, some monozygotic and others dizygotic, who were reared separately and reunited as adults. On the average the monozygotic twins resembled each other more strongly with regard to hobbies, vocational interests, answers on personality tests, political beliefs, job satisfaction, life satisfaction, probability of mental illness, consumption of coffee and fruit juices, and preference for awakening early in the morning or staying up late at night (Bouchard & McGue, 2003; DiLalla, Carey, Gottesman, & Bouchard, 1996; Hur, Bouchard, & Eckert, 1998; Hur, Bouchard, & Lykken, 1998; Lykken, Bouchard, McGue, & Tellegen, 1993; McCourt, Bouchard, Lykken, Tellegen, & Keyes, 1999). This pattern across a large number of individuals is more convincing than the anecdotes from any single pair. The implication is that genes influence a wide variety of behaviors.

Studies of Adopted Children

Another kind of evidence for heritability comes from studies of adopted children. Resemblance to their adopting parents implies an environmental influence. Resemblance to their biological parents implies a genetic influence.

However, the results are sometimes hard to interpret. For example, consider the evidence that many adopted children with an arrest record had biological mothers with a criminal history (Mason & Frick, 1994). The resemblance could indicate a genetic influence, but the mothers also provided the prenatal environment. Chances are many of the mothers with a criminal record smoked, drank alcohol, perhaps used other drugs, and in other ways endangered the fetus's brain development. Prenatal environment is sometimes an important influence on behavior that is

easily overlooked. For example, malnourished female rats give birth to babies that show learning impairments. In some cases even the grandchildren are impaired (Harper, 2005).

Another point to remember is that adoption agencies consistently place children in the best possible homes. That policy is certainly good for the children, but from a scientific standpoint, it means that we have little variance in the quality of adopting families. Does growing up with an alcoholic parent increase the probability of alcohol abuse? Probably, but we can't easily test this hypothesis with adopted children because few of their adopting parents are alcohol abusers (Stoolmiller, 1999).

 CONCEPT CHECK

4. Suppose someone studies a group of adopted children who developed severe depression and finds that many of their biological parents had depression, whereas few of their adopting parents did. One possible interpretation is that genetic factors influence depression more than family environment does. What is another interpretation? (Check your answer on page 162.)

How Genes Influence Behavior

Based on studies of twins and adopted children, researchers have found at least moderate heritability for almost every behavior they have examined, including loneliness (McGuire & Clifford, 2000), neuroticism (Lake, Eaves, Maes, Heath, & Martin, 2000), social attitudes (Posner, Baker, Heath, & Martin, 1996), time spent watching television (Plomin, Corley, DeFries, & Fulker, 1990), and religious devoutness (Waller, Kojetin, Bouchard, Lykken, & Tellegen, 1990). About the only behavior for which researchers have reported zero heritability is choice of religious denomination (Eaves, Martin, & Heath, 1990). That is, genes apparently influence how often you attend religious services but not which services you attend.

How could genes affect such complicated characteristics? Studies of twins and adopted children do not tell us about the mechanisms of genetic effects. Using modern technology researchers have identified genes that increase the risk of various diseases. You could have someone examine your chromosomes and tell you how likely you are to get various diseases and how soon (Gusella & MacDonald, 2000). The process would be more expensive than other kinds of fortune-tellers but vastly more accurate. The following Web site documents research on the identification of human genes: **www.ornl.gov/TechResources/Human_Genome/home.html.**

Researchers have also identified some of the genes that influence behavior. As we learn more about the various genes, we can understand their mechanisms better and perhaps modify the effects.

Direct and Indirect Influences

Genes control maturation of brain structures, production of neurotransmitters, and production of neurotransmitter receptors. For example, genes that control brain receptors for the hormone *vasopressin* determine whether male voles (similar to mice) desert their mates or stick around to help them rear babies (Hammock & Young, 2005). Genes control the types of color receptors in your eyes and the number of taste buds on your tongue. They also influence behavior by altering organs outside the nervous system. Consider dietary choices: Almost all infants can digest *lactose,* the sugar in milk. As they grow older, nearly all Asian children and many others lose the ability to digest it. (The loss depends on genes, not on how often the children drink milk.) They can still enjoy a little milk, and more readily enjoy cheese and yogurt, which are easier to digest, but they get gas and cramps from consuming too much milk or ice cream (Flatz, 1987; Rozin & Pelchat, 1988). Figure 5.8 shows how the ability to digest dairy products varies among ethnic groups. The point is that a gene can affect behavior—in this case consumption of dairy products—by altering chemical reactions outside the brain.

Genes also influence behaviors by altering body anatomy. Consider genes that make you unusually good-looking. Because many people smile at you, invite you to parties, and try to become your friend, you develop increased self-confidence and social skills. The genes changed your behavior by changing how other people treated you.

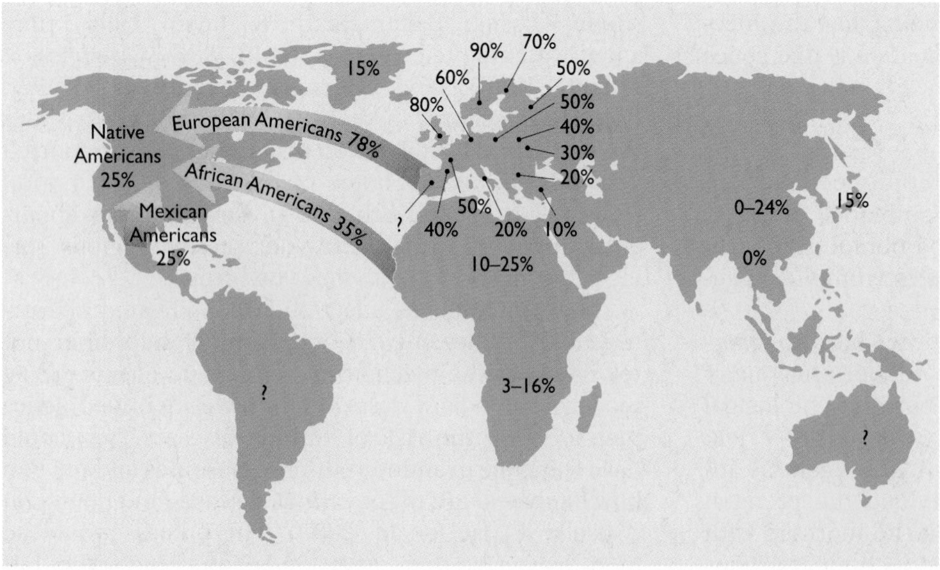

Interactions Between Heredity and Environment

A software program might run faster on one computer than another depending on their hardware. Similarly, the way you react to some experience can vary depending on your heredity. Statistically, this kind of effect is an **interaction**—*an instance in which the effect of one variable depends on some other variable.* For example, people with different genes react in different ways to marijuana and tobacco (Moffitt, Caspi, & Rutter, 2006).

One study found that the effect of social support on children's behavior depends on a gene that controls reuptake of the neurotransmitter serotonin. Recall from chapter 3 that a neurotransmitter, after its release from an axon, is taken back into that axon for reuse. A gene that controls this process comes in two forms, *long* and *short.* In children with the short form, social support decreases shyness. In children with the long form, social support *increases* shyness (Fox et al., 2005). We shall need more research to understand why this interaction occurs, but for present purposes the point is that sometimes neither heredity nor environment by itself has a predictable effect; the outcome depends on the combination.

Shyness is related to **temperament**—the *tendency to be active or inactive, outgoing or reserved, and to respond vigorously or quietly to new stimuli.* Temperament depends partly on genetics. Monozygotic twins resemble each other in temperament more than dizygotic twins do (Matheny, 1989). Monozygotic twins reared in separate environments generally develop similar temperaments (Bouchard, Lykken, McGue, Segal, & Tellegen, 1990). However, a genetically based temperament influences one's choice of environment. For example, someone who is inclined to be active and vigorous tends to choose outgoing friends and stimulating social situations. Someone with a more

FIGURE 5.8 Adult humans vary in their ability to digest lactose, the main sugar in milk. The numbers refer to the percentage of each population's adults that can easily digest lactose. *(Based on Flatz, 1987; Rozin & Pelchat, 1988)*

reserved temperament gravitates toward quiet activities and smaller social groups. Those choices of activities magnify or strengthen someone's original temperament.

As a result temperament is usually consistent over age. For example, infants who frequently kick and cry—termed "difficult" or "inhibited" (Thomas & Chess, 1980; Thomas, Chess, & Birch, 1968)—tend to be frightened by unfamiliar events at ages 9 and 14 months (Kagan & Snidman, 1991), and tend to be shy and nervous in a playground at age 7½ years (Kagan, Reznick, & Snidman, 1988). As adults, when confronted with photographs of unfamiliar people, they show enhanced responses in the amygdala, a brain area that processes anxiety-related information (Schwartz, Wright, Shin, Kagan, & Rauch, 2003) (see Figure 5.9). For another example, children who are rated "impulsive" at 30 months are likely to have more teenage sex partners than average (Zimmer-Bembeck, Siebenbruner, & Collins, 2004).

Here is another example: **Phenylketonuria (PKU)** is *an inherited condition that, if untreated, leads to mental retardation.* About 2% of people with European or Asian ancestry, and almost no Africans, have the recessive gene that leads to PKU, but because the gene is recessive, one copy produces no apparent harm. People with copies on both chromosomes (one from each parent) cannot metabolize *phenylalanine,* a common constituent of proteins. On an ordinary diet, an affected child accumulates phenylalanine in the brain and becomes mentally retarded. However, a diet low in phenylalanine protects the brain. Thus, a special diet prevents a disorder that would otherwise show high heritability.

 CONCEPT CHECK

5. Some people assume that if something is under genetic control, we can't do anything about it. Cite an example that contradicts this idea. (Check your answer on page 162.)

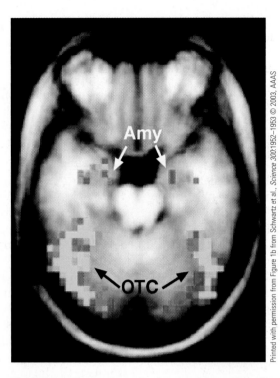

Printed with permission from Figure 1b from Schwartz et al., *Science 300:1952–1953* © 2003, AAAS

FIGURE 5.9 This horizontal section shows the result of functional magnetic resonance imaging (fMRI). Two brain areas were more active than average in adults with an inhibited temperament. Areas marked in red showed a large difference, and those in yellow showed an even larger difference. "Amy" indicates the area of the amygdala (on each side of the brain). OTC indicates the occipital and temporal areas of the cortex.

Evolution and Behavior

Why do you have the genes that you do? Simply, your parents had those genes and survived long enough to reproduce. So did your parents' parents and so on. Ancient people whose genes did not enable them to survive and reproduce failed to become your ancestors.

Let's say it in a different way: At any time individuals within any population of any species vary with regard to their genes. Gene mutations supply the population with new variations. Certain genes increase the probability of surviving and reproducing. Individuals who have those genes reproduce more than those with other genes, and the successful genes become more prevalent in the next generation. The consequence is *a gradual change in the frequency of various genes from one generation to the next,* otherwise known as **evolution.**

In a small population, a gene might spread accidentally, even if it is neutral or harmful. For example, imagine a population of insects on a small island. Some will reproduce more than others just because they happened to settle in a place with better food or one that their predators did not find. The ones that reproduced most successfully may or may not have had the best genes. You can see this in an Online Try It Yourself activity. Go to **www.thomsonedu.com/psychology/ kalat.** Navigate to the student website, then to the Online Try It Yourself section, and click Genetic Generations.

Online Try It Yourself

Still, a gene that has become common in a large population almost certainly had benefits in the past, though not necessarily today. Evolutionary psychologists try to infer the benefits that favored certain genes. For example, many people have genes that cause them to overeat and become obese, a clear disadvantage. Such genes might have been advantageous in previous times when food shortages were common. If food is often scarce, you should eat all you can when you can. We shall encounter other speculations like this later in the text. However, we need to be cautious, as some of the speculations are uncertain and difficult to test (de Waal, 2002). A widespread behavior might not depend on specific genes; it might be learned. Furthermore, most genes have multiple effects. One gene causes many older men to lose hair. Is baldness beneficial, or has it ever been? Not necessarily. Perhaps the gene produces baldness only as an accidental by-product of some other more important effect.

Nevertheless, evolutionary thinking helps us understand certain aspects of development that might not make sense otherwise (Bjorklund & Pellegrini, 2000). For example, consider a human infant's grasp reflex: An infant grasps tightly onto anything placed into the palm of the hand. As the infant grows older, that reflex becomes suppressed. It is certainly not a preparation for anything later in life; the reflex evolved to help the infant during infancy. For humans today, the function is far from obvious, but for our ancient ancestors, the grasp reflex helped the infant hold onto the mother as she traveled (Figure 5.10).

CONCEPT CHECK

6. Suppose we find that some gene that is widespread in the population appears to be disadvantageous. How can we explain the spread of a harmful gene? (Check your answer on page 162.)

The Fetus and the Newborn

Genes control development of the body, which in turn provides for behavior. Let's focus briefly on very early development, including the role of the prenatal environment.

During prenatal development everyone starts as a *fertilized egg cell,* or zygote, which develops through its first few stages until the stage of fetus *about 8 weeks after conception.* Even as soon as 6 weeks after conception, the brain is mature enough to produce the first few movements. By the 36th week, the brain can turn the head and eyes in response to sounds and alternates between waking and sleeping (Joseph, 2000). None of this behavior requires the cerebral cortex, which matures more slowly than the rest of the brain.

The growing body receives nutrition from the mother. If she takes drugs, the baby gets them too. If she is exposed to harmful chemicals, some of those chemicals reach the fetus's brain while it is developing and highly vulnerable (Hubbs-Tait, Nation, Krebs, & Bellinger, 2005). Undernourished mothers generally give birth to small babies (Figure 5.11). The lower the birthweight, the greater the risk of impaired cognitive ability later in life (Shenkin, Starr, & Deary, 2004). These facts are clear, but their meaning is not.

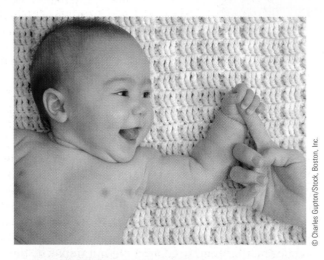

FIGURE 5.10 Human infants tightly grasp anything in the palm of their hands (top). Today, this reflex has no obvious value, but in our remote ancestors, it helped infants hold onto their mothers (bottom).

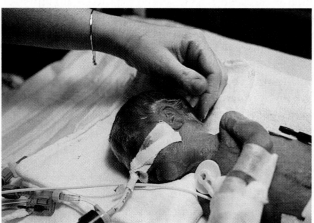

FIGURE 5.11 Babies with low birthweight are susceptible to physical and behavioral difficulties, but we cannot be sure that low birthweight causes the problems.

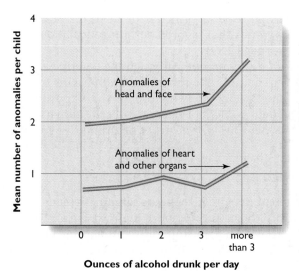

© George Steinmetz

FIGURE 5.12 (a) The more alcohol a woman drinks during pregnancy, the more likely her baby is to have anomalies of the head, face, and organs. *(Based on data of Ernhart et al., 1987)* (b) A child with fetal alcohol syndrome: Note the wide separation between the eyes, a common feature of this syndrome.

The apparently obvious interpretation is that low birthweight impairs brain development. However, in some cases the birthweight was low because the mothers were poorly nourished, unhealthy, victims of family violence, possibly smoking or drinking during pregnancy, and not receiving medical care (Garcia Coll, 1990; McCormick, 1985). In short, birthweight could correlate with brain development for several reasons.

One way to study the effect of birthweight separately from other influences is to examine pairs of twins where one twin was born heavier than the other. In most cases the one with lower birthweight develops about as well as the heavier one (R. S. Wilson, 1987). In short, low birthweight by itself may not be the problem.

A more severe risk arises if the fetus is exposed to alcohol or other substances. *If the mother drinks alcohol during pregnancy,* the infant may develop fetal alcohol syndrome, *a condition marked by stunted growth of the head and body; malformations of the face, heart, and ears; and nervous system damage, including seizures, hyperactivity, learning disabilities, and mental retardation* (Streissguth, Sampson, & Barr, 1989). In milder cases children appear normal but have moderate deficits in language, memory, and coordination (Mattson, Riley, Grambling, Delis, & Jones, 1998). The more alcohol the mother drinks during pregnancy, the greater the risk to the fetus (Figure 5.12).

The reason for the nervous system damage is now understood: Developing neurons require persistent excitation to survive. Without it they activate a self-destruct program. Alcohol interferes with the brain's main excitatory neurotransmitter (glutamate) and facilitates the main inhibitory neurotransmitter (GABA). It therefore decreases neurons' arousal and leads them to self-destruct (Ikonomidou et al., 2000).

Women who smoke during pregnancy have an increased probability that their babies will have health problems early in life. They also run an increased risk that their children, especially sons, eventually will develop *conduct disorder,* a condition marked by discipline problems both at school and at home and potentially criminal behavior in adulthood (Wakschlag, Pickett, Kasza, & Loeber, 2006). We cannot conclude that smoking caused these problems; perhaps the kind of women who smoke provide an environment in some other way that leads to antisocial behavior by their sons. Nevertheless, to be safe, pregnant women should avoid tobacco as well as other substances.

Still, it is remarkable that an occasional "high-risk" child—small at birth, exposed to alcohol or other drugs before birth, and from an impoverished or turbulent family—overcomes all odds and becomes a healthy, successful person. Resilience (the ability to overcome obstacles) is poorly understood and difficult to study (Luthar, Cicchetti, & Becker, 2000). Most people who overcome disadvantages have some special source of strength such as a close relationship with one or more supporting people, an effective school, a strong faith, some special skill, or just a naturally easygoing disposition (Masten & Coatsworth, 1998).

 CONCEPT CHECK

7. Tranquilizers and anti-anxiety drugs increase activity at GABA synapses. Why should a pregnant woman avoid taking them? (Check your answer on page 162.)

IN CLOSING

Getting Started in Life

Physicists say that the way the universe developed depended on its "initial conditions"—the array of matter and energy a fraction of a second after the start of the "big bang." The outcome of any experiment in physics or chemistry depends on the initial conditions—the type of matter, its temperature and pressure, and so forth. You had initial conditions too—your genetics and prenatal environment. Understanding those initial conditions is critical to understanding your special characteristics. However, even a thorough study of your initial conditions would not tell us much about your later development. At any point in your life, your behavior depends on a complex combination of your predispositions, the effects of past experiences, and all aspects of the current environment. ∎

Summary

- *Genes.* Genes, which are segments of chromosomes, control heredity. (page 153)
- *Sex-linked and sex-limited genes.* Genes on the X or Y chromosome are sex linked. An X-linked recessive gene will show its effects more frequently in males than in females. A sex-limited gene is present in both sexes, but it affects one more than the other. (page 154)
- *Heritability.* Researchers study twins and adopted children to estimate the heritability of various traits. However, the result of a gene can influence the environment in ways that magnify the effects of the gene; therefore, heritability estimates are sometimes misleading. (page 155)
- *Evidence for genetic influences.* Researchers estimate genetic contributions to behavior by comparing monozygotic and dizygotic twins, by comparing twins reared in separate environments, and by examining how adopted children resemble their biological and adoptive parents. (page 156)
- *How genes affect behavior.* Genes can affect behaviors by altering the chemistry of the brain. They also exert indirect effects by influencing some aspect of the body that in turn influences behavior. (page 157)
- *Interactions between heredity and environment.* In many cases the effect of a gene depends on some aspect of the environment. For example, social support increases shyness in people with one form of a particular gene and decreases shyness in people with a different form of the gene. The phenylketonuria gene would lead to mental retardation, but a special diet minimizes its effects. (page 158)
- *Evolution.* Genes that increase the probability of survival and reproduction become more common in the next generation. Psychologists try to under-

stand some aspects of behavior in terms of evolutionary trends that favored certain genes in our ancestors. (page 159)
- *Prenatal development.* Although the cerebral cortex is slow to mature, the rest of the brain begins to produce movements long before birth. Exposure to drugs such as alcohol decreases brain activity and releases neurons' self-destruct programs. (page 160)

Answers to Concept Checks

1. Both parents must lack the dominant gene that controls the ability to curl their tongues. Therefore, they can transmit only "noncurler" genes, and their children will be noncurlers also. (page 153)
2. The woman will pass a gene for normal color vision to all her children, so they will all have normal color vision. The man will pass a gene for deficient color vision on his X chromosome, so his daughters will be carriers for color vision deficiency. (page 155)
3. If all children had equally supportive environments, the heritability of behaviors would *increase.* Remember, heritability refers to how much of the difference among people is due to hereditary variation. If the environment is practically the same for all, then environmental variation cannot account for much of the variation in behavior. Whatever behavioral variation still occurs would be due mostly to hereditary variation. (Note one implication: Any estimate of heritability applies only to a given population.) (page 155)
4. Perhaps biological mothers who are becoming depressed eat less healthy foods, drink more alcohol, or in some other way impair the prenatal environment of their babies. (page 157)
5. Phenylketonuria is a genetic condition that would cause mental retardation, but a special diet minimizes the problem. (page 159)
6. Three possibilities: The disadvantageous gene could have spread randomly within a small population, perhaps because individuals with this gene happened to be in a good location. The gene could produce a mild disadvantage but spread because it also produces other, advantageous effects. Also, a gene that is disadvantageous now might have been beneficial at a previous time. (page 159)
7. These drugs decrease brain stimulation, and neurons that fail to receive enough stimulation self-destruct. (page 161)

Cognitive Development

* *How can we know about the sensations, memory, and other capacities of an infant?*
* *How do children's thought processes differ from adults'?*

The artwork of young children is amazingly inventive and revealing. One toddler, 1½ years old, showed off a drawing that consisted only of dots on a sheet of paper. Puzzled adults did not understand. It is a rabbit, the child explained, while making more dots: "Look: hop, hop, hop . . . ." (Winner, 1986). When my daughter, Robin, was 6 years old, she drew a picture of a boy and a girl drawing pictures (Figure 5.13). The overall drawing has features that may not be clear; for example, both children are wearing Halloween costumes. For the little girl's drawing, Robin pasted on some wildlife photos. This array, she maintained, was what the little girl had drawn. Now look at the little boy's drawing, which is just a scribble. When I asked why the little girl's drawing was so much better than the little boy's, Robin replied, "Don't make fun of him, Daddy. He's doing the best he can."

Sometimes, as in this case, a child's drawing expresses the child's worldview. As children grow older, their art changes. Certainly, it becomes more skillful, but it often becomes less expressive. The

As we grow older, we mature in our social and emotional behaviors. However, many revert quickly to childlike behaviors in situations where such behavior is acceptable.

point is this: As we grow older, we gain many new abilities and skills, but we lose something too.

Studying the abilities of young children is challenging. Often, they misunderstand our questions or we misunderstand their answers. Developmental psychologists have made progress by devising increasingly careful methods of measurement.

Infancy

Studying the infant's early attempts to understand the world is both fascinating and frustrating. A newborn is like a computer that is not attached to a monitor or printer: No matter how much information it processes, it cannot tell us about it. The

FIGURE 5.13 A drawing of two children drawing pictures, courtesy of 6-year-old Robin Kalat.

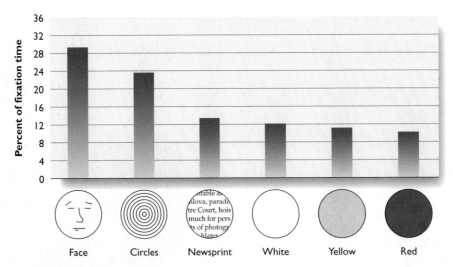

FIGURE 5.14 Infants pay more attention to faces than to other patterns. These results suggest that infants are born with certain visual preferences. *(Based on Fantz, 1963)*

challenge of studying the newborn is to figure out how to attach some sort of monitor to find out what is happening inside. To test infants' sensory and learning abilities, we must measure responses that they can control. About their only useful responses are eye and mouth movements, especially sucking.

Infants' Vision

William James, the founder of American psychology, said that as far as an infant can tell, the world is a "buzzing confusion," full of meaningless sights and sounds. Since James's time, psychologists have substantially increased their estimates of infants' vision.

One research method is to record the infant's eye movements. Even 2-day-old infants spend more time looking at drawings of human faces than at other patterns with similar areas of light and dark (Fantz, 1963) (see Figure 5.14). However, infants do not have the same concept of "face" that adults do. Figure 5.15 shows the results of distorting a face in various ways. Newborns gazed as long at a distorted face as at a normal face. However, they gazed longer at

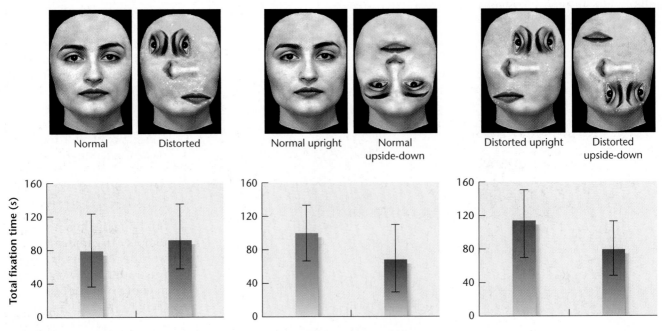

FIGURE 5.15 Infants gaze about equally long at normal and distorted faces. However, they stare longer at upright faces than those that are upside-down. *(Source: Cassia, Turati, & Simion, 2004)*

right-side-up faces than at upside-down faces, regardless of distortions. Evidently, the newborn's concept of face is simply an oval with most of its content toward the top (Cassia, Turati, & Simion, 2004). Even at age 3 to 4 months old, an infant's concept of face differs from an adult's: Infants at that age look longer at female than male faces and recognize female faces more easily than male faces (Ramsey-Rennels & Langlois, 2006). Presumably, the explanation is that most infants have more experience with seeing female than male faces.

Well beyond infancy, young children still do not see faces the same way adults do. In one study parents repeatedly read a storybook about "Johnny" and "Suzy," including photographs of the two children's faces from many angles, showing many expressions. After 2 weeks of becoming familiar with these photographs, 4-year-old children could easily recognize pictures of Johnny and Suzy in comparison to photos of different children. However, when they had to choose between a normal picture of Johnny or Suzy and one with altered spacing among the features, they guessed randomly (Mondloch, Leis, & Maurer, 2006). Most people 6 years old or older easily see the difference between the photos in Figure 5.16. Evidently, 4-year-olds do not.

FIGURE 5.16 These faces are the same except for the positions of the eyes, nose, and mouth. Four-year-olds do not recognize which of these faces is familiar. *("Recognizing the face of Johnny, Suzy, and me: Insensitivity to the spacing among features at 4 years of age." by C.J. Mondloch, A. Leis, A & D Maurer. (2006).* Child Development, *77, 234–243.)*

By the age of 5 months, infants have had extensive visual experience but almost no experience at crawling or reaching for objects. Over the next several months, they increase their control of arm and leg movements. They learn to pick up toys, crawl around objects, avoid crawling off ledges, and in other ways coordinate what they see with what they do. Apparently, they need experience of controlling their own movements before they show a fear of heights. Infants usually take a tumble or two before they develop a fear of heights (Adolph, 2000). Those who crawl early develop a fear of heights early; those who are late to crawl are also late to develop a fear of heights (Campos, Bertenthal, & Kermoian, 1992).

Infants' Hearing

It might seem difficult to measure newborns' responses to sounds because we cannot observe anything like eye movements. However, infants suck more vigorously when they are aroused, and certain sounds arouse them more than others do.

In one study the experimenters played a brief sound and noted how it affected infants' sucking rate (Figure 5.17). On the first few occasions, the sound increased the sucking rate. A repeated sound produced less and less effect. We say that the infant became *habituated* to the sound. **Habituation** is *decreased response to a repeated stimulus.* When the experimenters substituted a new sound, the sucking rate increased. Evidently, the infant was aroused by the unfamiliar sound. *When a change in a stimulus increases a previously habituated response,* we say that the stimulus produced **dishabituation.**

Psychologists monitor habituation and dishabituation to determine whether infants hear a difference between two sounds. For example, infants who have become habituated to the sound *ba* will increase their sucking rate when they hear the sound *pa* (Eimas, Siqueland, Jusczyk, & Vigorito, 1971). Apparently, even month-old infants notice the difference between *ba* and *pa,* an important distinction for later language comprehension.

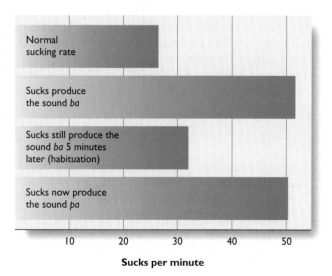

FIGURE 5.17 After repeatedly hearing a *ba* sound, the infant's sucking habituates. When a new sound, *pa,* follows, the sucking rate increases. *(Based on results of Eimas, Siqueland, Jusczyk, & Vigorito, 1971)*

Similar studies have shown that infants who have habituated to hearing one language, such as Dutch, dishabituate when they hear a different language, such as Japanese. At first they show no response to a shift between Dutch and English, presumably because the sounds and rhythms are similar. By age 5 months, however, they dishabituate when they hear a change from a British accent to an American accent (Jusczyk, 2002). Studies of this sort show that children discriminate relevant language sounds long before they know what the words mean.

 CONCEPT CHECK

8. Suppose an infant habituates to the sound *ba*, but when we substitute the sound *bla*, the infant fails to increase its sucking rate. What interpretation would be likely? (Check your answer on page 181.)

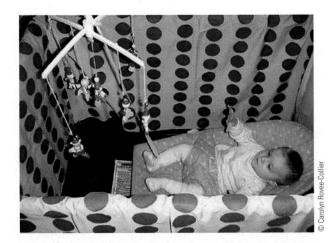

FIGURE 5.18 Two-month-old infants rapidly learn to kick to activate a mobile attached to their ankles with a ribbon. They remember how to activate the mobile when tested days later. *(From Hildreth, Sweeney, & Rovee-Collier, 2003)*

Infants' Learning and Memory

Although infants cannot describe their memories, they can change their responses based on previous experience, thereby displaying a memory. Several studies have begun with the observation that infants learn to suck harder on a nipple if their sucking turns on a sound. Investigators then tried to determine whether infants work harder for some sounds than others. In one study babies younger than 3 days old could turn on a tape recording of their mother's voice by sucking on a nipple at certain times or rates. By sucking at other times or at different rates, they could turn on a tape recording of another woman's voice. The results: They sucked more frequently to turn on recordings of their own mother's voice (DeCasper & Fifer, 1980). Apparently, even very young infants preferred their own mother's voice. Because they showed this preference so early—in some cases on the day of birth—psychologists believe that the infants display a memory of what they heard before birth.

 CONCEPT CHECK

9. Suppose a newborn sucks to turn on a tape recording of its father's voice. Eventually, the baby habituates and the sucking frequency decreases. Now the experimenters substitute the recording of a different man's voice. What would you conclude if the sucking frequency increased? What if it remained the same? What if it decreased? (Check your answers on page 181.)

Using somewhat older infants, Carolyn Rovee-Collier (1997, 1999) demonstrated an ability to re-

member a new response for days. She attached a ribbon to an ankle so that an infant could activate a mobile by kicking with one leg (Figure 5.18). Two-month-old infants quickly learned this response and generally kept the mobile going nonstop for a full 45-minute session. (Infants have little control over their leg muscles, but they don't need much control to keep the mobile going.) Once they have learned, they quickly remember what to do when the ribbon is reattached several days later—to the infants' evident delight. Six-month-old infants remembered the response for 2 weeks. Even after forgetting it, they could relearn it in 2 minutes and then retain it for an additional month or more (Hildreth, Sweeney, & Rovee-Collier, 2003).

Research Designs for Studying Development

As we move beyond the study of infancy, we begin to compare one age with another, and we encounter some special research problems that go beyond the general research issues raised in chapter 2. Do we study older and younger people at the same time (a cross-sectional design)? Or do we study one group of people when they are younger and then the same group again after they have grown older (a longitudinal design)? Each method has its strengths and limitations.

Cross-Sectional and Longitudinal Designs

A cross-sectional study *compares groups of individuals of different ages at the same time*. For example, we could compare the drawing abilities of 6-year-olds, 8-year-olds, and 10-year-olds. A weakness of cross-sectional studies is the difficulty of obtaining equivalent samples at different ages. For example, suppose you want to compare 20-year-olds and 60-year-olds. If you study 20-year-olds from the local college, where will you find a comparable group of 60-year-olds?

A **longitudinal study** *follows a single group of individuals as they develop.* For example, we could study one group of children as they age from, say, 6 to 12. Table 5.1 contrasts the two kinds of studies. Longitudinal studies face practical difficulties. A longitudinal study necessarily takes years, and not everyone who participates the first time is willing and available later.

Furthermore, those who remain in a study may differ in important ways from those who leave. Suppose a visitor from outer space observes that about 50% of young adult humans are males but that only 10 to 20% of 90-year-olds are males. The visitor concludes that, as humans grow older, most males transform into females. You know why that conclusion is wrong. Males—with a few exceptions—do not change into females, but on the average they die earlier, leaving a greater percentage of older females. **Selective attrition** is *the tendency for some kinds of people to be more likely than others to drop out of a study.* Psychologists can compensate by reporting the data for only the people who stayed to the end of the study.

A longitudinal study also faces the difficulty of separating the effects of age from the effects of changes in society. For example, suppose we found that most 20-year-olds in the United States in 1970 were politically liberal, but over the succeeding decades, most of them had become more conservative. We would not know whether they became more conservative because of age or because the country as a whole had become more conservative.

Nevertheless, certain questions logically require a longitudinal study. For example, to study the effects of divorce on children, researchers compare how each child reacts at first with how that same child reacts later. To study whether happy children are likely to become happy adults, we would follow a single group of people over time.

Sequential Designs

A sequential (or "cross-sequential") design combines the advantages of both cross-sectional and longitudinal designs. In a **sequential design,** *researchers start with groups of people of different ages, studied at the same time, and then study them again at one or more later times.* For example, imagine we study the drawings of 6-year-olds and 8-year-olds and then examine the drawings by those same children 2 years later:

First study	2 years later
Group A, age 6 years	Group A, now 8 years old
Group B, age 8 years	Group B, now 10 years old

TABLE 5.1 Cross-Sectional and Longitudinal Studies

	Description	Advantages	Disadvantages	Example
Cross-sectional	Several groups of subjects of various ages studied at one time	1. Quick 2. No risk of confusing age effects with effects of changes in society	1. Risk of sampling error by getting different kinds of people at different ages 2. Risk of cohort effects	Compare memory abilities of 3-, 5-, and 7-year-olds
Longitudinal	One group of subjects studied repeatedly as the members grow older	1. No risk of sampling differences 2. Can study effects of one experience on later development 3. Can study consistency within individuals over time	1. Takes a long time 2. Some participants quit 3. Sometimes hard to separate effects of age from changes in society	Study memory abilities of 3-year-olds, and of the same children again 2 and 4 years later

If Group A at age 8 resembles Group B at age 8, we can feel confident that the groups are comparable. We can then compare Group A at 6, both groups at 8, and Group B at 10.

Cohort Effects

If you had been a German during the Nazi era, how would you have acted? What if you had been a White person in the southern United States during the time of slavery? It is easy to say how you hope you would have acted, but you really don't know. If you had lived then, you would have developed differently. Your beliefs, attitudes, and even personality would have been different.

Consider something less drastic. Suppose you lived in the same place you now live, but 50 years earlier. You would have spent your childhood and adolescence with far less technology than you now take for granted: no Internet, computers, iPods, cell phones, televisions, air conditioners, automatic dishwashers, or appliances for washing and drying clothes. Long-distance telephone calls were a luxury. Women and minorities usually didn't go to college, and even if they did, their job opportunities were limited afterward. If you had lived then, how would you have been different?

People born in a given era differ from those of other eras in many ways, which psychologists call *cohort effects* (Figure 5.19). A **cohort** is *a group of people born at a particular time or a group of people who entered an organization at a particular time.*

Indeed, the era in which you grew up is one of the most important influences on your behavior, altering your personality, social behavior, and attitudes (Twenge, 2006). For example, people whose youth spanned the Great Depression and World War II learned to save money and to sacrifice their own pleasures for the needs of society as a whole. Even after the war was over and prosperity reigned, most remained thrifty and cautious (Rogler, 2002). In contrast the generation that has grown up since the early 1990s has had much more leisure time (Larson, 2001). Many aspects of intellect and personality differ between generations, as we shall examine in later chapters.

 CONCEPT CHECKS

10. Suppose you study the effect of age on artistic abilities, and you want to be sure that any apparent differences depend on age and not cohort effects. Should you use a longitudinal study or a cross-sectional study?

11. Suppose you want to study the effect of age on choice of clothing. What problems would arise with either a longitudinal study or a cross-sectional study?

12. At Santa Enigma College, the average first-year student has a C-minus average, and the average senior has a B-plus average. An observer concludes that, as students progress through college, they improve their study habits. Based on the idea of selective attrition, propose another possible explanation. (Check your answers on page 181.)

Jean Piaget's View of Cognitive Development

Now armed with an understanding of research methods for studying development, let's proceed with cognitive development. Attending a political rally can have a profound effect on a young adult, less effect on a preteen, and no effect on an infant. However, playing with a pile of blocks will be a more stimulating experience for a young child than for anyone older. The effect of any experience depends on someone's maturity and previous experiences. The theorist who made this point most influentially was Jean Piaget (pee-ah-ZHAY) (1896–1980).

FIGURE 5.19 Children of the 1920s, 1960s, and 1990s differed in their behavior because they grew up in different historical eras, with different education, nutrition, and health care. Differences based on such influences are called *cohort effects.*

 Jean Piaget (on the left) demonstrated that children with different levels of maturity react differently to the same experience.

Early in his career, while administering IQ tests to French-speaking children in Switzerland, Piaget was fascinated by their incorrect answers. He concluded that children and adults use qualitatively different thought processes. Piaget supported his conclusion with extensive longitudinal studies of children, especially his own.

CRITICAL THINKING
A STEP FURTHER

Children's Thinking

How could we know whether the difference in adult and child thought processes is qualitative or quantitative? Consider: A modern computer differs from an old one in purely quantitative ways—speed of processing and amount of memory. The basic principles of computing are the same. Yet the new computer runs programs that the old one cannot—a qualitative difference in results. Could the differences between child and adult thinking reflect speed of processing and amount of memory?

According to Piaget a child's intellectual development is not merely an accumulation of experience or a maturational unfolding. Rather, the child constructs new mental processes as he or she interacts with the environment.

In Piaget's terminology behavior is based on schemata (the plural of *schema*). A **schema** is *an organized way of interacting with objects in the world.* For instance, infants have a grasping schema and a sucking schema. Older infants gradually add new schemata to their repertoire and adapt their old ones. The adaptation takes place through the processes of assimilation and accommodation.

Assimilation means *applying an old schema to new objects or problems.* For example, a child who observes that animals move on their own may believe that the sun and moon are alive because they seem to move on their own. (Many ancient adult humans believed the same thing.) **Accommodation** means *modifying an old schema to fit a new object or problem.* For example, a child may learn that "only living things move on their own" is a rule with exceptions and that the sun and moon are not alive.

Infants shift back and forth between assimilation and accommodation. **Equilibration** is *the establishment of harmony or balance between the two,* and according to Piaget equilibration is the key to intellectual growth. A discrepancy occurs between the child's current understanding and some evidence to the contrary. The child accommodates to that discrepancy and achieves an equilibration at a higher level.

The same processes occur in adults. When you see a new mathematical problem, you try several methods until you hit upon one that works. In other words you assimilate the new problem to your old schema. However, if the new problem is different from any previous problem, you modify (accommodate) your schema until you find a solution. Through processes like these, said Piaget, intellectual growth occurs.

Piaget contended that children progress through four major stages of intellectual development:

1. *The sensorimotor stage* (from birth to almost 2 years)
2. *The preoperational stage* (from just before 2 to 7 years)
3. *The concrete operations stage* (from about 7 to 11 years)
4. *The formal operations stage* (from about 11 years onward)

The ages are variable, and not everyone reaches the formal operations stage. However, apparently everyone progresses through the stages in the same order. Let us consider children's capacities at each of Piaget's stages.

Infancy: Piaget's Sensorimotor Stage

Piaget called the first stage of intellectual development the **sensorimotor stage** because *at this early age (the first 1½ to 2 years) behavior is mostly simple motor responses to sensory stimuli—* for example, the grasp reflex and the sucking reflex. According to Piaget infants respond only to what they see and hear at the moment. In particular, he believed that children during this period fail to respond to objects they remember seeing even a few seconds ago. What evidence could he have for this view?

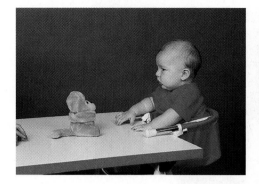

a   b

FIGURE 5.20 **(a)** A 6- to 9-month-old child reaches for a visible toy, but not one that is hidden behind a barrier **(b)** even if the child sees someone hide the toy. According to Piaget this observation indicates that the child hasn't yet grasped the concept of object permanence.

© Doug Goodman/Photo Researchers

CRITICAL THINKING
WHAT'S THE EVIDENCE?

The Infant's Thought Processes About Object Permanence

Piaget argued that infants in the first few months of life lack the concept of **object permanence**, *the idea that objects continue to exist even when we do not see or hear them.* That is, infants not only ignore what they don't see; they don't even know the objects still exist.

Piaget drew his inferences from observations of this type: Place a toy in front of a 6-month-old infant, who reaches out and grabs it. Later, place a toy in the same place, but before the infant has a chance to grab it, cover it with a clear glass. No problem; the infant removes the glass and takes the toy. Now repeat that procedure but use an opaque (nonclear) glass. The infant, who watched you place the glass over the toy, makes no effort to remove the glass and obtain the toy. Next, place a thin barrier between the infant and the toy. An infant who cannot see any part of the toy does not reach for it (Piaget, 1937/1954) (see Figure 5.20). Even at 9 months, a child who has repeatedly found a toy in one location will reach there again after watching you hide it in a neighboring location.

According to Piaget the infant *does not know* that the hidden toy continues to exist. However, the results vary depending on circumstances. For example, if you show a toy and then turn out the lights, a 7-month-old infant reaches out toward the unseen toy if it was a familiar toy but not if it was unfamiliar (Shinskey & Munakata, 2005). A study by Renee Baillargeon (1986) also suggests that infants show signs of understanding object permanence when they are tested differently.

Hypothesis. An infant who sees an event that would be impossible (if objects are permanent) will be surprised and therefore will stare longer than will an infant who sees a similar but possible event.

Method. Infants aged 6 or 8 months watched a series of events staged by the researcher. First, the child watched the experimenter raise a screen to show nothing blocking the track and then watched a toy car go down a slope and emerge on the other side, as shown below. This was called a "possible" event.

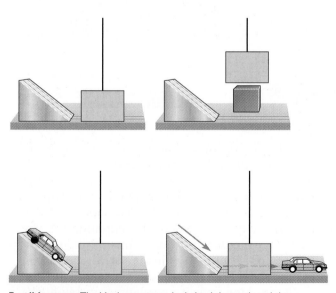

Possible event. The block appears to be behind the track, and the car passes by the block.

The researchers measured how long the child stared after the car went down the slope. They repeated the procedure until the child decreased his or her staring time for three trials in a row (showing habituation). Then the experimenters presented two kinds of events. One kind was the possible event as just described; the other was an impossible event like this:

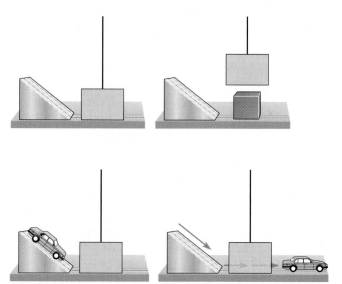

Impossible event. The raised screen shows a box on the track right where the car would pass. After the screen lowers, the car goes down the slope and emerges on the other side.

In an impossible event, the raised screen showed a box that was on the track where the car would pass. After the screen lowered, the car went down the slope and emerged on the other side. (The experimenters had pulled the box off the track after lowering the screen.) The experimenters measured each child's staring times after both kinds of events. They repeated both events two more times, randomizing the order of events.

Results. Figure 5.21 shows the mean looking times. Infants stared longer after seeing an impossible event than after seeing a possible event. They also stared longer after the first pair of events than after the second and third pairs (Baillargeon, 1986).

Interpretation. Why did the infants stare longer at the impossible event? The inference—and admittedly only an inference—is that the infants found the impossible event surprising. To be surprised the infants had to expect that the box would continue to exist where it was hidden and that a car could not go through it. If this inference is correct, even 6-month-old infants have

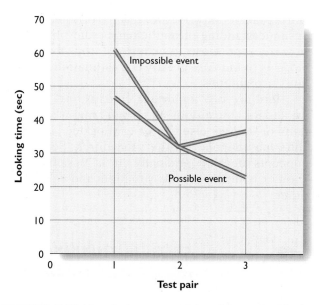

FIGURE 5.21 Mean looking times of 6- and 8-month-old infants after they had watched either possible or impossible events. *(From Baillargeon, 1986)*

some understanding of the permanence of objects, as well as elementary physics. A later study with a slightly different method again measured how long infants stared at possible and impossible events and demonstrated object permanence in infants as young as 3½ months (Baillargeon, 1987).

Still, remember that 9-month-olds failed Piaget's object permanence task of reaching out to pick up a hidden object. Do infants have the concept of object permanence or not? Evidently, the question is not well phrased. Infants use a concept in some situations and not others (Munakata, McClelland, Johnson, & Siegler, 1997). Even college students can pass a physics test and then fail to apply the laws of motion in a new situation or state a rule of grammar and yet make grammatical errors.

Many other psychologists have modified Baillargeon's procedure to test other aspects of infants' cognition. For example, researchers put five objects behind a screen, then added five more, and removed the screen. Nine-month-olds stared longer when they saw just five objects than when they saw ten, suggesting some understanding of addition (McCrink & Wynn, 2004). Researchers buried a ball in the sand and then retrieved apparently the same ball from the same or a different location. Infants stared longer when the ball emerged from the different location (Newcombe, Sluzenski, & Huttenlocher, 2005). This method assumes that staring means surprise and that surprise implies an understanding of mathematics and physics. If we accept those assumptions, this method leads us to increase greatly our estimation of infants' capabilities.

Here are two important conclusions: First, we should be cautious about inferring what infants or anyone else can or cannot do. The results may depend on the procedures. Second, concepts develop gradually. It is possible to show a concept in one situation and not another.

CRITICAL THINKING
A STEP FURTHER

Inferring "Surprise"

Suppose we play a series of musical notes and an infant stares longer toward the source of *do-re-mi-fa-so-la-ti* than *do-re-mi-fa-so-la-ti-do*. Should we infer that the infant is "surprised" by the absence of the final *do?*

Sense of Self

Another aspect of children's progress through the sensorimotor stage is that they appear to gain some concept of "self." The data are as follows: A mother puts a spot of unscented rouge on an infant's nose and then places the infant in front of a mirror. Infants younger than 1½ years old either ignore the red spot on the baby in the mirror or reach out to touch the mirror. At some point after age 1½ years, infants in the same situation touch themselves on the nose, indicating that they recognize themselves in the mirror (Figure 5.22). Infants show this sign of self-recognition at varying ages; the age when they start to show self-recognition is about the same as when they begin to act embarrassed (Lewis, Sullivan, Stanger, & Weiss, 1991). That is, they show a sense of self in both situations or neither.

FIGURE 5.22 If someone places a bit of unscented rouge on a child's nose, a 2-year-old shows self-recognition by touching his or her own nose. A younger child ignores the red spot or points at the mirror.

Before this time do they fail to perceive any distinction between self and other? Perhaps, but we cannot be sure. Before age 1½ we see no evidence for a sense of self, but absence of evidence is not evidence of absence. Perhaps younger infants would show a sense of self in some other test that we have not yet devised.

Early Childhood: Piaget's Preoperational Stage

By age 2, children are learning to speak. When a child asks for a toy, we no longer doubt that the child understands object permanence. Nevertheless, young children's understanding is not like that of adults. For example, they have difficulty understanding that a mother can be someone else's daughter. A boy with one brother will assert that his brother has no brother. Piaget refers to this period as the **preoperational stage** because *the child lacks operations, which are reversible mental processes.* For example, for a boy to understand that his brother has a brother, he must be able to reverse the concept of "having a brother." According to Piaget three typical aspects of preoperational thought are egocentrism, difficulty distinguishing appearance from reality, and lack of the concept of conservation.

Egocentrism: Understanding Other People's Thoughts

According to Piaget young children's thought is egocentric. By this term Piaget did *not* mean selfish. Instead, he meant that *a child sees the world as centered around himself or herself and cannot easily take another person's perspective.* If you sit opposite a preschooler with a complicated set of blocks between you, the child can describe how the blocks look from the child's side but not how they would look from your side.

Another example: Young children hear a story about a little girl, Lucy, who wants her old pair of red shoes. Part way through the story, Lucy's brother Linus comes into the room, and she asks him to bring her red shoes. He goes and brings back her new red shoes, and she is angry because she wanted the old red shoes. Young children hearing the story are surprised that he brought the wrong shoes because *they* knew which shoes she wanted (Keysar, Barr, & Horton, 1998). In this and other studies, children up to 4, 5, or 6 years old (depending on the details) seem to assume that whatever *they* know, other people will know too (Birch & Bloom, 2003).

However, even young children do understand another person's perspective on simple tasks. In one study 5- and 6-year-old children had to tell an adult to pick up a particular glass. If a child saw that the adult could see two glasses, the child usually said to pick up the "big" or "little" glass, so the adult could get the right one. If the child saw that the adult could see only one glass, the child often said just "the glass" (Nadig & Sedivy, 2002) (see Figure 5.23).

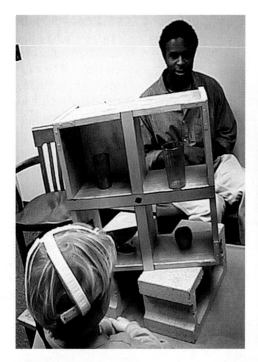

FIGURE 5.23 Sometimes, a child saw that the adult could see two glasses; other times, it was clear that the adult could see only one. If two glasses were visible, the child usually told the adult which glass to pick up, instead of just saying, "pick up the glass." *(Based on research by Nadig & Sedivy, 2002)*

 CONCEPT CHECK

13. Which of the following is the clearest example of egocentric thinking?
    a. A writer who uses someone else's words without giving credit.
    b. A politician who blames others for everything that goes wrong.
    c. A professor who gives the same complicated lecture to a freshman class that she gives to a convention of professionals. (Check your answer on page 181.)

To say that a child is egocentric means that he or she has trouble understanding what other people know and don't know. Psychologists say that a young child lacks, but gradually develops, **theory of mind,** which is *an understanding that other people have a mind too and that each person knows some things that other people don't know.* How can we know whether a child has this understanding? Here is one example of a research effort.

CRITICAL THINKING

WHAT'S THE EVIDENCE?

Children's Understanding of Other People's Knowledge

How and when do children first understand that other people have minds and knowledge? Researchers have devised some clever experiments to address this question.

Hypothesis. A child who understands that other people have minds will distinguish between someone who knows something and someone who could not.

Method. A 3- or 4-year-old child sat in front of four cups (Figure 5.24) and watched as one adult hid a candy or toy under one of the cups, although a screen prevented the child from seeing which cup. Then another adult entered the room. The "informed" adult pointed to one cup to show where he or she had just hidden the surprise; the "uninformed" adult pointed to a different cup. The child then had an opportunity to look under one cup for the treat.

This procedure was repeated 10 times for each child. The two adults alternated roles, but on each trial one or the other hid the treat while the other was absent. That is, one was informed and the other was not.

FIGURE 5.24 A child sits in front of a screen covering four cups and watches as one adult hides a surprise under one of the cups. Then that adult and another (who had not been present initially) point to one of the cups to signal where the surprise is hidden. Many 4-year-olds consistently follow the advice of the informed adult; 3-year-olds do not.

Results. Of the 4-year-olds, 10 of 20 consistently chose the cup indicated by the informed adult. (The other 10 showed no consistent preference.) That is, they understood who had the relevant knowledge and who did not. However, the 3-year-olds were as likely to follow the lead of the uninformed adult as that of the informed adult (Povinelli & deBlois, 1992).

Interpretation. Evidently, 4-year-olds are more likely than 3-year-olds to understand other people's knowledge (or lack of it).

Other experiments with different procedures have yielded related results. For example, one adult shows a child where she is hiding her "favorite toy" while she goes on an errand. During her absence another adult suggests playing a trick and moving the toy to another hiding place. Then the child is asked where the first person will look for her toy when she comes back. Most 5-year-olds say she will look in her original hiding place; most 3-year-olds say she will look in the new place; and 4-year-olds are about equally split between the two choices. That is, older children understand what someone else might or might not know, whereas younger children seem not to. Psychologists have found the same results for children in five cultures, so it appears to be a natural developmental process (Callaghan et al., 2005). However, the results depend on the procedure: If we *ask* where the returning person will look for her toy, 3-year-olds and half of 4-year-olds answer incorrectly. However, if we just say, "I wonder where she's going to look" and watch the children's eyes, even most 3-year-olds look toward the original hiding place (Clements & Perner, 1994). Again, you see that concepts develop gradually, and whether a child seems to understand something depends on how we do the test.

Distinguishing Appearance from Reality

Piaget and many other psychologists have contended that young children do not distinguish clearly between appearance and reality. For example, a child who sees you put a white ball behind a blue filter will say that the ball is blue. When you ask, "Yes, I know the ball *looks* blue, but what color is it *really?*" the child replies that it really *is* blue (Flavell, 1986). Similarly, a 3-year-old who encounters a sponge that looks like a rock probably will say that it really is a rock, but a child who says it is a sponge will also insist that it *looks like* a sponge.

However, other psychologists have argued that the 3-year-old's difficulty is more with language than with understanding the appearance–reality distinction.

(After all, 3-year-olds do play games of make-believe, so they sometimes distinguish appearance from reality.) In one study psychologists showed 3-year-olds a sponge that looked like a rock and let them touch it. When the investigators asked what it looked like and what it was *really,* most of the children said "rock" both times or "sponge" both times. However, if the investigators asked, "Bring me something so I can wipe up some spilled water," the children brought the sponge. And when the investigators asked, "Bring me something so I can take a picture of a teddy bear with something that looks like a rock," they again brought the sponge. So evidently, they did understand that something could be a sponge and look like a rock, even if they didn't say so (Sapp, Lee, & Muir, 2000).

Also consider this experiment: A psychologist shows a child a playhouse room that is a scale model of a full-size room. The psychologist hides a tiny toy in the small room while the child watches and explains that a bigger toy just like it is "in the same place" in the bigger room. (For example, if the little toy is behind the sofa in the little room, the big toy is behind the sofa in the big room.) Then the psychologist asks the child to find the big toy in the big room.

Most 3-year-olds look in the correct place and find the toy at once (DeLoache, 1989). Most 2½-year-old children, however, search haphazardly (Figure 5.25a). If the experimenter shows the child the big toy in the big room and asks the child to find the little toy "in the same place" in the little room, the results are the same: Most 3-year-olds find it, but most 2½-year-olds do not (DeLoache, 1989).

Before we conclude what a 2½-year-old cannot do, consider this clever follow-up study: The psychologist hides a toy in the small room while the child watches. Then both step out of the room, and the psychologist shows the child a "machine that can make things bigger." The psychologist aims a beam from the machine at the room and takes the child out of the way. They hear some chunkata-chunkata sounds, and then the psychologist shows the full-size "blown-up" room and asks the child to find the hidden toy. Even 2½-year-olds go immediately to the correct location (DeLoache, Miller, & Rosengren, 1997) (see Figure 5.25b). Evidently, they use one room as a map of the other if they think of them as "the same room." (Incidentally, hardly any of the children doubted that the machine had expanded the room. Many continued to

a A 2½-year-old is shown small room where stuffed animal is hidden.

Child is unable to find the stuffed animal in the larger room.

Child is told that the machine expands the room. Child stands out of the way during some noises and then returns.

b Child is shown small room where stuffed animal is hidden.

Child is able to find the stuffed animal in the blow n-up" room.

FIGURE 5.25 If an experimenter hides a small toy in a small room and asks a child to find a larger toy "in the same place" in the larger room, most 2½-year-olds search haphazardly **(a)**. However, the same children know where to look if the experimenter says this is the same room as before, but a machine has expanded it **(b)**.

believe it even after the psychologist explained what really happened!) The overall conclusion is that a child shows or fails to show an ability depending on how we ask the question.

Developing the Concept of Conservation

According to Piaget preoperational children lack the concept of conservation. They fail to *understand that objects conserve such properties as number, length, volume, area, and mass after changes in the shape or arrangement of the objects.* They cannot perform the mental operations necessary to understand the transformations. Table 5.2 shows typical conservation tasks. For example, if we show two glasses of the same size containing the same amount of water and then pour the contents of one glass into a taller, thinner glass, preoperational children say that the second glass contains more water (Figure 5.26).

I once thought perhaps the phrasing of the questions tricks children into saying something they do not believe. If you have the same doubts, borrow a 6-year-old child and try it yourself with your own wording. Here's my experience: Once when I was discussing Piaget in my introductory psychology class, I invited my son Sam, then 5½ years old, to take part in a class demonstration. I started with two glasses of water, which he agreed contained equal amounts of water. Then I poured the water from one glass into a wider glass, lowering the water level. When I asked Sam which glass contained more water, he confidently pointed to the tall, thin one. After class he complained, "Daddy, why did you ask me such an easy question? Everyone could see that there was more water in that glass! You should have asked me something harder to show how smart I am!" The following year I brought Sam, now 6½ years old, to class for the same demonstration. I poured the water from one of the tall glasses into a wider one and asked him which glass contained more water. He looked and paused. His face turned red. Finally, he whispered, "Daddy, I don't know!" After class he complained, "Why did you ask me such a hard question? I'm never coming back to any

of your classes again!" The question that used to be embarrassingly easy had become embarrassingly difficult.

The next year, when he was 7½, I tried again (at home). This time he answered confidently, "Both glasses have the same amount of water, of course. Why? Is this some sort of trick question?"

Later Childhood and Adolescence: Piaget's Stages of Concrete Operations and Formal Operations

At about age 7, children enter the stage of concrete operations and begin to understand the conservation of physical properties. The transition is gradual, however. For instance, a 6-year-old child may understand that squashing a ball of clay will not change its weight but may not realize until years later that squashing the ball will not change the volume of water it displaces when it is dropped into a glass.

TABLE 5.2 Typical Tasks Used to Measure Conservation

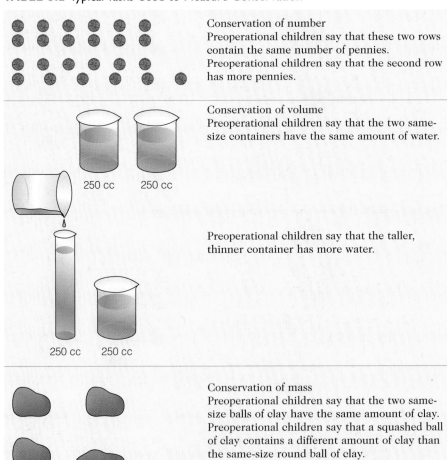

Conservation of number
Preoperational children say that these two rows contain the same number of pennies.
Preoperational children say that the second row has more pennies.

Conservation of volume
Preoperational children say that the two same-size containers have the same amount of water.

250 cc   250 cc

Preoperational children say that the taller, thinner container has more water.

250 cc   250 cc

Conservation of mass
Preoperational children say that the two same-size balls of clay have the same amount of clay.
Preoperational children say that a squashed ball of clay contains a different amount of clay than the same-size round ball of clay.

FIGURE 5.26 Preoperational children, usually younger than age 7, don't understand that the volume of water remains constant despite changes in its appearance. During the transition to concrete operations, a child finds conservation tasks difficult and confusing.

According to Piaget, during the **stage of concrete operations,** *children perform mental operations on concrete objects but still have trouble with abstract or hypothetical ideas.* For example, ask this question: "How could you move a 4-mile-high mountain of whipped cream from one side of the city to the other?" Older children think of imaginative answers, but children in the concrete operations stage are likely to complain that the question is silly.

Or ask, "If you could have a third eye anywhere on your body, where would you put it?" Children in this stage generally respond immediately that they would put it right between the other two, on their foreheads. Older children suggest more imaginative ideas such as on the back of their head, in the stomach (so they could watch food digesting), or on the tip of a finger (so they could peek around corners).

Finally, in Piaget's **stage of formal operations,** children develop *the mental processes that deal with abstract, hypothetical situations. Those processes demand logical, deductive reasoning and systematic planning.* According to Piaget children reach the stage of formal operations at about age 11. Later researchers found that many people reach this stage later or not at all, and like the other transitions, this one is gradual. Psychologists find that adolescents' thinking is not drastically different from children's thought. The main differences pertain to the adolescents' greater ability to make plans and to regulate their own behavior (Kuhn, 2006).

For example, we set up five bottles of clear liquid and explain that it is possible to mix some combination of them to produce a yellow liquid. The task is to find that combination. Children in the concrete operations stage plunge right in with no plan. They try combining bottles A and B, then C and D, then perhaps A, C, and E. Soon they have forgotten which combinations they've already tried.

Children in the formal operations stage approach the problem more systematically. They may first try all the two-bottle combinations: AB, AC, AD, AE, BC, and so forth. If those fail, they try three-bottle combinations: ABC, ABD, ABE, ACD, and so on. By trying every possible combination only once, they are sure to succeed.

Children do not reach the stage of formal operations any more suddenly than they reach the concrete operations stage. Reasoning logically about a particular problem requires some experience with it. A 9-year-old chess hobbyist reasons logically about chess problems and plans several moves ahead but reverts to concrete reasoning when faced with an unfamiliar problem. Table 5.3 summarizes Piaget's four stages.

☑ CONCEPT CHECK

14. You are given the following information about four children. Assign each of them to one of Piaget's stages of intellectual development.
    a. Child has mastered the concept of conservation; has trouble with abstract and hypothetical questions.
    b. Child performs well on tests of object permanence; has trouble with conservation.
    c. Child has schemata; does not speak in complete sentences; fails tests of object permanence.
    d. Child performs well on tests of object permanence, conservation, and hypothetical questions. (Check your answers on page 181.)

Are Piaget's Stages Distinct?

According to Piaget the four stages of intellectual development are distinct, and a transition from one stage to the next requires a major reorganization of

TABLE 5.3 Summary of Piaget's Stages of Cognitive Development

Stage and Approximate Age	Achievements and Activities	Limitations
Sensorimotor (birth to 1½ years)	Reacts to sensory stimuli through reflexes and other responses	Little use of language; seems not to understand object permanence in the early part of this stage
Preoperational (1½ to 7 years)	Develops language; can represent objects mentally by words and other symbols; can respond to objects that are remembered but not present	Lacks operations (reversible mental processes); lacks concept of conservation; focuses on one property at a time (such as length or width), not on both at once; still has trouble distinguishing appearance from reality
Concrete operations (7 to 11 years)	Understands conservation of mass, number, and volume; can reason logically with regard to concrete objects that can be seen or touched	Has trouble reasoning about abstract concepts and hypothetical situations
Formal operations (11 years onward)	Can reason logically about abstract and hypothetical concepts; develops strategies; plans actions in advance	None beyond the occasional irrationalities of all human thought

thinking, almost as a caterpillar metamorphoses into a chrysalis and a chrysalis metamorphoses into a butterfly. That is, intellectual growth has periods of revolutionary reorganization.

Later research has cast much doubt on this conclusion. If it were true, then a child in a given stage of development—say, the preoperational stage—should perform consistently at that level. In fact children fluctuate in their performance as a task is made more or less difficult. For example, consider the conservation-of-number task, in which an investigator presents two rows of seven or more objects, spreads out one row, and asks which row has more. Preoperational children reply that the spread-out row has more. However, when Rochel Gelman (1982) presented two rows of only three objects each (Figure 5.27) and then spread out one of the rows, even 3- and 4-year-old children usually answered that the rows had the same number of items. After much practice with short rows, most of the 3- and 4-year-olds also answered correctly that a spread-out row of eight items had the same number of items as a tightly packed row of eight.

Whereas Piaget believed children made distinct jumps from one stage to another, most psychologists today see development as gradual and continuous (Courage & Howe, 2002). That is, the difference between older children and younger children is not so much a matter of *having* or *lacking* some ability. Rather, younger children use their abilities only in simpler situations.

Differing Views: Piaget and Vygotsky

One implication of Piaget's findings is that children must discover certain concepts, such as the concept of conservation, mainly on their own. Teaching a concept means directing children's attention to the key aspects and letting them discover the concept. In contrast Russian psychologist Lev Vygotsky (1978) argued that educators cannot wait for children to rediscover the principles of physics and mathematics. Indeed, he argued, the distinguishing characteristic of human thought is that language and symbols enable each generation to profit from the experience of the previous ones.

However, when Vygotsky said that adults should teach children, he did not mean that adults should ignore the child's developmental level. Rather, every child has a **zone of proximal development**, which is *the distance between what a child can do alone and what the child can do with help*. Instruction should remain within that zone. For example, one should not try to teach a 4-year-old the concept of conservation of volume. However, a 6-year-old who does not yet un-

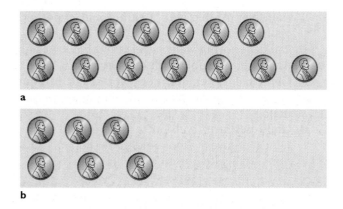

a

b

FIGURE 5.27 **(a)** With the standard conservation-of-number task, preoperational children answer that the lower row has more items. **(b)** With a simplified task, the same children say that both rows have the same number of items.

derstand the concept might learn it with help and guidance. Similarly, children improve their recall of a story when adults provide appropriate hints and reminders, and they can solve more complicated math problems with help than without it. Vygotsky compared this help to *scaffolding,* the temporary supports that builders use during construction: After the building is complete, the scaffolding is removed. Good advice for educators, therefore, is to be sensitive to a child's zone of proximal development and pursue how much further they can push a child.

 The zone of proximal development is the gap between what a child does alone and what the child can do with help.

✓ CONCEPT CHECK

15. What would Piaget and Vygotsky think about the feasibility of teaching the concept of conservation? (Check your answer on page 181.)

How Grown Up Are We?

Both Piaget and Vygotsky implied that we start with infant cognition and eventually attain adult thinking, which we practice from then on. Are they right, or do we still sometimes slip into childish ways of thought?

Consider egocentric thinking. Young children seem to assume that whatever they know or understand, other people will know or understand also.

Sometimes, adults make the same mistake. Suppose you say, "The daughter of the man and the woman arrived." Did one person arrive (the man and woman's daughter) or two people (the man's daughter and some other woman)? Presumably, you know what you meant, and you could use intonation to try to convey that meaning, but how many of your listeners would understand correctly? Most adults overestimate how well other people understand their meaning (Keysar & Henly, 2002).

Another example: You are sitting opposite another person. On each trial you are supposed to tell the person which of three cards to pick up, as quickly as possible. A fourth card is also present, which only you can see. Suppose the following arrangement, and suppose on this trial you are to direct the other person to the card on your far left:

Other person sits here

(barrier)

You sit here

All you need to say is "triangle" because the other person does not see the larger triangle that you see. However, adults often say, "the small triangle," as if the other person saw everything. Suppose we add the instruction not to give away any unnecessary information, because "the other person will try to guess the hidden card, and you will get rewards every time the other person guesses wrong." With these instructions people actually give away the unnecessary information even more than before. Evidently, their egocentric responding occurs automatically (Lane, Groisman, & Ferreira, 2006).

According to Piaget, after about age 7, we all understand conservation of number, volume, and so forth. True, if we show two equally tall thin containers of water and pour the water from one of them into a wider container, older children and adults confidently say that the two containers have equal amounts of water. However, suppose we test in a different way: We give people in a cafeteria a tall, thin glass or a short, wide glass and invite them to add as much juice as they want. Adults as well as children usually put more juice into the short, wide glass, while thinking that they are getting less juice than usual. Even professional bartenders generally pour more liquor into a short, wide glass than into a tall, thin one (Wansink & van Ittersum, 2003). Evidently, even adults don't fully understand conservation of volume if they are tested in this way.

Here is a different kind of childlike thinking in adults: Suppose you are given a stack of cards with designs varying in shape and color, including these:

First, you are told to sort them into stacks according to either shape or color. (The experimenter randomly assigns half the participants to each rule.) After you finish the experimenter shuffles the stack and asks you to sort them again but the other way. (If shape the first time, then color now.) Three-year-olds fail this task. After they sort the cards one way, they can't abandon that rule and sort by a different rule. Supposedly, children solve this task by age 4 or 5, and from then on they can switch from one sorting rule to the other. However, even college students are quicker when they sort the first time than when they have to sort the cards again by the other rule. When they switch back and forth between rules several times, they are a bit faster, on the average, whenever they use the same rule they used the first time (Diamond & Kirkham, 2005). In short, as we grow older, we learn to suppress our childlike ways of thinking and responding, but we don't lose them completely. A bit below the surface, there is a child's mind inside each of us.

  CONCEPT CHECK

16. How could you get someone to pour you a larger than average drink? (Check your answer on page 181.)

IN CLOSING

Developing Cognitive Abilities

Jean Piaget had an important influence on developmental psychology by calling attention to the ways in which infants and young children are different from adults. They are not just going through the same mental processes more slowly or with less information; they process information differently. Everything that we do develops over age, and we shall return to developmental issues repeatedly in later chapters. In particular, chapter 6 (learning) discusses the role of imitation in the development of social behaviors and personality; chapter 8 (cognition) discusses the development of language; and chapter 13 (social psychol-

ogy) includes the development of moral reasoning and prosocial behaviors.

However, Piaget was apparently wrong in his insistence that children go through distinct transitions from one stage to another, discarding previous types of cognition and adopting new ones. Whether an infant displays egocentric thinking, object permanence, theory of mind, the appearance–reality distinction, or conservation of number and volume depends on how we run the test. Even adults, who have supposedly mastered all these concepts, revert to childlike thinking at times. Cognitive development is not a matter of suddenly gaining concepts and then using them consistently. It is more a matter of gradually applying concepts more consistently and under a wider variety of conditions. ∎

Summary

- *Inferring infant capacities.* We easily underestimate newborns' capacities because they have so little control over their muscles. Careful testing procedures demonstrate that newborns see, hear, and remember more than we might have supposed. (page 163)
- *Infant vision and hearing.* Newborns stare at some visual patterns longer than others. Newborns habituate to a repeated sound but dishabituate to a slightly different sound, indicating that they hear a difference. (page 163)
- *Infant memory.* Newborns increase or alter their rate of sucking if a particular pattern of sucking turns on a specific recorded voice. They suck more vigorously to turn on a recording of their own mother's voice than some other woman's voice, indicating that they recognize the sound of the mother's voice. Infants just 2 months old learn to kick and move a mobile, and they remember how to do it several days later. (page 166)
- *Cross-sectional and longitudinal studies.* Psychologists study development by cross-sectional studies, which examine people of different ages at the same time, and by longitudinal studies, which look at a single group of people at various ages. A sequential design combines both methods. (page 166)
- *Cohort effects.* Many differences between young people and old people are not due to age but to time of birth. A group of people born in a particular era is called a cohort, and one cohort can differ from another in important ways. (page 168)
- *Piaget's view of children's thinking.* According to Jean Piaget, children's thought differs from adults' thought qualitatively as well as quantitatively. He believed children grew intellectually through accommodation and assimilation. (page 168)

- *Piaget's stages of development.* Children in the sensorimotor stage respond to what they see or otherwise sense at the moment. In the preoperational stage, according to Piaget, they lack reversible operations. In the concrete operations stage, children can reason about concrete problems but not abstractions. Adults and older children are in the formal operations stage, in which they can plan a strategy and can deal with hypothetical or abstract questions. (page 170)
- *Egocentric thinking.* Young children sometimes have trouble understanding other people's point of view. However, the results vary depending on the testing procedure. (page 172)
- *Appearance and reality.* Young children sometimes seem not to distinguish between appearance and reality. However, with a simpler task or different method of testing, they do distinguish. In many cases children do not fully have or lack a concept; they show the concept under some conditions and not others. (page 174)
- *Vygotsky.* According to Lev Vygotsky, children must learn new abilities from adults or older children, but we should be aware of their zone of proximal development. (page 178)
- *Adults.* Adults sometimes revert to childlike reasoning in some situations, if we observe carefully. (page 179)

Answers to Concept Checks

8. Evidently, the infant does not hear a difference between *ba* and *bla.* (This is a hypothetical result; the study has not been done.) (page 165)
9. If the frequency increased, we would conclude that the infant recognizes the difference between the father's voice and the other voice. If the frequency remained the same, we would conclude that the infant did not notice a difference. If it decreased, we would assume that the infant preferred the sound of the father's voice. (page 166)
10. Use a longitudinal study, which studies the same people repeatedly instead of comparing one cohort with another. (page 166)
11. With a longitudinal study, you would see clothing changes over time, and you would not know whether the changes were due to age or to changes in society. A cross-sectional study would have problems due to cohort effects. The older generation probably has always differed in its taste from the current younger generation. (page 166)
12. Another possible explanation is that the first-year students who have the lowest grades (and therefore pull down the grade average for first-year students) do not stay in school long enough to become seniors. (page 167)
13. c is the clearest case of egocentric thought, a failure to recognize another person's point of view. (page 173)
14. **a.** concrete operations stage; **b.** preoperational stage; **c.** sensorimotor stage; **d.** formal operations stage. (pages 170–177)
15. Piaget would recommend waiting for the child to discover the concept by himself or herself. According to Vygotsky the answer depends on the child's zone of proximal development. Some children could be taught the concept, and others are not yet ready for it. (page 178)
16. Ask the person to pour the drink into a short, wide glass. (page 179)

Social and Emotional Development

• *How do we change, socially and emotionally, as we grow older?*

You are a contestant on a new TV game show, *What's My Worry?* Behind the curtain is someone with an overriding concern. You are to identify that concern by questioning a psychologist who knows what it is. (You neither see nor hear the concerned person.) You must ask questions that can be answered with a single word or phrase. If you identify the worry correctly, you can win as much as $60,000.

Here's the catch: The more questions you ask, the smaller the prize. If you guess correctly after the first question, you win $60,000. After two questions you win $30,000 and so on. It would therefore be poor strategy to keep asking questions until you are sure. Instead, you should ask one or two questions and then make your best educated guess.

What would your first question be? Mine would be: "How old is this person?" The principal worries of teenagers are different from those of most 20-year-olds, which in turn differ from those of still older people. Each age has its own characteristic concerns, opportunities, and pleasures.

Erikson's Description of Human Development

Erik Erikson divided the human life span into eight periods that he variously called ages or stages. At each stage of life, he said, people have specific tasks to master, and each stage generates its own social and emotional conflicts. Table 5.4 summarizes Erikson's stages.

Erikson suggested that failure to master the task of a particular stage meant unfortunate consequences that would carry over to later stages. For example, the newborn infant deals with basic trust versus mistrust. An infant whose early environment is supportive, nurturing, and loving forms a strong parental attachment that positively influences future relationships with other people (Erikson, 1963). An infant who is mistreated fails to form a close, trusting relationship and has trouble developing close ties with anyone else later. We shall consider some of the relevant research later in this module.

In adolescence the key issue is identity. Most adolescents in Western societies consider many options of how they will spend the rest of their lives. It is possible to delay a decision or change one. Eventually, however, a decision becomes important. You can't achieve your goals until you set them.

According to Erikson the key decision of young adulthood is intimacy or isolation—that is, sharing your life with someone else or living alone. Here it is clear how a good decision benefits the rest of your life and how a poor decision hurts.

If you live a full life span, you will spend about half your life in "middle adulthood," where the issue is generativity (producing something important, e.g., children or work) versus stagnation (not producing). If all goes well, you can take pride in your success. If not, then the difficulties and disappointments are almost certain to continue into old age.

Is Erikson's view of development accurate? This question is unanswerable. You might or might not find his description useful, but it is not the kind of theory

TABLE 5.4 Erikson's Stages of Human Development

Stages	Main Conflict	Typical Question
Infant	Basic trust versus mistrust	Is my social world predictable and supportive?
Toddler (ages 1–3)	Autonomy versus shame and doubt	Can I do things by myself or must I always rely on others?
Preschool child (ages 3–6)	Initiative versus guilt	Am I good or bad?
Preadolescent (ages 6–12)	Industry versus inferiority	Am I successful or worthless?
Adolescent (early teens)	Identity versus role confusion	Who am I?
Young adult (late teens and early 20s)	Intimacy versus isolation	Shall I share my life with another person or live alone?
Middle adult (late 20s to retirement)	Generativity versus stagnation	Will I succeed in my life, both as a parent and as a worker?
Older adult (after retirement)	Ego integrity versus despair	Have I lived a full life or have I failed?

© Bettmann/CORBIS

Erik Erikson argued that each age group has its own special social and emotional conflicts.

that one can test scientifically. However, two of his general points do seem valid: Each stage has its own special difficulties, and an unsatisfactory resolution to the problems of one age carry over as an extra difficulty in later life.

Now let's examine in more detail some of the major social and emotional issues that confront people at different ages. Beyond the primary conflicts that Erikson highlighted, development is marked by a succession of other significant problems.

CRITICAL THINKING
A STEP FURTHER

Erikson's Stages

Suppose you disagree with Erikson's analysis. For example, suppose you believe that the main concern of young adults is not "intimacy versus isolation" but "earning money versus not earning money" or "finding meaning in life versus meaninglessness." How might you determine whether your theory or Erikson's is more accurate?

Infancy and Childhood

An important aspect of human life at any age is **attachment**—*a long-term feeling of closeness toward another person*—and one of the most important events of early childhood is forming one's first attachments. John Bowlby (1973) proposed that infants who develop one or more good attachments have a sense of security and safety. They can explore the world and return to their attachment figure when frightened or distressed. Those who do not develop strong early attachments may have trouble developing close relations later as well (Mikulincer, Shaver, & Pereg, 2003).

All that sounds fine in theory, but how can we measure strength of attachment to test and extend the theory? Most work has used the **Strange Situation** (usually capitalized), pioneered by Mary Ainsworth (1979). In this procedure *a mother and her infant* (typically 12 or 18 months old) *come into a room with many toys. Then a stranger enters the room. The mother leaves and then returns. A few minutes later, both the stranger and the mother leave; then the stranger returns, and finally, the mother returns.* Through a one-way mirror, a psychologist observes the infant's reactions to each of these events. Observers classify infants' responses in the following categories.

- *Securely attached.* The infant uses the mother as a base of exploration, often showing her a toy, cooing at her, or making eye contact with her. The infant shows some distress when the mother leaves but cries only briefly or not at all. When she returns, the infant goes to her with apparent delight, cuddles for a while, and then returns to the toys.
- *Anxious (or resistant).* Responses toward the mother fluctuate between happy and angry. The infant clings to the mother and cries profusely when she leaves, as if worried that she might not return. When she does return, the infant clings to her again but does not use her as a base to explore a room full of toys. A child with an anxious attachment typically shows many fears, including a strong fear of strangers.
- *Avoidant.* While the mother is present, the infant does not stay near her and does not interact much with her. The infant may or may not cry when she leaves and does not go to her when she returns.
- *Disorganized.* The infant seems not even to notice the mother or looks away while approaching her or covers his or her face or lies on the floor. The infant may alternate between approach and avoidance and shows more fear than affection.

The prevalence of the various attachment styles varies from one population to another, but these numbers are often cited as an approximation for North America: 65% secure, 10% anxious/resistant, 15% avoidant, 10% disorganized (Ainsworth, Blehar, Waters, & Wall, 1978). Of course, many children do not fit neatly into one category or another, so some who are classified as "secure" or "avoidant" are more secure or avoidant than others. Still, most children remain stable in their classification from one time to another (Moss, Cyr, Bureau, Tarabulsy, & Dubois-Comtois, 2005).

The Strange Situation also can be used to evaluate the relationship between child and father (Belsky,

1996), child and grandparent, or other relationships. As a rule the quality of one relationship correlates with the quality of others. For example, most children who have a secure relationship with the mother also have a secure relationship with the father, and chances are the parents are happy with each other as well (Elicker, Englund, & Sroufe, 1992; Erel & Burman, 1995). A secure attachment in early childhood correlates with favorable social relationships later. Most infants who have a secure relationship with their parents at age 12 months continue to have a close relationship with them decades later (Waters, Merrick, Treboux, Crowell, & Albersheim, 2000). Those who show a secure attachment in infancy are more likely than others to form high quality romantic attachments in adulthood (Roisman, Collins, Sroufe, & Egeland, 2005). They are also likely to form close and mutually supportive friendships, whereas those who had anxious or avoidant attachments worry excessively about rejection or fail to seek others' support in times of distress (Mikulincer et al., 2003).

Why do some children develop more secure attachments than others? One possibility is that children differ genetically in their tendency to fear the unfamiliar. Several studies with older children support this idea (McGuire, Clifford, Fink, Basho, & McDonnell, 2003; Schwartz et al., 2003). However, the variance in attachment style also depends on how responsive the parents are to the infants' needs, including such things as talking to the infant but also quite importantly holding and touching. Gentle touch can be very reassuring (Hertenstein, 2002). Programs that teach parents to be more responsive produce significant increases in secure attachments by the infants (Bakermans-Kranenburg, van IJzendoorn, & Juffer, 2003).

Extreme early experiences can also produce powerful effects. One study examined children adopted in Britain after living up to 2 years of life in Romanian orphanages, where they had received little attention. Many of them did not resemble any of the usual attachment styles. They might approach and cling to the stranger instead of the parent. Some of them approached the stranger in a friendly way at first and then withdrew, unlike typical children who avoid a stranger at first and then become friendlier (O'Connor et al., 2003).

The patterns of attachment are not entirely consistent across cultures. For example, in the United States, most mothers en-

courage their infants to be independent, and mothers who exert much physical control over their infants tend to be less sensitive to their infants, leading to an avoidant attachment style. In Puerto Rico, however, most mothers exert much physical control while nevertheless being warm and sensitive, leading to a secure attachment style (Carlson & Harwood, 2003). In Asia most mothers hold their infants much of the day and keep them in bed with the parents at night. If an Asian mother is persuaded to leave her infant with a stranger in the Strange Situation, it may be the first time the infant has been away from its mother, and it cries loud and long. By Western standards these children qualify as "anxiously attached," but the behavior means something different in its cultural context (Rothbaum, Weisz, Pott, Miyake, & Morelli, 2000).

 CONCEPT CHECK

17. If a child in the Strange Situation clings tightly to the mother and cries furiously when she leaves, which kind of attachment does the child have? Does the child's culture affect the answer?
18. What attachment style is most likely in a child who tends to have strong anxieties? (Check your answers on page 189.)

Social Development in Childhood and Adolescence

The social and emotional development of children depends largely on their friendships. "Popular" children have many friends and admirers. "Rejected" children are avoided by most other children. "Controversial" children are liked by some but avoided by others. In most cases a child's status as popular, rejected, or controversial is consistent from year to year (Coie & Dodge, 1983).

Adolescence begins when the body reaches *puberty,* the onset of sexual maturation. Adolescence merges into adulthood, and adulthood is more a state of mind than a condition of the body. Some 12-year-olds act like adults, and some 30-year-olds act like adolescents.

Adolescence is sometimes seen as a period of "storm and stress." Typically, teenagers report in-

Children learn social skills by interacting with brothers, sisters, and friends close to their own age.

© Doug Menuez/PhotoDisc./Getty Images

creased emotional intensity of their conflict with parents in early adolescence, but decreased frequency of conflicts in later adolescence (Laursen, Coy, & Collins, 1998). Comparisons of monozygotic and dizygotic twins suggest a genetic contribution to the conflicts (McGue, Elkins, Walden, & Iacono, 2005). Storm and stress also depend on family and culture (Arnett, 1999). Adolescents who receive sympathetic support experience less conflict with their parents (Lee, Su, & Yoshida, 2005).

Adolescence is also a time of risk-taking behaviors, not only in humans but in other species as well (Spear, 2000). In one study researchers asked people to play the video game Chicken, in which they guided a car on the screen. When a traffic light turned yellow, a participant could earn extra points by getting through the light but at the risk of a game-ending crash if the light turned red before the car got through the light. Adolescents age 13 and up were more likely than older participants to try to get through yellow lights, especially if several of their friends were watching (Gardner & Steinberg, 2005). No one will be surprised that peer pressure increases adolescents' risk taking, but this study provides a clever demonstration of the tendency. A review of the literature concluded that teaching adolescents to appraise the risks of their actions is futile. An adolescent who acts recklessly is in most cases already aware of the risk. The main difference between the adolescent and typical adults is that most adults would take the safe action habitually, without even considering the pros and cons of some risky action (Reyna & Farley, 2006).

In many nontechnological societies, most teenagers are married and working. In effect they move directly from childhood into adulthood. In Western culture our excellent health and nutrition have gradually lowered the average age of puberty (Okasha, McCarron, McEwen, & Smith, 2001), but our economic situation encourages people to stay in school and postpone marriage, family, and career (Arnett, 2000). The consequence is a long period of physical maturity without adult status. Imagine if our society decided that people should stay in college until age 30. Would this policy bring out the best behavior in 25- to 30-year-olds?

Identity Development

As Erikson pointed out, adolescence is a time of "finding yourself," determining "who am I?" or "who will I be?" It is when most people first construct a coherent "life story" of how they got to be the way they are and how one life event led to another (Habermas & Bluck, 2000).

In some societies most people are expected to enter the same occupation as their parents and live in the same town. The parents may even choose their children's marriage partners. Western society offers young people a vast variety of choices about education, career, marriage, political and religious affiliation, where to live, and activities regarding sex, alcohol, and drugs. Having a great deal of freedom to choose a life path can be invigorating, but it can also be more than a little frightening.

a

b

▍ **(a)** American teenagers are financially dependent on their parents but have the opportunity to spend much time in whatever way they choose. **(b)** In many nontechnological societies, teenagers are expected to do adult work and accept adult responsibilities.

An adolescent's *concern with decisions about the future and the quest for self-understanding* has been called an **identity crisis.** The term *crisis* implies more emotional turbulence than is typical. Identity development has two major elements: whether one is actively exploring the issue and whether one has made any decisions (Marcia, 1980). We can diagram the possibilities using the following grid:

	Has explored or is exploring the issues	Has not explored the issues
Decisions already made	Identity achievement	Identity foreclosure
Decisions not yet made	Identity moratorium	Identity diffusion

Those who have not yet given any serious thought to making any decisions and who have no clear sense of identity are said to have **identity diffusion.** They are not actively concerned with their identity at the moment. People in **identity moratorium** are *seriously considering the issues but not yet making decisions.* They experiment with various possibilities and imagine themselves in different roles before making a choice.

Identity foreclosure is a state of *reaching firm decisions without much thought.* For example, a young man might be told that he is expected to go into the family business with his father, or a young woman might be told that she is expected to marry and raise children. Decrees of that sort were once common in North America and Europe, and they are still common in other societies today. Someone who accepts such decisions has little reason to explore alternative possibilities.

Finally, **identity achievement** is *the outcome of having explored various possible identities and then making one's own decisions.* Identity achievement does not come all at once. For example, you might decide about your career but not about marriage. You might also reach identity achievement and then rethink a decision years later.

The "Personal Fable" of Teenagers

Answer the following items true or false:

- Other people may fail to realize their life ambitions, but I will realize mine.
- I understand love and sex in a way that my parents never did.
- Tragedy may strike other people, but probably not me.

- Almost everyone notices how I look and how I dress.

According to David Elkind (1984), teenagers are particularly likely to harbor such beliefs. Taken together, he calls them the "personal fable," the conviction that "I am special—what is true for everyone else is not true for me." Up to a point, this fable can help us maintain a cheerful, optimistic outlook on life, but it becomes dangerous when it leads people to take foolish chances.

According to David Elkind, one reason for risky behavior is the "personal fable," the secret belief that "nothing bad can happen to me."

For example, one study found that high school girls who were having sexual intercourse without contraception estimated that they had only a small chance of becoming pregnant through unprotected sex. Girls who were either having no sex or using contraception during sex estimated a much higher probability that unprotected sex would lead to pregnancy (Arnett, 1990). Because this was a correlational study, we do not know which came first—the girls' underestimation of the risk of pregnancy or their willingness to have unprotected sex. In either case the results illustrate the attitude, "it can't happen to me."

This attitude is hardly unique to teenagers, however. Most middle-aged adults regard themselves as more likely than other people to succeed on the job and as less likely than average to have a serious illness (Quadrel, Fischhoff, & Davis, 1993). They also overestimate their own chances of winning a lottery, especially if they get to choose their own lottery ticket

(Langer, 1975). That is, few people fully outgrow the personal fable.

Adulthood

From early adulthood until retirement, the main concern of most adults is, as Erikson noted, "What will I achieve and contribute to society and my family? Will I be successful?"

Adulthood extends from one's first full-time job until retirement—for most people, half or more of the total life span. We lump so many years together because it seems, at least superficially, that little is changing. During your childhood and adolescence, you grew taller each year. During adulthood, your hair might turn gray or you might gain a little weight, but the changes in your appearance are slow and subtle. From infancy until early adulthood, each new age brought new privileges, such as permission to stay out late, your first driver's license, the right to vote, and the opportunity to go to college. By early adulthood, you have already gained all the privileges, and one year blends into the next. Children and teenagers know exactly how old they are; sometimes, adults have to think about it.

However, on closer examination we find that important changes do occur during adulthood. Many or most of them are self-initiated. When adults describe the "turning points" in their lives, they most often mention the choices they made, such as getting married, having children, changing jobs, or moving to a new location (Rönkä, Oravala, & Pulkkinen, 2003).

The ways in which behavior changes during childhood depend mostly on the growth of new abilities. During adulthood, behavior changes mostly because new situations require people to assume new roles and change their priorities of how they spend their time. Daniel Levinson (1986) describes adult development in terms of a series of overlapping eras. After the transition into adulthood at about age 20, give or take a couple of years, early adulthood begins, which lasts until age 40 or 45. This is the time people make the biggest decisions in life concerning marriage, having children, and choosing a career. Once people have chosen a career, they usually stay with it or something related to it, as vocational interests are even more stable over time than personality is (Low, Yoon, Roberts, & Rounds, 2005). During early adulthood, people devote maximum energy to pursuing their goals. However, buying a house and raising a family on a young person's salary are usually difficult, and this is a period of much stress.

After early adulthood, according to Levinson (1986), people go through a **midlife transition,** *a time when they reassess their personal goals, set new ones,* *and prepare for the rest of life.* Many people become more accepting of themselves and others at this time and feel less tyrannized by job stress. During middle adulthood, extending from about age 40 to 65, physical strength and health may begin to decline but probably not enough to interfere with an active personal and professional life. At this point people have already achieved success at work or have come to accept whatever status they have. Their children are becoming adults themselves. Finally, people make the transition to late adulthood, which begins around age 65.

Let's consider the midlife transition a little further. It often occurs in response to a divorce, illness, death in the family, a turning point in the person's career, or some other event that causes the person to question past decisions and current goals (Wethington, Kessler, & Pixley, 2004). Just as the adolescent identity crisis is a bigger issue in cultures that offer many choices, the same is true for the midlife transition. If you lived in a society that offered no choices, you would not worry about the paths not taken! In Western society, however, you enter adulthood with high hopes. You hope to earn an advanced degree, excel at an outstanding job, marry a wonderful person, have marvelous children, become a leader in your community, run for political office, write a great novel, compose great music, travel the world . . . You know you are not working on all of your goals right now, but you tell yourself, "I'll do it later." As you grow older, you realize that you are running out of "later." Even if you could still achieve some of your dreams, time is passing.

People deal with their midlife transitions in many ways. Most of them abandon unrealistic goals and set new goals consistent with the direction their lives have taken. Others decide that they have been ignoring dreams that they are not willing to abandon. They quit their jobs and go back to school, set up a business of their own, or try something else they have always wanted to do. In one study middle-aged women who made major changes in their lives were happier and more successful than those who didn't (Stewart & Ostrove, 1998). Of course, we don't know whether the life changes made women happy and successful or whether happy, successful women are more likely than others to make changes.

The least satisfactory outcome is to decide, "I can't abandon my dreams, but I can't do anything about them either. I can't take the risk of changing my life, even though I am dissatisfied with it." People with that attitude become discouraged and depressed.

The advice is clear: To increase your chances of feeling good in middle age and beyond, make good decisions when you are young. If you really care about something, don't wait until you have a midlife crisis.

Get started now. If you fail, well, at least you won't always wonder what would have happened if you had tried. Besides, in the process of trying something, you might discover a related opportunity. And you never know: You might succeed.

 CONCEPT CHECK

19. How does a midlife transition resemble an adolescent identity crisis? (Check your answer on page 189.)

Old Age

People age in different ways. Some people, such as those with Alzheimer's disease, deteriorate rapidly in intellect, coordination, and ability to care for themselves. However, most people over 65 continue to work at full-time or part-time jobs, volunteer work, or hobbies. Many remain active and alert well into their 80s and 90s. On the average, memory declines in old age, but the results differ substantially among individuals. As you might guess, memory usually remains reasonably intact among older people who are healthy and active. Programs that increase older people's physical exercise lead to improvements in memory and cognition (Colcombe & Kramer, 2003).

Memory in old age also differs across situations. Everyone remembers interesting material better than something that seems unimportant, but the difference is larger for older people, who tend to focus their attention and resources more narrowly on topics likely to bring them pleasure or topics of practical importance to them. Thus, they overlook some details that a younger person would remember. When older people can't remember something in detail, they compensate by filling in the gaps with educated guesses of what "must have happened" (Hess, 2005). As you will see in the memory chapter, younger people do the same when they cannot remember the details; the difference is that older people face this difficulty more frequently.

As we shall see in chapter 12 (emotion), several kinds of evidence indicate that healthy older people are, on the average, happier and more satisfied with life than younger people are. That result may seem surprising. However, young people face many pressures from work and raising children, whereas older people have more leisure. Furthermore, older people deliberately focus their attention on family, friends, and other events that bring them pleasure (Carstensen, Mikels, & Mather, 2006).

Your satisfaction in old age will depend largely on how you live while younger. Some older people say, "I hope to live many more years, but even if I don't, I have lived my life well. I did everything that I really cared about." Others say, "I wanted to do so much that I never did." Feeling dignity in old age also depends on how people's families, communities, and societies treat them. Some cultures, such as Korea, observe a special ceremony to celebrate a person's retirement or 70th birthday (Damron-Rodriguez, 1991). African American and Native American families traditionally honor their elders, giving them a position of status in the family and calling on them for advice. Japanese families follow a similar tradition, at least publicly (Koyano, 1991).

In Tibet and many other cultures, children are taught to treat old people with respect and honor.

Although an increasing percentage of people over 65 remain in the work force, most people eventually retire. Retirement decreases stress, but it also brings a sense of loss to those whose lives had focused on their work (Kim & Moen, 2001). Loss of control becomes a serious issue when health begins to fail. Consider someone who spent half a century running a business and now lives in a nursing home where staff members make all the decisions. Leaving even a few of the choices and responsibilities to the residents improves their self-respect, health, alertness, and memory (Rodin, 1986; Rowe & Kahn, 1987).

The Psychology of Facing Death

A man who has not found something he is willing to die for is not fit to live.

—Martin Luther King Jr. (1964)

This is perhaps the greatest lesson we learned from our patients: LIVE, so you do not have to look back and say, "God, how I have wasted my life!"

—Elisabeth Kübler Ross (1975)

The worst thing about death is the fact that when a man is dead it's impossible any longer to undo the harm you have done him, or to do the good you haven't done him. They say: live in such a way as to be always ready to die. I would say: live in such a way that anyone can die without you having anything to regret.

—Leo Tolstoy (1865/1978, p. 192)

We commonly associate death with older people, although people die at any age. Just thinking about the fact that you will eventually die evokes distress. According to **terror-management theory**, *we cope with our fear of death by avoiding thoughts about death and by affirming a worldview that provides self-esteem, hope, and value in life* (Pyszczynski, Greenberg, & Solomon, 2000). That is, when something reminds you of your mortality, you do whatever you can to reduce your anxiety. You might reassure yourself that you still have many years to live, that your health is good, and that you will quit smoking, lose weight, or do whatever else would improve your health. You probably increase your ambitions temporarily, talking about the high salary you will earn and the exciting things you will do during the rest of your life (Kasser & Sheldon, 2000).

Still, even excellent health merely postpones death, so a reminder of death also redoubles your efforts to defend a belief that life is part of something eternal. You might restate strongly your belief in your religion or your patriotism or any other view that enables you to make sense of life and find meaning in it (Greenberg et al., 2003). You might also take pride in how you have contributed to your family, your profession, or something else that will continue after you are gone (Pyszczynski et al., 2000). Even a casual reference to death increases people's defenses of their beliefs, whatever those beliefs are.

IN CLOSING

Social and Emotional Issues Through the Life Span

Let's close by reemphasizing a key point of Erik Erikson's theory: Each age or stage builds on the previous ones. For example, the quality of your early attachments to parents and others correlates with your ability to form close, trusting relationships later. How well you handle the identity issues of adolescence affects your adult life. Certainly, your productivity during adulthood determines how satisfied you can feel with your life when you reach old age. Each of us has to master the tasks of an earlier stage before we can deal effectively with those of the next stage. Life is a continuum, and the choices you make at any age are linked with those you make before and after. ∎

Summary

* *Erikson's view of development.* Erik Erikson described the human life span as a series of eight ages or stages, each with its own social and emotional conflicts. (page 182)
* *Infant attachment.* Infants can develop several kinds of attachment to significant people in their lives, as measured in the Strange Situation. However, the results of studies in Western society do not apply equally well in other societies. (page 183)
* *Adolescent identity crisis.* Adolescents have to deal with the question "Who am I?" Many experiment with several identities before deciding. (page 185)
* *Adults' concerns.* One of the main concerns of adults is productivity in family and career. Many adults undergo a midlife transition when they reevaluate their goals. (page 187)
* *Old age.* Dignity and independence are key concerns of old age. (page 188)
* *Facing death.* People at all ages face the anxieties associated with the inevitability of death. A reminder of death influences people to set higher goals and to defend their worldviews. (page 189)

Answers to Concept Checks

17. In the United States, this pattern would indicate an anxious or insecure attachment. In Southeast Asia, however, this behavior is normal. (page 184)
18. A child with strong anxieties would probably show an anxious (or resistant) attachment style, clinging to the mother and being distressed when she leaves. (page 184)
19. In both cases people examine their lives, goals, and possible directions for the future. (page 187)

Diversity: Gender, Culture, and Family

- *What factors influence development of personality and social behavior?*

The start of the first module in this chapter began by asking how you would be different if we could go back and change just one of your genes. Suppose we changed you from male to female or female to male. Or suppose we changed you to a person with a different ethnicity or culture. Perhaps we switch you to a different family. Then how would you be different?

With such a drastic change, you might ask whether it would still be *you*. Gender, culture, and family are integral parts of any person's development and identity.

Gender Influences

Many popular books have stressed the differences between men and women, such as *Men Are from Mars, Women Are from Venus*. Comedians entertain us by exaggerating the differences. (I like the quip that "in a world full of men, all furniture would be in its original location.") But how big are the differences, really?

According to a review of the literature, gender differences with regard to most aspects of personality, cognition, intelligence, and self-esteem are close to zero (Hyde, 2005). Two areas in which people expect to find differences are language and mathematics. Men are more likely to enter careers in mathematics, physical sciences, and engineering, even in comparison to women with similar mathematical abilities (Benbow, Lubinski, Shea, & Efekhari-Sanjani, 2000). However, in terms of ability, the differences are small and depend on the task (Spelke, 2005). Females tend to have greater verbal fluency, while men on the average do slightly better on verbal analogies ("A is to B as C is to what?"). On the average females do better at arithmetic calculations, while males do better at mathematical word problems and some aspects of geometry, such as imagining how a display would look when rotated 90 degrees. However, even those differences are small and inconsistent (Levine, Vasilyeva, Lourenco, Newcombe, & Huttenlocher, 2005). Overall, females' grades in mathematics courses are at least the equal of males from elementary school through college (Spelke, 2005).

Males and females do differ, however, in miscellaneous regards. On the average boys are more active beginning at an early age, whereas girls have better

self-control (Else-Quest, Hyde, Goldsmith, & Van Hulle, 2006). On the average men, being larger and stronger, throw harder and get into fights more often (Hyde, 2005). Men are generally more likely to help a stranger change a flat tire, but women are more likely to provide long-term nurturing support (Eagly & Crowley, 1986). The more pairs of shoes you own, the higher is the probability that you are female.

When giving directions, men are more likely to use directions and distances—such as "go four blocks east . . ."—whereas women are more likely to use landmarks—such as "go until you see the library . . ." (Saucier et al., 2002). Figure 5.28 shows the relative frequency with which men and women used different ways of giving directions (Rahman, Andersson, & Govier, 2005). However, men are capable of following

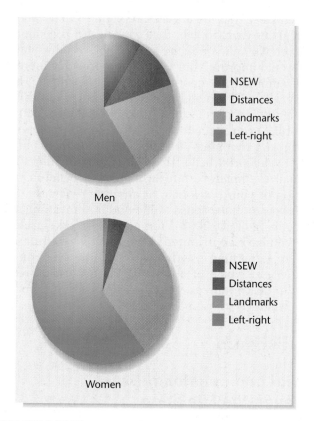

FIGURE 5.28 When giving directions, men refer to distances and north-south-east-west more often than women do. Women describe more landmarks. Men and women refer to left and right about equally. *(Based on data of Rahman, Andersson, & Govier, 2005)*

landmarks and women are capable of following directions and distances. When only one or the other is available, both men and women find their way (Spelke, 2005).

Why do men and women differ in this way? One interpretation is that men evolved greater attention to spatial relationships because men in early hunter-gatherer societies had to find their way home from hunting, whereas women spent more time close to home (Silverman et al., 2000). However, we know little for sure about prehistoric human life. An equally logical possibility is that women remember the landmarks better, so men are forced to rely on directions and distances (Levy, Astur, & Frick, 2005). In any case the difference is not unique to humans. In monkeys, mice, and several other species, males perform better than females in mazes without landmarks, whereas females remember the landmarks better (C. M. Jones, Braithwaite, & Healy, 2003; Williams, Barnett, & Meck, 1990).

Sex Roles and Androgyny

Within the topic of gender influences, the greatest research interest has focused on sex roles, *the different activities expected of males and females.* A few aspects of sex roles are biologically determined: For example, only women can nurse babies, and men are more likely than women to do jobs requiring physical strength. However, many of our sex roles are customs set by our society. Do you regard fire building as mostly men's work or women's? What about basket weaving? Planting crops? Milking cows? Your answers depend on the society in which you were reared. Some cultures regard each of these as men's work; others regard them as women's work (Wood & Eagly, 2002). Cultures also determine the relative status of men and women. Generally, if a culture lives in conditions that require hunting, vigorous defense, or other use of physical strength, men have greater status than women. When food is abundant and enemies are few, men and women have more equal status. However, a culture often maintains its traditions after the end of the conditions that established them (D. Cohen, 2001).

Nevertheless, customs do change. Within most technologically advanced countries since the 1960s, a much higher percentage of women have taken jobs in fields previously dominated by men—such as law, medicine, government, and business administration (Eagly, Johannesen-Schmidt, & van Engen, 2003). Simultaneously, most men have increased the amount of time they spend on child care (Barnett & Hyde, 2001).

Given that sex roles can be flexible, Sandra Bem (1974) proposed that the ideal would be a personality capable of alternating between stereotypically male and stereotypically female traits, depending on the situation. For example, you might be ambitious and assertive (male traits) but also sympathetic to the feelings of others (female). **Androgyny** is *the ability to display both male and female characteristics.* The word comes from the Greek roots *andr-,* meaning "man" (as in the words *androgen* and *android*), and *gyn-,* meaning "woman" (as in the word *gynecology*).

The idea sounds good, but the evidence has not strongly indicated that androgynous people are mentally healthier, more successful, or better adjusted than other people. Part of the problem has to do with measuring androgyny. Originally, the procedure was to give people a questionnaire about masculine traits (ambitious, competitive, independent, willing to take risks, etc.) and a questionnaire about feminine traits (affectionate, cheerful, loyal, sympathetic, etc.). An androgynous person was someone who checked about an equal number of masculine and feminine traits. The problem with this approach is that someone could be equal on both by being equally *low* on both! Imagine someone who is not ambitious, not independent, not cheerful, and not sympathetic.

Later researchers therefore defined androgyny as being above average on both masculine and feminine traits. However, another problem remains: Lists of masculine and feminine traits include both favorable and unfavorable items. Independence and ambition (masculine traits) are generally good, as are compassion and tolerance (feminine traits). However, selfishness is an undesirable masculine trait, and submissiveness is an undesirable feminine trait. Thus, an improved definition is that androgyny consists of being above average on both desirable masculine traits and desirable feminine traits. Using that definition psychologists find that androgynous people tend to be mentally healthy and to enjoy high self-esteem (Woodhill & Samuels, 2003).

However, that demonstration does not necessarily document the usefulness of the androgyny concept. Positive masculine traits (independence, ambition, etc.) are obviously beneficial. Positive feminine traits (compassion, tolerance, etc.) are also beneficial. So it is no surprise that having both positive masculine and positive feminine traits is beneficial. To be a useful concept, androgyny should provide a benefit above what the masculine and feminine characteristics provide. Researchers have occasionally demonstrated that androgynous people show much flexibility (Cheng, 2005), but most research suggests that the benefits of androgyny are simply the sum of the benefits from masculine and feminine traits (Marsh & Byrne, 1992; Spence, 1984).

CONCEPT CHECK

20. Research finds that androgynous people tend to be successful and mentally healthy. Why does this finding, by itself, fail to demonstrate the usefulness of the concept of androgyny? (Check your answer on page 198.)

Reasons Behind Gender Differences

It is easy to list differences between males and females but more difficult to explain them. Neither biological nor cultural influences act in isolation, but in combination with each other. On the one hand, the genders differ biologically. If nothing else, males are on the average taller and more muscular. The physical differences predispose each gender to certain behavioral differences, which alter the way other people react, and other people's reactions alter further behavior.

On the other hand, adults treat boys differently from girls. Even with 6- and 9-month-old infants, mothers talk to their daughters in a more conversational way and give more instructions to their sons, such as "come here" (Clearfield & Nelson, 2006). At this age the infants themselves are not talking, so the difference demonstrates the mother's own behavior, not her reaction to the infants' behavior.

In one fascinating study, researchers set up cameras and microphones to eavesdrop on families in a science museum. Boys and girls spent about equal time looking at each exhibit, and the parents spent about equal time telling boys and girls how to use each exhibit, but on the average they provided about three times as many scientific explanation to the boys as to the girls, regardless of how many questions the children themselves asked (Crowley, Callanen, Tenenbaum, & Allen, 2001).

Ethnic and Cultural Influences

Growing up as a member of a minority group poses special issues. For example, adolescence is for anyone a time of searching for identity. Minority group members have to consider not only their own identity but also how they feel about their group. For example, many African Americans and Hispanic Americans come to identify with their group more strongly during adolescence and to raise their estimation of their group. Increasing their group esteem is part of developing strong self-esteem (French, Seidman, Allen, & Aber, 2006). Minority youth also have to learn how to deal with prejudices so that they manage to succeed in spite of them.

Parents play an important part in this process. Adolescence is a time of strong peer pressure, and in many cases the peer culture of minority group adolescents has a risky impact. Researchers have found that improved parental supervision and communication help minority group youth to resist pressures for drug and alcohol use and early sexual activity (Brody et al., 2006).

Ethnic identity is especially salient for immigrants to a country. The pressures on immigrant children and adolescents can be intense. In addition to the usual difficulties of growing up, they face prejudices, questions about whether they have entered the country legally, and language problems. They also face the issue of how to deal with an unfamiliar culture. Immigrants, their children, and sometimes further generations experience **biculturalism,** *partial identification with two cultures.* For example, Mexican immigrants to the United States speak Spanish and follow Mexican customs at home but switch to the English language and U.S. customs in other places. Mexican American youth report difficulty understanding U.S. culture, problems of not fitting in with others at school, and either difficulties in school because of poor English or difficulties at home because of poor Spanish (Romero & Roberts, 2003). However, their situation is not entirely bleak. In many places bicultural youth tend to have low rates of substance use, delinquency, and depression (Coatsworth, Maldonado-Molina, Pantin, & Szapocznik, 2005). One reason is that their parents maintain close supervision, hoping that their children will maintain the best parts of their old cultures (Fuligni, 1998). Another reason is that by not feeling fully part of U.S. youth culture, bicultural adolescents are less subject to its peer pressures.

Many immigrants are bicultural, having reasonable familiarity with two sets of customs. These immigrant children attend middle school in Michigan.

At least to a small extent, nearly all of us learn to function in multiple subcultures. Unless you live in a small town where everyone has the same background, religion, and customs, you learn to adjust what you say and do in different settings and with different groups of people. The transitions are more noticeable and more intense for ethnic minorities.

Analogous to biculturalism is biracialism. A growing percentage of people in the United States have parents from different racial or ethnic origins, such as African and European, European and Hispanic, or Asian and Native American. People of biracial or multiracial backgrounds are especially common in Hawaii and California. Decades ago, psychologists speculated that biracial children and adolescents would be at a serious disadvantage, because they would not feel accepted by either group. The research, however, finds that most biracial people are pleased with their mixed background, which enables them to see the best in both cultures, to accept all cultures, and to overcome prejudice and discrimination. Some biracial youth (especially in the past) have indeed felt rejected by both groups, but in more recent surveys, most say they feel reasonably well accepted by both groups. They show no particular problems in either academic performance or mental health. The one problem they often mention is with regard to labeling. Sometimes, they have to fill out forms that ask them to indicate a racial/ethnic identity. They don't want to check just one identity because that would deny the other part of themselves (Shih & Sanchez, 2005). The U.S. Census form now permits an individual to check more than one category.

CONCEPT CHECK

21. In what way is biracialism similar to biculturalism? (Check your answer on page 198.)

The Family

In early childhood our parents and other relatives are the most important people in our lives. How do those early family experiences mold our personality and social behavior?

Birth Order and Family Size

You have no doubt heard people say that firstborn children are more successful in schoolwork and career accomplishments than later-borns. Firstborns also rate themselves as more ambitious, honest, and conscientious (e.g., Paulhus, Trapnell, & Chen, 1999). On the other hand, later-born children are said to be

more popular, more independent, less conforming, less neurotic, and possibly more creative.

Those generalizations are based on many studies, but most of them used flawed research methods (Ernst & Angst, 1983; Schooler, 1972). The simplest and most common way to do the research is this: You ask some large number of people to tell you their birth order and something else about themselves, such as their grade point average in school. Then you measure the correlation between the measurements. Do you see any possible problem here?

The problem is that many firstborns come from families with only one child, whereas later-born children necessarily come from larger families. On the average, highly educated and ambitious parents are more likely to have only one child and provide that child with many advantages. Therefore, what appears to be a difference between first- and later-born children could be a difference between small and large families (Rodgers, 2001).

A better research method is to compare first- and second-born children in families with at least two children, first- and third-born children in families with at least three children, and so forth. Figure 5.29 shows the results of one such study. As you can see, the average IQ is higher in small families than in large families. However, within a family of any given size, firstborns do about the same as later-borns on the average (Rodgers, Cleveland, van den Oord, & Rowe, 2000).

"But wait," you say. "The firstborn in my family does act different from the others, and most of the people I know see the same pattern in their own families." In a sense you are right: The firstborn takes

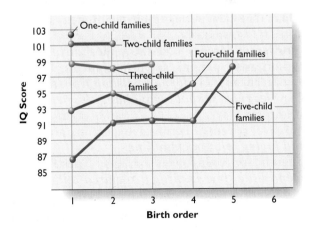

FIGURE 5.29 Children from small families tend to score higher on IQ tests than children from large families. However, within a family of a given size, birth order is not related to IQ. If we combine results for families of different sizes, firstborns have a higher mean score but only because many of them come from small families. *(From "Resolving the Debate Over Birth Order, Family Size, and Intelligence" by J. L. Rodgers, American Psychologist, 55(6), 2000, 599–612. Copyright © 2000 by the American Psychological Association. Adapted by permission of the author.)*

more responsibility, identifies more with the parents, bosses the younger children around, and in many other ways, acts differently from the later-born children *while at home*. However, the way people act at home is not necessarily the way they act among friends at school (Harris, 2000).

 CONCEPT CHECK

22. Suppose someone found that last-born children (those with no younger brothers or sisters) do better in school than second-to-last-borns. What would be one likely explanation? (Check your answer on page 198.)

Effects of Parenting Styles

If and when you have children of your own, will you be loving and kind or strict and distant? Will you give the children everything they want or make them work for rewards? Will you encourage their independence or enforce restrictions? Moreover, how much does your behavior matter?

Psychologists have done a great deal of research comparing parenting styles to the behavior and personality of the children. Much of this research is based on four parenting styles described by Diana Baumrind (1971):

Authoritative parents: These parents *set high standards and impose controls, but they are also warm and responsive to the child's communications.* They set limits but adjust them when appropriate. They encourage their children to strive toward their own goals.

Authoritarian parents: Like the authoritative parents, authoritarian parents set firm controls, but they tend to be *emotionally more distant from the child. They set rules without explaining the reasons behind them.*

Permissive parents: Permissive parents are *warm and loving but undemanding.*

Indifferent or uninvolved parents: These parents *spend little time with their children and do little more than provide them with food and shelter.*

Parenting styles are reasonably consistent within a family. For example, most parents who are permissive with one child are permissive with the others too (Holden & Miller, 1999). The research has found small but reasonably consistent links between parenting style and children's behavior. For example, most children of authoritative parents are self-reliant, cooperate with others, and do well in school. Children of authoritarian parents tend to be law-abiding but

distrustful and not very independent. Children of permissive parents are often socially irresponsible. Children of indifferent parents tend to be impulsive and undisciplined.

However, the interpretation of results is not as easy as it may appear. Many psychologists have drawn cause-and-effect conclusions—for example, assuming that parental indifference *leads to* impulsive, out-of-control children. However, as Judith Rich Harris (1998) pointed out, other explanations are possible. Maybe impulsive, hard-to-control children cause their parents to withdraw into indifference. Or maybe the parents and children share genes that lead to uncooperative behaviors. Similarly, the kindly behaviors of authoritative parents could encourage well-mannered behaviors in their children, but it is also possible that these children were well behaved from the start, thereby encouraging kindly, understanding behaviors in their parents.

A better approach is to study adopted children, who are genetically unrelated to the parents rearing them. One study of adult twins who had been adopted by separate families found that the parenting style described by one twin correlated significantly with the parenting style described by the other twin, especially for pairs of monozygotic twins (Krueger, Markon, & Bouchard, 2003). That is, if one twin reported being reared by kindly, understanding adoptive parents, the other usually did also. The reason is that the twins themselves had similar personalities, which affected their adopting parents, as well as affecting the twins' perceptions of their environments.

If we examine long-term personality traits of adopted children and their adopting parents, the results surprise most people: The personalities of the children correlate almost zero with the personalities of the parents (Heath, Neale, Kessler, Eaves, & Kendler, 1992; Loehlin, 1992; Viken, Rose, Kaprio, & Koskenvuo, 1994). For this reason Harris (1995, 1998) has argued that family life has little influence on most aspects of personality, except for what people do specifically at home. Much personality variation depends on genetic differences, and the rest of the variation, she argues, depends mostly on peer influences—that is, the other children in the neighborhood. If a researcher picks two children at random from the same classroom, they are more likely than children from different schools to resemble each other in a wide variety of behaviors (Rose et al., 2003). In short, peer influences are strong. For more information visit this Web site: **home.att.net/~xchar/tna/.**

As you can imagine, not everyone happily accepted Harris's conclusion. Psychologists who had spent a career studying parenting styles were not pleased to be told that their results were inconclusive. Parents were not pleased to be told that they had little influence on their children's personalities. Harris (2000), however, chose her words carefully. She did not say that it makes no difference how you treat your children. For one thing, obviously, if you treat your children badly, they won't like you!

Also, parents control where the children live and therefore influence their choice of peers, and parents influence some aspects of life that peers usually don't care about, such as religion and music lessons. Psychologists using improved research methods have shown real, though not huge, effects of parenting style (Collins, Maccoby, Steinberg, Hetherington, & Bornstein, 2000). For example, the quality of parenting is especially important for high-risk children, such as adopted children who spent the first few months of life in low-quality orphanages (Stams, Juffer, & van IJzendoorn, 2002). Parents do not have as much control over their children's psychological development as psychologists once assumed, but their effect is important nevertheless.

 CONCEPT CHECK

23. Why is a correlation between parents' behavior and children's behavior inconclusive concerning how parents influence their children? Why would a correlation between adoptive parents' behavior and that of their adopted children provide more useful information? (Check your answers on page 198.)

Parental Employment and Child Care

What is the normal way to rear infants and young children? The customs vary so widely that "normal" has no clear meaning. In many subsistence cultures, a mother returns to her usual tasks of gathering food and so forth shortly after giving birth, leaving her infant most of the day with other women, relatives, and older children (McGurk, Caplan, Hennessy, & Moss, 1993). In the Efe culture of Africa, a mother stays with her infant only about half of the day, although the infant is seldom alone. Within the first few months, the infant establishes strong attachments to several adults and children (Tronick, Morelli, & Ivey, 1992).

In many cultures it has long been the custom for a mother to leave her infant for much of the day with friends, relatives, and other children.

Still, many psychologists in Europe and North America had maintained that healthy emotional development required an infant to establish a strong attachment to a single caregiver—ordinarily, the mother. When more and more families began placing infants in day care so that both parents could return to work shortly after their infant's birth, a question arose about the psychological effects on those children.

Many studies compared children who stayed with their mothers and those who entered day care within their first year or two of life. The studies examined attachment (as measured by the Strange Situation or in other ways), adjustment and well-being, play with other children, social relations with adults, and intellectual development. The results were that most children develop satisfactorily, both intellectually and socially, if they receive adequate day care (Scarr, 1998). The quality of the day care is more important than the quantity. However, quantity does make a small difference also. If both parents return to work full time within the first year of an infant's life, the child later shows a slightly increased probability of problem behaviors toward both children and adults (Hill, Waldfogel, Brooks-Gunn, & Han, 2005; NICHD Early Child Care Research Network, 2006). As always, we cannot be sure about cause and effect from data such as these. Perhaps the families that use full-time day care in the first year are different from other families in additional ways that influence the results.

Older children are less affected, and perhaps positively affected, by having both parents employed. One longitudinal study of 2,402 low-income families examined preschoolers and older children before and after their mothers took jobs. The preschoolers showed no behavioral changes, and the older children showed slight benefits in some aspects of adjustment (Chase-Lansdale et al., 2003).

Nontraditional Families

Western society has considered a traditional family to be a mother, a father, and their children. A nontraditional family is, therefore, anything else. Psychologists have compared children reared by single mothers to those reared by a father and mother. On the average single mothers are more likely to have financial difficulties, and many are undergoing the emotional trauma of divorce. However, if we limit our attention to single mothers with good incomes and no recent divorce, their children show normal social and emotional development compared to those in two-parent homes (MacCallum & Golombek, 2004; Weissman, Leaf, & Bruce, 1987). Children reared by gay and lesbian parents also develop about the same as those reared by heterosexuals in terms of social and emotional development, psychological adjustment, and romantic relationships (Golombok et al., 2003; MacCallum & Golombok, 2004; Patterson, 1994; Silverstein & Auerbach, 1999; Wainright, Russell, & Patterson, 2004).

However, we should be cautious about our conclusions. The studies failing to find significant differences between children reared in traditional and nontraditional families have examined small numbers of children and have measured only limited aspects of behavior (Redding, 2001). At most we can say that being reared by a single parent or by gays or lesbians does not produce a big enough effect to be evident in small samples of people. We need more research before dismissing the possibility of any effect at all.

Parental Conflict and Divorce

In an earlier era, people in the United States considered divorce shameful. Political commentators attrib- uted Adlai Stevenson's defeat in the presidential campaign of 1952 to the fact that he was divorced. Americans would never vote for a divorced candidate, the commentators said. By 1980, when Ronald Reagan was elected president, voters hardly noticed his divorce and remarriage.

Most children who experience the divorce of their parents show a variety of academic, social, and emotional problems compared to other children. One reason is that these children receive less attention and suffer economic hardship. Also, many children in divorced families endure prolonged hostility between their parents (Amato & Keith, 1991). If the divorce takes place while the children are too young to realize what is happening, the effects are milder (Tschann, Johnston, Kline, & Wallerstein, 1990).

Mavis Hetherington and her associates conducted longitudinal studies of middle-class children and their families following a divorce (Hetherington, 1989). Compared to children in intact families, those in divorced families showed more conflicts with their parents and other children. They pouted and sought attention, especially in the first year after a divorce. The boys in particular became aggressive, both at home and at school. Distress was increased if a mother who had not worked before the divorce took a job immediately afterward—often by economic necessity.

In families where the mother remarried, the daughters were often indifferent or hostile to the stepfather and showed poorer adjustment than children of mothers who did not remarry (Hetherington, Bridges,

Many children today are reared by a single parent. Some are reared by gay parents. The research indicates that who rears the child has little influence on long-term personality development if the caregivers are loving and dependable.

Many sons of divorced parents go through a period when they act out their frustrations by starting fights.

& Insabella, 1998). Many of the girls rejected every attempt by their stepfathers to establish a positive relationship until eventually the stepfather gave up (Hetherington, 1989).

Hetherington's studies concentrated on White middle-class children, and the results differ for other cultures. Divorce is more common in Black families, but in most regards divorced Black women adjust better than White women do (McKelvey & McKenry, 2000). Many Black families ease the burden of single parenthood by having a grandmother or other relative help with child care. As in any other families, the more upset the mother is by the divorce, the more upset the children are likely to be (R. T. Phillips & Alcebo, 1986).

Exceptions occur to almost any generalization about the effects of divorce on children (Hetherington, Stanley-Hagan, & Anderson, 1989). Some children remain distressed for years, whereas others recover quickly. A few seem to do well at first but become more distressed later. Other children are resilient throughout their parents' divorce and afterward. They keep their friends, do all right in school, and maintain good relationships with both parents. In fact even some children who are seriously maltreated or abused develop far better than one might expect (Caspi et al., 2002).

Given the emotional difficulty associated with divorce, should parents stay together for the children's sake? Not necessarily. Children do not fare well if their parents are constantly fighting. For example, children who observe much conflict between their parents tend to be nervous, unable to sleep through the night (El-Sheikh, Buckhalt, Mize, & Acebo, 2006), and prone to violent and disruptive behaviors (Sternberg, Baradaran, Abbott, Lamb, & Guterman, 2006).

CONCEPT CHECK

24. You may hear someone say that the right way to rear children is with both a mother and a father. Based on the evidence, what would be a good reply? (Check your answer on page 198.)

IN CLOSING

Many Ways of Life

This module began with the question of how you would have been different if you had been born into a different gender, ethnic group, or family. In some ways it is obvious that the differences would have been drastic. You would have had different friends, different activities, and different experiences with sexism and racism. However, most of the research described in this module indicates that your intellect and many aspects of your personality would have been about the same. Our group identities affect us enormously in some regards and much less in others. ∎

Summary

- *Gender influences.* Women tend to do better than men on certain aspects of language, whereas men tend to solve spatial problems better. Men and women differ in miscellaneous other regards also. However, in most aspects of personality and intellect, the gender differences are close to zero. (page 190)
- *Androgyny.* Psychologists have proposed that people should benefit from androgyny, the ability to alternate between masculine and feminine traits. However, so far the demonstrated benefits of androgyny seem to be the sum of the benefits of masculinity and femininity. (page 191)
- *Ethnic and cultural differences.* Being a member of an ethnic minority raises special issues for identity development. Immigrant children have special difficulties as they try to participate in two cultures. However, bicultural children also have some advantages, as do biracial children. (page 192)
- *Birth order.* Most studies comparing firstborn versus later-born children do not separate the effects of birth order from the effects of family size. If we disregard families with only one child, most differences are small between firstborns and later-borns. (page 193)
- *Parenting styles.* Parenting style correlates with the behavior of the children. For example, caring, understanding parents tend to have well-behaved chil-

dren. However, children affect the parents as much as parents affect the children. Also, within biological families, children's behavior can correlate with parenting style because of genetic influences. (page 194)

• *Nontraditional child care.* A child's normal personality and social development require at least one caring adult, but the number of caregivers and their gender and sexual orientation apparently matter little. (page 195)

• *Effects of divorce.* Children of divorced parents often show signs of distress, but the results vary across families and over time. (page 196)

Answers to Concept Checks

20. Androgyny is defined as being above average on both favorable masculine traits and favorable feminine traits. It's obvious that the sum of two sets of favorable traits should be favorable. The important question is whether androgyny provides any benefit that goes beyond the sum of masculine and feminine. (page 191)

21. A bicultural person identifies to some extent with two cultures. A biracial person has two kinds of ethnic background and identifies to some extent with each. (page 193)

22. An only child is a last-born as well as a firstborn. A large sample of last-borns will include many children from single-child families, which are often characterized by high IQ and ambitions. Second-to-last-borns necessarily come from larger families. (page 193)

23. Children can resemble their parents' behavior because of either genetics or social influences. Adoptive children do not necessarily resemble their adopted parents genetically, so any similarity in behavior would reflect environmental influences. Of course, the question would remain as to whether the parents influenced the children or the children influenced the parents. (page 194)

24. According to the evidence so far, children reared by a single parent, divorced parents, or a gay couple develop about normally. (page 195)

CHAPTER ENDING

Key Terms and Activities

Key Terms

You can check the page listed for a complete description of a term. You can also check the glossary/index at the end of the text for a definition of a given term, or you can download a list of all the terms and their definitions for any chapter at this website:

www.thomsonedu.com/
psychology/kalat

accommodation (page 169)
androgyny (page 191)
assimilation (page 169)
attachment (page 183)
authoritarian parents (page 194)
authoritative parents (page 194)
biculturalism (page 192)
chromosome (page 153)
cohort (page 168)
conservation (page 176)
cross-sectional study (page 166)
dishabituation (page 165)
dizygotic twins (page 156)
dominant (page 154)
egocentric (page 172)

equilibration (page 169)
evolution (page 159)
fetal alcohol syndrome (page 161)
fetus (page 160)
gene (page 153)
habituation (page 165)
heritability (page 155)
identity achievement (page 186)
identity crisis (page 186)
identity diffusion (page 186)
identity foreclosure (page 186)
identity moratorium (page 186)
indifferent or uninvolved parents (page 194)
interaction (page 158)
longitudinal study (page 167)
midlife transition (page 187)
monozygotic twins (page 156)
multiplier effect (page 155)
object permanence (page 170)
operation (page 172)
permissive parents (page 194)
phenylketonuria (PKU) (page 159)
preoperational stage (page 172)

recessive (page 154)
schema (pl. schemata) (page 169)
selective attrition (page 167)
sensorimotor stage (page 170)
sequential design (page 167)
sex chromosomes (page 154)
sex-limited gene (page 155)
sex-linked (or X-linked) gene (page 155)
sex roles (page 191)
stage of concrete operations (page 177)
stage of formal operations (page 177)
Strange Situation (page 183)
temperament (page 158)
terror-management theory (page 189)
theory of mind (page 173)
X chromosome (page 154)
Y chromosome (page 154)
zone of proximal development (page 178)
zygote (page 160)

Suggestions for Further Reading

Twenge, J. M. (2006). *Generation Me.* New York: Free Press. Provocative description of generational differences, especially the effects on today's young adults.

Web/Technology Resources

Student Companion Website

www.thomsonedu.com/psychology/kalat

Explore the Student Companion Website for Online Try-It-Yourself activities, practice quizzes, flashcards, and more! The companion site also has direct links to the following websites.

Human Genome Project

www.ornl.gov/TechResources/Human_Genome/home.html

This is the definitive site for understanding the Human Genome Project, from the basic science to ethical, legal, and social considerations to the latest discoveries.

The Child Psychologist

www.childpsychology.com/

Rene Thomas Folse's site focuses on children with disorders or other causes for concern.

American Academy of Child & Adolescent Psychiatry

http://www.aacap.org

Check this site for information about common psychological disorders of children and teenagers.

The Nurture Assumption

home.att.net/~xchar/tna/

Judith Rich Harris maintains this Web page about her controversial book on the importance of peers and the relative unimportance of parenting styles.

The Child Artist Grown Up

www.robinka.com

Did you like Robin Kalat's drawing at the start of Module 5.2? Check out her adult art at this site.

For Additional Study

Kalat Premium Website

http://www.thomsonedu.com

For Critical Thinking Videos and additional Online Try-It-Yourself activities, go to this site to enter or purchase your code for the Kalat Premium Website.

ThomsonNOW!

http://www.thomsonedu.com

Go to this site for the link to ThomsonNOW, your one-stop study shop. Take a Pretest for this chapter, and Thomson-NOW will generate a personalized Study Plan based on your test reults. The Study Plan will identify the topics you need to review and direct you to online resources to help you master those topics. You can then take a Posttest to help you determine the concepts you have mastered and what you still need to work on.

Learning

Consider a toaster. You might adjust the settings on your toaster each day because you like your bread toasted medium, your English muffins a little lighter, and your bagels a little darker. Your sister readjusts the settings because she likes her bagels and English muffins light but her toast dark. Now imagine a toaster that could learn. You no longer need to change the settings because the toaster recognizes who is using it and the type of bread and adjusts its own settings.

Some machines, such as this chess computer, can learn. Similarly, animals long ago evolved the ability to alter their behavior based on experience.

Early in the evolution of life on Earth, animals must have been simple machines like today's toasters. The only way to change behavior was to alter their internal machinery through slow processes of evolution. At some point animals evolved the ability to learn. When circumstances changed, they could readjust quickly. The amazing process of learning provides enormous advantages.

Psychologists have devoted an enormous amount of research to learning, and in the process they developed and refined research methods that they now routinely apply in other areas of psychological investigation. This chapter is about the procedures that change behavior—why you lick your lips at the sight of tasty food, why you turn away from a food that once made you sick, why you get nervous if a police car starts to follow you, and why you shudder at the sight of someone charging toward you with a knife. In chapter 7 we proceed to the topic of memory. Obviously, any change in behavior implies some sort of memory, and any memory implies previous learning. Still, the study of learning is based on a different research tradition from that of memory.

Behaviorism

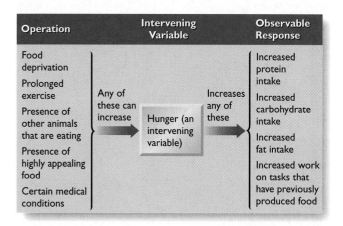

- *How and why did the behaviorist viewpoint arise?*
- *What is its enduring message?*

When you drop an object, why does it fall? In ancient times people said it falls because the ground is its natural resting place. It falls because it wants to be on the ground. Why is the water level about equal throughout a lake? According to the ancients, it is because nature abhors a vacuum. If a gap started to occur anywhere on the lake, water would rush in to prevent a vacuum.

Physicists of today do not talk about objects wanting to be on the ground or about nature abhorring a vacuum. Instead, they explain observations in terms of natural processes such as gravity and the motion of molecules. Beginning in the late 1800s, biologists and psychologists began applying the same approach to behavior. Instead of talking about what a dog, rat, or person thinks and wants, they sought to understand the natural mechanisms behind the behavior.

For example, consider this example of animal behavior: On one island off the coast of Florida, huge colonies of pelicans nest in trees right above equally huge colonies of cottonmouth snakes—so huge, in fact, that few humans will venture anywhere near the area. Why do the pelicans and snakes live so close together? When the pelicans feed fish to their young, they often drop pieces. The snakes lie there waiting for pieces of fish to rain from the sky. They get more food that way than they could by hunting for themselves. What's in the deal for the pelicans? The snakes scare away raccoons and other predators that might attack the pelicans or their eggs (Pennisi, 2004). (The cottonmouths are no threat to pelicans because they don't climb trees.) Now, have either the pelicans or the snakes chosen this strategy intelligently? Do they even understand the advantages of what they are doing?

Most psychologists who study animal learning and behavior seek simple explanations, such as trial-and-error learning, that do not require us to assume complicated mental processes. The **behaviorists,** who have dominated the study of animal learning, *insist that psychologists should study only observable, measurable behaviors, not mental processes.* Behaviorists seek the simplest possible explanation for any behavior and resist interpretations in terms of understanding or insight. At least, they insist, we should exhaust attempts at simple explanations before we adopt more complex ones. You will recognize this idea as the principle of parsimony from chapter 2.

The term *behaviorist* applies to theorists and researchers with quite a range of views (O'Donohue & Kitchener, 1999). Two major categories are *methodological behaviorists* and *radical behaviorists.* **Methodological behaviorists** *study only the events that they can measure and observe*—in other words the environment and the individual's actions—*but they sometimes use those observations to infer internal events* (Day & Moore, 1995). For example, depriving an animal of food, presenting it with very appealing food, or making it exercise increases the probability that the animal will eat, work for food, and so forth. From such observations a psychologist can infer an **intervening variable,** *something that we cannot directly observe but that links a variety of procedures to a variety of possible responses.* In this case the intervening variable is *hunger:*

Operation	Intervening Variable	Observable Response
Food deprivation Prolonged exercise Presence of other animals that are eating Presence of highly appealing food Certain medical conditions	Any of these can increase → Hunger (an intervening variable) → Increases any of these	Increased protein intake Increased carbohydrate intake Increased fat intake Increased work on tasks that have previously produced food

Similarly, one could use other observations to infer intervening variables such as thirst, sex drive, anger, and fear. We infer any of these intervening variables from behavior and never observe them directly. A methodological behaviorist will use such terms only after anchoring them firmly to observable procedures and responses—that is, after giving them a clear operational definition (as discussed in chapter 2). Many psychological researchers are methodological behaviorists, even if they do not use that term.

CRITICAL THINKING
A STEP FURTHER

Intervening Variables

Choose an intervening variable, such as fear or anger, and describe what measurements you could use to infer it. In the process do you establish an operational definition?

Radical behaviorists do not deny that private events such as hunger or fear exist. The distinguishing feature of radical behaviorists is that they *deny that hunger, fear, or any other internal, private event causes behavior* (Moore, 1995). For example, they maintain, if food deprivation leads to hunger and hunger leads to eating, why not just say that food deprivation leads to eating? What do we gain by introducing the word *hunger*? According to radical behaviorists, any internal state is caused by an event in the environment (or by the individual's genetics); therefore, the ultimate cause of any behavior lies in the observable events that led up to the behavior, not the internal states.

According to this point of view, discussions of mental events are just sloppy language. For example, as B. F. Skinner (1990) argued, when you say, "I *intend* to . . . ," what you really mean is "I am about to . . ." or "In situations like this, I usually . . ." or "This behavior is in the preliminary stages of happen-

ing . . . ." That is, any statement about mental experiences can be converted into a description of behavior.

CONCEPT CHECK

1. How does a radical behaviorist differ from a methodological behaviorist? (Check your answer on page 206.)

The Rise of Behaviorism

We should understand behaviorism within the historical context in which it arose. During the early 1900s, one highly influential group within psychology, the *structuralists* (see chapter 1), studied people's thoughts, ideas, and sensations by asking people to describe them. Behaviorists protested that it is useless to ask people to report their own private experiences. For example, if someone says, "My idea of roundness is stronger than my idea of color," we cannot check the accuracy of the report. We are not even certain what it means. If psychology is to be a scientific enterprise, behaviorists insisted, it must deal with observable, measurable events—that is, behavior and its relation to the environment.

Some behaviorists went to extremes to avoid any mention of mental processes. Jacques Loeb (1918/1973) argued that much of animal behavior, and perhaps human behavior as well, could be described in terms of simple responses to simple stimuli—for example, approaching light, turning away from strong smells, clinging to hard surfaces, walking toward or away from moisture, and so forth (see Figure 6.1). Complex behavior, he surmised, is the result of adding together many changes of speed and direction elicited by various stimuli. Loeb's view of behavior was an example of **stimulus–response psychology,** *the attempt to explain behavior in terms of how each stimulus triggers a response.*

Although the term *stimulus–response psychology* was appropriate for Loeb, it is a misleading description of today's behaviorists. Behaviorists believe that behavior is a product of not only the current stimuli but also the individual's history of stimuli and responses and their outcomes, plus the internal state of the organism, such as wakefulness or sleepiness (Staddon, 1999).

If behaviorists are to deal successfully with complex behaviors, the greatest challenge is to explain changes in behavior. The behaviorist movement became the heir to a tradition of animal learning research that began for other reasons. Charles Darwin's theory of evolution by natural selection inspired many early psychologists to study animal learning and intelligence (Dewsbury, 2000b). At first they were interested in

Behaviorists agree that all psychological investigations should be based on behavioral observations. A methodological behaviorist might observe facial expressions to make inferences about sadness. A radical behaviorist, however, would study the facial expressions and the events leading to them, without inferring internal processes.

© Owen Franken/CORBIS

comparing the intelligence of various species. By about 1930, however, most had lost interest in that topic because it seemed unanswerable. (A species that seems more intelligent on one task can be less intelligent on another.) Nevertheless, the behaviorists carried forth the tradition of experiments on animal learning, although they asked different questions.

If nonhumans learn in more or less the same way as humans do, behaviorists reasoned, then it should be possible to discover the basic laws of learning by studying the behavior of a convenient laboratory animal, such as a pigeon or a rat. This enterprise was ambitious and optimistic; its goal was no less than to determine the basic laws of behavior, analogous to the laws of physics. Most of the rest of this chapter will deal with behaviorists' research about learning.

▌ Behaviorists emphasize the role of experience in determining our actions—both our current experience and our past experiences in similar situations.

The Assumptions of Behaviorism

Behaviorists make several assumptions, including determinism, the ineffectiveness of mental explanations, and the power of the environment to select behaviors (Moore, 1995). Let's consider each of these points.

FIGURE 6.1 Jacques Loeb, an early student of animal behavior, argued that much or all of invertebrate behavior could be described as responses to simple stimuli, such as approaching light, turning away from light, or moving opposite to the direction of gravity.

Determinism

Behaviorists assume that we live in a universe of cause and effect; that is, they accept the idea of *determinism* as described in chapter 1. Given that our behavior is part of the universe, it too must have causes that we can study scientifically. Behavior must follow laws, such as "animals deprived of food will increase the rates of behaviors that lead to food." The goal of behaviorism is to determine more and more detailed laws of behavior.

The Ineffectiveness of Mental Explanations

In everyday life we commonly refer to our motivations, emotions, and mental state. However, behaviorists insist that such statements explain nothing:

Q: Why did she yell at that man?
A: She yelled because she was angry.
Q: How do you know she was angry?
A: We know she was angry because she was yelling.

Here, the reference to mental states lured us into circular reasoning. Behaviorists, especially radical behaviorists, avoid mental terms as much as possible. B. F. Skinner, the most famous and influential behaviorist, resisted using even apparently harmless words such as *hide* because they imply an intention (L. D. Smith, 1995). Skinner preferred simply to describe what the individuals *did* instead of inferring what they were *trying* to do.

The same insistence on description is central to the British and American legal systems: A witness is asked, "What did you see and hear?" An acceptable answer would be, "The defendant was sweating and trembling, and his voice was wavering." A witness should not say, "The defendant was nervous and worried," because that statement requires an inference that the witness is not entitled to make. (Of course, the jury might draw an inference.)

The Power of the Environment to Mold Behavior

Behaviors produce outcomes. Eating your carrots has one kind of outcome; insulting your roommate has another. The outcome determines how often the behavior will occur in the future. In effect our environment selects successful behaviors, much as evolution selects successful animals.

Behaviorists have been accused of believing that the environment controls practically all aspects of behavior. The most extreme statement of environmental determinism came from John B. Watson, one of the founders of behaviorism, who said,

> Give me a dozen healthy infants, well-formed, and my own specified world to bring them up in and I'll guarantee to take any one at random and train him to become any type of specialist I might select—doctor, lawyer, artist, merchant-chief, and yes, even beggar-man thief—regardless of his talents, penchants, tendencies, abilities, vocations, and race of his ancestors. I am going beyond my facts and I admit it, but so have the advocates of the contrary. (1925, p. 82)

Today, few psychologists would claim that variations in behavior depend entirely on the environment (or that they depend entirely on heredity, for that matter). Although behaviorists do not deny the importance of heredity, they generally emphasize how the environment selects one behavior over another, and their explanations of individual differences concentrate on people's different learning histories.

 CONCEPT CHECK

2. Why do behaviorists reject explanations in terms of thoughts? (Check your answer on this page.)

IN CLOSING

Behaviorism as a Theoretical Orientation

Many students dismiss behaviorism because, at least at first glance, it seems so ridiculous: "What do you *mean,* my thoughts and beliefs and emotions don't cause my behavior?!" The behaviorists' reply is, "Exactly right. Your thoughts and other internal states do not cause your behavior because events in your present and past environment caused your thoughts. The events that caused the thoughts are therefore the real causes of your behavior, and psychologists should spend their time trying to understand the influence of the events, not trying to analyze your thoughts." Don't be too quick to agree or disagree. Just contemplate this: If you believe that your thoughts or other internal states cause behaviors *independently* of your previous experiences, what evidence could you provide to support your claim? ∎

Summary

- *Methodological and radical behaviorists.* Behaviorists insist that psychologists should study behaviors and their relation to observable features of the environment. Methodological behaviorists use these observations to draw inferences about internal states. Radical behaviorists insist that internal states are of little scientific use and that they do not control behavior. The causes of the internal states themselves, as well as of the behaviors, lie in the environment. (page 203)
- *The origins of behaviorism.* Behaviorism began as a protest against structuralists, who asked people to describe their own mental processes. Behaviorists insisted that the structuralist approach was futile and that psychologists should study observable behaviors. (page 204)
- *Behaviorists' interest in learning.* Before the rise of the behaviorist movement, other psychologists had studied animal intelligence. Behaviorists adapted some of the methods used in previous studies but changed the questions, concentrating on the basic mechanisms of learning. (page 204)
- *Behaviorists' assumptions.* Behaviorists assume that all behaviors have causes (determinism), that mental explanations are unhelpful, and that the environment acts to select effective behaviors and suppress ineffective ones. (page 205)

Answers to Concept Checks

1. All behaviorists insist that conclusions must be based on measurements or observations of behavior. However, a methodological behaviorist will sometimes use behavioral observations to make inferences about motivations or other internal states. A radical behaviorist avoids discussion of internal events as much as possible and insists that internal events are never the cause of behavior. (page 204)

2. We cannot directly observe or measure thoughts or other internal events. We infer them from observed behaviors, and therefore, it is circular to use them as an explanation of behavior. (page 206)

Classical Conditioning

- *When we learn a relationship between two stimuli, what happens?*

You are sitting in your room when your roommate flicks a switch on the stereo. Your experience has been that the stereo is set to a deafening level. You flinch not because of the soft flicking sound of the switch itself but because of the loud noise it predicts.

You are driving on the highway when you see a car behind you with flashing lights. You get a sinking feeling in your stomach because you recognize the lights as the sign of a police car.

Many aspects of our behavior consist of learned responses to signals. We respond to what a signal means, what it predicts. However, even apparently simple responses to simple stimuli no longer seem as simple as they once did. Psychologists' efforts to understand learning have led them to conduct thousands of experiments on both humans and nonhumans.

For certain kinds of learning, such as birdsong learning, the results depend heavily on which species is studied, but for many other kinds of learning, the similarities among species are more impressive than the differences. Often, it is easier to study nonhumans because a researcher can better control all the variables likely to influence performance.

Pavlov and Classical Conditioning

In the late 1800s and early 1900s, behaviorism was becoming a dominant force within psychology. Researchers sought simple, mechanical explanations to displace what they considered unscientific accounts of thoughts, ideas, and other mental processes. The mood of the time was ripe for the theories of Ivan P. Pavlov, a Russian physiologist who had won a Nobel Prize in physiology in 1904 for his research on digestion. As Pavlov continued his digestion re-

search, one day he noticed that a dog would salivate or secrete stomach juices as soon as it saw the lab worker who customarily fed the dogs. Because this secretion undoubtedly depended on the dog's previous experiences, Pavlov called it a "psychological" secretion. He enlisted the help of other specialists, who then discovered that "teasing" a dog with the sight of food produced salivation that was as predictable and automatic as any reflex. Pavlov adopted the term *conditional reflex,* implying that he only *conditionally* (or tentatively) accepted it as a reflex (Todes, 1997). However, the term has usually been translated into English as *conditioned reflex,* and that term is now well established in the literature.

Pavlov's Procedures

Pavlov presumed that animals are born with certain *automatic connections*—called **unconditioned reflexes**—*between a stimulus such as food and a response such as secreting digestive juices.* He conjectured that animals acquire new reflexes by transferring a response from one stimulus to another. For example, if a neutral stimulus (e.g., a buzzer) always precedes food, an animal would respond to the buzzer as it responds to food. The buzzer would begin to elicit digestive secretions.

▌ Ivan P. Pavlov (with the white beard) with students and a dog. Pavlov devised simple principles to describe learned changes in the dog's behavior.

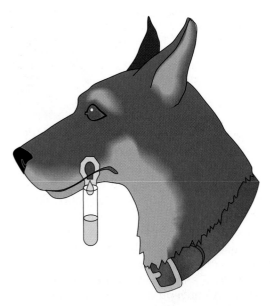

FIGURE 6.2 Pavlov used dogs for his experiments on classical conditioning and salivation. The experimenter rings a buzzer (CS), presents food (UCS), and measures the responses (CR and UCR). Pavlov collected saliva with a simple measuring pouch attached to the dog's cheek.

The *process by which an organism learns a new association between two paired stimuli—a neutral stimulus and one that already evokes a reflexive response*—is known as **classical conditioning,** or **Pavlovian conditioning.** (It is called classical because it has been known and studied for a long time.)

Pavlov used an experimental setup like the one in Figure 6.2 (Goodwin, 1991). First, he selected dogs with a moderate degree of arousal. (Highly excitable dogs would not hold still long enough, and highly inhibited dogs would fall asleep.) Then he attached a tube to one of the salivary ducts in the dog's mouth to measure salivation. He could have measured stomach secretions, but measuring salivation was easier.

Pavlov found that, whenever he gave a dog food, the dog salivated. The food → salivation connection was automatic, requiring no training. Pavlov called food the unconditioned stimulus, and he called salivation the unconditioned response. *If a particular stimulus consistently, automatically elicits a particular response,* we call that stimulus the **unconditioned stimulus (UCS),** and *the response to it* is the **unconditioned response (UCR).**

Next Pavlov introduced a new stimulus, such as a metronome. Upon hearing the metronome, the dog lifted its ears and looked around but did not salivate, so the metronome was a neutral stimulus with regard to salivation. Then Pavlov sounded the metronome a couple of seconds before giving food to the dog. After

a few pairings of the metronome with food, the dog began to salivate as soon as it heard the metronome (Pavlov, 1927/1960).

We call the metronome the **conditioned stimulus (CS)** because the dog's *response to it depends on the preceding conditions*—that is, the pairing of the CS with the UCS. The salivation that follows the metronome is the **conditioned response (CR).** The conditioned response is simply *whatever response the conditioned stimulus begins to elicit as a result of the conditioning (training) procedure.* At the start of the conditioning procedure, the conditioned stimulus does *not* elicit a conditioned response. After conditioning, it does.

In Pavlov's experiment the conditioned response (salivation) closely resembled the unconditioned response (also salivation). However, in some cases it is quite different. For example, the unconditioned response to an electric shock includes shrieking and jumping. The conditioned response to a stimulus paired with shock (i.e., a warning signal for shock) is a tensing of the muscles and lack of activity (e.g., Pezze, Bast, & Feldon, 2003).

To summarize, the *unconditioned stimulus* (UCS), such as food, automatically elicits the *unconditioned response* (UCR), such as salivating. A neutral stimulus, such as a sound, that is paired with the UCS becomes a *conditioned stimulus* (CS). At first this neutral stimulus elicits either no response or an irrelevant response, such as looking around. After some number of pairings of the CS with the UCS, the conditioned stimulus elicits the *conditioned response* (CR), which usually resembles the UCR. The key difference between the CR and UCR is that the CS (conditioned stimulus) elicits the CR (conditioned response) and the UCS (unconditioned stimulus) elicits the UCR (unconditioned response). Figure 6.3 diagrams these relationships.

All else being equal, conditioning occurs more rapidly if the conditioned stimulus is unfamiliar. For example, if you heard a tone many times (followed by nothing) and then started hearing the tone followed by a puff of air to your left eye, you would be slow to show signs of conditioning. Similarly, imagine two people who are bitten by a snake. One has never been near a snake before; the other has spent years tending snakes at the zoo. You can guess which one will develop a fear of snakes.

More Examples of Classical Conditioning

Here are more examples of classical conditioning:

- Your alarm clock makes a faint clicking sound a couple of seconds before the alarm goes off. At first the click by itself does not awaken you, but the

At first,

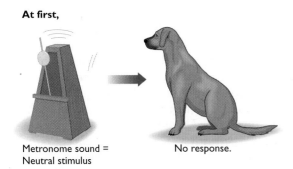

Metronome sound =
Neutral stimulus

No response.

FIGURE 6.3 A conditioned stimulus precedes an unconditioned stimulus. At first the conditioned stimulus elicits no response, and the unconditioned stimulus elicits the unconditioned response. After sufficient pairings the conditioned stimulus begins to elicit the conditioned response, which can resemble the unconditioned response.

During training,

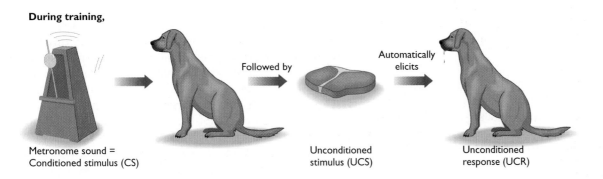

Metronome sound =
Conditioned stimulus (CS)

Followed by

Unconditioned stimulus (UCS)

Automatically elicits

Unconditioned response (UCR)

After some number of repetitions,

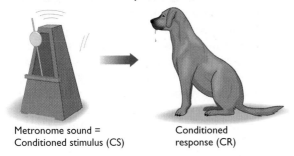

Metronome sound =
Conditioned stimulus (CS)

Conditioned response (CR)

alarm does. After a week or so, you awaken as soon as you hear the click.

Unconditioned stimulus = alarm → Unconditioned response = awakening

Conditioned stimulus = click → Conditioned response = awakening

- You hear the sound of a dentist's drill shortly before the unpleasant experience of the drill on your teeth. From then on the sound of a dentist's drill arouses anxiety.

Unconditioned stimulus = drilling → Unconditioned response = tension

Conditioned stimulus = sound of the drill → Conditioned response = tension

- A nursing mother responds to her baby's cries by putting the baby to her breast, stimulating the flow of milk. After a few days of repetitions, the sound of the baby's cry is enough to start the milk flowing.

Unconditioned stimulus = baby sucking → Unconditioned response = milk flow

Conditioned stimulus = baby's cry → Conditioned response = milk flow

Note the usefulness of classical conditioning in each case: It prepares an individual for likely events. In some cases, however, the effects can be unwelcome. For example, many cancer patients who have had repeated chemotherapy or radiation become nauseated when they approach or even imagine the building where they received treatment (Dadds, Bovbjerg, Redd, & Cutmore, 1997).

Unconditioned stimulus = chemotherapy or radiation → Unconditioned response = nausea

Conditioned stimulus = approaching the building → Conditioned response = nausea

Form an image of a lemon, a nice fresh juicy one. You cut it into slices and then suck on a slice. Imagine that sour taste. As you imagine the lemon, do you notice yourself salivating? If so, your imagination produced enough resemblance to the actual sight and taste of a lemon to serve as a conditioned stimulus.

 CONCEPT CHECK

3. At the start of training, the CS elicits ___ and the UCS elicits ___. After many repetitions of the CS followed by the UCS, the CS elicits ___ and the UCS elicits ___.
4. In this example identify the CS, UCS, CR, and UCR: Every time an army drill sergeant calls out "Ready, aim, fire," the artillery shoots, making a painfully loud sound that causes you to flinch. After a few repetitions, you tense your muscles after the word "fire," before the shot itself. (Check your answers on page 216.)

The Phenomena of Classical Conditioning

Let's start with laboratory studies and later discuss their application to some human experiences. The *process that establishes or strengthens a conditioned response* is known as **acquisition**. Figure 6.4 shows how the strength of a conditioned response increases after pairings of the conditioned and unconditioned stimuli.

Once Pavlov had demonstrated how classical conditioning occurs, curious psychologists wondered what would happen after various changes in the procedures. Their investigations have extended our knowledge of classical conditioning. Here are a few of the main phenomena.

Extinction

Suppose I sound a buzzer and then blow a puff of air into your eyes. After a few repetitions, you will start to close your eyes as soon as you hear the buzzer (Figure 6.5). Now I sound the buzzer repeatedly without the puff of air. What do you do?

You will blink your eyes the first time and perhaps the second and third times, but before long you will stop. This decrease of the conditioned response is called **extinction** (see Figure 6.4). *To extinguish a classically conditioned response, repeatedly present the conditioned stimulus (CS) without the unconditioned stimulus (UCS).* That is, acquisition of a response (CR) occurs when the CS predicts the UCS; extinction occurs when the CS no longer predicts the UCS.

Extinction is not the same as forgetting. Both weaken a learned response, but they arise in different ways. You forget during a long period with no relevant experience or practice. Extinction occurs as the result of a specific experience—perceiving the conditioned stimulus without the unconditioned stimulus.

Extinction does not erase the original connection between the CS and the UCS. We can regard acquisition as learning to do a response and extinction as learning to inhibit it. For example, suppose you have gone through original learning in which a tone regularly predicted a puff of air to your eyes. You learned to blink your eyes at the tone. Then you went through an extinction process in which you heard the tone many times but received no air puffs. You extinguished, so the tone no longer elicited a blink. Now, without hearing a tone, you get another puff of air to your eyes. As a result, the next time you hear the tone, you will blink your eyes. Extinction inhibited your response to the CS (here, the tone), but a sudden puff of air weakens that inhibition (Bouton, 1994).

Spontaneous Recovery

Suppose you are in a classical-conditioning experiment. At first you repeatedly hear a buzzer sound (CS) that precedes a puff of air to your eyes (UCS). Then the buzzer stops predicting an air puff. After a few trials, your response to the buzzer extinguishes. Now, suppose you sit there for a long time with nothing happening and then suddenly you hear another

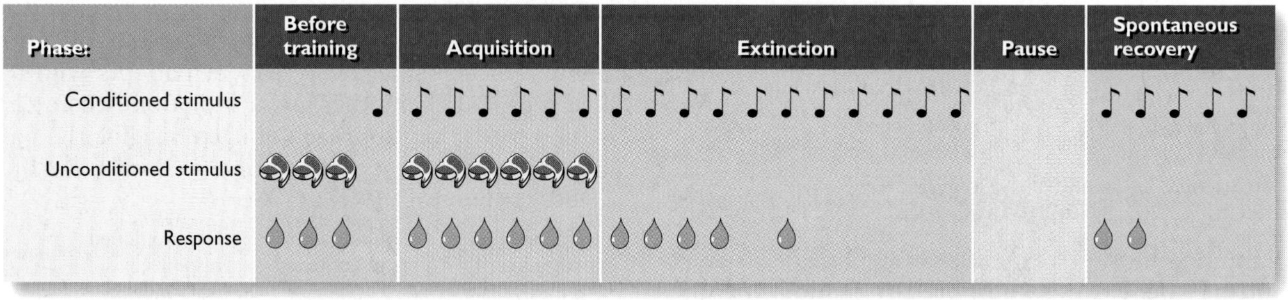

FIGURE 6.4 If the conditioned stimulus regularly precedes the unconditioned stimulus, acquisition occurs. If the conditioned stimulus is presented by itself, extinction occurs. A pause after extinction yields a brief spontaneous recovery.

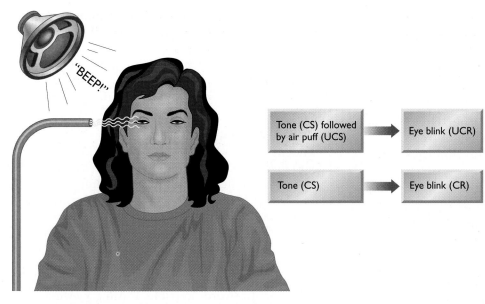

FIGURE 6.5 Classical conditioning of the eye-blink response.

tioned response from the training stimulus to similar stimuli.

This definition may sound pretty straightforward, but psychologists find it difficult to specify exactly what "similar" means (Pearce, 1994). For example, after a bee stings you, you might fear the sound of buzzing bees when you are walking through a forest but not when you hear the same sounds as part of a nature documentary on television. Your response depends on how similar the total configuration of stimuli is to the set on which you were trained, and that similarity is hard to measure.

buzzer sound. What will you do? Chances are, you will blink your eyes at least slightly. **Spontaneous recovery** is *this temporary return of an extinguished response after a delay* (see Figure 6.4). Spontaneous recovery requires no additional CS–UCS pairings.

Why does spontaneous recovery take place? Think of it this way: At first the buzzer predicted a puff of air to your eyes, and then it didn't. You behaved in accordance with the more recent experiences. Hours later, neither experience is much more recent than the other, and the effects of the original acquisition are almost as strong as those of extinction.

 CONCEPT CHECK

5. In Pavlov's experiment on conditioned salivation in response to a buzzer, what procedure could you use to produce extinction? What procedure could you use to produce spontaneous recovery? (Check your answers on page 216.)

Stimulus Generalization

Suppose a bee stings you. You quickly learn to fear bees. Now you see a similar large insect, such as a wasp or hornet. Will you fear that too?

You probably will. However, you probably will not show any fear of ants, fleas, or other insects that don't resemble bees. The more similar is a new stimulus to the conditioned stimulus, the more likely you are to show a similar response (Figure 6.6). **Stimulus generalization** is the *extension of a condi-*

Discrimination

Suppose your alarm clock makes one kind of click when the alarm is about to ring but you hear a different kind of click at other times. You will learn to **discriminate** between these two clicks: You will *respond differently because the two stimuli predicted different outcomes.* You awaken when you hear one click but not when you hear the other. Similarly, you discriminate between a bell that signals time for class to start and a different bell that signals a fire alarm. You might learn to discriminate between a poisonous snake and a similar looking, harmless snake.

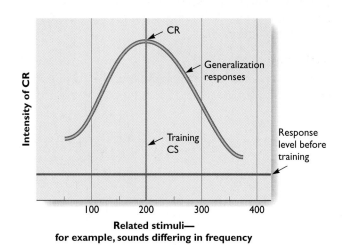

FIGURE 6.6 Stimulus generalization is the process of extending a learned response to new stimuli that resemble the one used in training. A stimulus similar to the training stimulus elicits a strong response; a less similar stimulus elicits a weaker response.

CRITICAL THINKING
A STEP FURTHER

Discrimination

We can easily determine how well human subjects discriminate between two stimuli. We simply ask, "Which note has the higher pitch?" or "Which light is brighter?" How could we determine how well a nonhuman discriminates between two stimuli?

CRITICAL THINKING
WHAT'S THE EVIDENCE?

Emotional Conditioning Without Awareness

In many situations conditioning occurs fastest when people are aware of the connection between the CS and UCS (Knuttinen, Power, Preston, & Disterhoft, 2001). (With laboratory animals, it is hard to ask!) However, emotional responses sometimes become conditioned without awareness. The implications are far-reaching. We shall examine one study in detail. In some ways this discussion will seem out of place: The whole idea of discussing attitudes, emotions, and so forth is contrary to the customs of radical behaviorism. Nevertheless, we see here how other psychologists have taken the idea of classical conditioning and applied it more broadly.

Hypothesis.   People will form favorable attitudes toward items paired with something they like

and unfavorable attitudes toward items paired with something they dislike, even if they are not aware of the connection (Olson & Fazio, 2001).

Method.   Forty-five female college students viewed a series of slides. Most included a Pokemon image, as shown in Figure 6.7, although a few were blank. Most of those with a Pokemon also included another picture or a word. Each student's task was to look for a particular "target" Pokemon and press a computer key whenever she saw it, ignoring all the other pictures and words. Most of the other Pokemon images were paired with neutral words and pictures, but one of them was always paired with something likable (e.g., a picture of tasty food or the word "excellent"), and one was always paired with something negative (e.g., a picture of a cockroach or the word "terrible"). After viewing all the slides repeatedly, each student was asked to look at all the Pokemon images (by themselves) and rate how pleasant or unpleasant they were. They were also asked whether they remembered what other items had paired with each Pokemon.

Results.   On the average the women gave a higher pleasantness rating to the Pokemon that had been associated with favorable words and pictures and lower ratings to the one associated with unfavorable words and pictures. However, they did not remember what words or pictures had been associated with each Pokemon. (They hadn't been told to remember those pairings, and they didn't.)

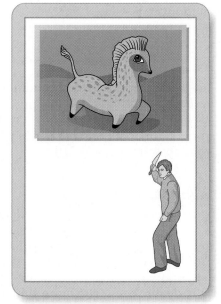

FIGURE 6.7 Each participant pressed a key whenever she saw a particular Pokemon image. Among the others, which she was to ignore, one was always paired with a pleasant word or image, another was always paired with something unpleasant, and the rest were not consistently paired with anything either pleasant or unpleasant.

Interpretation. These results show classical conditioning can alter people's emotional responses to pictures, even though people did not notice them enough to report explicit memories.

Additional research has shown conditioning of other kinds of emotional responses. In one study people saw words paired with pictures of faces, some of which were smiling or frowning. For some of the participants, personally relevant words (their name, their birth date, etc.) were consistently paired with smiling faces. As a result of this pairing, they showed increases in several measures of self-esteem! Evidently, the pairings enhanced emotional responses to reminders of the participants themselves (Baccus, Baldwin, & Packer, 2004).

Drug Tolerance as an Example of Classical Conditioning

Classical conditioning shows up in places you might not expect. One example is **drug tolerance**: *Users of certain drugs experience progressively weaker effects after taking the drugs repeatedly.* Some longtime users inject more heroin or morphine into their veins than it would take to kill a nonuser. Consequently, the users crave larger and larger amounts of the drug.

Drug tolerance results partly from automatic chemical changes that occur in cells throughout the body to counteract the drug's effects (Baker & Tiffany, 1985). It also depends partly on classical conditioning. Consider: When drug users inject themselves with morphine or heroin, the drug injection procedure is a complex stimulus that includes the time and place as well as the needle injection. This total stimulus predicts a second stimulus, the drug's entry into the brain, which triggers a variety of body defenses against its effects—for example, changes in hormone secretions, heart rate, and breathing rate.

First stimulus	→	**Second stimulus**	→	**Automatic response**
(Injection procedure)		(Drug enters brain)		(Body's defenses)

Whenever one stimulus predicts a second stimulus that produces an automatic response, classical conditioning can occur. The first stimulus becomes the CS, the second becomes the UCS, and its response is the UCR. So we can relabel as follows:

Conditioned stimulus	→	**Unconditioned stimulus**	→	**Unconditioned response**
(Injection procedure)		(Drug enters brain)		(Body's defenses)

If conditioning occurs here, what would be the consequences? Suppose the CS (drug injection) produces a CR that resembles the UCR (the body's defenses against the drug). As a result, as soon as the person starts the injection, before the drug enters the body, the body is already mobilizing its defenses against the drug. Therefore, the drug will have less effect—the body develops tolerance. Shepard Siegel (1977, 1983) conducted several experiments to confirm that classical conditioning occurs during drug injections. That is, after many drug injections, the injection procedure by itself evokes the body's antidrug defenses:

Conditioned stimulus	→	**Conditioned response**
(Injection procedure)		(Body's defenses)

One prediction was this: If the injection procedure serves as a conditioned stimulus, then the body's defense reactions should be strongest if the drug is administered in the usual way, in the usual location, with as many familiar stimuli as possible. (The whole experience constitutes the conditioned stimulus.)

The evidence strongly supports this prediction for a variety of drugs (Marin, Perez, Duero, & Ramirez, 1999; Siegel, 1983). For example, a rat that is repeatedly injected with alcohol develops tolerance, improving its balance while intoxicated. But if it is now tested in the presence of loud sounds and strobe lights, its balance suffers. Conversely, if it had practiced its balance while intoxicated in the presence of loud sounds and strobe lights, its balance suffers if it is tested *without* those stimuli (Larson & Siegel, 1998). In short, the tolerance depends on learning.

Why do some people die of a drug overdose that is no larger than the dose they normally tolerate? They probably took the fatal overdose in an unfamiliar setting. For example, someone who is accustomed to taking a drug at home in the evening could suffer a fatal reaction from taking it at a friend's house in the morning. Because the new setting did not serve as a CS, it failed to trigger the usual drug tolerance.

 CONCEPT CHECK

6. When an individual develops tolerance to the effects of a drug injection, what are the conditioned stimulus, the unconditioned stimulus, the conditioned response, and the unconditioned response?

7. Within the classical-conditioning interpretation of drug tolerance, what procedure should extinguish tolerance? (Check your answers on page 216.)

Explanations of Classical Conditioning

What is classical conditioning, really? As is often the case, the process appeared simple at first, but later investigation found it to be a more complex and more interesting phenomenon.

Pavlov noted that conditioning depended on the timing between CS and UCS, as shown here:

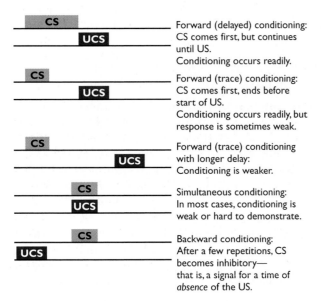

Forward (delayed) conditioning: CS comes first, but continues until US.
Conditioning occurs readily.

Forward (trace) conditioning: CS comes first, ends before start of US.
Conditioning occurs readily, but response is sometimes weak.

Forward (trace) conditioning with longer delay:
Conditioning is weaker.

Simultaneous conditioning:
In most cases, conditioning is weak or hard to demonstrate.

Backward conditioning:
After a few repetitions, CS becomes inhibitory—that is, a signal for a time of *absence* of the US.

In these displays read time left to right. Pavlov surmised that presenting the CS and UCS at nearly the same time caused a connection to grow in the brain so that the animal treated the CS as if it were the UCS. Figure 6.8a illustrates the connections before the start of training: The UCS excites a UCS center in the brain, which immediately stimulates the UCR center. Figure 6.8b illustrates connections that develop during conditioning: Pairing the CS and UCS develops a connection between their brain representations. After this connection develops, the CS excites the CS center, which excites the UCS center, which excites the UCR center and produces a response.

Later studies contradicted that idea. For example, a shock (UCS) causes rats to jump and shriek, but a conditioned stimulus paired with shock makes them freeze in position. They react to the conditioned stimulus as a danger signal, not as if they felt a shock. Also, in delay conditioning, where a delay separates the end of the CS from the start of the UCS, the animal does not make a conditioned response immediately after the conditioned stimulus but instead waits until almost the end of the usual delay between the CS and the UCS. Again, it is not treating the CS as if it were the UCS; it is using it as

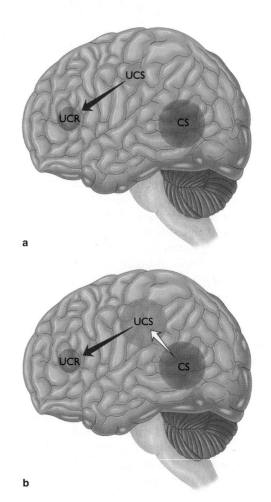

FIGURE 6.8 According to Pavlov, **(a)** at the start of conditioning, activity in the UCS center automatically activates the UCR center. **(b)** After sufficient pairings of the CS and UCS, a connection develops between the CS and UCS centers. Afterward, activity in the CS center flows to the UCS center and therefore excites the UCR center.

a predictor, a way to prepare for the UCS (Gallistel & Gibbon, 2000).

It is true, as Pavlov suggested, that the longer the delay between the CS and the UCS, the weaker the conditioning, other things being equal. However, just having the CS and UCS close together in time is not enough. It is essential that they occur more often together than they occur apart. That is, there must be some contingency or predictability between them. Consider this experiment: For rats in both Group 1 and Group 2, every presentation of a CS is followed by a UCS, as shown in Figure 6.9. However, for Group 2, the UCS also appears at many other times, without the CS. In other words, for this group, the UCS happens every few seconds anyway, and it isn't much more likely with the CS than without it. Group 1 learns a strong response to the CS; Group 2 does not (Rescorla, 1968, 1988).

Group 1

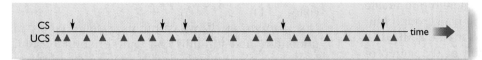

Group 2

FIGURE 6.9 In Rescorla's experiment the CS always preceded the UCS in both groups, but Group 2 received the UCS frequently at other times also. Group 1 developed a strong conditioned response to the CS; Group 2 did not.

 CONCEPT CHECK

8. If classical conditioning depended *entirely* on presenting the CS and UCS at nearly the same time, what result should the experimenters have obtained in Rescorla's experiment? (Check your answer on page 217.)

Now consider this experiment: One group of rats receives a light (CS) followed by shock (UCS) until they respond consistently to the light. (The response is to freeze in place.) Then they get a series of trials with both a light and a tone, again followed by shock. Do they learn a response to the tone? No. The tone always precedes the shock, but the light already predicted the shock, and the tone adds nothing new. The same pattern occurs with the reverse order: First rats learn a response to the tone and then they get light–tone combinations before the shock. They continue responding to the tone, but not to the light, again because the new stimulus predicted nothing that wasn't already predicted (Kamin, 1969) (see Figure 6.10). These results demonstrate the **blocking effect**: *The previously established association to one stimulus blocks the formation of an association to the added stimulus.* Again, it appears that conditioning depends on more than presenting two stimuli together in time. Learning occurs only when one stimulus predicts another. Later research has found that presenting two or more stimuli at a time often produces complex results that we would not have predicted from the results of single-stimulus experiments (Urushihara, Stout, & Miller, 2004).

Group 1

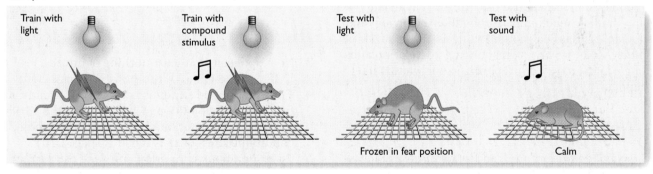

Group 2

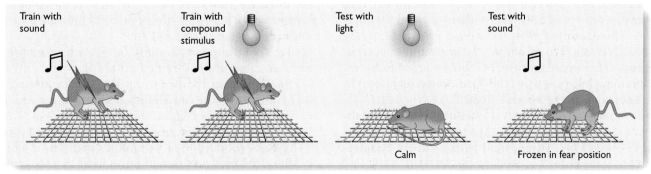

FIGURE 6.10 Each rat first learned to associate either light or sound with shock. Then it received a compound of both light and sound followed by shock. Each rat continued to show a strong response to the old stimulus (which already predicted shock) but little to the new one.

CONCEPT CHECK

9. Suppose you have already learned to flinch when you hear the sound of a dentist's drill. Now your dentist turns on some soothing background music at the same time as the drill. The background music is paired with the pain just as much as the drill sound is. Will you learn to flinch at the sound of that background music? (Check your answer on page 217.)

IN CLOSING

Classical Conditioning Is More Than Drooling Dogs

If someone had asked you, when you first decided to study psychology, to list the main things you hoped to learn, you probably would not have replied, "I want to learn how to make dogs salivate!" I hope you have seen that the research on dog salivation is just a way to explore fundamental mechanisms, much as genetics researchers have studied the fruit fly *Drosophila* or neurophysiologists have studied the nerves of squid. Classical conditioning plays an important role in a wide variety of important behaviors, ranging from emotional responses to drug tolerance.

People sometimes use the term "Pavlovian" to mean simple, mechanical, robotlike behavior. But Pavlovian or classical conditioning is not a mark of stupidity. It is a way of responding to relationships among events, a way of preparing us for what is likely to happen. ∎

Summary

• *Classical conditioning.* Ivan Pavlov discovered classical conditioning, the process by which an organism learns a new association between two stimuli that have been paired with each other—a neutral stimulus (the conditioned stimulus) and one that initially evokes a reflexive response (the unconditioned stimulus). The organism displays this association by responding in a new way (the conditioned response) to the conditioned stimulus. (page 207)

• *Extinction.* After classical conditioning has established a conditioned response to a stimulus, the response can be extinguished by repeatedly presenting that stimulus by itself. (page 210)

• *Spontaneous recovery.* If the conditioned stimulus is not presented at all for some time after extinction and is then presented again, the conditioned response may return to some degree. That return is called spontaneous recovery. (page 210)

• *Stimulus generalization.* An individual who learns to respond to one stimulus will respond similarly to stimuli that resemble it. However, it is difficult to specify how we should measure similarity. (page 211)

• *Discrimination.* If one stimulus is followed by an unconditioned stimulus and another similar stimulus is not, the individual will come to discriminate between these two stimuli. (page 211)

• *Emotional conditioning without awareness.* In many situations conditioning is strongest if the learner is aware of the CS–UCS connection. However, emotional responses can be conditioned even if the learner is not aware of the connection. (page 212)

• *Drug tolerance.* Drug tolerance is partly a form of classical conditioning in which the drug administration procedure comes to evoke defensive responses by the body. (page 213)

• *Basis for classical conditioning.* Pavlov believed that conditioning occurred because presenting two stimuli close to each other in time developed a connection between their brain representations. Later research showed that animals do not treat the conditioned stimulus as if it were the unconditioned stimulus. Also, being close in time is not enough; learning requires that the first stimulus predict the second stimulus. (page 214)

Answers to Concept Checks

3. No response (or at least nothing of interest) . . . the UCR . . . the CR . . . still the UCR. (page 210)

4. The conditioned stimulus is the sound "Ready, aim, fire." The unconditioned stimulus is the artillery shot. The unconditioned response is flinching; the conditioned response is tensing. (page 210)

5. To bring about extinction, present the buzzer repeatedly without presenting any food. To bring about spontaneous recovery, first bring about extinction; then wait hours or days and present the buzzer again. (page 211)

6. The conditioned stimulus is the injection procedure. The unconditioned stimulus is the entry of the drug into the brain. Both the conditioned response and the unconditioned response are the body's defenses against the drug. (page 213)

7. To extinguish tolerance, present the injection procedure (conditioned stimulus) without injecting the drug (unconditioned stimulus). Instead, inject water or salt water. Siegel (1977) demonstrated that repeated injections of salt water do reduce tolerance to morphine in rats. (page 213)

8. If classical conditioning depended entirely on presenting the CS and UCS at nearly the same time, the rats in both groups would have responded equally to the conditioned stimulus, regardless of how often they received the unconditioned stimulus at other times. (page 215)

9. No, you will not learn to flinch at the sound of the background music. Because the drill sound already predicted the pain, the new stimulus is uninformative and will not be strongly associated with the pain. (page 216)

Operant Conditioning

- *How do the consequences of our behaviors affect future behaviors?*

Sometimes, a simple idea, or at least one that sounds simple, can be amazingly powerful. In this module we consider the simple but powerful idea that behaviors become more likely or less likely because of their consequences. That is, we repeat or cease a behavior depending on the outcome.

Thorndike and Operant Conditioning

Shortly before Pavlov's research, Edward L. Thorndike (1911/1970), a Harvard graduate student, began training some cats in a basement. Saying that earlier experiments had dealt only with animal intelligence, never with animal stupidity, he devised a simple behaviorist explanation of learning. Thorndike put cats into puzzle boxes (Figure 6.11) from which they could escape by pressing a lever, pulling a string, or tilting a pole. Sometimes, he placed food outside the box. Usually, though, cats worked just to escape from the box. The cats learned to make whatever response opened the box, especially if the box opened quickly.

The learning was strictly trial and error. When a cat had to tilt a pole to escape from the box, it would first paw or gnaw at the door, scratch the walls, or pace back and forth. Eventually, it would bump against the pole by accident and the door would open. The next time, the cat would go through a similar repertoire of behaviors but might bump against the pole a little sooner. Over many trials the cat gradually and irregularly improved its speed of escaping from the box. Figure 6.12 shows a learning curve to represent this behavior. A learning curve is *a graph of the changes in behavior that occur over the course of learning.*

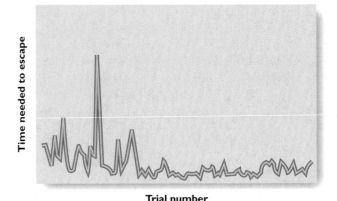

FIGURE 6.12 As the data from one of Thorndike's experiments show, a cat gradually and irregularly decreases the time it needs to escape from a box. Thorndike concluded that the cat did not at any point "get the idea." Instead, reinforcement gradually increased the probability of the successful behavior.

Had the cat discovered how to escape? Did it understand the connection between bumping against the pole and opening the door? No, said Thorndike. If the cat had gained a new insight at some point, its speed of escaping would have increased suddenly at that time. Instead, the cat's performance improved slowly and inconsistently, suggesting no point of insight or understanding.

Thorndike concluded that learning occurs only when certain behaviors are strengthened at the expense of others. An animal enters a given situation with a certain repertoire of responses such as pawing the door, scratching the walls, pacing, and so forth (labeled R_1, R_2, R_3, etc. in Figure 6.13). First, the animal engages in its most probable response for this situation (R_1). If nothing special happens, it proceeds to other responses, eventually reaching a response that opens the door—for example, bumping against the

FIGURE 6.11 Each of Thorndike's puzzle boxes had a device that could open it. Here, tilting the pole will open the door. *(Based on Thorndike, 1911/1970)*

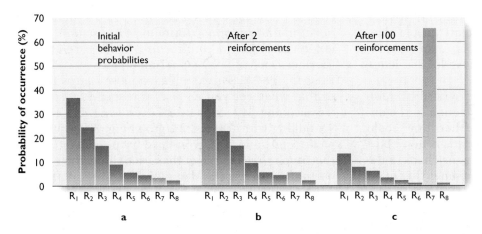

FIGURE 6.13 According to Thorndike, a cat starts with many potential behaviors in a given situation. When one of these, such as bumping against a pole, leads to reinforcement, the future probability of that behavior increases. We need not assume that the cat understands what it is doing or why.

pole (R_7 in this example). Opening the door serves as a reinforcement.

A **reinforcement** is *an event that increases the future probability of the most recent response.* Thorndike said that it "stamps in," or strengthens, the response. The next time the cat is in the puzzle box, it has a slightly higher probability of the effective response; after each succeeding reinforcement, the probability goes up another notch (Figure 6.13c).

Thorndike summarized his views in the **law of effect** (Thorndike, 1911/1970, p. 244): *"Of several responses made to the same situation, those which are accompanied or closely followed by satisfaction to the animal will, other things being equal, be more firmly connected with the situation, so that, when it recurs, they will be more likely to recur."* Hence, the animal becomes more likely to repeat the responses that led to favorable consequences even if it does not understand why. In fact it doesn't need to "understand" anything at all. A fairly simple machine could produce responses at random and then repeat the ones that led to reinforcement.

Thorndike revolutionized the study of animal learning, substituting experimentation for the collection of anecdotes. He also demonstrated the possibility of simple explanations for apparently complex behaviors (Dewsbury, 1998). On the negative side, his example of studying animals in contrived laboratory situations led researchers to ignore many interesting phenomena about animals' natural way of life (Galef, 1998).

The kind of learning that Thorndike studied is known as **operant conditioning** (because the subject *operates* on the environment to produce an outcome), or **instrumental conditioning** (because the subject's behavior is *instrumental* in producing the outcome). Operant or instrumental conditioning is *the process of*

changing behavior by providing a reinforcement after a response. The defining difference between operant conditioning and classical conditioning is the procedure: *In operant conditioning the subject's behavior determines an outcome and the outcome affects future behavior. In classical conditioning the subject's behavior has no effect on the outcome (the presentation of either the CS or the UCS).* For example, in classical conditioning the experimenter (or the world) presents two stimuli at particular times, regardless of what the individual does or doesn't do. In operant conditioning the individual has to make some response before it receives reinforcement.

In general the two kinds of conditioning also differ in the behaviors they affect. Classical conditioning applies primarily to **visceral responses** (i.e., *responses of the internal organs*), such as salivation and digestion, whereas operant conditioning applies primarily to **skeletal responses** (i.e., *movements of leg muscles, arm muscles, etc.*). However, this distinction sometimes breaks down. For example, if a tone consistently precedes an electric shock (a classical-conditioning procedure), the tone will make the animal freeze in position (a skeletal response) as well as increase its heart rate (a visceral response).

 CONCEPT CHECK

10. When I ring a bell, an animal sits up on its hind legs and drools; then I give it some food. Is the animal's behavior an example of classical conditioning or operant conditioning? So far, you do not have enough information to answer the question. What else would you need to know before you could answer? (Check your answer on page 230.)

Reinforcement and Punishment

What constitutes reinforcement? From a practical standpoint, a **reinforcer** is *an event that follows a response and increases the later probability or frequency of that response.* However, from a theoretical standpoint, we would like to have some way of predicting what would be a reinforcer and what would not. We might guess that reinforcers are biologically useful to the individual, but in fact many are not. For example, saccharin, a sweet but biologically useless chemical, can be a reinforcer. For many people alcohol and tobacco are stronger reinforcers than vitamin-rich vegetables. So biological usefulness doesn't define reinforcement.

In his law of effect, Thorndike described reinforcers as events that brought "satisfaction to the animal." That definition won't work either. How could you know what brings a rat or a cat satisfaction? Furthermore, people will work hard for a paycheck, a decent grade in a course, and other outcomes that often don't produce evidence of pleasure (Berridge & Robinson, 1995).

David Premack (1965) proposed a simple rule, now known as the **Premack principle**: *The opportunity to engage in frequent behavior* (e.g., eating) *will reinforce any less frequent behavior* (e.g., lever pressing). A great strength of this idea is its recognition that a reinforcer for one individual may not be for another. For example, if you love reading and hate watching television, someone could increase your television watching by reinforcing you with a new book for every 10 hours of television you watch. For someone else who loves television and seldom reads, the opposite procedure might work.

The limitation of the Premack principle is that opportunities for uncommon behaviors can also be reinforcing. What matters is not just how often you perform various behaviors usually but whether you have recently performed them as much as usual. For example, in an average week, you probably spend little or no time clipping your toenails. Still, if you have not had a chance to clip them for a long time, an opportunity to do so would be reinforcing. According to the **disequilibrium principle** of reinforcement, *each of us has a normal, or "equilibrium," state in which we spend a certain amount of time on each of various activities. If you have had a limited opportunity to engage in one of your behaviors, you are in disequilibrium, and an opportunity to increase that behavior, to get back to equilibrium, will be reinforcing* (Farmer-Dougan, 1998; Timberlake & Farmer-Dougan, 1991). For example, suppose that when you can do whatever you choose, you spend 30% of your day sleeping, 10% eating, 12% exercising, 11% reading, 9% talking with friends, 3% grooming, 3% playing the piano, and so forth. If you have been unable to spend this much time on one of those activities, then the opportunity to engage in that activity will be reinforcing.

 CONCEPT CHECK

11. Suppose you want to reinforce a child for doing chores around the house, and you don't know what would be a good reinforcer. According to the disequilibrium principle, how should you proceed? (Check your answer on page 230.)

Primary and Secondary Reinforcers

Psychologists distinguish between **primary reinforcers** (or *unconditioned reinforcers), which are reinforcing because of their own properties,* and **secondary reinforcers** (or *conditioned reinforcers), which became reinforcing because of previous experiences.* Food and water are primary reinforcers. Money (a secondary reinforcer) becomes reinforcing because it can be exchanged for food or other primary reinforcers. A student learns that good grades will win the approval of parents and teachers; an employee learns that increased sales will win the approval of an employer. In these cases *secondary* means "learned." It does not mean weak or unimportant. We spend most of our time working for secondary reinforcers.

What serves as a reinforcer for one person might not for another. Lucy Pearson (left) has collected over 110,000 hubcaps. Jim Hambrick (right) collects Superman items.

Many secondary reinforcers are surprisingly powerful. Consider, for example, how hard some children will work for a little gold star that the teacher pastes on an assignment.

Punishment

In contrast to a *reinforcer,* which increases the probability of a response, a **punishment** *decreases the probability of a response.* A reinforcer can be either the presentation of something (e.g., food) or the removal of something (e.g., pain). A punishment can be either the presentation of something (e.g., pain) or the removal of something (e.g., food).

Punishments are not always effective. For example, if the threat of punishment were always effective, the crime rate would be zero. B. F. Skinner (1938) tested punishment in a famous laboratory study. He first trained food-deprived rats to press a bar to get food and then stopped reinforcing their presses. For the first 10 minutes, some rats not only failed to get food but also had the bar slap their paws every time they pressed it. The punished rats temporarily suppressed their pressing, but in the long run, they pressed as many times as did the unpunished rats. Skinner concluded that punishment temporarily suppresses behavior but produces no long-term effects.

That conclusion, however, is an overstatement (Staddon, 1993). A better conclusion would have been that punishment does not greatly weaken a response when no other response is available. Skinner's food-deprived rats had no other way to seek food. Similarly, if someone punished you for breathing, you would continue breathing, but not because you were a slow learner.

Is physical punishment of children, such as spanking, a good or bad idea? Most American parents spank their children at times, whereas spanking is rare or illegal in many other countries. Many psychologists strongly discourage spanking, but the research findings are marred by several difficulties. Researchers almost always rely on parents' self-reports, which no doubt misstate the amount of spanking. Also, many studies do not distinguish adequately between mild spanking and physical abuse.

A review of the literature found that physical punishment had one clear benefit, which was immediate compliance. That is, if you want your child to stop doing something at once, a quick spank or slap on the hand will work (Gershoff, 2002). Punishment produces compliance especially if it is quick and predictable. If you *might* get punished a long time from now, the effects are weak and variable. The threat of punishment for crime is often ineffective because the punishment is uncertain and long delayed.

On the negative side, however, children who are spanked tend to be more aggressive than other children, more prone to antisocial and criminal behavior in both adolescence and later adulthood, and less healthy mentally. On the average they have a worse relationship with their parents, and they are more likely than others later to become abusive toward their own children or spouse (Gershoff, 2002).

Now, can we draw the conclusion that physical punishment produces these undesirable consequences? I hope you see that we cannot. A quick summary of the results is that parents who spank their children are more likely than others to have ill-behaved children. Sure, it is possible that spanking *caused* children to become violent and poorly adjusted, but it is also possible that ill-behaved children provoke their parents to spank them (Baumrind, Larzelere, & Cowan, 2002). (Similarly, the more time you spend as a hospital patient, the more likely you are to die soon, but we don't conclude that hospitals kill you.) If we compare children whose initial misbehaviors were similar, those who were spanked (mildly) behave no worse, and possibly better, than those who were not spanked (Larzelere, Kuhn, & Johnson, 2004).

Psychologists are virtually unanimous in recommending against severe punishment at any age. They also oppose spanking infants less than 18 months old or adolescents after the onset of puberty (Baumrind et al., 2002). On the issue of mild physical punishment for children between 18 months and puberty, opinions are strong, but the research results are not. You might contemplate the difficulty of experimental research, given the difficulty of randomly assigning children to be spanked or not spanked.

☑ **CONCEPT CHECK**

12. The U.S. government imposes strict punishments for selling illegal drugs. Based on what you have just read, why are those punishments ineffective for many people? (Check your answer on page 230.)

Categories of Reinforcement and Punishment

As mentioned, a reinforcer can be either the onset of something like food or the removal of something like pain. Of course, what works as a reinforcer for one person at one time may not work for another person or at another time. A punishment also can be either the onset or offset of something. Psychologists use different terms to distinguish these possibilities, as shown in Table 6.1.

Note that the upper left and lower right of the table both show reinforcement. Either gaining food or preventing pain *increases* the behavior. The items in the upper right and lower left are both punishment. Gaining pain or preventing food *decreases* the behavior. Food and pain are, of course, just examples; many other events serve as reinforcers or punishers. Let's go through these terms and procedures, beginning in the upper left of the table and proceeding clockwise.

Positive reinforcement is the *presentation of an event* (e.g., food or money) *that strengthens or increases the likelihood of a behavior.*

Punishment occurs when a response is followed by an event such as pain. The frequency of the response then decreases. For example, you put your hand on a hot stove, burn yourself, and learn to stop doing that. Punishment is also called **passive avoidance learning** because *the individual learns to avoid an outcome by being passive* (e.g., by *not* putting your hand on the stove).

Try not to be confused by the term negative reinforcement. **Negative reinforcement** is *a kind of reinforcement (not a punishment), and therefore, it increases the frequency of a behavior. It is "negative" in the sense that the reinforcement is the absence of something.* For example, you learn to apply sunscreen to avoid skin cancer, and you learn to brush your teeth to avoid tooth decay. With negative reinforcement the behavior increases and its outcome therefore decreases. Negative reinforcement is also known as **avoidance learning** *if the response prevents the outcome altogether* or **escape learning** *if it stops some outcome that has already begun.* Most people find the terms "escape learning" and "avoidance learning" easier to understand than "negative reinforcement," and the terms escape learning and avoidance learning show up in the titles of research articles four times more often than negative reinforcement does.

If reinforcement by avoiding something bad is negative reinforcement, then *punishment by avoiding something good* is **negative punishment**. If your parents punished you by taking away your allowance or privileges ("grounding you"), they were using negative punishment. Another example is a teacher punishing a child by a "time out" session away from classmates. Although this practice is common, the term negative punishment is not widely used. The practice is usually known simply as punishment or as **omission training** *because the omission of the response leads to restoration of the usual privileges.*

Classifying some procedure in one of these four categories is often tricky. If you adjust the thermostat in a

TABLE 6.1 Four Categories of Operant Conditioning

	Event Such as Food	Event Such as Pain
Behavior leads to the event	**Positive Reinforcement** *Result*: Increase in the behavior, reinforced by presentation of food. *Example*: "If you clean your room, I'll get you a pizza tonight."	**Punishment = Passive Avoidance Learning** *Result*: Decrease in the behavior, and therefore a decrease in pain. *Example*: "If you insult me, I'll slap you."
Behavior avoids the event	**Negative Punishment = Omission Training** *Result*: Decrease in the behavior, and therefore food continues to be available. *Example*: "If you hit your little brother again, you'll get no dessert."	**Negative Reinforcement = Escape or Avoidance Learning** *Result*: Increase in the behavior, and therefore a decrease in pain. *Example*: "If you go into the office over there, the doctor will remove the thorn from your leg."

cold room to increase the heat, are you working for increased heat (positive reinforcement) or decreased cold (negative reinforcement)? Because of this ambiguity, several authorities have recommended abandoning the term negative reinforcement (Baron & Galizio, 2005; Kimble, 1993). The ambiguity can get even worse: If you are told you can be suspended from school for academic dishonesty, you can think of it as being honest in order to stay in school (positive reinforcement), being honest to avoid suspension (negative reinforcement or avoidance learning), decreasing dishonesty to avoid suspension (punishment or passive avoidance), or decreasing dishonesty to stay in school (negative punishment or omission training). Sorry about that! We can often simplify matters by using just the terms reinforcement (to increase a behavior) and punishment (to decrease it). Nevertheless, you should understand all of the terms, as they appear in many psychological publications and conversations. Attend to how something is worded: Are we talking about increasing or decreasing some behavior and increasing or decreasing some outcome? Practice with the concept check that follows.

 CONCEPT CHECK

13. Identify each of the following examples using the terms in Table 6.1:
    a. Your employer gives you bonus pay for working overtime.
    b. You learn to stop playing your accordion at 5 A.M. because your roommate threatens to kill you if you do it again.
    c. You turn off a dripping faucet, ending the "drip drip drip" sound.
    d. You learn to drink less beer than you once did because you have felt sick after drinking too much.
    e. Your swimming coach says you cannot go to the next swim meet (which you are looking forward to) if you break a training rule.
    f. If you get a speeding ticket, you will temporarily lose the privilege of driving the family car.
    g. You learn to come inside when a storm is brewing to avoid getting wet. (Check your answers on page 230.)

 CRITICAL THINKING
A STEP FURTHER

Using Reinforcement

Your local school board proposes to improve class attendance by lowering the grades of any student who misses a certain number of classes. Might the board achieve the same goal more effectively by using positive reinforcement?

Additional Phenomena of Operant Conditioning

Recall the concepts of extinction, generalization, and discrimination in classical conditioning. The same concepts apply to operant conditioning, although the procedures are different.

Extinction

No doubt you are familiar with the saying, "If at first you don't succeed, try, try again." Better advice is, "Try again, but differently!" After all, you may be doing something wrong.

In operant conditioning extinction *occurs if responses stop producing reinforcements.* For example, you were once in the habit of asking your roommate to join you for supper. The last five times you asked, your roommate said no, so you stop asking. In classical conditioning extinction is achieved by presenting the CS without the UCS; in operant conditioning the procedure is response without reinforcement. Table 6.2 compares classical and operant conditioning.

TABLE 6.2 Classical Conditioning and Operant Conditioning

	Classical Conditioning	Operant Conditioning
Terminology	CS, UCS, CR, UCR	Response, reinforcement
Behavior	Does not control UCS	Controls reinforcement
Paired during acquisition	Two stimuli (CS and UCS)	Response and reinforcement (in the presence of certain stimuli)
Responses	Mostly visceral (internal organs)	Mostly skeletal muscles
Extinction procedure	CS without UCS	Response without reinforcement

Generalization

Someone who receives reinforcement for a response in the presence of one stimulus will probably make the same response in the presence of a similar stimulus. *The more similar a new stimulus is to the original reinforced stimulus, the more likely the same response.* This phenomenon is known as **stimulus generalization**. For example, you might reach for the turn signal of a rented car in the same place you would find it in your own car.

Here is a fascinating example of stimulus generalization in the animal world: Many harmless animals have evolved an appearance that resembles a poisonous animal, because any predator that learns to avoid the poisonous animal generalizes its learning and avoids the harmless animal also. Eastern Ecuador has two similar poisonous frog species and one harmless species that mimics their appearance. The frog on the left in Figure 6.14 is the more common and the more poisonous. The one in the middle is less common and less poisonous. In areas where all three species reside, the harmless frog closely resembles the *less* common and *less* toxic species. At first it would seem that the frog would have gained more advantage by resembling the more common, more dangerous species. However, researchers found the answer: The birds that try eating the more toxic species learn a strong avoidance, which they generalize to anything that looks remotely similar. The birds that attack the less toxic species form a weaker avoidance, which they generalize only to targets that are highly similar (Darst & Cummings, 2006). In short, the harmless frog gains an advantage by being even slightly similar to the more toxic species, but it has to be quite similar to the less toxic species to gain any advantage from it. The evolution of these frogs depended on the way birds generalize their learned responses.

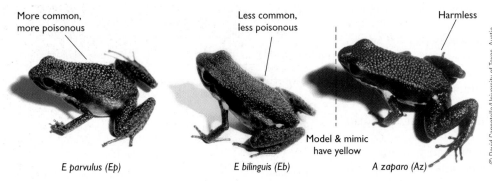

More common,
more poisonous

Less common,
less poisonous

Harmless

Model & mimic
have yellow

E parvulus (Ep)   *E bilinguis (Eb)*   *A zaparo (Az)*

© David Cannatella/University of Texas, Austin

FIGURE 6.14 The harmless frog evolved an appearance that resembles the less poisonous species, taking advantage of the way birds generalize their learned avoidance responses. *(Source: Darst & Cummings, 2006)*

Discrimination and Discriminative Stimuli

If reinforcement occurs for responding to one stimulus and not another, *the result is a* **discrimination** between them, yielding *a response to one stimulus and not the other.* For example, you smile and greet someone you think you know, but then you realize it is someone else. After several such experiences, you learn to recognize the difference between the two people.

A *stimulus that indicates which response is appropriate or inappropriate* is called a **discriminative stimulus.** A great deal of our behavior is governed by discriminative stimuli. For example, you learn ordinarily to be quiet in class but to talk when the profes-

sor encourages discussion. You learn to drive fast on some streets and slowly on others. Throughout your day one stimulus after another signals which behaviors will yield reinforcement, punishment, or neither. *The ability of a stimulus to encourage some responses and discourage others* is known as **stimulus control.**

What Makes Some Kinds of Learning Difficult?

Thorndike's cats learned to push and pull various devices in their efforts to escape from his puzzle boxes. But when Thorndike tried to teach them to scratch or lick themselves for the same reinforcement, they learned slowly and performed inconsistently. Why?

One possible reason is **belongingness** or "preparedness," the *concept that certain stimuli or responses "belong" together more than others do* (Seligman, 1970; Thorndike, 1911/1970). For example, a cat more easily associates opening a puzzle box with the response of pushing a door than with scratching its neck. Animals may have evolved this tendency because in the real world, pushing and shoving cause things to move. Scratching yourself ordinarily doesn't. Also, dogs readily learn that a sound coming from the left means "raise your left leg" and a sound coming from the right means "raise your right leg," but they are slow to learn that a ticking metronome means raise the left leg and a buzzer means raise the right leg (Dobrzecka, Szwejkowska, & Konorski, 1966) (see Figure 6.15). People learn more easily to turn a wheel clockwise to move something to the right and counterclockwise to move it to the left (as when turning the steering wheel of a car). Ergonomists do much research to find which procedures are easiest for people to learn so that machines can be designed to match people's tendencies.

However, we can imagine another explanation for why Thorndike's cats were slow to associate scratching themselves with escaping from a box: Perhaps a cat scratches itself only when it itches (Charlton, 1983). Suppose you could win a large prize in a saliva-swallowing contest. (I know it sounds ridiculous, but people compete at everything else, so why not.) You quickly swallow once, twice, maybe three times, but each successive swallow gets harder and

Try It Yourself

harder. (Go ahead and try it.) Some behaviors are just more difficult to produce without their normal stimulus (e.g., a mouthful of fluid or an itchy spot on the skin).

B. F. Skinner and the Shaping of Responses

The most influential radical behaviorist, B. F. Skinner (1904–1990), demonstrated many uses of operant conditioning. Skinner was an ardent practitioner of parsimony (chapter 2), always seeking simple explanations in terms of reinforcement histories rather than complex mental processes.

One problem confronting any student of behavior is how to define a response. For example, imagine watching a group of children and trying to count "aggressive behaviors." What is an aggressive act and what isn't? Psychologists studying intelligence, emotion, or personality spend much of their time trying to find the best method of measurement.

Skinner simplified the measurement by simplifying the situation (Zuriff, 1995): He set up a box, called an *operant-conditioning chamber* (or *Skinner box,* a term that Skinner himself never used), in which a rat presses a lever or a pigeon pecks an illuminated disk or "key" to receive food (Figure 6.16). He operationally defined the response as anything that the animal did to depress the lever or key. So if the rat pressed the lever with its snout instead of its paw, the response still counted; if the pigeon batted the key with its wing instead of pecking it with its beak, it still counted. The behavior was defined by its outcome, not by muscle movements.

Does that definition make sense? Skinner's reply was that it did, because it led to consistent results in his research. Skinner's procedures became standard in many laboratories. When deciding how to define a term (e.g., *response*), the best definition is the one that produces the clearest results.

Shaping Behavior

Suppose you want to train a rat to press a lever. If you put the rat in a box and wait, the rat might never press it. To avoid interminable waits, Skinner introduced a

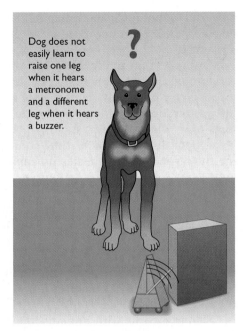

FIGURE 6.15 According to the principle of belongingness, some items are easy to associate with each other because they "belong" together. For example, dogs easily learn to use the direction of a sound as a signal for which leg to raise, but they have trouble using the type of sound as a signal for the same response.

FIGURE 6.16 B. F. Skinner examines one of his animals in an operant-conditioning chamber. When the light above the bar is on, pressing the bar is reinforced. A food pellet rolls out of the storage device (left) and down the tube into the cage.

powerful technique, called **shaping,** for *establishing a new response by reinforcing successive approximations to it.*

To *shape* a rat to press a lever, you might begin by reinforcing the rat for standing up, a common behavior in rats. After a few reinforcements, the rat stands up more frequently. Now you change the rules, giving food only when the rat stands up while facing the lever. Soon it spends more time standing up and facing the lever. (It extinguishes its behavior of standing and facing in other directions because those responses are not reinforced.)

Next you provide reinforcement only when the rat stands facing the correct direction while in the half of the cage nearer the lever. You gradually move the boundary, and the rat moves closer to the lever. Then the rat must touch the lever and, finally, apply weight to it. Through a series of short, easy steps, you shape the rat to press a lever.

Shaping works with humans too, of course. All of education is based on the idea of shaping: First, your parents or teachers praise you for counting your fingers; later, you must add and subtract to earn their congratulations; step by step your tasks become more complex until you are doing calculus.

Chaining Behavior

Ordinarily, you don't do just one action and then stop. You do a long sequence of actions. To produce sequences of learned behavior, psychologists use a procedure called **chaining.** Assume you want to train an animal, perhaps a guide dog or a show horse, to go through a sequence of actions in a particular order. You could *chain* the behaviors, *reinforcing each one with the opportunity to engage in the next one.* First, the animal learns the final behavior for a reinforcement. Then it learns the next to last behavior, which is reinforced by the opportunity to perform the final behavior. And so on.

For example, a rat might first be placed on the top platform as shown in Figure 6.17f, where it eats food. Then it is put on the intermediate platform with a ladder in place leading to the top platform. The rat learns to climb the ladder. After it has done so, it is placed again on the intermediate platform, but this time the ladder is not present. It must learn to pull a string to raise the ladder so that it can climb to the top platform. Then the rat is placed on the bot-

tom platform (Figure 6.17a). It now has to learn to climb the ladder to the intermediate platform, pull a string to raise the ladder, and then climb the ladder again. We could, of course, extend the chain still further. Each behavior is reinforced with the opportunity for the next behavior, except for the final behavior, which is reinforced with food.

People learn to make chains of responses too. First, you learned to eat with a fork and spoon. Later, you learned to put your own food on the plate before eating. Eventually, you learned to plan a menu, go to the store, buy the ingredients, cook the meal, put it on the plate, and then eat it. Each behavior is reinforced by the opportunity to engage in the next behavior.

To show how effective shaping and chaining can be, Skinner performed this demonstration: First, he trained a rat to go to the center of a cage. Then he trained it to do so only when he was playing a certain piece of music. Next he trained it to wait for the music, go to the center of the cage, and sit up on its hind

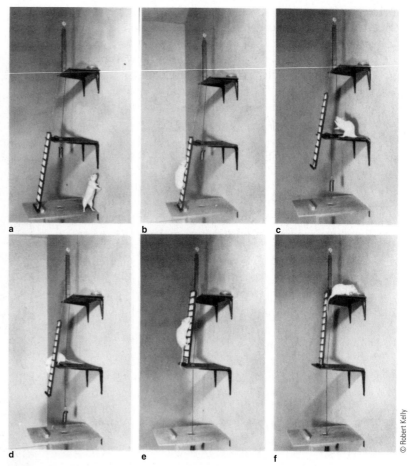

FIGURE 6.17 Chaining is a procedure in which the reinforcement for one behavior is the opportunity to engage in the next behavior. To reach food on the top platform, this rat must climb a ladder (**a, b**) and pull a string to raise the ladder (**c, d**) so that it can climb up again (**e, f**).

legs. Step by step he eventually trained the rat to wait for the music (which happened to be the "Star-Spangled Banner"), move to the center of the cage, sit up on its hind legs, put its claws on a string next to a pole, pull the string to hoist the U.S. flag, and then salute it. Only then did the rat get its reinforcement. Needless to say, a display of patriotism is not part of a rat's usual repertoire of behavior.

Schedules of Reinforcement

The simplest procedure in operant conditioning is to *provide reinforcement for every correct response,* a procedure known as **continuous reinforcement.** However, in the real world, unlike the laboratory, continuous reinforcement is not common.

Reinforcement for some responses and not for others is known as **intermittent reinforcement.** We behave differently when we learn that only some of our responses will be reinforced. Psychologists have investigated the effects of many **schedules of reinforcement,** which are *rules or procedures for the delivery of reinforcement.* Four schedules for the delivery of intermittent reinforcement are fixed ratio, fixed interval, variable ratio, and variable interval (see Table 6.3). A ratio schedule provides reinforcements depending on the number of responses. An interval schedule provides reinforcements depending on the timing of responses.

TABLE 6.3 Some Schedules of Reinforcement

Type	Description
Continuous	Reinforcement for every response of the correct type
Fixed ratio	Reinforcement following completion of a specific number of responses
Variable ratio	Reinforcement for an unpredictable number of responses that varies around a mean value
Fixed interval	Reinforcement for the first response that follows a given delay since the previous reinforcement
Variable interval	Reinforcement for the first response that follows an unpredictable delay (varying around a mean value) since the previous reinforcement

Fixed-Ratio Schedule

A **fixed-ratio schedule** *provides reinforcement only after a certain (fixed) number of correct responses have been made*—after every sixth response, for example. We see similar behavior among pieceworkers in a factory whose pay depends on how many pieces they turn out or among fruit pickers who get paid by the bushel.

A fixed-ratio schedule tends to produce rapid and steady responding. Researchers sometimes graph the results with a *cumulative record,* in which the line is flat when the animal does not respond, and it moves up with each response. For a fixed-ratio schedule, a typical result would look like this:

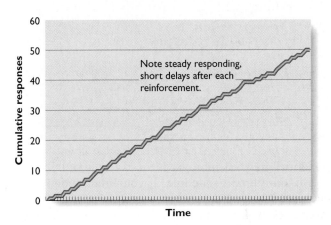

However, if the schedule requires a large number of responses for reinforcement, the individual pauses after each reinforced response. For example, if you have just completed 10 calculus problems, you may pause briefly before starting your next assignment. After completing 100 problems, you would pause even longer.

Variable-Ratio Schedule

A **variable-ratio schedule** is similar to a fixed-ratio schedule, except that *reinforcement occurs after a variable number of correct responses.* For example, reinforcement may come after as few as one or two responses or after a great many. Variable-ratio schedules generate steady response rates.

Variable-ratio schedules, or approximations of them, occur whenever each response has about an equal probability of success. For example, when you apply for a job, you might or might not be hired. The more times you apply, the better your chances, but you cannot predict how many applications you need to submit before receiving a job offer.

Fixed-Interval Schedule

A **fixed-interval schedule** *provides reinforcement for the first response made after a specific time interval.* For instance, an animal might get food for only the first response it makes after each 15-second interval. Then it would have to wait another 15 seconds before another response would be effective. Animals (including humans) on such a schedule learn to pause after each reinforcement and begin to respond again toward the end of the time interval. The cumulative record would look like this:

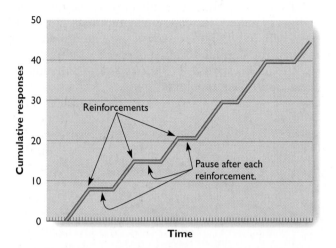

Checking your mailbox is an example of behavior on a fixed-interval schedule. If your mail is delivered at about 3 P.M., and you are eagerly awaiting an important package, you might begin to check around 2:30 and continue checking every few minutes until it arrives.

Variable-Interval Schedule

With a **variable-interval schedule**, *reinforcement is available after a variable amount of time has elapsed.* For example, reinforcement may come for the first response after 2 minutes, then for the first response after the next 7 seconds, then after 3 minutes 20 seconds, and so forth. You cannot know how much time will pass before your next response is reinforced. Consequently, responses on a variable-interval schedule occur slowly but steadily. Checking your e-mail is an example: A new message could appear at any time, so you check occasionally but not constantly.

Stargazing is also reinforced on a variable-interval schedule. The reinforcement for stargazing—finding a comet, for example—appears at unpredictable intervals. Consequently, both professional and amateur astronomers scan the skies regularly.

Extinction of Responses Reinforced on Different Schedules

Suppose you and a friend go to a gambling casino and bet on the roulette wheel. Amazingly, your first 10 bets are all winners. Your friend wins some and loses some. Then both of you go into a prolonged losing streak. Presuming the two of you have the same amount of money available and no unusual personality quirks, which of you is likely to continue betting longer?

Your friend is, even though you had a more favorable early experience. Responses extinguish more slowly after intermittent reinforcement (either a ratio schedule or an interval schedule) than after continuous reinforcement.

Consider another example. Your friend Beth has been highly reliable. Whenever she says she will do something, she does it. Becky, on the other hand, sometimes keeps her word and sometimes doesn't. Now both of them go through a period of untrustworthy behavior. With whom will you lose patience sooner? It's Beth. One explanation is that you notice the change more quickly. If someone has been unreliable in the past, a new stretch of similar behavior is nothing new.

 CONCEPT CHECK

14. Identify which schedule of reinforcement applies to each of the following examples:
    a. You attend every new movie that appears at your local theater, although you enjoy about one fourth of them.
    b. You phone your best friend and hear a busy signal. You don't know how soon your friend will hang up, so you try again every few minutes.
    c. You tune your television set to an all-news cable channel, and you look up from your studies to check the sports scores every 30 minutes.
15. Stargazing in the hope of finding a comet was cited as an example of a variable-interval schedule. Why is it not an example of a variable ratio?
16. A novice gambler and a longtime gambler both lose 20 bets in a row. Which one is more likely to continue betting? Why? (Check your answers on pages 230–231.)

Applications of Operant Conditioning

Although operant conditioning arose from purely theoretical concerns, it has a long history of applications. Here are three examples.

Animal Training

Most animal acts are based on training methods like Skinner's. To induce an animal to perform a trick, the trainer first trains it to perform something simple. Gradually, the trainer shapes the animal to perform more complex behaviors. Most animal trainers rely on positive reinforcement and seldom if ever use punishment.

Sometimes, what an animal learns is not exactly what the trainer intended (Rumbaugh & Washburn, 2003). Psychologists tried to teach a chimpanzee to

Monkeys can be trained to help people with disabilities. **(a)** Monkeys assist people with limited mobility. **(b)** This monkey is being trained to retrieve objects identified with a laser beam. Such training relies on shaping—building a complex response by reinforcing sequential approximations to it.

urinate in a pan instead of on the floor. They gave her some chocolate candy every time she used the pan. Quickly, she learned to urinate just a few drops at a time, holding out her hand for candy each time. When at last she could urinate no more, she *spat* into the pan and again held out her hand for candy!

Persuasion

How could you persuade someone to do something objectionable? To use an extreme example, could you convince a prisoner of war to cooperate with the enemy?

The best way is to start by reinforcing a slight degree of cooperation and then working up to the goal little by little. This principle has been applied by people who had probably never heard of B. F. Skinner, positive reinforcement, or shaping. During the Korean War, the Chinese Communists forwarded some of the letters written home by prisoners of war but intercepted others. (The prisoners could tell from the replies which letters had been forwarded.)

The prisoners suspected that they could get their letters through if they wrote something mildly favorable about their captors. So they began including occasional remarks that the Communists were not really so bad, that certain aspects of the Chinese system seemed to work pretty well, or that they hoped the war would end soon.

After a while the Chinese devised essay contests, offering a little extra food or other privileges to the soldier who wrote the best essay, in the captors' opinion. Most of the winning essays contained a statement or two that complimented the Communists on minor matters or admitted that "the United States is not perfect." Gradually, more and more soldiers started including such statements. Then the Chinese might ask, "You said the United States is not perfect. Could you tell us some of the ways in which it is not perfect, so that we can better understand your system?" Then they would ask the soldier to read aloud the lists of what was wrong with the United States. Gradually, without torture and with only modest reinforcements, the Chinese induced prisoners to denounce the United States, make false confessions, inform on fellow prisoners, and reveal military secrets (Cialdini, 1993).

The point is clear: Whether we want to get rats to salute the flag or soldiers to denounce it, the most effective training technique is to start with easy behaviors, reinforce those behaviors, and then gradually shape more complex behaviors.

Applied Behavior Analysis/ Behavior Modification

In one way or another, people are almost constantly trying to influence other people's behavior. Psychologists have applied operant conditioning to enhance influence procedures.

In **applied behavior analysis**, also known as **behavior modification**, a *psychologist tries to remove the reinforcers that sustain some unwanted behavior and provide suitable reinforcers for a more acceptable behavior.* For example, one man with mental retardation had a habit of "inappropriate" speech, including lewd sexual comments. Psychologists found that telling him to stop actually made things worse, because getting people's attention was reinforcing. So they switched to ignoring his inappropriate comments and responding attentively to all acceptable comments. The result was increased appropriate and decreased inappropriate comments (Dixon, Benedict, & Larson, 2001).

Another example: Many children hurt themselves on playgrounds, often by using equipment improperly, such as going down the slide head first. The reinforcement for such risky behavior is simply the thrill of it. To stop such behavior, a safety officer talked to elementary school classes about playground safety and offered rewards to the whole class if everyone shifted to safer playground behaviors. College students observed the children in the playground and reported instances of risky behavior. The reinforcements here were almost trivial, such as a blue ribbon for every student or a colorful poster for the door. Nevertheless, the result was decreased risky behaviors, and the improved safety continued for weeks afterward (Heck, Collins, & Peterson, 2001).

 CONCEPT CHECK

17. Of the procedures characterized in Table 6.1, which one applies to giving more attention to someone's appropriate speech? Which one applies to decreasing attention to inappropriate speech? (Check your answers on page 231.)

IN CLOSING

Operant Conditioning and Human Behavior

Suppose one of your instructors announced that everyone in the class would receive the same grade at the end of the course, regardless of performance on tests and papers. Would you study hard in that course? Probably not. Or suppose your employer said that all raises and promotions would be made at random, with no regard to how well you do your job. Would you work as hard as possible? Not likely. Our behavior depends on its consequences, just like that of a rat, pigeon, or any other animal. That is the main point of operant conditioning. ∎

Summary

* *Reinforcement.* Edward Thorndike introduced the concept of reinforcement. A reinforcement increases the probability that the preceding response will be repeated. (page 218)
* *Operant conditioning.* Operant conditioning is the process of controlling the rate of a behavior through its consequences. (page 219)
* *The nature of reinforcement.* If someone has recently been deprived of the opportunity to engage in some behavior, an opportunity for that behavior is reinforcing. Also, something that an individual can exchange for a reinforcer becomes a reinforcer itself. (page 220)
* *Reinforcement and punishment.* Behaviors can be reinforced (strengthened) by presenting favorable events or by omitting unfavorable events. Behaviors

can be punished (suppressed) by presenting unfavorable events or by omitting favorable events. (page 222)
* *Extinction.* In operant conditioning a response becomes extinguished if it is no longer followed by reinforcement. (page 223)
* *Shaping.* Shaping is a technique for training subjects to perform difficult acts by reinforcing them for successive approximations to the desired behavior. (page 225)
* *Schedules of reinforcement.* The frequency and timing of a response depend on the schedule of reinforcement. In a ratio schedule of reinforcement, an individual is given reinforcement after a fixed or variable number of responses. In an interval schedule of reinforcement, an individual is given reinforcement after a fixed or variable period of time. (page 227)
* *Applications.* People have applied operant conditioning to animal training, persuasion, and applied behavior analysis. (page 228)

Answers to Concept Checks

10. You would need to know whether the bell was always followed by food (classical conditioning) or whether food was presented only if the animal sat up on its hind legs (operant conditioning). (page 219)
11. Begin by determining how this person spends his or her time—for example, exercising, reading, watching television, visiting with friends. Then determine something that he or she has recently not had much opportunity to do. Activities for which one has only limited opportunities become good reinforcers. (page 220)
12. To be effective, punishments must be quick and predictable. Punishments for drug dealing are neither. Furthermore, punishment most effectively suppresses a response when the individual has alternative responses that can gain reinforcements. Many people who sell drugs have no alternative way to gain similar profits. (page 222)
13. **a.** positive reinforcement; **b.** punishment or passive avoidance; **c.** escape learning or negative reinforcement; **d.** punishment or passive avoidance; **e.** omission training or negative punishment; **f.** omission training or negative punishment; **g.** avoidance learning or negative reinforcement. (page 223)
14. **a.** variable ratio. (You will be reinforced for about one fourth of your entries to the theater but on an irregular basis.) **b.** variable interval. (Calling will become effective after some interval of time, but the length of that time is unpredictable.) **c.** fixed interval. (page 228)

15. In a variable-ratio schedule, the number of responses matters, but the timing does not. If you have already checked the stars tonight and found no comets, checking three more times tonight will probably be fruitless. Checking at a later date gives you a better chance. (page 228)

16. The longtime gambler will continue longer because he or she has a history of being reinforced for gambling on a variable-ratio schedule, which retards extinction. For the same reason, an alcoholic who has had both good experiences and bad experiences while drunk is likely to keep on drinking after several bad experiences. (page 228)

17. Increasing attention for appropriate speech is positive reinforcement. Decreasing attention for inappropriate speech is omission training or negative punishment. (If you called it "lack of positive reinforcement," you would not be wrong, and calling it simply "punishment" is acceptable for most purposes.) (page 230)

Other Kinds of Learning

- *What kinds of learning do not fit neatly into the categories of classical or operant conditioning?*
- *How do we learn from the successes and failures of others without trying every response ourselves?*

Thorndike, Pavlov, and the other pioneers of learning assumed that all learning was fundamentally the same. If so, researchers could study any convenient example of learning and discover all of its principles. Later researchers found some interesting examples of learning with some special features.

Conditioned Taste Aversions

If you eat something with an unfamiliar flavor and then feel ill, you quickly learn to avoid that flavor. The same process works in rats and other species. *Associating eating something with getting sick* is **conditioned taste aversion**, first documented by John Garcia and his colleagues (Garcia, Ervin, & Koelling, 1966). One of its special features is that it occurs reliably after a single pairing of food with illness, even with a long delay between them. For example, a rat drinks a saccharin solution, which it has never tasted before. Saccharin tastes sweet, and in moderate amounts it is neither healthful nor harmful. After the rat has drunk for a few minutes, the experimenter removes the bottle, waits minutes or even hours, and then injects a small amount of lithium or other substance that makes the rat moderately ill. The experi-

menter then waits days for the rat to recover and offers it a choice between the saccharin solution and unflavored water. The rat strongly prefers the unflavored water (Garcia et al., 1966). In contrast, rats that have not been given lithium, or that received it after drinking something else, strongly prefer the saccharin solution. In most other cases of either classical or operant conditioning, learning is greatest with a 1- or 2-second delay between the events to be associated, and it is hard to demonstrate at all with delays over 20 seconds (Kimble, 1961). With tastes followed by illness, animals learn rapidly despite delays of hours.

An animal that learns a conditioned taste aversion to a food treats it as if it tasted bad (Garcia, 1990). Some ranchers in the western United States have used this type of learning to deter coyotes from eating sheep (Figure 6.18). They offer the coyotes sheep meat containing enough lithium salts to produce nausea but not enough to be dangerous. Afterward, the coyotes become less likely to attack sheep, although they continue to hunt rabbits and other prey. One study reported that this method reduced coyotes' sheep kills to about half of what had occurred the previous year (Gustavson, Kelly, Sweeney, & Garcia, 1976). This technique has the potential of protecting sheep without killing the coyotes, which are a threatened species.

Conditioned taste aversions account for some of our choices of food and beverage. Mice that have trouble metabolizing alcohol get sick after drinking it and learn to avoid it (Broadbent, Muccino, & Cunningham,

© Stuart Ellins

FIGURE 6.18 This coyote previously fell ill after eating sheep meat containing a mild dose of lithium salts. Now it reacts toward both live and dead sheep as it would toward bad-tasting food.

2002). The same is true for people (Tu & Israel, 1995). Many women who get nauseated during pregnancy learn aversions to the foods they have been eating (Crystal, Bowen, & Bernstein, 1999), and many cancer patients learn aversions to foods they ate just prior to chemotherapy or radiation therapy (Bernstein, 1991).

Conditioned taste aversions are special in another regard as well: Recall that an animal can associate a food with feeling ill hours later. No doubt the animal had many other experiences between the food and the illness. Nevertheless, animals are predisposed to associate illness mostly with what they eat. In one classic experiment (Garcia & Koelling, 1966), rats were allowed to drink saccharin-flavored water from tubes that were set up to turn on a bright light and a loud noise whenever the rats licked the water. Some of the rats were exposed to x-rays (which induce nausea) while they drank. Others were given electric shocks to their feet when they drank. After the training was complete, each rat was tested separately with a tube of saccharin-flavored water and a tube of unflavored water that produced lights and noises. (Figure 6.19 illustrates the experiment.)

The rats that received x-rays avoided the flavored water. The rats that received shocks avoided the tube that produced lights and noises. Evidently, animals are predisposed to associate illness with what they eat or drink. They associate skin pain mostly with what they see or hear. This tendency is an example of preparedness, mentioned earlier in this chapter. Such predispositions are presumably beneficial because foods are more likely to cause internal events, and lights and sounds are more likely to signal external events.

One problem remains with all of this: I have described associations between food and illness, but some drugs that make the animal ill produce only

weak learned aversions, and some procedures such as x-rays that hardly make the animal ill at all produce powerful aversions to recently eaten foods. Rats will work for an opportunity to get into a running wheel, and they prefer to be in a distinctive cage associated with a running wheel instead of other cages. Nevertheless, running evidently produces some mild stomach distress (probably analogous to riding a roller coaster), and rats learn to avoid the taste of anything

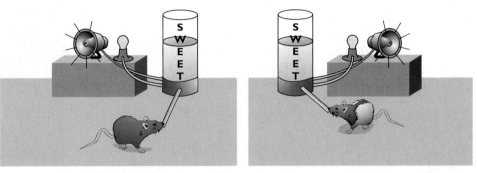

Rats drink saccharin-flavored water. Whenever they make contact with the tube, they turn on a bright light and a noisy buzzer.

Then

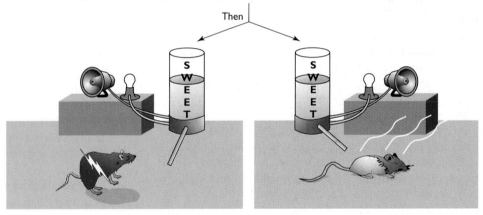

Some rats get electric shock.   Some rats are nauseated by x-rays.

Next day: Rats are given a choice between a tube of saccharin-flavored water and a tube of unflavored water hooked up to the light and the buzzer.

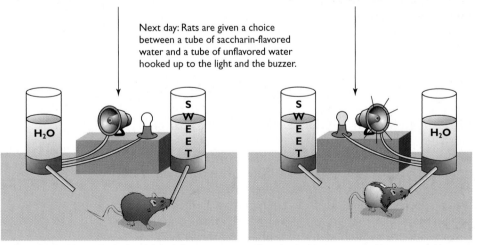

Rats that had been shocked avoid the tube with the lights and noises.

Rats that had been nauseated by x-rays avoid the saccharin-flavored water.

FIGURE 6.19 An experiment by Garcia and Koelling (1966): Rats "blame" an illness on what they ate. They blame pain on what they saw or heard or where they were.

they drank just before getting into the running wheel (Lett, Grant, Koh, & Smith, 2001). The fact that running in a wheel can simultaneously increase preference for the cage while decreasing preference for a food indicates that conditioned taste aversion is a special kind of learning. It also indicates that a single event can be reinforcing for one response and punishing for another!

 CONCEPT CHECK

18. Which kind of learning takes place despite a long delay between the events to be associated?
19. What evidence indicates that conditioned taste aversion is different from other kinds of learning? (Check your answers on page 239.)

Birdsong Learning

Birdsongs brighten the day for people who hear them, but they are earnest business for the birds themselves. For most species song is limited to males during the mating season. As a rule a song indicates, "Here I am. I am a male of species ___. If you're a female of my species, please come closer. If you're a male of my species, go away."

(Among the delights of birdsongs are the exceptions to the rule. Mockingbirds copy all the songs they hear and defend their territory against intruders of all species—sometimes even squirrels, cats, people, and automobiles. Carolina wrens sing male-and-female duets throughout the year. Woodpeckers don't sing but rely on the rhythm and loudness of their pecks to signal others. That woodpecker banging on the metal siding of your house in spring is *trying* to make a racket to impress the females. But on to more relevant matters.)

If you reared an infant songbird in isolation from others of its species, would it develop a normal song on its own? Pigeons and a few others would, but many would not. In many species, including some types of sparrows, a male develops a normal song only if he hears the song of his own species. He *learns most readily during a* sensitive period *early in his first year of life.* The young bird learns better from a live tutor, such as his father, than from a tape-recorded song in a laboratory (Baptista & Petrinovich, 1984; Marler & Peters, 1987, 1988). It will not learn at all from the song of another species. Evidently, it is equipped with mechanisms to produce approximately the right song and ways to identify which songs to imitate (Marler, 1997).

Birdsong learning resembles human language learning in that both take place in a social context, both occur most easily in early life, both start with babbling and gradually improve, and both deteriorate

A male white-crowned sparrow learns his song in the first months of life but does not begin to sing it until the next year.

gradually if the individual becomes deaf later (Brainard & Doupe, 2000). Song learning differs, however, from standard examples of classical and operant conditioning. During the sensitive period, the infant bird only listens. We cannot call the song he hears an unconditioned stimulus because it elicits no apparent response. At no time in this sensitive period does the bird receive any apparent reinforcement.

Nevertheless, he learns a representation of how his song should sound. The following spring, when the bird starts to sing, we see a trial-and-error process. At first his song is a disorganized mixture of sounds, somewhat like a babbling human infant. As time passes he eliminates some sounds and rearranges others until he matches the songs he heard the previous summer (Marler & Peters, 1981, 1982). But he receives no external reinforcement; the only reinforcer is knowing that he has sung correctly.

The point is that the principles of learning vary from one situation to another. If a situation poses special problems (e.g., food selection, song learning in birds, probably language learning in humans), we can expect to find that species have evolved their own special ways of learning (Rozin & Kalat, 1971).

 CONCEPT CHECK

20. What aspects of birdsong learning set it apart from classical and operant conditioning? (Check your answer on page 239.)

Social Learning

According to the **social-learning approach** (Bandura, 1977, 1986), *we learn about many behaviors before we try them. Much learning, especially in humans, results from observing the behaviors of others and from imagining the consequences of our own behavior.* For example, if you want to learn how to swim, paint pictures, or drive a car, you *could* try to learn strictly by trial and error, but you would probably start by watching someone who is already skilled. When you do try the task yourself, your attempt will be subject to reinforcement and punishment; therefore, it falls into the realm of operant conditioning. However, because you will be facilitated by your observations of others, we treat social learning as a special case.

Modeling and Imitation

If you visit another country with customs unlike your own, you may find much that seems bewildering. Even the way to order food in a restaurant may be unfamiliar. A hand gesture such as is considered friendly in some countries but rude and vulgar in others. Many visitors to Japan find the toilets confus-

According to the social-learning approach, we learn many behaviors by observing what others do, imitating behaviors that are reinforced and avoiding behaviors that are punished.

A Japanese toilet is a hole in the ground with no seat. Western visitors usually have to ask how to use it. (You squat.)

ing. With effort you learn foreign customs either because someone explains them to you or because you watch and copy. You *model* your behavior after others or *imitate* others. You also model or imitate the customs of a religious organization, fraternity or sorority, new place of employment, or any other group you join.

Why do we imitate? Sometimes, other people's behavior provides information. For example, if you go outside and see people carrying umbrellas, you assume they know something you don't, and you go back for your own umbrella. You also imitate because other people's behavior establishes a norm or rule. For example, you wear casual clothing where others dress casually and formalwear where others dress formally. You also imitate automatically in some cases. When you see someone yawn, you become more likely to yawn yourself. Even seeing a photo of an animal yawning may have the same result (Figure 6.20). You are not intentionally copying the animal, and the animal is not providing you with any information. You imitate just because seeing the yawn suggested the idea of yawning.

You automatically imitate many other actions that you see, often with no apparent motivation (Dijksterhuis & Bargh, 2001). If you see someone

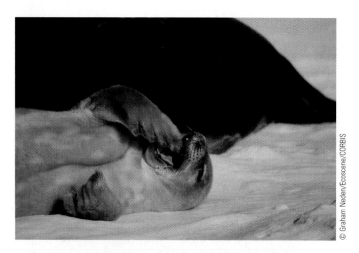

FIGURE 6.20 Does looking at this photo make you want to yawn?

smile or frown, you briefly start to smile or frown. Your expression may be just a quick, involuntary twitch, and an observer may have to watch carefully to see it, but it often does occur. Even newborns imitate facial expressions (Meltzoff & Moore, 1977, 1983) (see Figure 6.21).

Spectators at an athletic event sometimes move their arms or legs slightly in synchrony with what some athlete is doing. When expert pianists listen to a composition they have practiced, they start involuntarily tapping their fingers as if they were playing the music (Haueisen & Knösche, 2001). Similarly, people tend to copy the hand gestures they see (Bertenthal, Longo, & Kosobud, 2006). You can demonstrate this tendency by telling someone, "Please wave your hands" while you clap your hands. Many people copy your actions instead of following your instructions.

 Try It Yourself

Imitation relates to an exciting discovery in brain functioning known as **mirror neurons,** *which are activated while you perform a movement and also while you watch someone else perform the same movement,* such as reaching to grab an object. You identify with what someone else is doing, imagine what it would be like to make the same movement, and start activating cells that would make the movement (Fogassi et al., 2005; Gallese, Fadiga, Fogassi, & Rizzolatti, 1996). Something similar happens in other brain systems. Watching someone showing an expression of disgust activates the same brain areas as if you were feeling disgusted yourself (Wicker et al., 2003). Mirror neurons are probably important for imitation and other

social behaviors. However, we do not yet know how they develop. Are you born with mirror neurons, or do they develop as you learn how to identify with other people?

Albert Bandura, Dorothea Ross, and Sheila Ross (1963) studied the role of imitation for learning aggressive behavior. They asked two groups of children to watch films in which an adult or a cartoon character violently attacked an inflated "Bobo" doll. Another group watched a different film. They then left the children in a room with a Bobo doll. Only the children who had watched films with attacks on the doll attacked the doll themselves, using many of the same movements they had just seen (Figure 6.22). The clear implication is that children copy the aggressive behavior they have seen in others.

✓ CONCEPT CHECK

21. How may mirror neurons contribute to imitation?
22. Many people complain that they cannot find much difference between the two major political parties in the United States because so many American politicians campaign using similar styles and take similar stands on the issues. Explain this observation in terms of social learning. (Check your answers on page 239.)

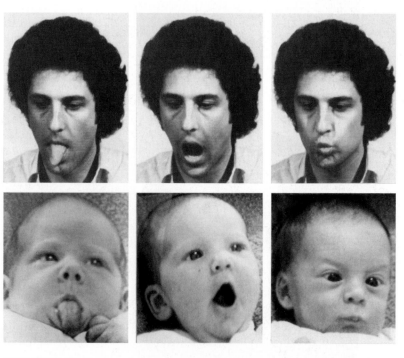

FIGURE 6.21 Newborn infants sometimes imitate people's facial expressions. *(Source: A.N. Meltzoff & M.K. Moore, "Imitation of facial and manual gestures by human neonates." Science, 1977, 198, 75–78.)*

FIGURE 6.22 This girl attacks a doll after seeing a film of a woman hitting it. Witnessing violence increases the probability of violent behavior.

other teams copy its style of play. When a television program wins high ratings, other producers are sure to present look-alikes the following year. Advertisers depend heavily on vicarious reinforcement; they show happy, successful people using their product, with the implication that if you use their product, you too will be happy and successful. The people promoting state lotteries show the ecstatic winners—never the losers!—suggesting that if you play the lottery, you too can win a fortune.

Vicarious Reinforcement and Punishment

Six months ago, your best friend quit a job with Consolidated Generic Products to open a restaurant. Now you are considering quitting your job and opening your own restaurant. How do you decide what to do?

You would probably start by asking how successful your friend has been. You imitate behavior that apparently has been reinforcing to someone else. That is, you learn by **vicarious reinforcement** or **vicarious punishment**—by *substituting someone else's experience for your own.*

Whenever a new business venture succeeds, other companies copy it. For example, the first few successful Internet companies were followed by a horde of imitators. When a sports team wins consistently,

CRITICAL THINKING
A STEP FURTHER

Vicarious Learning

Might vicarious learning lead to monotony of behavior and excessive conformity? How can we learn vicariously without becoming just like everyone else?

Vicarious punishment is generally less effective. If someone gets caught cheating, either in a classroom or in business, or if someone goes to prison for a crime, do other people quit those behaviors? Not necessarily. We are often reminded of the health risks associated with cigarette smoking, obesity, risky sex, lack of exercise, or failure to wear seat belts, but many people ignore the dangers. Even the death penalty, an extreme example of vicarious punishment, does not demonstrably lower the murder rate.

Why is vicarious punishment often so ineffective? To experience vicarious reinforcement, we identify with a successful person. To experience vicarious punishment, we have to identify with a loser, and most of us resist that identification.

Self-Efficacy in Social Learning

We primarily imitate people we regard as successful. So, when we watch an Olympic diver win a gold medal for a superb display of physical control, why do most of us *not* try to imitate those dives? We imitate someone else's behavior only if we have a sense of **self-efficacy**—*the perception of being able to perform the task successfully.* You consider your past successes and failures, compare yourself to the successful person, and estimate your chance of success.

We see this effect in children's life aspirations. Nearly anyone would like a high-paying, high-prestige profession, but many think they could

States that sponsor lotteries provide publicity and an exciting atmosphere for each big payoff. They hope this publicity will provide vicarious reinforcement that encourages other people to buy lottery tickets.

We tend to imitate the actions of successful people but only if we feel self-efficacy, a belief that we could perform the task well.

never rise to that level, so they don't try (Bandura, Barbaranelli, Caprara, & Pastorelli, 2001). One value of getting more women and minorities into high-visibility leadership jobs is that they provide role models, showing others that the opportunity is available.

Sometimes, people know that they cannot do much by themselves but gain confidence in what they can do with a group effort (Bandura, 2000). Even groups differ in their feeling of efficacy or nonefficacy. A group with confidence in its abilities accomplishes much more than a group with doubts.

Self-Reinforcement and Self-Punishment in Social Learning

We learn by observing others who are doing what we would like to do. If our sense of self-efficacy is strong enough, we try to imitate their behavior. But actually succeeding often requires prolonged efforts. People typically set a goal for themselves and monitor their progress toward that goal. They provide reinforcement or punishment for themselves, just as if they were training someone else. They say to themselves, "If I finish this math assignment on time, I'll treat myself to a movie and a new magazine. If I don't finish on time, I'll make myself clean the stove and the sink." (Nice threat, but people usually forgive themselves without imposing the punishment.)

We acquire a sense of self-efficacy mainly through our own successes but also partly by watching and identifying with role models.

Some therapists teach clients to use self-reinforcement. One 10-year-old boy had a habit of biting his fingernails, sometimes down to the skin and even drawing blood. He learned to keep records of how much nail-biting he did in the morning, afternoon, and evening, and then he set goals for himself. If he met the goals by reducing his nail-biting, he wrote compliments such as "I'm great! I did wonderful!" The penalty for doing worse was that he would return his weekly allowance to his parents. An additional reinforcement was that his father promised that if the son made enough progress, he would let the son be the "therapist" to help the father quit smoking. Over several weeks the boy quit nail biting altogether (Ronen & Rosenbaum, 2001).

One amusing anecdote shows how self-reinforcement and self-punishment can fail: Psychologist Ron Ash (1986) tried to teach himself to quit cigarettes by smoking only while he was reading *Psychological Bulletin* and other highly respected but tedious publications. He hoped to associate smoking with boredom. Two months later, he was smoking as much as ever, but he was starting to *enjoy* reading *Psychological Bulletin*!

IN CLOSING

Why We Do What We Do

Assembling a bicycle can be fairly complicated, with page after page of instructions. Still, when you're done, you're done. Assembling a person is never finished. Few of the brain's connections are permanent. Learning modifies almost everything we do. Indeed, you would have trouble listing much of what you did today that was not learned. ▮

Summary

- *Conditioned taste aversions.* Animals, including people, learn to avoid foods, especially unfamiliar ones, if they become ill afterward. This type of learning occurs reliably after a single pairing, even with a delay of hours between the food and the illness. Animals are predisposed to associate illness with what they eat or drink, not with other events. (page 232)

- *Birdsong learning.* Infant birds of some species must hear their songs during a sensitive period in the first few months of life if they are to develop a fully normal song the following spring. During the early learning, the bird makes no apparent response and receives no apparent reinforcement. (page 234)

- *Imitation.* We learn much by observing other people's actions and their consequences. Possibly because of mirror neurons, we automatically imitate some actions. (page 235)

- *Vicarious reinforcement and punishment.* We tend to imitate behaviors that lead to reinforcement for other people. We are less consistent in avoiding behaviors that lead to punishment. (page 237)

- *Self-efficacy.* Whether we decide to imitate a behavior depends on whether we believe we are capable of duplicating it and whether we believe we would be reinforced for it. (page 237)

- *Self-reinforcement and self-punishment.* Once people have decided to try to imitate a certain behavior, they set goals for themselves and may even provide their own reinforcements. (page 238)

Answers to Concept Checks

18. Conditioned taste aversions develop despite a long delay between food and illness. (page 234)

19. In addition to the fact that conditioned taste aversion occurs over long delays, animals are predisposed to associate foods and not other events with illnesses. Also, an event such as running in a wheel can be reinforcing for other responses but simultaneously decrease preference for a taste associated with it. (page 234)

20. The most distinctive feature is that birdsong learning occurs when the learner makes no apparent response and receives no apparent reinforcement. In certain sparrow species, birdsong learning occurs most readily during an early sensitive period, and the bird is capable of learning its own species' song but not the song of another species. (page 234)

21. When you see someone do something, mirror neurons become activated. They are also active when you make the movement itself. So watching a movement facilitates doing it. (page 236)

22. One reason that most American politicians run similar campaigns and take similar stands is that they all tend to copy the same models—candidates who have won recent elections. Another reason is that they all pay attention to the same public opinion polls. (page 236)

CHAPTER ENDING

Key Terms and Activities

Key Terms

You can check the page listed for a complete description of a term. You can also check the glossary/index at the end of the text for a definition of a given term, or you can download a list of all the terms and their definitions for any chapter at this website:

www.thomsonedu.com/ psychology/kalat

acquisition (page 210)
applied behavior analysis (or behavior modification) (page 229)
avoidance learning (page 222)
behaviorist (page 203)
belongingness (page 224)
blocking effect (page 215)
chaining (page 226)
classical conditioning (or Pavlovian conditioning) (page 208)
conditioned response (CR) (page 208)
conditioned stimulus (CS) (page 208)
conditioned taste aversion (page 232)
continuous reinforcement (page 227)
discrimination (pages 211, 224)

discriminative stimulus (page 224)
disequilibrium principle (page 220)
drug tolerance (page 213)
escape learning (page 222)
extinction (pages 210, 223)
fixed-interval schedule (page 227)
fixed-ratio schedule (page 227)
intermittent reinforcement (page 227)
intervening variable (page 203)
law of effect (page 219)
learning curve (page 218)
methodological behaviorist (page 203)
mirror neurons (page 236)
negative punishment (page 222)
negative reinforcement (page 222)
omission training (page 222)
operant conditioning (or instrumental conditioning) (page 219)
passive avoidance learning (page 222)
positive reinforcement (page 222)
Premack principle (page 220)
primary reinforcer (page 220)
punishment (page 221)
radical behaviorist (page 204)
reinforcement (page 219)

reinforcer (page 219)
schedule of reinforcement (page 227)
secondary reinforcer (page 220)
self-efficacy (page 237)
sensitive period (page 234)
shaping (page 226)
skeletal responses (page 219)
social-learning approach (page 235)
spontaneous recovery (page 211)
stimulus control (page 224)
stimulus generalization (pages 211, 223)
stimulus–response psychology (page 204)
unconditioned reflex (page 207)
unconditioned response (UCR) (page 208)
unconditioned stimulus (UCS) (page 208)
variable-interval schedule (page 228)
variable-ratio schedule (page 227)
vicarious reinforcement (or vicarious punishment) (page 237)
visceral responses (page 219)

Suggestions for Further Reading

Bandura, A. (1986). *Social foundations of thought and action.* Upper Saddle River, NJ: Prentice Hall. A review of social learning by its most influential investigator.

Kroodsma, D. (2005). *The singing life of birds.* New York: Houghton Mifflin. Thorough account of research on a fascinating kind of animal learning.

Staddon, J. (1993). *Behaviorism.* London: Duckworth. A critique of both the strengths and weaknesses of Skinner's views.

 Web/Technology Resources

Student Companion Website

www.thomsonedu.com/psychology/kalat

Explore the Student Companion Website for Online Try-It-Yourself activities, practice quizzes, flashcards, and more! The companion site also has direct links to the following websites.

Positive Reinforcement

server.bmod.athabascau.ca/html/prtut/reinpair.htm

Lyle K. Grant of Athabasca University helps students understand what does and what does not constitute positive reinforcement. Be sure you understand the examples before you begin the practice exercise.

B. F. Skinner

http://www.bfskinner.org/bio.asp

Skinner's daughter provides a biography of a highly influential psychologist.

Albert Bandura

www.ship.edu/~cgboeree/bandura.html

C. George Boeree of Shippensburg University provides a short biography of Albert Bandura, a pioneer in the field of social learning.

 For Additional Study

Kalat Premium Website

http://www.thomsonedu.com

For Critical Thinking Videos and additional Online Try-It-Yourself activities, go to this site to enter or purchase your code for the Kalat Premium Website.

ThomsonNOW!

http://www.thomsonedu.com

Go to this site for the link to ThomsonNOW, your one-stop study shop. Take a Pretest for this chapter, and ThomsonNOW will generate a personalized Study Plan based on your test results. The Study Plan will identify the topics you need to review and direct you to online resources to help you master those topics. You can then take a Posttest to help you determine the concepts you have mastered and what you still need to work on.

Memory

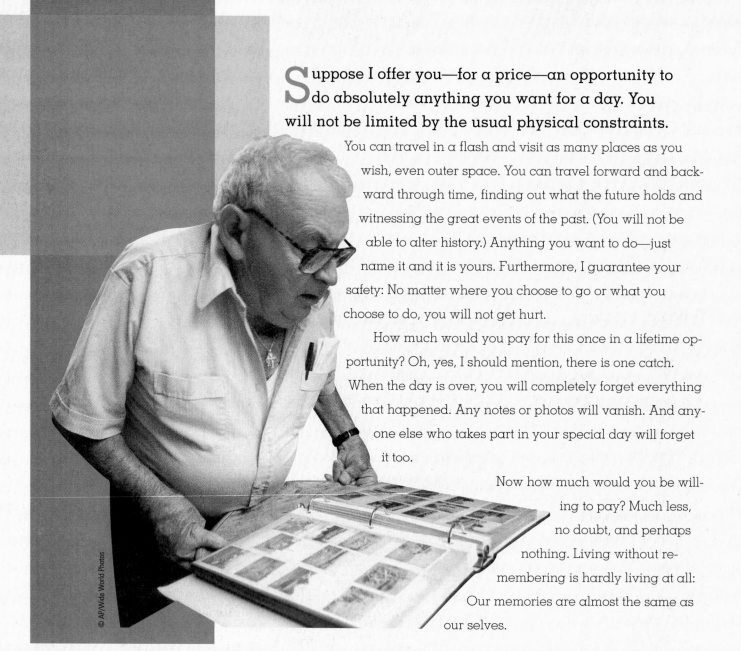

Suppose I offer you—for a price—an opportunity to do absolutely anything you want for a day. You will not be limited by the usual physical constraints.

You can travel in a flash and visit as many places as you wish, even outer space. You can travel forward and backward through time, finding out what the future holds and witnessing the great events of the past. (You will not be able to alter history.) Anything you want to do—just name it and it is yours. Furthermore, I guarantee your safety: No matter where you choose to go or what you choose to do, you will not get hurt.

How much would you pay for this once in a lifetime opportunity? Oh, yes, I should mention, there is one catch. When the day is over, you will completely forget everything that happened. Any notes or photos will vanish. And anyone else who takes part in your special day will forget it too.

Now how much would you be willing to pay? Much less, no doubt, and perhaps nothing. Living without remembering is hardly living at all: Our memories are almost the same as our selves.

With a suitable reminder, you will find that you remember some events quite distinctly, even after a long delay. Other memories, however, are lost or distorted.

Types of Memory

- *Do we have different kinds of memory?*
- *If so, what is the best way to describe those differences?*

Every year, people compete in the World Memory Championship in Britain. It is like a mental Olympic competition. (You can read about it at this Web site: http://www.worldmemorychampionship.com/). One event is speed of memorizing a shuffled deck of 52 cards. The all-time record is 32.13 seconds. Another is memorizing a string of binary digits (11110011011001 . . .) within 30 minutes. The record total is 3,705 digits. People also compete at memorizing dates of fictional events, names of unfamiliar faces in photos, and so forth. Dominic O'Brien, the seven-time world champion, gives speeches and writes books about how to train your memory. However, he admits that one time while he was practicing card memorization, an irate friend called from an airport to complain that O'Brien had forgotten to pick him up. O'Brien apologized and drove to London's Gatwick Airport, practicing card memorization along the way. When he arrived, he remembered that his friend was at Heathrow, London's other major airport (Johnstone, 1994).

Anyone—you, me, or Dominic O'Brien—remembers some information and forgets the rest. Let's define memory broadly. **Memory** refers to *the retention of information*. It includes skills such as riding a bicycle or eating with chopsticks. It also includes facts that never change (your birthday), facts that seldom change (your mailing address), and facts that frequently change (where you last parked your car). You remember repeated events, most of the important events of your life, and some of the less important events. You remember many of the most interesting and important facts you were taught in school and a few of the less useful ones. (I remember learning that "Polynesians eat poi and breadfruit," although I seldom meet a Polynesian person, and I wouldn't recognize poi or breadfruit if I saw it.)

Dominic O'Brien, seven-time winner of the World Memory Championship and author of several books on training your memory, admits he sometimes forgets practical information, such as promising to meet a friend at Heathrow Airport.

© Rupert Watts

Human memory is analogous to that of a computer in some ways, but it also differs in important ways (Bjork & VanHuele, 1992). If you press the Store key on your computer, it will store the information without pausing to consider whether it is boring. If you retrieve something from your computer, it will give it to you precisely. In contrast, if you try to recall an event from your childhood, you remember better at some times than others, and you remember some parts correctly while losing or distorting others. You might even claim to remember events that never happened.

A few words of advice: This chapter, like chapters 4 and 8, includes many Try It Yourself activities. You will gain much more from this chapter if you take the time to try each of them.

Ebbinghaus's Pioneering Studies of Memory

Suppose you wanted to study memory, but no one had ever done memory research before, so you couldn't copy anyone else's procedure. Where would you start? Some of the earliest psychological researchers asked people to describe their memories. The obvious problem was that the researchers did not know when the memories had formed, how many times they had been rehearsed, or even whether they were correct. German psychologist Hermann Ebbinghaus (1850–1909) got around these problems by an approach that was completely original at the time, although we now take it for granted: He taught new material, so that he knew exactly what someone had learned and when, and then measured memory after various delays. To be sure the material was totally new, he used lists of nonsense syllables, such as GAK or JEK. He wrote

FIGURE 7.1 Hermann Ebbinghaus pioneered the scientific study of memory by observing his own capacity for memorizing lists of nonsense syllables.

out 2,300 syllables, assembled them randomly into lists (Figure 7.1), and then set out to study memorization. He had no cooperative introductory psychology students to enlist for his study or friends eager to memorize nonsense syllables, so he ran all the tests on himself. For 6 years he memorized thousands of lists of nonsense syllables. (He was either very dedicated to his science or uncommonly tolerant of boredom.)

Many of his findings were hardly surprising. For example, as shown in Figure 7.2, the longer a list of nonsense syllables, the more slowly he memorized it. "Of course!" you might scoff. But Ebbinghaus was not just demonstrating the obvious. He measured *how much* longer it took to memorize a longer list. You might similarly object to the law of gravity: "Of course the farther something falls, the longer it takes to hit the ground!" Nevertheless, measuring the acceleration of gravity was essential to progress in physics. In

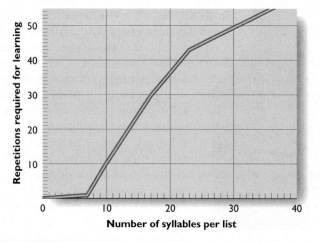

FIGURE 7.2 Ebbinghaus counted how many times he had to read a list of nonsense syllables before he could recite it once correctly. For a list of seven or fewer, one reading was usually enough. Beyond seven, the longer list, the more repetitions he needed. *(From Ebbinghaus, 1885/1913)*

the same way, measuring how long it takes to learn a list enables researchers to compare learning under different conditions: Do adults learn faster than children? Do we learn some kinds of lists faster than others? Ebbinghaus's approach led to all the later research on memory, including findings that were not so obvious.

Memory for Lists of Items

Unlike Ebbinghaus, most current memory researches use meaningful words instead of nonsense syllables. Still, they often use his method of presenting words in a list. If you read a list of words, you are more likely to remember some kinds of words than others. To illustrate, read the following list, close the book, and write as many of the words as you can. The demonstration would work better if you saw the words one at a time on a screen. You can approximate that procedure by covering the list with a sheet of paper and pulling it down to reveal one word at a time.

*Try It
Yourself*

LEMON
GRAPE
POTATO
COCONUT
CUCUMBER
TOMATO
BROCCOLI
APPLE
SPINACH
TOMATO
ORANGE
LETTUCE
CARROT
STRAWBERRY
BANANA
TOMATO
PHILADELPHIA
LIME
PEACH
PINEAPPLE
TURNIP
MANGO
TOMATO
BLUEBERRY
TOMATO
APRICOT
WATERMELON

I hope you tried the demonstration. If so, TOMATO was probably one of the words you remembered, because it occurred five times instead of just once. Other things being equal, repetition helps. You probably remembered LEMON and WATERMELON,

Bob Williams was one of 40 aging former paratroopers who reenacted his parachute jump on the 50th anniversary of D-day. We forget most events from 50 years ago but remember the distinctive ones.

taken, or all the teachers you have ever had, you will probably include both the earliest ones and the most recent.

You probably also remembered CARROT and PHILADELPHIA. The word CARROT was distinctive because of its size, color, and font. PHILADELPHIA stood out as the only item on the list that was neither a fruit nor a vegetable. In a list of mostly similar items, the distinctive ones are easier to remember. We also tend to remember unusual people and those with unusual names. If you meet several men of ordinary appearance with similar names, like John Stevens, Steve Johnson, and Joe Stevenson, you will have trouble learning their names. You will more quickly remember a 7-foot-tall, redheaded man named Stinky Rockefeller.

On the other hand, if you are like most Americans, you probably didn't remember MANGO. Although that word might stand out as unusual, you probably didn't grow up eating mangoes in early childhood. People find it easier to remember words they learned in early childhood (e.g., APPLE, ORANGE, and BANANA) than words they learned later (Juhasz, 2005). However, if your parents introduced you to mangoes early, your chance of remembering the word increases. Similarly, if you grew up watching *Sesame Street,* you can probably name the characters Bert, Ernie, and Oscar the Grouch more quickly than many characters you have watched on television more recently.

Another effect would be fun to demonstrate with a series of slides: Suppose you see these words on the screen, one at a time, and right after the word LIME you see, to your surprise, a photo of two attractive naked people. At the end you don't have to include "Naked people" on your memory list, but something else happens: You probably do *not* remember the word PEACH, and probably not PINEAPPLE either. The naked people distracted you so much that you did not concentrate on the next word or two (Schmidt, 2002).

because they were the first and last items on the list. The **primacy effect** *is the tendency to remember well the first items.* The **recency effect** *is the tendency to remember the final items.* The primacy and recency effects are robust for almost any type of memory, not just word lists. If you try to list all the people you have ever dated, all the long-distance trips you have ever

CONCEPT CHECK

1. What are some factors that increase or decrease your probability of remembering a word on a list? (Check your answer on page 258.)

Methods of Testing Memory

Nearly everyone occasionally has a tip-of-the-tongue experience (Brown & McNeill, 1966). You want to remember someone's name, and all you can think of is a similar name that you know isn't right. You will probably think of the correct name later, and you are sure you would recognize it if you heard it.

In other words memory is not an all-or-none thing. You might seem to remember or seem to forget depending on how someone tests you. Let's survey the main ways of testing memory.

Free Recall

The simplest method for the tester (though not for the person tested) is to ask for **free recall**. To recall something is *to produce a response, as you do on essay tests or short-answer tests.* For instance, "Please name all the children in your second-grade class." You probably will not name many, partly because you confuse the names of the children in your second-grade class with those you knew in other grades.

Cued Recall

You will do better with **cued recall**, in which you *receive significant hints about the material.* For example, a photograph of the children in your second-grade class (Figure 7.3) or a list of their initials will help you

FIGURE 7.3 Can you recall the names of the students in your second-grade class? Trying to remember without any hints is *free recall*. Using a photo or a list of initials is *cued recall*.

remember many names. Try this: Cover the right side of Table 7.1 with a piece of paper and try to identify the authors of each book on the left. (This method is free recall.) Then uncover the right side, revealing each author's initials, and try again. (This method is cued recall.)

Try It Yourself

Recognition

With **recognition**, a third method of testing memory, someone is *offered several choices and asked to select the correct one.* People usually recognize more items than they recall. For example, I might give you a list of 60 names and ask you to check off the correct names of children in your second-grade class. Multiple-choice tests use the recognition method.

Savings

A fourth method, the **savings method** (also known as the **relearning method**), detects weak memories *by comparing the speed of original learning to the speed of relearning.* Suppose you cannot name the children in your second-grade class and cannot even pick out their names from a list of choices. You would nevertheless learn a correct list of names faster than a list of people you had never met. That is, you save time when you relearn material that you learned in the past. The amount of time saved (time needed for original learning minus the time for relearning) is a measure of memory.

TABLE 7.1 The Difference Between Free Recall and Cued Recall

Instructions: First try to identify the author of each book listed in the left column while covering the right column (free recall method). Then expose the right column, which gives each author's initials, and try again (cued recall).

Book	Author
Moby Dick	H. M.
Emma and *Pride and Prejudice*	J. A.
Hercule Poirot stories	A. C.
Sherlock Holmes stories	A. C. D.
I Know Why the Caged Bird Sings	M. A.
War and Peace	L. T.
This textbook	J. K.
The Canterbury Tales	G. C.
The Origin of Species	C. D.
Gone with the Wind	M. M.
Les Misérables	V. H.

(For answers see page 258, answer A.)

Implicit Memory

Free recall, cued recall, recognition, and savings are tests of **explicit memory (or direct memory)**. That is, *someone who states an answer regards it as a product of his or her memory.* In **implicit memory (or indirect memory)**, *an experience influences what you say or do even though you might not be aware of the influence.* If you find that definition unsatisfactory, you are not alone (Frensch & Rünger, 2003). Defining something in terms of a vague concept like "awareness" is not a good habit. So this definition is tentative until we develop a better one.

The best way to explain implicit memory is by example: Suppose you are in a conversation while other people nearby are discussing something else. You ignore the other discussion, but a few words from that background conversation probably creep into your own. You do not even notice the influence, although an observer might.

Here is a demonstration of implicit memories. For each of the following three-letter combinations, fill in additional letters to make any English word:

CON___
SUP___
DIS___
PRO___

You could have thought of any number of words—the dictionary lists well over 100 familiar CON___

words alone. Did you happen to write any of the following: *conversation, suppose, discussion,* or *probably?* Each of these words appeared in the paragraph before this demonstration. *Reading or hearing a word temporarily* primes *that word and increases the chance that you will use it yourself,* even if you are not aware of the influence (Graf & Mandler, 1984; Schacter, 1987). However, this demonstration works better if you listen to spoken words than if you read them. To get a better sense of priming, try an Online Try It Yourself activity. Go to **http://www.thomsonedu.com/psychology/kalat.** Navigate to the student Web site, then to the Online Try It Yourself section, and click Implicit Memories. Table 7.2 contrasts the various memory tests.

The brain stores implicit memories differently from explicit memories. People with various kinds of brain damage show impaired explicit memory despite normal implicit memory (such as priming) or impaired implicit memory and normal explicit memory (Gabrieli, Fleischman, Keane, Reminger, & Morrell, 1995; Levy, Stark, & Squire, 2004). If people hear a few words repeatedly while they are anesthetized for surgery, the experience primes them to think of those words afterward (an implicit memory), even though they have no explicit memory of hearing those words (Jelicic, Bonke, Wolters, & Phaf, 1992).

Procedural memories, *memories of motor skills* such as walking and talking, are another kind of implicit memories. Psychologists distinguish procedural

TABLE 7.2 Several Ways to Test Memory

Title	Description	Example
Recall	You are asked to say what you remember.	Name the Seven Dwarfs.
Cued recall	You are given significant hints to help you remember.	Name the Seven Dwarfs. Hint: One was always smiling, one was smart, one never talked, one always seemed to have a cold . . .
Recognition	You are asked to choose the correct item from among several items.	Which of the following were among the Seven Dwarfs: Sneezy, Sleazy, Dopey, Dippy, Hippy, Happy?
Savings (relearning)	You are asked to relearn something: If it takes you less time than when you first learned that material, some memory has persisted.	Try memorizing this list: Sleepy, Sneezy, Doc, Dopey, Grumpy, Happy, Bashful. Can you memorize it faster than this list: Sleazy, Snoopy, Duke, Dippy, Gripey, Hippy, Blushy?
Implicit memory	You are asked to generate words, without necessarily regarding them as memories	You hear the story "Snow White and the Seven Dwarfs." Later you are asked to fill in these blanks to make any words that come to mind: _ L _ _ P _ _ N _ _ Z _ _ _ C _ O _ EY _ R _ _ P _ _ _ P P _ _ A _ H _ U _

memories from **declarative memories,** *memories we can readily state in words.* To illustrate the difference, take some motor skill you have mastered—such as riding a bicycle, using in-line skates, or tying a necktie—and try explaining it in words (no gestures!) to someone who has never done it before. You will quickly discover how much you do without thinking about it verbally. Also, if you type, you know the locations of the letters well enough to press the right key at the right time, but can you state that knowledge explicitly? For example, which letter is directly to the right of C? Which is directly to the left of P?

 CONCEPT CHECK

2. For each of these examples, identify the type of memory test—free recall, cued recall, recognition, savings, or implicit.
   a. Although you thought you had forgotten your high school French, you do better in your college French course than your roommate, who never studied French before.
   b. You are trying to remember the phone number of the local pizza parlor without looking it up in the phone directory.
   c. You hear a song on the radio without paying much attention to it. Later, you find yourself humming a melody, but you don't know what it is or where you heard it.
   d. You forget where you parked your car, so you scan the parking lot hoping to pick yours out among all the others.
   e. Your friend asks, "What's the name of our chemistry lab instructor? I think it's Julie or Judy something."
3. Is remembering how to tie your shoes a procedural memory or a declarative memory? Is remembering the color of your shoes a procedural or a declarative memory? (Check your answers on page 258.)

Application: Suspect Lineups as Recognition Memory

Suppose you witness a crime, and now the police want you to identify the guilty person. They ask you to look at a few suspects in a lineup or to examine a book of photos. Your task is a clear example of recognition memory, as you are trying to identify the correct item among some distracters.

The task raises a problem, familiar from your own experience. When you take a multiple-choice test— another example of recognition memory—you pick the best available choice. Sometimes, you think none of the choices is exactly right, but you select the best one available. Now, imagine doing the same with a book of photos. You look through the choices, eliminate most, and pick the one that looks most like the perpetrator of the crime. You tell the police you think suspect 42 is the guilty person. "Think?" the police ask. "Your testimony won't be worth much in court unless you're sure." You look again, eager to cooperate. Finally, you say yes, you're sure. The police say, "Good, that's the person we thought did it." You testify in court, and the suspect is convicted. But is justice done? Since the advent of DNA testing, investigators have identified many innocent people who were convicted by the testimony of a confident witness.

Memory researchers have proposed ways to improve suspect lineups, and most U.S. police investigators now follow these recommendations. One is to avoid any hint of agreeing with a tentative choice (Wells, Olson, & Charman, 2003; Zaragoza, Payment, Ackil, Drivdahl, & Beck, 2001). Any sign of agreement adds to a witness's confidence, regardless of whether the witness's report was right or wrong (Semmler, Brewer, & Wells, 2004). Another recommendation is to present the lineup sequentially—that is, one suspect at a time (Wells et al., 2000). For each suspect the witness says "yes" or "no." As soon as the witness says yes, the procedure is finished. After all, there is no point in looking at additional suspects if the witness has already decided. Most important, the witness should have no opportunity to go back and reexamine photos after rejecting them. The witness should make a definite decision or none at all, not just choose the best among those available.

 CRITICAL THINKING
A STEP FURTHER

Lineups and Multiple-Choice Testing

What would happen if classroom multiple-choice tests were done with sequential answers? That is, after each question you would have to say yes or no to each answer before reading the next answer.

The Information-Processing View of Memory

Over the years psychologists have repeatedly tried to explain the mechanisms of behavior by analogy to the technologies of their time. In the 1600s René Descartes compared animal behavior to the actions of a hydraulic pump. Psychologists of the early 1900s suggested that learning worked like a telephone switchboard. Later, they compared memory to a computer. A computer has three kinds of memory. First, if you type letters faster than the screen can show them, the computer stores a few letters in a temporary buffer until it can display them. Older computers showed this effect more often than today's faster models. Second, the material you have written without saving it is in random access memory (RAM). RAM is vulnerable, as you learned if you ever had a power outage while writing something. Finally, you can save something to a disk that stores huge amounts of information in a stable, almost permanent way.

According to the **information-processing model**, human memory resembles that of a computer in this regard: *Information that enters the system is processed, coded, and stored* (Figure 7.4). According to a popular version of this model, information first enters a sensory store (like the computer's buffer). Some of that information is stored in short-term memory (like RAM), and some short-term memory transfers into long-term memory (like a hard disk). Eventually, a cue from the environment prompts the system to retrieve stored information (Atkinson & Shiffrin, 1968). Let's examine each part of this model.

The Sensory Store

Close your eyes and turn your head. Then blink your eyes open and shut. You will have a sudden impression that you

Try It Yourself

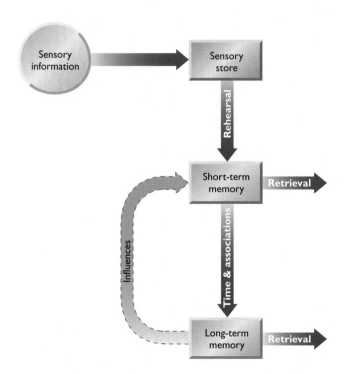

FIGURE 7.4 The information-processing model of memory resembles a computer's memory system, including temporary and permanent memory.

can still see "in your mind's eye" much detail from what you just saw. However, you cannot describe it all, mainly because the image fades faster than you can describe it. It fades even faster if you look at something else instead of keeping your eyes shut.

© Joe McDonald/CORBIS

A bolt of lightning flashes through the sky for a split second, but you can visualize it in detail for a short time afterward. Your sensory store momentarily holds the image.

This *momentary storage of sensory information* is called the **sensory store,** also known as iconic memory (for visual information) and echoic memory (for auditory). George Sperling (1960) found a way to demonstrate visual sensory store. He flashed an array like the one shown in Figure 7.5 onto a screen for 50 milliseconds. When he asked viewers to report what they saw, they recalled a mean of only about four items. If he had stopped his experiment at that point, he might have concluded that viewers stored only a few items. However, he surmised that the sensory store was probably fading while people were describing it. So he told viewers he would ask them to report only one row of the array, varying which row.

After flashing an array on the screen, he immediately used a high, medium, or low tone to signal which row to recall. Frequently, people could name all the items in whichever row he indicated. Evidently, the whole array was briefly available to memory. When he waited for even 1 second before signaling which row to recall, though, recall was poor. That is, for the sensory store, "use it or lose it," and you need to use it fast.

You can try a version of Sperling's experiment in an Online Try It Yourself activity, Sperling Effect. However, this is a fragile effect (as opposed to a robust effect, which occurs under most circumstances). The effect improves with practice. It also varies from one person to another and from one com-

Online Try It Yourself

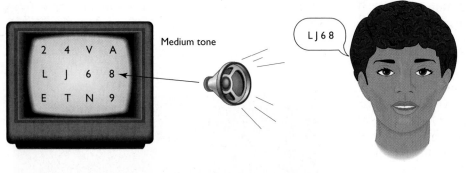

Medium tone

LJ68

Stimulus array flashed on screen for 0.05 seconds

Tone within the next 0.3 seconds indicates which row to speak

Participant says the correct row

FIGURE 7.5 George Sperling (1960) flashed arrays like this on a screen for 50 milliseconds. After the display went off, a signal told the viewer which row to recite.

puter to another depending on their speed. Give it a try, but don't be dismayed if your results don't match the predictions.

Is the sensory store really memory, or is it perception? It is a little of both. Not everything falls neatly into our human-made categories.

 CONCEPT CHECK

4. Would viewers probably remember as many items if Sperling had flashed pictures of objects instead of numbers and letters? (Check your answer on page 258)

 CRITICAL THINKING
A STEP FURTHER

Sensory Storage

Sperling demonstrated the capacity of the sensory store for visual information. How could you demonstrate the capacity of the sensory store for auditory information?

Short-Term and Long-Term Memory

Of all the information you see, hear, or feel, most fades at once, you deal with a little of it temporarily, and you store even less permanently. The traditional version of information-processing theory distinguishes between **short-term memory,** *temporary storage of recent events,* and **long-term memory,** *a relatively permanent store.* For example, while you are playing tennis, the current score is in your short-term memory, and the rules of the game are in your long-term memory.

Psychologists distinguish two major types of long-term memory: semantic and episodic. **Semantic**

memory is *memory of general principles and facts*—like nearly everything you learn in school. **Episodic memory** is *memory for specific events in a person's life* (Tulving, 1989). For example, your memory of the law of gravity is a semantic memory, whereas remembering the time you dropped your grandmother's vase is an episodic memory. Remembering the rules of tennis is a semantic memory; your memory of the time you beat your roommate at tennis is an episodic memory.

Most episodic memories are more fragile than semantic memories. For example, if you don't play tennis for a few years, you will still remember the rules, but you will forget most of the specific times you played tennis. Older people are especially likely to forget specific episodes while retaining semantic memories (Piolino, Desgranges, Benali, & Eustache, 2002).

People also frequently remember some fact they have heard (a semantic memory) but forget where they heard it (an episodic memory). *Forgetting where or how you learned something* is called **source amnesia.** Therefore, people confuse reliable information with the unreliable. ("Did I hear this idea from my professor or was it on *South Park?* Did I read about brain transplants in *Scientific American* or in the *National Enquirer?*") As a result you might dismiss an idea at first because you know it came from an unreliable source, but later remember it, forget where you heard it, and start to take it seriously (M. K. Johnson, Hashtroudi, & Lindsay, 1993; Riccio, 1994). In chapter 13 on social psychology, we return to this phenomenon, known as the *sleeper effect.*

Psychologists have traditionally drawn several distinctions between short- and long-term memory, including capacity, dependence on retrieval cues, and decay over time (Table 7.3). However, on closer examination we can find exceptions at least to the latter two. Let us consider these comparisons between short- and long-term memory (see Table 7.3).

Differences in Capacity

Long-term memory has a vast, hard-to-measure capacity. Asking how much information you could store in long-term memory is like asking how many books you could fit into a library. The answer depends on how big the books are, how you arrange them, and so forth. Short-term memory in contrast has a small, easily measured capacity. Read each of the following sequences of letters and then look away and try to re-

TABLE 7.3 Sensory Store, Short-Term Memory, and Long-Term Memory

	Sensory Store	Short-Term Memory	Long-Term Memory
Capacity	Whatever you see or hear at one moment	7 ± 2 items in healthy adults	Vast, uncountable
Duration	Fraction of a second	A period of seconds if not rehearsed	Perhaps a lifetime
Example	You see something for an instant and then recall a detail about it	You look up a telephone number, remember it long enough to dial it	You remember the house where you lived when you were 7 years old

peat them from memory. Or read each aloud and ask a friend to repeat it.

Try It Yourself

E H G P H
J R O Z N Q
S R B W R C N
M P D I W F B S
Z Y B P I A F M O

Most normal adults can repeat a list of about seven letters, numbers, or words. Some can remember eight or nine; others, only five or six. George Miller (1956) referred to the short-term memory capacity as "the magical number seven, plus or minus two." When people try to repeat a longer list, however, they may fail to remember even the first seven items. It is like trying to hold objects in one hand: If you try to hold too many, you drop them all.

Short-term memory is like a handful of eggs; it can hold only a limited number of items at a time.

The limit of short-term memory depends partly on how long it takes to say a word. If you were equally fluent in English and Welsh, you would display a greater short-term memory for numbers when tested in English, just because you can say English numbers like *five* and *seven* faster than Welsh numbers like *pedwar* and *chwech* (Ellis & Hennelley, 1980). For similar reasons you would have a greater short-term memory capacity for numbers in Chinese than in German (Lüer et al., 1998) and greater capacity in spoken English than in American sign language (Boutla, Supalla, Newport, & Bavelier, 2004). Of course, if you were more fluent in one language than another, you would show less short-term memory in your second language. Short-term memory capacity falls to five or fewer when people try to remember complex visual patterns because they have to attend to many details in each pattern (Alvarez & Cavanagh, 2004).

Kutbidin Atamkulov travels from one Central Asian village to another singing from memory the tale of the Kirghiz hero, Manas. The song, which lasts 3 hours, has been passed from master to student for centuries.

You can store more information in short-term memory by coding it efficiently through a process called **chunking**—*grouping items into meaningful sequences or clusters* (Figure 7.6). For example, the sequence "ventysi" has seven letters, at the limit of most people's short-term memory capacity. However, "seventysix" with three additional letters can be easily remembered as "76," a two-digit number. "Seventeenseventysix" is even longer, but if you think of it as 1776, one important date in U.S. history, it now is just a single item to store.

One college student in a lengthy experiment initially could repeat about seven digits at a time, the same as average (Ericsson, Chase, & Faloon, 1980). Over a year and a half, working 3 to 5 hours per week, he gradually improved until he could repeat 80 digits, as shown in Figure 7.7, by using elaborate strategies for chunking. He was a competitive runner, so he might store the sequence "3492 . . ." as "3 minutes, 49.2 seconds, a near world-record time for running a mile." He might store the next set of numbers as a good time for running a kilometer, a mediocre marathon time, or a date in history. With practice he started recognizing larger and larger chunks. However, when he was tested on his ability to remember a

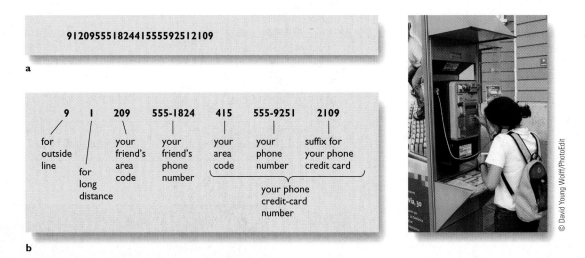

a

9 1 209 555-1824 415 555-9251 2109

9	1	209	555-1824	415	555-9251	2109

for outside line — for long distance — your friend's area code — your friend's phone number — your area code — your phone number — suffix for your phone credit card

your phone credit-card number

b

FIGURE 7.6 You might remember a 26-digit number by breaking it into a series of chunks.

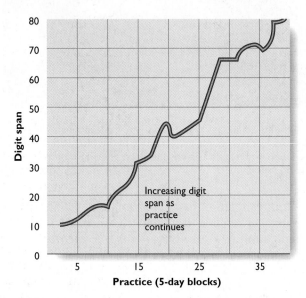

FIGURE 7.7 One college student gradually increased his ability to repeat a list of numbers. However, his short-term memory for letters or words did not increase. *(From Ericsson, Chase, & Faloon, 1980)*

list of letters, his performance was only average because he had not developed any chunking strategies for letters.

One cautionary point before we proceed: We talk about "storing" a memory as if you were holding objects in your hand or placing books on a library shelf. These are only loose analogies. The brain does not store a memory like an object in one place. Memory depends on changes in synapses spread out over a huge population of cells.

Dependence on Retrieval Cues

When you form a long-term memory and try to find it later, you need a **retrieval cue** (*associated information*

that might help you regain the memory). For example, if someone asks you what *demand characteristics* are, you might say you have no idea. Then the person says, "I think they have something to do with research methods in psychology." Still, you don't remember. "Do you remember an experiment in which people were in an ordinary room, but they thought they were in sensory deprivation, so they reported hallucinations. . . ?" Suddenly, you remember the concept.

Traditionally, psychologists have regarded retrieval cues as irrelevant to short-term memory. For example, if you fail to recall a telephone number that you heard a minute ago, no reminder will help. The results are different, though, with more meaningful materials. Suppose you hear a list of words, including "closet," and then recall as many of the words as you can. If you don't recall "closet," but someone gives you the reminder "broom . . . ," you might say, "Oh, yes, 'closet.'" So retrieval cues are helpful for some short-term memories, even if not for all (D. L. Nelson & Goodmon, 2003).

Decay of Memories over Time

A well-learned memory can last a lifetime. Harry Bahrick (1984) found that people who had studied Spanish 1 or 2 years ago remembered more than those who had studied it 3 to 6 years ago, but beyond 6 years the retention appeared to be stable (Figure 7.8). If you ask your grandparents to get out an old photo album, they will recall events they had not thought about in decades. Although the photographs may have faded, it is not certain that the memories themselves fade. They gradually become harder to retrieve, mainly because of interference from other memories.

Short-term memories do fade, however. In fact neuroscientists have identified a protein that the

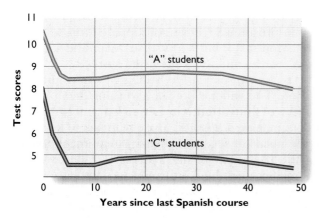

FIGURE 7.8 Spanish vocabulary as measured by a recognition test declines in the first few years but then becomes stable. The students who received an "A" performed better, but each group showed similar rates of forgetting. *(From Bahrick, 1984)*

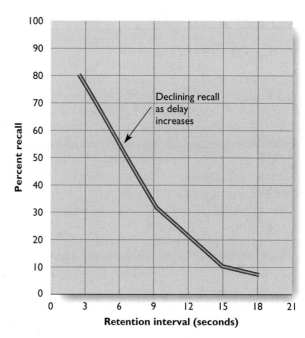

FIGURE 7.9 In a study by Peterson and Peterson (1959), people remembered a set of letters well after a short delay, but their memory faded quickly if they were prevented from rehearsing.

brain makes after an experience that weakens the memory trace, presumably to avoid permanently storing unimportant information (Genoux et al., 2002). Obviously, the effects of that protein can be canceled if the information is repeated. It can also be canceled by emotional arousal, which mobilizes epinephrine (adrenalin) and thereby strengthens memory formation (LaLumiere, Buen, & McGaugh, 2003).

Here is the classic behavioral demonstration of the fading of short-term memories: Lloyd Peterson and Margaret Peterson (1959) wanted to present a meaningless sequence of letters, like HOXDF, and then test people's memory after various delays. However, most adults rehearse, "HOXDF, HOXDF, . . ." To prevent rehearsal, the experimenters gave a competing task. They simultaneously presented the letters and a number, such as 231. The instruction was to start with that number and count backward by 3s, such as "231, 228, 225, 222, 219, . . ." until the end of the delay and then say the letters.

Figure 7.9 shows the results. Note that only about 10% of the participants could recall the letters after 18 seconds. In other words an unrehearsed short-term memory decays rapidly. You can demonstrate this phenomenon yourself with an Online Try It Yourself activity, Decay of Short-Term Memory.

Online Try It Yourself

Do not take that figure of 18 seconds too seriously. Peterson and Peterson were dealing with nonsense information, such as HOXDF. They presented a long series of trials, and the answer to each one would interfere with the others. People sometimes remember meaningful short-term memories much longer. Certainly, you should not imagine that every memory either fades within seconds (short-term memory) or lasts a lifetime (long-term). You have many memories that you keep as long as they are current, updating them with new information as often as necessary (Altmann & Gray, 2002). For example, if you are playing basketball, you remember the score, approximately how much time is left in the game, what defense your team is using, what offense, how many fouls you have committed, and so forth. You won't (and wouldn't want to) remember that information for the rest of your life, but you also don't need to rehearse it constantly to prevent it from fading within seconds. Similarly, right now you probably remember approximately how much money is in your wallet, where and when you plan to meet someone for dinner, what you plan to do next weekend, how long until your next psychology test, and much other information you need to store until you update it with new information. Not all memories fade quickly.

CONCEPT CHECK

5. Is your memory of your mailing address a semantic memory or an episodic memory? What about your memories of the day you moved to your current address?

6. How does the capacity of short-term memory compare with that of long-term memory? (Check your answers on page 258.)

Working Memory

Originally, psychologists described short-term memory as the way you store something while you are moving it into long-term storage. That is, you gradually **consolidate** your memory by *converting a short-term memory into a long-term memory*. Many memories do indeed strengthen over time, becoming less vulnerable to disruption. However, consolidation no longer appears to be a simple, single process as psychologists once assumed (Meeter & Murre, 2004) and neither does short-term memory.

One problem for the simple consolidation idea is that *how long* information remains in short-term memory is a poor predictor of whether it becomes a long-term memory. For example, you might watch a hockey game in which the score remains 1-0 for 2 hours, but you don't store that score as a permanent memory. In contrast, if someone tells you, "Your sister just had a baby," you form a lasting memory quickly.

Today, most researchers emphasize temporary memory storage as the information you are working with at the moment, regardless of whether you ever store it as a more permanent memory. To emphasize this different perspective, they speak of *working* memory instead of short-term memory.

Working memory is *a system for working with current information*. It is almost synonymous with someone's current sphere of attention. Different psychologists have used the term in different ways, and some have broadened the term until it is almost synonymous with intelligence (Oberauer, Süss, Wilhelm, & Wittman, 2003).

Working memory includes at least four major components (Baddeley, 2001; Baddeley & Hitch, 1994; Repovš & Baddeley, 2006):

• A *phonological loop*, which stores and rehearses speech information. The phonological loop, similar to the traditional view of short-term memory, enables us to repeat seven or so items immediately after hearing them. It is essential for understanding a long sentence; you have to remember the words at the start of the sentence long enough to connect them to the words at the end.

• A *visuospatial sketchpad,* which stores and manipulates visual and spatial information, providing for vision what the phonological loop provides for speech (Luck & Vogel, 1997). You would use this process for recognizing pictures or for imagining what an object looks like from another angle.

Researchers distinguish between the phonological and visuospatial stores because you can do an auditory word task and a visuospatial task at the same time without much interference but not two auditory tasks or two visuospatial tasks (Baddeley & Hitch,

1974; Hale, Myerson, Rhee, Weiss, & Abrams, 1996). People presumably have additional stores for touch, smell, and taste, but so far researchers have concentrated on the auditory and visual stores.

• *A central executive,* which governs shifts of attention. The hallmark of good working memory is the ability to shift attention as needed among different tasks. Imagine a hospital nurse who has to keep track of the needs of several patients, sometimes interrupting the treatment of one patient to take care of an emergency and then returning to complete the first patient. Also imagine yourself driving a car, watching the oncoming traffic, the cars in front of you and behind, the gauges on your dashboard, sometimes a map, and possibly a conversation with a passenger.

• *An episodic buffer,* which binds together the various parts of a meaningful experience. Psychologists struggled with the fact that you can repeat only about seven items from the supposed phonological loop, but you can easily repeat a sentence of 10–20 words. Your memory must have some way of linking items into meaningful wholes. Also, you can remember what you saw and felt at the time you heard something. The episodic buffer is the hypothetical device that puts these items together. Because this component was proposed more recently than the others, it has not yet been the topic of much research or theory.

Psychologists have not defined "central executive" or "episodic buffer" precisely, so measuring them is difficult (Logan, 2003). (The same issue arises for "intelligence" and many other terms in psychology.) Here is one simple way to measure shifting attention, which is considered a major component of the central executive: Recite aloud some poem, song, or other passage that you know well. (If you can't think of a more interesting example, you can recite the alphabet.) Time how long it takes. Then measure how long it takes you to say the same thing silently. Finally, time how long it takes you to alternate—the first word aloud, the second silent, the third aloud, and so forth. Alternating takes longer because you keep shifting attention.

Try It Yourself

Here is another way to measure executive processes: You hear a list of words such as *maple, elm, oak, hemlock, chestnut, birch, sycamore, pine, redwood, walnut, dogwood, hickory.* After each word you are supposed to say the *previous* word. So after "maple, elm," you should say "maple." After "oak" you reply "elm." If you do well on that task, you proceed to a more difficult version: You should repeat what you heard *two* words ago. So you wait for "maple, elm, oak" and reply "maple." Then you hear "hemlock" and reply "elm." You need to shift back and forth between listening to the new word and repeating something from memory.

Another example: An investigator flashes on the screen a simple arithmetic question and a word, such as

$$(2 \times 3) + 1 = 8? \quad \text{SPRING}$$

As quickly as possible, you should read the arithmetic question, answer it yes or no, and then say the word. As soon as you do, you will see a new question and word; again, you answer the question and say the word. After a few such items, the investigator stops and asks you to say all the words in order. To do well you have to shift your attention between doing the arithmetic and memorizing the words. This is a difficult task. Some people have trouble remembering even two words under these conditions. Remembering five or six is an excellent score.

People vary in their performance on tasks like this partly for genetic reasons (Parasuraman, Greenwood, Kumar, & Fossella, 2005). Those who do well on this task are considered to have a "high capacity" of working memory. Because of their ability to control attention, they generally do well on many other tasks, including intelligence tests (Engle, Tuholski, Laughlin, & Conway, 1999; Süss, Oberauer, Wittman, Wilhelm, & Schulze, 2002), suppressing unwanted thoughts (Brewin & Beaton, 2002), and understanding other people's point of view (Barrett, Tugade, & Engle, 2004). They are more likely than other people to prefer a large reward later instead of a smaller reward now (Hinson, Jameson, & Whitney, 2003).

What enables some people to have a greater than average capacity of working memory? According to one study, the key is attention. Participants were instructed to watch two displays on a screen and say whether the red rectangles were the same for the two displays, ignoring the blue rectangles. Brain recordings indicated that the people with less working memory responded to both the red and blue rectangles, while those with more working memory screened out the blue ones, as if they weren't there at all (Vogel, McCollough, & Machizawa, 2005). That is, good working memory requires attending to the relevant and screening out the irrelevant.

Interestingly, if people have to perform an additional constantly distracting task, such as tapping a rhythm with their fingers, everyone's performance suffers, but those with the best working memory suffer the most (Kane & Engle, 2000; Rosen & Engle, 1997). They still perform better than people with less working memory but not by as much as usual. Of course, one reason is that those with poor working memory weren't doing well anyway, so they had less room to get worse. Another reason is that people with good working memory usually do well because they direct their attention to the important aspects of the task. When they are distracted, they lose that advantage.

 ✓ **CONCEPT CHECK**

7. Some students like to listen to music while studying. Is the music likely to help or impair their study? (What might the answer depend on?) (Check your answers on page 258.)

IN CLOSING

Varieties of Memory

Although researchers cannot clearly say what memory is, they agree about what it is *not*: Memory is not a single store into which we simply dump things and later take them out. When Ebbinghaus conducted his studies of memory in the late 1800s, he thought he was measuring the properties of memory, period. We now know that the properties of memory depend on the type of material memorized, the individual's experience with similar materials, the method of testing, and the recency of the event. Memory is not one process, but many. ∎

Summary

- *Ebbinghaus's approach.* Hermann Ebbinghaus pioneered the experimental study of memory by testing his own ability to memorize and retain lists of nonsense syllables. (page 245)
- *Methods of testing memory.* The free recall method reveals only relatively strong memories. Progressively weaker memories can be demonstrated by the cued recall, recognition, and savings methods. Implicit memories are changes in behavior under conditions in which the person cannot verbalize the memory or is unaware of the influence. (page 248)
- *Suspect lineups.* Suspect lineups are an example of the recognition method of testing memory. Unfortunately, witnesses sometimes choose the best available choice and then decide they are sure. Psychologists have recommended ways of improving lineups to decrease inaccurate identifications. (page 250)
- *The information-processing model.* According to the information-processing model of memory, information progresses through stages of a sensory store, short-term memory, and long-term memory. (page 250)
- *Differences between short-term and long-term memory.* Long-term memory requires elicitation by

a retrieval cue, whereas short-term memory does not. Short-term memory has a capacity of only about seven items in normal adults, although chunking can enable us to store much information in each item. Long-term memory has a huge capacity. Short-term memories fade over time if not rehearsed, whereas some long-term memories last a lifetime. (page 252)

- *Working memory.* As an alternative to the traditional description of short-term memory, current researchers identify working memory as a system for dealing with current information, including the ability to shift attention back and forth among several tasks as necessary. (page 256)

Answers to Concept Checks

1. Memory is enhanced by repetition, distinctiveness, and being either first or last on a list. We also tend to remember words we learned early in life more easily than those we learned later. Anything that distracts attention decreases memory of the next one or more items. (page 246)
2. **a.** savings; **b.** free recall; **c.** implicit; **d.** recognition; **e.** cued recall. (page 248)
3. Remembering how to tie your shoes is a procedural memory. Remembering their appearance is a declarative memory (one you could express in words). (page 249)
4. If we assume that it would take longer to name objects than numbers or letters, people would probably name fewer. The longer it takes for people to answer, the more their sensory store fades. (page 251)
5. Your memory of your current address is a semantic memory. Your memory of the events of moving day is an episodic memory. (page 252)
6. Short-term memory has a capacity limited to only about seven items in the average adult, whereas long-term memory has a huge, difficult-to-measure capacity. (page 252)
7. If the music requires any attention at all or evokes any response, such as singing along or tapping a foot, it will impair attention. The difference will be most noticeable for the best students. However, background music with no words and no tendency to evoke responses might provide a slight benefit if it prevents the student from noticing other sounds that might be more distracting. (page 257)

Answers to Other Question in the Module

A. Herman Melville, Jane Austen, Agatha Christie, Arthur Conan Doyle, Maya Angelou, Leo Tolstoy, James Kalat, Geoffrey Chaucer, Charles Darwin, Margaret Mitchell, Victor Hugo. (page 248)

Long-Term Memory

MODULE 7.2

- *How can we improve our memories?*

Have you ever felt distressed that you can't remember some experience from your past? One woman reports feeling distressed that she can't stop remembering! If she just sees or hears a date—such as April 27, 1994—a flood of memories descends on her. "That was Wednesday. . . . I was down in Florida. I was summoned to come down and to say goodbye to my grandmother who they all thought was dying but she ended up living. My Dad and my Mom went to New York for a wedding. Then my Mom went to Baltimore to see her family. I went to Florida on the 25th, which was a Monday. This was also the weekend that Nixon died. And then I flew to Florida and my Dad flew to Florida the next day. Then I flew home and my Dad flew to Baltimore to be with my Mom." (Parker, Cahill, & McGaugh, 2006, p. 40). Tell her another date, and she might describe where she went to dinner, and with whom, as well as the major news event of that day. The researchers studying her checked her reports against her extensive diaries and a book of news events and found she was almost always correct for any date since she was 11 years old. For one test they asked her to give the date (e.g., April 7) for every Easter between 1980 and 2003. She was right on all but one and later corrected herself on that one. What makes this feat even more impressive is that she is Jewish and therefore doesn't celebrate Easter (Parker et al., 2006).

You might not want to have the detailed autobiographical memory of this woman, who says her memories so occupy her that she can hardly focus on the present. Still, it would be good to improve your memory for the items you want to remember. The main point of this module is simple: To improve your memory, improve the way you study.

Meaningful Storage and Levels of Processing

If you want to memorize a definition, what would you do? Repeat it over and over? Other things being equal, repetition helps, but repetition by itself is a poor study method.

To illustrate, examine Figure 7.10, which shows a real U.S. penny and 14 fakes. If you live in the United

▌ Most actors preparing for a play spend much time thinking about the meaning of what they will say (a deep level of processing) instead of just repeating the words.

States, you have seen pennies countless times, but can you now identify the real one? Most U.S. citizens guess wrong (Nickerson & Adams, 1979). (If you do not have a penny in your pocket, check answer B on page 266. If you are not from the United States, try drawing the front or back of a common coin in your own country.) In short, mere repetition, such as looking at a coin many times, does not guarantee a strong memory.

Suppose you read two articles of equal length from the sports pages of a newspaper. One is about a sport you follow closely, and the other is about a sport that has never interested you. Even though you spend the same amount of time reading each article, you will remember more from the article you care about. The more you already know about any topic, the easier it is to learn still more (Hambrick & Engle, 2002). You notice the important points and you associate the details to other facts you already know.

According to the **levels-of-processing principle** (Craik & Lockhart, 1972), *how easily you retrieve a memory depends on the number and types of associations you form.* The associations establish retrieval cues. By analogy, for every new book in the library, a librarian enters information into the retrieval system so that anyone who knows the title, author, or topic can find the book. The more items the librarian enters, the easier it will be for someone to find that book later. Your memory is similar.

259

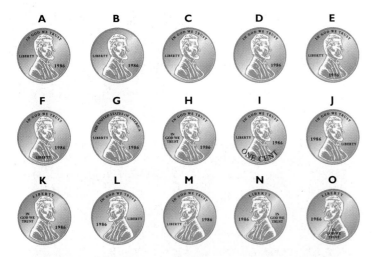

FIGURE 7.10 Can you spot the genuine penny among 14 fakes? *(Based on Nickerson & Adams, 1979)*

When you read something—this chapter, for example—you might simply read over the words, giving them little thought. We call that kind of study "shallow processing," and you will remember almost nothing at test time. Alternatively, you might stop and consider various points that you read, relate them to your own experiences, and think of your own examples of the principles. The more ways you think about the material, the "deeper" your processing is and the more easily you will remember later. Table 7.4 summarizes this model.

Imagine several groups of students who study a list of words in different ways. One group simply reads the list over and over, and a second counts the letters in each word. Both procedures yield poor recall later. A third group tries to think of a synonym for each word or tries to use each word in a sentence. These students form many associations and later recall the words better than the first two groups. Students in the fourth group ask about each word, "How does it apply to some experience in my own life?" This group does better yet. For a while psychologists thought that relating words to yourself produces a special kind of

TABLE 7.4 Levels-of-Processing Model of Memory

Superficial processing	Simply repeat the material to be remembered: "Hawk, Oriole, Tiger, Timberwolf, Blue Jay, Bull."
Deeper processing	Think about each item. Note that two start with T and two with B.
Still deeper processing	Note that three are birds and three are mammals. Also, three are major league baseball teams and three are NBA basketball teams. Use whichever associations mean the most to you.

strengthening, but later research found equally strong memories in students who tried to relate each word to their mothers (Symons & Johnson, 1997). The conclusion is that memory grows stronger when people elaborate and organize the material and relate it to anything they know and care about.

✓ **CONCEPT CHECK**

8. Many students who get the best grades in a course read the assigned text chapters more slowly than average. Why? (Check your answer on page 265.)

Encoding Specificity

If encoding something in a variety of ways improves recall under varied circumstances, then encoding it in just one way means that only a few retrieval cues will stimulate the memory later. Those few cues, however, can be highly effective.

According to the **encoding specificity principle** (Tulving & Thomson, 1973), *the associations you form at the time of learning will be the most effective retrieval cues* (Figure 7.11). Here is an example (modified from Thieman, 1984). First, read the pairs of words (which psychologists call *paired associates*) in Table 7.5a. Then turn to Table 7.5b on page 262. For each of the words on that list, try to recall a related word on the list you just read. *Do this now.* (The answers are on page 266, answer C.)

Most people find this task difficult. Because they initially coded the word *cardinal* as a type of clergy-

FIGURE 7.11 According to the principle of encoding specificity, how you code a word during learning determines which cues will remind you of that word later. When you hear the word *queen*, if you think of *queen bee*, then the cue *playing card* will not remind you of it later. If you think of the *queen of England*, then *chess piece* will not be a good reminder.

TABLE 7.5A

Clergyman—Cardinal	Geometry—Plane
Trinket—Charm	Tennis—Racket
Type of wine—Port	Music—Rock
U.S. politician—Bush	Magic—Spell
Inch—Foot	Envelope—Seal
Computer—Apple	Graduation—Degree

man, for example, they do not think of it when they see the retrieval cue *bird*. If they had thought of it as a bird, then *clergyman* would not have been a good reminder.

The principle of encoding specificity extends to other aspects of experience at the time of storage. For example, if you return to a place where you haven't been in years, you may remember events that happened there. In one study college students who were fluent in both English and Russian were given a list of words such as *summer, birthday,* and *doctor,* some in English and some in Russian. For each word they were asked to describe any related event they remembered. In response to Russian words, they recalled mostly events that happened when they were speaking Russian. In response to English words, they recalled mostly events when they were speaking English (Marian & Neisser, 2000).

More examples: If you experience something while you are sad, you will remember it better when you are sad again (Eich & Macaulay, 2000). If you learn something while frightened, you will remember it better when you are frightened again, and if you learn while calm, you will remember better when calm (Lang, Craske, Brown, & Ghaneian, 2001). Strong drugs can induce this effect also. **State-dependent memory** is *the tendency to remember something better if your body is in the same condition during recall as it was during the original learning.* State-dependent memory, however, is a fragile effect, difficult to demonstrate (Eich, 1995).

The encoding specificity principle has clear implications. If you want to remember something at a particular time and place, make your study conditions similar to the conditions when you will try to remember. On the other hand, if you want to remember the material for life, under many conditions, then you should vary your study habits.

 CONCEPT CHECK

9. Suppose someone cannot remember what happened at a party last night. What steps might help improve the memory? (Check your answer on page 265.)

The Timing of Study Sessions

If you have an upcoming test, should you study a little at a time or wait until shortly before the test? If you sometimes wait until just before the test, you know this strategy is risky. An unexpected interruption might prevent you from studying at all. Let's change the question in a way that makes the answer less obvious: Suppose you don't wait until the day before the test, but you nevertheless study the material all at once when you have plenty of time and no distractions. Will your result be better, worse, or about the same than if you had studied a little at a time over several days?

The answer is that studying all at once is worse, for many reasons (Cepeda, Pashler, Vul, Wixted, & Rohrer, 2006). First, if you study all at once, you overestimate how well you will remember it. Consequently, most students overestimate their probable grade (Cann, 2005). Below-average students are especially likely to overestimate (Dunning, Johnson, Ehrlinger, & Kruger, 2003). For example, you have just read about the encoding specificity principle. What do you estimate is your percent probability of remembering the idea a minute from now? One week from now? Presumably, you estimated a higher probability for a minute than for next week—maybe 90% in a minute and 50% next week. However, if I had asked you about next week without first asking about

© Paul A. Souders/CORBIS

▌ People need to monitor their understanding of a text to decide whether to continue studying or whether they already understand it well enough. Most readers have trouble making that judgment correctly.

TABLE 7.5B

Instructions: For each of these words, write one of the second of the paired terms from the list in Table 7.5a.

Animal—	Stone—
Part of body—	Personality—
Transportation—	Write—
Temperature—	Bird—
Crime—	Harbor—
Shrubbery—	Fruit—

1 minute—that is, without calling your attention to the time difference—you might have estimated 90% for next week. In one study researchers asked different groups of students to estimate how well they would recall something immediately, tomorrow, or next week. All three groups made the same estimates on the average (Koriat, Bjork, Sheffer, & Bar, 2004). That is, it is easy to disregard the fact that you are likely to forget. Because you think you will remember, you prematurely stop studying.

A second reason for spreading out your study is that to improve your memory of something, you need to practice retrieving the memory—that is, finding it. When you study something all at once, it is fresh in your working memory. Holding it there by reading it over and over provides no practice at retrieving it. If you go away and come back later, you need some effort to refresh the ideas.

You can accomplish some of that same advantage by alternating between reading and testing yourself. A test forces you to generate the material instead of passively reading it. Students in one experiment read a page about sea otters. Half of them spent the whole time rereading it. The other half spent part of their time reading it and part taking a test (on which they received no feedback). Two days later, the group that took the test remembered more of the material (Roediger & Karpicke, 2006). The act of generating answers helped solidify their memories.

A third reason for spreading out your study is that if you study under a variety of conditions, you establish a variety of retrieval cues and therefore remember under more conditions (Schmidt & Bjork, 1992). Varying the conditions slows the original learning and makes the task seem more difficult, but in the long run, it helps. In one experiment a group of 8-year-old children practiced throwing a small beanbag at a target on the floor 3 feet away. Another group practiced with a target sometimes 2 feet away and sometimes 4 feet away, but never 3 feet away. Then both groups were tested with the target 3 feet away. The children who had been practicing with the 3-foot target missed it by a mean of 8.3 inches. The children who had been practicing with 2-foot and 4-foot targets actually did better, missing by a mean of only 5.4 inches, even though they were aiming at the 3-foot target for the first time (Kerr & Booth, 1978). In another experiment young adults practiced a technique for mentally squaring two-digit numbers—for example, $23 \times 23 = 529$. Those who practiced with a small range of numbers learned the technique quickly but forgot it quickly. Those who practiced with a wider range of numbers learned more slowly but remembered better later (Sanders, Gonzalez, Murphy, Pesta, & Bucur, 2002).

The conclusions: (a) It is hard to judge how well you have learned something if you haven't waited long enough to see whether you will forget. (b) Studying something once is seldom effective. (c) You will remember better if you pause to test yourself. (d) Varying the conditions of studying improves long-term memory.

 CONCEPT CHECK

10. Based on this section, why is it advantageous to stop and answer Concept Checks like this one? (Check your answer on page 265.)

The SPAR Method

One systematic way to organize your study is the SPAR method:

Survey. Get an overview of what the passage is about. Scan through it; look at the boldface headings; try to understand the organization and goals of the passage.

Process *meaningfully.* Think about how you could use the ideas or how they relate to other things you know. Evaluate the strengths and weaknesses of the argument. The more you think about what you read, the better you will remember it.

Ask *questions.* If the text provides questions, like the Concept Checks in this text, answer them. Then pretend you are the instructor, write questions you would ask on a test, and answer them yourself. In the process you discover which sections of the passage you need to reread.

Review. Wait a day or more and retest your knowledge. Spreading out your study over time increases your ability to remember it.

 CONCEPT CHECK

11. If you want to do well on the final exam in this course, what should you do now—review this chapter or review the first three chapters in the book?

12. How does the advice to spread out your study over a long time instead of doing it all at one sitting fit or contrast with the encoding specificity principle? (Check your answers on pages 265-266.)

Emotional Arousal and Memory Storage

People usually remember emotionally arousing events. Chances are you vividly remember your first day of college, your first kiss, the time your team won the big game, and times you were extremely frightened.

The effects of arousal on memory have been known for centuries. In England in the early 1600s, when people sold land, they did not yet have the custom of recording the sale on paper. Paper was expensive and few people could read anyway. Instead, local residents would gather while someone announced the sale and instructed everyone to remember it. Of all those present, whose memory of the sale was most important? The children, because they would live the longest. And of all those present, who were least interested? Right, again, it's the children. To increase the chances that the children would remember, the adults would kick them while telling them about the business deal. The same idea persisted in the custom, still common in the early 1900s, of slapping schoolchildren's hands with a stick to make them pay attention.

Many people report intense, detailed "flashbulb" memories of hearing highly emotional news, in which they remember where they were, what they were doing, and even the weather and other irrelevant details. However, although flashbulb memories are intense, they are not always accurate. In one study Israeli students were interviewed 2 weeks after the assassination of Israel's Prime Minister, Itzhak Rabin, and again 11 months later. About 36% of the memories they confidently reported at the later time differed from what they had reported earlier (Nachson & Zelig, 2003). In another study U.S. students reported their memories of where they were, what they were doing, and so forth at the time of hearing about the terrorist attacks on September 11, 2001. They reported their memories on the day after the attacks and then again weeks or months later. Over time the students continued to report highly vivid memories, but their accuracy gradually declined (Talarico & Rubin, 2003).

If you read a list of words, you will recall emotional words (e.g., "hate") better than neutral words, and you will recall swear words and taboo words better yet, including irrelevant aspects such as the color of ink or their location on the screen (Kensinger & Corkin, 2003; MacKay & Ahmetzanov, 2005). Emotional arousal enhances memory in at least two ways.

Do you remember the first time you saw a comet? Most people recall emotionally arousing events, sometimes in great detail, although not always accurately.

First, emotional arousal increases the release of the hormones cortisol and epinephrine (adrenaline) from the adrenal gland. Moderate increases in cortisol and epinephrine stimulate the *amygdala* and other brain areas that enhance memory storage, although still greater increases are ineffective (Andreano & Cahill, 2006). As a result people remember emotional events better than neutral ones; however, their memory is less reliable when emotional arousal verges on panic.

Second, if you feel emotion when you recall something, the emotion increases your confidence that the memory must be right. In one study people first viewed a series of neutral and unpleasant photos. Then they examined another series of photos and tried to identify which ones had been in the first set and which ones were new. They were equally accurate at identifying neutral and unpleasant photos, but they reported greater confidence in their memory for the unpleasant ones (Sharot, Delgado, & Phelps, 2004).

 CONCEPT CHECK

13. Most people with posttraumatic stress disorder have lower than normal levels of cortisol. What would you predict about their memory? (Check your answer on page 266.)

Mnemonic Devices

If you needed to memorize something lengthy and not especially exciting—for example, a list of all the bones in the body—how would you do it? One effective strategy is to attach systematic retrieval cues to each

A parachute lets you coast down slowly, like the parasympathetic nervous system.

If the symphony excites you, it arouses your sympathetic nervous system.

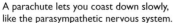

FIGURE 7.12 A simple mnemonic device is to think of a short story or image that will remind you of what you need to remember. Here you might think of images to help remember functions of different parts of the nervous system.

term so that you can remind yourself of the terms when you need them.

A **mnemonic device** is *any memory aid that relies on encoding each item in a special way.* The word *mnemonic* (nee-MAHN-ik) comes from a Greek root meaning "memory." (The same root appears in the word *amnesia,* "lack of memory.") Some mnemonic devices are simple, such as "Every Good Boy Does Fine" to remember the notes EGBDF on the treble clef in music. If you have to remember the functions of various brain areas, you might try links like those shown in Figure 7.12 (Carney & Levin, 1998).

Suppose you had to memorize a list of Nobel Peace Prize winners (Figure 7.13). You might try making up a little story: "Dun (Dunant) passed (Passy) the Duke (Ducommun) of Gob (Gobat) some cream (Cremer). That made him internally ILL (Institute of International Law). He suited (von Suttner) up with some roses (Roosevelt) and spent some money (Moneta) on a Renault (Renault) . . ." You still have to study the names, but your story helps.

Another mnemonic device is the **method of loci** (method of places). *First, you memorize a series of places, and then you use a vivid image to associate each of these locations with something you want to remember.* For example, you might start by memorizing every location along the route from your dormitory room to, say, your psychology classroom. Then you link the locations, in order, to the names.

Suppose the first three locations you pass are the desk in your room, the door to your room, and the corridor. To link the first Nobel Peace Prize winners,

Dunant and Passy, to your desk, you might imagine a Monopoly game board on your desk with a big sign "DO NOT (Dunant) PASS (Passy) GO." Then you link the second pair of names to the second location, your door: A DUKE student (as in Ducommun) is standing at the door, giving confusing signals. He says "DO COME IN (Ducommun)" and "GO BACK (Gobat)." Then you link

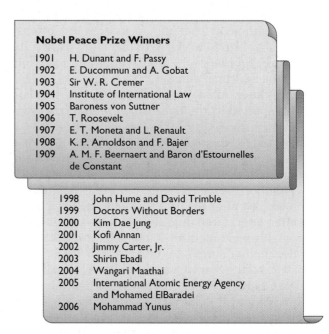

Nobel Peace Prize Winners	
1901	H. Dunant and F. Passy
1902	E. Ducommun and A. Gobat
1903	Sir W. R. Cremer
1904	Institute of International Law
1905	Baroness von Suttner
1906	T. Roosevelt
1907	E. T. Moneta and L. Renault
1908	K. P. Arnoldson and F. Bajer
1909	A. M. F. Beernaert and Baron d'Estournelles de Constant

1998	John Hume and David Trimble
1999	Doctors Without Borders
2000	Kim Dae Jung
2001	Kofi Annan
2002	Jimmy Carter, Jr.
2003	Shirin Ebadi
2004	Wangari Maathai
2005	International Atomic Energy Agency and Mohamed ElBaradei
2006	Mohammad Yunus

FIGURE 7.13 A list of Nobel Peace Prize winners: Mnemonic devices can be useful when people try to memorize long lists like this one.

FIGURE 7.14 With the method of loci, you first learn a list of places, such as "my desk, the door of my room, the corridor, . . ." Then you link each place to an item on a list of words or names, such as a list of the names of Nobel Peace Prize winners.

the corridor to Cremer, perhaps by imagining someone has spilled CREAM (Cremer) all over the floor (Figure 7.14). You continue in this manner until you have linked every name to a location. Now, if you can remember all those locations in order and if you have good visual images for each one, you will be able to recite the list of Nobel Peace Prize winners.

Regardless of whether you use such elaborate mnemonic devices, simpler ones can be helpful in many cases, such as remembering people's names. For example, you might remember someone named Harry Moore by picturing him as "more hairy" than everyone else. If you want to recite a traditional wedding vow by memory, you might remember "BRISTLE," to remind you of "**B**etter or worse, **R**icher or poorer, **I**n **S**ickness and health, **T**o **L**ove and to cherish."

IN CLOSING

Improving Your Memory

You have probably heard of people taking ginkgo biloba or other herbs or drugs to try to improve their memory. These chemicals do produce small but measurable memory benefits for people with impaired blood flow to the brain (Gold, Cahill, & Wenk, 2002; McDaniel, Maier, & Einstein, 2002). However, no one has demonstrated any benefits for healthy people. To improve your memory, by far the best strategy is to think carefully about anything you want to remember, study it under a variety of conditions, and review frequently. ∎

Summary

* *Levels of processing.* A memory becomes stronger and easier to recall if you think about the meaning of the material and relate it to other material. (page 259)
* *Encoding specificity.* When you form a memory, you store it with links to the way you thought about it at the time. When you try to recall the memory, a cue is most effective if it resembles the links you formed at the time of storage. (page 260)
* *Timing of study.* Spreading out your study is more effective than a single session for several reasons. During a single session, you underestimate how much you will forget later, and you ordinarily do not get to practice retrieving a memory because it is still fresh. Also, studying at several times provides a variety of cues that will be helpful in retrieval. (page 261)
* *The SPAR method.* One method to improve study is to Survey, Process meaningfully, Ask questions, and Review. (page 262)
* *Emotional arousal.* Emotionally exciting events tend to be remembered more vividly, though not always more accurately, than neutral events. (page 263)
* *Mnemonics.* Specialized techniques for establishing systematic retrieval cues can help people remember ordered lists of names or terms. (page 264)

Answers to Concept Checks

8. Students who read slowly and frequently pause to think about the meaning of the material are engaging in deep processing and are likely to remember the material well, probably better than those who read through the material quickly. (page 260)
9. Sometimes, someone who claims not to remember simply does not want to talk about it. However, presuming the person really wants to remember, it would help to return to the place of the party, with the same people present, perhaps even at the same time of day. If he or she used alcohol or other drugs, take them again. The more similar the conditions of original learning and later recall, the better the probability of remembering. (page 264)
10. Practicing retrieving a memory strengthens it. In one study students who spent part of their study time answering test questions did better than those who spent the whole time reading. (page 262)
11. To prepare well for the final exam, you should review all the material at irregular intervals. Thus, you might profit by skimming over chapters 1, 2, and 3 right now. Of course, if you have a test on chapter 7 in a day or two, your goal and your strategy are different. (page 262)

12. If you study all at one sitting, the memory will be encoded specifically to what you are thinking about at that time. If you study at several times, the memory will attach to a greater variety of retrieval cues instead of being specific to just one set. (pages 260, 262)

13. Because of the lower cortisol levels, they should have trouble storing memories and therefore report frequent memory lapses. (page 263)

Answers to Other Questions in the Module

B. The correct coin is A. (page 259)

C. Animal—Seal; Part of body—Foot; Transportation—Plane; Temperature—Degree; Crime—Racket; Shrubbery—Bush; Stone—Rock; Personality—Charm; Write—Spell; Bird—Cardinal; Harbor—Port; Fruit—Apple. (page 260)

Memory Retrieval and Error

- *Why is memory retrieval sometimes difficult?*
- *Why do we sometimes report confident but inaccurate memories?*

Imagine that you have written a term paper on your computer, and when you click the icon to retrieve it, the computer gives you this error message: "I know it's around here somewhere, but I just can't find it. Try asking me again in a few hours." Or suppose it displays, not the correct term paper, but another one that you wrote the previous semester. Or odder yet, it prints out an elaborate, complicated term paper that you never wrote! A computer doesn't make those errors, but human memory does.

Retrieval and Interference

Human memory sometimes confuses the sought material with similar information. The first experimental demonstration of this principle was accidental. Remember Hermann Ebbinghaus, who pioneered memory research. Ebbinghaus measured how long he could remember various lists of 13 nonsense syllables. The results appear as the green line on Figure 7.15. On the average he forgot more than half of each list within the first hour (Ebbinghaus, 1885/1913). What a discouraging graph! If people typically forget that fast, then education would be pointless. However, most college students remember nearly 90% of a list of non-

sense syllables 24 hours later, as shown in the purple line of Figure 7.15 (Koppenaal, 1963).

Why do you suppose most college students remember a list so much better than Ebbinghaus did? You may be tempted to say that college students are very intelligent. Well, yes, but Ebbinghaus was no dummy either. Or you might suggest that college students "have had so much practice at memorizing nonsense." (Sorry if you think so.) But the explanation is the opposite: Ebbinghaus had memorized *too much* nonsense—thousands of lists of syllables. If you memorize large amounts of similar material, your memory becomes like a cluttered room: The clutter doesn't prevent you from bringing in still more clutter, but it interferes with finding the item you want. Ebbinghaus forgot new lists quickly because of interference from older lists.

If you learn several sets of related materials, the old interferes with the new and the new interferes with the old. The *old materials increase forgetting of*

Ebbinghaus quickly forgot new lists of nonsense syllables because of interference from all the previous lists he had learned.

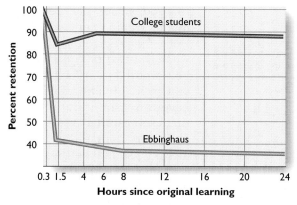

FIGURE 7.15 Recall of lists of syllables by Ebbinghaus (1885/1913) and by college students after delays of various lengths *(based on Koppenaal, 1963)*. Ebbinghaus learned as fast as other people but forgot faster.

the new materials through **proactive interference** (acting forward in time); the *new materials increase forgetting of the old materials* through **retroactive interference** (acting backward in time). Figure 7.16 shows the distinction between these two kinds of interference.

Interference is a major cause of forgetting. You may forget where you parked your car because of proactive interference from all the previous times you parked in the same lot. You may forget last week's French vocabulary list because of retroactive interference from this week's list.

Consider the relevance to a classic study we considered earlier in this chapter: On the average short-term memories appear to decay quickly if you don't rehearse them. For example, if you read the letters BKLRE and then count backward by 3s from 228, you probably will forget the letters within seconds. Although that result is correct on the average over many trials, it is *not* true on the first trial. On the first trial, you have no interference from previous letter sequences, and you can remember the letters well (Keppel & Underwood, 1962). Evidently, short-term memories fade fast because of proactive interference from similar materials.

 CONCEPT CHECK

14. Professor Tryhard learns the names of his students every semester. After several years he learns them as quickly as ever but forgets them faster. Does he forget because of retroactive or proactive interference?

15. Remember the concept of spontaneous recovery from chapter 6? Can you explain it in terms of proactive interference? (Hint: Original learning comes first and extinction comes second. What would happen if the first interfered with the second?)

16. How does interference explain the primacy effect and recency effect in list learning? (Check your answers on page 276.)

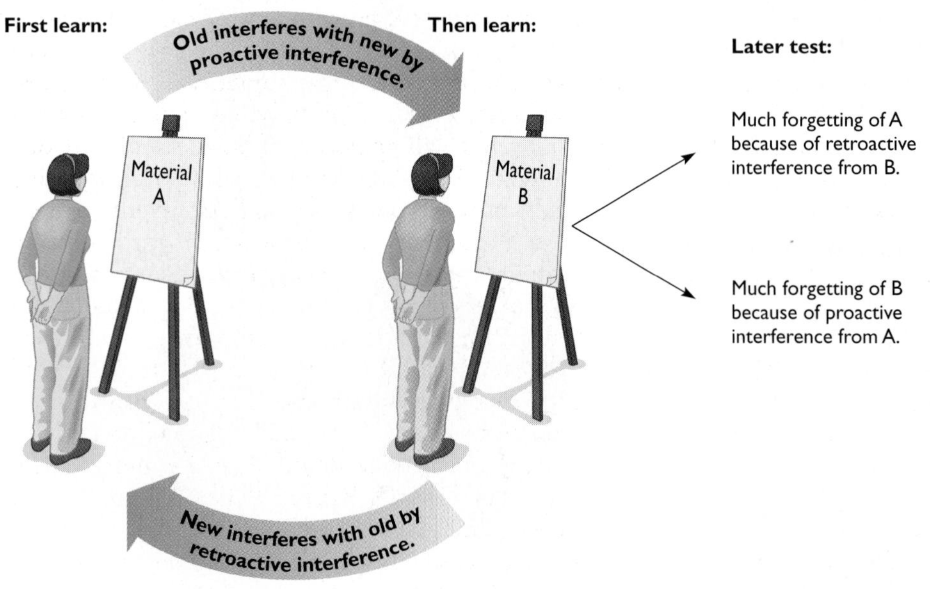

Reconstructing Past Events

If you try to retrieve a memory of some experience, you will start with the details that you remember clearly and **reconstruct** the rest to fill in the gaps: *During an original experience, we construct a memory. When we try to retrieve that memory, we reconstruct an account based partly on surviving memories and partly on our expectations of what must have happened.* For example, you might recall studying in the library three nights ago. With a little effort, you might remember where you sat, what you were reading, who sat next to you, and where you went for a snack afterward. If you aren't quite sure, you fill in the gaps with what usually happens during an evening at the library. Within weeks you gradually forget that evening, and if you try to remember it, you will rely more and more on "what must have happened," omitting more and more details (Schmolck, Buffalo, & Squire, 2000). However, if you happen to fall in love with the person who sat next to you that evening, the events will become a lifetime memory. Still, when you try to recall it, you will have to reconstruct the details. You might remember where you went for a snack and some of what the two of you said, but if you wanted to recall the book you were reading, you would have to reason it out: "Let's see, that semester I was taking a chemistry course that took a lot of study, so maybe I was reading a chemistry book. No, wait, I remember. When we went out to eat, we talked about politics. So maybe I was reading my political science text."

First learn: *Old interferes with new by proactive interference.*   **Then learn:**

Material A

Material B

Later test:

Much forgetting of A because of retroactive interference from B.

Much forgetting of B because of proactive interference from A.

New interferes with old by retroactive interference.

FIGURE 7.16 If you learn similar sets of materials, each interferes with retrieval of the other.

Reconstruction and Inference in List Memory

Try this demonstration: Read the words in list A once; then turn away from the list, pause for a few seconds, and write as many of the words as you can remember. Repeat the same procedure for lists B and C. *Please do this now, before reading the following paragraph.*

List A	List B	List C
bed	candy	fade
rest	sour	fame
weep	sugar	face
tired	dessert	fake
dream	salty	date
wake	taste	hate
snooze	flavor	late
keep	bitter	mate
doze	cookies	rate
steep	fruits	
snore	chocolate	
nap	yummy	

After you have written out your lists, check how many of the words you got right. If you omitted many, you are normal. The point of this demonstration is not how many you got right but whether you included *sleep* on the first list, *sweet* on the second, or *fate* on the third. Many people include one or more of these (which are not on the lists), and some do so with confidence (Deese, 1959; Roediger & McDermott, 1995). Apparently, while learning the individual words, people also learn the gist of what they are all about, and when they are trying to retrieve the list later, they reconstruct a memory of a word that the list implied (Seamon et al., 2002). Up to 65% of people report the implied but absent word (Watson, Balota, & Roediger, 2003). Warning people about this effect reduces but does not eliminate it (Roediger & McDermott, 2000; Westerberg & Marsolek, 2006). Evidently, we reconstruct what "must have" been on the list.

In list B *sweet* is related to the other words in meaning; in list C *fate* resembles the others in sound. In list A *sleep* is related to most of the words in meaning, but the list also includes three words that rhyme with sleep (*weep, keep,* and *steep*). This combined influence is even more effective, producing false recall in a higher percentage of people. Young children are particularly prone to the effects of rhyming words and less sensitive to words of related meaning (Dewhurst & Robinson, 2004).

If you did not include *sleep, sweet,* or *fate,* try an Online Try It Yourself activity, False Memories. Hearing a list (as you can with the online demonstration) produces a bigger effect than reading a list.

The effect occurs mostly when people have neither a strong nor a very weak memory, but something intermediate. If a list is short or if you have a chance to learn it well, you are unlikely to infer an extra word not on the list. On the other hand, if you had such a defective memory that you could not remember any of the words on the list, you could not use them to infer another word on the list, and again you would not show a false memory (Schacter, Verfaellie, Anes, & Racine, 1998). Many older people have trouble remembering the individual items on the list and therefore compensate by relying on the gist, becoming more likely to report words implied by the list (Jacoby & Rhodes, 2006; Lövdén, 2003).

✓ CONCEPT CHECK

17. If you studied a list such as "candy, sour, sugar, dessert, salty, taste, . . ." thoroughly instead of hearing it just once, would you be more likely or less likely to include "sweet," which isn't on the list? Why? (Check your answers on page 276.)

Reconstructing Stories

Suppose you listen to a story about a teenager's day, including a mixture of normal events (watching television) and oddities (clutching a teddy bear and parking a bicycle in the kitchen). Which would you remember better—the normal events or the oddities? It depends. If you are tested immediately, while your memory is still strong, you will remember the unusual and distinctive events best. However, as you start forgetting the story, you begin to omit the unlikely events, reconstructing a more typical day for the teenager, including likely events that the story omitted, such as "the teenager went to school in the morning." In short, the less certain your memory is, the more you rely on your expectations (Heit, 1993; Maki, 1990). If you retell something repeatedly—either a story you heard or an event from your own experience—the retellings gradually become more coherent and make more sense (Ackil, Van Abbema, & Bauer, 2003; Bartlett, 1932). They make more sense because you rely more on the gist, keeping the details that fit the overall theme and omitting or distorting those that do not.

In a study that highlights the role of expectations, U.S. and Mexican adults tried to recall three stories.

Some were given U.S. versions of the stories, and others were given Mexican versions. (For example, in the "going on a date" story, the Mexican version had the man's sister go along as a chaperone.) On the average U.S. participants remembered the U.S. versions better, whereas Mexicans remembered the Mexican versions better (R. J. Harris, Schoen, & Hensley, 1992).

CONCEPT CHECK

18. When you read an account of history, it often seems that one event led to another in a logical order, whereas in everyday life events often seem illogical, unconnected, and unpredictable. Why? (Check your answer on page 276.)

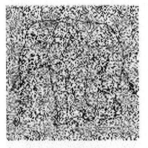

Hindsight Bias

Three weeks before the impeachment trial of U.S. President Clinton in 1999, college students were asked to predict the outcome. On the average they estimated the probability of a conviction at 50.5%. A week and a half after Clinton was not convicted, they were asked, "What would you have said 4½ weeks ago was the chance [of a conviction]?" On the average they reported a 42.8% estimate (Bryant & Guilbault, 2002). Their behavior illustrates **hindsight bias,** *the tendency to mold our recollection of the past to fit how events later turned out.* Something happens and we then say, "I *knew* that was going to happen!"

Another example: As you can see in Figure 7.17,

FIGURE 7.17 At what point in this sequence do you think the average person would recognize it as an elephant? *(Source: From Bernstein, Atance, Loftus, & Meltzoff, 2004)*

an image gradually morphs from a blur to an elephant. At what point do you think the average person would identify it as an elephant? It is hard to imagine not knowing it will be an elephant. On this and similar sequences, most people overestimate how soon people will recognize the image (Bernstein, Atance, Loftus, & Meltzoff, 2004). That is, they show hindsight bias.

Hindsight bias can affect judgments in legal cases. In one study community adults were told about possible hazards of a train going around a mountain track. Some participants were asked whether the company should cease operations for safety reasons. One third said yes. The other participants were told, in addition, that a train had derailed, spilling toxic chemicals into a river. They were asked whether the company should pay punitive damages for irresponsibly continuing operations in spite of foreseeable dangers. Two thirds said yes (Hastie, Schkade, & Payne, 1999). That is, after people knew about the accident, they thought it was foreseeable.

Hindsight bias is not altogether irrational. When you are making a prediction, you receive a huge array of information, some of it unimportant or wrong. When you get the final outcome, you reasonably conclude that the information that had pointed in the correct direction was the best. You want to focus on that information so you can pay more attention to it in the future (Hoffrage, Hertwig, & Gigerenzer, 2000). In the process you accidentally convince yourself that you were already strongly influenced by that information.

CRITICAL THINKING
A STEP FURTHER

Hindsight Bias

Can you interpret people's beliefs that they had a "psychic hunch" in terms of hindsight bias?

The "Recovered Memory" Versus "False Memory" Controversy

Occasionally, someone tells a therapist about vague unpleasant feelings, and the therapist replies, "Symptoms like yours are usually found among people who were abused, especially sexually abused, in childhood. Do you think you were?" In some cases, although the client says "no," the therapist persists: "The fact that you can't remember doesn't mean that it didn't happen. It may have been so painful that you repressed the memory." The therapist may recommend hypnosis, repeated attempts to remember, or other techniques. A few sessions later, the client may say, "It's starting to come back to me. . . . I think I do remember. . . ." Most therapists would not use such aggressive techniques to try to recover old memories, but some do. *Reports of long-lost memories, prompted by clinical techniques, are known as* **recovered memories.**

Sexual abuse in childhood does occur, and no one knows how often. Some abused children develop long-lasting psychological scars. But when people claim to recover long-forgotten memories, has the therapist uncovered the truth, distorted the truth, or convinced the client to believe something that never happened? Since the early 1990s, this issue has been one of the most heated debates in psychology. When a commission of respected therapists and researchers met to consider the evidence, they disagreed on many points and issued competing reports (Alpert, Brown, & Courtois, 1998; Ornstein, Ceci, & Loftus, 1998).

Some reports are bizarre. In one case two sisters accused their father of raping them many times, both vaginally and anally; bringing his friends over on Friday nights to rape them; and forcing them to participate in satanic rituals that included cannibalism and the slaughter of babies (Wright, 1994). The sisters had not remembered any of these events until repeated sessions with a therapist. In another case a group of 3- and 4-year-old children, after repeated urgings from a therapist, accused their Sunday school teacher of sexually abusing them with a curling iron, forcing them to drink blood and urine, hanging them upside down from a chandelier, dunking them in toilets, and killing an elephant and a giraffe during Sunday school class (M. Gardner, 1994). There was no physical evidence to support the claims, such as scarred tissues or giraffe bones.

Even when recovered-memory claims are much less bizarre, their accuracy is uncertain. If a 30-year-old woman claims that her father sexually abused her when she was 8, that she told no one about it at the time, and in fact forgot it until now, how could anyone check her accuracy? One might consult old school records for any mention of physical and emotional scars, but even the best of such records are incomplete.

Some related questions are, however, testable: When people have abusive experiences, are they likely to forget them for years? And is it possible to persuade someone to "remember" an event that never actually happened just by suggesting it?

Memory for Traumatic Events

Sigmund Freud, whom we shall consider more fully in a later chapter, introduced the term **repression** as *the process of moving an unbearably unacceptable memory or impulse from the conscious mind to the unconscious mind.* Although many therapists continue to use the concept of repression, researchers have found no clear evidence for the idea (Holmes, 1990). Experiments designed to demonstrate repression have produced small effects that one could explain without the concept of repression. Many clinicians now prefer the term **dissociation,** referring to *memory that one has stored but cannot retrieve* (Alpert et al., 1998). However, most of the doubts about the term *repression* also apply to the similar concept of *dissociation.*

Do people forget traumatic events? It depends. Partly, it depends on what we mean by "forget." Someone with a painful memory might avoid thinking or talking about it and might say, "I don't remember" to avoid talking about it (Pope, Hudson, Bodkin, & Oliva, 1998).

In general, however, people seldom forget traumatic events. One study examined 16 children who had witnessed the murder of one of their parents. All had recurring nightmares and haunting thoughts of the experience, and none had forgotten (Malmquist, 1986). Other studies have examined prisoners of war who had been severely mistreated (Merckelbach, Dekkers, Wessel, & Roefs, 2003), children who had been kidnapped or forced to participate in pornographic movies (Terr, 1988), and others who had additional horrible experiences. People almost always remembered the events, or they forgot only about as much as one might expect for childhood events. Evidently, if repression of traumatic experiences occurs at all, it does so only under rare and undefined circumstances.

Memory for a traumatic experience depends on someone's age at the time of the event, its severity, and the reaction of other family members. In one study investigators interviewed 129 young adult women who had been brought to a hospital emergency ward because of sexual assault at ages 1 to 12 years. Most reported remembering the sexual assault, although 38% did not (L. M. Williams, 1994). Generally, those who were at least 7 years old at the time of the attack remembered better than those who were younger.

In two similar studies, researchers interviewed hundreds of young adults who had been victims of criminally prosecuted child sexual abuse. Of these, the vast majority remembered the events well, although a few claimed that they had been false reports and some people refused to answer questions about childhood sexual abuse (Alexander et al., 2005; Goodman et al., 2003). In both studies memory was better among those who were older at the time of the offense, those who had more severe or repeated abuse, and those who received more family support and encouragement. These results suggest that early traumatic memories are similar to other memories. They also suggest that repression of such memories is rare, if it occurs at all.

Areas of Agreement and Disagreement

Psychologists agree that some people cannot remember abusive childhood experiences. However, in most of these cases, the abusive events happened in early childhood, a period that most people remember poorly or not at all. Even when someone does forget a horrible experience, the question is why. Many clinicians believe that repression or dissociation is a possible explanation. If so, then attempts to recover the memory are at least a theoretical possibility (Alpert et al., 1998). (Whether recovering them would be *beneficial* is uncertain.) The alternative view, favored by most memory researchers, is that traumatic memories are like other memories: If we don't think about something for a long time, we find it harder to retrieve, and if we try to reconstruct the event later, the result will be a mixture of truth and distortion.

 CONCEPT CHECK

19. Based on material earlier in this chapter, why should we expect traumatic events to be remembered better than most other events? (Check your answer on page 276.)

 CRITICAL THINKING
WHAT'S THE EVIDENCE?

Suggestions and False Memories

Critics of attempts to recover lost memories have suggested that a therapist who repeatedly encourages a client to recall lost memories can unintentionally implant a **false memory** (or false report), *a report that someone believes to be a memory but that does not correspond to real events* (Lindsay & Read, 1994; Loftus, 1993). Let's examine three representative experiments.

FIRST STUDY

Hypothesis. If people are asked questions that suggest or presuppose some fact, many people will later report remembering that "fact," even if it never happened.

Method. Elizabeth Loftus (1975) asked two groups of students to watch a videotape of an automobile accident. Then she asked one group but not the other, "Did you see the children getting on the school bus?" The videotape did not show

a school bus. A week later, she asked both groups 20 new questions about the accident, including this one: "Did you see a school bus in the film?"

Results. Of the group who were asked about seeing children get on a school bus, 26% reported that they had seen a school bus; of the other group, only 6% said they had seen a school bus.

Interpretation. The question "Did you see the children getting on the school bus?" implies that there was a school bus. Some of the students who heard that question reconstructed events by combining what they actually saw, what they believed must have happened, and what the researcher suggested.

SECOND STUDY

The first experiment demonstrated that suggestions distort memories. But could suggestions implant memories of experiences that never occurred?

Hypothesis. People who are told about a childhood event will come to remember it as something they experienced, even if in fact they did not.

Method. The participants, aged 18 to 53, were told that the study concerned their childhood memories. Each participant was given paragraphs describing four different events. Three of the events had actually happened. (The experimenters had contacted parents to get descriptions of childhood events.) A fourth event was a plausible but false story about getting lost. An example for one Vietnamese woman: "You, your Mom, Tien, and Tuan, all went to the Bremerton Kmart. You must have been 5 years old at the time. Your Mom gave each of you some money to get a blueberry ICEE. You ran ahead to get into the line first, and somehow lost your way in the store. Tien found you crying to an elderly Chinese woman. You three then went together to get an ICEE." After reading the four paragraphs, each participant was asked to write whatever additional details he or she could remember of the event. Participants were asked to try again 1 week later and then again after another week (Loftus, Feldman, & Dashiell, 1995).

Results. Of 24 participants 6 reported remembering the suggested false event. Participants generally described these events in fewer words than their correct memories, but some did provide additional details. The woman in the foregoing example said, "I vaguely remember walking around Kmart crying and looking for Tien and Tuan. I thought I was lost forever. I went to the shoe department, because we always spent a lot of time there. I went to the handkerchief place because we were there last. I circled all over the store it seemed 10 times. I just remember walking around crying. I do not remember the Chinese woman, or the ICEE (but it would be raspberry ICEE if I was getting an ICEE) part. I don't even remember being found."

Interpretation.   A suggestion can provoke some people to report a personal experience in moderate detail, even though the event never happened. Granted, the suggestion influenced only a quarter of the people tested, and most of them reported only vague memories. Still, the researchers achieved this effect after only a single brief suggestion. In a similar study, 13 of 47 participants reported detailed false memories of getting lost or getting attacked by an animal or another child, and 18 more participants reported partial recollection (Porter, Birt, Yuille, & Lehman, 2000).

One objection is that perhaps this "false" memory was not entirely false. Maybe this young woman was lost at some point—if not in a Kmart at age 5, then somewhere else at some other age. In later studies researchers suggested virtually impossible events. For example, college students read fake advertisements for Disneyland that depicted people meeting and shaking hands with Bugs Bunny, a Warner Brothers character who would never appear at Disneyland. About 30% of those who read this ad later reported that they too had met Bugs Bunny at Disneyland. Some reported touching his ears or tail (Loftus, 2003). In another study British students who were asked to imagine certain experiences later reported that they actually remembered those experiences, including "having a nurse remove a skin sample from my little finger"—a procedure that British physicians never use (Mazzoni & Memon, 2003). In short, suggestions can lead people to report memories of events that never happened.

THIRD STUDY

Some therapists recommend that their clients examine photographs from their childhood to help evoke old memories. They are certainly right that photographs bring back memories. The question, however, is whether old photographs might also prompt a report of false memories.

Hypothesis.   A false suggestion about a childhood event will evoke more memory reports if people have examined photographs from that time period.

Method.   The researchers contacted the parents of 45 college students and asked each to provide a report of some event that happened while these students were in third or fourth grade and another that happened in fifth or sixth grade. Both were supposed to be events that the student might or might not remember, rather than events that the family had repeatedly discussed. The researchers also asked the parents to confirm that the following "false memory" event—the one they planned to suggest—had *not* happened: In the first grade, the child took a "Slime" toy to school, and then she and another child slid it into the teacher's desk and received a mild punishment later. Finally, the researchers asked the parents for copies of class photographs from first grade, third or fourth, and fifth or sixth.

After all these preparations, they brought in the students and briefly described for each student the two correct events (provided by the parents) and the one false event. For each they asked the students to provide whatever additional information they remembered. Half of them (randomly selected) were shown their class photographs and half were not. At the end of the session, they were asked to think about the first-grade event for the next week and try to remember more about it. Those in the photograph group took the photo with them. A week later, the students returned and again reported whatever they thought they remembered (Lindsay, Hagen, Read, Wade, & Garry, 2003).

Results.   Most students reported clear memories of the two real events. For the false event of first grade, Figure 7.18 shows the percentage of students who reported the event in the first and second sessions. Memories increased from the first to the second session, and students who saw the

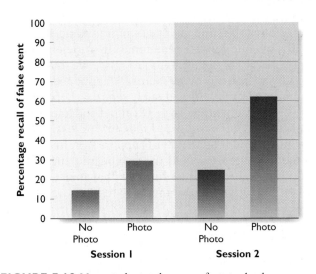

FIGURE 7.18 More students who saw a first-grade class photograph reported remembering the suggested (false) event. *(D. S. Lindsay, L. Hagen, J. D. Read, K. A. Wada, and M. Garry. True photographs and false memories. Psychological Science. Copyright 2004 Blackwell Publishing. Reprinted with permission.)*

photographs reported more memories than those who did not see photographs. By the second session, almost two thirds of the students who saw a class photograph reported some memory of the false event.

At the end of the study, the researchers explained that the first-grade event did not really happen. Many of the students expressed surprise, such as, "No way! I remember it! That is so weird!" (Lindsay et al., 2004, p. 153).

Interpretation. Examining an old photograph evokes old memories but also increases suggestibility for false memories. Looking at the photo helps the person remember, "Oh, yes, that's what my first-grade teacher looked like. And that was my closest friend back then . . ." If the person tries to remember acting with a friend to pull a prank on the teacher, the visual image becomes more vivid and more convincing.

In related studies researchers manipulated photos by computers, showing childhood pictures of people having tea with Prince Charles of England or riding with their families in a hot-air balloon—false events for each of the participants. Many of the participants claimed to remember the events and provided additional details (Strange, Sutherland, & Garry, 2004; Wade, Garry, Read, & Lindsay, 2002).

The question still remains, however, about clinicians' reports of recovering lost memories of early trauma. Many clinicians object that the kinds of false memories implanted in research settings (being lost in a mall, first-grade mischief, etc.) are different from emotionally intense memories of sexual abuse. To this criticism researchers reply that ethical concerns prevent them from suggesting memories of traumatic abuse.

If someone reports remembering some event after many years of not remembering it, we may never know whether the event actually happened. No one recommends rejecting all such reports (Pope, 1996). The recommendation is to withhold judgment about the accuracy of a recovered memory unless someone has independent evidence to support it. A further recommendation is to avoid using repeated suggestions, photographs, or other techniques that might increase the probability of a false memory report.

 CONCEPT CHECK

20. In what way is hindsight bias similar to an implanted "false memory"? (Check your answer on page 276.)

Children as Eyewitnesses

Finally, should we trust the reports of young children who are witnesses or victims of a crime? Research here can be tricky. No ethical researcher would abuse children or tell children they had been abused. A better approach is to ask a child to recall a medical or dental examination, where a stranger probed various parts of the body. How well can the child report what happened?

In such studies researchers found that children as young as 3 years old report accurately under proper conditions. They volunteer very little when asked, "Tell me what happened." However, what they do report is generally accurate. They usually also answer correctly to specific questions such as, "Did the doctor shine a light in your eyes?" (yes) and "Did the doctor cut your hair?" (no). Preschool children's accuracy is reasonably good even 6 weeks after the physical exam (Baker-Ward, Gordon, Ornstein, Larus, & Clubb, 1993).

Several factors influence the accuracy of young children's reports:

- **The delay between event and questioning.** Imagine a doctor who usually takes a child's temperature during a physical exam but did not do so in the most recent exam. A child who is asked about this exam within the next few weeks will probably report correctly that the doctor did not take a temperature. However, if asked at a much later time, the child reports that the doctor did take the child's temperature. Evidently, a child confuses the most recent exam with the usual exam (Ornstein et al., 1998).
- **Suggestive questions.** To an invitation such as, "Tell me what happened," a young child's answer is usually short but accurate. To a suggestive question such as, "Did he touch you under your clothing?" the probability of a false report increases (Lamb & Fauchier, 2001).
- **Hearing other children.** Children respond strongly to social influences. A child who hears other children reporting a false memory is likely to report the same event (Principe, Kanaya, Ceci, & Singh, 2006).
- **Repetition of the question.** If someone asks a child the same question two or three times, the child often changes answers (Krähenbühl & Blades, 2006; Poole & White, 1993). Apparently, the child assumes, "I must have been wrong the first time, so I'll try something else." Children are especially likely to change their answers on opinion questions. Also, if they said "I don't know" the first time, they may guess the second time.

However, asking a question again a few days later does not ordinarily prompt the child to change answers and may help the child remember. That procedure can help if a child has to testify in court at a later date (Poole & White, 1995).

• **Use of doll props.** Because children's reports are limited by their small vocabulary, some psychologists try to help them by providing anatomically detailed dolls and asking them to act out what happened. The idea sounds reasonable, but when researchers ask children to act out a doctor's exam (where we know what happened), they act out many events that did not happen (Greenhoot, Ornstein, Gordon, & Baker-Ward, 1999). In fact, if you point to a child's elbow and ask the child to find the doll's elbow, many young children cannot. Interpreting a child's doll play is a very uncertain matter (Ceci, 1995; Koocher et al., 1995).

• **Understandability of the questions.** Three-year-olds who understand a question will usually answer correctly. When they don't understand, they seldom say they don't understand. Instead, they usually answer "yes" (Imhoff & Baker-Ward, 1999).

Sometimes, an adult thinks a child understands when the child does not. Once my son and his wife took my granddaughter, then 3 years old, on a trip. They told her they would stop at a barbecue restaurant for dinner. She was so excited that she could hardly wait. She spent most of the trip asking, "Now how long till barbecue?" As they finally approached the restaurant, she asked, "Will other children be there too, with their Barbies?"

The general recommendations for children's eyewitness testimony are simple: If a child is asked simple questions, without suggestions or pressure and reasonably soon after the event, even children as young as 3 years can be believed (Ceci & Bruck, 1993). However, a young child can be highly influenced by suggestions.

CRITICAL THINKING

A STEP FURTHER

Unlikely Memory Reports

Some people claim to have been abducted by aliens from another planet. Apparently, most of these people are neither mentally ill nor deliberately lying (Banaji & Kihlstrom, 1996). Presuming that they were not actually abducted by aliens, how might we explain their reports?

IN CLOSING

Memory Distortions

Memory distortions are sometimes a serious problem, but they are by-products of a useful process. That process is our ability to focus on the essential gist.

When we are reasoning and making decisions, we may or may not need the details (Brainerd & Reyna, 2002). The older some experience is, the less likely we are to need its details. If we do need the details, we can usually reason them out well enough for most purposes. So memory distortions are not evidence of something going wrong. They are a necessary consequence of the way our memory normally works. The following dialogue illustrates our tendency to forget details:

He: We met at nine.
She: We met at eight.
He: I was on time.
She: No, you were late.
He: Ah, yes! I remember it well. We dined with friends.
She: We dined alone.
He: A tenor sang.
She: A baritone.
He: Ah, yes! I remember it well. That dazzling April moon!
She: There was none that night. And the month was June.
He: That's right! That's right!
She: It warms my heart to know that you remember still the way you do.
He: Ah, yes! I remember it well.
　　　　—"I Remember It Well" from the musical *Gigi* by Alan Jay Lerner and Frederick Loewe ▌

Summary

- *Interference.* When someone learns several similar sets of material, the earlier ones interfere with retrieval of later ones by proactive interference. The later ones interfere with earlier ones by retroactive interference. (page 267)
- *Reconstruction.* When remembering stories or events from their own lives, people recall some of the facts and fill in the gaps based on logical inferences of what must have happened. They rely heavily on inferences when their memory is uncertain. (page 268)
- *Reconstructions from a word list.* If people read or hear a list of related words and try to recall them, they are likely to include closely related words that were not on the list. They have remembered the gist and reconstructed what else must have been on the list. (page 269)
- *Story memory.* Someone who tries to retell a story after memory of the details has faded will rely on the gist and therefore leave out some details that seemed irrelevant and add or change other facts to fit the logic of the story. (page 269)
- *Hindsight bias.* People often revise their memories of what they previously expected, saying that how

events turned out was what they had expected all along. (page 270)

- *The "recovered memory" vs. "false memory" debate.* Some therapists have used hypnosis or suggestions to try to help people remember painful experiences. Suggestions can induce people to distort memories or report events that did not happen. It is difficult to distinguish accurate memories from distorted or false ones. (page 270)
- *Children as eyewitnesses.* Even preschool children can correctly report events if they are asked simple questions without pressure soon after the event. However, suggestive questions can lead them astray. (page 274)

Answers to Concept Checks

14. It is due to proactive interference—interference from memories learned earlier. (page 267)

15. First, someone learns the response; the second learning is the extinction of the response. If the first learning proactively interferes with the later extinction, spontaneous recovery will result. (page 267)

16. The first item on a list is spared from proactive interference. The last is spared from retroactive interference. However, low interference is not the only explanation for these effects. (page 267)

17. You would be less likely to add a word not on the list. We rely on inferences mostly when the actual memory is weak. (page 269)

18. Long after the fact, a historian puts together a coherent story based on the gist of events, emphasizing details that fit the pattern and omitting others. In your everyday life, you are aware of all the facts, including those that do not fit any pattern. (page 269)

19. Emotionally arousing memories are usually more memorable than other events. Any emotionally arousing event stimulates cortisol release and in other ways activates the amygdala, a brain area that helps store memories. (page 271; see also page 263)

20. In a case of hindsight bias, something that you learn later operates like a suggestion, so that when you try to remember what you previously thought, you are influenced by that suggestion and change your reported memory to fit it. (pages 270, 272)

Amnesia

• *Why do some people have severe memory problems?*

Imagine you defied the advice given to computer owners and passed your computer through a powerful magnetic field. Chances are you would erase the memory, but suppose you found that you had erased only the text files and not the graphics files. Or suppose the old memories were intact but you could no longer store new ones. From the damage you would gain hints about how your computer's memory works.

The same is true of human memory. Various kinds of brain damage impair one kind of memory but not another, enabling us to draw inferences about how memory is organized.

Amnesia After Damage to the Hippocampus

Amnesia is a *loss of memory.* Even in the most severe cases, people don't forget everything they ever learned. For example, they don't forget how to walk, talk, or eat. (If they did, we would call it *dementia,* not amnesia.) Amnesia results from many kinds of brain damage, including damage to the hippocampus.

In 1953 a man with the initials H. M. was suffering from many small daily epileptic seizures and about one major seizure per week. He did not respond to any antiepileptic drugs, so in desperation surgeons removed most of his **hippocampus,** *a large forebrain structure in the interior of the temporal lobe* (Figure 7.19), where they believed his epileptic seizures were originating. They also removed some surrounding brain areas. At the time researchers knew very little about the hippocampus and did not know what to expect. Had they known the behavioral outcome, H. M. almost certainly would have preferred to continue having epileptic seizures instead of undergoing this operation.

The surgery greatly decreased the frequency and severity of H. M.'s seizures. His personality remained the same, but he became more passive (Eichenbaum, 2002). His IQ score increased slightly, presumably because he had fewer epileptic seizures. However, he suffered severe memory problems (Corkin, 1984; Milner, 1959). H. M. suffered a massive **anterograde** (ANT-eh-ro-grade) **amnesia,** *inability to store new long-term memories.* For years after the operation, he cited the year as 1953 and his own age as 27. Later, he took wild guesses (Corkin, 1984). He would read the same issue of a magazine repeatedly without recog-

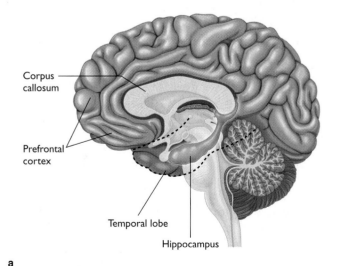

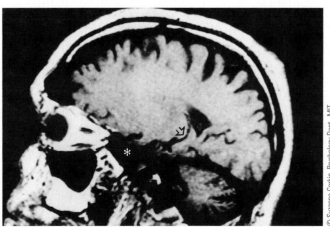

a   b

FIGURE 7.19 **(a)** The hippocampus is a large subcortical structure of the brain. **(b)** The photo shows a scan of the brain of H. M. formed by magnetic resonance imaging. The asterisk indicates the area from which the hippocampus is missing. The arrow indicates a portion of the hippocampus that is preserved. *(Photo courtesy of Suzanne Corkin and David Amaral)*

nizing it. He could not even remember where he had lived. He also suffered a moderate **retrograde amnesia,** *loss of memory for events that occurred shortly before the brain damage* (Figure 7.20). That is, he had some trouble recalling events that had happened within the last 1 to 3 years before the operation. Any loss of consciousness, such as after a concussion or excessive alcohol intake, can produce retrograde amnesia, although seldom as extensive as 1 to 3 years (Riccio, Millin, & Gisquet-Verrier, 2003).

FIGURE 7.20 Brain damage induces retrograde amnesia (loss of old memories) and anterograde amnesia (difficulty storing new memories).

H. M. could form normal short-term memories, such as repeating a short list of words or numbers, and he could retain them as long as he kept rehearsing them. However, a brief distraction would eliminate the memory. For example, he might tell the same person the same story several times within a few minutes, each time forgetting that he had told it before (Eichenbaum, 2002).

Like Rip van Winkle (the story character who slept for 20 years and awakened to a vastly changed world), H. M. became more and more out of date with each passing year (Gabrieli, Cohen, & Corkin, 1988; M. L. Smith, 1988). He did not recognize people who became famous after the mid-1950s, although when given a famous person's name—such as John Glenn or Mikhail Gorbachev—he could provide a bit of more-or-less correct information (O'Kane, Kensinger, & Corkin, 2004). He did not understand the meaning of words and phrases that entered the English language after his surgery. For example, he treated *Jacuzzi* and *granola* as nonwords (Corkin, 2002). He guessed that *soul food* means "forgiveness" and that a *closet queen* might be "a moth" (Gabrieli et al., 1988).

In spite of H. M.'s massive memory difficulties, he could still acquire and retain new skills. Recall the distinction between procedural memory (skills) and declarative memory (facts). H. M. learned to read material written in mirror fashion (N. J. Cohen & Squire, 1980), such as shown below. However, he could not remember having learned this skill or any of the others he acquired and always expressed surprise at his success.

He could read sentences written backwards, like this.

The results for H. M. led researchers to study both people and laboratory animals with similar damage. The following points have emerged:

- The hippocampus is active during both storage and retrieval of most long-term memories, although people can retrieve old memories despite damage to the hippocampus (Eldridge, Engel, Zeineh, Bookheimer, & Knowlton, 2005).
- The hippocampus is more important for explicit memory than for implicit memory and more important for difficult tasks than for easy tasks (Reed & Squire, 1999; Ryan, Althoff, Whitlow, & Cohen, 2000).
- Declarative memory requires the hippocampus. Procedural memories do not.
- The hippocampus is necessary for remembering details. One man with hippocampal damage could sketch the general layout of his home neighborhood but could not identify photos of houses and other landmarks within the neighborhood (Rosenbaum et al., 2000).

CONCEPT CHECK

21. Which kinds of memory are most impaired in H. M.? Which kinds are least impaired? (Check your answers on page 281.)

Amnesia After Damage to the Prefrontal Cortex

Damage to the prefrontal cortex also produces amnesia (see Figure 7.19). Because the prefrontal cortex receives extensive input from the hippocampus, the symptoms of prefrontal cortex damage overlap those of hippocampal damage. However, some special deficits also arise.

Prefrontal cortex damage can be the result of a stroke, head trauma, or **Korsakoff's syndrome,** *a condition caused by a prolonged deficiency of vitamin B_1 (thiamine), usually as a result of chronic alcoholism.* This deficiency leads to widespread loss or shrinkage of neurons, especially in the prefrontal cortex. Patients suffer apathy, confusion, and amnesia (Squire, Haist, & Shimamura, 1989). If given a list of words to remember, they forget those at the beginning of the list before they reach the end and soon forget those at the end also (Stuss et al., 1994).

Patients with prefrontal cortex damage answer many questions with **confabulations,** *which are attempts to fill in the gaps in their memory.* Most confabulations include out-of-date information (Schnider, 2003) and usually replace the current reality with something more pleasant from the past (Fotopoulou, Solms, & Turnbull, 2004). For example, an aged hospitalized woman might insist that she had to go home to feed her baby. Confabulations are not exactly attempts to hide an inability to answer a question, as Korsakoff's patients almost never confabulate on a question such as "Where is Premola?" or "Who is Princess Lolita?" (Schnider, 2003). That is, someone who never knew the answer freely admits not knowing. The following interview is a typical example (Moscovitch, 1989, pp. 135–136). Note the mixture of correct information, confabulations that were correct at some time in the past, and imaginative attempts to explain the discrepancies between one answer and another:

Psychologist: How old are you?
Patient: I'm 40, 42, pardon me, 62.
Psychologist: Are you married or single?
Patient: Married.
Psychologist: How long have you been married?
Patient: About 4 months.
Psychologist: What's your wife's name?
Patient: Martha.
Psychologist: How many children do you have?
Patient: Four. (He laughs.) Not bad for 4 months.
Psychologist: How old are your children?
Patient: The eldest is 32; his name is Bob. And the youngest is 22; his name is Joe.
Psychologist: How did you get these children in 4 months?
Patient: They're adopted.
Psychologist: Who adopted them?
Patient: Martha and I.
Psychologist: Immediately after you got married you wanted to adopt these older children?
Patient: Before we were married we adopted one of them, two of them. The eldest girl Brenda and Bob, and Joe and Dina since we were married.
Psychologist: Does it all sound a little strange to you, what you are saying?
Patient: I think it is a little strange.
Psychologist: I think when I looked at your record it said that you've been married for over 30 years. Does that sound more reasonable to you if I told you that?
Patient: No.
Psychologist: Do you really believe that you have been married for 4 months?
Patient: Yes.

Patients with prefrontal cortex damage confidently defend their confabulations and often maintain the same confabulation from one time to the next. Actually, the same is true of normal people who have learned some-

thing poorly. In one study college students listened to complicated 2-minute descriptions of topics they knew little about and then answered detailed questions. Once a week for the next 4 weeks, they heard the same description and answered the same questions. Most people repeated the same incorrect guesses from one week to the next (Fritz, Morris, Bjork, Gelman, & Wickens, 2000).

Why do people with prefrontal damage confabulate so much more than the rest of us? According to Morris Moscovitch (1992), the prefrontal cortex is necessary for *working with memory*, the strategies we use to reconstruct memories that we cannot immediately recall. For example, if you are asked what is the farthest north that you have ever traveled or how many salads you ate last week, you have to reason out your answer. People with prefrontal cortex damage have difficulty making reasonable inferences.

Despite their impoverished memory in other regards, people with brain damage perform well on most tests of implicit memory. For example, after hearing a list of words, a patient may not be able to say any of the words on the list and may not even remember that there was a list. However, when given a set of three-letter stems such as CON—, the patient completes them to make words that were on the list (Hamann & Squire, 1997).

Blue Planet Software, Inc. Tetris © Elorg 1987–2002

People who spend many hours playing the game Tetris report seeing images of Tetris blocks, especially as they are falling asleep. So do people with severe amnesia, even though they don't remember playing the game.

Another example: After patients repeatedly practiced playing the video game Tetris, they said they did not remember playing the game before, although they did improve from one session to the next. When they closed their eyes to go to sleep at night, they said they saw little images of blocks but did not know what they were (Stickgold, Malia, Maguire, Roddenberry, & O'Connor, 2000).

One important conclusion emerges from all the studies of brain damage and amnesia: We have several different types of memory. It is possible to impair one type without equally damaging another.

 CONCEPT CHECK

22. Although confabulation is a kind of false memory, how does it differ from the suggested false memories discussed in the previous module? (Check your answer on page 281.)

Memory Impairments in Alzheimer's Disease

A more common cause of memory loss is **Alzheimer's** (AHLTZ-hime-ers) **disease**, *a condition occurring mostly in old age, characterized by increasingly severe memory loss, confusion, depression, disordered thinking, and impaired attention.* Although several genes have been linked to an onset of Alzheimer's disease before age 60, more than 99% of the people with Alzheimer's disease have a later onset, and most cases of the late-onset form are not linked with any identified gene. Moreover, the genes' effects are not inevitable. The Yoruba people of Nigeria almost never get Alzheimer's disease, even if they have the genes that predispose Americans to this disease (Hendrie, 2001). Which aspect of their culture shields them from Alzheimer's is uncertain, although diet is a likely candidate.

Alzheimer's disease is marked by a gradual accumulation of harmful proteins in the brain and deterioration of brain cells, leading to a loss of arousal and attention. The memory problem includes both anterograde and retrograde amnesia. Because the areas of damage include the hippocampus and the prefrontal cortex, their memory deficits overlap those of H. M. and patients with Korsakoff's syndrome. For example, like Korsakoff's patients, they often confabulate (Nedjam, Dalla Barba, & Pillon, 2000). Like H. M., as a rule they learn new skills and other implicit memories much better than new explicit memories. For example, they can be taught to use a mobile phone (Lekeu, Wojtasik, Van der Linden, & Salmon, 2002). However, even their implicit memory is deficient in some cases (McGeorge, Taylor, Della Sala, & Shanks, 2002). Their

mixture of memory problems should not be surprising, given the overall decrease of arousal and attention. Weak arousal and impaired attention cause problems for almost any aspect of memory.

 CONCEPT CHECK

23. What kinds of memory are impaired in Alzheimer's disease? (Check your answer on page 282.)

Infant Amnesia

Can you recall events from when you were 6 years old? How about age 4? Age 2? Although 2- and 3-year-olds can describe events that happened months ago, these memories fade over time, and most adults report only a few fragmentary memories of early childhood or none at all (Bauer, Wenner, & Kroupina, 2002; K. Nelson & Fivush, 2004). The *scarcity of early declarative memories* is known as **infant amnesia,** or **childhood amnesia.** People retain procedural memories from early childhood, such as memory of how to walk, but of course they have practiced those skills from then on. Although psychologists have proposed many theories of infant amnesia, none are fully persuasive (Howe & Courage, 1997).

In what may have been the earliest proposal on this issue, Sigmund Freud suggested that children go through emotionally difficult experiences at ages 4 to 5 that are so disturbing that a child represses everything experienced at that time or before. However, neither Freud nor anyone else has provided persuasive evidence for this idea.

A more modern proposal is that the hippocampus, known to be important for memory, is slow to mature, so memories from the first few years are not stored well (Moscovitch, 1985). A weakness of that suggestion is that young children do form long-term memories. Patricia Bauer (2005) provided some novel experiences to preschool children of various ages and tested their recollections later. Although children of all ages showed good initial learning, the youngest children forgot fastest. That is, the problem is not that young children fail to form memories, as we might expect if they have an immature hippocampus. The problem is that they forget rapidly.

Another proposal is that a permanent memory of an experience requires a "sense of self" that develops between ages 3 and 4 (Howe & Courage, 1993). One difficulty with this idea is that the offset of childhood amnesia is gradual. Even for ages 5 and 6, many people report relatively few memories. Also, rats, pigeons, and other nonhuman species develop long-lasting memories. If we want to avoid saying that rats have more sense of self than 3-year-old children, we could argue that rats' memories aren't the same as the kind of memory we are discussing for adult humans. However, at best, this idea is not convincing.

Another possibility is that after we come to rely on language, we lose access to memories encoded earlier. That idea will not explain why a 4-year-old can describe what happened at age 3, whereas a 7-year-old cannot. Still, some interesting research supports the onset of language as one factor in infant amnesia: Psychologists let some 3-year-olds play with a "magic shrinking machine." A child could place a large toy into a slot, crank a handle, and then see a smaller version of the same toy come out, as if the machine had shrunk the toy. When the children returned 6 months or a year later, they clearly remembered the machine and how to work it. However, when they were asked to describe how the machine worked or to name the toys that it shrank, the children described their experience using only the words they had known at the time they originally played with the machine (Simcock & Hayne, 2002). For example, a child who knew the word "teddy bear" at age 3 would use it later, but a child who did not know the term at age 3 would not, even after learning it in the meantime. In a similar study, 2-year-old children learned that only one color of fluid would operate a "magic" bubble machine. Of those who did not know the name of that color at the time, but who learned it within the next 2 months, 30% could then name the color that operated the machine (Morris & Baker-Ward, in press). So it appears that children sometimes apply newly learned words to old memories.

One more possibility is that infant amnesia relates to encoding specificity. If we learn something in one time, place, physiological condition, or state of mind, we remember it more easily under the same or similar conditions. Maybe we forget our early years just because we don't have enough of the right retrieval cues to find those infant memories.

At this point none of these hypotheses is well established. Infant amnesia probably has several explanations, not just one.

 CONCEPT CHECK

24. What evidence indicates that infant amnesia is not due to a failure to establish long-term memories? (Check your answer on page 282.)

IN CLOSING

What Amnesia Teaches Us

We could distinguish among types of memory in many ways. Studies of amnesia show us that some of these distinctions are natural. It is possible to impair ex-plicit memory without impairing implicit memory or to damage declarative memory without loss of procedural memory. Therefore, those distinctions relate to the way the brain organizes memory.

Amnesia also shows us that human memory is not much like computer memory. You could delete one file from your computer without harming any of the others. You could even delete one word or one letter from a computer file without altering the rest of the file. In human memory amnesia never wipes out just a single memory. People with memory problems have diffuse difficulties with many memories, not just one or a few, and they generally have problems with other aspects of life too, such as emotional control or motivation (Kopelman, 2000). Memory is closely linked to everything we do. ∎

Summary

- *Amnesia after damage to the hippocampus.* H. M. and other patients with damage to the hippocampus have great difficulty storing new long-term declarative memories, although they form normal short-term, procedural, and implicit memories. (page 277)
- *Damage to the prefrontal cortex.* Patients with damage to the prefrontal cortex give confident wrong answers, known as confabulations. Most confabulations were correct information earlier in the person's life. (page 278)
- *Alzheimer's disease.* Patients with Alzheimer's disease, a condition that occurs mostly after age 60 to 65, have a variety of memory problems, although implicit and procedural memory are more intact than explicit, declarative memory. Their problems stem largely from impairments of arousal and attention. (page 280)
- *Infant amnesia.* Most people remember little from early childhood, even though preschoolers have clear recollections of experiences that happened months or even years ago. No one explanation is fully convincing. (page 280)

Answers to Concept Checks

21. H. M. is greatly impaired at forming new declarative memories. His short-term memory is intact, as is his memory for events long before the operation and his ability to form new procedural memories. (page 277)
22. Most confabulated statements were true at one time, though not now. Also, people with brain damage seldom confabulate answers to questions they never could have answered in the past. That is, they seldom make up totally new information. (page 279)

23. Patients with Alzheimer's disease have weaknesses in almost all types of memory, although they show better implicit than explicit memory. (page 280)

24. Young children remember events that happened months or even years ago. However, a few years later, they lose those memories. (page 280)

CHAPTER ENDING

Key Terms and Activities

Key Terms

You can check the page listed for a complete description of a term. You can also check the glossary/index at the end of the text for a definition of a given term, or you can download a list of all the terms and their definitions for any chapter at this website:

www.thomsonedu.com/ psychology/kalat

Alzheimer's disease (page 280)
amnesia (page 277)
anterograde amnesia (page 277)
chunking (page 253)
confabulations (page 278)
consolidation (page 256)
cued recall (page 248)
declarative memory (page 250)
dissociation (page 271)
encoding specificity principle (page 260)

episodic memory (page 252)
explicit memory (or direct memory) (page 249)
false memory (page 272)
free recall (page 248)
hindsight bias (page 270)
hippocampus (page 277)
implicit memory (or indirect memory) (page 249)
infant amnesia (or childhood amnesia) (page 280)
information-processing model (page 251)
Korsakoff's syndrome (page 278)
levels-of-processing principle (page 259)
long-term memory (page 252)
memory (page 245)
method of loci (page 264)
mnemonic device (page 264)
primacy effect (page 247)

primes (page 249)
proactive interference (page 268)
procedural memory (page 249)
recency effect (page 247)
recognition (page 248)
reconstruction (page 268)
recovered memory (page 271)
repression (page 271)
retrieval cue (page 254)
retroactive interference (page 268)
retrograde amnesia (page 278)
savings method (or relearning method) (page 248)
semantic memory (page 252)
sensory store (page 251)
short-term memory (page 252)
source amnesia (page 252)
SPAR method (page 262)
state-dependent memory (page 261)
working memory (page 256)

Suggestions for Further Reading

Eichenbaum, H. (2002). *The Cognitive Neuroscience of Memory*. New York: Oxford University Press. An engaging account of memory and its impairments.

Schacter, D. L. (1996). *Searching for Memory*. New York: Basic Books. Discusses current theories and research in an accessible manner.

 ## Web/Technology Resources

Student Companion Website

www.thomsonedu.com/psychology/kalat

Explore the Student Companion Website for Online Try-It-Yourself activities, practice quizzes, flashcards, and more! The companion site also has direct links to the following websites.

The Magic Number Seven, Plus or Minus Two

www.well.com/user/smalin/miller.html

This is George Miller's classic article about the limits of short-term memory, complete with graphs and references, as it originally appeared in the *Psychological Review* in 1956.

 ## For Additional Study

Kalat Premium Website

http://www.thomsonedu.com

For Critical Thinking Videos and additional Online Try-It-Yourself activities, go to this site to enter or purchase your code for the Kalat Premium Website.

ThomsonNOW!

http://www.thomsonedu.com

Go to this site for the link to ThomsonNOW, your one-stop study shop. Take a Pretest for this chapter, and Thomson-NOW will generate a personalized Study Plan based on your test reults. The Study Plan will identify the topics you need to review and direct you to online resources to help you master those topics. You can then take a Posttest to help you determine the concepts you have mastered and what you still need to work on.

Cognition and Language

Consider the statement, "This sentence is false." Is the statement itself true or false? Declaring the statement true agrees with its own assessment that it is false. But declaring it false would make its assessment correct. A sentence about itself, called a *self-referential* sentence, can be confusing, like the one above, or true (like this one!). It can also be false ("Anyone who reads this sentence will be transported suddenly to the planet Neptune"), untestable ("Whenever no one is reading this sentence, it changes into the passive voice"), or amusing ("This sentence no verb" or "This sentence sofa includes an unnecessary word").

In this chapter you will be asked to think about thinking, talk about talking, and read about reading. Doing so is self-referential, and if you try to "think about what you are thinking now," you can go into a confusing loop like the one in "This sentence is false." Psychological researchers focus as much as possible on results obtained from carefully controlled experiments, not just on what people say that they think about their own thought processes.

Cognitive psychology studies how people think and what they know.

Attention and Categorization

• *What is attention? What are concepts? How can we measure them?*

Cognition means *thinking, gaining knowledge, and using knowledge.* Cognitive psychologists also deal with how people organize their thoughts into language. Cognition begins with focusing on something (attending to it) and determining what it is (categorization). This module will concentrate mostly on attention and categorization. But how can researchers learn about them? During the era when behaviorists heavily dominated experimental psychology, researchers devoted little effort to cognition or other unobservable processes. Since about 1970, research has increased substantially, as psychologists developed methods for inferring the unobservable.

Research in Cognitive Psychology

Perhaps it seems that cognitive psychology should be simple. "If you want to find out what people think or what they know, why not ask them?" Sometimes, psychologists do ask, but people can't always describe their own thought processes. Recall, for example, implicit memory as discussed in chapter 7: Sometimes, you see or hear something that influences your behavior although you don't realize it.

People often say they answered some question by forming a detailed visual image. However, that image is not always accurate. To illustrate, imagine a simple cube balanced with one point (corner) on a table and the opposite point straight up. Imagine that you are holding the highest point with one finger. Now, using a finger of the opposite hand, point to all the remaining corners of the cube (not counting the one touching the table). How many corners do you touch?

You probably will say that you answered this question by "picturing" a cube in your mind as if you were actually seeing it. However, most people answer the question incorrectly, and few get it right quickly (Hinton, 1979). (Check answer A on page 299.)

In short, we should not simply accept people's self-reports about their thinking. So how *can* we measure thinking? Let's consider one of the first experiments that showed a way to measure a mental process.

CRITICAL THINKING
WHAT'S THE EVIDENCE?

Mental Imagery

Roger Shepard and Jacqueline Metzler (1971) reasoned that if people visualize mental images, then the time it takes them to rotate a mental image should be similar to the time needed to rotate a real object.

Hypothesis. When people have to rotate a mental image to answer a question, the farther they have to rotate it, the longer it will take them to answer the question.

Method. Participants examined pairs of drawings of three-dimensional objects, as in Figure 8.1, and indicated whether the two drawings represented different objects or one object and a rotated view of it. (Try to answer this question yourself before reading further.)

Try It Yourself

People pulled one lever to indicate *same* and another lever to indicate *different.* When the correct answer was *same,* someone might determine that answer by rotating a mental image of the first picture until it matched the second. If so, the delay should depend on how far the image had to be rotated.

Results. Participants answered almost 97% of the items correctly. As predicted, their reaction time when they responded *same* depended on the angular difference in orientation between the two views. For example, if the first image of a pair had to be rotated 30 degrees to match the second image, people needed a certain amount of time to pull the *same* lever. If an image had to be rotated 60 degrees to match the other, they took twice as long to pull the lever. That is, they reacted as if they were watching a model of the object rotate; the more the object needed to be rotated, the longer they took to determine the answer.

Interpretation. Viewing a mental image is at least partly like real vision. So in this case, common sense appears to be correct. However, the main point is that it is possible for researchers to

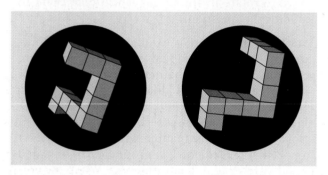

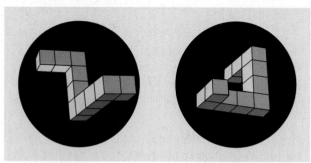

FIGURE 8.1 Examples of pairs of drawings used in an experiment by Shepard and Metzler (1971). Do the drawings for each pair represent the same object being rotated, or are they different objects? (See answer B on page 299.) *(From "Mental rotation of three-dimensional objects" by R. N. Shepard and J. N. Metzler from* Science, *1971, pp. 701–703. Copyright © 1971. Reprinted with permission from AAAS.)*

infer thought processes from someone's delay in answering a question. Most research in cognitive psychology relies on measurements of accuracy and timing of responses. Less frequently, some researchers use brain scans to measure brain activation during cognitive activities.

CRITICAL THINKING

A STEP FURTHER

Auditory Imagery

Some people report that they have auditory images as well as visual images. They "hear" words or songs "in their head." What kind of evidence would we need to test this claim?

Attention

Human cognition cannot deal with all the information that the world provides. You are constantly bombarded with sights, sounds, smells, and other stimuli. **Attention** is *your tendency to respond to some stimuli more than others at any given time or to remember some more than others.* Attention shifts, enabling you to respond to different kinds of information at different times.

To illustrate, recall that the fovea of your retina receives the most detail. Ordinarily, the information striking your retina is the most memorable and has the greatest impact on your behavior. However, it is possible to direct your attention elsewhere. For example, if you don't want someone to know you are watching, you look off to the side but nevertheless concentrate on that person. You can demonstrate your ability to shift attention with the following. Fixate your eyes on the x in the center and then, without moving your eyes, read the letters in the circle around it clockwise:

Try It Yourself

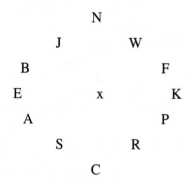

As you see, focusing your attention away from the center of your vision is difficult but possible. You can even attend to two nonadjacent spots at once—for example, the places occupied by **A** and **F** in the display above. When you increase your attention to something in your visual field, the part of your visual cortex sensitive to that area becomes more active and receives more blood flow (Müller, Malinowski, Gruber, & Hillyard, 2003) Also, if you plan to pay extra attention to the color or motion of the next object to be shown on the screen, then the brain areas sensitive to color or motion become more active, even before the object appears (Driver & Frith, 2000). So attention is a process of increasing the brain's response to selected stimuli. Our conscious memory is virtually limited to the material that has held attention (Lachter, Forster, & Ruthruff, 2004).

Attentive and Preattentive Processes

In the example just described, you deliberately shifted your attention from one letter to another. Often, however, objects grab your attention automatically. Seeing or hearing your own name or seeing your photograph is almost sure to attract your attention (Brédart, Delchambre, & Laureys, 2006; K. L. Shapiro, Caldwell, & Sorensen, 1997). Your attention also flows to moving objects (Abrams & Christ, 2003) and to anything unusual. I once watched a costume contest in which people were told to dress so distinctively that their friends could find them in a crowd as quickly as possible. The winner was a young man who came onto the stage naked. Although I concede that he earned the prize, there is a problem with this contest: The most distinctive clothing (or lack of it) depends on what everyone else is wearing. A naked person would be easy to spot in a shopping mall but not at a nudist beach. Our

FIGURE 8.2 Demonstration of preattentive processes: The one whooping crane stands out immediately among the sandhill cranes. You would find it just as fast in a larger or smaller flock of sandhill cranes.

attention is drawn to the unusual, but what is unusual depends on the context. Ordinarily, we notice something that is flashing on and off, but if almost everything is flashing on and off, something that isn't flashing draws our attention (Pashler & Harris, 2001). If almost everything is moving, we notice the one thing that isn't (Theeuwes, 2004).

To illustrate how an unusual object draws attention, examine Figure 8.2, which shows a huge flock of sandhill cranes and one whooping crane, which looks different. Find the whooping crane. That was easy, wasn't it? When an object differs drastically from those around it in size, shape, color, or movement, we find it by a **preattentive process,** *meaning that it stands out immediately. We don't have to shift attention from one object to another.* Because the distinctive item jumps out preattentively, the number of sandhill cranes is irrelevant. If some of them departed or more arrived, you would find the whooping crane just as fast.

Contrast that task with Figure 8.3. Here, all the birds are marbled godwits. Most of them are facing to your left; your task is to find the one that is facing to your right. The difference between facing left and facing right is not salient enough to attract your attention automatically. You have to check each bird separately, and the more birds present, the longer you will probably need to find the unusual one. (You might find it quickly if you are lucky enough to start your search in the correct corner of the photograph.) You had to rely

Try It Yourself

on an **attentive process**—*one that requires searching through the items in series* (Enns & Rensink, 1990; Treisman & Souther, 1985). The *Where's Waldo* books are an excellent example of a task requiring an attentive process. Studies of brain activity confirm that when we search through a complex display for an item that is hard to find, we shift the brain's responsiveness from one area of the display to another (Woodman & Luck, 2003).

The distinction between attentive and preattentive processes has practical applications. Imagine yourself as an ergonomist (human factors psycholo-

FIGURE 8.3 Demonstration of attentive processes: Find the marbled godwit that is facing to the right. In this case you need to check the birds one at a time.

gist) designing machinery with several gauges. When the apparatus is running safely, the first gauge should read about 70, the second 40, the third 30, and the fourth 10. If you arrange the gauges as in the top row of Figure 8.4, then people using this machine must check each gauge separately to find anything dangerous. In the bottom row of Figure 8.4, the gauges are arranged so that all the safe ranges are on the right. Now someone can glance at the display and quickly (preattentively) notice anything out of position.

 CONCEPT CHECK

1. Suppose you are in a field full of brownish bushes and one motionless brown rabbit. Will you find the rabbit by attentive or preattentive processes? If the field has many motionless rabbits and one that is hopping, will you find the active one by attentive or preattentive processes? (Check your answers on page 298.)

The Stroop Effect

Here is another example of something that grabs our attention automatically: Read the following instructions and then examine Figure 8.5:

 Try It Yourself

> Notice the blocks of color at the top of the figure. Scanning from left to right, give the name of each color as fast as you can. Then notice the nonsense syllables printed in different colors in the center of the figure. Instead of pronouncing them, say the color of each one as fast as possible. Then turn to the real words at the bottom. Instead of reading them, quickly state the color of each one.

Most people find it difficult to ignore the words at the bottom of the figure, unless they blur their vision, say the colors in a different language, or somehow manage to regard the color words as meaningless (Raz, Kirsch, Pollard, & Nitkin-Kaner, 2006). After all of your years of reading, you can hardly bring yourself to look at **RED** and say "green." *The tendency to read the word, instead of saying the color of ink as instructed,* is known as the **Stroop effect**, after the psychologist who discovered it.

As a possible explanation, you might imagine that words always take priority over colors. Try the following: Go back to Figure 8.5 and notice the red, green, blue, and yellow patches at the four corners. This time, instead of saying anything, point to the correct color patch. First, try pointing to the color patch corresponding to the color of the ink; that is, when you come to **RED**, point to the blue patch in the lower left. Then try it again but point to the color corresponding to the meaning of the word. That is, when you come to **RED**, point to the red patch in the upper left. Try it now.

 Try It Yourself

You probably found it easy to point to the patch that matches the color of the ink and harder to point to the color matching the word meaning (Durgin, 2000). When you are speaking, you are primed to read the words you see, but when you are pointing, you are more primed to attend to something nonverbal, such as ink color. In either case one response dominates, and it interferes with the less dominant response.

Limitations of Attention

We have considered how an object can grab your attention and how you can deliberately shift it from one item to another. Now let's consider the limitations of your attention. How much can your attention hold at once? For example, imagine yourself in the control room of the Three Mile Island nuclear power plant, the site of a nearly disastrous accident in 1979. Figure 8.6 shows a small portion of the room as it appeared then, with an enormous number of knobs and gauges. Furthermore, in certain cases the knob controlling something and the gauge measuring it were in different places. Since then the controls have been redesigned to simplify the task. The design of good controls requires an understanding of human attention and its limitations.

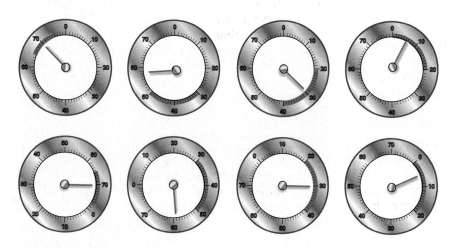

FIGURE 8.4 Each gauge represents a measurement of a different variable in a machine. For the top row, the operator must check gauges one at a time. In the bottom row, all the safe ranges are in the same direction. The operator detects an unsafe reading preattentively.

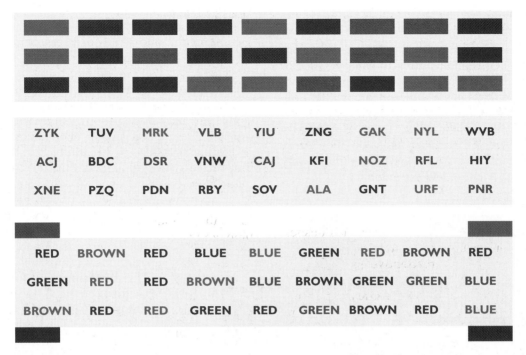

FIGURE 8.5 Read (left to right) the color of the ink in each part. Try to ignore the words themselves.

Change Blindness

If you look out your window, do you see the whole scene at once? Recall the concept of *sensory store* from chapter 7: If a display disappears but a signal immediately calls your attention to part of the display, you can say what had been there. So in a sense, you saw the whole scene. However, if nothing calls your attention to a particular spot, how well could you recall it? If you scan the scene, briefly fixating everything, do you know everything in the scene?

Most people think they do, and they believe they would notice anything that changed. However, movie directors discovered long ago that if they shot different parts of a story on different days, few viewers noticed the changes in background props or the actors' clothes (Simons & Levin, 2003).

Psychologists have named this phenomenon **change blindness**—*the frequent failure to detect changes in parts of a scene.* If anything moves or changes its appearance suddenly, it automatically draws your attention. However, if a similar change occurs slowly or while you are blinking or moving your eyes, you might not notice (Henderson & Hollingworth, 2003b). You are especially unlikely to notice if your working memory is occupied with other matters (Todd, Fougnie, & Marois, 2005). Have you ever seen one of those puzzles that ask you to "find ten differences between these two pictures"? The difficulty of finding them indicates that you don't simultaneously pay at-

tention to everything you see. To experience this effect, see an Online Try It Yourself activity. Go to **www.thomsonedu. com/psychology/kalat.** Navigate to the student website, then to the Online Try It Yourself section, and click Change Blindness. In one experiment people looked at a screen that alternated between two views of a scene, as shown in Figure 8.7. Each view appeared for 560 milliseconds (ms), followed by a blank screen for 80 ms, and then the other view for 560 ms, with the sequence repeating until the viewer detected how the two scenes differed. Generally, viewers found differences in important features of the scene faster than changes in less central details, but on the average they took almost 11 seconds to find a difference, and up to 50 seconds or more for some pairs of pictures (Rensink, O'Regan, & Clark, 1997).

CONCEPT CHECK

2. Did viewers in this study detect the changes by a preattentive or an attentive mechanism? (Check your answer on page 298.)

People also have change deafness for sounds. In one study students tried to repeat the words that someone spoke. After a 1-minute rest break, the procedure continued but with a new voice speaking the words. Only about half of the students noticed the change (Vitevitch, 2003).

Overall, the apparent conclusion is that you do not maintain a detailed representation of what you see or hear. You hold a few details, but those details vary from one time to another. That's what we mean by attention. You retain the gist of the rest of the scene but not the details (Becker & Pashler, 2002; Tatler, Gilchrist, & Rusted, 2003). Recall a similar conclusion about story memory from chapter 7: We ordinarily remember only the gist of the story and a few extra details.

Shifting Attention

Attending to one thing detracts from attending to something else (Pashler, 1994). Can you do two things at once? Yes, you can *do* two things at once, such as walk and chew gum. However, if you closely watch someone who is walking and chewing at the same time, you may notice that the activities are synchronized. The person might chew once per footstep, twice per footstep, or two times per three footsteps, but the activities are linked. Furthermore, you cannot *plan* two actions at once. To illustrate, put a pen or pencil in each of your two hands. Now draw ∪ with one hand and ⊃ with the other hand. Either you will draw them slowly, or you will draw at least one of them sloppily. You can't plan separate movements by your two hands at once (Lien, Ruthruff, & Johnston, 2006). However, after you have carefully drawn ∪ and ⊃, you can easily trace one with the left hand and the other with the right. When you trace, you follow the guide of what you see.

Try It Yourself

Even simple activities interfere with each other. For example, if you write with one hand while tapping the other in time with a song, the faster the song, the less coherent will be the content of your writing. Suppose you see symbols on a computer screen. Every time you see a letter, you are supposed to say the letter and type it on the keyboard. If you know what the next letter will be—D, for example—you can say it and type it at once, just as quickly as if you were doing one or the other. However, if you don't know the letter in advance, you will be slower to say it and type it than if you were doing just one or the other (Ruthruff, Pashler, & Hazeltine, 2003; Ruthruff, Pashler, & Klaassen, 2001). To experience this attentional bottleneck, visit this website: **http://dualtask.org/.**

Many years ago, when automobile radios were introduced, people worried that listening to the radio would distract drivers and cause accidents. We no longer worry so much about radio, but we do worry about drivers using cell phones, and some states and countries have outlawed driving while holding a cell phone. Even if you don't have to hold the phone, listening with a phone on one ear tends to shift your attention toward that side of the body instead of straight ahead (Spence & Read, 2003). Also, conversations require more attention than a radio,

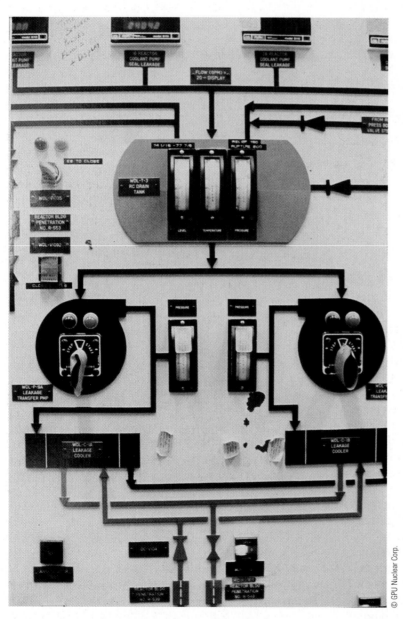

© GPU Nuclear Corp.

FIGURE 8.6 The Three Mile Island TMI-2 nuclear power plant had a complex and confusing control system, a small portion of which is shown here. Some of the important gauges were not easily visible, some were poorly labeled, and many alarm signals had ambiguous meanings. After the accident in 1979, the control system was redesigned and simplified.

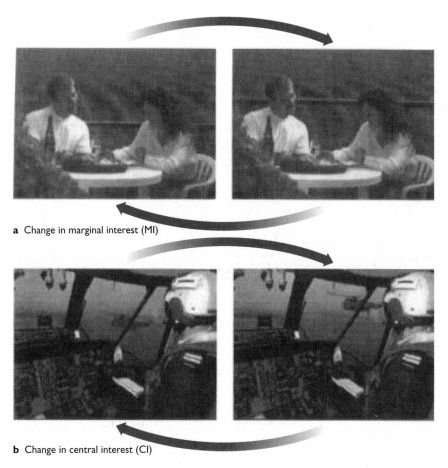

a Change in marginal interest (MI)

b Change in central interest (CI)

FIGURE 8.7 How quickly can you find the difference in each pair of pictures? If you need help, check answer C, page 299.

2003). Not much is known yet about this process, but it opens the way for further research: Might certain kinds of video games be either helpful or harmful to people with disorders of attention?

The Attentional Blink

Just as we don't attend equally to every point in space, we don't attend equally at all points in time. It takes time to shift attention from one item to another, as we see in the **attentional blink**: *During a brief time after perceiving one stimulus, it is difficult to attend to something else.* Just as you don't see anything during a brief blink of the eyes, you don't attend to something during the attentional "blink." For example, suppose you watch a screen that displays a series of letters, one at a time for 90 ms each. Every series includes one letter in blue ink, and it may or may not include the letter T. Your task is to name the blue letter and say whether or not a T appeared. Here are two series and their correct answers:

D S R B J A O E C V "B, no."
Y L H F X G W K T Q "G, yes."

In the second example, most people miss the T (and say "no") because it appeared during a period between 100 to 700 ms after the blue letter. Similar results occur with many other kinds of stimuli and several variations of this procedure (Visser, Bischof, & DiLollo, 1999). The difficulty relates to attention, not memory: You could easily remember "G W K T Q" after seeing or hearing them one at a time. However, if you have to select particular ones, such as the blue G, your attention gets so absorbed in one letter that it does not shift easily to another one (Nieuwenstein & Potter, 2006).

Note that calling this phenomenon the attentional blink does not explain it. Why do we not notice a second stimulus 100 to 700 ms after the first one? "Because of the attentional blink." How do we know there is such a thing as an attentional blink? "Because we ignore a second stimulus 100 to 700 ms after the first one." One hypothesis is that while the brain is binding the first stimulus into a single object, it cannot bind the second one and therefore does not fully perceive it (Raymond, 2003). Clearly, much more research is needed here.

and a cell-phone conversation is more distracting than one with a passenger in the car, because most passengers pause a conversation when they see that driving conditions are difficult. Research on simulated driving finds that a cell-phone conversation decreases a driver's attention to signs and increases the risk of accidents (Strayer, Drews, & Johnston, 2003). Even such a simple task as saying whether you heard one tone or two significantly slows drivers' responses when they need to hit the brakes (Levy, Pashler, & Boer, 2006).

The way you divide your attention among tasks is not fixed from birth. You can change it—perhaps unintentionally. For example, people who spend much time playing complex action video games learn to divide their attention widely over the video screen (Trick, Jaspers-Fayer, & Sethi, 2005). That division of attention helps while playing the games, and probably in some real-life situations too, but on the other hand, it impairs the ability to concentrate on just one item. That is, habitual video game players tend to be distracted by irrelevant stimuli in their peripheral vision that most other people ignore (C. S. Green & Bavelier,

☑ CONCEPT CHECK

3. Suppose you are playing a video game and you see two signals, about a quarter-second apart, telling you to do two things. You respond to the first one but not to the second. Why? (Check your answer on page 298.)

CRITICAL THINKING
A STEP FURTHER

The Attentional Blink

When you read or listen to someone talk, one word or syllable follows another with very short delays. Why doesn't the attentional blink stop you from hearing or reading some of the words?

Attention-Deficit Disorder

People vary in their ability to maintain attention, as in anything else. Attention-deficit disorder (ADD) is characterized by *easy distraction, impulsiveness, moodiness, and failure to follow through on plans* (Wender, Wolf, & Wasserstein, 2001). Attention-deficit hyperactivity disorder (ADHD) is *the same except with excessive activity and "fidgetiness."* Both are obviously a matter of degree, and it is often difficult to distinguish them from normal high energy (Panksepp, 1998). After all, how natural is it for a 6-year-old to sit still in school for hours at a time? Several brain areas are known to relate to impulsivity and its control (S. M. Brown, Manuck, Flory, & Hariri, 2006), and brain scans show minor abnormalities in these areas for most people diagnosed with ADD or ADHD (Seidman, Valera, & Makris, 2005). However, none of the abnormalities is consistent enough to help with diagnosis.

In the United States, the ADD or ADHD diagnosis is applied to an estimated 3 to 10% of children, about 70% of them boys. Some of them "outgrow" the problem, but many have problems that persist into adulthood, impairing social behavior and job performance (Mannuzza, Klein, Bessler, Malloy, & LaPadula, 1998).

The causes include both genetic and environmental influences. Researchers have identified several genes that influence impulsivity and attention (Blasi et al., 2005). The environmental causes include fetal alcohol exposure, lead poisoning, epilepsy, sleep deprivation, emotional stress, and several kinds of mild brain damage (Pearl, Weiss, & Stein, 2001). For most individuals the causes are unknown.

The most common treatment is stimulant drugs such as methylphenidate (Ritalin) (Elia, Ambrosini, & Rapoport, 1999). Stimulant drugs improve school performance and everyday behaviors (de Wit, Crean, & Richards, 2000; Jerome & Segal, 2001). However, the fact that stimulant drugs appear to help a given child does not confirm a diagnosis of ADD or ADHD. Stimulant drugs also increase the attention span of normal children (R. Elliott et al., 1997; Zahn, Rapoport, & Thompson, 1980).

Researchers would like to clarify what they mean by "attention deficit." The deficit is *not* a short attention span. Many people with ADD or ADHD pay attention to a video game for hours. The problem lies more with controlling or shifting attention. For example, recall the attentional blink. After detecting a target on a screen, anyone has trouble detecting another target a half-second later, but many people with ADD or ADHD have trouble for a full second or more (Hollingsworth, McAuliffe, & Knowlton, 2001). In other words they cannot quickly shift their attention from one item to another. Here are two more tasks sensitive to attention-deficit disorder:

- **The Choice-Delay Task** Would you prefer a small reward now or a bigger reward later? Obviously, your answer depends on *how much* bigger and *how much* later. To make the task more challenging, researchers put a cookie in front of a child and explain that the child can have the cookie now or wait 15 minutes and receive two cookies. Many find it difficult to resist while looking at the cookie. On the average people with ADD or ADHD are more likely than other people to opt for the immediate reward (Solanto et al., 2001). Researchers found that 4-year-olds who choose the immediate reward have difficulties with attention and self-control both at age 4 and during adolescence (Eigsti et al., 2006).

- **The Stop Signal Task** Suppose your task is to press a button whenever you see a circle on the screen, as fast as possible, but if you hear a "beep" shortly after you see the circle, then you should not press. If the circle and beep occur simultaneously, you can inhibit your urge to press the button. If the beep occurs after you have already started to press, it's too late. The interesting results are with short delays: After how long a delay could you still manage to stop your finger from pressing the button? Most people with ADD or ADHD have trouble inhibiting their response, even after short delays (Rubia, Oosterlaan, Sergeant, Brandeis, & v. Leeuwen, 1998;

Online Try It Yourself

Solanto et al., 2001). Try the Online Try It Yourself exercise Stop Signal Task.

The Choice-Delay task and Stop Signal task measure different types of attentional problems. Some children show impairments on one task but not the other. Those with impairments on both are the most likely to be diagnosed with ADD or ADHD (Solanto et al., 2001; Sonuga-Barke, 2004).

For links to many kinds of information about ADHD, visit this website: www.add-adhd.org/.

 CONCEPT CHECK

4. Describe one of the behavioral tests used to measure deficits of attention or impulse control. (Check your answer on page 298.)

Categorization

After you have attended to something, you want to know what it is. That is, you put it into a category of some type, such as *building, tree,* or *river*. Any category includes items that differ from one another in many ways. Indeed, the ancient Greek philosopher Heraclitus said that you cannot step into the same river twice. He referred to the fact that the river changes, so that the Mississippi River now is not the same as what we call the Mississippi River a short time later. Even you change: The "you" that steps into a river now is different from the "you" of a short time later. Nevertheless, to think and communicate about anything, we have to group items into categories, and the formation of categories or concepts is a major step in cognition.

Ways to Describe a Category

Do we look up our concepts in a mental dictionary to determine their meaning? A few words have simple, unambiguous definitions. For example, we think of the term *bachelor* as an unmarried man. Because we would not apply the term to a young child or to a Catholic priest, we might refine the definition to "a man who has not yet married but could." That definition explains the concept.

Many concepts are harder to define, however. For example, you can recognize country music, but try defining it. Or imagine a man who loses one hair from his head. Is he bald? Of course not. Then he loses one more hair, then another, and another. Eventually, he *is* bald. So at what point did losing one more hair make him bald? Similar problems arise if we try to classify everyone as depressed or not, schizophrenic or not, or alcoholic or not. Almost everything comes in degrees.

Eleanor Rosch (1978; Rosch & Mervis, 1975) argued that many categories are best described by *familiar or typical examples* called **prototypes**. We decide whether an object belongs to a category by determining how well it resembles the prototypes of that category. For example, we define the category "vehicle" by examples: *car, bus, train, airplane, boat,* and *truck.* Is an *escalator* also a vehicle? What about *water skis*? These items resemble the prototypes in some ways but not others, so they are marginal members of the category.

However, some categories cannot be described by prototypes (Fodor, 1998). For example, we can think about "bug-eyed monsters from outer space" without ever encountering a prototype of that category.

Conceptual Networks and Priming

Try to think about one word and nothing else. It's impossible. You can't think about anything without relating it to something else. For example, when you think about *bird,* you link it to more specific terms, such as *sparrow,* more general terms, such as *animals,* and related terms, such as *flight* and *eggs.*

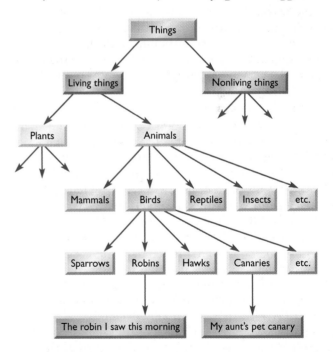

We naturally organize items into hierarchies, such as animal as a higher level category, bird as intermediate, and sparrow as a lower level category. Researchers demonstrate the reality of this kind of hierarchy by measuring the delay for people to

Try It Yourself

answer various questions (A. M. Collins & Quillian, 1969, 1970). Answer the following true–false questions as quickly as possible:

- Canaries are yellow.
- Canaries sing.
- Canaries lay eggs.
- Canaries have feathers.
- Canaries have skin.

All five items are true, but you may have answered some faster than others. Most people answer fastest on the *yellow* and *sing* items, slightly slower on the *eggs* and *feathers* items, and still slower on the *skin* item. Why? Yellowness and singing are distinctive characteristics of canaries. Because you do not think of eggs or feathers specifically as canary features, you reason, "Canaries are birds, and birds lay eggs. So canaries must lay eggs." Skin is not even distinctive of birds, so you have to reason, "Canaries are birds and birds are animals. Animals have skin, so canaries must have skin." This way of categorizing things saves you enormous effort overall. When you learn some new fact about birds or animals in general, you don't have to learn it again separately for every individual species.

 CONCEPT CHECK

5. Which would people answer faster: whether politicians give speeches or whether they sometimes eat spaghetti? Why? (Check your answers on page 299.)

We also link a word or concept to related concepts. Figure 8.8 shows a possible network of conceptual links that someone might have at a particular moment (A. M. Collins & Loftus, 1975). Suppose this network describes your own concepts. *Thinking about one of the concepts shown in this figure will activate, or prime, the concepts linked to it* through a process called spreading activation (A. M. Collins & Loftus, 1975). For example, if you hear *flower,* you are primed to think of *rose, violet,* and other flowers. If you also hear *red,* the combination of *flower* and *red* strongly primes you to think of *rose.* You might think of the word spontaneously, and you would recognize it more easily than usual if it were flashed briefly on a screen or spoken very softly.

The idea of priming a concept is analogous to priming a pump: If you put some water in the pump to get it started, you can continue using the pump to draw water from a well. Similarly, *priming a concept gets it started. A small reminder of a concept makes it easier for someone to think of it.* Priming is important during reading. When you come to a word that

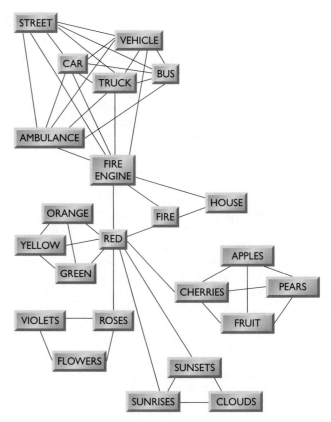

FIGURE 8.8 We link each concept to a variety of other related concepts. Any stimulus that activates one of these concepts will also partly activate (or prime) the ones that are linked to it. *(From "A spreading-activation theory of semantic processing" by A. M. Collins and E. F. Loftus in* Psychological Review *1975, pp. 407–428. Reprinted by permission of Elizabeth Loftus.)*

you barely know, you find it easier to understand if the preceding sentences were about closely related concepts (Plaut & Booth, 2000). In effect they provide hints about the meaning of the new word.

Priming occurs in many situations. After men watch television commercials that depict women as sex objects, they are primed to use words like "babe" and "bimbo" more than usual (Rudman & Borgida, 1995). If you were asked what you plan to do tomorrow, the odor of cleaning fluid in the room would prime you to think of cleaning your room, even if you were not conscious of the odor (Holland, Hendriks, & Aarts, 2005). If you view photos of famous people, you will more easily remember the name Brad Pitt if you had recently thought about cherry pits, just because of the similarity between pit and Pitt (Burke, Locantore, Austin, & Chae, 2004). If you look at pictures and try to identify the people or objects in the foreground, you will find the task easier if the background primes the same answer as the object in the foreground (Davenport & Potter, 2004) (see Figure 8.9).

FIGURE 8.9 A football stadium background primes identification of "football player," and a church primes identification of "priest/clergyman." When the people are placed in the opposite settings, they are harder to identify. *(From Davenport & Potter, 2004)*

Here is an illustration that can be explained in terms of spreading activation. Quickly answer each of the following questions (or ask someone else):

Try It Yourself

1. How many animals of each kind did Moses take on the ark?
2. What was the famous saying uttered by Louis Armstrong when he first set foot on the moon?
3. Some people pronounce St. Louis "saint loo-iss" and some pronounce it "saint loo-ee." How would you pronounce the capital city of Kentucky?

You can check answer D at the end of this module, page 299. Many people miss these questions and are then embarrassed or angry. Figure 8.10 offers an explanation in terms of spreading activation (Shafto & MacKay, 2000): The question about Louis Armstrong activates a series of sounds and concepts that are linked to one another and to other items. The sound *Armstrong* and the ideas *first astronaut on the moon* and *famous sayings* are all linked to "One small step for a man . . ." Even the name *Louis Arm-* *strong* is loosely linked to *Neil Armstrong* because both are famous people. The combined effect of all these influences automatically triggers the answer, "One small step for a man . . ." The name *Louis* in the second question helps prime the answer *Louisville* in the third.

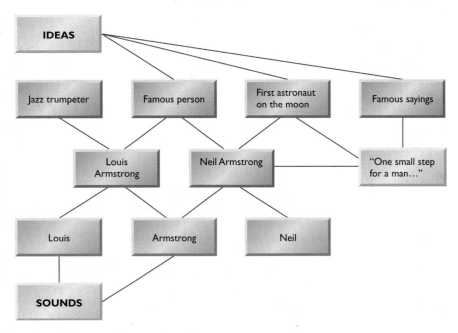

FIGURE 8.10 According to one explanation, the word *Armstrong* and the ideas *astronaut, first person on the moon,* and *famous sayings* all activate the linked saying "One small step for a man . . ."

CONCEPT CHECK

6. Suppose someone says "cardinal" and then briefly flashes the word *bird* on a screen. Some viewers identify the word correctly, suggesting priming, and some do not. Considering both priming and the encoding specificity idea from chapter 7, how might you explain why some people and not others identified the word *bird?* (Check your answer on page 299.)

IN CLOSING

Thinking About Attention and Concepts

Behaviorists have traditionally avoided the topic of cognition because thinking and knowledge are unobservable. Although I hope this module has demonstrated that scientific research on cognition is possible and leads to new understanding, I also hope you see that the behaviorists' objections were not frivolous. Research on cognition is difficult, and each advance requires many experiments to check and recheck each conclusion and compare alternative explanations. The results can have practical as well as theoretical benefits. For example, the better we can specify what we mean by "attention," for example, the better we can deal with those who have attention deficits. ∎

Summary

- *Research methods in cognitive psychology.* Researchers cannot directly observe thinking or knowledge, but they can make inferences from observations such as people's delays in answering various questions. (page 287)
- *Mental imagery.* Mental images resemble vision in certain respects. For example, the time required to answer questions about a rotating object depends on how far the object would actually rotate between one position and another. (page 287)
- *Attentive and preattentive processes.* We quickly notice items that are unusual in certain salient ways, regardless of potential distracters. Noticing less distinct items requires attention to one possible target after another. (page 288)
- *The Stroop effect.* Sometimes, it is difficult to avoid attending to certain stimuli. For example, it is difficult to state the color of the ink in which words are written while ignoring the words themselves, especially if they are color names. (page 290)

- *Attention limits.* Ordinarily, we notice only a small portion of a scene, perceiving and remembering just a gist of the rest. We often fail to detect changes in a scene if they occur slowly or during an eye blink or eye movement. We also frequently fail to detect a stimulus that appears 100 to 700 ms after a first stimulus that required attention. (page 291)
- *Shifting attention.* Attending to one stimulus or activity detracts from attention to another. However, repeated practice at video games alters the degree to which someone divides attention across objects. (page 292)
- *Attention-deficit disorder.* Researchers are trying to specify more precisely what problems characterize people with attention-deficit disorder. Three common measures of attention problems are the attentional blink, the Choice-Delay task, and the Stop Signal task. (page 294)
- *Categorization.* People use many categories that are hard to define. We determine whether something fits the category by how closely it resembles familiar examples. Many items are marginal examples of a category, so we cannot insist on a yes–no decision. (page 295)
- *Conceptual networks.* We represent words or concepts with links to related concepts. Hearing or thinking about one concept will temporarily prime the linked concepts, and hearing several concepts can strongly prime another. (page 295)

Answers to Concept Checks

1. Finding a motionless brown rabbit in a field full of brown objects will require attentive processes, but you could use preattentive processes to find a hopping rabbit in a field where nothing else is moving. (For this reason small animals in danger of predation stay motionless when they can.) (page 289)
2. The changes did not jump out by a preattentive mechanism. People had to use an attentive process to check each part of the scene one at a time. (page 291)
3. The second fell within the attentional blink. (page 293)
4. Tests of attentional blink present a stream of signals, requiring the person to respond to particular targets. After detecting a target, most people fail to detect a second one a half-second later. Some people fail to detect a second target even a second later. In the Choice-Delay task, the question is under what conditions someone will sacrifice a reward now for a larger one later. In the Stop Signal task, one signal calls for a response and a second signal cancels the first signal; the question is under

what circumstances a person can inhibit the response. (page 294)

5. It would take longer to answer whether politicians sometimes eat spaghetti. Giving speeches is a distinctive feature of politicians; eating spaghetti is not. To answer the second question, you have to reason that politicians are people, and most people sometimes eat spaghetti. (page 295)

6. People who heard "cardinal" and thought of it as a bird would have spreading activation to prime the word *bird*. However, other people who thought of "cardinal" as an officer in the Catholic church would have spreading activation to prime a very different set of words and not *bird*. (page 297)

Answers to Other Questions in the Module

A. The cube has six (not four) remaining corners. (page 287)

B. The objects in pair a are the same; in b they are the same; and in c they are different. (page 288)

C. In the top scene, a horizontal bar along the wall has changed position. In the lower scene, the location of the helicopter has changed. (page 293)

D. (1) None. Moses didn't have an ark; Noah did. (2) Louis Armstrong never set foot on the moon; it was Neil Armstrong. (3) The right pronunciation of Kentucky's capital is "frank-furt." (Not "loo-ee-ville"!) (page 297)

Problem Solving, Decision Making, and Expertise

- *How do we solve problems?*
- *What are some common errors of thinking?*
- *Why do we sometimes make decisions that leave us dissatisfied?*
- *How does someone become an expert?*

Ultimately, the thought processes that begin with attention and categorization, as discussed in the previous module, lead to practical outcomes such as solving problems. Here is an example of creative problem solving: A college physics exam asked how to use a barometer to determine the height of a building. One student answered that he would tie a long string to the barometer, go to the top of the building, and carefully lower the barometer until it reached the ground. Then he would cut the string and measure its length.

When the professor marked this answer incorrect, the student asked why. "Well," said the professor, "your method would work, but it's not the method I wanted you to use." When the student objected, the professor offered as a compromise to let him try again.

"All right," the student said. "Take the barometer to the top of the building, drop it, and measure the time it takes to hit the ground. Then, from the formula for the speed of a falling object, using the gravitational constant, calculate the height of the building."

"Hmmm," replied the professor. "That too would work. And it does make use of physical principles. But it still isn't the answer I had in mind. Can you think of another way?"

"Another way? Sure," he replied. "Place the barometer next to the building on a sunny day. Measure the height of the barometer and the length of its shadow. Also measure the length of the building's shadow. Then use the formula

height of barometer ÷ height of building = length of barometer's shadow ÷ length of building's shadow

The professor was impressed but still reluctant to give credit, so the student persisted with another method:

"Measure the barometer's height. Then walk up the stairs of the building, marking it off in units of the barometer's height. At the top take the number of barometer units and multiply by the height of the barometer to get the height of the building."

The professor sighed: "Give me one more way—any other way—and I'll give you credit, even if it's not the answer I wanted."

"Really?" asked the student with a smile. "*Any* other way?"

"Yes, any other way."

"All right," said the student. "Go to the man who owns the building and say, 'Hey, buddy, if you tell me how tall the building is, I'll give you this cool barometer!'"

Whenever we face a new problem, we must devise a new solution. Sometimes, people develop creative, imaginative solutions like the ones that the physics student proposed. In other cases, they make consistent and even predictable errors. They sometimes make good decisions, and sometimes make decisions they regret. With enough practice and experience, people develop expertise that enables them to solve most problems quickly in their field of specialization. Psychologists study problem-solving behavior, error, decision making, and expertise partly to understand the thought processes and partly to look for ways to help people reason more effectively.

Problem Solving

According to George Polya (1957), problem solving can be described in terms of four phases: (a) understanding the problem, (b) devising a plan, (c) carrying out the plan, and (d) looking back (Figure 8.11). Let's discuss these four phases.

Understanding a Problem

Some problems are straight-forward and clearly stated—for example, "What's the best route for a truck

▌ How would you carry 98 water bottles—all at once, with no vehicle? When faced with a new problem, sometimes people find a novel and effective solution, and sometimes they do not. (© *David Burnett/Contact Press Images*)

FIGURE 8.11 Four steps to solving a problem.

to take from Boston to Seattle?" or "What is an effective treatment for migraine headaches?" At least you can recognize a good answer when you have found it. In other cases you may hardly know where to begin—for example, "What should I do with my life?" In still other cases ("insight" problems), you may not see a way to start on the problem. When a problem is complex, you need to start by trying to understand it more clearly.

Sometimes, a solution is easy once we recognize the problem. For years airport terminals listed incoming and outgoing flights in order of time. You can imagine the struggle to find your flight: You might remember that it was supposed to depart somewhere between 10 and 10:30, but you didn't remember exactly when (and planes seldom leave exactly on time anyway), so you would have to sort through listings of many irrelevant flights to find the right one. Eventually, someone recognized the problem: People look for "the flight to San Jose," not "the flight at 10:27." Once the problem was recognized, the solution was obvious (Figure 8.12).

When we don't know how to solve a problem, a good strategy is to start with a simpler version. For example, here is what may appear to be a difficult, even impossible, problem: A professor hands

Try It Yourself

back students' test papers at random. On the average how many students will accidentally receive their own paper?

Note that the problem does not specify how many students are in the class. If you don't see how to approach the problem, try simpler cases: How many students will get their own paper back if there is only one student in the class? One, of course. What if there are two students? There is a 50% chance that both will get their own paper back and a 50% chance that neither will, for an average of one student getting the correct paper. What if there are three students? Each student then has one chance in three of getting his or her own paper. A one-third chance times three students means that on the average one student will get the correct paper. Now you see the pattern: If there are n students, each student has one chance in n of getting his or her own paper back. No matter how many students are in the class, on the average one student gets his or her paper back.

Certain "insight" problems are especially difficult to understand, and after you understand one clearly, the correct answer might occur to you suddenly (an "Aha!" reaction). Here is an example (M. Gardner, 1978): Figure 8.13 shows an object that was made by cutting and bending an ordinary piece of cardboard. How was it made? If you think you know, take a piece of paper and try to make it yourself. (The solution is on page 315, answer E.)

Try It Yourself

Devising a Plan

After you have understood or simplified a problem, you devise a plan to solve it. Depending on the problem, you might have a single plan, or your plan might con-

FIGURE 8.12 Years ago, airports listed flights in order of their scheduled times, as shown here. The current method—listing destinations—simplifies the problem of finding one's flight.

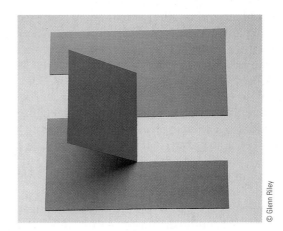

FIGURE 8.13 This object was made by cutting and folding an ordinary piece of cardboard with nothing left over. How was it done?

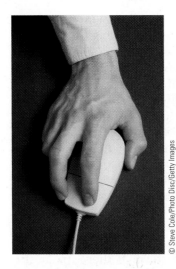

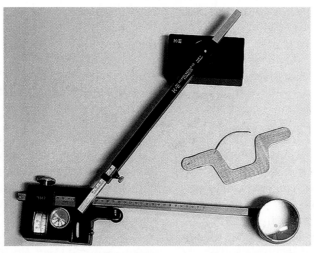

FIGURE 8.14 The computer mouse was invented by a computer scientist who thought he could modify an engineering device called a planimeter for use with computers. Most people find it difficult to generalize a solution from one task to another.

sist of several hypotheses to test. In some cases you can test every possible hypothesis. For example, suppose you want to connect your television to stereo amplifiers, a VCR, and a DVD player, but you have lost the instruction manuals. You have several cables, and each device has input and output channels. You could simply connect the cables by trial and error, testing every possibility until you find one that works. *A mechanical, repetitive procedure for solving a problem or testing every hypothesis* is called an **algorithm**. In most cases, however, such as finding the cause of schizophrenia or improving your company's business, you generate as many ideas as you can, with no algorithm to guide you.

You can solve a problem more quickly if you recognize it as similar to one you had solved before (De Corte, 2003). In that case you would quickly choose an appropriate plan or a correct hypothesis. However, people often fail to recognize the similarity between one problem and another (Figure 8.14). For example, if you have learned to use a formula in mathematics, you might not recognize that the same formula applies to some problem in a physics class (Barnett & Ceci, 2002; Gick & Holyoak, 1980).

For an example of the failure to transfer a concept from one situation to another, consider Figure 8.15a, which shows a coiled garden hose. When the water spurts out, what path will it take? (Draw it.) Figure 8.15b shows a curved gun barrel. When the bullet comes out, what path will it take? (Draw it.)

Try It Yourself

Almost everyone draws the water coming straight out of the garden hose, but most draw a bullet coming out of a gun in a curved path, as if the bullet remembered the curved path it had just taken (Kaiser, Jonides, & Alexander, 1986). The physics is the same

in both situations: Except for the effects of gravity, both the water and the bullet follow a straight path.

Here is another example in which people correctly answer one version of the problem but not another. Let's start with the harder version: Each of the following cards has a letter on one side and a number on the other. Your task is to test the hypothesis that "any card that has a vowel on one side has an even number on the other." Which cards do you need to turn over to test the hypothesis?

Try It Yourself

| A | | T | | 4 | | 7 |

One choice is easy, if you understand the instructions: You have to turn over the card with an A. Most people, however, turn over the card with a 4, which is unnecessary. (Either a vowel or a consonant on the back of the 4 would be okay, according to the hypothesis.) But a vowel on the back of the 7 would contradict the hypothesis, and most people do not check the 7 (Wason, 1960).

Change the task, however, and it becomes easier. Now you are told that each card represents a person.

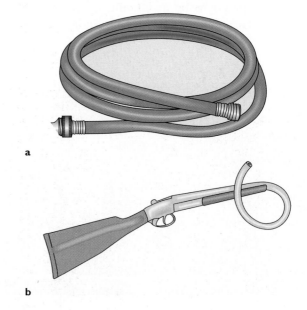

FIGURE 8.15 (a) Draw the trajectory of water as it flows out of a coiled garden hose. **(b)** Draw the trajectory of a bullet as it leaves a coiled gun barrel.

One side indicates the person's age and the other is what kind of beverage the person is drinking. You are supposed to test the hypothesis that everyone under age 21 is drinking nonalcoholic beverages. Which of these cards do you need to turn over to check the hypothesis?

Age 18	Age 30	Drinking Ginger Ale	Drinking Wine

With this version the answer is obvious: Check the 18-year-old and the person drinking wine, but not the other two (Cosmides, 1989). As we saw in the discussion of children's thinking (chapter 5), a concept isn't something you either have or don't have. You can have it to a greater or lesser degree, find it easy or difficult to use, and use it frequently or infrequently (Siegler, 2000).

CRITICAL THINKING
A STEP FURTHER

Logical Reasoning

Why was this version so much easier than the first? Some psychologists believe we are specialized to think more clearly about human social situations than about anything else. Try writing the question in some other way that pertains to realistic nonhuman events. Is your phrasing as easy as the human drinking example, as difficult as the letter–vowel example, or intermediate?

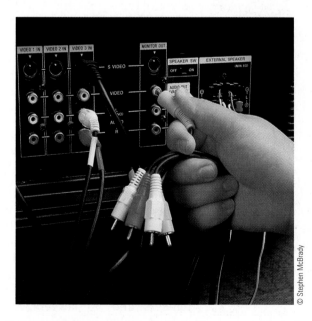

To find the right way to connect the cables, you could use the simple algorithm of trying every possible combination.

CONCEPT CHECK

7. Suppose you are a traveling salesperson who must visit several cities and then return home. Your task is to find the shortest route. What would be the appropriate algorithm? (Check your answer on page 314.)

Carrying Out the Plan

After you have selected a plan, or a series of hypotheses to test, you need to try out your ideas to see how well they work. Sometimes, an idea looks good in principle until someone tries it in practice. One inventor applied for a patent on the "perpetual motion machine" shown in Figure 8.16. Rubber balls, being lighter than water, rise in a column of water and flow over the top. The balls are heavier than air, so they fall, thus moving a belt and generating energy. At the bottom they reenter the water column. Do you see why this system could never work? You would if you tried to build it. (Check answer F on page 315.)

Looking Back

After you think you have solved a problem, check it and double-check it. Scientists are seldom satisfied with the results of a single experiment, even if it was

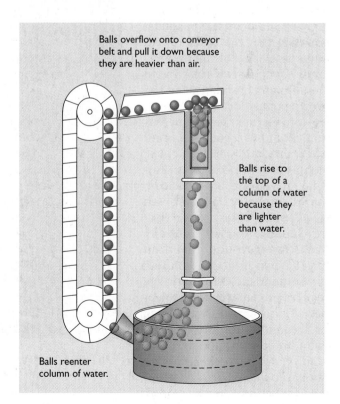

Balls overflow onto conveyor belt and pull it down because they are heavier than air.

Balls rise to the top of a column of water because they are lighter than water.

Balls reenter column of water.

FIGURE 8.16 What is wrong with this perpetual motion machine?

conducted well and the results seem clear. The procedure might have had some hidden flaw, and to be safe, researchers should find a different procedure for testing the same hypothesis.

If the solution to a problem seems valid, you might then consider other uses for it. Can you use the same solution for additional problems?

Reasoning by Heuristics

Often, you don't have time to go through Polya's four steps for solving a problem, or you don't even care about finding the "correct" solution. The question may be so complicated—e.g., "What should I do with my life?"—that fully analyzing all the options is not practical. In other situations the question may not be complicated, but you need to act quickly. You want a "good enough" answer or one that works most of the time. **Heuristics** are *strategies for simplifying a problem and generating a satisfactory guess*. Often, these strategies are quick and unconscious, not deliberate. They provide guidance when you have to make quick decisions with limited information, although they sometimes lead to error. For example, one heuristic is that if you want to guess which child is oldest, choose the tallest. That heuristic is usually correct with children, but some children also try applying the heuristic to adults, assuming that the taller of two adults is older. For another example, suppose we ask you to guess which of two cities has the larger population. Sometimes, they are German cities, such as Munich and Cologne, and other times, they are American cities, such as San Diego and San Antonio. If you are an American, you will probably do better with the German cities, and if you are German, you will probably do better with the American cities! When in doubt, you rely on the heuristic, "The city I've heard of probably has more people." That heuristic works fine for a country you know a little about but less well for your own country, where both cities are familiar (Goldstein & Gigerenzer, 2002). Let's consider other heuristics that usually work, but sometimes lead to error.

In 2002 Princeton psychologist Daniel Kahneman won the Nobel Prize for Economics. (There is no Nobel Prize in psychology.) Although others have won Nobel Prizes for research related to psychology, Kahneman was the first winner who had a PhD in psychology.

The Representativeness Heuristic and Base-Rate Information

Although heuristic thinking is often helpful, it leads us astray when we rely on it inappropriately. In 2002 Daniel Kahneman won the Nobel Prize for Economics for research showing how heuristics and biases sometimes lead to illogical decisions. For example, consider the saying: "If something looks like a duck, waddles like a duck, and quacks like a duck, chances are it's a duck." This saying is an example of the **representativeness heuristic**, *the assumption that an item that resembles members of some category is probably another member of that category*. This heuristic is usually correct, but it leads us astray when we deal with uncommon categories. If you see something that looks, walks, and sounds like a rare bird, you should check carefully to make sure it isn't a similar, more common species. In general, to decide whether something belongs in one category or another, you should consider how closely it resembles the two categories and also the **base-rate information**—that is, *how common the two categories are*.

When people apply the representativeness heuristic, they frequently overlook base-rate information. For example, consider the following question (modified from Kahneman & Tversky, 1973):

> Psychologists have interviewed 30 engineers and 70 lawyers. One of them, Jack, is a 45-year-old married man with four children. He is generally conservative, cautious, and ambitious. He shows no interest in political and social issues and spends most of his free time on home carpentry, sailing, and solving mathematical puzzles. What is the probability that Jack is one of the 30 engineers in the sample of 100?

Most people estimate a rather high probability—perhaps 80 or 90%—because the description sounds more like engineers than lawyers. That estimate isn't wrong, as we do not know the true probability. The key point is that if some people are told the sample included 30 engineers and 70 lawyers, and others are told it included 70 engineers and 30 lawyers, both groups make about the same estimate for Jack (Kahneman &

Tversky, 1973). Certainly, the base-rate information should have some influence.

Here is another example of misuse of the representativeness heuristic:

> Linda was a philosophy major. She is 31, bright, outspoken, and concerned about issues of discrimination and social justice.

What would you estimate is the probability that Linda is a bank teller? What is the probability that she is a feminist bank teller? (Answer before you read on.)

The true probabilities, hard to estimate, are not the point. The interesting result is that most people estimate a higher probability that Linda is a *feminist* bank teller than the probability that she is a bank teller (A. Tversky & Kahneman, 1983). However, every feminist bank teller is a bank teller. Apparently, people regard this description as fairly typical for a feminist and thus for a feminist bank teller (or feminist anything else) but not typical for bank tellers in general (Shafir, Smith, & Osherson, 1990).

 CONCEPT CHECK

8. A device was built to protect airplanes by detecting explosives in people's luggage. It detects 95% of bombs. When luggage has no explosives, it has a false alarm (falsely detecting a bomb) 5% of the time. Is this device good enough to use? (Hint: Think about the base-rate probability of the presence of a bomb.) (Check your answer on page 315.)

The Availability Heuristic

When you estimate how common something is, you generally start by trying to think of examples. Usually this approach works. If, at the end of a semester, you remember enjoying your astronomy class more times than you remember enjoying any other class, probably that astronomy class really was interesting. If you remember many summer days when mosquitoes bit you, and few or no winter days when they bit you, it is reasonable to conclude that mosquitoes are more common in summer than winter. However, this heuristic sometimes leads us astray when uncommon events are easier to remember than common events. Try this question: Does the English language have

more words that start with *k* or more words with *k* as the third letter? Most people guess that more words start with *k*. They start by thinking of words that start with *k*: "king, kitchen, kangaroo, key, knowledge, . . ." Those were pretty easy. Then they try to think of words with *k* as the third letter: "ask, ink, . . . uh . . ." They rely on the **availability heuristic,** *the strategy of assuming that how easily one can remember examples of some kind of item indicates how common the item itself is* (Table 8.1). In fact many more words have *k* as the third letter.

Because the news media tend to emphasize the spectacular, our use of the availability heuristic leads us to overestimate some dangers and underestimate others. For example, during the months after the terrorist attacks of September 11, 2001, most Americans avoided air travel and drove their cars instead. The *increase* in the number of people dying in automobile crashes over the next 3 months exceeded the number of people who died in the terrorist attacks themselves (Gigerenzer, 2004).

Another example: How would you feel if your favorite team wins its next game? How would you feel if you missed your bus? How would you feel if your professor complimented you on good work? Most people overestimate how good they would feel after good events and how bad they would feel after bad events, because the most extreme memories are easily available. You remember the most intense joy you ever felt when your team won a big game, the worst you ever felt when you missed the bus, and so forth (Morewedge, Gilbert, & Wilson, 2005). Therefore, you overestimate your emotion from the next such event.

More examples: Would you rate yourself a better than average, average, or worse than average driver? Most Americans rate themselves above average. They also rate themselves as better organized than average, more hardworking, fairer, healthier, and more polite (Chambers & Windschitl, 2004). In a way these self-ratings might be defensible: Remember the example from module 2.4 that almost everyone you know has

TABLE 8.1 The Representativeness Heuristic and the Availability Heuristic

	A Tendency to Assume That	Leads Us Astray When	Example of Error
Representativeness Heuristic	An item that resembles members of a category probably belongs to that category.	Something resembles members of a rare category.	Something looks like it might be a UFO, so you decide it is.
Availability Heuristic	The more easily we can think of members of a category, the more common the category is.	One category gets more publicity than another or is more memorable.	You remember more reports of airplane crashes than car crashes so you think air travel is more dangerous.

a greater than average number of arms and legs. The average (mean) number of arms or legs is 1.99 . . . because a few people have had amputations. Similarly, if a few people are extremely bad drivers, extremely unfair, extremely rude, and so forth, it is possible for most people to be "better than average." Still, it seems likely that most of us are fooling ourselves. We are motivated to see ourselves in a good light, but in addition, it is easy to remember the worst drivers we have seen, the rudest people we have encountered, and so forth. Therefore, by the availability heuristic, we misestimate what is typical.

Finally, consider the widespread belief that "you should always stick with your first impulse on a multiple-choice test." Researchers have evaluated this claim repeatedly and have consistently found it to be wrong (J. J. Johnston, 1975; Kruger, Wirtz, & Miller, 2005). Changing your answer is likely to help for several reasons. You might discover that you misread a question the first time or that you wrote down the wrong answer accidentally. Sometimes, a question later in the test reminds you of the correct answer to an earlier item. Why, then, do students widely believe that their first impulse is correct? Think of what happens when you get your test back. You look closely at all the questions you got wrong, and therefore, you notice anything you changed from right to wrong. You don't notice the ones you changed from wrong to right. Your availability heuristic leads you to believe that changing your answers hurt you.

Other Common Errors in Human Cognition

In addition to relying inappropriately on the representativeness heuristic and availability heuristic, people make several other kinds of errors consistently. For decades college professors have emphasized **critical thinking,** *the careful evaluation of evidence for and against any conclusion.* However, even the sincerest advocates of critical thinking sometimes find themselves repeating nonsense that they should have questioned. For example, I myself used to repeat the rumors—only I thought they were facts—that "glass flows as a very slow liquid," that "when the lemming population gets very high, some of them jump off cliffs," and that "Thomas Crapper invented the flush toilet." I later learned that all these claims were false. (Wallace Reyburn started the story about Crapper with a partly true, partly fictitious biography, *Flushed with Pride.* Crapper manufactured toilets, but didn't invent them. Everyone might have continued to believe Reyburn's hoax if he hadn't followed it with a less plausible book, *Bust Up,* a biography of Otto Titzling, who allegedly invented the bra!)

Why do intelligent people sometimes come to false conclusions or accept conclusions without adequate evidence? Here are a few of the reasons.

Overconfidence

Try the following ten questions. Few people know any of the answers exactly, but you need only an approximation. For each, give a range within which you are 90% sure the correct answer lies. For example, consider this question: In the 2000 summer Olympics, how many silver medals did China win? You might decide that you would be surprised if they won fewer than 5 or more than 25, so you guess "5 to 25." If so, you would be right, because China won 16 silver medals. Okay, that's the idea. Now fill in your answers:

Your estimate (as a 90% confidence range)

1. How old was Martin Luther King Jr. at the time of his death? __ to __
2. How long is the Nile River? __ to __
3. How many countries belong to OPEC? __ to __
4. How many books are in the Old Testament? __ to __
5. What is the diameter of the moon? __ to __
6. What is the weight of an empty Boeing 747? __ to __
7. In what year was Mozart born? __ to __
8. What is the gestation period of an Asian elephant? (in days) __ to __
9. How far is London from Tokyo? __ to __
10. What is the deepest known point in the ocean? (in feet or meters) __ to __

Now turn to answer G on page 315 to check your answers (Plous, 1993). How many of your ranges included the correct answer? Because you said you were 90% confident of each answer, you should be right on about nine of the ten. However, most people miss more than half. That is, they were **overconfident;** *they believed their estimates were more accurate than they actually were.* These were, of course, difficult questions. On easy questions the trend is reversed and people tend to be underconfident (Erev, Wallsten, & Budescu, 1994; Juslin, Winman, & Olsson, 2000). You can try additional items with the Online Try It Yourself exercise Overconfidence.

Philip Tetlock (1994) studied government officials and consultants, foreign policy professors, newspaper columnists, and others who make their living by analyzing and predicting world events. He asked them to predict world events over the next several years—such as what would happen in Korea, the Middle East, Eastern Europe, and Cuba—and to state their confidence in their predictions (e.g., 70%). Five years later, he compared predictions to actual results and found very low accuracy, especially among those who were the most confident and those with a strong liberal or conservative point of view. That is, those who saw both sides of a question were more likely to be right.

Most people are overconfident of how well they understand complex physical processes. In one study college students rated how well they understood how various devices work, including a speedometer, zipper, flush toilet, cylinder lock, helicopter, quartz watch, and sewing machine. Then the researchers asked them to explain four of the devices and answer questions, such as "How could someone pick a cylinder lock?" and "How does a helicopter go from hovering to forward flight?" After producing what were obviously weak answers, nearly all students lowered their ratings of understanding for these four devices (Rozenblit & Keil, 2002). However, curiously, some insisted that except for the devices that the experimenters happened to choose, they understood the other ones well!

Attractiveness of Valuable but Unlikely Outcomes

If people are faced with choices A and B, and on the average A is worth $1 and on the average B is also worth $1, then theoretically, people should like both choices equally. In reality people don't behave that way.

Try It Yourself

Which would you rather have:

- $100,000 for sure or a 10% chance of winning $1 million?
- $10,000 or a 1% chance at $1 million?
- $1,000 or a 0.1% chance at $1 million?
- $100 or a 0.01% chance at $1 million?
- $10 or a 0.001% chance at $1 million?
- $1 or a 0.0001% chance at $1 million?

If you are like most people, you chose the $100,000 over a 10% chance at a million. However, at some point before you reached the final choice, you switched to preferring the gamble. In fact almost half of college students said they would forego $10 to have one chance in a million of winning a million—a gamble of bad odds (Rachlin, Siegel, & Cross, 1994). A later study, using an Internet sample of thousands of people from 44 countries, confirmed this tendency to prefer a long-shot bet over a small but sure gain (Birnbaum, 1999), so it is not unique to one culture.

Why do people prefer a slim chance at a fortune to a small but sure gain? First, for most people $10 would not raise your standard of living. A million dol-

lars would. Second, although you understand the difference between a 10% chance and a 1% chance, it is hard to grasp the differences among a 0.001% chance, a 0.0001%, and a 0.000001% chance. If you experience something actually happening one time in a million, you appropriately discount its likelihood, but the verbal description "one chance in a million" sounds like a possible outcome (Hertwig, Barron, Weber, & Erev, 2004). You think, "Someone is going to win, and it might be me." In fact the unlikelihood of winning is part of the appeal: People report more pleasure from a surprising gain than from an expected one (Mellers, Schwartz, Ho, & Ritov, 1997). That is, a surprising gambling win is a bigger thrill than money you knew you were going to gain.

Confirmation Bias

We often err by *accepting a hypothesis and then looking for evidence to support it, instead of considering other possibilities.* This tendency is the **confirmation bias.** For example, examine the poorly focused photo in Figure 8.17a and guess what it depicts. Then see Figures 8.17b and 8.17c on the following pages. Seeing the extremely out-of-focus photo makes it harder to identify the second photo. When people see the first photo, they form a hypothesis, probably a wrong one, which interferes with correctly perceiving a later photo (Bruner & Potter, 1964).

Try It Yourself

Peter Wason (1960) asked students to discover a certain rule he had in mind for generating sequences of numbers. One example of the numbers the rule

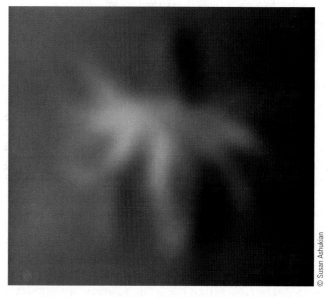

FIGURE 8.17a Guess what this shows. Then examine parts **b** and **c** on pages 309 and 311.

might generate, he explained, was "2, 4, 6." He told the students that they could ask about other sequences, and he would tell them whether or not those sequences fit his rule. They should tell him as soon as they thought they knew the rule.

Most students started by asking, "8, 10, 12?" When told "yes," they proceeded with "14, 16, 18?" Each time, they were told, "Yes, that sequence fits the rule." Soon most of them guessed, "The rule is three consecutive even numbers." "No," came the reply. "That is not the rule." Many students persisted, trying "20, 22, 24?" "26, 28, 30?" "250, 252, 254?" They continued testing sequences that fit their rule, ignoring other possibilities. The rule Wason had in mind was, "Any three positive numbers of increasing magnitude." For instance, 1, 2, 3, would be acceptable, and so would 21, 25, 24601.

A special case of confirmation bias is **functional fixedness,** *the tendency to adhere to a single approach or a single way of using an item.* Here are three examples:

Try It Yourself

1. You are provided with a candle, a box of matches, some thumbtacks, and a tiny piece of string, as shown in Figure 8.18. Using no other equipment, find a way to mount the candle to the wall so that it can be lit.

FIGURE 8.18 Given only these materials, what is the best way to attach the candle to a wall so that it can be lit?

2. Consider an array of nine dots:

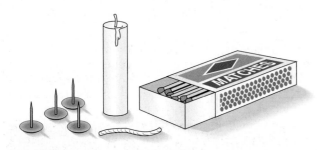

Connect all nine dots with a series of connected straight lines, such that the end of one line is the start of the next. For example, one way would be:

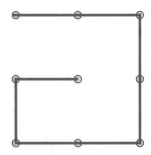

But use the fewest lines possible.

3. There are some students in a room. All but two of them are psychology majors, all but two are chemistry majors, and all but two are history majors. How many students are present? (If your first impulse is to say "two of each," try it out: It doesn't work.) Now here's the interesting part: There are two possible solutions. After you have found one solution, discard it and find another. After you have either found solutions or given up, check answer H on page 315. (Solve these problems before reading further.)

Question 1 was difficult because most people think of the matchbox as a container for matches, not as a potential tool on its own. The box is "functionally fixed" for one way of using it. A similar question was put to people in a subsistence society with few tools. They were given a set of objects and asked how they could use them to build a tower to reach a person in distress. If the objects included an empty box, they used it, but if the box contained other objects, they didn't quickly think of emptying the box and using it (German & Barrett, 2005).

Question 2 was difficult because most people assume that the lines must remain within the area defined by the nine dots. On question 3 it is difficult to think of even one solution, and after thinking of it, it is hard to abandon it to think of an entirely different approach.

Framing Questions

A truly logical person would give the same answer to a question no matter how it was worded. However, most people change their answers depending on the wording of the questions, as you may recall from the discussion of surveys in chapter 2.

For example, answer the following: "What's the probability that Sunday will be hotter than every other day next week?" (Please answer before you read on.)

Try It Yourself

Many people answer "50%" because it seems there are two possibilities—it will be hotter, or it won't. But now consider this rewording: "What's the probability that next week, the hottest day of the week will be Sunday?" With this wording most people switch to the correct answer, one seventh, because they see that 7 days have an equal chance of being the hottest (Fox & Rottenstreich, 2003).

For another example, suppose you have been appointed head of the Public Health Service, and you need to choose a plan to deal with a disease that has endangered the lives of 600 people. If you adopt plan A, you will save the lives of 200 people. If you adopt plan B, you have a 33% chance to save all 600 and a 67% chance to save no one. *Choose plan A or B before reading further.*

Now another disease breaks out, and again, you must choose between two plans. If you adopt plan C, 400 people will die. If you adopt plan D, there is a 33% chance that no one will die and a 67% chance that 600 will die. *Choose plan C or D now.*

Figure 8.19 shows the results for a large group of people. Most chose A over B and D over C. However, plan A is exactly the same as C (200 live, 400 die), and plan B is exactly the same as D. Why then did so many people choose both A and D? According to Tversky and Kahneman (1981), most people avoid taking a risk to gain something (e.g., saving lives) but willingly take a risk to avoid loss (e.g., not letting people die). *The tendency to answer a question differently when it is framed (phrased) differently* is called the framing effect. For an additional example of a framing effect, see the Online Try It Yourself activity Framing Effect.

Try It Yourself

Online Try It Yourself

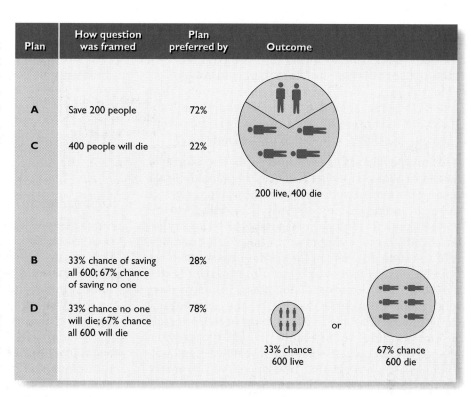

Plan	How question was framed	Plan preferred by	Outcome
A	Save 200 people	72%	
C	400 people will die	22%	200 live, 400 die
B	33% chance of saving all 600; 67% chance of saving no one	28%	
D	33% chance no one will die; 67% chance all 600 will die	78%	33% chance 600 live or 67% chance 600 die

FIGURE 8.19 Most people chose plan A over B and D over C, although A produces the same result as C and B produces the same result as D. Amos Tversky and Daniel Kahneman (1981) proposed that most people play it safe to gain something but accept a risk to avoid a loss.

The Sunk Cost Effect

The sunk cost effect is a special case of the framing effect. Consider some examples:

- You have bought a $200 plane ticket to Wonderfulville and a $500 ticket to Marvelousville. Too late,

CRITICAL THINKING

A STEP FURTHER

Framing a Question

People will take more risks to avoid a loss than to increase a gain. Can you use this principle to explain why many gamblers on a losing streak will continue betting, sometimes increasing their bets? Is there a different way to think about the situation to decrease the temptation to continue gambling?

FIGURE 8.17b

© Susan Ashukian

you realize that they are both for the same weekend, and both are nonrefundable. You think you would prefer Wonderfulville, but you paid more for the ticket to Marvelousville. Where will you go?

- Months ago, you bought an expensive ticket to a football game, but the game is today and the weather is miserably cold. You wish you hadn't bought the ticket. Do you go to the game?

Many people say they would go to Marvelousville instead of Wonderfulville, because the Marvelousville ticket was more expensive and they don't want to waste the money. Many also say they will go to the football game in the bad weather, again because they don't want to waste the money. These examples illustrate the **sunk cost effect,** *the willingness to do something because of money or effort already spent* (Arkes & Ayton, 1999). This tendency arises in many situations. Someone gambles weekly on the state lottery, losing huge sums, but keeps betting because to quit without winning would admit that all the previous bets were a mistake. A company invests vast amounts of money in a project that now appears to be a mistake but doesn't want to cancel the project and admit it has wasted so much money. A professional sports team gives someone a huge signing bonus, and later finds the player's performance disappointing, but keeps using that player anyway to avoid wasting the money.

 CONCEPT CHECK

9. When students estimate their grades for the coming semester or athletic coaches estimate their teams' success for the coming year, what mistake is likely?
10. Someone says, "More than 90% of all college students like to watch late-night television, but only 20% of older adults do. Therefore, most watchers of late-night television are college students." What error in thinking has this person made?
11. Someone tells me that if I say "abracadabra" every morning, I will stay healthy. I say it daily and, sure enough, I stay healthy. I conclude that this magic word ensures health. What error of thinking have I made?
12. Which of the following offers by your professor would probably be more persuasive? **(a)** "If you do this extra project, there's a small chance I will add some points to your grade." **(b)** "I'm going to penalize this whole class for being inattentive today, but if you do this extra project, there's a chance I won't subtract anything from your grade." (Check your answers on page 315.)

Decision Making

Ultimately, we use our reasoning to make decisions. When you have to make a choice, people sometimes advise you to make a list of the pros and cons of each possible option. In contrast many psychologists have concluded that people often make good decisions unconsciously, perhaps relying on unstated heuristics, but certainly not on well-defined algorithms.

Unconscious Decision Making

Suppose you are registering for next semester's courses, and you are debating between a course in anthropology and one in economics. You receive a flood of information: The anthropology course sounds more interesting, it meets at a more convenient time, and your boyfriend or girlfriend is planning to take it, but the textbook is more expensive and the class meets in a building that is a long walk from your room. The economics course is probably more useful for your career plans, your adviser recommends it, your roommate liked the course last semester, and the class size is smaller, but the professor teaching the course next semester has a reputation for being boring. How do you decide?

Researchers gave participants a series of scenarios like this. Sometimes, they asked for a quick decision; sometimes, they let a person think about it deliberately for 3 minutes; and sometimes, they distracted the person for 3 minutes, allowing time for unconscious processing. On the average people made the best decisions when they processed the information unconsciously during a 3-minute distraction. The decisions were best according to two criteria: People were more likely to choose the item with more positive features and fewer negatives, as counted by the researchers. Also, when asked about their choice later, the participants were more likely to be happy with their choices. When making a conscious decision, participants usually focused on a single attribute that was easy to defend, such as "the economics course is better for my career plans," whereas unconscious heuristic thinking weighed a combination of factors (Dijksterhuis & Nordgren, 2006).

 CONCEPT CHECK

13. Sometimes, people say they are going to "sleep on it" before making a decision. For what kind of decision might that be a good strategy? (Check your answer on page 315.)

Maximizing and Satisficing

Sometimes, you face a choice among a huge number of options. If your cable system offers hundreds of channels, do you channel-surf through all of them to find the program you like best, or do you check just until you find one that looks interesting? When shopping for clothes, do you go from store to store in search of the best item possible, or do you buy the first one that you like? People follow two strategies. **Maximizing** means *thoroughly considering every possibility to find the best one.* **Satisficing** is *searching only until you find something that is good enough (satisfactory).* The maximizing strategy approximates the use of an algorithm. Satisficing is more of a heuristic approach.

Some people rely mostly on maximizing, and others prefer satisficing, although of course you might switch from one to the other depending on the importance of a decision. Researchers classify people as mainly maximizers or satisficers based on questions of the following type (Schwartz et al., 2002). For each item rate yourself from 1 (not at all true) to 7 (definitely true):

- When I listen to the car radio, I frequently check other stations.
- I shop at many stores before deciding which clothes to buy.
- I expect to interview for many jobs before I accept one.

Researchers find that high maximizers usually make better choices, at least according to certain criteria. For example, they get jobs with higher starting pay than do satisficers, in spite of being about equal in their college grade-point average. However, they are *less* satisfied with their choices! Satisficers look for something "good enough" and find it. Maximizers look for "the best" and continue to wonder whether they were right (Iyengar, Wells, & Schwartz, 2006). Also, whatever they choose, maximizers regret the other opportunities they missed. In short, seeking the best possible choice sets you up for disappointment.

In a society like the United States today, the maximizing strategy makes life difficult, just because of the huge number of choices available in clothing, food, careers, and almost anything else. In one study, researchers set up a booth offering free

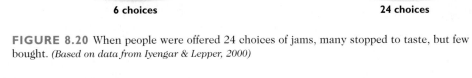

FIGURE 8.20 When people were offered 24 choices of jams, many stopped to taste, but few bought. *(Based on data from Iyengar & Lepper, 2000)*

tastes of jams at a supermarket. Sometimes, they offered 6 kinds of jam; at other times, 24. As shown in Figure 8.20, the offering of 24 jams attracted more people to stop and taste, but almost none of them bought any. With fewer choices to try, more people selected one to buy. Similarly, when students at one college were offered an opportunity to write a short paper for extra credit, more wrote a paper if they were offered 6 possible topics than if they had to choose from among 30 (Iyengar & Lepper, 2000). The point is that too many choices inhibit people from making any decision at all, especially people who are looking for the best possible choice (Schwartz, 2004).

 CONCEPT CHECK

14. Who would be more likely to feel depressed, a maximizer or a satisficer? (Check your answer on page 315.)

FIGURE 8.17c

Expertise

How can we overcome all the errors of human reasoning? Although all of us make mistakes in our reasoning, some develop expertise within a given field that enables them to solve problems quickly with a minimum of error. They learn to apply the appropriate algorithms quickly, and they recognize which heuristics work in a particular situation and which ones do not. Reaching that point requires enormous effort. For example, when computer programmers tried to build "expert machines" to answer people's questions, they discovered a need to build in a huge number of facts (C. Thompson, 2001). A website to advise people about travel plans should be able to say, "Because you are claustrophobic, you should avoid taking the Channel Tunnel from England to France." But to do so, the program needs to be told that:

- Claustrophobic people dislike long tunnels.
- The Channel Tunnel is 31 miles long.
- In this context anything more than 50 feet is considered "long."
- 31 miles is longer than 50 feet.

Here are some facts the programmers had to tell a machine for other kinds of expert systems:

- Water is wet.
- Every person has a mother.
- You should carry a glass of water open end up.
- When people die, they stay dead.
- If you melt a statue, it is no longer a statue.

These facts are so obvious that stating them seems humorous. The point is that even everyday life requires an enormous amount of learning. Expertise requires vastly more.

Practice Makes (Nearly) Perfect

Expert performance is extremely impressive. An expert crossword puzzle solver not only completes *The New York Times* Sunday crossword—an impressive feat in itself—but also tries to make it more interesting by racing against others. An expert bird watcher views a blurry photo and identifies not only the bird's species but also its subspecies and whether it is male or female, juvenile or adult, and in summer or winter plumage.

It is tempting to assume that experts were born with special talent or intelligence. Not so, say psychologists who have studied expertise. Remember the World Memory Championship from the start of chapter 7? Winning contestants memorize a shuffled deck of cards in less than 40 seconds or a 300-digit number in 5 minutes. Psychologists tested 10 of the top performers and found that their mean IQ score was 111 (Maguire, Valentine, Wilding, & Kapur, 2003). That score is above the population average of 100 but hardly unusual. These people had developed their skills by practicing mnemonic devices. They were no better than anyone else at remembering a series of photographs—a memory task they had not practiced because it is not part of the contest.

Similarly, in fields ranging from chess to sports to violin playing, the rule is that expertise requires about 10 years of intense practice (Ericsson & Charness, 1994; Ericsson, Krampe, & Tesch-Römer, 1993). The top violin players say they have practiced 3 to 4 hours every day since early childhood. A world-class tennis player spends hours working on backhand shots; a golfer spends similar efforts on chip shots. Novelist John Irving is dyslexic and says he always took longer

Judit Polgar confirmed her father's confidence that prolonged effort could make her an expert chess player. At age 15 years and 5 months, she beat Bobby Fisher's previous record for being the youngest grand master.

© Yves Forestier/CORBIS SYGMA

than others to complete assignments in school. By his own assessment, he succeeded without special talent and only because of hard work and a willingness to undertake many revisions (Amabile, 2001). In short, experts are made, not born. In fact, the very brightest people—the top 1% of the top 1%—seldom become experts at anything because they get bored with the repetition.

Hungarian author Laszlo Polgar set out to demonstrate his conviction that almost anyone can achieve expertise with sufficient effort. He devoted enormous efforts to nurturing his three daughters' chess skills. All three became outstanding chess players, and one, Judit, was the first woman and the youngest person ever to reach grand master status.

Some psychologists have argued that expertise depends *entirely* on practice, regardless of inborn predispositions. That claim is certainly an overstatement (H. Gardner, 1995). For obvious examples, short slow people will not become basketball stars no matter how hard they practice, and blind people will not become expert photographers. Also, those who show early success in any field are most likely to devote the necessary effort to achieve expertise. The main point, however, is that even someone born with talent (whatever that means) needs years of hard work to develop expertise.

Would you like to become an expert at something? In fields such as chess, violin, or basketball, the greatest performers invariably start practicing during early childhood, so if you haven't already been working at it, your chances of catching up are slim. Still, you have a choice among fields where almost no one starts in childhood—psychology, for example. However, do not underestimate the effort required. Judit Polgar became a grand master by practicing chess 8 hours a day from age 5 to 15, missing most of the usual childhood activities. Thomas Young, a great 19th-century scientist, worked 16 hours a day, 7 days a week, including the day he died. His wife complained that she could not get pregnant because he almost never found time for sex (Martindale, 2001).

When we look at brain anatomy, we find that developing expertise expands the axons, dendrites, and probably, cell bodies in the brain areas relevant to a skill. For example, professional musicians show expansions in the brain areas important for hearing (Schneider et al., 2002) and timing (Gaser & Schlaug, 2003). The areas representing finger sensations expand in people who read Braille (Pascual-Leone, Wasserman, Sadato, & Hallett, 1995). The longer someone has been a London taxi driver, the larger the posterior hippocampus, which is important for spatial memory (Maguire et al., 2000).

Brain autopsies have shown that people with more education or greater mental activity in their daily lives tend to have greater branching in their dendrites (Jacobs, Schall, & Scheibel, 1993). However, although it is possible that education and mental activity promote brain growth, it is also possible that people who started with more dendritic branching succeeded well in their education and were drawn to more intellectual activities. Older adults who spend much time on crossword puzzles and similar activities improve their performance on those tasks, but not on other tasks, and do not reduce their likelihood of mental decline (Salthouse, 2006). In short, practice of any skill improves performance of that skill, at any age, but we have no clear evidence that mental exercise improves performance of skills one has not practiced.

Expert Pattern Recognition

What exactly do experts do that sets them apart from others? Primarily, experts can look at a pattern and recognize its important features quickly.

In a typical experiment (de Groot, 1966), chess experts and novices briefly examined pieces on a chessboard, as in Figure 8.21, and then tried to recall the positions. When the pieces were arranged as they might be in an actual game, expert players recalled 91% of the positions correctly, whereas novices recalled only 41%. When the pieces were arranged randomly, however, the expert players did no better than average. That is, on the average they do not have a superior memory overall, but through long practice they have learned to recognize common chessboard patterns, so that they show excellent memory in their field of expertise. (Recall the concept of chunking from the previous chapter—the process of recognizing a large cluster of items and then remembering them as a unit.) The top players do almost as well in blitz chess—where they have only a few seconds to choose each move—as in normal chess. That is, they make

a   b

FIGURE 8.21 Master chess players quickly recognize and memorize chess pieces arranged as they might occur in a normal game (a). However, they are no better than average at memorizing a random pattern (b).

most of their moves by memory, not reasoning (Burns, 2004).

In a wide variety of other areas, from bird identification to reading x-rays to judging gymnastic competitions, experts learn to recognize important details that other observers overlook (Murphy & Medin, 1985; Ste-Marie, 1999). For example, if you practiced identifying one species of wading bird from another, you would learn to spot the differences quickly (Tanaka, Curran, & Sheinberg, 2005).

 CONCEPT CHECK

15. The introduction to module 7.1 mentioned the World Memory Championship, in which contestants compete at memorizing long lists of words, numbers, or cards. How would practice enable them to develop this kind of expertise? That is, what must they do differently from other people? (Check your answer on page 315.)

IN CLOSING

Successful and Unsuccessful Problem Solving

In this module we have considered thinking at its best and worst—expertise and error. Experts polish their skills through extensive practice. Of course, we all have to make decisions about topics in which we are not experts. Without insisting on perfection, we can at least hold ourselves to the standard of not doing anything foolish. Perhaps if we become more aware of common errors, we can be more alert to avoid them. ▌

Summary

* *Steps for solving a problem.* Problem solving can be described as a series of steps: understanding the problem, devising a plan, carrying out the plan, and looking back. (page 300)
* *Algorithms.* People solve some problems by using algorithms (repetitive means of checking every possibility). (page 302)
* *Generalizing.* People who have learned how to solve a problem often fail to apply that solution to a similar problem. (page 302)
* *Thinking by heuristics.* Heuristics are strategies to simplify complex problems and help us find quick answers that are correct most of the time. However, relying on them inappropriately leads to errors. (page 304)

* *Representativeness heuristic and base-rate information.* If something resembles members of some category, we usually assume it too belongs to that category. However, that assumption is risky if the category is a rare one. (page 304)
* *Availability heuristic.* We generally assume that the more easily we can think of examples of some category, the more common that category is. However, some rare items are easy to think of because they get much publicity or because they stand out emotionally. (page 305)
* *Critical thinking.* Even people who try conscientiously to evaluate the evidence for every claim sometimes find themselves repeating a nonsensical statement that they know they should have doubted. (page 306)
* *Reasons for errors.* People tend to be overconfident about their own judgments on difficult questions. They are attracted to high-payoff gambles even when the chance of winning is extremely low. They tend to look for evidence that supports their hypothesis instead of evidence that might reject it. They answer the same question differently when it is phrased differently. They sometimes take unpleasant actions to avoid admitting that previous actions were a waste of time or money. (page 306)
* *Unconscious decision making.* When confronted with many kinds of competing information, we sometimes make better decisions by thinking about the problem unconsciously while doing other things than by debating the possibilities directly. (page 310)
* *Maximizing and satisficing.* People who follow the "maximizing" strategy of carefully considering all options usually make good choices, but tend to be less pleased with their choices than people who use the "satisficing" strategy of searching only until they find something good enough. (page 311)
* *Becoming an expert.* Experts are made, not born. Becoming an expert requires years of practice and effort. (page 312)
* *Expert pattern recognition.* Experts recognize and memorize familiar and meaningful patterns more rapidly than less experienced people do. (page 313)

Answers to Concept Checks

7. You could check each possible route: For your home city (H) and three other cities (1, 2, and 3), the possible routes would be H-1-2-3-H, H-1-3-2-H, and H-2-1-3-H. (Three other routes that you could generate would be the mirror images of these three and therefore are not necessary to consider.) However, as the number of cities increases, the number of possible routes rises

rapidly. If you had to visit 10 cities, your algorithm would have to consider almost 2 million routes. You would therefore need to restrict yourself to checking the routes that appear most plausible. (page 302)

8. A false-alarm rate of 5% is far too high. Imagine a plane with 100 innocent passengers, each checking two bags. Of the 200 innocent bags, this device will identify 5%—that is, 10 bags—as containing a bomb! Speer (1989) estimated that this device (which the Federal Aviation Administration considered using) would have 5 million false alarms for every bomb it found. (page 304)

9. Both are likely to overestimate their success. Generally, the weakest students are most likely to overestimate their success. However, the straight-A students can hardly overestimate and are therefore more likely to underestimate. (page 306)

10. Failure to consider the base rate: 20% of all older adults is a larger number than 90% of all college students. (page 304)

11. The confirmation bias: failing to test the hypothesis that one could stay healthy without the magic word. (page 307)

12. Probably (b). People are generally more willing to take a risk to avoid losing something than to gain something. (page 309)

13. It might be a good strategy for someone who needs to weigh large quantities of information about several choices. (page 310)

14. Researchers find that maximizers are less satisfied with their lives and more likely to feel depressed. One hypothesis is that by setting their standards so high, they constantly regret their choices and what they missed. However, the data are correlational, so other explanations are possible. Perhaps people who are already depressed tend to become maximizers, in hopes of overcoming their current bad feelings. (page 311)

15. As with other kinds of expertise, experts at memorizing learn to recognize patterns. Whereas most people would see "king of hearts, two of spades, three of clubs, seven of clubs, ace of diamonds" as five items, someone who has practiced memorizing cards might see this as a single familiar pattern or as part of an even larger pattern. (page 313)

Answers to Other Questions in the Module

E. This illustration shows how to cut and fold an ordinary piece of paper or cardboard to match the figure with nothing left over. (page 301)

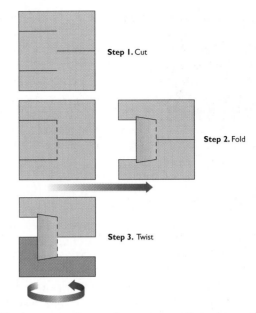

F. Any membrane heavy enough to keep the water in would also keep the rubber balls out. (page 303)

G. (1) 39 years. (2) 4,187 miles, or 6,738 kilometers. (3) 13 countries. (4) 39 books. (5) 2,160 miles, or 3,476 kilometers. (6) 390,000 pounds, or 177,000 kilograms. (7) 1756. (8) 645 days. (9) 5,959 miles, or 9,590 kilometers. (10) 36,198 feet, or 11,033 meters. (page 306)

H. (1) The best way to attach the candle to the wall is to dump the matches from the box and thumbtack the side of the box to the wall, as shown in this picture. The tiny piece of string is irrelevant.

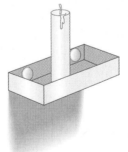

(2) The dots can be connected with four lines:

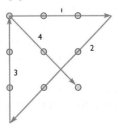

(3) One answer is three students: one psychology major, one chemistry major, and one history major. The other possibility is two students who are majoring in something else—music, for example. (If there are two music majors, all but two of them are indeed majoring in psychology etc.) (page 308)

Language

• *How do we learn language?*

Language is a complicated and impressive product of human cognition. It enables us to learn from the experiences of people who lived far away or long ago. Languages have the property of **productivity**, *the ability to combine our words into new sentences that express an unlimited variety of ideas* (Deacon, 1997). Every day, you say and hear a few stock sentences like, "Nice weather we're having," or "I can't find my keys," but you also invent new sentences that no one has ever said or heard before.

You might ask, "How do you know that no one has ever said that sentence before?!" Well, of course, no one can be certain that a particular sentence is new, but we can be confident that many sentences are new (without specifying which ones), because of the vast number of possible ways to rearrange words. Imagine this exercise (but don't really try it unless you have nothing else to do with your life): Pick a sentence of more than 10 words from any book you choose. How long would you need to keep reading, in that book or any other, until you found the exact same sentence again?

In short, we do not memorize all the sentences we use. Not even infants do. Instead, we learn rules for making and understanding sentences. The famous linguist Noam Chomsky (1980) described those rules as a **transformational grammar**, *a system for converting a deep structure into a surface structure*. The deep structure is the underlying logic or meaning of a sentence. The surface structure is the sequence of words as they are actually spoken or written (Figure 8.22). According to this theory, whenever we speak, we transform the deep structure of the language into a surface structure.

Two surface structures can resemble each other without representing the same deep structure, or conversely, they can represent the same deep structure without resembling each other. For example, "John is easy to please" has the same deep structure as "pleasing John is easy" and "it is easy to please John." These sentences represent the same idea. In contrast consider the sentence, "Never threaten someone with a chain saw." The surface structure of that sentence maps into two deep structures, as shown in Figure 8.23.

Language researcher Terrence Deacon once presented a talk about language to his 8-year-old's elementary school class. One child asked whether other ani-

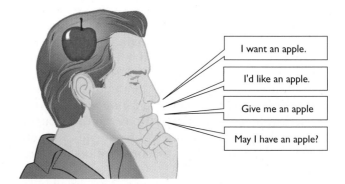

FIGURE 8.22 According to transformational grammar, we can transform a sentence with a given deep structure into any of several other sentences with different surface structures.

mals have their own languages. Deacon explained that other species communicate but without the productivity of human language. The child persisted, asking whether other animals had at least a *simple* language, perhaps one with only a few words and short sentences. No, he replied, they do not have even a simple language.

Then another child asked, "Why not?" (Deacon, 1997, p. 12). Deacon paused. Why not, indeed. This 8-year-old had asked a profound question. If language is so extremely useful to humans, why haven't other

Deep Structure No. 1:
You are holding a chain saw. Don't threaten to use it to attack someone!

Deep Structure No. 2:
Some deranged person is holding a chain saw. Don't threaten him!

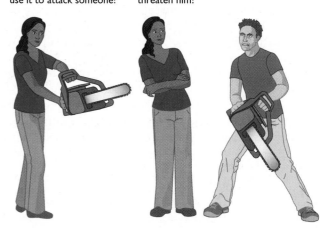

FIGURE 8.23 The sentence "Never threaten someone with a chain saw" has one surface structure but two deep structures, corresponding to different meanings.

species evolved at least a little of it? And what makes humans so good at learning language?

Nonhuman Precursors to Language

One way to examine humans' language specialization is to ask how far another species could progress toward language. Beginning in the 1920s, several psy-chologists reared chimpanzees in their homes and tried to teach them to talk. The chimpanzees learned many human habits (Figure 8.24) but understood no more words than a dog might.

Chimpanzees make sounds while inhaling, not exhaling. (Try to speak while inhaling!) However, chimpanzees do make hand gestures in nature. R. Allen Gardner and Beatrice Gardner (1969) taught a chimpanzee named Washoe to use the sign language of the American deaf (Ameslan).

a

b

c

d

e

FIGURE 8.24 Psychologists have tried to teach chimpanzees to communicate with gestures or symbols. (a) One of the Premacks' chimps arranges plastic chips to request food. (b) Viki in her human home, helping with the housework. She learned to make a few sounds similar to English words. (c) Kanzi, a bonobo, presses symbols to indicate words. (d) A chimp signing *toothbrush.* (e) Roger Fouts with Alley the chimp, who is signing *lizard.*

Images Courtesy of Ann Premack

Washoe eventually learned the symbols for about 100 words.

How much do these gestures resemble language? Washoe and other chimpanzees trained in this way used their symbols almost exclusively to make requests, not to describe, and rarely in original combinations (Pate & Rumbaugh, 1983; Terrace, Petitto, Sanders, & Bever, 1979; C. R. Thompson & Church, 1980). By contrast a human child with a vocabulary of 100 words or so links them into short sentences and frequently uses words to describe.

The results have been different, however, for another species, *Pan paniscus*, sometimes known as the pygmy chimpanzee (a misleading term because these animals are almost as large as common chimpanzees) and also known as the bonobo. Bonobos' social behavior resembles that of humans in several regards: Males and females form strong attachments; females are sexually responsive outside their fertile period; males contribute to infant care; and adults often share food with one another.

Several bonobos have used symbols in impressive ways, sometimes just to name or describe objects that they are not requesting. They use the symbols to describe past events. One with a cut on his hand explained that his mother had bit him. Also, they frequently make original, creative requests, such as asking one person to chase another.

The most proficient bonobos seem to comprehend symbols about as well as a 2- to 2½-year-old child understands language (Savage-Rumbaugh et al., 1993). They have also shown considerable understanding of spoken English, following even such odd commands such as "bite your ball" and "take the vacuum cleaner outside" (Savage-Rumbaugh, 1990; Savage-Rumbaugh, Sevcik, Brakke, & Rumbaugh, 1992). They also passed the test of responding to commands issued over earphones, eliminating the possibility of unintentional "Clever Hans"-type signals, as discussed in chapter 2 (Figure 8.25).

Why have bonobos been more successful than common chimpanzees? Apparently, bonobos have a greater predisposition for this type of learning. Also, they learned by observation and imitation, which

FIGURE 8.25 Kanzi, a bonobo, points to answers on a board in response to questions he hears through earphones. Experimenter Rose Sevcik sits with him but does not hear the questions, so she cannot signal the correct answer.

promote better understanding than the formal training methods that previous studies used (Savage-Rumbaugh et al., 1992). Finally, the bonobos began their language experience early in life. Humans learn language more easily when they are young, and bonobos probably do too.

CONCEPT CHECK

16. Based on the studies with bonobos, can you offer advice about how to teach language to children with impaired language learning? (Check your answer on page 329.)

Human Specializations for Learning Language

Humans are clearly more adapted for language than any other species is, including bonobos. Why do we learn language so easily, when other species do not?

Language and General Intelligence

Did we evolve language as an accidental by-product of evolving big brains and great intelligence? The idea sounds appealing, but several observations argue strongly against it. Dolphins and whales have larger brains than humans have but do not develop language. They communicate but not in a flexible system resembling human language. Some people with massive brain damage have less total brain mass than a chimpanzee but continue to speak and understand language.

Also, people in one family, having a particular gene, develop normal intelligence except for language (Fisher, Vargha-Khadem, Watkins, Monaco, & Pembrey, 1998; Lai, Fisher, Hurst, Vargha-Khadem, & Monaco, 2001). Their pronunciation is poor and they do not fully master even simple rules, such as how to form plurals of nouns. So normal human brain size and normal intelligence do not automatically produce language.

At the opposite extreme, consider **Williams syndrome,** *a genetic condi-*

tion characterized by mental retardation in most re-gards but skillful use of language. Before the discovery of Williams syndrome, psychologists assumed that language was impossible without normal intelligence. One 14-year-old with Williams syndrome wrote creative stories and songs but in other ways performed like a 5- to 7-year-old and could not be left alone without a baby-sitter. Another child with Williams syndrome, when asked to name as many animals as he could, started with "ibex, whale, bull, yak, zebra, puppy, kitten, tiger, koala, dragon . . ." Another child could sing more than 1,000 songs in 22 languages (Bellugi & St. George, 2000). However, these children prefer 50 pennies to 5 dollars and, when asked to estimate the length of a bus, give answers such as "3 inches or 100 inches, maybe" (Bellugi, Lichtenberger, Jones, Lai, & St. George, 2000). Again, the conclusion is that language ability is not synonymous with overall intelligence.

Language Learning as a Specialized Capacity

Susan Carey (1978) calculated that children between the ages of 1½ and 6 learn an average of nine new words per day. But how do they infer the meanings of all those words? Suppose you are in Japan and someone points to a pillow and says "makura." You infer that *makura* is the Japanese word for *pillow.* But logically, it could have meant "soft thing," "throwable thing," or "*this particular* pillow." How did you make the correct inference that the word referred to the category *pillow*? More important, how did you know the sound meant anything at all?

Noam Chomsky has argued that people learn language so easily that children must begin with preconceptions, such as the idea that words *mean* something. Children also make essential distinctions, such as between actors and actions (i.e., nouns and verbs), actors and recipients of action, singular and plural, same and different, and so forth. They have to learn how to express those relationships in their particular language, but they do not have to learn the concepts that language expresses. Chomsky and his followers therefore suggest that people are born with a **language acquisition device** or "language instinct," *a built-in mechanism for acquiring language* (Pinker, 1994).

However, it is difficult to specify exactly what is built in. Are we born with a primitive grammar or just a good ability to learn it? What kind of predisposition do we have that facilitates language? The predisposition could be far removed from the details of language itself (Deacon, 1997; Seidenberg, 1997).

Here is one study suggesting an innate predisposition: Adult German speakers were asked to learn a little of Italian or Japanese, which were unfamiliar to

them before the experiment. In all cases the experimenters used real Italian or Japanese words, but they taught some people real grammatical rules (which are unlike those of German) and other people some made-up rules unlike those of any known language. For example, one made-up rule was, "to make a sentence negative, add the negative word (*no* in Italian, *nai* in Japanese) after the third word of the sentence, whatever that word may be." Another fake rule was "to make a statement into a question, say the words in reverse order." So *"Paolo mangia la pera"* (the Italian for "Paul eats the pear") would become *"Pera la mangia Paolo?"* ("Does Paul eat the pear?"). Those who learned either Italian or Japanese with real grammar showed increased activity in the brain areas usually associated with language. Those learning with the fake rules showed increased activity in other brain areas but not in the circuits usually important for language (Musso et al., 2003). Evidently, some grammars seem "natural" even when they are unfamiliar, whereas other grammars are recognized as "not real language."

But what conclusion do we draw? It would be a vast overstatement to say that we are literally born knowing the grammars of all possible languages. A more reasonable conclusion is that we are predisposed to learn some relationships more easily than others (Saffran, 2003). For example, making questions by inverting the order of entire sentences would be difficult. Learning the rule would be easy, but applying it would tax one's memory, especially with a long sentence.

Is it possible that infants learn all the complexities of word meanings and grammar from the apparently meager information they receive? Perhaps the information is better than we imagined. Parents throughout the world simplify the language-learning task by speaking to their infants in "parentese"—a pattern of speech that prolongs the vowels, making clearer than usual the difference between words such as *cat* and *cot* (Kuhl et al., 1997). Infants listen more intently to parentese than to normal speech and learn more from it. We also speak slowly, distinctly, and in simple words to someone who barely understands our language. To those who know the language well, we can speak rapidly in a noisy environment and still expect understanding (Calvin & Bickerton, 2000).

Several studies have found that even infants younger than 1 year old detect the regularities of the language they hear (Marcus, Vijayan, Rao, & Vishton, 1999; Saffran, 2003). For example, when adults speak they usually run all their words together without pausing between them: "Lookattheprettybaby." The infant detects which sounds go together as words by statistical relations. For example, the infant frequently hears the two-syllable combination "pre-tty" and frequently hears "ba-by" but less often hears the combination "ty-ba" and concludes that the word break comes between *pretty* and *baby*. We can infer that infants draw this conclusion because infants react to "ty-ba" as a new, attention-getting sound and don't react the same way to "pretty" or "baby" (Saffran, Aslin, & Newport, 1996). In short, infants learn the basics of language from regularities in what they hear.

Adults go through a similar process when trying to learn a foreign language (Cutler, Demuth, & McQueen, 2002). If you heard someone say, "vogubarilatusomatafikogovogurasu...," you would infer that the first word is either "vo," "vog," "vogu," or something longer because no word in any language is shorter than one syllable. (Whether we are born with that assumption or learn it is not known.) Because "vogu" was repeated within this utterance, but "voguba" was not, you might infer that "vogu" is a word of this language.

Language and the Human Brain

What aspect of the human brain enables us to learn language so easily? Studies of people with brain damage have long pointed to two brain areas as particularly important for language. People with damage in the frontal cortex, including *Broca's area* (Figure 8.26), develop **Broca's aphasia,** *a condition characterized by difficulties in language production*. The patient speaks slowly and inarticulately—and is no better with writing or typing—and is especially impaired with both using and understanding grammatical devices, such as prepositions, conjunctions, word endings, and complex sentence structures. For example, one patient who was asked about a dental appointment slowly mumbled, "Yes . . . Monday . . . Dad and Dick . . . Wednesday nine o'clock . . . 10 o'clock . . . doctors . . . and . . . teeth" (Geschwind, 1979, p. 186). People with an intact brain sometimes have similar difficulties putting together a clear grammatical sentence if they try to talk while concentrating on some other very trying task (Blackwell & Bates, 1995).

People with damage in the temporal cortex, including *Wernicke's area* (see Figure 8.26), develop **Wernicke's aphasia,** *a condition marked by difficulty recalling the names of objects and impaired comprehension of language*. These two problems fit together: If you have trouble remembering what something is called, you will have trouble processing a sentence based on that word. Because these people try to speak without using many nouns, their speech is usually nonsensical even when it is grammatical. For example, one patient responded to a question about his health, "I felt worse because I can no longer keep in mind from the mind of the minds to keep me from mind and up to the ear which can be to find among ourselves" (J. Brown, 1977, p. 29).

However, language did not evolve simply by adding a language module to a chimpanzee brain. The

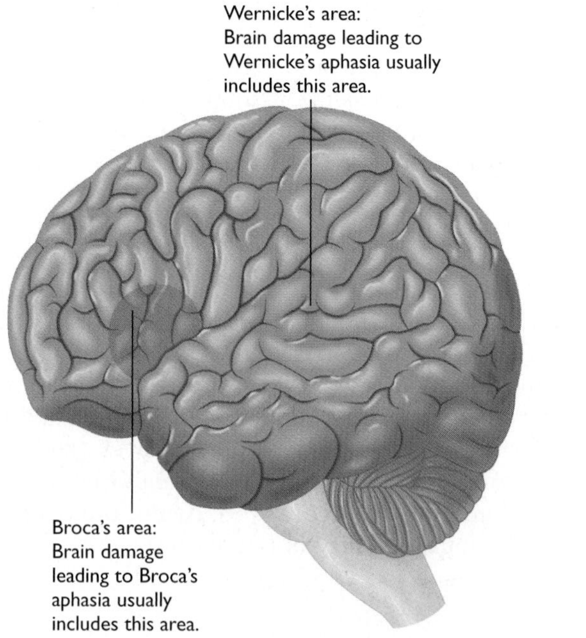

FIGURE 8.26 Brain damage that produces major deficits in language usually includes the left-hemisphere areas shown here. However, the deficits are severe only if the damage is more extensive, including these areas but extending to others as well.

brain areas important for language are critical for many other processes as well, including music (Patel, 2003) and some aspects of memory (Tyler et al., 2002). Brain damage that seriously impairs language extends well beyond Broca's or Wernicke's area. Indeed, the nature of the language deficit varies from one person to another, and the location of the damage does not accurately predict the language problems. Evidently, each person's language cortex is organized somewhat differently from everyone else's. Furthermore, brain recordings show widespread activation during speech (Just, Carpenter, Keller, Eddy, & Thulborn, 1996). It is hardly an exaggeration to say that the whole human brain is specialized to make language possible.

Language Development

Having a brain that is specialized for language is important, but not sufficient. Children develop language, in a process that is amazing, when you stop to think about it. Parents who might not know how to teach a dog to do simple tricks teach children one of the most complicated skills one can imagine, without much effort.

Language in Early Childhood

Table 8.2 lists the average ages at which children reach various stages of language ability (Lenneberg, 1969; Moskowitz, 1978). Progression through these

TABLE 8.2 Stages of Language Development

Age	Typical Language Abilities (Much Individual Variation)
3 months	Random vocalizations.
6 months	More distinct babbling.
1 year	Babbling that resembles the typical sounds of the family's language; probably one or more words including "mama"; language comprehension much better than production.
1½ years	Can say some words (mean about 50), mostly nouns; few or no phrases.
2 years	Speaks in two-word phrases.
2½ years	Longer phrases and short sentences with some errors and unusual constructions. Can understand much more.
3 years	Vocabulary near 1,000 words; longer sentences with fewer errors.
4 years	Close to adult speech competence.

stages depends largely on maturation, not just extra experience (Lenneberg, 1967, 1969). Parents who expose their children to as much language as possible increase the children's vocabulary, but they hardly affect the rate of progression through language stages (Figure 8.27). At the other extreme, hearing children of deaf parents are exposed to much less spoken language, and at first they start "babbling" with rhythmic hand gestures (Petitto, Holowka, Sergio, & Ostry, 2001). However, with even modest exposure to spoken language, their language development progresses on schedule.

Deaf infants babble as much as hearing infants do for the first 6 months and then start to decline. At first, hearing infants babble only haphazard sounds, but soon they start repeating the sounds that are common in the language they have been hearing. Thus, a 1-year-old babbles a variety of sounds that resemble whatever language the family speaks (Locke, 1994).

One of the first sounds an infant can make is *muh*, and that sound or something similar has been adopted by most of the world's languages to mean "mother." Infants also make the sounds *duh, puh,* and *buh*. In many languages the word for father is similar to *dada* or *papa*. *Baba* is the word for grandmother in several languages. In effect infants tell their parents what words to use for important concepts. Languages have evolved to be easy for children to learn (Deacon, 1997).

By age 1½ most toddlers have a vocabulary of about 50 words, but they seldom link words together. A toddler will say "Daddy" and "bye-bye" but not "Bye-bye, Daddy." In context parents can usually discern considerable meaning in these single-word utterances. *Mama* might mean, "That's a picture of Mama," "Take me to Mama," "Mama went away and left me here," or "Mama, I'm hungry." Toddlers do, however, combine a word with a gesture, such as pointing at something while saying "mine" (Iverson & Goldin-Meadow, 2005). The word plus gesture constitute a primitive kind of sentence.

Toddlers "learn how to learn" word meanings. If they are given careful practice with the idea that names refer to the shapes of objects—for example, being taught that *box* always refers to a particular shape, regardless of the color or size—they start increasing their vocabulary faster, particularly their vocabulary of the names of objects (L. B. Smith, Jones, Landau, Gershkoff-Stowe, & Samuelson, 2002).

By age 2 children start producing telegraphic phrases of two or more words, such as "more page" (read some more), "allgone sticky" (my hands are now clean), and "allgone outside" (someone has closed the door). Note the originality of such phrases; it is unlikely that the parents ever said "allgone sticky"!

By age 2½ to 3 years, most children generate full sentences but with some idiosyncrasies. For example, many young children have their own rules for forming negative sentences. A common one is to add *no* or *not* to the beginning or end of a sentence, such as, "No I want to go to bed!" One little girl formed her negatives just by saying something louder and at a higher pitch; for instance, if she shrieked, "I want to share my toys!" she really meant, "I do *not* want to share my toys." Presumably, she had learned this "rule" by remembering that people screamed at her when they told her not to do something. My son Sam made negatives for a while by adding the word *either* to the end of a sentence: "I want to eat lima beans either." Apparently, he had heard people say, "I don't want to do that either."

© Stephen Rapley

FIGURE 8.27 Some overeager parents try to teach their children language early. The child may enjoy the attention, but the activity has little effect on the child's language development.

Young children act as if they were applying grammatical rules. (I say "as if" because they cannot state the rules. By the same token, baseball players chasing a high fly ball act as if they understood calculus.) For example, a child may learn the word *feet* at an early age and then, after learning other plurals, abandon *feet* in favor of *foots*. Later, the child begins to compromise by saying "feets," "footses," or "feetses" before eventually returning to "feet." Children at this stage say many things they have never heard anyone else say, such as "the womans goed and doed something." Clearly, they are applying rules for how to form plurals and past tenses, although they *overregularize* or *overgeneralize* the rules. My son David invented the word *shis* to mean "belonging to a female." (He had apparently generalized the rule "He–his, she–shis.") These inventions imply that children are learning rules, not just repeating what they have heard.

Apparently, we have an "optimal period" for learning language in early childhood. The start and finish of this period are gradual, but language learning is easiest in early childhood (Werker & Tees, 2005). Much of the evidence for this conclusion comes from people who learn a second language. Adults learn the vocabulary of a second language faster than children do, but children learn the pronunciation better, as well as difficult aspects of the grammar. Even those who overheard another language in childhood without paying much attention to it learn it more easily later in life (Au, Knightly, Jun, & Oh, 2002). However, researchers find no sharp age cutoff when language becomes more difficult. That is, learning a second language is easier for 2-year-olds than 4-year-olds but also easier for 13-year-olds than 16-year-olds (Hakuta, Bialystok, & Wiley, 2003; Harley & Wang, 1997).

  CONCEPT CHECK

17. At what age do children begin to string words into combinations they have never heard before? Why do psychologists believe that even very young children learn some of the rules of grammar? (Check your answers on page 329.)

Children Exposed to No Language or Two Languages

Would children who were exposed to no language at all make up a new one? In rare cases an infant who was accidentally separated from other people grew up in a forest without human contact until discovered years later. Such children not only fail to show a language of their own but also fail to learn much language after they are given the chance (Pinker, 1994). However, their development is so abnormal and their early life so unknown that we should hesitate to draw conclusions.

The best evidence comes from studies of children who are deaf. Children who cannot hear well enough to learn speech and who are not taught sign language invent their own sign language (Senghas, Kita, & Özyürek, 2004). Observations in Nicaragua found that sign language had evolved over the decades. Deaf people learned sign language and taught it to the next generation, who, having learned it from early childhood, elaborated on it, made it more expressive, and then taught the enhanced sign language to the next generation, and so on (Senghas & Coppola, 2001).

Most sign languages share some interesting similarities. For example, most include a marker to distinguish between a subject that is acting on an object ("the mouse eats the cheese") and a subject that is acting without an object ("the mouse is moving"). The sign languages invented by children in Taiwan resemble those of children in the United States, even though the spoken languages of those countries—Chinese and English—have very different grammars (Goldin-Meadow & Mylander, 1998).

If a deaf child starts to invent a sign language and no one responds to it, because the child meets no other deaf children and the adults fail to or refuse to learn, the child gradually abandons it. If such a child is exposed to sign language much later, such as age 12, he or she struggles to develop signing skills and never catches up with those who started earlier (Harley & Wang, 1997; Mayberry, Lock, & Kazmi, 2002). This observation is our best evidence for the importance of early development in language learning: A child who doesn't learn a language while young is permanently impaired at learning one.

Some children grow up in a **bilingual** environment, *learning two languages about equally well.* Bilingualism is especially common among immigrant children, who are generally bicultural as well, learning both their parents' customs and those of their new country. The brain areas responding to words in one language are the same as those for words of the other language (Paradis, 1990; Solin, 1989). As a result parts of the left hemisphere grow thicker than average among people who develop high fluency in two or more languages from childhood onward (Mechelli et al., 2004). However, if the brain representations of the two languages overlap heavily, how do bilingual people keep their two languages separate? They don't, at least not completely (Francis, 1999). However, one brain area, the caudate nucleus, is strongly activated while the person shifts from one language to the other (Crinion et al., 2006). Evidently, it primes one set of word representations and inhibits the other.

Bilingualism has two disadvantages: Children take longer to master two languages than to master one (of course), and even adult bilinguals occasionally confuse words from the two languages. The primary advantage is obvious: If you learn a second language, you can communicate with more people. A second advantage is subtle: A bilingual person gains extra cognitive flexibility by learning that there are different ways of expressing the same idea. For example, children younger than 6 years old who speak only one language apparently believe that every object has only one name. If an adult gestures toward a cup and a gyroscope and says, "Please bring me the gyroscope," a child who knows the word *cup* will immediately bring the gyroscope, assuming that if one object is the cup, the other one must be the gyroscope. But the child would also fetch the gyroscope if asked to bring the *vessel*, the *chalice*, or any other synonym for *cup* that the child did not know. A bilingual child, however, is more likely to hesitate or ask for help, understanding that an unfamiliar word could refer to the cup just as easily as the other object (Davidson, Jergovic, Imami, & Theodos, 1997).

CONCEPT CHECK

18. What is the most convincing evidence that early exposure to language is necessary for language development? (Check your answer on page 329.)

Understanding Language

When we think about a child learning language, we tend to focus first on what the child says. Understanding the language is just as important, if not more so. On a trip to Norway some years ago, I consulted my Norwegian phrase book and asked directions to the men's room: "Hvor er toalettet?" When the man answered—in Norwegian, of course—I suddenly realized the problem: It doesn't do me any good to speak the language unless I understand the answers!

Understanding a Word

We customarily describe the word *cat* as being composed of three sounds, *kuh, ah,* and *tuh*. However, the first sound in *cat* is not quite the same as the consonant sound in *kuh*; the sounds *a* and *t* are different also. Each letter changes its sound depending on the other sounds that precede and follow it. What we hear also depends on the context and our expectations, which prime us to perceive the relevant word. For example, a computer generated a sound halfway between a normal *s* sound and a normal *sh* sound. When this intermediate sound replaced the *s* sound at the end of the word *embarrass*,

people heard it as an *s* sound, but when the same sound replaced the *sh* at the end of *abolish*, people heard the same sound as *sh* (Samuel, 2001).

We use lipreading more than we realize to understand what we hear. If lip movements do not match the sound, we sometimes perceive something that is a compromise between what we saw and what we heard (McGurk & MacDonald, 1976). To experience this phenomenon, go to the Online Try It Yourself activity McGurk Effect (**www.thomsonedu.com/psychology/kalat**). The McGurk effect depends especially on seeing the right side of the speaker's mouth, which moves more than the left side when most people speak (Nicholls, Searle, & Bradshaw, 2004). We watch head movements, too. It is slightly easier to understand people if we can see their head movements while they speak (Munhall, Jones, Callan, Kuratate, & Vatikiotis-Bateson, 2004).

Online Try It Yourself

In one study students listened to a tape recording of a sentence with a sound missing (Warren, 1970). The sentence was, "The state governors met with their respective legislatures convening in the capital city." However, the sound of the first *s* in the word *legislatures*, along with part of the adjacent *i* and *l*, had been replaced by a cough or a tone. The students were asked to listen to the recording and try to identify the location of the cough or tone. None of the 20 students identified the location correctly, and half thought the cough or tone interrupted one of the other words on the tape. They all claimed to have heard the *s* plainly. In fact even those who had been told that the *s* sound was missing insisted that they had heard the sound. Apparently, the brain uses the context to fill in the missing sound.

Many English words have different meanings in different contexts. *Rose* can refer to a flower, or it can be the past tense of the verb *to rise*. Consider the word *mean* in this sentence: "What did that mean old statistician mean by asking us to find the mean and mode of this distribution?" Just as we hear the word *legislatures* as a whole, not as a string of separate letters, we interpret a sequence of words as a whole, not one at a time. Suppose you hear a tape-recorded word that is carefully engineered to sound halfway between *dent* and *tent*. The way you perceive it depends on the context:

1. When the *ent in the fender was well camouflaged, we sold the car.
2. When the *ent in the forest was well camouflaged, we began our hike.

Most people who hear sentence 1 report the word *dent*. Most who hear sentence 2 report *tent*. Now consider two more sentences:

3. When the *ent was noticed in the fender, we sold the car.

4. When the *ent was noticed in the forest, we stopped to rest.

For sentences 3 and 4, the context comes too late to help. People are as likely to report hearing *dent* in one sentence as in the other (Connine, Blasko, & Hall, 1991). Consider what this means: In the first two sentences, the fender or forest showed up three syllables after *ent. In the second pair, the fender or forest appeared six syllables later. Evidently, when you hear an ambiguous sound, you can hold it in a temporary "undecided" state for about three syllables for the context to help you understand it. Beyond that point it is too late. You hear it one way or the other and stick with your decision.

Although a long-delayed context cannot help you hear an ambiguous word correctly, it can help you understand its meaning. Consider the following sentence from Karl Lashley (1951):

> Rapid righting with his uninjured hand saved from loss the contents of the capsized canoe.

If you hear this sentence spoken aloud, so that spelling is not a clue, you are likely at first to interpret the second word as *writing*, until you reach the final two words of the sentence. Suddenly, the phrase *capsized canoe* changes the scenario; we understand that *righting* meant "pushing with a paddle." In summary only the immediate context can influence what you hear, but even a delayed context can change the word's meaning.

Understanding Sentences

Making sense of language requires knowledge about the world. For example, consider the following sentences (from Just & Carpenter, 1987):

- That store sells horse shoes.
- That store sells alligator shoes.

You interpret *horse shoes* to mean "shoes for horses to wear," but you don't interpret *alligator shoes* as "shoes for alligators to wear." Your understanding of the sentences depended on your knowledge of the world, not just the syntax of the sentences.

Here is another example:

- I'm going to buy a pet hamster at the store, if it's open.
- I'm going to buy a pet hamster at the store, if it's healthy.

Nothing about the sentence structure told you that *it* refers to the store in the first sentence and the hamster in the second sentence. You understood because you know that stores but not hamsters can be open, whereas hamsters but not stores can be healthy.

In short, understanding a sentence depends on your knowledge of the world and all the assumptions that you share with the speaker or writer of the sentence. Sometimes, you even have to remember where you are because the meaning of a word differs from one place to another (Figure 8.28).

FIGURE 8.28 In England a *football coach* is a bus full of soccer fans. In the United States it's the person who directs a team of American football players.

Now consider this sentence: *While Anna dressed the baby played in the crib.* Quickly: Whom did Anna dress? And who played in the crib? The addition of a comma would simplify the sentence, but even without it, English grammar prohibits "baby" from being both the object of *dressed* and the subject of *played*. If the baby played in the crib (as you no doubt answered), Anna must have dressed herself. Nevertheless, many people misunderstand and think Anna dressed the baby (Ferreira, Bailey, & Ferraro, 2002). Remember the example from earlier in the chapter about how many animals Moses took on the ark? That was another example in which many people overlook the details of the sentence and construct a "good enough" interpretation of the sentence's meaning based on their knowledge and reasonable expectations. That strategy occasionally misleads us, but it usually works, such as in the sentences about alligator shoes or buying a hamster at the store.

Try It Yourself

Limits to Our Language Understanding

Some sentences that follow the rules of grammar are nevertheless nearly incomprehensible. One example is a doubly embedded sentence—a sentence within a sentence within a sentence. A singly embedded sentence is understandable, though not simple:

The dog the cat saw chased a squirrel.
The squirrel the dog chased climbed the tree.

In the first sentence, "the cat saw the dog" is embedded within "the dog chased a squirrel." In the second, "the dog chased the squirrel" is embedded within "the squirrel climbed the tree." So far, so good, but now consider a doubly embedded sentence:

The squirrel the dog the cat saw chased climbed the tree.

Doubly embedded sentences overburden our memory. In fact, if your memory is already burdened with other matters, you may have trouble understanding a singly embedded sentence (Gordon, Hendrick, & Levine, 2002).

Double negatives are also difficult to understand. "I would not deny that . . ." means that I agree. "It is not false that . . ." means that something is true. People can understand such sentences, but with difficulty. Have you ever seen a multiple-choice test item that asks "Which of the following is not true . . ." and then one of the choices has a *not* in it? With such items confusion is almost certain.

Triple negatives are still worse. Consider the following sentence, which includes *four* negatives (emphasis added): "If you do *not* unanimously find from your consideration of all the evidence that there are *no* mitigating factors sufficient to *preclude* the imposition of a death sentence, then you should sign the verdict requiring the court to impose a sentence *other than* death." In Illinois a judge reads those instructions to a jury in a capital punishment case to explain how to decide between a death penalty and life in prison. Do you think many jurors understand?

With a single negative, people understand the sentence but often seem not to fully accept the meaning of the word *not*. Suppose you are trying to decide whether to buy a product at the supermarket. The package says, "Contains no cyanide or rat pieces!" Does that notice encourage you to buy the product? Hardly! It is as if you do not fully believe the "no." After all, why would the manufacturer mention the absence of something unless it might be present? I was once on an airplane that turned around shortly after departure because one of its two engines failed. The attendant told the passengers what was happening, but until she said "Please don't panic," we didn't realize there was any reason to panic.

In one clever experiment, students watched an experimenter pour sugar into two jars. The students were then told to label one jar "sucrose, table sugar" and the other "not sodium cyanide, not poison." Then the experimenter made two cups of Kool-Aid, one from each jar of sugar, and asked the students to choose one cup to drink (Figure 8.29). Almost half expressed no preference, but of the 44 who did have a preference, 35 wanted Kool-Aid made from the jar marked "sucrose," not from the one that denied cyanide and poison (Rozin, Markwith, & Ross, 1990).

Reading

As you will recall, 10 years of intensive practice produces expertise, enabling someone to recognize complex patterns at a glance. You have intensively practiced reading for more than 10 years, so you qualify as an expert reader. You may not think of yourself as an expert because we usually reserve the term *expert* for someone who is far more skilled than others. Nevertheless, your years of reading enable you to recognize words instantaneously, like an expert who recognizes chess patterns at a glance.

Word Recognition

Consider the following experiment: The investigator flashes a letter on a screen for less than a quarter-second, then shows an interfering pattern, and asks, "Was it C or J?" Then the experimenter flashes an entire word on the screen for the same length of time and asks, "Was the first letter of the word C or J?" (Figure 8.30). Which question would be easier to answer? Most people can *identify the letter more accurately when it is part of a whole word than when it is presented by itself* (Reicher, 1969; Wheeler, 1970). This is known as the **word-superiority effect**.

Online Try It Yourself

FIGURE 8.29 Most students preferred Kool-Aid made with sugar labeled "sugar" instead of sugar labeled "not cyanide," even though they had placed the labels themselves. Evidently, people don't always believe or don't always trust the word "not." *(Based on results of Rozin, Markwith, & Ross, 1990)*

FIGURE 8.30 Either a word or a single letter flashed on a screen and then an interfering pattern. The observers were asked, "Which was presented: *C* or *J*?" More of them identified the letter correctly when it was part of a word.

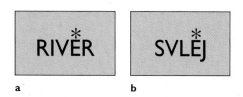

FIGURE 8.31 Students identified an indicated letter better when they focused on an entire word **(a)** than on a single letter in a designated spot **(b)**.

You can experience it yourself with the Online Try It Yourself activity Word-Superiority Effect.

In further research James Johnston and James McClelland (1974) briefly flashed words on the screen and asked students to identify one letter (whose position was marked) in each word (Figure 8.31). On some trials the experimenters told the students to try to see the whole word. On other trials they showed the students exactly where the critical letter would appear on the screen and told them to focus on that spot and ignore the rest of the screen. Most students identified the critical letter more successfully when they looked at the whole word than when they focused on just the letter itself. This benefit occurs only with a real word, like COIN, not with a nonsense combination, like CXQF (Rumelhart & McClelland, 1982).

You may have experienced the word-superiority effect yourself. To pass time on long car trips, people sometimes try to find every letter of the alphabet on the billboards. It is usually easier to spot a letter by reading complete words than by checking letter by letter.

What accounts for the word-superiority effect? Ac-

cording to one model (McClelland, 1988; Rumelhart, McClelland, & the PDP Research Group, 1986), our perceptions and memories are represented by vast numbers of connections among "units," presumably corresponding to sets of neurons. Each unit connects to other units (Figure 8.32). Any activated unit excites some of its neighbors and inhibits others. Suppose units corresponding to the letters C, O, I, and N are moderately active. They excite a higher order unit corresponding to the word COIN. Although none of the four letter units sends a strong message by itself, the collective impact is strong (McClelland & Rumelhart, 1981). The perception COIN then feeds excitation back to the individual letter-identifying units and confirms their tentative identifications.

This model helps explain our perception of Figure 8.33. Why do you see the top word in that figure as *RED* instead of *PFB*? After all, in the other words, those letters do look like *P, F,* and *B*. But in the top word, one ambiguous figure activates some *P* units

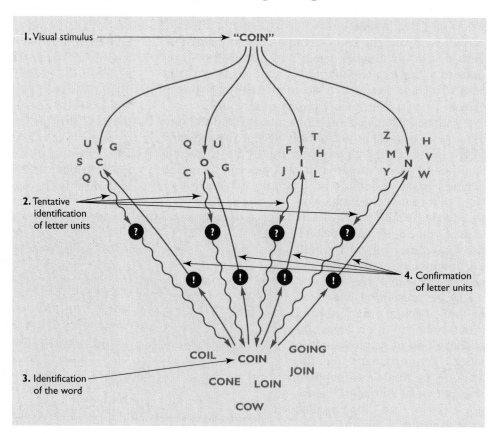

FIGURE 8.32 According to one model, a visual stimulus activates certain letter units, some more strongly than others. Those letter units then activate a word unit, which in turn strengthens the letter units that compose it. For this reason we recognize a whole word more easily than a single letter.

FIGURE 8.33 The combination of possible letters enables us to identify a word. Word recognition in turn helps to confirm the letter identifications. (From "Parallel Distributed Processing: Explorations in the Microstructure of Cognition," Vol. 1: Foundations, by David E. Rumelhart et al., p. 8, figure 2. [Series in Computational Models of Cognition and Perception.] Copyright 1986 by MIT Press. Used by permission of the publisher.)

and some *R* units; the next figure activates *E* and *F* units, and the third figure activates *D* and *B* units. All of those units in turn activate other units corresponding to *RFB*, *PFB*, *PFD*, and *RED*. As you tentatively perceive the word as *RED* (the only English word among those choices), the feedback strengthens the activity of the *R*, *E*, and *D* units.

Reading and Eye Movements

In an alphabetical language such as English, the printed page consists of letters that form familiar clusters that in turn form words and sentences. One kind of cluster is a **phoneme**, *a unit of sound*. A phoneme can be a single letter, such as *f*, or a combination, such as *sh*. Good reading requires mastering phonics—the relationship between letters and sounds (Rayner, Foorman, Perfetti, Pesetsky, & Seidenberg, 2001). Another kind of cluster is a **morpheme**, *a unit of meaning*. For example, the noun *thrills* has two morphemes (*thrill* and *s*). The final *s* is a unit of meaning because it indicates that the noun is plural (Figure 8.34).

 CONCEPT CHECK

19. How many phonemes are in the word thoughtfully? How many morphemes? (Check your answers on page 329.)

Psychologists have arranged devices to monitor eye movements during reading. One discovery was that a reader's eyes move in a jerky fashion. You can move your eyes steadily to follow a moving object, but when you are scanning a stationary object, such as a page of print, you alternate between *fixations, when your eyes are stationary*, and *quick eye movements called saccades* (sa-KAHDS) *that take your eyes from one fixation point to another.*

You read during your fixations, but you are virtually blind during the saccades. To illustrate this point, try the following demonstration: Look at yourself in the mirror and focus on your left eye. Then move your focus to the right eye. Can you see your eyes moving in the mirror? (Go ahead; try it.) People generally agree that they do not see their eyes move.

Try It Yourself

"Oh, but wait," you say. "That movement in the mirror was simply too quick and too small to see." Wrong. Get someone else to look at your left eye and then shift gaze to your right eye. Now you do see the other person's eye movement. Go back and try your own eyes in the mirror again and observe the difference. You can see someone else's eyes moving, but you cannot see your own eyes moving in the mirror.

Why not? First, certain areas in the parietal cortex monitor impending eye movements and send a message to the visual cortex, in effect saying, "The eyes are about to move, so decrease activity for a moment." Even in total darkness, the visual cortex decreases its activity during saccadic eye movements (Burr, Morrone, & Ross, 1994; Paus, Marrett, Worsley, & Evans, 1995). Second, anything you do see during the saccade is blurry, and the stationary view at the end of a saccade interferes with the blurry view (Matin, Clymer, & Matin, 1972).

In short, we see during fixations and not during saccades. An average adult reading a magazine article fixates each point for about 200 to 250 milliseconds (ms). Good readers generally have briefer fixations than poor readers do, and everyone has briefer fixations on familiar words like *girl* than on harder words like *ghoul*. We also tend to pause longer on words with more than one meaning, like *bark* or *lie* (Rodd, Gaskell, & Marslen-Wilson, 2002). After each fixation the next saccade lasts 25 to 50 ms. Thus, most readers have about four fixations per second (Rayner, 1998).

How much can a person read during one fixation? Many people believe they see quite a bit of the page at each instant. However, research indicates that we read only about 11 characters—one or two words—at a time. To demonstrate this

Phonemes
(units of sound):

Morphemes
(units of meaning):

FIGURE 8.34 The word *shamelessness* has nine phonemes (units of sound) and three morphemes (units of meaning).

limitation, focus on the letter *i* marked by an arrow (↓) in the two sentences below.

↓
1. This is a sentence with no misspelled words.

↓
2. Xboc tx zjg rxunce with no mijvgab zucn.

If you permit your eyes to wander back and forth, you quickly notice the gibberish in sentence 2. But as long as you dutifully keep your eyes on the fixation point, the sentence looks all right. You can read the letter on which you fixated plus about three or four characters (including spaces) to the left and about seven to the right; the rest is a blur. Therefore, you see —*ce with no m*—, or possibly —*nce with no mi*—.

This limit of about 11 letters depends partly on the lighting. In faint light your span decreases to as little as 1 or 2 letters, and your reading ability suffers accordingly (Legge, Ahn, Klitz, & Luebker, 1997). The limit does not depend on how much fits into the fovea of your eyes. In the following display, again focus on the letter *i* in each sentence and check how many letters you can read to its left and right:

↓
This is a sentence with no misspelled words.

↓
This is a sentence with no misspelled words.

↓
is a sentence with no misspelled

If your reading span were limited by how many letters can fit into the fovea of your retina, you could read fewer letters as the print gets larger. In fact you do at least as well, maybe even better, with larger print (up to a point).

What we can see at a glance also depends on our habits of reading. In Japanese and Chinese, where each character conveys more information than English letters do, readers see fewer letters per fixation (Rayner, 1998). In Hebrew and Farsi, which are written right to left, readers read more letters to the left of fixation and fewer to the right (Brysbaert, Vitu, & Schroyens, 1996; Faust, Kravetz, & Babkoff, 1993; Malamed & Zaidel, 1993).

Often, our 11-character window of reading includes one word plus a fragment of another. For example, suppose you have fixated on the point shown by an arrow in the following sentence:

↓
The government made serious mistakes.

Readers can see the word *serious* plus about the first three letters of *mistakes*. Three letters do not identify the word. From what the reader knows, the next word could be *misspellings, misbehavior, missiles, mishmash,* or any of a number of other *mis-*things that a government might make.

Does the preview of the next word facilitate reading? Yes. In one study college students again read passages on a computer screen while a machine monitored their eye movements. The computer correctly displayed the word the student fixated on plus the next zero, three, or four letters. So the display might look like this:

or like this:

Students who could preview the first three or four letters of the next word read significantly faster than those who could not (Inhoff, 1989). Evidently, while we are reading one word, we are previewing the next. Our preview helps guide the next eye movement and primes us to identify the next word (Inhoff, Radach, Eiter, & Juhasz, 2003).

You might wonder how speed-readers differ from normal readers. An average adult reader has about four or five fixations per second with occasional backtracks, for an overall rate of about 200 words per minute. Speed-readers have briefer fixations with fewer backtracks. With practice people can double or triple their reading speed with normal comprehension. Some claim that they see more than 11 characters per fixation, and unfortunately, researchers haven't tested this possibility. However, reading speed has some physical limits. Each saccadic eye movement lasts 25 to 50 ms, and reading does not occur during saccades. Thus, it would be impossible to exceed 20 to 40 fixations per second, even if each fixation lasted no time at all! If people could average 2 words per fixation, the theoretical maximum would be 20 to 80 words per second, or 1,200 to 4,800 words per minute. And remember, this calculation unrealistically assumes a fixation time of zero. Yet some people claim to read 5,000 to 10,000 words per minute. They must be fixating some words and inferring the rest. A combination of reading and inference produces fast reading and adequate comprehension of books with predictable content, like a James Bond novel. However, speed-readers do miss details. When they read college textbooks, they either slow their reading (Just & Carpenter, 1987) or fail the tests (Homa, 1983).

CONCEPT CHECK

20. Why can we sometimes read two or three short words at a time, whereas we need a saccade or two to read the same number of longer words?

21. If a word is longer than 11 letters, will a reader need more than one fixation to read it? (Check your answers on page 330.)

IN CLOSING

Language and Humanity

At the start of this module, we considered the question, "If language is so useful to humans, why haven't other species evolved at least a little of it?" None of the research answers this question, but we can speculate. Certain adaptations are much more useful on a large scale than on a small scale. For example, skunks survive because of their stink. Being slightly stinky wouldn't help much. Porcupines survive because of their long quills. Having a few short quills could be slightly helpful, but not very. Similarly, a little bit of language development is probably an unstable condition, evolutionarily speaking. Once a species such as humans had evolved a little language, those individuals with still better language abilities would have a huge selective advantage over the others. ▐

Summary

- *Language productivity.* Human languages enable us to create new words and phrases to express new ideas. (page 316)
- *Language training in nonhumans.* Bonobos, and to a lesser extent other chimpanzees, have learned certain aspects of language. Human evolution evidently elaborated on potentials found in our apelike ancestors but developed that potential further. (page 317)
- *Language and intelligence.* It is possible to have intelligence without language or language without other aspects of intelligence. Therefore, many psychologists regard language as a specialized capacity, not just a by-product of overall intelligence. (page 318)
- *Predisposition to learn language.* Noam Chomsky and others have argued that the ease with which children acquire language indicates that they are born with a predisposition that facilitates language. (page 319)
- *Brain organization and aphasia.* Brain damage, especially in the left hemisphere, can impair people's

ability to understand or use language. However, many brain areas contribute to language in varied ways. (page 320)

- *Stages of language development.* Children advance through several stages of language development, probably reflecting maturation of brain structures necessary for language and not just the total amount of experience. From the start children's language is creative, using the rules of language to make new word combinations and sentences. (page 320)
- *Children exposed to no language or two.* If deaf children are not exposed to language, they invent a sign language of their own. However, a deaf child who has no opportunity to use sign language in childhood will be impaired on learning it or any other language later. Children in a bilingual environment sometimes have trouble keeping the two languages separate but gain the ability to converse with many people and in certain ways show extra cognitive flexibility. (page 322)
- *Understanding language.* Much of speech is ambiguous; we understand words and sentences in context by applying the knowledge we have about the world in general. (page 323)
- *Limits to our language understanding.* Many sentences are difficult to understand, especially those with embedded clauses or more than one negative. Difficult grammar places a burden on our working memory. (page 324)
- *Reading.* When we read, we have fixation periods separated by eye movements called saccades. We read during the fixations, not the saccades. Even good readers can read only about 11 letters per fixation; people increase their speed of reading by increasing the number of fixations per second. (page 325)

Answers to Concept Checks

16. Start language learning when a child is young. Rely on imitation as much as possible, instead of providing direct reinforcements for correct responses. (page 318)

17. Children begin to string words into novel combinations as soon as they begin to speak two words at a time. We believe that they learn rules of grammar because they overgeneralize those rules, creating such words as *womans* and *goed*. (page 321)

18. Deaf children who cannot learn spoken language and who have no opportunity to communicate with signs early in life are permanently disadvantaged in learning sign language. (page 322)

19. *Thoughtfully* has seven phonemes: th-ough-t-f-u-ll-y. (A phoneme is a unit of sound, not necessar-

ily a letter of the alphabet.) It has three morphemes: thought-ful-ly. (Each morpheme has a distinct meaning.) (page 327)

20. Two or three short words fall within the window of about 11 letters that we can fixate. If the words are longer, it may be impossible to see them all at once. (page 328)

21. Sometimes, but not always. Suppose your eyes fixate on the fourth letter of *memorization*. You should be able to see the three letters to its left and the seven to its right—that is, all except the final letter. Because there is only one English word that starts *memorizatio-*, you already know the word. (page 328)

CHAPTER ENDING

Key Terms and Activities

Key Terms

You can check the page listed for a complete description of a term. You can also check the glossary/index at the end of the text for a definition of a given term, or you can download a list of all the terms and their definitions for any chapter at this website:

**www.thomsonedu.com/
psychology/kalat**

algorithm (page 302)
attention (page 288)
attention-deficit disorder (ADD) (page 294)
attention-deficit hyperactivity disorder (ADHD) (page 294)
attentional blink (page 293)

attentive process (page 289)
availability heuristic (page 305)
base-rate information (page 304)
bilingual (page 322)
Broca's aphasia (page 320)
change blindness (page 291)
cognition (page 287)
confirmation bias (page 307)
critical thinking (page 306)
fixation (page 327)
framing effect (page 309)
functional fixedness (page 308)
heuristics (page 304)
language acquisition device (page 319)
maximizing (page 311)
morpheme (page 327)

overconfident (page 306)
phoneme (page 327)
preattentive process (page 289)
priming (page 296)
productivity (page 316)
prototype (page 295)
representativeness heuristic (page 304)
saccade (page 327)
satisficing (page 311)
spreading activation (page 296)
Stroop effect (page 290)
sunk cost effect (page 310)
transformational grammar (page 316)
Wernicke's aphasia (page 320)
Williams syndrome (page 318)
word-superiority effect (page 325)

Suggestions for Further Reading

Pinker, S. (1999). *Words and rules: The ingredients of language.* New York: Basic Books. A discussion of language by a writer with a keen eye for excellent examples.

Schwartz, B. (2004). *The paradox of choice: Why more is less.* New York: HarperCollins. Fascinating, entertaining discussion of why too many choices or too much effort to find the best choice can work to our disadvantage.

Web/Technology Resources

Student Companion Website

www.thomsonedu.com/psychology/kalat

Explore the Student Companion Website for Online Try-It-Yourself activities, practice quizzes, flashcards, and more! The companion site also has direct links to the following websites.

Attention

http://dualtask.org/

You can try some demonstrations that show how hard it is to plan two actions at once.

Human Language

http://www.ilovelanguages.com

This site has links to many sources of information about languages.

For Additional Study

Kalat Premium Website

http://www.thomsonedu.com

For Critical Thinking Videos and additional Online Try-It-Yourself activities, go to this site to enter or purchase your code for the Kalat Premium Website.

ThomsonNOW!

http://www.thomsonedu.com

Go to this site for the link to ThomsonNOW, your one-stop study shop. Take a Pretest for this chapter, and Thomson-NOW will generate a personalized Study Plan based on your test results. The Study Plan will identify the topics you need to review and direct you to online resources to help you master those topics. You can then take a Posttest to help you determine the concepts you have mastered and what you still need to work on.

Intelligence

Alan Turing, a famous mathematician and pioneer in computer science, bicycled to and from work each day. Occasionally, the chain fell off his bicycle, and he had to replace it. Eventually, Turing kept records and noticed that the chain fell off at regular intervals, after exactly a certain number of turns of the front wheel. He calculated that this number was the product of the number of spokes in the front wheel times the number of links in the chain times the number of cogs in the pedal. He deduced that the chain came loose whenever a particular link in the chain came in contact with a particular bent spoke on the wheel. He identified that spoke, repaired it, and never again had trouble with his bicycle (I. Stewart, 1987).

Turing's solution to his problem is impressive, but hold your applause. Your local bicycle mechanic could have solved the problem quickly without using mathematics at all. So, you might ask, what's my point? Was Turing unintelligent? Of course not. If you have a complicated, unfamiliar problem to solve, you should take it to someone like Turing, not your local bicycle mechanic. The point is that intelligence includes both general abilities and practiced skills. The term *intelligence* refers to the highly practiced skills shown by a good bicycle mechanic, a Micronesian sailor, a hunter-gatherer of the Serengeti Plain, or anyone else with extensive experience. Intelligence also refers to the generalized problem-solving ability that Turing showed. Even that sort of ability develops gradually, reflecting many kinds of experience.

■ To repair a bicycle, you could use general problem-solving skills or specific expertise about bicycles. Either approach shows a kind of intelligence.

Intelligence and Intelligence Tests

- *What do we mean by "intelligence"?*
- *Is there more than one kind of intelligence?*

Is there intelligent life in outer space? For decades people have pointed huge arrays of dishes toward the stars, hoping to detect signals that aliens have sent toward us. If we did intercept some signals, would we make any sense of them? The whole enterprise assumes that intelligent life in outer space would be in some way similar to us. It is a remarkable assumption, considering how different human intelligence is from that of, say, dolphins here on Earth.

What Is Intelligence?

Intelligence clearly has something to do with learning, memory, and cognition—the topics of the last three chapters. Defining it more precisely is not easy. Here are examples of proposals for defining intelligence (Kanazawa, 2004; Sternberg, 1997; Wolman, 1989):

- The mental abilities that enable one to adapt to, shape, or select one's environment.
- The ability to deal with novel situations.
- The ability to judge, comprehend, and reason.
- The ability to understand and deal with people, objects, and symbols.
- The ability to act purposefully, think rationally, and deal effectively with the environment.

Note that these definitions use such terms as *judge, comprehend, understand,* and *think rationally*—terms that are just as poorly defined as intelligence. An alternative is to avoid any concept of ability and to consider intelligence as an assortment of useful behaviors (Schlinger, 2003).

To advance our understanding, we need research on the processes that contribute to whatever we mean by intelligence. Psychological researchers have followed a circuitous route: They began with tests of intellectual abilities, or the ability to do well in school. Then they conducted research to answer questions about those tests: Do the tests measure something useful? If so, do they measure a single skill or a variety of separate skills? Finally, they used the results of the research to draw inferences about intelligence itself and then to improve the tests.

This procedure may strike you as odd—starting with measurements of something before figuring out what that something is. However, physicists used the same approach with electricity, magnetism, and other observable phenomena.

Spearman's Psychometric Approach and the *g* Factor

One of the earliest research studies in psychology was Charles Spearman's (1904) psychometric approach to intelligence, based on *the measurement of individual differences in performance.* Spearman began by measuring how well a group of people performed various tasks, such as following directions, judging musical pitch, matching colors, and doing arithmetic. He found that performance on any of his tasks correlated positively with performance on any of the others. He therefore inferred that all the tasks have something in common. To perform well on any test of mental ability, Spearman argued, people need a *"general" ability,* which he called *g*. The symbol *g is* italicized and always lowercase, like the mathematical terms *e* (the base of natural logarithms) and *i* (the square root of -1).

To account for the fact that performances on various tasks do not correlate perfectly, Spearman suggested that each task also requires a *"specific" ability, s* (Figure 9.1). Thus, intelligence consists of a general ability plus an unknown number of specific abilities, such as mechanical, musical, arithmetical, logical, and spatial abilities. Spearman called his theory a "monarchic" theory of intelligence because it included a dominant ability, or monarch (*g*), which ruled over the lesser abilities.

Later researchers confirmed that scores on virtually all kinds of cognitive tests correlate positively with one another under nearly all circumstances, within any representative sample of the population (W. Johnson, Bouchard, Krueger, McGue, & Gottesman, 2004). You have probably noticed this trend yourself: A student who does well in one course probably will do well in another course. Exceptions do occur—sometimes strikingly—but the principle holds as a general rule. Researchers have reported the same trend even in mice: The mice that learn well in one situation generally learn quickly in another, even with

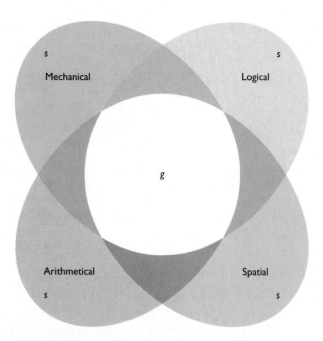

FIGURE 9.1 According to Spearman (1904) all intelligent abilities have an area of overlap, which he called *g* (for "general"). Each ability also depends partly on an *s* (for "specific") factor.

FIGURE 9.2 Measurements of sprinting, long jumping, and high jumping correlate with one another because they all depend on the same leg muscles. Similarly, the *g* factor that emerges in IQ testing could reflect a single ability.

different responses, different reinforcers, and different kinds of stimuli (Matzel et al., 2003). Only under special conditions do the individuals who perform well on one test tend to score below average on another. For example, in one study rural Kenyan children who did well on an academic test did poorly on a test of knowledge about traditional herbal medicines, and those who did well on the test of herbal medicines did poorly on the academic test (Sternberg et al., 2001). Presumably, the two groups of children had been exposed to different types of experience.

Possible Explanations for *g*

The observations underlying *g* indicate that whatever causes people to do well on one test also increases their probability of doing well on almost any other test. But what contributes to good performance on so many kinds of tests? The simplest and most popular interpretation is that all the tasks measure a single underlying ability. Consider an analogy with the tasks shown in Figure 9.2: Most people who excel at running a 100-meter race also do well at the high jump and the long jump. We can hardly imagine an outstanding high jumper who could not manage a better than average long jump. The reason for this high correlation is that all three events depend on the same leg muscles. An injury that impaired performance on one event would impair performance on all three.

Similarly, people might perform well on a variety of intellectual tests because all the tests depend on

one underlying skill. What might that skill be? One possibility is that all intellectual tests depend on "mental speed" (Luo, Thompson, & Detterman, 2003). Another is that *g* represents how easily one's neurons change in response to altered experiences (Garlick, 2003). Other possibilities include attentional resources and speed of visual processing. An increasingly popular position is that *g* depends mainly on working memory or some aspect of it (Ackerman, Beier, & Boyle, 2005; Friedman et al., 2006; Gray, Chabris, & Braver, 2003; Oberauer, Schulze, Wilhelm, & Süss, 2005; Polderman et al., 2006). For almost any intellectual task, holding information in memory is important, as is the ability to shift attention from one part of the task to another. Those are the key elements of working memory.

An alternative explanation for *g* is that we have several kinds of intelligence that correlate because they grow in the same ways (Petrill, Luo, Thompson,

& Detterman, 1996). By analogy consider the lengths of three body parts—the left leg, the right arm, and the left index finger: As a rule most people with a long left leg also have a long right arm and left index finger. However, although the three lengths correlate strongly, they do not measure the same thing. Amputating one of them would not affect the others. Lengths of leg, arm, and finger correlate because the factors that increase the growth of one of them also increase the growth of the others—factors such as genes, health, and nutrition. Similarly, all forms of intelligence depend on genes, health, nutrition, and education. Most people who have good support for developing one intellectual skill also have good support for developing others.

Which of these examples is more like intelligence? Do the various intellectual skills correlate with one another because they all measure a single underlying ability (as do running and jumping, which require good leg muscles) or because they all grow together (as do your arms, legs, and fingers)?

To some extent both hypotheses are probably correct. Most intellectual tasks activate the brain areas responsible for attention and working memory (Duncan et al., 2000), and g probably depends on attention and working memory. On the other hand, the genes, nutrition, health, and other factors that cause any brain area to develop have similar effects on other areas, so independent brain functions do correlate with one another for reasons of health, nutrition, and so forth.

 CONCEPT CHECK

1. What evidence did Spearman have in favor of the concept of g?
2. What are two possible explanations for g? (Check your answers on page 343.)

Hierarchical Models of Intelligence

Although Spearman and most later psychologists have regarded g as the key to intelligence, it does not account for everything. Spearman suggested the existence of specific (s) factors, but the task fell to other researchers to try to describe those specific factors.

One proposed distinction is between fluid intelligence and crystallized intelligence (Cattell, 1987). The analogy is to water: Fluid water fits into any shape of container, whereas an ice crystal fits only one shape. **Fluid intelligence** is *the power of reasoning and using information*. It includes the ability to perceive relationships, solve unfamiliar problems, and gain new knowledge. **Crystallized intelligence** consists of *acquired skills and knowledge and the ability to apply that knowledge in specific situations*. For example,

fluid intelligence is the ability to learn new skills in a new job, whereas crystallized intelligence includes the job skills that someone has acquired over years. Expertise, as discussed in chapter 8, is an example of crystallized intelligence. Even memory experts—those who win competitions for memorizing shuffled decks of cards or long numbers—achieve that expertise through practice at specific skills, not through a high overall g (Maguire, Valentine, Wilding, & Kapur, 2003). Standard IQ tests focus mainly on fluid intelligence because each person has a different kind of crystallized intelligence, and no test could do justice to that variety.

Fluid intelligence reaches its peak before age 20, remains nearly steady for decades, and declines on the average in old age, although more in some people than others (Horn, 1968). Crystallized intelligence, on the other hand, continues to increase as long as people are active and alert (Cattell, 1987; Horn & Donaldson, 1976). A 20-year-old may be more successful than a 65-year-old at solving a new, unfamiliar problem, but the 65-year-old will excel on problems in his or her area of specialization. However, the distinction between fluid and crystallized intelligence is sharper in theory than in practice. Any task taps both crystallized and fluid intelligence to some extent.

Other researchers have described intelligence in terms of a hierarchy, or a series of levels. According to one view, g consists of eight or more subabilities, including fluid intelligence (reasoning), crystallized intelligence, memory, visual perception, auditory perception, retrieval fluency, cognitive speed, and processing speed (Carroll, 1993, 2003). Other researchers, noting that many of these subabilities correlate strongly with one another, proposed a simpler hierarchy, in which g consists of three major subabilities: verbal processing (language), perceptual processing (dealing with vision and hearing), and image rotation (spatial relationships). Each of these major abilities could be subdivided into a large number of even more specific abilities (W. Johnson & Bouchard, 2005).

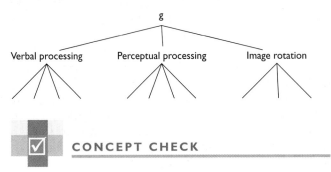

 CONCEPT CHECK

3. Was Alan Turing's solution to the slipping bicycle chain, from the introduction to this chapter, an example of fluid or crystallized intelligence? Would the solution provided by a bicycle mechanic be an example of fluid or crystallized intelligence?

❚ According to Howard Gardner, we have many intelligences, including mathematical ability, artistic skill, muscle skills, and musical abilities.

4. What kind of evidence indicates how many subabilities compose *g*? (Check your answers on page 343.)

Gardner's Theory of Multiple Intelligences

Certain critics propose to dispense with, or at least deemphasize, the concept of *g*. According to this view, scores on all kinds of intellectual tests correlate with one another for extraneous reasons, such as the fact that all of the tests require the use of language or all of them require logical reasoning. According to Howard Gardner (1985, 1999), if we could test intellectual abilities in pure form, we might find multiple intelligences—*unrelated forms of intelligence,* consisting of language, musical abilities, logical and mathematical reasoning, spatial reasoning, ability to recognize and classify objects, body movement skills, self-control and self-understanding, and sensitivity to other people's social signals. Gardner argues that people can be outstanding in one type of intelligence but not others. For example, an athlete can excel at body movement skills but lack musical abilities, an outstanding musician can be insensitive to other people, and so forth. Someone who seems intelligent in one way may be mediocre or worse in another, because different skills require not only different kinds of practice but also, perhaps, different brain specializations.

Gardner certainly makes the important point that each person has different

❚ In Garrison Keillor's fictional *Lake Wobegon,* "all the children are above average." Although that description sounds impossible, in one sense it is true: Almost everyone is above average at something.

valuable skills. However, to make the case that we have separate kinds of intelligence, research must show that various abilities do not correlate with one another. Demonstrating that point might be difficult even if it is true: Remember the idea that unrelated abilities or behaviors can correlate with one another just because the health, nutrition, and education that promote the development of any one ability probably also promote the development of many others. Researchers who have attempted to test Gardner's theory have reported that all the kinds of intelligence he reported do seem to correlate with one another, with the exception of body movement skills and possibly music (Visser, Ashton, & Vernon, 2006). (It was hard to be sure about music because the tests they used for music turned out to be unsatisfactory.) At this point Gardner's theory is an appealing idea without solid evidence to support it.

Sternberg's Triarchic Theory of Intelligence

Regardless of exactly why *g* emerges or what it means, we often need to know about more than overall ability. For example, many children labeled "learning disabled" have serious difficulties on one or two kinds of skills while performing at an average or above-average level on others. To help these children, psychologists and teachers want to determine exactly *why* a child is struggling (Conners & Schulte, 2002; Das, 2002).

Spearman's concept of intelligence has been called "monarchic" because it proposes *g* as a "monarch" that rules over the more specialized abilities. Robert Sternberg (1985) attempted to go beyond this view by proposing a **triarchic theory** that deals with *three aspects of intelligence: (a) cognitive processes, (b) identifying situations that require intelligence, and (c) using intelligence in the external world.* He tried to analyze the cognitive processes into smaller components. For example, he suggested that when solving certain kinds of problems we go through several stages, including encoding the information, drawing inferences, mapping relationships, and applying the knowledge. If so, it might make sense for intelligence tests to measure each of these processes separately. The goal was an intelligence test that had some theoretical relationship to cognitive psychology. Unfortunately, when Sternberg tried to develop tests of encoding, inferring, mapping, and so forth, he found that all the measures correlated fairly highly with each other (Deary, 2002). In other words he had rediscovered *g*.

Sternberg has explored other possible distinctions among types of intelligence. He has argued that we have at least three types of intelligence: *analytical* (or academic), *creative* (planning approaches to new problems), and *practical* (actually doing something). While criticizing standard IQ tests for concentrating only on analytical intelligence, Sternberg has tried to develop new tests that tap creative and practical aspects as well. Controversy persists regarding the status of creative and practical intelligence. On the one hand, we have all known people who seem high in academic intelligence but not in creativity or practical intelligence. On the other hand, thinking of examples is not enough; the question is whether *in general* analytical intelligence is strongly or weakly correlated with creativity and practical intelligence. Furthermore, measuring creativity and practical intelligence is easier said than done.

Sternberg and his colleagues have argued that their tests of creative and practical intelligence are better predictors of intelligence in everyday life than are standard IQ tests (Sternberg, 2002). However,

many other researchers remain unconvinced, arguing as follows (Brody, 2003; Gottfredson, 2003):

- The tests that claim to measure analytical, creative, and practical intelligence produce scores that correlate highly with one another, so it is not clear that they are measuring different processes. Sternberg may have rediscovered *g* again.
- The scores on analytical, creative, and practical tests also correlate highly with the scores on more traditional IQ tests.
- The analytical scores (similar to standard IQ tests) predict people's creative and practical behaviors about as well as scores on the creative and practical tests do. Again, what are claimed to be three different kinds of tests seem to be measuring the same processes.

However, the possibility remains that new tests will overcome these criticisms. Sternberg and colleagues have developed a new variation of the SAT based on his triarchic theory, and the early results show reason to be encouraged about its potential. (Sternberg & the Rainbow Project Collaborators, 2006).

Table 9.1 summarizes four theories of intelligence.

 CONCEPT CHECK

5. What evidence would we need to determine whether music, mathematics, social sensitivity, and so forth are really different kinds of intelligence or just different aspects of a single type? (Check your answer on page 343.)

IQ Tests

We have been discussing intelligence and IQ tests in general, and the idea of IQ tests is no doubt familiar to you, as such tests are commonplace in education through most of the developed world. However, the

TABLE 9.1 Four Theories of Intelligence

Theory	Theorist	Key Ideas and Terms
Psychometric approach	Charles Spearman	*g* factor: general reasoning ability *s* factor: specific ability required for a given task
Fluid and crystallized intelligence	Raymond Cattell	Fluid intelligence: solving unfamiliar problems Crystallized intelligence: highly practiced skills
Multiple intelligences	Howard Gardner	Music, social attentiveness, dancing, mathematics, and all other skills that society values
Triarchic theory	Robert Sternberg	Analytical, creative, and practical intelligence

time has come to examine several examples in more detail.

Let's start with this analogy: You have just been put in charge of choosing the members of your country's next Olympic team. However, the Olympic rules have been changed: Each country will send only 30 men and 30 women, and each athlete must compete in every event. Furthermore, the Olympic committee will not describe those events until all the athletes have been chosen. Clearly, you cannot hold the usual kind of tryouts, but neither will you choose people at random. How will you proceed?

Your best bet would be to devise a test of "general athletic ability." You might measure the abilities of applicants to run, jump, change direction, maintain balance, throw and catch, kick, lift weights, respond rapidly to signals, and perform other athletic feats. Then you would choose the applicants with the best scores.

No doubt, your test would be imperfect. Any test would be. But if you want your team to do well, you need some way to measure athletic ability. Later, other people begin to use your test also. Does its wide acceptance mean that athletic ability is a single quantity, like speed or weight? Of course not. You found it useful to treat athletic ability as a single quantity, but you know that most great basketball players are not great swimmers or gymnasts. Does your test imply that athletic ability reflects innate talent? No, it merely measures athletic skills. It says nothing about how they developed.

Intelligence tests resemble our imaginary test of athletic ability. If you were in charge of choosing which applicants a college should admit, you would want to select those who would learn the most. Because students may be studying subjects that they have never studied before, it makes sense to measure a range of skills, not just knowledge of a single topic.

The original goal of intelligence tests was to identify the *least* capable children, who could not learn from ordinary schooling. Later, the tests were also used to identify the best students, who would profit from accelerated classes. Similar tests were used for selecting among applicants to colleges and professional schools. Teachers' recommendations are useful up to a point, but teachers have their own biases, and objective measures help compare students from different classes and different schools.

Intelligence quotient (IQ) tests attempt to *measure an individual's probable performance in school and similar settings.* (The term *quotient* dates from when IQ was determined by dividing mental age by chronological age and then multiplying by 100. For example, an 8-year-old who performed like an average 10-year-old would have a mental age of 10, a chronological age of 8, and an IQ of 10 / 8 × 100 = 125. That

method is now obsolete, but the term remains.) Two French psychologists, Alfred Binet and Theophile Simon (1905), devised the first IQ tests. The French Ministry of Public Instruction wanted a fair way to identify children who had such serious intellectual deficiencies that they should not be placed in the same classes with other students. The task of identifying such children had formerly been left to medical doctors, but the school system wanted an impartial test. Binet and Simon's test measured the skills that children need for success in school, such as understanding and using language, computational skills, memory, and the ability to follow instructions.

Their test and others like it do make reasonably accurate predictions. But suppose a test correctly predicts that one student will perform better than another in school. Can we then say that the first student did better in school *because of* a higher IQ score? No, an IQ score does not explain school performance any more than a basketball player's shooting average explains how many shots he makes. An IQ score, like a shooting average, is a measurement, not an explanation.

The Stanford-Binet Test

The test that Binet and Simon designed was later modified for English speakers by Lewis Terman and other Stanford psychologists and published as the **Stanford-Binet IQ test.** School psychologists are carefully trained on how to administer the test items and score the answers. The test's items are designated by age (Table 9.2). An item designated as "age 8," for example, will be answered correctly by 60 to 90% of 8-year-olds. (A higher percentage of older children answer it correctly and a lower percentage of younger children.)

A psychologist testing an 8-year-old might start with the items designated for 7-year-olds. Unless the child missed many of the 7-year-old items, the psychologist would give credit for all the 6-year-old items without testing them. If the child answered most of the 7-year-old items correctly, the psychologist would proceed to the items for 8-year-olds, 9-year-olds, and so forth, until the child began to miss most items. At that point the psychologist would end the test. This method is known as *adaptive testing.* Individuals proceed at their own pace, usually finishing in somewhat over an hour (McCall, Yates, Hendricks, Turner, & McNabb, 1989).

Stanford-Binet IQ scores are computed from tables set up to ensure that a given IQ score means the same at different ages. The mean IQ at each age is 100. A 6-year-old with an IQ score of, say, 116 has performed better on the test than 84% of other 6-year-olds; similarly, an adult with an IQ score of 116 has

TABLE 9.2 Examples of the Types of Items on the Stanford-Binet Test

Age	Sample Test Item
2	Test administrator points at pictures of everyday objects and asks, "What is this?" "Here are some pegs of different sizes and shapes. See whether you can put each one into the correct hole."
4	"Why do people live in houses?" "Birds fly in the air; fish swim in the ____."
6	"Here is a picture of a horse. Do you see what part of the horse is missing?" "Here are some candies. Can you count how many there are?"
8	"What should you do if you find a lost puppy?" "Stephanie can't write today because she twisted her ankle. What is wrong with that?"
10	"Why should people be quiet in a library?" "Repeat after me: 4 8 3 7 1 4."
12	"What does regret mean?" "Here is a picture. Can you tell me what is wrong with it?"
14	"What is the similarity between high and low?" "Watch me fold this paper and cut it. Now, when I unfold it, how many holes will there be?"
Adult	"Make up a sentence using the words *celebrate, reverse,* and *appointment.*" "What do people mean when they say, 'People who live in glass houses should not throw stones' "?

Source: Modified from Nietzel and Bernstein, 1987.

FIGURE 9.3 Most IQ tests are administered individually. Here, a psychologist (left) records the responses by a participant (right).

performed better than 84% of other adults. The original Binet IQ tests provided just a total score. Today, because psychologists recognize several subabilities within the hierarchy that composes intelligence, the Stanford-Binet provides subscores reflecting visual reasoning, short-term memory, and other specialized skills (Daniel, 1997; McCall et al., 1989).

As shown in Table 9.2, the Stanford-Binet test has questions for children as young as 2 years old. At that age scores have low reliability. Nevertheless, behavioral measurements at ages as young as 4 months do correlate positively, though not very highly, with later IQ measurements (Bornstein et al., 2006).

The Wechsler Tests

Two IQ tests originally devised by David Wechsler, and later modified by others, known as the **Wechsler Adult Intelligence Scale–Third Edition (WAIS–III)** and the **Wechsler Intelligence Scale for Children–Fourth Edition (WISC–IV)**, produce the same average, 100, and almost the same distribution of scores as the Stanford-Binet. The WISC is given to children up to age 16; the WAIS is for everyone older. As with the Stanford-Binet, the Wechsler tests are administered to one person at a time. The Stanford-Binet and Wechsler tests are the most widely used IQ tests in the English language.

A Wechsler test provides an overall score and several subscores representing components of intelligence. For example, the WISC-IV has four composite scores. One is the Verbal Comprehension Index, based on such items as "Define the word *letter,*" and "How are a peach and a plum similar?" A second part is the Perceptual Reasoning Index, which calls for nonverbal answers. For example, the examiner might arrange four blocks in a particular pattern and then ask the child to arrange four other blocks to match the pattern (Figure 9.3).

A third part, the Working Memory Index, includes such items as "Listen to these numbers and then repeat them: 3 6 2 5," and "Listen to these numbers and repeat them in reverse order: 4 7 6." The fourth part is Processing Speed. An example of an item is "Here is a page full of shapes. Put a slash (/) through all the circles and an X through all the squares." In this case the task itself is simple; the question is how much of the page a child can complete within a short time limit.

△ ○ □ ▱ ○ △ ▱ □ ○

Each part of the WISC–IV or the WAIS–III begins with the simplest questions and progresses to increasingly difficult ones. The inclusion of several subscores calls attention to someone's specific strengths and weaknesses. For example, a child who learned English as a second language might do poorly on the Verbal Comprehension Index but much better on Perceptual Reasoning and Processing Speed, which do not re-

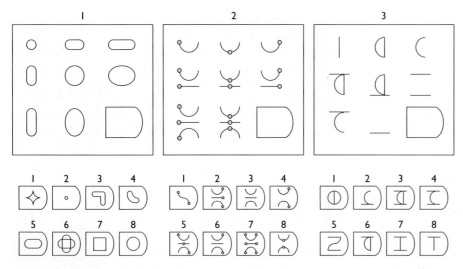

FIGURE 9.4 Items similar to those in Raven's Progressive Matrices test. Each pattern has a piece missing. From the choices provided, select the one that completes the pattern, both going across and going down. (You can check your answers against answer A on page 343.)

quire verbal answers. People with certain disabilities perform slowly on the Processing Speed tasks but do well on other parts of the test. Sometimes, a low score on one part of the WISC helps identify a problem for which teachers can provide help or special consideration. Unfortunately, the memory scale does not include enough difficult items to identify people with extraordinary strength in this area (Uttl, 2005).

Culture-Reduced Testing

The Stanford-Binet and Wechsler tests, though useful for many purposes, have one major limitation: Because they require use and comprehension of the English language, they are unfair to immigrants, people with hearing impairments, and anyone else who does not speak English well. "Why not simply translate the tests into other languages, including sign language?" you might ask. Psychologists sometimes do, but a translated item may be easier or harder than the original. For example, one part of the Stanford-Binet presents words and asks for words that rhyme with them. Generating rhymes is moderately easy in English, easier in Italian, but almost impossible in Zulu (M. W. Smith, 1974).

To overcome such problems, psychologists have tried to devise a culture-fair or culture-reduced test. No task is free of cultural influences (Rosselli & Ardila, 2003). However, a test with no language is at least fairer to more people, including immigrants and people who are deaf, than are most other tests. *The most widely used culture-reduced test* is the **Progressive Matrices** test devised by John C. Raven. These matrices, which *progress* gradually from easy to difficult

items, attempt to measure abstract reasoning. To answer the questions, a person must generate hypotheses, test them, and infer rules (Carpenter, Just, & Shell, 1990). Figure 9.4 presents three matrices similar to those on this test. The first is relatively easy, the second is harder, and the third is harder still.

The Progressive Matrices test requires no verbal responses or factual information, and the instructions are simple. It therefore gives a non-English speaker a better opportunity than most other IQ tests do. The main disadvantage is that this test provides only a single overall score, instead of identifying an individual's strengths and weaknesses.

How culture-fair is the Progressive Matrices test? It requires less information than the Wechsler or Stanford-Binet tests, but it does assume familiarity with pencil-and-paper, multiple-choice tests. The Progressive Matrices test has less cultural content than the other tests, but no test can be totally free of cultural influence.

 CONCEPT CHECK

6. What is one advantage of the Wechsler IQ tests over Raven's Progressive Matrices? What is an advantage of the Progressive Matrices? (Check your answers on page 343.)

IN CLOSING

Measuring Something We Don't Fully Understand

The standard IQ tests were devised by trial and error long before most of the discoveries about memory and cognition that we discussed in the last two chapters. We still have only a limited theoretical understanding of intelligence. Can we measure intelligence without understanding it? Possibly so; physicists measured gravity and magnetism long before they understood them theoretically. Maybe psychologists can do the same with intelligence.

Or maybe not. Physicists of the past measured not only gravity and magnetism but also "phlogiston," a substance that they later discovered does not exist. Measuring a poorly understood phenomenon is risky.

Many psychologists who are dissatisfied with the current tests are striving toward better ones. However, producing a significantly improved IQ test is not as easy as it may sound.

In the meantime the current tests have both strengths and weaknesses. An IQ test, like any other tool, can be used in constructive or destructive ways. The next module explores ways of evaluating IQ tests and their uses. ∎

Summary

- *Defining intelligence.* Intelligence is difficult to define, given our current understanding. Psychological researchers have begun by trying to measure it, hoping to learn something from the measurements. (page 335)
- *g factor.* People's scores on almost any test of "intelligent" abilities correlate positively with scores on other tests. The overlap among tests is referred to as g, meaning the general factor in intelligence. (page 335)
- *Possible explanations for g.* Many psychologists believe the g factor corresponds to an ability that underlies all kinds of intelligence, such as mental speed or working memory. Another possibility is that all kinds of intellectual abilities correlate with one another because the same growth factors that promote any one of them also support the others. (page 336)
- *Fluid and crystallized intelligence.* Psychologists distinguish between fluid intelligence (a basic reasoning ability that can be applied to any problem, including unfamiliar ones) and crystallized intelligence (acquired abilities to solve familiar types of problems). (page 337)
- *Intelligence as a hierarchy.* The g factor can be subdivided into more specific categories, such as verbal, perceptual, and image rotation. (page 337)
- *Abilities that make up intelligence.* Some psychologists define intelligence narrowly in terms of academic skills. Others include such abilities as social attentiveness, musical abilities, and motor skills. According to the theory of multiple intelligences, people possess many independent types of intelligence. (page 338)
- *Triarchic theory.* According to Sternberg's triarchic theory, intelligence consists of analytical, creative, and practical abilities. (page 338)
- *IQ tests.* The Stanford-Binet and other IQ tests were devised to predict the level of performance in school. (page 339)
- *Wechsler IQ tests.* The Wechsler IQ tests measure verbal comprehension, perceptual reasoning, working memory, and processing speed. (page 341)
- *Culture-reduced tests.* Culture-reduced tests such as Raven's Progressive Matrices can be used to test people who are unfamiliar with English. However, every test is based on familiarity with some customs that are more common in one culture than in another. (page 342)

Answers to Concept Checks

1. Scores on many different kinds of tests correlate positively with one another. (page 335)
2. Different kinds of intellectual tests may all tap the same underlying ability, such as working memory. Or they may depend on different abilities that tend to develop together because they all depend on the same influences, including health, nutrition, education, and genetics. (page 336)
3. Turing's solution reflected fluid intelligence, a generalized ability that could apply to any topic. The solution provided by a bicycle mechanic reflected crystallized intelligence, an ability developed in a particular area of experience. (page 337)
4. Researchers determine which skills correlate with one another. Those that correlate should be grouped into major components of g. The number of components is the number of clusters, where items within a cluster correlate with each other, but each cluster does not correlate strongly with the others. (page 337)
5. We would need to determine whether ability at each kind of intelligence correlates highly with the others. If they all correlate highly with one another, they are simply different aspects of g. If they do not, and if the differences reflect more than just different amounts of practice at different skills, then they are separate kinds of intelligence. (page 338)
6. The Wechsler tests provide separate scores for different tasks and therefore identify someone's strengths and weaknesses. Raven's Progressive Matrices are fairer for someone who is not a native speaker of English. (page 342)

Answers to Other Question in the Module

A. 1. (8); 2. (2); 3. (4) (page 342)

Evaluation of Intelligence Tests

- *How accurate, useful, and fair are the IQ tests?*
- *Why do some people score higher than others?*

> Whatever exists at all exists in some amount.
> —E. L. Thorndike (1918, p. 16)

> Anything that exists in amount can be measured.
> —W. A. McCall (1939, p. 15)

> Anything which exists can be measured incorrectly.
> —D. Detterman (1979, p. 167)

All three of these quotes apply well to intelligence: If intelligence exists, it must exist in some amount, and therefore, it must be measurable, but it can also be measured incorrectly. The challenge is to evaluate the accuracy, usefulness, and fairness of IQ tests. Because much is at stake here, the conclusions are often controversial.

Standardization of IQ Tests

In the first module, we considered examples of IQ tests. To evaluate them, or any other test, we need to go beyond impressions of whether they look reasonable. The evaluation begins with **standardization**, *the process of establishing rules for administering a test and interpreting the scores.* One main step is to find the **norms**, which are *descriptions of how frequently various scores occur.* Psychologists try to standardize a test on a large sample of people who are as representative as possible of the entire population.

The Distribution of IQ Scores

Binet, Wechsler, and the other pioneers who devised the first IQ tests chose items and arranged the scoring method to establish a mean score of 100, with a standard deviation of 15 for the Wechsler test, as Figure 9.5 shows, and 16 for the Stanford-Binet. (Recall from chapter 2 that the standard deviation measures the variability of performance. It is small if most scores are close to the mean and large if scores vary widely.) The scores of almost any population approximate a *normal distribution,* or bell-shaped curve, as shown in Figure 9.5. The distribution is symmetrical, and most scores are close to the mean.

In any normal distribution, 68% of all people fall within 1 standard deviation above or below the mean,

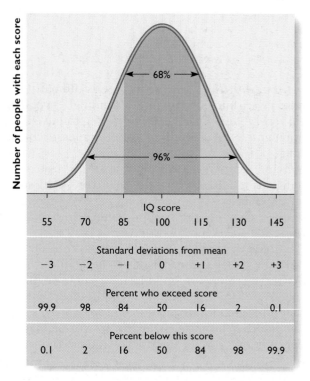

FIGURE 9.5 The curve shown here represents scores on the Wechsler IQ test, with a standard deviation of 15 (15 points above and below the mean, which is 100).

and about 95% are within 2 standard deviations. Someone with a score of 115 on the Wechsler test exceeds the scores of people within 1 standard deviation from the mean, plus all of those more than 1 standard deviation below the mean—a total of 84%, as shown in Figure 9.5. We say that such a person is "in the 84th percentile." Someone with an IQ score of 130 is in the 98th percentile, with a score higher than those of 98% of others.

Psychologists sometimes refer to people more than 2 standard deviations above the mean—with an IQ of 130 or more—as "gifted." However, being gifted requires more than a high IQ score. Gifted children learn rapidly and without much help, seek to master knowledge, ask deep philosophical questions, and develop new ideas (Winner, 2000a). Many develop a single ability, such as mathematics, far beyond their other abilities (Sweetland, Reina, & Taffi, 2006). Often, they have trouble finding friends their own age with similar interests, and they spend most of their time alone. Most grow up to be successful adults in fields such as law and medicine, although few become the highly creative leaders who revolutionize a field (Winner, 2000b).

Psychologists and educators classify people more than 2 standard deviations below the mean as mentally challenged or disabled. Again, the cutoff is arbitrary, and a psychologist considers other observations of the person's level of functioning before making a diagnosis. In the United States, the Individuals with Disabilities Education Act requires public schools to provide "free and appropriate" education for all children, regardless of their limitations. Children with mild physical or intellectual disabilities are mainstreamed as much as possible—that is, placed in the same classes as other children but given special consideration. The results of mainstreaming have been mixed. On the plus side, some studies have found that children included in mainstream classes develop better language abilities than those in classes limited to children with disabilities (Laws, Byrne, & Buckley, 2000). However, most children with disabilities have few friends, especially as they advance to the later grades (Hall & McGregor, 2000).

Since the first IQ tests, psychologists have found that girls tend to do better than boys on certain kinds of language tasks, especially relating to verbal fluency, as well as certain memory tests. Boys tend to do better than girls on visuospatial rotations. On attention tasks the genders tend to differ in strategy, with males more often focusing on one item at a time and females spreading their attention more broadly (W. Johnson & Bouchard, 2007). None of these differences are huge. By loading IQ tests with one type of item or another, test authors could have produced results showing that girls are smarter than boys or that boys are smarter than girls. Instead, they balanced various types of items to ensure that the mean scores of both females and males would be 100, and they continue to be equal today (Colom, Juan-Espinosa, Abad, & García, 2000).

Males show greater individual variability. On several intellectual measures, more males than females appear at the extreme top and bottom parts of the range, even though males and females have nearly the same means (Arden & Plomin, 2006; Hedges & Nowell, 1995). (*Why* males are more variable, we do not know.)

Restandardizations and the Flynn Effect

In 1920 a question that asked people to identify Mars was considered difficult because most people knew little about the planets. Today, the same question is easy. Researchers periodically restandardize tests to keep the mean score from rising or falling.

Those who restandardized the IQ tests eventually realized that they were consistently making the questions more difficult to keep the mean score from rising. That is, *decade by decade, generation by generation, people's raw scores on IQ tests have gradually increased, and test makers have had to make the tests harder to keep the mean score at 100.* This tendency is known as the **Flynn effect**, after James Flynn, who called attention to it (Flynn, 1984, 1999). The results vary across countries, tests, and periods of time, but a typical figure is 3 to 4 IQ points per 10 years. So if you took the same IQ test as your parents, and your parents are about 25 years older than you, then your score might be almost 10 points higher than theirs. If you took an IQ test from your grandparents' era, your score would be still higher.

One consequence is that if you take an IQ test and later take a restandardized form, your score will probably drop! Although you did not deteriorate, you are being compared to a higher standard. For most people a few points' change makes little difference, but for people at the lower end of the distribution, the loss of a few points might qualify them for special services (Kanaya, Scullin, & Ceci, 2003).

The Flynn effect—increase in IQ scores over generations—has occurred across ethnic groups (Raven, 2000), over many decades, and in every country for which we have data, including the United States, Canada, Britain, Australia, New Zealand, Israel, Japan, all of continental Europe, and urban areas of Brazil and China (Flynn, 1998). It has occurred even in rural Kenya, where people live mainly by subsistence farming (Daley, Whaley, Sigman, Espinosa, & Neumann, 2003). However, several studies suggest that

Many children with low IQ scores can be mainstreamed in regular classes. Those with more severe disabilities are taught in special classes.

© Bob Daemmrich/The Image Works

the Flynn effect was strongest in the early and middle 1900s and that it has slowed or stopped since the 1990s, at least in parts of Europe (Sundet, Barlaug, & Torjussen, 2004; Teasdale & Owen, 2005).

The effect has been reported for a wide variety of IQ tests, including the Wechsler tests (Kaufman, 2001), Raven's Progressive Matrices (Pind, Gunnarsdóttir, & Jóhannesson, 2003), and others (Colom & García-López, 2003). However, researchers have found no change over generations in speed of responding (Nettelbeck & Wilson, 2004). On conservation of volume and weight tasks, like those that Jean Piaget studied (chapter 5), researchers reported *decreased* performance between 1976 and 2003 (Shayer, Ginsburg, & Coe, in press). So not all mental abilities have improved.

What accounts for the Flynn effect? Psychologists have no consensus. One hypothesis is improved education and test-taking skills (W. M. Williams, 1998). However, the IQ gains have been greatest on Raven's Progressive Matrices and similar reasoning tests and weakest on tests of factual knowledge (Flynn, 1999; Rodgers & Wänström, 2006). Besides, the IQ improvement is evident in 6-year-old children and in rural Kenyan children, who have had little schooling (Daley et al., 2003).

A stronger hypothesis is improved health and nutrition (Lynn, 1998; Sigman & Whaley, 1998). After all, people have been getting taller over the years also, and a likely explanation for that trend is advances in health and nutrition. Improved nutrition is a particularly appealing explanation for the decrease in mental retardation over the years. However, improved health and nutrition are probably not the full explanation (Martorell, 1998).

Another possibility is exposure to increasing technology, beginning with movies and radio in the early 1900s and progressing through television, video games, and the Internet. These kinds of experience stimulate visuospatial thinking, probably related to performance on Raven's Progressive Matrices and similar tests (Neisser, 1997). Even in rural Kenya, the least technological place in which the Flynn effect has been demonstrated, some homes now have television (Daley et al., 2003).

For years psychologists dismissed genetics as a contributing factor. Evolution simply does not operate fast enough to explain changes from one decade to another. However, a different kind of genetic explanation is possible (Mingroni, 2004): **Heterosis** *is improvement due to outbreeding.* We don't know much about the genes that influence intelligence, but apparently, a great many genes have small effects (Plomin & Kovas, 2005). Imagine a series of genes—call them A, B, C, and so forth—and suppose in each case the dominant form of the gene promotes higher IQ development.

Genetic diversity is limited in any small village or community, so if people mate with others nearby, many couples will have similar genes. For example, both the man and the woman might have two dominant forms of gene A (AA), two recessive forms of B (bb), and so forth. Now, if people start traveling farther, choosing partners from other villages, maybe even other countries or other ethnic groups, then someone with dominant forms of A and recessive forms of B might mate with someone who has the recessive forms of A (aa) and the dominant forms of B (BB). Their children therefore have a dominant form of both genes (Aa and Bb). As a result the children might develop higher IQ scores, on the average, than either parent. The same explanation could account for increased height over generations.

Here is one observation that heterosis explains and other hypotheses do not: If a couple has children born many years apart, the oldest might be, say, 10 years older than the youngest, but on the average the youngest child does *not* have a higher IQ than the oldest (nor a lower IQ, for that matter). If the Flynn effect were due to improved health, nutrition, or technology over the years, we should expect the latest-born to have an advantage. But if the effect depends on heterosis, birth order within a family should have no effect.

Although IQ test performance has been increasing, actual intelligence may not have been. It is possible to argue that young adults today are somewhat smarter than young adults of previous generations (Cocodia et al., 2003; Howard, 1999; Schooler, 1998). However, it is difficult to believe that today's young people deserve IQ scores 20 points higher than those of 50 or 60 years ago. Flynn (1998) therefore argued that we have seen an increase in IQ scores, but not intelligence, over time. If so, what exactly do IQ scores mean? At a minimum we should beware of comparing two people's scores unless they grew up in the same era and took the same test at about the same time.

Evaluation of Tests

Have you ever complained about a test in school that seemed unfair? *Seeming* unfair doesn't necessarily make a test unfair—and seeming fair doesn't necessarily make it fair. When psychologists want to evaluate the accuracy or fairness of a test, they examine specific kinds of evidence. The main ways of evaluating any test are to check its reliability and validity.

Reliability

The **reliability** of a test is defined as *the repeatability of its scores* (T. B. Rogers, 1995). A reliable test produces consistent, repeatable results. To determine the reliability of a test, psychologists calculate a correlation coefficient. (Recall from chapter 2 that a correlation coefficient measures how accurately we can use one measurement to predict another.) Psychologists may test the same people twice, either with the same test or with equivalent versions of it, and compare the two sets of scores. Or they may compare the scores on the first and second halves of the test or the scores on the test's odd-numbered and even-numbered items. If all items measure approximately the same thing, one set of scores should correlate highly with the other set. Any correlation coefficient can theoretically range from +1 to –1. In the real world, however, a reliability coefficient is always either zero or positive. A negative reliability would mean that most people who score high the first time they take the test do worse than average the second time. That pattern simply never happens. Figure 9.6 illustrates **test–retest reliability,** *the correlation between scores on a first test and a retest.*

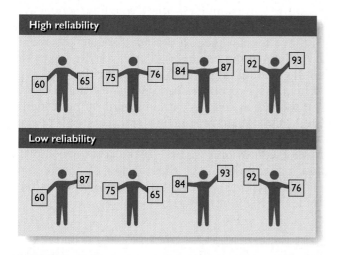

FIGURE 9.6 On a test with high reliability, people who score high the first time will score high when they take the test again. On a test with low reliability, scores fluctuate randomly.

If a test's reliability is perfect (+1), the person who scores the highest on the first test will also score highest on the retest, the person who scores second highest on the first test will also score second highest on the retest, and so forth. If the reliability is 0, scores vary randomly from one test to another. The reliability of the WISC, Stanford-Binet, Progressive Matrices, and other commonly used intelligence tests is above .9.

Whatever it is that IQ tests measure, it is reasonably stable over time for most individuals. Many studies have found correlations over .9 for people taking the same test at two times 10 years apart, and one study found that IQ scores at age 11 correlate .63 with scores at age 77 (Deary, Whalley, Lemmon, Crawford, & Starr, 2000).

Reliability

Try to imagine a test with 0 reliability. What kind of questions would such a test include?

CONCEPT CHECK

7. I have just devised a new "intelligence test." I measure your intelligence by dividing the length of your head by its width and then multiplying by 100. Would that test be reliable?
8. Most students find that their scores on any standardized test increase the second time they take it. Does the improvement indicate that the test is unreliable? (Check your answers on page 356.)

Validity

A test's **validity** is defined as *the degree to which evidence and theory support the interpretations of test scores for its intended purposes* (Joint Committee on Standards, 1999). In simpler terms validity is a determination of how well the test measures what it claims to measure. To determine the validity of a test, researchers examine five types of evidence:

Content. The content of a test should match its stated purposes. For example, a test given to job applicants should include only tasks that are important for that job. A test to determine which children have successfully completed fifth grade should correspond to the most important aspects of the fifth-grade curriculum.

Response processes. If a test claims to measure a certain skill, then the test-takers should need to use that skill to answer the questions. This criterion seems obvious, but cases arise in which people find shortcuts to answering questions. For example, some tests of reading comprehension include a paragraph or two to read, followed by multiple-choice questions about the reading. In some cases people can rely on previous knowledge to guess the correct answer without reading the passage (Katz, Lautenschlager, Blackburn, & Harris, 1990). Unfortunately, few research studies have examined the processes that people use to answer test questions (Braden & Niebling, 2005).

Internal structure. If a test claims to measure a single skill or process, such as working memory, then all the items should correlate with one another. That is, people who answer one item correctly should be more likely than average to answer any other item correctly. However, if a test claims to test two or more somewhat independent abilities, then we should expect to find clusters of items that correlate strongly with others of their own cluster and not with items of other clusters.

Relation to other variables. If a test is valid, the scores predict other kinds of performance that we care about. Scores on an interest inventory should predict which jobs or other activities someone would enjoy. Results of a personality test should predict which people might develop anxiety problems or depression. Scores on an IQ test should predict grades in school. In fact they do; the scores correlate positively with grades and achievement tests in all academic subjects (Deary, Strand, Smith, & Fernandes, 2007). Other personal factors are important in school also. One study found that eighth graders' performance in school correlated highly with questionnaire measurements of their self-discipline (Duckworth & Seligman, 2005). That is, having strong abilities is not enough; success also requires hard work.

IQ tests were designed to predict school performance. Later results showed that they predicted other outcomes as well, to the surprise of almost everyone, including the authors of the tests. People with high scores on standard intelligence tests average fewer automobile accidents than others do (O'Toole, 1990) and are less likely to suffer post-traumatic stress disorder (Vasterling et al., 2002). They do better than others at reading maps, understanding order forms, reading a bus schedule, and taking their medicines correctly (Gottfredson, 2002a). They even live longer than average (Deary & Der, 2005). Many of these correlations are small and their explanations unclear. Nevertheless, they indicate that IQ scores relate to real-world outcomes outside the classroom.

IQ tests also predict success on a variety of jobs, especially if combined with other information, such as a structured interview or a work sample (Schmidt & Hunter, 1998). According to Linda Gottfredson (2002b, pp. 25, 27), "The general mental ability factor—*g*—is the best single predictor of job performance . . . [It] enhances performance in all domains of work." According to Frank Schmidt and John Hunter (1981, p. 1128), "Professionally developed cognitive ability tests are valid predictors of performance on the job . . . for all jobs . . . in all settings." That is probably an overstatement. (It could hardly be an understatement!) For example, if you wanted to predict who would have a successful career as a singer or professional athlete, I doubt you would bother to give applicants an IQ test. For some aspects of job performance, personality factors such as conscientiousness are important predictors, al-

though difficult to measure (Wagner, 1997). Still, for many jobs, using some type of cognitive test score to select employees increases the chances that those who are hired will learn their jobs quickly and succeed at them.

Consequences of testing. Finally, we need to consider IQ tests' costs and benefits. Test publishers claim that their tests enable schools to choose the right students for advanced placement courses, help colleges admit the best applicants, and help employers fill jobs. Do the tests actually accomplish those goals? In some cases yes, but in other cases a test seems not worth the bother. For example, one college required all applicants to take both the general part of the SAT and the SAT achievement tests. Because the two scores correlated highly with each other, the college could predict grades just as well from one score as from both (Baron & Norman, 1992).

Critics raise other issues about the consequences of testing. For example, in the U.S. public school system, students' scores on end-of-grade tests determine whether they advance to the next grade. The scores also influence the teachers' salaries for the next year and the amount of government support that comes to a school. As a result the best qualified teachers don't want to work at schools with low-performing students (Tuerk, 2005). Many students and teachers concentrate heavily on preparing for the tests at the expense of other educational goals. Do the tests accomplish enough good to outweigh these costs? Although opinions are strong, good research on these issues is rare (Braden & Niebling, 2005).

▌ In some countries test scores determine a student's future almost irrevocably. Students who perform well are almost assured of future success; those who perform poorly will have very limited opportunities.

Special Problems in Measuring Validity

Measuring the validity of a test can be tricky. For example, consider data for the Graduate Record Examination (GRE), a test taken by applicants to most graduate schools in the United States. Grades for first-year graduate students in physics correlated .13 with their GRE quantitative scores and .19 with their verbal scores. That is, their verbal scores were better predictors than their quantitative scores. For first-year students in English, the pattern was reversed. Their grades correlated .29 with their quantitative scores and .23 with their verbal scores (Educational Testing Service, 1994). These scores surprise most people because physics is such a quantitative field and English is such a verbal field.

How can we explain the results? Simply. Almost all graduate students in physics have about the same (very high) score on the quantitative test, and almost all English graduate students have the same (very high) score on the verbal test. If almost all the students in a department have nearly the same score, their scores cannot predict which students will succeed. A test has a high predictive validity only for a population whose scores vary over a substantial range.

 CONCEPT CHECK

9. Can a test have high reliability and low validity? Can a test have low reliability and high validity?

10. If physics graduate departments tried admitting some students with low quantitative scores on the GRE and English departments tried admitting some students with low verbal scores, what would happen to the predictive validity of the tests?

11. Would you expect the SAT scores to show higher predictive validity at a college with extremely competitive admissions standards or at a college that admits almost every applicant? (Check your answers on page 356.)

Interpreting Fluctuations in Scores

Suppose on the first test in your psychology course you get 94% correct. On the second test (which was equally difficult), your score is only 88%. Does that score indicate that you studied harder for the first test than for the second test? Not necessarily. Whenever you take tests that are not perfectly reliable, your scores are likely to fluctuate. The lower the reliability, the greater the fluctuation.

When people lose sight of this fact, they sometimes draw unwarranted conclusions. In one study Harold Skeels (1966) tested infants in an orphanage and identified those with the lowest IQ scores. He then had those infants transferred to an institution that provided more personal attention. Several years later, most of them showed major increases in their IQ scores. Should we conclude, as many psychologists did, that the extra attention improved the children's IQ performances? Not necessarily (Longstreth, 1981). IQ tests for infants have low reliability. The scores fluctuate widely from one time to another, even from one day to the next. If someone selects infants with low scores and retests them later, their mean IQ score is almost certain to improve simply because the scores had nowhere to go but up.

 CRITICAL THINKING
A STEP FURTHER

Score Fluctuations

What would be the proper control group for the study by Skeels?

Are IQ Tests Biased?

In addition to being reliable and valid, any test should also be unbiased—that is, equally fair for all groups. A biased test *overstates or understates the true performance of one or more groups.* We cannot insist that all groups must do equally well on a test. If groups really do differ, the test should report that fact, and we should not blame the test for what it tells us. However, it should not exaggerate a difference or give unfair advantages to one group or another.

Because this concept is easily misunderstood, let's illustrate with an example. Imagine a store that sells DVDs. The management determines that the best salespeople are those who know the most about contemporary popular culture. So the company develops a test of knowledge about contemporary movies, television, and music and offers sales jobs only to people who do well on this test. Suppose we find—as we almost certainly would—that on the average young adults do better on this test than older adults. Is this test, therefore, biased against older adults?

This is an empirical question—that is, one to be decided by the evidence—but the answer is probably no. Most older adults have below-average scores on the test but only because they really do not know as much about popular culture. Using the test to select employees at this store is not biased if the test results correctly predict who will be good salespeople. Note that it does not prevent all older people from getting the job. Those older adults who do know much about popular culture will succeed on both the test and the job.

But now suppose an employer down the street takes this "unbiased" test and uses it to select em-

AP/Wide World Photos

❚ Women who return to school after age 25 usually get better grades than their test scores predict. That is, the tests are "biased" against them in the sense of underpredicting their performance.

ployees for a shoe store. Again, someone should collect data instead of assuming what the results would be, but a reasonable prediction is that this test, which is unbiased for choosing employees at a DVD store, will be highly biased for choosing salespeople at a shoe store. How much you know about popular culture is important for selling DVDs but not for selling shoes. Therefore, the test would unfairly penalize older job applicants at the shoe store. Furthermore, the older adults who did well on the test, and therefore got hired, would in fact be no better qualified for this job than the ones the test rejected.

The point is that bias means unfairness for a particular purpose. Researchers need to determine the bias, or lack of it, for any potential use of any test.

So, for what purposes, if any, are the IQ tests biased? For one example, women who enter college or graduate school after age 25 generally receive better grades than their test scores predict (Swinton, 1987). Therefore, the tests are biased against them, even though in fact most of them have good test scores. The tests are biased against them in the sense that a given score means something different for a 25-year-old woman than for a 20-year-old. Why do the older women get better grades than their test scores predict? Here are three hypotheses: (a) Because they have been away from school for a while, their test-taking skills are rusty. (b) Anyone who returns to school at that point must have strong motivation, whereas some younger students do not. (c) A few extra years of experiences give them some advantages.

To determine whether a test is biased against any group, psychologists conduct several kinds of research. They try to identify bias both in individual test items and in the test as a whole.

Evaluating Possible Bias in Single Test Items

Suppose on a test with 100 items, one of the items is the 10th easiest for one group but only the 42nd easiest for another group. This pattern suggests that the item taps information or skills that are more available to one group than the other and therefore is biased (Schmitt & Dorans, 1990). For example, Figure 9.7, an item that once appeared on the SAT, diagrams an American football field and asks for the ratio of the distance between the goal lines to the distance between the sidelines. For men this was one of the easiest items on the test. Many women missed it, including some of the brightest women who missed almost no other questions.

The reason was that some women had so little interest in football that they did not know which were the goal lines and which were the sidelines. The publishers of the SAT determined that this item was biased and removed it from the test.

© Shelly Gazin/CORBIS

© Warner Bros./courtesy of Everett Collection

❚ "Students will rise to your level of expectation," says Jaime Escalante (left), the high school teacher portrayed by Edward James Olmos (right) in *Stand and Deliver*. The movie chronicles Escalante's talent for inspiring average students to excel in calculus.

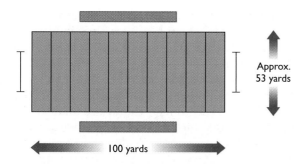

The diagram above represents a football field. What is the ratio of the distance between the goal lines to the distance between the sidelines?

a. 1.89
b. 1.53
c. 0.53
d. 5.3
e. 53

FIGURE 9.7 This item was eliminated from the SAT when researchers determined that it was biased against women. Some women who did very well on the rest of the test did not know which were the goal lines and which were the sidelines.

Evaluating Possible Bias in a Test as a Whole

By definition a biased test systematically misestimates the performance by members of some group. For example, if an IQ test is biased against Black students, then Black students who score, say, 100 will do *better* in school than White students with the same score.

However, the evidence indicates that Black students with a given IQ score generally do about the same in school as do White students with the same score (Jensen, 1980). The same is true for SAT scores (McCornack, 1983). A few exceptions have been reported, but only with small samples (Lawlor, Richman, & Richman, 1997). The unpleasant fact is that over many years White students have usually had better grades in school than Black students. The difference in IQ scores correlates with that difference in performance. The tests are reporting a difference, not creating one.

Since about 1970 Black students have increased their scores on IQ tests. In comparison to the mean of 100 for White children, the mean for Black students increased from about 83 in 1970 to 88 or 89 in 2000, according to the Stanford-Binet and Wechsler tests, as shown in Figure 9.8 (Dickens & Flynn, 2006). On the average, Black students have also increased their grades in school during the same time (Grissmer, Williamson, Kirby, & Berends, 1998). The fact that grades and test scores improved simultaneously supports the idea that the tests predict performance validly. The improvement of Black students' IQ scores and grades presumably relates to improved educational and occupational opportunities for most Black families.

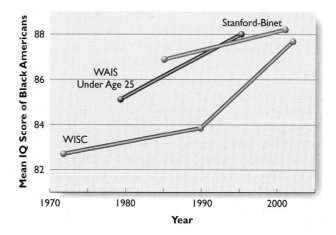

FIGURE 9.8 The mean IQ scores of Black students increased relative to White students from 1970 to 2000, according to the results of the two most widely used IQ tests. *(Modified from Dickens & Flynn, 2006)*

Saying the tests are unbiased tells us nothing about the cause of any difference between groups. In particular it offers no implications about genetic or environmental contributions. The conclusion is merely that whatever causes Black students to do less well in school also leads them to do less well on the IQ tests. Researchers still need to uncover the underlying reasons, which could include not only the more obvious factors relating to poverty and prenatal health but also subtle influences such as lower expectations and aspirations.

 CONCEPT CHECK

12. A test of driving skills includes items requiring good vision. People with visual impairments score lower than people with good vision. Is the test therefore biased against people with visual impairments?
13. Suppose on some new IQ test tall people generally get higher scores than short people. How could we determine whether this test is biased against short people? (Check your answers on pages 356–357.)

 CRITICAL THINKING
WHAT'S THE EVIDENCE?

Stereotype Threat

The possible bias of a test depends not only on the test's questions but also on how the test is administered. For example, if members of one group feel especially nervous or uncomfortable, their performance will suffer unfairly. In some studies (though not all), children who were tested by an interviewer of their own ethnic group scored higher than those tested by someone of another group (Kim, Baydar, & Greek, 2003).

A related but subtler influence is what Claude Steele termed **stereotype threat**—*people's perceived risk of performing poorly and thereby supporting an unfavorable stereotype about their group.* For example, Black students who take an IQ test may fear that a poor score would support prejudices against Blacks in general. They may become distracted and upset, or they may decide not to try. Let's examine Steele's study and its results.

Hypothesis. Suppose a group of Black students are about to take a test. If they believe that this is the kind of test on which Black students in general do not perform well, then they will worry that their own performance may reflect poorly on their group. As a result they will fail to perform up to their abilities. However, if they are freed from this kind of worry, their performance may improve.

Method. Participants were 20 Black and 20 White undergraduate students at Stanford University, a prestigious and highly selective institution. They were given a set of 27 difficult verbal questions from the Graduate Record Exam, a test similar to the SAT but intended for college seniors applying to graduate schools. Prior to starting the test, different groups (randomly assigned) received different instructions. Those in the "nondiagnostic" group were told that the research was an attempt to study the psychological factors related to solving difficult verbal problems and was not an attempt to evaluate anyone's abilities. In contrast participants in the "diagnostic" group were told that the research was an attempt to find each participant's "strengths and weaknesses" in solving verbal problems. This latter instruction was an attempt to increase students' nervousness about being evaluated.

Results. Instead of simply presenting the number of correct answers for each group, the researchers adjusted the scores based on participants' SAT scores. The results in Figure 9.9 show the number of correct answers for

each group *relative to the scores predicted by their SAT scores.* The mean for these Black students on the SAT was 603, and the mean for these White students was 655. So, if the Black and White students both did as well as their SAT scores predicted, the graph would show equal performances on the test, even though the White students answered a slightly higher percentage correctly.

The results for the "nondiagnostic" group do in fact show this pattern. However, for students who were given the "diagnostic" instructions, Black students had significantly lower scores than their SAT scores predicted. Black students given the "diagnostic" instructions answered fewer questions overall, and answered fewer correctly, than Black students given the "nondiagnostic" instructions. The type of instructions did not significantly affect the White students.

When interviewed afterward, the Black students who received the "diagnostic" instructions said that they felt strongly aware of the stereotype about Black students taking ability tests. They also said they felt self-doubts and worries about possibly conforming to this stereotype (Steele & Aronson, 1995). An additional study by the same researchers found that even when all participants received equal instructions, simply asking participants to indicate their race prior to the test produced a significant decrease in Black students' performances (Steele & Aronson, 1995).

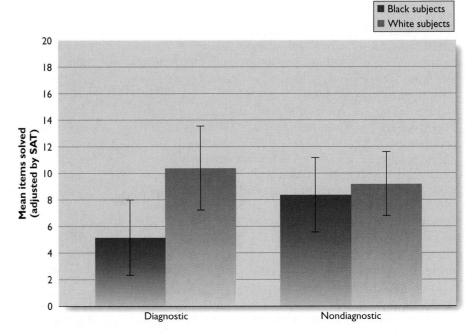

FIGURE 9.9 Black students who believed the test would identify their strengths and weaknesses failed to live up to their abilities. *(From Claude M. Steele and Joshua Aronson, 1995. "Stereotype threat and the intellectual test performance of African Americans."* Journal of Personality and Social Psychology, 69, 797–811.)

Interpretation. The results confirmed that many Black students are sensitive to any suggestion that they are taking an ability test on which Black students in general do not excel. Presumably, the worry distracts from their ability to concentrate on the problems.

The idea of stereotype threat has been confirmed in other studies, including some with other groups. Several studies have found that, on the average, women's performance on a math test deteriorates if someone highlights the stereotype that women don't do well at math. After a discussion of that stereotype, many women reported that throughout the test, they were distracted by thoughts such as "I hate math" or "I'm poor at math" (Cadinu, Maass, Rosabianca, & Kiesner, 2005). However, women with a strong interest in math dismiss the stereotype about women as irrelevant or wrong and perform well (Lesko & Corpus, 2006).

Three fascinating studies presented math problems to Asian women. For some of the women, the researchers primed their attention to being female by first giving them a questionnaire about being female. Those women did less well than usual on the test. For other women the researchers primed their attention to being Asian. (The stereotype is that women are not so good at math, but Asians are quite good.) Focusing their attention on being Asian improved their math performance in two of the three studies (Ambady, Shih, Kim, & Pittinsky, 2001; Cheryan & Bodenhausen, 2000; Shih, Pittinsky, & Ambady, 1999).

Given the goal of having all people live up to their abilities, how can we combat stereotype threat? One approach is simply to tell people about stereotype threat! In one study researchers described math problems as diagnostic of abilities that differ between men and women. But then they told some of the women (randomly assigned) about stereotype threat and urged them not to let the stereotype bother them. Those women performed as well as men did on the average (Johns, Schmader, & Martens, 2005). In another study researchers presented math problems as diagnostic of people's abilities but then instructed some of the women to engage in "self-affirmation" by briefly writing about their most valuable characteristic, such as creativity, social skills, or

sense of humor. These women approached the test with confidence and performed well (Martens, Johns, Greenberg, & Schimel, 2006).

 CONCEPT CHECK

14. How would a decrease in stereotype threat affect the validity of a test? (Check your answer on page 357.)

Individual Differences in IQ Scores

Why do some people score higher than others on IQ tests? The obvious possibilities are differences in heredity and environment. The British scholar Francis Galton (1869/1978)[1] was the first to argue for the importance of heredity. His evidence was that politicians, judges, and other eminent and distinguished people generally had distinguished relatives. I assume you will quickly see why this evidence does not justify a conclusion about the importance of genetics. Let's consider the evidence we have today, which is certainly stronger than it was in Galton's time.

Family Resemblances

Figure 9.10, based on a literature review by Thomas Bouchard and Matthew McGue (1981), shows the correlations of IQ scores for people with various degrees

[1] Remember, a slash like this indicates original publication date and the date of a revised printing. It does not represent Galton's birth and death dates.

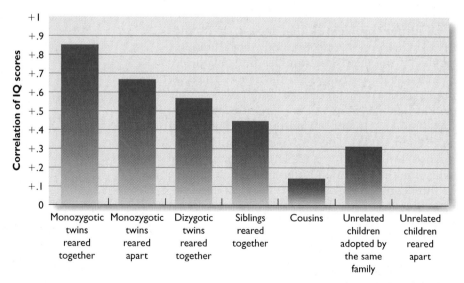

FIGURE 9.10 Mean correlations for the IQs of children with various degrees of genetic and environmental similarity. (Siblings are nontwin children in the same family.) *(From "Familial Studies of Intelligence: A Review" by T. Bouchard and M. McGue from* Science, *1981, pp. 1055–1059. Copyright © 1981. Reprinted by permission of AAAS.)*

of genetic relationship. These data are based mostly on middle-class European American families.

Because no IQ test has perfect reliability, someone taking a test on two occasions will get slightly different scores. The scores of monozygotic ("identical") twins correlate with each other about .85, not much below the reliability of the test (McGue & Bouchard, 1998). Monozygotic twins resemble each other in overall IQ, as well as in brain volume (Posthuma et al., 2002) and in specific skills such as working memory and processing speed (Luciano et al., 2001). They continue to resemble each other throughout life, even beyond age 80 (Petrill et al., 1998). Dizygotic twins and nontwin siblings resemble each other but less closely than monozygotic twins (Bishop et al., 2003). The greater similarity between monozygotic twins implies a probable genetic basis.

Monozygotic Twins Reared Apart

In Figure 9.10 note the high correlation between monozygotic twins reared apart. That is, monozygotic twins who have been adopted by different parents and reared in separate environments strongly resemble each other in IQ scores (Bouchard & McGue, 1981; Farber, 1981).

These results imply a genetic contribution, but they may overstate its size. Recall the multiplier effect from chapter 5: Slightly better than average performance early in life, perhaps genetically based, leads to encouragement and support, which leads to still better performance. So, if twins begin life with a small intellectual advantage, their environment may encourage and magnify that effect, making an initially small advantage a larger one (Dickens & Flynn, 2001).

A further problem is that most twin studies rely primarily on data from middle-class families. Studies of impoverished families find much less evidence for a genetic influence. That is, monozygotic twins in those families resemble each other no more than dizygotic twins do (Turkheimer, Haley, Waldron, D'Onofrio, & Gottesman, 2003). The probable meaning is this: For people living in a terrible environment, the genes don't make much difference. Their chance for intellectual development is limited. However, for people in a satisfactory environment, genetic differences have more impact.

Twins and Single Births

In Figure 9.10 notice that dizygotic twins resemble each other more closely than single-birth siblings do. This finding, consistent across several studies but not all (Bishop et al., 2003),

suggests an influence from being born at the same time. Presumably, twins have extra resemblance because they shared a greater amount of their environment, including their prenatal environment. Sharing prenatal environment means having the same nutrition, body temperature, alcohol or tobacco effects, and so forth during key moments in brain development (Devlin, Daniels, & Roeder, 1997).

Adopted Children

In Figure 9.10 note the positive correlation between unrelated children adopted into the same family. An extensive, more recent study found a slightly lower correlation, .26 (Segal, 2000). These correlations indicate an influence from shared environment. However, this correlation is lower than the correlation between biological brothers or sisters. The IQs of young adopted children correlate moderately with those of their adoptive parents. As the children grow older, their IQ scores gradually correlate more with those of their biological parents and less with those of their adoptive parents (Loehlin, Horn, & Willerman, 1989; Plomin, Fulker, Corley, & DeFries, 1997) (see Figure 9.11).

These results seem to imply a genetic influence from the biological parents. However, another interpretation is possible. Many of the low-IQ parents who put their children up for adoption are impoverished and probably do not provide good prenatal care. The mother may have poor nutrition, may smoke and drink, and may in other ways put her infant at risk for reasons other than genetics. Poor prenatal care correlates with decreased IQ for the offspring throughout life (Breslau, Dickens, Flynn, Peterson, & Lucia, 2006).

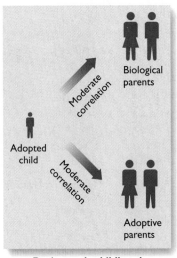
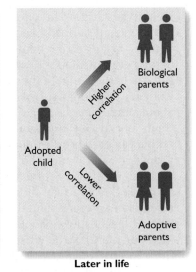

During early childhood   **Later in life**

FIGURE 9.11 As adopted children grow older, their IQs begin to correlate more strongly with those of their biological parents.

Gene Identification

The strongest line of evidence is a demonstration that different forms of particular genes are associated with higher or lower IQ scores. The Human Genome Project and related research now make it possible to seek exactly that kind of evidence.

The outline of the research is to determine whether any gene is more common among those with higher scores than those with lower scores. Similar research has been done with laboratory animals, comparing fast learners to slow learners. Dozens of genes have been found to correlate with human performance, and dozens in mice, some of them the same genes that were identified in humans. However, most of the identified genes have only small effects (Goldberg et al., 2003; Morely & Montgomery, 2001; Plomin et al., 2001). Evidently, intelligence depends on the combined influence of many genes, as well as environmental influences. The task now is to learn more about *how* various genes contribute and *which* environmental influences are most important. A few genes have been identified that influence IQ through effects on specific neurotransmitter receptors in the brain (Bertolino et al., 2006; de Quervain & Papassotiropoulos, 2006).

The heritability of variations in IQ scores does not mean that genes dictate people's intellectual accomplishments. Obviously, if we gave every child either an extremely good or extremely bad environment, we could raise or lower all their IQ scores. Positive heritability of IQ scores merely means that when children grow up in the same environment, some do better than others, and part of that difference relates to genetics.

Environmental Interventions

Although psychologists widely agree that both heredity and environment are important for intellectual development, we do not know much in detail about the critical aspects of the environment. If simply growing up in a family of people with high IQ scores were a major influence, we should expect to find a higher correlation between the IQs of adopting parents and

Many immigrants to the United States settle in ethnic neighborhoods where they can use their original language. Most first-generation immigrants do not score highly on English-language intelligence tests; as a rule their children and grandchildren get higher scores.

their adopted children. Other aspects of the environment need more careful research attention, including the role of prenatal health and nutrition.

A variety of programs have attempted to take children from extremely deprived homes and give them special intervention to improve their intellectual development. People who hoped that brief intervention might lead to huge long-term gains have been disappointed. Just as no one gene produces a huge effect, no single environmental intervention does either. However, intensive programs occupying many hours per week for several years do produce significant, lasting benefits (Ramey & Ramey, 1998). One interesting intervention is music lessons. In one study 6-year-olds who were randomly assigned to receive music lessons showed a gain of 1 to 2 IQ points, on the average, compared to other children (Schellenberg, 2004). Additional research indicates that children with music training show IQ advantages beyond what we can explain in terms of parental income and education (Schellenberg, 2006).

Interventions work best if they start early. Some orphanages provide a particularly deprived environment, including poor nutrition and minimal intellectual stimulation. Most children who remain in the orphanages perform poorly on tests and in school. Those who leave the orphanages and enter adoptive families show clear improvement, with the greatest improvement evident among children adopted before age 6 months (Beckett et al., 2006; van IJzendoorn, Juffer, & Poelhuis, 2005).

 CONCEPT CHECK

15. What types of evidence support a genetic contribution to individual differences in IQ scores? What are some reasons to suspect that the evidence overstates the role of genetics?

16. Under what circumstances do environmental interventions most strongly influence intellectual development? (Check your answers on page 357.)

IN CLOSING

Consequences of Testing

Regardless of what we think of intelligence theoretically, testing continues for practical reasons. Just as a coach tries to choose the best players for an athletic team, colleges and employers try to choose the applicants who will learn the fastest. If people are going to make those judgments—as they no doubt will—we want them to use the best available tests and evaluate the results accurately.

Testing has consequences for the individuals who take them and the institutions that evaluate the scores, but it can have another kind of consequence also: If we begin to better understand the factors that influence intelligence, we may be able to do something about them. As a society we would like to intervene early to help children develop as well as possible, but to make those interventions work, we need research. How important are prenatal health and early childhood nutrition? Which kinds of environmental stimulation are most effective? Are different kinds of stimulation better for different kinds of children? To answer these questions, we need good measurements—measurements that can come only from testing of some kind. ▌

Summary

* *Standardization.* To determine the meaning of a test's scores, the authors of a test determine the mean and the distribution of scores for a random or representative sample of the population. IQ tests are revised periodically. (page 344)
* *Distribution of IQ scores.* IQ tests have a mean of 100 and a standard deviation of about 15 or 16, depending on the test. (page 344)
* *The Flynn effect.* To keep the mean score at 100, authors of IQ tests have had to revise the tests periodically, always making them more difficult. That is, raw performance has been increasing steadily. The reasons for this trend are unknown. (page 345)
* *Reliability and validity.* Tests are evaluated in terms of reliability and validity. Reliability is a measure of the repeatability of a test's scores. Validity is a determination of how well a test measures what it claims to measure. (page 346)
* *Measuring validity.* To evaluate a test's validity for a given purpose, researchers examine its content, the response processes people use while taking the test, the internal structure of the test, the scores' relationship to other variables, and the consequences of using the test. (page 347)
* *Test bias.* Bias means inaccuracy of measurement. Psychologists try to remove from a test any item that tends to be easy for one group of people to answer but difficult for another. They also try to evaluate whether the test as a whole makes equally accurate predictions for all groups. (page 349)
* *Test anxiety and stereotype threat.* Many Black students perform worse on tests after any reminder of the stereotype of Black students scoring poorly on such tests. However, some simple procedures can weaken this threat. (page 351)
* *Hereditary and environmental influences.* Several kinds of evidence point to both hereditary and environmental influences on individual differences in IQ performance. (page 353)

Answers to Concept Checks

7. Yes! To say that a test is "reliable" is simply to say that its scores are repeatable. My test would give highly reliable (repeatable) scores. True, they would be useless, but reliability does not measure usefulness. (page 347)
8. No. An individual's score may be higher on the retest either because of practice at taking the test or because of additional months of education. But the rank order of scores does not change much. That is, if some people retake the test, all of them are likely to improve their scores, but those who had the highest scores the first time will probably still have the highest scores the second time. (page 347)
9. Yes, a test can have high reliability and low validity. A measure of intelligence determined by dividing head length by head width has high reliability (repeatability) but presumably no validity. A test with low reliability cannot have high validity, however. Low reliability means that the scores fluctuate randomly. If the test scores cannot even predict a later score on the same test, then they can hardly predict anything else. (page 347)
10. The predictive validity of the tests would increase. The predictive validity tends to be low when almost all students have practically the same score; it is higher when students' scores are highly variable. (page 349)
11. The predictive validity of SAT scores will be higher at the university that admits almost anyone. At the university with extremely competitive admissions standards, almost all students have nearly the same SAT scores, and the slight variation in scores cannot predict which students will get the best grades. (page 349)
12. No, this test is not biased against people with visual impairments. It correctly determines that they are likely to be poor drivers. A *difference* be-

tween groups does not constitute bias; only an *inaccurate* difference in scores constitutes bias. (page 349)

13. We would need to determine whether the test accurately predicts the school performances of both short and tall people. If short people with, say, an IQ score of 100 perform better in school than tall people with the same score, then the test underpredicts the short people's performances, and inaccurate prediction means bias. (The fact that tall people do better on this test is not *in itself* evidence of bias.) (page 349)

14. A decrease in stereotype threat should enable participants to perform closer to their abilities. Because the scores will become more accurate, the validity will increase. (page 353)

15. One type of evidence is that monozygotic twins resemble each other in IQ more than dizygotic twins do. However, this observation may overstate the role of genetics because twins that show early talent in some area such as academics, possibly for genetic reasons, receive encouragement to develop that ability, so environmental factors strengthen the early tendency. A second type of evidence is that IQs of adopted children correlate significantly with those of their biological parents. The limitation here is that the biological mother provides the prenatal environment as well as genetics. (page 354)

16. Environmental interventions are most effective if they start early, preferably before age 6 months. (page 355)

CHAPTER ENDING

Key Terms and Activities

Key Terms

You can check the page listed for a complete description of a term. You can also check the glossary/index at the end of the text for a definition of a given term, or you can download a list of all the terms and their definitions for any chapter at this website:

www.thomsonedu.com/ psychology/kalat

bias (page 349)
crystallized intelligence (page 337)

fluid intelligence (page 337)
Flynn effect (page 345)
g (page 335)
heterosis (page 346)
intelligence quotient (IQ) tests (page 340)
multiple intelligences (page 338)
norms (page 344)
Progressive Matrices (page 342)
psychometric approach (page 335)
reliability (page 346)
s (page 335)

standardization (page 344)
Stanford-Binet IQ test (page 340)
stereotype threat (page 352)
test–retest reliability (page 347)
triarchic theory (page 339)
validity (page 347)
Wechsler Adult Intelligence Scale–Third Edition (WAIS–III) (page 341)
Wechsler Intelligence Scale for Children–Fourth Edition (WISC–IV) (page 341)

Suggestions for Further Reading

Neisser, U., et al. (1996). Intelligence: Knowns and unknowns. *American Psychologist, 51,* 77–101. Although much dispute surrounds the meaning of IQ scores and the reasons individuals differ, psychologists have also found areas of agreement. This article describes the consensus of most psychologists, the evidence behind their conclusions, and the unanswered questions.

Web/Technology Resources

Student Companion Website

www.thomsonedu.com/psychology/kalat

Explore the Student Companion Website for Online Try-It-Yourself activities, practice quizzes, flashcards, and more! The companion site also has direct links to the following websites.

Sample IQ Tests

2h.com/

Take a variety of IQ and personality tests. Some are serious and some are obviously fake. None of these are the best established tests, but you might find them interesting.[2]

The Flynn Effect

http://pespmc1.vub.ac.be/FLYNNEFF.html

Read about research concerning the Flynn effect, including data from various countries.

For Additional Study

Kalat Premium Website

http://www.thomsonedu.com

For Critical Thinking Videos and additional Online Try-It-Yourself activities, go to this site to enter or purchase your code for the Kalat Premium Website.

ThomsonNOW!

http://www.thomsonedu.com

Go to this site for the link to ThomsonNOW, your one-stop study shop. Take a Pretest for this chapter, and Thomson-NOW will generate a personalized Study Plan based on your test results. The Study Plan will identify the topics you need to review and direct you to online resources to help you master those topics. You can then take a Posttest to help you determine the concepts you have mastered and what you still need to work on.

---

[2] Any psychological test that is readily available to the public, while entertaining and possibly informative, should not be used to make important decisions. The most powerful, valid, and reliable psychological assessment devices are usually kept under the tight control of their creators or copyright holders.

Consciousness

Today's computers play chess, predict the weather, and perform many other tasks as well as or better than people can. Still, we can list areas in which we greatly outperform the machines—such as in recognizing faces, expressing sympathy when people get hurt, and understanding humor. Suppose some future computer masters all these tasks. Would it then be conscious? Most of us assume it still would not be, but how would we know? Indeed, how do you know that I am conscious, or how do I know that you are? I don't! I infer that other people are conscious because they look and act much like me, but I cannot be certain. Ask me at what point before or after birth an infant first becomes conscious, or ask me which nonhuman animals (if any) are conscious, and I shall have to admit uncertainty.

Because consciousness is unobservable, many psychologists have despaired of any scientific approach to it. As Karl Lashley (1923) observed, some psychologists have gone so far as to imply that consciousness does not exist at all. Some philosophers have suggested wishfully that a future psychology may dispense altogether with any concept of mind or consciousness so that we shall not need to explain them (Churchland, 1986).

Nevertheless, researchers have begun to answer a few questions about consciousness. Although we cannot say much about what it is, we can answer a few questions about the conditions necessary for its occurrence. We also know some of the ways in which it varies during sleep, dreams, and hypnosis. This chapter attempts to answer a variety of scientific questions but leaves unanswered this fundamental philosophical question: In a universe composed of matter and energy, why is there such a thing as consciousness?

Sleep and dreams are alterations of consciousness.

Conscious and Unconscious Processes

- *What brain activity is necessary for consciousness?*
- *How does consciousness relate to action?*

What is consciousness, anyway? As William James (1892/1961) said about consciousness, "Its meaning we know so long as no one asks us to define it" (p. 19).

If we do try to define it, we start with the general agreement that it is a process, not an object (James, 1904). Just as fire is a continuous change in an object that reacts with oxygen at high temperatures, consciousness is a series of changes in a brain. Consciousness is an awareness of sensations—either current ones, remembered ones, or imagined ones. Therefore, we might define **consciousness** as *the subjective experience of perceiving oneself and other entities.* This definition is only marginally useful, however, as it relies on the undefined phrase "subjective experience." At this point we don't understand consciousness well enough to define it except in terms of synonyms.

Brain Mechanisms Necessary for Consciousness

Brain activity and consciousness, which seem so different, are inseparable. Any new experience increases activity in some brain area, and stimulation of activity in any brain area alters one's sensory experience. A decrease in brain activity accompanies a decrease or loss of consciousness.

Nevertheless, not all nervous system activity is conscious. Your spinal cord controls many reflexes, your hypothalamus regulates body temperature, and many other brain processes occur without your awareness. Even among the sensory stimuli striking your receptors at any moment, you are conscious of only a few. For example, right now you are looking at these words, but what else do you see among objects that surround this page? What do you hear? Do you smell or taste anything? What sensation do you feel in your left leg? Your right elbow? The back of your neck? As you turn your attention to one sensation after another, you become aware of much that had been present but unconscious until then (Lambie & Marcel, 2002).

In terms of brain activity, how does a stimulus that becomes conscious differ from one that remains unconscious? To conduct research on this question, psychologists use the operational definition that you are conscious of something if you can report it in words. Presumably, you are not conscious of something that you can't report. This definition works only for people who speak. One-year-olds do not talk, but we don't assume they are unconscious. Similarly, non-human animals do not talk, nor do adults with brain damage, people when they are dreaming, or monks of certain religious orders. In such cases silence does not necessarily mean unconsciousness.

A good research design is to present some stimulus under conditions where people report it (conscious) and the same stimulus under conditions where they cannot report it (unconscious). Brain scans then measure what is different about brain activity under the two conditions. Participants in one study watched as words were flashed on a screen for just 29 milliseconds each. On some trials a blank screen preceded and followed the word:

Under those conditions people usually identified the word, even though it flashed so briefly. On other trials a masking pattern preceded and followed the word:

Under those conditions people almost always say they saw no word at all. Under both conditions the light struck the retina for 29 ms, so we can ask what happened to the information during that period and after. Brain recordings indicated that the stimuli activated the same areas of the visual cortex in both conditions but produced greater activation on trials when people became conscious of the word. Also, on those trials the activation spread from the visual cortex to more of the rest of the brain (Dehaene et al., 2001).

These data imply that consciousness of a stimulus depends on the amount of brain activity. At any moment a variety of stimuli compete for your attention (Dehaene & Changeux, 2004). You become conscious of something when its information takes over much of your brain's activity.

Let's consider another example. What you see in your left eye remains separate from the vision from your right eye until the axons reporting this information converge in the cerebral cortex. Each cell in the visual cortex receives input from one part of the left retina and a corresponding part of the right retina—two retinal areas that ordinarily focus on the same point in space. Under normal conditions the input coming from the left retina is almost the same as that coming from the right retina. However, examine Figure 10.1 to see what happens when the retinal images conflict.

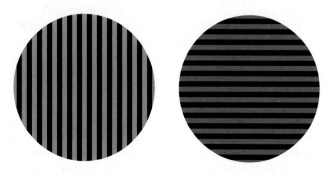

FIGURE 10.1 To produce binocular rivalry, look through tubes and change the way you focus your eyes until the two circles seem to merge. You will alternate between seeing red lines and green lines.

Find or make tubes like those in a roll of paper towels, so your left eye can look through one and your right eye can look *Try It* through the other. For a quick shortcut, *Yourself* you could cup your two hands to form viewing tubes. Look through the tubes at the circles in Figure 10.1. Adjust the focus of your eyes until the two circles appear to overlap. First, you will be conscious of what one eye sees—such as red and black lines. Gradually, that perception fades and you start seeing green and black lines from the other eye. You can't see both at the same time in the same place because your brain can't see "greenish red." So your brain alternates between the two conscious perceptions. Some people shift very slowly between the two, whereas others shift more frequently. So far, no one seems to have investigated the reason for this individual difference. With effort you can voluntarily direct attention toward the red lines or the green lines, but you cannot maintain control for long, and soon the other pattern emerges again (Blake & Logothetis, 2002). The *alternation between seeing the pattern in the left retina and the pattern in the right retina* is known as **binocular rivalry**.

Researchers use fMRI and similar devices to measure the resulting brain activity, as described in chapter 3. To make the patterns easy to identify, they might make the green and black pattern flash, say, 4 times per second while the red and black pattern flashes 9 times per second. Then they can look for patterns of brain activity that are flashing 4 or 9 times per second. When people say they see one pattern, researchers see the associated level of flashing over a large portion of the brain (Cosmelli et al., 2004; Lee, Blake, & Heeger, 2005). As that perception fades and the other replaces it, the other frequency of flashing spreads over the brain. In short, a conscious perception controls the activity over a large portion of the brain. We begin to understand why it is hard to be conscious of several things at the same time: At any moment, a large portion of your brain is occupied with whatever is at that time conscious.

Consciousness as a Threshold Phenomenon

Is consciousness a gradual thing? For example, suppose some stimulus produces a very low level of brain activity that is not conscious. If the activity slowly increases, might you first report being a "little bit" conscious of it and then more and more? A fascinating study suggests on the contrary that consciousness is an all-or-none process. Words were presented for various brief times (less than a twentieth of a second) with various degrees of masking, such as mere and кот A related study used the attentional blink procedure described in chapter 8 to make a word hard to identify. Both studies adjusted the procedures such that people identified the words sometimes but not always. Researchers asked not only what each word was but also, "On a scale from 0 to 100, how visible was the word?" The key result was that most people rated nearly every word either 0 or 100 (Sergent & Dehaene, 2004). People seldom said they were partly aware of a word. Theoretically, these results suggest that brain activity below a certain threshold is unconscious. Above that threshold it spreads, reverberates, occupies much of the brain, and becomes conscious.

CRITICAL THINKING

A STEP FURTHER

Animal Consciousness

Now that we see what kind of brain activity is necessary for consciousness, could we examine brain activity to determine the presence of consciousness in nonhuman animals, newborn infants, and others who cannot speak?

1. How did researchers present the same stimulus and let it become conscious on some trials and not others?
2. What evidence suggests that consciousness is an all-or-none matter? (Check your answers on page 370.)

Consciousness as a Construction

When you see or hear something, you believe that you are seeing it or hearing it *as it happens.* However, if you think about the experiments with very brief presentations of stimuli, you can see a reason to doubt that assumption: Suppose a word flashes on the screen for 29 ms, with interfering stimuli before, after, or superimposed on the word, such that you are not aware of seeing any word. Now the experimenter presents new words with similar interference but extends the duration from 29 to 50 ms. With this longer presentation, you will see the word. More important, you see it for the whole 50 ms. It is not as if you had 29 ms of unconscious perception and 21 ms of conscious perception. Rather, the final part of that 50 ms presentation enabled you to become conscious of the first part retroactively! In some way your brain constructed an experience of a 50 ms stimulus, even though it had to wait until the second half of the stimulus to perceive the first part at all.

Here is a related phenomenon. Suppose you see a light alternating between two locations, like this:

With proper timing between the lights, you will experience an *illusion of the light moving back and forth between the two locations,* known as the **phi effect.** Some signs in front of restaurants or motels use this effect. Moreover, the light appears to move smoothly and gradually. You "see" the light moving through intermediate positions, even though it was never there.

The illusion can become more elaborate: Suppose you see a small bright line alternating with a longer bright line:

You will perceive the line not only as moving back and forth but also growing gradually longer and shorter (Jancke, Chavane, Naaman, & Grinvald, 2004). So, when the longer line appears, you construct a conscious perception of an intermediate length line *earlier* than the long line. Similarly, if a red light alternates with a green light, side by side, you will perceive the red light moving, changing color to green, and then continuing its movement. Then it moves partway back, changes back to red, and continues to the first location (Kolers & von Grünau, 1976).

In each of these cases, the later stimulus changes your perception of what came before it. Evidently, consciousness does not always occur at exactly the same time as the events; we construct a conscious perception of events that already happened. This observation raises the fascinating question of whether our consciousness constantly fluctuates between being virtually up to date and being 30 ms or so behind. Further, it is possible that visual consciousness and auditory consciousness lag behind the events to different degrees.

3. What is the phi effect and what does it tell us about consciousness? (Check your answer on page 370.)

Unconscious Perception

Given that only some of the information reaching the brain becomes conscious, what happens to the rest of it? The brain does use it to a limited degree. First, recall subliminal perception from chapter 4: Although you might not consciously detect a brief, faint stimulus, it temporarily primes you to detect something similar. Also recall the discussion of implicit memory from chapter 7: You might not remember seeing or hearing some word, but nevertheless, you become more likely than usual to think of that word and use it. We shall encounter additional examples in later chapters.

Spatial Neglect

Particularly striking examples of unconscious perception arise in patients with damage to parts of the right hemisphere, who show **spatial neglect**—*a tendency to* *ignore the left side of the body, the left side of the world, and the left side of objects.* Information from the left side reaches the brain without becoming conscious, indicating that parts of the right hemisphere are necessary for attention to the left side of the body and the world. (Damage in the left hemisphere seldom yields neglect of the right side. Apparently, an intact right hemisphere can attend to both sides of the world.) The exact location of the damage within the right hemisphere varies, as do the details of what the person neglects (Hillis et al., 2005; Husain & Rorden, 2003; Karnath, Ferber, & Himmelbach, 2001). Symptoms are usually severest shortly after someone has a right-hemisphere stroke, with partial recovery over the next few weeks (Farnè et al., 2006).

Many people with neglect eat food from only the right side of the plate, ignore people who approach from the left side, read only the right side of the page, and sometimes read only the right side of words. When copying a picture, they might draw only the right side of the object (Driver & Mattingley, 1998). Some also ignore much of what they hear in the left ear and feel in the left hand, especially if they simultaneously feel something in the right hand. They may put clothes on only the right side of the body. If asked to point "straight ahead," most of them point to the right of center (Richard, Honoré, Bernati, & Rousseaux, 2004).

Although some patients have a partial loss of sensation from the left side, the problem for most patients is mainly one of attention. For example, if asked to close their eyes and describe something from memory, they describe only the right side of the scene. Someone who fails to report touch sensations on the left hand may begin to attend to them if you pull the left hand to the right side of the person's body, as in Figure 10.2 (Aglioti, Smania, & Peru, 1999).

One person was shown a letter E, composed of small Hs, as in Figure 10.3c. She identified it as a big E composed of small Hs, indicating that she saw the whole figure. However, when she was then asked to cross off all the Hs, she crossed off only the ones on the right. When she was shown the figures in Figure 10.3e and f, she identified them as an O composed of little Os and an X composed of little Xs. Apparently, she saw both halves of both figures, but when she was asked to cross off all the elements, she crossed off only the ones on the right (Marshall & Halligan, 1995).

So these patients see the whole scene but usually attend to only half of it. What would it be like to have this experience?

You can demonstrate something similar for yourself. Stare straight ahead and describe what you see, *without moving your eyes.* After you finish hold a white napkin, small piece of paper, or similar object a little more than a finger's length in front of your eyes so that it covers the center of your vision. Now describe again what you see without moving your eyes. You will find yourself including more of the objects in the periphery of your view. You saw them before, but you were attending so much to the objects in the center that you ignored those around the sides.

Try It Yourself

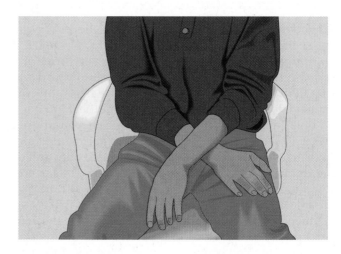

FIGURE 10.2 A person who ordinarily neglects the left arm gives it more attention if it crosses over or under the right arm.

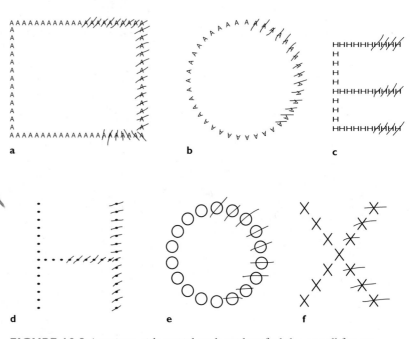

FIGURE 10.3 A patient with spatial neglect identified the overall figures implying that she saw both sides. However, when she tried to cross off the elements within each letter, she crossed off only the parts on the right. *(Source: Marshall & Halligan, 1995)*

Patients with neglect show similar tendencies. They report the objects on the left when they see nothing on the right. They also briefly attend to the left side when someone asks them to, just as you can look straight ahead but make a special effort to attend to objects in the periphery. They increase attention to what they see on the left while someone touches them on the left, while they hear something on the left, or while they tilt the body to the left (Driver & Mattingley, 1998; Frassinetti, Pavani, & Làdavas, 2002; Vaishnavi, Calhoun, & Chatterjee, 2001). These results exaggerate a tendency present in all of us. If you hear something or feel something on one side, it shifts your attention so that you will pay more than the usual amount of attention to what you see on that side (Kennett, Eimer, Spence, & Driver, 2001). The same is true for other animal species (Winkowski & Knudsen, 2006).

Blindsight

Here is another example of behavioral influence by unconscious sensations. After damage to the primary visual cortex (see Figure 3.8), people lose conscious access to visual information from part or all of the visual field. Although their eyes are intact, they cannot see. They are said to have *cortical blindness.* Depending on the amount of damage, the area of blindness may extend over a large or small area of the visual field. Nevertheless, some people with cortical blindness show **blindsight,** *an ability to respond to visual information in certain ways without being conscious of it.* For example, if an object moves, they may turn their eyes toward it, while continuing to insist that they see nothing (Cowey, 2004; Weiskrantz, Warrington, Sanders, & Marshall, 1974).

The explanation remains uncertain. The eyes have connections to other brain areas besides the visual cortex (Morland, Lê, Carroll, Hoffmann, & Pambakian, 2004). Perhaps those areas control eye movements, whereas the visual cortex is necessary for conscious vision. Another possibility is that people with blindsight may have islands of undamaged neurons within the visual cortex, with enough cells to direct eye movements but not enough to generate the reverberating activity that results in consciousness (Fendrich, Wessinger, & Gazzaniga, 1992; Wüst, Kasten, & Sabel, 2002). Several types of evidence support each hypothesis, so both may be true for different people (Ro, Shelton, Lee, & Chang, 2004).

 CONCEPT CHECK

4. What evidence indicates that spatial neglect is a matter of decreased attention instead of impaired sensation?

5. After damage to the visual cortex, what aspect of vision sometimes remains intact despite conscious blindness? (Check your answers on page 370.)

Other Phenomena of Consciousness

In passing let's briefly examine two interesting but poorly understood conditions related to consciousness.

The **déjà vu experience** is the *sense that an event is uncannily familiar.* Because it takes several forms, a single explanation probably will not suffice. Occasionally, someone is in some place for the first time and sees everything as familiar, as if he or she had been there before. A reasonable hypothesis is that the person really had seen something similar, possibly in a movie or photo, but forgot when and where. However, many people report déjà vu when they know they are in a familiar setting. You might be sitting in your room, walking down a familiar road, or having an everyday conversation, when you suddenly feel, "This has happened before!" In a sense, of course it has happened before, because you are doing a familiar task in a familiar location; however, your sense is not of having an experience similar to previous ones, but instead, it seems *this particular* event has happened before. As people talk, you feel, "I knew they were going to say that!" You probably could not really have predicted the words, but after you hear them, you feel that you had been *about to* predict them. For this type of déjà vu experience, psychologists have offered several hypotheses, but so far little evidence supports any of them (A. S. Brown, 2003). Apparently, something is triggering the brain to signal "familiar" in a strong way but for unknown reasons. We do know that the experience is fairly common in young adults and becomes progressively less frequent as people grow older (A. S. Brown, 2003). We also know that déjà vu is common and particularly intense in some people with damage to the temporal cortex of the brain (Moulin, Conway, Thompson, James, & Jones, 2005).

At the opposite extreme, some people report a feeling of unfamiliarity for something that should be familiar. In a rare condition called **Capgras syndrome,** *someone regards relatives and close friends as unfamiliar, insisting that these people are impostors who just resemble the real people.* Most people with Capgras syndrome have either brain damage or psychological disorders such as schizophrenia, and many have difficulties recognizing faces (Feinberg & Roane, 2003). However, most people with facial recognition problems still recognize their loved ones based on sound of voice and other signals. People with Capgras syndrome ignore all types of evidence and continue insisting that these familiar people are unfamiliar. One person insisted that the picture on her ID card was not her but rather some impostor (Grignon, 2005).

Possible Functions of Consciousness

Given that some sensory information becomes conscious and other information doesn't, but the unconscious information still influences behavior, the question arises: Exactly what does consciousness do, if anything? Is it responsible for our decisions and actions?

 CRITICAL THINKING

WHAT'S THE EVIDENCE?

Consciousness and Action

Each of us has the impression that "I make a conscious decision, and then I act." But does your consciousness *cause* your actions? In a scientifically and philosophically important study, researchers measured the time when someone made a conscious decision to act, the time when brain activity in preparation for the movement started, and the time when the act itself started. What would you guess was the order of the three events in time?

Hypothesis. In this study researchers were interested in three hypotheses, any one of which would be interesting if confirmed: (a) A person becomes aware of a conscious decision to act before relevant brain activity begins, (b) awareness occurs at the same time as the brain activity, and (c) the brain activity responsible for a movement starts before any conscious awareness of a decision.

Method. People were instructed to make a simple movement—flexion of the wrist. Although they had no choice over the type of movement, they had complete freedom over the timing. The instruction was to flex the wrist whenever they decided to, but as spontaneously as possible, with no advance planning. While waiting for that spontaneous urge to occur, they were to watch a special clock like the one in Figure 10.4, on which a spot of light moved around the edge every 2.56 seconds. At whatever time they suddenly decided to flex the wrist, they were to note the exact position of the light at that moment, so they could report it later. In this way the study measured, as well as anyone knows how to, the time of the conscious decision. Meanwhile, researchers used electrodes on the scalp to detect

increased activity in the motor cortex (see Figures 3.8 and 3.10), which is the brain area responsible for initiating muscle movements. *The increased motor cortex activity prior to the start of the movement* is known as the **readiness potential**. Researchers also measured the time the wrist muscles began to flex. On certain trials the participants were told to report when they felt the wrist actually start to flex, instead of the time they felt the intention to move it.

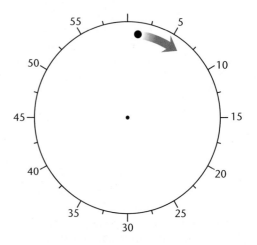

FIGURE 10.4 A spot of light rotated around the clock once every 2.56 seconds. Participants made a spontaneous decision to flex the wrist and noted the location of the light at the time of the decision. They remembered that time and reported it later. *(From Libet, Gleason, Wright, & Pearl, 1983)*

Results. It is not easy to report the exact moment when you form an intention, and the results varied from person to person and from trial to trial. The results in Figure 10.5 show the means for a large sample. On the average people reported forming an intention of movement 200–300 ms before the movement (Libet, Gleason, Wright, & Pearl, 1983). (They noted the time on the clock then; they did not report it until later.) For example, someone might report that he or she formed an intention when the light was at location 25 on the clock, 200 ms before the movement began at location 30. (Remember, the light zooms around the circle in 2.56 seconds.) In contrast the readiness potential in the brain began 300–800 ms before the reported intention. Several other laboratories have replicated the observation that the readiness potential comes before the awareness of conscious intention (Haggard & Eimer, 1999; Lau, Rogers, Haggard, & Passingham, 2004; Trevena & Miller, 2002).

Recall that on certain trials the participants reported the time of the wrist motion. The purpose of those trials was to measure the accuracy of people's reports of time. On these trials people

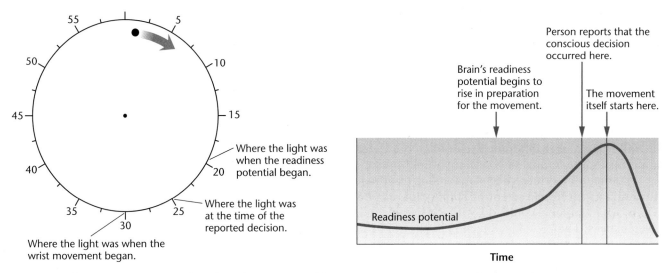

FIGURE 10.5 On the average the brain's readiness potential began 300 ms or more prior to the reported decision, which occurred 200–300 ms before the movement.

usually reported feeling the movement within 100 ms of the actual time (Lau et al., 2004; Libet et al., 1983). From this finding the researchers concluded that people can report the time of an experience with moderate accuracy.

Interpretation.   These results indicate that your brain is starting to produce a voluntary movement before you are consciously aware of it. If so, your conscious decision does not cause your action. Rather, you become conscious of your decision after the brain activity leading to the action is already well underway. Most people find this idea surprising, and both psychologists and philosophers have tried to find a way to challenge the conclusion. One legitimate criticism is that the task requires people to make a decision and then shift their attention to noting the position of a spot on the clock. Shifting attention takes time, and for that reason and others, people cannot precisely report when they made their decision (Haggard & Libet, 2001; Lau, Rogers, & Passingham, 2006; Wundt, 1862/1961). However, the onset of the readiness potential precedes the reported decision by at least 300 ms, often more, and it is unlikely that people's reports are inaccurate by that much. Consider that their reports of feeling the wrist movement are within 100 ms of the actual time. That judgment also requires shifting attention.

What happens to the concept of free will? It depends on what you mean by free will. This study does not conflict with the idea that you make a voluntary decision. The choice of when to flex your wrist definitely originates within you. However, the results imply that the voluntary de-

cision is at first *unconscious*. Earlier in this module, we considered evidence that a sensory stimulus must produce a certain strength of brain activity to become conscious; presumably, the same is true for an intention to make a movement. In support of this idea, one study found that mild electrical stimulation of certain brain areas caused people to report "feeling an urge" to make some movement, and slightly stronger stimulation caused actual movements (Fried et al., 1991).

However, if the brain activity responsible for movement precedes conscious awareness of intending a movement, we have to ask what consciousness is good for, if anything. If we become conscious of a decision to act only after the brain is preparing to make the movement, consciousness seems more of a spectator than an actor. For people with damage in part of the parietal cortex (see Figure 3.5), that conclusion is even truer: They report an intention to act only after the muscles have started to move (Sirigu et al., 2004). That is, they have no sense of intending or planning a movement prior to the movement itself.

 CONCEPT CHECK

6. In this experiment on the timing of consciousness, what did participants report, and when did they report it?
7. What was the order of these events: Conscious decision to move, brain activity relevant to movement, and the movement itself? (Check your answers on page 370.)

The Role of Consciousness

Which nonhuman animals are conscious, if any? Some biologists and psychologists have argued in favor of nonhuman consciousness (Griffin, 2001), but others remain doubtful. If we ever resolve this question, will it make any difference scientifically? Determining that some animal is conscious would presumably influence our ethical decisions about treatment of the animal, but from a scientific standpoint, it is not obvious what anyone could do with the concept of consciousness. That is, consciousness might not be an explanation for anything else.

On the other hand, any advance we make toward answering questions about consciousness is evidence of significant progress in research methods. Since the dawn of psychology, most researchers have considered consciousness an impossible topic to research. As you have read in this module, it is a very difficult topic, but it no longer seems impossible. ∎

Summary

- A single stimulus presented under different conditions may become conscious in some cases and not others. When it becomes conscious, it activates the same brain areas as when it is unconscious, but it activates them more strongly. The strong activation then reverberates through other brain areas. (page 363)
- In binocular rivalry we see how two stimuli compete for conscious awareness and for dominance of brain activity. (page 364)
- If a stimulus is detected on some trials and not others, on any given trial people rate it either completely visible (100%) or not visible at all (0%). These results suggest that consciousness requires a stimulus to pass an all-or-nothing threshold. (page 364)
- Unconscious stimuli also influence behavior in several ways. (page 365)
- Some people with damage in parts of the right hemisphere seem to be unconscious of the left side of their world, but it is possible to direct their attention to information on the left and make it conscious. (page 365)
- Some people with damage to the visual cortex experience blindsight, an ability to direct eye movements toward an object that they do not perceive consciously. (page 367)

- In déjà vu people experience a sense of extreme familiarity for a new event. Individuals with Capgras syndrome report unfamiliarity with people they have known for a long time. (page 367)
- People's reports of the time of onset of a conscious decision place it later than the time when brain activity in preparation for the movement begins. Evidently, the intention to move must reach a certain level of strength before it becomes conscious. (page 368)

Answers to Concept Checks

1. Researchers presented a stimulus, such as a word, for a small fraction of a second. When they simply presented the word, most people identified it consciously. In other cases researchers put interfering patterns before and after the stimulus, added a masking pattern to the stimulus, or used the attentional blink procedure to distract attention from the stimulus. In those cases people typically could not identify the stimulus consciously. (page 363)
2. Participants viewed words under difficult conditions and reported how visible they were. People usually reported a word as either 0% or 100% visible; they rarely reported partial consciousness of a stimulus. (page 364)
3. The phi effect is an illusion of movement when a stimulus alternately blinks on and off in two locations. The fact that we perceive gradual movement between the two locations implies that the later perception induced a conscious perception prior to itself. That is, we sometimes experience consciousness retroactively, not simultaneously with the events. (page 365)
4. People with spatial neglect ignore the left side of objects that they imagine, as well as those they see. Also, simply crossing someone's left hand to the right side of the body increases attention to it. (page 366)
5. People with damage to the visual cortex sometimes turn their heads toward a moving object in the part of the world they do not consciously see. (page 367)
6. Participants watched a special fast clock and noted the time when they made a spontaneous decision to flex the wrist. They reported it a few seconds later. (page 368)
7. Measurable brain activity came first, then the perception of the conscious decision, and then the movement. (page 368)

Sleep and Dreams

- *Why do we sleep?*
- *What accounts for the content of our dreams?*

Consciousness and alertness cycle daily between wakefulness and sleep. During sleep we become less aware of our surroundings. Dreams take us to a fantasy world where impossible events seem possible. Why do we have these periods of altered consciousness?

Our Circadian Rhythms

Animal life shows many biological cycles. Consider hibernation. Ground squirrels hibernate during the winter, when they would have trouble finding food. The females awaken in spring as soon as food becomes available. The males also need to eat, but they have a reason to awaken earlier: The females are ready to mate as soon as they come out of their winter burrows, and each female mates only once a year. Any male who awakens after the females pays for his extra rest by missing his only mating opportunity for the *entire year*. Males don't take any chances. They awaken from hibernation a week before the females do. And then they spend that week waiting—with no females, nothing to eat, and little to do except fight with one another (French, 1988).

The point is that animals have evolved internal timing mechanisms to prepare them for predictable needs. Male ground squirrels awaken not in response to their current situation but in preparation for what will happen a few days later. Similarly, most migrating birds start south in the fall well before their northern homes become inhospitable.

Humans also have mechanisms that prepare us for activity during the day and sleep at night. We, like other animals, generate a **circadian rhythm,** a *rhythm of activity and inactivity lasting about a day.* (The term *circadian* comes from the Latin roots *circa* and *dies,* meaning "about a day.") The rising and setting of the sun provide cues to reset our rhythm each day. In an environment with no cues for time, such as near-polar regions in summer or winter, most people generate a waking–sleeping rhythm a little longer than 24 hours, which gradually drifts out of phase with the clock (Palinkas, 2003).

Many people in the Scandinavian countries have sleep difficulties (Ohayon & Partinen, 2002).

The genes that control circadian rhythms vary, like any other gene. Some people have a gene that causes their circadian rhythm to run faster than normal (Toh et al., 2001). They consistently go to sleep earlier than other people and wake up earlier. Whereas most people enjoy weekends and vacations as an opportunity to stay up later than usual, people with these fast-running rhythms enjoy the opportunity to go to bed even earlier than usual! Most people with this condition are depressed (Xu et al., 2005). Sleep and mood are closely linked.

Sleepiness and alertness depend on one's position within the circadian rhythm. If you have ever gone all night without sleep—as most college students do at one time or another—you probably grew very sleepy between 2 and 6 A.M. But if you were still awake the next morning, you began feeling less sleepy, not more. You became more alert because of your circadian rhythm, even though your sleep deprivation had continued.

In one study volunteers went without sleep for three nights. An experimenter periodically took their temperature and measured their performance on reasoning tasks. Both temperature and reasoning de-

The rising and setting of the sun do not produce our daily rhythm of wakefulness and sleepiness, but they synchronize the rhythm. We adjust our internally generated cycles so that we feel alert during the day and sleepy at night.

clined during the first night and then increased the next morning. During the second and third nights, temperature and reasoning decreased more than on the first night, but they rebounded again the next day (Figure 10.6). Thus, sleep deprivation produces a pattern of progressive deterioration superimposed on the normal circadian cycle of rising and falling body temperature and alertness (Babkoff, Caspy, Mikulincer, & Sing, 1991). In short, sleepiness apparently depends partly on how long one has gone without sleep and partly on the time of day (i.e., circadian rhythm).

Morning People and Evening People

People vary in their circadian rhythms. "Morning people" awaken easily, become alert quickly, and do their best work before noon. "Evening people" take longer to warm up in the morning (literally as well as figuratively) and do their best work in the afternoon or evening (Horne, Brass, & Pettitt, 1980). Most people are consistent, and you probably know whether you are a morning person, evening person, or somewhere in between.

Most young adults are either evening people or neutral (about equally alert at all times), whereas nearly all people over age 65 are morning people. If you ask people at what time they like to go to bed on days when they have no obligations, their mean answer shifts later and later during the teenage years, reaches a peak of about 1–2 A.M. at age 20, and then starts reversing, slowly and steadily over decades (Roenneberg et al., 2004). If the shift toward earlier bedtimes after age 20 were entirely a reaction to job requirements, we might expect it to be a sudden change, and we should predict a reversal of the trend at retirement. The fact that the trend continues gradually over a lifetime suggests a biological basis.

The age differences in circadian rhythms are relevant to research methods on several topics. For example, researchers have often reported memory losses in older people. But as with much of the rest of psychology, a great deal of the research is done by graduate students. How old are graduate students? Most are in their 20s. At what time do they choose to conduct their research? Most prefer late afternoon, a fine time for young adults but not for the elderly. Researchers in one study compared the memories of young adults (18–22 years old) and older adults (66–78 years old) at different times of day. Early in the morning, the older adults did about as well as the younger ones. However, as the day went on, the younger adults remained steady or improved, whereas the older adults deteriorated (May, Hasher, & Stoltzfus, 1993). Figure 10.7 shows the results. The deterioration over the day represents a loss of alertness, and

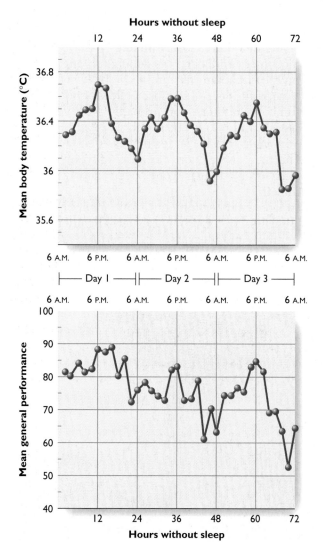

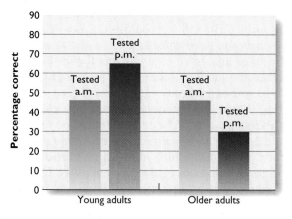

FIGURE 10.6 Cumulative effects of three nights without sleep: Both body temperature and reasoning decrease each night and increase the next morning. They also deteriorate from one day to the next. *(From Babkoff, Caspy, Mikulincer, & Sing, 1991)*

FIGURE 10.7 If tested early in the morning, older people perform as well as younger people on memory tasks. As the day progresses, young people improve and older people deteriorate.

older people can improve their afternoon performance by drinking caffeinated beverages (Ryan, Hatfield, & Hofstetter, 2002) or by exercising. Curiously, although explicit memory declines when people are at the less alert stage of their circadian rhythm, implicit memory improves when people are less alert (May, Hasher, & Foong, 2005).

The relationship between age and morning or evening arousal is apparently not specific to our culture or even our species. Young rats are about equally able to perform difficult tasks at all times of day, but aged rats do best shortly after they wake up and then deteriorate as the day goes on (Winocur & Hasher, 1999).

CRITICAL THINKING
A STEP FURTHER

Morning and Evening People

Are most college classes offered in the early morning or late afternoon? Is that because most students want to take them at that time or because their aging professors want to schedule them then?

Shifting Sleep Schedules

Ordinarily, the light of early morning resets the body's clock each day to keep it in synchrony with the outside world. If you travel across time zones, the light in your new location will eventually reset your clock to the new time, but until it does, your internal rhythms will be out of phase with your new environment. For example, if you travel from California to France, it will be 7 A.M. (time to wake up) when your body says it is 10 P.M. (getting close to bedtime). You will experience jet lag, *a period of discomfort and inefficiency while your internal clock is out of phase with your new surroundings.*

Most people find it easier to adjust when flying west, where they go to bed later, than when flying east, where they go to bed earlier. Thus, east-coast people adjust to west-coast time faster than west-coast people adjust to east-coast time (Figure 10.8).

It is possible to have an experience like jet lag without leaving town. Suppose you stay up late on Friday night and wake up late on Saturday morning. You stay up late again on Saturday and wake up late on Sunday. By Monday morning your circadian rhythm has reset, so when your clock says 7 A.M., it feels like 5 A.M., as if you had traveled a couple of time zones west.

Some businesses run three work shifts, such as midnight–8 A.M., 8 A.M.–4 P.M., and 4 P.M.–midnight. Because few people want to work regularly on the mid-

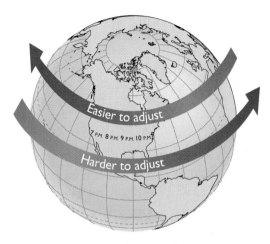

FIGURE 10.8 People traveling east suffer more serious jet lag than people traveling west.

night–8 A.M. shift, many companies rotate their workers among the three shifts. Suppose you worked the 8 A.M.–4 P.M. shift today but tomorrow you are scheduled for midnight–8 A.M. You can't get to sleep at 4 in the afternoon, so you show up for work at midnight without having slept. You are likely to make many mistakes during the night, and when you drive home the next morning, you will be as impaired as if you were legally drunk (Dawson & Reid, 1997). Even people who work the night shift month after month continue feeling groggy on the job and unable to sleep soundly during the day.

Employers can ease this burden on their workers in two ways: First, when they transfer workers from one shift to another, they should transfer workers to a *later* shift (Czeisler, Moore-Ede, & Coleman, 1982) (see Figure 10.9). That is, someone working the 8 A.M.–4 P.M. shift should switch to the 4 P.M.–midnight shift (equivalent to traveling west) instead of the midnight–8 A.M. shift (equivalent to traveling east).

Second, employers can help workers adjust to the night shift by providing bright lights that resemble sunlight. In one study young people exposed to very bright lights at night adjusted well to working at

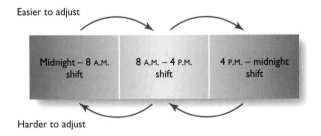

FIGURE 10.9 The graveyard shift is aptly named: Serious industrial accidents usually occur at night, when workers are least alert. As in jet lag, the direction of change is critical. Moving forward—clockwise—is easier than going backward.

night and sleeping during the day. Within 6 days their circadian rhythms had shifted to the new schedule. Another group who worked the same schedule under dimmer lights showed no indications of altering their circadian rhythms (Czeisler et al., 1990).

 CONCEPT CHECK

8. Suppose you are the president of a company in the United States. You are negotiating a difficult business deal with someone from the opposite side of the world. Should you prefer a meeting place in Europe or on an island in the Pacific Ocean? (Check your answer on page 385.)

 CRITICAL THINKING

A STEP FURTHER

Sleep Cycles

Imagine someone who cannot get to sleep until 3 A.M. For months she has been trying to get to bed earlier but failing. What advice would you offer? (Hint: Remember that our internal clocks can shift more easily to a later time than to an earlier time.)

Brain Mechanisms of Circadian Rhythms

The circadian rhythm of sleep and wakefulness is generated by a tiny structure at the base of the brain known as the *suprachiasmatic nucleus.* If that area of the brain is damaged, the body's activity cycles become erratic (Rusak, 1977). If cells from that area are kept alive outside the body, they generate a 24-hour rhythm on their own (Earnest, Liang, Ratcliff, & Cassone, 1999; Inouye & Kawamura, 1979). Cells in other body areas also produce daily rhythms, but those in the suprachiasmatic nucleus are sufficient by themselves to produce daily rhythms of activity and inactivity (Sujino et al., 2003). In short, this brain area is the body's clock (Figure 10.10).

The suprachiasmatic nucleus exerts its control partly by regulating the pineal gland's secretions of the hormone *melatonin,* which induces drowsiness. Ordinarily, the human pineal gland starts increasing its release of melatonin at about 8 to 10 P.M., so people find it easy to fall asleep about 2 or 3 hours later. If you take a melatonin pill in the evening, you will notice little if any effect because you were already producing increased melatonin at that time. However, if you have just flown a few time zones east and want to get to bed in a couple of hours, but you're not sleepy yet, then a melatonin pill can help (Deacon & Arendt, 1996).

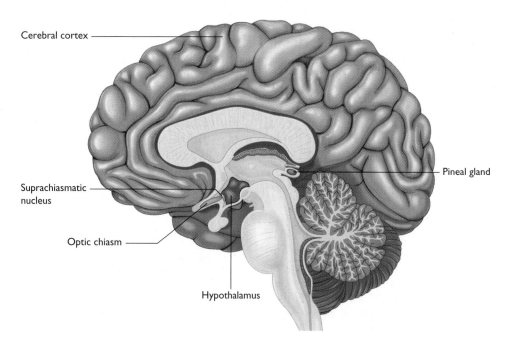

FIGURE 10.10 The suprachiasmatic nucleus, a small area at the base of the brain, produces the circadian rhythm. Information from the optic nerves resets the circadian rhythm but is not necessary for its generation.

CONCEPT CHECK

9. Suppose you are required to work the midnight–8 A.M. shift, and you would like to go to sleep at 4 P.M. to be well rested before starting work. Would a melatonin pill help? If so, when should you take it? (Check your answers on page 385.)

Why We Sleep

We would not have evolved a mechanism that forces us to spend one third of our lives sleeping unless sleep did us some good. But what good does it do? Scientists have identified several benefits.

The simplest is that sleep saves energy. When NASA sent a robot to explore Mars, they programmed it to shut down at nights, when exploration would only waste energy. Presumably, our ancient ancestors evolved sleep for the same reason. During sleep mammals and birds lower their body temperatures, and all animals decrease muscle activity. The result is a substantial saving of energy. When food is scarce, people conserve even more energy by sleeping longer and lowering their body temperature more than usual (Berger & Phillips, 1995).

Various animal species differ in their amount of sleep per day, in ways that make sense based on their way of life (Campbell & Tobler, 1984; Siegel, 2005). Predatory animals, including cats and bats, spend most of the day asleep. They get all the nutrition they need from brief, energy-rich meals, and they face little danger of being attacked during their sleep. In contrast prey species like horses need to spend many hours grazing, and their survival depends on running away from attackers, even at night (Figure 10.11). They sleep fewer hours and rouse easily. (Woody Allen once wrote, "The lion and the calf shall lie down together, but the calf won't get much sleep.")

Animals show many other specializations of sleep. Migratory birds forage for food during the day and do their migratory flying at night. That schedule leaves little time for sleep, and furthermore, they would have trouble finding a safe place to sleep at unfamiliar sites along their migratory route. Their solution is simple: They hardly sleep at all during migration. If a member of a migratory species is kept in a cage, it almost stops sleeping during the migration season. Instead, it paces back and forth nervously in its cage, all day and all night. These birds show no sign of sleep deprivation. In some way—which we haven't figured out how to bottle and sell—they actually decrease their need for sleep (Rattenborg et al., 2004).

Whales and dolphins face a different problem: Being mammals, they have to breathe while they sleep, and breathing requires swimming to the surface. Their solution is to sleep in half of the brain at a time so that one half or the other is always alert enough to enable breathing (Lyamin et al., 2002; Rattenborg, Amlaner, & Lima, 2000). During the first month or more after a baby whale or dolphin is born, it doesn't sleep at all, and neither does its mother (Lyamin, Pryaslova, Lance, & Siegel, 2005). Evidently, like migratory birds, they have found the secret to decreasing the need for sleep.

In addition to saving energy, we have evolved to accomplish other functions during sleep. Sleep provides an occasion for restorative functions in the brain. People who don't get enough sleep suffer. If you are not doing well in school or if you are frequently ill, consider

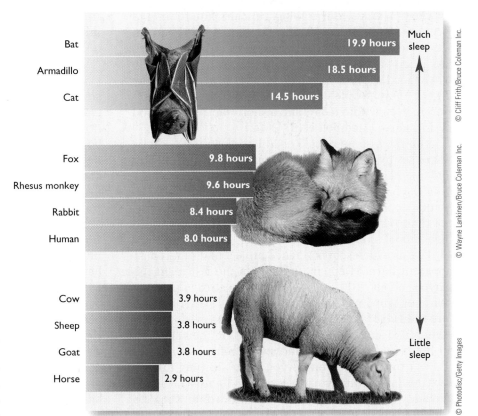

FIGURE 10.11 Predatory mammals sleep more than prey animals. Predators are seldom attacked during their sleep, but prey species need to arouse quickly from sleep to avoid being attacked. (*Based on data from Zepelin & Rechtschaffen, 1974*)

San Diego Historical Society

FIGURE 10.12 Even near the end of Randy Gardner's 264 consecutive sleepless hours, he performed tasks requiring strength and skill. Observers dutifully recorded his every move.

the possibility that you are not sleeping enough. Sleep deprivation leads to irritability, impairs attention, and weakens the immune system (Dement, 1972; Everson, 1995; Rechtschaffen & Bergmann, 1995). People who are sleep deprived make poor decisions, especially when faced with unexpected events (Harrison & Horne, 2000). Many people's alertness and performance deteriorate even within a day, and a short nap restores good performance (Mednick et al., 2002).

However, some people need less sleep than others. Some get by fine with 3 or 4 hours of sleep per night, and one healthy 70-year-old woman slept only about 1 hour each night (Meddis, Pearson, & Langford, 1973). Some people also tolerate sleep deprivation much better than others (Figure 10.12). In 1965 a San Diego high school student, Randy Gardner, stayed awake for 11 days as a high school science project and suffered no apparent harm (Dement, 1972). On the last night, he played about 100 arcade games against sleep researcher William Dement and won every game. Just before the end of the 264 hours, he held a television press conference and handled himself well. He then slept for 14 hours and 40 minutes and awoke refreshed.

If a torturer prevented you from sleeping for the next 11 days, would you do as well as Randy Gardner? Probably not, for two reasons: First, Gardner knew he could quit if necessary. A sense of control makes any experience less stressful. Second, people vary in their ability to tolerate sleep deprivation. We heard about Gardner only because he tolerated it so well. We have

no idea how many other people tried to deprive themselves of sleep for many days but gave up.

Sleep also strengthens learning and memory, including both motor skills and language-related tasks (Marshall, Helgadóttir, Mölle, & Born, 2006; Stickgold, 2005). If you learn something today, your memory of it will improve tomorrow if you get a good night's sleep (Fenn, Nusbaum, & Margoliash, 2003; Stickgold, Whidbee, Schirmer, Patel, & Hobson, 2000). When people learn a difficult new motor task, such as a video game skill, the brain areas active during the learning also become activated during sleep that night. Furthermore, a high level of activity in those areas during sleep predicts significant improvement of the skill the next day (Huber, Ghilardi, Massimini, & Tononi, 2004; Maquet et al., 2000; Peigneux et al., 2004). Sleep also helps people reanalyze their memories: In one study people who had just practiced a complex task were more likely to perceive a hidden rule (an "aha" experience) after a period of sleep than after a similar period of wakefulness (Wagner, Gais, Haider, Verleger, & Born, 2004). In short, sleep helps store and reorganize several types of learning and memory.

Stages of Sleep

In the mid-1950s American and French researchers independently discovered a stage of sleep called *paradoxical sleep,* or **rapid eye movement (REM) sleep** (Dement & Kleitman, 1957a, 1957b; Jouvet, Michel, & Courjon, 1959). *During this stage of sleep, the sleeper's eyes move rapidly back and forth under the closed lids.* (All other stages of sleep are known as non-REM, or NREM, sleep.) A paradox is an apparent contradiction; REM sleep is paradoxical because it is light in some ways and deep in others. It is light because the brain is active and the body's heart rate, breathing rate, and temperature fluctuate substantially (Parmeggiani, 1982). It is deep because the large muscles of the body that control posture and locomotion are deeply relaxed. Indeed, the nerves to those muscles are virtually paralyzed at this time. REM also has some features that are hard to classify as deep or light, such as penis erections and vaginal lubrication.

William Dement's early research indicated that people who were awakened during REM sleep usually reported they had been dreaming, but people who were awakened during any other period seldom reported dreaming. So at first REM sleep was thought to be almost synonymous with dreaming. Later research has weakened that link, however. Adults who are awakened during REM sleep report dreams about 85 to 90% of the time, whereas those awakened during NREM sleep report dreams on 50 to 60% of occasions (Foulkes, 1999). REM dreams are on the average longer, more complicated, and more visual, but not always. REM dreams include more violent themes and more incidents of the dreamer taking action, instead of viewing passively or receiving other people's actions (McNamara, McLaren, Smith, Brown, & Stickgold, 2005). Furthermore, some people with brain damage have REM sleep but no dreams, and others have dreams but no REM sleep (Solms, 1997). Thus, REM is not synonymous with dreaming (Domhoff, 1999).

Sleep Cycles During the Night

Decades ago, almost everyone assumed that brain activity nearly shut down during sleep. In fact neurons' metabolic rate, spontaneous activity, and responsiveness to stimuli decrease less than 20% during sleep (Hobson, 2005). The main characteristic is an increase of inhibitory messages, preventing most brain messages from reverberating to other neurons for long (Massimini et al., 2005). However, the inhibition is not constant. Over the course of the night, the nature of the sleep experience changes repeatedly.

Sleep researchers distinguish among sleep stages by recording brain waves with electrodes attached to the scalp (Figure 10.13). *A device* called an **electroencephalograph (EEG)** *measures and amplifies tiny electrical changes on the scalp that reflect patterns of brain activity.* Sleep researchers *combine an EEG measure with a simultaneous measure of eye movements to produce a* **polysomnograph** (literally, "many-sleep measure"), as shown in Figure 10.14. Upon falling asleep one enters non-REM stage 1, when the eyes are nearly motionless and the EEG shows many short, choppy waves, as shown in Figure 10.14a. These small waves indicate a fair amount of brain activity, with brain cells firing out of synchrony with one another. Because they are out of synchrony, their activities nearly cancel each other out, like the sound of many people talking at the same time.

As sleep continues a person progresses into non-REM stages 2, 3, and 4, as shown in Figure 10.14b–e. These stages are most easily distinguished by the number of long, slow waves. Stage 2 has the fewest and stage 4 has the most. These large waves indicate synchrony among neurons, which occurs during *decreased* brain activity. The waves grow larger from one stage to the next because the brain has little stim-

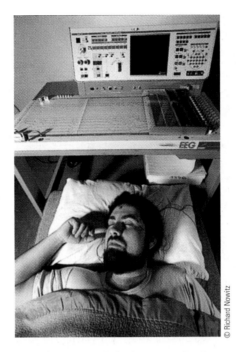

FIGURE 10.13 Electrodes monitor the activity in a sleeper's brain, and an EEG then records and displays brain-wave patterns.

© Richard Nowitz

ulation, so the little activity that does occur drives many neurons in synchrony. The eyes remain nearly motionless in each of these stages.

After stage 4 a sleeper gradually moves back through stages 3 and 2. After stage 2, the sleeper enters REM sleep, not stage 1. In Figure 10.14f the EEG in REM sleep resembles that of stage 1, but the eyes are steadily moving. At the end of REM sleep, the sleeper cycles through stages 2, 3, 4, and then back to 3, 2, and REM again. In a healthy young adult, each cycle lasts 90 to 100 minutes on average. As shown in Figure 10.15, over the course of the night, stages 3 and 4 become shorter while REM and stage 2 increase in duration. Figure 10.15 represents sleep under quiet, undisturbed conditions. Someone who sleeps in an uncomfortable room will have many awakenings and little stage 3 or 4 sleep (Velluti, 1997).

Sleep Stages and Dreaming

The interest in REM sleep prompted sleep investigators to awaken people during REM sleep and ask for dream reports to answer some basic questions. For example, does everyone dream? Adults who claim they do not dream have been taken into the laboratory and attached to a polysomnograph, which revealed normal periods of REM sleep. When they were awakened during a REM period, they usually reported dreaming, to their own surprise. Apparently, they dream but quickly forget their dreams.

Another question: How long do dreams last? William Dement and Edward Wolpert (1958) awakened people after REM periods of various durations and asked them to describe their dreams. Someone awakened after 1 minute of REM usually told a brief story; someone awakened after 5 minutes of REM usually told a story about 5 times as long and so on. That is, a dream is not over in a split second; if a dream seemed to last several minutes, it probably did.

 CONCEPT CHECK

10. Is dreaming more common toward the end of the night's sleep or toward the beginning? (Check your answer on page 385.)

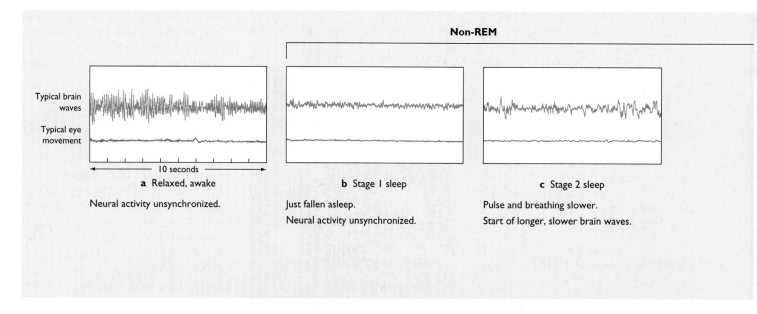

FIGURE 10.14 During sleep people progress through stages of varying brain activity. The blue line indicates brain waves, as shown by an EEG. The red line shows eye movements. REM sleep resembles stage 1 sleep, except for the addition of rapid eye movements. *(Six panels of EEG's reprinted by permission of T. E. LeVere.)*

FIGURE 10.15 This sleeper had five cycles of REM and non-REM sleep and awakened (A) briefly three times during the night. Stage 4 occupies more time early in the night than later. REM becomes more prevalent as the night progresses. *(From Dement, 1972)*

The Functions of REM Sleep

Given that people spend 20 to 25% of an average night in REM sleep, REM presumably serves an important function, but what? The most direct way to approach this question is to deprive people of REM sleep and study how this deprivation affects their health or behavior.

In one study Dement (1960) monitored the sleep of eight young men for seven consecutive nights and awakened them for a few minutes whenever their EEG and eye movements indicated the onset of REM sleep. He awakened the members of a control group equally often but at random times so that he did not necessarily interrupt their REM sleep. Over the course of 1 week, Dement found it harder and harder to prevent REM sleep in the experimental group—and harder to keep them from quitting the experiment. On the first night, the average participant had to be awakened 12 times; by the seventh night, 26 times. During the day REM-deprived participants experienced anxiety, irritability, and impaired concentration. However, in this and related studies, the effects of REM deprivation were not catastrophic. Furthermore, drugs called monoamine oxidase inhibitors inhibit REM but produce none of the problems attributed to REM deprivation (Siegel, 2005).

A second approach is to determine which people get more REM sleep than others. One clear pattern is that infants get more REM sleep than children and children more than adults. From that observation many researchers have inferred that REM sleep serves a function that is more acute in younger people. However, infants not only get more REM sleep but also more total sleep (Figure 10.16). If we compare species, we find that the species that get the most sleep (e.g., cats) also generally have the greatest percentage of REM sleep.

Among adult humans those who sleep 9 or more hours per night spend a large percentage of that time in REM sleep; those who sleep 6 hours or fewer also get less REM sleep. In short, those who sleep the most spend the greatest percentage of that time in REM. It is as though a certain amount of *non*-REM sleep is necessary each night, and additional amounts of REM sleep are added if sleep continues long enough (Horne, 1988).

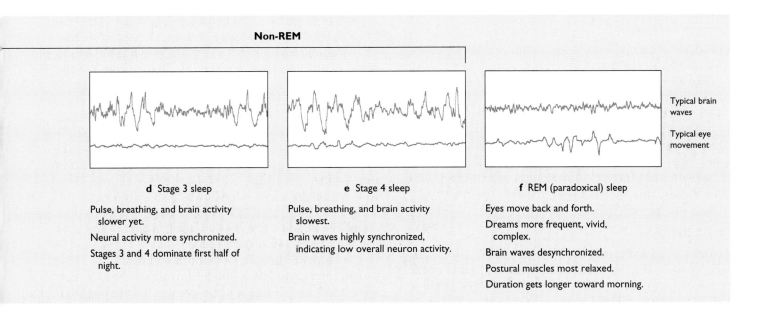

Non-REM

Typical brain waves

Typical eye movement

d Stage 3 sleep

Pulse, breathing, and brain activity slower yet.

Neural activity more synchronized.

Stages 3 and 4 dominate first half of night.

e Stage 4 sleep

Pulse, breathing, and brain activity slowest.

Brain waves highly synchronized, indicating low overall neuron activity.

f REM (paradoxical) sleep

Eyes move back and forth.

Dreams more frequent, vivid, complex.

Brain waves desynchronized.

Postural muscles most relaxed.

Duration gets longer toward morning.

3 A.M.   4 A.M.   5 A.M.   6 A.M.   7 A.M.

2 3 2   REM   1 2 3 2 A 1   REM   A 1 A 2   REM

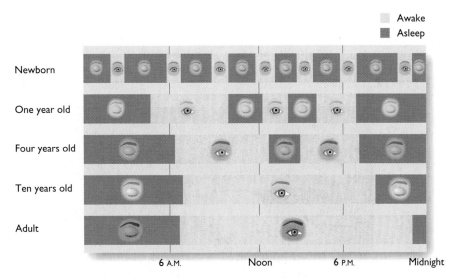

Awake
Asleep

Newborn

One year old

Four years old

Ten years old

Adult

6 A.M.   Noon   6 P.M.   Midnight

FIGURE 10.16 Newborns' sleep alternates between wakefulness and naps throughout the day. Within a few months, infants consolidate most of their sleep into one longer period at night, although they continue having one or two naps during the day. As people grow older, the amount of sleep per day decreases. *(Based on Kleitman, 1963)*

Abnormalities of Sleep

Comedian Steven Wright says that someone asked him, "Did you sleep well last night?" He replied, "No, I made a few mistakes."

We laugh because sleep isn't the kind of activity on which you make mistakes. Sometimes, however, we fail to sleep, fail to feel rested afterward, or have bad dreams. We would not call these experiences "mistakes," but our sleep is not what we wanted it to be.

For more information in general about sleep disorders, visit this website: www.thesleepsite.com/.

Insomnia

Insomnia literally means "lack of sleep." However, some people feel well rested after fewer than 6 hours of sleep per night; others feel poorly rested after 9 hours. A better definition of **insomnia** is *not enough sleep for the person to feel rested the next day.* Insomnia can result from a huge number of causes, including noise, worries, indigestion, uncomfortable temperatures, use of alcohol or caffeine, and medical or psychological disorders (Ohayon, 1997). If you experience persistent insomnia, consult a physician, but for occasional or minor insomnia, you can try a few things yourself (Hauri, 1982; Lilie & Rosenberg, 1990):

- Keep a regular time schedule for going to bed and waking up each day.
- Avoid caffeine, nicotine, and other stimulants, especially in the evening.
- Don't rely on alcohol or tranquilizers to fall asleep. After repeated use you may become dependent on them and unable to get to sleep without them.
- Keep your bedroom cool and quiet.
- Exercise daily but not shortly before bedtime.

Sleep Apnea

One type of insomnia is sleep apnea (AP-nee-uh). *Apnea* means "no breathing." Many people have irregular breathing or occasional periods of 10 seconds or so without breathing during their sleep. People with **sleep apnea**, however, *fail to breathe for a minute or more and then wake up gasping for breath.* When they manage to breathe during their sleep, they generally snore. They may lie in bed for 8 to 10 hours per night but sleep less than half that time. During the following day, they feel sleepy and may have headaches.

Although many people with sleep apnea have mild brain abnormalities (Macey et al., 2002), some of the brain abnormalities are probably the result of years of poor sleep rather than the cause of it. The most common cause of apnea is obstructions in the breathing passages. When someone with a very large abdomen—usually, a middle-aged man—lies on his back, the abdomen's weight interferes with the diaphragm muscles that control breathing. Also the airways become narrow, especially while lying down to sleep (Mezzanotte, Tangel, & White, 1992). Sleep apnea is reported in about 8% of adult men, 4% of adult women, and 2 or 3% of children (Moorcroft, 2003).

Treatment includes recommendations to lose weight and avoid alcohol and tranquilizers, which slow breathing. Surgeons can remove tissue to widen the airways. Some people with sleep apnea use a device that pumps air into a mask covering the nose and mouth during sleep, forcing the person to breathe.

Narcolepsy

People with **narcolepsy** experience *sudden attacks of extreme, even irresistible, sleepiness in the middle of the day.* They also experience sudden attacks of muscle weakness or paralysis and occasional dreamlike experiences while awake. These symptoms could be interpreted as a sudden intrusion of REM sleep into the waking period of the day (Guilleminault, Heinzer, Mignot, & Black, 1998).

Narcolepsy also occurs in dogs with a particular gene. Researchers discovered that this gene controls the brain receptors for a transmitter called *orexin*, also known as *hypocretin* (Lin et al., 1999). Other researchers found that preventing the production of orexin causes narcolepsy in mice (Chemelli et al., 1999). People with narcolepsy have fewer than the normal number of neurons that produce orexin (Thanickal et al., 2000). Orexin does not wake people up, but it helps keep them awake (M. G. Lee, Hassani, & Jones, 2005). People lacking orexin alternate between wakefulness and sleepiness repeatedly over a day, instead of remaining awake during the day and remaining asleep at night (Mochizuki et al., 2004).

Insomnia is identified by how sleepy the person is the following day.

© Tony Hutchings/Getty Images

A combination of stimulant and antidepressant drugs maintains wakefulness during the day and blocks the attacks of muscle weakness. Future research may develop medications based on orexin, but none are available currently.

Sleep Talking, Sleepwalking, Nightmares, and Night Terrors

Many people, whether or not they suffer from insomnia, have unsettling experiences during their sleep. Sleep talking is the most common and least troublesome. Most people talk in their sleep more often than they realize because they do not remember sleep talking and usually no one else hears them. Sleep talking is most common during stage 2 sleep, but it can occur during any stage (Moorcroft, 2003). It ranges from a single indistinct word to a clearly articulated paragraph. Sleep talkers sometimes pause between utterances, as if they were carrying on a conversation with someone else. In fact it is possible to engage some sleep talkers in a dialogue. Sleep talking is not related to any mental or emotional disorder, and sleep talkers rarely say anything that they would be embarrassed to say when awake.

Sleepwalking tends to run (walk?) in families. True sleepwalking occurs mostly in children during stage 4 sleep and lasts fewer than 15 minutes. Few children hurt themselves when sleepwalking, and most children outgrow it (Dement, 1972). Some adults sleepwalk also, mostly during the first half of the night's sleep. Apparently, the brain arouses partly but not fully. The person engages in clumsy, apparently purposeless movements with only limited responsiveness to surroundings. Awakening a sleepwalker is not dangerous, but it is not particularly helpful either (Moorcroft, 2003). A better idea is to guide the person gently back to bed.

Other concerns include nightmares and night terrors. Nightmares are merely unpleasant dreams, common for anyone. A night terror, however, causes someone to awaken screaming and sweating with a racing heart rate, sometimes flailing with the arms and pounding the walls. Night terrors occur during stage 3 or stage 4 sleep, not REM, and their dream content is usually simple, like a single image rather than a story. Sometimes, people report no dream content at all. Comforting or reassuring people during a night terror is futile, and the terror simply has to run its course. Night terrors are fairly common in young children and occur in nearly 3% of adults (Mahowald & Schenck, 2005). Treatments include psychotherapy, antidepressant and anti-anxiety drugs, and advice to minimize stress. Children with night terrors are particularly advised to avoid frightening movies (Vgontzas & Kales, 1999).

Leg Movements While Trying to Sleep

Have you ever lain in bed, trying to fall asleep, when suddenly one of your legs kicked? An occasional leg jerk while trying to fall asleep is common and no cause for concern. In contrast some people have *prolonged "creepy-crawly" sensations in their legs, accompanied by repetitive leg movements strong enough to awaken the person, especially during the first half of the night* (Moorcroft, 1993). This condition, known as **periodic limb movement disorder** (or more informally as restless leg syndrome), interrupts sleep in many people over age 50. The causes are unknown, and the best advice is to avoid factors that make the condition worse, such as caffeine, stress, or fatigue. Tranquilizers sometimes suppress these leg movements (Schenck & Mahowald, 1996).

 CONCEPT CHECK

11. Why would sleepwalking be unlikely or impossible during REM? (Check your answer on page 385.)

The Content of Our Dreams

> Even a saint is not responsible for what happens in his dreams.
>
> —*St. Thomas Aquinas*

What do we dream about and why? People once believed that dreams foretold the future. Occasionally, of course, they do, either by coincidence or because the dreamer had a reason to expect some outcome. Today, psychologists do not expect dreams to tell us about the future, but some look to dreams to tell us something about the dreamer. Even that effort is controversial, however.

Freud's Approach

The Austrian physician and founder of psychoanalysis, Sigmund Freud, maintained that dreams reveal the dreamer's unconscious thoughts and motivations. To understand a dream, he said, one must probe for hidden meanings. Each dream has a **manifest content**—*the content that appears on the surface*—and a **latent content**—*the hidden ideas that the dream experience represents symbolically.*

For example, Freud (1900/1955) once dreamed that one of his friends was his uncle. He worked out these associations: Both this friend and another one had been recommended for an appointment as professor at the university. Both had been turned down, probably because they were Jews. Freud himself had been recently recommended for the same appointment, but he feared that he too would be rejected for the same reason. Freud's only uncle had once been convicted of illegal business dealings. Freud's father had said, however, that the uncle was not bad, but just a simpleton.

How did the two friends relate to the uncle? One of the friends was in Freud's judgment a bit simpleminded. The other had once been accused of sexual misconduct, although he was not convicted. By linking these two friends to his uncle, Freud interpreted the dream as meaning, "Maybe they didn't get the university appointment because one was a simpleton (like my uncle) and the other was regarded as a criminal (like my uncle). If so, my being Jewish might not stop me from getting the appointment."

In some cases Freud relied on individual associations, as in the dream just described, but often, he assumed that certain elements have predicable meanings, regardless of whether the dreamer agrees. For example, he claimed that the number three in a dream represented a man's penis and testes. Anything long, such as a stick or pole, represented the penis. So did anything that could penetrate the body, such as a knife or gun; anything from which water flows; anything that can be lengthened; almost any tool; and anything that can fly or float—because rising is like an erection (Freud, 1935). He admitted that if you dream about a knife or an airplane, you really might be dreaming about a knife or airplane instead of a penis, but he was confident that a skilled psychoanalyst could tell the difference (even if the dreamer could not).

One of Freud's most famous dream analyses concerned a man who reported remembering a dream from when he was 4 years old (!) in which he saw six or seven white dogs with large tails sitting motionless in a tree outside his window. (The actual dream was of spitz dogs, although Freud wrote about them as wolves.) After a laborious line of reasoning, Freud concluded that the child had dreamed about his parents in their bedclothes—presumably white, like the dogs in the dream. The dogs' lack of motion represented its opposite—frantic sexual activity. The big tails also represented their opposite—the boy's fear of having his penis cut off. In short, said Freud, the boy had dreamed about watching his parents have sex—doggy style. Decades later, researchers located the man who had told this dream to Freud. He reported that (a) he regarded Freud's interpretation of his dream as far-fetched and (b) Freud's treatment did him no apparent good, as he spent many later years in continued treatment (Esterson, 1993).

Regardless of Freud's interpretations, the key question is whether *anyone* can listen to dreams and determine hidden aspects of the dreamer's motivations and personality. Undoubtedly, many therapists

do offer dream interpretations that their clients find meaningful. However, psychoanalysts offer no evidence to back their conclusions. Freud's approach to dream analysis, popular for many years, is now on the decline because of its untestable interpretations (Domhoff, 2003).

 CONCEPT CHECK

12. Are Freud's ideas on dreaming falsifiable in the sense described in chapter 2? (Check your answer on page 385.)

The Activation-Synthesis Theory

A modern theory relates dream content to spontaneous activity that arises in the brain during REM sleep. According to the **activation-synthesis theory of dreams,** *input arising from the pons (see Figure 3.3) activates the brain during REM sleep. The cortex takes that haphazard activity plus whatever stimuli strike the sense organs and does its best to synthesize a story that makes sense of this activity* (Hobson & McCarley, 1977). The activation-synthesis theory does not regard our dreams as meaningless. Even if dreams begin with random brain activity, the dreamer's interpretations of this activity reflect his or her personality, motivations, and previous experiences. Still, the activation-synthesis theory sees meaning as a by-product of other processes, not the cause of the dream.

Some aspects of dreams appear to relate to the spontaneous activity of the brain during REM sleep. For a basic example, input from the pons activates the visual areas of the brain during REM sleep, especially during the first minutes of a REM period, and nearly all dreams include visual content (Amzica & Steriade, 1996). Also, when people dream of using a toilet or trying to find a toilet, they often awake and discover that they really do need to use a toilet. Many people occasionally dream of flying or falling, probably because the vestibular system detects the body's horizontal position and the brain interprets this sensation as floating or flying (Hobson & McCarley, 1977; Velluti, 1997).

Have you ever dreamed that you are trying to walk or run away, but you cannot move? One explanation is that the major postural muscles are really paralyzed during REM sleep. Thus, your brain could send messages telling your muscles to move but then receive sensory feedback indicating that they have not moved at all.

The main problem with the activation-synthesis theory is that it does not make clear, testable predictions. For example, people almost always sleep horizontally but only occasionally dream of flying or falling. Why not always? Our muscles are always paralyzed during REM sleep. Why don't we always dream that we can't move? *After* a dream the activation-synthesis theory can provide explanations, but it offers few predictions. It does predict that sounds and other stimuli in the room might be incorporated into the dream, but in fact few dreams show any connection to such stimuli.

The Neurocognitive Theory

Sometimes, you may have a dream that strikes you as so strange that you never would have thought of such a thing in waking life. Nevertheless, you did think of it while dreaming. The **neurocognitive theory** *treats dreams as a kind of thinking that occurs under special conditions* (Domhoff, 2001; Foulkes, 1999; Solms, 2000). These conditions include:

- persisting activity of much of the cortex
- great reduction of sensory stimulation, including reduced activity in the primary sensory areas of the brain
- loss of voluntary self-control of thinking

As a result the brain is active enough to engage in imagination, which sensory information does not override. According to this theory, REM sleep is not necessary for dreaming, although the arousal associated with REM intensifies dreams. Arousal in the temporal lobe of the cortex adds emotional content to most dreams (Maquet et al., 1996).

Researchers working within this framework have attempted to describe people's dreams. Sometimes, people keep dream diaries or report the most recent dream they remember. Sometimes, researchers awaken people in the laboratory and ask for immediate dream reports (Domhoff, 2003). Table 10.1 lists common dream themes of college students in the United States and Japan in 1958 and Canada in 2003 (Griffith, Miyagi, & Tago, 1958; Nielsen et al., 2003). Note the similarity across the three samples. Note also that many dreams deal with "things that could go wrong," such as falling, being chased, or being unable to do something. The most common emotion in adult dreams is apprehension or fear. Dreams include more misfortune than good fortune (Domhoff, 1996; Hall & Van de Castle, 1966). Men have violent dreams more often than women, but both have a fair number (Schredl, Ciric, Bishop, Gölitz, & Buschtöns, 2003). People occasionally awaken with disappointment that it was only a dream, but more often with relief. Curiously, 11- to 13-year-olds have the happiest dreams on the average (Foulkes, 1999).

Although some memorable dreams are bizarre, most are commonplace and similar to the interests of

TABLE 10.1 Percentages of College Students Who Reported Certain Dream Topics

Dream Topic	U.S. 1958	Japan 1958	Canada 2003
Falling	83%	74%	74%
Being attacked or pursued	77%	91%	82%
Trying to do something again and again	71%	87%	54%
Schoolwork	71%	86%	67%
Sex	66%	68%	76%
Arriving too late	64%	49%	60%
Eating delicious food	62%	68%	31%
Frozen with fright	58%	87%	41%
Loved one dying	57%	42%	54%

Based on Griffith et al. (1958); Nielsen et al. (2003)

everyday life (Domhoff, 1996; Hall & Van de Castle, 1966). For example, preteens seldom dream about the opposite sex, but teenagers do (Strauch & Lederbogen, 1999). Blind people frequently dream about difficulties in locomotion or transportation (Hurovitz, Dunn, Domhoff, & Fiss, 1999). In one study young adults checked off from a list the topics (e.g., marriage, family, friends, and hobbies) those that were concerns to them and others that were matters of indifference. Then they reported their dreams over three nights. They frequently dreamed of the concerns and very rarely of the indifferent topics (Nikles, Brecht, Klinger, & Bursell, 1998). However, we do not dream about everything we do in daily life. People seldom dream about reading, writing, using a computer, or watching television (Schredl, 2000). For the best research on the content of dreams, visit this website: **http://psych.ucsc.edu/dreams/**.

The ability to dream requires cognitive maturity (Foulkes, 1999). Even infants have a great deal of REM sleep, but children younger than 5 years old who are awakened during REM sleep seldom report a clear dream. It is hard to know whether they don't have dreams or just can't report them. The dreams that young children report are mostly of unmoving images. Even somewhat older children report dreams in fewer than half of their REM awakenings. Those with the strongest visuospatial abilities, such as the ability to solve puzzles, generally report the clearest dreams. Table 10.2 outlines stages of the development of dreaming in children.

You might try keeping a dream diary and checking the content of your dreams. Do you in fact dream mostly about the topics that you think about while you are awake?

Try It Yourself

TABLE 10.2 Stages in the Development of Dreaming in Children

Age	Frequency of Dream Reports if Awakened During REM Sleep	Median Length of Dream Report	Typical Dream Content
3–5 years	15%, including many questionable reports	14 words	A single motionless image; many reports of animals; almost none about the self; almost no emotions
5–7 years	31%	41 words	Simple event with some motion; self seldom does anything
7–9 years	43%	72 words	More complex stories, including many with active self; mostly happy with some fear

Based on Foulkes (1999)

SLOW WAVE

SLOW WAVE

These comic strips represent actual dreams as described to the artist. Dreams often mix possible with impossible events and frequently explore the theme of "things that could go wrong." *(Reprinted with permission of Jesse Reklaw.)*

Many other questions about dreaming are difficult to answer. For example, how accurately do we remember our dreams? Well, how would we find out? With real events we compare people's memories to what actually happened, but we have no way to compare reported dreams to the originals. Or consider this apparently simple question: Do we dream in color? The fact that people ask this question reveals why it is difficult to answer: They ask because they do not remember whether their dreams were in color. But how could an investigator determine whether people dream in color except by asking them to remember? The best evidence we have is that, when people are awakened during REM sleep, when their recall should be as sharp as possible, they report color at least half of the time (Herman, Roffwarg, & Tauber, 1968; Padgham, 1975). This result does not mean that their other dreams are in black and white. Perhaps the colors in those dreams were not memorable.

You might wonder whether people who are blind have visual dreams. It depends. People who experienced eye damage after about age 5 to 7 continue to have visual dreams. However, people who were born blind or who became blind in early childhood have no visual imagery in their dreams; instead, they dream of sounds, touch, smells, and taste (Hurovitz et al., 1999). Sighted people rarely dream of smells or tastes (Zadra, Nielsen, & Donderi, 1998). People who become blind because of damage to the visual cortex lose visual dreaming as well as visual imagery.

✓ CONCEPT CHECK

13. According to the neurocognitive theory of dreaming, how does dreaming differ from other thinking? (Check your answer on page 385.)

IN CLOSING

The Mysteries of Sleep and Dreams

Sleep and dreams are not a state of unconsciousness, but a state of reduced or altered consciousness. For example, a parent will awaken at the sound of a child softly crying. The brain is never completely off duty, never completely relaxed.

Although our understanding of sleep and dreams continues to grow, major questions remain. Even such basic issues as the function of REM sleep remain in doubt. People have long found their dreams a source of wonder, and researchers continue to find much of interest and mystery. ▮

Summary

- *Circadian rhythms.* Sleepiness depends on the time of day. Even in an unchanging environment, people become sleepy in cycles of approximately 24 hours. (page 371)
- *The need for sleep.* Sleep serves several functions, including conservation of energy, an occasion for restorative functions in the brain, and an occasion for strengthening of memories, especially of motor skills. (page 375)
- *Sleep stages.* During sleep people cycle through sleep stages 1 through 4 and back through stages 3 and 2 to 1 again. The cycle beginning and ending with stage 1 lasts about 90 to 100 minutes. (page 376)
- *REM sleep.* A special stage known as REM sleep replaces many of the stage 1 periods. REM sleep is characterized by rapid eye movements, a high level of brain activity, and relaxed muscles. People usually dream during this stage but dream in other stages also. The function of REM sleep is uncertain. (page 376)
- *Insomnia.* Insomnia—subjectively unsatisfactory sleep—can result from many influences, including sleep apnea and narcolepsy. (page 380)
- *The content of dreams.* Freud proposed that dreams are the product of unconscious wishes. The activation-synthesis theory claims that dreams are an accidental by-product of arousal during REM sleep. The neurocognitive theory states that dreaming is just thinking, except that it occurs under conditions of low sensory input and no voluntary control of thinking. (page 381)

Answers to Concept Checks

8. You should prefer to schedule the meeting on a Pacific island so that you will travel west and the other person will travel east. (page 373)
9. Try a melatonin pill 2 or 3 hours before your desired bedtime. (page 374)
10. REM sleep and dreaming are more common toward the end of the night's sleep. (page 377)
11. During REM sleep the major postural muscles of the body are completely relaxed. (pages 376, 381)
12. No. A falsifiable theory makes specific predictions so that we could imagine evidence that would contradict it. Freud's theories about dreams make no clear predictions. (page 382)
13. According to the neurocognitive theory, dreaming is like other thinking, except that it occurs during a time of decreased sensory input and loss of voluntary control of thinking. (page 383)

Hypnosis

- *What can hypnosis do?*
- *What are its limitations?*

Truth is nothing but a path traced between errors.[1]

—*Franz Anton Mesmer*

If a hypnotist told you that you were 4 years old and you suddenly starting acting like a 4-year-old, we would say that you are a good hypnotic subject. If the hypnotist told you that your cousin was sitting in the empty chair in front of you and you said that you see her, then again we would remark on the depth of your hypnotism.

But what if you had *not* been hypnotized and you suddenly started acting like a 4-year-old or insisted that you saw someone in that empty chair? In this case psychologists would suspect that you were suffering from a serious psychological disorder. Hypnosis induces a temporary state that is sometimes bizarre. No wonder we find it so fascinating.

Hypnosis is *a condition of increased suggestibility that occurs in the context of a special hypnotist–subject relationship.* The term *hypnosis* comes from Hypnos, the Greek god of sleep, although the similarity between hypnosis and sleep is superficial. People in both states lose initiative, and hypnotized people, like dreamers, accept contradictory information without protest. Hypnotized people, however, walk around and respond to objects in the real world. Also, their EEG is not like that of sleepers. It is more like that of a relaxed wakeful person (Rainville, Hofbauer, Bushnell, Duncan, & Price, 2002).

Hypnosis was introduced by Franz Anton Mesmer (1734–1815), an Austrian physician. When treating medical problems, Mesmer would pass a magnet back and forth across the patient's body to redirect the flow of blood, nerve activity, and undefined "fluids." Some patients reported dramatic benefits. Later, Mesmer discovered that he could dispense with the magnet and use only his hand. From this observation you or I would conclude that the phenomenon related to the power of suggestion instead of magnetism. Mesmer, however, drew the quirky conclusion that he did not need a magnet because *he himself* was a magnet. With that claim he gave us the term "animal magnetism."

After his death others studied "animal magnetism" or "Mesmerism," eventually calling it "hypnotism." By that time many physicians and scientists had already associated hypnosis with charlatans and hocus-pocus. Even today, some stage performers use hypnosis for entertainment. We should carefully distinguish the exaggerated claims from the legitimate use of hypnosis by licensed therapists.

Ways of Inducing Hypnosis

Mesmer thought hypnosis was a power emanating from his own body. If so, only special people could hypnotize others. Today, we believe that becoming a successful hypnotist requires practice but no unusual powers or personality.

The first step toward being hypnotized is agreeing to give it a try. Contrary to what you may have heard, no one can hypnotize an uncooperative person. The hypnotist tells you, for example, to sit down and relax,

Although Mesmer is often depicted as irresistibly controlling people, hypnosis depends on the person's willingness.

© Mary Evans Picture Library

---

[1] Does this seem profound? Or is it nonsense? Many statements sound profound until we try to figure out exactly what they mean.

and you do so because you would like to experience hypnosis. The whole point of hypnosis is doing what the hypnotist suggests, and by sitting down and relaxing, you are already starting to follow suggestions.

A hypnotist might then monotonously repeat something like, "You are starting to fall asleep. Your eyelids are getting heavy. Your eyelids are getting very heavy. They are starting to close. You are falling into a deep, deep sleep." In another technique (Udolf, 1981) the hyp-

A hypnotist induces hypnosis by repeating suggestions, relying on the hypnotized person's cooperation and willingness to accept suggestions.

notist suggests, "After you go under hypnosis, your arm will begin to rise automatically." (Some people, eager for the hypnosis to succeed, shoot their arm up immediately and have to be told, "No, not yet. Just relax; that will happen later.") Then the hypnotist encourages you to relax and suggests that your arm is starting to feel lighter, as if it were tied to a helium balloon.

The hypnotist might suggest that your arm is beginning to feel strange and is beginning to twitch. The timing of this suggestion is important because when people stand or sit in one position long enough, their limbs really do feel strange and twitch. If the hypnotist's suggestion comes at just the right moment, you think, "Wow, that's right. My arm does feel strange. This is starting to work!" Believing that you are being hypnotized is a big step toward actually being hypnotized.

The Uses and Limitations of Hypnosis

Hypnosis can produce relaxation, concentration, and changes in behavior, some of which persist after the end of the hypnotic state. Hynotizability is similar to ordinary suggestibility. If I asked you to imagine a bright, sunny day, you almost certainly would, even without being hypnotized. If I asked you to please stand and put your hands on your head, you probably would (if I asked nicely), again without being hypnotized. If I asked you to stand, flap your arms, and cluck like a chicken, you might or might not. People vary in how far they will follow suggestions without hypnosis, and suggestibility without hypnosis correlates with hypnosis. You might follow suggestions a little more with hypnosis than without, but only a little (J. Kirsch & Braffman, 2001). If you are highly hypnotizable and highly suggestible, you probably also re-

spond strongly to books and movies, reacting almost as if the events were really happening. That is, hypnotizability is a variation on people's normal suggestibility.

What Hypnosis Can Do

One well-established effect of hypnosis is to inhibit pain. Some people can undergo medical or dental surgery with only hypnosis and no anesthesia. The benefits of hypnosis are most easily demonstrated for acute (sudden) pains, but hypnosis can help with chronic pains too if carefully administered (Patterson, 2004). Hypnosis is particularly helpful for people who react unfavorably to anesthetic drugs and those who have developed a tolerance for painkilling opiates.

Recall from chapter 4 that pain has both sensory and emotional components. Hypnosis alters mostly the emotional components. Even when a hypnotized person says that he or she feels no pain, the heart rate and blood pressure still increase substantially (Hilgard, 1973). Under hypnotic suggestion to feel no unpleasantness, a person subjected to painful stimuli shows high arousal in the parietal cortex areas responsive to

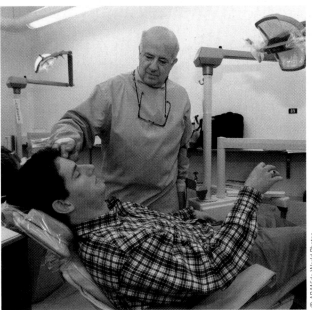

Some dentists have used hypnosis to relieve pain, even for tooth extractions and root canal surgery.

body sensations but not in the frontal cortex areas responsive to unpleasant emotions (Rainville, Duncan, Price, Carrier, & Bushnell, 1997) (see Figure 10.17).

Another potentially constructive use of hypnosis is the **posthypnotic suggestion,** *a suggestion to do or experience something after coming out of hypnosis.* For example, people who are told to forget what happened during hypnosis often do forget, although careful testing can reveal that the memory is not completely obliterated (David, Brown, Pojoga, & David, 2000).

In one study adults already known to be easily hypnotized were randomly assigned to different groups. One group was handed a stack of 120 addressed stamped postcards and asked (without being hypnotized) to mail one back each day until they exhausted the stack. Another group was given a posthypnotic suggestion to mail one card per day. The nonhypnotized group actually mailed back more cards, but they reported that they had to remind themselves each day to mail a card. Those given the posthypnotic suggestion said they never made a deliberate effort. The idea of mailing a card just "popped into mind," providing a sudden compulsion to mail one (Barnier & McConkey, 1998).

Many therapists have given cigarette smokers a posthypnotic suggestion that they will not want to smoke. The results are mixed. Some studies report significant benefits, but placebo treatments also produce benefits (Elkins, Marcus, Bates, Rajab, & Cook, 2006; J. P. Green & Lynn, 2000). That is, much of the improvement depends on expectations.

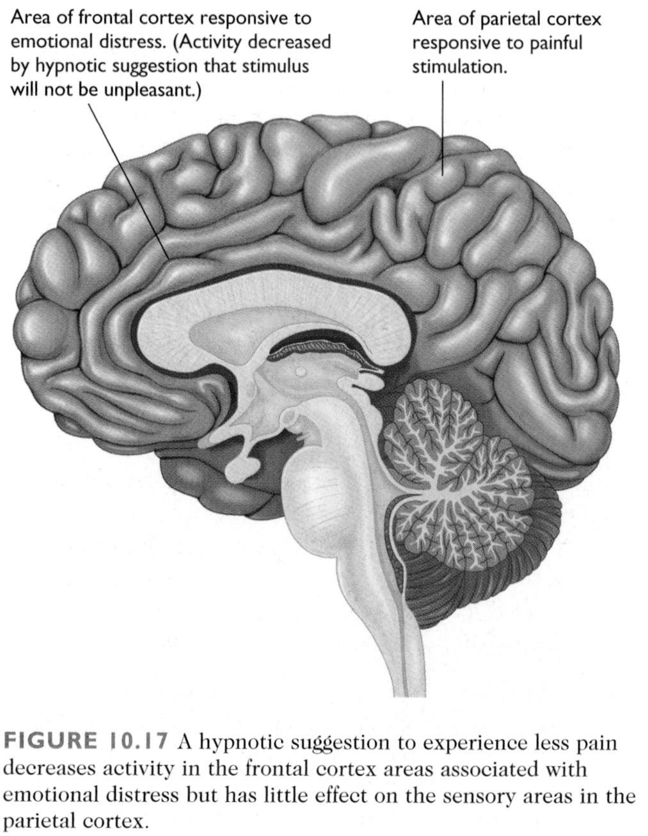

Perceptual Distortions Under Hypnosis

A few people report visual or auditory **hallucinations** *(sensory experiences not corresponding to reality)* under hypnosis, and many report touch hallucinations after being told, "your nose itches" or "your left hand feels numb" (Udolf, 1981). When hypnotized people report hallucinations, are they telling the truth or are they just saying what the hypnotist wants them to say?

At least sometimes, people are telling the truth. In one study researchers performed brain scans while people listened to sounds, imagined sounds, or hallucinated them under hypnotic suggestion. The hypnotic experiences activated some of the same brain areas as actual sounds did, but imagining sounds did not (Szechtman, Woody, Bowers, & Nahmias, 1998). Evidently, hypnotic hallucinations are more like real experiences than like imagination.

However, when hypnotized people claim that they don't see or hear something, careful testing demonstrates that the information does register partly. In one study people who were highly susceptible to hypnosis looked at the optical illusion shown in Figure 10.18a. They were hypnotized and told not to see the radiating lines but to see only the two horizontal ones. Those who said that they no longer saw the radiating lines still perceived the top line as longer than the bottom one, as in the usual optical illusion (R. J. Miller, Hennessy, & Leibowitz, 1973). If the radiating lines had truly disappeared, they would have seen something like Figure 10.18b, where the horizontal lines look equal. So these people did see the radiating lines, at least unconsciously.

Area of frontal cortex responsive to emotional distress. (Activity decreased by hypnotic suggestion that stimulus will not be unpleasant.)

Area of parietal cortex responsive to painful stimulation.

FIGURE 10.17 A hypnotic suggestion to experience less pain decreases activity in the frontal cortex areas associated with emotional distress but has little effect on the sensory areas in the parietal cortex.

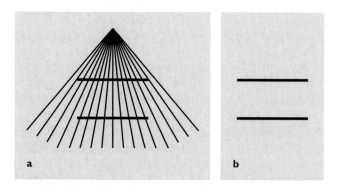

FIGURE 10.18 Horizontal lines of equal length in **(a)** the Ponzo illusion and **(b)** without the optical illusion. Researchers employ such visual stimuli to determine how hypnosis may alter sensory perception.

What Hypnosis Cannot Do

Many of the spectacular claims made for the power of hypnosis turn out to be less impressive on closer scrutiny. For instance, as in Figure 10.19, people under hypnosis can balance their head and neck on one chair and their feet on another chair and even allow someone to stand on their body! Amazing? Not really. It's easier than it looks, with or without hypnosis. Give it a try. (But don't invite someone to stand on you. Someone who does not balance correctly could injure you.)

Try It Yourself

Many people have attempted to use hypnosis to enhance memory. For example, a distressed person tells a psychotherapist, "I don't know why I have such troubles. Maybe I had some bad experience when I was younger. I just can't remember." Or a witness to a crime says, "I saw the culprit for a second or two, but now I can't give you a good description." Therapists and police officers have sometimes turned to hypnotism in the hope of uncovering lost memories. However, hypnotized people are highly sug-

FIGURE 10.19 The U.S. Supreme Court ruled in 1987 that criminal defendants may testify about details they recalled under hypnosis. Its decision sparked this protest by the magician known as The Amazing Kreskin, who borrowed a stunt commonly used to demonstrate the power of hypnosis—standing on a person suspended between two chairs.

gestible. When given a suggestion such as "you will remember more than you told us before," hypnotized people report more information, some of it correct and some of it incorrect, with increased confidence in both the correct and the incorrect (Fligstein, Barabasz, Barabasz, Trevisan, & Warner, 1998; Green & Lynn, 2005; Wagstaff et al., 2004). If they are also asked misleading questions, such as "Did the woman have one or two children?" (when in fact she had none), hypnotized people are easily influenced into reporting false information (Scoboria, Mazzoni, Kirsch, & Milling, 2002). Let's consider one typical study.

CRITICAL THINKING
WHAT'S THE EVIDENCE?

Hypnosis and Memory

The design of this study and many like it is simple: The experimenter presents a large array of material, tests people's memory of it, and then retests some people under hypnosis and other people without hypnosis to see how the hypnosis changes their memory (Dywan & Bowers, 1983).

Hypothesis. People will remember some of the material without hypnosis and more of it after hypnosis.

Method. Fifty-four people looked at a series of 60 slides of black-and-white drawings of simple objects (e.g., pencil, hammer, or bicycle), one every 3.5 seconds. Then they were given a sheet with 60 blank spaces and asked to recall as many of the items as possible. The slides were presented a second and third time, and after each session the participants had another chance to recall items. Each day for the next week, they again wrote a list of all the items they could remember (but without seeing the slides again). Finally, a week after the original slide sessions, they returned to the laboratory. Half of them, selected at random, were hypnotized and the others were just told to relax. Then all were asked to recall as many of the drawings as possible.

Results. Figure 10.20 shows the means for the two groups. The hypnotized people reported some items that they had not recalled before and more than the nonhypnotized group did. However, the hypnotized group reported more incorrect items than the nonhypnotized group did.

Interpretation. These results show no evidence that hypnosis improves memory. Rather, it decreases people's usual hesitance about reporting uncertain or doubtful memories. It may also cause people to confuse imagination with reality.

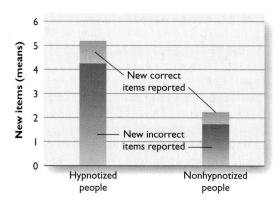

FIGURE 10.20 Hypnosis increased people's recall of items they had not recalled before. However, most of the new "memories" they confidently reported were incorrect. *(From "The Use of Hypnosis to Aid Recall" by J. Dywan and K. Bowers in* Science, *1981, pp. 184–185. Copyright © 1981. Reprinted by permission of AAAS.)*

You might note that this study is an example of the signal-detection issue discussed in chapter 4: A reported new memory is a "hit," but the number of hits, by itself, is useless information unless we also know the number of "false alarms"—reported memories that are incorrect.

Many other studies have produced similar conclusions: Hypnosis sometimes increases the number of correct items recalled, but it also increases the number of incorrect items recalled. People who have been hypnotized continue to report both the correct and incorrect items with high confidence, long after the hypnotic session (Steblay & Bothwell, 1994).

In response to such findings, a panel appointed by the American Medical Association (1986) recommended that courts of law should refuse to admit any testimony that was elicited under hypnosis, although hypnosis might be used as an investigative tool if all else fails. For example, if a hypnotized witness reports a license plate number, and the police track down the car and find blood on it, the blood is certainly admissible evidence, even if the hypnotized report is not. Success stories of that type are rare.

However, professional hypnotists have objected to having their work rejected by the courts, and some judges do admit hypnotically induced testimony, provided that the hypnotic session was fully recorded so that opposing attorneys could watch it. The result is sometimes, shall we say, questionable. In one case a truck crashed into a car in an intersection, killing the driver and seriously wounding a passenger in the backseat, whose head injury left him dazed, confused, and unable to remember the accident. Three eyewitnesses testified that the car had entered the intersection on a red light and that the truck driver was not to blame. *After* the backseat passenger collected damages from the driver's insurance company, and almost

2 years after the accident, he contacted a hypnotist to help him remember more of how the accident happened. Under hypnosis he reported that just before the accident he leaned forward and saw that the light was green, thus implying that the accident was the truck driver's fault. Although it is extremely doubtful that hypnosis could reinstate a 2-year-old memory of an event that caused head injury and confusion, the judge ruled that because the hypnotic session had been carefully recorded, it could be admitted as evidence. A few days later, the truck company settled the suit for hundreds of thousands of dollars (Karlin, 1997).

An even more doubtful claim is that hypnosis can help people recall their early childhood. A hypnotist might say, "You are getting younger. It is now the year . . . ; now it is . . . ; now you are only 6 years old." A hypnotized person may act like a young child, playing with teddy bears and blankets (Nash, Johnson, & Tipton, 1979). But is he or she reliving early experiences? Evidently not.

- The reported memories, such as the names of friends and teachers and the details of birthday parties, are generally inaccurate, according to records that parents or others have kept (Nash, 1987).
- Someone who has presumably regressed under hypnosis to early childhood retains spelling and other skills learned later in life. When asked to draw a picture, he or she does not draw as children draw but as adults imagine that children draw (Orne, 1951) (see Figure 10.21).
- Hypnotized subjects who are given a suggestion that they are growing older give a convincing performance of being an older person and report memories of what has happened to them in old age (Rubenstein & Newman, 1954). Because their reports of the future can only be imagination, we should assume the same for their past.

You may even encounter the astounding claim that hypnosis can help someone recall memories from a previous life. Hypnotized young people who claim to be recollecting a previous life most often describe the life of someone similar to themselves and married to someone remarkably similar to their current boyfriend or girlfriend. If they are asked whether their country (in their past life) is at war or what kind of money is in use, their guesses are seldom correct (Spanos, 1987–1988).

 CONCEPT CHECK

14. List two practical uses of hypnosis that the evidence supports and one that it does not. (Check your answer on page 393.)

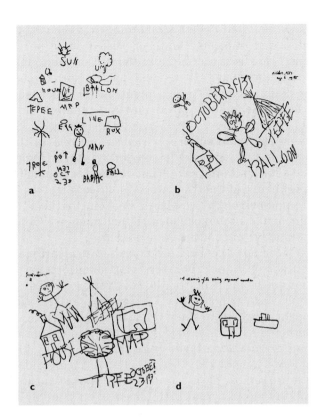

FIGURE 10.21 One person made drawing **(a)** at age 6 and the other three drawings **(b, c, & d)** as a college student while hypnotized and told to regress to age 6. Orne (1951) concluded that hypnotized students drew as they thought a child would.

CRITICAL THINKING
WHAT'S THE EVIDENCE?

Hypnosis and Risky Acts

Most hypnotists agree, "You don't have to worry. People will not do anything under hypnosis that they would ordinarily refuse to do." That reassurance is an important strategy in persuading you to agree to hypnosis. But is it true? How would anyone know? Do you suppose hypnotists ask clients to perform criminal or immoral acts, meet with repeated refusals, and then report the results of these unethical experiments? Not likely. Furthermore, when investigators have in fact asked hypnotized people to perform dangerous acts, the results have been hard to interpret. Here is an example.

Hypothesis. Hypnotized people will sometimes perform acts that people would refuse to do otherwise.

Method. Eighteen college students were randomly assigned to three groups. The investigator hypnotized those in one group, instructed the second group to pretend they were hypnotized, and asked the third group to participate in the study, without mentioning hypnosis. Each student was then asked to perform three acts: First, pick up a poisonous snake from a box. The snake really was poisonous, and anyone who got too close was restrained at the last moment. Second, reach into a vat of fuming nitric acid to retrieve a coin (which was already starting to dissolve). Here there was no last-second restraint. Anyone who followed the instructions was told to wash his or her hands in warm soapy water immediately afterward. (Today's ethical procedures would prevent this study.) Third, throw the nitric acid into the face of the hypnotist's assistant. While the participant was washing hands, the researcher had replaced the nitric acid with water, but the participant had no way of knowing that.

Results. Five of the six hypnotized students followed all three directions (Orne & Evans, 1965). Moreover, so did all six of those who were pretending to be hypnotized! So did two of the six who were just told to take these actions as part of an experiment, with no mention of hypnosis. (Nonhypnotized subjects did, however, hesitate much longer than the hypnotized subjects.)

Why would people do such extraordinary things? They explained that they simply trusted the experimenter: "If he tells me to do something, it can't really be dangerous."

Interpretation. We do not have adequate evidence to decide whether people under hypnosis will do anything that they would refuse to do otherwise, because it is difficult to find anything that people will refuse to do!

Notice the importance of control groups: We cannot simply assume what people would do without hypnosis. We need to test them.

Will hypnotized people do anything that they would otherwise refuse to do? The problem is that nonhypnotized people will sometimes perform some strange and dangerous acts, either because an experimenter asked them to or on their own.

Is Hypnosis an Altered State of Consciousness?

If a hypnotist tells you, "Your hand is rising; you can do nothing to stop it," your hand might indeed rise. If you were later asked why, you might reply that you lost control over your own behavior. Still, you were not a puppet. Was the act voluntary, involuntary, or something in between? To put the question differently, is hypnosis really different from normal wakefulness?

At one extreme, some psychologists regard hypnosis as a special state of consciousness characterized by increased suggestibility. At the other extreme, some psychologists emphasize the similarities between hypnosis and normal wakeful consciousness, including the fact that people who respond well to hypnosis also respond strongly to suggestions without hypnosis. Most psychologists take intermediate positions, noting that hypnotized people are neither "pretending to be hypnotized" nor under a hypnotist's control. That is, hypnosis is a special state in some ways but not others (I. Kirsch & Lynn, 1998).

One way to determine whether hypnosis is a special state of consciousness is to find out whether nonhypnotized people can do everything that hypnotized people do. How convincingly could you act like a hypnotized person?

How Well Can Someone Pretend to Be Hypnotized?

In several experiments some college students were hypnotized and others pretended they were hypnotized. An experienced hypnotist then examined them and tried to determine which ones were really hypnotized.

Fooling the hypnotist turned out to be easier than expected. The pretenders tolerated sharp pain without flinching and pretended to recall old memories. They made their bodies as stiff as a board and lay rigid between two chairs. When standing people were told to sit down, they did so immediately (as hypnotized people do) without first checking to make sure they had a chair behind them (Orne, 1959, 1979). When told to experience anger or another emotion, they exhibited physiological changes such as increased heart rate and sweating, just as hypnotized people do (Damaser, Shor, & Orne, 1963). Even experienced hypnotists could not identify the pretenders.

However, a few differences between the hypnotized people and pretenders did emerge (Orne, 1979). The pretenders failed to match some of the behaviors of hypnotized people, simply because they did not know how a hypnotized subject would act. For instance, when the hypnotist suggested, "You see Professor Schmaltz sitting in that chair," people in both

groups reported seeing the professor. Some of the hypnotized subjects, however, asked with puzzlement, "How is it that I see the professor there, but I also see the chair?" Pretenders never reported seeing this double reality. At that point in the experiment, Professor Schmaltz walked into the room. "Who is that entering the room?" asked the hypnotist. The pretenders would either say they saw no one, or they would identify Schmaltz as someone else. The hypnotized subjects would say, "That's Professor Schmaltz." Some then said that they were confused about seeing the same person in two places. For some of them, the hallucinated professor faded at that moment. Others continued to accept the double image.

One study reported a way to distinguish hypnotized people from pretenders more than 90% of the time. But it might not be the way you would expect. Simply ask people how deeply hypnotized they thought they were, how relaxed they were, and whether they were aware of their surroundings while hypnotized. People who rate themselves as "extremely" hypnotized, "extremely" relaxed, and so forth are almost always pretenders. Those who were really hypnotized rate themselves as only mildly influenced (Martin & Lynn, 1996).

So, what is our conclusion? Is hypnosis an altered state, or are hypnotized people just playing a role? Apparently, people pretending to be hypnotized can mimic almost any effect of hypnosis that they know about. However, hypnosis is ordinarily not just role-playing. The effects that role-players learn to imitate happen spontaneously for the hypnotized people.

 CONCEPT CHECK

15. Does hypnosis give people the power to do anything they could not do otherwise? Does it cause them to do anything they would be unwilling to do otherwise? (Check your answers on page 393.)

Meditation as an Altered State of Consciousness

Hypnosis is not the only method of inducing a relaxed and possibly altered state of consciousness. **Meditation,** *a systematic procedure for inducing a calm, relaxed state through the use of special techniques,* follows traditions that have been practiced in much of the world for thousands of years. The methods vary from concentrating on a single image or sound (e.g. "om") to opening one's attention to a rapidly changing variety of images. Meditators may observe their own thoughts, attempt to modify them, or distance themselves from certain thoughts. Goals of meditation vary

Meditation excludes the worries and concerns of the day and thereby induces a calm, relaxed state.

from the development of wisdom to general well-being (Walsh & Shapiro, 2006).

Many studies document that meditation decreases heart rate, breathing rate, blood pressure, and EEG arousal (e.g., Travis & Wallace, 1999). It can also improve attention, calmness, and concern for others (Walsh & Shapiro, 2006). However, most studies depend on short-term self-reports and fail to control for participants' expectations of benefits. Few studies have used double-blind procedures. So far, the medical and psychological benefits appear attributable to relaxation (Holmes, 1987).

IN CLOSING

The Nature of Hypnosis

Researchers agree on a few general points: Hypnosis is not faking or pretending to be hypnotized, and it does not give people mental or physical powers that they otherwise lack. Hypnosis enables people to relax, concentrate, and follow suggestions better than they usually do. Be skeptical of anyone who claims much more than that for hypnosis. ▌

Summary

- *Nature of hypnosis.* Hypnosis is a condition of increased suggestibility that occurs in the context of a special hypnotist–subject relationship. Psychologists try to distinguish the genuine phenomenon, which deserves serious study, from exaggerated claims. (page 386)

- *Hypnosis induction.* To induce hypnosis a hypnotist asks a person to concentrate and then makes repetitive suggestions. The first steps toward being hypnotized are the willingness to be hypnotized and the belief that one is becoming hypnotized. (page 386)

- *Uses.* Hypnosis can alleviate pain, and through posthypnotic suggestion, it can sometimes help people combat bad habits. (page 387)

- *Sensory distortions.* Hypnosis can induce hallucinations and other sensory distortions. However, when hypnotized people are told not to see something, even when they claim not to see it, enough aspects of the information get through to the brain to influence other perceptions. (page 388)

- *Nonuses.* Hypnosis does not give people special strength or unusual powers. When asked to report their memories under hypnosis, people report a mixture of correct and incorrect information with much confidence. (page 389)

- *Uncertain limits.* Although many hypnotists insist that hypnotized people will not do anything that they would refuse to do when not hypnotized, little evidence is available to support this claim. (page 391)

- *Hypnosis as an altered state.* Controversy continues about whether hypnosis is a special state of consciousness. (page 392)

- *Meditation.* Meditation induces a highly relaxed condition that one might regard as an altered state of consciousness. (page 392)

Answers to Concept Checks

14. Supported by the evidence: Hypnosis can decrease pain. Weakly supported by the evidence: Posthypnotic suggestions can sometimes help people break bad habits. Not supported: Hypnosis does not improve people's memories. (Nor does it give them added strength.) (page 387)

15. No evidence indicates that hypnosis empowers people to do anything they could not do otherwise if sufficiently motivated. That is, people pretending to be hypnotized can imitate what hypnotized people do, and the only exceptions are things that the imitators did not know about. As to whether hypnosis can make people do something they would ordinarily refuse to do, we do not know. In certain experiments hypnotized people have done some strange things, but so have nonhypnotized people. (page 391)

CHAPTER ENDING

Key Terms and Activities

Key Terms

You can check the page listed for a complete description of a term. You can also check the glossary/index at the end of the text for a definition of a given term, or you can download a list of all the terms and their definitions for any chapter at this website:

www.thomsonedu.com/ psychology/kalat

activation-synthesis theory of dreams (page 382)
binocular rivalry (page 364)

blindsight (page 367)
Capgras syndrome (page 367)
circadian rhythm (page 371)
consciousness (page 363)
déjà vu experience (page 367)
electroencephalograph (EEG) (page 377)
hallucination (page 388)
hypnosis (page 386)
insomnia (page 380)
jet lag (page 373)
latent content (page 381)
manifest content (page 381)

meditation (page 392)
narcolepsy (page 380)
neurocognitive theory (page 383)
periodic limb movement disorder (page 381)
phi effect (page 365)
polysomnograph (page 377)
posthypnotic suggestion (page 388)
rapid eye movement (REM) sleep (page 376)
readiness potential (page 368)
sleep apnea (page 380)
spatial neglect (page 365)

Suggestions for Further Reading

Domhoff, G. W. (2003). *The scientific study of dreams.* Washington, DC: American Psychological Association. A review of the best research on dreams.

Koch, C. (2004). *The quest for consciousness.* Englewood, CO: Roberts. A scientific approach to the mind–brain issue.

Moorcroft, W. (2003). *Understanding sleep and dreaming.* New York: Kluwer. An excellent review of research on many aspects of sleep and dreams.

Web/Technology Resources

Student Companion Website

www.thomsonedu.com/psychology/kalat

Explore the Student Companion Website for Online Try-It-Yourself activities, practice quizzes, flashcards, and more! The companion site also has direct links to the following websites.

Binocular Rivalry

http://www.psy.vanderbilt.edu/faculty/blake/rivalry/BR.html

Demonstrations and discussion of binocular rivalry and its implications for consciousness.

Sleep Disorders

www.thesleepsite.com/

Learn more about sleep disorders and treatment.

Dream Research

http://psych.ucsc.edu/dreams/

The best scientific work on the content of dreams.

Sleep Research

www.sleepfoundation.org/

Links to all kinds of information about sleep.

For Additional Study

Kalat Premium Website

http://www.thomsonedu.com

For Critical Thinking Videos and additional Online Try-It-Yourself activities, go to this site to enter or purchase your code for the Kalat Premium Website.

ThomsonNOW!

http://www.thomsonedu.com

Go to this site for the link to ThomsonNOW, your one-stop study shop. Take a Pretest for this chapter, and Thomson-NOW will generate a personalized Study Plan based on your test results. The Study Plan will identify the topics you need to review and direct you to online resources to help you master those topics. You can then take a Posttest to help you determine the concepts you have mastered and what you still need to work on.

Motivated Behaviors

During the summer of 1996, the proprietors of London's Kew Gardens announced that an unusual plant, native to Sumatra and rarely cultivated elsewhere, was about to bloom for the first time since 1963. If you had been in London then, with enough time available, would you have made a point of visiting Kew Gardens to witness this rare event? No? What if I told you that it was a truly beautiful flower? With a lovely, sweet smell. Still no?

This flower is seldom cultivated, for good reasons. Would you stand in line to visit it?

Then what if I told you the truth—that it has the nastiest, most obnoxious smell of any plant on Earth—that the flower is called the *stinking lily*, or *corpse plant*, because it smells like a huge, week-old carcass of rotting meat or fish. One whiff of it can make a strong person retch. Now would you want to visit it? If so, you would have to wait in line. When Kew Gardens announced that the stinking lily was about to bloom, an enormous crowd gathered, forming a line that stretched to the length of a soccer field (MacQuitty, 1996). (The first day that the flower bloomed, it had hardly begun to stink. Disappointed visitors vowed to return later.)

Although the visitors' behavior may seem puzzling, it is not that unusual. People frequently seek new and interesting experiences, just for curiosity. Even motivations with obvious biological value, such as hunger and sex, sometimes produce puzzling behaviors. Researchers have nevertheless made progress in understanding many aspects of motivation. We begin this chapter with an overview of general principles of motivation. Then we shall explore three representative and obviously important motivations: hunger, sex, and work.

General Principles of Motivation

- *What is motivation?*
- *What is the difference between motivated and nonmotivated behaviors?*

You are sitting quietly, reading a book, when suddenly you hear a loud noise. You jump a little and gasp. Was your action motivated? "No," you say. "I jumped involuntarily." Now I tell you that I want to do a little experiment. As soon as you hear me tap my pencil, you should try to jump and gasp just as you did the first time. I tap my pencil, and sure enough, you jump and gasp. Was that action motivated? "Yes," you reply.

So, what appears to be approximately the same behavior can be motivated at one time and nonmotivated at another time. Can we trust people to tell us whether their behavior was motivated or not? No, we can't. Someone accused of murder says, "I didn't mean to kill. It was an accident." Your friend, who promised to drive you somewhere and then left without you, says, "I didn't do it on purpose. I just forgot." We need to study how motivated behaviors differ from nonmotivated behaviors, but even then we will frequently be uncertain whether someone's behavior was motivated or accidental.

Properties of Motivated Behavior

What, if anything, do various motivated behaviors have in common? That is, what distinguishes a motivated act from a reflex? Motivated behaviors vary from time to time and from person to person. For example, on a cold day, you might sit by the fireplace and drink hot chocolate, or you might put on heavy clothing or become more active. Someone else might find other strategies for keeping warm. The foremost characteristic of motivated behaviors is that they are goal directed. If you are motivated to accomplish something, you try one approach after another until you succeed. If necessary, you set up subgoals you need to meet on your way to the final goal (Austin & Vancouver, 1996). For example, if you were motivated to improve your house, you might start by listing the items that need repair and the tools you will need.

These criteria are good in principle. However, nearly all behaviors combine elements of motivation

and reflex. For example, walking depends on leg reflexes that maintain balance. Eating requires reflexes of digestion. Fixating your eyes on a target depends on reflexive movements of eye muscles.

 CRITICAL THINKING
A STEP FURTHER

Motivations and Reflexes

A frog flicks its tongue at a passing insect, captures it, and swallows it. The behavior satisfies the frog's need for food, so we might guess that it is motivated. However, the behavior appears to be as constant as a reflex. How might you determine whether this behavior is motivated?

Views of Motivation

Like many other important terms in psychology, motivation is difficult to define. Let's consider several possibilities: "Motivation is what activates and directs behavior." That description fits many examples, but it also fits some nonmotivational phenomena. For instance, light activates and directs the growth of plants, but we would hardly say that light motivates plants.

"Motivation is what makes our behavior more vigorous and energetic." The problem with that definition is that some motivated behavior is not vigorous at all. For example, you might be highly motivated to spend the next few hours sleeping.

How about this: Based on the concept of reinforcement from chapter 6, we could define **motivation** as *the process that determines the reinforcement value of an outcome.* In more everyday language, motivation is what makes you want something more at one time and less at another. For example, something to eat or drink is more reinforcing at some times than others. Thus, we say that motivation for them has increased or decreased. Note the close relationship between learning and motivation.

That definition works as a description, although it offers no theory. Few psychologists today spend much time debating the true nature of motivation, but let's briefly consider a few influential theories, with their strengths and weaknesses.

Motivation as an Energy

Motivation, which comes from the same root as *motion,* is literally something that "moves" a person. So we might think of it as a type of energy. According to Konrad Lorenz (1950), a pioneer in the study of animal behavior, animals engage in instinctive acts when specific energies reach a critical level. For example, a male stickleback fish has no specific energy for mating outside the breeding season, so it does not respond sexually. At the start of the breeding season, it has a small amount of mating energy, so it courts females and attacks males. At the height of the breeding season, it has a great amount of mating energy, so it courts females vigorously, as well as wood models that resemble females.

Figure 11.1 illustrates Lorenz's model. A specific kind of energy builds up in the reservoir and flows into the tray below. The outlets in that tray represent ways of releasing this energy. If conditions are right, the energy is released through the lowest outlet—for example, the male stickleback mates with a female. If that opportunity is absent, the outlet is blocked and energy continues to build up until it spills through one of the higher, less preferred outlets. However, Lorenz's theories are based on the idea of specific energies for specific tasks—an idea that neuroscience research has disconfirmed. He believed that every impulse had to be carried out in some way to use up the energy. We now know that an individual can simply inhibit an impulse.

Drive Theories

A related set of theories describe motivation as a **drive,** *a state of unrest or irritation that energizes one behavior after another until one of them removes the irritation* (Hull, 1943). For example, when you get a splinter in your finger, the discomfort motivates you to try various actions until you remove the splinter.

According to the *drive-reduction theory* that was popular among psychologists of the 1940s and 1950s, humans and other animals strive to reduce their needs and drives as much as possible. They eat to reduce their hunger, drink to reduce their thirst, have sexual activity to reduce their sex drive, and so forth. This view implies that if we satisfy all our needs, we would then become inactive. People's search for new experiences—riding roller coasters or smelling odd flowers, for example—is a problem for this view.

Another flaw in drive theory is that it ignores the role of external stimulation. For example, your interest in food depends not only on hunger (an internal drive) but also on what foods are available. Similarly, interest in sex depends partly on an internal drive and partly on the presence of a suitable partner.

Homeostasis

One important advance upon the idea of drive reduction is the concept of **homeostasis,** *the maintenance of an optimum level of biological conditions within an organism* (Cannon, 1929). The idea of homeostasis recognizes that we are motivated to seek a state of equilibrium, which is not zero stimulation. For example, people maintain a nearly constant body temperature, resisting either an increase or decrease. We also work to maintain a fairly steady body weight, a nearly constant amount of water in the body, a moderate amount of sensory experience, and so on.

Unlike a rock, which remains static only because nothing is acting upon it, the homeostasis of the body is more like a spinning top; it needs additional energy from time to time to keep it spinning. For example, we maintain constant body temperature partly by shivering, sweating, and other involuntary physiological responses and partly by putting on extra clothing, taking off excess clothing, or finding a more comfortable location.

Human motivated behaviors differ from the actions of a thermostat, because our behavior often anticipates future needs. For example, you might eat a large breakfast even though you are not hungry, just because you know you are going to be too busy to stop for lunch. If you are angry or frightened, you start sweating before you begin the vigorous actions that might heat your body. (We call this phenomenon a "cold sweat.") Furthermore, the optimum level of a condition varies. Your body raises its temperature in midafternoon and lowers it at night. Many animals put on extra fat and fur to protect against winter's cold weather and then lose weight and shed the extra fur in spring. For many purposes a better concept than

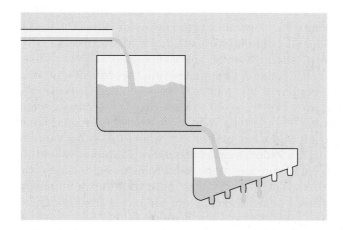

FIGURE 11.1 According to Konrad Lorenz, energy (represented as a fluid) builds up in a reservoir and needs to be discharged. For example, if your sex-specific energy cannot discharge through its normal outlets, it builds up until it discharges through some other outlet. *(After Lorenz, 1950)*

homeostasis is **allostasis**, defined as *maintaining certain levels of biological conditions that vary according to an individual's needs and circumstances.*

Incentive Theories

The homeostasis concept of motivation overlooks the power of new stimuli to arouse behaviors. For example, why do you sometimes eat tasty-looking foods even when you are not hungry? Why do we seek opportunities to enjoy music and art? Many strong motivations correspond to no apparent need.

Evidently, motivation includes more than the internal forces that push us toward certain behaviors. It also includes **incentives**—*external stimuli that pull us toward certain actions.* Most motivated behaviors are controlled by a combination of drives and incentives. You eat because you are hungry (a drive) and because you see appealing food in front of you (an incentive). You jump into a swimming pool on a hot day to cool your body (a drive) and because you will enjoy splashing around in the water with friends (an incentive).

Intrinsic and Extrinsic Motivations

Similar to the distinction between drives and incentives, psychologists also distinguish between intrinsic and extrinsic motivations. An **intrinsic motivation** is *a motivation to do an act for its own sake;* an **extrinsic motivation** is *based on the reinforcements and punishments that the act may bring.* For example, reading a book for enjoyment displays an intrinsic motivation; reading a book to pass a test depends on an extrinsic motivation. The two kinds of motivation frequently combine. For instance, an artist paints for the joy of creation (intrinsic) and for the hope of profit (extrinsic). Even if you read a book because it is assigned—this one, for example—you might also enjoy it. We seldom do anything for just one reason.

Does a combination of intrinsic and extrinsic motivations lead to more persistent and effective performance than, say, intrinsic motivation alone? Not always. In a classic study, researchers let monkeys play with a device like the one in Figure 11.2. To open it a monkey had to remove the pin, lift the hook, and then lift the hasp. The monkeys played with the device for 10 days, apparently just for fun (an intrinsic motivation). Then the device was placed over a food well containing a raisin. If they opened the device, they could get the raisin (an extrinsic motivation). Suddenly, their ability to open the device deteriorated. Instead of patiently removing the pin, the hook, and the hasp as before, they attacked the hasp forcefully. They took longer to open the device for food than they did for play. Later, when they were offered the device by itself with no food available, they played with it less than before (Harlow, Harlow, & Meyer, 1950). The device had become work, not play.

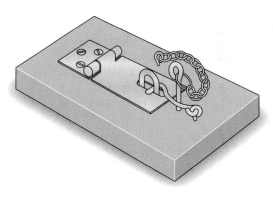

FIGURE 11.2 Monkeys learned to remove the pin, hook, and hasp to open this device. When they started receiving a raisin instead of opening it just for fun, their performance deteriorated.

Does the same principle apply to human behavior? In a typical experiment, college students were asked to try to arrange seven plastic pieces with complex shapes to match figures in a drawing. At one point halfway through the experiment, students in the experimental group were paid $1 for each correct match. (Students in the control group did not know that the experimental group was being paid.) Later, the experiment continued without pay for anyone. After pay was suspended, the experimental group decreased their efforts (Deci, 1971). As with the monkeys, once you have been paid, the task becomes work and not play.

© Michael Speaker (both photos)

▌ The artist who created this wooden cow probably hoped for recognition and money (an extrinsic motivation) but also must have enjoyed the creative process itself (an intrinsic motivation). The back of the cow folds out to reveal a desk.

Results such as these illustrate the **overjustification effect:** *When people are given more extrinsic motivation than necessary to perform a task, their intrinsic motivation declines.* The same principle works for both rewards and punishments. You could work hard to get a reward or to avoid a punishment. In either case, after you finished what you had to do, you probably would stop working on the task, even if it was something you previously enjoyed (Ryan & Deci, 2000).

One explanation for the overjustification effect is that after working extra hard on a task, you become tired of it. However, even after a rest period, people still often show a decreased interest in the task. According to another explanation, people ask themselves, "Why am I doing this?" They then answer, "It's not because I enjoy the task. It's because I'm being paid." (Or "Because I'll be punished if I stop.") Therefore, they no longer do it for the sheer joy of it.

The overjustification effect applies under some conditions but not others, and it is sometimes a weak effect (Eisenberger & Cameron, 1996). For example, would you guess that praising a child for work well done would strengthen intrinsic motivation, or would it act like a payment does and decrease intrinsic motivation? The results vary from one study to another (Henderlong & Lepper, 2002). As a rule praise helps if the recipient thinks the praise was deserved. If the praise appears insincere, it accomplishes nothing. Someone who is praised after a mediocre effort may conclude, "They expected very little of me."

Table 11.1 summarizes four views of motivation.

CONCEPT CHECK

1. Suppose you want to encourage your younger cousin to continue taking piano lessons. Based on the overjustification effect, would it be wise to pay him for practicing? (Check your answer on page 403.)

Delay of Gratification

Often, a motivation requires you to choose a less pleasant behavior now to have a more pleasant opportunity later. People differ in how well they can *defer gratification*—that is, choose the action that produces the bigger payoff later instead of the smaller pleasure now (Simpson & Vuchinich, 2000). Recall the Choice-Delay task from chapter 8: You might be offered a choice between a small, immediate reward and a larger, delayed one. You might know that the delayed reward is better, and you would like to wait for it, but that immediate reward is tempting. Think of some examples: If you study hard now, you will get a good grade later, but you would really like to do something fun right now. If you eat just a light meal tonight, you will start losing weight, but you would really enjoy that triple cheeseburger and a hot fudge sundae.

One way to overcome the temptation to choose the immediate reward is to commit yourself to an action well in advance. For example, suppose you expect that you would choose an immediate $500 over

TABLE 11.1 Four Views of Motivation

View	Basic Position	Major Weaknesses
Energy Theories According to energy theories, motivation is a kind of energy that builds up until it finds a release.	Motivations are energies that accumulate; each energy specifies a preferred action, although it might spill over into a less preferred outlet.	Based on obsolete view of the nervous system.
Drive Theories According to drive theories, motivation is an irritation that continues until we find a way to reduce it.	Motivations are based on needs or irritations that we try to reduce; they do not specify particular actions.	Implies that we always try to reduce stimulation, never to increase it. Also overlooks importance of external stimuli.
Homeostasis (plus anticipation) Homeostasis is the process of maintaining a variable such as body temperature within a set range.	Motivations tend to maintain body states near some optimum intermediate level. They may react to current needs and anticipate future needs.	Overlooks importance of external stimuli.
Incentive Theories Incentives are external stimuli that attract us even if we have no biological need for them.	Motivations are responses to attractive stimuli.	Incomplete theory unless combined with drive or homeostasis.

$1,000 a year later. Economically, that is a poor choice, as 100% interest over one year is outstanding. You can make the wiser decision if you choose far in advance. For example, which would you prefer, $500 a year from now or $1,000 two years from now? You know that when you get to one year from now, you will wish you could have the $500 right away, but if you choose now, you can commit yourself to the better but delayed reward.

Similarly, suppose someone offers to pay you a reasonable price to do a somewhat unpleasant job a year from now. This far in advance, you can agree to the deal. When you get close to the actual time, you start thinking more about the unpleasant details, and if you could make the decision anew, you probably would find excuses to refuse (Trope & Liberman, 2003). However, having already committed yourself, you keep the deal.

Although we generally prefer a reward now to a bigger one later, the reverse occurs if the reward will be emotionally exciting. Most people would prefer a passionate kiss from their favorite movie star a few days from now instead of right now (Loewenstein, 1987). Presumably, they enjoy the anticipation, the opportunity to look forward to an emotionally exciting event. Conversely, most would prefer to receive a painful, unavoidable shock today than 10 years from now. It feels better to get it over with than to dread it for so long. Similarly, most people don't object to waiting a couple of weeks to receive good news, but they want to know bad news as quickly as possible (Lovallo & Kahneman, 2000). The period of dreading the bad news only makes it worse.

 CONCEPT CHECK

2. If you want to invite someone to be a guest speaker for your favorite organization, should you make the invitation long in advance or wait until close to the time of the talk? Why?
3. Can you explain why many people would prefer to bet on a lottery than a roulette wheel, which produces immediate results? (Check your answers on page 403.)

IN CLOSING

Many Types of Motivation

People frequently puzzle over why a person did something that has no apparent benefit. Often, it is a combination: curiosity, the desire to have something unusual to talk about with friends, perhaps even a desire for fame. As you will see in later modules of this chapter, even clearly adaptive behaviors such as hunger and sex are based on multiple and complex motives.

Summary

- *Characteristics of motivated behaviors.* Motivated behaviors vary from time to time, from situation to situation, and from person to person. They persist until the individual reaches the goal. (page 399)
- *Motivation as energy or drive reduction.* Viewing motivation as a type of energy is an analogy that should not be taken too seriously. Some aspects of motivation can be described as drive reduction, but people strive for new experiences that do not reduce any apparent drive. (page 400)
- *Motivation as a way of maintaining homeostasis.* Many motivated behaviors tend to maintain body conditions and stimulation at a near-constant, or homeostatic, level. This view of motivation can account for much behavior if we also assume that behaviors anticipate future needs instead of just responding to current needs. (page 400)
- *Motivation as incentive.* Motivations are partly under the control of incentives—external stimuli that pull us toward certain actions. Both drives and incentives control most motivated behaviors. (page 401)
- *Delayed gratification.* People vary in how well they can postpone pleasure, choosing a larger reward later over a smaller one now. It is often easier to make the economically logical decision if you make it far in advance. Although people usually prefer a reward now instead of later, they reverse that preference if the reward has high emotional value so they can enjoy the anticipation. (page 402)

Answers to Concept Checks

1. According to the overjustification effect, you should not pay him enough so that he starts practicing just for the reward. However, sincere verbal praise would be good. (page 402)
2. Make the invitation far in advance. Far in advance, it is easy to see that the advantages of an action outweigh the disadvantages. When the time is close, the details of the task become more salient, and people will find an excuse for not participating. (page 403)
3. Someone who bets on a lottery can enjoy the long period of anticipation of how exciting the win might be. If the payoff from a gamble comes quickly, that long anticipation is not possible. (page 403)

Hunger Motivation

• *How do we decide how much to eat and when?*

Small birds eat only what they need at the moment, storing almost no fat at all. The advantage is that they remain light and fast enough to escape predators. The disadvantage is that they starve if they have trouble finding food for a few days. Bears follow a different strategy. They find abundant food when nuts and berries are in season, but at other times, they go days or weeks with nothing to eat. Their evolved strategy is to eat as much as they can whenever they can and then live off their stored fat.

Few humans eat as gluttonously as bears, but we too have apparently evolved a strategy of eating more than we need at the moment in case food is scarce tomorrow, as it frequently has been during human history. Today, however, prosperous countries have abundant, tasty food every day, and the result is much overeating (Pinel, Assanand, & Lehman, 2000).

Mealtime is more than just an opportunity to satisfy hunger: It is an occasion to bring the family and sometimes friends together, to share a pleasant experience, to discuss the events of the day, and even to pass on cultural traditions from one generation to the next.

How much we eat and what and when we eat also depend on social motives. Imagine you visit your boyfriend's or girlfriend's family and you want to make a good impression. "Dinner's ready!" someone calls. You go into the dining room and find a huge meal spread out before you, which your hosts clearly expect you to enjoy. Do you explain that you are not hungry because you already made a pig of yourself at lunch? Probably not.

The Physiology of Hunger and Satiety

Hunger is a partly homeostatic drive that keeps fuel available for the body. When supplies begin to drop, specialized brain mechanisms trigger behaviors that lead to eating. But how does your brain know how much fuel you have and how much more you need?

The problem is more complex than keeping enough fuel in your car's gas tank. When the fuel gauge shows that the tank is running low, you fill it with gas. By contrast your stomach and intestines are not the only places where you store fuel. Fuel is present in every cell of your body, and more circulates in your blood, ready to enter cells that need it. Fat cells and liver cells store still more fuel. If necessary, your body can break down muscle tissues for additional fuel.

How do you know how much to eat, considering that each meal has a different density of nutrients from any other? Fortunately, you don't have to get it exactly right. You have one set of mechanisms that control short-term changes in hunger and separate long-term mechanisms that correct for short-term fluctuations in your intake.

Short-Term Regulation of Hunger

Under most circumstances the main factor for ending a meal is distension of the stomach and intestines. We feel full because the digestive system is literally full (Seeley, Kaplan, & Grill, 1995). With familiar foods we also calibrate approximately how much nutrition we are getting per amount swallowed (Deutsch & Gonzalez, 1980), and receptors in our intestines detect sugars in the food (Lavin et al., 1996).

The main factor responsible for the onset of hunger and the start of a meal is a drop in how much glucose enters the cells (Figure 11.3). **Glucose,** *the most abundant sugar in your blood, is an important source of energy for all parts of the body and almost*

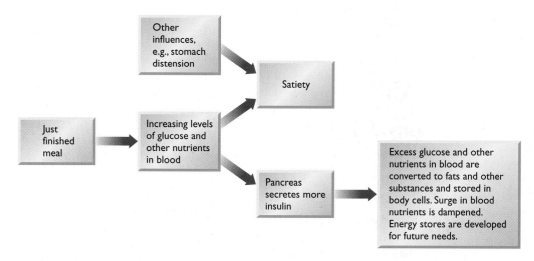

FIGURE 11.3 Varying secretions of insulin regulate the flow of nutrients from the blood into the cells or from storage back into the blood.

the only source for the brain. We could say, with only mild oversimplification, that hunger is a homeostatic mechanism that motivates you to supply enough glucose. The body can make glucose from almost any food. If you eat too much, your body converts excess blood glucose into fats and other stored fuels. If you eat too little, you convert stored fuels back into blood glucose. The flow of glucose from the blood into cells depends on insulin, a hormone released by the pancreas.

The hormone **insulin** *increases the flow of glucose and several other nutrients into body cells.* At the beginning of a meal, before the nutrients have even started entering the blood, the brain sends messages to the pancreas to increase its secretion of insulin. Insulin promotes the movement of glucose and other nutrients out of the blood and into both the cells that need fuel and the cells that store the nutrients as fats and other supplies.

As the meal continues, the digested food enters the blood, but almost as fast as it enters, insulin helps to move excess nutrients out of the blood and into the liver or fat cells. In that manner the insulin holds down the surge of glucose and other nutrients in the blood (Woods, 1991). Hours after a meal, when blood glucose levels begin to drop, the pancreas secretes another hormone, *glucagon,* which stimulates the liver to release stored glucose back into the blood.

As insulin levels rise and fall, hunger decreases and increases, as shown in Figure 11.4. Insulin affects hunger partly by controlling the flow of glucose, but it also has a more direct effect. Insulin in the brain stimulates neurons that signal satiety (Brüning et al., 2000). The importance of insulin has a consequence for dieting. Since about 1970, companies that produce soft drinks and packaged foods have been using high-fructose corn syrup as a sweetener.

Fructose has the advantage that it tastes sweeter than other sugars, so you need fewer calories of fructose to achieve the same taste. The disadvantage is that fructose does not stimulate insulin release nearly as much as other sugars do (Teff et al., 2004). Therefore, people consuming fructose do not quickly feel satiated. The increased use of fructose is a possible explanation for the increased prevalence of obesity since 1970 (Bray, Nielsen, & Popkin, 2004).

 CONCEPT CHECK

4. Insulin levels fluctuate cyclically over the course of a day. Would they be higher in the middle of the day, when people tend to be hungry, or late at night, when most are less hungry? (Check your answer on page 413.)

Long-Term Regulation of Hunger

Stomach distension and the other mechanisms for ending a meal are far from perfect. Depending on the caloric density of your next meal, you may eat a bit more or less than you need. If you misjudged in the same direction meal after meal, you would soon have a problem.

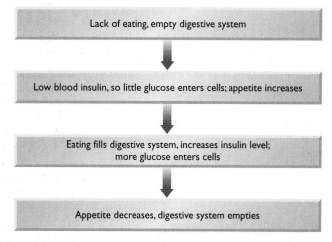

FIGURE 11.4 A feedback system between eating and insulin levels maintains homeostatic control of nutrition.

However, you have long-term mechanisms to correct short-term errors. If you overeat for several meals, you will feel less hungry until you get back to about your normal weight. Conversely, if you undereat for a few meals, you will start feeling hungrier than usual until you get back to normal. Most people's weight fluctuates from day to day but remains remarkably stable from month to month, even if they seldom check the scales.

That mean weight is referred to as a **set point**— *a level that the body works to maintain* (Figure 11.5). The mechanism for this correction is now partly understood (J. M. Friedman, 2000). *The body's fat cells produce a hormone called* **leptin** *in amounts proportional to the total amount of fat.* When the body gains fat, the extra leptin alters activity in parts of the hypothalamus (an area of the brain), causing meals to satisfy hunger faster. That is, leptin is your fat cells' way of telling the brain "you have enough fat already, so eat less." Among the other effects of leptin, it triggers the start of puberty: When the body reaches a certain size and weight, the increased leptin levels combine with other forces to induce the hormonal changes of puberty (Chehab, Mounzih, Lu, & Lim, 1997). Not coincidentally, as young people have tended to become heavier over the last several generations, puberty has been starting at younger and younger ages (Gilger, Geary, & Eisele, 1991).

FIGURE 11.5 For most people weight fluctuates around a set point, just as a diving board bounces up and down from a central position.

Those few people who lack the genes to produce leptin do become obese (Farooqi et al., 2001). Their brains get no signals from their fat supplies, so they act as if they have no fat and are starving. They also fail to enter puberty (Clément et al., 1998). Leptin injections greatly reduce obesity for these few people (D. A. Williamson et al., 2005). Most obese people produce large amounts of leptin but apparently fail to respond to it. Injections of even larger amounts decrease their appetite somewhat, but at the risk of inducing Type II diabetes (B. Cohen, Novick, & Rubinstein, 1996).

 CONCEPT CHECK

5. What two hormones influence appetite, and which body parts release them? (Check your answer on page 413.)

Brain Mechanisms

Your appetite at any moment depends on the taste and appearance of the food, the contents of your stomach and intestines, the availability of glucose to the cells, and your body's fat supplies. It also depends on your health, body temperature, time of day, and social influences. The key areas for integrating all this information and thereby determining your hunger level include several parts of the hypothalamus (Figure 11.6).

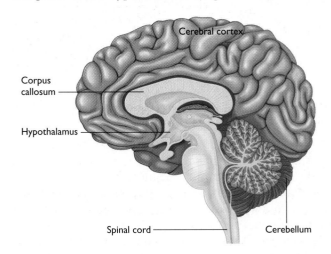

FIGURE 11.6 The hypothalamus, a small area on the underside of the brain, helps regulate eating, drinking, sexual behavior, and other motivated activities.

Within the hypothalamus an area called the arcuate nucleus has one set of neurons that receive hunger signals (e.g., "the food looks good" and "my stomach is empty") and other neurons that receive satiety signals (e.g., "my insulin level is high" and "my fat cells are supplying plenty of leptin"). These signals come from both hormones and neurotransmitters. The combined output from the arcuate nucleus directs other parts of the hypothalamus to enhance or weaken the taste of food, salivation responses, swallowing, and digestion. Damage in the hypothalamus can lead to severe undereating or overeating. Figure 11.7 shows an example of a rat with damage to one part of the hypothalamus, the ventromedial nucleus.

The areas of the hypothalamus that control feeding use many neurotransmitters that are used in few if any other parts of the brain (Horvath, 2005). The consequence is that medical researchers have many possibilities for developing weight-control drugs, although the drugs marketed so far have been disappointing in their effectiveness.

 CONCEPT CHECK

6. Many young ballet dancers and other female athletes who exercise heavily and keep their weight low are slower to start puberty than most other girls. Why?

Reeves & Plum, "Hyperphagia, rage, and dementia accompanying a ventromedial hypothalamic neoplasm," *Archives of Neurology* 1969, Vol. 20, no. 616-624

FIGURE 11.7 A rat with a damaged ventromedial hypothalamus (left) has a constantly high insulin level that causes it to store most of each meal as fat. Because the nutrients do not circulate in the blood, the rat quickly becomes hungry again. This rat's excess fat prevents it from grooming its fur.

7. After damage to the ventromedial hypothalamus, an animal's weight eventually reaches a higher than usual level and then fluctuates around that amount. What has happened to the set point? (Check your answers on page 413.)

Social and Cultural Influences on Eating

Physiological mechanisms account for only part of our eating habits. In the United States and much of the rest of the world, obesity is a growing problem. Our physiology and eating strategies evolved long ago, when life required much physical activity and food was often scarce. We seem unprepared for a world of abundant high-calorie foods and sit-at-a-desk jobs.

Social factors significantly influence our eating. When you eat with friends, you linger over the meal. You eat a few more bites after you thought you were done, and later a few more. Someone wants to have dessert, so you have one too. On the average you will sit at the table two or three times as long with a group of friends as you would alone (Bell & Pliner, 2003), and you will eat almost twice as much food (de Castro, 2000). Exceptions occur, of course. If you think someone is watching how much you eat and likely to scold you for overeating, you show restraint (Herman, Roth, & Polivy, 2003).

Overeating has spread in other cultures as they became, as some people put it, "Coca-Colonized" by Western cultures (J. M. Friedman, 2000). The strongest example comes from the Native American Pima of Arizona (Figure 11.8). Most Pima adults are seriously obese, probably because of several genes (Norman et al., 1998), and most also have high blood pressure and Type II (adult-onset) diabetes. However, their ancestors—with the same genes—were not obese. They ate the fruits and vegetables that grow in the Sonoran Desert, which are available only briefly during the year. To survive they had to eat as much as they could whenever they could and conserve their energy as much as possible. Beginning in the 1940s, they switched to the same diet as other Americans, which is richer in calories and available year-round. The Pima still eat massive quantities and conserve their energy by being relatively inactive, and the result is weight gain. We see here a superb example of

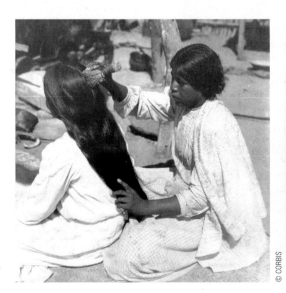

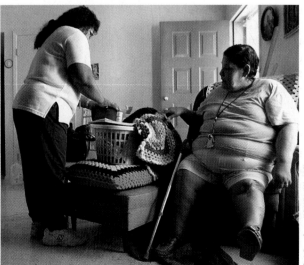

FIGURE 11.8 Until the 1940s the Native American Pima ate their traditional diet of desert plants and remained thin. Today, they eat the typical U.S. diet while remaining relatively inactive, and the result is high prevalence of obesity.

408 CHAPTER 11 Motivated Behaviors

the combined influence of genetics and environment. The Pima became obese because of a combination of their genes and the change in diet, whereas neither by itself would have this effect.

Eating Too Much or Too Little

Obesity has become widespread but not universal. Why do some people become obese whereas others do not? And at the other extreme, why do some people eat too little? Abnormal eating reflects a combination of social and physiological influences.

Obesity

Obesity is *the excessive accumulation of body fat.* Physicians calculate a *body mass index,* defined as weight in kilograms divided by height in meters squared (kg / m²). A ratio over 25 is considered overweight; over 30, obese; over 40, extremely obese (National Institutes of Health, 2000). A current estimate is that 30% of U.S. adults are obese, and another 35% are overweight (Marx, 2003). Obesity increases the risk of diabetes, coronary heart disease, cancer, sleep apnea, and other diseases (P. G. Kopelman, 2000). For information about obesity in general, visit this website: **www.obesity.org.** People become seriously overweight because they take in more calories than they use. But *why* do they do that?

The Limited Role of Emotional Disturbances

Emotional distress produces temporary fluctuations in eating and body weight for almost anyone. Nearly half of adults say that they overeat at least three times per month because of feeling nervous, tired, lonely, or sorry for themselves (Edelman, 1981). An eating binge distracts them from their worries (Heatherton & Baumeister, 1991). Eating binges are particularly common among people who have been dieting to lose weight (Greeno & Wing, 1994). Evidently, dieters actively inhibit their desire to eat until a stressful experience breaks their inhibitions and releases a pent-up desire to eat.

If distress provokes eating binges, could psychological distress be the cause of obesity? The evidence indicates only a small influence. In one study 19% of the people with a history of serious depression became obese compared to 15% of other people (McIntyre, Konarski, Wilkins, Soczynska, & Kennedy, 2006). However, many people report psychological distress *after* becoming obese as a result of being treated unkindly by other people (M. A. Friedman & Brownell, 1996).

Genetics and Energy Output

Researchers have identified genes that increase the probability of obesity (Herbert et al., 2006), and twin studies suggest that many other genes increase the probability of impulsive or unrestrained eating (Mergen, Mergen, Ozata, Oner, & Oner, 2001; Tholin, Rasmussen, Tynelius, & Karlsson, 2005). But how do those genes alter behavior?

Many overweight people who claim to eat only normal amounts of food eat more than they admit, maybe even more than they admit to themselves. In one admirably simple study, researchers collected supermarket receipts and found that overweight families bought more food per person than average and especially more high-fat food (Ransley et al., 2003). However, in addition to consuming more energy, they also have low energy output, including a low metabolic rate.

One group of investigators compared the infants of twelve overweight mothers and six normal-weight mothers over their first year of life. All the babies weighed about the same at birth, but six of the babies of the overweight mothers were inactive compared to the other babies and became overweight within their first year. During their first 3 months, they expended about 20% less energy per day than the average for other babies (Roberts, Savage, Coward, Chew, & Lucas, 1988).

Low energy expenditure is a good predictor of weight gain in adults as well. Researchers found that mildly obese people are less active than other people and spend more time sitting, even after they lose weight (Levine et al., 2005). Evidently, inactivity is a long-term habit, not a reaction to being heavy.

Portion Size

If a restaurant brings you more food than you wanted, do you feel obligated to eat as much as you can, so it won't go to waste? If you dine at an all-you-can-eat buffet (sometimes called an "all night buffet"), do you try to eat a little of everything, so you can

Many people with obesity feel distressed and suffer from low self-esteem because of how other people treat them.

© Dennis MacDonald/PhotoEdit

get your money's worth? One contributor to the problem of obesity is the availability of large quantities of tasty food.

A puzzling observation is that the French have less cardiovascular disease than Americans do, despite eating a diet much richer in fats. One of the likeliest explanations is meal size. On the average French restaurants serve smaller meals than American restaurants, even when they are part of the same international chain, such as McDonald's or Pizza Hut (Rozin, Kabnick, Pete, Fischler, & Shields, 2003). French supermarkets also sell items in smaller sizes. People seem to have a predisposition—you might call it a default setting—to eat one portion of a food, whatever the size of that portion might be. According to this view, the French tend to eat less just because they are given smaller portions. To explore the role of portion size, researchers tried offering free snacks in the lobby of a building, varying the size of the snacks from one day to another. When they offered soft pretzels, most people ate one pretzel. When researchers offered pretzels already cut in half, most people ate half a pretzel. Similarly, in the lobby of a different building, the researchers sometimes offered 3-g Tootsie Rolls and sometimes 12-g Tootsie Rolls. On the average people ate more, by weight, on the days with big Tootsie Rolls (Geier, Rozin, & Doros, 2006).

Losing Weight

People trying to lose weight have a conflict between the motive to enjoy eating now and the motive to feel good about losing weight later. Clinical psychologists who work with people trying to lose weight report frequent frustrations as people repeatedly lose weight and then gain it back (Polivy & Herman, 2002). Most interventions to prevent or treat obesity produce only small or temporary benefits (Stice, Shaw, & Marti, 2006). However, you probably know some people who did manage to diet and then keep to a moderate weight. The reason we hear about more dieting failures than successes is simple: Most of the people who lose weight and keep it off don't keep talking about it and seeking help (Schachter, 1982). The people who show up at one weight-loss clinic after another have repeatedly failed to lose weight. In other words the difficult patients seem disproportionately common.

Many approaches are available for those seeking help in losing weight. A survey of weight-loss experts found that they disagreed about much but did agree on a few recommendations (Schwartz & Brownell, 1995):

- Almost anyone who needs to lose weight should include increased exercise as part of the strategy.
- Only people with severe, life-threatening obesity should even consider surgical removal of fat.

- Programs such as Overeaters Anonymous (OA) help people who feel comfortable with the spiritual focus and the emphasis on overeating as an addiction or disease. However, not everyone feels comfortable with this approach.
- Private counseling is useful mostly for people with other psychological problems in addition to their weight problem.

Effect of Weight Loss on Appetite

Are you satisfied with your weight? In the United States, women in particular are likely to be dissatisfied with their own appearance, and the percentage of women expressing dissatisfaction has increased gradually over decades. Concern about weight is common among both White and Black women (Grabe & Hyde, 2006) and often begins at an early age. We live with constant pressures to be thin and attractive, beginning with such things as Barbie dolls. Barbie's waist to height ratio is thinner than would be possible, even on a starvation diet. A woman that thin at the waist would have no breast development, even if she could stay alive. Researchers have found that repeated exposure to the doll causes 5- to 7-year-old girls to express increased dissatisfaction with their own bodies (Dittmar, Halliwell, & Ive, 2006).

Dissatisfaction about one's body often translates into worries about eating. Before we proceed try these questions. In each case circle one of the choices.

Try It Yourself

- *Ice cream* belongs best with: delicious   fattening
- *Chocolate cake* belongs best with: guilt   celebration
- *Heavy cream* belongs best with: whipped   unhealthy
- *Fried eggs* belong best with: breakfast   cholesterol

On questions like these, U.S. people, especially women, are more likely to circle *fattening, guilt, unhealthy,* and *cholesterol*—indicating food worries—whereas people in Japan, Belgium, and France usually circle *delicious, celebration, whipped,* and *breakfast.* On a wide range of questions, U.S. people indicate great interest in eating highly healthful foods but have serious worries about their diet (Rozin, Fischler, Imada, Sarubin, & Wrzesniewski, 1999).

April Fallon and Paul Rozin (1985) asked women to indicate on a diagram which body figure they thought men considered most attractive. The investigators also asked men which female figure *they* considered most attractive. As Figure 11.9 shows, women thought that men preferred thinner women than most men actually do. (The same study also found that men

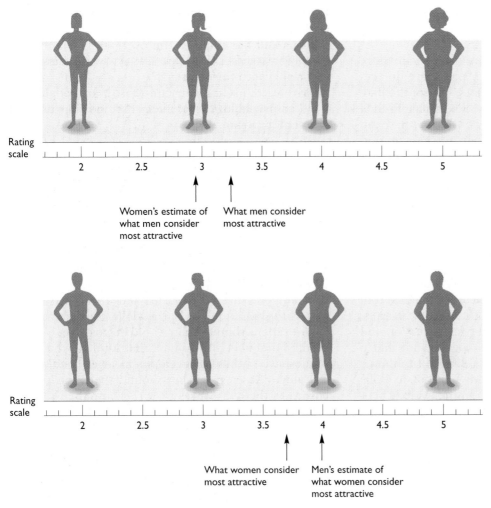

FIGURE 11.9 In a study by Fallon and Rozin (1985), women and men were asked which figure they considered most attractive and which figure they believed the opposite sex considered most attractive. Each sex misestimated the other's preferences.

thought women preferred heavier men than most women actually do.)

Anorexia Nervosa

The Duchess of Windsor once said, "You can't be too rich or too thin." She may have been right about too rich, but she was definitely wrong about too thin. Some people are so strongly motivated to be thin that they threaten their health.

Anorexia nervosa is *a condition in which someone refuses to eat enough to maintain a stable weight, intensely fears gaining weight, and misperceives his or her body as fatter than it actually is.* Most people with anorexia also exercise heavily. *Anorexia* means "loss of appetite," although the problem here is more a refusal to eat than a loss of appetite. The term *nervosa*, meaning "for reasons of the nerves," distinguishes this condition from disorders of the digestive system. Anorexia nervosa occurs in about 0.3% of young women about age 15 to 24 in the United States

and Europe, with much lower incidence in men and older women (Hoek & van Hoeken, 2003). As with other psychological conditions, anorexia nervosa comes in all degrees, but in its most severe form, it can fatally damage the heart muscle.

The prevalence of anorexia seems to have increased over the last several decades, presumably in response to social pressures. However, the increase has been slow, and it is difficult to know how much of the increase is real and how much is due to increased recognition and improved recordkeeping (Lindberg & Hjern, 2003).

At the outset the person may have decided to lose weight for health reasons, to become a ballet dancer or model, or for some other reason. Unlike people who are food deprived for other reasons, people with anorexia run long distances, compete at sports, work diligently on their school assignments, and sleep little. Most are perfectionists who take pride in the extreme self-control they demonstrate by refusing to eat (Halmi et al., 2000). The perfectionist personality probably contributes to anorexia, although it could hardly be the whole explanation.

The causes of anorexia are unknown. Many biochemical abnormalities have been demonstrated in the brains of people with anorexia, but the abnormalities are probably more the result than the cause of severe weight loss (Ferguson & Pigott, 2000). After weight returns to normal, most of the biochemical measures do too. Similarities between monozygotic twins imply a genetic contribution, although the route of the genes' effects is not yet known (Klump, Miller, Keel, McGue, & Iacono, 2001). Anorexia is reported more often in upper-middle-class families, although part of the explanation is that people from poorer families are less likely to get help and therefore less likely to show up in the statistics (Becker, Franko, Speck, & Herzog, 2003). Anorexia is also somewhat more common among families with a parent who has a psychiatric disorder (Lindberg & Hjern, 2003). However, most people with anorexia have no psychiatric history themselves before the onset of anorexia.

One hypothesis is that anorexia reflects impairment of the brain's hunger mechanisms. However, most people with anorexia enjoy the taste of food and even enjoy preparing it. The problem is more a fear of eating than a lack of hunger. Some even refuse to lick postage stamps for fear that the glue might contain some tiny fraction of a calorie. People with anorexia usually deny or understate their problem. Even when they become dangerously thin, they often describe themselves as "looking fat" and "needing to lose weight."

A fun house mirror temporarily distorts anyone's appearance. People with anorexia nervosa report a similar distortion of body image at all times, describing themselves as much fatter than they really are.

Cultural influences are strong but not the whole story. Western culture today puts strong pressure, especially on young women, to be thin, and dieting in response to that pressure can lead to anorexia. However, society's pressure cannot be the complete explanation, as most women who go on severe diets do not develop anorexia. Anorexia is more common in cultures that emphasize thinness, such as the United States, Canada, and northern Europe. Immigrants from southern Europe, Africa, or the Arab countries have increased risk of anorexia after living in one of the cultures with higher incidence (Lindberg & Hjern, 2003). However, occasional cases of anorexia nervosa

have been documented in non-Westernized cultures of Africa and Southeast Asia, as well as in Europe hundreds of years ago, long before the emphasis on being thin to be beautiful (Keel & Klump, 2003). In some of those cases, society had other kinds of pressures, such as fasting for religious reasons. So the cultural influences that contribute to anorexia vary, but we need to explain why some people react so much more strongly than others.

This teenage girl, posing with her mother, was elected "best body in the senior class" during the worst period of her anorexia. Society encourages women to be extremely, even dangerously, thin.

 CONCEPT CHECK

8. In what way is a patient with anorexia strikingly different from typical starving people? (Check your answer on page 413.)

Bulimia Nervosa

Another eating disorder is **bulimia nervosa** (literally, "ox hunger"), in which people—again, mostly women—alternate *between self-starvation and frequent periods of excessive eating when they feel they have lost their ability to control themselves. To compensate for the overeating, they may force themselves to vomit or use laxatives or enemas, or they may go* *through long periods of dieting and exercising.* That is, they "binge and purge." In extreme eating binges, people have been known to consume up to 20,000 calories at a time (Schlesier-Stropp, 1984). A meal of a "regular size" cheeseburger, regular fries, and a milkshake constitutes about 1,000 calories, so imagine eating that meal 20 times at one sitting. However, most binges feature sweets and fats with little protein (Latner, 2003), so a better illustration of 20,000 calories would be 10 liters of chocolate fudge topping.

In the United States, about 1% of adult women and about 0.1% of adult men have bulimia nervosa (Hoek & van Hoeken, 2003). One study found that, 6 years after women were treated for bulimia, 60% were fully recovered, 30% still had moderate problems, and 10% had serious disorders or were dead (Fichter & Quadflieg, 1997).

The incidence of bulimia nervosa has increased steadily over the last few decades. Whenever the numbers seem to go up or down, the question arises as to whether the actual incidence has changed or whether psychiatrists have changed their diagnoses. In this case, however, we have a special kind of evidence: The more recently a woman was born, the higher her risk of ever developing bulimia nervosa, even when all women are evaluated at the same time and according to the same criteria. That is, bulimia is more common among young women today than it ever was in their mothers' and grandmothers' generations (Kendler et al., 1991).

Culture is a major contributor to bulimia nervosa. Bulimia was rare and perhaps nonexistent until a few decades ago, and it has not been recorded in any cultures without a strong Western influence (Keel & Klump, 2003). Of course, eating binges are impossible without huge amounts of tasty food, and that availability is a recent historical development.

The most spectacular example comes from the Fiji Islands, where women have traditionally been heavy but content with their bodies. The idea of dieting to lose weight was unknown until the introduction of television, with many American programs, in 1995. Since then, many have begun dieting, self-induced vomiting, and binge eating. Many said they were trying to lose weight to be more like the women they saw on television (Becker, Burwell, Gilman, Herzog, & Hamburg, 2002; Becker, Burwell, Navara, & Gilman, 2003).

One hypothesis has been that either anorexia or bulimia might result from sexual abuse early in life, low self-esteem, or depression (Bardone, Vohs, Abramson, Heatherton, & Joiner, 2000; Fairburn, Welch, Doll, Davies, & O'Connor, 1997). However, the research has found no consistent link between any of these factors and the onset of eating disorders. The disorders do tend to persist longer in depressed people (Stice, 2002).

Another hypothesis is that people with bulimia starve themselves for a while, fight their persistent feelings of hunger, and then go on an eating binge (Polivy & Herman, 1985). That idea may be on the right track, but it is incomplete. Of the people who starve themselves for days or weeks, some do develop eating binges, but others do not (Stice, 2002).

The results may depend on what someone eats after a period of deprivation. Whereas most people who end a fast begin the next meal with meat, fish, or eggs, people with bulimia start with dessert or snack foods (Latner, 2003). One hypothesis compares bulimia to drug addiction (Hoebel, Rada, Mark, & Pothos, 1999). Overeating can provide a "high" similar to that from drugs, and some drug users withdrawing from a drug turn to overeating as a substitute. Moreover, when an addict abstains from a drug for a while and then returns to it, the first new use of the drug can be highly reinforcing. By this reasoning the cycles of abstention and overeating become addictive because the first big meal after a period of abstention is extremely reinforcing.

To test this idea, researchers put laboratory rats on a regimen of no food for 12 hours, including the first 4 hours of their waking day, followed by a meal of a sweet, syrupy liquid. With each repetition of this schedule, the rats ate more and more of that rich meal. Furthermore, if they were then deprived of this accustomed meal, they shook their heads and chattered their teeth in a pattern much like that of rats going through morphine withdrawal (Colantuoni et al., 2001, 2002). Obviously, the rats in this study do not fully model the complexities of human bulimia, but they suggest that a pattern of deprivation followed by overeating can provide strong reinforcement that overwhelms other motivations.

 CONCEPT CHECK

9. Under what circumstances would an eating binge be likely to produce an experience similar to taking an addictive drug? (Check your answer on page 413.)

IN CLOSING

The Complexities of Hunger

The research on nearly every topic in this module underscores the idea that our motivations are controlled by a complex mixture of physiological, social, and cognitive forces. For example, people become overweight (or falsely perceive themselves as overweight) for a variety of reasons relating to everything from genetics to culture, and they then try to lose weight mostly for social reasons, such as trying to look attractive. Sometimes, the physiological factors and the social factors collide, as when normal-weight people try to make themselves thinner and thinner.

The overall point is this: All our motivations interact and combine. How much we eat and what and when we eat depend not only on our need for food but also on social needs and the need for self-esteem. ▮

Summary

- *Short-term regulation of hunger.* Meals are ended by several mechanisms, principally distension of the stomach and intestines. Hunger resumes when the cells begin to receive less glucose and other nutrients. The hormone insulin regulates the flow of nutrients from the blood to storage. (page 404)

- *Long-term regulation of hunger.* An individual meal can be larger or smaller than necessary to provide the energy that the body needs. The body's fat cells secrete the hormone leptin in proportion to their mass; an increase of leptin decreases hunger, and a decrease of leptin increases hunger. (page 405)

- *Causes of being overweight.* Some people are predisposed to obesity for genetic reasons. Whether they become obese or how obese they become depends on the kinds and amounts of food available. Obese people tend to be inactive and remain so even after losing weight. (page 408)

- *Weight-loss techniques.* Many people resort to a variety of strategies to lose weight, ranging from diet-

ing to surgery. Increased exercise is a good idea for almost anyone wishing to lose weight. (page 409)

- *Anorexia nervosa and bulimia nervosa.* People suffering from anorexia nervosa deprive themselves of food, sometimes to the point of starvation. People suffering from bulimia nervosa alternate between periods of strict dieting and brief but spectacular eating binges. The cultural pressure to become thin is a contributor to both conditions but not a sufficient explanation of either. (page 410)

Answers to Concept Checks

4. Insulin levels are higher in the middle of the day (LeMagnen, 1981). As a result much of the food you eat is stored as fats, and you become hungry again soon. Late at night, when insulin levels are lower, some of your fat supplies are converted to glucose, which enters the blood. (page 405)

5. Leptin, released by fat cells, and insulin, released by the pancreas. (pages 405, 406)

6. By keeping their fat levels very low, they also keep their leptin levels low, and leptin is one of the triggers for puberty. (page 406)

7. The set point has increased. (page 406)

8. Unlike typical starving people, those with anorexia have high levels of activity. Also, they refuse to eat in the presence of tasty foods. (page 410)

9. Eating a meal high in sweets and fats right after a deprivation period apparently produces an experience comparable to those produced by addictive drugs. (page 412)

Sexual Motivation

- *What do people do sexually?*
- *Why do some people's sexual interests differ from others'?*

If you have any doubts about people's interest in sex, take a look at television listings, popular books and magazines, and films. Sexual activity occupies a small percentage of most people's time but a great deal of their interest.

Sexual motivation, like hunger, depends on both a physiological drive and available incentives. Also like hunger, the sex drive increases during times of deprivation, at least up to a point, and it can be inhibited for social and symbolic reasons, including religious ones. However, the sex drive differs from hunger in important ways. We do not need to be around food to feel hungry, but many people do need a partner to feel sexual arousal. We eat in public, but we have sexual activities in private.

Ultimately, of course, hunger and sex serve important biological functions that we ordinarily don't even think about during the acts themselves. We eat because we enjoy eating, and we evolved mechanisms that make us enjoy eating because eating keeps us alive. Similarly, we enjoy sex, and we evolved mechanisms that make sex feel good because it leads to reproduction.

What Do People Do, and How Often?

Researchers have many reasons for inquiring about the frequency of various sexual behaviors. For example, if we want to predict the spread of AIDS, we need to know how many people are having unsafe sex and with how many partners. In addition to the scientific and medical reasons for studying sex, let's admit it: Most of us are curious about what other people do.

The Kinsey Survey

The first important survey of human sexual behavior was conducted by Alfred C. Kinsey, an insect biologist who agreed to teach the biological portion of Indiana University's course on marriage. When he found that the library included very little information about human sexuality, he decided to conduct a survey. What started as a small-scale project for teaching purposes grew into a survey of 18,000 people.

Alfred C. Kinsey, who pioneered survey studies of sexual behavior, was an outstanding interviewer. He put people at ease so they could speak freely but was also alert to probable lies. However, he did not obtain a random or representative sample of the population.

Although Kinsey's sample was large, it was neither random nor representative. He obtained most of his interviews by going to organizations, ranging from fraternities to nunneries, and asking everyone in the organization to talk to him. He interviewed mostly midwestern European Americans who belonged to organizations that agreed to cooperate, and the percentages he reported do not generalize to other populations.

Nevertheless, he did document the variability of human sexual behavior (Kinsey, Pomeroy, & Martin, 1948; Kinsey, Pomeroy, Martin, & Gebhard, 1953). He found some people who had rarely or never experienced orgasm. At the other extreme, he found one man who reported an average of four or five orgasms per day over the preceding 30 years (with a wide variety of male, female, and nonhuman partners) and several women who sometimes had 50 or more orgasms within 20 minutes.

Kinsey found that most people were unaware of the great variation in sexual behavior in the population. When he asked people whether they believed that "ex-

Sexual customs vary sharply from one society to another. At a Hmong festival, unmarried women toss tennis balls to potential suitors.

cessive masturbation" causes physical and mental illness, most said yes. (We now know it does not.) He then asked what would constitute "excessive." For each person excessive meant a little more than what he or she did. One young man who masturbated once a month said he thought three times a month would cause mental illness. A man who masturbated three times daily said he thought five times daily would be excessive. (In reaction to these findings, Kinsey defined a *nymphomaniac* as "someone who wants sex more than you do.")

Contemporary Surveys

Kinsey did not try to interview a random sample of the population because he assumed that most people would refuse to cooperate. He may have been right in the 1940s, but in the 1980s and beyond, researchers identified random samples and managed to get cooperation from most of the people they approached (Fay, Turner, Klassen, & Gagnon, 1989; Laumann, Gagnon, Michael, & Michaels, 1994). Unfortunately, people's self-reports are not entirely accurate. Even when they try to be honest, their memories about frequency of sexual activity grow blurry, and they often overstate their consistency of practicing safe sex (Garry, Sharman, Feldman, Marlatt, & Loftus, 2002).

(Some advice if anyone ever asks you to participate in a sex survey: Legitimate researchers carefully present their credentials to show their affiliation with a research institute. They also take precautions to guarantee the confidentiality of responses. If "researchers" who want to ask you about your sex life fail to show their credentials or seem unconcerned about your confidentiality, do not trust them. Be wary of sex surveys by telephone. Some sex researchers do conduct research by telephone, but it is hard to distinguish a legitimate sex survey from an obscene phone call in disguise.)

A survey of a random sample of almost 3,500 U.S. adults (Laumann et al., 1994) explored what people would like to be doing. Figure 11.10 shows the percentage of men and women who describe various sexual activities as "very appealing." The most popular sexual activity is vaginal intercourse, followed by watching one's partner undress and then by oral sex. Other possible options lag well behind. Note an ambiguity in certain responses: When 13% of men say they find group sex "very appealing," do they mean they have frequently enjoyed doing it or that they have fantasies about it?

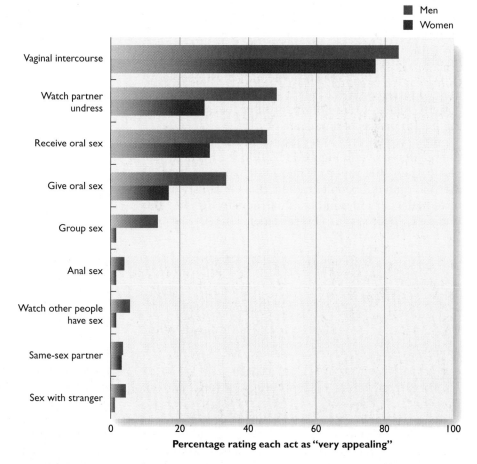

FIGURE 11.10 The percentage of U.S. adults who rate various sexual activities as "very appealing" as opposed to "somewhat appealing," "not appealing," or "not at all appealing." *(Based on data of Laumann, Gagnon, Michael, & Michaels, 1994)*

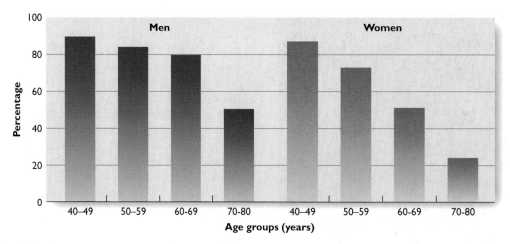

FIGURE 11.11 In a survey of four countries, the percentage of people reporting at least occasional sexual intercourse declines with advancing age. *(From Brock et al., 2003)*

Note that more men than women report enjoying every activity on the graph. A broader survey of 27,500 people in 29 countries found that in every country, a higher percentage of men than women reported pleasure and satisfaction with their sex life (Laumann et al., 2006).

Figure 11.11 presents the results from a large-scale international survey of sexual behavior. As the figure shows, sexual activity declines gradually with age, but even beyond age 70, about half of men and nearly a quarter of women remain sexually active (Brock et al., 2003). Even in old age, most people remain interested in sex. Much of the decline in sexual activity relates to loss of opportunity because of failing health or loss of a partner.

A survey in the United States in the 1990s found the results shown in Figure 11.12. On the average people in their 40s reported more sex partners in their lifetime than did people in their 50s. Obviously, if you have had a certain number of partners by age 40, your total can't decrease as you get older. The 40-year-olds

were different people from the 50-year-olds, and they had been young during an era of greater sexual freedom. This is a cohort effect, like the ones described in chapter 5.

 CONCEPT CHECK

10. Why did Kinsey's results differ from those of later surveys? (Check your answer on page 425.)

Sexual Behavior in the Era of AIDS

During the 1980s a new factor entered into people's sexual motivations: the fear of **acquired immune deficiency syndrome (AIDS),** *a sexually transmitted disease that attacks the body's immune system.* For HIV (human immunodeficiency virus)—the virus that causes AIDS—to spread from one person to another, it must enter the other person's blood. (The virus does not survive long outside body fluids.) The three common routes of transmission are transfusions of contaminated blood, sharing needles used for intravenous injections of illegal drugs, and sexual contact. Of types of sexual contact, anal intercourse is the riskiest, but vaginal intercourse is risky also. Touching and kissing do not spread the virus unless both people have open wounds that exchange blood.

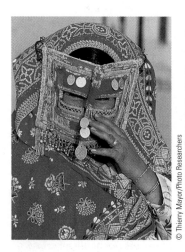

▌ Different cultures have very different standards regarding public display of the human body and premarital sex.

Courtesy of San Francisco AIDS Foundation

▌ To prevent AIDS use condoms during sex and don't share injection needles. Advertisements such as this have prompted many people to change their behavior.

For generations people have known how to avoid contracting syphilis, gonorrhea, and other sexually transmitted diseases: Don't have sex with someone who might be infected or use a condom. If people had consistently followed this advice, we could have eliminated those diseases long ago. The same advice is now offered to combat AIDS, and the amount of compliance varies. Information campaigns have produced clear benefits but not enough to eradicate the disease.

In the United States, AIDS spread first among male homosexuals and later among heterosexuals as well. In some parts of Africa, it affects one fifth or more of the adult population. One difficulty is that people remain symptom-free for years, so they can spread the virus long before they know they have it and before their partners have reason to suspect it.

Sexual Arousal

Sexual motivation depends on both physiological and cognitive influences—that is, not just the "plumbing" of the body but also the presence of a suitable partner, a willingness to be aroused, and a lack of anxiety. William Masters and Virginia Johnson (1966), who pioneered the study of human sexual response, discovered similarities in physiological arousal between men and women.

They observed hundreds of people masturbating or having sexual intercourse in a laboratory and monitored their physiological responses, including heart rate, breathing, muscle tension, blood engorgement of the genitals and breasts, and nipple erection. Masters and Johnson identified four physiological stages in sexual arousal (Figure 11.13).

During the first stage, *excitement,* a man's penis becomes erect and a woman's vagina becomes lubricated. Breathing becomes rapid and deep. Heart rate and blood pressure increase. Many people experience a flush of the skin, which sometimes resembles a measles rash. Women's nipples become erect, and the breasts swell slightly for women who have not nursed a baby. Although this stage is referred to as excitement,

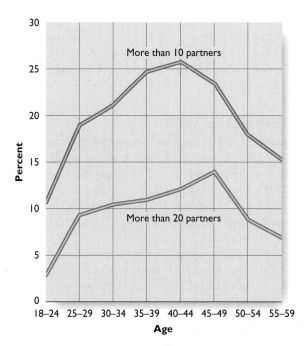

FIGURE 11.12 The percentage of U.S. men and women reporting more than 10 or 20 sex partners in their lives. *(Based on data of Laumann et al., 1994)*

nervousness interferes with it, as do stimulant drugs, including coffee.

During the second stage, called the *plateau,* excitement remains fairly constant. This stage lasts for varying lengths of time depending on a person's age and the intensity of the stimulation. Excitement becomes intense in the third stage, until a sudden release of tension known as *climax* or *orgasm,* which is felt throughout the entire body. During the fourth and final stage, *resolution,* the person relaxes.

As Figure 11.13 shows, the pattern of excitation varies from one person to another. During a given episode, a woman may experience no orgasm, one, or many. Most men do not experience multiple consecu-

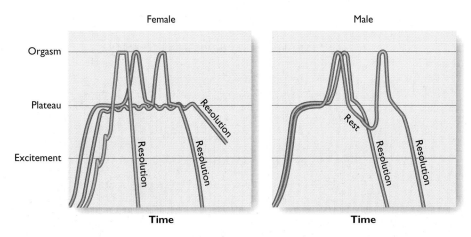

FIGURE 11.13. Sexual arousal usually proceeds through four stages—excitement, plateau, orgasm, and resolution. Each color represents the response of a different individual. Note the variation. *(After Masters & Johnson, 1966)*

tive orgasms, although they can achieve orgasm again following a rest (or refractory) period. Among individuals in both genders, the intensity of the orgasm ranges from something like a sigh to an extremely intense experience.

Sexual Dysfunction

The pattern just described is common but hardly universal. Many people experience sexual difficulties of one sort or another at some point in life (Laumann et al., 2003). One problem, for example, is a decreased interest in sex. People with decreased interest miss an opportunity for pleasure and risk jeopardizing their relationship with a partner.

Many people—more women than men—experience sexual arousal without orgasm. That is, they go through Masters and Johnson's first two stages without reaching the third. In some cases the lack of orgasm relates to psychological depression, but in most cases the cause is unknown (Laumann et al., 2003).

Some men cannot produce or maintain an erection. A man's erection requires relaxation of the smooth muscles controlling blood flow to the penis. The drug sildenafil (trade name Viagra) relaxes those muscles and thereby facilitates an erection (Rowland & Burnett, 2000). Other men, especially young men, have premature ejaculations, advancing from excitement to orgasm sooner than they or their partners wish. Unfortunately, most people hesitate to discuss sexual problems with their physicians, and physicians seldom ask. Consequently, most difficulties go untreated.

Sexual Anatomy and Identity

Gender identity is *the sex that a person regards him- or herself as being.* Most people with male genitals have a male identity, and most with female genitals have a female identity, but exceptions do occur.

In the earliest stages of development, the human fetus has a "unisex" appearance (Figure 11.14). One structure subsequently develops into either a penis or a clitoris. Another structure develops into either a scrotum or labia. The direction of development depends on hormonal influences during prenatal development. Beginning in the seventh or eighth week after conception, genetic *male fetuses generally secrete higher levels of the hormone* **testosterone** *than do females* (although both sexes produce some), and over the next couple of months, the testosterone causes the tiny fetal structures to grow into a penis and a scrotum. In genetic female fetuses, with lower levels of testosterone, the structures develop into clitoris and labia instead. Levels of *the hormone* **estrogen** *increase more in females than in males* at this time. Estrogen is important for internal female development but has little effect on the external anatomical development of penis versus clitoris and scrotum versus labia.

Remember: In humans and other mammals, high testosterone levels produce a male

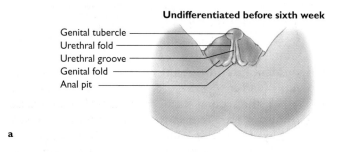

Undifferentiated before sixth week

Genital tubercle
Urethral fold
Urethral groove
Genital fold
Anal pit

a

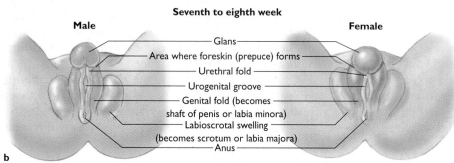

Seventh to eighth week

Male — Female

Glans
Area where foreskin (prepuce) forms
Urethral fold
Urogenital groove
Genital fold (becomes shaft of penis or labia minora)
Labioscrotal swelling (becomes scrotum or labia majora)
Anus

b

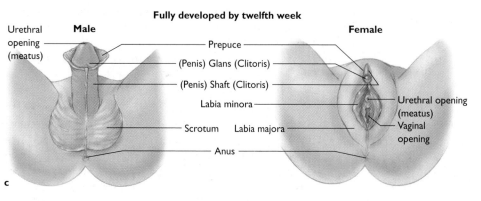

Fully developed by twelfth week

Urethral opening (meatus)   Male   Female

Prepuce
(Penis) Glans (Clitoris)
(Penis) Shaft (Clitoris)
Labia minora
Scrotum   Labia majora
Anus

Urethral opening (meatus)
Vaginal opening

c

FIGURE 11.14 The human genitals look the same in male and female fetuses for the first 6 or 7 weeks after conception **(a).** Differences begin to emerge over the next couple of months **(b)** and are clear at birth **(c).**

external anatomy; low testosterone levels produce a female anatomy. Within normal limits the amount of circulating estrogen does not determine whether one develops a male or female appearance.

About 1 child in 2,000 is born with genitals that are hard to classify as male or female, and 1 or 2 in 100 have a slightly ambiguous external anatomy (Blackless et al., 2000). The most common cause is overactive adrenal glands in a genetic female. Adrenal glands secrete testosterone, as well as other hormones, and if a genetic female is exposed to elevated amounts of testosterone during prenatal development, she develops a sexual anatomy that looks intermediate between male and female (Money & Ehrhardt, 1972). Less frequently, a genetic male develops an intermediate appearance because of an alteration in the gene that controls testosterone receptors (Misrahi et al., 1997). *People with an anatomy that appears intermediate between male and female* are known as intersexes (Figure 11.15). The Intersex Society of North America (www.isna.org) is devoted to increasing understanding and acceptance of people with ambiguous genitals.

How should parents and others treat intersexed people? For decades the standard medical recommendation has been, when in doubt, call the child female and perform surgery to make her anatomy look female. This surgery includes creating or lengthening a vagina and reducing the ambiguous penis/clitoris to the size of an average clitoris. Many cases require repeated surgery to obtain a satisfactory appearance.

This recommendation was based on the assumption that, if a child looks like a girl and is treated like a girl, she will develop psychologically as a girl. Physi-

A group of intersexed adults gathered to provide mutual support and protest against involuntary surgical intervention for intersexes. To emphasize that they do not consider intersexuality shameful, they requested that their names be used. Left to right: Martha Coventry, Max Beck, David Vandertie, Kristi Bruse, and Angela Moreno.

Courtesy of Intersex Society of North America

cians never had much evidence for their assumption, and later experience has contradicted it. Follow-up studies on girls who were partly masculinized at birth, but reared as females, have found that they are more likely than other girls to prefer boy-typical toys (cars, guns, and tools) to girl-typical toys (dolls, cosmetics, dishes), despite their parents' attempts to encourage interest in the girl-typical toys (Berenbaum, Duck, & Bryk, 2000; Nordenström, Servin, Bohlin, Larson, & Wedell, 2002; Pasterski et al., 2005). At adolescence most continue to have male-typical interests (Berenbaum, 1999). An unusually high percentage report *no* sexual fantasies—neither heterosexual nor homosexual (Zucker et al., 1996).

There is, of course, nothing wrong with a girl being interested in boys' activities or being uninterested in sex. The point is that we can't count on rearing patterns to control psychological development. Prenatal hormones evidently influence interests and activities in addition to external anatomy. Male and female brains differ on the average in many ways, although none are consistent across all individuals. One part of your brain might be "male typical" whereas another is "female typical" (Woodson & Gorski, 2000). Evidently, genetically female brains exposed to the prenatal influence of male hormones develop several male-typical aspects.

Furthermore, the genital surgery—reducing or removing the penis/clitoris—decreases sexual pleasure and the capacity for orgasm (Minto, Liao, Woodhouse, Ransley, & Creighton, 2003). An artificial vagina may be satisfactory to a male partner, but it provides no sensation or pleasure to the woman, and it requires frequent attention to prevent scar tissue. Finally, intersexed individuals object that, in many cases, physicians lied to them about the surgery and the reasons

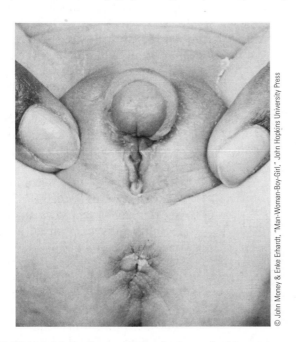

© John Money & Enke Erhardt, "Man-Woman-Boy-Girl", John Hopkins University Press

FIGURE 11.15 External genitals of a 3-month-old genetic female who was masculinized before birth by excess androgens from the adrenal gland.

for it. Today, more and more physicians recommend that parents raise the child as the gender the genitals most resemble and perform no surgery until and unless the individual requests it. Many intersexed individuals prefer to remain as they are, without surgery (Dreger, 1998).

CONCEPT CHECK

11. If a human fetus were exposed to very low levels of both testosterone and estrogen throughout prenatal development, how would the sexual anatomy appear?

12. If a human fetus were exposed to high levels of both testosterone and estrogen throughout prenatal development, how would the sexual anatomy appear? (Check your answers on page 425.)

Sexual Orientation

Sexual orientation is *someone's tendency to respond sexually to male or female partners or both or neither.* People vary in their sexual orientations, just as they do in their food preferences and other motivations. Those who prefer partners of their own sex have a homosexual (gay or lesbian) orientation.

Evidence has gradually accumulated that sexual orientation varies in many nonhuman species also. Homosexual or bisexual behavior has been observed in hundreds of animal species, although it is apparently absent in many others. It has been extensively documented and investigated in sheep (Perkins, Fitzgerald, & Moss, 1995). Biologists used to assume that animal homosexuality occurred only in captivity, only if an individual could not find a partner of the other sex, or only in hormonally abnormal animals, but the evidence has refuted each of these hypotheses (Bagemihl, 1999). So, if "natural" means that something occurs in nature, then homosexuality is natural.

How many people have a homosexual orientation? You may have heard people confidently assert "10%." That number is derived from Kinsey's report that about 13% of the men and 7% of the women he interviewed in the 1940s and 1950s stated a predominantly homosexual orientation. The often-quoted figure of 10% is the mean of Kinsey's results for men and women. However, Kinsey's data were based on a nonrandom sample of the population.

In a random sample of 3,500 U.S. adults, 2.8% of men and 1.4% of women described themselves as having a homosexual (gay or lesbian) orientation (Laumann et al., 1994). More people describe a homosexual experience if they answer on a computer than if they fill out a piece of paper, presumably because the computer answer is more clearly anonymous (Turner et al., 1998). However, even with the greatest assurances of anonymity, the descriptions of homosexuality don't increase much.

As Figure 11.16 demonstrates, the prevalence of homosexuality depends on the phrasing of the question. Many people who do not consider themselves gay or lesbian have had at least one adult homosexual experience, and still more (especially males) had one in early adolescence (Laumann et al., 1994). Even higher percentages say they have felt some attraction to a member of their own sex at some time in their life (Dickson, Paul, & Herbison, 2003).

If you have frequently heard the prevalence of homosexual orientations estimated at 10%, you may be skeptical of the report that only 1 to 3% of people identify themselves as gay or lesbian. However, three other large surveys reported that 1 to 2%, 3%, or 6% of U.S. men were either gay or bisexual (Billy, Tanfer, Grady, & Klepinger, 1993; Cameron, Proctor, Coburn, & Forde, 1985; Fay et al., 1989). Surveys in other countries have reported similar or slightly lower percentages, as shown in Figure 11.17 (Izazola-Licea, Gortmaker, Tolbert, De Gruttola, & Mann, 2000; Sandfort, de Graaf, Bijl, & Schnabel, 2001; Spira et al., 1993; Wellings, Field, Johnson, & Wadsworth, 1994).

Attitudes toward homosexual relationships have varied among cultures and among historical eras.

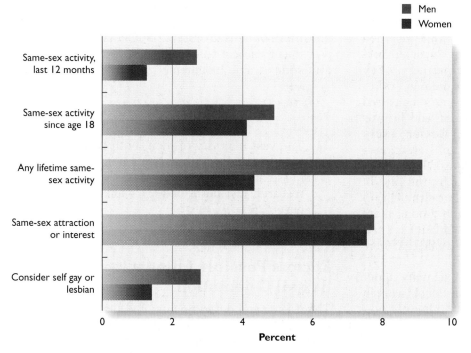

FIGURE 11.16 The percentages of U.S. adults who report sexual activity or interest in sexual activity with people of their own sex. *(Based on data of Laumann et al., 1994)*

Differences Between Men and Women

In Figure 11.16 notice that although men report more homosexual activity than women do, women are as likely as men to report some "same-sex attraction or interest." Let's focus on sexual attraction. In one study homosexual and heterosexual men and women watched a series of short pornographic films while the experimenters measured penis erection in the men and vaginal secretions by the women. (They tested people one at a time, so don't picture a mixed group watching these films with devices attached to their genitals.) Some of the films showed two men; some showed two women, and some showed a man and a woman. Among men the results were clear: Heterosexual men showed the greatest arousal while watching two women, secondarily to watching a woman and a man, and little or no arousal while watching two men. Homosexual men showed the reverse—greatest arousal while watching two men. Women's responses were much less clear. Most women, both lesbians and heterosexuals, showed nearly equal

responses to watching either men or women (Chivers, Rieger, Latty, & Bailey, 2004).

A related study asked people to rate the strength of their sex drive and their degree of attraction to men and women. For heterosexual men greater sex drive meant greater attraction to women but no increase in attraction to men. For gay men greater sex drive correlated with greater attraction to men but no increased interest in women. However, the pattern was different for women. For heterosexual women a strong sex drive correlated with increased interest in men but also increased interest in women. For lesbian women a strong sex drive correlated with increased interest in women but also increased interest in men (Lippa, 2006). These correlations describe averages, and you should certainly not conclude that any woman with a strong sex drive is bisexual. Still, the results suggest that for women, increased sex drive in-

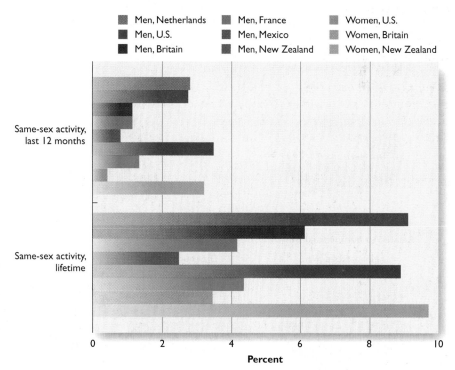

FIGURE 11.17 Comparisons of the results of surveys conducted in six countries, in which people were asked about homosexual experiences. *(Based on data of Dickson, Paul, & Herbison, 2003; Izazola-Licea, Gortmaker, Tolbert, De Gruttola, & Mann, 2000; Laumann, Gagnon, Michael, & Michaels, 1994; Sandfort, de Graaf, Bijl, & Schnabel, 2001; Spira et al., 1993; Wellings, Field, Johnson, & Wadsworth, 1994)*

creases the probability of response to both kinds of partners.

Another study focused on men who regarded themselves as bisexual. All had a history of sexual experiences with both male and female partners. They watched films of sex acts between two men and other films of two women, while the researchers measured penis erections. Although each of them said he was sexually interested in both men and women, every one of them showed strong arousal—penis erection—to just one or the other. Most were aroused by the film of men, although a few were aroused by the film of women. The researchers concluded that although bisexual behavior is moderately common among men, very few men have equally strong sexual fantasies and excitement about both male and female partners (Rieger, Chivers, & Bailey, 2005).

In contrast some women respond sexually about equally to both males and females, and such women sometimes switch between being predominantly heterosexual and predominantly lesbian (Cameron & Cameron, 2002; Diamond, 2003a; Dickson et al., 2003). Some are in love with a person of one sex while being sexually attracted to someone of the other sex (Diamond, 2003b).

The general principle, according to some psychologists, is that women tend to be more flexible. For example, a woman who changes male partners is more likely to accept the preferences of her new partner than a man is to alter his pattern to suit a new female partner (Baumeister, 2000). We don't know why women are more flexible. (Is being more flexible an advantage or a disadvantage? You could argue it either way, but it is best to take it as a description without attaching a value judgment.)

 CONCEPT CHECK

13. The vast majority of men, both homosexual and heterosexual, say they could not imagine switching sexual orientations. How does that fit with the research just described? (Check your answer on page 425.)

Factors Possibly Influencing Sexual Orientation

The origins and determinants of sexual orientation are not well understood. Most adults, especially men, report that their sexual orientation was apparent to them from as young as they can remember. The available research, based on only a few studies, suggests that genetic factors contribute toward sexual orientation for both men and women. Figure 11.18 shows the results of studies concerning homosexuality in twins and other relatives of adult gays and lesbians (Bailey & Pillard, 1991; Bailey, Pillard, Neale, & Agyei, 1993). Note that homosexuality is more prevalent in their monozygotic (identical) twins

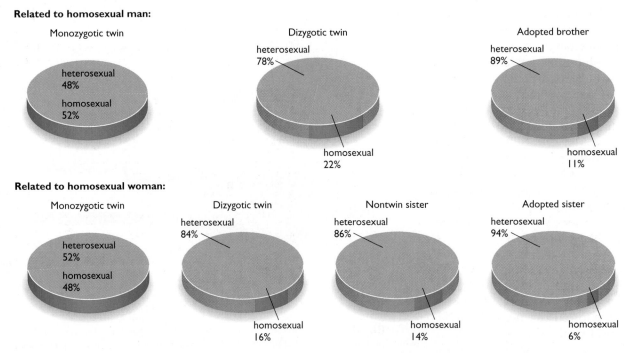

FIGURE 11.18 The probability of a homosexual orientation is higher among monozygotic twins of adult homosexuals than among their fraternal twins. The probability is higher among dizygotic twins than among adopted brothers or sisters who grew up in the same family. These data suggest a possible genetic role in sexual orientation. *(Based on results of Bailey & Pillard, 1991; Bailey, Pillard, Neale, & Agyei, 1993)*

than in their dizygotic (fraternal) twins. Another study with a smaller sample showed the same trends (Kendler, Thornton, Gilman, & Kessler, 2000).

That trend suggests a genetic influence toward homosexuality, although a gene could hardly be the only factor. If it were, then monozygotic twins would always have the same orientation. Furthermore, a genetic explanation raises an evolutionary question: If a gene has a major effect, how does it remain at a moderate frequency in the population? Ordinarily, any gene that decreases the probability of having children becomes rare. We don't know the explanation, but one study found that the female relatives of gay men tend to have larger than average families (Camperio-Ciani, Corna, & Capiluppi, 2004). A gene that decreases the probability of reproduction by men but increases the probability in their sisters could remain at a stable frequency in the population.

Another contributing factor is biological but not genetic: The probability of a homosexual orientation is slightly elevated among men who have an older brother. Having an older sister doesn't make a difference, nor does having an older adopted brother. It also doesn't make any difference whether the older brother lived in the same house with the younger brother or somewhere else. What matters is whether the mother had previously given birth to another son (Bogaert, 2006). One hypothesis to explain this tendency is that the first son sometimes causes the mother's immune system to build up antibodies that alter development of later sons (Bogaert, 2003).

Regardless of whether the original basis is genetics, prenatal environment, or something else, the question arises of what, if anything, is different in the body. Adult hormone levels are *not* different. On the average adult homosexual people are similar to heterosexual people in their levels of testosterone and estrogen. Altering someone's hormone levels can alter the strength of the sex drive but not sexual orientation (Tuiten et al., 2000). By analogy changing your insulin or glucose levels can affect your hunger but has little effect on what you consider good food.

However, it is possible that prenatal sex hormones influence later sexual orientation (Lalumière, Blanchard, & Zucker, 2000). Presumably, if they do, they have some effect on the brain. One widely quoted and often misunderstood study reported a small but measurable difference between the brains of homosexual and heterosexual men. Let's examine the evidence.

CRITICAL THINKING

WHAT'S THE EVIDENCE?

Sexual Orientation and Brain Anatomy

Animal studies have demonstrated that one section of the anterior hypothalamus is generally larger in males than in females. This brain area is necessary for the display of male-typical sexual activity in many mammalian species, and its size depends on prenatal hormones. Might part of the anterior hypothalamus differ between homosexual and heterosexual men?

Hypothesis. INAH3, a particular cluster of neurons in the anterior hypothalamus, will be larger on average in the brains of heterosexual men than in the brains of homosexual men or heterosexual women.

Method. Simon LeVay (1991) examined the brains of 41 adults who died at ages 26–59. AIDS was the cause of death for all 19 of the homosexual men in the study, 6 of the 16 heterosexual men, and 1 of the 6 heterosexual women. No brains of homosexual women were available for study. LeVay measured the sizes of four clusters of neurons in the anterior hypothalamus, including two clusters for which sex differences are common and two that are the same between the sexes.

Results. Three of the four neuron clusters did not consistently vary in size among the groups LeVay studied. However, area INAH3 was on the average about twice as large in heterosexual men as it was in homosexual men and about the same size in homosexual men as in heterosexual women. Figure 11.19 shows results for two representative individuals. The size of this area was about the same in heterosexual men who died of AIDS as in heterosexual men who died of other causes, so AIDS probably did not control the size of this area.

Interpretation. These results suggest that the size of the INAH3 area of the anterior hypothalamus may be related to heterosexual versus homosexual orientation, at least for some individuals. Note, however, that each group had much variation. The anatomy does not correlate perfectly with the behavior.

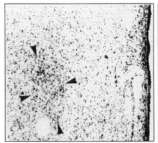

a   b

FIGURE 11.19 One section of the anterior hypothalamus (marked by arrows) is larger on the average in the brains of heterosexual men (**a**) than in the brains of homosexual men (**b**) or heterosexual women *(LeVay, 1991)*. Review Figure 11.6 for the location of the hypothalamus.

Like most studies, this one has its limitations: As with any study, we do not know whether the people that LeVay studied were typical of others. One later study found that the INAH3 of homosexual men was intermediate in size between that of heterosexual men and heterosexual women (Byne et al., 2001). That study extended our knowledge by finding that the INAH3 varied among people because of differences in the size of neurons there, not the number of neurons.

Another limitation is that LeVay's study does not tell us whether brain anatomy influenced people's sexual orientation or whether their sexual activities altered brain anatomy. As mentioned in chapter 3, extensive experience modifies some aspects of brain anatomy, even in adults.

You might recall the observations of homosexual behavior in sheep mentioned earlier. Researchers have found an area in sheep brains, possibly corresponding to INAH3 in humans, which is larger in rams that mount female sheep than in rams that mount other rams (Roselli, Larkin, Resko, Stellflug, & Stormshak, 2004). Further research on sheep may shed light on the relationship between this brain area and sexual orientation.

So where do all these studies leave us? At this point the evidence points to genetics and prenatal environment, which probably alter certain aspects of brain anatomy in small ways. However, we need to know far more about how these biological factors interact with experience. At this point we don't even know what kinds of experience are most relevant.

Uncertainty and tentative conclusions are not unusual in psychology. If you decide to become a psychologist, you will need to get used to the words "maybe" and "probably." As mentioned in chapter 2, most psychologists avoid the word "prove." Results merely increase or decrease their confidence in a conclusion.

 CONCEPT CHECK

14. Most studies find that gay men have approximately the same levels of testosterone in their blood as heterosexual men of the same age. Do such results conflict with the suggestion that prenatal hormonal conditions can predispose certain men to homosexuality? (Check your answer on page 425.)

The Biology and Sociology of Sex

What do studies of sexual motivation tell us about motivation in general? One point is that important motives have multiple determinants, both biological and social. We engage in sexual activity because it feels good, and we have evolved mechanisms that make it feel good because sex leads to reproduction. On the other hand, it often makes good biological sense to postpone reproduction until a safer time, so it is no wonder that nervousness decreases sexual arousal. We also engage in sexual activity because it cements a relationship with another person. Sex is one of the most powerful ways of drawing people together or tearing their relationship apart.

Because of its power, society regulates sexual behavior strictly. The rules vary from one culture to another, but every culture has definite expectations about what people will do, when, and with whom. In short, we cannot make much sense of complex human behaviors without considering a range of biological and social influences. ∎

Summary

- *Variability in human sexual behavior.* Alfred Kinsey, who conducted the first extensive survey of human sexual behavior, found that sexual activity varies more widely than most people realize. (page 414)

- *More recent surveys.* Both men and women choose vaginal intercourse as their most preferred sexual activity. Most people remain sexually active even into their 70s if they remain healthy and have a healthy, willing partner. (page 415)

- *Sexual arousal.* Sexual arousal proceeds through four stages: excitement, plateau, orgasm, and resolution. (page 417)

- *Development of genitals.* In the early stages of development, the human fetus possesses anatomical structures that may develop into either male genitals (if testosterone levels are high enough) or female genitals (if testosterone levels are lower). (page 418)

- *Prevalence of homosexuality.* According to surveys in several countries, about 2 to 4% of adult men and somewhat fewer women regard themselves as primarily or exclusively homosexual. Sexual orientation varies in degree from exclusively homosexual to exclusively heterosexual, with many intermediate gradations. (page 420)

- *Differences between men and women.* Nearly all men show a strong sexual response to either males or females but not both. Increasing their sex drive increases their interest in whichever kind of partner they already desired, without noticeable effects on their attraction to the other sex. In contrast many women seem capable of at least some response to both men and women, and increased sex drive enhances both kinds of response. (page 421)

- *Origins of sexual orientation.* Genetic influences and prenatal environment can apparently influence sexual orientation. On the average heterosexual and homosexual men differ in the size of one structure in the hypothalamus that contributes to certain aspects of sexual behavior. Less is known about the role of experience in the development of sexual orientation. (page 422)

Answers to Concept Checks

10. Kinsey interviewed a nonrandom, nonrepresentative sample of people. (page 415)

11. A fetus exposed to very low levels of both testosterone and estrogen throughout prenatal development would develop a female appearance. (page 418)

12. A fetus exposed to high levels of both testosterone and estrogen would develop a male appearance. High levels of testosterone lead to male anatomy; low levels lead to female anatomy. The level of estrogen does not play a decisive role. (page 418)

13. Studies of physiological arousal indicate that nearly all men respond either just to men or just to women. Although many men engage in sexual activities with both men and women, the orientation seems to be strongly one way or the other. (page 421)

14. Not necessarily. The suggestion is that prenatal hormones can alter early brain development. In adulthood hormone levels are normal, but certain aspects of brain development have already been determined. (page 424)

Work Motivation

• *Why do some people try harder than others?*

Most people like to compete against others, at least if they think they have a chance of winning. Archeologists once excavated an ancient human civilization from about 1400 B.C. and discovered, to their surprise, a ball court complete with nets (Hill, Blake, & Clark, 1998). People also strive to improve on their own previous performance. In effect they compete against themselves: Can I run farther, or bicycle faster, than last time?

Striving for excellence on the job resembles competing at sports: People exert great efforts to outdo a competitor or to reach their own goals *if* they think they have a chance of succeeding. One of the key interests of both employers and industrial/organizational psychologists is to understand what motivates workers to put their full efforts into their jobs. We shall consider "work" and "jobs" broadly. Although most research focuses on employment, the same principles apply to schoolwork.

Goals and Deadlines

People who strive for excellence usually set goals for themselves, and employers striving for excellence set goals for their employees, including deadlines. If you did not have deadlines to meet, how hard would you work? For example, if one of your instructors said you could turn in your papers and take your tests whenever you wanted, how would you react? When you have deadlines, do you sometimes wait until shortly before the deadline to start working in earnest? For example, are you reading this chapter now because you have to take a test on it tomorrow? (If so, don't feel too embarrassed. I wouldn't be sitting here revising this chapter late at night except for the deadline my publisher gave me! People never outgrow their need for deadlines.)

Procrastination (putting off work until tomorrow) is a problem for many students and for workers on the job as well. Here is an experiment that beautifully illustrates the phenomenon:

CRITICAL THINKING
WHAT'S THE EVIDENCE?

The Value of Deadlines

A professor set firm deadlines for one class and let the other class choose their own deadlines to see whether those with evenly spaced deadlines would outperform those who had the opportunity to procrastinate (Ariely & Wertenbroch, 2002).

Hypothesis. Students who are required, or who require themselves, to spread out their work over a semester will do better than those with an opportunity to wait until the end.

Method. A professor taught two sections of the same course. Students were not randomly assigned to sections, but the students in the two sections had about equal academic records. The professor told one class that they had to write three papers, the first due after one third of the semester, the second after two thirds, and the third at the end of the semester. The other class was told that they could choose their own deadlines. They might make their papers due at one third, two thirds, and the end of the semester or all three at the end of the semester or whatever else they chose. However, they had to make a decision by the second day of class, and whatever deadlines they chose would be enforced. That is, a paper that missed a deadline would be penalized, even though the student could have chosen a later deadline.

At the end of the course, the professor graded all the papers, blind to when they had been submitted.

Results. If you were in the class that could choose their deadlines, what would you do? Twelve of the fifty-one students set all three deadlines on the final day of the semester. Presumably, they reasoned that they could still try to finish papers at one third, two thirds, and the end, but if for any reason they needed extra time, they would have as much as possible. That is, they gave themselves built-in extensions on their due dates. Other students, however, saw that if they set their deadlines at the end, they would expose themselves to a temptation that would be hard to resist, so they imposed earlier deadlines. Some spaced the deadlines evenly at one third, two thirds, and the end of the semester, but others compromised, setting deadlines for the first two papers later than one third and two thirds but not at the end of the semester.

On average the students in the section with assigned deadlines got better grades than those who were allowed to choose their own deadlines. Of those permitted to choose their own deadlines, those who set their deadlines at approximately one third, two thirds, and the end of the semester did about the same as those with assigned deadlines and much better than those who set all their deadlines at the end.

Interpretation. By itself the fact that those who spread out their deadlines evenly did better than those who set late deadlines would tell us nothing. It could mean that early deadlines help, but it could also mean that better students set earlier deadlines. However, the early-deadline students merely matched the assigned-deadline students, whereas the late-deadline students did significantly worse. Therefore, the conclusion follows that setting deadlines does help. If you are required to do part of your work at a time, you manage your time to accomplish it. If your deadlines are all at the end, you face a powerful temptation to delay your work.

CONCEPT CHECK

15. What conclusion would have followed if the early-deadline students did better than the late-deadline students but that class as a whole did as well as the assigned-deadline students? (Check your answer on page 432.)

Overcoming Procrastination

Given the importance of working steadily toward a goal, how can we overcome the temptation to procrastinate? Part of the answer is confidence. The people most worried about failing are the ones most likely to postpone getting started. For people who tend to procrastinate writing assignments, a little positive feedback on their writing often helps (Fritzsche, Young, & Hickson, 2003).

The other answer to overcoming procrastination is to form a specific plan. Try this: First identify some activity that you do occasionally but less often than you think you should—such as flossing your teeth or calling your grandparents. *Please choose an activity.* Now, estimate how likely you are to complete that activity at least once in the next week. *Please make that estimate.* If you have followed instructions, you have just increased your actual probability of engaging in that behavior! *Simply estimating your probability of doing something—if it is something desirable—*

increases the probability of that action (Levav & Fitzsimons, 2006). Psychologists call this phenomenon the **mere measurement effect.**

Try It Yourself

In addition to stating your probability of doing something, you increase your likelihood even more if you state a definite plan of when, where, and how you will do it. For example, suppose you set a goal that you will exercise more and eat a healthier diet. Fine, but if you really mean it, you should make a specific plan. Decide what kind of exercise you will do and when. If you want to eat a healthier diet, decide to eat a salad instead of a hamburger for lunch tomorrow, or vow to buy fruits and vegetables the next time you go to the supermarket. If you set specific plans, then the relevant situation will evoke the behavior (Milne, Orbell, & Sheeran, 2002; Verplanken & Faes, 1999).

CONCEPT CHECK

16. How could you increase your probability of getting a good start on writing a term paper?
17. How could someone use the mere measurement effect to persuade you to do something? (Check your answers on page 432.)

High and Low Goals

If you are going to set goals, what goals are best? For an academic example, at the start of a semester, which of these goals would be best?

- I will work for an A in every course (a difficult goal).
- I will work for at least a C average (an easy goal).
- I will do my best (a vague goal).

The research says that a vague "do your best" goal is no better than no goal at all. Although it sounds nice, you are never behind schedule on achieving the goal, so it doesn't motivate extra work.

The most effective goals are difficult but realistic (Locke & Latham, 2002). For example, a goal of an A in every course would be effective for someone who had a mix of As and Bs last semester but not for a student who is likely to become discouraged because the goal is way out of reach. A goal of a C average would be too low a goal for most students, but perhaps appropriate for a student working a full-time job while going to school or struggling for some other reason.

The same principles apply at work. Suppose a company announces that it will provide a generous bonus for all employees if profits increase by 10% this year. The employees will work to reach that level if they see a realistic chance of achieving it. If they think that an extraordinary effort could achieve only a 7 or 8% increase, and that nothing less than 10% will qualify for the bonus, they are likely to give up. On the other hand, if business is booming and a 10% increase will be easy, that goal won't motivate increased efforts.

For any goal to be effective, certain conditions are necessary (Locke & Latham, 2002). One is to take the goal seriously, preferably by committing to it publicly. If you want to get better grades next semester, tell your friends about it. If a company wants greater profits, it needs its employees to agree to the goal. Another condition for success is that you get frequent feedback about your progress. If you are aiming for all As and you get a B on a test in one course, you know you have to study harder in that course. If you want to increase profits by 10% and you learn that they are currently up 9%, you know you need to work just a little harder. One final condition is that you have to believe that the reward at the end will be worth your effort. Some students believe a high grade point average is worth the effort, but others don't. Some employees trust their bosses to pay the bonuses they promised. Others consider their bosses lying, cheating scoundrels (Craig & Gustafson, 1998) (see Figure 11.20).

A word of caution about setting goals: When people work hard toward a goal, they subordinate everything else. That is, they stop doing activities that don't lead to the goal. If you own a store and you convince your sales staff to try to increase sales, they may spend *less* effort than before on cleaning the floor, neatly arranging the shelves, or anything else that does not immediately increase sales. In 1995 the Australian government set a goal for the faculty at the national universities. It said the faculty should increase their number of publications, and henceforth, their salary increases would depend on their number of professional publications. Can you guess what happened? Over the next few years, the Australian faculty members greatly increased their *number* of publica-

tions, but mostly in seldom-read journals that were willing to publish minor findings (Butler, 2002). As the saying goes, be careful what you wish for, because you might get it.

 CONCEPT CHECK

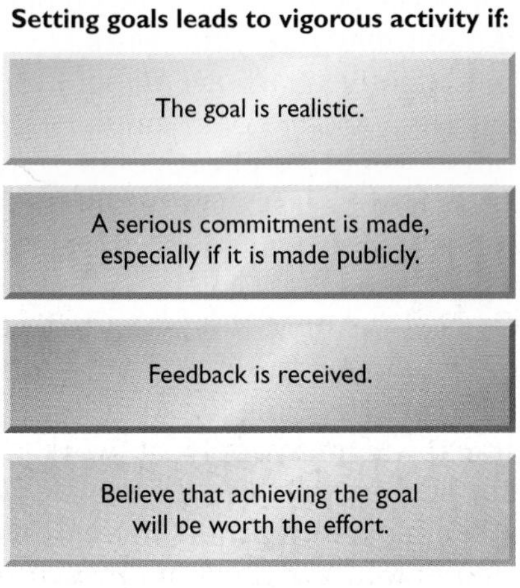

18. Under what conditions would people be most likely to keep their New Year's resolutions? (Check your answer on page 432.)

Realistic Goals

Given that the best goals are high but realistic, do you have any trouble deciding what goal is realistic? Most people, especially Americans, tend to be excessively optimistic. They regard themselves as healthier than average, smarter, more creative, and better than average at handling social situations. As part of this optimism, they underestimate how long they will need to complete a complex task. So do most companies, organizations, and governments (Dunning, Heath, & Suls, 2005). For example, most people underestimate the time needed for holiday shopping, writing a term paper, or remodeling their kitchen. Companies often underestimate how long they will need to bring a product to market, reorganize their sales staff, or finish a building. Governments underestimate the time and cost to construct bridges and other projects. The Sydney Opera House in Australia was expected to be complete by 1963 at a cost of $7 million. It was finally completed in 1973 at a cost of $102 million.

One group of senior college students were asked to estimate "realistically" the date they would finish writing their senior honors thesis—a major research paper. They were also asked what would be the latest time they might finish if everything went wrong. On the average they actually finished their papers 1 week *later* than what they said was the worst-case scenario (Buehler, Griffin, & Ross, 1994).

One reason we underestimate how long a task will take is that we also underestimate how long such tasks have taken in the past. We remember the best occasions, when everything went smoothly, and take those occasions as typical (Roy, Christenfeld, & McKenzie, 2005). However, that memory bias is not sufficient to explain our underestimates of future tasks, as our estimates of the future are more distorted than our reports about the past. Even when people remember that in the past they always waited until the last minute and just barely finished their projects on time, they still insist, "this time will be different" (Griffin & Buehler, 2005).

The message from this research is not to become discouraged but to allow yourself more time than you

Setting goals leads to vigorous activity if:

The goal is realistic.

A serious commitment is made, especially if it is made publicly.

Feedback is received.

Believe that achieving the goal will be worth the effort.

FIGURE 11.20 The conditions under which goals are most effective in motivating vigorous efforts.

think you need—and get started more quickly than you think necessary. Major tasks usually take more work than we expected.

✓ CONCEPT CHECK

19. If you are supervising some employees who say they can finish a challenging new job in 6 weeks, should you promise them a bonus for finishing in 6 weeks or would 5 or 7 be more appropriate? (Check your answer on page 432.)

Job Design and Job Satisfaction

People work harder, more effectively, and with more satisfaction at some jobs than at others. Why?

Two Approaches to Job Design

Imagine that you are starting up or reorganizing a company, and you must decide how to divide the workload. Should you make the jobs challenging and interesting at the risk of being difficult? Or should you make them simple and foolproof at the risk of being boring?

The answer depends on what you assume about the workers and their motivations. *According to the scientific-management approach* to job design, also known as *Theory X, most employees are lazy, indifferent, and uncreative.* Therefore, employers should make the work as foolproof as possible and supervise the workers to make sure they are doing each task the right way to save time and avoid injury (Figure 11.21). The employer leaves nothing to chance or to the worker's own initiative (McGregor, 1960).

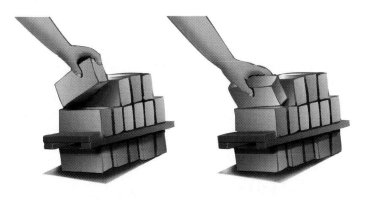

FIGURE 11.21 Psychologists have conducted research to determine the best, safest, most efficient ways to perform even simple tasks. For example, the drawing on the left shows the right way to lift a brick, and the drawing on the right shows the wrong way, according to Gilbreth (1911).

According to an alternative view, the human-relations approach to job design, also known as *Theory Y, employees like variety in their job, a sense of accomplishment, and a sense of responsibility* (McGregor, 1960). Therefore, employers should enrich the jobs, giving each employee responsibility for meaningful tasks. For example, a financial services corporation that followed the scientific-management approach would have each employee keep just one kind of records for many clients, developing expertise at a narrow task. The same company, reorganized according to the human-relations approach, might put each employee in charge of fewer clients, keeping track of all the information about those clients, and seeing how all the pieces come together. Employees with enriched jobs generally report greater satisfaction (Campion & McClelland, 1991). From the employer's standpoint, the enriched jobs have many advantages but two disadvantages: It takes longer to train the workers than it would with simpler jobs, and the workers performing enriched jobs expect to be paid more!

So which approach is better? It depends. Consider an analogy to education: Professor X tells students exactly what to read on which day, what facts to study for each test, and precisely what to do to get a good grade. (This course is analogous to the scientific-management approach.) Professor Y outlines the general issues to be discussed, provides a list of suggested readings, lets the students control class discussion, and invites students to create their own ideas for projects. (This course is analogous to the human-relations approach, though perhaps more extreme.) Which class would you like better?

If you are highly interested in the topic and have ideas of your own, you would love Professor Y's course and would consider Professor X's course tedious and insulting. But if you are taking the course just to satisfy a requirement, you might appreciate the precise structure of Professor X's class. The same is true of jobs. Some workers, especially the younger and brighter ones, thrive on the challenge of an enriched job, but others prefer a simple, secure, stable set of tasks (Arnold & House, 1980; Campion & Thayer, 1985; Hackman & Lawler, 1971).

✓ CONCEPT CHECK

20. "I want my employees to enjoy their work and to feel pride in their achievements." Does that statement reflect a belief in the human-relations approach or the scientific-management approach? (Check your answer on page 432.)

Job Satisfaction

Your choice of career profoundly affects the quality of your life. Between the ages 20 and 70, you will spend about half of your waking hours on the job. You do not want to spend it on work you find unimportant. In turn how much you like your job correlates moderately well with how well you perform it (Judge, Thoresen, Bono, & Patton, 2001). The causation probably goes in several directions: High job satisfaction improves performance, good performance improves job satisfaction, and qualities such as a conscientious personality improve job performance and also help develop a contented personality (Judge et al., 2001; Tett & Burnett, 2003).

You can probably imagine several explanations for why job satisfaction correlates only moderately with performance. For example, some people with excellent job performance are not highly satisfied because they think they deserve a promotion.

Obviously, job satisfaction depends largely on the job itself, including the interest level, the pay, coworkers, and management. It also depends on the worker's personality. Some people are just easier to please than others. Comparisons of identical and fraternal twins indicate that job satisfaction is highly heritable (Arvey, McCall, Bouchard, Taubman, & Cavanaugh, 1994). That is, if your close relatives say they are happy with their jobs, you probably will be also, even though you have a different job. You don't inherit your job, but you inherit your disposition. Some people find things to like about their jobs, and others find things to complain about (Ilies & Judge, 2003; Judge & Laarsen, 2001; Thoresen, Kaplan, Barsky, Warren, & de Chermont, 2003). People who are prone to unpleasant feelings become exhausted with their work faster than others do and are likely to complain of "job burnout" (Houkes, Janssen, de Jonge, & Nijhuis, 2001; Maslach, 2003).

On the average older workers express higher job satisfaction than younger workers do (Pond & Geyer, 1991) (see Figure 11.22). One possible explanation is that older workers have better, higher paying jobs. Another is that today's young people are harder to satisfy than their elders ever were (Beck & Wilson, 2000). Another possibility is that many young workers start in the wrong job and find a more suitable one later. Yet another is that many young people are still considering the possibility of changing jobs. By middle age most people have reconciled themselves to whatever jobs they have.

Pay and Job Satisfaction

An employer who wants to keep workers satisfied must pay careful attention to the pay scale. Obviously, workers want to be paid well, and the more pay the better, but in addition they need to perceive the pay scale as fair. In one classic experiment, some workers were led

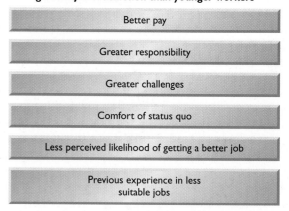

Possible reasons why older workers report greater job satisfaction than younger workers

Better pay
Greater responsibility
Greater challenges
Comfort of status quo
Less perceived likelihood of getting a better job
Previous experience in less suitable jobs

FIGURE 11.22 *Psychologists propose several reasons why most older workers report higher job satisfaction than younger workers do.*

to believe that they had been hired in spite of less than average qualifications for the job. They worked harder than average, apparently to convince the employer that they deserved the job, but perhaps also to convince themselves that they earned their pay (Adams, 1963).

Employees expect their bosses to be honest and open with them and to follow fair procedures in determining salaries. Those who perceive their bosses as operating unfairly often start looking for another job. They also stop doing the "good citizen" behaviors that help the company even though the worker isn't paid to do them, such as keeping the building tidy, helping other workers, and attending extra meetings after working hours (Simons & Roberson, 2003). At the opposite extreme, some workers develop an emotional commitment to their company or organization, which leads them to work loyally and energetically, well beyond what they are paid to do (Meyer, Becker, & Vandenberghe, 2004; Seo, Barrett, & Bartunek, 2004).

Money is certainly part of anyone's work motivation. Presumably, you would quit your job if your employer stopped paying you. However, pay is not the whole motivation. Many people take a lower paying job because it offers a greater sense of accomplishment or more pleasant working conditions than some higher paying job. Even after people retire, many find that they miss the work. For many people work is an enjoyable, important part of who they are. As with other behaviors, we work because of multiple motives.

 CONCEPT CHECK

21. What are some factors that contribute to high job satisfaction? (Check your answer on page 432.)

Leadership

How hard you are motivated to work also depends on how you perceive the leadership of your organization. Some employers inspire deep loyalties and intense efforts, whereas others can barely get their workers to do the minimum. (The same is true of college professors, athletic coaches, and political leaders.)

Can we measure the qualities of an effective leader or give advice on how to become one? It is certainly not easy. For example, industrial/organizational psychologists have been trying to measure "leader-member exchange," which more or less means trust, attention, and sensitivity by the leader toward subordinates. Over the years the questionnaires for measuring it have changed repeatedly, as has the description of exactly what the questionnaires are trying to measure, so it is difficult to compare any set of results to any other (Schriesheim, Castro, & Cogliser, 1999).

One prominent idea is the distinction between transformational and transactional leadership styles. A **transformational leader** *articulates a vision of the future, intellectually stimulates subordinates, and motivates them to use their imagination to raise the organization to a new level.* A **transactional leader** *tries to make the organization more efficient at doing what it is already doing by providing rewards (mainly pay) for effective work.* A leader can be either of these, both, or neither. People who are perceived as transformational leaders are also perceived as effective in almost any organization (Lowe, Kroeck, & Sivasubramaniam, 1996). This result should not be surprising. You would hardly describe your leader as "a visionary who intellectually stimulates me and motivates me to reach my potential" if you thought your leader were doing a bad job overall. Workers are more likely to describe their immediate supervisors—the people they interact with every day—as transformational leaders than they are the top people in the organization, whom they seldom meet. Transactional leaders are also effective under some circumstances, mainly in organizations where activities stay the same from year to year (Lowe et al., 1996).

 CONCEPT CHECK

22. Do transformational leaders emphasize intrinsic or extrinsic motivation? Which do transactional leaders emphasize? (Check your answers on page 432.)

IN CLOSING

Work as Another Kind of Motivation

In this chapter we have considered hunger, sex, and work. People have many other motivations, of course, but we can understand the basic principles without going through additional examples. Work motivation has important points in common with hunger, sex, and other motivations. For example, they are all marked by persistent and varied behaviors to reach a goal. However, work also has some special features. One is the aspect of striving for excellence. Work is often competitive in a way that eating and sex are not. (Oh, I suppose you could compete at eating or sex, but ordinarily, we don't.) Striving for excellence is never fully satisfied. Those who achieve their goals in business or other competitive endeavors usually respond by setting new, higher goals. In short, any kind of motivation requires a kind of striving, but each kind of striving has its own special features. ▪

Summary

- *Deadlines.* In general, people who are forced to meet deadlines manage their time to do so. If it is possible to postpone all work until later, many find it hard to resist that temptation. Setting deadlines for parts of one's own work can help. (page 426)
- *Overcoming procrastination.* People get started toward their goals if they set specific plans about what they will do, when, and where. (page 427)
- *Effectiveness of goal setting.* Setting a work goal motivates strong effort if the goal is high but realistic. Other important factors include making a serious commitment to the goal, receiving feedback on progress, and believing that the goal will bring a fair reward. (page 427)
- *Making goals realistic.* People tend to underestimate how much time and effort they will need to achieve their goals. It is best to plan for more time and resources than seem necessary and to start as quickly as possible. (page 428)
- *Job design.* According to the scientific-management approach, jobs should be made simple and foolproof. According to the human-management approach, jobs should be made interesting enough to give workers a sense of achievement. (page 429)
- *Job satisfaction.* Job satisfaction is moderately correlated with good performance on the job for several reasons. People with a happy disposition are more likely than others to be satisfied with their jobs, as are older workers in general. Job satisfac-

tion also requires a perception that the pay scale is fair. (page 430)

- *Leadership.* Leaders who are perceived as inspiring their associates to fulfill a vision are also perceived as effective in almost any organization. Those perceived as using rewards to get employees to do their work efficiently are effective in some situations, mainly when the business is stable. (page 431)

Answers to Concept Checks

15. If students in the two sections had equal performance overall, we could not conclude that deadlines help. Instead, the conclusion would be that brighter students tend to set earlier deadlines. (page 427)

16. First, find some way to enhance your confidence. Then make specific plans, such as, "I will spend Monday night at the library looking for materials." (page 427)

17. If someone asks you how likely you are to vote for a candidate, give money to a charity, or buy a new car, answering the question increases your probability of doing so. (page 427)

18. A New Year's resolution is like any other goal: People are more likely to keep it if it is realistic, if they state the resolution publicly, and if they receive feedback on how well they are doing. (page 428)

19. If your employees predict they can finish in 6 weeks, don't count on it. They are likely to be underestimating how long the task will take, and a goal of finishing in 6 weeks may be unrealistic. You might offer a bonus for finishing in 6 weeks, but you should also offer a decent incentive for finishing in 7. (page 428)

20. It reflects the human-relations approach. (page 429)

21. Among factors associated with high job satisfaction are high ability to perform the job, a happy personality, a perception that the pay scale is fair, and old age. (page 430)

22. A transformational leader emphasizes intrinsic motivation, the desire to achieve excellence. A transactional leader applies rewards to get workers to do their current jobs efficiently and so emphasizes extrinsic motivation. (page 431)

CHAPTER ENDING

Key Terms and Activities

Key Terms

You can check the page listed for a complete description of a term. You can also check the glossary/index at the end of the text for a definition of a given term, or you can download a list of all the terms and their definitions for any chapter at this website:

www.thomsonedu.com/
psychology/kalat

acquired immune deficiency syndrome (AIDS) (page 416)
allostasis (page 401)

anorexia nervosa (page 410)
bulimia nervosa (page 411)
drive (page 400)
estrogen (page 418)
extrinsic motivation (page 401)
gender identity (page 418)
glucose (page 404)
homeostasis (page 400)
human-relations approach (page 429)
incentive (page 401)
insulin (page 405)
intersexes (page 419)
intrinsic motivation (page 401)

leptin (page 406)
mere measurement effect (page 427)
motivation (page 399)
obesity (page 408)
overjustification effect (page 402)
scientific-management approach (page 429)
set point (page 406)
sexual orientation (page 420)
testosterone (page 418)
transactional leader (page 431)
transformational leader (page 431)

Suggestions for Further Reading

Diamond, J. (1997). *Why is sex fun?* New York: Basic Books. Exploration of the "why" of sex. Why did we evolve to reproduce sexually? Why is human sex in several ways different from that of other animals?

 ## Web/Technology Resources

Student Companion Website

www.thomsonedu.com/psychology/kalat

Explore the Student Companion Website for Online Try-It-Yourself activities, practice quizzes, flashcards, and more! The companion site also has direct links to the following websites.

Obesity

www.obesity.org

Check all kinds of information about this serious problem.

Sexual Behavior

www.indiana.edu/~kinsey/

See the latest research reports by the research institute that Kinsey founded.

Intersexes

www.isna.org/

Information from a support group for people with ambiguous genitalia.

 ## For Additional Study

Kalat Premium Website

http://www.thomsonedu.com

For Critical Thinking Videos and additional Online Try-It-Yourself activities, go to this site to enter or purchase your code for the Kalat Premium Website.

ThomsonNOW!

http://www.thomsonedu.com

Go to this site for the link to ThomsonNOW, your one-stop study shop. Take a Pretest for this chapter, and Thomson-NOW will generate a personalized Study Plan based on your test results. The Study Plan will identify the topics you need to review and direct you to online resources to help you master those topics. You can then take a Posttest to help you determine the concepts you have mastered and what you still need to work on.

Emotional Behaviors, Stress, and Health

Suppose you are the first astronaut to land on a planet where the inhabitants experience no emotions at all (but who conveniently speak English). They gather around and ask you, their first visitor from Earth, "What is emotion?" What do you tell them?

"Well," you might say, "emotion is how you feel when something surprisingly good or surprisingly bad happens to you." "Wait a minute," they reply. "We don't understand these words *feel* and *sur-prisingly*." "All right, how about this: Emotions are experiences like anger, fear, happiness, sadness . . . " "*Anger, fear . . .* what do those terms mean?" they ask.

Could you explain them? Could you even explain how to measure emotions? (After all, you could show people who are blind how to measure color vision, even if they never had the experience themselves.) Emotions are hard to define except by showing examples, and the examples mean nothing to someone who does not experience them. In this chapter we consider what psychologists have learned so far about emotions, despite the difficulties of definition and measurement.

▌ *Would you make more intelligent decisions if you could thoroughly suppress your emotions, like the fictional character Spock? After brain damage that impairs emotion, people make worse than average decisions.*

© Paramount Pictures/Getty Images

436

The Nature of Emotion

- *How does arousal relate to emotion?*
- *How many kinds of emotions do people have?*
- *In what ways do emotions influence our thinking?*

Imagine keeping a list of all the emotions you feel during a day. At one time or another, you might feel frightened, angry, sad, joyful, disgusted, worried, bored, ashamed, frustrated, contemptuous, embarrassed, surprised, and confused. But which of those states are really emotions? And which of them are *different* emotions, instead of overlapping or synonymous conditions?

To answer even such basic questions, we need research. For decades most psychologists considered emotion too subjective or vague a topic for serious research. Many still do. Almost everyone agrees, though, that emotions are interesting and important. It is difficult to imagine what life would be like without them.

Although most people think they know what they mean by the term *emotion*, defining it is difficult. Psychologists usually define it in terms of a combination of cognitions, physiology, feelings, and actions (Keltner & Shiota, 2003; Plutchik, 1982). For example, you might have the *cognition* "he was unfair to me," *physiological* changes that include increased heart rate, a *feeling* you call anger, and *behaviors* including a clenched fist. However, these different kinds of elements don't always go together. You might have the cognition of being unfairly treated, without any feeling of anger. At another time you might feel angry without any cognition of why (Berkowitz, 1990). For the way most people use the term emotion, the key component is the feeling. A robot could calculate "someone was unfair," generate a physiological change, and direct a behavior, but if the robot doesn't *feel* something, we would not say it had an emotion.

Measuring Emotions

Recall from chapter 1 that research progress depends on good measurement. Psychologists measure emotions by self-reports, behavioral observations, and physiological measures. Each method has its strengths and weaknesses.

Self-Reports

Psychologists often measure emotions by asking people how happy they are, how nervous, and so forth. Self-reports are quick, easy, and almost the only choice for measuring an unobservable state like happiness. However, their accuracy is questionable. For example, if you rate your current anger 3 on a scale of 1 to 7, and I rate my anger 3 on the same scale, your anger may not be equal to mine.

Behavioral Observations

Although we cannot observe emotion directly, we infer it from someone's behavior and its context. For example, if we see one person make a fist while another person shrieks and runs away, we infer that the second person is afraid. Indeed, when you were an infant, your parents must have inferred your emotions before you started to report them verbally. They had to in order to teach you the words for emotions! At some point you screamed and someone said you were "afraid," and at some other time you smiled and someone said you were "happy."

One behavior that we watch closely is facial expressions. People can smile or frown when they do not feel an emotion or suppress smiles and frowns when they do. However, *very brief, involuntary expressions of fear, anger, or other emotions,* called **microexpressions,** are harder to control. For example, someone who is pretending to be calm or happy may show occasional brief signs of anger, fear, or extreme sadness (Ekman, 2001). With practice (or a videotape that can be played slowly), psychologists sometimes identify emotions that people would like to hide.

Physiological Measures

Originally, the term *emotion* referred to any sort of turbulent motion. Centuries ago, people described thunder as an "emotion of the atmosphere." Eventually, people limited the term to body motions and their associated feelings, but the idea still includes turbulence and vigorous arousal.

Any stimulus that arouses an emotion alters the activity of the **autonomic nervous system,** *the section of the nervous system that controls the functioning of the internal organs.* The word *autonomic* means "in-

437

Ordinarily, an emotional state elicits a tendency toward vigorous action, even if we suppress that tendency. Here, a soldier disarms a mine during the war in the former Yugoslavia.

dependent" (autonomous); biologists once believed that the autonomic nervous system was independent of the brain and the spinal cord. We now know that the brain and spinal cord can alter the activity of the autonomic nervous system, but the term *autonomic* remains.

The autonomic nervous system has two branches: the sympathetic and the parasympathetic nervous systems (Figure 12.1). *Two chains of neuron clusters just to the left and right of the spinal cord* make up the sympathetic nervous system, *which arouses the body for vigorous action*. Traditionally, it has been called the "fight-or-flight" system because it increases your heart rate, breathing rate, production of sweat, and flow of epinephrine (EP-i-NEF-rin; also known as adrenaline), thereby preparing you for intense activity. However, different situations activate different

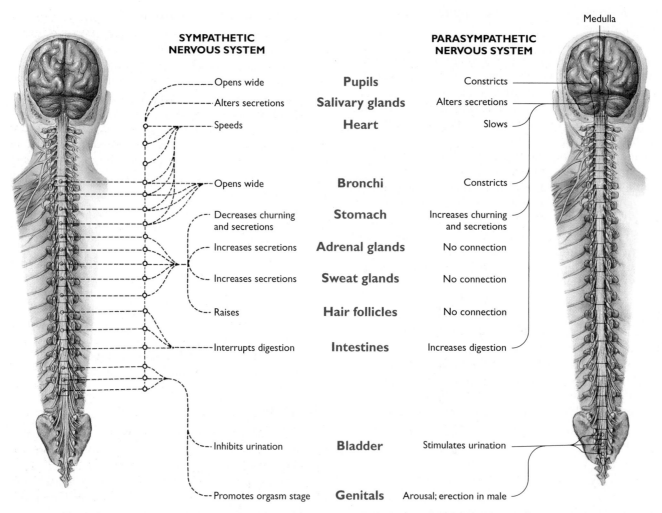

FIGURE 12.1 The autonomic nervous system consists of the sympathetic and parasympathetic nervous systems, which sometimes act in opposing ways and sometimes cooperate. The sympathetic nervous system readies the body for emergency action; the parasympathetic nervous system supports digestive and other nonemergency functions.

❚ The sympathetic nervous system prepares the body for a vigorous burst of activity.

parts of the sympathetic nervous system to facilitate different kinds of intense activity.

The **parasympathetic nervous system** consists of *neurons whose axons extend from the medulla* (see Figure 12.1) *and the lower part of the spinal cord to neuron clusters near the internal organs. The parasympathetic nervous system decreases the heart rate, promotes digestion, and in general supports nonemergency functions.* Both the sympathetic and parasympathetic systems send axons to the heart, the digestive system, and other organs. A few organs, such as the adrenal gland, receive input from only the sympathetic nervous system.

Both systems are constantly active, although one system can temporarily dominate. An emergency that demands a vigorous response activates mostly the sympathetic system, whereas a restful situation activates mostly the parasympathetic system. Many situations activate parts of both systems (Berntson, Cacioppo, & Quigley, 1993). For example, a frightening situation may increase your heart rate and sweating (sympathetic responses) and also promote bowel and bladder evacuation (parasympathetic responses). Do you remember ever being so frightened that you thought you might lose your bladder control?

Researchers often measure activity of the sympathetic nervous system as an indicator of emotional arousal. For example, moment-by-moment changes in the electrical conductivity across the skin indicate instantaneous changes in the amount of sweating, a sympathetic nervous system response that reflects emotional arousal. Strong emotions also make people breathe faster (Gomez, Zimmermann, Guttormsen-Schär, & Danuser, 2005). However, remember that the sympathetic nervous system is the fight-*or*-flight sys-

tem, so its responses could indicate anger, fear, or any other intense emotion. Physiological measurements do not tell us *which* emotion someone is feeling.

Brain measurements are somewhat more specific, but not much. Figure 12.2 summarizes the results of many studies using PET and fMRI brain scans (see chapter 3) to measure which brain areas became active when five different emotions were aroused in various ways (Phan, Wager, Taylor, & Liberzon, 2002). As you can see, the areas aroused by a given emotion largely overlap those aroused by other emotions.

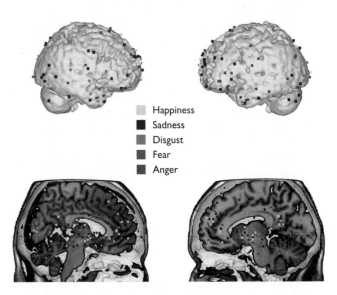

▢	Happiness
■	Sadness
▨	Disgust
▣	Fear
▦	Anger

FIGURE 12.2 Researchers aroused emotions in various ways and then used PET or fMRI scans to identify which brain areas became aroused. No brain area appears specific to one type of emotion. *(Source: Phan, Wager, Taylor, & Liberzon, 2002)*

CONCEPT CHECK

1. Why should we not insist on verbal reports to infer or measure emotions?
2. Why are physiological measurements more helpful for determining the intensity of an emotion than for identifying which emotion is present? (Check your answers on page 453.)

Emotion, Arousal, and Actions

If an emotion includes cognitions, feelings, behavior, and arousal, how do those parts relate to one another? William James, the founder of American psychology, proposed one of psychology's first theories.

The James-Lange Theory of Emotions

Common sense suggests that you feel sad and therefore you cry; you become afraid and therefore you tremble; you feel angry and therefore your face turns red. In 1884 William James and Carl Lange independently proposed to turn this concept around. According to the James-Lange theory, *your interpretation of a stimulus directly evokes autonomic changes and sometimes muscle actions. Your perception of those changes is the feeling aspect of the emotion.* In James's original article, he said simply that the situation (e.g., the sight of a bear) gives rise to an action (e.g., running away), and your perception of the action is the emotion. That is, you don't run away because you are afraid; you feel afraid because you perceive yourself running away. In response to his critics, he clarified his view (James, 1894): Obviously, the sight of a bear doesn't automatically cause you to run away. You first appraise the situation. If it is a caged bear or a trained circus bear, you do not run. If it appears dangerous, you do run. So your appraisal of the total situation is the cognitive aspect of the emotion. Your perception of yourself running away, with heart rate and breathing rate soaring, is what you *feel* as the emotion. That is,

Situation →	Appraisal →	Actions →	Perception of the actions
	= cognitive aspect of the emotion	= physiological and behavioral aspects	= feeling aspect of the emotion

Given this interpretation, the James-Lange theory seems reasonable. Indeed, it is hard to imagine where the feeling aspect would come from if the body didn't react in some physical way. Furthermore, much evidence supports the theory. The two main types of evidence are that people who feel little reaction to an event feel little emotion, and people who feel a stronger reaction feel an enhanced emotion.

Effects of Decreased Perceived Arousal

According to the James-Lange theory, people with weak physiological responses can still identify an emotional situation cognitively, but they should have little emotional feeling. People with paralyzed muscles because of spinal cord injuries report normal or nearly normal emotions (Cobos, Sánchez, García, Vera, & Vila, 2002). However, the results differ after loss of autonomic responses. In **pure autonomic failure**, *an uncommon condition with unknown cause, the autonomic nervous system stops regulating the organs.* That is, nothing in the nervous system influences heart rate, breathing rate, and so forth. One effect is that a patient who stands up quickly faints, because none of the usual reflexes kick in to prevent gravity from drawing most of the blood from the head. With regard to emotions, affected people still recognize which situations call for anger, fear, sadness, and the like, but they report that their emotions feel much less intense than before (Critchley, Mathias, & Dolan, 2001). That is, the cognitive aspect of emotion remains, but the feeling aspect is weak, exactly as the James-Lange theory predicts.

Effects of Increased Perceived Arousal

Suppose a researcher induced you to attack someone. Would you then feel angry? Researchers steer away from anything so ethically doubtful, but milder approaches are available. Suppose researchers molded your posture and breathing pattern into a pattern typical of a given emotion. Would you then feel that emotion? Have someone read these instructions to you, or read them to someone else and check what happens emotionally:

Try It Yourself

> Lower your eyebrows toward your cheeks. Sigh. Close your mouth and push your lower lip slightly upward. Sigh again. Sit back in your chair and draw your feet under the chair. Be sure you feel no tension in your legs or feet. Sigh again. Fold your hands in your lap, cupping one in the other. Drop your head, letting your rib cage fall, letting most of your body go limp, except for a little tension in the back of your neck and across your shoulder blades. Sigh again.

Most people who follow these directions report starting to feel sad (Flack, Laird, & Cavallaro, 1999; Philippot, Chapelle, & Blairy, 2002). Instructions to hold the posture and breathing pattern characteristic of happiness, anger, or fear induce those emotions too, although the instructions for fear sometimes induce anger and those for anger sometimes induce fear. Fear and anger are physiologically similar.

With studies like this, one worry is that the participants may guess what the experimenter is trying to demonstrate. (Remember the issue of "demand characteristics" from chapter 2.) One group of researchers found a clever way to conceal the expectation of the study. They told participants that the experiment related to how people learn to write after amputation or paralysis of their arms. The participants were told to hold a pen either with their teeth or with their protruded lips, as Figure 12.3 shows. Then they were to use the pen in various ways, such as drawing lines between dots and making check marks to rate the funniness of cartoons.

CONCEPT CHECK

3. According to the James-Lange theory, do you run away from something because you are afraid of it?
4. What happens to emotions in people with medical conditions that weaken their autonomic responses to a situation? What happens when people adopt postures and breathing patterns characteristic of a particular emotion? How do these results relate to the James-Lange theory? (Check your answers on page 453.)

a   b

FIGURE 12.3 Facial expression can influence mood. When people hold a pen with their teeth (**a**), they rate cartoons as funnier than when they hold it with their protruded lips (**b**).

When they held the pen with their teeth, their face was forced into a near smile, and they rated the cartoons as very funny. When they held the pen with protruded lips, a smile was impossible, and they rated the cartoons as less funny (Strack, Martin, & Stepper, 1988). Try holding a pen one way and then the other while reading newspaper cartoons. Do you notice any difference?

Try It Yourself

In a similar study, researchers said they were studying people's ability to do a motor task and a cognitive task at once. The motor task was to hold together the tips of two golf tees, which they attached to the participants' eyebrows. The only way to hold them together was to frown; so without saying "frown," they got people to frown. The cognitive task was to rate the pleasantness of photos. While people were frowning, they usually rated the photos less pleasant than people usually do (Larsen, Kasimatis, & Frey, 1992).

Schachter and Singer's Theory of Emotions

All right, once you get your body into a hunched-over posture with tension only in your neck and you are constantly sighing, you feel sad. But how did you get into that posture in the first place? Your appraisal of the situation had to enter into the process somewhere.

Furthermore, how can you tell whether you are angry or frightened? As mentioned, the breathing pattern, heart rate pattern, and other physiological activities are almost the same for anger and fear. Even extreme joy can elevate heart rate like anger and fear. Your autonomic changes tell you how strong your emotional feeling is, but the autonomic responses do not tell you which emotion you are experiencing (Lang, 1994).

Because of such considerations, Stanley Schachter and Jerome Singer (1962) proposed a theory of how we identify one emotion from another. According to **Schachter and Singer's theory of emotions** (Figure 12.4), *the intensity of the physiological state—that is, the degree of sympathetic nervous system arousal—determines the intensity of the emotion, but a cognitive appraisal of the situation identifies the type of emotion.* That is, a given type of arousal might feel like fear, anger, joy, or none of these depending on the situation. Schachter and Singer saw their theory as an alternative to the James-Lange theory, but it really addresses a different question.

The ideal test of Schachter and Singer's theory would be to wire you to another person so that when-

FIGURE 12.4 According to Schachter and Singer's theory, physiological arousal determines the intensity of an emotion, but a cognitive appraisal determines which emotion one feels.

ever the other person's heart rate, breathing rate, and so forth changed, yours would too, at the same time and to the same degree. Then, when the other person felt an emotion, researchers would ask whether you feel it too. That procedure is impossible with current technology so Schachter and Singer (1962) tried a simpler procedure.

CRITICAL THINKING
WHAT'S THE EVIDENCE?

The Cognitive Aspect of Emotion

Hypothesis. A drug that increases physiological arousal will enhance whatever emotion the situation arouses, but the type of emotion will depend on the situation.

Method. The experimenters put college students into different situations but gave some of them injections of epinephrine (adrenaline) to induce (they hoped) the same physiological condition regardless of the situation. (Epinephrine mimics the effects of the sympathetic nervous system.) They tried to influence some participants to attribute their increased arousal to the situation and others to attribute it to the injection.

Specifically, the experimenters told some participants that the injections were vitamins that would have no easily noticed effects. These par-

ticipants would presumably notice their arousal and attribute it to the situation, feeling intense emotions. Others were told to expect side effects, including increased heart rate, butterflies in the stomach, and so forth. When these people felt the changes, they would presumably attribute them to the injections and not consider them emotional experiences. Additional participants were given one set of instructions or the other but injected with a placebo instead of epinephrine.

Participants were then placed in different situations to elicit euphoria or anger. Each student in the euphoria situation was asked to wait in a room with a very playful young man who flipped paper wads into a trash can, sailed paper airplanes, built a tower with manila folders, shot paper wads at the tower with a rubber band, played with a Hula-Hoop, and tried to get the other student to join his play. Each participant in the anger situation was asked to answer a questionnaire full of such insulting items as these:

Which member of your immediate family does not bathe or wash regularly?

With how many men (other than your father) has your mother had extramarital relationships?

4 or fewer   5–9   10 or more

Results. Many students in the euphoria situation joined the playful partner (Figure 12.5). One jumped up and down on the desk, and another opened a window and threw paper wads at passersby. The anger situation was less effective than expected, although a few students muttered angry comments or refused to complete the questionnaire.

Recall that some of the participants had been informed beforehand that the injections would produce certain autonomic effects, including tremors and increased heart rate. No matter which situation they were in, they showed only slight emotional responses. When they felt themselves sweating and their hands trembling, they said to themselves, "Aha! I'm getting the side effects, just as they said I would."

Interpretation. Unfortunately, this experiment has some problems that limit the conclusions. Recall that some participants were given one set of instructions or the other and placed in one situation or the other but injected with a placebo instead of epinephrine. These participants showed about as much euphoria in the euphoria situation and as much anger in the anger situation as did the participants injected with epinephrine. Therefore, the epinephrine injections apparently had nothing to do with the results. If so, we are left with this unexciting summary of the results: People in a situation designed to induce euphoria act happy; those in an anger situation act angry (Plutchik & Ax, 1967). However, if they attribute their arousal to an injection, their response is more restrained.

Despite the problems in Schachter and Singer's experiment, the idea behind it is reasonable, and other research since then has supported it in many though not all cases. That idea, to reiterate, is that the arousal you perceive in yourself determines the intensity of the emotion, although not the identity of the emotion itself. To illustrate with one example, young heterosexual men were asked to rate the attractiveness of each woman in the *Sports Illustrated* swimsuit issue. (They participated in the name of science, of course.) While they were viewing each photo, they heard sounds. Some were told (correctly) that they were listening to random sounds, and others were told (incorrectly) that they were hearing their own heartbeat. The rate of the sounds fluctuated haphazardly. The men who thought they were hearing their own heartbeats gave high ratings to the women they were examining when they thought their heartbeat was accelerating (Crucian et al., 2000). That is, a man who thought his heart was beating faster assumed he was excited about a particular woman. Experiments like this suggest that what emotion (if any) we perceive depends on a cognitive attribution we make based on the situation. However, results of such experiments vary depending on details of the procedure (Reisenzein, 1983).

 CONCEPT CHECK

5. You are going on a first date with someone you hope will find you exciting. According to Schachter and Singer's theory, should you plan a date walking through an art gallery or riding on roller coasters? (Check your answer on page 453.)

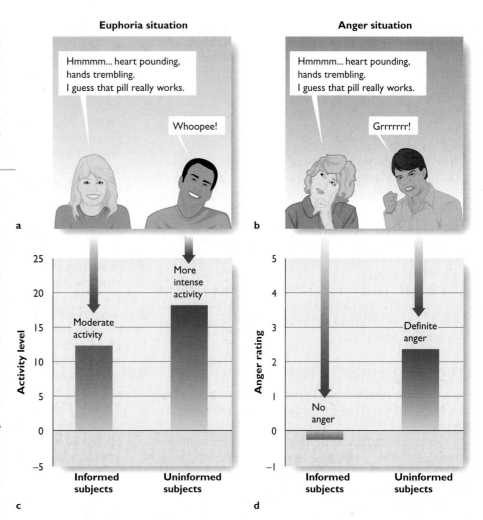

FIGURE 12.5 (**a** and **b**) In Schachter and Singer's experiment, people who were uninformed about the effects of epinephrine reported strong emotions appropriate to the situation. (**c** and **d**) According to Schachter and Singer, autonomic arousal controls the strength of an emotion, but cognitive factors tell us which emotion we are experiencing.

The Range of Emotions

How many different emotions do humans experience? Do we have a few "basic" emotions that combine to form other experiences, like the elements of chemistry? Some psychologists have proposed a short list, such as happiness, sadness, anger, fear, disgust, and surprise. Others add more candidates, such as contempt, shame, guilt, interest, hope, pride, relief, frustration, love, awe, boredom, jealousy, regret, and embarrassment (Keltner & Buswell, 1997). Japanese people list among the emotions *amae,* translated as "the pleasant feeling of depending on someone else," or "the feeling of comfort in another person's acceptance." The Japanese believe that people in other cultures have this emotional experience but fail to notice or emphasize it, and research does find that Americans and Japanese react similarly to amae-type situations (Doi, 1981; Niiya, Ellsworth, & Yamaguchi,

2006). Hindus include heroism, amusement, peace, and wonder (Hejmadi, Davidson, & Rozin, 2000).

How can we decide what is a basic emotion (if there is such a thing)? Psychologists generally consider the following criteria:

- Basic emotions should emerge early in life without requiring much experience. For example, nostalgia and pride emerge slowly and seem less basic than fear, anger, or joy (M. Lewis, 1995). The problem is that all emotional expressions emerge gradually. Infants' expressions at first do not distinguish among distress, anger, and fear (Messinger, 2002).
- Basic emotions should be similar across cultures. Because most emotions are recognizably similar throughout human cultures, this criterion does not eliminate much.
- Each basic emotion should have its own facial expression and characteristic physiology. We shall explore facial expressions more fully because of the extensive research.

Producing Facial Expressions

Does each emotion have its own special expression? And why do we have facial expressions of emotions anyway?

Quite simply, the function of facial expressions is communication. Primates (humans, apes, and monkeys) communicate their emotional states through gestures and facial expressions (Redican, 1982) (see Figure 12.6), and we humans also rely on nonverbal expressions when possible. For example, you wink, nod, or smile to show a possible romantic interest; you withhold such expressions to indicate a lack of interest. (You *could* tell a stranger "I find you sexually attractive" or "I find you boring," but facial expressions are at least as effective and much less risky.)

Emotional expressions occur mostly in a social context. For example, Olympic medal winners generally smile if they are waiting for the awards ceremony with others but not if they are waiting alone (Fernández-Dols & Ruiz-Belda, 1997). Even 10-month-old infants smile more when their mothers are watching than when they are not (S. S. Jones, Collins, & Hong, 1991). Laughter occurs mainly in social settings, and we laugh mostly when others are laughing. Robert Provine (2000) spent many hours in shopping malls and elsewhere recording and observing laughter. He found that people laughed almost entirely when they were with friends and that the speakers laughed more than the listeners. Most of the time people laughed while saying something that wasn't even funny, such as, "Can I join you?" or "It was nice meeting you too." The laughter was a way to express friendliness.

Voluntary smiles, frowns, and other facial expressions seldom exactly match the appearance of spontaneous expressions. For example, the smile of a truly happy person includes movements of the mouth muscles and the muscles surrounding the eyes (Figure 12.7a). Voluntary smiles (Figure 12.7b) generally do not include the muscles around the eyes (Ekman & Davidson, 1993). *The full expression including the muscles around the eyes* is called the Duchenne smile, named after Duchenne de Boulogne, the first person to describe it.

Because the Duchenne smile is hard to produce voluntarily, it is a good indicator of someone's true feelings. Researchers have found that women with a Duchenne smile in their college yearbooks were more likely than other women to have happy, long-lasting marriages and to report feeling happy and competent

FIGURE 12.6 Chimpanzees and humans have very special facial expressions.

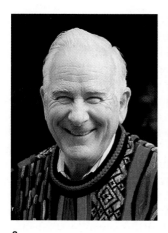

a

b

© John Boykin

FIGURE 12.7 A spontaneous, happy smile (a) uses both the mouth muscles and the muscles surrounding the eyes. This expression is sometimes called the *Duchenne smile*. A voluntary smile (b) ordinarily includes only the mouth muscles. Most people cannot voluntarily activate the eye muscles associated with the Duchenne smile.

© Eibl-Eibesfeldt

FIGURE 12.9 A boy who has been blind since birth covers his face in embarrassment. He prevents others from seeing his face, even though he has never experienced sight himself. *(From Eibl-Eibesfeldt, 1973)*

© Eibl-Eibesfeldt

FIGURE 12.8 This laughing girl was born deaf and blind. *(From Eibl-Eibesfeldt, 1973)*

decades after graduation from college (Harker & Keltner, 2001).

Understanding Facial Expressions

Do we learn how to make appropriate facial expressions, or are they part of our biological heritage? One way to approach this question is through naturalistic observations.

Charles Darwin (1872/1965) asked missionaries and other people in remote places to describe the facial expressions of the people they saw. He reported that people everywhere had similar facial expressions, including expressions of grief, determination, anger, surprise, terror, and disgust. A century later, Irenäus Eibl-Eibesfeldt (1973, 1974) photographed people in various cultures, documenting smiling, frowning, laughing, and crying throughout the world, even in children who were born deaf and blind (Figures 12.8 and 12.9). Evidently, at least some of our facial expressions develop without any need for imitation.

Eibl-Eibesfeldt also found that people everywhere expressed a friendly greeting by briefly raising their eyebrows (Figure 12.10). The mean duration of that expression is the same in all cultures: one third of a second from start to finish.

To move beyond naturalistic observations, researchers typically use photos of people showing the presumed "basic" facial expressions, as shown in Figure 12.11. Look at each face and try to name its expression. (Please try now.)

Try It Yourself

© Eibl-Eibesfeldt

FIGURE 12.10 Like this man from New Guinea, people throughout the world raise their eyebrows as a greeting. *(From Eibl-Eibesfeldt, 1973)*

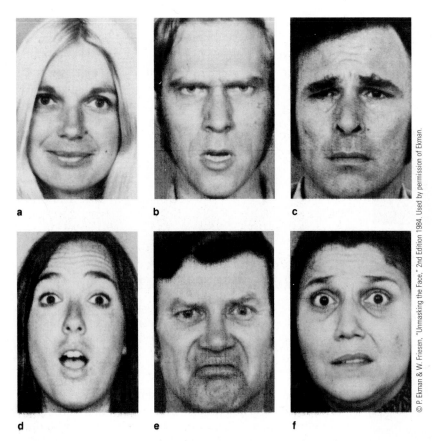

a   b   c

d   e   f

FIGURE 12.11 Paul Ekman has used these faces in experiments testing people's ability to recognize emotional expressions. Can you identify them? Check answer A on page 454.

© P. Ekman & W. Friesen, "Unmasking the Face," 2nd Edition 1984. Used by permission of Ekman.

Then look at each and match the expressions to the following labels (one face per label): anger, disgust, fear, happiness, sadness, and surprise. Most people can match all six expressions to their labels.

Try It Yourself

After researchers translated the labels into other languages, people in other cultures also matched them, though somewhat less accurately (Ekman, 1992). What should we conclude? Evidently, these facial expressions have nearly the same meaning throughout the world (Ekman, 1994). Variations in the expressions have been compared to regional "accents." For example, the Chinese tend to restrain their expressions of both pride and disgust, whereas Americans express them more fully (Camras, Chen, Bakeman, Norris, & Cain, 2006; Stipek, 1998). Just as you understand the speech from your own region better than that from elsewhere, you recognize facial expressions a bit more accurately among people from your own culture (Marsh, Elfenbein, & Ambady, 2003). Still, most people identify expressions fairly accurately even when viewing faces from an unfamiliar culture (Ekman & Friesen, 1984; Russell, 1994). Try the online activity Universal Emotions.

Online Try It Yourself

The research has some difficulties, however, and the results may either overestimate or underestimate how easy it is to recognize emotional expressions. Imagine yourself as the researcher. Suppose you show people the faces in Figure 12.11, and someone looks at the "fear" picture and calls it "worry" or "distress." Is that answer right or wrong? To make the scoring more objective, psychologists usually list the six emotions and ask people to choose one. But then anyone who identifies five of them gets the sixth one by process of elimination. Even identifying one or two faces improves one's chance of guessing the others (Russell, 1994). So the matching method overestimates people's accuracy.

On the other hand, asking people to identify emotions from a still photograph underestimates their abilities. We do better with films than with photographs (Ambadar, Schooler, & Cohn, 2005), and ordinarily, we supplement facial information by noticing gestures, posture, smell, context, and tone of voice (Edwards, 1998; Leppänen & Hietanen, 2003). Furthermore, the six faces in Figure 12.11 are all looking directly at the viewer. From the standpoint of experimental design, putting all the faces in the same position seems right. However, sad people almost always look down, not directly at you. Frightened people look directly at you only if they are afraid of *you*, and why would they be afraid of you—especially when you are sitting there calmly, as you probably are right now? Examine the photos in Figure 12.12. Which expression is easier to identify? Most observers identify sad or frightened expressions faster when they see someone looking away (Adams &

Try It Yourself

Fear

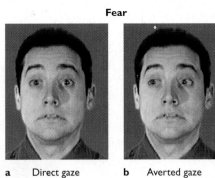

a   Direct gaze   b   Averted gaze

© Reginald Adams, Jr.

FIGURE 12.12 What emotions are these faces expressing? Most people identify fearful expressions more easily when the person is looking away.

Kleck, 2003). In contrast happy and angry expressions are easier to identify if the person is looking directly forward (Adams & Kleck, 2005).

CONCEPT CHECK

6. Researchers often show a set of photographs and ask observers to pair each with the name of an emotion. In what way might this procedure overestimate or underestimate accuracy of recognizing emotions? (Check your answer on page 453.)

Do Facial Expressions Indicate Basic Emotions?

Let's return to the question of how many basic emotions people have. Suppose we agree that people throughout the world recognize facial expressions of joy, sadness, fear, anger, disgust, and surprise. Can we then conclude that people have six basic emotions? No. First, people can, with a little less accuracy but still better than chance, identify several other facial expressions too. Try to identify the expression in Figure 12.13, for example, and then check answer B on page 454. People can also readily identify expressions of pride from facial expres-

FIGURE 12.13 Can you identify this emotional expression? Check answer B on page 454. *(Source: Rozin, Lowery, Imada, & Haidt, 1999)*

sion and posture (Tracy & Robins, 2004; Tracy, Robins, & Lagattuta, 2005). From videotapes, though not from still photographs, most people can identify expressions of "peace" and "heroism," which Hindu people generally list as emotions (Hejmadi et al., 2000). So if the ability to identify an expression is evidence for a basic emotion, our list should grow.

Second problem: We readily identify the facial expression in Figure 12.14 as "sleepiness," although few people regard sleepiness as an emotion. We can also identify expressions of "confusion," although confusion is at best a debatable example of an emotion (Keltner & Shiota, 2003; Rozin & Cohen, 2003). So the fact that we recognize facial expressions of surprise and disgust is not necessarily evidence that surprise and disgust are emotions.

FIGURE 12.14 Simple point: We easily recognize expressions of sleepiness, although we do not regard sleepiness as an emotion. So recognizing expressions of disgust or surprise does not necessarily qualify them as emotions either.

An Alternative to Basic Emotions

Not all psychologists are convinced that anger, fear, and so forth are psychological "elements." For several reasons many question whether it makes sense to talk about basic emotions at all (Barrett, 2006). First, the components of an emotion often occur piecemeal. For example, you might have the cognition "that person treated me unfairly" without feeling anger, or you might feel angry without any appropriate cognition. Furthermore, what we experience as anger is a compound of several experiences that can occur separately. As shown in Figure 12.15, you widen your eyes for a novel, surprising event. You turn down the corners of your mouth to indicate displeasure and furrow your eyebrows to indicate a desire to change something. You compress your lips when you feel in control of a situation. The expression we call anger is the sum of these compo-

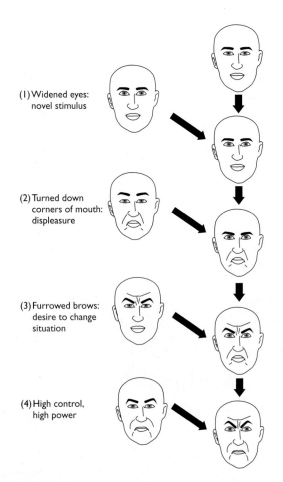

(1) Widened eyes: novel stimulus

(2) Turned down corners of mouth: displeasure

(3) Furrowed brows: desire to change situation

(4) High control, high power

FIGURE 12.15 What we usually regard as a single expression—in this case anger—may be analyzed as a compound of several parts. *(Figure 5.3 from Scherer, K. R. (1992), "What does facial expression express?" In K. T. Strongman (ed.), International Review of Studies on Emotion (Vol. 2, pp. 139–165). Chichester, England: Wiley.)*

nents, rather than an element by itself (Ortony & Turner, 1990; Scherer, 1992).

A second problem with the basic emotions idea is that the emotions overlap. People often feel angry and frightened at the same time or sad and frightened. In fact feeling just one emotion may be the exception rather than the rule. Third, the various emotions have similar physiological responses.

An alternative to the idea of basic emotions is a system of emotional dimensions. According to the "circumplex" model, all emotions range on a continuum from pleasure to misery and along another continuum from arousal to sleepiness (Russell, 1980). Figure 12.16 shows this idea. Note that this model deals with the feeling aspect of emotion, not the cognitive aspects. For example, both anger and fear would fit near "distress" on this graph, even though we associate anger and fear with different cognitions. Other psychologists have proposed slightly different descriptions but maintain the idea that emotions range along a couple of continuous dimensions (D. Watson, Wiese, Vaidya, & Tellegen, 1999).

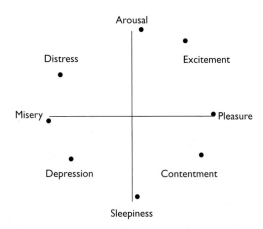

FIGURE 12.16 According to the circumplex model of emotion, all emotional feelings occur along a continuum of arousal and another continuum of pleasure. *(Figure 1 from Russell, J. A. (1980). "A circumplex model of affect," Journal of Personality and Social Psychology, 39, 1161–1178.)*

 CONCEPT CHECK

7. In what way does research on facial expressions support the idea of basic emotions?
8. In what way does research on facial expressions fail to support the idea of basic emotions? (Check your answers on page 453.)

Usefulness of Emotions

Are emotions *useful* for anything? Presumably, they must be, or we would not have evolved the capacity to feel them. One function is that emotions focus our attention on important information. If you see an array of stimuli, your eyes and your attention turn at once toward the strongly pleasant or unpleasant images instead of the neutral ones (Calvo & Avero, 2005; Nummenmaa, Hyönä, & Calvo, 2006; Phelps, Long, & Carrasco, 2006). You also remember emotionally arousing information better than neutral information (Levine & Pizarro, 2004). When you are distracted, you forget much of what you see and hear, but if you see or hear something frightening, you usually remember it despite the distraction (Kern, Libkuman, Otani, & Holmes, 2005).

Emotions or moods also adjust our priorities. If you see something frightening, you concentrate on the danger and virtually ignore everything else, as if you hardly saw it at all (Adolphs, Denburg, & Tranel, 2001; Mathews & Mackintosh, 2004). If you are running away from a mad attacker with a chainsaw, you don't stop to smell the roses. However, when you are in a happy mood, you expand the focus of your attention. According to Barbara Fredrickson's (2001) **broaden-and-build hypothesis** of positive emotions, *a* *happy mood increases your readiness to explore new ideas and opportunities.* You explore new possibilities, think creatively, notice the details in the background that you ordinarily overlook, and increase your chance for good new experiences that will help maintain your happy mood (Fredrickson & Losada, 2005).

Although major depression seriously impairs reasoning, a mildly sad mood is helpful under some conditions. As discussed in the last chapter, most people overestimate their own abilities and underestimate how long a task will take. People in a happy mood are especially prone to that error. Sad people tend to be more cautious and examine the evidence more carefully before making a decision. In one study students listened to a weaker and a stronger argument concerning possible increases in student fees at their university. Students in a sad mood were more persuaded by the stronger argument, whereas students in a happy mood found both arguments about equally persuasive (Bless, Bohner, Schwarz, & Strack, 1990). In another study slightly sad people were less likely than average to form "false memories," as described in chapter 7 (Storbeck & Clore, 2005).

Why might people in a sad mood evaluate the evidence more carefully? Perhaps the setbacks that make you feel sad also impair your self-confidence. Happy people are confident and therefore accept their first impulse. Sad people have more doubts and therefore delay making a decision until they have considered the facts more fully (Tiedens & Linton, 2001).

 CONCEPT CHECK

9. What is one apparent "advantage" of feeling sad? (Check your answer on page 454.)

Emotions and Moral Reasoning

People often advise us not to let our emotions get in the way of our decisions. Emotions can impair our decisions, but they sometimes help (Beer, Knight, & D'Esposito, 2006). In particular they often provide a guide when we have to make a quick decision about right and wrong.

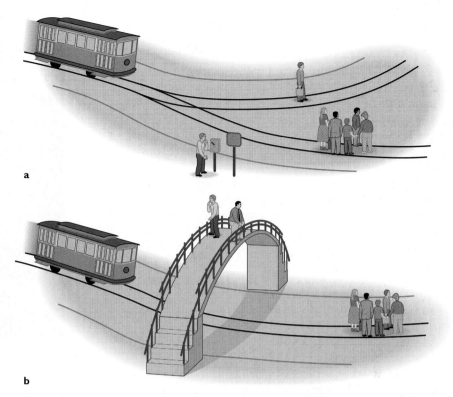

FIGURE 12.17 (a) Should you flip a switch so the trolley goes down a track with one person instead of five? **(b)** Should you push a fat person off a bridge to save five people?

Let's begin with two moral dilemmas. These are difficult decisions on which well-meaning people can disagree.

The Trolley Dilemma. A trolley car with defective brakes is coasting downhill toward five people standing on the tracks. You could throw a switch to divert the trolley onto a different track, where one person is standing. That is, if you flip the switch, the trolley will kill one instead of five. Should you do it?

The Footbridge Dilemma. Another trolley with defective brakes is coasting downhill and about to kill five people. This time you are standing on a footbridge over the track. You see a way to save those five people: A fat person is beside you, leaning over. If you push him off the bridge, he will land on the track and block the trolley. (You are, let's assume, too thin to block it yourself.) Again your action would kill one to save five. Should you do it? (See Figure 12.17.)

Most people say "yes" to flipping the switch in the first dilemma, but either say "no" or hesitate for a long time in the second dilemma (J. D. Greene, Sommerville, Nystrom, Darley, & Cohen, 2001). Logically, the answer should be the same because you kill one person to save five. Of course, the situations are not quite comparable. The instruction says you can save five people by pushing a man off a bridge, but you will not feel sure. What if you pushed him to his death and the trolley killed the others anyway? What if you pushed him and then the others jumped out of the way so that killing him was unnecessary? However, even if you were fully confident that pushing one man off a bridge would save five others, it would still be difficult to do. The idea of putting your hands on someone to push him to his death is emotionally repulsive, *as it should be!* In a bizarre case like this, maybe it makes sense to push a stranger off a bridge, but ordinarily it does not, and your emotional reaction is a quick guide to making a decision that is almost always right.

Let's try another scenario. Here you don't have to make a decision. You just decide whether the decision two people already made is acceptable: Mark and his sister Julie are college students. During one summer they traveled together, and one night they stayed at a cabin in the woods. They decided it would be fun to have sex together, so they did. Julie was taking birth-control pills, but Mark used a condom anyway just to be sure. Both enjoyed the experience and neither felt hurt in any way. They decided not to do it again, but to keep it as their little secret. They feel closer than ever as brother and sister. Was their action okay?

Almost everyone reacts vigorously and immediately that the decision was wrong. Why? Mark and Julie used two reliable methods of birth control, and both said they enjoyed the experience and did not feel hurt. So if their act was wrong, why was it wrong? Regardless of whether you can state a logical reason, you react that brother–sister sex *feels* emotionally repulsive (Haidt, 2001). Again, your emotions are a good guide to behavior. Even if Mark and Julie weren't hurt—and I understand if you doubt that claim!—they would be an extremely rare exception to a dependable rule.

Decisions by People with Impaired Emotions

Antonio Damasio (1994) described patients who suffered impoverished or inappropriate emotions following brain damage. One was the famous patient Phineas Gage, who survived an accident in 1848 in which an iron bar shot through his head. Nearly one-and-a-half centuries later, researchers examined his skull (which is still on display in a Boston museum) and reconstructed the route that the bar must have taken through his brain (H. Damasio, Grabowski, Frank, Galaburda, & Damasio, 1994). As you can see in Figure 12.18, the accident damaged part of his prefrontal cortex. As a result Gage often showed little emotion, and what emotion he did show was inappropriate. He seemed to lose his former values, becoming unreliable in both his work and his personal habits. He made rude sexual advances and used profanities that people had not heard him say before. He followed each whim of the moment, without any long-term plans.

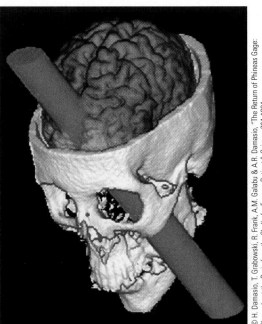

FIGURE 12.18 In the 1990s researchers used modern technology to reconstruct the path that an iron bar must have made through the brain of Phineas Gage, who survived this injury in 1848. The damage impaired Gage's judgment and decision-making ability.

A more recent example is known to us as "Elliot" (A. R. Damasio, 1994). Elliot too suffered damage to his prefrontal cortex as a result of surgery to remove a brain tumor. After the operation he showed almost no emotional expression, no impatience, no frustration, no joy from music or art, and almost no anger. He described his brain surgery and the resulting deterioration of his life with calm detachment, as if describing events that happened to a stranger. Besides his impaired emotions, he had great difficulty making or following reasonable plans. If given an array of information, he discussed the probable outcome of each possible decision but still had trouble deciding. As a result Elliot could not keep a job, invest his money intelligently, or maintain normal friendships.

According to Damasio (1994), Elliot's impaired decision making stemmed from his weak emotions. Ordinarily, when you and I consider possible decisions, we contemplate the possible outcomes and briefly experience how each outcome might feel. For example, if you consider a job offer from a company that recently fired your best friend, you imagine the unpleasant scene when you face your friend and reject the offer. Elliot can hardly imagine feeling good after one outcome or bad after another. If nothing feels good or bad, then it doesn't seem to matter what you do. As Damasio (1999, p. 55) said, "Emotions are inseparable from the idea of good and evil." If you cannot even imagine happiness or unhappiness, you will make bad decisions.

CONCEPT CHECK

10. In what way does prefrontal cortex damage interfere with decision making? (Check your answer on page 454.)

Emotional Intelligence

Is reasoning about emotional issues different from reasoning about anything else? The observations on patient Elliot imply a difference, as he can answer questions normally as long as they have nothing to do with emotional consequences. Casual observations in everyday life also suggest that reasoning about emotional topics might be special. Some people usually seem to know the right thing to say to make someone else feel better. They notice subtle signals in people's facial expressions that indicate who needs a pat on the back or a kind word. They know when a smile is sincere or fake. They foresee whether their romantic attachments are going well or about to break up.

Many psychologists therefore speak of **emotional intelligence,** *the ability to perceive, imagine, and understand emotions and to use that information in making decisions* (Mayer & Salovey, 1995, 1997). Part of emotional intelligence is detecting other people's emotions and knowing the right thing to say to manage emotional situations. Another aspect is being aware of one's own emotions, managing them, and expressing or restraining them depending on the situation (Mayer, 2001; Swinkels & Giuliano, 1995).

The idea of emotional intelligence quickly became popular, although the evidence behind the idea is not strong. If the concept is going to be useful, emotional intelligence must have enough in common with other kinds of intelligence to deserve being called intelligence. However, it should not overlap too heavily with academic intelligence, or we would have no reason to talk about it separately. To make any progress, the first step has to be finding a way to measure emotional intelligence.

Psychologists usually measure personality variables by asking people to rate themselves. For example, you might rate how extraverted you are or how conscientious. Self-reports of emotional intelligence do correlate moderately well with several aspects of personality (Engleberg & Sjöberg, 2004; Hemmati, Mills, & Kroner, 2004; Warwick & Nettelbeck, 2004). However, psychologists note some remarkable exceptions. To the question, "How sensitive are you to other people's feelings," some people whom others regard as insensitive rate themselves as highly sensitive (Carney & Harrigan, 2003). Apparently, they do not realize how insensitive they are.

If emotional intelligence is more like intelligence than like a personality trait, psychologists should be able to measure it as they do other abilities. Several psychologists have devised pencil-and-paper tests. Here are examples of some questions, reworded slightly (Mayer, Caruso, & Salovey, 2000):

1. A middle-aged man has been so busy at work that he spends little time with his wife and daughter. He feels guilty for spending so little time with them, and they feel hurt. Recently, a relative who lost her job moved in with them. A few weeks later, they told her she had to leave because they needed their privacy.
On a scale from 1 to 5, where 5 is highest, rate how much this man feels:
Depressed _____
Frustrated _____
Guilty _____
Energetic _____
Liking _____
Joyous _____
Happy _____

2. A driver hit a dog that ran into the street. The driver and the dog's owner hurried to check on the dog.
On a scale from 1 to 5, where 5 means "extremely likely" and 1 means "extremely unlikely," how would the driver and the dog's owner probably feel?
The owner would feel angry at the driver _____
The owner would feel embarrassed at not training the dog better _____
The driver would feel guilty for not driving more carefully _____
The driver would feel relieved that it was dog and not a child _____

3. Someone you know at work seems worried. You and he have lunch alone at a quiet restaurant. He confides in you that he lied on his application to get his job, and now he is afraid of getting caught. *What do you do?*

To each of these questions, you would probably answer, "It depends!" You need more information about the people and the situation. Indeed, one of the key aspects of emotional intelligence is to know what additional information to request. Still, you could do your best to answer these questions as stated. The problem then is, gulp, what are the correct answers? In fact *are there* any correct answers, or do they vary depending on culture and individual circumstances?

One way to determine the right answers is "consensus": Ask many people each question and take

Men often fail to read other people's emotions. (© *ZITS PARTNERSHIP, King Features Syndicate. Reprinted by permission.*)

their most common answer as correct. However, a test that relies on consensus scoring cannot have any difficult questions to identify people with special talent. All it could do is identify people who fail to answer questions that most people get right. That by itself is worth something. People with certain kinds of brain damage or psychiatric disorders do poorly even on easy questions about emotional situations (Adolphs, Baron-Cohen, & Tranel, 2002; Blair et al., 2004; Edwards, Jackson, & Pattison, 2002; Townshend & Duka, 2003). So the test could identify "emotional stupidity," even if it didn't identify emotional intelligence.

An alternative is to ask experts to identify the correct answers. Tests of mathematics use that approach, of course. However, mathematical experts are easy to identify. Who are the experts on emotional intelligence? If we assume that psychologists who have done years of research on emotion are experts on emotional intelligence, then according to the experts' scoring key, men on the average get higher emotional intelligence scores than women. That result should be surprising. Many studies show that from childhood on, girls and women are better than boys and men at detecting emotions from nonverbal signals (Chen & Haviland-Jones, 2000; Hall & Matsumoto, 2004). If men are told to try hard to pay attention to emotions, they narrow the gap, but they don't catch up (Ciarrochi, Hynes, & Crittenden, 2005). Guess what? All of the emotion researchers who determined the expert scoring key were men (Roberts et al., 2001).

A third approach is to use "targets"—people who have had particular experiences. For example, in the question about a driver who hit a dog that ran into the street, we might ask people who had this experience exactly how they felt. This approach requires finding those people and requires assuming that they can remember their emotions and report them accurately. This approach has much potential, but researchers have not used it much so far.

In short, emotional intelligence is an interesting idea, but researchers have a long way to go. The currently available tests of emotional intelligence have decent reliability (Mayer, Salovey, Caruso, & Sitarenios, 2001), but their validity is less certain. The self-report questionnaires about emotional intelligence correlate strongly with personality profiles (Gannon & Ranzijn, 2005). The ability tests correlate more strongly with academic performance (Zeidner, Shani-Zinovich, Matthews, & Roberts, 2005). If we know about people's personality (e.g., how conscientious they are) and we know their academic performance, how much do their scores on emotional intelligence tests add? So far, the answer appears to be little or nothing (Amelang & Steinmayr, 2006; Gannon & Ranzijn, 2005). So either emotional intelligence is not a useful concept, or we have not yet found a good way to measure it.

 CONCEPT CHECK

11. How does consensus scoring differ from expert scoring? (Check your answer on page 454.)

IN CLOSING

Research on Emotions

Research on emotions is fascinating but difficult. Of the various components of emotion, the cognitive and phenomenological (feeling) aspects are the hardest to measure. Behavioral and physiological measures are more objective but have their own problems. The best solution, therefore, is to approach each problem in multiple ways. Any one kind of study has flaws and limitations, but if several different kinds of research point to the same conclusion, we gain confidence in the overall idea. That principle is, indeed, important throughout psychology: Seldom is any study fully decisive, so we strive for independent lines of research that converge on the same conclusion. ▮

Summary

- *Measuring emotions.* Emotions are inferred, not observed directly. Researchers rely on self-reports, observations of behavior, and measurements of physiological changes. (page 437)
- *Emotions and autonomic arousal.* Most emotions are associated with increased arousal of the sympathetic nervous system, although some parts of the parasympathetic nervous system increase their activity also. The sympathetic nervous system readies the body for emergency action. (page 437)
- *James-Lange theory.* According to the James-Lange theory of emotions, the feeling aspect of an emotion is the perception of a change in the body's physiological state. (page 440)
- *Evidence supporting the James-Lange theory.* People who lose control of their autonomic responses generally report weakened emotional feelings. Also, molding someone's posture and breathing pattern into the pattern typical for some emotion tends to elicit that emotion. (page 440)
- *Schachter and Singer's theory.* According to Schachter and Singer's theory, autonomic arousal determines the intensity of an emotion but does not determine which emotion occurs. We identify an emotion on the basis of how we perceive the situation. (page 441)
- *Range of emotions.* Psychologists do not fully agree on which emotions, if any, are basic. (page 443)
- *Facial expressions.* People produce facial expressions of emotion as a means of communicating their probable social behaviors. (page 444)
- *Understanding facial expressions.* Many human facial expressions have similar meanings in cultures throughout the world. (page 445)
- *Alternative views.* Instead of speaking of a list of basic emotions, an alternative is to consider emotions as varying along continuous dimensions. (page 447)
- *Usefulness of emotions.* Emotions call our attention to important information and adjust our priorities to our situation in life. (page 448)
- *Emotions and moral decisions.* When we face a moral decision, we often react emotionally for or against one of the choices. Those quick emotional feelings may be an evolved mechanism to steer our behavior toward what is usually the right choice. (page 449)
- *Effects of brain damage.* We make many decisions by imagining the emotional consequences of the possible outcomes. People with brain damage that impairs their emotions have trouble making good decisions. (page 450)
- *Emotional intelligence.* People need skills to judge other people's emotions and the probable emotional outcomes of their own actions. The ability to handle such issues may constitute an "emotional intelligence." However, much work needs to be done to improve our measurements of emotional intelligence. (page 451)

Answers to Concept Checks

1. It would be impossible to teach a child (or anyone else) the words for emotions unless we had already inferred the emotions from the individual's behavior. (page 437)
2. The sympathetic nervous system is aroused by either anger or fear (fight or flight), and therefore, its arousal indicates strength of one or the other but does not identify which one. Brain measurements show overlap among the various emotions; that is, the areas excited by one emotion can be aroused by other emotions as well. (page 439)
3. No. According to the James-Lange theory, you feel fear because you are running away. (page 440)
4. People with pure autonomic failure have no systematic autonomic changes, and their emotions feel weak. People who adopt postures and breathing patterns characteristic of a certain emotion become more likely to feel that emotion, at least slightly. These results confirm the predictions of the James-Lange theory. (page 440)
5. According to Schachter and Singer's theory, you should plan a date riding roller coasters. If your date gets emotionally excited, he or she may attribute the arousal to you. (However, if you are dating someone who gets excited at art galleries and nauseated on roller coasters, you should change your strategy!) (page 442)
6. The matching procedure can overestimate accuracy because someone who identifies one or more correctly has an improved chance of guessing the others by the process of elimination. However, the use of still photographs underestimates people's accuracy because we ordinarily have many other cues, such as change over time, gestures, tone of voice, and context. Also, it is easier to recognize expressions of sadness and fear if the person looks down or to the side. (page 446)
7. Because people throughout the world can recognize the meaning of a few facial expressions, they appear to be universal among humans. (page 445)
8. A facial expression, such as that for anger, can be described as a combination of independent components, instead of being an element by itself. (page 447)

9. In some regards sad people are more realistic and more likely to consider evidence slowly and carefully before making a decision. (page 449)
10. People with damage to the prefrontal cortex cannot imagine feeling good or bad after various outcomes, and therefore, they see little reason to prefer one outcome over another. (page 450)
11. Consensus scoring takes the most common answer to the question as correct. Expert scoring uses the decision of a group of experts to determine the correct answer. (page 452)

Answers to Other Questions in the Module

A. faces express (a) happiness, (b) anger, (c) sadness, (d) surprise, (e) disgust, and (f) fear. (page 446)
B. Most people describe this expression as contempt. (page 447)

A Survey of Emotions

- *What makes people frightened, angry, happy, or sad?*
- *How do our emotions affect our actions?*

The field of emotions includes difficult theoretical questions, but we do not have to wait until we answer them. We can proceed to issues of practical importance to almost everyone, especially clinical psychologists: How can we control our fear and anger and increase our happiness?

Fear and Anxiety

Fear and anxiety feel about the same. *Fear* generally refers to the response to an immediate danger, whereas *anxiety* is a vague, long-lasting sense that "something bad might happen." Clinical psychologists spend much of their time dealing with people's excessive anxieties.

Is there a "right" level of anxiety? It depends on the situation. Presumably, evolution enabled us to readjust our anxiety based on our dangerous experiences.

Measuring Anxiety

Most emotion research relies on self-reports, but anxiety researchers also use an operational definition based on behavior: **Anxiety** is *an increase in the startle reflex.* The startle reflex is the quick, automatic response that almost any animal makes after a sudden loud noise. Within a fifth of a second after the noise, you tense your muscles, especially your neck muscles, close your eyes, and mobilize your sympathetic nervous system to prepare for escape if necessary. The startle reflex itself is automatic, but experiences and context can modify it.

For example, imagine yourself sitting with friends in a familiar place on a nice, sunny day when suddenly you hear a loud noise. You startle, but not very strongly. Now imagine yourself walking alone that night through a graveyard when you think you see someone walking toward you . . . and then you hear the same loud noise. Your startle response will be much greater. The increase in the startle reflex is a reliable, objective measurement of your anxiety. As you would expect, the startle reflex is enhanced for people with anxiety disorders, especially posttraumatic stress disorder (Grillon, Morgan, Davis, & Southwick, 1998; Pole, Neylan, Best, Orr, & Marmar, 2003).

Learned associations can also alter the startle reflex in laboratory animals. Suppose a rat frequently sees a "danger" stimulus—say, a light—before receiving a shock. Now that danger stimulus enhances the startle reflex to any loud noise. The increase in the startle reflex is taken as a measure of anxiety, and research based on this measure has identified the amygdala (uh-MIG-duh-luh), as shown in Figure 12.19, as

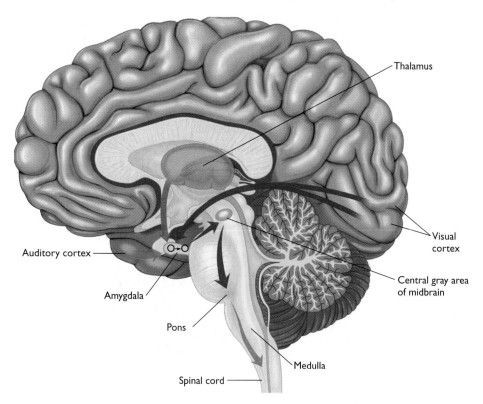

FIGURE 12.19 Structures in the pons and medulla control the startle response to a sudden loud sound. The amygdala sends information that modifies activity in the pons and medulla. This drawing is of a human brain, although the key research was conducted with rats.

the key brain area for this kind of learning. The figure shows a human brain, although much of the research has been conducted with rodents. For example, rats with damage to the amygdala still show a startle reflex, but a danger signal does not increase it (R. G. Phillips & LeDoux, 1992). Rats with such damage also lose their fear of cats (Berdoy, Webster, & Macdonald, 2000; McGregor, Hargreaves, Apfelbach, & Hunt, 2004).

People with amygdala damage report that they still feel fear and other emotions (Anderson & Phelps, 2002). However, they no longer respond quickly the way other people do to subtle or complicated signals about emotions (Baxter & Murray, 2002; Whalen, 1998). For example, they are impaired at recognizing facial expressions of emotion (Anderson & Phelps, 2000) and have trouble inferring other people's emotions from their tone of voice (Scott et al., 1997). They rate all faces about equally trustworthy (Adolphs, Tranel, & Damasio, 1998) and almost all drawings about equally attractive (Adolphs & Tranel, 1999). Most people remember emotionally disturbing pictures better than emotionally neutral ones, but people with amygdala damage remember both kinds of photos about equally (LaBar & Phelps, 1998).

CONCEPT CHECK

12. What method could one use to compare anxiety levels of nonhuman animals, preverbal children, or others who cannot answer in words? (Check your answer on page 464.)

Anxiety, Arousal, and Lie Detection

Let's consider an attempt to use physiological measurement of an emotion for a practical purpose: The **polygraph**, or "lie-detector test," *simultaneously records several indications of sympathetic nervous system arousal, such as blood pressure, heart rate, breathing rate, and electrical conduction of the skin* (Figure 12.20). (Slight sweating increases electrical conduction of the skin.) The assumption is that when people lie, they feel nervous and therefore increase their sympathetic nervous system arousal.

(A bit of trivia: William Marston, the inventor of the polygraph, was also the originator of the *Wonder Woman* cartoons. Wonder Woman used a "lasso of truth" to force people to stop lying.)

The polygraph sometimes accomplishes its goal simply because an accused person hooked up to a polygraph confesses, "Oh, what's the use. You're going to figure it out now anyway, so I may as well tell you. . . ." But if people do not confess, how effectively does a polygraph detect lying?

In one study investigators selected 50 criminal cases where two suspects had taken a polygraph test and one suspect had later confessed to the crime (Kleinmuntz & Szucko, 1984). Thus, they had data from 100 people who were considered equally plausible suspects at the time, of whom 50 were later shown to be guilty and 50 shown to be innocent. Six professional polygraph administrators examined all the polygraph results and judged which suspects appeared to be lying. Figure 12.21 shows the results. The polygraph administrators identified 76% of the guilty suspects as liars but also classified 37% of the innocent suspects as liars.

Other research on the polygraph has produced varying results. In an ideal study, some suspects are innocent and others are guilty, all are seriously worried about being convicted, and the investigators eventually determine for certain who was guilty. Few such studies have been done, and those few have produced unimpressive results. Although many police officers still believe in polygraph testing, most researchers regard the accuracy as too uncertain for important decisions (Fiedler, Schmid, & Stahl, 2002). Polygraph results are almost never admissible as evidence in U.S. or European courts. The U.S. Congress passed a law in 1988 prohibiting private employers from giving polygraph tests to employees or job applicants, except under special circumstances, and a commission of the U.S. National Academy of Sciences

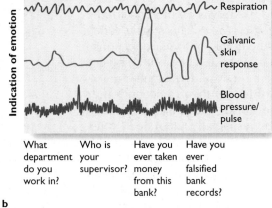

FIGURE 12.20 A polygraph operator **(a)** asks a series of nonthreatening questions to establish baseline readings of the subject's autonomic responses **(b)** and then asks questions relevant to an investigation.

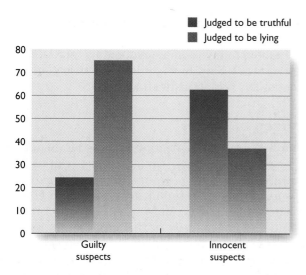

FIGURE 12.21 Polygraph examiners correctly identified 76% of guilty suspects as lying. However, they also identified 37% of innocent suspects as lying. *(Based on data of Kleinmuntz & Szucko, 1984)*

in 2002 concluded that polygraphs should not be used for national security clearances.

Alternative Methods of Detecting Lies

If polygraphs are unsatisfactory, what would work better? Researchers have reported that most people who are nervous about telling a lie show increased blood flow to the face, thereby radiating heat that a thermal camera can detect, as in Figure 12.22. This technique has the advantage that it can be used without attaching any instruments to the person's body; in fact, except for laws and ethics, it could be used without even telling someone. Preliminary results suggest this procedure would work at least as accurately as a polygraph (Pavlidis, Eberhardt, & Levine, 2002). However, doing just as well as a polygraph is not a great recommendation. Similarly, brain scans show that certain brain areas tend to become more active when people lie, but again, the accuracy is probably not high enough to use for any important decisions (Kozel, Padgett, & George, 2004).

The **guilty-knowledge test**, *a modified version of the polygraph test,* produces more accurate results by *asking questions that should be threatening only to someone who knows the facts of a crime that have not been publicized* (Lykken, 1979). Instead of asking, "Did you rob the gas station?" the interrogator asks, "Was the gas station robbed at 8 P.M.? At 10:30? At midnight? At 1:30 in the morning? Did the robber carry a gun? A knife? A club? Was the getaway car green? Red? Blue?" Someone who shows heightened arousal only in response to the correct details of the crime is presumed to have "guilty knowledge" that only the guilty person or someone who had talked to

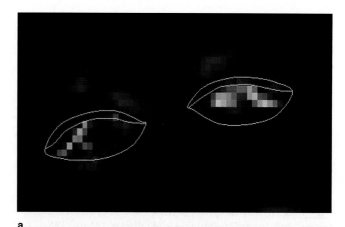

b

FIGURE 12.22 Thermal images show ordinary blood flow to the face **(a)** and increased blood flow just after the person lied to an interviewer **(b)**. *(Source: Pavlidis, Eberhardt, & Levine, 2002).*

the guilty person would possess. The guilty-knowledge test, when properly administered, identifies most guilty people and only rarely classifies an innocent person as guilty (Iacono & Patrick, 1999).

CRITICAL THINKING

A STEP FURTHER

The Guilty-Knowledge Test

How might the results of the guilty-knowledge test be biased by a questioner who knows the correct details of the crime? How should the test be administered to minimize that bias?

Another approach is to avoid technology and simply improve the way we observe others. Paul Ekman (2001) conducted extensive research to see how people react when they lie. For example, he asked people to watch either a pleasant movie or a disturbing documentary about burns and amputations and then, regardless of the content of the movie, to say they found the movie pleasant. So they all said the same words, but some were lying. Based on this and similar designs, Ekman found that people who are lying try to maintain a calm, happy expression but show microexpressions (brief involuntary emotional expressions), such as slight expressions of fear or a brief partial shrug of the shoulders. These microexpressions identify liars more accurately than the polygraph does. Researchers also report that when people lie, they tend to provide fewer details than when the same people are telling the truth, perhaps to avoid saying something that could be shown to be wrong (DePaolo et al., 2003).

One final comment: All these methods of detecting lying, from the polygraph to microexpressions, assume that people are nervous about lying. They fail with experienced, confident liars or people who have come to believe their own lies.

 CONCEPT CHECK

13. What does a polygraph measure?
14. What is the main objection to polygraph tests? (Check your answers on page 464.)

Anger and Aggressive Behavior

During World War II, nearly all the industrialized nations were at war, the Nazis were exterminating the Jews, and the United States was preparing a nuclear bomb that it later dropped on Japan. Meanwhile, Mohandas K. Gandhi was in jail for leading a nonviolent protest march against British rule in India. The charge against Gandhi was, ironically, "disturbing the peace." Someone asked Gandhi what he thought of Western civilization. He replied that he thought it might be a good idea.

Human beings are capable of ghastly acts of cruelty but also of nobility, heroism, and courageous opposition to violence. The struggle to understand violence is among the most important goals facing humanity in general and psychology in particular.

Relationship of Anger to Aggression

Anger is an emotion associated with a desire to harm people or drive them away. Aggressive behavior is easy to observe in nonhuman animals—or in little boys on a playground—but most adults learn to restrain their physical aggression. Surveys across a variety of cultures have found that people experience anger frequently but seldom even consider striking anyone (Ramirez, Santisteban, Fujihara, & Van Goozen, 2002).

Participants in one study kept an "anger diary" for a week (Averill, 1983). A typical entry was, "My roommate locked me out of the room when I went to the shower." They also described how they reacted, such as, "I talked to my roommate about it," or "I did nothing about it." Very few admitted to threatening violence, much less actually attacking.

Causes of Anger

According to the **frustration-aggression hypothesis,** *the main cause of anger (and therefore aggression) is frustration—an obstacle that stands in the way of doing something or obtaining some expected reinforcer* (Dollard, Miller, Doob, Mowrer, & Sears, 1939). Many instances of anger easily fit this description. However, frustration makes you angry only when you believe the other person acted intentionally. For example, you might feel angry at someone who ran down the hall and bumped into you but probably not at someone who slipped on a wet spot and bumped into you.

Leonard Berkowitz (1983, 1989) proposed a more comprehensive theory: Any unpleasant event—frustration, pain, heat, foul odors, bad news, whatever—excites both the impulse to fight and the impulse to flee. That is, it excites the sympathetic nervous system and its fight-or-flight response. Your choice between fight and flight depends on the circumstances, especially the expected result of attacking. If you have won many fights, have seldom been punished, and think the person who just spilled coffee on you looks easy to beat, you may threaten or even strike. If you think you have little chance of winning a fight, you suppress your anger. And if the one who bumped into you is your boss or the loan and scholarship officer at your college, you smile and apologize for being in the way.

Individual Differences in Anger and Aggression

Why are some people angry or aggressive more often than others? One hypothesis has been that low self-esteem leads to violence. According to this idea, people who think little of themselves try to build themselves up by tearing someone else down. The data on this point are mixed. Some studies find a small but significant relationship between aggressive behaviors and low self-esteem (Donnellan, Trzesniewski, Robins, Moffitt, & Caspi, 2005). Other studies find little effect or find a relationship between aggressiveness and narcissism—excessive self-centeredness (Baumeister, Campbell, Krueger, & Vohs, 2003; Baumeister, Smart, & Boden, 1996). One study found that most aggressive children greatly overestimate their popularity among their classmates (David & Kistner, 2000).

Another hypothesis not consistently supported is any strong link between violence and mental illness. Drug and alcohol abuse are highly associated with violence, and many mental patients abuse alcohol or other drugs. However, those without drug or alcohol abuse are no more likely than average to be violent (Hodgins, Mednick, Brennan, Schulsinger, & Engberg, 1996).

If low self-esteem and mental illness do not predict violence, what does? The answer is a combination of genetics and environment. Researchers have linked violence to childhood maltreatment in combination with one form of the gene controlling the brain protein monoamine oxidase (MAO). People with low levels of the protein respond more vigorously than average to childhood maltreatment. Figure 12.23 shows the results of one study (Caspi et al., 2002). Of boys who had both childhood maltreatment and a low level of monoamine oxidase, more than 80 percent developed conduct disorder, a condition marked by aggressive and antisocial behaviors. A much smaller percentage of boys in the overall population develop conduct disorder (Shaffer et al., 1996). Childhood maltreatment by itself had little effect, and the gene by itself had little effect, but the combination led to problems.

Several other factors are associated with a tendency toward violent behavior (Davidson, Putnam, & Larson, 2000; D. O. Lewis et al., 1985; Lynam, 1996; Osofsky, 1995; Raine, Lencz, Bihrle, LaCasse, & Colletti, 2000):

- Growing up in a violent neighborhood
- Not feeling guilty after hurting someone
- Weaker than normal physiological responses to arousal
- Smaller than average prefrontal cortex and decreased release of serotonin to this area

- A history of suicide attempts
- Frequently watching violence on television

Culture is also a powerful influence. A fascinating study documented the influence of culture on aggressive behavior even in nonhuman primates. Researchers observed one troop of baboons over 25 years. At one point all the most aggressive males in the troop tried to take food from a neighboring troop. The food happened to be contaminated, and all the aggressive males died. The troop then consisted of females, juveniles, and the least aggressive males. They got along well, stress levels decreased, and health improved. Over the years new males occasionally entered the troop and adopted this troop's customs. Today, none of the original males remain there, but the troop continues its nonaggressive tradition (Sapolsky & Share, 2004).

 CONCEPT CHECK

15. Is low self-esteem a good predictor of violent behavior? Is mental illness? What is? (Check your answers on page 464.)

Sexual Aggression and Violence in Relationships

Most acts of violence occur between people who know each other well, including romantic couples. A review of the extensive research within heterosexual couples reported that women commit *more* acts of violence against men than men do against women (Archer, 2000). Almost everyone finds that result surprising. After all, we have heard of battered women's clinics but not battered men's clinics. The explanation is that most researchers defined violence to include slaps, pushes, and other minor acts. On the average men inflict more serious injuries. Ordinarily, the men who most frequently and severely attack their romantic partners have a long history of criminal and violent behavior toward other people as well (Holtzworth-Munroe, 2000).

Rape is *sexual activity without the consent of the partner.* It includes cases in which someone uses violence or threats of violence to force a woman into submission. It also includes cases in which someone could not resist because of the influence of alcohol or other drugs. In one survey about 10% of adult women reported that they had been forcibly raped, and another 10% said they had involuntary sex while incapacitated by alcohol or other drugs (Testa, Livingston, Vanzile-Tamsen, & Frone, 2003). However, the statistics vary considerably from one study to another. Recall from chapter 2 that slight changes in the wording

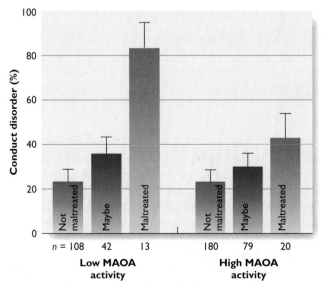

FIGURE 12.23 Children with low MAO type A levels who are maltreated have a high probability of showing aggressive and antisocial behaviors. *(Figure 2A, page 852, from Caspi, A., McClay, J., Moffitt, T. E., Mill, J. Martin, J., Craig, I. W., et al (2002). "Role of genotype in the cycle of violence in maltreated children,"* Science, 297, 851–854.)

of a survey question can enormously influence people's answers. Surveys that ask about "unwanted" sex report very high numbers because many people interpret "unwanted" to include times when one person wasn't in the mood but agreed to sex to please a partner (Hamby & Koss, 2003). Not only most women but also most men say they have sometimes had sex when they did not want to (Struckman-Johnson, Struckman-Johnson, & Anderson, 2003).

Even with a narrowly worded definition, surveys find rape to be far more widespread than the crime statistics indicate. Of all sexual assaults that legally qualify as rape, only about half the victims call the experience rape, and far fewer report the event to the police (Fisher, Daigle, Cullen, & Turner, 2003). Most women who have involuntary sex with a boyfriend or other acquaintance do not call the event rape, especially if alcohol was involved (Kahn, Jackson, Kully, Badger, & Halvorsen, 2003). In some cases the man does not realize that the woman considered his behavior abusive.

What kind of man commits rape? Most who commit violent rape have a history of other violent acts against both men and women (Hanson, 2000). Unlike most other men, rapists find the idea of forcible sex appealing and enjoy violent pornography (Donnerstein & Malamuth, 1997). That is, they display hostility toward women. One survey of admitted "date rapists" or "acquaintance rapists" found that they too reported anger against women and a wish to dominate them (Lisak & Roth, 1988).

Another element in rape is extreme self-centeredness, or lack of concern for others (Dean & Malamuth, 1997). Also, sexually aggressive men tend not to believe women who say they do not want to have sex (Malamuth & Brown, 1994).

Controlling Anger and Violence

Animals that live in social groups do much to restrain fighting. For example, if two members of a chimpanzee troop fight, they usually patch up their relationship afterward, and if they don't, another chimpanzee drags them together (de Waal, 2000). After one of these reconciliation ceremonies, they become less likely to fight. People also frequently reconcile with each other after a fight, especially if they know they will continue to see each other or work together.

If someone gets angry too frequently, psychologists have worked out methods of **anger management training,** *which are techniques for decreasing or restraining displays of anger.* Typical methods include relaxation, distraction, improved communication with others, and learning to reinterpret other people's actions as less threatening or insulting (Dahlen & Deffenbacher, 2001).

CONCEPT CHECK

16. Psychologists often study the causes of aggression by putting one person at a time in a laboratory and testing the effects of some experience on that person's willingness to flip a switch that supposedly shocks another person. Which aspect of aggression does that procedure probably overlook? (Check your answer on page 464.)

Happiness, Joy, and Positive Psychology

Happiness, unlike fear and anger, does not prime us for vigorous activity. The physiological responses associated with it are slight. We indicate happiness with a smile, but a happy mood often lasts much longer than a smile. Because the behavioral and physiological measures are so meager, researchers rely almost entirely on people's self-reports to measure happiness or **subjective well-being,** *which is a self-evaluation of one's life as pleasant, interesting, and satisfying* (Diener, 2000). **Positive psychology** is *the study of the features that enrich life, such as happiness, hope, creativity, courage, spirituality, and responsibility* (Seligman & Csikszentmihalyi, 2000).

What factors influence happiness or subjective well-being? Pose these questions to your friends. You can ask everyone question 1, but for some people add just question 2, and for other people question 3.

Try It Yourself

1. How would you rate your happiness on a scale where 0 means extremely unhappy and 10 means extremely happy?
2. What would make you happier than you are now?
3. What makes you happy?

On the first question, most Americans rate themselves on the positive side of the scale, calling themselves happy. The same is true in most other countries, except those overrun by poverty, war, or disease (Diener & Diener, 1996). Happiness is generally greatest in countries that respect individual rights and that accord women economic and political opportunities similar to men's (Basabe et al., 2002).

To the question of what would make you happier, most U.S. students mention money, a good job, more time to relax, or a boyfriend or girlfriend (or a "better" boyfriend or girlfriend). To the question of what makes you happy, common answers include relationships with friends and family, exercise, music, a sense of accomplishing something well, religious faith, and enjoyment of nature.

Influence of Wealth

Although many people say more money would make them happier, few say their money does make them happy. How important is money for happiness?

To find out we could ask rich people and poor people how happy they usually feel, or we could use a different, probably more accurate, measure of happiness: Researchers equip people with devices that buzz them at various unpredictable times to indicate their subjective well-being at the moment. On the average low-income people report feeling happy almost as frequently as high-income people. A likely reason is that your well-being, at least with this method of measurement, depends on how you spend your time. Many wealthy people spend many hours at work-related activities, and fewer hours on leisure (Kahneman, Krueger, Schkade, Schwarz, & Stone, 2006).

Wealth is not irrelevant, however. First, although wealth does not greatly increase happiness, extreme poverty produces unhappiness (Myers, 2000), especially if people compare themselves to relatives or neighbors who are doing better. Impoverished people are particularly unhappy if they are also in poor health (D. M. Smith, Langa, Kabeto, & Ubel, 2005). Evidently, you can be happy while poor or while sick, but not while both poor and sick.

Another way to examine the effect of wealth is to interview people who recently became wealthy. As you might guess, people who have just won a lottery call themselves very happy. As you might not guess, people who won a lottery a few months ago no longer rate themselves unusually happy (Diener, Suh, Lucas, & Smith, 1999; Myers, 2000). One explanation is that lottery winners get used to a new level of happiness, so a given rating doesn't mean what it used to. Also, people are greedy. According to one newspaper survey, people earning $25,000 a year thought $50,000 a year would make them happy, but those earning $50,000 a year said they would need $100,000 a year, and those earning $100,000 a year wanted $200,000 (Csikszentmihalyi, 1999). Furthermore, winning a lottery backfires for many people. Some lottery winners spend more than they won; many quit their jobs and lose all sense of accomplishment; and many encounter conflicts with relatives and friends who expect a share of the winnings.

CONCEPT CHECK

17. Many people think wealth would make them happy. In what way are they right, and in what way are they wrong? (Check your answer on page 464.)

Other Influences

If wealth does not predict happiness, what does? We might guess that weather would make a difference. Shouldn't people in sunny California be happier than those in Michigan, with its long, cold winters? On the average they are not, if we trust their self-reports (Schkade & Kahneman, 1998). Pleasant weather in spring improves people's mood temporarily, but people get used to the climate wherever they live (Keller et al., 2005).

One of the strongest influences is people's temperament or personality. In one study twins' ratings of happiness correlated only slightly with their wealth, education, job prestige, and so forth. In most cases both twins reported about the same level of happiness (Lykken & Tellegen, 1996). Some people tend to be gloomy while others tend to be cheerful, and most events change the level of happiness for no more than a month or two (Pavot & Diener, 1993). Recall the concept of set point from the last chapter. You have a set point for happiness and remain near it most of the time (Diener, Lucas, & Scollon, 2006).

A few major events provide exceptions, however. For example, people who get divorced show a gradual decrease in happiness in the years leading up to the divorce. On the average they recover slowly and incompletely over the next few years (Diener & Seligman, 2004; Lucas, 2005). People who lose a spouse through death also show decreased happiness leading up to the event, because of the spouse's failing health, and they recover slowly and incompletely afterward. Figure 12.24 shows the mean results. Naturally, the results vary from one person to another. Losing a job is a similar blow to life satisfaction, and many people do not fully recover (Lucas, Clark, Georgellis, & Diener, 2004).

Many aspects of life correlate with happiness or subjective well-being. In the following list, remember that correlations do not demonstrate causation, so alternative explanations are possible.

- Married people tend to be happier than unmarried people (DeNeve, 1999; Myers, 2000), and college students with close friendships and romantic attachments are usually happier than those without such attachments (Diener & Seligman, 2002). At least two explanations are likely. One is that close social contacts are helpful in many ways (Cacioppo, Hawkley, & Berntson, 2003). The other is that people who are already happy are more likely than sad people to develop strong attachments to others (Lyubomirsky, King, & Diener, 2005).
- Happy people are more likely than unhappy people to have goals in life. The only goal *not* correlated with happiness is making money (Csikszentmihalyi, 1999; Diener et al., 1999). One reason that goal does not lead to happiness is that most people who strive

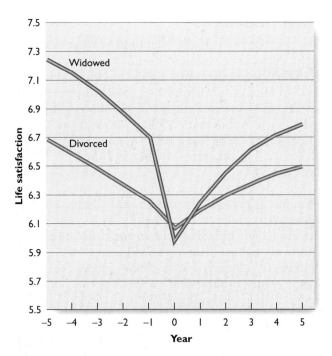

FIGURE 12.24 For each person, 0 marks the year of loss of a spouse through divorce or death. On the average life satisfaction declines until the loss and gradually but incompletely recovers afterward. *(From "Beyond money: Toward an economy of well-being" by E. Diener and M. E. P. Seligman from* Psychological Science in the Public Interest, 5, 1–31. Copyright © 2004 Blackwell Publishing. *Reprinted by permission.)*

to be rich do not succeed! Those who strive for wealth and achieve it are reasonably happy (Nickerson, Schwarz, Diener, & Kahneman, 2003).

- Generally, health and happiness go together (DeNeve, 1999; Myers, 2000). Health improves happiness, and a happy disposition probably improves the chances of long-term health. Even when happy and unhappy people develop the same illness, unhappy people complain more (Salovey & Birnbaum, 1989).
- Religious people tend to be happier than nonreligious people (Myers, 2000). Again, alternative explanations are possible. Faith probably supports favorable attitudes, and in addition unhappy people may be more critical of religious teachings and less likely to accept them.
- Happy people are more likely to trust others, to be emotionally stable, to be conscientious workers, and to enjoy being in control of a situation (DeNeve, 1999; DeNeve & Cooper, 1998). Again, you can no doubt imagine alternative explanations.

If you want to improve your happiness, your best chance is to change your activities. In one study researchers identified students who said they had recently had a major improvement in their living circumstances (e.g., more money or a better roommate) and other students who reported a recent improve-

ment in their activities (e.g., joining a club or starting better study habits). Both groups reported about equal happiness at first, but by the end of the semester, those who had changed their activities were happier than those who changed their circumstances (Sheldon & Lyubomirsky, 2006).

Among the possible activities that might make you happier, here are two with well-documented benefits: First, take out time once a week to list five things about which you feel grateful. In one study people who wrote about feeling grateful improved their life satisfaction, optimism, health, and exercise habits (Emmons & McCullough, 2003). Second, make it a point to perform a random act of kindness for someone you don't know once a week (Sheldon & Lyubomirsky, 2004). In the words of a Chinese proverb, if you want happiness for an hour, take a nap. If you want happiness for a day, go fishing. If you want happiness for a year, inherit a fortune. If you want happiness for a lifetime, help somebody.

Age

Other things being equal, would you expect people to become happier as they grow older, become less happy, or remain the same? Given that you would probably prefer to be young, you may be surprised to learn that, compared to younger people, most people over age 65 report more happiness and less fear, anger, and sadness. They continue showing that trend as long as they remain healthy (Mroczek, 2004; Mroczek & Spiro, 2005). Researchers have reported these results for the United States and Europe; we don't have comparable data for other parts of the world.

Brain studies confirm these self-reports. In one study young and old adults viewed emotional photos while investigators recorded their brain activity. The amygdala of young adults responded more strongly to sad or frightening photos, whereas that of older adults responded more strongly to pleasant photos (Mather et al., 2004). Correspondingly, when people view emotional photos, young adults remember the unpleasant ones as well as or better than the pleasant ones, but older adults remember the pleasant ones better (Charles, Mather, & Carstensen, 2003).

What accounts for these trends? The most popular hypothesis is that older people deliberately regulate their mood. That is, they intentionally attend to happy events and screen out unpleasant ones (Isaacowitz, 2006; L. M. Williams et al., 2006). While much evidence supports that view, an additional possibility is that the autonomic nervous system becomes less able to sustain the strong responses necessary for intense fear or anger.

Sadness

If you ask people what makes them happy, you get many answers, but if you ask what makes them sad, most answers fit a pattern: People feel sad from a sense of loss. It could be death of a loved one, breakup of a romantic relationship, failure of health, or financial setbacks, but whatever someone has lost, they see little prospect of recovering it. (People who can still avoid the loss feel fear or anger.)

Crying

Severely sad people often react by crying. Just as cultures differ in their attitudes toward loud public laughter, they also differ in attitudes about adult crying. Adults in the United States cry—or at least admit to crying—far more often than those in China. Women report crying more than men in each of the 30 cultures in one survey (Becht & Vingerhoets, 2002).

Many people say that crying relieves tension and makes them feel better, but the evidence says otherwise. While people are crying, sympathetic nervous system arousal and other signs of tension visibly increase. Relaxation occurs when people *stop* crying (Gross, Fredrickson, & Levenson, 1994). Even then, they may be no more relaxed than if they had not cried at all. In one experiment one group was encouraged to cry and another was instructed to hold back their tears while watching a very sad film. Contrary to the idea that crying relieves tension, the two groups had equal tension at the end, and those who cried reported more depression (Kraemer & Hastrup, 1988).

Crying is an interesting mystery in another regard too. Although many other species howl or whimper after an injury or during separation from their group, the shedding of tears seems to be a human specialization. Its function is not at all clear, unless it is simply to attract more attention and perhaps sympathy.

 CONCEPT CHECK

18. What evidence conflicts with the idea that crying relieves tension? (Check your answer on page 464.)

Other Emotions

As mentioned in the previous module, psychologists have no consensus on how many types of emotion people have. Indeed, they may not form an enumerable list. We can list all the elements of chemistry, but not everything comes in distinct elements. Here, very briefly, let us consider a few other important emotional experiences.

Many psychologists list surprise among the emotions. It occurs when events do not match expectations. When people are surprised, they become more sensitive to dangers and turn their attention toward anything that suggests a threat (Schützwohl & Borgstedt, 2005). Beyond that, researchers have little to say about surprise.

Anger, disgust, and contempt are reactions to different kinds of offenses. Anger occurs when someone interferes with your rights or expectations. Disgust is literally *dis* (bad) + *gust* (taste). In the English language, we use the term loosely to refer to almost anything displeasing (Royzman & Sabini, 2001), but narrowly speaking, **disgust** refers to *a reaction to something that would make you feel contaminated if it got into your mouth* (Rozin, Lowery, et al., 1999). Most people find the idea of eating feces or insects highly disgusting. In contrast **contempt** is *a reaction to a violation of community standards,* such as our reaction when someone fails to do a fair share of the work or claims credit for something that another person did (Rozin, Lowery, et al., 1999).

Embarrassment, shame, guilt, and pride are regarded as "self-conscious" emotions because they occur when you think about how other people regard or might regard you if they knew what you had done. The distinctions among embarrassment, shame, and guilt are not sharp, and different cultures draw the distinctions in different ways. For example, the Japanese use a word we translate as *shame* far more often than the word we translate as *embarrassment* (Imahori & Cupach, 1994). For English speakers most causes of **embarrassment** fall into three categories (Sabini, Siepmann, Stein, & Meyerowitz, 2000):

- *mistakes,* such as wearing casual clothes to a formal event or thinking someone was flirting with you when in fact they were flirting with the person right behind you.
- *being the center of attention,* such as having people sing "Happy Birthday" to you.
- *sticky situations,* such as having to ask someone for a major favor.

Sometimes, people also feel embarrassed out of sympathy for someone else who is in an embarrassing situation (Shearn, Spellman, Straley, Meirick, & Stryker, 1999). Simply imagining how the other person feels causes you embarrassment too.

Emotions and the Richness of Life

We try to feel happy as much as possible and try to avoid feeling sad, angry, or frightened, right? Well, usually, but not always. People voluntarily go to movies that they know will make them sad or frightened. They ride roller coasters that advertise how scary they are. Some people seem to enjoy being angry. Alcoholics and drug abusers experience wild swings of emotion, and many who quit say that although life is better since they quit, they miss the emotional swings. All of our emotions, within limits, provide richness to our experiences. ∎

Summary

- *Fear and anxiety.* Anxiety can be measured objectively by variations in the startle reflex after a loud noise. Processing emotional information, including that related to anxiety, depends on a brain area called the amygdala. (page 455)
- *Polygraph.* The polygraph measures the activity of the sympathetic nervous system through such variables as heart rate, breathing rate, blood pressure, and electrical conductance of the skin. The polygraph is sometimes used as a "lie detector." However, because the responses of honest people overlap those of liars, the polygraph makes many mistakes. (page 456)
- *Anger.* People experience anger frequently, although it seldom leads to violence. Anger arises when we perceive that someone has done something intentionally that blocks our intended actions. (page 458)
- *Individual differences in aggression.* One identified gene increases the probability of aggressive behavior, but mainly among those who had abusive experiences in childhood. (page 459)
- *Happiness and joy.* Most studies of happiness rely on questionnaires and self-ratings. Happiness level appears to be a fairly stable aspect of personality despite changes in people's lives. However, happiness decreases for years, sometimes permanently, after death of a close loved one, divorce, or loss of a job. (page 460)
- *Increasing happiness.* Increased wealth usually has only a temporary effect on happiness. More lasting benefits come from finding things to feel grateful about and helping other people. Changing one's activities boosts happiness in a more lasting way than most events do. (page 461)
- *Sadness.* Sadness is a reaction to a loss. Crying is a way of communicating sadness or distress to others. (page 463)
- *Other emotions.* Anger, disgust, and contempt are reactions to different types of offenses. Embarrassment, shame, guilt, and pride arise in social contexts based on how we believe others will react to our actions. (page 463)

Answers to Concept Checks

12. One could measure the strength of the startle reflex. (page 455)
13. The polygraph measures several aspects of sympathetic nervous system activity, such as heart rate, breathing rate, and sweating. (page 456)
14. A polygraph too often identifies an innocent person as lying. (page 456)
15. Low self-esteem is not a good predictor of violent behavior and neither is mental illness. Violence shows a stronger link to a combination of childhood mistreatment and low levels of MAOA activity. (page 458)
16. It would overlook reconciliation. (page 460)
17. Increased wealth does make people happier temporarily, and it increases well-being for those who were impoverished. However, for most people increased wealth has little effect on happiness in the long run. (page 461)
18. People who cried during a sad movie had no less tension than people who restrained their crying, and they reported feeling more depressed. (page 463)

Stress, Health, and Coping

- *What is stress and how does it affect health?*
- *How can we deal more effectively with stress?*

Imagine you meet a man suffering from, say, multiple sclerosis. Would you say, "It's his own fault. He's being punished for his sins"? I presume not. However, many people in previous times believed just that. We congratulate ourselves today on having learned not to blame the victim.

Or have we? We think that cigarette smokers are at least partly at fault if they develop lung cancer. We note that AIDS is most common among people with a history of intravenous drug use or unsafe sex. If women drink alcohol during pregnancy, we hold them partly to blame if their infants have deformities or mental retardation. As we learn more and more about the causes of various illnesses, we expect people to accept more responsibility for their own health.

However, we can easily overstate how much people's behavior influences their health. Even if you are as careful as possible about your diet, exercise regularly, and have healthy habits, you could become ill anyway. Your actions do influence your health but only to a certain extent. **Health psychology** *is concerned with how people's behavior can enhance health and prevent illness and how behavior contributes to recovery from illness.* It deals with such issues as why people smoke, why they sometimes ignore their physician's advice, and how to reduce pain. In this module we focus on stress, the effects of stress on health, and means of coping with stress.

Stress

Have you ever gone without sleep several nights in a row trying to meet a deadline? Or waited in a dangerous area for someone who was supposed to pick you up? Or had a close friend suddenly not want to see you anymore? Or tried to explain why you no longer want to date someone? All of those experiences and countless others cause stress.

Selye's Concept of Stress

Hans Selye, an Austrian-born physician who worked at McGill University in Montreal, noticed that a wide variety of illnesses produce many of the same symptoms—fever, inactivity, sleepiness, and lack of appetite. He noted that stressful experiences sometimes produce those same symptoms. He inferred that these symptoms were the body's response to an illness or challenge, its way of fighting the difficulty. Ac-

▌ Our emotions affect physiological processes and thereby influence health.

465

cording to Selye (1979), **stress** is *the nonspecific response of the body to any demand made upon it.* All demands on the body evoke generalized responses that prepare the body to fight some kind of problem.

When people say, "I've been under a lot of stress lately," they usually refer to unpleasant experiences. Selye's concept of stress is broader, including any experience that brings about change in a person's life. For example, getting married and being promoted are presumably pleasant experiences, but they also require changes in your life, so in Selye's sense they produce stress. Note, however, that Selye's definition does not include the effects of poverty, racism, or a lifelong disability because they are unchanging over time. In that sense Selye's definition is too limited. For example, the experience of African Americans of being insulted, avoided, excluded from opportunities, and so on certainly appears to be stressful, and it aggravates the medical problems associated with stress (Clark, Anderson, Clark, & Williams, 1999; Contrada et al., 2000). A better definition of stress is *"an event or events that are interpreted as threatening to an individual and which elicit physiological and behavioral responses"* (McEwen, 2000, p. 173). Because this definition highlights what an individual interprets as threatening, it recognizes that some event might be stressful to you and not someone else or to you at one time and not another. For example, seeing a snake in your backyard could terrify you but not bother someone who recognizes it as a harmless species. A critical word from your boss might disturb you, but less so if you know why your boss is in a bad mood today.

Measuring Stress

To do research on stress, we need a way to measure it. One approach is to give people a checklist of presumably stressful experiences. For example, the Social Readjustment Rating Scale lists 43 life-change events (Holmes & Rahe, 1967). The authors of this test asked a group of people to rate how stressful each event would be, and on that basis they assigned each event a certain number of points, such as 100 for death of a spouse and 11 for a traffic ticket. If you answered this questionnaire, you would check each event you have experienced recently, and then the psychologist administering the test would total your points to determine how stressful your life has been.

A later revision of this checklist changed and clarified many of the items (Hobson et al., 1998; Hobson & Delunas, 2001). However, checklists of this sort have serious problems. One is the assumption that a series of small stressors adds to the same as one large stressor. For example, graduating from college, getting unexpected money, moving to a new address, and starting a new job are all considered stressors. According to the checklist, this combination rates almost twice as many points as you would get from a divorce. That assumption is implausible. Another problem is the ambiguity of many items. You can get 44 points for "change in health of a family member." You would certainly check that item if you discovered that your 5-year-old son or daughter had diabetes. Should you also check it if your aunt, whom you seldom see, recovered nicely from a bout of influenza? Apparently, you get to decide what counts and what doesn't.

Moreover, a given event has different meanings for different people depending on how they interpret the event and what they can do about it (Lazarus, 1977). Becoming pregnant is not equally stressful to a 27-year-old married woman as to an unmarried 16-year-old. Losing a job may be a disaster to a 50-year-old, a minor annoyance to a 17-year-old with a summer job, and a nonevent for an actor who works in many plays each year and never expects any of them to last long. How would you feel about winning a silver

The stressfulness of an event depends on how we interpret it. For example, most people would be delighted to finish second or third in an Olympic event, but someone who was expecting to finish first may consider any lesser result a defeat.

medal in the Olympics? Most of us assume we would feel great, but researchers who watched facial expressions found that many silver medal winners looked sad. Presumably, they were disappointed because they almost won the gold medals (Medver, Madey, & Gilovich, 1995). In short, what matters is not the event itself but what it means to an individual.

The effects of stress depend not only on the unpleasant events ("hassles") that we have to deal with but also the pleasant events ("uplifts") that brighten our day and help to cancel out the unpleasant events (Kanner, Coyne, Schaefer, & Lazarus, 1981). Table 12.1 presents one example of this approach. Given that the stressfulness of an event depends on our interpretation of the event, the best way to measure someone's stress is through a careful, well-structured interview that can evaluate all the pluses and minuses in someone's life (G. W. Brown, 1989).

TABLE 12.1 Ten Common Hassles and Uplifts

Hassles	Uplifts
1. Concerns about weight	1. Relating well with your spouse or lover
2. Health of a family member	2. Relating well with friends
3. Rising prices of common goods	3. Completing task
4. Home maintenance	4. Feeling healthy
5. Too many things to do	5. Getting enough sleep
6. Misplacing or losing things	6. Eating out
7. Yard work or outside home maintenance	7. Meeting your responsibilities
8. Property, investment, or taxes	8. Visiting, phoning, or writing someone
9. Crime	9. Spending time with family
10. Physical appearance	10. Home (inside) pleasing to you

Source: Adapted from "Comparison of Two Modes of Stress Measurement: Daily Hassles and Uplifts Versus Major Life Events," by A. D. Kanner, J. C. Coyne, C. Schaefer, and R. S. Lazarus, *Journal of Behavioral Medicine*, 1981, *4*, 14. Copyright © 1981 Plenum Publishing Corporation.

 CONCEPT CHECK

19. According to Selye's definition of stress, would getting married be stressful? Would constant quarreling with your family be stressful?
20. Why are checklists an unsatisfactory way to measure stress? (Check your answers on page 474.)

How Stress Affects Health

People who have recently endured severe stress, such as the death of a husband or wife, have an increased risk of medical problems, ranging from life-threatening illnesses to tooth decay (Hugoson, Ljungquist, & Breivik, 2002; Lillberg et al., 2003; Manor & Eisenbach, 2003). How does stress lead to health problems?

Indirect Effects

Sometimes, stress acts indirectly by altering people's behavior. For example, people who have just lost a husband or wife lose their appetite (Shahar, Schultz, Shahar, & Wing, 2001). They don't sleep well, they forget to take their medications, and some—especially men—increase their alcohol intake (Byrne, Raphael, & Arnold, 1999). One study examined adults who had endured serious stress during childhood, such as physical or sexual abuse. These childhood experiences correlated strongly with risk-taking behaviors in adulthood, such as smoking, drinking excessively, using illegal drugs, overeating, and having unsafe sex. As a result they had multiple health problems (Felitti et al., 1998). Evidently, the childhood stress led to risky adult behaviors, and the behaviors led to health problems.

Stress can also impair health in strange, roundabout ways: Back in the 1940s, a midwife delivered three female babies on a Friday the 13th and announced that all three were hexed and would die before their 23rd birthday. The first two did die young. As the third woman approached her 23rd birthday, she checked into a hospital and informed the staff of her fears. The staff noted that she dealt with her anxiety by extreme hyperventilation (deep breathing). Shortly before her birthday, she hyperventilated to death.

How did this happen? Ordinarily, when people do not breathe voluntarily, they breathe reflexively; the reflex is triggered by carbon dioxide in the blood. By extreme hyperventilation this woman had exhaled so much carbon dioxide that she did not have enough left to trigger reflexive breathing. When she stopped breathing voluntarily, she stopped breathing altogether ("Clinicopathologic Conference," 1967). This is a clear example of a self-fulfilling prophecy and an indirect effect of emotions on health: The fact that she believed the hex caused its fulfillment.

Direct Effects

Stress can also affect health more directly. An angry shouting match or similar stressful event arouses your sympathetic nervous system, readying your body for vigorous activity. You increase your heart rate, your breathing rate, and your secretions of epinephrine (adrenaline). This is known as your "fight-or-flight system," which evolved as a way to deal with attackers and similar emergencies. However, your body reacts differently to a prolonged stressor. Perhaps you have a miserable job. Perhaps you live near a nuclear power plant and worry that it might have an accident. Perhaps you live in a war zone. If you have a nearly constant problem, your fight-or-flight system gives up, and you instead activate your adrenal glands to release higher amounts of the *hormone cortisol, which enhances metabolism and increases the availability of sugar and other fuels to the cells.* The increased fuel supply to the cells enables them to sustain a high, steady level of activity to endure prolonged stress. A moderate increase in cortisol, for a limited period of time, also enhances brain activity and improves memory (Abercrombie, Kalin, Thurow, Rosenkranz, & Davidson, 2003). Finally, cortisol activates parts of your immune system, preparing it to fight anything from infections to tumors (Benschop et al., 1995; Connor & Leonard, 1998). Presumably, the reason is that throughout our evolutionary history, stressful situations often lead to injury, so your immune system must be ready to fight off infections. Part of the way your immune system fights infections is to produce a fever because most bacteria do not reproduce well at elevated temperatures (Kluger, 1991). Your immune system also conserves your energy by making you sleepy, decreasing your activity, and decreasing your appetite. Note the result: Stress *by itself*, acting through the immune system, can lead to fever, fatigue, and sleepiness (Maier & Watkins, 1998). These symptoms will convince you that you are ill, even though the only illness is the stress response.

With prolonged stress and prolonged release of cortisol, you develop more serious problems. High levels of cortisol damage your hippocampus, a key brain area for memory, and produce memory loss (deQuervain, Roozendaal, Nitsch, McGaugh, & Hock, 2000; Kuhlmann, Piel, & Wolf, 2005). You feel withdrawn, your performance declines, and you complain about low quality of life (Evans, Bullinger, & Hygge, 1998). Furthermore, prolonged stress exhausts the immune system. High cortisol levels cause the body to break down proteins for extra fuel, and eventually—unless you have a great deal of protein in your diet—your body starts breaking down its own muscles for protein and stops making new proteins, including those of the immune system itself. With a weakened immune system, you become more vulnerable to illness (S. Cohen et al., 1998).

CONCEPT CHECK

21. How do the short-term effects of cortisol differ from the effects of prolonged cortisol? (Check your answer on page 474.)

Heart Disease

An upholsterer repairing the chairs in a physician's waiting room once noticed that the fronts of the seats wore out before the backs. To figure out why, the physician began watching patients in the waiting room. He noticed that his heart patients habitually sat on the front edges of their seats, waiting impatiently to be called in for their appointments. This observation led the physician to hypothesize a link between heart disease and an impatient, success-driven personality, now known as the Type A personality (Friedman & Rosenman, 1974).

People with **Type A personality** are *highly competitive; they believe that they must always win. They are impatient, always in a hurry, and often angry and hostile.* By contrast people with **a Type B personality** are *relatively easygoing, less hurried, and less hostile.* Are you a Type A or a Type B? Test yourself by answering the questions in Figure 12.25.

Measuring the Type A Personality

_____ 1. Do you find it difficult to restrain yourself from hurrying others' speech (finishing their sentences for them)?

_____ 2. Do you often try to do more than one thing at a time (such as eat and read simultaneously)?

_____ 3. Do you often feel guilty if you use extra time to relax?

_____ 4. Do you tend to get involved in a great number of projects at once?

_____ 5. Do you find yourself racing through yellow lights when you drive?

_____ 6. Do you need to win in order to derive enjoyment from games and sports?

_____ 7. Do you generally move, walk, and eat rapidly?

_____ 8. Do you agree to take on too many responsibilities?

_____ 9. Do you detest waiting in lines?

_____ 10. Do you have an intense desire to better your position in life and impress others?

FIGURE 12.25 If you answer "yes" to most of these items, Friedman and Rosenman (1974) would say that you probably have a Type A personality. But they would also take into account how you explain your answers, so this questionnaire gives only a rough estimate of your personality. *(From* Type A Behavior and Your Heart, *by Meyer Friedman and Ray H. Rosenman, copyright © 1974 by Meyer Friedman. Used by permission of Alfred A. Knopf, a division of Random House, Inc.)*

Statistically, a link does exist between heart disease and Type A behavior, especially with hostility, but the link is weak (Eaker, Sullivan, Kelly-Hayes, D'Agostino, & Benjamin, 2004). The best way to conduct the research is to measure hostility now and heart problems later. A study of that kind found a correlation of only .08 (Rutledge & Hogan, 2002). Even that weak effect may not indicate an emotional influence. Many people with high hostility also smoke,

a   b

People in some cultures (a) live at a frantic pace: People walk fast, talk fast, and push one another around. In other cultures (b) no one is sure what time it is and no one cares. The risk of heart disease is greatest in cultures and subcultures characterized by a hectic pace.

drink excessively, and eat a high-fat diet. Each of those behaviors also increases the risk of heart problems (Krantz, Sheps, Carney, & Natelson, 2000).

The strongest known psychological influence on heart disease is social support. People with strong friendships and family ties usually take better care of themselves and keep their heart rate and blood pressure under control (Uchino, Cacioppo, & Kiecolt-Glaser, 1996). People who learn techniques for managing stress also lower their blood pressure and decrease their risk of heart disease (Linden, Lenz, & Con, 2001).

Variations in the prevalence of heart disease across cultures may have behavioral influences (Levine, 1990). Some cultures have a hurried pace of life; people walk fast; they talk fast; almost everyone wears a watch; storekeepers pay prompt attention to their customers. Other cultures have a more relaxed pace of life; people are seldom in a rush; few people wear watches; the buses and trains seldom arrive on schedule but no one seems to care. As you might guess, heart disease is more common in countries with a hurried pace of life.

  CONCEPT CHECK

22. People with a Type A personality have an increased risk of stress-related heart disease. Yet, when they fill out the Social Readjustment Rating Scale, their scores are often low. Why might that scale understate the stress levels of Type A people? (Check your answer on page 474.)

Cancer

Behavior can also influence the onset and spread of cancer, at least indirectly. For example, women who examine their breasts regularly can detect breast can-

cer at an early stage, when treatment is more likely to be successful. Most women do not conduct regular, competent self-examinations, either because they do not know how, because they are fearful, or because they doubt a checkup would help (S. M. Miller, Shoda, & Hurley, 1996). Latina women in the United States have a higher rate of cervical cancer than other women, partly because they are less likely than other women to see doctors regularly for Pap smear tests (Meyerowitz, Richardson, Hudson, & Leedham, 1998). Preventing or treating cancer requires behavioral as well as medical interventions.

Does stress contribute directly to cancer? Stress and depression probably increase the risk of cancer, but the influence is weak. For example, one study of 673 breast-cancer patients found no relationship between stressful events prior to the disease and the patients' survival times (Maunsell, Brisson, Mondor, Verreault, & Deschênes, 2001). Social support does, however, strengthen the immune system (S. Cohen, Doyle, Turner, Alper, & Skoner, 2003) and improve both the survival time and the quality of life for cancer patients. That is, even if stress is not a clear cause of cancer, decreased stress is a good weapon for fighting cancer (Fawzy, Fawzy, Arndt, & Pasnau, 1995).

Posttraumatic Stress Disorder

A profound result of severe stress is **posttraumatic stress disorder (PTSD)**. *People who have endured extreme stress feel prolonged anxiety and depression.* This condition has been recognized in postwar periods throughout history under such terms as "battle fatigue" and "shell shock." It also occurs in rape or assault victims, torture victims, survivors of life-threatening accidents, and witnesses to a murder.

People with posttraumatic stress disorder suffer from frequent nightmares, outbursts of anger, unhappiness, and guilt. A brief reminder of the tragic experience can trigger a flashback that borders on panic. Mild problems seem unduly stressful, even years after the original event (Solomon, Mikulincer, & Flum, 1988).

However, most people who suffer severely traumatic events do not develop PTSD. Most suffer badly for the first few weeks and then gradually recover (McFarlane, 1997). Many psychologists have assumed that the more intense the initial reaction to a stressful event, the more likely the person is to develop PTSD. If so, then an immediate intervention, such as talking to a therapist right after a traumatic event, should help reduce the likelihood of PTSD. However, although this idea sounds reasonable, the evidence does not support it. The intensity of someone's response in the first week or so after a trauma is a poor predictor of PTSD (Harvey & Bryant, 2002), and most studies find that talking to a therapist right after a traumatic event has no measurable effect on the development of PTSD (McNally, Bryant, & Ehlers, 2003). Some studies find that it makes people feel worse (Bootzin & Bailey, 2005).

One possibility is that some people are simply more vulnerable than others. Most PTSD victims have a smaller than average hippocampus, and their brains differ on the average from those of other people in several other ways (Stein, Hanna, Koverola, Torchia, & McClarty, 1997; Yehuda, 1997). Given that stress releases cortisol and high levels of cortisol damage the hippocampus, it would seem likely that the smaller hippocampus was a result of high stress. However, one study compared identical male twins in which one twin had developed PTSD after combat experiences in war and the other had not been in battle and had not developed PTSD. The results: The more severe the symptoms of PTSD, the smaller the hippocampus of *both* the twin with PTSD and the twin without it (Gilbertson et al., 2002). These results imply that the hippocampus was already small before the combat trauma, perhaps for genetic reasons. Thus, some people are more vulnerable than others to PTSD.

People who devote a short time each day to deliberate relaxation report diminished stress. Exercise can work off excess energy, allowing greater relaxation.

 CONCEPT CHECK

23. What conclusion would follow if researchers had found that the twin without PTSD had a normal size hippocampus? (Check your answer on page 474.)

Coping with Stress

How you react to an event depends not only on the event itself but also on how you interpret it (Frijda, 1988; Lazarus, Averill, & Opton, 1970). Was it better or worse than you had expected? Better or worse than what happened to other people? Was it a one-time event or the start of a trend? How you feel about an event also depends on your personality. Some people manage to keep their spirits high even in the face of tragedy; others are devastated by minor setbacks. Coping with stress is the process of developing ways to decrease its effects and to get through difficult tasks despite the stress.

People cope with stress in many ways. Most coping methods can be grouped into three categories. One category is **problem-focused coping**, *in which people do something to control the situation.* Another is **reappraisal**, *or reinterpreting a situation to make it seem less threatening.* The third category is **emotion-focused coping**, *in which people try to weaken their emotional reaction.* For example, suppose you are nervous about an upcoming test. Studying harder would be a problem-focused method of coping. The problem-focused methods are generally the most effective, when possible (Gross, 2001). Deciding that your grade on this test is not important would be an example of reappraisal. Deep breathing exercises would be an emotion-focused method.

The distinction is not a firm one, however (Skinner, Edge, Altman, & Sherwood, 2003). For example, one way of coping is to seek help and support from friends. Their support helps calm emotions (emotion-focused) but also may help deal with the problem itself (problem-focused).

Problem-Focused Coping

Gaining any sense of control over a situation makes it less stressful. Consider two hypothetical situations. First, imagine some torturer is keeping you awake 24 hours per day. You have no way of escaping and no way of knowing how long the torture will last, but in fact it lasts 3 days until someone liberates you. Contrast that experience with an experiment in which you agree to go without sleep for 3 days. You could quit if you wanted, but in fact you don't.

Another comparison: A huge snowstorm has trapped you in a small cabin. You have enough food and fuel, but you have no idea how long you will be stuck. The snow melts 5 days later, enabling you to leave. Contrast a case where you decide to isolate yourself in a cabin for 5 days so you can finish a painting.

In both cases the physical circumstances are the same—3 days without sleep or 5 days without leaving a cabin. But if you are doing something voluntarily, you know what to expect, you know that you can quit, and you feel much less stress.

When hospital patients or nursing-home residents are told what to expect and are given the chance to make some decisions for themselves, they feel better, their alertness and memory improve, and on the average they live longer (Rodin, 1986; D. H. Shapiro, Schwartz, & Astin, 1996). Many people find that religious faith helps them cope with stress by giving them some sense of control over matters that are otherwise uncontrollable.

Why does a predictable or controllable event produce less stress than an unpredictable or uncontrollable event? One reason is that we fear an unpredictable, uncontrollable event may grow so intense that it will eventually become unbearable. If we have some control, we tell ourselves that we can do something if the situation becomes unbearable. A second reason is that, when an event is predictable, we can prepare for it at the appropriate time and relax at other times.

Thinking that you have control is calming, even if you really don't. In several studies people had to sit through painfully loud noises while doing a cognitive task. Those who were told they could press an "escape button" to turn off the noise did significantly better

than those without an escape button, even though almost none of them pressed the button—and therefore did not know whether the button worked (Glass, Singer, & Pennebaker, 1977; Sherrod, Hage, Halpern, & Moore, 1977).

People can gain a sense of control over a future problem by rehearsing it in their imagination. For example, you might imagine what someone might say or do and then how you might respond (Sanna, 2000). The better you can predict the situation, the more easily you can rehearse your responses. In one study pregnant women described what would happen as they went through labor and delivery. Those with the most accurate and detailed descriptions showed the least anxiety (G. P. Brown, MacLeod, Tata, & Goddard, 2002).

Many self-help books advise you to "visualize yourself succeeding" at something. The research says that visualizing yourself getting good grades, winning prizes, or receiving honors accomplishes nothing. What helps is to visualize yourself doing the work that will achieve the desired result. You might visualize yourself performing some athletic feat because visualizing the act is a kind of practice. As a student you might visualize yourself studying in the library or writing a long research paper. By imagining the work, you start on it sooner, organize your time better, and finish sooner (Taylor, Pham, Rivkin, & Armor, 1998). You also gain a feeling of control, which makes the task less stressful.

A stressful experience is less disturbing if you know what to expect, but it is hard to know what to expect if you have not been through the experience before. Sometimes, a good solution is to get a small-scale preview of a stressful experience that you may face later. In other words you can "inoculate" or immunize yourself against stressful experiences.

One way to **inoculate** yourself against stressful events is *by exposing yourself to small amounts of such events beforehand* (Janis, 1983; Meichenbaum, 1985; Meichenbaum & Cameron, 1983). For example, many armies have soldiers practice combat skills under realistic conditions, even under actual gunfire. Another way is through role-playing. A police trainee might pretend to intervene while two people act like a husband and wife having a violent quarrel. If you are nervous about going to your landlord with a complaint, you might get a friend to play the part of the landlord and then practice what you plan to say. Inoculation has proved successful with young people suffering from "dating anxiety." Some young people are so nervous about saying or doing the wrong thing that they avoid all opportunities to go out on a date. By means of role-playing, they can practice dating behaviors with assigned partners and thus feel less apprehensive about dating (Jaremko, 1983).

© Cindy Charles

Practicing self-defense serves as a kind of inoculation against fear. The thought of being attacked is less frightening when we have some idea of how to handle a situation.

 CONCEPT CHECK

24. Which would disrupt your studying more, your own radio or your roommate's radio? Why?
25. Suppose you are nervous about giving a speech before a group of 200 strangers. How could you inoculate yourself to reduce the stress? (Check your answers on page 474.)

Coping by Reappraisal

Sometimes, you are in a situation that offers no control. You applied for admission to graduate school, and now you are waiting for the replies. You underwent some medical tests, and you are nervously waiting for the results. While you are waiting, with no ability to control the outcome, what can you do? Another example: You already received the results, and they look bad. Every graduate school rejected you, or your medical tests indicate that you have a dreadful illness.

An effective approach is to reappraise the situation: "Here is an opportunity for me to rise to the occasion, to show how strong I can be. Even if the news is bad, I can still make the best of this situation." People who recover well from tragedies and defeats say that they always try to see the positive side of any event (Tugade & Fredrickson, 2004).

Here is an example of reappraisal: Students were asked to restrain their emotions by whatever means they chose, while examining a series of pictures that included some disturbing images, such as injured people and crying children. Those who restrained their emotions most successfully relied on reinterpreting the pictures. For example, they might regard a picture of an injured person as "someone about to receive good medical care" (Jackson, Malmstadt, Larson, & Davidson, 2000).

Emotion-Focused Coping

Emotion-focused strategies do not attempt to solve the underlying problems, but they help us manage our reactions to them. Three common methods are relaxation, exercise, and distraction.

Relaxation is one good way to reduce unnecessary anxiety. Here are some suggestions (Benson, 1985):

- Find a quiet place. Do not insist on absolute silence; just find a spot where the noise is least disturbing.
- Adopt a comfortable position, relaxing your muscles. If you are not sure how to do so, start with the opposite: *Tense* all your muscles so you become fully aware of how they feel. Then relax them one by one, starting from your toes and working systematically toward your head.
- Reduce sources of stimulation, including your own thoughts. Focus your eyes on a simple, unexciting object. Or repeat something over and over—a sentence, a phrase, a prayer, perhaps the Hindu syllable *om*—whatever feels comfortable to you.
- Don't worry about anything, not even about relaxing. If worrisome thoughts keep popping into your head, dismiss them with "oh, well."

Some people call this practice meditation. People who practice this technique report that they feel less stress. Many of them improve their overall health (Benson, 1977, 1985). One study found that people who went through a 12-week meditation program had a long-lasting decrease in anxiety and depression compared with a control group who spent the same amount of time listening to lectures about how to reduce stress (Sheppard, Staggers, & John, 1997).

Exercise also can help reduce stress. It may seem contradictory to say that both relaxation and exercise reduce stress, but exercise helps people relax. Suppose you are tense about something that you have to do tomorrow. Your sympathetic nervous system becomes highly aroused, but you cannot actually do anything. Under those conditions your best approach may be to put your energy to use, exercise, and relax afterward.

People in good physical condition react less strongly than other people do to stressful events (Crews & Landers, 1987). An event that would elevate the heart rate enormously in other people elevates it only moderately in a person who has been exercising regularly. The exercise should be consistent over days and weeks, but it does not need to be vigorous. In addition to the physical benefits of exercise, it provides distraction from the source of anxiety.

Distraction in general is a third powerful emotion-focused strategy (Cioffi, 1991). For example, many people find that they can reduce dental or postsurgical pain by playing video games or by watching comedies on television. The Lamaze method teaches pregnant women to suppress the pain of childbirth by concentrating on breathing exercises. Hospitalized patients can handle their pain better if they can distract themselves with a view or pleasant music (Fauerbach, Lawrence, Haythornthwaite, & Richter, 2002). Many people report that they distract themselves from stressful events by going shopping (Hama, 2001).

The effectiveness of distraction depends partly on people's expectations. In one experiment college students were asked to hold their fingers in ice water until the sensation became too painful to endure (Melzack, Weisz, & Sprague, 1963). Some of them listened to music of their own choice and were told that listening to music would lessen the pain. Others also listened to music but were given no suggestion that it would ease the pain. Still others heard nothing but were told that a special "ultrasonic sound" was being transmitted that would lessen the pain. The group that heard music and expected it to lessen the pain tolerated the pain better than either of the other two groups. Evidently, neither the music nor the suggestion of reduced pain is as effective as both are together.

 CONCEPT CHECK

26. Some people control anxiety with tranquilizers. In which of the three categories of coping strategy do these drugs belong? (Check your answer on page 474.)

 CRITICAL THINKING

A STEP FURTHER

Placebos

Many experiments report that a placebo alone serves as an effective painkiller for certain patients. Why might that be true?

IN CLOSING

Health Is Both Psycho and Somatic

In this module we have considered the ways people try to deal with stressful situations, but how well do these strategies work? The answer is that they work well for many people but at a cost. The cost is that coping with serious stressors requires energy. Many people who have had to cope with long-lasting stressors break their diets, resume smoking and drinking habits that they had abandoned long ago, and find it difficult to concentrate on challenging cognitive tasks (Muraven & Baumeister, 2000).

Still, in spite of the costs, an amazing number of people say that the experience of battling a chronic illness, tending to a loved one with a severe illness, or dealing with other painful experiences has brought them personal strength and an enhanced feeling of meaning in life (Folkman & Moskowitz, 2000). They found positive moments even in the midst of fear and loss. Not everyone rises to the occasion, but we should admire those who do. ▮

Summary

- *Selye's concept of stress.* According to Hans Selye, stress is "the nonspecific response of the body to any demand made upon it." Any event, pleasant or unpleasant, that brings about change in a person's life produces some measure of stress. One problem with this definition is that it omits lifelong problems, such as coping with racism. (page 465)
- *Difficulties of measuring stress.* Stress checklists are problematic because many items are ambiguous. Also, the stressfulness of an event depends on the person's interpretation of the event and ability to cope with it. (page 466)
- *Indirect effects on health.* Stress affects health indirectly because people exposed to stressful events often change their eating, sleeping, and drinking habits. (page 467)
- *Direct effects on health.* Stress causes increased secretion of the hormone cortisol. Brief, moderate elevations of cortisol enhance memory and immune system responses. However, prolonged cortisol damages health by impairing the hippocampus and by exhausting the immune system. (page 467)
- *Heart disease and cancer.* Research has found only a small link between emotional responses and the onset of heart disease. Any link to the onset of cancer remains uncertain, but social support that decreases stress improves survival times and the quality of life of people with cancer. (page 468)

- *Posttraumatic stress disorder.* After severe traumatic experiences, some people have long-lasting changes in experience. Some people may be more vulnerable than others to this outcome. (page 469)
- *Coping styles.* Most strategies for dealing with stress fall into three major categories: trying to fix the problem, reappraisal, and trying to control emotions. (page 470)
- *Prediction and control.* Events are generally less stressful when people think they can predict or control them. (page 471)
- *Reappraisal.* Interpreting a situation in a new, less threatening way reduces tension. (page 472)
- *Emotion-focused coping.* Relaxation, exercise, and distraction reduce excess anxiety. (page 473)

Answers to Concept Checks

19. By Selye's definition getting married produces stress because it requires a change in one's life. However, constant quarreling with one's family would not be stressful because it is not a change in one's life. (page 466)

20. Items on stress checklists are often ambiguous, and therefore, the results have low reliability and validity. Also, a given event can be more stressful for one person than another. (page 466)

21. Short-term, moderate increases in cortisol enhance memory and increase immune responses. Prolonged cortisol damages the hippocampus, impairs memory, and exhausts the immune system. (page 468)

22. The Social Readjustment Rating Scale measures events that change a person's life; it does not measure constant sources of stress such as the pressures of work. The scale also fails to measure impatience, competitiveness, and hostility, which are typical of people with Type A personality. (page 468)

23. If the twin without PTSD had a normal hippocampus, the conclusion would be that severe stress had damaged the hippocampus of the twin with PTSD. (page 470)

24. Your roommate's radio would be more disruptive. You can turn your own radio on or off, switch stations, or reduce the volume. You have no such control over your roommate's radio (unless your roommate happens to be very cooperative). (page 471)

25. Practice giving your speech to a small group of friends. If possible, practice giving the speech in the room where you will ultimately deliver it. (page 471)

26. Using tranquilizers is an example of emotion-focused coping. (page 472)

CHAPTER ENDING

Key Terms and Activities

Key Terms

You can check the page listed for a complete description of a term. You can also check the glossary/index at the end of the text for a definition of a given term, or you can download a list of all the terms and their definitions for any chapter at this website:

www.thomsonedu.com/psychology/kalat

anger management training (page 460)
anxiety (page 455)
autonomic nervous system (page 437)
broaden-and-build hypothesis (page 448)

contempt (page 463)
cortisol (page 468)
disgust (page 463)
Duchenne smile (page 444)
embarrassment (page 463)
emotion-focused coping (page 470)
emotional intelligence (page 451)
frustration-aggression hypothesis (page 458)
guilty-knowledge test (page 457)
health psychology (page 465)
inoculation (page 471)
James-Lange theory (page 440)
microexpressions (page 437)
parasympathetic nervous system (page 439)
polygraph (page 456)

positive psychology (page 460)
posttraumatic stress disorder (PTSD) (page 469)
problem-focused coping (page 470)
pure autonomic failure (page 440)
rape (page 459)
reappraisal (page 470)
Schachter and Singer's theory of emotions (page 441)
stress (page 466)
subjective well-being (page 460)
sympathetic nervous system (page 438)
Type A personality (page 468)
Type B personality (page 468)

Suggestions for Further Reading

Damasio, A. (1999). *The feeling of what happens.* New York: Harcourt Brace. Ambitious treatment of the role of emotions in thinking and consciousness.

Kalat, J. W., & Shiota, M. (2007). *Emotion.* Belmont, CA: Wadsworth. A textbook covering contemporary research on emotion.

Provine, R. (2000). *Laughter.* New York: Viking Press. Pioneering observations of who laughs, when, and why. Highly recommended.

 Web/Technology Resources

Student Companion Website

www.thomsonedu.com/psychology/kalat

Explore the Student Companion Website for Online Try-It-Yourself activities, practice quizzes, flashcards, and more! The companion site also has direct links to the following websites.

MINCAVA: Global Links on Violence

http://www.mincava.umn.edu/

The Minnesota Center Against Violence and Abuse (MINCAVA) maintains hundreds of links to sites that provide information about all forms of violence.

Emotions and Artificial Intelligence

http://www.aaai.org/aitopics/html/emotion.html

Would it be possible to build a robot with emotions? Here is a site for people who like to think about that question.

 *For Additional Study*

Kalat Premium Website

http://www.thomsonedu.com

For Critical Thinking Videos and additional Online Try-It-Yourself activities, go to this site to enter or purchase your code for the Kalat Premium Website.

ThomsonNOW!

http://www.thomsonedu.com

Go to this site for the link to ThomsonNOW, your one-stop study shop. Take a Pretest for this chapter, and Thomson-NOW will generate a personalized Study Plan based on your test results. The Study Plan will identify the topics you need to review and direct you to online resources to help you master those topics. You can then take a Posttest to help you determine the concepts you have mastered and what you still need to work on.

13

Social Psychology

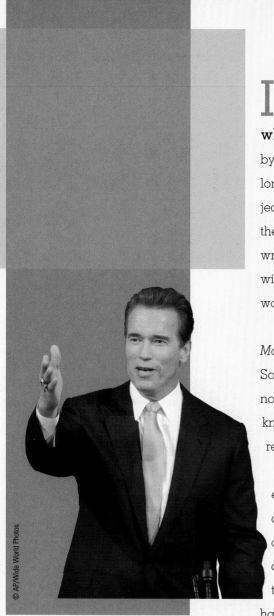

In the *Communist Manifesto*, Karl Marx and Friedrich Engels wrote, "Mankind are more disposed to suffer, while evils are sufferable, than to right themselves by abolishing the forms to which they are accustomed. But when a long train of abuses and usurpations, pursuing invariably the same object, evinces a design to reduce them under absolute despotism, it is their right, it is their duty, to throw off such government." Fidel Castro wrote, "A little rebellion, now and then, is a good thing." Do you agree with those statements? Why or why not? Can you think of anything that would change your mind?

Oh, pardon me. . . . That first statement is not from the *Communist Manifesto*. It is from the United States' Declaration of Independence. Sorry. And that second statement is a quotation from Thomas Jefferson, not Castro. Do you agree more with these statements now that you know they came from democratic revolutionaries instead of communist revolutionaries?

What kinds of influences alter your opinions? This question is one example of the issues that interest **social psychologists**—*the psychologists who study social behavior and how individuals influence other people and are influenced by other people.* Social psychology can be described as a broad field because it includes the study of attitudes, persuasion, self-understanding, and almost all everyday behaviors of relatively normal people in their relationships with others. It can also be criticized as a narrow field because so much of its research deals with North American college students in laboratory settings (Rozin, 2001). As you will see, social psychologists have studied some fascinating phenomena, but major questions remain.

Influence depends not only on what someone says but also on what the listeners think of the speaker.

Cooperation and Competition

- *What determines whether we cooperate with or compete with others?*

The custom of living in groups dates back to before the origin of the human species, as almost all primates (monkeys and apes) live in groups. Group life has many advantages. Groups have better defense against predators and better ability to protect their food and supplies from potential raiders. Another advantage is easily overlooked: A band of females, or a band of females with a few "friendly" males, provides protection against sexually aggressive males (Brereton, 2004). All of these advantages and more probably played important roles in primitive human societies.

Human societies provide another feature not seen in other mammals: an extraordinary division of labor. If you had to make your own shelter and clothing, find your own food and water, and tend to your own medical problems, how long would you survive? Each of us learns to specialize in a job that would be useless without the cooperation of many other people. Together, we accomplish vastly more than any of us could alone.

Furthermore, people go beyond mere cooperation. Most of us at least occasionally give to charity, volunteer our time for worthy projects, offer directions to a stranger who appears lost, and in other ways help people who will never pay us back. We even help other species. If you see a turtle on a busy road, you might pull your car to the side, pick up the turtle, and carry it to safety.

Why do we (sometimes) engage in **altruistic behavior**—*accepting some cost or risk to help others?* It seems so natural that we take it for granted, but altruism is uncommon among other animal species. Let's qualify that: In almost every species, animals devote great energies and risk their lives to help their children and sometimes other relatives. But they seldom spend much effort to help unrelated individuals. For example, although chimpanzees cooperate when working toward a common goal (Melis, Hare, & Tomasello, 2006), they only occasionally provide altruistic help (Warneken & Tomasello, 2006).

In one study each chimpanzee had a choice between two ropes. In one condition, if it pulled one rope it got food and if it pulled the other it got nothing. Under those conditions a chimp almost always chose the rope with food. In another condition one rope brought food to the chimp, and the other rope brought food to *both* itself and a familiar but unrelated chimp in another cage. The one in control seemed indifferent to whether the other chimp got food, even when the other chimp made begging gestures. Usually, the chimp just pulled whichever rope was on the right, regardless of whether it fed the other chimp or not (Silk et al., 2005).

Given how uncommon altruism is in the rest of the animal kingdom, why do people go out of their way to help one another? You may reply that it feels good to help others. Yes, but why does it feel good? We also have sex because it feels good, but we see why we evolved to enjoy sex. (It increases our chances of passing on our genes.) Could we have evolved genes that make altruistic behavior feel good? If so, why? No one has found such a gene, but regardless of finding one or not, a theoretical mystery remains of how natural selection could favor such a gene. If you have a gene that increases your probability of helping your relatives, you help spread the genes that you have in common with them, including this gene for altruism. However, if a gene increases your altruism toward unrelated people, you increase the other people's probability of surviving and spreading their genes, which are unlike your own. You don't increase, and you may slightly decrease, the probability of spreading your own genes, including the one for altruism. So your society would benefit, but the gene causing the benefit would not spread. If we consider the issue in nongenetic terms, the same problem arises: If you learn a habit of helping others, including people who are not altruistic themselves, they profit and you do not. Why would you learn to act that way? We shall consider two answers.

The Prisoner's Dilemma and Similar Situations

Researchers find that very few people are consistently altruistic (Fehr & Fischbacher, 2003). Do you cooperate with others and help others generously? For most of us, the honest answer is "it depends." To investigate how situations evoke cooperation or competition, many researchers in psychology and economics have used the **prisoner's dilemma,** *a situation where people choose between a cooperative act and a competitive act that benefits themselves but hurts others.* Let's start with the original version of this dilemma: You and a partner are arrested and charged with armed robbery. The police take you into separate rooms and ask each of you to confess. If neither confesses, the police do not have enough evidence to convict you of armed robbery, but they can convict you of a lesser offense with a sentence of 1 year in prison. If either confesses and testifies against the other, the confessor goes free and the other gets 20 years in prison. If you both confess, you each get 5 years in prison. Each of you knows that the other person has the same options. Figure 13.1 illustrates the choices.

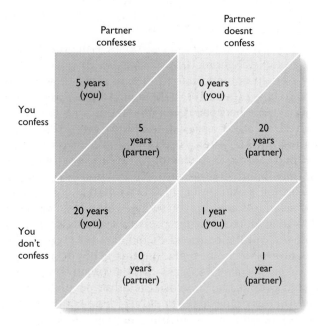

FIGURE 13.1 In the prisoner's dilemma, each person considering the choice alone finds it beneficial to confess. But if both people confess, they suffer worse consequences than if both had refused to confess.

If your partner does not confess, then you can confess and go free. (Your partner will get 20 years in prison, but let's assume you care only about yourself.) If your partner does confess, it is still to your advantage to confess because you will get only 5 years in prison instead of 20. So you confess. Your partner, reasoning the same way, also confesses, and you both get 5 years in prison. If you had both kept quiet, you would have served only 1 year in prison. The situation led both people to uncooperative behavior.

If you and your partner could have discussed your strategy, you would have agreed not to confess. Then, when the police took you to separate rooms, you would each hope that the other would keep the bargain. But can you be sure? Maybe your partner will double-cross you and confess. If so, you should con-

fess too. And if your partner does keep the bargain, what should you do? Again, it's to your advantage to confess! We're back where we started.

The two of you are most likely to cooperate if you can stay in constant communication (Nemeth, 1972). If you can overhear each other, you know that, as soon as one confesses, the other will retaliate. This kind of situation occurs in real life, among nations as well as individuals. During the arms race between the United States and the Soviet Union, both sides wanted an agreement to stop building nuclear weapons. However, if one country kept the agreement while the other "cheated" by making additional weapons, the cheater could build a huge military advantage. The only way to forge an agreement was to allow each side to inspect the other. Each side needed to observe the other but also needed to be observed (even to be spied upon, to some extent) to reassure the other side that it was not cheating. If either side doubted that the other was keeping its word, the agreement would be lost.

The prisoner's dilemma can also be stated in terms of gains. Suppose you and another person have a choice between two moves, which we call *cooperate* and *compete.* Depending on your choices, here are the payoffs:

Here are the payoffs:

	Other person cooperates	Other person competes
You cooperate	Both win $1	Other person gains $2; you lose $2
You compete	You gain $2; other person loses $2	Both lose $1

Suppose you will play this game only once with someone you will never meet. Both of you will reveal your answers by telephone to some third person. Which move do you choose? If the other person cooperates, your winning choice is *compete* because you will get $2 instead of $1. If the other person competes, again you gain by competing because you will lose just $1 instead of $2. Logically, you should choose to compete, and so should the other person. Therefore, you both lose $1.

Effective Strategies

If you and another person play repeatedly, the strategy changes drastically, and cooperation overtakes competition. The most dependable strategy is reciprocity, also called "tit for tat": Start with the *cooperate* move. If the other person cooperates too, then continue cooperating. If the other person makes a *compete* move, retaliate with a *compete* move on your next turn. (Your retaliation should teach the other person not to try to take advantage of you.) You can try this strategy and others at this website, where you compete against a computer opponent: **http://serendip.brynmawr.edu/bb/pd.html.**

If you use the tit-for-tat strategy, you will never beat the other person, but both of you will do reasonably well. Business deals work like this in real life. You offer to sell me something, so I send you the money. If we both keep our promises, we are willing to do business again.

Most individuals do cooperate in prisoner's dilemma-type situations, especially when real rewards are at stake. Culture makes some difference; for example, Chinese people cooperate more than Americans on the average (Wong & Hong, 2005). Curiously, when people make decisions as groups, groups are more likely to compete with one another instead of cooperating (Wildschut, Pinter, Vevea, Insko, & Schopler, 2003). Think, for example, of the conflicts between nations or the ways in which competing political parties sometimes treat each other.

Let's consider another situation of cooperation versus competition known as the Trust game. The researchers give you (player A) $10 (or euros, pesos, or whatever) and the same amount to player B. Now you can, if you choose, transfer any or all of that money to player B. If so, it will be doubled, so that B gains $20. B then has an opportunity to transfer $0–10 back to you, which will be doubled. If you each transfer the full amount, you both gain $20. However, how much do you trust B? If you transfer $10 and B transfers nothing, B goes home with $30 and you get nothing. A further complication: You play anonymously. That is, you don't know who B is, and B doesn't know who you are. Also, you will play repeatedly with a variety of partners, sometimes in the role of player A and sometimes as player B. How would you behave? Most people start off by cooperating. Player A transfers most of the $10 to B, and B returns the same or almost as much to A. After the first round, your behavior depends on how people have treated you in the past. Whenever people cooperate with you or treat you kindly, in this situation or any other, you become more likely to trust and help other people (Bartlett & DeSteno, 2006). However, if someone cheats you—for example, you transfer $10 to B, who returns nothing to you—you become less trusting and less cooperative. You stop transferring money when you are player A, and you return less when you are player B. Cheating spreads within the population, and soon, no one transfers any money (Fehr & Fischbacher, 2003).

Why don't business deals break down like that in real life? Unlike these games people in real life are not anonymous. You develop a reputation and so do others. You learn to cooperate with people who cooperate, and you refuse to do business with those who don't (Nowak & Sigmund, 2005; D. S. Wilson, Near, & Miller, 1996). Thus, here is our first explanation for why people act altruistically: *They want a reputation for being fair and helpful.* As a result other people will be pleased to deal with them and offer them help when they need it.

Why is altruistic behavior uncommon among nonhumans? For reputations to develop, individuals must recognize one another over long delays (Burtsev & Turchin, 2006). Recall from chapter 4 that people have an amazing ability to recognize other people's faces, even after delays of many years. Why have we evolved that ability? It is to keep track of whom to trust and whom to avoid. Most other species have poorer ability to recognize other individuals.

Cultural Transmission

If you have been thinking about why people help one another, one answer that you probably generated is that other people teach us to cooperate. Again, researchers have demonstrated this tendency with games. One version is the Public Goods game. Imagine that you and three others are playing this game anonymously. The researcher gives each of you $20 (or 20 euros or whatever) to start. Each of you can contribute as much of it as you choose to the common pool. After all have made their contributions, the researchers will increase the amount in the common pool by 60% and then divide it equally among all four players, regardless of how much each contributed. That is, if each of you contributes the full $20, the total of $80 becomes $128 ($80 × 1.6), and each person's share is $32, a nice profit over your original $20. However, a cheater or free-rider could keep the $20 and take one fourth of the wealth earned by other people's contributions. You play this game repeatedly, and each time you are in a different group, so you never interact with the same person twice. How much would you contribute? Most people contribute less and less as the game continues.

However, the results change if we alter the rules: At the end of each round, each of you learns how much each other player contributed. You then have the option to punish anyone. For a charge of $1 to yourself, you can subtract $3 from the player you want to punish. If you contributed most of your money to the common pool, and so did two of the others, you might be willing to pay for the opportunity to punish the greedy, uncooperative person who contributed little or nothing. It is considered "altruistic punishment," because the punisher gains nothing, except a feeling of justice. The punished person might learn a lesson, but if so, the benefit is to the next group of people that he or she plays with. Most people do administer punishments, and the result is a high level of cooperation across almost all individuals. No one wants to be the lowest contributor to the common pool for fear of being punished (Fehr & Gächter, 2002). Researchers using similar games have found that people in every society they tested will at least occasionally pay to punish the uncooperative players, and the societies with the greatest amount of altruism tend also to be the ones with the greatest amount of altruistic punishment (Henrich et al., 2006). So we have identified a second reason for human altruistic behavior: *We learn to cooperate because others who cooperate will punish us if we don't.* It is interesting what goes together here: Our ability to cooperate, which we consider a noble trait, is possible only because of our eagerness to wreak revenge (a rather base motive) when someone else behaves selfishly.

 CONCEPT CHECK

1. Theoretically, how can we explain why people sometimes act altruistically toward people they have never met? Why do they tend to be even more cooperative with people they have known for a long time?
2. You have read two explanations for humans' altruistic behavior. Why do both of them require individual recognition? (Check your answers on page 487.)

Accepting or Denying Responsibility Toward Others

Other people can encourage us to do something we would not have done on our own. They can also inhibit us from doing something that we would have done on our own. We look around to see what others are doing—or *not* doing—and we say, "Okay, I'll do that too." Why do people sometimes work together and sometimes ignore the needs of others?

Bystander Helpfulness and Apathy

Suppose while you are waiting at a bus stop, you see me trip and fall down, just 10 meters away. I am not screaming in agony, but I don't get up either, so you are not sure whether I need help. Would you come over and offer to help? Or would you stand there and ignore me? Before you answer try imagining the situation in two ways: First, you and I are the only people in sight. Second, many other people are nearby, none of them rushing to my aid. Does the presence of those other people make any difference to you? (It doesn't to me. I am in the same pain, regardless of how many people ignore me.)

Late one night in March 1964, Kitty Genovese was stabbed to death near her apartment in Queens, New York. A newspaper article at the time reported that 38 of her neighbors heard her screaming more than half an hour, but none of them called the police, each either declining to get involved or assuming that someone else had already called the police. Later investigations of the crime indicated that this report was greatly exaggerated. When Genovese was first attacked, probably only one person saw the attack and a few others heard her screams. At least one did call the police, who did not act. A few witnesses saw Genovese slowly walk away and turn the corner as the attacker drove away. She collapsed inside the hallway of the rear entrance to the building. Half an hour later, the attacker returned to complete the murder, by which time she was too weak to scream loudly. At most a few people saw or heard the second attack, by which time it was too late to help her. (This website provides detailed information: **http://www.oldkewgardens.com/kitty_genovese-001.html.**)

Although the original newspaper article was largely erroneous, it prompted widespread interest in why people often fail to aid a person in distress. Are we less likely to act just because we know that someone else could act on the same information? Bibb Latané and John Darley (1969) proposed that being in a crowd decreases our probability of action because of **diffusion of responsibility**: *We tend to feel less responsibility to act when other people are equally able to act.*

In an experiment designed to test this hypothesis, a young woman ushered one or two students into a room and asked them to wait for the start of a market research study (Latané & Darley, 1968, 1969). She went into the next room, closing the door behind her. There she played a tape recording that sounded as though she had climbed onto a chair and fallen off. For about 2 minutes, she could be heard crying and moaning, "Oh . . . my foot . . . I can't move it. Oh . . . my ankle . . ." Of the participants who were waiting alone, 70% went next door and offered to help. Of the participants who were waiting with someone else, only 13% offered to help.

In another study investigators entered 400 Internet chat groups of different sizes and in each one asked, "Can anyone tell me how to look at someone's profile?" (That is, how can I check the autobiographical sketch that each chat room user posts?) The researchers found that the more people in a chat room at the time, the longer the wait before anyone answered the question. In large groups the researchers sometimes had to post the same question repeatedly (Markey, 2000).

Diffusion of responsibility is one possible explanation. Each person thinks, "It's not my responsibility to help any more than someone else's." A second possi-

People watch other people's responses to help decide how they should respond. When a group of sidewalk Santas—who had gathered in Manhattan to promote a back-rub business—came to the aid of an injured cyclist, a few Santas made the first move and the others followed.

ble explanation is that the presence of other people who are also doing nothing provides information (or misinformation). At first the situation is ambiguous: "Do I need to act or not?" Other people's inaction implies that the situation requires no action. In fact the others are just as uncertain as you are, and they draw conclusions from *your* inaction. Social psychologists use the term **pluralistic ignorance** to describe *a situation in which people say nothing and each person falsely assumes that everyone else has a better informed opinion*. Notice that the presence of other people exerts both normative and informational influences: Their inactivity implies that doing nothing is acceptable (a norm) and that the situation is not an emergency (information).

Social Loafing

When you take a test, you are required to work alone, and your success depends entirely on your own effort. In many other cases, however, you work as part of a team. For example, if you work for a company that gives workers a share of the profits, your rewards depend on other workers' productivity as well as your own. Do you work as hard when the rewards depend on the group's productivity as when they depend on your own efforts alone?

In many cases you do not. In one experiment students were told to scream, clap, and make as

much noise as possible, like cheerleaders at a sports event. Sometimes, each student screamed and clapped alone; sometimes, students acted in groups; and sometimes, they acted alone but *thought* other people were screaming and clapping too. (They wore headphones so they could not hear anyone else.) Most of the students who screamed and clapped alone made more noise than those who were or thought they were part of a group (Latané, Williams, & Harkins, 1979). Social psychologists call this phenomenon **social loafing**—*the tendency to "loaf" (or work less hard) when sharing work with other people.*

Social loafing has been demonstrated in many situations. For example, suppose you were asked to "name all the uses you can think of for a brick" (e.g., crack nuts, anchor a boat, use as a doorstop, etc.) and write each one on a card. You would probably fill many cards by yourself but fewer if you were tossing cards into a pile along with other people's suggestions to be evaluated as a group (Harkins & Jackson, 1985). You probably wouldn't bother submitting ideas that you assume other people had already suggested.

At this point you may be thinking, "Wait a minute. When I'm playing basketball or soccer, I try as hard as I can. I don't think I loaf." You are right; social loafing is rare in team sports. The reason is that observers, including teammates, watch your performance. People work hard in groups if they expect other people to notice their effort or if they think they can contribute something that other group members cannot (Shepperd, 1993; K. D. Williams & Karau, 1991). People also give full effort if it appears that the benefit to the group will be large compared to the cost to themselves (Goren, Kurzban, & Rapoport, 2003).

During a catastrophe people abandon their usual tendencies toward bystander apathy and social loafing.

✓ CONCEPT CHECK

3. Given what we have learned about social loafing, why are most people unlikely to work hard to clean the environment?
4. In a typical family, one or two members have jobs, but their wages benefit all. Why do those wage earners *not* engage in social loafing? (Check your answers on page 487.)

Learning Morality and Cooperation

Regardless of whether our potential for altruistic, cooperative behavior depends on a genetic predisposition, experiences, or a combination of the two, it has to develop in some way. Infants don't do much to help anyone else, but at some point in life, people do begin to cooperate. How do we acquire a tendency to cooperate or a sense of moral behavior? Psychologists once regarded morality as a set of arbitrary, learned rules, such as learning to stop at a red light and go at a green light. Lawrence Kohlberg (1969; Kohlberg & Hersh, 1977) proposed instead that moral reasoning is a process that naturally matures through a series of stages. For example, children younger than about 6 years old say that accidentally breaking something valuable is worse than intentionally breaking something of less value. Older children and adults attend more to people's intentions. The change is a natural unfolding, according to Kohlberg, not a matter of memorizing rules.

Kohlberg argued that moral reasoning should not be evaluated according to someone's decision but according to the reasons behind it. For example, do you think designing nuclear bombs is a moral way to make a living? According to Kohlberg the answer depends on someone's reasons for taking the job. Hugh Gusterson (1992) interviewed nuclear bomb designers at the Lawrence Livermore National Laboratory. When he asked them about the morality of their actions, nearly everyone said something like, "You're lucky you chose me to interview, because I, unlike all the others, think deeply about these matters." Nearly all insisted that the weapons' only function was to threaten an enemy and thereby prevent wars. If you doubt that assumption, you might disagree with the morality of the bomb designers' *actions*, but you could still respect their moral *reasoning*.

To measure the maturity of someone's moral judgments, Kohlberg devised a series of moral dilemmas— *problems that pit one moral value against another.*

Each dilemma is accompanied by a question such as, "What should this person do?" or "Did this person do the right thing?" Kohlberg was not concerned about the choices people make, because well-meaning people disagree on the right answer. More revealing are their explanations, which are categorized into six stages, grouped into three levels (Table 13.1). Because few people respond consistently at stage 6, many authorities combine stages 5 and 6. To emphasize: Kohlberg's stages do not represent moral or immoral decisions but only moral and less moral *reasons* for a decision.

CRITICAL THINKING
A STEP FURTHER

Kohlberg's Stages

Suppose a military junta overthrows a democratic government and sets up a dictatorship. In which of Kohlberg's stages of moral reasoning would you classify the members of the junta? Would your answer depend on their reasons for setting up the dictatorship?

People begin at Kohlberg's first stage and then progress through the others in order, although few reach the highest stages. (The order of progression is an important point: If people were just as likely to progress in the order 3-5-4 as in the order 3-4-5, then we would have no justification for calling one stage higher than another.) People seldom skip a stage or revert to an earlier stage after reaching a higher one. Although people fluctuate from one time to another, we can classify people in terms of their average level.

✓ CONCEPT CHECK

5. For the moral dilemma described at the top of Table 13.1, suppose someone says that Heinz was wrong to steal the drug to save his wife's life. Which level of moral reasoning is characteristic of this judgment? (Check your answer on page 487.)

Limitations of Kohlberg's Views

Kohlberg's theory is based on several uncertain assumptions. Let us consider two major issues: (a) justice versus caring orientations to morality and (b) the relationship between moral reasoning and behavior.

Moral Reasoning Not Centered on Justice

Kohlberg assumed that most judgments of right and wrong depend on "justice." In many non-Western cultures, such as the Hindu culture of India, people sel-

TABLE 13.1 Responses to One of Kohlberg's Moral Dilemmas by People at Six Levels of Moral Reasoning

The dilemma: Heinz's wife was near death from cancer. A druggist had recently discovered a drug that might be able to save her. The druggist was charging $2000 for the drug, which cost him $200 to make. Heinz could not afford to pay for it, and he could borrow only $1000 from friends. He offered to pay the rest later. The druggist refused to sell the drug for less than the full price paid in advance: "I discovered the drug, and I'm going to make money from it." Late that night, Heinz broke into the store to steal the drug for his wife. Did Heinz do the right thing?

Level/Stage	Typical Answer	Basis for Judging Right from Wrong	Description of Stage
The Level of Preconventional Morality			
1. Punishment and obedience orientation	"No. If he steals the drug, he might go to jail." "Yes. If he can't afford the drug, he can't afford a funeral, either."	Wrong is equated with punishment. What is good is whatever is in the man's immediate self-interest.	Decisions are based on their immediate consequences. Whatever is rewarded is "good" and whatever is punished is "bad." If you break something and are punished, then what you did was bad.
2. Instrumental relativist orientation	"He can steal the drug and save his wife, and he'll be with her when he gets out of jail."	Again, what is good is whatever is in the man's own best interests, but his interests include delayed benefits.	It is good to help other people, but only because they may one day return the favor: "You scratch my back and I'll scratch yours."
The Level of Conventional Morality			
3. Interpersonal concordance, or "good boy/nice girl" orientation	"People will understand if you steal the drug to save your wife, but they'll think you're cruel and a coward if you don't."	Public opinion is the main basis for judging what is good.	The "right" thing to do is whatever pleases others, especially those in authority. Be a good person so others will think you are good. Conformity to the dictates of public opinion is important.
4. "Law and order" orientation	"No, because stealing is illegal." "Yes. It is the husband's duty to save his wife even if he feels guilty afterward for stealing the drug."	Right and wrong can be determined by duty or by one's role in society.	You should respect the law—simply because it *is* the law—and work to strengthen the social order that enforces it.
The Level of Postconventional or Principled Morality			
5. Social-contract legalistic orientation	"The husband has a right to the drug even if he can't pay now. If the druggist won't charge it, the government should look after it."	Laws are made for people's benefit. They should be flexible. If necessary, we may have to change certain laws or allow for exceptions to them.	The "right" thing to do is whatever people have agreed is the best thing for society. As in stage 4, you respect the law, but in addition recognize that a majority of the people can agree to change the rules. Anyone who makes a promise is obligated to keep the promise.
6. Universal ethical principle orientation	"Although it is legally wrong to steal, the husband would be morally wrong not to steal to save his wife. A life is more precious than financial gain."	Right and wrong are based on absolute values such as human life. Sometimes these values take precedence over human laws.	In special cases it may be right to violate a law that conflicts with higher ethical principles, such as justice and respect for human life. Among those who have obeyed a "higher law" are Jesus, Mahatma Gandhi, and Martin Luther King, Jr.

Source: Kohlberg, 1981.

dom talk about justice. They speak instead of a natural sense of duty toward others (Shweder, Mahapatra, & Miller, 1987). Even in Western cultures, we don't always reason in terms of justice. Carol Gilligan (1977, 1979) pointed out that we sometimes rely on a "caring" orientation—that is, what would help or hurt other people. For example, at one point during the Vietnam War, a group of soldiers were ordered to kill unarmed civilians. One soldier, who regarded the order as immoral, refused to shoot. In terms of "justice," he acted at a high moral level, following a higher law that required him not to kill. However, his actions made no difference, as other soldiers killed all the civilians. In terms of "caring," he would have been more moral if he had found a way to hide a few of the victims (Linn & Gilligan, 1990).

Sometimes, the two "voices" of moral reasoning—justice and caring—conflict with each other. From a caring standpoint, you want to help someone in distress. From a justice standpoint, you may think it wrong to encourage begging.

Moral Reasoning and Moral Behavior

The movie *Schindler's List* portrays a German man who risked his life to save Jewish people from the Nazi Holocaust. We all agree he did the right thing. But if you and I had been Germans at the time, would we have done the same? I don't know. Stating the right thing is not the same as doing it.

Kohlberg's approach concentrated on moral reasoning, not behavior. People are, at best, moderately consistent in their answers to hypothetical questions about moral dilemmas. They are less consistent in their reasoning about real-life decisions and still less consistent in actual behavior. Recall the vignette in chapter 12 about Mark and Julie, the brother and sister who had sex together. Nearly everyone says, "That was wrong!" and then tries to think of a good reason it was wrong. Researchers find that people usually act first and then suggest moral reasons to justify their behavior. Consequently, moral reasoning, as evaluated by Kohlberg's methods, correlates poorly with actual behavior (Krebs & Denton, 2005).

Although many people give answers that qualify as stages 4, 5, and 6, moral *behavior* at those levels is uncommon, and we can understand why (Krebs, 2000). Most behavior follows reasoning at stages 1, 2, and 3: Seek rewards, avoid punishments, cooperate with others who cooperate with you, and punish those who don't cooperate—the kinds of motives easily demonstrated in the prisoner's dilemma and related situations. Behavior at stages 4, 5, and 6 benefits other people whom you will never meet. You might gain indirectly because you build a reputation, but you don't gain immediately.

Still, most people recognize a moral imperative, even if they know their behavior falls short of it. As you read about the prisoner's dilemma, you may have reacted, "Yes, that's very interesting about developing a reputation, but that's not the whole reason I help others. When I see someone in pain, it hurts as if it happened to me. I help because I *want* to help. I *want* to behave morally."

Imagine the following: You and another student show up for a research study. The researchers explain that two studies are available. One study sounds interesting and pleasant. The other is difficult and painful. You are invited to flip a coin, examine it yourself in private, and then announce who gets to be in the pleasant study. In this situation nearly 90% of students claim they won the toss and get to be in the pleasant experiment. Obviously, many are lying. However, suppose you were asked whether you want to flip the coin and announce the results or let the experimenter do it. Now most people say, "let the experimenter do it" (Batson & Thompson, 2001). They avoid putting themselves in a situation in which they know they will be tempted to cheat.

IN CLOSING

Is Cooperative Behavior Logical?

Given that people frequently help one another, some explanation must be possible. Either we have evolved a tendency to help, or we learn to. The research on the prisoner's dilemma and similar games attempts to demonstrate that cooperation and mutual aid are logical under certain conditions. You cooperate to develop a good reputation so that others will cooperate with you and not penalize you. You develop your tendency toward altruistic, cooperative behavior gradually, as Kohlberg demonstrated, although you probably never reach the point of being completely altruistic in every situation.

All this is persuasive and impressive, but you might not find it completely satisfactory. Sometimes, you make an anonymous contribution to a worthy cause, with no expectation of any personal gain, not even an improvement of your reputation. You simply wanted to help that cause. You occasionally help someone you'll never see again while no one else is watching. Perhaps these acts require no special explanation. You have developed habits of helping for all the reasons that investigators have identified. Once you developed those habits, you generalize them to other circumstances, even when they do you no good. Yes, perhaps. Or maybe researchers are still overlooking something. Conclusions in psychology are almost never final. You are invited to think about these issues yourself and develop your own hypotheses. ∎

Summary

- *The prisoner's dilemma.* In the prisoner's dilemma, two people can choose to cooperate or compete. The *compete* move seems best from the individual's point of view, but it is harmful to the group. (page 479)
- *Effective strategies.* If someone plays the prisoner's dilemma repeatedly with the same partner, an effective strategy is tit for tat: Cooperate unless the other person competes, and then retaliate. (page 480)
- *Reasons for cooperation.* Studies of the prisoner's dilemma and other situations demonstrate two rational reasons for cooperation: A cooperative person enhances his or her reputation and therefore gains cooperation from others. Also, people who cooperate often punish those who do not. (page 481)
- *Bystander apathy.* People are less likely to help someone if they see other people who are in an equally good position to help. (page 482)
- *Social loafing.* Most people work less hard when they are part of a group than when they work alone, except when they think they can make a unique contribution or if they think others are evaluating their contribution. (page 483)
- *Kohlberg's view of moral reasoning.* From infancy through adulthood, people gradually develop their

tendencies toward altruistic and cooperative behavior. According to Lawrence Kohlberg, moral reasoning should be evaluated on the basis of the reasons someone gives for a decision rather than the decision itself. (page 484)
- *Challenges to Kohlberg's views.* Kohlberg concentrated on "justice," ignoring a "caring" orientation that sometimes gives a conflicting view. People's answers to Kohlberg's dilemmas correlate only weakly with their actual behavior. (page 484)

Answers to Concept Checks

1. Even with a stranger, you behave altruistically to develop a reputation for cooperating. With a familiar person, you know the person will return your favors and probably retaliate if you fail to cooperate. (page 479)
2. One explanation is that cooperating builds a reputation, and a reputation requires individuals to recognize one another. The other explanation is that people who cooperate will punish those who do not. Again, to retaliate they need to recognize who has failed to cooperate. (page 481)
3. Social loafing is likely because many one-person contributions, such as picking up litter, would not earn individual credit or recognition. Also, each person thinks, "What good could one person do with such a gigantic problem?" (page 483)
4. The main reason is that the wage earners see they can make a special contribution that the others (children, injured, or retired) cannot. Also, their contributions are easily observed by the others. (page 483)
5. Not enough information is provided to answer this question. In Kohlberg's system any judgment can represent either a high or a low level of moral reasoning; we evaluate a person's moral reasoning by the explanation, not by the decision itself. (page 484)

Social Perception and Cognition

- *What factors influence our judgments of others?*
- *How can we measure stereotypes that people do not want to admit?*
- *How do we explain the causes of our own behavior and that of others?*

People generally measure their own success by comparing themselves to others. To decide whether you are satisfied with your grades in school, your salary on the job, or the morality of your behavior, you compare yourself to other people similar to yourself. You cheer yourself up by noting that you are doing better than some of your friends; you motivate yourself to try harder by comparing yourself to someone more successful (Suls, Martin, & Wheeler, 2002).

To make these comparisons, we need accurate information about other people. We also need that information to form expectations about how others will act, whom we can trust, and so forth. **Social perception and cognition** are *the processes we use to gather and remember information about others and to make inferences from that information.* Social perception and cognition, like any other perception and cognition, influence our observations, memory, and thinking.

First Impressions

Other things being equal, *the first information we learn about someone influences us more than later information does* (Belmore, 1987; E. E. Jones & Goethals, 1972). This tendency is known as the **primacy effect.** For example, if a professor makes a good impression on the first day of class, your favorable attitude helps you discount a lackluster performance later in the semester. A professor who seems dull at first will have a

If you were a new patient of Dr. Balamurali Ambati, the world's youngest doctor (at age 17), what would your first impression probably be? An impression based only on his youthful appearance could be greatly mistaken.

© Bettmann/CORBIS

hard time impressing you later. Similarly, your professor's early impression of you can have lasting effects.

We form first impressions with amazing speed. In one study researchers flashed photographs of unfamiliar people on a screen for one tenth of a second each and asked observers to judge each person's attractiveness, likability, competence, and so forth. Judgments made in this split second correlated better than .5 with judgments made at leisure (Willis & Todorov, 2006). In another study researchers flashed photographs for just 13 milliseconds, with interfering patterns before and after. Under these circumstances people were not conscious of seeing a face at all, but when they were asked to guess how attractive the unseen face was, their guesses agreed moderately well with the judgments other people made after viewing each face for as long as they wanted (Olson & Marshuetz, 2005). You may have heard the expression, "You only have one chance to make a first impression." These results suggest that you have only a split second to make that first impression!

Why are first impressions so influential? If your first impression of someone is unfavorable, you may not spend enough time with that person to change your view. Also, once you have formed an impression, it alters your interpretation of later experiences. Suppose your first impression of someone is that he talks about himself too much. Later, whenever he talks about himself, you take his comments as supporting your initial impression.

Our first impressions can become **self-fulfilling prophecies,** *expectations that change one's own behavior in such a way as to increase the probability of the predicted event.* Suppose a psychologist hands you a telephone receiver and asks you to talk with someone, while showing you a photo supposedly of that person. Unknown to you and to the person you are talking to, the psychologist hands some people a photo of a very attractive member of the opposite sex and hands other people a much less attractive photo. Not surprisingly, you act friendlier to someone you regard as attractive. More interesting, if you think you are talking to someone attractive, that person reacts to you by becoming more cheerful and talkative. In short, your first impression changes how you act and influences the other person to live up to (or down to) your expectations (M. Snyder, Tanke, & Berscheid, 1977).

CRITICAL THINKING
A STEP FURTHER

First Impressions

In a criminal trial, the prosecution presents its evidence first. Might that give the jury an unfavorable first impression of the defendant and increase the probability of a conviction?

☑ CONCEPT CHECK

6. Why do some professors avoid looking at students' names when they grade essay exams? Why is it more important for them to avoid looking at the names on tests given later in the semester than on the first test? (Check your answers on page 497.)

Stereotypes and Prejudices

A stereotype is *a generalized belief or expectation about a group of people.* It is possible to develop false stereotypes because of our tendency to remember the unusual. If we see an unusual person doing something unusual, the event is doubly memorable. For example, you might remember one left-handed redhead who cheated you and then form a false stereotype about left-handed redheads—an illusory correlation, as discussed in chapter 2. As a result many stereotypes about people of various nationalities are wrong (McCrae & Terracciano, 2006).

Stereotypes can also be based on overstatements of correct observations. In particular, people tend to exaggerate the positions of their political opponents (Chambers, Baron, & Inman, 2006; Robinson & Keltner, 1996).

However, some stereotypes are correct. For example, who do you think gets into more fistfights on the average—men or women? If you answered "men," you are supporting a stereotype, but you are correct.

Similarly, who do you think is more likely to be sensitive to the subtle social connotations in everyday conversation—a liberal arts major or an engineering major? Again, if you said "liberal arts major," you are endorsing a stereotype, but the research supports you (Ottati & Lee, 1995).

Indeed, whenever we say that culture influences behavior, we imply that members of those cultures behave differently on the average and therefore that a stereotype about them is partly correct. In some cases members of both cultures agree on the stereotypes but express them in different words. For example, many Americans describe the Chinese as "inhibited," whereas Chinese call themselves "self-controlled." U.S. businesspeople complain that Mexicans "don't show up on time," whereas Mexicans complain that people from the United States "are always in a rush" (Lee & Duenas, 1995).

However, agreeing that a stereotype is correct on the average does not mean that it fits all individuals (Banaji & Bhaskar, 2000). For example, most 20-year-olds are more athletic than most 80-year-olds, but some 80-year-olds are in better shape than some 20-year-olds. Also, believing that a stereotype is usually correct does not mean that we have to let it influence the way we treat people. Ideally, we should strive to know people as individuals and treat them accordingly.

Although most people agree to that idea in principle, stereotypes affect us in subtle, unconscious ways. Imagine yourself in this experiment: You are given sets of five words to arrange into sentences. Here are three examples:

CAR REPAIRS OLD THIS NEEDS
CLOUDY GRAY SKY THE WAS
OFFER GAMES SMALL BINGO PRIZES

Easy, right? You think the experiment is over, and now you are walking out. The real point of the experiment is to watch you walk out! People in one experimental condition—the one you were in—unscrambled sentences that all included words associated with the stereotype of old people, such as *old, gray, bingo,* and so forth. On the average people who have just been thinking about old people tend to walk more slowly than usual, like their stereotype of old people (Bargh, Chen, & Burrows, 1996). In a similar study, students who had just been thinking about old people before filling out an attitude questionnaire expressed attitudes more consistent with their stereotypes of old people, such as defending more government support for health care (Kawakami, Dovidio, & Dijksterhuis, 2003). If stereotypes can prime such unintentional behavior as this, you can see the potential for far-reaching effects.

The stereotype of old people as inactive has many exceptions.

Aversive Racism

A **prejudice** is *an unfavorable attitude toward a group of people.* It is usually associated with **discrimination,** which is *unequal treatment of different groups,* such as minority groups, women, the physically disabled, people who are obese, or gays and lesbians. Decades ago, many Americans admitted their prejudices and discriminated openly. Today, most people are ashamed of such feelings and deny having them. They *consciously express the idea that all people are equal, but nevertheless harbor negative feelings and unintentionally discriminate.* When these conflicting feelings pertain to race, psychologists use the term **aversive racism,** also known as subtle prejudice, modern racism, symbolic racism, and racial ambivalence (Sears & Henry, 2003). This kind of racism is called "aversive" because it is unpleasant to the person who acts this way. In a similar way, many people have **ambivalent sexism,** *an overt belief in equal treatment of the sexes joined with a lingering belief that women should be treated differently* (Glick & Fiske, 2001).

Subtle, unstated prejudices are less harmful than the overt hostility of previous eras, but they can take their toll nevertheless. For example, if you are a victim of prejudice, you might be excluded from conversations among fellow students or workers (S. T. Fiske, 2002). People might smile at you less, offer you less

help, and give you less benefit of the doubt in an uncertain situation (Crandall & Eshleman, 2003). If they see you frowning slightly, they may overestimate your hostility (Hugenberg & Bodenhausen, 2003). When you fail to get a job, promotion, or other opportunity, you may not know whether you were rejected because of something you did wrong or because of prejudices against your group (Major, Quinton, & McCoy, 2002). If you are convicted of a crime, you might get a harsher than average sentence (Eberhardt, Davies, Purdie-Vaughns, & Johnson, 2006).

Stereotypes and prejudices can also become self-fulfilling prophecies. Recall the idea of *stereotype threat* from chapter 9: African American students' test performance suffers if they are told, "Your group usually doesn't do well on this kind of test." In general, people perform below their abilities when they believe their group is at a disadvantage, especially on difficult tasks (Steele, Spencer, & Aronson, 2002). Perhaps they simply don't try very hard, or maybe they are distracted from the task.

Researchers have tried to measure aversive racism (unintentional, unconscious discrimination). Here is an example (Dovidio & Gaertner, 2000): Each White college student was asked to evaluate the folder for one person applying for a job as a peer counselor. One third of the applications described strong experience and qualifications for the job, one third were marginal, and one third had weak qualifications. Of each kind of application (strong, marginal, or weak), half mentioned membership in a nearly all-White fraternity, and the other half mentioned membership in the Black Student Union. So each student read what appeared to be a strong White, strong Black, marginal White, marginal Black, weak White, or weak Black application. The following graph shows the mean results: Note that the students were slightly more generous with well-qualified or poorly qualified Black applicants than with equally qualified Whites. The big difference, however, was for the marginal applications.

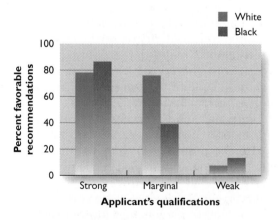

The students favorably recommended 77% of the marginal White applicants but only 40% of the marginal Black applicants (Dovidio & Gaertner, 2000). Without realizing it the students evaluated the ambiguous qualifications more positively if they thought they applied to White applicants. Later studies have found similar results (Vanman, Saltz, Nathan, & Warren, 2004).

Implicit Measures of Stereotypes and Prejudice

Most people in the United States believe in fair treatment for everyone, or so they say. But if all people are all as unprejudiced as they claim to be, where do the racism, sexism, and so forth come from? Researchers have sought methods of measuring subtle prejudices that people do not want to admit, not even to themselves.

One method uses the Implicit Association Test. Recall from chapter 9 the idea of priming: Immediately after reading or hearing a word, such as *red,* you are quicker than usual to identify a related word, such as *cherry.* The fact that one word primes the other indicates that you see the two words as related. The **Implicit Association Test** *measures your reactions to combinations of two categories, such as flower and pleasant.* If you respond quickly, you probably see the two categories as related.

Imagine this example: You rest your left and right forefingers on a computer keyboard. When you hear a word, you should press with your left finger if it is an unpleasant word, such as *death, fail,* or *shame,* and press with your right finger if it is a pleasant word, such as *joy, love,* or *success.* After you have practiced this procedure, the instructions change. Now you should press the left key if you hear the name of an insect and the right key if you hear the name of a flower. Next you have to combine two categories: Press the left key for unpleasant words or insects and the right key for pleasant words or flowers. Then the pairings switch: Press the left key for unpleasant words or flowers and the right key for pleasant words or insects. The experimenter repeats the procedure, alternating between the two instructions.

Most people respond faster to the combination "pleasant or flowers" than to "pleasant or insects." The conclusion is that most people like flowers more than insects. The procedure may seem more trouble than it is worth, as people readily tell us that they like flowers and not insects. However, after

we have established the validity of the method, we can use it to measure preferences that people did not want to admit, perhaps not even to themselves (Greenwald, Nosek, & Banaji, 2003).

Imagine yourself in this experiment: You are seated in front of a computer screen that sometimes shows a photo and sometimes a word. If it is a photo of a Black person or a pleasant word, press the left key. If it is a photo of a White person or an unpleasant word, press the right key. After you respond that way for a while, the rule switches to the opposite pairing.

Figure 13.2 illustrates the procedures and Figure 13.3 summarizes the results for a group of White college students. Most responded faster to the combinations *Black/unpleasant* and *White/pleasant.* That is, even though most of the participants claimed to have no racial prejudices, they evaluated White faces more favorably than Black faces (Phelps et al., 2000). A similar study reported that White students found it easier to pair pleasant words with White names, such as *Andrew* and *Brandon,* and unpleasant words with Black names, such as *Lamar* and *Jamal* (Dasgupta, McGhee, Greenwald, & Banaji, 2000). This implicit preference of White people toward other White people is stable from childhood to adulthood (Baron & Banaji, 2006), and it correlates positively, though not strongly, with people's behavior in real-world situations (Cunningham, Preacher, & Banaji, 2001; Greenwald, Nosek, & Sriram, 2006).

FIGURE 13.2 Procedures for an Implicit Association Test to measure prejudices.

Implicit Association Test

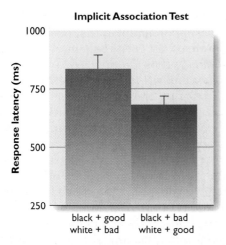

FIGURE 13.3 On the average White students who claimed to have no racial prejudice responded faster if they had to make one response for "Black face or unpleasant word" and a different response for "White face or pleasant word" than if the pairings were reversed—Black and pleasant, White and unpleasant. *(From "Performance on Indirect Measures of Race Evaluation Predicts Amygdala Activation" by E. A. Phelps, K. J. O'Connor, W. A. Cunningham, E. S. Funayama, J. C. Gatenby, J. C. Gore & M. R. Banaji, Journal of Cognitive Neuroscience, 2000, 12, 729–738. Copyright © 2000 MIT Press. Reprinted by permission.)*

Researchers made available a simplified version of the Implicit Association Test on a website, which you can try yourself: **https://implicit.harvard.edu/implicit/demo/**.

Online Try It Yourself

Psychologists analyzed the results for more than 600,000 people who have visited this website over the years (Nosek, Banaji, & Greenwald, 2002). People who visit a website are, of course, not a representative sample of the population, but they do vary in age, geographical region, and education. (Most research studies use college students, who are an even less representative sample.) The results were that White participants on the average linked White–pleasant, Black–unpleasant more easily than White–unpleasant, Black–pleasant, even though most of them denied having any racial prejudice.

What results would you predict for Black participants? Although most stated that their explicit attitude was more favorable to Blacks than to Whites, the Implicit Association Test results indicated almost equal responses to Blacks and Whites, or a slight implicit attitude favoring Whites. That is, they linked White–pleasant, Black–unpleasant slightly more readily than White–unpleasant, Black–pleasant.

Research on gender preferences indicates that women show a strong implicit preference for women over men. Men, however, show an almost equal preference for women versus men (Nosek & Banaji, 2001; Rudman & Goodwin, 2004). Evidently, women like other women more than men like other men.

These results are important for showing that even well-meaning people can have prejudices that operate without their awareness (Greenwald & Banaji, 1995). That result is important to remember when people insist that we should evaluate college applicants or job applicants "entirely on the basis of their qualifications." The problem is that we may be influenced by stereotypes and prejudices that we do not even recognize, especially when the qualifications are hard to evaluate (Crosby, Iyer, Clayton, & Downing, 2003). Perhaps it is better to recognize our stereotypes and compensate for them than to deny their existence.

On the other hand, it may also be that the Implicit Association Test overstates people's prejudices. In a related task, called the **bona fide pipeline**, *people alternate between looking at different kinds of faces, such as Black and White, and reading words that they need to classify as pleasant or unpleasant.* The assumption is that someone who is prejudiced against Black people will answer "unpleasant" faster after seeing a Black face than after seeing a White face. However, the results depend on the instructions. If White students just look at the faces with the expectation of trying to recognize them later, then seeing a Black or White face has little effect on how fast they say "pleasant" or "unpleasant" to the next word. If, however, they have to count the number of Black faces so that they are forced to pay attention to race, then the predicted results do occur, with faster "unpleasant" responses after seeing Black faces (Olson & Fazio, 2003). Hence, the bona fide pipeline, and presumably also the Implicit Association Test, show implicit prejudice if the instructions ask people to pay attention to race. Without such urging, people may react to the faces as individuals with less evidence of prejudice.

 CONCEPT CHECK

7. What is the advantage of the Implicit Association Test over simply asking people about their racial prejudices?
8. Under what condition are the Implicit Association Test and bona fide pipeline most likely to show evidence of implicit prejudice? (Check your answers on pages 497–498.)

Overcoming Prejudice

After prejudices and hostility have arisen between two groups, what can anyone do to break down the barriers? Simply increasing contact between the groups usually decreases prejudice, but not always (Tropp & Pettigrew, 2005). A more effective technique is to get the two groups to work toward a common goal, to consider themselves part of a combined group (Dovidio & Gaertner, 1999).

Many years ago, psychologists demonstrated the power of this technique using two arbitrarily chosen groups (Sherif, 1966). At a summer camp at Robbers' Cave, Oklahoma, 11- to 12-year-old boys were divided into two groups in separate cabins. The groups competed for prizes in sports, treasure hunts, and other activities. With each competition the antagonism between the two groups grew more intense. The boys made threatening posters, shouted insults, and engaged in food fights. Each group showed clear prejudice and hostility toward the other.

Up to a point, the "counselors" (experimenters) allowed the hostility to take its course, neither encouraging nor prohibiting it. Then they tried to reverse it by stopping the competitions and setting common goals. First, they asked the two groups to work together to find and repair a leak in the water pipe that supplied the camp. Then they had the two groups pool their treasuries to rent a movie that both groups wanted to see. Later, they had the boys pull together to get a truck out of a rut. Gradually, hostility turned into friendship—except for a few holdouts who nursed their hatred to the bitter end! The point is that competition leads to hostility, and cooperation leads to friendship.

© James Wilson/Woodfin Camp & Associates

▌ People who work together for a common goal can overcome prejudices that initially divide them.

Attribution

We want to understand why people behave as they do. Yesterday, you won $1 million in the state lottery, and today, classmates who previously ignored you want to be your friends. You draw inferences about their reasons. **Attribution** is *the set of thought processes we use to assign causes to our own behavior and that of others.*

Internal Versus External Causes

Fritz Heider, the founder of attribution theory, emphasized the distinction between internal and external causes of behavior (Heider, 1958). **Internal attributions** are *explanations based on someone's individual characteristics, such as attitudes, personality traits, or abilities.* **External attributions** are *explanations based on the situation, including events that presumably would influence almost anyone.* An example of an internal attribution is that your brother walked to work this morning "because he likes the exercise." An external attribution would be that he walked "because his car wouldn't start." Internal attributions are also known as *dispositional* (i.e., something about the person's disposition led to the behavior). External attributions are also known as *situational* (i.e., something about the situation led to the behavior).

You make internal attributions when someone does something that you think most people would not do. For example, if I say I would like to visit Hawaii, you draw no conclusions about me. However, if I say I would like to visit northern Norway in midwinter, you wonder what is special about my personality or interests (Krull & Anderson, 1997).

This tendency sometimes leads to misunderstandings between members of different cultures. Each person views the other's behavior as "something I would not have done" and therefore as grounds for making an attribution about personality. For example, some cultures expect people to cry loudly at funerals, whereas others expect people to show more restraint. People who are unfamiliar with other cultures may attribute a behavior to someone's personality, when in fact it is a dictate of the culture.

Harold Kelley (1967) proposed that we rely on three types of information when deciding whether to make an internal or an external attribution for someone's behavior:

- **Consensus information** *(how the person's behavior compares with other people's behavior).* If someone behaves the same way you believe other people would in the same situation, then you make an external attribution. That is, you recognize that the situation led to the behavior. If someone's behavior seems unusual, you look for an internal attribution pertaining to the person instead of the situation. (You can easily be wrong if you misunderstand the situation.)
- **Consistency information** *(how the person's behavior varies from one time to the next).* If someone almost always seems friendly, for example, you would make an internal attribution ("a friendly person"). If someone's friendliness varies, you look for an external attribution, such as an event that elicited a good or bad mood.
- **Distinctiveness** *(how the person's behavior varies from one situation to another).* If your friend is pleasant to everybody except one person, you assume that person has done something to irritate your friend (an external attribution).

❚ We sometimes attribute a behavior to personality, when in fact people are acting according to the customs of their culture. In the United States, a funeral usually calls for reserved behavior. Many other places expect loud wailing.

 CONCEPT CHECK

9. Classify the following as either internal or external attributions:
   a. She contributed money to charity because she is generous.
   b. She contributed money to charity because she wanted to impress her boss, who was watching.
   c. She contributed money to charity because she owed a favor to the man who was asking for contributions.

10. Juanita returns from watching *The Return of the Son of Sequel Strikes Back Again Part 2* and says it was excellent. Most other people that you know disliked the movie. Will you make an internal or external attribution for Juanita's opinion? Why? (Distinctiveness, consensus, or consistency?) (Check your answers on page 498.)

The Fundamental Attribution Error

A common error is *to make internal attributions for people's behavior even when we see evidence for an external influence on behavior.* This tendency is known as the **fundamental attribution error** (Ross, 1977). It is also known as the *correspondence bias*, meaning a tendency to assume a strong similarity between someone's current actions and his or her dispositions.

Imagine yourself in a classic study demonstrating this phenomenon. You are told that U.S. college students were randomly assigned to write essays praising or condemning Fidel Castro, the communist leader of Cuba. You read an essay that defends Castro, criticizes the United States for its long embargo against Cuba, and compares Cuba favorably to other Latin American countries. What's your guess about the actual attitude of the student who wrote this essay?

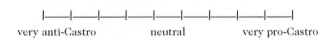

very anti-Castro   neutral   very pro-Castro

Most U.S. students in one study guessed that the author of a pro-Castro essay was at least mildly pro-Castro, even though they were informed, as you were, that the author had been required to praise Castro (E. E. Jones & Harris, 1967). In a later study, experimenters explained that one student in a creative writing class had been assigned to write a pro-Castro essay and an anti-Castro essay at different times in the course. Then the participants read the two essays and estimated the writer's true beliefs. Most thought that the writer had changed attitudes between the two essays (Allison, Mackie, Muller, & Worth, 1993). That is, even when people are told of a powerful external reason for someone's behavior, they seem to believe the person probably had internal reasons as well (McClure, 1998).

 CONCEPT CHECK

11. How would the fundamental attribution error affect people's attitudes toward actors and actresses who portrayed likable and contemptible characters? (Check your answer on page 498.)

Cultural Differences in Attribution and Related Matters

The fundamental attribution error relates to culture. In general, people of Western cultures rely more on internal (personality) attributions, whereas people in China and other Asian countries tend to rely more on external (situational) attributions. For example, how would you explain the behavior of the fish designated with an arrow in this drawing? Most Americans say this fish is leading the others, whereas many Chinese say the other fish are chasing it (Hong, Morris, Chiu, & Benet-Martinez, 2000). That is, the cultures differ in whether they think the fish controls its own behavior or obeys the influence of the others.

Try It Yourself

Richard Nisbett and his colleagues noted other cases in which Asian people tend to focus more on the situation, and less on individual personality, than do most people in Western cultures (Nisbett, Peng, Choi, & Norenzayan, 2001). As a result they expect more change and less consistency in people's behavior from one situation to another. Asians are also more likely to accept contradictions and look for compromises, instead of viewing one position as correct and another as incorrect. Here are a few examples:

- When given a description of a conflict, such as one between mother and daughter, Chinese students are more likely than Americans to see merit in both arguments, instead of siding with one or the other (Peng & Nisbett, 1999).
- Far more Chinese than English-language proverbs include apparent self-contradictions, such as "beware of your friends, not your enemies" and "too humble is half proud" (Peng & Nisbett, 1999).
- Chinese people are more likely than Americans to expect events to change and to predict that current trends—whatever they might be—will reverse themselves. For example, if life seems to have been getting better lately, most Americans predict that things will continue getting better, whereas Chinese predict that things will get worse (Ji, Nisbett, & Su, 2001).
- In one study people were told about some event and then told the final outcome. Americans often expressed surprise when Koreans said the outcome was to be expected. That is, in this study the Koreans showed a stronger hindsight bias (chapter 7)—the tendency to say, "I knew it all along" (Choi & Nisbett, 2000).

The reported differences are interesting. Still, an important question remains: To the extent that Asian people respond differently from Western-culture people, is that difference due to ancient traditions or current conditions? Perhaps Asians notice the influence of their environment more just because their environment looks different from that of Western countries. Most Asian cities are more cluttered than American and European cities (Figure 13.4). Researchers found that Japanese students tended to notice the background of photographs more than Americans, who focused heavily on objects in the foreground. However, after Americans viewed a series of pictures of Japan-

FIGURE 13.4 On the average Asian cities are more crowded and cluttered than U.S. and European cities.

© Justin Guariglia/ National Geographic/ Getty Images

© Ryuchi Sato/ Amana Images/ Getty Images

ese cities, they too began paying more attention to the backgrounds (Miyamoto, Nisbett, & Masuda, 2006). The question remains whether Asians pay more attention to backgrounds because of the way they build their cities or whether they build their cities that way because of a cultural tendency in their perception and thinking.

The Actor-Observer Effect

Here is another common bias related to the fundamental attribution error: *People are more likely to make internal attributions for other people's behavior and more likely to make external attributions for their own* (E. E. Jones & Nisbett, 1972). This tendency is called the **actor-observer effect.** You are an "actor" when you try to explain the causes of your own behavior and an "observer" when you try to explain someone else's behavior.

In one study investigators asked college students to rate themselves, their fathers, their best friends, and Walter Cronkite (a television news announcer at the time) on several personality traits. For each trait (e.g., "leniency"), the participants were given three choices: (a) the person possesses the trait, (b) the person possesses the opposite trait, and (c) the person's behavior "depends on the situation." Participants checked "depends on the situation"—an external attribution—most frequently for themselves, less frequently for their fathers and friends, and least often for Walter Cronkite (Nisbett, Caputo, Legant, & Marecek, 1973). Figure 13.5 shows the results.

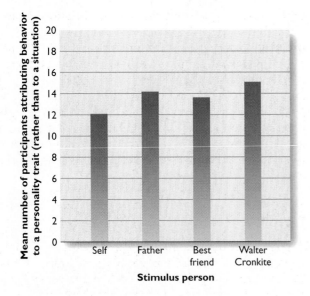

FIGURE 13.5 Participants were most likely to say that their own behavior depended on the situation and least likely to say "it depends" for the person they knew the least. *(Based on data of Nisbett, Caputo, Legant, & Marecek, 1973)*

Why do we tend to explain our own behavior differently from that of others? We are aware of how our own behavior varies from one situation to another. The less well we know someone else, the less aware we are of variations from situation to situation. If I have an emergency and I am rushing to get somewhere, I might honk at other drivers and pass every one I can. Because they don't know me or my situation, they might assume I am always rude and aggressive.

Another reason is perceptual. We see other people as objects in our visual field, and we tend to think that whatever we are watching is the cause of the action. The perceptual explanation for the actor-observer effect has an interesting implication: If you became an object in your own visual field, you might explain your own behavior in terms of internal traits, as you do with others. Researchers have found that if you watch a videotape of your own behavior, you do tend to explain your behavior in terms of personality factors more than situational factors (Storms, 1973).

A further application of this idea: Suppose you watch a videotape of a conversation between two people. The actual conversation is planned so that both people participate equally. However, you are randomly given one of two versions of the videotape, with the camera focused on one person or the other. You will tend to perceive that the person you are watching dominates the conversation and influences the other person. Similarly, if you watch a videotape of an interrogation between a detective and a suspect, you will judge the suspect's confession to be more voluntary if the camera focuses on the suspect and more coerced if the camera focuses on the detective (Lassiter, Geers, Munhall, Ploutz-Snyder, & Breitenbecher, 2002).

Using Attributions to Manage Perceptions of Ourselves

Even if you generally attribute your own behavior largely to external causes, you probably vary your attributions to try to present yourself in a favorable light. For example, you might credit your good grades to your intelligence and hard work (an internal attribution) but blame your bad grades on unfair tests (an external attribution). *Attributions that we adopt to maximize our credit for our success and minimize our blame for our failure* are called **self-serving biases** (D. T. Miller & Ross, 1975; van der Pligt & Eiser, 1983). Self-serving biases are robust. Even students who have learned about them usually think the biases apply to other people more than themselves (Pronin, Gilovich, & Ross, 2004).

People also protect their images with **self-handicapping strategies,** in which they *intentionally put themselves at a disadvantage to provide an ex-*

cuse for possible failure. Suppose you fear you will do poorly on a test. You go to a party the night before and stay out late. Now you can blame your low score on your lack of sleep without admitting that you might have done poorly anyway.

In an experiment on self-handicapping strategies, Steven Berglas and Edward Jones (1978) asked some college students to work on solvable problems and asked others to work on a mixture of solvable and unsolvable problems. (The students did not know that some of the problems were impossible.) The experimenters told all the students that they had done well. The students who had been given solvable problems (and had solved them) felt good about their success. Those who had worked on unsolvable problems were unsure in what way they had "done well." They had no confidence that they could continue to do well.

Next the experimenters told the participants that the purpose of the experiment was to investigate the effects of drugs on problem solving and that they were now going to hand out another set of problems. The participants could choose between taking a drug that supposedly impaired problem-solving abilities and another drug that supposedly improved them. The participants who had worked on unsolvable problems the first time were more likely than the others to choose the drug that supposedly impaired performance. Because they did not expect to do well on the second set of problems anyway, they provided themselves with a convenient excuse.

 CONCEPT CHECK

12. Who is more likely to make the fundamental attribution error, Americans or Chinese?
13. If, instead of watching someone, you close your eyes and imagine yourself in that person's position, will you be more likely to explain the behavior with internal or external attributions? Why?
14. Why would people sometimes intentionally do something likely to harm their own performance? (Check your answers on page 498.)

IN CLOSING

How Social Perceptions Affect Behavior

We are seldom fully aware of the reasons for our own behavior, much less someone else's, but we make our best guesses. If someone you know passes by without saying hello, you might attribute that person's behavior to absent-mindedness, indifference, or hostility. You might attribute someone's friendly response to your own personal charm, the other person's extraverted personality, or that person's devious and manipulative personality. The attributions you make are sure to influence your own social behaviors. ∎

Summary

- *First impressions.* Other things being equal, we pay more attention to the first information we learn about someone than to later information. (page 488)
- *Stereotypes.* Stereotypes are generalized beliefs about groups of people. Stereotypes influence our behavior in subtle ways, often without our awareness. (page 489)
- *Prejudice.* A prejudice is an unfavorable stereotype. Many people do not admit their prejudices, even to themselves. Through indirect measures researchers have found ways to demonstrate subtle effects of prejudices even in people who deny having them. (page 490)
- *Attribution.* Attribution is the set of thought processes by which we assign internal or external causes to behavior. According to Harold Kelley, we are likely to attribute behavior to an internal cause if it is consistent over time, different from most other people's behavior, and directed toward a variety of other people or objects. (page 493)
- *Fundamental attribution error.* People frequently attribute people's behavior to internal causes, even when they see evidence of external influences. (page 494)
- *Cultural differences.* People in Asian cultures are less likely than those in Western cultures to attribute behavior to consistent personality traits and more likely to attribute it to the situation. (page 495)
- *Actor-observer effect.* We are more likely to attribute internal causes to other people's behavior than to our own. (page 496)
- *Self-serving bias and self-handicapping.* People sometimes try to protect their self-esteem by attributing their successes to skill and their failures to outside influences. They can also intentionally place themselves at a disadvantage to provide an excuse for their expected failure. (page 496)

Answers to Concept Checks

6. They want to avoid being biased by their first impressions of the students. This procedure is less important with the first test because they have not yet formed strong impressions. (page 488)
7. The Implicit Association Test can reveal prejudices that people don't want to admit, perhaps even to themselves. (page 491)

8. They are most likely to show evidence of implicit prejudice if the instructions ask people to pay attention to the race of the people in the photos. (page 492)

9. **a.** internal; **b.** and **c.** external. An internal attribution relates to a stable aspect of personality or attitudes; an external attribution relates to the current situation. (page 493)

10. You probably will make an internal attribution because of *consensus*. When one person's behavior differs from others', we make an internal attribution. (page 493)

11. Because of the fundamental attribution error, people would tend to think that performers who portrayed likable characters were themselves likable, and those who played contemptible people probably resembled those characters. (page 494)

12. Americans and others from Western cultures are more likely to make the fundamental attribution error because the Chinese tend to attribute behavior more to situational factors than do Westerners. (page 495)

13. You will be more likely to give an external attribution because you will become more like an actor and less an observer. (page 496)

14. People sometimes do something to harm their own performance to give themselves an excuse for doing poorly, especially if they thought they might do poorly anyway. (page 496)

Attitudes and Persuasion

- *What are some effective ways to influence people's attitudes?*

"If you want to change people's behavior, you have to change their attitudes first." Do you agree? Suppose you do. Now answer two more questions: (a) What is your attitude about paying higher taxes? (b) If the government raises taxes, will you pay them?

I assume you said that you have an unfavorable attitude about paying higher taxes, but if the taxes are raised, you will pay them. Thus, by changing the law, the government could change your behavior without changing your attitude. Frequently, behaviors change more easily than attitudes.

So, what effects do attitudes have on behavior? And what leads people to change their attitudes?

Attitudes and Behavior

An **attitude** is *a like or dislike that influences our behavior toward someone or something* (Allport, 1935; Petty & Cacioppo, 1981). Your attitudes include an evaluative or emotional component (how you feel about something), a cognitive component (what you know or believe), and a behavioral component (what you are likely to do). *Persuasion* is an attempt to alter your attitudes or behavior.

Attitude Measurement

One common way of measuring attitudes (and thus the effectiveness of persuasion) is through attitude scales. On a Likert scale (named after psychologist Rensis Likert), you would check a point along a line ranging from 1, meaning "strongly disagree," to 7, meaning "strongly agree," for each of several statements about a topic, as illustrated in Figure 13.6.

The attitudes that people report do not always relate closely to their behaviors. For example, many people report attitudes about cigarettes, alcohol, safe sex, wearing seat belts in a car, studying hard for tests, and so forth that do not match their behavior. Why? One reason is that people sometimes answer attitude questionnaires impulsively, especially on questions they regard as unimportant (van der Pligt, de Vries, Manstead, & van Harreveld, 2000). A second reason is that people's answers to an attitude question fluctuate (Lord & Lepper, 1999). For example, what is your attitude toward politicians on a scale from 1 (very unfavorable) to 7 (very favorable)? If you are thinking about the public servants you admire most, you might rate politicians favorably. Later, however, you might be thinking about corrupt or incompetent politicians, and you would answer differently.

Your attitudes are most likely to match your behavior if you have had much personal experience with the topic of the attitude (Glasman & Albarracín, 2006). For example, if you have had extensive experience dealing with mental patients, then you know how you react to them, and you can state your attitude accordingly. Someone with less experience is stating a hypothetical attitude, which might change readily.

Indicate your level of agreement with the items below, using the following scale:

	Strongly disagree		Neutral			Strongly agree
1. Labor unions are necessary to protect the rights of workers.	1 2	3	4	5	6	7
2. Labor union leaders have too much power.	1 2	3	4	5	6	7
3. If I worked for a company with a union, I would join the union.	1 2	3	4	5	6	7
4. I would never cross a picket line of striking workers.	1 2	3	4	5	6	7
5. Striking workers hurt their company and unfairly raise prices for the consumer.	1 2	3	4	5	6	7
6. Labor unions should not be permitted to engage in political activity.	1 2	3	4	5	6	7
7. America is a better place for today's workers because of the efforts by labor unions in the past.	1 2	3	4	5	6	7

Note: Items 2, 5, and 6 are scored the opposite of 1, 3, 4, and 7.

FIGURE 13.6 This Likert scale assesses attitudes toward labor unions.

15. What test or method mentioned earlier in this chapter could demonstrate mixed or contradictory attitudes? (Check your answer on page 507.)

Cognitive Dissonance and Attitude Change

Much research asks whether people's attitudes change their behavior. The theory of cognitive dissonance reverses the direction: It holds that a change in people's behavior alters their attitudes (Festinger, 1957). **Cognitive dissonance** is *a state of unpleasant tension that people experience when they hold contradictory attitudes or when their behavior is inconsistent with their attitudes, especially if they are distressed about the inconsistency.*

For example, if you pride yourself on honesty and find yourself saying something you do not believe, you feel tension. You can reduce that tension in three ways: You can change what you are saying to match your attitudes, change your attitude to match what you are saying, or find an explanation that justifies your behavior under the circumstances (Wicklund & Brehm, 1976) (see Figure 13.7). Although all of these options are possible, most research has focused on how cognitive dissonance changes people's attitudes.

Imagine yourself as a participant in this classic experiment on cognitive dissonance (Festinger & Carlsmith, 1959). The experimenters explain that they are studying motor behavior. They show you a board full of pegs. Your task is to take each peg out of the board, rotate it one fourth of a turn, and return it to the board. When you finish all the pegs, you start over, rotating all the pegs again as quickly and accurately as possible for an hour. As you proceed an experimenter silently takes notes. You find your task immensely tedious. In fact the researchers intentionally chose this task because it was so boring.

At the end of the hour, the experimenter thanks you for participating and "explains" to you (falsely) that the study's purpose was to determine whether people's performances are influenced by their attitudes toward the task. You were in the neutral-attitude group, but those in the positive-attitude group are told before they start that they will enjoy this experience.

In fact, the experimenter continues, right now the research assistant is supposed to give that instruction to the next participant, a young woman waiting in the next room. The experimenter excuses himself to find the research assistant and then returns distraught.

The assistant is nowhere to be found, he says. He turns to you and asks, "Would you be willing to tell the next participant that you thought this was an interesting, enjoyable experiment? If so, I will pay you." Assume that you consent, as most students in the study did. After you tell that woman in the next room that you enjoyed the study, what would you actually think of the study, assuming the experimenter paid you $1? What if he paid you $20? (This study occurred in the 1950s. In today's money that $20 would be worth more than $100.)

After you have told the woman how much fun the experiment was, you leave, believing the study is over. As you walk down the hall, a representative of the psychology department greets you and explains that the department wants to find out what kinds of experiments are being conducted and whether they are educationally worthwhile. (The answers to these questions are the real point of the experiment.) You are asked how enjoyable you considered the experiment and whether you would be willing to participate in a similar experiment later.

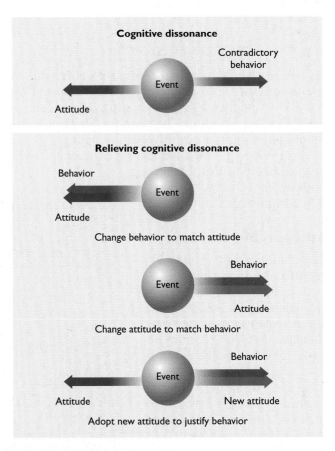

FIGURE 13.7 Cognitive dissonance is a state of tension that arises when people perceive that their attitudes do not match their behavior. They can resolve this discrepancy by changing their attitudes or their behavior or by developing a new attitude to explain the discrepancy.

In this experiment the students who received $20 said they thought the experiment was boring and that they wanted nothing to do with another such experiment. However, contrary to what you might guess, those who received $1 said they enjoyed the experiment and would be willing to participate again (Figure 13.8).

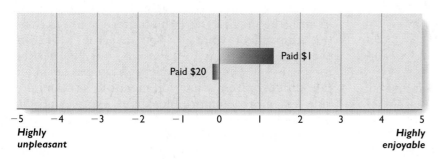

−5   −4   −3   −2   −1   0   1   2   3   4   5
Highly unpleasant   *Highly enjoyable*

FIGURE 13.8 In a classic experiment demonstrating cognitive dissonance, participants were paid either $1 or $20 for telling another subject that they enjoyed an experiment (which was actually boring). Later, they were asked for their real opinions. Participants who were paid the smaller amount said that they enjoyed the study more than the others. *(Based on data from Festinger & Carlsmith, 1959)*

Why? According to the theory of cognitive dissonance, if you accepted $20 to tell a lie, you experienced little conflict. You knew you were lying, but you knew you were doing it for the $20. However, if you told a lie for only $1, you felt a conflict between your true attitude and what you had said about the experiment. The small payment provided little reason for lying, so you experienced cognitive dissonance—an unpleasant tension. You did not want to feel bad about telling a lie, so you reduced your tension by changing your attitude, deciding that the experiment really had been interesting after all. ("I learned a lot of interesting things about myself, like . . . uh . . . how good I am at rotating pegs.")

The idea of cognitive dissonance attracted much attention and inspired a great deal of research (Aronson, 1997). Here are two examples:

- An experimenter left a child in a room with toys but forbade the child to play with one particular toy. If the experimenter threatened the child with severe punishment for playing with the toy, the child avoided it but still regarded it as desirable. However, if the experimenter merely said that he or she would be disappointed if the child played with that toy, the child avoided the toy and said (even weeks later) that it was not a good toy (Aronson & Carlsmith, 1963).

- The experimenter asked college students to write an essay defending a position that the experimenter knew, from previous information, was contrary to the students' beliefs. For example, college students who favored freer access to alcohol might be

asked to write essays on why the college should increase restrictions on alcohol. Those who were told they must write the essays did not change their views significantly, but those who were asked to "please" write the essay and were also reminded that they did so voluntarily generally came to agree with what they wrote (Croyle & Cooper, 1983).

The general principle is that, if you entice people to do something by means of a minimum reward or a tiny threat so that they are acting almost voluntarily, they change their attitudes to support what they are doing and reduce cognitive dissonance. This procedure is a powerful method of attitude change because people are actively participating, not just listening.

So, if you want to change people's behavior, do you have to change their attitudes first? The results of cognitive dissonance experiments tell us quite the opposite: If you start by changing people's behavior, their attitudes will change too.

 CONCEPT CHECK

16. Suppose your parents pay you to get a good grade in a course that you consider boring. According to cognitive dissonance theory, are you more likely to develop a positive attitude toward your studies if your parents pay you $10 or $100? (Check your answer on page 507.)

Central and Peripheral Routes of Attitude Change and Persuasion

We sometimes form our attitudes after pondering the evidence carefully, but some of our attitudes have only a superficial basis. Richard Petty and John Cacioppo (1981, 1986) proposed the following distinction: *When people take a decision seriously, they invest the necessary time and effort to evaluate the evidence and logic behind each message.* Petty and Cacioppo call this logical approach the **central route to persuasion**. In contrast, *when people listen to a message on a topic they consider unimportant, they attend to such factors as the speaker's appearance and reputation or the sheer number of arguments presented, regardless of their quality.* This superficial approach is the **peripheral route to persuasion**.

CONCEPT CHECK

17. You listen to a debate about raising tuition at Santa Enigma Junior College. Later, you listen to a debate about raising tuition at your own college. In which case will you follow the central route to persuasion? (Check your answer on page 507.)

Delayed Influence

Some messages have no apparent influence at first but an important effect later. We consider two reasons.

The Sleeper Effect

Suppose you reject a message because of peripheral route influences. For example, you hear some idea but then learn that the person who suggested it has poor qualifications. Weeks or months later, you may forget where you heard the idea (*source amnesia*) and remember only the idea itself. If you are highly motivated to think about the idea, its persuasive impact may increase (Kumkale & Abarracín, 2004). If you completely forget the source, you might even claim it as your own idea! Psychologists use the term **sleeper effect** to describe *delayed persuasion by an initially rejected message*.

Minority Influence

Delayed influence also occurs when a minority group, especially one that is not widely respected, proposes a worthwhile idea: The majority rejects the idea at first but reconsiders it later. The minority could be an ethnic minority, and a group that mixes Black and White students tends to consider a wider range of ideas than a group with Black or White students alone (Antonio et al., 2004). However, similar effects emerge with political minorities or any other outnumbered group.

If a minority group continually repeats a single simple message and its members seem united, it has a good chance of eventually influencing the majority's decision. The minority's uncompromising stance forces the majority to wonder, "Why won't they conform? Maybe their idea is better than we thought." The minority's influence often increases gradually, even if the majority hesitates to admit that the minority has swayed them (Wood, Lundgren, Ouellette, Busceme, & Blackstone, 1994). A minority, by expressing its views, can also prompt the majority to generate new ideas of its own (Nemeth, 1986). That is, by demonstrating the possibility of disagreement, the minority opens the way for other people to offer suggestions different from the original views of both the majority and the minority. You may notice this effect yourself. You disagree with what everyone else seems to be saying, but you hesitate to speak out. Then someone else voices an objection different from what you meant to say, and now you feel more comfortable about expressing your own idea.

One powerful example of minority influence is that of the Socialist Party of the United States, which ran candidates for elective offices from 1900 through the 1950s. The party never received more than 6% of the vote in any presidential election. No Socialist candidate was elected senator or governor, and only a few were elected to the House of Representatives (Shannon, 1955). Beginning in the 1930s, the party's support dwindled, until eventually the party stopped nominating candidates. Was that because they had failed? No! Most of their major proposals had been enacted into law (Table 13.2). Of course, the Democrats and Republicans who voted for these changes claimed credit for the ideas. The Socialist Party, without winning elections, exerted an enormous influence.

TABLE 13.2 Political Proposals of the U.S. Socialist Party, Around 1900

Proposal	Eventual Fate of Proposal
Women's right to vote	Established by 19th Amendment to U.S. Constitution; ratified in 1920
Old-age pensions	Included in the Social Security Act of 1935
Unemployment insurance	Included in the Social Security Act of 1935; also guaranteed by the other state and federal legislation
Health and accident insurance	Included in part in the Social Security Act of 1935 and in the Medicare Act of 1965
Increased wages, including minimum wage	First minimum-wage law passed in 1938; periodically updated since then
Reduction of working hours	Maximum 40-hour workweek (with exceptions) established by the Fair Labor Standards Act of 1938
Public ownership of electric, gas, and other utilities and of the means of transportation and communication	Utilities not owned by government but heavily regulated by federal and state government since the 1930s
Initiative, referendum, and recall (mechanisms for private citizens to push for changes in legislation and for removal of elected officials)	Adopted by most state governments

Sources: Foster, 1968; and Leuchtenburg, 1963.

CONCEPT CHECK

18. At a meeting of your student government, you suggest a new method of testing and grading students. The other members immediately reject your plan. Should you become discouraged and give up? If not, what should you do? (Check your answers on page 507.)

Ways of Presenting Persuasive Messages

The influence of an attempt at persuasion can depend on many factors that we hardly notice. For example, a television ad may become more effective because of its pleasant background music. Advertisers, politicians, and many others attend closely to the details of how they present their messages.

Influence of Similarity

Other things being equal, a persuasive message is more effective if the speaker conveys the message, "I resemble you." In one striking illustration of the influence of similarity, students were asked to read a very unflattering description of Grigory Rasputin, the "mad monk of Russia," and then rate Rasputin on sev-

© Hulton-Deutsch Collection/CORBIS

Grigory Rasputin's unsavory influence on the czar of Russia led to the Communist revolution. However, people who are told Rasputin resembled them, even in trivial ways, soften their criticisms.

eral scales such as pleasant to unpleasant, effective to ineffective, and strong to weak. All students read the same description except for Rasputin's birth date: In some cases Rasputin's birth date had been changed to match the student's own birth date. Students who thought Rasputin had the same birth date as their own were more likely than others to rate him as "strong" and "effective" (Finch & Cialdini, 1989).

In another study people read arguments in favor of higher taxes. People who were sad responded best to an argument based on sadness. (For example, if we don't pass this tax, then impoverished, sick children will suffer.) People who were angry responded best to an argument that highlighted anger. (For example, if we don't pass this tax, you will have to wait even longer than now in traffic jams.) The general point is that persuasion is most effective if the listener identifies with it personally (DeSteno, Petty, Rucker, Wegener, & Braverman, 2004).

Influence of Group Endorsement

Imagine some preposterous idea that you reject vigorously. Now imagine that some group you respect endorses the idea. Would you suddenly like the idea better?

In one study psychologists used a questionnaire to identify the most politically liberal and the most conservative students. Then they gave each student one of two versions of what they said was a proposed law about welfare for the unemployed. One version offered extraordinarily generous benefits, including $800 per month for up to 8 years, plus full medical care, $2,000 in food stamps, subsidies for housing and day care, job training, full tuition at a community college, and more. Although this policy goes far beyond what the most liberal U.S. politicians have recommended, if students were told that the Republicans (the more conservative party) endorsed it, conservative students said they supported it too, and liberal students opposed it. Other students were told about a stingy proposed law, which offered only $250 per month, with an 18-month limit, and no other benefits. Ordinarily, almost anyone would consider this policy inadequate, but if students were told that the Democrats (the more liberal party) endorsed it, liberal students supported it, and conservatives did not. When students were asked the reasons for their decisions, almost none admitted that endorsement by one party or the other was a significant influence. They insisted that they decided on their own (G. L. Cohen, 2003).

CONCEPT CHECK

19. A salesperson calls at your door and says that several of your neighbors (whom the salesperson names) have bought the product and recom-

mended you as another possible customer. What techniques of persuasion is this salesperson using? (Check your answer on page 507.)

Audience Variables

Some people are more easily persuaded than others are, and someone may be more easily influenced at some times than at others. The ease of persuading someone depends on both the person and the situation.

Intelligence and Interest

Who would you guess would be persuaded more easily—more intelligent or less intelligent people? It depends. The peripheral route to persuasion is more likely to persuade less intelligent people of an illogical or poorly supported idea (Eagly & Warren, 1976). The central route to persuasion is generally more effective with highly intelligent people, who are better able to understand complicated evidence.

However, the effectiveness of the central or peripheral route also depends on people's level of interest. Even if you are very intelligent, you won't devote much effort to an issue that seems unimportant. A clever salesperson gauges a client's interests and adjusts the message accordingly. Today, it is possible to tailor Internet ads to the individual. Computers store information about you and change the emphasis of an ad depending on what kinds of information are most likely to interest and persuade you (Kreutzer & Holt, 2001).

Heightened Resistance

Once you have formed an attitude or opinion, you are likely to stick with it. People are often quite willing to read or hear about ideas they dislike, but they argue against them and resist changing their attitudes (Eagly, Kulesa, Chen, & Chaiken, 2001). In one study students read a research paper indicating that capital punishment deters murder and a second paper that found capital punishment ineffective. Students who supported capital punishment saw the flaws in the research that found capital punishment ineffective, and students who opposed capital punishment saw the flaws in the research reporting it effective (Lord, Ross, & Lepper, 1979).

Simply informing people that they are about to hear a persuasive speech activates their resistance and weakens the effect of the persuasion (Petty & Cacioppo, 1977). This tendency is called the **forewarning effect**. Actually, the results are somewhat complex. Suppose you have a strongly unfavorable attitude toward something—increased tuition at your college, for example. Now someone tells you that a well-informed person is going to try to persuade you

in favor of higher tuition. At once, before the speech even begins, your attitudes shift slightly in that direction, toward favoring higher tuition! Exactly why is unclear; perhaps you are telling yourself, "I guess there must be some good reason for that opinion." Then when you hear the speech itself, it does have some influence, and your attitudes will shift still further toward favoring it (or at least toward neutrality), but your attitudes do not shift as much as those of someone who had not been forewarned. The warning alerts you to resist the persuasion, to criticize weak arguments, and to reject weak evidence (Wood & Quinn, 2003).

In the closely related **inoculation effect**, *people first hear a weak argument and then a stronger argument supporting the same conclusion.* After they have rejected the first argument, they usually reject the second one also. In one experiment people listened to speeches *against* brushing their teeth after every meal. Some of them heard just a strong argument (e.g., "Brushing your teeth too frequently wears away tooth enamel, leading to serious disease"). Others first heard a weak argument and then the strong argument 2 days later. Still others first heard an argument *for* tooth-brushing and then the strong argument against it. Only those who heard the weak argument against brushing resisted the influence of the strong argument. The other two groups found it highly persuasive (McGuire & Papageorgis, 1961). So if you want to convince people, start with your strong evidence.

 CONCEPT CHECK

20. If you want your children to preserve the beliefs and attitudes you try to teach them, should you give them only arguments that support those beliefs or should you also expose them to attacks on those beliefs? Why? (Check your answers on page 508.)

Strategies of Persuasion

People representing anything from worthless products to noble charities will sometimes ask you to give more of your time or money than you would rationally choose to spend. You should understand several of their techniques so that you can resist these appeals.

One technique is to start with a modest request, which the person accepts, and then follow it with a larger request. This procedure is called the **foot-in-the-door technique**. When Jonathan Freedman and Scott Fraser (1966) asked suburban residents in Palo Alto, California, to put a small "Drive Safely" sign in their windows, most agreed to do so. A couple of weeks later, other researchers asked the same residents to let them set up a large "Drive Safely" billboard in their front yards for 10 days. They also made the request to some residents who had not been approached by the first researchers. Of those who had already agreed to display the small sign, 76% agreed to the billboard. Only 17% of the others agreed. Even agreeing to make as small a commitment as signing a petition to support a cause significantly increases the probability that people will later donate money to that cause (Schwarzwald, Bizman, & Raz, 1983).

In another approach, called the **door-in-the-face technique** (Cialdini et al., 1975), *someone follows an outrageous initial request with a more reasonable second one,* implying that if you refused the first request, you should agree to the second. For example, I once received a telephone call from a college alumni association asking me to show my loyalty by contributing $1,000. When I apologetically declined, the caller acted sympathetic (as if to say, "It's sad that you don't have a high-paying job like all our other alumni . . .") and then asked whether I could contribute $500. And if not $500, how about $200? The implication was that, after I had refused the original request, I should "compromise."

Robert Cialdini and his colleagues (1975) demonstrated the power of the door-in-the-face technique with a clever experiment. They asked one group of college students, chosen randomly, to chaperone a group from the juvenile detention center on a trip to the zoo. Only 17% agreed to do so. They asked other students to spend 2 hours per week for 2 years working as counselors with juvenile delinquents. Not surprisingly, all of them refused. But then the researchers asked them, "If you won't do that, would you chaperone a group from the juvenile detention center on one trip to the zoo?" Half of them said they would. Apparently, they thought it was only fair to meet halfway.

Someone using the **bait-and-switch technique** *first offers an extremely favorable deal, gets the other person to commit to the deal, and then makes additional demands.* Alternatively, the person might offer a product at a very low price to get customers to the store but then claim to be out of the product and try to sell them something else. For example, a car dealer offers you an exceptionally good price on a new car and a generous price for the trade-in of your old car. The deal seems too good to resist. After you have committed yourself to buying this car, the dealer checks with the boss, who rejects the deal. Your salesperson comes back saying, "I'm so sorry. I forgot that this car has some special features that raise the value. If we sold it for the price I originally quoted, we'd lose

money." So you agree to a higher price. Then the company's used car specialist looks at your old car and "corrects" the trade-in value to a lower amount. Still, you have already committed yourself, so you don't back out. Eventually, you leave with a deal that you would not have accepted at the start.

In the **that's-not-all technique,** *someone makes an offer and then improves the offer before you have a chance to reply.* The television announcer says, "Here's your chance to buy this amazing combination paper shredder and coffeemaker for only $39.95. But wait, there's more! We'll throw in a can of dog deodorant! Also this handy windshield wiper cleaner and a solar-powered flashlight and a subscription to *Modern Lobotomist!* If you call now, you can get this amazing offer, which usually costs $39.95, for only $19.95! Call this number!" People who hear the first offer and then the "improved" offer are more likely to comply than are people who hear the "improved" offer from the start (Burger, 1986).

You may notice a similarity among the four techniques just mentioned. In the foot-in-the-door, door-in-the-face, bait-and-switch, and that's-not-all techniques, the persuader starts with one proposal and then switches to another. The first one changes the listener's state of mind for the second one.

 CONCEPT CHECK

21. Identify each of the following as an example of the foot-in-the-door technique, the door-in-the-face technique, or the that's-not-all technique.
    a. Your boss says, "We need to cut costs drastically. I'm afraid I'm going to have to cut your salary in half." You protest vigorously. Your boss replies, "Well, I suppose we could cut expenses some other way. Maybe I can give you just a 5% cut." "Thanks," you reply. "I can live with that."
    b. A store marks its prices "25% off" and then scratches that out and marks them "50% off!"
    c. A friend asks you to help carry some supplies over to the elementary school for an afternoon tutoring program. When you get there, the principal says that one of the tutors is late and asks whether you could take her place until she arrives. You agree and spend the rest of the afternoon tutoring. The principal then talks you into coming back every week as a tutor.

22. The effort to avoid cognitive dissonance leads to consistency in behavior. Use that principle to explain the foot-in-the-door technique. (Check your answers on page 508.)

The Role of Fear

Usually people who are trying to persuade you of something rely on enticements of possible rewards, but sometimes they use fear also. Some appeals for money use threats, such as, "If you don't send money to support our cause, our political opponents will gain power and do terrible things." One organization sent out appeals with a message on the envelope, "Every day an estimated 800 dolphins, porpoises, and whales will die . . . unless you act now!" Other things being equal, stronger fear increases the persuasion (Dillard & Anderson, 2004), but people disregard statements that seem exaggerated or unrealistic (Leventhal, 1970).

A fear message is effective only if people believe they can easily reduce the danger. For example, a message about the dangers of influenza motivates many people to get immunized. Messages about the dangers of AIDS are less effective in motivating people to practice safe sex (Albarracín et al., 2005), perhaps because using condoms consistently is more difficult than getting a flu shot once a year. Messages about global warming are seriously frightening, but few people change their behavior significantly because they doubt that one person's behavior can have a big effect.

Fear messages sometimes backfire. For example, an antidrug campaign might say that drug use is spreading wildly, or a conservation organization might say that pollution and destruction of the environment are out of control. The intended message is, "Take this problem seriously and act now." The unintended message that people sometimes receive is, "Drug use, pollution, etc. are normal." Another unintended message is, "The problem is hopeless" (Cialdini, 2003).

Coercive Persuasion

Finally, let's consider the most unfriendly kinds of persuasion. Suppose the police suspect you of a crime, and they are trying to get you to confess. You agree to waive your rights to an attorney and talk with them. After all, what do you have to lose? You're innocent, so you have nothing to hide. First the police claim your crime is horrendous and you face a stiff sentence. Then they offer sympathy and excuses, implying that if you confess, you can get a much lighter sentence. They claim to have solid evidence of your guilt anyway, so you may as well confess because they can convict you even if you don't. They tell you that you failed a polygraph test. You stay in isolation, without food or sleep for many hours, with no promise of when, if ever, this ordeal will end. Apparently, the only way you can get them to stop badgering you is to confess. Might you con-

fess, even though you are innocent? You think, "Oh, well, eventually they will realize their mistake. They can't really convict me, because they won't have any other evidence."

Many innocent people do confess under these conditions. Unfortunately, juries consider a confession extremely strong evidence, even if they know it was coerced and the prosecution has no other evidence (Kassin & Gudjonsson, 2004). To test the effects of coercive persuasion, researchers set up the following experiment: They asked pairs of students to work independently on logic problems. For half of the pairs, one of them (a confederate of the experimenter) asked for help, which the first person usually gave. Later, they were told that offering help was considered cheating. For the other pairs, the confederate did not ask for help and therefore no cheating occurred. After both completed the problems, the experimenter entered the room and accused the participant of cheating. For some, the experimenter merely made the accusation and asked for a confession. Under those conditions 46% of the guilty students and 6% of the innocent ones signed a confession. (Why any innocent students confessed here is a mystery.) Other students were exposed to coercive techniques. The experimenter threatened to report the student to the professor, who would deal with this event as harshly as any other case of academic cheating. However, the experimenter suggested they could settle the problem quickly if the student signed a confession. Under these circumstances 87% of the guilty students and 43% of the innocent ones agreed to confess, as illustrated in Figure 13.9 (Russano, Meissner, Narchet, & Kassin, 2005). The message is that coercive techniques increase confessions by guilty people, and also by innocent people, and therefore make the confessions unreliable evidence.

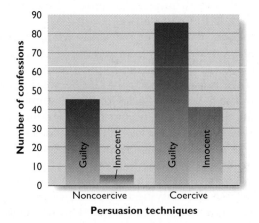

FIGURE 13.9 Coercive persuasion techniques increased the number of confessions by both guilty and innocent people. *(Based on data of Russano, Meissner, Narchet, & Kassin, 2005)*

CRITICAL THINKING
A STEP FURTHER

Coercive Persuasion

What implication do these results have for military investigators who are trying to get suspected terrorists to reveal information?

IN CLOSING

Persuasion and Manipulation

Broadly defined, attitudes influence almost everything we do. When you form an attitude about something of little consequence to you, it is understandable that you will follow the peripheral route, paying little attention to the complexities of the evidence. When you are dealing with important matters, however, such as how you will spend your time and money, you will almost certainly follow the central route, examining the facts as carefully as you can. It is important to be alert to some of the influences that might throw you off course, such as the foot-in-the-door technique, bait-and-switch, and cognitive dissonance. Advertisers, politicians, and others try to polish their techniques of persuasion, and not everyone has your best interest at heart. ∎

Summary

- *Attitudes.* An attitude is a like or dislike of something or somebody that influences our behavior toward that thing or person. (page 499)
- *Cognitive dissonance.* Cognitive dissonance is a state of unpleasant tension that arises from contradictory attitudes or from behavior that conflicts with a person's attitudes. When people's behavior does not match their attitudes, they try to eliminate the inconsistency by changing either their behavior or their attitudes. (page 500)
- *Two routes to persuasion.* When people consider a topic of little importance to them, they are easily persuaded by the speaker's appearance and other superficial factors. When people care about the topic, they pay more attention to logic and to the quality of the evidence. (page 501)
- *Sleeper effect.* When people reject a message because of their low regard for the person who proposed it, they sometimes forget where they heard the idea and later come to accept it. (page 502)
- *Minority influence.* Although a minority may have little influence at first, it can, through persistent repetition of its message, eventually persuade the majority to adopt its position or consider other alternatives. (page 502)

- *Influence of group endorsement.* People tend to accept a position endorsed by a political party or other group they favor, even if they would ordinarily doubt that position. (page 503)
- *Forewarning and inoculation effects.* If people have been warned that someone will try to persuade them of something, or if they have previously heard a weak version of the persuasive argument, they tend to resist the argument. (page 504)
- *Strategies of persuasion.* Several procedures can influence people to do something they would not have done otherwise. These include starting with a tiny request and then increasing it, starting with an enormous request and offering to compromise, offering a generous deal and then demanding more, and offering a moderate deal and then adding inducements. (page 504)
- *Influence of fear-inducing messages.* Messages that appeal to fear are effective if people perceive the danger as real and think they can do something about it. (page 506)
- *Coercive persuasion.* Techniques designed to pressure a suspect into confessing decrease the reliability of the confession, because under these circumstances many innocent people confess also. (page 506)

Answers to Concept Checks

15. Some people express one attitude openly but demonstrate another attitude on the Implicit Association Test. (page 491)
16. You will come to like your studies more if you are paid $10 than if you are paid $100. If you are paid only $10, you won't be able to tell yourself that you are studying harder only for the money. Instead, you will tell yourself that you must be really interested. The theory of intrinsic and extrinsic motivation leads to the same prediction: If you study hard in the absence of any strong external reason, you will perceive that you have internal reasons for studying. (page 501)
17. You will pay more attention to the evidence and logic, following the central route to persuasion, for the debate about your own college because it is worth your effort to evaluate the evidence carefully. (page 501)
18. The fact that your idea was overwhelmingly rejected does not mean that you should give up. If you and a few allies continue to present this plan in a simple way, showing apparent agreement among yourselves, the majority may eventually endorse a similar plan—but probably without giving you credit for it. (page 502)
19. The salesperson is relying on endorsement by a group that you presumably like and trust. Also,

you are likely to be persuaded by people similar to yourself. (page 503)

20. You should expose them to weak attacks on their beliefs so that they will learn how to resist such attacks. (page 504)

21. **a.** door-in-the-face technique; **b.** that's-not-all technique; **c.** foot-in-the-door technique. (page 504)

22. Once you have agreed to a small request, you can maintain consistency (decrease dissonance) by agreeing to similar requests in the future. (page 500)

Interpersonal Attraction

- *How do we choose our partners?*
- *Do men and women choose for the same reasons?*

William Proxmire, a former U.S. senator, used to give Golden Fleece Awards to those who, in his opinion, most flagrantly wasted the taxpayers' money. He once bestowed an award on psychologists who had received a federal grant to study how people fall in love. According to Proxmire the research was pointless because people do not want to understand love. They prefer, he said, to let such matters remain a mystery.

This module presents the information Senator Proxmire thought you did not want to know.

Establishing Relationships

Of all the people you meet, how do you choose those who become your friends or romantic attachments? How do they choose you? Some influences apply mainly to romantic relationships, and some apply to friendships as well.

Proximity and Familiarity

Proximity means *closeness*. (It comes from the same root as *approximate*.) Not surprisingly, *we are most likely to become friends with people who live or work in close proximity and become familiar to us.* At the start of a school year, Robert Hays (1985) asked college students to name two other students with whom they thought they might become friends. After 3 months he found that more of the potential friends who lived close together had become friends than had those who lived farther apart.

One reason proximity is important is that people who live nearby have frequent opportunities to discover what they have in common. Another reason is the **mere exposure effect,** the principle that *the more often we come in contact with someone or something, the more we tend to like that person or object* (Saegert, Swap, & Zajonc, 1973; Zajonc, 1968). You can think of exceptions, of course. Frequent contact with a disease will not make you like it. Exactly why we prefer familiar things is not known.

Physical Attractiveness

What characteristics do you look for in a potential romantic partner? You might reply that you want "someone who is intelligent, honest, easy to talk to, with a good sense of humor." Now imagine a friend says, "Hey, you're not doing anything this weekend, right? How about going on a blind date with my cousin who is visiting for the weekend?" "Well, I don't know. Tell me about your cousin." "My cousin is intelligent, honest, easy to talk to, and has a good sense of humor." That description matches what you said you wanted, but you are skeptical. Your friend did not mention the cousin's appearance, so you assume the worst. Were you being dishonest when you said you wanted someone intelligent, honest, and easy to talk to? Not really. You did not mention appearance because you assumed anyone would take that for granted. (You also didn't say that you hope your date speaks English. You don't mention the obvious.) Attractiveness also matters in nonromantic relationships. Close friends usually resemble each other in level of attractiveness.

In one study social psychologists arranged blind dates for 332 freshman couples for a dance before the start of classes. They asked participants to fill out questionnaires, but then the experimenters ignored the questionnaires and paired students at random. Midway through the dance, the experimenters separated the men and women and asked them to rate how much they liked their dates. The only factor that influenced the ratings was physical attractiveness (Walster, Aronson, Abrahams, & Rottman, 1966). Similarities of attitudes, personality, and intelligence counted for almost nothing. Surprising? Hardly. During the brief time they had spent together at the dance, the couples had little opportunity to learn about each other. Intelligence, honesty, and other character values do become important in a lasting relationship, but less so on the first date or two, and certainly not in the first hour (Keller, Thiessen, & Young, 1996).

Possible Biological Value of Attractiveness: Birds

Why do we care about physical appearance? We take its importance so much for granted that we don't even understand why there is a question, so for a moment let's consider other species.

509

FIGURE 13.10 In some bird species, males with long tails attract more mates. Only a healthy male can afford this trait that impairs his flying ability.

In many bird species, early in the mating season, females shop around and choose a brilliantly colored male that sings vigorously from the treetops. In several species females also prefer males with especially long tails (Figure 13.10). From an evolutionary standpoint, aren't these choices foolish? The most popular males are those that risk their lives by singing loudly from the treetops, where they call the attention of hawks and eagles. They also waste enormous energy by growing bright feathers. (It takes more energy to produce bright than dull colors.) A long tail may look pretty, but it interferes with flying. Why does the female prefer a mate who wastes energy and endangers his life?

Biologists eventually decided that wasting energy and risking life were precisely the point (Zahavi & Zahavi, 1997). Only a healthy, vigorous male has enough energy to make bright, colorful feathers (Blount, Metcalfe, Birkhead, & Surai, 2003; Faivre, Grégoire, Préault, Cézilly, & Sorci, 2003). Only a strong male can fly despite a long tail, and only a strong male

would risk predation by singing from an exposed perch. In effect a colorful, singing male is showing off: "Look at me! I am so healthy and vigorous that I can afford to take crazy risks and waste energy!" The female, we presume, does not understand why she is attracted to colorful, loud, active males. She just is because, throughout her evolutionary history, most females who chose such partners reproduced more successfully than those who chose dull-colored, less active males.

So it would seem, theoretically. The problem is that although a male's bright colors and vigorous singing do indicate health, his health depends more on his luck in finding a good feeding place than on his genes. The same is true for fish as well as birds (Brooks, 2000; Cunningham & Russell, 2000).

Possible Biological Value of Attractiveness: Humans

Although individual preferences vary somewhat, most people agree rather closely on which faces are attractive and which are not (Hönekopp, 2006). Are attractive people more likely than others to be healthy and fertile? Theoretically, they should be. Certainly, many illnesses decrease people's attractiveness. Also, *good-looking* generally means *normal*, and normal appearance probably indicates *good genes*. Suppose a computer takes photographs of many people and averages their faces. The resulting composite face has about an average nose, average distance between the eyes, and so forth, and most people rate this face "highly attractive" (Langlois & Roggman, 1990; Langlois, Roggman, & Musselman, 1994; Rhodes, Sumich, & Byatt, 1999) (see Figure 13.11). The average person may not be

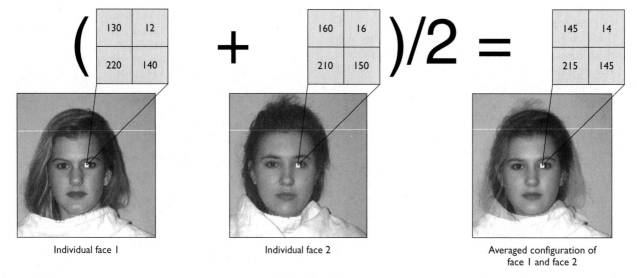

Individual face 1   Individual face 2   Averaged configuration of face 1 and face 2

FIGURE 13.11 A computer measured the gray value of each point on each picture. It then produced a new picture with the average of the grays at each point. This set of photos illustrates the procedure for two original faces. The numbers are for illustrative purposes only. Most people rate the resulting face as highly attractive. *(From Langlois, Roggman, & Musselman, 1994)*

highly attractive, but a highly attractive person has approximately average features. An attractive face has few irregularities—no crooked teeth, skin blemishes, or asymmetries, and no facial hair on women (Fink & Penton-Voak, 2002).

Why is normal attractive? One reason is that normal implies healthy. Presumably, the genes for an average face spread in the population because of their link to success. Any face far different from the average might indicate a genetic mutation. Another reason is that we like anything that is familiar. People tend to think "average-looking" dogs, birds, and wristwatches are attractive (Halberstadt & Rhodes, 2000). That evidence by itself is not convincing. For example, presumably the reason average-looking wristwatches look attractive is that manufacturers usually choose the most attractive design they can find for their products. More persuasive evidence is that if you have recently seen many faces that are thinner than usual, fatter than usual, or in some other way distorted, your judgment of "attractive" is shifted slightly in the direction of the faces you have just seen (Rhodes, Jeffery, Watson, Clifford, & Nakayama, 2003).

The best way to address this issue is to see whether attractive people tend to be healthier or more fertile than others. In one study researchers obtained photos of hundreds of teenagers from long ago. They asked other people to rate the faces for attractiveness, and they obtained medical records for the people in the photos. The ratings of attractiveness did not correlate reliably with health. People who were rated attractive were more likely to marry, and especially to marry early, but unattractive people who did marry were just as likely to have children as the more attractive people (Kalick, Zebrowitz, Langlois, &

Johnson, 1998). Evidently, at least for this sample, attractiveness did not predict health or fertility. Other studies have found a low but statistically reliable correlation between facial attractiveness and health for women, but not for men (Weeden & Sabini, 2005).

If facial attractiveness is a weak cue to health, what about the rest of the body? People with much abdominal fat are considered less attractive, and they tend to be less healthy (Weeden & Sabini, 2005). Theorists have proposed a more precise hypothesis, that men should prefer women with a narrow waist and wide hips—a waist-to-hip ratio of about 0.7—because medical researchers believe women with that ratio are most likely to be healthy and fertile. Examine the drawings of women's figures in Figure 13.12. Which one do you consider most attractive? Most people in the United States rate thinner women as the most attractive (Tassinary & Hansen, 1998). In non-Westernized cultures of Tanzania and southeastern Peru, most men regarded heavier women as the most attractive (Marlowe & Wetsman, 2001; Yu & Shepard, 1998). In short, preferences for female shape vary somewhat across cultures and do not necessarily match what researchers consider healthy or fertile.

Where do all these studies leave us? Theoretically, it would make sense for good appearance to represent "truthful advertising" of healthful genes. However, so far researchers have not found a strong link between good appearance and healthful genes. Still, even a weak relationship means something. An animal that wants to choose a partner can rely on appearance, which is probably a weak indicator of health and good genes, or on no information at all. We see how a preference for good appearance might have evolved.

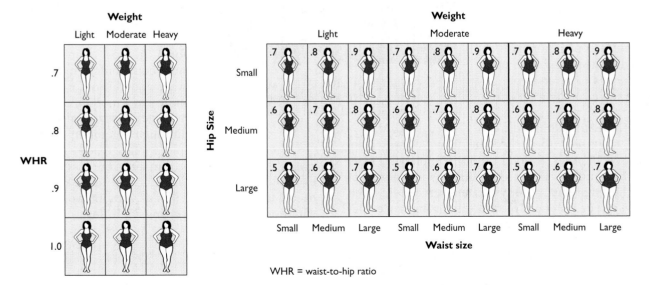

FIGURE 13.12 Which of these female figures do you find most attractive? Average ratings vary across cultures. *(From "A Critical Test of the Waist-to-Hip-Ratio Hypothesis of Female Physical Attractiveness" by L. G. Tassinary & K. A. Hansen, Psychological Science, 1998, 9, 150–155. Copyright © 1998 Blackwell Publishers. Reprinted by permission.)*

CONCEPT CHECK

23. According to the evolutionary theory, attractiveness is a sign of good health. Why would it be difficult for an unhealthy individual to produce "counterfeit" attractiveness? (Check your answer on page 516.)

Similarity

Although physical appearance is important, it is clearly not enough. You will find yourself physically attracted to many people who would be unsuitable as your long-term partner. As you get to know someone, your reaction to his or her personality alters your appraisal of physical attractiveness. That is, someone whom you come to respect and admire seems more attractive than before. Someone whom you find deceitful and cruel begins to look unattractive (Kniffin & Wilson, 2004).

Most romantic partners and close friends resemble each other in age, physical attractiveness, political and religious beliefs, intelligence, education, and attitudes (Laumann, 1969; Rushton & Bons, 2005). Similarity with someone helps counteract a negative first impression. Ordinarily, if you dislike someone at first, you avoid contact and therefore don't change your impression. However, if you have much in common, you accidentally encounter each other often enough to reverse your initial negative opinion (Denrell, 2005).

As a relationship between people matures, they become even more alike (Anderson, Keltner, & John, 2003). People who have much in common enjoy the relationship more because they share many activities and agree more often than disagree. Members of minority groups face special difficulties. If your ethnic or religious group is greatly outnumbered where you live, your choice of potential friends or romantic partners may be limited to members of your group who do not share your interests or members of other groups who do (Hamm, 2000).

Do you like people better when you learn that their beliefs and attitudes resemble yours? This ques-

Even when friends differ in some ways, they generally have much in common, such as interests, attitudes, and level of education.

tion is more complex than it sounds. You probably like most of the people you meet until you have a reason to alter your judgment. If you think at all about a new acquaintance's beliefs and attitudes, you probably assume that he or she shares your own beliefs and attitudes—because most people do, don't they? After all, you believe your opinions and actions are normal and correct (Alicke & Largo, 1995). Therefore, finding a disagreement with someone *lowers* your regard more than finding an agreement with someone *raises* your regard (Rosenbaum, 1986).

The Equity Principle

According to **exchange** or **equity theories,** *social relationships are transactions in which partners exchange goods and services.* In some cases the businesslike nature of a romantic relationship is unmistakable. In the Singles' Ads of many newspapers, people seeking a relationship describe what they have to offer and what they expect in return. Most people who describe themselves as attractive or wealthy describe high expectations for a mate. People who have less to offer make fewer demands (Waynforth & Dunbar, 1995).

As in business, a relationship is most stable if both partners believe the deal is fair. It is easiest to establish a fair deal if the partners are about equally attractive and intelligent, contribute about equally to the finances and the chores, and so forth. In most couples one partner contributes more in one way, and the other contributes more in another way. Those arrangements can also seem fair, although arguments do arise.

The equity principle applies readily in the early stages of friendships or romances but less so later. For example, you might nurse your spouse or lifelong friend through a long illness without worrying about whether you are still getting a fair deal.

CONCEPT CHECK

24. Someone your own age from another country moves next door. Neither of you speaks the other's language. What factors will tend to strengthen the likelihood of your becoming friends? What factors will tend to weaken it? (Check your answers on page 517.)

Special Concerns in Selecting a Mate

Choosing a partner for marriage or long-term partnership has special features because of the extra dimension of raising children. Yes, I know, not everyone wants to get married, not all married couples want children, and many unmarried people rear children. The following discussion does not apply to everyone— almost nothing in psychology does!—but it applies to those who hope to marry and have children.

Imagine that two people have expressed a desire to date you, and you have reason to believe the date could lead to a long-term relationship and eventual marriage. You have to choose between the two, and you cannot date both. Here are the choices for women: Man A is extraordinarily good-looking. He works as a waiter at a small restaurant and has no ambition to do anything more. Man B is about average looking. He patented an invention and sold it for a fortune. He was recently accepted to a prestigious medical school, and he is said to have an outstanding career ahead as a medical researcher.

The choices for men: Woman A is extraordinarily good-looking. She works as a waitress at a small restaurant and has no ambition to do anything more. Woman B is about average looking. She patented an invention and sold it for a fortune. She was recently accepted to a prestigious medical school, and she is said to have an outstanding career ahead as a medical researcher.

I have offered these choices to my own classes, and you probably can guess the results: Nearly all of the women chose man B. The men were divided, but most chose woman A. (Curiously, secret ballots gave different results from a show of hands, but the trend was in the same direction.)

The same trends occur in all cultures for which we have data (Buss, 2000). Both men and women prefer a physically attractive partner, if possible, but women have the additional concern of preferring a partner who can be a good provider. Most men are less concerned about a woman's potential job success.

Another trend found worldwide is that many men will accept almost any partner for a short-term sexual relationship, whereas most women either refuse a short-term sexual relationship or accept only a very appealing partner (Buss, 2000). Another is that men are more interested

in sexual variety. As shown in Figure 13.13, in all of the 52 nations that were surveyed, more men than women hoped for more than one sexual partner (Schmitt et al., 2003). Still another trend pertains to jealousy: In most cultures men insist that women be sexually faithful more than women require fidelity from men. In China men and women are equally insistent on the other's sexual fidelity, and in Sweden both seem equally tolerant of infidelity, but researchers have found no culture where women demand more fidelity from men than men demand from women (Buss, Larsen, Westen, & Semmelroth, 1992; Buunk, Angleitner, Oubaid, & Buss, 1996).

Those trends are well confirmed, but the explanation is not. One hypothesis is that we have evolved to act this way (Bjorklund & Shackelford, 1999; Buss, 2000; Gangestad, 2000; Geary, 2000). The argument

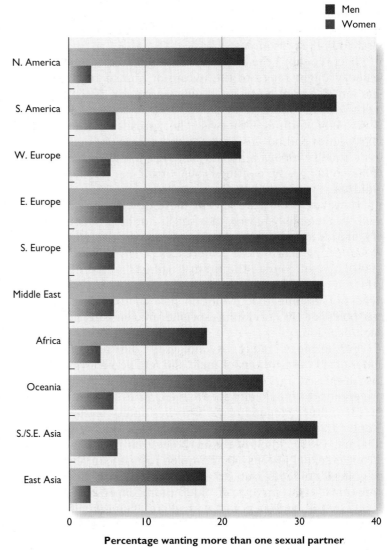

FIGURE 13.13 More than 16,000 people in 52 nations throughout the world were asked how many sexual partners they hoped to have in the next month. In all countries a higher percentage of men than women wanted more than one. *(Source: Based on data of Schmitt et al., 2003)*

goes as follows. First, consider short-term sexual relationships: A man who has a quick sexual relationship has some chance of spreading his genes if the woman becomes pregnant and manages to rear the child successfully. Therefore, a hypothetical gene that caused men to act this way would spread in the population. For a woman, having sex with many partners cannot give her more babies than sex with one partner. So a gene causing her to have sex with many partners would provide no advantage.

A man's other way of spreading his genes is to devote his energies to supporting one woman and her children (presumably his, too). However, this strategy succeeds only if the woman he marries is fertile. A young woman will be fertile for a long time, and an attractive woman is perhaps more likely to be fertile. So men increase their probable contribution to the gene pool if they marry young, attractive women. In contrast a woman can be less concerned about the age of her partner because men remain fertile into old age. However, she should prefer a man who can provide food and other resources.

Theoretically, the reported difference in sexual jealousy might relate to the nature of human reproduction. If a man mates with one woman for life and helps rear her children, he should make sure that she is sexually faithful. Otherwise, he spreads another man's genes and not his own. A woman does not need to be equally jealous if her husband has a brief sexual affair, so long as he continues supporting her and her children.

However, even if we accept these descriptions of male and female behavior, they might not be products of genetics and natural selection. An alternative view is that people learn these preferences (Eagly & Wood, 1999). Yes, of course, the brain is subject to natural selection just as much as any other organ, but we need not assume that evolution has micromanaged our behavior by developing specific mechanisms for each decision.

Furthermore, many psychologists question the generalized descriptions of male and female behavior just discussed. For example, the strength of women's preference for financially secure men varies from culture to culture, depending on women's ability to earn money and control resources of their own (Kasser & Sharma, 1999). Much of the evidence that men have stronger sexual jealousy than women rests on surveys of college students who are discussing hypothetical situations. Most surveys of older, more experienced people report that men and women are about equally angry over a partner's sexual infidelity and about equally hurt if a partner forms an emotional attachment to someone else (M. C. Green & Sabini, 2006).

Finally, is it really true that women gain nothing from having sex with multiple partners? Sarah Hrdy

(2000) has pointed out a number of potential benefits, including the following:

- Her husband might be infertile.
- Another man might have better genes than her husband and give her better children.
- The other man may provide her with additional resources and protection.
- If she has sex with many men, all of them may provide a modest amount of care and protection for her children.
- She might be able to "trade up," leaving her husband and joining the new partner.

A general point is that we cannot reconstruct the social life of our ancestors with great confidence. Mating customs vary from one human culture to another and even from one chimpanzee troop to another (Parish & deWaal, 2000). So reconstructing the evolution of human social behavior is uncertain. The case for evolutionary influence on mate choices would be stronger if someone found a gene that alters preferences. (For example, imagine a gene that caused men to prefer older women or women to prefer impoverished men.) Without evidence of genetic variation in mate choice, discussions of the evolution of social behavior remain speculative.

 CONCEPT CHECK

25. Suppose astronauts discover humanlike beings on another planet, whose biology and culture resemble ours except that all men have exactly the same wealth and women remain fertile all their lives instead of losing their fertility at menopause. What would an evolutionary theorist predict about the mate preferences of men and women on this planet? (Check your answer on page 517.)

Marriage

A couple that decides to marry pledges to stay together as long as they both shall live, but a distressing percentage of marriages end in divorce. What goes wrong?

Many couples date each other for a long time before exploring certain issues that become critical during a life together. Questionnaire studies have found that, as couples continue to date, their estimates of each other's interests, attitudes, sexual histories, and so forth become more *confident* without becoming more *accurate* (Swann & Gill, 1997). Answer the following questions, first for yourself and second *as you think your current dating partner would answer them.* (Several questions assume a heterosexual relationship; disregard any items that do not apply to you.)

1. After you marry or establish another long-term relationship, how often would you want to visit your parents? Your in-laws?
2. How many children do you want to have? How soon?
3. If you have children, should one partner stay home with the children while they are young? Should both partners share the responsibility for child care? Should the children be placed in a day-care center as soon as possible?
4. Suppose the two of you are offered good jobs in cities far apart. Neither of you can find a satisfactory job in the other's city. How would you decide where to live?
5. Suppose a sudden financial crisis strikes. Where would you cut expenses to balance the budget: Clothes? Food? Housing? Entertainment?
6. How often do you plan to attend religious services?
7. Where do you like to spend your vacations?
8. How often would you expect to spend an evening with friends, apart from your partner?

Were you uncertain about how your dating partner would answer any of these questions? If so, you are in the majority. Disagreements about such issues are common reasons for relationship conflicts. I do not suggest that you ask people to fill out this questionnaire on a first date. However, before you get far into a relationship, you should discuss anything that is important to you.

Sometimes, couples change in ways they could not have foreseen, but many breakups are predictable. First, people with a happy disposition are more likely to have successful marriages than people who are often unhappy (Lucas, 2005). Second, most couples who divorce have troubles with their relationship from the start. Psychologists studied recently married couples and related their observations to how the marriages developed later. In most cases a couple that divorced within 7 years showed mixed feelings and made frequent negative comments about each other, even early in their marriage. Any sign of contempt—such as rolling the eyes or being sarcastic—is a particularly bad sign. Apparently, they married in the hope of working out their problems, but matters just grew worse. Most couples who divorced after more than 7 years started on stronger terms and did not express hostility early in their marriage but also did not show as much love and affection as other couples whose marriages were going to last (Gottman, Coan, Carrere, & Swanson, 1998; Gottman & Levenson, 2000; Huston, Niehuis, & Smith, 2001).

Apparently, other subtle cues, hard to quantify, also distinguish successful from less successful marriages. In one fascinating study, various people watched 3-minute videotaped conversations between married couples and estimated how satisfied each couple was. Their estimates were then compared to reports by the couples themselves. People who reported that their own marriages were either highly satisfying or highly unsatisfying were the best at judging the quality of other couples' marriages. Marriage counselors and marriage researchers lagged behind, as did unmarried people (Ebling & Levenson, 2003).

Marriages That Last

When you hear about how many marriages end in divorce, it is easy to despair, but many marriages remain strong for a lifetime. Most characteristics of successful marriages are what you would probably expect (Howard & Dawes, 1976; Karney & Bradbury, 1995; Thornton, 1977). The following list is based on studies mainly in the United States in the late 20th century, so we do not know how they might differ for other times and places:

- The husband and wife have similar attitudes and personalities.
- They have sexual relations frequently and arguments infrequently.
- They have an adequate income.
- The husband has a good enough job to maintain self-respect.
- The wife was not pregnant before they married.
- The couple's parents also had successful marriages.

A successful marriage changes over the years, just as individual lives do. At first the couple has the intense excitement of learning about each other and do-

In a mature, lasting relationship, a couple can count on each other for care and affection through both good and bad times.

ing new things together. Sexual desire, romance, and friendship increase in parallel with one another. As the years pass, the physical desire tends to decline, but the companionship and friendship aspects of the relationship continue to increase (Berscheid, 1983; Gonzaga, Turner, Keltner, Campos, & Altemus, 2006).

Trying to Save a Marriage

Many couples with troubled marriages seek help from marriage counselors. Marriage counseling is more effective than no treatment at all on the average, but the amount of benefit is often disappointing (Shadish & Baldwin, 2005). One reason is that the fully open communication advocated by many counselors often backfires. "Open communication" sounds like a good thing, but venting hostile emotions toward your spouse is almost always harmful. The other person feels hurt and retaliates with equally insulting remarks (Fincham, 2003). If you have a complaint against your partner—an annoying habit, for example—yes, of course, you should state it. However, state it politely, not angrily. And if the other person expresses hostile emotions, you are better off if you restrain your reaction.

In several studies dating or married couples recorded their emotional reactions toward each other during a single conversation or on a daily basis; then each person reported what emotions they thought their partner had expressed. Happy couples expressed negative emotions only occasionally, and even then, the other usually did not notice it (Gable, Reis, & Downey, 2003; Simpson, Oriña, & Ickes, 2003). In other words successful couples limit both their expression and perception of negative emotions.

 CONCEPT CHECK

26. Why does the advice to "fully express your emotions" sometimes backfire in marriage counseling? (Check your answer on page 517.)

IN CLOSING

Choosing Your Partners Carefully

Few people enjoy living as a hermit, isolated from others. In prisons one of the harshest forms of punishment is solitary confinement. Almost any social contact is better than none at all. However, many people may choose their friends and their spouses poorly. In the second module of this chapter, we considered social perception—how we form impressions of other people. Finding friends and romantic partners is a

special case, where more is at stake, but the processes are the same. In some regards forming impressions of romantic partners is especially difficult. A person you date is probably trying to make a good impression, and you *hope* to like the person. As the relationship progresses, another factor kicks in: Remember from the section on persuasion that anyone you like tends to be highly persuasive. In short, it is easy to form an attachment and later regret it.

Life is like a roller-coaster ride in the dark: It has lots of ups and downs, and you never know what is going to happen next. Be sure you are riding with someone you like and trust. ∎

Summary

- *Forming relationships.* People generally choose friends and romantic partners who live near them and resemble them. Relationships are most likely to thrive if each person believes that he or she is getting about as good a deal as the other person is. (page 509)
- *Physical attractiveness.* In many nonhuman species, physical attractiveness is a reliable cue to the individual's health and therefore desirability as a mate. However, the relationship to genetics is unclear. In humans attractiveness is a powerful determinant of mate choice but only a weak predictor of health. (page 509)
- *Men's and women's preferences in marriage partners.* In every human culture, men prefer young, attractive women and women prefer men who are good providers. Evolutionary theorists believe humans evolved to have these preferences to improve chances of reproducing. However, it is also plausible that people learn these preferences. (page 513)
- *Marriage.* Marriage and similar relationships often break up because of problems that were present from the start. Marriages are successful when the partners have much in common and find ways to satisfy each other's needs. They are unsuccessful if the partners express too much hostility. (page 514)

Answers to Concept Checks

23. Attractive features such as bright feathers in a bird or large muscles in a man require much energy. It would be difficult for an unhealthy individual to devote enough energy to produce such features. (page 510)
24. Proximity and familiarity will strengthen the likelihood of your becoming friends. The similarity principle will weaken it. Because of the difference in languages, you will have little chance, at least at first, to discover any similarities in interests or

attitudes. In fact proximity will probably not be as potent a force as usual, because it serves largely as a means of enabling people to discover what they have in common. (page 509)

25. If all men are equally wealthy, women would select men on some other basis, such as appearance. If women's fertility lasts as late in life as men's does, then the men on this planet should not have a strong preference for younger women. (page 514)

26. If the spouses exchange hostile comments, their relationship deteriorates. Better advice would be to discuss complaints or difficulties calmly. (page 516)

Interpersonal Influence

- *How are we influenced by other people's actions or inactions?*

People influence us constantly. First, they provide us with *information* (or misinformation). For example, if you approach a building and find crowds quickly fleeing from it, they probably know something that you don't. Second, people set *norms* that define the expectations of a situation. For example, you learn rules of politeness, such as "do not interrupt," "raise your hand if you want to speak," and "wait in line." You are especially likely to imitate people whom you like, the ones you would like to resemble. Third, people influence us just by suggesting a possible action. Often, seeing people yawn makes you feel like yawning too. Why? They haven't given you any new information, and you don't necessarily wish to resemble them. You copy their yawn just because seeing a yawn suggested the possibility.

Conformity

Conformity means *maintaining or changing one's behavior to match the behavior or expectations of others.* The pressure to conform often exerts an overwhelming normative influence. For example, Koversada, Croatia, is a small nudist town (although people there sometimes dress for dinner at an elegant restaurant). If a first-time visitor walks around the city wearing clothes, other people stop and stare, shaking their heads with disapproval. The visitor feels as awkward and self-conscious as a naked person would be in a city of clothed people. Most visitors quickly undress (Newman, 1988).

If you exclaim, "I wouldn't conform," compare your own clothing right now to what others around you are wearing. Professors have sometimes noted the irony of watching a class full of students in blue jeans insisting that they do not conform to other people's style of dress (C. R. Snyder, 2003).

Conformity to an Obviously Wrong Majority

Early research suggested that we conform our opinions mostly in ambiguous situations where we are unsure of our own judgment (Sherif, 1935). Would we

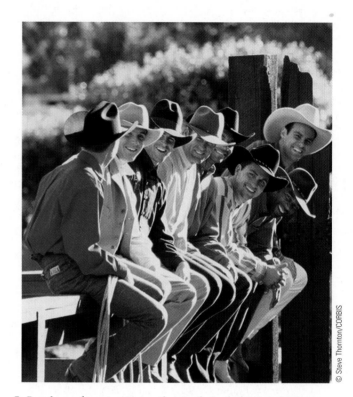

People conform to one another in their clothing and other customs.

also conform if we saw that everyone else was wrong? To answer that question, Solomon Asch (1951, 1956) conducted a now-famous series of experiments. He asked groups of students to look at a vertical bar, as shown in Figure 13.14, which was defined as the model. He showed them three other vertical bars (right half of Figure 13.14) and asked them which bar was the same length as the model. As you can see, the task is simple. Asch asked the students to give their

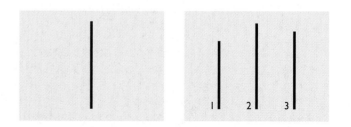

FIGURE 13.14 In Asch's conformity studies, a participant was asked which of three lines matched another line. Before answering, the participant heard other people answer incorrectly.

answers aloud. He repeated the procedure with 18 sets of bars.

Only one student in each group was a real participant. All the others were confederates who had been instructed to give incorrect answers on 12 of the 18 trials. Asch arranged for the real participant to be the next-to-last person in the group to announce his answer so that he would hear most of the confederates' incorrect responses before giving his own (Figure 13.15). Would he go along with the crowd?

FIGURE 13.15 Three of the participants in one of Asch's experiments on conformity. The one in the middle looking uncomfortable is the real participant. The others are the experimenter's confederates. *(From Asch, 1951)*

To Asch's surprise 37 of the 50 participants conformed to the majority at least once, and 14 conformed on most of the trials. When faced with a unanimous wrong answer by the other group members, the mean participant conformed on 4 of the 12 trials. Asch (1955) was disturbed by these results: "That we have found the tendency to conformity in our society so strong . . . is a matter of concern. It raises questions about our ways of education and about the values that guide our conduct" (p. 34).

Why did people conform so readily? When they were interviewed after the experiment, some said they thought the rest of the group was correct or they guessed that an optical illusion was influencing the appearance of the bars. Others said they knew their "conforming" answers were wrong but went along with the group for fear of ridicule. That is, they were subject to a normative influence even without any informational influence. The nonconformists were interesting too. Some were nervous but felt duty bound to say how the bars looked to them. A few seemed socially withdrawn. Still others were supremely self-confident, as if to say, "I'm right and everyone else is wrong. It happens all the time." Asch (1951, 1955) found that the amount of conforming influence depended on the size of the opposing majority. In a series of studies, he varied the number of confederates who gave incorrect answers from 1 to 15. He found that people conformed to a group of 3 or 4 just as readily as to a larger group (Figure 13.16). However, a

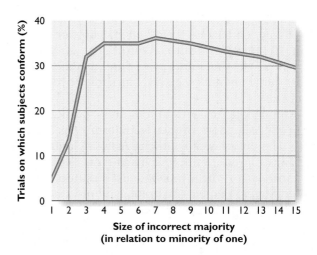

FIGURE 13.16 Asch found that conformity became more frequent as group size increased to about three, and then it leveled off. *(Adapted from "Opinion and Social Pressure" by Solomon Asch,* Scientific American, *November 1955. Copyright © 1955 by* Scientific American, Inc. *All rights reserved.)*

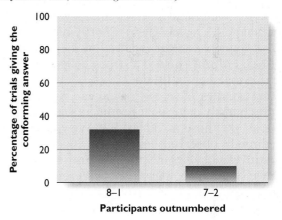

FIGURE 13.17 In Asch's experiments participants who were faced with a unanimous incorrect majority conformed on 32% of trials. Participants who had one "ally" giving the correct answer were less likely to conform.

participant conformed much less if he or she had an "ally." Being a minority of one is painful, but being in a minority of two is not as bad (Figure 13.17).

 CONCEPT CHECK

27. Are you more likely to conform to a group when you are outnumbered 5 to 1, 10 to 1, or 10 to 2? (Check your answer on page 525.)

Variation in Conformity

Over the years since Asch's experiments, many similar studies have been conducted. In the United States, most studies show a decrease in the amount of conformity since the 1950s. In most Asian countries, the percentage of conforming answers tends to be relatively high, partly because people are trying to be polite and not embarrass the others by pointing out their error (R. Bond & Smith, 1996). That is, when researchers use the same procedure in different cultures, they may not be testing the same psychological processes.

Are people in certain cultures, particularly in southern Asia, more prone to conformity as a general rule? The cultures of southern Asia, including China and Japan, are often described as more "collectivist" in contrast to the "individualist" cultures of the United States, Canada, Australia, and most of Europe. According to this view, Western culture encourages originality, competition, and individual freedom, whereas Eastern culture favors subordination of the individual to the welfare of the family or society. Originally, this contrast was based on observations of the Japanese during and shortly after World War II. However, Japan is a far different place today from what it was then. Acting collectively is a common response of any country when under attack or recovering from attack (Takano & Osaka, 1999). Shortly after terrorists crashed four passenger planes on September 11, 2001, U.S. citizens showed a strong collectivist "we're all in this together" attitude.

Many studies have contrasted Japanese and U.S. attitudes, mostly using college students and relying on questions like those in Table 13.3. A few investigators have directly observed conformist, cooperative, and competitive behaviors in various countries. Most studies have found no significant difference between Japanese and American attitudes, and some have even found Japanese students slightly *more* individu-

TABLE 13.3 Examples of Questions to Measure Collectivist Versus Individualist Attitudes

T	F	I take pride in accomplishing what no one else can accomplish.
T	F	It is important to me that I perform better than others on a task.
T	F	I am unique—different from others in many respects.
T	F	I like my privacy.
T	F	To understand who I am, you must see me with members of my group.
T	F	I would help, within my means, if a relative were in financial difficulty.
T	F	Before making a decision, I always consult with others.
T	F	I have respect for the authority figures with whom I interact.

Note: The first four items measure individualism; the second four measure collectivist attitudes.
Source: From Oyserman, Coon, & Kemmelmeier, 2002.

alistic than Americans (M. H. Bond, 2002; Oyserman, Coon, & Kemmelmeier, 2002; Takano & Osaka, 1999).

Some researchers therefore suggest that the "collectivist" notion is wrong, at least with regard to modern-day Japan (Takano & Osaka, 1999). Others point out that each country has multiple subcultures, and no generalization holds for an entire country (A. P. Fiske, 2002). Also, we need to measure collectivism or individualism more carefully and distinguish different aspects of each (M. H. Bond, 2002). For example, you can probably find fault with some of the items in Table 13.3. In any case we should avoid the generalization that all Asian cultures tend to be collectivist or conformist.

CONCEPT CHECK

28. What is one possible explanation for why collectivism may have been a more prominent aspect of Japanese thinking in the past than it is today? (Check your answer on page 525.)

Obedience to Authority

Ordinarily, if someone ordered you to hurt another person, you would refuse. However, certain situations exert a powerful pressure.

Decades ago, psychologist Philip Zimbardo and his colleagues paid college students to play the roles of guards and prisoners for 2 weeks during a vacation period. The researchers set up the basement of a university building as a prison but gave the students only minimal instructions on how to conduct themselves. Within 6 days the researchers had to cancel the study because many of "guards" were physically and emotionally bullying the "prisoners" (Haney, Banks, & Zimbardo, 1973). Why? None of the students were habitually cruel in everyday life. However, in this situation they could get away with cruelty without any penalties or retaliation. Also, they presumably inferred that cruelty was expected. After all, what would be the point of "playing prison" for 2 weeks while behaving politely?

Although we should beware of drawing too broad a conclusion from this single study, as the results would differ with changes in instructions or procedure, we can see parallels in real life. In 2003 American soldiers admitted brutally degrading Iraqi prisoners at the Abu Ghraib prison. Early speculation attributed their actions to "a few bad apples" among the soldiers. Later, it became apparent that none of them were habitually cruel. They were ill-trained as prison guards, lightly supervised, under constant stress and discomfort, and in almost constant danger.

Further, they had the usual military custom of obedience to authority and conformity to their peers. No one can excuse their terrible actions, but the actions probably stemmed more from the evil situation than from inherently evil people (S. T. Fiske, Harris, & Cuddy, 2004).

CRITICAL THINKING
WHAT'S THE EVIDENCE?

The Milgram Experiment

A more extensive series of studies examined how people would react if an experimenter asked them to deliver shocks to another person, starting with weak shocks and progressing to stronger ones. At what point, if any, would they refuse? This research by Stanley Milgram (1974) was inspired by reports of atrocities in the Nazi concentration camps during World War II. People who had committed the atrocities defended themselves by saying that they were only obeying orders. International courts rejected that defense, and outraged people throughout the world told themselves, "If I had been there, I would have refused to follow such orders" and "It couldn't happen here."

What do you think? Could it happen here?

Hypothesis. When an authority figure gives normal people instructions to do something that might hurt another person, some of them will obey.

Method. Two adult male participants arrived at the experimental room—the real participant and a confederate of the experimenter pretending to be a participant. They were not college students. The experimenters wanted results that would generalize to a broad population. They also wanted to minimize the risk that the participants would suspect the true purpose of the experiment. The experimenter told the participants that in this study on learning, one participant would be the "teacher" and the other the "learner." The teacher would read lists of words through a microphone to the learner, who would sit in a nearby room. The teacher would then test the learner's memory for the words. Whenever the learner made a mistake, the teacher was to deliver an electric shock as punishment.

The experiment was rigged so that the real participant was always the teacher and the confederate was always the learner. The teacher watched as the learner was strapped into the escape-proof shock device (Figure 13.18). The learner never received any shocks, but the teacher was led to believe that he did. In fact, be-

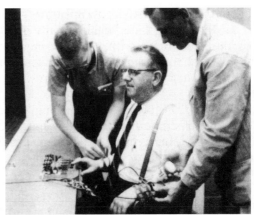

FIGURE 13.18 In Milgram's experiment a rigged selection chose a confederate of the experimenter to be the "learner." Here the learner is strapped to a device that supposedly delivers shocks.

fore the start of the study, the experimenter had the teacher feel a sample shock from the machine.

At the start of the experiment, the teacher read the words and the learner made many mistakes. The teacher operated a shock generator with levers to deliver shocks ranging from 15 volts to 450 volts in 15-volt increments (Figure 13.19). The experimenter instructed the teacher to begin by punishing the learner with the 15-volt switch for his first mistake and increase by 15 volts for each successive mistake.

As the voltage went up, the learner in the next room cried out in pain and kicked the wall. In one version of the experiment, the learner complained that he had a heart condition. If a teacher asked who would take responsibility for any harm done to the learner, the experimenter replied that he, the experimenter, would take responsibility but insisted, "while the shocks may be painful, they are not dangerous." When the shocks reached 150 volts, the learner called out in pain and begged to

FIGURE 13.19 The "teacher" in Milgram's experiment flipped switches on this box, apparently delivering stronger and stronger shocks for each successive error that the "learner" made. Although the device looked realistic, it did not actually shock the learner.

be let out of the experiment, complaining that his heart was bothering him. Beginning at 270 volts, he responded to shocks with agonized screams. At 300 volts he shouted that he would no longer answer any questions. After 330 volts he made no response at all. Still, the experimenter ordered the teacher to continue asking questions and delivering shocks. Remember, the learner was not really being shocked. The screams of pain came from a tape recording.

Results. Of 40 participants, 25 delivered shocks all the way to 450 volts. Most of those who quit did so fairly early. Anyone who continued beyond 330 volts persisted all the way to 450. Those who delivered the maximum shock were not sadists but normal adults recruited from the community through newspaper ads. They were paid a few dollars for their services, and those who asked were told that they could keep the money even if they quit. (Not many asked.) People from all walks of life obeyed the experimenter's orders, including blue-collar workers, white-collar workers, and professionals. Most of them grew upset and agitated while they were supposedly delivering shocks to the screaming learner.

Interpretation. The level of obedience Milgram observed depended on certain factors of the situation. One was that the experimenter agreed to take responsibility. (Remember the diffusion of responsibility principle.) Another influence was that the experimenter started with a small request, asking the participant to press the lever for a 15-volt shock, and then gradually progress to stronger shocks.

Figures 13.20 and 13.21 illustrate the results of some variations in procedure. Participants

© Stanley Milgram, from the 1965 film "Obedience," distributed by Pennsylvania State University Audio Visual Services

FIGURE 13.20 In one variation of the standard procedure, the experimenter asked the teacher to hold the learner's hand on the shock electrode. This close contact with the learner decreased obedience to less than half its usual level. *(From Milgram's 1965 film,* Obedience*)*

were more obedient to an experimenter who remained in the same room than to one who left. They were less obedient if they needed to force the learner's hand back onto the shock plate. If additional "teachers" divided the task—the other "teachers" being confederates of the experimenter—a participant was likely to obey if the others obeyed, but unlikely if the others did not.

Still, the remarkable conclusion remains that, under a variety of conditions, many normal people followed orders from an experimenter they had just met, even though they thought they might hurt or even kill someone. Imagine how much stronger the pressure to obey orders from a government or military leader would be.

Ethical Issues. Milgram's experiment told us something about ourselves that we did not want to hear. No longer could we say, "What happened in Nazi Germany could never happen here." We found that most of us do follow orders, even offensive ones. We are indebted to Milgram's study for this important, if unwelcome, information.

However, although I am glad to know about Milgram's results, I doubt that I would have enjoyed participating in his experiment. Most people were emotionally drained, and some were visibly upset to discover how readily they had obeyed orders to deliver dangerous shocks to another person.

Milgram's study prompted psychology researchers to establish clear rules about what an experimenter can ethically ask someone to do. Today, before the start of any psychological experiment—even the simplest and most innocuous—the experimenter must submit a plan to an institutional committee that can approve or reject the ethics of the experiment.

If anyone today submitted a proposal to conduct research similar to Milgram's study, the local institutional committee would presumably refuse permission or require changes in procedure. However, if the same rules had been in place *at the time* of Milgram's study, a committee might not have objected. Before the research almost no one expected his results to turn out as they did. Milgram asked various psychologists and psychiatrists to predict the results, and nearly all replied that only a rare psychopathic weirdo would press levers to deliver severe shocks. The distress experienced by so many participants underscores just how surprising Milgram's results were.

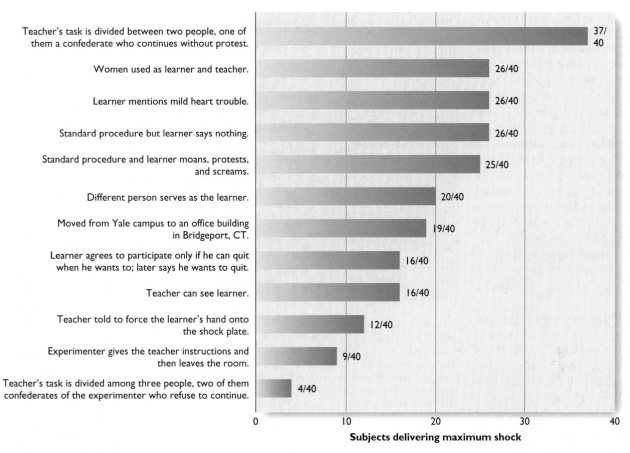

FIGURE 13.21 Milgram varied his procedure in many ways. Division of responsibility increased obedience. An implication of personal responsibility decreased obedience.

CONCEPT CHECK

29. In what way did the obedience in Milgram's experiment resemble the foot-in-the-door procedure? How did it resemble Skinner's shaping procedure? (Check your answers on page 525.)

CRITICAL THINKING

A STEP FURTHER

Modifying Obedience

Here is one version of the experiment that Milgram never tried: At the start of the experiment, we announce that the teacher and the learner will trade places halfway through the experiment so that the previous learner will start delivering shocks to the teacher. How do you think the teachers would behave then? What other changes in procedure can you imagine that might influence the degree of obedience?

Group Decision Making

An organization that needs to reach a decision often sets up a committee to consider the issues and make recommendations. A committee has more time, more information, and fewer peculiarities than any individual has. Research finds that a group generally makes better decisions than the average individual. However, the advantage of a group over an individual is often not as great as we might expect (Sorkin, Hays, & West, 2001). Groups sometimes rush to a decision, and many groups show social loafing. Some individuals conform to the majority opinion and discard their own, possibly better, opinions.

Group Polarization

If nearly all the people who compose a group lean in the same direction on a particular issue, then a group discussion will move the group as a whole even further in that direction. This phenomenon is known as **group polarization**. Note that it requires a fairly homogeneous group. If the group has several disagreeing factions, the trends are less predictable (Rodrigo & Ato, 2002).

The term *polarization* does not mean that the group breaks up into fragments favoring different positions. Rather, it means that the members of a group move *together* toward one pole (extreme position) or the other. For example, a group of people who are opposed to abortion or in favor of animal rights or opposed to gun regulations will, after discussing the issue among themselves, generally become more extreme in their views than they had been at the start (Lamm & Myers, 1978).

Group polarization demonstrates both informational and normative influences (Isenberg, 1986). During the discussion, if most of the members were already leaning in the same direction, they hear new arguments favoring that side of the issue and few or none for the opposition (Kuhn & Lao, 1996). Also, as the members of the group become aware of the consensus during the discussion, the pressure to conform is especially powerful for those who do not feel fully accepted by the group (Noel, Wann, & Branscombe, 1995).

Many organizations try to resist the tendency toward groupthink, which stifles dissenting views. During the Renaissance European kings sometimes called on a "fool" (or court jester) to describe some proposal in a fresh and possibly amusing light. In a court composed largely of yes-men, the fool was the only one who could point out the folly of a proposed action without fear of reprisals.

  CONCEPT CHECK

30. Is a jury more likely to reach a biased or extreme decision than a single individual would be? (Check your answer on page 525.)

Groupthink

An extreme form of group polarization, known as groupthink, occurs when *the members of a group suppress their doubts about a group's decision for fear of making a bad impression or disrupting group harmony* (Janis, 1972, 1985). The main elements leading to groupthink are overconfidence by the leadership, underestimation of the problems, and pressure to conform. Sometimes, dissenters conform on their own, and sometimes, the leadership actively urges them to conform.

A dramatic example of groupthink led to the Bay of Pigs fiasco of 1962. President John F. Kennedy and his advisers were considering a plan to support a small-scale invasion of Cuba at the Bay of Pigs. They assumed that a small group of Cuban exiles could overwhelm the Cuban army and trigger a spontaneous rebellion of the Cuban people against their government. Most of the advisers who doubted this assumption kept quiet. The one who did express doubts was told that he should loyally support the president. Within a few hours after the invasion began, all the invaders were killed or captured. The decision makers then wondered how they could have made such a stupid decision.

Groupthink often occurs in business decisions, especially in highly prosperous and successful companies. The leaders become overconfident and their critics become hesitant to speak up. For example, after British Airways discovered that 60% of its passengers were non-British, its leaders decided to remove the British flag from the tailfins of the planes. This decision not only angered the British public but also outraged the employees who resented what seemed a pointless expense of £60 million to change the company's logo while the company was firing workers to save costs (Eaton, 2001).

Groupthink is not easy to avoid. We generally admire government or business leaders who are decisive and confident. Groupthink occurs when they become *too* decisive and confident, failing to consider all the risks. One strategy is for a leader to consult with advisers individually so they are not influenced by what they hear other advisers saying. A message for all of us is to be concerned when anyone in power seems too sure of success.

IN CLOSING

Fix the Situation, Not Human Nature

If we want to prevent people from panicking when a fire breaks out in a crowded theater, the best solution is to build more exits. Similarly, it is difficult to teach people to behave ethically or intelligently when they are under strong pressure to conform. For example, the more shocks you have already given someone in Milgram's obedience study, the harder it is to quit. In a group where everyone else seems united behind the leader's decision, it is hard to speak up in opposition. To avoid the temptation to make bad decisions, we need to choose our situations carefully. ▊

Summary

- *Social influence.* People influence our behavior by offering information and by setting norms of expected conduct. We also follow others' examples just because they suggested a possible action. (page 518)
- *Conformity.* Many people conform to the majority view even when they are confident that the majority is wrong. An individual is as likely to conform to a group of three as to a larger group, but an individual with an ally is less likely to conform. (page 518)
- *Cultural differences.* Although some cultures tend to be more collectivist or conforming than others, it is an overgeneralization to regard all Asian cultures as collectivist or to assume that all members of a society are equally collectivist. (page 519)
- *Obedience.* In Milgram's obedience study, many people followed directions in which they thought they were delivering painful shocks to another person. (page 521)
- *Group polarization.* Groups of people who lean mostly in the same direction on a given issue often make more extreme decisions than most people would have made on their own. (page 523)

- *Groupthink.* Groupthink occurs when members of a cohesive group fail to express their opposition to a decision for fear of making a bad impression or harming the cohesive spirit of the group. (page 524)

Answers to Concept Checks

27. You would be about equally likely to conform when outnumbered 5 to 1 or 10 to 1. Any group of 3 or more produces about the same urge to conform. However, having even one ally decreases the pressure, so you would be less likely to conform when outnumbered 10 to 2. (page 519)
28. During and shortly after World War II, the people of Japan were under attack or recovering from attack. In that situation people of any country are motivated to work collectively. (page 520)
29. As with the foot-in-the-door procedure, Milgram started with a small request (give a small shock) and then built up. Skinner's shaping procedure also starts with an easy task and then builds to something more difficult. (page 521)
30. It depends. Group polarization would probably move a nearly unanimous jury toward a unanimous verdict. However, a jury that starts out divided would not experience group polarization. Most research has found that juries and similar groups are no more extreme than the average individual (Kerr, MacCoun, & Kramer, 1996). (page 523)

CHAPTER ENDING

Key Terms and Activities

Key Terms

You can check the page listed for a complete description of a term. You can also check the glossary/index at the end of the text for a definition of a given term, or you can download a list of all the terms and their definitions for any chapter at this website:

www.thomsonedu.com/ psychology/kalat

actor-observer effect (page 496)
altruistic behavior (page 479)
ambivalent sexism (page 490)
attitude (page 499)
attribution (page 493)
aversive racism (page 490)
bait-and-switch technique (page 505)
bona fide pipeline (page 492)
central route to persuasion (page 501)
cognitive dissonance (page 500)

conformity (page 518)
consensus information (page 493)
consistency information (page 493)
diffusion of responsibility (page 482)
discrimination (page 490)
distinctiveness (page 493)
door-in-the-face technique (page 505)
exchange (or equity) theories (page 512)
external attribution (page 493)
foot-in-the-door technique (page 504)
forewarning effect (page 504)
fundamental attribution error (page 494)
group polarization (page 523)
groupthink (page 524)
Implicit Association Test (page 491)
inoculation effect (page 504)
internal attribution (page 493)

mere exposure effect (page 509)
moral dilemma (page 484)
peripheral route to persuasion (page 501)
pluralistic ignorance (page 483)
prejudice (page 490)
primacy effect (page 488)
prisoner's dilemma (page 480)
proximity (page 509)
self-fulfilling prophecy (page 488)
self-handicapping strategies (page 496)
self-serving biases (page 496)
sleeper effect (page 502)
social loafing (page 483)
social perception and cognition (page 488)
social psychologists (page 478)
stereotypes (page 489)
that's-not-all technique (page 505)

Suggestions for Further Reading

Cialdini, R. B. (1993). *Influence: Science and practice* (Rev. ed.). New York: William Morrow. One of the most enjoyable books in psychology, this would be suitable for vacation reading.

Milgram, S. (1975). *Obedience to authority.* New York: Harper & Row. Describes Milgram's classic experiments on obedience.

Web/Technology Resources

Student Companion Website

www.thomsonedu.com/psychology/kalat

Explore the Student Companion Website for Online Try-It-Yourself activities, practice quizzes, flashcards, and more! The companion site also has direct links to the following websites.

Social Psychology Network

www.socialpsychology.org/

This huge database includes more than 13,000 links to resources about social behavior.

Prisoner's Dilemma

serendip.brynmawr.edu/bb/pd.html

Play the prisoner's dilemma game with a computer opponent. Try different strategies to see which works best.

Implicit Association Test

https://implicit.harvard.edu/implicit/demo/

Test your own responses on the Implicit Association Test.

For Additional Study

Kalat Premium Website

http://www.thomsonedu.com

For Critical Thinking Videos and additional Online Try-It-Yourself activities, go to this site to enter or purchase your code for the Kalat Premium Website.

ThomsonNOW!

http://www.thomsonedu.com

Go to this site for the link to ThomsonNOW, your one-stop study shop. Take a Pretest for this chapter, and Thomson-NOW will generate a personalized Study Plan based on your test results. The Study Plan will identify the topics you need to review and direct you to online resources to help you master those topics. You can then take a Posttest to help you determine the concepts you have mastered and what you still need to work on.

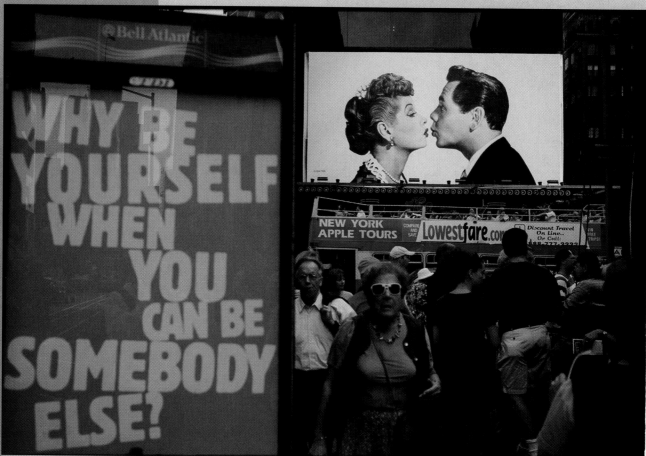

Personality

© AP/Wide World Photos

This three-dimensional jigsaw puzzle of the ocean liner Titanic consists of 26,000 pieces. Understanding personality is an even more complex puzzle.

everal thousand people have the task of assembling the world's largest jigsaw puzzle, which contains more than a trillion pieces. Connie Conclusionjumper scrutinizes 20 pieces, stares off into space, and announces, "When the puzzle is fully assembled, it will be a picture of the Sydney Opera House!" Prudence Plodder says, "Well, I don't know what the whole puzzle will look like, but I think I've found two little pieces that fit together."

Which of the two has made the greater contribution to completing the puzzle? We could argue either way. Clearly, the task requires an enormous number of little, unglamorous accomplishments like Prudence's. But if Connie is right, her flash of insight will be extremely valuable for assembling all the pieces. Of course, if the puzzle turns out to be a picture of a sailboat at sunset, then Connie will have misled us and wasted our time.

Some psychologists have offered grand theories about the nature of personality. Others have tried to classify personality types and understand why people act differently in specific situations. In this chapter we explore several methods of approaching personality ranging from large-scale theories to small-scale descriptions. In the first module, we consider some famous personality theorists, including Sigmund Freud. The second module concerns descriptions of personality. Any description is, of course, a theory, but it differs from the kinds of theories in the first module. The final module describes measurements of personality.

Personality Theories

• *How can we best describe the overall structure of personality?*

> Every individual is virtually an enemy of civilization. . . . Thus civilization has to be defended against the individual. . . . For the masses are lazy and unintelligent . . . and the individuals composing them support one another in giving free rein to their indiscipline.
>
> —Sigmund Freud (1927/1961)

> It has been my experience that persons have a basically positive direction. In my deepest contacts with individuals in therapy, even those whose troubles are most disturbing, whose behavior has been most antisocial, whose feelings seem most abnormal, I find this to be true.
>
> —Carl Rogers (1961)

What is human nature? The 17th-century philosopher Thomas Hobbes argued that humans are by nature selfish. Life in a state of nature, he said, is "nasty, brutish, and short." We need the government to protect ourselves from one another. The 18th-century political philosopher Jean-Jacques Rousseau disagreed, maintaining that people are naturally good and that governments are the problem, not the solution. Rational people acting freely, he maintained, would advance the welfare of all.

The debate between those two viewpoints survives in theories of personality (Figure 14.1). Sigmund Freud held that people are born with sexual and destructive impulses that must be held in check if civilization is to survive. Carl Rogers believed that people

seek good and noble goals after they have been freed from unnecessary restraints.

Which point of view is correct? Way down deep, are we good, bad, both, or neither? We cannot expect a firm scientific answer, but psychologists have developed many approaches to exploring personality.

The term *personality* comes from the Latin word *persona*, meaning "mask." In the plays of ancient Greece and Rome, actors wore masks to indicate their characters. Unlike a mask, however, the term *personality* implies something stable. **Personality** consists of *all the consistent ways in which the behavior of one person differs from that of others, especially in social situations.* (Differences in learning, memory, sensation, or muscle control are generally not considered personality.)

In this module we concentrate largely on the theory of Sigmund Freud, which has been so influential outside psychology as well as within. You should evaluate it carefully before you decide how seriously to take it.

Sigmund Freud and the Psychodynamic Approach

Sigmund Freud (1856–1939), an Austrian physician, developed the first psychodynamic theory. *A psychodynamic theory relates personality to the interplay of conflicting forces within the individual, including un-*

Hobbes	Rousseau
Government is required for protection	Humans are good
Humans are selfish	Government is a corrupting influence
Freud	**Rogers**
Natural impulses are detrimental to society	Natural impulses are noble and good

FIGURE 14.1 Sigmund Freud, like the philosopher Thomas Hobbes, stressed the more destructive aspects of human nature. Carl Rogers, like Jean-Jacques Rousseau, emphasized the more favorable aspects.

▌ Sigmund Freud interpreted dreams, slips of the tongue, and so forth to infer unconscious thoughts and motivations. Most researchers today, however, are skeptical of Freud's interpretations.

conscious ones. That is, we are being pushed and pulled by internal forces that we do not fully understand.

Freud's influence extends into sociology, literature, art, religion, and politics. And yet, here we are, more than three fourths of the way through this text on psychology, and until now I have barely mentioned Freud. Why?

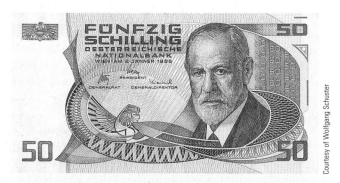

▌ The fame of Sigmund Freud far exceeds that of any other psychologist. His picture has even appeared on the Austrian 50-schilling bill and bimetal millennial coin.

The reason is that Freud's influence within psychology has declined substantially. According to one psychologist, Frederick Crews (1996, p. 63), "independent studies have begun to converge toward a verdict that was once considered a sign of extremism or even of neurosis: that there is literally nothing to be said, scientifically or therapeutically, to the advantage of the entire Freudian system or any of its constituent dogmas." Think about that: *nothing* to be said in favor of *any* of Freud's theories. Needless to say, not everyone agrees with that statement. Still, the decline of Freud's influence is striking.

Freud's Search for the Unconscious

Freud would have preferred to be a professor of cultural history or anthropology. In Austria at the time, however, universities offered few positions to Jews. The only professions readily open to him were law, business, and medicine. Freud chose medicine, but his interests within medicine were highly theoretical.

Early in his career, Freud worked with the psychiatrist Josef Breuer, who was treating a young woman

with a fluctuating variety of physical complaints. As she talked with Breuer about her past, she remembered various emotionally traumatic experiences. Breuer, and later Freud also, said that remembering these experiences produced **catharsis,** *a release of pent-up emotional tension,* thereby relieving her illness. However, later scholars who reexamined the medical records found that this woman who was so central to the history of psychoanalysis showed little or no benefit from the treatment (Ellenberger, 1972).

Regardless of whether the "talking cure" had been successful, Freud began applying it to other patients. He referred to *his method of explaining and dealing with personality, based on the interplay of conscious and unconscious forces,* as **psychoanalysis.** To this day psychoanalysts remain loyal to some version of Freud's methods and theories, although their views have of course developed over the decades.

Psychoanalysis started as a simple theory: Each of us has an unconscious mind and a conscious mind (Figure 14.2). The **unconscious** is *the repository of memories, emotions, and thoughts, many of them illogical, that affect our behavior even though we cannot talk about them.* Traumatic experiences force thoughts and emotions into the unconscious (theoretically). The goal of psychoanalysts is to bring those memories back to consciousness, producing catharsis and enabling the person to overcome irrational impulses.

As Freud listened to his patients, however, he became convinced that the traumatic events they recalled could not account for their abnormal behavior. Some patients reacted strongly to events that others took in stride. Why? At first, in the early 1890s, Freud attributed their overreactions to sexual difficulties

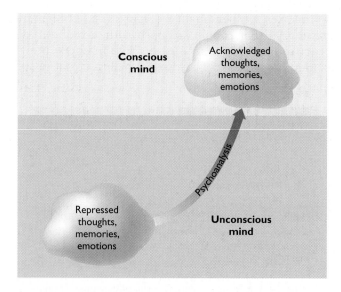

FIGURE 14.2 Freud believed that psychoanalysis could bring parts of the unconscious into the conscious mind, where the client could deal with them.

(Macmillan, 1997). For a while Freud recommended increased sexual activity as a cure for certain kinds of anxiety disorders. In contrast people suffering from nervous exhaustion, he said, were suffering from the results of masturbation. His evidence for this idea was that all his patients who were suffering from nervous exhaustion had masturbated (!). You can see the problem with this evidence.

A few years later, however, Freud abandoned these hypotheses and suggested instead that the ultimate cause of psychological disorders was traumatic childhood sexual experiences, either seduction by other children or sexual abuse by adults. Freud's patients did not report any such memories, but Freud put together parts of the patients' dream reports, slips of the tongue, and so forth and claimed that they pointed to early sexual abuse.

At this point Freud's problems with evidence became serious. His ideas about inadequate sex or too much masturbation may have been wrong but at least they were testable. But how was anyone to determine whether the childhood events that Freud inferred had actually happened?

A few years later, he abandoned the idea that psychological disorders resulted from childhood sexual abuse. According to Freud's own description of these events, he decided that his patients had "misled" him into believing they were sexually abused in early childhood, whereas in fact, Freud said, their claims were wishes and fantasies (Freud, 1925). Why did Freud abandon his early theory? According to one view (Masson, 1984), Freud simply lost the courage to defend his theory. According to other scholars, however, Freud never had any evidence for it (Esterson, 2001; Powell & Boer, 1994; Schatzman, 1992). Freud had inferred his patients' sexual abuse from their symptoms and dreams despite their own denials of abuse. It was hardly fair, therefore, to complain that the patients had misled him into believing they had been abused.

When he abandoned his ideas about early sexual abuse, he replaced them with theories about early sexual fantasies—which were even harder to test scientifically. Although he did not fully develop his views of girls' early sexual development, he was explicit about boys: During early childhood every boy goes through an **Oedipus complex**, *when he develops a sexual interest in his mother and competitive aggression toward his father.* (Oedipus—EHD-ah-puhs—in the ancient Greek play by Sophocles unknowingly murdered his father and married his mother.) Most boys negotiate through this stage and emerge with a healthy personality, but some have sexual fantasies that they fail to resolve, leading to long-term personality difficulties.

What evidence did he have for this view? Again, he had none. He reconsidered the same statements his patients made to him earlier and reinterpreted them. Just as his patients denied having been sexually abused in childhood, they also denied what he inferred about their childhood sexual fantasies. Freud considered his patients' protests to be signs of emotional resistance and therefore confirmation that his interpretations were correct. Freud's main evidence for his interpretations was simply that he could construct a coherent story linking a patient's symptoms, dreams, and so forth to the sexual fantasies that Freud inferred (Esterson, 1993).

Consider another example of Freud's use of evidence: A patient described as "Dora" came to Freud at the insistence of her father. Since about age 8, Dora had suffered from headaches, coughing, and shortness of breath, all of which Freud interpreted as psychological in nature. She had also avoided a certain friend of her father, Mr. K, ever since she was 14, when he grabbed her and kissed her lips.

Freud wrote that Dora surely experienced sexual pleasure at this time because K's presumably erect penis must have rubbed up against her clitoris and excited it. Freud described Dora's disgust as "entirely and completely hysterical" (Freud, 1905/1963, p. 44). He then proceeded to try to trace Dora's behavior to her presumed love for both K and her father and her homosexual attraction to Mrs. K. As one reads Freud's elaborate discussion, one wonders what was wrong with Dora's simpler explanation—that she found the sexual advances of this middle-aged man repulsive.

Stages of Psychosexual Development in Freud's Theory of Personality

Right or wrong, Freud's theory is so well known that you should understand it. One of his central points was that psychosexual interest and pleasure begin in infancy. He used the term **psychosexual pleasure** broadly to include *all strong, pleasant excitement arising from body stimulation.* He maintained that how we deal with our psychosexual development influences nearly all aspects of our personality. According to Freud young children experience sexual pleasure not only from stimulation of the genitals but also from the mouth and anus.

According to Freud (1905/1925), people have a *psychosexual energy,* which he called **libido** (lih-BEE-doh), from a Latin word meaning "desire." Normally, libido is focused in an infant's mouth and flows to other body parts as the child grows older. Children go through five stages of psychosexual development, and each leaves its mark on the adult personality. If normal sexual development is blocked or frustrated at any stage, Freud said, part of the libido becomes **fixated** at that stage, and the person *continues to be pre-*

TABLE 14.1 Freud's Stages of Psychosexual Development

Stage (approximate ages)	Sexual Interests	Effects of Fixation at This Stage
Oral stage (birth to 1 year)	Sucking, swallowing, biting	Lasting concerns with dependence and independence; pleasure from eating, drinking, and other oral activities
Anal stage (1 to 3 years)	Expelling feces, retaining feces	Orderliness or sloppiness, stinginess or wastefulness, stubbornness
Phallic stage (3 to 5 or 6 years)	Touching penis or clitoris; Oedipus complex	Difficulty feeling closeness. Males: fear of castration Females: penis envy
Latent period (5 or 6 to puberty)	Sexual interests suppressed	—
Genital stage (puberty onward)	Sexual contact with other people	—

occupied *with the pleasure area associated with that stage.* Table 14.1 summarizes these stages.

The Oral Stage

In the **oral stage,** from birth to about age 2, *the infant derives intense psychosexual pleasure from stimulation of the mouth, particularly while sucking at the mother's breast.* According to Freud someone fixated at this stage continues to receive great pleasure from eating, drinking, and smoking and may also have lasting concerns with dependence and independence.

The Anal Stage

At about 2 years of age, children enter the **anal stage,** when *they get psychosexual pleasure from the sensations of bowel movements.* Someone fixated at this stage goes through life "holding things back"—being orderly, stingy, and stubborn—or less commonly, may go to the opposite extreme and become messy and wasteful.

The Phallic Stage

Beginning at about age 3, in the **phallic stage,** children begin to *play with their genitals* and according to Freud become sexually attracted to the opposite-sex parent. Freud claimed that boys are afraid of being castrated, whereas girls develop "penis envy." These ideas have always been controversial. Some girls report

fantasies about what it would be like to be a boy (Linday, 1994), but having a fantasy about being a boy is hardly the same as penis envy, and we have no evidence that such fantasies play a major role in personality development. Similarly, few boys show clear fears of castration.

The Latent Period

From about age 5 or 6 until adolescence, Freud said, most children enter a **latent period** in which they *suppress their psychosexual interest.* At this time they play mostly with peers of their own sex. The latent period is evidently a product of European culture and does not appear in all societies.

The Genital Stage

Beginning at puberty young people *take a strong sexual interest in other people.* This is known as the **genital stage.** According to Freud anyone who has fixated a great deal of libido in an earlier stage has little libido left for the genital stage. But people who have suc-

According to Freud, if normal sexual development is blocked at the oral stage, the child will seek pleasure from drinking and eating and later from kissing and smoking. Perhaps this smoker's mother weaned him too quickly—or let him nurse too long. Like most of Freud's ideas, this one is difficult to test.

cessfully negotiated the earlier stages can now derive primary satisfaction from sexual intercourse.

Evaluation of Freud's Stages

Freud's theory is vague and difficult to test (Grünbaum, 1986; Popper, 1986). When it has been tested, the results have been mostly inconclusive. For example, the characteristics of being orderly, stingy, and stubborn, which Freud described as due to anal fixation, correlate with one another, suggesting that they relate to a single personality trait. However, we have no evidence connecting them to toilet training (Fisher & Greenberg, 1977).

Freud's Description of the Structure of Personality

Personality, Freud claimed, consists of three aspects: id, ego, and superego. (Actually, he used German words that mean *it, I,* and *over-I.* A translator used Latin equivalents instead of English words.) The **id** consists of *all our biological drives,* such as sex and hunger, that demand immediate gratification. The **ego** is *the rational, decision-making aspect of the personality.* The **superego** contains *the memory of rules and prohibitions we learned from our parents and the rest of society,* such as, "Nice little boys and girls don't do that." Sometimes, the id produces sexual or other motivations that the superego considers repugnant, thus evoking feelings of guilt. However, most psychologists today find it difficult to imagine the mind in terms of three warring factions and therefore regard Freud's description as only a metaphor.

 CONCEPT CHECK

1. If someone has persistent problems with independence and dependence, Freud would suggest a fixation at which psychosexual stage?
2. What kind of behavior would Freud expect of someone with a strong id and a weak superego? What behavior would Freud expect of someone

FIGURE 14.3 The ego, or "rational I," defends itself against anxiety, that apprehensive state named for the Latin word meaning "to strangle."

with an unusually strong superego? (Check your answers on page 544.)

Defense Mechanisms Against Anxiety

According to Freud *the ego defends itself against conflicts and anxieties by relegating unpleasant thoughts and impulses to the unconscious.* Among the **defense mechanisms** that the ego employs are repression, denial, rationalization, displacement, regression, projection, reaction formation, and sublimation (Figure 14.3). He saw these as normal processes that sometimes went to extremes. His daughter, Anna, developed and elaborated descriptions of these mechanisms.

Repression

The defense mechanism of **repression** is *motivated forgetting*—rejecting unacceptable thoughts, desires, and memories and banishing them to the unconscious. For example, someone sees a murder and later fails to remember it, or someone has an unacceptable sexual impulse and becomes unaware of it.

Researchers have struggled to find clear evidence of repression. As discussed in chapter 7, most people who endure miserable experiences remember them well, unless they were very young at the time. Laboratory investigators have exposed participants to unpleasant or threatening experiences in the expectation that repression would interfere with their memories. Even when people did forget, alternative explanations were available that did not include repression (Holmes, 1990). If repression occurs at all, it occurs rarely or under circumstances we have not yet specified.

Denial

The refusal to believe information that provokes anxiety ("This can't be happening") *is denial.* Whereas repression is the motivated forgetting of information, denial is an assertion that the information is incorrect. For example, someone with an alcohol problem may insist, "I'm not an alcoholic. I can take it or leave it." A patient who is told that he or she has a fatal illness may refuse to accept the diagnosis.

Rationalization

When people *attempt to prove that their actions are rational and justifiable and thus worthy of approval,* they are using **rationalization.** For example, a student who wants to go to the movies says, "More studying won't do me any good anyway." Someone who misses a deadline to apply for a job says, "I didn't really want that job."

Displacement

By diverting a behavior or thought away from its natural target toward a less threatening target, **displacement** lets people engage in the behavior with less anxiety. For example, someone who is angry with a boss or professor might yell at someone who seems less dangerous.

Regression

A *return to a more immature level of functioning,* **regression** is an effort to avoid the anxiety of facing one's current role in life. By adopting a childish role, a person can escape responsibility and return to an earlier, perhaps more secure, way of life. For example, after a new sibling is born, an older child may cry or pout. An adult who has just gone through a divorce or business loss may move in with his or her parents.

Projection

The attribution of one's own undesirable characteristics to other people is known as **projection.** In theory suggesting that other people have those faults might make the faults seem less threatening. For example, someone who secretly enjoys pornography might accuse other people of enjoying it. However, the research finds that people using projection do not ordinarily decrease their anxiety or their awareness of their own faults (Holmes, 1978; Sherwood, 1981). If so, projection is not an effective defense.

Reaction Formation

To keep undesirable characteristics repressed, people may use **reaction formation** to *present themselves as the opposite of what they really are to hide the unpleasant truth either from themselves or others.* In other words they go to the opposite extreme. For example, a man troubled by doubts about his religious faith may try to convert others to the faith. Someone with unacceptable aggressive tendencies may join a group dedicated to preventing violence. (He did not mean that everyone who proselytizes for a faith has deep doubts about it or that everyone who tries to prevent violence is secretly violent. Different people have different reasons for the same actions.)

Sublimation

The transformation of sexual or aggressive energies into culturally acceptable, even admirable, behaviors is **sublimation.** According to Freud sublimation lets someone express an impulse without admitting its existence. For example, painting and sculpture may represent a sublimation of sexual impulses. Someone may sublimate aggressive impulses by becoming a surgeon. However, if the true motives of a painter are sexual and the true motives of a surgeon are violent, they are well hidden indeed. Sublimation is the one proposed defense mechanism that is associated with socially constructive behavior.

 CONCEPT CHECK

3. Match the Freudian defense mechanisms in this list with the situations that follow: repression, regression, denial, projection, rationalization, reaction formation, displacement, sublimation.
   a. A man who is angry with his neighbor goes deer hunting.
   b. A smoker insists there is no convincing evidence that smoking impairs health.
   c. A woman who doubts her religious faith tries to convert others to her religion.
   d. A man who beats his wife writes a book arguing that people have an instinctive need for aggressive behavior.
   e. A woman forgets a doctor's appointment for a test for cancer.
   f. Someone who has difficulty dealing with others resorts to pouting and crying.

g. A boss takes credit for an employee's idea because "If I get the credit, our department will look good and all employees will benefit."

h. Someone with an impulse to shout obscenities writes novels. (Check your answers on page 544.)

Freud's Legacy

Undeniably, Freud was a great pioneer in identifying new questions. The validity of his answers is less certain, however. He drew inferences from what his patients said and did without testing the validity of those inferences. A growing number of psychologists contend that Freud decided on conclusions and then looked for data to fit them, instead of collecting observations and then seeing what conclusions followed from them.

Freud's own couch is now part of our history. What is the future of the psychoanalytic couch?

It is conceivable, of course, that someone might draw correct conclusions even from weak data. One reviewer of the literature (Westen, 1998) identifies the following ideas as Freud's enduring contributions to psychology:

- Much of mental life is unconscious. We don't always know why we're doing something.
- People often have conflicting motives.
- Childhood experiences are important for the development of personality and social behavior.
- Our relationships with other people can resemble the relationships we had with other people in the past, such as our parents.
- People develop through stages of psychosexual interest and relationships with the social world.

However, a critic can reply that these comments are "damning with faint praise." That is, Freud's goal was not to make generalizations such as "people often have conflicting motives" or "childhood is important"—ideas

that were hardly original. Freud thought he had found a way to uncover people's unconscious thoughts and motives. Furthermore, the kinds of unconscious processes that current data support are very different from Freud's concepts. For example, implicit memory (chapter 7) and priming (chapters 7 and 8) are unconscious in the sense that people are unaware of certain influences on their behavior. However, these processes are unconscious because of weak stimuli, not because of repression. Freud's ideas about the unconscious did not lead to research on implicit memory or priming. If anything, they may have discouraged research on unconscious processes. In short, how much credit we should give Freud is a matter of opinion.

Neo-Freudians

Psychologists known as **neo-Freudians** *remained faithful to parts of Freud's theory while modifying other parts.* One of the most influential was the German physician Karen Horney (HOR-nigh; 1885–1952), who believed that Freud exaggerated the role of the sex drive in human behavior and misunderstood women's motivations. She believed, for example, that children had conflict with their parents because of parental intimidation, not because of sexual desires. Horney emphasized the social and cultural influences on personality that spur anxiety. Still, she maintained many Freudian concepts such as repression. Her views were more a revision than a rejection of Freud's theories.

Karen Horney, a neo-Freudian, revised some of Freud's theories and paid greater attention to cultural influences. She pioneered the study of feminine psychology.

Other theorists, including Carl Jung and Alfred Adler, broke more sharply with Freud. Although Jung and Adler were at one time associates of Freud, each broke with Freud's theory in substantial ways and should not be classified as neo-Freudians.

Carl Jung and the Collective Unconscious

Carl G. Jung (YOONG; 1875–1961), a Swiss physician, was an early member of Freud's inner circle. Freud regarded Jung like a son, the "heir apparent" or "crown prince" of the psychoanalytic movement, until their father–son relationship deteriorated (Alexander, 1982).

 Carl G. Jung rejected Freud's concept that dreams hide their meaning from the conscious mind: "To me dreams are a part of nature, which harbors no intention to deceive, but expresses something as best it can" (Jung, 1965).

Jung's own theory of personality emphasized people's search for a spiritual meaning in life and the continuity of human experience, past and present. In contrast to Freud, who traced much of adult personality to the events of childhood, Jung stressed the possibility of personality changes in adulthood, under the influence of the goals people set.

Jung believed that every person has not only a conscious mind and a "personal unconscious" (equivalent to Freud's unconscious) but also a collective unconscious that could influence many aspects of personality. You could think of it as a "group mind." The personal unconscious results from each person's own experience. The **collective unconscious,** present at birth, represents *the cumulative experience of preceding generations.* Because all humans share common ancestors, all have the same collective unconscious. The collective unconscious contains **archetypes,** which are *vague images that we inherited from the experiences of our ancestors.* As evidence for this view, Jung pointed out that similar images emerge in the art of cultures throughout the world (Figure 14.4) and that similar themes emerge in various religions, myths, and folklore.

Those images and themes also appear in dreams and hallucinations. So, for example, if you dream about a beetle, Jung might relate your dream to the important role that beetles have played in human mythology dating back at least to the ancient Egyptians. Given modern views of genetics, Jung's ideas are hard to defend. You cannot inherit your ancestors' memories. Jung's alternative to a genetic explanation was that perhaps archetypes exist on their own, independent of time, space, and brains. That idea is difficult to understand, much less test. In short, Jung's views of the collective unconscious and archetypes are mystical (Neher, 1996).

CRITICAL THINKING

A STEP FURTHER

Archetypes

Jung believed that the similarities in artworks throughout the world indicated that people inherited images or archetypes for those shapes.

Can you suggest a simpler, more parsimonious explanation?
_____
_____

☑ **CONCEPT CHECK**

4. How does Jung's idea of the collective unconscious differ from Freud's idea of the unconscious? (Check your answer on page 544.)

Alfred Adler and Individual Psychology

Alfred Adler (1870–1937), an Austrian physician who, like Jung, had been one of Freud's early associates, broke with Freud because he believed Freud overemphasized the sex drive and neglected other influences. They parted company in 1911, with Freud insisting that women experience "penis envy" and Adler replying that women were more likely to envy men's status and power.

Alfred Adler emphasized the ways in which personality depended on people's goals, especially their way of striving for a sense of superiority.

Adler founded a rival school of thought, which he called **individual psychology.** To Adler this term did not mean "psychology of the individual." Rather, it meant *"indivisible psychology," a psychology of the person as a whole rather than a psychology of parts,* such as id, ego, and superego. Adler emphasized the importance of conscious, goal-directed behavior and deemphasized (but did not deny) unconscious influences.

Adler's Description of Personality

Several of Adler's early patients were acrobats who had suffered childhood injuries to an arm or leg. After they worked to overcome their disabilities, they continued until they developed unusual strength and coordination. Perhaps, Adler surmised, people in general try to overcome weaknesses and transform them into strengths (Adler, 1932/1964).

As infants, Adler noted, we are small, dependent creatures who strive to overcome our inferiority. Normal experiences with failure goad people to try harder.

FIGURE 14.4 Carl Jung was fascinated that similar images appear in the artwork of different cultures. One recurring image is the circular mandala, a symbol of unity and wholeness. These mandalas are: **(a)** a Hindu painting from Bhutan; **(b)** a mosaic from Beth Alpha Synagogue, Israel; **(c)** a tie-dye tapestry created in California; and **(d)** a Navajo sand painting from the southwestern United States.

However, persistent failures and excessive criticism can produce an **inferiority complex,** *an exaggerated feeling of weakness, inadequacy, and helplessness.*

According to Adler everyone has a natural **striving for superiority,** *a desire to seek personal excellence and fulfillment.* Each person creates a **style of life,** or *master plan for achieving a sense of superiority.* One style of life is to seek success in business,

sports, or other competitive activities. People can also strive for success in other ways. For example, someone who withdraws from life may gain a sense of accomplishment or superiority from being uncommonly self-sacrificing. Someone who constantly complains about illnesses or disabilities may win a measure of control over friends and family. Or someone may commit crimes to savor the attention the crimes bring. People also sometimes get a feeling of superiority by making excuses. If you marry someone who is likely to thwart your ambitions, perhaps your underlying motivation is to maintain an illusion: "I could have been a great success if my spouse hadn't prevented me." Failure to study can have a similar motivation: "I could have done well on this test, but my friends talked me into partying the night before." Adler recognized that people are not always aware of their own style of life and the assumptions behind it. They may engage in self-defeating behavior because they have not admitted to themselves their real goals.

Adler tried to determine people's real motives. For example, he would ask someone who complained of a backache, "How would your life be different if you could get rid of your backache?" Those who eagerly said they would become more active were presumably trying to overcome their ailment. Those who said they could not imagine how their life would change, or said only that they would get less sympathy from others, were presumably exaggerating their discomfort if not imagining it.

 CONCEPT CHECK

5. In Adler's theory what is the relationship between striving for superiority and style of life? (Check your answer on page 544.)

Adler's View of Psychological Disorders

According to Adler what counts most is not how successful you are but the way in which you strive for success. Seeking success for yourself alone is unhealthy, he said (Adler, 1928/1964). The healthiest goal is to seek success for a larger group, such as your family, your community, your nation, or better yet all of humanity. Adler was ahead of his time, and many psychologists since then have rediscovered this idea (Crocker & Park, 2004).

According to Adler people's needs for one another require a social interest, *a sense of solidarity and identification with other people.* Note that social interest does not mean a desire to socialize. It means an interest in the welfare of society. People with social interest want to cooperate, not compete. In equating mental health with social interest, Adler saw mental health as a positive state, not just a lack of impairments. In Adler's view people with excessive anxieties are not suffering from an illness. Rather, they have set immature goals, are following a faulty style of life, and show little social interest. Their re-

sponse to new opportunity is, "Yes, but . . ." (Adler, 1932/1964).

For example, one of Adler's patients was a man who lived in conflict with his wife because he was constantly trying to impress and dominate her (Adler, 1927). When discussing his problems, the man revealed that he had been slow to mature and did not reach puberty until age 17. Other teenagers had ignored him or treated him like a child. Though he was now physically normal, he was overcompensating for those years of feeling inferior by trying to seem bigger and more important than he really was.

Adler's Legacy

Adler's influence exceeds his fame, and he probably would be glad for that. His concept of the inferiority complex has become part of the common culture. He was the first to talk about mental health as a positive state rather than merely the absence of impairments. Many later forms of therapy drew upon Adler's emphasis on understanding the assumptions that people make and how those assumptions influence behavior. Many psychologists also followed Adler by urging people to take responsibility for their own behavior. According to Adler the key to a healthy personality was not just freedom from disorders but social interest, a desire for the welfare of other people.

The Learning Approach

How did you develop your personality? You learn much of it on a situation-by-situation basis (Mischel, 1973, 1981). Consequently, if we observe you in several situations, your personality may seem inconsistent. You might be honest about returning a lost wallet to its owner but lie to your professor about why your paper is late. The learning approach helps explain variations among individuals and among situations for a given individual.

As described in the Social Learning section of chapter 6, we learn much by imitation or by vicarious reinforcement and punishment. That is, we copy behaviors that were successful for other people and avoid behaviors that failed for others. We behave like the people whom we respect and want to resemble.

Let's consider how this idea applies to masculine and feminine tendencies. As we learn people's expectations for us, we develop a gender role, *the pattern of behavior that a person is expected to follow because of being male or female.* A gender role is the psychological aspect of being male or female, as opposed to sex, which is the biological aspect. We know that gender role is at least partly learned because of the variation among cultures (Figure 14.5). For example, some cultures define cooking as women's work, and others define it as men's work. Men wear their hair short in some cultures and long in others.

To say that children learn their gender role does not mean that anyone teaches it deliberately. People teach mainly by example. Boys tend to imitate men, and girls tend to imitate women. In one experiment children watched adults choose between an apple and a banana. If all the men chose one fruit and all the women chose the other, the boys wanted what the men had and the girls wanted what the women had (Perry & Bussey, 1979). Even more powerfully, boys and girls learn their gender roles from older children. In short, the learning approach focuses on specific behaviors and attempts to relate them to specific experiences.

FIGURE 14.5 Gender roles vary greatly among cultures and even from one time period to another for a single culture. Here a Palestinian man **(a)** and a Vietnamese woman **(b)** plow the fields. Men in Bangladesh **(c)** and women in Thailand **(d)** do the wash.

▌ Children learn gender roles partly by imitating adults, but they probably learn more from other children.

Humanistic Psychology

Another perspective on personality, **humanistic psychology,** *deals with consciousness, values, and abstract beliefs, including spiritual experiences and the beliefs that people live and die for.* According to humanistic psychologists, personality depends on people's beliefs and perceptions of the world. If you *believe* that a particular experience was highly meaningful, then it *was* highly meaningful. A psychologist can understand you only by asking you to interpret and evaluate the events of your life. (In theology a *humanist* glorifies human potentials, generally denying or de-emphasizing a supreme being. The term *humanistic psychologist* implies nothing about someone's religious beliefs.)

Humanistic psychology emerged in the 1950s and 1960s as a protest against behaviorism and psychoanalysis, the dominant psychological viewpoints at the time (Berlyne, 1981). Behaviorists and psychoanalysts often emphasize the less noble, or at least morally neutral, aspects of people's thoughts and actions, whereas humanistic psychologists see people as essentially good and striving to achieve their potential. Also, behaviorism and psychoanalysis, despite their differences, both assume *determinism* (the belief that every behavior has a cause) and *reductionism* (the attempt to explain behavior in terms of its component elements).

Humanistic psychologists do not try to explain behavior in terms of its parts or hidden causes. They claim that people make deliberate, conscious decisions. For example, people might devote themselves to a great cause, sacrifice their own well-being, or risk their lives. To the humanistic psychologist, ascribing such behavior to past reinforcements or unconscious thought processes misses the point.

Humanistic psychologists generally study the special qualities of a given individual as opposed to studying groups. Their research consists mostly of recording narratives, more like a biographer than like a scientist. Their data are qualitative, not quantitative, and often difficult to evaluate.

Carl Rogers and the Goal of Self-Actualization

Carl Rogers, an American psychologist, studied theology before turning to psychology, and the influence of those early studies is apparent in his view of human nature. Rogers became the most influential humanistic psychologist.

Rogers (1980) regarded human nature as basically good. He said people have a natural drive toward **self-actualization,** *the achievement of one's full potential.* According to Rogers it is as natural for

Carl Rogers maintained that people naturally strive toward positive goals without special urging. He recommended that people relate to one another with unconditional positive regard.

© Bettmann/CORBIS

people to strive for excellence as it is for a plant to grow. The drive for self-actualization is the basic drive behind the development of personality. Rogers's concept of self-actualization is similar to Adler's concept of striving for superiority. Adler was a forerunner of humanistic psychology.

Children evaluate themselves and their actions beginning at an early age. They learn that their actions can be good or bad. They develop a **self-concept,** *an image of what they really are,* and an **ideal self,** *an image of what they would like to be.* Rogers measured self-concept and ideal self by handing someone a stack of cards containing statements such as "I am honest" and "I am suspicious of others." The person would then sort the statements into piles representing *true of me* and *not true of me* or arrange them in a continuum from *most true of me* to *least true of me.* (This method is known as a *Q-sort.*) Then Rogers would provide an identical stack of cards and ask the person to sort them into two piles: *true of my ideal self* and *not true of my ideal self.* In this manner he could compare someone's self-concept to his or her ideal self. People who perceive much discrepancy between the two generally feel distress. Humanistic psychologists try to help people overcome their distress by improving their self-concept or by revising their ideal self.

To promote human welfare, Rogers maintained that people should relate to one another with **unconditional positive regard,** a relationship that Thomas Harris (1967) described as "I'm OK—You're OK." Unconditional positive regard is *the complete, unqualified acceptance of another person as he or she is,* much like the love of a parent for a child. If you feel unconditional positive regard, you might disapprove of someone's actions or intentions, but you would still accept and love the person. (This view resembles the Christian advice to "hate the sin but love the sinner.") The alternative is *conditional positive regard,* the attitude that "I shall like you only if . . . ." People who are treated with conditional positive regard feel restrained about opening themselves to new ideas or activities for fear of losing someone else's support.

Abraham Maslow and the Self-Actualized Personality

Abraham Maslow, another founder of humanistic psychology, complained that most psychologists concentrate on disordered personalities, assuming that personality is either normal or worse than normal. Maslow insisted that personality can differ from normal in positive, desirable ways. He proposed that people's highest need is *self-actualization,* the fulfillment of an individual's potential. That is, of course, a difficult concept, as we have no way to know people's potential or whether they have achieved it.

As a first step toward describing the self-actualized personality, Maslow (1962, 1971) made a list of people

Abraham Maslow, one of the founders of humanistic psychology, introduced the concept of a "self-actualized personality," a personality associated with high productivity and enjoyment of life.

© Bettman/CORBIS

Harriet Tubman (1823– 1913)
nurse, spy and scout

© CORBIS

Harriet Tubman, identified by Maslow as having a self-actualized personality, was a leader of the Underground Railroad, a system for helping slaves escape from the southern states before the Civil War. Maslow defined the self-actualized personality by first identifying admirable people, such as Tubman, and then determining what they had in common.

who in his opinion were approaching their full potential. His list included people he knew personally as well as some from history. He sought to discover what, if anything, they had in common.

According to Maslow (1962, 1971), people with a self-actualized (or self-actualizing) personality show the following characteristics:

- An accurate perception of reality: They perceive the world as it is, not as they would like it to be. They accept uncertainty and ambiguity.
- Independence, creativity, and spontaneity: They make their own decisions, even if others disagree.
- Acceptance of themselves and others: They treat people with unconditional positive regard.
- A problem-centered outlook rather than a self-centered outlook: They think about how to solve problems, not how to make themselves look good. They concentrate on significant philosophical or political issues, not just on getting through the day.
- Enjoyment of life: They are open to positive experiences, including "peak experiences" when they feel truly fulfilled and content.
- A good sense of humor.

Critics have noted that, because Maslow's description is based on his own choice of examples, it may simply reflect the characteristics that he himself admired. That is, his reasoning was circular: He defined certain people as self-actualized and then inquired what they had in common to figure out what "self-actualized" means (Neher, 1991). In any case Maslow paved the way for other attempts to define a healthy personality as something more than a personality without disorder.

 CONCEPT CHECK

6. What does humanistic psychology have in common with the ideas of Alfred Adler? (Check your answer on page 544.)

IN CLOSING

In Search of Human Nature

The three most comprehensive personality theorists—Freud, Jung, and Adler—lived and worked in Austria in the early 1900s. Here we are, a century later, and most specialists in personality research neither accept those theories nor try to replace them with anything better. The whole idea of a single theory of personality seems at best premature. Even the breakdown into psychodynamic, learning, humanistic, and trait approaches (discussed in the next module) strikes many psychologists as obsolete (J. D. Mayer, 2005). The future will not lie with competing grand theories but with an approach that combines all kinds of research about the organization and development of personality.

Recall from chapter 1 that a good research question is interesting and answerable. Fundamental questions about human nature are extraordinarily interesting but not easily answerable. Most researchers today try to answer smaller questions about specific, measurable aspects of behavior, as the next two modules will describe. After researchers answer many of the smaller questions, perhaps they may return to the big questions of "what makes people tick?" ∎

Summary

- *Personality theories as views of human nature.* Personality consists of the stable, consistent ways in which each person's behavior differs from that of others. Theories of personality relate to conceptions of whether people are naturally good or bad (page 531)
- *Psychodynamic theories.* Several historically influential theories have described personality as the outcome of unconscious internal forces. (page 531)
- *Freud.* Sigmund Freud, the founder of psychoanalysis, proposed that much of what we do and say has hidden meanings. Critics say he twisted his evidence to fit his theories instead of deriving theories from the evidence itself. (page 531)
- *Freud's psychosexual stages.* Freud believed that many unconscious thoughts and motives are sexual in nature. He proposed that people progress through stages or periods of psychosexual development—oral, anal, phallic, latent, and genital—and that frustration at any stage fixates the libido at that stage. (page 533)
- *Defense mechanisms.* Freud and his followers argued that people defend themselves against anxiety by such mechanisms as denial, repression, projection, and reaction formation. (page 535)

- *Jung.* Carl Jung believed that all people share a collective unconscious that represents the entire experience of humanity. (page 537)
- *Adler.* Alfred Adler proposed that people's primary motivation is a striving for superiority. Each person adopts his or her own method of striving, and to understand people we need to understand their goals and beliefs. (page 538)
- *Adler's view of a healthy personality.* According to Adler the healthiest style of life is one that emphasizes social interest—that is, concern for the welfare of others. (page 540)
- *The learning approach.* The behaviors that constitute personality can be learned through individual experience or by vicarious reinforcement and punishment. (page 540)
- *Humanistic psychology.* Humanistic psychologists emphasize conscious, deliberate decision making. (page 542)

Answers to Concept Checks

1. Freud would interpret this behavior as a fixation at the oral stage. (page 534)
2. Someone with a strong id and a weak superego could be expected to give in to a variety of sexual and other impulses that other people would inhibit. Someone with an unusually strong superego would be unusually inhibited and dominated by feelings of guilt. (page 535)
3. **a.** displacement; **b.** denial; **c.** reaction formation; **d.** projection; **e.** repression; **f.** regression; **g.** rationalization; **h.** sublimation. (page 535)
4. Jung's collective unconscious is the same for all people and is present at birth. Freud believed the unconscious developed from repressed experiences. (page 538)
5. In Adler's theory a style of life is a method of striving for superiority. (page 539)
6. Adler emphasized the importance of people's beliefs and the possibility of a better than normal personality. Humanistic psychology is based on Adler's approach. (page 542)

Personality Traits

• *What traits provide the best description of personality?*

• *Why do people differ in their personalities?*

With regard to human personality, which would you say?

a. Every person is different from every other.
b. Way down deep, we're all the same.
c. It depends.

I vote for "it depends." The answer depends on our purposes. By analogy in some ways every rock is unique. If you want to know the fair market value of a rock, you cannot treat diamonds the same as granite, and if you want to predict how well a rock will conduct electricity or how easily you could break it, you need to know about the content of the rock. However, if you want to predict how fast a rock will fall if you drop it or what will happen when you throw it against a window, one kind of rock is about the same as another.

Similarly, people are alike in some ways and not others. Psychologists study personalities in two ways, called the nomothetic and the idiographic approaches. The word *nomothetic* (NAHM-uh-THEHT-ick) comes from the Greek *nomothetes,* meaning "legislator," and the **nomothetic approach** *seeks general laws about various aspects of personality* based on studies of groups of people. For example, we might make the nomothetic statement that people vary in a trait called *extraversion,* and the more extraverted someone is, the more likely that person will introduce himself or herself to a stranger.

In contrast the word *idiographic* is based on the root *idio-,* meaning "individual." The **idiographic approach** concentrates on *intensive studies of individ-*

Like this man playing the role of a woman in Japanese kabuki theater, actors can present personalities that are very different from their private ones. All of us occasionally display temporary personalities that are different from our usual selves.

uals (Allport, 1961). For example, a psychologist might study one person's goals, moods, and reactions. The conclusions would apply to this person and perhaps no one else.

Personality Traits and States

Meteorologists distinguish between climate (the usual conditions) and weather (the current conditions). For example, the climate in Scotland is moister and cooler than the climate in Texas, but on a given day, the weather could be warm in Scotland and cool in Texas. Similarly, psychologists distinguish between long-lasting personality conditions and temporary fluctuations.

A consistent, long-lasting tendency in behavior, such as shyness, hostility, or talkativeness, is known as a **trait.** In contrast a **state** is *a temporary activation of a particular behavior.* For example, being afraid right now is a state; being nervous most of the time is a trait. Being quiet in a library is a state; being quiet habitually is a trait. A trait, like a climatic condition, manifests itself as an average over time. Both traits and states are descriptions of behavior, not explanations. To say that someone is nervous and quiet does not explain anything. It merely describes what we are trying to explain.

 CONCEPT CHECK

7. Suppose someone becomes nervous as soon as he sits down in a dentist's chair. Is this experience "trait anxiety" or "state anxiety"? (Check your answer on page 553.)

The Search for Broad Personality Traits

According to the **trait approach to personality**, *people have consistent characteristics in their behavior.* Psychologists have described, studied, and measured many personality traits. Let's consider one example: belief in a just world. People who have a strong **belief in a just world** *maintain that life is fair and people usually get what they deserve* (Lerner, 1980). Here are examples of questions to measure this belief, reworded from a standard questionnaire (Lipkus, 1991). Indicate your degree of agreement from 1 (complete disagreement) to 6 (complete agreement). The higher your score, the greater your belief in a just world:

People usually get the rewards and punishments they deserve.
Most people who meet with misfortune did something to bring it on themselves.
Most of the lucky breaks I get are earned.
Promotions go to the people who work hardest.
People who have no job or no money have only themselves to blame.
Only rarely does an innocent person go to prison.

It is comforting to believe that life is fundamentally fair, that good deeds are rewarded and bad deeds punished. People with a strong belief in a just world usually handle stressful situations well, confident that things will turn out favorably after all (Bègue & Muller, 2006; Otto, Boos, Dalbert. Schöps, & Hoyer, 2006). They are more likely than average to offer help to a person in distress or to seek revenge against whoever caused the harm, presumably to restore a sense of justice (Furnham, 2003; Kaiser, Vick, & Major, 2004). However, if someone has been harmed and cannot be helped, people with a strong belief in a just world feel threatened, and to defend their belief, they often blame the victim (Hafer & Bègue, 2005). ("She shouldn't have been walking in that neighborhood." "He shouldn't have been out so late at night.") The point is that a personality trait—in this case belief in a just world—can manifest itself in many ways.

 CONCEPT CHECK

8. Accident victims often respond, "It could have been worse." How might this reaction relate to a belief in a just world? (Check your answer on page 553.)

Issues in Personality Measurement

In personality as in other areas of psychology, research progress depends on good measurement. The problem in measuring personality is that behavior fluctuates substantially depending on the situation. For example, if we tried to measure risk taking, we would find that many people take risks in one situation but not other situations. Some people gamble extensively but don't regard their habit as especially risky. Cigarette smokers are risking their health, but many of them avoid risks in other situations (Hanoch, Johnson, & Wilke, 2006). If we want to observe how people act in general, we would have to watch them in a wide variety of situations. Instead, researchers use questionnaires to ask people how they usually behave.

Devising and evaluating a useful questionnaire are more difficult than you might think. Recall the discussion of reliability and validity from chapter 9. Reliability means consistency of scores; validity means usefulness of the scores for predicting something else. Determining the reliability of a personality questionnaire is the first step. If the reliability is low, then the questions are probably not worded well. Validity is more difficult to determine. When people rate their own personality, can we trust them to be accurate? For example, most Americans describe their own intelligence as well above average, whereas the British are more modest, and the Japanese are still more modest, although on actual IQ tests the British do at least as well as Americans and the Japanese usually do better (Furnham, Hosoe, & Tang, 2002). On personality questionnaires also, people presumably vary in how accurately they describe themselves.

One way to check the validity of a personality questionnaire is to compare questionnaire results to behaviors recorded in diary form. In one study 170 college students filled out questionnaires about several personality dimensions, including aggressiveness and spontaneity. Then they kept daily records of such behaviors as yelling at someone (aggression) and buying something on the spur of the moment (spontaneous behavior). Both kinds of data rely on self-reports, but the daily behavior records are more detailed, closer in time to the actual events, and presumably more accurate. The questionnaire results correlated about .4 with daily reports of aggressive behavior but less well with reports of spontaneous acts (Wu & Clark, 2003). That is, the questionnaire results were moderately accurate.

In another study 10- to 11-year-old girls filled out a questionnaire about conscientiousness (tendency to follow the rules and keep one's promises) and a year later reported whether they had engaged in any risky sexual behaviors. Conscientiousness correlated −.42 with risky sexual behaviors. That is, the girls lowest in conscientiousness were the most likely to engage in risky activities (Markey, Markey, & Tinsley, 2003). Again, it appears that the personality questionnaire measures an important aspect of behavior—not perfectly, but moderately well.

An Example of Measurement Problems: Self-Esteem

For some years a popular goal among both psychologists and the general public was to raise people's self-esteem. The belief was that low self-esteem led to self-destructive activities and violence toward others, whereas high self-esteem led to satisfaction, productivity, and other good outcomes. That belief was only a hypothesis, however, and researchers needed to test it. When psychologists developed programs to raise people's self-esteem, the results were often disappointing. On the plus side, people who increased their self-esteem were less likely to feel depressed (Watson, Suls, & Haig, 2002) and better able to cope with stressors and defeats (Creswell et al., 2005; Marsh & Craven, 2006). However, raising people's self-esteem generally had little effect on aggressive behavior and sometimes *decreased* school and job performance (Baumeister, Campbell, Krueger, & Vohs, 2003). Evidently, people who hear "you're doing great" see little need to try harder!

One problem is that different questionnaires measure self-esteem differently (Blascovich & Tomaka, 1991). Here is one set of items from a self-esteem questionnaire:

- I feel that I have a number of good qualities.
- I am able to do things as well as most other people.
- At times I think I'm no good at all.
- I'm a failure.

An answer of "true" to the first two or "false" to the second two would count as points toward a high self-esteem score. Contrast those to the following items from a different self-esteem questionnaire, on which you are to answer from 1 (rarely or never) to 5 (usually or always):

- I feel that I am a beautiful person.
- I think that I make a good impression on others.
- I think that I have a good sense of humor.
- I feel that people really like me very much.

Would you call those items self-esteem, self-evaluation, or bragging? Certainly, they highlight a different aspect of self-regard.

Now consider these additional true–false items:

- There are lots of things about myself I'd change if I could.
- I'm often sorry for the things I do.
- I'm not doing as well in school as I'd like.
- I wish I could change my physical appearance.

A "true" answer on any of those items would count as a point toward low self-esteem. Do these answers indicate low self-esteem or high goals? Someone who says "true" is presumably striving for self-improvement. Someone who says "false" is satisfied

with current performance, whatever that might be. In short, some of the self-esteem questionnaires might not be measuring what they are designed to measure.

Here is another problem: Most Americans rate themselves above average in intelligence, personality, self-esteem, and almost anything else. Therefore, if you rate yourself "average," you are considered to have *below-average* self-esteem! Next, a survey asks what you think of minority groups or foreigners. Most Americans claim to have a "very high" opinion of minority groups and foreigners, so if you rate them "about average," you are considered to have a *below-average* opinion of them! Using these methods, some studies have reported that "people with low self-esteem tend to be prejudiced," when a better statement of the data would be "people who rate themselves average rate other people average too" (Baumeister et al., 2003).

 CONCEPT CHECK

9. If someone's questionnaire results indicate "low self-esteem," what else might the results actually mean other than low self-esteem? (Check your answer on page 553.)

The Big Five Model of Personality

Psychologists have devised questionnaires to measure belief in a just world, self-esteem, and hundreds of other traits. Measuring hundreds of traits is impractical. Remember the principle of parsimony from chapter 2: If we can adequately describe personality with, say, five or ten traits, we should not measure more.

One way to begin is to examine our language. The English language probably has a word for every important personality trait. Although this assumption is not a logical necessity, it seems reasonable considering how much attention people pay to other people's personalities. Gordon Allport and H. S. Odbert (1936) plodded through an English dictionary and found almost 18,000 words that might be used to describe personality. They deleted from this list words that were merely evaluations, such as *nasty,* and terms referring to temporary states, such as *confused.* (At least we hope that being confused is temporary.) In the remaining list, they looked for clusters of synonyms, such as *affectionate, warm,* and *loving,* and kept only one of these terms. When they found opposites, such as *honest* and *dishonest,* they also kept just one term. (*Honesty* and *dishonesty* are different extremes of one dimension, not separate traits.) After eliminating synonyms and antonyms, Raymond Cattell (1965) narrowed the original list to 35 traits.

Derivation of the Big Five Personality Traits

Although some of the 35 personality traits that Cattell identified are not exactly synonyms or antonyms of one another, many of them overlap. To determine which traits correlate with one another, psychologists use a method called *factor analysis*. For example, if measurements of warmth, gregariousness, and assertiveness correlate strongly with one another, we can cluster them together as a single trait. But if this combined trait does not correlate highly with self-discipline, then self-discipline (and anything that correlates strongly with it) is a separate trait.

Using this approach researchers found major clusters of personality traits, which they call the **big five personality traits**: *neuroticism, extraversion, agreeableness, conscientiousness, and openness to new experience* (McCrae & Costa, 1987). The case for these five traits is that (a) each correlates with many personality dimensions for which our language has a word and (b) none of these traits correlates highly with any of the other four, so they are not measuring the same thing.

The big five dimensions are described in the following list (Costa, McCrae, & Dye, 1991). Note that the first two, neuroticism and extraversion, are the "biggest" of the big five. Even psychologists who are skeptical of the big five model agree that neuroticism and extraversion are powerful traits relevant to much of human behavior (Block, 1995).

Neuroticism is *a tendency to experience unpleasant emotions frequently.* Some personality researchers prefer to use the term *emotional stability,* which is the mirror image of neuroticism. That is, anyone who is high in one is low in the other, so we could use either term equally well. Neuroticism correlates positively with anxiety, hostility, depression, and self-consciousness. In one study college students kept a diary in which they recorded the most stressful event of the day. Students who scored high on a neuroticism questionnaire were more likely than other students to identify their most stressful event as a conflict with another person. They were also more likely than other students to rate the experience as highly distressing and less likely to deal effectively with it (Gunthert, Cohen, & Armeli, 1999).

Extraversion is *a tendency to seek stimulation and to enjoy the company of other people.* The opposite of extraversion is introversion. Extraversion is associated with warmth, gregariousness, assertiveness, impulsiveness, and a need for excitement. Extraverted people tend to be risk takers, and the unpleasant side of extraversion is an increased risk of alcohol abuse and similar problems (Martsh &

Miller, 1997). The pleasant side is that extraverts tend to be happy (Francis, Brown, Lester, & Philipchalk, 1998). In one study participants reported five times a day for 2 weeks what they had been doing and how they were feeling. Generally, they reported feeling happy at the same times when they had been talkative, energetic, and adventuresome. Furthermore, people who were *instructed* to act in an extraverted way reported feeling happier afterward (Fleeson, Malanos, & Achille, 2002).

Active, outgoing behavior ⟷ Happy feelings

Agreeableness is *a tendency to be compassionate toward others.* It implies a concern for the welfare of other people and is closely related to Adler's concept of social interest. People high in agreeableness generally trust other people and expect other people to trust them.

Conscientiousness is *a tendency to show self-discipline, to be dutiful, and to strive for achievement and competence.* People high in conscientiousness usually work hard and complete the tasks they say they will perform (Judge & Ilies, 2002). Highly conscientious people tend to exercise, eat a healthy diet, and avoid tobacco, excessive alcohol, risky sex, and other dangers (Bogg & Roberts, 2004).

Openness to experience, the big five trait that is usually the least variable and hardest to observe, is *a tendency to enjoy new intellectual experiences and new ideas.* People high in this trait enjoy modern art, unusual music, thought-provoking films and plays, and so forth. They enjoy meeting different kinds of people and exploring new ideas and opinions (McCrae, 1996). When young people meet, one of the first questions they usually explore is taste in music. In one study people listed their favorite 10 songs. Then another person listened to those songs and tried to guess the personality of the person who chose them. From music alone they could guess the person's openness to experience with a correlation above .6 (Rentfrow & Gosling, 2006).

 CONCEPT CHECK

10. Some psychologists suggest that we should divide extraversion into two traits—which they call *ambition* and *sociability*—changing the big five into the big six. How should psychologists determine whether to do so?

The Japanese artist Morimura Yasumasa re-creates famous paintings, substituting his own face for the original. Some people love his work; others dislike it. People high in "openness to experience" delight in new, unusual forms of art, literature, and music.

11. If you wanted to predict someone's happiness, which personality trait would you measure? What if you wanted to predict how long someone would live? (Check your answers on page 553.)

Criticisms and Problems

The research methods could overlook certain personality traits because of quirks of the English language. For example, we identify extraversion–introversion as a big factor because it relates to so many words in the English language—sociability, warmth, friendliness, adventuresomeness, gregariousness, happiness, and so forth. Sense of humor does not emerge as a major personality trait because the language has few synonyms for it. Critics of the big five approach point to nine personality dimensions that the big five model seems to overlook (Paunonen & Jackson, 2000): religiousness, manipulativeness, honesty, sexiness, thriftiness, conservativeness, masculinity–femininity, snobbishness, and sense of humor. None of these correlates strongly with one another or with the big five.

On the other end, some critics believe that five is more traits than we need. Openness to experience has

a modest positive correlation with extraversion, and conscientiousness correlates negatively with neuroticism, so perhaps we could get by with just neuroticism, extraversion, and agreeableness (Eysenck, 1992).

Cross-cultural studies offer partial, but only partial, support to the big five approach. Some studies have used translations of English words or an array of personality descriptions from other languages. Others have shown pictures of people in various activities and asked, "How likely would you be to do this?" The picture approach makes it easy to test people of various cultures without first thoroughly studying their language (Paunonen, Zeidner, Engvik, Oosterveld, & Maliphant, 2000). Many researchers have found results consistent with the big five model (McCrae & Costa, 1997). However, some studies did find cross-cultural differences (Panayiotou, Kokkinos, & Spanoudis, 2004). A study in China identified traits corresponding approximately to extraversion, neuroticism, conscientiousness, and "loyalty to Chinese traditions" (Cheung et al., 1996).

Overall, how should we evaluate the five-factor description? The answer depends on our purposes. The five-factor description accounts for enough of the variability in human behavior to be useful, although for some purposes three factors may be enough and for other purposes more may be necessary. It depends on how much precision we want in describing and predicting people's behavior.

The Origins of Personality

A description of personality differences is not an explanation. What makes some people more extraverted, neurotic, agreeable, conscientious, or open to experience than other people are?

Heredity and Environment

If you want evidence that heredity can influence personality, you need look no further than the nearest pet dog. For centuries people have selectively bred dogs for certain personalities, ranging from the friendliest lap dogs to those capable of furious attacks.

To measure the influences of heredity and environment on human personality, researchers have relied mostly on the same kinds of data as in other areas of psychology (Bouchard & McGue, 2003). First, they compare the similarities between identical twins and fraternal twins. As Figure 14.6 shows, five studies conducted in separate locations indicated much greater similarities in extraversion between identical pairs than fraternal pairs (Loehlin, 1992). Studies in Australia and the United States found a similar pattern for neuroticism, with identical twins resembling each other much more than fraternal twins, who resembled each other no

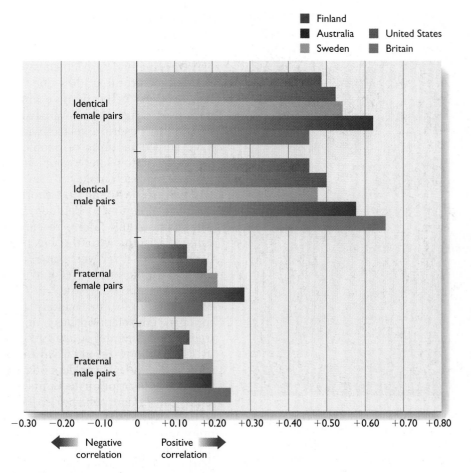

FIGURE 14.6 Five studies—conducted in Great Britain, the United States, Sweden, Australia, and Finland—found larger correlations between the extraversion levels of monozygotic (identical) twins than those of dizygotic (fraternal) twins. *(Based on data summarized by Loehlin, 1992)*

more than brothers or sisters born at different times (Lake, Eaves, Maes, Heath, & Martin, 2000).

Modern methods make it possible to search for specific genes linked to particular personality traits. Several studies have identified genes apparently linked to neuroticism or to the specific aspect of neuroticism known as *harm avoidance* or anxiety-proneness (Fullerton et al., 2003). However, each of the genes identified so far makes only a small contribution.

Also, researchers compare the personalities of parents, their biological children, and their adopted children. As Figure 14.7 shows, parents' extraversion levels correlate moderately with those of their biological children but hardly at all with their adopted children. Similarly, biologically related brothers or sisters growing up together resemble each other moderately in personality, and unrelated children adopted into the same family do not (Loehlin, 1992). The results shown in Figures 14.6 and 14.7 pertain to extraversion; other studies provide a largely similar pattern for other personality traits (Heath, Neale, Kessler, Eaves, & Kendler, 1992; Loehlin, 1992; Viken, Rose, Kaprio, & Koskenvuo, 1994).

The low correlations between adopted children and adoptive parents imply that children learn rather little of their personalities by imitating their parents. (Recall from chapter 5 that Judith Harris made this same point.) Many researchers believe that much of the variation among people's personalities relates to the **unshared environment,** *the aspects of environment that differ from one individual to another, even within a family.* Unshared environment includes the effects of a particular playmate, a particular teacher, an injury or illness, or any other isolated experience. Because of its idiosyncratic nature, unshared environment is difficult to investigate.

 CONCEPT CHECK

12. What evidence would indicate an important role of the *shared environment*—the influences that are the same for all children within a family? (Check your answer on page 553.)

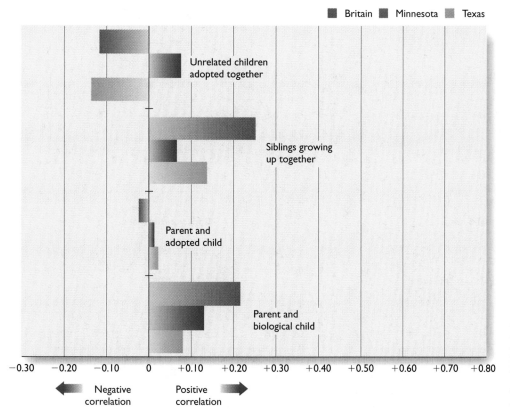

Britain ■ Minnesota ■ Texas

Unrelated children
adopted together

Siblings growing
up together

Parent and
adopted child

Parent and
biological child

−0.30 −0.20 −0.10 0 +0.10 +0.20 +0.30 +0.40 +0.50 +0.60 +0.70 +0.80

◄ Negative
correlation

Positive ►
correlation

FIGURE 14.7 Researchers in Britain, Minnesota, and Texas measured extraversion in hundreds of families. Each found moderate positive correlations among relatives but near-zero correlations between parents and adopted children. *(Based on data summarized by Loehlin, 1992)*

Influences of Age, Culture, and Cohort

Do you think your personality now resembles what it was in childhood? In some aspects it probably does. In one study investigators observed the behavior of 3-year-old children and followed them longitudinally until age 26. Children who were fearful and easily upset at age 3 were more nervous and inhibited than others at age 26. Those who were impulsive and restless at age 3 tended to have trouble with others from then on and to feel alienated from society. Those who were confident, friendly, and eager to explore their environment at 3 tended to be confident adults, eager to take charge of events (Caspi et al., 2003).

Will your personality change much in the next few years? According to the research, the older people get, the more slowly they change. In childhood answers on a personality questionnaire correlate a modest .34 with a second test given 6 or 7 years later. By college age the correlation is .54. It increases to .64 at age 30 and .74 at age 60 (Roberts & DelVecchio, 2000). Why personality becomes more fixed as we grow older is not known, but you can probably imagine a few hypotheses.

Although the differences that occur over age are not large, they are fairly consistent. One trend is that as people grow older, they become more conscientious. In every culture that has been studied through-

out the world, middle-aged people are more likely to be highly conscientious—that is, to do what they promise they will do—than are teenagers (McCrae et al., 2000). A simple hypothesis is that adults are forced, whether they like it or not, to hold a job, pay the bills, repair the house, care for children, and take responsibility in other ways.

Most people reach their peak of social vitality and sensation seeking during adolescence or early adulthood and then decline gradually with further age (Roberts, Walton, & Viechtbauer, 2006). Again, this trend occurs across cultures (Labouvie-Vief, Diehl, Tarnowksi, & Shen, 2000). Older people also tend to be less neurotic—that is, more emotionally stable—and more agreeable (Cramer, 2003; McCrae et al., 2000). In the United States, young adults on the average score higher on openness to new experience than older people (Roberts et al., 2006). This trend is no surprise; we see that young people enjoy new types of music, new kinds of food, new styles of clothing, and so forth (Sapolsky, 1998), whereas older people stay with old habits. In some other cultures, however, openness to experience shows no clear trend over age (McCrae et al., 2000). Figure 14.8 shows mean changes in six aspects of personality over age (Roberts et al., 2006). Note that this research distinguished between two aspects of extraversion—social vitality and social dominance.

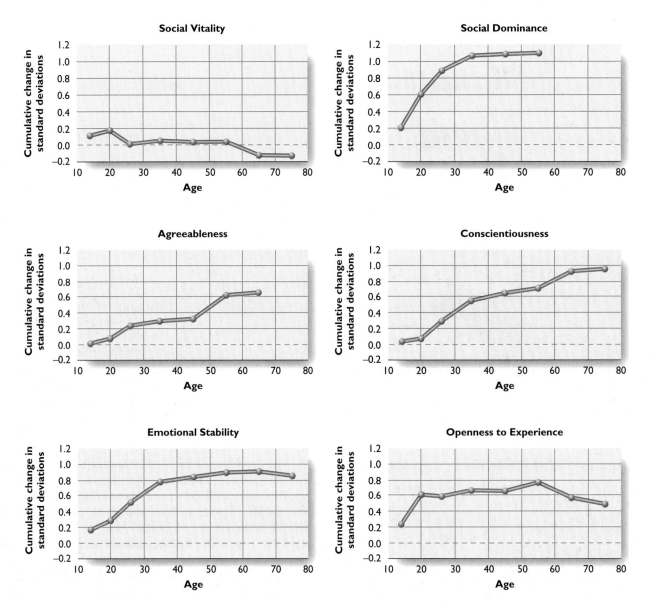

FIGURE 14.8 Six aspects of personality show different patterns of change over age, based on the means of longitudinal research studies. The numbers along the vertical axis represent changes from the earliest age tested, measured in terms of standard deviations. *(From Roberts, Walton, & Viechtbauer, 2006)*

Does personality vary among cultures or countries? That is, might the typical or average personality in one country differ from that in another? The differences among people within a country are certainly larger than the differences between one country and another, but differences do occur among countries. For example, Europeans and North Americans tend to be high in extraversion and openness to experience, while Asians and Africans tend to be higher in agreeableness. In general, people in neighboring countries usually resemble one another. For example, average scores on personality inventories are similar for Canadians and U.S. citizens; Germans resemble Austrians; and Spaniards resemble the Portuguese (Allik & McCrae, 2004).

Finally, does personality change from one generation to the next? Remember the Flynn effect from chapter 9: Over the years people's performance on IQ tests has gradually increased so that each generation does better on the tests than the previous generation. Researchers have also found generational differences in personality. For example, over the years, beginning in the 1950s, measurements of anxiety have steadily increased (Twenge, 2000). On the Child Manifest Anxiety Scale, the mean score in the 1950s was 15.1, and the mean for children in mental hospitals was 20.1. By the 1980s the mean for *all* children was 23.3! Do we really have that much more anxiety than in past generations? Perhaps people's answers do not mean what they used to. The more disturbing possibility is that we really do live in an age of anxiety. Compared to past generations, more children today have to live through their parents' divorce, and fewer live in a neighborhood with many friends and relatives. Might those social changes have raised the average anxiety level to what used to characterize the top 10%? The answer is uncertain, but today's researchers worry about why people worry so much.

IN CLOSING

The Challenges of Classifying Personality

Personality descriptions refer to averages over time. We don't expect anyone to be equally extraverted at all times, equally neurotic, or anything else. What you do at any moment depends largely on the situation. In a sufficiently novel situation, you may be surprised by the actions of people you know well and even by your own behavior. The variation across situations makes the measurement of general tendencies difficult. Research progress always depends on good measurement, and you can see why progress in understanding personality is slow. ▮

Summary

* *Nomothetic and idiographic research.* Nomothetic studies examine large numbers of people briefly, whereas idiographic studies examine one or a few individuals intensively. (page 545)
* *Traits and states.* Traits are personality characteristics that persist over time; states are temporary tendencies in response to particular situations. (page 545)
* *Measurement problems.* Personality researchers rely mostly on self-reports, which are not entirely accurate. (page 546)
* *Five major traits.* Much of personality can be explained by these five traits: neuroticism, extraversion, agreeableness, conscientiousness, and openness to new experience. However, several other important dimensions may have been overlooked. (page 548)
* *Determinants of personality.* Studies of twins and adopted children indicate that heredity contributes to the observed differences in personality. Family environment evidently contributes rather little.

Much of personality relates to unshared environment, the special experiences that vary from one person to another even within a family. (page 549)
* *Changes over age.* Compared to younger people, older people tend to be higher in conscientiousness and agreeableness. They are somewhat lower in extraversion and neuroticism. Openness to experience decreases with age in the United States, but several other countries do not show this trend. (page 551)
* *Changes over generations.* Measurements of anxiety have gradually increased over the decades so that normal people now report anxiety levels that used to characterize people in mental hospitals. (page 552)

Answers to Concept Checks

7. This nervousness is state anxiety because it is evoked by a particular situation. Trait anxiety is a tendency to become nervous in many situations. (page 545)
8. It seems unjust for an innocent person to sustain an injury. Minimizing the damage makes the injustice seem less. (page 546)
9. Depending on the questionnaire items, what appears to be low self-esteem might indicate high goals and therefore lack of satisfaction with one's current performance. Also, rating one's intelligence and personality as "average" could simply mean that the person tends to use the middle part of the rating scale. (page 547)
10. They should determine whether measures of ambition correlate strongly with measures of sociability. If so, then ambition and sociability can be considered two aspects of a single trait, extraversion. If not, then they are indeed separate personality traits. (page 548)
11. Extraversion correlates significantly with happiness. To predict longevity you could measure someone's conscientiousness. Conscientious people tend to follow recommendations about good diet, exercise, and avoiding risky behaviors. (page 548)
12. If the personalities of adopted children within a family correlated highly with one another, we would conclude that the similarity reflected the shared environment. The weakness of such correlations is the main evidence for the importance of the unshared environment. (page 550)

Personality Assessment

• *What inferences can we draw from the results of a personality test?*

A new P. T. Barnum Psychology Clinic has just opened at your local shopping mall and is offering a grand opening special on personality tests. You have always wanted to know more about yourself, so you sign up. Here is Barnum's true–false test:

Questionnaire for Universal Assessment of Zealous Youth (QUAZY)

1. I have never met a cannibal I didn't like.   T F
2. Robbery is the only felony I have ever committed.   T F
3. I eat "funny mushrooms" less frequently than I used to.   T F
4. I don't care what people say about my nose-picking habit.   T F
5. Sex with vegetables no longer disgusts me.   T F
6. This time I am quitting glue-sniffing for good.   T F
7. I generally lie on questions like this one.   T F
8. I spent much of my childhood sucking on computer cables.   T F
9. I find it impossible to sleep if I think my bed might be clean.   T F
10. Naked bus drivers make me nervous.   T F
11. I spend my spare time playing strip solitaire.   T F

You turn in your answers. A few minutes later, a computer prints out your personality profile:

> You have a need for other people to like and admire you, and yet you tend to be critical of yourself. While you have some personality weaknesses, you are generally able to compensate for them. You have considerable unused capacity that you have not turned to your advantage. Disciplined and self-controlled on the outside, you tend to be worrisome and insecure on the inside. At times, you have serious doubts as to whether you have made the right decision or done the right thing. You prefer a certain amount of change and variety and become dissatisfied when hemmed in by restrictions and limitations. You also pride yourself as an independent thinker and do not accept others' statements without satisfactory proof. But you have found it unwise to be too frank in revealing yourself to others. At times you are extraverted, affable, and so-

ciable, while at other times you are introverted, wary, and reserved. Some of your aspirations tend to be rather unrealistic. (Forer, 1949, p. 120)

Do you agree with this assessment? Did it capture your personality? Several experiments have been conducted along these lines with psychology classes (Forer, 1949; Marks & Kammann, 1980; Ulrich, Stachnik, & Stainton, 1963). Students started by filling out a questionnaire that looked reasonable, not like the ridiculous questions here (which were included just to amuse you). Several days later, each student received a sealed envelope with his or her name on it. Inside was a personality profile supposedly based on the student's answers to the questionnaire. The students were asked, "How accurately does this profile describe you?" About 90% rated it as good or excellent. Some expressed amazement at its accuracy: "I didn't realize until now that psychology was an exact science." None of them realized that everyone had received exactly the same personality profile—the same one you just read.

▌ People tend to accept almost any personality assessment, especially if it is stated in vague terms that people can interpret to fit themselves.

The students accepted this personality profile partly because it vaguely describes almost everyone, like newspaper horoscopes, and partly because people accept almost *any* statement that a psychologist makes about them (Marks & Kammann, 1980). This *tendency to accept vague descriptions of our personality is known as the* **Barnum effect,** named after P. T. Barnum, the circus owner who specialized in fooling people out of their money.

The conclusion: Psychological testing must be done carefully. If we want to know whether a particular test measures a particular person's personality, we cannot simply ask that person's opinion or the opinion of the psychologist who gave the test. Psychologists need to design a test carefully and then determine its reliability and validity.

Standardized Personality Tests

A **standardized test** is *one that is administered according to rules that specify how to interpret the results.* One important step for standardizing a test is to determine the distribution of scores. We need to know the mean score and the range of scores for a representative sample of the population and how they differ for special populations, such as people with severe depression. Given such information we can determine whether a particular score on a personality test is within the normal range or whether it is more typical of people with some disorder.

Most of the tests published in popular magazines have not been standardized. A magazine may herald an article: "Test Yourself: How Good Is Your Marriage?" or "Test Yourself: How Well Do You Control the Stress in Your Life?" After you compare your answers to the scoring key, the article may tell you that "if your score is greater than 80, you are doing very well . . . if it is below 20, you need to work on improving yourself!"—or some such nonsense. Unless the magazine states otherwise, you can assume that the author pulled the scoring norms out of thin air, with no supporting research.

Over the years psychologists have developed an enormous variety of tests to measure normal and abnormal personality. We shall examine a few prominent examples and explore possibilities for future personality measurement.

An Objective Personality Test: The Minnesota Multiphasic Personality Inventory

Some of the most widely used personality tests use simple pencil-and-paper responses. The most widely used personality test, the **Minnesota Multiphasic Personality Inventory** (mercifully abbreviated **MMPI**), consists of *true–false questions intended to measure certain personality dimensions and clinical conditions such as depression.* The original MMPI, developed in the 1940s and still in use, has 550 items. *The second edition, MMPI–2,* published in 1990, has 567. Example items are "my mother never loved me" and "I think I would like the work of a pharmacist." (The items stated in this text are rewordings of actual items.)

The MMPI was devised *empirically*—that is, based on evidence rather than theory (Hathaway & McKinley, 1940). The authors wrote hundreds of questions that they thought might relate to personality. They put these questions to people with various psychological disorders and to a group of hospital visitors, who were assumed to be psychologically normal. The researchers selected the items that most of the people in any clinical group answered differently from most of the normal people. They assumed, for example, that if your answers resemble those of people with depression, you probably are depressed also. The MMPI had scales for depression, paranoia, schizophrenia, and others. The result was a test that worked fairly well. For example, most people with scores above a certain level on the Depression scale are in fact depressed.

Some of the items on the MMPI made sense theoretically, and others did not. For example, some items on the Depression scale asked about feelings of helplessness or worthlessness, which are an important part of depression. But two other items were "I attend religious services frequently" and "occasionally I tease animals." If you answered *false* to either of those items, you would get a point on the Depression scale! These items were included simply because more depressed people than others answered *false*. The reason is not obvious. Perhaps people with depression do not tease animals because they seldom do anything just for fun.

Revisions of the Test

The MMPI was standardized in the 1940s. As time passed the meaning of certain items or their answers changed. For example, how would you respond to the following item?

I believe I am important.   T   F

In the 1940s fewer than 10% of all people marked *true*. At the time the word *important* meant about the same thing as *famous*, and people who called themselves important were thought to have an inflated view of themselves. Today, we stress that every person is important.

What about this item?

I like to play drop the handkerchief.   T   F

Drop the handkerchief, a game similar to tag, fell out of popularity in the 1950s. Most people today have never heard of the game, much less played it.

To bring the MMPI up to date, psychologists eliminated obsolete items and added new ones to deal with drug abuse, suicidal thoughts, and other issues (Butcher, Graham, Williams, & Ben-Porath, 1990). Then they tried out the new MMPI–2 on a large repre-

TABLE 14.2 The 10 MMPI–2 Clinical Scales

Scale	Typical Item
Hypochondria (Hs)	I have chest pains several times a week. (T)
Depression (D)	I am glad that I am alive. (F)
Hysteria (Hy)	My heart frequently pounds so hard I can hear it. (T)
Psychopathic Deviation (Pd)	I get a fair deal from most people. (F)
Masculinity–Femininity (Mf)	I like to arrange flowers. (T = female)
Paranoia (Pa)	There are evil people trying to influence my mind. (T)
Psychasthenia (Obsessive–Compulsive) (Pt)	I save nearly everything I buy, even after I have no use for it. (T)
Schizophrenia (Sc)	I see, hear, and smell things that no one else knows about. (T)
Hypomania (Ma)	When things are dull I try to get some excitement started. (T)
Social Introversion (Si)	I have the time of my life at parties. (F)

sentative sample of the U.S. population. That is, they restandardized the test. Psychologists also developed a new form, the MMPI–A, intended for use with adolescents.

The MMPI–2 has 10 clinical scales, as shown in Table 14.2. Other psychologists have selected other items from the same test to measure other personality traits (Sellbom & Ben-Porath, 2005). The items of any type are scattered throughout the test so that people won't see that "oh, this seems to be a set of items about depression." Most people get at least a few points on each scale. A score above a certain level indicates a probable difficulty. Figure 14.9 shows how MMPI–2 scores are plotted.

Culture and the MMPI

Can a single test measure personality for all kinds of people? In particular is the MMPI (or MMPI–2 or MMPI–A) a fair measure of personality for people of different ethnic and cultural backgrounds?

In general, the means and ranges on each scale are about the same for many ethnic groups, even after translation into different languages (Negy, Leal-Puente, Trainor, & Carlson, 1997). However, differences do occur. For example, Mexicans are more likely than U.S. people to say *true* to "Life is a constant strain for me." Presumably, the reason is that life really is more difficult for many people in Mexico. On several scales of the MMPI–2, the Mexican means differ from the U.S. means (Lucio, Ampudia, Durán, León, & Butcher, 2001). Consequently, the scoring standards for a personality test should differ from one country to another. Even within a country, psychologists need to be cautious when interpreting scores for ethnic minorities (Gynther, 1989).

Detection of Deception

If you were taking the MMPI or another personality test, could you lie to make yourself look mentally healthier than you really are? Yes. Could someone catch your lies? Probably.

The designers of the MMPI and MMPI–2 included items designed to identify lying (Woychyshyn, McElheran, & Romney, 1992). For example, consider the items "I like every person I have ever met" and "occasionally I get angry at someone." If you answer *true* to the first question and *false* to the second, you are either a saint or a liar. The test authors, convinced that liars outnumber saints, count such answers on a scale of lies. If you get too many points on that scale, a psychologist distrusts your answers to the other items. Strangely enough, some people lie to try to look bad. For example, a criminal defendant might want to be classified as mentally ill. The MMPI includes items to detect that kind of faking also (Bagby, Nicholson, Bacchiochi, Ryder, & Bury, 2002).

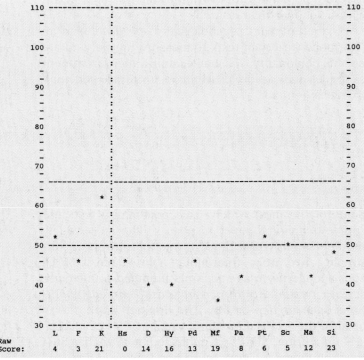

FIGURE 14.9 This is the MMPI–2 profile of a middle-aged man with no psychological problems. Someone with a disorder would have a score above 65 on one or more scales. *(Source: Minnesota Multiphasic Personality Inventory–2, © by the Regents of the University of Minnesota. Data courtesy of R. J. Huber.)*

Several other questionnaires also try to detect deception. For example, suppose an employer's questionnaire asks you how much experience you have had at various skills including "determining myopic weights for periodic tables." You're not sure what that means, but you want the job. Do you claim to have had extensive experience? If so, your claimed expertise will count *against* you because "determining myopic weights for periodic tables" is nonsense. The employer asked about it just to see whether you were exaggerating your qualifications on other items. According to the results of one study, almost half of all job applicants claimed to have experience with one or more nonexistent tasks (Anderson, Warner, & Spencer, 1984). Some claimed they had not only performed the tasks but had also trained others!

CRITICAL THINKING
A STEP FURTHER

Assessing Honesty

Could you use this strategy in other situations? Suppose a political candidate promises to increase aid to college students. You are skeptical. How could you use the candidate's statements on other issues to help you decide whether to believe this promise?

 CONCEPT CHECK

13. Suppose a person thinks "True or false, black is my favorite color" would be a good item for the Depression scale of the MMPI. How would a researcher decide whether to include it?
14. Why does the MMPI include some items that ask about common flaws, such as, "Sometimes I think more about my own welfare than that of others"? (Check your answers on page 563.)

Projective Techniques

The MMPI and similar personality tests are easy to handle statistically, but they limit people's answers. In hopes of learning more, psychologists ask open-ended questions. However, to the inquiry "tell me about yourself," many people are reluctant to confide embarrassing information. Many people prefer to discuss their problems in the abstract. A person seeking help might say, "Let me tell you about my friend's problem and ask what my friend should do." They then describe their own problem. They are "projecting" their problem onto someone else in Freud's sense of the word—that is, attributing it to someone else.

Rather than discouraging projection, psychologists often make use of it with **projective techniques,** which are *designed to encourage people to project their personality characteristics onto ambiguous stimuli.* Let's consider two well-known projective techniques: the Rorschach Inkblots and the Thematic Apperception Test.

 CONCEPT CHECK

15. Which of the following is a projective technique?
    a. A psychologist gives a child a set of puppets with instructions to act out a story about a family.
    b. A psychologist hands you a stack of cards, each containing one word, and asks you to sort the cards into a stack that applies to you and a stack that does not. (Check your answers on page 563.)

The Rorschach Inkblots

The **Rorschach Inkblots,** *a projective technique based on people's interpretations of 10 ambiguous inkblots,* is the most famous and most widely used projective personality technique. It was created by Hermann Rorschach (ROAR-shock), a Swiss psychiatrist, who showed people inkblots and asked them to say whatever came to mind (Pichot, 1984). Rorschach was impressed that his patients' interpretations of the blots differed from his own. In a book published in 1921 (English translation 1942), he presented the 10 symmetrical inkblots that still constitute the Rorschach Inkblot Technique. (Originally, he used a larger number, but the publisher insisted on cutting the number to 10 to reduce printing costs.) Other psychiatrists and psychologists gradually developed the Rorschach into the projective technique we know today.

Administering the Rorschach

The Rorschach Inkblot Technique consists of cards similar to the one in Figure 14.10. Five are in black and white and five are in color. A psychologist hands you a card and asks, "What might this be?" The in-

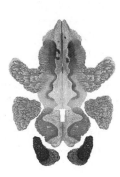

FIGURE 14.10 In the Rorschach Inkblot Technique, people examine an abstract pattern and say what it looks like.

structions are intentionally vague on the assumption that anything you do in an ill-defined situation reveals something about your personality.

Sometimes, people's answers are revealing, either immediately or in response to a psychologist's probes. Here is an example (Aronow, Reznikoff, & Moreland, 1995):

Client: Some kind of insect; it's not pretty enough to be a butterfly.
Psychologist: Any association to that?
Client: It's an ugly black butterfly, no colors.
Psychologist: What does that make you think of in your own life?
Client: You probably want me to say "myself." Well, that's probably how I thought of myself when I was younger—I never thought of myself as attractive—my sister was the attractive one. I was the ugly duckling—I did get more attractive as I got older.

Evaluation of the Rorschach

It is true that personality makes a bigger difference in an ill-defined situation than when people receive specific instructions. The question is how accurately a psychologist can interpret the responses to that ambiguous situation. When you describe what you see in a picture, your answer has some relation to your experiences and concerns. But would anyone else guess the connection?

In the 1950s and 1960s, certain psychologists called the Rorschach "an x-ray of the mind." Their exaggerated claims provoked vigorous criticism. The main problem was that different psychologists drew different conclusions from the same answer depending on their theoretical expectations. To a particular blot, one man said, "It looks like a bat that has been squashed on the pavement under the heel of a giant's boot" (Dawes, 1994, p. 149). Psychologist Robyn Dawes initially was impressed with how the Rorschach had revealed this client's sense of being overwhelmed and crushed by powers beyond his control. However, Dawes later realized that he had already known the client was depressed. If a client with a history of violence had made the same response, he would have focused on the aggressive nature of the giant's foot stomp. For a hallucinating or paranoid client, he would have made still other interpretations. Psychologists often believe the Rorschach gave them an insight, when in fact it just confirmed an opinion they already had (Wood, Nezworski, Lilienfeld, & Garb, 2003). The result can be an illusory correlation, as described in chapter 2: People remember individual cases in which the results seemed to be useful and then conclude that the test works in general (Garb, Wood, Lilienfeld, & Nezworski, 2005).

James Exner (1986) developed methods to standardize the interpretations of Rorschach responses. Using Exner's system a psychologist counts the number of times a client mentions certain kinds of themes, such as aggression, how often the response refers to the whole blot or just part of it, and several other reasonably objective measurements. From comparison to standards that presumably represent normal people, a psychologist derives measures of certain possible problems. Experienced clinicians using this system achieve a reasonably high level of agreement in their interpretations (Viglione & Taylor, 2003). Most individuals' scores are consistent over time (Grønnerød, 2003), and the test shows no evidence of bias against minority groups (Meyer, 2002).

However, serious problems with the Rorschach remain (Garb et al., 2005; Lilienfeld, Wood, & Garb, 2000; Wood et al., 2003):

- The standardization sample must have been strange because the test identifies *most* people as psychologically disturbed.
- People are asked to give as many answers as they wish on each blot, but psychologists count the *total number* of pathological answers. Highly intelligent or talkative people give more answers than other people do, and the more total answers you give, the more likely you are to say something that counts as "disturbed."
- Although the test is valid for some purposes—such as detecting thought disorder and predicting the outcome of therapy—several other scales of the test appear to be invalid, and many of the scales have never been tested for validity.
- Finally and most important, the Rorschach rarely gives information that could not be obtained more easily in other ways. One study did find that Rorschach scores slightly but significantly improved psychologists' ability to predict juvenile delinquency in comparison to using parental descriptions of their children (Janson & Stattin, 2003). However, in most cases psychologists who are given biographical and MMPI information plus Rorschach results make no better personality judgments than psychologists who are given the biographical and MMPI information alone.

Critics of the Rorschach stop short of calling it completely invalid. Their point is that it is not valid enough to make important decisions about an individual, such as which parent should get custody of a child or which prisoners should get parole (Wood et al., 2003). They also question whether its usefulness justifies training psychologists to use it. Other psychologists continue to defend the Rorschach, insisting that when it is used properly, its reliability and validity are comparable to those of other psychological tests (Society for Personality Assessment, 2005). The problem is that many of the other tests also have validity too low for making important decisions about people. Personality measurement is, frankly, difficult. The controversy will surely continue.

CONCEPT CHECK

16. Why are highly talkative people more likely than others to have their Rorschach answers considered disturbed? (Check your answer on page 563.)

The Thematic Apperception Test

The **Thematic Apperception Test (TAT)** consists of pictures like the one shown in Figure 14.11. *The person is asked to make up a story for each picture, describing what events led up to this scene, what is happening now, and what will happen in the future.* Christiana Morgan and Henry Murray devised this test to measure people's needs. It was revised and published by Murray (1943) and later revised by others. It includes 31 pictures, including some showing women, some showing men, some with both or neither, and one that is totally blank. A psychologist selects a few cards to use with a given client (Lilienfeld et al., 2000).

FIGURE 14.11 In the Thematic Apperception Test, people tell a story about what is going on in a picture, including what led up to this event, what is happening now, and what will happen in the future. *(From the* Thematic Apperception Test *by Henry A. Murray, 1943. © 1971 by the President and Fellows of Harvard College.)*

The assumption is that when you tell a story about a person in the drawing, you probably identify with the person and so the story is really about yourself. You might describe events and concerns in your own life, including some that you might be reluctant to discuss openly. For example, one young man told the following story about a picture of a man clinging to a rope:

> This man is escaping. Several months ago he was beat up and shanghaied and taken aboard ship.

Since then, he has been mistreated and unhappy and has been looking for a way to escape. Now the ship is anchored near a tropical island and he is climbing down a rope to the water. He will get away successfully and swim to shore. When he gets there, he will be met by a group of beautiful native women with whom he will live the rest of his life in luxury and never tell anyone what happened. Sometimes he will feel that he should go back to his old life; but he will never do it. (Kimble & Garmezy, 1968, pp. 582–583)

This young man had entered divinity school to please his parents but was unhappy there. He was wrestling with a secret desire to escape to a new life with greater worldly pleasures. In his story he described someone doing what he wanted to do.

Psychologists use the TAT in various inconsistent ways. Many therapists interpret the results according to their clinical judgment, without any clear rules. If you took the TAT with two psychologists, they might reach different conclusions about you (Cramer, 1996). As with the Rorschach, one criticism is that the test seldom provides information that goes beyond what we could get in other ways (Lilienfeld et al., 2000).

The TAT is also used to measure people's need for achievement by counting all the times they mention achievement. The test is similarly used to measure power and affiliation needs. These results are useful for research purposes, although not necessarily for making decisions about an individual (Lilienfeld et al., 2000).

Handwriting as a Projective Technique

Based on the theory that your personality affects everything you do, some psychologists (and others) have tried analyzing people's handwriting. For example, perhaps people who dot their i's with a dash— *i* —are especially energetic, or perhaps people who draw large loops above the line—as in *allow* —are highly idealistic. Carefully collected data, however, show only random relationships between handwriting and personality (Tett & Palmer, 1997).

Possible Implicit Personality Tests

The research provides only weak support for the projective tests, but the motivation behind them remains: Psychologists would like to measure personality aspects that people cannot or will not discuss openly. So the search for another kind of personality test continues.

Recall from chapter 7 the distinction between explicit and implicit memory. If you listen to a list of words and then try to repeat them, what you recall is explicit memory. If you unknowingly use words from the list in your later conversation, your use of those words constitutes implicit memory. Implicit memory occurs even when you are not aware of remembering something.

Many researchers are trying to develop an implicit personality test—one that measures some aspect of your personality without your awareness. One example is the Implicit Association Test. In the last chapter, we considered how this test could be used to measure prejudices that people do not want to admit. It can also be used to detect other emotional reactions. For example, someone who is nervous around other people might pair social words (*party, friend, companion*) more readily with unpleasant words than with pleasant words. Someone with an intense fear of spiders might pair spiders with unpleasant words more strongly than most others do (Ellwart, Rinck, & Becker, 2006).

Another example of an implicit personality test is the Emotional Stroop Test. Recall the Stroop effect from chapter 8: People are asked to look at a display like this and read the color of the ink instead of reading the words:

> purple brown green blue yellow purple yellow red brown

In the **Emotional Stroop Test**, *someone examines a list of words, some of which relate to a possible source of worry or concern, and tries to say the color of the ink of each word.* For example, say the color of the ink of each of these words as fast as you can:

> cancer venom defeat hospital rattler failure fangs blood loser slither nurses bite jobless cobra inadequate disease

If you have a snake phobia, might you pause longer when you try to read the color of snake-related words—*venom, rattler, fangs, slither, bite, cobra?* You can collect results for yourself at the Online Try It Yourself activity Emotional Stroop Test.

Online Try It Yourself

Let's examine a representative study.

CRITICAL THINKING

WHAT'S THE EVIDENCE?

The Emotional Stroop Test and Suicidal Anxieties

The Emotional Stroop Test is sometimes called the Personal Stroop Test because the items are individualized to concerns that some person might have. In this case the research dealt with people who had attempted suicide (Becker, Strohbach, & Rinck, 1999).

Hypothesis. It is always somewhat difficult to look at a word and say the color of ink instead of reading the word. It may be especially difficult if the word has a strong emotional meaning. In this case the hypothesis is that people who have attempted suicide will be slower than other people to read the color of words that relate to suicide.

Method. The experimenters asked 31 suicide attempters and 31 other people to look at four cards with 12 words each and say the color of ink for each word. One card had words with *positive* connotations, such as *talent* and *love*. Another card had words with *negative* connotations, such as *jail* and *stupidity*. A third card had words with *neutral* connotations, such as *anklebone* and *square*. The final card had *suicide-related* words such as *grave, coldness,* and *darkness.* Different people looked at the cards in different orders. The experimenters timed how long each person took to say the ink colors of words on each card.

Results. Previous suicide attempters took slightly longer to read the suicide-related words. Other people took about equal times with all four cards. Here are the means for the two groups:

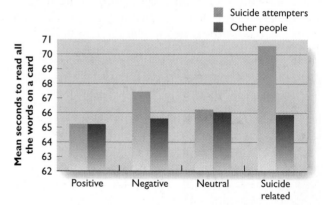

Interpretation. The previous suicide attempters apparently were distracted by the suicide-related words. The difference was not large, however. In its present form, the Emotional Stroop Test reports differences between groups, but it is not reliable enough to make decisions about an individual.

The Emotional Stroop Test has similarly shown that violent offenders have long delays on words like *anger* and *hate* (P. Smith & Waterman, 2003), that pain sufferers respond slowly for words related to pain (Crombez, Hermans, & Adriaensen, 2000), and that drug addicts have delays on words related to addiction (Cox, Fadardi, & Pothos, 2006). However, an extra delay on a word does not necessarily mean that the word reflects a fear or worry. In one study pessimistic people were slow to read the colors of unpleasant words like *germ, loser,* and *failure,* whereas optimistic people were slower with pleasant words like *joy, smile,* and *accomplish* (Segerstrom, 2001). Evidently, people were slow with words that grabbed their attention for whatever reason. Furthermore, if you are slow to read *venom, slither,* and *cobra,* your delay might indicate an emotional reaction, or it might simply reflect the fact that these are uncommon words (Larsen, Mercer, & Balota, 2006). In short, the results are often difficult to interpret.

 CONCEPT CHECK

17. On the preceding sample items of an Emotional Stroop Test, if you had the greatest delay in naming the ink color for *cancer, hospital, blood, nurses,* and *disease,* what would these results imply about your emotions? (Check your answer on page 563.)

Uses and Misuses of Personality Tests

Before any drug company can market a new drug in the United States, the Food and Drug Administration (FDA) requires that it be carefully tested. If the FDA finds the drug safe and effective, it approves the drug for certain purposes and requires a warning label stating how it is to be used. However, after the drug is approved, physicians can prescribe it for purposes the FDA did not consider.

Personality tests are a little like prescription drugs: They should be used with caution and only for the purposes for which they have demonstrable usefulness. At a minimum they help psychologists "break the ice" and begin a conversation with a client. However, a test score by itself can be misleading. For example, suppose someone has an MMPI personality profile that resembles the profile typical for schizophrenia. Identifying schizophrenia or any other unusual condition is a signal-detection problem, as we discussed in chapter 4:

We want to report a stimulus when it is present but not when it is absent. Suppose (realistically) people without schizophrenia outnumber people with schizophrenia by 100 to 1. Suppose further a particular personality profile on the MMPI–2 is characteristic of 95% of people with schizophrenia and only 5% of other people. As Figure 14.12 shows, 5% of the normal population is a larger group than 95% of the population with schizophrenia. Thus, if we labeled as "schizophrenic" everyone with a high score, we would be wrong more often than right. (Recall the representativeness heuristic and the issue of base-rate information, discussed in chapter 8: Someone who seems representative of people in a rare category does not necessarily belong to that category.) Therefore, a conscientious psychologist looks for evidence beyond the test score before drawing a conclusion.

Personality Tests in Action: Criminal Profiling

When we hear about a cruel crime, we wonder, "What kind of person could have done such a thing?" Although you might not have thought of it this way, psychological profiling of criminals is an application of personality testing. It assumes that people who commit similar crimes have similar personalities or backgrounds. A few spectacular anecdotes have been reported. In 1956 a psychiatrist helped New York police find the "mad bomber" who had planted more than 30 bombs over 16 years. He examined the evidence and told police the mad bomber was probably unmarried,

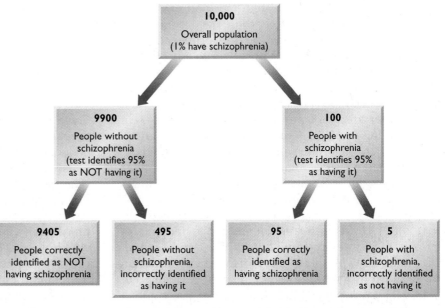

FIGURE 14.12 Assume that a certain profile occurs in 95% of people with schizophrenia and 5% of other people. If we relied entirely on this test, we would correctly identify 95 schizophrenic people and misidentify 495 normal people.

foreign, self-educated, paranoid, 50–60 years old, living in Connecticut, and hating the local power company. That evidence led police to a suspect, who confessed (Winerman, 2004).

However, what we need is systematic evidence, not just a few anecdotes. Certainly, it is possible to draw inferences from a crime, and experienced investigators learn to notice important clues (Alison, Bennell, & Mokros, 2002; Scott, Lambie, Henwood, & Lamb, 2003). For example, if a rapist broke into the house through a window, he was probably someone the victim would not have invited to enter through the door. If he removed all trace of his semen from the scene of the crime, he probably knows something about police investigative techniques and may have been arrested for similar crimes in the past. However, these statements are based on probability, not certainty. For example, someone might know about police investigative techniques from watching crime shows on television, not from a previous arrest. Based on other facts of the crime, investigators draw many inferences with varying degrees of confidence (Turvey, 1999).

Can a psychologist infer a criminal's personality and background in enough detail to aid a police investigation? If so, we should be surprised. Personality testing is far from an exact science, even when psychologists test cooperative people. A few studies have tried to collect data about the relationship between the crime and the criminal. For example, one study of sex-related murders categorized some crimes as deliberate and cruel, some as motivated more by sex than violence, others as "furious" and possibly revenge-based, and still others as antisocial and perverse. The kinds of people who committed one kind of murder differed on the average from those who committed other kinds. However, most of the crimes the researchers examined did not fit neatly into any of these categories, and those that did fit were so few that the apparent links to personal characteristics could have been due to chance (Kocsis, Cooksey, & Irwin, 2002).

Another study examined 100 cases of rape by a stranger. Researchers found no consistent relationship between the crimes and the convicted offenders. That is, men who committed apparently similar crimes were no more likely than others to be similar in age, ethnic group, education, marital status, employment records, or criminal records (Mokros & Alison, 2002). However, a study of murders found one relationship between the offender and the type of crime: Drug addicts were more likely than other murderers to steal from the victim (Hakkanen & Laajasalo, 2006). These results suggest that we can make only a few inferences about criminals from their crimes, but probably not as many as we might hope.

A few studies have measured the accuracy of criminal profilers. Unfortunately, sample sizes have been small because most profilers declined to be tested. In one study five professional profilers and larger numbers of police officers, psychologists, college students, and self-declared psychics were given extensive details about a murder case, including photos of the crime scene, information about the victim, and various laboratory reports. Then they were asked to guess the sex, height, age, religion, and so forth of the murderer in 30 multiple-choice questions. Researchers compared the answers to facts about the actual murderer, who had in fact been caught, although the participants did not know about him. The number of choices per item varied from 2 to 9. Random guessing would have produced 8.1 correct answers out of the 30 items. However, even an uninformed person should do better than chance by knowing, for example, that men commit more crimes than women and by guessing a common religion instead of a rare one. Of the tested groups, professional profilers did the best, at 13.8 correct, and psychics did the worst, at 11.3, but the differences were small and none of the groups did well (Kocsis, Irwin, Hayes, & Nunn, 2000). It is possible to object that this test was not representative of what profilers usually do, but if so, someone needs to propose a better test.

A similar study compared police officers with varying levels of experience and college students with no relevant experience. In this case the college students slightly outperformed the police officers, although the students averaged only 12.4 correct out of 30 (Kocsis, Hayes, & Irwin, 2002). One conclusion from this study is that police experience by itself does not enable someone to guess what kind of person committed a crime.

We should not conclude that criminal profiling is impossible. However, the results of the research so far are unimpressive. Why, then, do many police investigators insist they find criminal profiles useful? Many actual (as opposed to television) profiles of criminals include vague statements that apply to many people: The criminal is about the same age as the victim, average in appearance, does not look out of context in the area, possibly unemployed, has a pornography collection, and is probably a very confused person. (Alison, Smith, & Morgan, 2003). In one study researchers gave police officers a criminal profile that an FBI profiler had prepared for the investigation of a particular murder, plus a description of the actual murderer (who had been caught), and asked the officers how well the profile fit the actual criminal. Most rated it between 5 and 6 on a scale of 1 to 7. The researchers then gave a different group of police officers the same profile, plus a completely different, fictional description of the murderer, changing his age, relationship to the victim, childhood history, and everything else. Most of this group also rated it between 5 and 6 (Alison et al., 2003). In short, the actual facts about the criminal made little difference to how highly the police rated the profile.

 CONCEPT CHECK

18. In what way does criminal profiling illustrate the representativeness heuristic, as described in chapter 8? (Check your answer on page 563.)

IN CLOSING

Possibilities and Limits of Personality Tests

One of most people's main topics of conversation could be described uncharitably as "gossip" or more kindly as "understanding other people." Knowing about other people is important. You need to know whom to trust and whom to distrust.

Given this focus on personality, most of us tend to believe that personality is highly stable and governs a great deal of behavior. If so, someone should be able to look at a crime scene and infer the personality of the perpetrator. Psychologists should be able to listen to people's answers to the Rorschach Inkblots and discern their innermost secrets. So it might seem, but the research suggests we should be cautious. Personality is somewhat consistent over time and situations, but it is like climate—a trend over a long period of time and not always a good guide to what is happening at the moment. Our actions depend on our situations at least as much as they depend on our personalities. ∎

Summary

* *People's tendency to accept personality test results.* Because most people accept almost any interpretation of their personality based on a personality test, tests must be carefully scrutinized to ensure that they are measuring what they claim to measure. (page 554)
* *Standardized personality tests.* A standardized test is administered according to explicit rules, and its results are interpreted in a prescribed fashion based on the norms for the population. (page 555)
* *The MMPI.* The MMPI, a widely used personality test, consists of a series of true–false questions selected in an effort to distinguish among various personality types. The MMPI–2 is a modern version. (page 555)
* *Detection of lying.* The MMPI and other tests guard against lying by including items about common faults and rare virtues. Anyone who denies common faults or claims rare virtues is probably lying. (page 556)

* *Projective techniques.* A projective technique, such as the Rorschach Inkblots or the Thematic Apperception Test, lets people describe their concerns indirectly while talking about ambiguous stimuli. The results from projective techniques have unimpressive validity for making decisions about any individual. (page 557)
* *Implicit personality tests.* The Emotional Stroop Test measures people's delays in naming the color of ink on the assumption that they will pause longer if the word has emotional meaning to them. So far, such tests are useful for research but not for decisions about an individual. (page 560)
* *Uses and misuses of personality tests.* Personality tests can help assess personality, but their results should be interpreted in conjunction with other evidence. (page 561)
* *Criminal profiling.* Some psychologists try to aid police investigations by constructing personality profiles of the kind of person who would commit a certain crime. Research has been limited, and so far, it suggests low accuracy of personality profiles. (page 561)

Answers to Concept Checks

13. Researchers would determine whether people with depression were more likely than other people to answer *true*. If so, the item could be included. If people with depression answer about the same as others, the item would be discarded. (page 555)
14. Such items are intended to detect lying. If you answered *false*, you would get a point on a lying scale. (page 556)
15. The puppet activity could be a projective technique if the child projects his or her own concerns onto the puppets. Sorting cards is an objective measure, not a projective test. (page 557)
16. The psychologist administering the test counts the total number of answers that are considered abnormal or disturbed. The more answers someone gives, the greater the probability of saying something that seems disturbed. (On the other hand, if you give very few answers, you will be considered unimaginative.) (page 558)
17. The results would suggest that you are worried about health-related matters. (page 560)
18. The representativeness heuristic is the assumption that if something resembles category A, then it is a member of category A. In this case the idea is that someone who resembles others who have committed a particular type of crime is a likely suspect. This reasoning is risky if many people fit that description. (page 561)

CHAPTER ENDING

Key Terms and Activities

Key Terms

You can check the page listed for a complete description of a term. You can also check the glossary/index at the end of the text for a definition of a given term, or you can download a list of all the terms and their definitions for any chapter at this website:

www.thomsonedu.com/
psychology/kalat

agreeableness (page 548)
anal stage (page 534)
archetypes (page 538)
Barnum effect (page 554)
belief in a just world (page 546)
big five personality traits (page 548)
catharsis (page 532)
collective unconscious (page 538)
conscientiousness (page 548)
defense mechanism (page 535)
denial (page 536)
displacement (page 536)
ego (page 535)
Emotional Stroop Test (page 560)
extraversion (page 548)

fixation (page 533)
gender role (page 540)
genital stage (page 534)
humanistic psychology (page 542)
id (page 535)
ideal self (page 542)
idiographic approach (page 545)
individual psychology (page 538)
inferiority complex (page 539)
latent period (page 534)
libido (page 533)
Minnesota Multiphasic Personality
    Inventory (MMPI) (page 555)
MMPI–2 (page 555)
neo-Freudians (page 537)
neuroticism (page 548)
nomothetic approach (page 545)
Oedipus complex (page 533)
openness to experience (page 548)
oral stage (page 534)
personality (page 531)
phallic stage (page 534)
projection (page 536)
projective techniques (page 557)
psychoanalysis (page 532)

psychodynamic theory (page 531)
psychosexual pleasure (page 533)
rationalization (page 536)
reaction formation (page 536)
regression (page 536)
repression (page 535)
Rorschach Inkblots (page 557)
self-actualization (page 542)
self-concept (page 542)
social interest (page 540)
standardized test (page 555)
state (page 545)
striving for superiority (page 539)
style of life (page 539)
sublimation (page 536)
superego (page 535)
Thematic Apperception Test (TAT)
    (page 559)
trait (page 545)
trait approach to personality
    (page 546)
unconditional positive regard
    (page 542)
unconscious (page 532)
unshared environment (page 550)

 *Suggestions for Further Reading*

Crews, F. C. (1998). *Unauthorized Freud.* New York: Viking Press. Devastating criticisms of Sigmund Freud's use and misuse of evidence.

Freud, S. (1924). *Introductory lectures on psychoanalysis.* New York: Boni and Liveright. Read Freud's own words and form your own opinion.

 *Web/Technology Resources*

Student Companion Website

www.thomsonedu.com/psychology/kalat

Explore the Student Companion Website for Online Try-It-Yourself activities, practice quizzes, flashcards, and more! The companion site also has direct links to the following websites.

Personality Measures and the Big Five

personality-project.org/personality.html

This site offers a wealth of information about personality traits and research, including links to many research sites.

 *For Additional Study*

Kalat Premium Website

http://www.thomsonedu.com

For Critical Thinking Videos and additional Online Try-It-Yourself activities, go to this site to enter or purchase your code for the Kalat Premium Website.

ThomsonNOW!

http://www.thomsonedu.com

Go to this site for the link to ThomsonNOW, your one-stop study shop. Take a Pretest for this chapter, and Thomson-NOW will generate a personalized Study Plan based on your test results. The Study Plan will identify the topics you need to review and direct you to online resources to help you master those topics. You can then take a Posttest to help you determine the concepts you have mastered and what you still need to work on.

Abnormality, Therapy, and Social Issues

Over the past 4 months, George has injured dozens of people whom he hardly knew. Two of them had to be sent to the hospital. George expresses no guilt, no regrets. He says he would hit every one of them again if he got the chance. What should society do with George?

1. Send him to jail.
2. Commit him to a mental hospital.
3. Give him an award for being the best defensive player in the league.

A protestor who spends years of his life picketing the White House in search of peace is statistically abnormal and puts himself at risk of harm. Still, most of us would not call him psychologically abnormal.

You cannot answer the question unless you know the context of George's behavior. Behavior that seems normal at a party might seem bizarre in a business meeting. Behavior that earns millions for a rock singer might earn a trip to the mental hospital for a college professor.

Even knowing the context of someone's behavior may not tell us whether it is normal. Suppose your rich Aunt Tillie starts passing out money to strangers on the street corner and plans to continue until she has exhausted her fortune. Should the court commit her to a mental hospital and make you the trustee of her estate?

A man claiming to have a message from God asks permission to address the United Nations. A psychiatrist is sure that antipsychotic drugs can relieve this man of his disordered thinking, but the man insists that he is perfectly sane. Should we force him to take the drugs, ignore him, or place his speech on the agenda of the United Nations?

Abnormal Behavior: An Overview

• *What do we mean by "abnormal" behavior?*

Many students in medical school contract what is known as "medical students' disease." Imagine reading a medical textbook that describes, say, Cryptic Ruminating Umbilicus Disorder (CRUD): "The symptoms are hardly noticeable until the condition becomes hopeless. The first symptom is a pale tongue." (You go to the mirror. You can't remember what your tongue is supposed to look like, but it *does* look a little pale.) "Later, a hard spot forms in the neck." (You feel your neck. "Wait! I never felt *this* before! I think it's something hard!") "Just before the arms and legs fall off, there is shortness of breath, increased heart rate, and sweating." (Already distressed, you *do* have shortness of breath, your heart *is* racing, and you *are* sweating profusely.)

Sooner or later, most medical students misunderstand the description of some disease and confuse it with their own normal condition. When my brother was in medical school, he diagnosed himself as having a rare, fatal illness, checked himself into a hospital, and wrote out his will. (He finished medical school and is still doing fine today, decades later.)

Students of psychological disorders are particularly vulnerable to medical students' disease. As you read this chapter and the next one, you may decide that you are suffering from one of the disorders you read about. Perhaps you are, but recognizing a little of yourself in the description of a psychological disorder does not mean that you have the disorder. All of us feel nervous occasionally, and most of us have mood swings, bad habits, or beliefs that strike other people as odd. A diagnosis of a psychological disorder should be reserved for people whose problems seriously interfere with their lives.

Defining Abnormal Behavior

How should we define abnormal behavior? To try to be completely objective, we might define it as any behavior significantly different from the average. However, by that definition unusually happy or successful people are abnormal, and severe depression would be normal if it became common enough.

Another way to define abnormal would be to let people decide for themselves whether they are troubled. That is, anyone who complains of feeling miserable has a problem, even if it is not apparent to anyone else. Fair enough, but what about certain people who insist that they do *not* have a problem? Imagine

What we consider abnormal depends on the context. (a) People dressed as witches ski down a mountain as part of an annual festival in Belalp, Switzerland, in which dressing as witches is supposed to chase away evil spirits. (b) A woman walks through a public park carrying a snake. We don't know why, but unusual behavior is not necessarily a sign of psychological disorder.

a woman who babbles incoherently, urinates and defecates in the street, insults strangers, begs for $1 bills and then sets them on fire, while claiming to be obeying messages from another planet. Most of us would call her behavior abnormal, even if she does not.

The American Psychiatric Association (1994) defined abnormal behavior as any behavior that leads to distress (including distress to others), disability (impaired functioning), or an increased risk of death, pain, or loss of freedom. This definition may be too inclusive. For example, when Dr. Martin Luther King Jr. fought for the rights of African Americans, he risked death, pain, and loss of freedom, but we regard his acts as heroic, not abnormal. Presumably, we want to limit our concept of "abnormal behavior" to conditions that are clearly undesirable. Social scientists hate to admit that they make value judgments, but calling a behavior abnormal seems to be one, perhaps unavoidably.

CRITICAL THINKING
A STEP FURTHER

What Is Abnormal?

How would *you* define abnormal behavior?

Cultural Influences on Abnormality

Each time and place has its own view about abnormal behavior and what it means. People in the Middle Ages, for example, regarded peculiar behavior as a sign of demon possession and treated it with religious rituals. In part of Sudan some years ago, women had low status and very limited rights. If a woman's husband mistreated her, she had no defense. However, people in this society believed that a woman could be possessed by a demon who caused her to lose control and scream all sorts of "crazy" things that she "could not possibly believe," including insults against her own husband (!). Her husband could not scold or punish her because, after all, it was not she but the demon who was speaking. The standard way to remove the demon was to provide the woman with luxurious food, new clothing, an opportunity to spend much time with other women, and almost anything else she demanded until the demon departed. You can imagine how common demon possession became (Constantinides, 1977).

More examples: *Brain fag syndrome*, marked by headache, dizziness, eye fatigue, and inability to concentrate, is a common complaint among students in sub-Saharan Africa (Morakinyo & Peltzer, 2002). You might ask your own professor to excuse you from your next test because of brain fag syndrome, but unless you live in sub-Saharan Africa, I doubt that your explanation will do you much good. *Koro*, said to be common in China, is a fear that a man's penis will retract into the body, causing death. Some men have been known to hold onto their penis constantly to prevent it from disappearing into the body (Bracha, 2006). Japanese psychiatrists recognize a condition called *karoshi*, in which someone who has just been humiliated in public suffers a fatal heart attack (Bracha, 2006).

You have probably heard the expression "to run amok." *Running amok* is an abnormal behavior in parts of Southeast Asia, where someone (usually a young man) runs around engaging in indiscriminate violent behavior (Berry, Poortinga, Segal, & Dasen, 1992). Such behavior is considered an understandable reaction to psychological stress. Does running amok remind

Edvard Munch (1864–1944), *Self Portrait, The Night Wanderer*, 1923–1924, Munch Museum, Oslo, Norway. The uncurtained windows and the bare room emphasize the feeling of loneliness and isolation.

© 2002 The Munch Museum/Munch Willingsen Group. Artists Rights Society (ARS) NY/Erich Lessing/Art Resource, NY.

Fans sometimes celebrate a major sports victory with a destructive rampage. In some ways this behavior is like "running amok." It is an abnormal behavior copied from other people's example.

Chris Sizemore, whose story was told in *The Three Faces of Eve,* exhibited a total of 22 personalities, including her final, permanent identity.

you of anything common in North America or Europe? How about the celebrations that occur after a sports team wins a major championship? Like running amok, people often regard such wild displays as temporary responses to overwhelming emotion.

The point is that just as we learn from other people how to behave normally, we also learn some of the possible ways to behave abnormally. For a Western culture example, one Australian psychiatrist found that three mental patients in a hospital had cut off one of their ears. Assuming that this behavior must be a common symptom of mental illness, he contacted other psychiatrists to ask how often they had seen the same thing, but he found that ear removal was occurring only at his own hospital. Apparently, after one patient cut off his ear, the other two copied (Alroe & Gunda, 1995). (Why they copied is, of course, an interesting question.)

Suggestion may also be a major influence in **dissociative identity disorder (DID)**, previously known as **multiple personality disorder**, in which *someone alternates among two or more distinct personalities.* (Alternating among different personalities is *not* schizophrenia, although the media often mislabel it as such.) Dissociative identity disorder was extremely rare before the 1950s, when a few cases received much publicity. Chris Sizemore was featured in the book and movie *The Three Faces of Eve,* written by her psychiatrists (Thigpen & Cleckley, 1957). Sizemore ("Eve") eventually told her own story, which was very different from her psychiatrists' version (Sizemore & Huber, 1988; Sizemore & Pittillo, 1977). A few other cases of dissociative identity disorder also received extensive publicity, such as the celebrated case *Sybil,* although one of the psychiatrists associated with that case later said he thought the author of

the book about Sybil had distorted the facts to improve sales of the book (Borch-Jacobsen, 1997). In the 1970s through the 1990s, therapists reported far more cases than anyone had seen before. One hypothesis is that the publicity about Eve and Sybil led to the increased prevalence. Some therapists suggested to patients with vague symptoms that perhaps they had other personalities. In some cases they used hypnosis to explore that possibility, inadvertently implanting a suggestion while people were in a state of increased suggestibility (Lilienfeld et al., 1999). The suggestions may have exaggerated small tendencies until they became full-blown disorders.

CONCEPT CHECK

1. In what way might dissociative identity disorder resemble brain fag syndrome, koro, and running amok? (Check your answer on page 575.)

The Biopsychosocial Model

In Western cultures today, the predominant view is the **biopsychosocial model**, which emphasizes that *abnormal behavior has three major aspects: biological, psychological, and sociological.* Many researchers and therapists focus more on one aspect than another, but few deny that all three are important.

The *biological* roots of abnormal behavior include genetic factors, which can lead to abnormal brain development, excesses or deficiencies in the activity of various neurotransmitters or hormones, and so forth. Additional influences include brain damage, infectious diseases, brain tumors, poor nutrition, inadequate sleep, and the overuse of drugs, including non-prescription medications.

The *psychological* component of abnormality includes a person's vulnerability to stressful events. For example, people who are known to have been physically or sexually abused in childhood are more likely than others to develop psychological problems in adulthood (J. G. Johnson, Cohen, Brown, Smailes, & Bernstein, 1999).

Finally, the behavior must be understood in a *social* and cultural context. People are greatly influenced by other people's expectations. Many people with strange behavior have disordered families or social networks.

 CONCEPT CHECK

2. Of the three aspects of the biopsychosocial model, which one would be most prominent in explanations of brain fag syndrome and running amok? (Check your answer on page 575.)

Classifying Psychological Disorders

To determine the best kinds of therapy for psychological disorders, researchers need to measure the effects of various treatments on a large number of people suffering from similar problems. For example, suppose researchers in various places want to study depression. If they define depression differently, or disagree about which people should be considered depressed, they won't make much progress. To standardize their definitions, psychiatrists and psychologists developed *a reference book called* the ***Diagnostic and Statistical Manual of Mental Disorders (DSM)***—now in its fourth edition and therefore known as *DSM–IV*—which *sets specific criteria for each psychological diagnosis,* including depression, alcohol intoxication, exhibitionism, pathological gambling, anorexia nervosa, sleepwalking disorder, stuttering, and hundreds of others. The latest edition of this book is called a Text Revision of *DSM–IV* and therefore is labeled *DSM–IV–TR* (American Psychiatric Association, 2000).

TABLE 15.1 Some Major Categories of Psychological Disorders According to Axis I of DSM–IV

Category	Examples and Descriptions
Disorder usually first evident in childhood	*Attention deficit hyperactivity disorder:* impulsivity, impaired attention *Tourette's disorder:* repetitive movements such as blinking, twitching, chanting sounds or words *Elimination disorders:* bedwetting, urinating or defecating in one's clothes *Stuttering:* frequent repetition or prolongation of sounds while trying to speak
Substance-related disorders	Abuse of alcohol, cocaine, opiates, or other drugs
Schizophrenia	Deterioration of daily functioning along with a combination of hallucinations, delusions, or other symptoms
Delusional (paranoid) disorder	Unjustifiable beliefs, such as "everyone is talking about me behind my back"
Mood disorders	*Major depressive disorder:* Repeated episodes of depressed mood and lack of energy *Bipolar disorder:* Alternation between periods of depression and mania
Anxiety disorders	*Panic disorder:* Repeated attacks of intense terror *Phobia:* Severe anxiety and avoidance of a particular object or situation
Somatoform disorders	*Conversion disorder:* Physical ailments caused partly by psychological factors but not faked *Hypochondriasis:* Exaggerated complaints of illness *Somatization disorder:* Complaints of pain or other ailments without any physical disorder
Dissociative disorders	Loss of personal identity or memory without brain damage
Sexual disorders	*Pedophilia:* Sexual attraction to children *Voyeurism:* Sexual arousal primarily from watching others undress or have sexual relations *Exhibitionism:* Sexual arousal from exposing one's genitals in public
Eating disorders	*Anorexia nervosa:* Refusal to eat, fear of fatness *Bulimia nervosa:* Binge eating alternating with severe dieting
Sleep disorders	*Sleep terror disorder:* Repeated sudden awakenings in a state of panic *Insomnia:* Frequently not getting enough sleep to feel well rested the next day
Impulse control disorders	Frequently acting on impulses that others would inhibit, such as stealing, gambling foolishly, or hitting people

DSM-IV *Classifications*

The clinicians and researchers who use *DSM–IV* classify each client along five separate *axes* (lists). A person may have one disorder, several, or none at all. The axis that gets the most attention is *Axis I, clinical disorders*. Table 15.1 lists the major categories of disorder listed on Axis I. Each disorder on Axis I represents in some way a deterioration of functioning. Previous chapters discussed eating disorders and sleep disorders, which are listed on Axis I. In chapter 16 we shall concentrate on the most common Axis I disorders—anxiety disorders, substance-abuse disorders, and depression—as well as schizophrenia, a less common but often disabling condition.

Axis II includes personality disorders and mental retardation, as listed in Table 15.2. One distinction between Axis I and Axis II disorders is that Axis II disorders tend to be lifelong, whereas Axis I disorders represent a deterioration of functioning. However, that rule has many exceptions. For example, the personality disorders listed in Axis II change from time to time more than psychologists used to assume (Lenzenweger, Johnson, & Willett, 2004). The main reason for distinguishing Axis II from Axis I is that Axis II disorders are generally less spectacular and less likely to be the main reason for consulting a therapist. By listing Axis II disorders separately, *DSM–IV* encourages the therapist to notice them. That is, a therapist fills out a diagnosis on Axis I and then comes to the question of what, if anything, to list on Axis II.

It is possible to list "no diagnosis," but at least the therapist pauses to consider the possibilities.

A **personality disorder** is *a maladaptive, inflexible way of dealing with the environment and other people,* such as being unusually self-centered. Some personality disorders are widespread. For example, one survey found that 5% of people had avoidant personality disorder, and about 2% each had paranoid and histrionic personality disorders (Torgerson, Kringlen, & Cramer, 2001). Most people do not seek treatment for their personality disorders, except when other people insist on it. Treatment is usually slow and difficult, as it requires changing someone's personality.

Axis III, general medical conditions, lists physical disorders, such as diabetes, head trauma, or alcoholic cirrhosis of the liver. A psychotherapist needs to know about these disorders because they influence behavior and sometimes interfere with treatment. *Axis IV, psychosocial and environmental problems*, indicates how much stress the person has had to endure. Stress can intensify a psychological disorder and thus affect the course of treatment. *Axis V, global assessment of functioning*, evaluates a person's overall level of functioning on a scale from 1 (serious attempt at suicide or complete inability to take care of oneself) to 100 (happy, productive, with many interests). Some people with a psychological disorder are able to proceed with their normal work and social activities, but other people are not.

TABLE 15.2 Some Major Categories of Psychological Disorders According to Axis II of *DSM–IV*

Category and Examples	Descriptions
Mental Retardation	Intellectual functioning significantly below average; inability to function effectively and independently
Personality Disorders	
Paranoid personality disorder	Suspiciousness, habitual interpretation of others' acts as threatening
Schizoid personality disorder	Impaired social relations and emotional responses
Schizotypal personality disorder	Poor relationships with other people; odd thinking; neglect of normal grooming. (Similar to schizophrenia but less severe.)
Antisocial personality disorder	Lack of affection for others; high probability of harming others without feeling guilty; apparent weakness of most emotions
Borderline personality disorder	Lack of stable self-image; trouble establishing lasting relationships or maintaining lasting decisions; repeated self-endangering behaviors
Histrionic personality disorder	Excessive emotionality and attention seeking
Narcissistic personality disorder	Exaggerated opinion of one's own importance and disregard for others. (Narcissus was a figure in Greek mythology who fell in love with his own image.)
Avoidant personality disorder	Avoidance of social contact; lack of friends
Dependent personality disorder	Preference for letting other people make decisions; lack of initiative and self-confidence
Obsessive-compulsive personality disorder	Preoccupation with orderliness and perfectionism. (Similar to obsessive-compulsive disorder, but less severe.)

Criticisms of *DSM-IV*

DSM–IV has helped standardize psychiatric diagnoses, but even its most loyal defenders admit it has flaws. One criticism is that *DSM–IV* includes many minor disorders. A reply is that recognizing and treating minor problems may help prevent major problems (Kessler et al., 2003). However, some of the problems that therapists diagnose pose little threat of developing into anything serious (Kutchins & Kirk, 1997). For example, if you don't enjoy sex as much as most other people seem to, you might seek help. To receive help you will be diagnosed with *hypoactive sexual desire disorder*. If you are a woman with enough premenstrual distress that you would like help dealing with it, a therapist might diagnose you with *premenstrual dysphoric disorder* (Daw, 2002). Any diagnosis implies that you have a mental illness, so the result is that almost anyone who wants a little help can be labeled mentally ill. Partly because of the large number of diagnoses, surveys have found that about a quarter of all people in the United States qualify for a psychiatric diagnosis in any given year, and almost half qualify at some time in life (Kessler, Berglund, et al., 2005; Kessler, Chiu, Demler, & Walters, 2005). The most common disorders are anxiety disorders, mood disorders (e.g., depression), impulse control problems (including attention-deficit disorder and conduct disorder), and substance abuse, as shown in Figure 15.1.

A more fundamental question concerns *DSM–IV*'s assumption that disorders occur in categories. That is, if you have a disorder, it must be depression, schizophrenia, panic disorder, or one of the other items on the list. Therapists' goal has been to put each patient into a discrete category, just as physicians do for other kinds of illness. If you report to a physician with a cough and fever, the physician runs tests to determine whether you have pneumonia, bronchitis, tuberculosis, or some other illness and then recommends a treatment based on the illness. However, psychiatric disorders may or may not fit into such neat categories (Ahn, Flanagan, Marsh, & Sanislow, 2006). So far, no laboratory test separates one psychiatric disorder from another. Behavioral symptoms are often ambiguous too. A typical client fits several diagnoses partly and none perfectly (Kupfer, First, & Regier, 2002). Of all people with any psychiatric diagnosis, nearly half qualify for at least one additional diagnosis, and people with a serious disorder are especially likely to have additional disorders (Kessler, Chiu, et al., 2005).

The problem is even more acute for the personality disorders. Because the personality disorders overlap significantly, most people who meet the criteria for one of them meet the standards for others (Lenzenweger et al., 2004). Many psychologists and psychiatrists predict that the next diagnostic manual—*DSM–V*, to be published in 2010 or later—will include a major revision for the personality disorders. Instead of listing categories, it may list dimensions, such as neuroticism, antagonism, social withdrawal, and compulsiveness. A therapist would rate a patient on each of those dimensions independently (Watson & Clark, 2006).

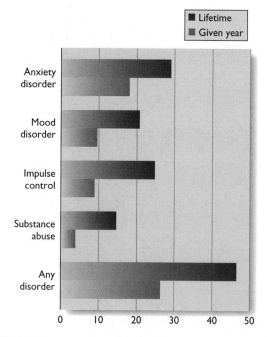

FIGURE 15.1 In this survey just over a quarter of U.S. adults suffer a psychological disorder in any given year, and nearly half do at some time in life. This figure combines results for men and women of all adult ages. *(Based on data of Kessler, Berglund, et al., 2005; Kessler, Chiu, Demler, & Walters, 2005)*

▌ Almost everyone has an unpleasant mood or behaves strangely once in a while. Many people who qualify for a *DSM–IV* diagnosis are not very different from other people.

CONCEPT CHECK

3. How does Axis I of *DSM–IV* differ from Axis II?
4. What are some criticisms of *DSM–IV*? (Check your answers on page 575.)

IN CLOSING

Is Anyone Normal?

According to the studies described in this module, nearly half of all people in the United States will have a *DSM–IV* disorder at some point in life. If those statistics are even close to accurate, one implication is obvious: Most of the people who qualify for a psychological diagnosis are not a rare group who would stand out immediately from everyone else. At some point in your life, you may have a bout of some kind of psychological distress. If so, remember that you have plenty of company. ▌

Summary

- *Normal and abnormal behavior.* The American Psychiatric Association defines behavior as abnormal if it leads to distress, disability, or increased risk of harm. However, any definition of abnormal behavior has difficulties. (page 569)
- *Cultural influences on abnormality.* Every culture provides examples not only of how to behave normally but also of how to behave abnormally. (page 570)
- *Multiple causes of abnormal behavior.* Abnormal behavior is the result of various combinations of biological factors, early experiences, and learned responses to a stressful or unsupportive environment. (page 571)
- *The Diagnostic and Statistical Manual.* Psychological disorders are classified in the *Diagnostic and Statistical Manual of Mental Disorders, Fourth Edition (DSM–IV).* This manual classifies disorders along five axes. Axes I and II contain psychological disorders; Axis III lists physical ailments that can affect behavior; Axes IV and V provide the means of evaluating a person's stress level and overall functioning. (page 573)
- *Axis I disorders.* Axis I of *DSM–IV* lists a wide variety of disorders, including anxiety disorders, substance abuse, and depression. (page 573)
- *Axis II disorders.* Axis II of *DSM–IV* lists mental retardation and various personality disorders. (page 573)
- *Personality disorders.* Personality disorders are stable characteristics that impair a person's effectiveness or ability to get along with others. Examples of personality disorders are excessive dependence on others and excessive self-centeredness. (page 573)
- *Criticisms of DSM–IV.* *DSM–IV* has been criticized for giving psychiatric labels to people with minor difficulties or understandable reactions to stressful situations. A fundamental question is whether disorders occur as discrete categories. Many people have some but not all of the typical symptoms of several disorders. (page 574)

Answers to Concept Checks

1. In each case people are reacting to real problems, but the way they react follows suggestions or expectations from other people. (page 571)
2. The social aspect would certainly be prominent because these disorders occur only in cultures that have made them seem like options. However, the people showing these symptoms may have biological and psychological problems as well. (page 571)
3. Axis I lists disorders that in most cases represent a deterioration of functioning. Axis II includes mental retardation and personality disorders, which are in most cases lifelong conditions. Also, personality disorders are easy to overlook because a client seldom comes to a therapist complaining about them. (page 573)
4. One criticism is that *DSM–IV* lists many minor problems and risks giving too many people the stigma of a mental illness. Also, many of the disorders overlap, especially the personality disorders. It is not clear that we should treat psychological disorders as discrete categories. (page 574)

Psychotherapy: An Overview

- *What methods do therapists use to combat psychological disorders, and how effective are they?*

Observation

If I don't drive around the park, I'm pretty sure to make my mark.

If I'm in bed each night by ten, I may get back my looks again.

If I abstain from fun and such, I'll probably amount to much.

But I shall stay the way I am, Because I do not give a damn.

—Dorothy Parker (1944)[1]

Psychotherapy is *a treatment of psychological disorders by methods that include a personal relationship between a trained therapist and a client.* But psychotherapy does little good unless the client gives the proverbial damn.

Psychotherapy is used for people with the disorders listed in *DSM–IV* and also for people who just need to talk about some concern or worry. Some psychotherapy clients are virtually incapacitated by their problems, but others are reasonably happy, successful people who would like to function even more successfully.

The discussion here focuses on psychotherapy as it is practiced in the United States and Europe. Most Chinese would consider it shameful to discuss personal or family matters with a stranger (Bond, 1991). Psychologists in India adapt their practice to local customs. For example, to maintain a close relationship with a client, they have to respect beliefs in astrology and other concepts that most Western psychologists would dismiss (Clay, 2002).

Historical Trends in Psychotherapy

Psychotherapy has changed greatly since the mid-1900s for both scientific and economic reasons (Sanchez & Turner, 2003). Before World War II, almost all psychotherapists were psychiatrists. In the 1940s and 1950s, most therapists used Freudian methods and expected to see each patient frequently, perhaps even

daily, for months or years. No one had done much research to determine whether the treatment was effective, mainly because therapists had little incentive to undertake such research. People who wanted therapy had to pay for it themselves, as almost no one had health insurance that covered psychiatric visits. Most didn't have health insurance at all. Therefore, few people other than the wealthy received psychotherapy. At this time almost no research had been done concerning the effectiveness of psychotherapy, so clients had little choice but to trust whatever their therapists claimed. Some clients received a diagnosis such as depressed or schizophrenic, but many were given either no diagnosis at all or a vague diagnosis like "neurotic" or "psychotic."

Today, all of that has changed. In addition to psychiatrists, clinical psychologists, social workers, and others provide services for distressed people. Although some continue to rely on Freud's methods, most have turned to other procedures. Many other changes can be traced to the influence of health maintenance organizations (HMOs) and other health insurance programs that now pay for mental health care. HMOs try to restrain costs and make sure that money is spent effectively. If the man down the street pays for his own treatment, no one will object if he sees his therapist every day for the rest of his life for something that strikes most of us as a quack treatment. However, if he is under the same health insurance program that you are, then you are helping to pay his fees. Suddenly, you and your insurance company want to know whether his treatment is effective enough to justify the cost. Generally, insurance companies will pay for more treatment if someone has a diagnosed mental disorder. They limit the treatment to a moderate number of sessions and support only therapies that appear effective according to the best available evidence. The consequences have been, as you might guess:

- Therapists have listed more and more diagnoses of mental disorder so that more clients can qualify for insurance help. The previous module mentioned the huge number of diagnoses listed in *DSM–IV,* and now you understand why.
- Therapists try to streamline the process to achieve good results in a few sessions if possible, extending the treatment only if necessary.
- Psychologists have conducted extensive research on the effectiveness of psychotherapy. In particular

[1]Quote from "Observation" by Dorothy Parker, copyright 1928, renewed © 1956 by Dorothy Parker from *The Portable Dorothy Parker,* by Dorothy Parker, introduction by Brendan Gill. Used by permission of Viking Penguin, a division of Penguin Books USA Inc.

they have worked to determine **evidence-based treatments,** *which are therapies demonstrated to be helpful* (APA Presidential Task Force on Evidence-Based Practice, 2006). Many therapists follow published manuals that specify exactly how to treat various disorders.

- In many cases HMOs have also produced unwelcome changes to psychological care because they sometimes refuse to support treatment or insist on inexpensive, minimum care—for example, directing a patient with drug abuse to enter a 3-day outpatient program instead of longer, but probably much more effective, inpatient treatment at a rehabilitation center. That is, sometimes HMOs stand in the way of good care instead of facilitating it.

Table 15.3 summarizes these changes.

Psychotherapists today employ a great variety of methods. Different therapists treating the same problem approach it in strikingly different ways. We shall review some of the most common types of therapy, exploring what they have in common as well as how they differ.

TABLE 15.3 Changes in Psychotherapy Between the 1950s and the 21st Century

	1950s	Early 21st Century
Payment	By the patient or family	By health insurance
Types of therapist	Psychiatrists	Psychiatrists, clinical psychologists, others
Types of treatment	Mostly Freudian	Many types; emphasis on evidence-based treatments
Duration of treatment	Usually long, often years	A few sessions if effective; more if necessary
Diagnoses	Usually vague, such as "neurosis" or "psychosis." Often, no diagnosis.	Many diagnoses. Each clearly described in *DSM–IV*.
Treatment decisions	By the therapist and patient	Sometimes by the HMO

Psychoanalysis, the first of the "talk" therapies, is *a method based on identifying unconscious thoughts and emotions and bringing them to consciousness to help people understand their thoughts and actions.* Psychoanalysis is therefore an "insight-oriented therapy" in contrast to therapies that focus on changing thoughts and behaviors (Figure 15.2). Psychoanalysis was the dominant form of psychotherapy in the United States in the mid-1900s. Over the years it has declined in popularity and influence in the United States, although it remains more widespread in parts of Europe.

Freud believed that psychological problems result from unconscious thought processes and that the way to control self-defeating behavior is to make those

 CONCEPT CHECK

5. How has treatment of psychological disorders changed since the 1950s?
6. What is one major reason psychotherapists have added so many diagnoses to *DSM–IV*? (Check your answers on page 589.)

Psychoanalysis

Psychodynamic therapies *attempt to relate personality to the interplay of conflicting impulses within the individual, including some that the individual may not consciously recognize.* For example, both Sigmund Freud's procedure (looking for sexual motives) and Alfred Adler's procedure (looking for power and superiority motives) are considered psychodynamic despite the differences between them. Here we focus on the procedure developed by Freud, although its practitioners have modified and developed it further since Freud's time.

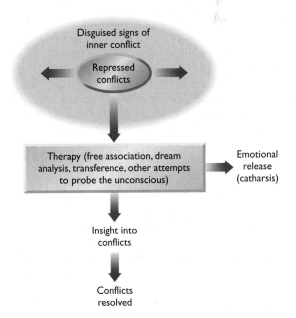

FIGURE 15.2 The goal of psychoanalysis is to resolve psychological problems by bringing to awareness the unconscious thought processes that created the difficulty. *Analysis* literally means "to loosen or break up, to look at the parts."

processes conscious. Bringing them to consciousness, he thought, would produce **catharsis,** *a release of pent-up emotions associated with unconscious thoughts and memories.* To bring unconscious material to consciousness, Freud used dream analysis, as discussed in chapter 10, free association, and transference.

Free Association

In free association the client starts *thinking about a particular symptom or problem and then reports everything that comes to mind—a word, a phrase, a visual image.* The client is instructed not to omit or censor anything or even try to speak in complete sentences. The psychoanalyst listens for links and themes that might tie the patient's fragmentary remarks together. The assumption is that nothing happens without a cause, and every jump from one thought to another reveals a relationship between them.

Here is a paraphrased excerpt from a free-association session:

> A man begins by describing a conference he had with his boss the previous day. He did not like the boss's policy, but he was in no position to contradict the boss. He dreamed something about an ironing board, but that was all he remembered of the dream. He comments that his wife has been complaining about the way their maid irons. He thinks his wife is being unfair; he hopes she does not fire the maid. He complains that his boss did not give him credit for some work he did recently. He recalls a childhood episode: He jumped off a cupboard and bounced off his mother's behind while she was leaning over to do some ironing. She told his father, who gave him a spanking. His father never let him explain; he was always too strict. (Munroe, 1955, p. 39)

To a psychoanalyst the links in this story suggest that the man is associating his wife with his mother. His wife was unfair to the maid about the ironing, just as his mother had been unfair to him. Moreover, his boss is like his father, never giving him a chance to explain his errors and never giving him credit for what he did well.

Transference

Some clients express love or hatred for their therapist because he or she unconsciously reminds them of someone else. Psychoanalysts call this inappropriate

A psychotherapist, like this military psychologist in a Haitian refugee camp, tries to help people overcome problems.

reaction **transference;** they mean that clients are *transferring onto the therapist the behaviors and feelings they originally established toward their father, mother, or another important person in their lives.* Transference often provides clues to the client's feelings about that person.

Psychoanalysts offer **interpretations** of what the client says—that is, they *explain the underlying meaning*—and may even argue with the client about interpretations. They may regard the client's disagreement as resistance. For example, a client who has begun to touch on an extremely anxiety-provoking topic may turn the conversation to something trivial or may simply "forget" to come to the next session.

Psychoanalysts today modify Freud's approach in many ways. The goal is still to bring about a major reorganization of the personality, changing a person from the inside out, by helping people understand the hidden reasons behind their actions.

 CONCEPT CHECK

7. What methods do psychoanalysts use to try to gain access to the unconscious? (Check your answer on page 589.)

Behavior Therapy

Behavior therapists assume that human behavior is learned and that someone who has learned an abnormal behavior can extinguish it or learn a competing response. They identify the behavior that needs to be changed, such as a fear or bad habit, and then set about changing it through reinforcement and other principles of learning. They may try to understand the causes of the behavior as a first step toward changing it, but unlike psychoanalysts, they are more interested in changing behaviors than in understanding their hidden meanings.

Behavior therapy *begins with clear, well-defined behavioral goals, such as eliminating test anxiety, and then attempts to achieve those goals through learning.* Setting clear goals enables the therapist to judge whether the therapy is succeeding. If the client

FIGURE 15.3 A small device called a Potty Pager fits into a child's underwear and vibrates when it becomes moist. This awakens the child, who then learns to awaken when the bladder is full.

Courtesy of Ideas for Living, Inc.

shows no improvement after a few sessions, the therapist tries a different procedure.

One example of behavior therapy is for children who continue wetting the bed after the usual age of toilet training. Occasionally, this problem lingers to age 5, 10, or even into the teens. Many bedwetters have small bladders and thus have difficulty getting through the night without urinating. Also, many are unusually deep sleepers who do not wake up when they need to urinate (Stegat, 1975).

The most effective procedure uses classical conditioning to train the child to wake up at night when the bladder is full (Houts, Berman, & Abramson, 1994). A small battery-powered device is attached to the child's underwear at night (Figure 15.3). When the child urinates, the device detects the moisture and produces a pulsing vibration that awakens the child. (Alternative devices work on the same principle but produce loud noises.) The vibration acts as an unconditioned stimulus (UCS) that evokes the unconditioned response (UCR) of waking up. In this instance the body itself generates the conditioned stimulus (CS): the sensation produced by a full bladder (Figure 15.4). Whenever that sensation is present, it serves as a signal that the vibration is imminent. After a few pairings (or more), the sensation of a full bladder is enough to wake the child.

Actually, the situation is a little more complicated because the child is positively reinforced with praise for waking up to use the toilet. Thus, the process includes both classical and operant conditioning. Training with an alarm or vibration eliminates bedwetting in most children, sometimes after as little as one night.

 CONCEPT CHECK

8. Contrast the goals and methods of behavior therapy with those of psychoanalysis. (Check your answer on page 589.)

Therapies That Focus on Thoughts and Beliefs

Suppose someone asks for your opinion on something and then asks someone else also. How do you react? You might think, "It's perfectly reasonable to get several opinions." Or you might feel hurt by the implication that your opinion wasn't trusted or wasn't good enough. Suppose someone invites several of your friends to a party but not you. Do you shrug your shoulders or do you take it as an insult? Your emotions depend not just on the events of life but also on how you interpret them. Some therapists focus on the thoughts and beliefs that underlie emotional reactions. Unlike psychoanalysts, these therapists are more concerned about what their clients are thinking right now than about the early experiences that led to those thoughts.

Cognitive Therapies

Cognitive therapy seeks to improve people's psychological well-being by changing their thoughts and beliefs—their cognitions (Beck, 1976; Hollon & Beck,

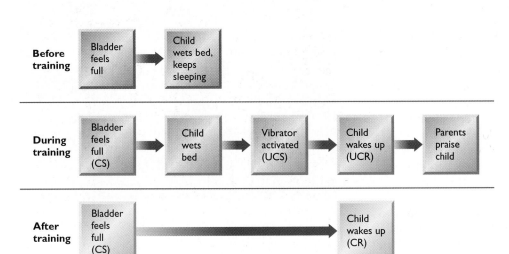

FIGURE 15.4 A child can be trained not to wet the bed by using classical conditioning techniques. At first the sensation of a full bladder (the CS) produces no response, and the child wets the bed. This causes a vibration or other alarm (the UCS), and the child wakes up (the UCR). By associating the sensation of a full bladder with the vibration, the child soon begins waking up to the sensation of a full bladder alone.

1979). A cognitive therapist identifies distressing thoughts and encourages the client to explore the evidence behind them. Usually, the client discovers that the beliefs are unjustified. Cognitive therapy also encourages people to monitor their daily activities and determine which ones provide opportunities for pleasure or a sense of accomplishment. The therapist helps the client overcome specific problems, develop better social skills, and take a more active role in life.

A related approach, **rational-emotive behavior therapy,** *assumes that thoughts (rationality) lead to emotions. The problem therefore is not the unpleasant emotions themselves, but the irrational thoughts that lead to them.* Rational-emotive therapists believe that abnormal behavior often results from irrational "internal sentences" such as these (Ellis, 1987):

- I must perform certain tasks successfully.
- I must perform well at all times.
- I must have the approval of certain people at all times.
- Others must treat me fairly and with consideration.
- I must live under easy, gratifying conditions.

The word *must* makes these beliefs irrational. Rational-emotive therapists try to identify irrational beliefs (which people may never have verbalized) and then contradict them. They urge clients to substitute other more realistic internal sentences. Here is an excerpt from a rational-emotive therapy session with a 25-year-old physicist:

Client: The whole trouble is that I am really a phony. I am living under false pretenses. And the longer it goes on, the more people praise me and make a fuss over my accomplishments, the worse I feel.

Therapist: What do you mean you are a phony? I thought that you told me, during our last session, that your work has been examined at another laboratory and that some of the people there think your ideas are of revolutionary importance.

Client: But I have wasted so much time. I could be doing very much better. . . . Remember that book I told you I was writing . . . it's been three weeks now since I've spent any time on it. And this is simple stuff that I should be able to do with my left hand while I am writing a technical paper with my right. I have heard Bob Oppenheimer reel off stuff extemporaneously to a bunch of newspaper reporters that is twice as good as what I am mightily laboring on in this damned book!

Therapist: Perhaps so. And perhaps you're not quite as good—yet—as Oppenheimer or a few other outstanding people in your field. But the real point, it seems to me, is that . . . here you are, at just

twenty-five, with a Ph.D. in a most difficult field, with an excellent job, much good work in process, and what well may be a fine professional paper and a good popular book also in progress. And just because you're not another Oppenheimer or Einstein quite yet, you're savagely berating yourself.

Client: Well, shouldn't I be doing much better than I am?

Therapist: No, why the devil should you? As far as I can see, you are not doing badly at all. But your major difficulty—the main cause of your present unhappiness—is your utterly perfectionistic criteria for judging your performance. (Ellis & Harper, 1961, pp. 99–100)

 CONCEPT CHECK

9. How does the concept behind rational-emotive therapy compare to the James-Lange theory of emotions discussed in chapter 12? (Check your answer on page 589.)

Cognitive-Behavior Therapy

Many therapists combine important features of both behavior therapy and cognitive therapy to form **cognitive-behavior therapy.** *Cognitive-behavior therapists set explicit goals for changing people's behavior, but they place more emphasis than most behavior therapists do on changing people's interpretation of their situation.* For example, most of us become very upset if we see a video news report showing a fatal au-

Fictional tragedies in films, like the one in *Con Air,* are far less disturbing than real ones. The impact of any event depends not just on the event itself but also on its context and how we interpret it.

tomobile accident; we would be much less upset if someone told us that the film was a special-effects simulation (Meichenbaum, 1995). Similarly, cognitive-behavior therapists try to help clients distinguish between serious problems and imagined or exaggerated problems. They help clients change their interpretations of past events, current concerns, and future possibilities. Cognitive-behavior therapy has become one of the most widespread forms of therapy in the United States.

Humanistic Therapy

As we saw in chapter 14, humanistic psychologists believe that people can decide deliberately what kind of person to be and that we naturally strive to achieve our full potential. However, people sometimes learn to dislike themselves because they feel criticism and rejection. They become distressed by the **incongruence** *(mismatch) between their perceptions of their real self and their ideal self.* That incongruence becomes a problem, causing people to lose confidence in their ability to cope. According to humanistic therapists, once people are freed from the inhibiting influences of a rejecting society, they can solve their own problems.

The best-known version of humanistic therapy, pioneered by Carl Rogers, is **person-centered therapy,** or *nondirective* or *client-centered* therapy. *The therapist listens to the client with total acceptance and unconditional positive regard.* Most of the time, the therapist paraphrases and clarifies what the client has said, conveying the message, "I'm trying to understand your experience from your point of view." The therapist strives to be genuine, empathic, and caring, rarely offering any interpretation or advice. Here is an example (shortened from Rogers, 1951, pp. 46–47):

Client: I've never said this before to anyone. This is a terrible thing to say, but if I could just find some glorious cause that I could give my life for I would be happy. I guess maybe I haven't the guts—or the strength—to kill myself—and I just don't want to live.

Counselor: At the present time things look so black to you that you can't see much point in living.

Client: Yes. I wish people hated me, because then I could turn away from them and could blame them. But no, it is all in my hands. I either fight whatever it is that holds me in this terrible conflict, or retreat clear back to the security of my dream world where I could do things, have clever friends, be a pretty wonderful sort of person.

Counselor: It's really a tough struggle, digging into this like you are, and at times the shelter of your dream world looks more attractive and comfortable.

Client: My dream world or suicide.

Counselor: Your dream world or something more permanent than dreams.

Client: Yes. (A long pause. Complete change of voice.) So I don't see why I should waste your time. I'm not worth it. What do you think?

Counselor: It's up to you, Gil. It isn't wasting my time. I'd be glad to see you, whenever you come, but it's how you feel about it. If you want to come twice a week, once a week, it's up to you.

Client: You're not going to suggest that I come in oftener? You're not alarmed and think I ought to come in every day until I get out of this?

Counselor: I believe you are able to make your own decision. I'll see you whenever you want to come.

Client: I don't believe you are alarmed about . . . I see. I may be afraid of myself, but you aren't afraid for me.

The therapist provides an atmosphere in which the client freely explores feelings of guilt, anxiety, and hostility. By accepting the client's feelings, the therapist conveys the message, "You can make your own decisions. Now that you are more aware of certain problems, you can deal with them constructively yourself." Few therapists today rely purely on person-centered therapy, but most users of other therapy methods have adopted its emphasis on the close, caring, honest relationship between therapist and client (Hill & Nakayama, 2000).

 CONCEPT CHECK

10. Answer the following questions with reference to psychoanalysis, cognitive therapy, humanistic therapy, and behavior therapy.
    a. With which type of therapy is the therapist least likely to offer advice and interpretations of behavior?
    b. Which type focuses more on changing what people do than on exploring what they think?
    c. Which two types of therapy try to change what people think? (Check your answers on page 589.)

Family Systems Therapy

In **family systems therapy,** *the guiding assumptions are that most people's problems develop in a family setting and that the best way to deal with them is to improve family relationships and communication.* Family systems therapy is not an alternative to other forms of therapy; a family therapist uses behavior

For example, a young woman with anorexia nervosa may have excessively demanding parents or other family difficulties. Treating only the woman with anorexia would be pointless. A therapist needs to enlist her parents' help to monitor her eating without blame, criticism, or dominance (Eisler et al., 2000).

For another example, a young man who had been caught stealing a car was taken to a family therapist who asked to talk with the parents as well. As it turned out, the father had been a heavy drinker until his boss pressured him to quit drinking and join Alcoholics Anonymous. Until then the mother had made most of the family decisions in close consultation with her son, who had be-

■ At one stage in therapy for anorexia nervosa, patients have to eat a "fear food," such as Pop-Tarts or doughnuts and then describe their feelings.

therapy, cognitive therapy, or other techniques. What distinguishes family therapists is that they prefer to talk with two or more members of a family together. Even when they talk with someone alone, they focus on how the individual fits into the family and how other family members react. Solving most problems requires changing the family dynamics as well as any individual's behavior (Clarkin & Carpenter, 1995; Rohrbaugh, Shoham, Spungen, & Steinglass, 1995).

come almost a substitute husband. When the father quit drinking, he began to resume his authority within the family, and his son came to resent him. The mother felt less needed and grew depressed. Each member of the family had problems that they could not resolve separately. The therapist helped the father improve his relationships with his son and his wife and helped all three find satisfying roles within the family (Foley, 1984).

TABLE 15.4 Comparison of Five Types of Psychotherapy

Type of Psychotherapy	Theory of What Causes Psychological Disorders	Goal of Treatment	Therapeutic Methods	Role of Therapist
Psychoanalysis	Unconscious thoughts and motivations	To bring unconscious thoughts to consciousness to achieve insight	Free association, dream analysis, and other methods of probing the unconscious mind	To interpret associations
Cognitive therapies	Irrational beliefs and unrealistic goals	To establish realistic goals, expectations, and interpretations of a situation	Dialog with the therapist	To help the client reexamine assumptions
Humanistic (person-centered) therapy	Reactions to a rejecting society; incongruence between self-concept and ideal self	To enable client to make personal decisions; to promote self-acceptance	Client-centered interviews	To focus the client's attention; to provide unconditional positive regard
Behavior therapy	Learned inappropriate maladaptive behaviors	To change behaviors	Positive reinforcement and other learning techniques	To develop, direct, and evaluate the behavior therapy program
Family system therapy	Distorted communication and confused roles within a family	To improve the life of each individual by improving functioning of the family	Counseling sessions with the whole family or with the individual talking about life in the family	To promote better family communication and understanding

Trends in Psychotherapy

Hundreds of types of therapy are available, including some that are quite different from the five discussed thus far (Table 15.4). About half of U.S. psychotherapists profess no strong allegiance to any single form of therapy. Instead, they practice **eclectic therapy,** meaning that they *use a combination of methods and approaches* (Wachtel, 2000). An eclectic therapist might use behavior therapy with one client and rational-emotive therapy with another or might start with one therapy and then shift to another if the first is ineffective. The therapist would use insights from several approaches, including person-centered therapy's emphasis on a caring relationship between therapist and client.

Because health insurance companies insist on limiting costs, psychotherapists have sought methods for quick and inexpensive help, such as brief therapy and group therapy. Self-help groups provide a no-cost alternative.

Brief Therapy

Some types of psychotherapy require a major commitment of time and money. In psychoanalysis you might see a therapist for a 50-minute session as many as five times a week. The cost of a session varies, but it is not cheap. A physician who sees many patients per hour—a dermatologist, for example—might charge a moderate amount per visit, but a therapist who sees just one person per hour charges more. A therapy that continues "as long as necessary" might drag on for years.

However, most clients do not need such prolonged treatment. About half of all people who enter psychotherapy show significant improvement within 8 sessions, and three fourths improve within 26 sessions (Howard, Kopta, Krause, & Orlinsky, 1986). As a result many therapists place limits on the duration of therapy. At the start of **brief therapy,** or time-limited

therapy, *the therapist and client reach an agreement about what they can expect from each other and how long the treatment will last*—such as once per week for 2 months (Koss & Butcher, 1986). As the deadline approaches, both therapist and client are strongly motivated to reach a successful conclusion. (The same issue arose in the motivation chapter. Without deadlines few people apply themselves diligently.)

Moreover, clients who know the deadline in advance do not feel deserted or rejected when the therapy ends. They may return for an occasional extra session months later, but for a time they must get along without help. Most clients with mild to moderate problems respond well to brief therapy.

Unfortunately, however, many HMOs insist on extremely brief therapy, in some cases as few as three sessions. Even a few sessions might be better than none, so the HMOs do make help available for many distressed people (Hoyt & Austad, 1992). However, many need more help than their insurance provides.

Group Therapy

The pioneers of psychotherapy saw their clients individually. Individual treatment has advantages, such as privacy. However, therapists today frequently treat clients in groups. **Group therapy** is *administered to several people at once*. It first became popular as a method of providing help to people who could not afford individual sessions. (Spreading the costs among five to ten people reduces the cost for each.) Soon therapists found that group therapy has other advantages as well. Just meeting other people with similar problems can be reassuring. People learn, "I am not so odd after all." Also, many clients seek help because of failed relationships or because they have trouble dealing with other people. A group therapy session lets them examine how they relate to others, practice social skills, and receive feedback (Ballinger & Yalom, 1995).

a   b

(a) Individual therapy offers complete privacy and the opportunity to pursue individual problems in depth.
(b) In group therapy participants can explore how they relate to other people.

Consider an analogy to education. Would you prefer your professor to teach you privately instead of in a large class? If so, the cost of your tuition would skyrocket. Besides, discussions with your fellow students are a valuable part of your education.

Self-Help Groups

A **self-help group**, such as Alcoholics Anonymous, *operates much like group therapy, except without a therapist.* Each participant both gives and receives help. People who have experienced a problem can offer special insights to others with the same problem. They are especially well prepared when someone says, "You just don't understand." They reply, "Oh, yes, we do!" Self-help groups have another advantage: The members can call one another for help at almost any time without an appointment. Furthermore, the service is supported by voluntary contributions, so each person pays only what he or she can afford.

Some self-help groups are composed of current or former mental patients. The members feel a need to talk to others who have gone through a similar experience, either in addition to or instead of seeing a therapist. The Mental Patients' Association in Canada consists of former patients who were frustrated about their treatment (or lack of treatment) in mental hospitals (Chamberlin, 1978). Members share experiences, provide support, and work together to defend the rights and welfare of mental patients.

The ultimate in self-help is to deal with your own problems without any therapist or group. In a series of studies, James Pennebaker and his colleagues have found that people with mild problems can do themselves an amazing amount of good just by organizing their thoughts about their emotional difficulties. Research participants are randomly assigned to two groups. One group writes about their intense and difficult emotional experiences for 15 minutes on 3 or more days. The other group spends the same time writing about unemotional events. The people writing about their emotions consistently show improved mental and physical health over the next few months, especially those with much variation and flexibility in what they write (Campbell & Pennebaker, 2003; Pennebaker & Seagal, 1999). Apparently, writing about a difficult experience helps people make sense of it and eventually put it behind them. In many cases writing about emotions prompts people to make decisions and change their way of life.

CONCEPT CHECK

11. Brief therapy is a goal or policy for many therapists. Why would it be less important in self-help groups? (Check your answer on page 589.)

CRITICAL THINKING
WHAT'S THE EVIDENCE?

How Effective Is Psychotherapy?

The rise of HMOs and other insurance programs heightened interest in measuring the effectiveness of psychotherapy. Hans Eysenck (1952) pointed out that most people who receive no therapy nevertheless improve in a year or two. (Most psychological crises are temporary.) *Improvement without therapy* is called **spontaneous remission.** Psychotherapy is effective only if it does better than what we could expect by spontaneous remission.

In other chapters most What's the Evidence? sections highlighted one or two studies. Here, the section highlights a general research approach. Hundreds of research studies similar to this have been conducted, although they vary in their details (Kazdin, 1995).

Hypothesis. Psychologically troubled people who receive psychotherapy will show greater im-

▌ Because everyone's moods and effectiveness fluctuate over time, an apparent improvement between (a) the start of therapy and (b) the end is hard to interpret. How much of the improvement is due to the therapy and how much would have occurred without it?

provements in their condition than similar people who do not receive therapy.

Method. For the results to be meaningful, participants must be randomly assigned to the therapy and nontherapy groups. Comparing people who sought therapy to those who did not seek it would be improper because the two groups might differ in the severity of their problems or their motivation for overcoming them. In the best studies, people who contact a clinic about receiving therapy are all given a preliminary examination and then randomly assigned to receive therapy at once or to be placed on a waiting list for therapy later. A few months later, the investigators compare the amount of improvement shown by the therapy group and the waiting-list group. Because of ethical considerations, such research is usually limited to people with mild to moderate problems. It would be difficult to ask someone with a severe problem to wait several months for treatment.

How should the investigators measure the amount of improvement? They cannot rely on the therapists' judgments any more than someone could ask professors to evaluate the effectiveness of their own courses. For similar reasons researchers cannot ask the clients for an unbiased opinion. Most clients exaggerate how much they improved (Safer & Keuler, 2002). Therefore, the researchers may ask a "blind" observer to evaluate each client without knowing who has received therapy and who has been on the waiting list. Or they may ask each person to take a standardized personality test, such as the MMPI. None of these measures are perfect, of course, and they probably overlook some kinds of improvement.

Many experiments compare a group that received therapy to a control group that was on the waiting list. Other experiments, however, have compared groups receiving different kinds of therapy or different frequencies of therapy.

Results. Here, we do not focus on the results of any one study. Most experiments have included only a modest number of people, such as 10 or 20 receiving therapy and a similar number on the waiting list. To draw a conclusion, we need to pool the results from a great many similar experiments. Psychologists use a method called **meta-analysis,** *taking the results of many experiments, weighting each one in proportion to the number of participants, and determining the overall average effect.* According to one meta-analysis that pooled the results of 475 experiments, the average person in therapy shows greater improvement than 80% of similarly trou-

bled people who do not receive therapy (M. L. Smith, Glass, & Miller, 1980). Figure 15.5 illustrates this effect.

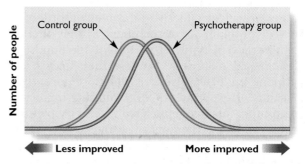

FIGURE 15.5 According to one review of 475 studies, the average person receiving psychotherapy shows more improvement than do 80% of similar, randomly assigned people who are not in therapy. This comparison lumps together all kinds of therapy and all kinds of disorders. (*From* The Benefits of Psychotherapy, *by M. L. Smith, G. V. Glass and T. I. Miller, Copyright © 1980 The Johns Hopkins University Press. Reprinted by permission.*)

Interpretation. Even a collection of 475 studies has limitations. In particular most research has dealt with mild disorders. Most research has used brief treatments because it is hard to keep anyone on a waiting list for long. Also, most of the research has examined behavior therapy or cognitive therapy because these methods use consistent methods and set specific goals. It is more difficult to evaluate psychoanalysis or person-centered therapy.

One could easily complain that investigators have invested a great deal of effort for rather little payoff. After 475 experiments we can confidently say that therapy is usually better than no therapy for mild psychological disorders. This conclusion is like saying that medicine is usually better than no medicine, or education is usually better than no education. However, even if the conclusion seems unimpressive, it does pave the way for further, more detailed studies about how therapy produces its benefits and so forth. It also tells us something about the magnitude of psychotherapy's effects: The effects are real but usually not huge. Most clients benefit, but not enormously.

 CONCEPT CHECK

12. Although well-designed experiments on psychotherapy use a blind observer to rate clients' mental health, double-blind studies are difficult or impossible. Why? (Check your answer on page 589.)

Comparing Therapies and Therapists

Next, of course, we would like to know which kinds of therapy are most effective for which disorders. The practical problem for researchers is that therapists use hundreds of types of treatment for hundreds of psychological disorders. To test the effect of each treatment on each disorder would require tens of thousands of experiments, not counting replications. Furthermore, many clients have several problems, not just one, and most therapists use an eclectic trial-and-error approach instead of a single well-defined therapy (Goldfried & Wolfe, 1996).

Many studies have proceeded despite these difficulties, and they lead to a stunningly simple conclusion: For the disorders studied, researchers find only small differences in effectiveness between one type of therapy and another (Leichsenring & Leibing, 2003; Lipsey & Wilson, 1993; Stiles, Shapiro, & Elliott, 1986; Wampold et al., 1997). Even those differences are sometimes hard to interpret. For example, in some studies one kind of treatment produced better immediate benefits and another produced greater long-term benefits, so the apparent advantage depended on the time of measurement (Sandell et al., 1999). Most research so far has dealt with mild to moderate disorders and behavioral or cognitive therapies. The effectiveness of psychoanalysis remains more controversial.

In chapter 16 we shall encounter examples in which one type of therapy appears to have the advantage, such as behavior therapy for phobias and cognitive therapy for depression. However, even in these cases, the differences between one form of therapy and another are small, and the interesting point remains that therapies differing widely in their assumptions and methods produce results far more similar than most psychologists had expected.

Researchers also have compared the effectiveness of therapists with different kinds of training. The U.S. magazine *Consumer Reports* (1995) surveyed its readers about their mental health and their contact with psychotherapy. Of the thousands who said they had sought help for a mental-health problem within the previous 3 years, most said they were satisfied with the treatment and thought it had helped them. For measuring the effectiveness of

psychotherapy, this study has some obvious problems: the lack of a random sample, the lack of a control group, and reliance on clients to evaluate their own improvement (Jacobson & Christensen, 1996). Nevertheless, the results indicated that people reported about equal satisfaction and benefits from talking with a psychiatrist, a psychologist, or a social worker (Seligman, 1995). They reported somewhat less satisfaction from consulting a marriage counselor or a general-practice physician (Figure 15.6). A later survey of psychotherapy clients in Germany yielded similar results (Hartmann & Zepf, 2003).

The same general pattern emerged in a variety of other studies with different research methods: The type of therapist is not critical to the amount of improvement. Even the amount of therapist experience makes little difference in most studies (Christensen & Jacobson, 1994; Dawes, 1994).

Is the conclusion, then, that if you are psychologically troubled, you may as well talk to your next-door neighbor as to a psychotherapist? No, for several reasons:

- The research comparing nonprofessionals to experienced therapists has examined clients with mild problems. We cannot assume that the same results would hold for more disabling conditions.
- Few of us know someone with enough patience to listen to hours of personal ramblings.
- Conversation with a professional psychotherapist is confidential (except under special circumstances, such as if you tell your therapist you are planning to kill someone). You are less sure that a friend will keep your secrets.

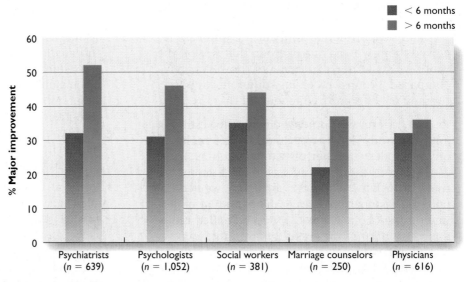

FIGURE 15.6 The percentage of *Consumer Reports* respondents who said they experienced great improvement in the problem that led them to treatment. *(From "The Effectiveness of Psychotherapy: The Consumer Reports Study" by M. E. P. Seligman, American Psychologist, 1995, 50, 965–974. Copyright © 1995 by the American Psychological Association. Reprinted by permission.)*

Just talking to a sympathetic listener, even someone without training, is helpful for many people with mild to moderate problems.

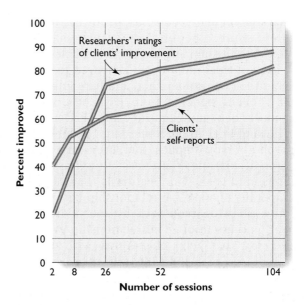

FIGURE 15.7 The relationship of the number of psychotherapy sessions to the percentage of clients who improved. *(From "The Dose-Effect Relationship in Psychotherapy" by K. I. Howard et al, American Psychologist, 1986, 41, 159–164. Copyright © 1986 by the American Psychological Association. Reprinted by permission of the author.)*

- A well-trained psychotherapist can recognize symptoms of a brain tumor or other medical disorder and can refer you to an appropriate medical specialist.

Is More Treatment Better?

If seeing a therapist once per week for 3 months is helpful, would meeting twice per week for a year help even more? How much is the right amount?

Respondents in the *Consumer Reports* (1995) study were asked how much treatment they received and how much it helped them. Generally, those who received longer treatment reported that it helped them more. However, perhaps those who stayed in treatment the longest were those with the greatest problems at the start and therefore had the greatest room for improvement.

A somewhat better research design examines a single group of clients repeatedly as all of them progress through a given number of therapy sessions. Figure 15.7 shows the results of one such study. According to both the researchers and the clients themselves, most clients showed fairly rapid progress at first and then gradual additional progress (Howard et al., 1986). Evidently, prolonged treatment is somewhat more beneficial than brief treatment on the average.

A 5-year study conducted at Fort Bragg, North Carolina, examined the effects of extensive treatment. A government-supported program provided free clinical services for every teenager or child who needed psychological help and who had a parent in the military.

Each client had a case manager who determined what treatment plan was best, made sure the client received every necessary type of help, and coordinated all the service providers to make sure that each one knew what the others were doing. The goal was to demonstrate that a well-planned, integrated program would be highly effective and perhaps save money by avoiding a wasteful overlap of services. Results were compared to those in a similar community that offered the usual less coordinated services. The result? The integrated program at Fort Bragg was no more beneficial, just more expensive (Bickman, 1996). We should not draw too strong a conclusion from this study or from any other single study. Still, most people had expected the integrated program to show clear advantages, and the results seem to imply that more therapy is not always better.

Similarities Among Psychotherapeutic Methods

What should we conclude from the observation that different forms of psychotherapy seem to be similar in their effectiveness? Consider an analogy to education: Suppose researchers found that, on the average, students learn about equally from lecture courses as from discussion classes, from experienced professors as from first-time instructors, and from one textbook as another. I, personally, would not be thrilled with that finding. As a professor and textbook author, I like to think that students learn *much* more from my lectures and textbook than from anyone else's! However, I should not be terribly surprised by the results. How much a student learns depends mainly on the student. A better lecture, a better class organization, or a better textbook presumably makes some difference, but it is surely a small difference compared to the difference between one student and another. Similarly, how much a client benefits from psychotherapy varies enormously depending on the client (Bohart, 2000).

The similarity in outcomes among different forms of psychotherapy implies that they have much in common despite the differences in their assumptions, methods, and goals. One feature is that all rely on a "therapeutic alliance"—a relationship between therapist and client characterized by acceptance, caring, respect, and attention. The relationship provides social support that helps clients deal with their problems and acquire social skills that they can apply to other relationships (Krupnick et al., 1994).

Moreover, in nearly all forms of therapy, clients talk openly and honestly about their beliefs and emotions, relationships with family members, and other issues that people ordinarily keep secret. They examine aspects of themselves that they usually take for granted. The mere fact of entering therapy improves clients' morale. The therapist conveys the message "you are going to get better." Clients gain confidence. The expectation of improvement can lead to improvement.

Finally, every form of therapy requires clients to commit themselves to changes in their lifestyle. Simply by coming to the therapy session, they reaffirm their commitment to feel less depressed, to overcome their fears, or to conquer some bad habit. They make an effort so that they can report at the next session, "I've been doing a little better lately." Improvement probably depends more on what clients do between sessions than on anything in the sessions themselves.

 CONCEPT CHECK

13. Name four ways in which nearly all forms of psychotherapy are similar. (Check your answer on page 589.)

Advice for Potential Clients

At some point you or someone close to you may be interested in seeing a psychotherapist. If so, here are some points to remember:

- Consulting a therapist does not mean that something is wrong with you. Many people merely want to talk with someone about difficulties they are facing.
- If you live in the United States, you can look in the white pages of your telephone directory for the

Mental Health Association. Call and ask for a recommendation. You can specify how much you can pay, what kind of problem you have, and even what kind of therapist you prefer.
- Other things being equal, you may do best with a therapist from your own cultural background (Sue, 1998). Therapists are trained to be sensitive to people from different backgrounds, but a communication barrier often remains nevertheless. Even if a therapist from a different background feels comfortable talking with you, you might not feel comfortable talking with the therapist.
- You might prefer a therapist who shares your religious beliefs or lack of them (Worthington, Kurusu, McCullough & Sandage, 1996).
- Be skeptical of any therapist who seems overconfident. Clinical experience does not give anyone quick access to your private thoughts.
- Expect at least some improvement within 6 to 8 weeks. If you do not seem to be making progress, ask your therapist why. If you do not receive a convincing answer, consider seeing someone else.

IN CLOSING

Trying to Understand Therapy

As you have seen, therapists differ enormously in their assumptions and methods. A psychoanalyst hopes to uncover your unconscious thoughts, memories, and motives, on the assumption that knowing about them will help solve your problems. A cognitive or behavior therapist is more interested in changing your current thoughts and actions than in dwelling on the past. A person-centered therapist provides a warm, supportive setting, in which you can set your own goals and decide for yourself how to achieve them. Despite these major differences, all the common forms of therapy are almost equally effective. It is as if researchers found that when you are sick, one kind of medicine is as good as another.

Psychotherapy began with psychiatry, a branch of medicine, and we still treat it as analogous to medicine. That is, a client comes with a disorder, the therapist provides a treatment, and health insurance pays the bills. In some ways this analogy fails, and therapy is more like education. A client is like a student, and the therapist is like an instructor who tries to provide direction, but the amount of progress depends on the client's own efforts. This is not to say that the therapist is irrelevant. However, the variation between one client and another is greater than the typical difference between one treatment and another. ∎

Summary

- *Psychoanalysis.* Psychoanalysts try to uncover the unconscious reasons behind self-defeating behaviors. To bring the unconscious to consciousness, they rely on free association, dream analysis, and transference. (page 577)

- *Behavior therapy.* Behavior therapists set specific goals for changing a client's behavior and use learning techniques to help a client achieve those goals. (page 578)

- *Cognitive therapies.* Cognitive therapists try to get clients to give up their irrational beliefs and unrealistic goals and to replace defeatist thinking with more favorable views of themselves and the world. Many therapists combine features of behavior therapy and cognitive therapy, attempting to change people's behaviors by altering how they interpret the situation. (page 579)

- *Humanistic therapy.* Humanistic therapists, including person-centered therapists, assume that people who accept themselves as they are can solve their own problems. Person-centered therapists listen with unconditional positive regard and seldom offer interpretations or advice. (page 581)

- *Family systems therapy.* In many cases an individual's problem is part of an overall disorder of family communications and expectations. Family systems therapists try to work with a whole family. (page 581)

- *Eclectic therapy.* About half of all psychotherapists today call themselves eclectic. That is, they use a combination of methods depending on the circumstances. (page 583)

- *Brief therapy.* Many therapists set a time limit for treatment. Brief therapy is typically about as successful as long-term therapy if the goals are limited. (page 583)

- *Group therapies and self-help groups.* Psychotherapy is sometimes provided to people in groups, often composed of individuals with similar problems. Self-help groups provide sessions similar to group therapy but without a therapist. (page 583)

- *Effectiveness of psychotherapy.* The average troubled person in therapy improves more than at least 80% of the troubled people not in therapy. In general all therapies appear effective, and the differences among them are small. Psychiatrists, psychologists, and social workers provide approximately equal benefits on the average. (page 584)

- *Similarities among therapies.* A wide variety of therapies share certain features: All rely on a caring relationship between therapist and client. All promote self-understanding. All improve clients' morale. And all require a commitment by clients to try to make changes in their lives. (page 587)

Answers to Concept Checks

5. In the 1950s psychiatrists conducted almost all psychotherapy. Today, clinical psychologists and other specialists also provide treatment. Today's therapists use a variety of evidence-based treatments, with much less reliance on Freudian methods. Therapists try to achieve good results in just a few sessions, when possible, instead of proceeding for months or years. Today's therapists provide diagnoses for more disorders and define their diagnoses more carefully. (page 576)

6. It is possible to get health insurance to pay for treatment if someone has a diagnosed disorder. (page 576)

7. Psychoanalysts use free association and transference to infer the contents of the unconscious. They also use dream analysis, as discussed in chapter 10. (page 578)

8. Psychoanalysts try to infer unconscious thoughts and motives and try to trace current behavior to experiences of long ago. Behavior therapists pay little attention to thoughts, conscious or unconscious. They set specific goals and try to change current behavior regardless of whether they understand how the behavior originated. (page 578)

9. Rational-emotive therapy assumes that many thoughts lead to emotions. This assumption is the reverse of the James-Lange theory, which argues that emotion-related changes in the body give rise to thoughts. (page 580)

10. **a.** humanistic therapy; **b.** behavior therapy; **c.** psychoanalysis and cognitive therapy. (page 577)

11. One advantage of brief therapy is that it limits the expense. Expense is not an issue for self-help groups because they charge nothing, other than a voluntary contribution toward rental of the facilities. (page 584)

12. A double-blind design requires that neither the subjects nor the observers know which subjects received the experimental treatment and which ones were in the control group. It is not possible to prevent subjects from knowing whether they have received psychotherapy. (It is, of course, possible to use a treatment believed to be ineffective and call it psychotherapy.) (page 585)

13. Nearly all forms of psychotherapy include a "therapeutic alliance" (a close relationship between client and therapist), an effort to understand oneself and discuss personal difficulties openly, an expectation of improvement, and a commitment to make changes in one's life. (page 588)

Social and Legal Aspects of Treatment

- *How should society deal with psychological disorders?*

Some nearsighted people lost in the woods were trying to find their way home. One of the few who wore glasses said, "I think I know the way. Follow me." The others burst into laughter. "That's ridiculous," said one. "How could anybody who needs glasses be our leader?"

In 1972 the Democratic Party nominated Senator Thomas Eagleton for vice president of the United States. Shortly after his nomination, he revealed that he had once received psychiatric treatment for depression. He was ridiculed mercilessly: "How could anybody who needed a psychiatrist be our leader?"

Although many people today receive psychiatric care, it still carries a stigma, and most people who have a disorder decline to seek help from a psychologist or psychiatrist (Wang et al., 2005). All of us need to consider our reactions toward the idea of psychiatric help. We also need to deal with other issues. Who, if anyone, should receive psychiatric treatment involuntarily? Should mental patients have the right to refuse treatment? Under what circumstances, if any, should a criminal defendant be acquitted because of "insanity"? Can society as a whole take steps to prevent psychological disorders?

Deinstitutionalization

In the 1800s and early 1900s, growing numbers of people with severe psychological disturbances were confined in large mental hospitals supported by the government (Torrey & Miller, 2001). Most of these hospitals were understaffed and overcrowded. Residents included not only mental patients but also elderly people with Alzheimer's disease and others who could not care for themselves (Leff, 2002). Hospital attendants cooked all the food, washed the laundry, and did other chores but did not try to teach residents the skills they would need if they were ever to leave. Some hospitals were better than others, but most were grim places.

Since the 1950s more and more hospitals moved toward **deinstitutionalization,** *the removal of patients from mental hospitals,* to give them the least restric-

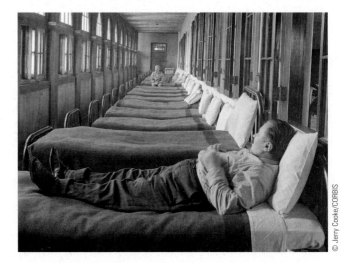

Most mental hospitals of the mid-1900s were unpleasant warehouses that provided minimal care.

tive care possible. Much of the decrease in population of the mental hospitals was due to *re*institutionalization, as elderly people moved from mental hospitals to nursing homes. In addition, mental hospitals began a policy of keeping people for shorter times, unless they were dangerous to themselves or others. Most patients were expected to live at home and receive outpatient care at community mental health centers, which are usually cheaper and more effective than large mental hospitals (Fenton, Hoch, Herrell, Mosher, & Dixon, 2002; Fenton, Mosher, Herrell, & Blyler, 1998). The idea was that troubled people should receive appropriate supervision and care but should also have as much contact as possible with their home community. As a result of deinstitutionalization policies, as well as the advent of antidepressant and antipsychotic medications, the number of long-term mental patients declined substantially. For example, England and Wales had 130 psychiatric hospitals in 1975 but only 12 in 2000 (Leff, 2002).

Unfortunately, many of the patients discharged from mental hospitals became homeless, especially those who had lost contact with their relatives and those with substance-abuse problems (Odell & Commander, 2000). Some ended in nursing homes or prisons. Deinstitutionalization was and is a good idea in principle, but only if implemented well, including good opportunities for community health care.

Deinstitutionalization moved people out of mental hospitals, but many received little or no treatment after their release.

 CONCEPT CHECK

14. Why did deinstitutionalization seem like a good idea? For what reason has it often not worked well? (Check your answers on page 594.)

Involuntary Commitment and Treatment of Potentially Dangerous Patients

Suppose a family moves into the house next to yours, and their adult son, who lives at home, is a current or former mental patient. Are you in danger? If so, how much? The most extensive study of this question was conducted in Sweden, where researchers had access to all the medical and crime records of the whole country. They found that 6.6% of people with severe mental illnesses committed violent crimes compared to 1.8% of everyone else. Another way of putting it is that people with severe mental illnesses, who constituted about 1.4% of the population, committed about 5% of the violent crimes (Fazel & Grann, 2006). If we know a little more about the person who moved in next door to you, we can specify the risk more precisely. A mental patient who does not abuse alcohol or other drugs is much less dangerous than one who does (Monahan, 1992; Wallace, Mullen, & Burgess, 2004).

Someone who is socially withdrawn is generally not dangerous (Swanson et al., 2006).

Suppose a particular person with a history of mental illness does appear to be dangerous. Should it be possible to require him or her to accept treatment or should everyone have the right to refuse? Should it be possible to require someone to enter a mental hospital? In the United States, the law varies from state to state, but typically, a judge can order a mental patient who is dangerous to be involuntarily confined to a mental hospital (Weiner & Wettstein, 1993). However, that judgment is difficult. How extensive a history of offenses should be necessary, and under what circumstances could the person be released from the hospital?

Most states also permit involuntary commitment to a mental hospital for nondangerous patients who have become incompetent to make their own decisions or take care of their daily needs. That judgment is also difficult. Imagine someone who mutters incoherently, cannot keep a job, does not take care of personal hygiene, and harasses the neighbors. Is that person sufficiently incompetent to justify an involuntary commitment? If not, what would constitute incompetence? The problem is that, on the one hand, some seriously disordered people fail to recognize that they have a problem. On the other hand, some families have been known to commit annoying relatives to mental hospitals just to get them out of the way, and some psychiatrists have given strong medications to people with minor problems, doing more harm than good.

Even after involuntary commitment to a mental hospital, a patient still has the right to refuse medications or other treatments (Appelbaum, 1988). According to psychiatrists most of the people who refuse treatment are hostile, emotionally withdrawn, and prone to disorganized thinking (Marder et al., 1983). According to the patients themselves, they have good reason to be hostile and withdrawn, as the hospital staff is trying to force dangerous treatments upon them. Either can be right in a given case.

 CRITICAL THINKING

A STEP FURTHER

Involuntary Treatment

Thomas Szasz (1982) proposed that people should write a "psychiatric will," specifying what treatments are acceptable or unacceptable if they ever develop a severe psychological disorder. If you wrote such a will, what would you include? Or would you prefer to trust your judgment later?

The Duty to Protect

Suppose someone tells his psychotherapist that he plans to kill his former girlfriend. The therapist doubts the threat and ignores it. However, a few days later, the client really does kill his ex-girlfriend, who happens to be your sister. Should your family be able to sue the therapist and collect damages?

Before you answer "yes," consider the following. First, psychotherapy is based on a trusting relationship in which the therapist promises to keep the client's comments secret. Second, therapists are seldom certain about which clients are dangerous. Suppose you are a therapist. Last week, three of your patients said they were so angry they could kill somebody. How do you decide which ones, if any, to take seriously? (Have you yourself ever said you were so angry you could kill someone?) If in fact one of those patients does attack someone, other people can claim that of course you should have seen that this patient was the dangerous one. Recall the phenomenon of hindsight bias—the tendency to reinterpret past signals based on how events turned out later.

In 1976 a California court ruled in the **Tarasoff** case that *a therapist who has reason to believe that a client is dangerous must break the pledge of confidentiality and warn the endangered person.* Since then the rule has become widely accepted in the United States and Canada, although its application remains unclear in many cases (Quattrocchi & Schopp, 2005). A therapist should warn someone whom the patient has threatened to attack, but what happens if the patient seems likely to attack *someone,* but we don't know whom? The therapist might alert the patient's employer—at the risk that the patient becomes unemployed—or perhaps the police. The therapist might attempt to get the patient committed to a mental hospital, but commitment is not always appropriate. Often, the situation poses a difficult and confusing decision.

The Insanity Defense

Suppose, in the midst of an epileptic seizure, you flail your arms about and accidentally knock someone down the stairs, who dies from the fall. Should you be convicted of murder? Of course not. You intended no harm. Now suppose, in the midst of severely disordered thinking and perception, you attack and kill what looks to you like a giant cockroach. However, you were wrong; it was a human being. Again you intended no harm. You didn't even know you were attacking a person. Should you be convicted of murder?

The tradition since Roman times has been that you would be "not guilty by reason of insanity." You should go to a mental hospital, not a prison. Most people agree with that principle in extreme cases. The problem is where to draw the line. Under what conditions is someone legally insane? *Insanity* is a legal term, not a psychological or medical term, and its definition is based on politics more than science.

One point of agreement is that the crime itself, no matter how atrocious, does not demonstrate insanity. Jeffrey Dahmer, arrested in 1991 for murdering and cannibalizing several men, was ruled sane and sentenced to prison. Theodore Kaczynski, arrested for mailing bombs over two decades, refused to plead insanity and probably would not have been ruled insane anyway. Bizarre crimes do not, in themselves, demonstrate insanity. In fact each of these murderers knew what he was doing and tried to avoid capture.

In many cases a decision about sanity or insanity is difficult. Lawyers, physicians, and psychologists have long struggled to establish a clear definition of insanity. The most famous definition, the **M'Naghten rule,** written in Great Britain in 1843, states:

> To establish a defense on the ground of insanity, it must be clearly proved that, at the time of the committing of the act, the party accused was laboring under such a defect of reason, from disease of the mind, as not to know the nature and quality of the act he was doing; or if he did know it, that he did not know he was doing what was wrong. (Shapiro, 1985)

a   b

Theodore Kaczynski **(a)**, a brilliant mathematician who once had a promising career, became **(b)** a recluse who mailed bombs that killed 3 and injured 23 others. However, committing bizarre acts of violence does not qualify someone as legally insane.

In other words, *to be regarded as insane under the M'Naghten rule, people must be so disordered that they do not understand what they are doing.* Presumably, they would continue the act even if a police officer were standing nearby. Many observers consider that rule too narrow and would like to broaden it. However, either a broad or a narrow definition of insanity requires a difficult judgment about the defendant's state of mind at the time of the act. To help make that judgment, psychologists and psychiatrists are called as expert witnesses. If all the experts agree the defendant is insane, the prosecution ordinarily accepts the insanity plea. If the experts agree the defendant is not insane, the defense abandons the plea. Therefore, the only insanity cases that come to a jury trial are the difficult ones in which the experts disagree. Those cases are rare. In the United States, fewer than 1% of accused felons plead insanity, and of those only about 25% are found not guilty (Lymburner & Roesch, 1999). However, those few cases generally receive much media attention, and because people hear about them, they assume such cases are common. (Remember the availability heuristic from chapter 8.) The insanity defense is equally rare in other countries.

Another common misconception is that defendants found not guilty by reason of insanity simply go free, where they are apt to commit further attacks. People found not guilty by reason of insanity are almost always committed to a mental hospital, and they usually stay at least as long in the hospital as they would have in prison (Silver, 1995).

Several states in the United States have experimented with allowing a verdict of "guilty but mentally ill," intended as a compromise between guilty and not guilty. However, the defendant receives the same sentence as if he or she had been found guilty and is no more likely to receive psychiatric care in prison than any other convicted person (Lymburner & Roesch, 1999). In short, the guilty but mentally ill verdict is the same as a guilty verdict. An appealing alternative proposal is to specify that anyone found not guilty by reason of insanity must be temporarily hospitalized and, when eventually released, must abide by certain conditions and restrictions, like those of a prisoner released on parole (Linhorst & Dirks-Linhorst, 1999).

For more information about cases using the insanity defense, as well as other legal cases relevant to psychology, visit this website: **bama.ua.edu/~jhooper/tableofc.html.**

 CONCEPT CHECK

15. Someone who has been involuntarily committed to a mental hospital escapes and commits a murder. Will this person be judged not guilty by reason of insanity? (Check your answer on page 595.)

Preventing Mental Illness

Which would you prefer, a treatment that relieves you of a disorder or a procedure that prevents you from developing one at all? Traditionally, psychologists and psychiatrists have focused on treatment, but prevention would be even better. **Prevention** is *avoiding a disorder from the start.* For example, in one study of "pessimistic" college students and another study with children of depressed parents, half of the participants received cognitive therapy and half did not. In both studies fewer people in the therapy group became depressed over the next 2 or 3 years (Clarke et al., 2001; Seligman, Schulman, DeRubeis, & Hollon, 1999).

Let's distinguish prevention from intervention and maintenance. **Intervention** is *identifying a disorder in its early stages and relieving it,* and **maintenance** is *taking steps to keep it from becoming more serious.* For an example of maintenance, therapists identify people showing early signs of schizophrenia and try to block further deterioration (McGorry et al., 2002).

Just as our society puts fluoride into drinking water to prevent tooth decay and immunizes people against contagious diseases, it can take action to prevent certain types of psychological disorders (Albee, 1986; Wandersman & Florin, 2003). Here are some examples:

- **Ban toxins.** The sale of lead-based paint has been banned because children who eat flakes of it sustain brain damage. Other toxins in the air and water have yet to be controlled.
- **Educate pregnant women about prenatal care.** For example, the use of alcohol or other drugs during pregnancy damages the brain of a fetus, and bacterial and viral infections during pregnancy can impair fetal brain development.
- **Outlaw smoking in public places and educate people about the risks of smoking.** Improvements in physical health can improve psychological well-being too.
- **Help people get jobs.** People who lose their jobs lose self-esteem and increase their risk of depression and substance abuse.
- **Provide child care.** Improved, affordable day-care services would relieve stress for both parents and children.
- **Improve educational opportunities.** Programs that get young people interested in their schoolwork help to decrease juvenile delinquency.

These techniques are aimed at prevention for the entire community. Community psychologists, who *focus on the needs of large groups rather than those of individuals,* have been among the leaders in seeking prevention. Unfortunately, prevention is often more difficult than it might seem. For example, many programs designed to teach young people to avoid illegal drugs have produced no measurable benefits. Many attempts to prevent PTSD by counseling tragedy victims and urging them to discuss their feelings have increased the rate of PTSD (Bootzin & Bailey, 2005). Group therapy for juvenile delinquents also increases the problem compared to a no-treatment control group (Bootzin & Bailey, 2005; Poulin, Dishion, & Burraston, 2001). Evidently, associating with an all-delinquent group provides bad role models and does more harm than good. Of programs intended to prevent women from developing anorexia or bulimia nervosa, some have been effective, some ineffective, and some counterproductive (Mann et al., 1997; Stice & Shaw, 2004; C. B. Taylor et al., 2006).

Attempts have been made to combat suicide, especially teenage suicide, by television programs about suicide and the pain it causes to friends and relatives. These programs have never decreased the suicide rate; in fact the research controversy is about how much the programs *increased* the suicide rate (Joiner, 1999). One study compared suicidal patients receiving brief crisis intervention to others receiving more prolonged therapy. Those receiving more help had a *higher* rate of suicide (Moller, 1992). The general point is that we cannot take it for granted that a procedure intended to help will succeed. Sometimes, talking about a behavior problem makes it more likely.

 CONCEPT CHECK

16. Why is it important to do careful research before initiating a new program to prevent a psychological disorder? (Check your answer on page 595.)

IN CLOSING

The Science and Politics of Mental Illness

Suppose you are a storekeeper. Someone dressed as Batman stands outside your store every day shouting gibberish at anyone who comes by. Your once-thriving business draws fewer and fewer customers each day. The disturbing man outside does not seem to be breaking any laws. A psychologist consults *DSM–IV* and finds a couple of possible diagnoses. However, the man is not obviously dangerous or incompetent, just annoying, and he wants nothing to do with psychologists or psychiatrists. Should he nevertheless be forced to accept treatment for his odd behavior? If not, what happens to your rights as a storekeeper?

Similarly, the insanity defense and all the other issues in this module are complicated questions that require political decisions by society as a whole, not just the opinions of psychologists or psychiatrists. Regardless of what career you enter, you will be a voter and potential juror, and you will have a voice in deciding these issues. The decisions deserve serious, informed consideration. ∎

Summary

- *Deinstitutionalization.* Today, few patients stay very long in mental hospitals. However, many states have released patients from mental hospitals without providing adequate community mental health facilities. (page 590)
- *Involuntary commitment.* Laws on involuntary commitment to mental hospitals vary, but typically, people can be committed if they are judged to be dangerous or incompetent. It is difficult to frame laws that ensure treatment for those who need it while also protecting the rights of those who have good reasons for refusing it. (page 591)
- *Duty to warn.* The courts have ruled that a therapist who is convinced that a client is dangerous should warn the endangered person. Applying this rule in practice is difficult, however, because judging dangerousness is difficult. (page 592)
- *The insanity defense.* Some defendants accused of a crime are acquitted for reasons of insanity, which is a legal rather than a medical or psychological concept. The criteria for establishing insanity are controversial. (page 592)
- *Prevention of psychological disorders.* Psychologists and psychiatrists are increasingly concerned about preventing psychological disorders. Many preventive measures require the cooperation of society as a whole. Methods of prevention based on good intentions do not always succeed. (page 593)

Answers to Concept Checks

14. Deinstitutionalization appears to be a good idea because treatment in a community mental health center is more effective and less costly than treatment in a mental hospital. However, many states removed people from mental hospitals

without providing adequate alternative care. (page 590)

15. Not necessarily. Having a psychological disorder, even a severe one, does not automatically qualify a person as insane in the legal sense. The judge or jury must also find that the psychological disorder prevented the person from knowing what he or she was doing or made law-abiding behavior impossible. (page 592)

16. In many cases a program intended for prevention has proved to be ineffective or counterproductive. It is important to test the effectiveness of a program before setting it up on a large scale. (page 594)

CHAPTER ENDING

Key Terms and Activities

Key Terms

You can check the page listed for a complete description of a term. You can also check the glossary/index at the end of the text for a definition of a given term, or you can download a list of all the terms and their definitions for any chapter at this website:

www.thomsonedu.com/ psychology/kalat

behavior therapy (page 578)

biopsychosocial model (page 571)

brief therapy (page 583)

catharsis (page 578)

cognitive therapy (page 579)

cognitive-behavior therapy (page 580)

community psychologist (page 594)

deinstitutionalization (page 590)

Diagnostic and Statistical Manual of Mental Disorders, Fourth Edition (DSM–IV) (page 572)

dissociative identity disorder (page 571)

eclectic therapy (page 583)

evidence-based treatments (page 577)

family systems therapy (page 581)

free association (page 578)

group therapy (page 583)

incongruence (page 581)

interpretation (page 578)

intervention (page 593)

maintenance (page 593)

meta-analysis (page 585)

M'Naghten rule (page 592)

person-centered therapy (page 581)

personality disorder (page 573)

prevention (page 593)

psychoanalysis (page 577)

psychodynamic therapies (page 577)

psychotherapy (page 576)

rational-emotive behavior therapy (page 580)

self-help group (page 584)

spontaneous remission (page 584)

Tarasoff (page 592)

transference (page 578)

Suggestions for Further Reading

Lilienfeld, S. O., Lynn, S. J., & Lohr, J. M. (Eds.) (2003). *Science and pseudoscience in clinical psychology*. New York: Guilford Press. Most clinical psychologists today use evidence-based treatments. This book surveys some of the faddish quack treatments that are not based on evidence.

Porter, R., & Wright, D. (Eds.). (2003). *The confinement of the insane*. Cambridge, England: Cambridge University Press. A review of mental hospitals and the treatment of people with disorders from 1800 through the middle of the 20th century.

Seligman, M. E. P. (1993). *What you can change . . . and what you can't*. New York: Fawcett Columbine. Description of both the possibilities and the limitations of psychotherapy.

 ## Web/Technology Resource

Student Companion Website

www.thomsonedu.com/psychology/kalat

Explore the Student Companion Website for Online Try-It-Yourself activities, practice quizzes, flashcards, and more! The companion site also has direct links to the following websites.

Landmark Cases in Forensic Psychiatry

bama.ua.edu/~jhooper/tableofc.html

In his excellent Forensic Psychiatry Resource Page, James Hooper offers brief summaries of criminal and civil cases in which mental disorders became an issue.

 ## For Additional Study

Kalat Premium Website

http://www.thomsonedu.com

For Critical Thinking Videos and additional Online Try-It-Yourself activities, go to this site to enter or purchase your code for the Kalat Premium Website.

ThomsonNOW!

http://www.thomsonedu.com

Go to this site for the link to ThomsonNOW, your one-stop study shop. Take a Pretest for this chapter, and Thomson-NOW will generate a personalized Study Plan based on your test results. The Study Plan will identify the topics you need to review and direct you to online resources to help you master those topics. You can then take a Posttest to help you determine the concepts you have mastered and what you still need to work on.

Specific Disorders and Treatments

In the 1700s and 1800s, medical science was primitive by today's standards. Most physicians made no effort to distinguish one illness from another. They recommended general all-purpose "tonics," suggested bed rest, sometimes applied leeches to withdraw blood, and so forth. Medical progress since then has been marked by an increasing ability to apply specific treatments aimed at specific disorders.

Psychotherapists have been trying to move in the same direction. They would like to provide specific treatments for each disorder. However, not everyone is convinced that we can or should. As discussed in the previous chapter, researchers find that many types of therapy are about equally effective for a variety of problems. If the type of therapy doesn't matter, then careful diagnosis may not be important either (Messer & Wampold, 2002).

The distinctiveness of each psychological disorder is an empirical question—that is, one to be decided by the evidence. In the first three modules of this chapter, we consider research on the most commonly diagnosed psychological disorders: anxiety disorders, substance abuse, and depression. The final module is about schizophrenia, which is less common but often disabling. As you will see, each disorder has its own special features, but each overlaps with the others as well.

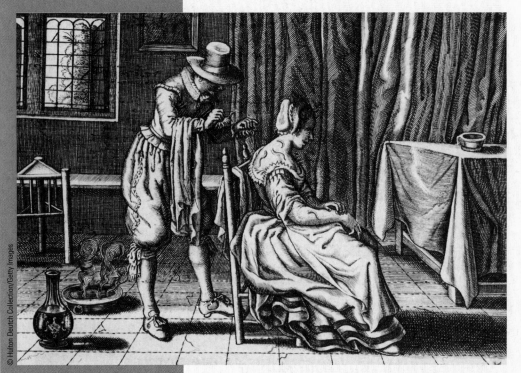

In the early days of medicine, physicians provided the same treatments for all diseases (e.g., applying leeches to draw blood, as shown). Progress depended on differentiating particular disorders and developing individual treatments for each. Can we also find specific treatments for specific psychological disorders?

© Hulton Deutch Collection/Getty Images

Anxiety Disorders

- *Why do some people develop exaggerated fears?*
- *Why do some people develop strange habits of thought and action?*

You go to the beach, looking forward to an afternoon of swimming and surfing. Will you go in the water if someone tells you that a shark attacked two swimmers yesterday? What if the shark attack was a month ago? What if someone saw a small shark a few days ago, which did not attack anyone?

How much fear and caution are normal? Staying out of the water because you see a large shark is reasonable. Staying out because a small shark was present a few days ago is less sensible. If you refuse even to look at ocean photographs that might *remind* you of sharks, you have a serious problem. Excessive fear and caution are linked to some common psychological disorders.

Disorders with Excessive Anxiety

Many psychological disorders are marked by anxiety and attempts to avoid anxiety. Anxiety, unlike fear, is not generally associated with a specific situation. You might be afraid of a growling dog, but your fear subsides when you get away. Anxiety is an apprehensive feeling that something might go wrong. We also talk of anxieties about dying or anxieties about a personal deficiency. The key is that you cannot escape from anxieties as easily as you could from the growling dog.

How much anxiety is normal? It depends. If you live in constant danger in a war-torn country, a high level of anxiety makes sense. If you live in a quiet small town, your anxiety should be lower. You have an anxiety disorder if your anxiety is more extreme than your circumstances warrant and great enough

■ Many situations evoke anxiety or tension in almost anyone. Anxiety becomes a problem only if it is frequently more intense than the situation justifies.

to interfere with your life. We already considered post-traumatic stress disorder in chapter 12. Here, let's consider additional anxiety disorders.

Generalized Anxiety Disorder (GAD)

People with **generalized anxiety disorder (GAD)** are *almost constantly plagued by exaggerated worries.* They worry that "I might get sick," "My daughter might get sick," "I might lose my job," or "I might not be able to pay my bills." Although they have no more reason for worry than anyone else, they grow so tense, irritable, and fatigued that they have trouble working or enjoying life. About 5% of all people experience generalized anxiety disorder at some point in life (Wittchen, Zhao, Kessler, & Eaton, 1994). Because anxiety is a common symptom of so many other disorders, most people with the symptoms of GAD have (or have had or will have) other disorders too, such as depression, panic disorder, or phobia (Bruce, Machan, Dyck, & Keller, 2001). GAD responds fairly well to both antidepressant drugs (Rivas-Vazquez, 2001) and cognitive-behavior therapy (Mitte, 2005).

Panic Disorder (PD)

People with **panic disorder (PD)** *have frequent periods of anxiety and occasional attacks of panic—rapid breathing, increased heart rate, chest pains, sweating, faintness, and trembling.* A panic attack usually lasts only minutes, but it is intense during that time. During and after an attack, people worry about fainting, having a heart attack, or becoming insane.

Panic disorder occurs in 1 to 3% of adults at some time during their lives throughout the world. It is more common in women than men (Weissman, Warner, Wickramaratne, Moreau, & Olfson, 1997) and more common in young adults than older ones. Indeed, anxiety in general weakens

601

with age. One study found that 8 of 24 people with panic disorder recovered completely within 11 years, while all of the others had less frequent panic attacks than before (Swoboda, Amering, Windhaber, & Katschnig, 2003).

Several studies have indicated a genetic contribution, although the results do not point strongly to any one gene (Crowe et al., 2001; Hamilton et al., 2003; Hettema, Neale, & Kendler, 2001). A few studies have found a high overlap between panic disorder and *joint laxity* (the ability to bend fingers farther than usual, popularly called "double-jointedness"), which is believed to have a genetic basis (Bulbena et al., 2004; Gratacòs et al., 2001).

Psychologists have proposed several theories of panic disorder, but so far the evidence does not strongly support any of them (Roth, Wilhelm, & Pettit, 2005). One is that people start having strong autonomic responses, such as rapid heartbeat, and interpret the arousal as a heart attack or other emergency. Their anxiety about the attack increases the arousal, thus further increasing the anxiety (Austin & Richards, 2001). Another theory is that a panic attack begins with **hyperventilation**, *rapid deep breathing.* Almost anything that causes hyperventilation makes the body react as if it were suffocating, thereby triggering other sympathetic nervous system responses such as sweating and increased heart rate (Coplan et al., 1998; Klein, 1993). If you became aroused after exercise, you would not react emotionally because you would attribute your arousal to the exercise (Esquivel, Schruers, Kuipers, & Griez, 2002). However, if you suddenly increase your breathing rate and don't know why, you may worry about the next attack and worry that it may embarrass you in public. Your worry increases the risk of further attacks (McNally, 2002). People who have repeated panic attacks start to associate them with places, events, activities, and internal states. Any situation that resembles those of previous panic attacks may trigger a new panic attack as a conditioned response (Bouton, Mineka, & Barlow, 2001).

The usual treatment for panic disorder is cognitive-behavior therapy, which was discussed in the previous chapter. The procedures include teaching the patient to control breathing, countering the start of a panic with pleasant imagery, and learning to relax. For many, just knowing that a panic attack does not mean they are "losing their minds" or having a heart attack helps greatly. Therapists also try to identify the thoughts and situations that trigger panic attacks and help a patient deal with those triggers. Also, they help the person experience sweating and increased heart rate in a controlled setting, so the person learns that these physiological changes do not have to lead to a full-scale panic attack. Although this therapy may require several months, researchers find that at least

three fourths of patients can stop their panic attacks altogether (Butler, Chapman, Forman, & Beck, 2006).

Many people with panic disorder also have **social phobia,** *a severe avoidance of other people and a fear of doing anything in public,* where they might become embarrassed. Common types of social phobia include fear of talking to strangers or large groups and fear of feeling rejected or ridiculed by others (Stein, Torgrud, & Walker, 2000). Social phobia is partly related to growing up in an overprotective family, with much criticism. It can be treated with antidepressant drugs, antianxiety drugs, or cognitive-behavior therapy (Coupland, 2001).

Many people with panic disorder also have **agoraphobia** (from *agora,* the Greek word for "marketplace"), *an excessive fear of open or public places,* although it is also possible to have agoraphobia without panic disorder (Wittchen, Reed, & Kessler, 1998). Most psychologists believe that people with panic disorder develop their social phobia or agoraphobia because they are afraid of being incapacitated or embarrassed by a panic attack in a public place. In a sense they are afraid of their own anxiety (McNally, 1990). To avoid the prospect of a public panic attack, they stay home as much as possible.

 CONCEPT CHECK

I. Some psychologists advise people with panic attacks to adopt the attitude, "If it happens, it happens." Why would they make this recommendation? (Check your answer on page 611.)

Disorders with Exaggerated Avoidance

People learn to avoid punishment, as we saw in chapter 6. In some cases their efforts become so extreme and persistent that they interfere with daily activities.

Let's begin by discussing avoidance learning, which is relevant to the later discussion of phobias and compulsions. If you learn to do something for positive reinforcement, your responses extinguish when reinforcements cease, as discussed in chapter 6. Avoidance behaviors are different. Suppose you learn to press a lever to avoid electric shocks. Soon you are responding consistently and receiving no shocks. Now the experimenter disconnects the shock generator without telling you. The extinction procedure has begun, and you no longer need to press the lever. What will you do? You will continue pressing, of course. As far as you can tell, nothing has changed; the response still works. *Avoidance behaviors are highly resistant to extinction.* Once someone learns a response to avoid mishap, the response continues long after it ceases to be necessary.

You can see how this tendency would support superstitions. Suppose you believe that Friday the 13th is dangerous, so you are very cautious on that day. If nothing goes wrong, your caution seemed to work. If a misfortune happens anyway, it confirms your belief that Friday the 13th is dangerous, and you suspect you were not cautious enough. As long as you continue an avoidance behavior, you never learn whether it is useful or not!

 CONCEPT CHECK

2. Suppose you are an experimenter, and you have trained someone to press a lever to avoid shocks. Now you disconnect the shock generator. Other than telling the person what you have done, how could you facilitate extinction of the lever pressing? (Check your answer on page 611.)

Phobias

Terror is the only thing that comes close to how I feel when I think of moths. Their willowy, see-through wings always seem filthy. I remember being stuck in a car with a huge moth and my date, not knowing how terrified I was of moths, thought I was kidding when I told him I was afraid. It was terrible! I can feel it right now . . . feeling trapped and the moth with its ugly body flitting around so quickly, I couldn't anticipate where it would go next. Finally that creature hit me in the arm and I screamed—it felt dirty and sleazy and then it hit me in the face and I began to scream uncontrollably. I had the terrible feeling it was going to fly into my mouth while I was screaming, but I couldn't stop. (phobia patient quoted by Duke & Nowicki, 1979, p. 244)

A **phobia** is *an extreme, persistent fear that interferes with normal living.* A phobia is often described as an irrational fear. However, fearing snakes is not irrational, and neither is a fear of heights or most other objects of phobia. What is irrational is the excessive degree of the fear, which leads to avoidance behaviors and panic in the presence of the feared object. Confronting the object can

lead to sweating, trembling, rapid breathing, and elevated heart rate, similar to a panic attack. In most cases people with phobias are not so much afraid of the object itself but of their own reactions (Beck & Emery, 1985). They fear that they will have a heart attack or that they will embarrass themselves by trembling or fainting.

Prevalence

According to an extensive study of U.S. adults, about 11% of people suffer a phobia at some time in life, and 5 to 6% have a phobia at any given time (Magee, Eaton, Wittchen, McGonagle, & Kessler, 1996). However, phobias vary from mild to extreme, so their apparent prevalence depends on how many marginal cases we include. As with other anxiety disorders, phobias are more common in women than men (Burke, Burke, Regier, & Rae, 1990).

Here are some common objects of phobias (Cox, McWilliams, Clara, & Stein, 2003):

- Open, public places (*agoraphobia*)
- Public speaking
- Heights (including elevators, being on a high floor of a building)
- Not being on solid ground (being in the air or on the water)
- Being with or being observed by strangers (*social phobia*)
- Being alone
- Dangers or reminders of dangers (snakes, spiders, other animals, blood, injections, storms, etc.)

Figure 16.1 shows the prevalence of phobias by age. As with panic disorder, phobias are most common in young adults and less common with age.

❚ Many people who watched the famous shower scene in the movie *Psycho* became afraid to take showers. Actress Janet Leigh, who portrayed the woman killed in that scene, subsequently avoided showers herself.

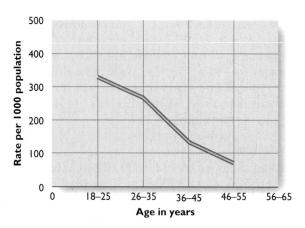

FIGURE 16.1 Most phobias do not last a lifetime. Young people with phobias often lose them by middle age. *(Based on the data of Burke, Burke, Regier, & Rae, 1990)*

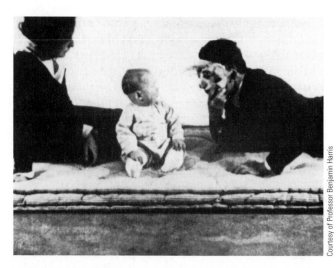

FIGURE 16.2 John B. Watson first demonstrated that little Albert showed little fear of small animals. Then Watson paired a white rat with a loud, frightening noise. Albert became afraid of the white rat, as well as other small animals and odd-looking masks.

Acquiring Phobias

Infants are born with a fear of sudden loud noises, and most of them so quickly show a fear of abandonment that we could suspect that fear of being built-in, too. In contrast all phobias are acquired—no one is born with a phobia—although some people may be more predisposed than others to acquire them. The more closely related you are to someone with a phobia or similar disorders, the more likely you are to develop a phobia yourself (Kendler, Myers, Prescott, & Neale, 2001; Skre, Onstad, Torgerson, Lygren, & Kringlen, 2000).

Still, regardless of genetic predispositions, people with phobias had to acquire them. How? Some phobias can be traced to a specific event. For example, one child got locked in a trunk and developed a phobia of closed spaces. Another person developed a phobia of water after diving into a lake and finding a corpse (Kendler et al., 1995).

However, these experiences may determine the object of the phobia rather than the fact of having a phobia. In one study researchers located pairs of twins in which at least one had a phobia. Some of them could trace their phobia to a particular experience, but others could not. The probability of phobia was just as great in the twins of people who remembered an event as in twins of people who could not (Kendler, Myers, & Prescott, 2002). In other words, the genetic predisposition seemed to account for the probability of phobia independently of the experiences.

John B. Watson, one of the founders of behaviorism, was the first to demonstrate the possibility of learning fears (Watson & Rayner, 1920). Today, we would consider it unethical to try to teach a child an intense fear, but Watson felt less restraint. He and Rosalie Rayner studied an 11-month-old child, "Albert B.," who had previously shown no fear of white rats or other animals (Figure 16.2). They set a white rat in front of him and then struck a large steel bar behind him with a hammer. The sound made Albert whimper and cover his face. After a few repetitions, the mere sight of the rat made Albert cry and crawl away. Watson and Rayner declared that they had created a strong fear similar to a phobia. Unfortunately, they made no attempt to extinguish Albert's fear.

Watson and Rayner's explanation of phobias ignored some important questions: Why do many people develop phobias toward objects that have never injured them? Why are some phobias much more common than others? And why are phobias so persistent? Although Watson and Rayner's study was unsatisfactory scientifically as well as ethically (B. Harris, 1979; Samelson, 1980), it led the way for later research.

 CONCEPT CHECK

3. In classical conditioning terms, what was the CS in Watson and Rayner's experiment? The UCS? The CR? The UCR? (Check your answers on page 611.)

 CRITICAL THINKING

WHAT'S THE EVIDENCE?

Learning Fear by Observation

As noted in the discussion of social learning in chapter 6, we learn much by watching or listening to others. Perhaps we learn our fears and phobias from other people. That hypothesis sounds reasonable, but how can we test it? Susan Mineka and her colleagues demonstrated that monkeys learn fears by observing other monkeys (Mineka, 1987; Mineka, Davidson, Cook, & Keir, 1984). Her research shows how animal studies can shed light on important human issues.

EXPERIMENT 1

Hypothesis. Monkeys that have seen other monkeys avoid a snake will develop a similar fear themselves.

Method. Nearly all monkeys born in the wild show a fear of snakes, but laboratory monkeys do not. Mineka put a laboratory-reared monkey with a wild-born monkey and let them both see a snake (Figure 16.3a). The lab monkey watched the wild monkey show signs of fear. Later, Mineka tested the lab monkey by itself to see its response to a snake.

Results. When the lab monkey saw how frightened its partner was of the snake, it became frightened too (Figure 16.3b). It continued to be afraid of the snake when tested by itself, even months later.

Interpretation. The lab monkey may have learned a fear of snakes because it saw that its partner was afraid of snakes. But Mineka also considered another interpretation: Perhaps seeing the other monkey's fear simply heightened the lab monkey's fear in general, including its fear of snakes (which happened to be the only fear that was tested). What was the critical experience—seeing the other monkey show fear *of snakes* or seeing the other monkey show fear *of anything?* To find out, Mineka conducted a second experiment.

EXPERIMENT 2

Hypothesis. A monkey that does not see the object that another monkey fears will not develop a fear itself.

Method. A monkey reared in a lab watched a monkey reared in the wild through a plate-glass window. The wild monkey could look through another window, where it saw a snake. Thus, when the wild monkey shrieked and ran away from the snake, the lab monkey saw the wild monkey's fear but did not know what it was afraid of. Later, the lab monkey was placed close to a snake to see whether it would show fear.

Results. The lab monkey showed no fear of the snake.

Interpretation. To develop a fear of snakes, the observer monkey needed to see that the other

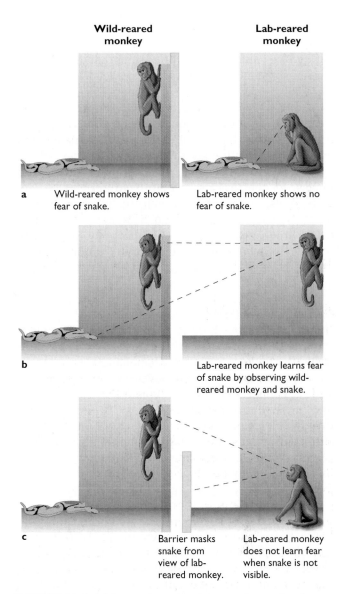

Wild-reared monkey   **Lab-reared monkey**

a   Wild-reared monkey shows fear of snake.   Lab-reared monkey shows no fear of snake.

b   Lab-reared monkey learns fear of snake by observing wild-reared monkey and snake.

c   Barrier masks snake from view of lab-reared monkey.   Lab-reared monkey does not learn fear when snake is not visible.

FIGURE 16.3 A lab-reared monkey learns to fear snakes from the reactions of a wild-reared monkey. But if the snake is not visible, the lab-reared monkey learns no fear.

monkey was frightened of snakes, not just that it was frightened (Figure 16.3c).

Note that the observer monkey had to see *what* the other monkey feared but not *why* it was afraid of the snake. Humans not only observe one another's fears but also explain why.

Why Some Phobias Are More Common Than Others

Imagine that you survey your friends. You can actually survey them, if you wish, but it's easy enough to imagine the results. You ask them:

• Are you afraid of snakes?
• Are you afraid of cars?

- Have you ever been bitten by a snake or seen someone else bitten?
- Have you ever been injured in a car accident or seen someone else injured?

I think you know what to expect. Far more people have been injured or seen someone injured by cars than by snakes, but far more are afraid of snakes than cars. Common phobias include open spaces, closed spaces, heights, lightning and thunder, animals, and illness. In contrast few people have phobias of cars, guns, tools, or electricity—even though they produce many injuries. When my son Sam was a toddler, at least three times he stuck his finger into an electric outlet. He even had a name for it: "Smoky got me again." (I worried about him!) But he never developed a fear of electricity or gadgets.

Why do people develop fears of some objects more readily than other objects? One explanation is that although we are not born with many fears, we may be evolutionarily prepared to learn certain fears more easily than others (Öhman & Mineka, 2003; Seligman, 1971). Nearly every infant develops a fear of heights and of strangers, especially unfamiliar men. Heights and unfamiliar adult males have been dangerous throughout mammalian evolution. Less universal but still widespread are the fears of snakes, darkness, and confined spaces, which have been dangerous throughout primate (monkey and ape) evolution, though not for all mammals. Cars, guns, and electricity became dangerous only within the last few generations of humans, a tiny amount of time in evolutionary terms. Our predisposition to develop fears and phobias corresponds to how long various items have been dangerous in our evolutionary history (Bracha, 2006).

Evidence supporting this view comes from both monkey and human studies. Monkeys who watch a videotape of another monkey running away from a snake learn to fear snakes; monkeys who watch another monkey running away from a flower learn no fear of flowers (Mineka, 1987). People who receive electric shocks paired with pictures of snakes quickly develop a strong and persistent response to snake pictures; people who receive shocks paired with pictures of houses show a much weaker response (Öhman, Eriksson, & Olofsson, 1975).

However, we need to consider other possible explanations (Mineka & Zinbarg, 2006). For example, we have many safe experiences with cars and tools that outweigh the bad experiences. Most people have few safe experiences with snakes, spiders, or falling from high places. One study found that people who had extensive experiences with tarantulas lost their fears (Kleinknecht, 1982).

Another possible explanation is that people generally develop phobias of objects that they cannot pre-

Many people are afraid of extreme heights, partly because the danger is hard to control and partly because we have few safe experiences with heights.

dict or control. If you are afraid of spiders, for example, you must be constantly on the alert. Because you never know where those tiny little critters might be, you can never completely relax. Lightning is also unpredictable and uncontrollable. In contrast you don't have to worry that hammers, saws, or electric outlets will take you by surprise. You must be on the alert for cars when you are near a road but not at other times.

 CONCEPT CHECK

4. Give three explanations for why more people develop phobias of snakes and spiders than cars and guns. (Check your answer on page 611.)

Behavior Therapy for Phobias

Well-established phobias can last many years. Remembering the discussion about avoidance learning, you can see why phobias are so difficult to extinguish: If you have learned to press a lever to avoid shock, you may not stop pressing long enough to find out that such a response is no longer necessary. Similarly, if you stay away from snakes or heights or closed places, you will never learn that your fear is exaggerated. That is, you will not extinguish your fear.

Recall the concept of behavior therapy from chapter 15: A therapist sets a specific goal and uses learning techniques to help the client achieve that goal. One common and usually successful type of behavior therapy for phobia is **systematic desensitization,** *a method of reducing fear by gradually exposing people to the object of their fear* (Wolpe, 1961). Someone with a phobia of snakes, for example, is first trained in relaxation methods. When the client is fully relaxed, the therapist asks the client briefly to imagine a small black-and-white photo of a snake, then to imagine a

FIGURE 16.4 Systematic desensitization is an effective therapy for phobia. A therapist gradually exposes a client to the object of the phobia, first in imagination and later in reality. Exposure therapy is a similar procedure. The therapist demonstrates fearlessness in the presence of the object and encourages the client to do the same.

FIGURE 16.5 Some therapists use virtual reality to let a patient with a phobia of heights experience heights under carefully controlled conditions.

color photo, and then to imagine a real snake. After the client has successfully visualized all those images, the same sequence is repeated with real photos and eventually with a view of a real snake (Figure 16.4).

The process resembles Skinner's shaping procedure (see chapter 6). The person is given time to master each step before going on to the next. The client can say "stop" if the distress becomes threatening; the therapist then goes back several steps and repeats the sequence. Some people complete the whole procedure in a single 1-hour session; others need more time. Systematic desensitization can easily be combined with social learning: The person with a phobia watches other people who display a fearless response to the object.

However, most therapists do not keep handy a supply of snakes, spiders, and so forth. Instead, they use virtual reality, which proves effective in most cases (Garcia-Palacios, Hoffman, Carlin, Furness, & Botella, 2002): The client is equipped with a helmet that displays a virtual-reality scene, as shown in Figure 16.5. Then, without leaving the office, the therapist can expose the client to the feared object or situation. For example, a client with a phobia of heights can go up a glass elevator in a hotel or cross a narrow bridge over a chasm (Rothbaum et al., 1995). This technology gives the therapist control of the situation, including the option of turning off the display if the client becomes too fearful.

Flooding (or **implosion** or **intensive exposure therapy**) is *a treatment that exposes the person to the object of the phobia suddenly rather than gradually* (Hogan & Kirchner, 1967; Rachman, 1969). (This treatment is called *flooding* because the patient is

flooded with fear.) If you had a phobia of rats, for example, you might be told to imagine that you were locked in a room full of rats crawling all over you and viciously attacking you. The image arouses your sympathetic nervous system enormously, and your heart and breathing rates soar (Lande, 1982). The human sympathetic nervous system cannot maintain a panic for long, however, so within a few minutes, your heart and breathing rates begin to decline. A little later, you report feeling more relaxed, even though the therapist continues to suggest gory images of what rats are doing to you. Once you have reached this point, the battle is half won. People with phobias fear that they will have a heart attack or other catastrophic reaction. When they learn that they can withstand even the most frightening experience, they become less afraid of their own responses.

 CONCEPT CHECK

5. How does systematic desensitization resemble extinction of a learned shock-avoidance response?
6. How does the flooding procedure relate to the James-Lange theory of emotions that was discussed in chapter 12? (Check your answers on page 611.)

Obsessive-Compulsive Disorder

People with **obsessive-compulsive disorder** have two kinds of problems. An **obsession** is a *repetitive, unwelcome stream of thought.* For example, some people find themselves constantly imagining gruesome scenes, worrying that they are about to kill someone, dwelling on doubts about their religion, or thinking, "I hate my sister. I hate my sister." A **compulsion** is a *repetitive, almost irresistible action.* Obsessions generally lead to compulsions, as an itching sensation leads to scratching. For example, someone obsessed about dirt and disease develops compulsions of continual cleaning and washing. Someone with obsessive worries about doing something shameful develops compulsive rituals that maintain excessive self-control. That is, the compulsion is an attempt to reduce the distress that the obsession caused.

An estimated 2 to 3% of all people in the United States suffer from obsessive-compulsive disorder at some time in life, mostly to a mild degree (Karno, Golding, Sorenson, & Burnam, 1988). More than half have obsessions without compulsions. Most have additional disorders, such as depression or generalized anxiety disorder (Torres et al., 2006). The disorder occurs most frequently among hardworking, perfectionist people of average or above-average intelligence. It usually develops between the ages of 10 and 25. Nearly all people with obsessive-compulsive disorder realize that their thoughts and rituals are inappropriate. However, that understanding does not bring relief.

DSM–IV lists obsessive-compulsive disorder with the anxiety disorders, but it is associated with guilt at least as much as with anxiety. People with obsessive-compulsive disorder say they feel guilt and anxiety over persistent impulses—perhaps an impulse to engage in a sexual act that they consider shameful, an impulse to hurt someone, or an impulse to commit suicide. They decide, "Oh, what a terrible thought. I don't want to think that ever again." And so they resolve to avoid that thought or impulse.

However, trying to block out a thought only makes it more intrusive. As a child, the Russian novelist Leo Tolstoy once organized a club with a most unusual qualification for membership: A prospective member had to stand alone in a corner *without thinking about a white bear* (Simmons, 1949). If you think that sounds easy, try it. Ordinarily, you go months between thoughts about polar bears, but when you try *not* to think about them, you can think of little else.

Try It Yourself

In one experiment college students were asked to tape-record everything that came to mind during 5 minutes but to try *not* to think about white bears. If they did, they were to mention it and ring a bell. Participants reported thinking about bears a mean of more than six times during the 5 minutes (Wegner, Schneider, Carter, & White, 1987). Afterward, they reported that almost everything in the room reminded them of white bears. Evidently, attempts to suppress a thought are likely to backfire, even with an emotionally trivial thought. You can imagine how hard it is with severely upsetting thoughts.

❚ Most people seldom think about polar bears. But if you try to avoid thinking about them, you can think of little else.

People with obsessive-compulsive disorder have any of several kinds of compulsions. Some collect things. One man collected newspapers under his bed until they raised the bed so high it almost touched the ceiling. Others have odd habits, such as touching everything they see, trying to arrange objects in a completely symmetrical manner, or walking back and forth through a doorway nine times before leaving a building. One person with obsessive-compulsive disorder could not go to sleep at night until he had counted the corners of every object in the room to make sure that the total number of corners was evenly divisible by 16. If it was not, he would add or remove objects until the room had an acceptable total of corners. (The Obsessive-Compulsive Foundation produces a button that reads, "Every Member Counts"!) The most common compulsions are cleaning and checking.

Cleaning Compulsion

Many religions recommend ritual washing to clean one's soul after any foul action or thought, and many people use compulsive cleaning as a way to improve their sense of purity. Consider the following study: You are asked to fill in missing letters to form English words in items like these:

S _ _ P
W _ _ H

Each of the items could be completed in more than one way to make a common word. At the end of the task, you get to choose either a pencil or an antiseptic wipe as your token reward for participation. The manipulation is this: Before the fill-in-the-letters task, some people are asked to recall a good deed from their past, and others are asked to recall something shameful they did. If you were in the "shameful" group, you would be more likely to fill in letters to form "cleaning" words, such as SOAP and WASH, and more likely to choose the antiseptic wipe instead of the pencil (Zhong & Liljenquist, 2006).

Here is a description of a severe cleaning compulsion (Nagera, 1976): "R.," a 12-year-old boy, had a longstanding habit of prolonged bathing and hand washing, dating from a film about germs he had seen in the second grade. At about age 12, he started to complain about "being dirty" and having "bad thoughts," but he would not elaborate. His hand washing and bathing became longer and more frequent. When he bathed he carefully washed himself with soap and washcloth all over, including the inside of his mouth and the inside of each nostril. He even opened his eyes in the soapy water and carefully washed his eyeballs. The only part he did not wash was his penis, which he covered with a washcloth as soon as he entered the tub.

In addition to his peculiar bathing habits, he developed some original superstitions. Whenever he did anything with one hand, he immediately did the same thing with the other hand. Whenever anyone mentioned a member of his family, he would mention the corresponding member of the other person's family. He always walked to school by the same route but was careful never to step on any spot where he had ever stepped before. You can imagine the strain on his memory. At school he would wipe the palm of his hand on his pants after any "good" thought; at home he would wipe his hand on his pants after any "bad" thought.

Checking Compulsion

An obsessive-compulsive checker double-checks everything. Before going to bed at night, he or she makes sure that all the doors and windows are locked and that all the water faucets and gas outlets are turned off. But then the question arises, "Did I *really* check them all, or did I only imagine it?" So everything has to be checked again. And again. "After all, maybe I accidentally unlocked one of the doors while I was checking it." Obsessive-compulsive checkers can never decide when to stop checking; they may go on for hours and even then not be satisfied.

Obsessive-compulsive checkers have been known to check every door they pass to see whether anyone has been locked in, to check trash containers and bushes to see whether anyone has abandoned a baby, to call the police every day to ask whether they have committed a crime that they have forgotten, and to drive back and forth along a street to see whether they ran over any pedestrians the last time through (Pollak, 1979; Rachman & Hodgson, 1980).

Why do they go on checking? Part of the explanation is that they feel a strong responsibility to prevent harm to others. They continue checking to make sure nothing has gone wrong (Rachman, 2002; Szechtman & Woody, 2004). Another reason is that they do not

trust their own memory. In one study obsessive-compulsive patients took a memory test and estimated how many questions they answered correctly. Their actual percentage correct was as good as average, but their estimates of their own performance were well below average (Dar, Rish, Hermish, Taub, & Fux, 2000). So perhaps obsessive-compulsive patients continue checking because they do not trust their memory that they have already checked.

Why do they distrust their own memory? One study found that repeated checking makes the memories less distinct! Normal college students were asked to turn on and off the gas rings of a "virtual gas stove" on a computer. One group did it just once; the other group turned the rings on and off repeatedly. At the end both groups were asked which rings they had turned off on the most recent trial. Those who had manipulated the controls repeatedly answered as correctly as the others but expressed less confidence in their answers. That is, the authors of this study suggest a vicious cycle: Not trusting your memory causes you to check repeatedly, and repeated checking makes the memory less distinct (van den Hout & Kindt, 2003).

Table 16.1 summarizes key differences between obsessive-compulsive cleaners and checkers. Table 16.2 lists some items from a questionnaire on obsessive-compulsive tendencies (Rachman & Hodgson, 1980). Try answering these questions yourself, or try guessing how a person with obsessive-compulsive disorder would answer them. (The few items listed here are not sufficient to diagnose someone as obsessive-compulsive. So don't obsess about it if you agree with all the obsessive-compulsive answers.)

Try It Yourself

TABLE 16.1 Obsessive-Compulsive Cleaners and Checkers

	Cleaners	Checkers
Sex distribution	Mostly female	About equally male and female
Dominant emotion	Anxiety, similar to phobia	Guilt, shame
Speed of onset	Usually rapid	More often gradual
Life disruption	Dominates life	Usually does not disrupt job and family life
Ritual length	Less than 1 hour at a time	Some go on indefinitely
Feel better after rituals?	Yes	Usually not

Source: From *Obsessions and Compulsions*, by Stanley J. Rachman and Ray J. Hodgson. Copyright © 1980 by Prentice-Hall, Inc. Reprinted by permission.

TABLE 16.2 Obsessive-Compulsive Tendencies

1. I avoid public telephones because of possible contamination.	T F
2. I frequently get nasty thoughts and have difficulty getting rid of them.	T F
3. I usually have serious thoughts about the simple everyday things I do.	T F
4. Neither of my parents was very strict during my childhood.	T F
5. I do not take a long time to dress in the morning.	T F
6. One of my major problems is that I pay too much attention to detail.	T F
7. I do not stick to a very strict routine when doing ordinary things.	T F
8. I do not usually count when doing a routine task	T F
9. Even when I do something very carefully, I often feel that it is not quite right.	T F

Check typical answers on page 611.
Source: From *Obsessions and Compulsions*, by Stanley J. Rachman and Ray J. Hodgson. Copyright © 1980 by Prentice-Hall, Inc. Reprinted by permission.

Therapies for Obsessive-Compulsive Disorder

Most people with obsessive-compulsive disorder improve over time, with or without treatment (Skoog & Skoog, 1999). Still, no one wants to wait years for spontaneous recovery. One effective treatment is *exposure therapy,* which resembles systematic desensitization for phobias: The person with obsessive-compulsive disorder is exposed to a situation in which he or she ordinarily performs certain rituals but is prevented from performing them. For example, someone might be prevented from cleaning the house or checking the doors and windows more than once before going to sleep. The point is to demonstrate that nothing catastrophic occurs if one leaves a little mess in the house or runs a slight risk of leaving a door unlocked. Antidepressant drugs are also helpful in many cases (Greist, Jefferson, Kobak, Katzelnick, & Serlin, 1995).

 CONCEPT CHECK

7. In what way do people with obsessive-compulsive disorder have an abnormal memory?
8. Suppose someone reports that a long-term therapy, lasting 10 years, cures many people of obsessive-compulsive disorder. Should we be impressed? Why or why not? (Check your answers on page 611.)

IN CLOSING

Emotions and Avoidance

Phobia and obsessive-compulsive disorder illustrate some of the possible links between emotions and cognitions. At the risk of seriously oversimplifying, we could say that people with phobias experience emotional attacks because of their cognitions about a particular object, whereas people with obsessive-compulsive disorder experience repetitive cognitions for emotional reasons. In both conditions most people know that their reactions are exaggerated, but mere awareness of the problem does not correct it. Dealing with such conditions requires attention to emotions, cognitions, and the links between them. ∎

Summary

- *Generalized anxiety disorder and panic disorder.* People with generalized anxiety disorder experience excessive anxiety much of the day, even when actual dangers are low. Panic disorder is characterized by episodes of disabling anxiety, high heart rate, and rapid breathing. (page 601)
- *Persistence of avoidance behaviors.* A learned shock-avoidance response can persist long after the possibility of shock has been removed. As with shock-avoidance responses, phobias and obsessive-compulsive disorder persist because people do not discover that their avoidance behaviors are unnecessary. (page 602)
- *Phobia.* A phobia is a fear so extreme that it interferes with normal living. Phobias are learned through observation as well as through experience. (page 603)
- *Common phobias.* People are more likely to develop phobias of certain objects (e.g., snakes) than of others (e.g., cars). The most common objects of phobias have menaced humans throughout evolutionary history. They pose dangers that are difficult to predict or control, and we generally have few safe experiences with them. (page 606)
- *Systematic desensitization of phobias.* A common therapy for phobia is systematic desensitization. The patient is taught to relax and is then gradually exposed to the object of the phobia. Flooding is similar, but the person is exposed to the object suddenly. (page 606)
- *Obsessive-compulsive disorder.* People with obsessive-compulsive disorder try to avoid thoughts or impulses that cause distress. They also perform repetitive behaviors. (page 607)
- *Types of obsessive-compulsive disorder.* Two common compulsions are cleaning and checking.

Cleaners try to avoid any type of contamination. Checkers constantly double-check themselves and invent elaborate rituals. (page 608)

Answers to Concept Checks

1. Worrying about anything—even panic attacks themselves—increases the risk of another panic attack. (page 602)
2. Temporarily prevent the person from pressing the lever. Only by ceasing to press it does the person discover that pressing is not necessary. (page 602)
3. The CS was the white rat. The UCS was the loud noise. The CR and the UCR were a combination of crying and other fear reactions. (page 604)
4. People may be born with a predisposition to learn fears of objects that have been dangerous throughout our evolutionary history. We more readily learn to fear objects that we cannot predict or control. We more readily learn to fear objects with which we have few safe experiences. (page 606)
5. To extinguish a learned shock-avoidance response, prevent the response so that the individual learns that a failure to respond is not dangerous. Simi-larly, in systematic desensitization the patient is prevented from fleeing the feared stimulus. He or she learns that the danger is not as great as imagined. (page 606)
6. The flooding procedure is compatible with the James-Lange theory of emotions, which holds that emotions follow from perceptions of body arousal. In flooding, as arousal of the autonomic nervous system decreases, the person perceives, "I am calming down. I must be less frightened than I thought I was." (page 607)
7. People with obsessive-compulsive disorder do not trust their memory, although its accuracy is normal. (page 609)
8. We should not be impressed. Over a long enough time, most people recover from obsessive-compulsive disorder, even without treatment. (page 610)

Answers to Other Questions in the Module

Typical answers for people with obsessive-compulsive disorder (page 610): 1. T; 2. T; 3. T; 4. F; 5. F; 6. T; 7. F; 8. F; 9. T

Substance-Related Disorders

- *Why do people abuse alcohol and other drugs?*
- *What can be done to help people with substance-related disorders?*

How would you like to volunteer for a little experiment? I want to implant into your brain a little device that will automatically lift your mood. There are still a few kinks in it, but most people who have tried say that it makes them feel good at least some of the time, and some people say they like it a great deal.

I should tell you about the possible risks. My device will endanger your health and reduce your life expectancy. Some people believe it causes brain damage, but they haven't proved that charge, so I don't think you should worry about it. Your behavior will change a good bit, though. You may have difficulty concentrating, for example. The device affects some people more than others. If you happen to be strongly affected, you will have difficulty completing your education, getting or keeping a job, and carrying on a satisfactory personal life. But if you are lucky, you can avoid all that. Anyway, you can quit the experiment anytime you decide. You should know, though, that the longer the device remains in your brain, the harder it is to remove.

I cannot pay you for taking part in this experiment. In fact *you* will have to pay *me*. But I'll give you a bargain rate: only $5 for the first week and then a little more each week as time passes. One other thing: Technically speaking, this experiment is illegal. We probably won't get caught, but if we do, we could both go to jail.

What do you say? Is it a deal? I presume you will say "no." I get very few volunteers. And yet, if I change the term *brain device* to *drug* and change *experiment* to *drug deal,* it is amazing how many volunteers come forward.

In chapter 3 we examined the effects of drugs on the brain and behavior. In this module the focus is on the process of addiction.

Substance Dependence (Addiction)

Use and abuse of alcohol and other drugs come in all degrees, from the social drinker, to the person whose use occasionally interferes with other goals, to the person whose problems become ruinous. People who *find it difficult or impossible to quit a self-destructive habit* are said to have a **dependence** on it or an **addiction** to it. Two major questions are what causes occasional drug use to develop into an overwhelming craving, and why some people are more vulnerable than others.

Addictions vary in many ways, and many people convince themselves that they are not addicted because they still fulfill their daily activities—usually. In fact many people with alcoholism or other addictions keep their jobs and do them well at times. Many go days or weeks without using the substance. To decide whether you are addicted, ask, "Does the substance cause troubles in my life, and do I often take more than I had decided I would?"

Nearly all the drugs that commonly produce addictions stimulate dopamine receptors in a small brain area called the *nucleus accumbens,* apparently critical for attention and habit formation (Berridge & Robinson, 1998; Koob & LeMoal, 1997). Figure 16.6 shows its location. Some people have assumed this area is the brain's pleasure center. However, the synapses respond to almost any surprising event, even unpleasant ones, but hardly at all to pleasant but expected events (Waelti, Dickinson, & Schultz, 2001; Young, Joseph, & Gray, 1993). They also become active when a person or animal starts seeking a drug, long before receiving the effects of it (Phillips, Stuber, Heien, Wightman, & Carelli, 2003). So the role of the nucleus accumbens may relate more to attention than to pleasure. Indeed, it is reasonable to describe addiction as something that monopolizes people's attention (Robinson & Berridge, 2000).

Moreover, it is probably not helpful to say that something becomes addictive *because* it stimulates the nucleus accumbens. One could just as well say that it stimulates the nucleus accumbens because it has become addictive. For example, gambling and video game playing do not automatically stimulate the nucleus accumbens—they can't, because they aren't "substances"—but after people develop a strong gambling or video game habit, the activities come to stimulate the nucleus accumbens (Koepp et al., 1998).

Many substances can be addictive under certain circumstances—or, at least, can satisfy an addiction that had already formed. In a hospital ward where alcoholics were being treated, one patient moved his

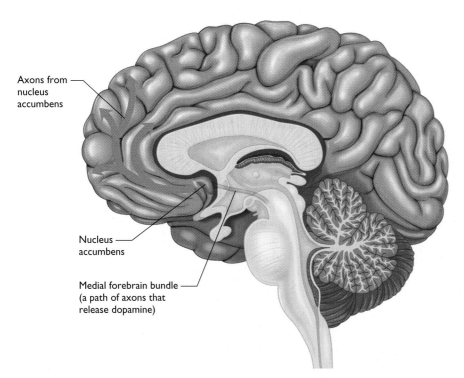

Axons from
nucleus
accumbens

Nucleus
accumbens

Medial forebrain bundle
(a path of axons that
release dopamine)

FIGURE 16.6 The nucleus accumbens is a small brain area that is critical for the motivating effects of many experiences, including drugs, food, and sex. Most abused drugs increase the activity of the neurotransmitter dopamine in this area.

bed into the men's room (Cummings, 1979). At first the hospital staff ignored this curious behavior. Then, one by one, other patients moved their beds into the men's room. Eventually, the staff discovered what was happening. These men, deprived of alcohol, had discovered that by drinking about 30 liters (7.5 gallons) of water per day and urinating the same amount (which was why they moved into the men's room), they could alter the acid-to-base balance of their blood enough to produce a sensation similar to drunkenness. (Do *not* try this yourself. Some people have died from an overdose of water!)

 CONCEPT CHECK

9. Why is it probably pointless to distinguish between substances that are and are not addictive? (Check your answer on page 619.)

What Motivates Addictive Behavior?

After someone has become addicted, what motivation sustains the repetitive and insistent drug seeking? The motivation for trying a drug once is to seek a new and presumably pleasant experience. If it is indeed pleasant, then the motivation for trying it a second time is to repeat the experience. However, most peo-ple who have become addicted to a drug no longer report great pleasure. So why do they continue despite the costs and risks?

One possibility is that they really are still seeking pleasure. Even if the experience usually is not good, sometimes it is, and you may remember from chapter 6 that behavior on a partial reinforcement schedule is highly persistent. In particular the first use of a drug after a period of abstention produces intense effects, so the user learns to return to the substance after any attempt to quit (Hoebel, Rada, Mark, & Pothos, 1999; Hutcheson, Everitt, Robbins, & Dickinson, 2001).

An alternative hypothesis, not contradictory to the first, is that the motivation is to escape unpleasant feelings. Even for someone in the early stages of addiction, a brief period of abstention produces withdrawal symptoms, marked by discomfort and depression. Withdrawal symptoms from prolonged alcoholism include sweating, nausea, sleeplessness, and in severe cases hallucinations and seizures (Mello & Mendelson, 1978). With opiate drugs, withdrawal symptoms include anxiety, restlessness, vomiting, diarrhea, and sweating (Mansky, 1978). A user learns to take the drug to escape these feelings. Someone who *uses a drug to reduce unpleasant withdrawal symptoms* is said to have a **physical dependence**. A **psychological dependence** is a *strong repetitive desire for something without physical symptoms of withdrawal*. For example, habitual gamblers have a psychological dependence on placing bets, even though abstaining from gambling produces no withdrawal symptoms. A psychological dependence can be extremely insistent, and it is often pointless to decide whether someone's dependence is physical or psychological.

However, many people report strong drug cravings long after the end of withdrawal symptoms, so we need to look further to explain addiction. One hypothesis is that a drug user learns to associate the drug with relief from internal distress. That is, at first someone takes a drug to relieve withdrawal symptoms but later learns to use it to relieve other kinds of displeasure. Support for this idea comes from the observation that people who have quit drugs are most likely to relapse during periods of financial or social difficulties (Baker, Piper, McCarthy, Majeskie, & Fiore, 2004).

The relief-from-distress explanation is plausible, so far as it goes, but leaves the question of why addiction produces such obsessive use. After all, many people deal with stress by exercising, but few continue until they collapse and lose consciousness. Many cope with stress by shopping, but not to the point of bankruptcy.

To account for the persistence of drug use far beyond what seems necessary for escape from distress, Terry Robinson and Kent Berridge (2000, 2001) distinguish between "liking" and "wanting." Addicted drug users rarely get intense pleasure ("liking") from a drug, but they continue to want it anyway. By analogy someone who plays video games by the hour *wants* to play but probably does not feel great pleasure. The process of becoming addicted changes the organization of several brain areas that are important for motivation, attention, and learning (Kalivas, Volkow, & Seamans, 2005; Liu, Pu, & Poo, 2005; Volkow et al., 2006). Eventually, the drug monopolizes the person's attention (Laviolette & van der Kooy, 2004; Robinson & Berridge, 2001).

 CONCEPT CHECK

10. According to one of the theories just described, how do people first learn to use drugs when they are feeling bad? (Check your answer on page 620.)

Is Substance Dependence a Disease?

You have no doubt heard people call alcoholism or drug abuse a disease. It is hard to confirm or deny that statement, however, without a clear definition of *disease*. Medical doctors assign it no precise meaning.

When people call alcoholism or drug dependence a disease, they apparently mean that people who abuse alcohol or other drugs should feel no guiltier about their condition than they would about having pneumonia. Although the disease label is reassuring, the concept has some questionable implications. For example, it suggests an all or none distinction between people with the disease and those without it. The evidence suggests a continuum from no problem to severe problems (W. R. Miller & Brown, 1997; Polcin, 1997).

Also, because many untreated diseases grow worse over time, the disease concept suggests that alcoholism or drug dependence becomes worse over time. In fact the outcome varies. Some individuals deteriorate, some remain steady, some improve, and still others fluctuate (Sartor, Jacob, & Bucholz, 2003).

Furthermore, to regard substance dependence as a disease suggests a need for medical intervention. One of the most effective treatments for alcoholism or drug dependence is family therapy, which is not a

medical intervention (Stanton & Shadish, 1997). By improving the person's family life, possibly improving the job situation, and helping the person to develop new interests, family therapy decreases the person's compulsion for alcohol or drug use.

Nicotine Dependence

You have no doubt heard that the cigarette smoking habit depends on nicotine addiction. One type of evidence for this conclusion is that people find it easier to quit cigarettes if they have a replacement source of nicotine, such as a nicotine patch, nicotine chewing gum, or nicotine nasal spray (Rose, 1996).

"If so," you may have wondered, "why have so many smokers switched to low-tar, low-nicotine cigarette brands? Wouldn't those brands fail to satisfy a nicotine craving?" Yes, they would, *if* they delivered low nicotine! Most low-tar, low-nicotine cigarettes have the same kind of tobacco as other cigarettes but have a filter with a row of little air holes, as shown at the top of Figure 16.7. The idea is that air entering these holes will dilute the tobacco smoke coming through the barrel of the cigarette. However, many smokers wrap their fingers around the air holes, either accidentally or intentionally. Regardless of whether people cover the holes, those who switch to low-nicotine cigarettes generally inhale more deeply than they did when smoking regular cigarettes, and

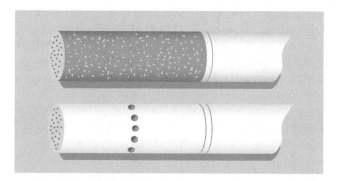

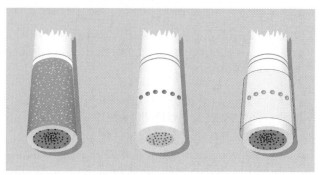

FIGURE 16.7 "Low-nicotine" cigarettes have a row of holes in the filter to let room air dilute the tobacco smoke. However, many smokers cover the holes with their fingers.

they smoke more cigarettes per day. Consequently, people smoking low-nicotine cigarettes inhale about as much tar and nicotine per day as people smoking regular cigarettes and incur the same health risks (Benowitz et al., 2005; Kozlowski, Frecker, Khouw, & Pope, 1980).

Alcoholism

Although most people drink alcohol in moderation, some let alcohol ruin their lives. **Alcoholism** is *the habitual overuse of alcohol.* Treating alcoholism is difficult and often unsuccessful. If we could identify the problem earlier, or identify young people who are at great risk for alcoholism, perhaps we could initiate effective prevention. At least psychologists would like to try.

Genetics and Family Background

Twin studies indicate a strong genetic basis for alcoholism (True et al., 1999). However, most alcoholics are also heavy cigarette smokers and many abuse other drugs too, so the genes that predispose to alcoholism may not be specific to alcohol. Rats that were selectively bred for high alcohol consumption also show a stronger than average motivation for pressing a lever to inject nicotine into their veins (Lê et al., 2006). That is, certain genes may predispose to several kinds of addictive behavior.

A genetic predisposition contributes mainly to early-onset alcoholism. Late-onset or **Type I alcoholism** *develops gradually over the years, affects about as many women as men, is generally less severe, and depends more on life experiences than genetics.* That is, Type I alcoholism often occurs in people with no family history. Early-onset or **Type II alcoholism** *develops rapidly, usually by age 25, is much more common in men than women, is usually more severe, and shows a stronger genetic basis* (Devor, Abell, Hoffman, Tabakoff, & Cloninger, 1994; McGue, 1999). Table 16.3 summarizes this distinction. Naturally, not every person with alcoholism fits neatly into one category or the other.

The incidence of alcoholism is greater than average among people who grew up in families marked by conflict, hostility, and inadequate parental supervision of the children (Schulsinger, Knop, Goodwin, Teasdale, & Mikkelsen, 1986; Zucker & Gomberg, 1986). Women who were sexually abused in childhood are at increased risk for alcoholism (Kendler, Bulik, et al., 2000). Culture also plays an important role. For example, alcoholism is more prevalent in Irish culture, which tolerates it, than among Jews or Italians, who emphasize drinking in moderation (Cahalan, 1978; Vaillant & Milofsky, 1982).

Italian and Jewish cultures, which stress moderation, have much alcohol use but not much abuse.

Still, individuals differ. Not all children of alcoholic parents become alcoholics themselves, and not all children who grow up in a culture that tolerates heavy drinking become alcoholics. Can we identify people who are highly vulnerable to alcoholism?

CRITICAL THINKING
WHAT'S THE EVIDENCE?

Ways of Predicting Alcoholism

Perhaps people's behavior might indicate who is more likely to develop alcoholism. One way to find such clues is to record the behaviors of young people and then, many years later, examine their alcohol use. However, this procedure

TABLE 16.3 Type I and Type II Alcoholism

	Severity	Gender Distribution	Genetics Basis	Onset
Type I (or Type A)	Generally less severe; better long-term outcome	Both males and females	Weaker genetic contribution	Gradual onset later in life
Type II (or Type B)	More severe, more likely to be associated with aggressive behavior and antisocial personality	Almost exclusively males	Strong evidence for genetic contribution	Rapid onset in teens or early 20s

requires decades of research and a huge sample of participants.

A more feasible approach is to compare children of an alcoholic parent with children who have no alcoholic relatives. From previous studies we know that more children of alcoholics will become alcoholics. Therefore, behaviors that are significantly more prevalent among the children of alcoholics may predict vulnerability to alcoholism. In the first study that we consider, experimenters tested whether alcohol might provide more than the usual amount of reward to the sons of alcoholics (Levenson, Oyama, & Meek, 1987).

EXPERIMENT I

Hypothesis. Drinking alcohol will provide relief for almost anyone in a stressful situation. It will provide more relief to the adult sons of alcoholic fathers than to other men of the same age.

The researchers did not study sons of alcoholic mothers because they focused on genetics, not prenatal environment. If a mother drinks heavily during pregnancy, especially early pregnancy, she increases the risk of alcohol abuse in her children regardless of genetics (Alati et al., 2006; Baer, Sampson, Barr, Connor, & Streissguth, 2003).

Method. Half of the participants were sons of alcoholic fathers and the others were from families with no known alcoholics. The young men were told that, at a certain time, they would receive an electric shock and later they would have to give a 3-minute speech entitled "What I Like and Dislike About My Body." (You can imagine the embarrassment and stress of that assignment.) They watched a clock tick off the waiting time. Alcohol was offered to half of each group at the start of the waiting period, and all of them drank it.

Results. All of the men showed considerable stress, as measured by heart rate, restlessness, and self-reports. Those who drank alcohol showed a lower heart rate and reported less anxiety. The easing of stress was more pronounced in those with an alcoholic father (Figure 16.8).

Interpretation. Men who are genetically vulnerable to alcoholism experience greater stress-reducing effects from alcohol than other men of the same age. Why that is true, we do not know, but we might use the stress-reducing effects to predict vulnerability to alcoholism.

EXPERIMENT 2

Several other studies found that young men who are vulnerable to alcoholism have difficulty estimating their own degree of intoxication. This study tested whether young drinkers who underestimate their degree of intoxication are more likely than others to become alcoholics later in life (Schuckit & Smith, 1997).

Hypothesis. Men who underestimate their intoxication after moderate drinking will be more likely than others to develop alcoholism later.

Method. This study was limited to 18- to 25-year-old men with a close relative who was alcoholic. After each of them drank a fixed amount of alcohol, they were asked to walk and describe how intoxicated they felt. Experimenters measured the stagger or sway when the men walked. Ten years later, the experimenters located as many of these men as possible, interviewed them, and determined which ones had become alcoholics.

Results. Of those who either did not sway much when walking or stated that they did not feel intoxicated, 51 of 81 (63%) became alcoholics within 10 years. Of those who clearly swayed and reported that they felt intoxicated, 9 of 52 (17%) became alcoholics.

Interpretation. Men who neither act nor feel intoxicated after a moderate amount of drinking are likely to continue drinking and to become alcoholics. By watching and interviewing young drinkers, psychologists can identify a high-risk population.

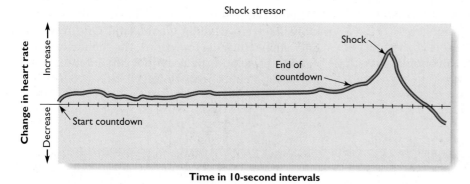

FIGURE 16.8 Changes in stress over time for a typical subject: The line goes up to indicate an increase in heart rate. Alcohol suppressed the signs of stress, especially for the sons of alcoholics. (*From "Greater Reinforcement from Alcohol for Those At Risk: Parental Risk, Personality Risk, and Sex," by Levenson et al.,* Journal of Abnormal Psychology, 1987, 96, 242–253. *Copyright © 1987 by the American Psychological Association. Reprinted by permission of the author.*)

Any research study has limitations, and one limitation of these studies is clear: They examined only men. One study of a small sample of women found that daughters of alcoholics, like sons of alcoholics, tend to feel less intoxicated and show less body sway after drinking alcohol (Schuckit et al., 2000). Whether that tendency predicts later alcoholism in women as well as it does in men, we do not yet know.

 CONCEPT CHECK

11. What are two ways in which sons of alcoholics differ from sons of nonalcoholics? (Check your answer on page 620.)

Treatments

> My mind is a dark place, and I should not be left alone there at night.
>
> —Participant at Alcoholics Anonymous Meeting

Of all the people who try to quit alcohol or other drugs on their own, an estimated 10 to 20% manage to succeed (S. Cohen et al., 1989), though not necessarily on the first try. Some people quit and relapse many times before eventual success. In many cases, however, people with a substance-abuse problem find that they cannot quit on their own. Eventually, they "hit bottom," discovering that they have damaged their health, their ability to hold a job, and their relationships with friends and family. At that point they turn to either a mental health professional or a self-help group such as Alcoholics Anonymous. Combating alcoholism is difficult but not hopeless. Let's consider several approaches and controversies.

Alcoholics Anonymous

The most popular treatment for alcoholism in North America is **Alcoholics Anonymous (AA)**, *a self-help group of people who are trying to abstain from alcohol use and help others do the same.* AA meetings are held regularly in community halls, church basements, and other available spaces. The meeting format varies but often includes study of the book *Alcoholics Anonymous* (Anonymous, 1955) and discussions of participants' individual problems. Some meetings feature an invited speaker. The group has a strong spiritual focus, including a reliance on "a Power greater than ourselves," but no affiliation with any particular religion. Although AA imposes no requirements on its members other than making an effort to quit alcohol, new members are strongly encouraged to attend 90 meetings during the first 90 days. Those who miss a day or two can compensate by attending extra meetings on another day. The idea is to make a strong commitment. From then on members attend as often as they like.

Millions of people have participated in the AA program. One reason for its appeal is that all its members have gone through similar experiences. If someone tries to make an excuse for drinking, saying, "You just don't understand how I feel," others can retort, "Oh, yes we do!" A member who feels the urge to take a drink can call a fellow member day or night for support. The only charge is a voluntary contribution toward the cost of renting the meeting place. AA has inspired other "anonymous" self-help groups whose purpose is to help drug addicts, compulsive gamblers, compulsive eaters, and others.

Although AA members themselves have confidence in the program, research on its effectiveness has been scarce. One reason is that the organization is serious about its members' anonymity. It does not provide a list of members, and many of its meetings are closed to nonmembers. A further problem is that people cannot be assigned randomly to an AA group and a control group. AA participation is voluntary, and the members undoubtedly differ in many ways from those who decline to participate.

Antabuse

In addition to or instead of attendance at AA meetings, some individuals with alcoholism seek medical treatment. Many years ago, investigators noticed that the workers in a certain rubber manufacturing plant drank very little alcohol. The investigators eventually linked this behavior to *disulfiram,* a chemical that was used in the manufacturing process. Ordinarily, the liver converts alcohol into a toxic substance, *acetaldehyde* (ASS-eh-TAL-de-HIDE) and then converts acetaldehyde into a harmless substance, *acetic acid.* Disulfiram, however, blocks the conversion of acetaldehyde to acetic acid. Whenever the workers exposed to disulfiram drank alcohol, they accumulated acetaldehyde and became ill. Over time they learned to avoid alcohol.

Disulfiram, available under the trade name **Antabuse,** is now sometimes used in the treatment of alcoholism, for which it is regarded as only moderately effective (Hughes & Cook, 1997). *Alcoholics who take a daily Antabuse pill become sick whenever they have a drink.* They develop headache, nausea, blurred vision, anxiety, and a sensation of heat in the face. The threat of sickness is more effective than the sickness itself (Fuller & Roth, 1979). By taking a daily Antabuse pill, a recovering alcoholic renews the decision not to drink. Those who do take a drink in spite of the threat become quite ill, at which point they decide either not to drink again or not to take the pill again!

CONCEPT CHECK

12. About 50% of Southeast Asians have a gene that makes them unable to convert acetaldehyde to acetic acid. Would such people be more likely or less likely than others to become alcoholics? (Check your answer on page 620.)

Harm Reduction

Most physicians agree with Alcoholics Anonymous that the only hope for an alcoholic is abstinence. Drinking in moderation, they insist, is out of the question. A few psychologists doubt that abstention is a realistic goal for everyone (Peele, 1998). The **harm reduction** approach *concentrates on decreasing the frequency of drug use and minimizing the harmful consequences to health and well-being,* even if the person does not abstain (MacCoun, 1998). Critics charge that the idea of reduced drinking discourages people from making a serious effort at abstinence. Defenders reply that when people find that they cannot quit, we should not give up on helping them.

Contingency Management

Another approach is a form of behavior therapy known as *contingency management.* Practitioners monitor alcohol use by a Breathalyzer or other drugs by urine samples. Whenever the test shows no alcohol or drugs, a therapist provides an immediate reinforcement. For example, teenagers might receive a movie pass or a voucher for a pizza (Kaminer, 2000).

A major strength of this approach is that many people who are not motivated to try other approaches do agree to receive rewards for being free of alcohol and drugs. The effectiveness of contingency management is surprising, as the rewards are small. That is, people could have abstained from alcohol and drugs and then used the money they saved to give themselves the same or greater rewards. Evidently, there is something powerful about testing negative for drugs and then receiving an immediate reinforcement.

Opiate Dependence

Prior to 1900 opiate drugs such as morphine and heroin were considered less dangerous than alcohol (Siegel, 1987). In fact many doctors urged their patients with alcoholism to switch from alcohol to morphine. Then, around 1900, opiates became illegal in the United States, except by prescription to control pain. Since then research on opiate use has been limited by the fact that only lawbreakers use opiates.

Opiate dependence often has a rapid onset in contrast to alcohol and tobacco dependence, which develop more slowly. Like alcoholism, opiate abuse shows a hereditary tendency. That is, the closer your genetic relationship to an opiate abuser, the higher your probability of developing the same problem (Kendler, Karkowski, Neale, & Prescott, 2000).

Treatments

Some users of heroin and other opiates try to break their habit by going "cold turkey"—quitting completely, sometimes under medical supervision. Many people, however, experience a recurring urge to take the drug long after the withdrawal symptoms have subsided. To combat that urge, they can turn to self-help groups, contingency management, and other treatments. Cognitive-behavior therapists emphasize the importance of identifying the locations and situations in which a person has the greatest cravings and the greatest temptation to relapse into drug use. Therapists then teach the person how to minimize exposure to those situations and how to handle the situations when avoiding them is impossible (Witkiewitz & Marlatt, 2004).

For those who cannot quit, researchers have sought to find a nonaddictive substitute that would satisfy the craving for opiates without harmful side effects. (Heroin was originally introduced as a substitute for morphine before physicians discovered that it is even more troublesome!)

The drug **methadone** (METH-uh-don) *is sometimes offered as a less dangerous substitute for opiates.* Methadone, which is chemically similar to morphine and heroin, can itself be addictive. (Table 16.4 com-

Heroin withdrawal resembles a week-long bout of severe flu, with aching limbs, intense chills, vomiting, and diarrhea. Unfortunately, even after people have endured withdrawal, they still sometimes crave the drug.

TABLE 16.4 Comparison of Methadone with Morphine

	Morphine	Methadone By Injection	Methadone Taken Orally
Addictive?	Yes	Yes	Weakly
Onset	Rapid	Rapid	Slow
"Rush"?	Yes	Yes	No
Relieves craving?	Yes	Yes	Yes
Rapid withdrawal symptoms?	Yes	Yes	No

pares methadone and morphine.) When methadone is taken as a pill, however, it enters the bloodstream gradually and departs gradually (Dole, 1980). (If morphine or heroin is taken as a pill, much of it is digested and never reaches the brain.) Thus, methadone does not produce the "rush" associated with injected opiates. Although methadone satisfies the craving for opiates, it does not eliminate the addiction. If the dosage is reduced, the craving returns.

A more recent alternative to methadone is *buprenorphine,* which attaches to the same receptors as heroin and morphine but attaches to them for long times and stimulates them less strongly. Thus, it prevents heroin or similar drugs from attaching to those receptors. Most buprenorphine users decrease their use of heroin and other drugs, decrease their criminal activities, and improve their health (Teesson et al., 2006).

 CONCEPT CHECK

13. Many heroin users report withdrawal symptoms when they take buprenorphine. Why? (Check your answer on page 620.)

IN CLOSING

Substances, the Individual, and Society

Substance dependence is costly to society as well as to the individual. The United States and many other countries have tried to control the problem by issuing stiff prison sentences for those who use or sell certain drugs. The result? Hard to say; drug use continues to be widespread, but we do not know what it would be without the legal prohibitions. We do know that law enforcement itself is costly. Prisons are crowded with those whose only offense was drug possession, and many drug users turn to theft as a way of getting drugs. The Netherlands has experimented with greatly de-

creased penalties against the use of marijuana and other drugs. The results are favorable in some ways but not others. Overall, it is impossible to generalize about what might happen if other countries tried the same approach (Mac-Coun & Reuter, 1997). Substance abuse will continue to be a problem for many individuals, and for society as a whole. ∎

Summary

- *Substance dependence.* People who find it difficult or impossible to stop using a substance are said to be dependent on it or addicted to it. (page 612)
- *Addictive substances.* Nearly all addictive substances stimulate dopamine synapses in a brain area that is apparently associated with attention. (page 612)
- *Motivations behind addiction.* Some people continue using drugs frequently despite little apparent pleasure. One hypothesis is that they use the drugs to escape displeasure. Another is that frequent use of a drug modifies brain circuits to make the drug dominate attention. (page 613)
- *The disease concept.* Whether or not substance abuse is considered a disease depends on what we mean by disease. (page 614)
- *Predisposition to alcoholism.* People at risk for alcoholism find that alcohol relieves their stress more than it does for other people. People who underestimate their level of intoxication are more likely than others to become alcoholics later. (page 616)
- *Alcoholics Anonymous.* The self-help group Alcoholics Anonymous provides the most common treatment for alcoholism in North America. (page 617)
- *Antabuse.* Some alcoholics are treated with Antabuse, a prescription drug that makes them ill if they drink alcohol. (page 617)
- *Harm reduction.* A controversial approach to alcoholism or drug addiction is to try to minimize the harm instead of insisting or abstinence. (page 618)
- *Opiate abuse.* Some opiate users quit using opiates, suffer through the withdrawal symptoms, and manage to abstain from further use. Others substitute methadone or buprenorphine under medical supervision. (page 618)

Answers to Concept Checks

9. Some people show addictions to gambling or video games, which are not substances at all. Some have managed to abuse water. (page 612)

10. At first, they learn to use the drug to escape withdrawal symptoms caused by abstention from the drug itself. Later, they learn to use the drug to escape from other kinds of distress. (page 613)

11. Alcohol gives them more than the average amount of relief from stress, and they do not appear or feel as drunk as other people do after a moderate amount of drinking. (page 616)

12. They are less likely than others to become alcoholics. This gene is considered the probable reason that relatively few Asians become alcoholics (Harada, Agarwal, Goedde, Tagaki, & Ishikawa, 1982; Reed, 1985). (page 617)

13. Buprenorphine attaches to the opiate receptors in the brain but excites them less than heroin or morphine would. Therefore, the user gets less than the accustomed amount of effect and enters withdrawal. (page 619)

Mood Disorders

- *What causes severe mood swings, and what can be done to relieve them?*

Ordinarily, most people feel happy when life is going well and sad when it is not. Some people, however, feel extremely bad or (less often) extremely good for weeks or months regardless of the events in their lives. Why?

Depression

People who say "I'm depressed," often mean "I'm sad. Life isn't going well for me right now." A **major depression** is a more *extreme condition, persisting most of each day for at least 2 weeks, usually more, while the person experiences little interest, pleasure, motivation, or activity.* People who are depressed cannot even imagine anything that would make them happy. They have trouble concentrating. They no longer enjoy food or sex. A profound sadness is characteristic of depression, but lack of happiness may be even more characteristic. In one study people had a beeper that alerted them at unpredictable times to make a note in their journal of what they were doing and how they felt about it. People with depression reported about an average number of sad experiences but far fewer than average happy experiences (Peters, Nicolson, Berkhof, Delespaul, & deVries, 2003).

Nearly all depressed people experience sleep abnormalities (Carroll, 1980; Healy & Williams, 1988) (see Figure 16.9). They enter REM sleep within 45 minutes after falling asleep—an unusually short time for most people—and have more frequent eye movements during their REM periods. Most depressed people wake up early and cannot get back to sleep. When morning comes, they feel poorly rested. In fact they usually feel most depressed early in the morning.

Depression is common from adolescence through old age. Almost 10% of adults are depressed within any given year (Kessler, Chiu, Demler, & Walters, 2005),

and about 20% are depressed at some time in life (Kessler, Berglund, Demler, Jin, & Walters, 2005). Most people with depression say they had difficulties off and on for years before they first visited a therapist (Eaton et al., 1997). Some reports indicate that depression has been growing more common over the decades, although the research is mixed on this point (Murphy, Laird, Monson, Sobol, & Leighton, 2000). It is difficult, of course, to distinguish between changes in prevalence and changes in standards of diagnosis.

The good news is that few people remain permanently depressed. Typically, people have an episode of depression that lasts a few months (less commonly for years) and then recover. The bad news is that depression is likely to return. Later episodes tend to be briefer but more frequent (Solomon et al., 1997). A common pattern is that an intensely stressful event triggers the first episode of depression, but later episodes seem to occur on their own, with little evidence of stress. Later episodes also become more difficult to treat. It is as if the brain learns how to become depressed. It gets better and better at becoming depressed (Monroe & Harkness, 2005; Post, 1992). The same is true for epilepsy and migraine headaches: The more episodes one has had, the easier it is to have another one. An implication is that early treatment is important for depression. It may not only help at the moment, but it also decreases the risk of additional episodes later.

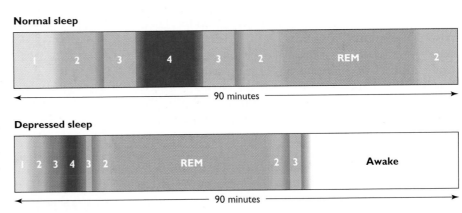

FIGURE 16.9 When most people go to sleep at their usual time, they progress slowly to stage 4 and then back through stages 3 and 2, reaching REM sleep toward the end of their first 90-minute cycle. Depressed people enter REM sooner than average and awaken frequently during the night.

In a variant form of depression known as seasonal affective disorder (SAD), or depression with a seasonal pattern (Figure 16.10), *people repeatedly become depressed during a particular season of the year.* It is common in Scandinavia, which has huge differences between summer and winter (Haggarty et al., 2002), and almost universal among explorers who spend long times in Antarctica (Palinkas, 2003). Although annual winter depressions receive the most publicity, annual summer depressions also occur (Faedda et al., 1993). Unlike other depressed patients, most people with seasonal affective disorder sleep and eat excessively during their depressed periods (Jacobsen, Sack, Wehr, Rogers, & Rosenthal, 1987). They tend to fall asleep late and awaken late in contrast to other depressed patients who generally get sleepy early and wake up early (Teicher et al., 1997).

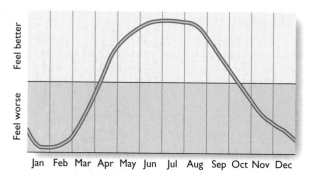

FIGURE 16.10 Most people feel better during the summer than during the winter, when there are fewer hours of sunlight. The differences are greater for people with seasonal affective disorder (SAD).

Seasonal affective disorder can be relieved by sitting in front of a bright light for a few hours each day. Although the effects of light therapy are poorly understood, they are powerful and reliable, with relatively little cost and no side effects (Wirz-Justice, 1998). Light therapy is also helpful for many people with other kinds of depression. Although research has been sparse, preliminary results suggest that light therapy is also effective for nonseasonal depression, producing results at least as good as drugs or psychotherapy and showing the benefits more quickly (Kripke, 1998; Putilov, Pinchasov, & Poljakova, 2005). To find more information about seasonal affective disorder and light therapy, visit this website: **http://www.sada .org.uk/.**

Bipolar disorder, previously known as *manic-depressive disorder,* is a related condition in which someone *alternates between periods of depression and periods of mania, which are opposite extremes.* We shall consider bipolar disorder in more detail later.

  CONCEPT CHECK

14. How does major depression differ from ordinary sadness or discouragement? (Check your answer on page 631.)

Genetics

Your probability of becoming depressed is higher if you have close biological relatives with depression, especially if they became depressed before age 30 (Kendler, Gardner, & Prescott, 1999; Lyons et al., 1998). In that regard depression resembles many other psychological and neurological disorders: People with an early onset are more likely than those with a later onset to have relatives with the same disorder. However, no gene appears to be specific to depression. People with depression are more likely than other people to have relatives with substance abuse, antisocial personality disorder, attention-deficit disorder, bulimia nervosa, migraine headaches, and a variety of other disorders (Fu et al., 2002; Hudson et al., 2003; Kendler et al., 1995). Evidently, certain genes magnify the risk of many problems, but other circumstances dictate which problem arises. Your risk of depression is also increased, but not as much, if you have adoptive relatives with depression (Figure 16.11). That is, depression depends on both hereditary and family influences, as well as experiences outside the family setting.

People with a genetic predisposition show some early indications relating to depression before developing clear symptoms. For example, recall that most

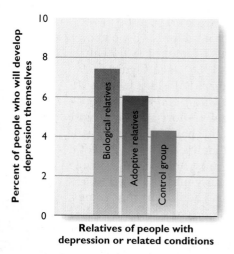

FIGURE 16.11 Genetic relatives of depressed people, substance-dependent people, and suicidal people have an increased risk of depression, as do adopted relatives to a lesser extent. *(Based on data of Weissman, Kidd, & Prusoff, 1982)*

people with depression have sleep abnormalities. Many show the sleep abnormalities long before becoming depressed (Modell, Ising, Holsboer, & Lauer, 2005).

While seeking to identify genes related to depression, researchers found inconsistent results from one study to another. Then researchers considered the possibility that the effect of a gene might depend on the environment. Maybe certain genes increase the risk of depression only for people who have faced highly stressful conditions. Figure 16.12 shows the results for a study examining different alleles (forms) of a gene controlling levels of the neurotransmitter serotonin. One allele is called s (short), and the other is l (long). A person can have two s alleles (s/s), two l alleles (l/l), or one of each (s/l). Researchers compared people with different levels of stress, counting only major stressors such as divorce and job loss. For young adults reporting no major stressors, the risk of depression was low regardless of the genes. For those who had undergone stressful experiences, people with the s/s combination had the greatest probability of depression, and those with the l/l combination had the least. The greater the number of stressful experiences, the greater the effect of the genetic difference (Caspi et al., 2003). That is, the s allele magnified the depressive influence of stressful experiences. Another study replicated this tendency (S. E. Taylor et al., 2006). Further studies found that when people with the s/s combination become depressed, their depression tends to be more severe, and their episodes more frequent, compared to people with the other genes (Zalsman et al., 2006). These results illustrate an interaction between heredity and environment.

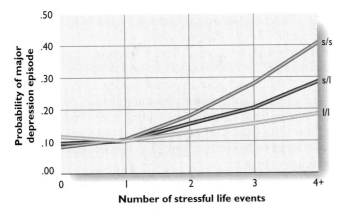

FIGURE 16.12 People with the *s/s* genes controlling serotonin levels have the greatest risk of depression, and those with the *l/l* genes have the least. The importance of the genes depends on how many serious stressful experiences a person has had. *(From Caspi et al., 2003)*

Gender Differences

Depression is uncommon before adolescence, but from adolescence on it occurs about twice as often in women as in men, and the ratio is even higher for severe depression. Women experience depression more than men in all cultures for which we have data (Culbertson, 1997; Cyranowski, Frank, Young, & Shear, 2000; Silberg et al., 1999).

Why is depression more common in women than in men? On the average depressed women have about the same hormonal levels as other women (Roca, Schmidt, & Rubinow, 1999), so hormones are apparently not the answer. One hypothesis is that females encounter more negative events than males do (Hankin & Abramson, 2001). For example, severe sexual abuse in childhood increases the risk of later depression, and more girls than boys are sexually abused. The strongest evidence for the effects of sexual abuse comes from a study that compared pairs of twins in which one reported childhood sexual abuse and the other did not. On the average the twin reporting sexual abuse had more depression than the other twin (E. C. Nelson et al., 2002). Of course, this conclusion presumes that both twins accurately reported childhood events.

Susan Nolen-Hoeksema (1990, 1991) has suggested that the excess of depression among women relates to how people react to emotional distress: When men start to feel sad, they generally try to distract themselves. They play basketball or watch a movie or do something else instead of thinking about how they feel. Women are more likely to ruminate—to think about why they are depressed, to talk with others about their feelings, even to have a long cry. According to Nolen-Hoeksema, ruminating about depression only makes it worse. The ruminative thoughts interfere with useful problem solving and bias a person toward a pessimistic appraisal of the situation. This explanation has the advantage of suggesting ways to help women (and men) avoid or minimize their depression. It does not, however, explain *why* women ruminate more and distract themselves less than men do. Another difficult question: Do the ruminative thoughts *lead to* depression? Or are they just an early symptom of depression?

Although ruminating about your unpleasant feelings tends to make them worse, thinking about the problem that led to the feelings can be helpful and sometimes necessary. The advice is to think about the problem as an outside observer might. Consider what events made you sad, angry, or frightened, and what you might do about them, rather than thinking about what emotions you feel (Kross, Ayduk, & Mischel, 2005).

Events That Precipitate Depression

As a rule people become depressed when bad things happen to them. Depression is particularly likely after events that leave people feeling not only sad but also humiliated and guilty, taking the blame for some bad event (Kendler, Hettema, Butera, Gardner, & Prescott, 2003). However, the event itself is not the sole cause of depression; when various people have roughly the same experience, some become depressed and others do not. For example, of the people who lived in New York City during the terrorist attack on the World Trade Center in 2001, about 9% became seriously depressed within the next 6 months. Most of those were people with many other stressful events in their lives and a history of previous traumatic events (Person, Tracy, & Galea, 2006). Thus, depression usually results from a sequence of events, not a single event.

One study followed students at a California university who had answered a questionnaire about their mental health 2 weeks before a major earthquake. Psychologists asked the same students to fill out the questionnaires again 10 days and 7 weeks after the earthquake. The results showed that students who were already somewhat depressed before the earthquake became and remained depressed, whereas students who had not been depressed recovered rapidly (Nolen-Hoeksema & Morrow, 1991). Hence, a stressful event has its strongest effects on people who were already somewhat depressed.

Depression is most common among people who have little social support.

CONCEPT CHECK

15. What might you observe about people to determine which ones were most likely to become depressed later?
16. Why might a particular gene appear to be linked to depression in one sample of people and not in another?
17. What is the relationship between depression and precipitating events? (Check your answers on page 631.)

Cognitive Aspects of Depression

Suppose you fail a test. Choose your probable explanation:

- The test was difficult. Probably other students did poorly too.
- I had a weak background in this topic from my previous education, compared to others.
- I didn't get a good chance to study.
- I'm just stupid. I always do badly, no matter how hard I try.

Any of the first three explanations would not leave you depressed. They attribute your failure to something temporary, specific, or correctable. However, the fourth attribution applies to you always and everywhere. If you make that attribution—and if your grades are important to you—you are likely to feel depressed (Abramson, Seligman, & Teasdale, 1978; C. Peterson, Bettes, & Seligman, 1985).

In a given situation, you might have a good reason for one attribution or another. For example, if you get a low grade on a French test, perhaps you are the only one in your class who did not take high school French. Still, everyone has an **explanatory style,** *a tendency to accept one kind of explanation for success or failure more often than others.* Recall from chapter 13 that an *internal attribution* cites a cause within the person. ("I failed because I studied poorly.") An *external attribution* identifies causes outside the person. ("I failed because the test was so hard.") Most people vary in how they explain their successes, but they are more consistent in how they explain their failures (Burns & Seligman, 1989).

Blaming yourself isn't always wrong, of course. However, taking the blame too consistently constitutes a *pessimistic* explanatory style, especially if your attributions for failure are global (applying to all situations) and stable (applying to all times). People with a pessimistic style are more likely than others to have been depressed in the past and more likely to become depressed in the future (Alloy et al., 1999; Haeffel et al., 2005). Indeed, according to Aaron Beck (1973, 1987), people with depression put unfavorable interpretations on almost all their experiences. If someone walks by without comment, their likely response is, "See, people ignore me. They don't like me." After any kind of defeat, "I'm hopeless." They lack confidence in their relationships with other people and frequently seek reassurances of love or support (Joiner & Metalsky, 2001).

Researchers have also gauged the explanatory styles of famous people, even dead people, by reading their speeches and writings to see what explanations they offered for successes and failures. Using this method psychologists have found that pessimistic political leaders tend to be cautious, indecisive, and inactive. Leaders with an optimistic explanatory style take bold, risky actions (Satterfield & Seligman, 1994; Zullow, Oettingen, Peterson, & Seligman, 1988). Athletes with a pessimistic style tend to give up and try less after a defeat. Athletes with a more optimistic style try harder after a defeat because they believe they can overcome their defeats with hard work (Seligman, Nolen-Hoeksema, Thornton, & Thornton, 1990). (How do you react after a disappointment? Do you try harder or do you give up?)

 CONCEPT CHECK

18. Would depressed people be more or less likely than others to buy a lottery ticket? (Check your answer on page 631.)

Treatments

Most people with major depression receive psychotherapy, antidepressant drugs, or both. Of people with depression who have no treatment or only a placebo, about one third will improve significantly over the next few months. Improvement without treatment is called spontaneous recovery. Of those who get interpersonal or cognitive-behavior psychotherapy, more than half will improve. Psychodynamic therapy, including psychoanalysis, has been tested less often but appears less effective. Of those who take antidepressant drugs, more than half improve (Hollon, Thase, & Markowitz, 2002). Figure 16.13 shows the results. Psychotherapy and antidepressant drugs appear to help about the same percentage of people. Note that many of the people who recover with either psychotherapy or medication would have recovered spontaneously without treatment. A combination of psychotherapy and antidepressant drugs boosts the mean benefit but still leaves many people not responding. Treatments are in general considerably less effective for children and adolescents

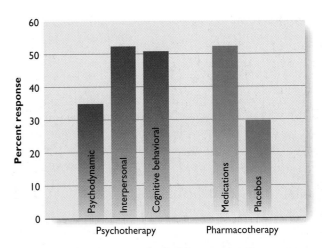

FIGURE 16.13 About one third of depressed patients recover without treatment, many others recover with treatment, and more than one third respond poorly to treatment. *(From Figure 3, p. 53 from Hollon, S. D., Thase, M. E., and Markowitz, J. C. (2002). Treatment and prevention of depression.* Psychological Science in the Public Interest, 3, *39–77.)*

with depression than for adults (Weisz, McCarty, & Valeri, 2006). In short, we have much reason to hope for improvements in the treatment for depression.

Psychotherapy

Most of the research on psychotherapy for depression focuses on interpersonal therapy and cognitive therapy, as shown in Figure 16.13. **Interpersonal therapy** *focuses on improving interpersonal relationships and on coping with difficulties someone has faced in the present or recent past, such as death of a loved one, divorce, unemployment, and lack of social skills* (Hollon et al., 2002). The therapist tries to understand the difficulties and help the client develop a strategy and skills to deal with them.

Cognitive therapy, as discussed in chapter 15, focuses on changing people's thoughts and beliefs and encouraging a more active life. According to Aaron Beck, a pioneer in cognitive therapy, depressed people are guided by certain thoughts or assumptions of which they are only dimly aware. He refers to the "negative cognitive triad of depression":

- I am deprived or defeated.
- The world is full of obstacles.
- The future is devoid of hope.

Based on these "automatic thoughts," people who are depressed interpret ambiguous situations to their own disadvantage. When something goes wrong, they habitually blame themselves (Beck, 1991). The therapist focuses on a belief, such as "no one likes me," points out that it is a hypothesis, and invites the client to collect evidence to test the hypothesis and if possible discard or modify it.

In addition to the focus on changing thoughts and beliefs, cognitive therapy also encourages people to become more active, to take part in more activities that might bring pleasure or a sense of accomplishment. The therapist helps the person improve social skills or overcome any unfortunate habits that stand in the way of greater activity. Research has found that giving depressed people just this guidance toward greater activity produces about the same antidepressant effect as the complete cognitive therapy treatment (Jacobson et al., 1996). Think about a parallel finding in chapter 14: Extraverted personality consists of friendly, active, outgoing behavior and enjoyment of life. Introverts who pretend to be extraverted, talking more and being more outgoing for the time being, report feeling happier. The same applies here: Just getting people to become more active helps relieve depression.

Antidepressant Medications

The common antidepressants include tricyclics, serotonin reuptake inhibitors, and monoamine oxidase inhibitors. **Tricyclic drugs** (e.g., imipramine, trade name Tofranil) *block the reabsorption of the neurotransmitters dopamine, norepinephrine, and serotonin after they are released by an axon's terminal* (Figure 16.14). Thus, tricyclics prolong the effect of these neurotransmitters on the receptors of the postsynaptic cell. Although they are effective for many people, they produce unpleasant side effects, including dry mouth, difficulty urinating, heart irregularities, and drowsiness (Horst & Preskorn, 1998). Many people quit the drugs or reduce the dosage because of the side effects.

Selective serotonin reuptake inhibitors (SSRIs) (e.g., fluoxetine, trade name Prozac) are similar to tricyclic drugs but more specific in their effects. They *block the reuptake of the neurotransmitter serotonin.* Their side effects are usually limited to mild nausea or headache (Feighner et al., 1991). Other common drugs in this category are sertraline (Zoloft), fluvoxamine (Luvox), citalopram (Celexa), and paroxetine (Paxil or Seroxat).

Monoamine (MAHN-oh-ah-MEEN) **oxidase inhibitors (MAOIs)** (e.g., phenelzine, trade name Nardil) *block the metabolic breakdown of released dopamine, norepinephrine, and serotonin* by the enzyme monoamine oxidase (MAO) (Figure 16.14c). Thus, MAOIs also prolong the ability of released neurotransmitters to stimulate the postsynaptic cell. MAOIs are usually less effective than the other antidepressant drugs, but they help some people who do not respond to other drugs (Thase, Trivedi, & Rush, 1995).

Other antidepressant drugs have little in common with each other except that they do not fit into the first three groups. These **atypical antidepressants** *are about as effective, on the average, as other antidepressants and produce milder side effects.* They act primarily on dopamine or norepinephrine synapses rather than serotonin, although their mechanism of effect is not entirely certain. The most common is buproprion, also known by the trade name Wellbutrin (Thase et al., 2005). Two studies found that 25 to 30% of patients who did not respond to one of the SSRI drugs improved after switching to one of the atypical antidepressants or a combination of an SSRI and an atypical antidepressant for an additional 12 to 14 weeks (Rush et al., 2006; Trivedi et al., 2006). However, neither study had a control group to consider the possibility that these patients might have improved spontaneously during that period of time.

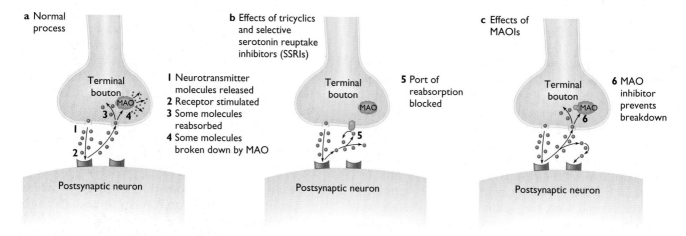

FIGURE 16.14 **(a)** Ordinarily, after the release of a neurotransmitter, some of the molecules are reabsorbed by the terminal bouton, and some are broken down by the enzyme monoamine oxidase (MAO). **(b)** Selective serotonin reuptake inhibitors (SSRIs) prevent reabsorption of serotonin. Tricyclic drugs prevent reabsorption of dopamine, norepinephrine, and serotonin. **(c)** MAO inhibitors (MAOIs) block the enzyme monoamine oxidase and thereby increase the availability of the neurotransmitter.

You have probably heard about St. John's wort, *an herb with antidepressant effects.* It contains several chemicals that block the reuptake of dopamine and serotonin, as other antidepressant drugs do. Because St. John's wort is a naturally occurring substance, it is inexpensive and available without a doctor's prescription. Researchers are not yet in agreement about its effectiveness (Linde, Berner, Egger, & Mulrow, 2005), but it has drawbacks. First, because the Food and Drug Administration does not regulate the sale of herbs, the purity and strength vary from one batch to another. Second, it has side effects, including gastrointestinal distress, drowsiness, and painful sensitivity to light (Wong, Smith, & Boon, 1998). Third, it has an additional unusual side effect: It activates a liver enzyme that breaks down a wide variety of toxic plant chemicals. Helping to break down toxins sounds like a benefit, and indeed, it can be. However, that enzyme also breaks down most medications. Therefore, taking St. John's wort decreases the effectiveness of cancer drugs, AIDS drugs, and even birth-control pills (Moore et al., 2000). How much it impairs those other drugs varies from one person to another. Thus, the advice is to consider St. John's wort only if you take no other medications.

 CONCEPT CHECK

19. Which type of antidepressant drug has effects similar to methylphenidate (Ritalin), discussed in chapter 3?
20. If someone takes prescription antidepressant drugs, would it help to take St. John's wort also? (Check your answers on page 631.)

The effects of antidepressant drugs develop gradually. Nearly any benefit within the first 2 weeks is a *placebo effect,* which depends on the person's expectation of feeling better (Stewart et al., 1998). The effects of the drug itself begin after 2 to 3 weeks and increase over the next few weeks (Blaine, Prien, & Levine, 1983). Even then, part of the apparent drug effect is also a placebo effect or an effect of the passage of time. That is, many of the people showing improvement over that time also would have improved without the drug (Kirsch & Sapirstein, 1998).

The fact that antidepressant drugs alter synaptic activity within an hour or so but need weeks to improve someone's mood tells us that the explanation in terms of synapses must be incomplete. One promising hypothesis concerns cell growth. In several brain areas, neurons' cell bodies shrink visibly—well, visibly under a microscope—when people become depressed (Cotter, Mackay, Landau, Kerwin, & Everall, 2001).

Antidepressants stimulate neuronal growth, which is evidently necessary for the improvement of mood (Saarelainen et al., 2003).

Choosing Between Psychotherapy and Antidepressant Drugs

Cognitive therapy produces no side effects, and its benefits generally persist longer than do those of antidepressant drugs (Robinson, Berman, & Neimeyer, 1990). That is, people who quit taking antidepressant drugs are likely to relapse into another depressive episode sooner than are people who had psychotherapy. Why, then, would anyone choose the drugs over psychotherapy?

Two reasons are convenience and cost. If a depressed person has enough time and money (or a generous insurance program), then psychotherapy is a good idea. However, antidepressant pills are cheaper and require only a few seconds a day plus an occasional checkup at the doctor's office.

Ideally, therapists would like to identify whether a particular patient is more likely to respond well to psychotherapy or drugs. Some preliminary progress has been reported. According to one study, patients who reported major traumatic experiences in early childhood—such as death of their parents or prolonged neglect—responded better to psychotherapy than to drugs (Nemeroff et al., 2003). Another study found a genetic test that predicted which patients would respond well to SSRIs (McMahon et al., 2006).

Electroconvulsive Shock Therapy

Another treatment for depression is **electroconvulsive therapy (ECT)** (Figure 16.15): *A brief electrical shock is administered across the patient's head to induce a*

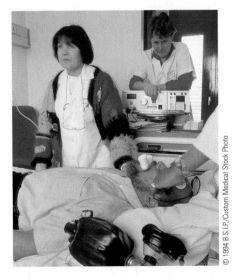

FIGURE 16.15 Electroconvulsive therapy is administered today only with the patient's informed consent. ECT is given in conjunction with muscle relaxants and anesthetics to minimize discomfort.

convulsion similar to epilepsy. ECT was first used in the 1930s and became popular in the 1940s and 1950s as a treatment for many psychiatric disorders. It then fell out of favor, partly because of the advent of antidepressant drugs and partly because ECT had been widely abused. Some patients were subjected to ECT hundreds of times without informed consent, and sometimes, ECT was used more as a punishment than as a therapy.

Beginning in the 1970s, ECT made a comeback in modified form, mostly for severely depressed people who fail to respond to antidepressant drugs, whose thinking is seriously disordered, or who have strong suicidal tendencies (Scovern & Kilmann, 1980). For suicidal patients ECT has the advantage of taking effect rapidly, generally within 1 week. When a life is at stake, rapid relief is important. However, about half of those who show a good response will relapse into depression within 6 months unless they receive some other therapy to prevent it (Riddle & Scott, 1995).

ECT is now used only with patients who have given their informed consent. The shock is less intense than it used to be, and the patient is given muscle relaxants to prevent injury and anesthetics to reduce discomfort. As a rule the procedure is applied every other day for about 2 weeks. Then the psychiatrist evaluates the progress and either stops the treatment or repeats it a few more times.

How ECT works is uncertain (Fink, 2000). The data do not support the idea that it relieves depression by causing people to forget depressing thoughts and memories. ECT that is administered to just the frontal part of the brain or just the right hemisphere is as effective as the usual whole-brain ECT, but without significant memory loss (Lisanby, Maddox, Prudic, Devanand, & Sackeim, 2000; Sackeim et al., 2000).

Other Treatments

Several other kinds of treatment have shown significant benefits, although the research is less extensive. Each of these has the advantages of being inexpensive or free and of producing few if any side effects. One method, already mentioned, is the use of bright lights. A second is to get some consistent aerobic exercise, such as jogging, brisk walking, or dancing. Exercise increases blood flow to the brain and improves overall mood (Leppämäki, Partonen, & Lönnqvist, 2002).

A third method is to maintain a regular sleep schedule (Wehr et al., 1998). People who are depressed have sleep problems, and sleep problems increase the risk of depression. Also, to almost everyone's surprise, a full night's sleep deprivation provides quick relief for about 60% of people with depression. The benefits usually last only until the next night's sleep but sometimes last a few days (Wirz-Justice & Van den Hoofdakker, 1999). Sleep deprivation, bright light, or exercise can be combined with psychotherapy or antidepressant drugs to increase the benefits (Martiny, Lunde, Undén, Dam, & Bech, 2005; Putilov et al., 2005).

CONCEPT CHECK

21. What would be one major advantage of combining one night's sleep deprivation with either psychotherapy or antidepressant drugs? (Check your answer on page 631.)

Bipolar Disorder

People with bipolar disorder (formerly called manic-depressive disorder) alternate between the extremes of mania and depression. In many respects **mania** is the *opposite of depression.* When in the depressed phase, people are inactive and inhibited. In the manic phase, they are *constantly active and uninhibited.* People with a mild degree of mania ("hypomania") are energetic, life-of-the-party types, but people with more severe mania are dangerous to themselves and others. Some mental hospitals have to disable the fire alarms in certain wards because manic patients impulsively pull the alarm again and again. People feel helpless, guilt ridden, and sad during a depressed phase. When they are manic, they are either excited or irritable. In either phase they have problems with attention and memory (Quraishi & Frangou, 2002). Typically, episodes of depression alternate with briefer episodes of mania. Psychologists distinguish two types of bipolar disorder. People with **bipolar I disorder** *have had at least one episode of mania.* People with **bipolar II disorder** *have had episodes of major depression and hypomania, which is a milder degree of mania.* In the past about 1% of all adults in the United States were diagnosed with bipolar disorder (Robins et al., 1984), but the diagnosis is applied more broadly today.

Twin studies indicate a strong hereditary component for bipolar disorder. It does not typically show up in the same families as unipolar (noncycling) depression, so the genetic basis is different (McGuffin et al., 2003). In cases of monozygotic twins in which one has bipolar disorder and the other does not, brain research suggests that the twin without bipolar disorder strongly activates parts of the frontal cortex to control mood and fight off distress. That is, both twins are vulnerable, but one has found a way to be resilient (Krüger et al., 2006).

Many artists, writers, and composers have suffered from bipolar disorder. To test whether creative skills increase or decrease over phases of the bipolar cycle, Robert Weisberg (1994) examined the works of classical composer Robert Schumann, who had bipolar disorder. Schumann produced more works during his manic phases than during his depressed phases. However, the compositions written during the depressed phases have been performed and recorded as often as those written during the manic phases on average. That is, the works that Schumann composed during his depressed phases became about as popular as those of his manic phases.

A Self-Report

Mania can become so serious that it makes normal life impossible. Theatrical director Joshua Logan has described his own experiences with depression and mania. A few excerpts follow.

Depressive Phase

First, Logan describes life in his depressed phase.

> I had no faith in the work I was doing or the people I was working with. . . . It was a great burden to get up in the morning and I couldn't wait to go to bed at night, even though I started not sleeping well. . . . I thought I was well but feeling low because of a hidden personal discouragement of some sort—something I couldn't quite put my finger on. . . . I just forced myself to live through a dreary, hopeless existence that lasted for months on end. . . .

> My depressions actually began around the age of thirty-two. I remember I was working on a play, and I was forcing myself to work. . . . I can remember that I sat in some sort of aggravated agony as it was read aloud for the first time by the cast. It sounded so awful that I didn't want to direct it. I didn't even want to see it. I remember feeling so depressed that I wished that I were dead without having to go through the shame and defeat of suicide. I couldn't sleep well at all, and sleep meant, for me, oblivion, and that's what I longed for and couldn't get. I didn't know what to do and I felt very, very lost. (Fieve, 1975, pp. 42–43)

Manic Phase

Here, Logan describes his manic experiences:

> Finally, as time passed, the depression gradually wore off and turned into something else, which I didn't understand either. But it was a much pleasanter thing to go through, at least at first. Instead of hating everything, I started liking things—liking them too much, perhaps. . . . I put out a thousand ideas a minute: things to do, plays to write, plots to write stories about. . . .

> I decided to get married on the spur of the moment. . . . I practically forced her to say yes. Suddenly we had a loveless marriage and that had to be broken up overnight. . . .

> I can only remember that I worked constantly, day and night, never even seeming to need more than a

few hours of sleep. I always had a new idea or another conference. . . . It was an exhilarating time for me.

> It finally went too far. In the end I went over the bounds of reality, or law and order, so to say. I don't mean that I committed any crimes, but I could easily have done so if anyone had crossed me. I flew into rages if contradicted. I began to be irritable with everyone. Should a man, friend or foe, object to anything I did or said, it was quite possible that I could poke him in the jaw. I was eventually persuaded by the doctors that I was desperately ill and should go into the hospital. But it was not, even then, convincing to me that I was ill.

> There I was, on the sixth floor of a New York building that had special iron bars around it and an iron gate that had slid into place and locked me away from the rest of the world. . . . I looked about and saw that there was an open window. I leaped up on the sill and climbed out of the window on the ledge on the sixth floor and said, "Unless you open the door, I'm going to climb down the outside of this building." At the time, I remember feeling so powerful that I might actually be able to scale the building. . . . They immediately opened the steel door, and I climbed back in. That's where manic elation can take you. (Excerpts from Joshua Logan in *Moodswing,* by Ronald R. Fieve. Copyright © 1975 by Ronald R. Fieve. Published by William Morrow & Co.)

 CONCEPT CHECK

22. What are the similarities and differences between seasonal affective disorder and bipolar disorder? (Check your answer on page 631.)

Drug Therapies

Many years ago, researcher J. F. Cade proposed that uric acid might be effective for treating mania. To dissolve uric acid in water, he mixed it with lithium salts. The resulting mixture proved effective, but researchers soon discovered that the benefits depended on the lithium salts, not the uric acid.

Lithium salts were adopted quickly in the Scandinavian countries but only later in the United States. One reason was that drug manufacturers had no interest in marketing lithium, which is a natural substance and not available for patents. A second reason was that the lithium dosage must be carefully monitored. A dose too low is useless, and one too high produces nausea, blurred vision, and tremors.

Properly regulated dosages of lithium are now a common and effective treatment for bipolar disorder (Baldessarini & Tondo, 2000). People take the recommended doses of lithium for years without suffering unfavorable consequences (Schou, 1997). Anticonvulsant drugs, such as valproate (Depakene, Depakote), also used for bipolar disorder, are about equal to lithium in effectiveness (Hilty, Brady, & Hales, 1999). Researchers do not yet know how lithium or the anticonvulsant drugs alleviate bipolar disorder. One promising hypothesis is that the drugs act by blocking the synthesis of a chemical called *arachidonic acid,* which is produced mostly during times of brain inflammation (Rapoport & Bosetti, 2002). Another way to counteract arachidonic acid is to increase intake of fish oils, and researchers find that people who eat about a pound (0.45 kg) of seafood per week have a decreased probability of bipolar disorder (Noaghiul & Hibbeln, 2003).

Psychotherapy can help bipolar patients cope with life difficulties and is an important supplement to the drug treatments (Hollon et al., 2002).

Mood Disorders and Suicide

Most severely depressed people and people with bipolar disorder consider suicide, and many attempt it. Suicides also occur for other reasons, though. Some people commit suicide because they feel guilt or disgrace. Some have committed suicide because of obedience to a cult leader (Maris, 1997). Others have a painful terminal illness and wish to hasten the end.

One survey in the United States reported that more than 13% of adults had considered suicide and more than 4% had survived a suicide attempt (Kessler, Borges, & Walters, 1999). Across cultures more men die by suicide, often by violent means, although women make more attempts, often trying something like a drug overdose, which is less likely to be fatal (Canetto & Sakinofsky, 1998; Cross & Hirschfeld, 1986). Many people, especially women, who attempt suicide are probably crying out for help without really intending to die. Unfortunately, some do die and others become disabled.

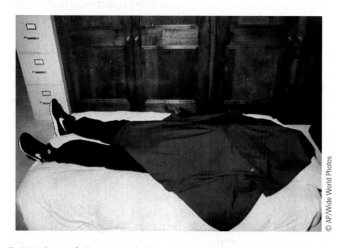

❚ Members of the Heaven's Gate cult in San Diego committed mass suicide in 1997 because their leader assured them that death was the route to being rescued by an alien spacecraft that tailed the comet Hale-Bopp.

TABLE 16.5 People Most Likely to Attempt Suicide

- People who have recently endured the death of a spouse or a child, and men who recently have been divorced or separated (Blumenthal & Kupfer, 1986; Qin & Mortensen, 2003)
- People who have had major recent setbacks in their job, finances, or social life (Hendin, Maltsberger, Lipschitz, Haas, & Kyle, 2001)
- People with depression or bipolar disorder, especially those not in treatment and those who feel hopeless (Baldessarini, Tondo, & Hennen, 2001; Beck, Steer, Beck, & Newman, 1993)
- People who have made previous suicide attempts (Beck, Steer, & Brown, 1993)
- Drug or alcohol abusers (Beck & Steer, 1989)
- People who, during their childhood or adolescence, lost a parent by death or divorce (Adam, 1986)
- People with guns in their home (Brent, 2001)
- People whose relatives committed suicide (Blumenthal & Kupfer, 1986)

Suicide has no dependable pattern. Some people give warning signals well in advance, but many do not, and some firmly deny they are considering suicide (Fawcett, 2001). One study found that most of the people who attempted suicide made the decision impulsively within 24 hours of the attempt (Peterson, Peterson, O'Shanick, & Swann, 1985). However, anyone who admits to having a plan of how to commit suicide is at serious risk. Table 16.5 lists additional risk factors. Similar patterns have been found in the United States and China, so they are apparently not culture specific (Cheng, 1995).

If you suspect that someone you know is thinking about suicide, what should you do? Treat the person like a normal human being, who needs social support and friendship. Don't assume that he or she is so fragile that one wrong word will be disastrous.

IN CLOSING

Mood and Mood Disorders

The capacity to feel emotions, even negative emotions, is important. If you never felt sad under any circumstances, you might make disastrous decisions. If you never acted embarrassed or guilty, you would anger those around you. Depression can be seen as the result of normal, useful mechanisms that have gone to an extreme (Allen & Badcock, 2003). Depression distorts thinking and mood so badly that people who have been depressed insist you can't really understand how miserable it is if you haven't been through it yourself. We need research to find further weapons to fight this monster. ❚

Summary

- *Symptoms of depression.* People with depression find little interest or pleasure in life, have trouble sleeping, lose interest in sex and food, and cannot concentrate. (page 621)
- *Episodes.* Depression occurs in episodes. Although the first episode is usually triggered by a stressful event, later episodes occur faster and more easily. (page 621)
- *Seasonal affective disorder.* People with seasonal affective disorder become depressed during one season of the year. Bright light usually relieves this condition. (page 622)
- *Predispositions.* Certain genes magnify the depressive effects of stressful experiences. That is, people with these genes are more likely than other people to become depressed after a stressful experience. (page 622)
- *Gender differences.* Psychologists are uncertain why more women than men become depressed. One hypothesis is that women are more likely to ruminate about their depression, and therefore aggravate it, whereas men find ways to distract themselves. (page 623)
- *Cognitive factors.* People who consistently blame themselves for their failures are likely to become depressed. (page 624)
- *Treatments.* About one third of depressed patients recover spontaneously within a few months. About half recover with either psychotherapy or antidepressant drugs. (page 625)
- *Psychotherapy.* Interpersonal therapy helps depressed people deal with current life problems, such as the death of a loved one, a bad marriage, and so forth. Cognitive therapy attempts to change people's self-defeating thoughts and encourages more active participation in life. The increased activity is a powerful antidepressant procedure by itself. (page 625)
- *Antidepressant drugs.* Several kinds of drugs prolong the activity of dopamine or serotonin at synaptic receptors. Although the drugs affect the synapses within an hour or so, their behavioral effects begin after 2 or 3 weeks of treatment. (page 626)
- *Advantages and disadvantages.* Psychotherapy's effects usually last longer and are more likely to produce long-lasting benefits, but antidepressant drugs remain popular because of their convenience and lower cost. (page 627)
- *Other treatments.* Electroconvulsive therapy (ECT) has a history of abuse. In modified form it helps many depressed people who fail to respond to antidepressant drugs. Additional treatments include exercise, bright light, and altered sleep schedules. (page 627)
- *Bipolar disorder.* People with bipolar disorder alternate between periods of depression and mania, when they engage in constant, uninhibited activity. Lithium salts are an effective treatment, as are certain anticonvulsant drugs. (page 628)
- *Suicide.* Although it is difficult to know who will attempt suicide, several warning signs are associated with an increased risk. (page 630)

Answers to Concept Checks

14. Major depression is more severe than sadness and lasts months. Also, a person with major depression can hardly imagine anything that would be enjoyable. (page 621)
15. You could examine sleep patterns. Depressed people show certain sleep abnormalities, such as REM periods soon after going to sleep, and some of these sleep abnormalities occur long before depression itself. (page 623)
16. Certain genes increase the risk of depression among people who have experienced severe stress. Such genes would show no clear link to depression in people who had less stress. (page 623)
17. Unpleasant events make anyone sad, but most people recover soon. People who were already sad and predisposed to depression may go into an episode of major depression. (page 624)
18. Depressed people are less likely than others to buy a lottery ticket because they regard their chances of success as remote on any task. (page 624)
19. The effects of methylphenidate (Ritalin) resemble those of buproprion (Wellbutrin). Both block the reuptake of dopamine. Buproprion, like methylphenidate, is sometimes prescribed for attention-deficit disorder. The effects of methylphenidate also overlap those of tricyclics. (page 626)
20. Possibly, but it would be risky. St. John's wort activates the enzyme that inactivates many drugs, probably including the antidepressant drug itself. (page 627)
21. Sleep deprivation produces rapid relief, but its effects do not last long. Psychotherapy and antidepressant drugs take effect more slowly, but their benefits last longer. (page 628)
22. Both conditions have repetitive cycles. However, people with bipolar disorder swing back and forth between depression and mania, whereas people with seasonal affective disorder alternate between depression and normal mood. (page 628)

Schizophrenia

- *What is schizophrenia and what can be done about it?*

Would you like to live in a world all your own? You can be the supreme ruler, who tells other people—and even inanimate objects—what to do. Your fantasies become realities.

Perhaps that world sounds like heaven to you. It might not feel that way for long. Most of us enjoy the give and take of interactions with other people. We enjoy struggling to achieve our fantasies more than we would enjoy their immediate fulfillment.

Some people with schizophrenia live practically in a world of their own, confusing fantasy with reality. Some retreat into a private existence and pay little attention to others.

Symptoms

The widely misunderstood term *schizophrenia* is based on Greek roots meaning "split mind." However, the term does *not* refer to a split into two minds or personalities. Many people use the term *schizophrenia* when they really mean *dissociative identity disorder,* or *multiple personality,* a condition in which people alternate among different personalities. The "split" in the term schizophrenia does not refer to a split between personalities but to a split between the intellectual and emotional aspects of one personality, as if the intellect were no longer in contact with the emotions (Figure 16.16). Someone suffering from schizophrenia may express strong emotion for no apparent reason or fail to show it when it seems appropriate. This separation of intellect and emotions is no longer considered a key feature of schizophrenia, but it does occur. A person with schizophrenia also has a "split" in the sense of a split from reality.

To be diagnosed with schizophrenia, according to *DSM–IV, someone must exhibit a deterioration of daily activities, including work, social relations, and self-care. He or she must also exhibit at least two of the following: hallucinations, delusions, disorganized speech, grossly disorganized behavior, or a loss of normal emotional responses and social behaviors* (American Psychiatric Association, 1994). However, if someone's hallucinations or delusions are severe, then no other symptoms are necessary. The

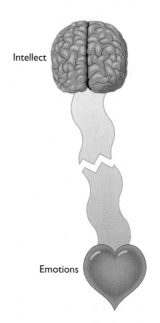

Intellect

Emotions

FIGURE 16.16 The term *schizophrenia*, derived from Greek roots meaning "split mind," refers to a split between the intellectual and emotional aspects of a single personality.

definition of schizophrenia calls for two or more symptoms from a list of five. Consequently, it is possible for two people diagnosed with schizophrenia to have no symptoms in common. What we have traditionally lumped together as one disorder may consist of several conditions.

Before assigning a diagnosis of schizophrenia, a therapist must rule out other conditions that produce similar symptoms, including drug abuse, brain damage, neurological diseases, niacin deficiency, and food allergies. About half of all people with schizophrenia have substance abuse as well, and nearly half are depressed.

Positive and Negative Symptoms

Psychologists distinguish between positive and negative symptoms of schizophrenia. In this case *positive* means *present* and *negative* means *absent;* they do not mean *good* and *bad.* **Positive symptoms** are *behaviors that are notable by their presence,* such as hallucinations and delusions. **Negative symptoms** are *behaviors notable for their absence,* including a lack of speech and emotional expression, a lack of ability to feel pleasure, and a general inability to take care of oneself.

Patients with mostly negative symptoms may differ from those with mostly positive or a mixture of positive and negative symptoms (Kirkpatrick, Buchanan, Ross,

& Carpenter, 2001). Their symptoms tend to be more consistent over time and more difficult to treat (Arndt, Andreasen, Flaum, Miller, & Nopoulos, 1995). People with many negative symptoms have an earlier onset of the disorder and worse performance in school and on the job (Andreasen, Flaum, Swayze, Tyrrell, & Arndt, 1990). They also have different kinds of brain abnormalities (Palmer et al., 1997).

Hallucinations

Hallucinations are *perceptions that do not correspond to anything in the objective world.* The most common hallucination is to hear voices or other sounds that no one else hears. The voices may speak nonsense, or they may direct the person to do something. Hallucinating people sometimes think the voices are real, sometimes know the voices are unreal, and sometimes are not sure (Junginger & Frame, 1985). Auditory hallucinations occur at the same time as spontaneous activity in the auditory cortex and related brain areas (Shergill, Brammer, Williams, Murray, & McGuire, 2000).

Have you ever heard a voice when you knew you were alone? I once asked my class this question. At first just a few people hesitantly raised their hands, and then more and more, until about one fourth of the class—and I myself—admitted to hearing a voice at least once. In most cases, the experience occurred while the person was lying in bed, not asleep but not fully awake either. Having an occasional auditory hallucination does not mean you are losing your mind. However, hearing voices frequently and insistently during the day, as some people with schizophrenia do, can be very troubling.

Delusions

Delusions are *unfounded beliefs that are strongly held despite a lack of evidence for them.* Three common types are delusions of persecution, grandeur, and reference. A **delusion of persecution** is *a belief that dangerous enemies are persecuting you.* A **delusion of grandeur** is *a belief that you are unusually important,* perhaps a special messenger from God or a person of central importance to the future of the world. A **delusion of reference** is *a tendency to interpret all sorts of messages as if they were meant for oneself.* For example, someone may interpret a newspaper head-

line as a coded message or take a television announcer's comments as personal insults.

However, it is hazardous to diagnose someone with schizophrenia if the only symptoms are delusions. For example, suppose someone constantly sees evidence of government conspiracies in everyday events. Is that belief a delusion of persecution or merely an unusual opinion? Might it even be correct? Many elderly people have occasional delusions, as do patients receiving pain medication (Östling & Skoog, 2002). Most people who believe they have been abducted by outer-space aliens seem to be normal in most other regards. Even if we confidently label their beliefs as false, we should not consider them mentally ill (Clancy, 2005). Members of some religious minorities also have beliefs that other people regard as strange. Don't most of us have a belief or two that someone might consider unjustifiable?

Disordered Thinking

Even those people with schizophrenia who have normal or above-average intelligence are impaired on tasks requiring selective attention or executive functions. Cognitive impairments are a more consistent finding in schizophrenia than any measured abnormality of the brain (Heinrichs, 2005). For example, the Wisconsin Card Sorting Task asks people to sort a stack of cards by one rule (e.g., piles by color) and then shift to a different rule (e.g., number or shape). People with schizophrenia have trouble shifting, as do people with frontal cortex damage. In addition people with schizophrenia are impaired at recognizing other people's emotional expressions (Hempel, Hempel, Schönknecht, Stippich, & Schröder, 2003). They also have trouble perceiving the kinds of faces shown in Figure 16.17 (Uhlhaas et al., 2006).

FIGURE 16.17 Patterns like these are known as Mooney faces. Most people with schizophrenia are slow to see the faces.

The impaired attention may relate to the tendency of patients with schizophrenia to loose associations, somewhat like the illogical leaps that occur in dreams. For example, one man used the words *Jesus, cigar,* and *sex* as synonyms. He explained that they were the same because Jesus has a halo around his head, a cigar has a band around it, and during sex people put their arms around each other.

The following excerpt from a letter by a patient to his mother provides another example of loose associations. Notice also the rambling quality, with no apparent overall idea:

> I am writing on paper. The pen which I am using is from a factory called "Perry & Co." This factory is in England. I assume this. Behind the name of Perry & Co. the city of London is inscribed; but not the city. The city of London is in England. I know this from my school-days. Then, I always liked geography. My last teacher in that subject was Professor August A. He was a man with black eyes. I also like black eyes. There are also blue and gray eyes and other sorts, too. I have heard it said that snakes have green eyes. All people have eyes. There are some, too, who are blind. These blind people are led about by a boy. It must be very terrible not to be able to see. There are people who can't see and, in addition, can't hear. I know some who hear too much. (Bleuler, 1911/1950, p. 17)

Another characteristic of schizophrenic thought is difficulty using abstract concepts. For instance, many people with schizophrenia have trouble sorting objects into categories. Many also give strictly literal responses when asked to interpret the meaning of proverbs. Here are some examples (Krueger, 1978, pp. 196–197):

Proverb: People who live in glass houses shouldn't throw stones.
Interpretation: "It would break the glass."
Proverb: All that glitters is not gold.
Interpretation: "It might be brass."
Proverb: A stitch in time saves nine.
Interpretation: "If you take one stitch for a small tear now, it will save nine later."

People with schizophrenic thought disorder often misunderstand simple statements because of their tendency to interpret everything literally. Upon being taken to the admitting office of a hospital, one person said, "Oh, is this where people go to admit their faults?"

 CONCEPT CHECK

23. If someone alternates between one personality and another, is that a case of schizophrenia?
24. What are typical "positive" and "negative" symptoms of schizophrenia? (Check your answers on page 640.)

Types and Prevalence

Depending on which symptoms are most prominent, psychiatrists and psychologists distinguish five major types of schizophrenia. These distinctions are useful for descriptive purposes, although they do not identify the underlying causes.

Types of Schizophrenia

Catatonic schizophrenia is characterized by a *prominent movement disorder, including either rigid inactivity or excessive activity.* Periods of extremely rapid, repetitive activity alternate with periods of total inactivity. During the inactive periods, the person may hold a rigid posture and resist attempts to alter it (Figure 16.18). Despite the inactivity, the brain is alert and the person may complain later about comments someone said at the time. Catatonic schizophrenia is diagnosed less often today than decades ago (Stompe, Ortwein-Swoboda, Ritter, Schanda, & Friedmann, 2002), although periods of catatonia sometimes occur in patients with disorders other than schizophrenia (Moskowitz, 2004).

FIGURE 16.18 Someone with catatonic schizophrenia alternates between periods of rigidity and periods of frantic activity.

Disorganized schizophrenia is characterized by *incoherent speech, absence of social relationships, and "silly" or odd behavior.* Here is a conversation with someone suffering from disorganized schizophrenia (Duke & Nowicki, 1979, p. 162). Note the "clanging" associations based on sound instead of meaning:

Interviewer: How does it feel to have your problems?
Patient: Who can tell me the name of my song? I don't know, but it won't be long. It won't be

short, tall, none at all. My head hurts, my knees hurt—my nephew, his uncle, my aunt. My God, I'm happy . . . not a care in the world. My hair's been curled, the flag's unfurled. This is my country, land that I love, this is the country, land that I love.

Interviewer: How do you feel?

Patient: Happy! Don't you hear me? Why do you talk to me? (barks like a dog).

Paranoid schizophrenia is characterized by *elaborate hallucinations and delusions, especially delusions of persecution and delusions of grandeur.* As a rule people with paranoid schizophrenia are more cognitively intact than those with other forms. They can generally take care of themselves well enough to get through the activities of the day. Some manage to complete college work and take good jobs.

Undifferentiated schizophrenia is characterized by the *basic symptoms—deterioration of daily functioning plus some combination of hallucinations, delusions, inappropriate emotions, thought disorders, and so forth.* However, the person does not have any of the special features that would qualify for the catatonic, disorganized, or paranoid types.

Residual schizophrenia is a diagnosis for people *who have had an episode of schizophrenia and who are partly recovered.* That is, the person has some mild lingering symptoms but nothing severe.

Many people fall on the margin between two or more types of schizophrenia, perhaps switching back and forth between them. Switching is especially common between undifferentiated schizophrenia and the other types (Kendler, Gruenberg, & Tsuang, 1985).

 CONCEPT CHECK

25. Why are people more likely to switch between undifferentiated schizophrenia and one of the other types than, say, between disorganized schizophrenia and another type? (Check your answer on page 640.)

Prevalence

About 1% of Americans have schizophrenia at some point in life (Kendler, Gallagher, Abelson, & Kessler, 1996). Some sources cite higher or lower figures depending on how many marginal cases they include. As well as researchers can reconstruct from historical records, the incidence of schizophrenia and severe mental illness in general began to increase in the late 1700s, especially in England and Ireland,

and later in the United States. For generation after generation, people tried to convince themselves that mental illness wasn't really becoming more common but that it just appeared to increase because previous generations had not kept good records (Torrey & Miller, 2001). Nevertheless, they kept building new mental hospitals, which quickly became crowded to overflowing, despite their uninviting accommodations. Since about 1950 the incidence of schizophrenia has stopped increasing. It appears to be decreasing in some parts of the world (Suvisaari, Haukka, Tanskanen, & Lönnqvist, 1999) and increasing in others (Healy et al., 2001). Part of the fluctuation is probably due to changes in patterns of diagnosis (Ösby et al., 2001). However, it is also likely that the incidence really does vary from one time and place to another, and if we can understand why, we may get major clues to the causes of schizophrenia (Torrey & Miller, 2001). Note that either an increase or decrease in incidence from one era to another implies nongenetic influences. (Evolution doesn't occur that fast.)

Schizophrenia occurs in all ethnic groups, but it is less common and usually less severe in Third World countries (El-Islam, 1982; Leff et al., 1987; Torrey, 1986; Wig et al., 1987). It is more common in crowded cities than in small towns and farms (Torrey, Bowler, & Clark, 1997). One explanation is that mentally ill people move from small towns and farms to big cities where they can get more help. Another is that some aspect of life in crowded and technologically advanced countries increases the risk of schizophrenia. A third possibility is that people in small towns and Third World countries receive more social support from nearby relatives and friends. Still another is that most people in Third World countries eat less sugar and saturated fats than people who consume the typical Western diet. A diet high in sugar and fat decreases the prospect of recovery from schizophrenia and may be among the causes of its onset (Peet, 2004).

Schizophrenia is most frequently diagnosed in young adults in their teens or 20s. It is more common in men than women by a ratio of about 7 to 5. Men are also more likely to be diagnosed younger and to have more severe symptoms (Aleman, Kahn, & Selten, 2003).

Schizophrenia's onset can be sudden but is usually gradual. Most people with schizophrenia are described as having been strange children with a short attention span, who made few friends and often disrupted their class (Arboleda & Holzman, 1985; Parnas, Schulsinger, Schulsinger, Mednick, & Teasdale, 1982). Many had minor psychological disorders as adolescents before developing schizophrenia (Weiser et al., 2001).

CRITICAL THINKING

A STEP FURTHER

Retrospective Accounts

If you try to recall the childhood behavior of someone who later developed schizophrenia, what kinds of memory errors are you likely to make and why? (Recall the issues raised in the chapters on memory and cognition.)

Causes

Schizophrenia probably develops from a variety of influences. Genetics and prenatal environment are prime candidates.

Genetics

The evidence for a genetic basis rests primarily on studies of twins and adopted children. If one member of a pair of monozygotic (identical) twins develops schizophrenia, the probability is almost 50% that the other will too (Cardno et al., 1999; Gottesman, 1991) (see Figure 16.19). Adopted children who develop schizophrenia have more biological relatives than adoptive relatives with schizophrenia (Kety et al., 1994). However, the data on adopted children are ambiguous with regard to genetics. A child's biological mother influences her baby's brain development not only through genes but also through prenatal environment. Many women with schizophrenia smoke and drink during pregnancy and fail to eat a good diet. Therefore, if some of their children develop schizophrenia, we cannot assume a genetic explanation.

The most persuasive evidence would be a demonstration linking schizophrenia to a specific gene. So far the results have been unimpressive. Identifiable genetic abnormalities have been found for childhood schizophrenia, an uncommon condition that differs from adult-onset schizophrenia in several regards (Burgess et al., 1998; Nopoulos, Giedd, Andreasen, & Rapoport, 1998). For the more common adult-onset version, researchers have found links to several genes, but each appears to have only a small effect (Callicott et al., 2005; Fanous et al., 2005; Gurling et al., 2006; Millar et al., 2005). For example, investigators found that one gene occurs in 70% of people with schizophrenia and 60% of everyone else (Saleem et al., 2001).

If schizophrenia does have a genetic basis, we need to explain why natural selection has not eliminated the gene. People with schizophrenia are less likely than others to have children, and their unaffected brothers and sisters do not compensate by reproducing more than average (Haukka, Suvisaari, & Lönnqvist, 2003). So it is difficult to imagine how genes that lead to schizophrenia could remain common enough to affect 1% of the population.

Brain Damage

Much evidence points to mild brain abnormalities in many, though not all, people with schizophrenia. Brain damage could occur for either genetic or nongenetic reasons. Indications of brain abnormalities have been reported in patients in cultures as different as the United States and Nigeria (Ohaeri, Adeyinka, & Osuntokun, 1995) and in patients who have not yet taken any medications (Torrey, 2002). Brain scans indicate that the hippocampus and several areas of the cerebral cortex are a few percent smaller than normal in people with schizophrenia, especially those with the greatest behavioral deficits (Kasai et al., 2003; Velakoulis et al., 1999; Wright et al., 2000). The cerebral ventricles, which are fluid-filled cavities in the brain, are larger than normal in people with schizophrenia (Wolkin et al., 1998; Wright et al., 2000). Figure 16.20 shows an example of enlarged cerebral ventricles.

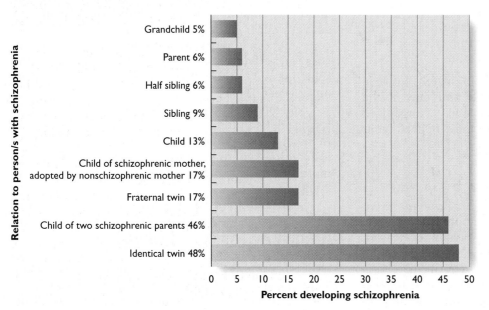

FIGURE 16.19 The relatives of a person with schizophrenia have an increased probability of developing schizophrenia themselves. *(Based on data from Gottesman, 1991)*

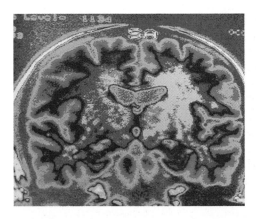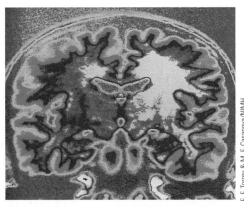

FIGURE 16.20 The twin on the left has schizophrenia; the twin on the right does not. Note that the ventricles (near the center of each brain) are larger in the twin with schizophrenia. The ventricles are fluid-filled cavities. An enlargement of the ventricles implies a loss of brain tissue. *(Photos courtesy of E. F. Torrey & M. F. Casanova / NIMH)*

Most people with schizophrenia also have smaller than average neurons (Pierri, Volk, Auh, Sampson, & Lewis, 2001; Weinberger, 1999) and fewer than the average number of synapses, especially in the prefrontal cortex (Glantz & Lewis, 1997, 2000). They also have less than the average amount of myelin, a material that surrounds and insulates many axons (K. L. Davis et al., 2003). One area of the cortex with consistent impairments, the dorsolateral prefrontal cortex, is important for those aspects of working memory that are consistently impaired in schizophrenia, and it is one of the slowest areas of the brain to mature. Therefore, its malformation supports the view that schizophrenia is related to impaired brain maturation (Gur et al., 2000; Pearlson, Petty, Ross, & Tien, 1996; Sowell, Thompson, Holmes, Jernigan, & Toga, 1999).

However, these results must be interpreted cautiously. Many people with schizophrenia abuse alcohol or other drugs, and people with both schizophrenia and alcohol abuse have greater indications of brain damage than those with schizophrenia alone (Deshmukh, Rosenbloom, Pfefferbaum, & Sullivan, 2002; Mathalon, Pfefferbaum, Lim, Rosenbloom, & Sullivan, 2003; Sullivan et al., 2000). Unfortunately, most studies have not attempted to separate the effects of schizophrenia from those of alcohol abuse.

 CONCEPT CHECK

26. Suppose someone argues that the brain abnormalities in schizophrenia indicate that brain damage causes schizophrenia. What is an alternative explanation? (Check your answer on page 640.)

The Neurodevelopmental Hypothesis

Research results conflict about the time course of the brain damage associated with schizophrenia. Many studies indicate that the brain abnormalities develop early and remain steady over the years (Benes, 1995; Heaton et al., 2001). Other studies, however, report gradual shrinkage of neurons during adulthood (Cahn et al. 2002; Hulshoff et al., 2001). In either case the results do not show progressive cell death on a scale comparable to Parkinson's disease or other deteriorative conditions. That is, most of the brain abnormality is present from the time of the first diagnosis.

If the abnormalities are present in young adults, perhaps they were present from infancy. According to the **neurodevelopmental hypothesis**, *schizophrenia originates with nervous system impairments that develop before or around the time of birth, for either genetic or other reasons* (McGrath, Féron, Burne, Mackay-Sim, & Eyles, 2003; Weinberger, 1996). The probability of schizophrenia is higher than normal in the following cases:

- The patient's mother had a difficult pregnancy, labor, or delivery (Hultman, Öhman, Cnattingius, Wieselgren, & Lindström, 1997).
- The mother was poorly nourished during pregnancy (Dalman, Allebeck, Cullberg, Grunewald, & Köstler, 1999; Susser et al., 1996).
- The mother had an infection, and presumably a high fever, during pregnancy (Buka et al., 2001).
- The mother had an Rh-negative blood type and her baby was Rh-positive. The risk of schizophrenia is more than 2% for her second and later Rh-positive children, especially boys (Hollister, Laing, & Mednick, 1996).
- The patient was unusually small at birth (Wahlbeck, Forsén, Osmond, Barker, & Eriksson, 2001).
- The patient had a serious head injury in early childhood (AbdelMalik, Husted, Chow, & Bassett, 2003).
- The patient was infected during childhood with the parasite *Toxoplasma gondii,* which attacks parts of the brain. The usual route of infection with this parasite is handling cat feces (Leweke et al., 2004; Torrey & Yolken, 2005).

Furthermore, *a person born in the winter or early spring is slightly more likely to develop schizophre-*

nia than a person born at other times (Bradbury & Miller, 1985; Davies, Welham, Chant, Torrey, & McGrath, 2003). Investigators have demonstrated this **season-of-birth effect** only in the northern climates, not near the equator. Evidently, something about the weather contributes to some people's vulnerability to schizophrenia. No other psychological disorder has this characteristic.

One possible explanation relates to the fact that influenza and other epidemics are most common in the fall and early winter. If a woman catches influenza or another infection during the second trimester of pregnancy, her illness can impair critical stages of brain development in her fetus at that time. A virus does not cross the placenta into the fetus (Taller et al., 1996), so the problem is not the virus itself but probably the mother's fever, which can impair the development of fetal neurons (Laburn, 1996). Researchers have found a small but significant increase in schizophrenia among people born 2 to 3 months after an epidemic of influenza or measles (Adams, Kendell, Hare, & Munk-Jorgensen, 1993).

You might ask, "If brain damage occurs before or near the time of birth, why do the symptoms emerge so much later?" One answer is that certain brain areas, especially the prefrontal cortex, go through a critical stage of development during the second trimester of pregnancy but do not become fully functional until adolescence. As the brain begins to rely more on those areas, the effects of early damage become more evident (Weinberger, 1987).

Therapies

Before the discovery of effective drugs to combat schizophrenia, the outlook was bleak. Many people spent years or decades in mental hospitals, growing more disoriented. Matters are better now, although far from ideal. Psychotherapy helps, presumably by controlling the stress that often aggravates schizophrenia (Sensky et al., 2000). However, nearly all patients with schizophrenia receive drugs as part of their treatment.

Medications

During the 1950s researchers discovered the first effective **antipsychotic drug**—*that is, a drug that can relieve schizophrenia.* That drug was chlorpromazine (klor-PRAHM-uh-ZEEN, trade name Thorazine). Chlorpromazine and other antipsychotic drugs, including haloperidol (HAHL-o-PAIR-ih-dol, trade name Haldol), have enabled many people to live active and productive lives. Although the drugs do not cure the disorder, a daily pill helps control it, much as insulin shots control diabetes.

Antipsychotic drugs take effect gradually and produce variable degrees of recovery. As a rule the greater someone's deterioration before drug treatment begins, the less the recovery will be. Most of the improvement emerges in about a month (Szymanski, Simon, & Gutterman, 1983). When affected people stop taking the drugs, the symptoms return (Figure 16.21).

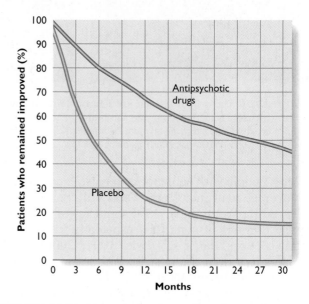

FIGURE 16.21 After recovery from schizophrenia, the percentage of schizophrenic patients who remained improved for the next 2½ years was higher in the group that received continuing drug treatment than in the placebo group. *(Based on Baldessarini, 1984)*

Typical antipsychotic drugs block dopamine synapses in the brain. Their therapeutic effectiveness is nearly proportional to their ability to block those synapses (Seeman & Lee, 1975). Furthermore, large doses of amphetamines, cocaine, or other drugs that stimulate dopamine activity produce the positive symptoms of schizophrenia. These observations led to the **dopamine hypothesis of schizophrenia**—that *the underlying cause of schizophrenia is excessive stimulation of certain types of dopamine synapses.* People with schizophrenia do not overproduce dopamine, but they could have increased release or increased numbers of dopamine receptors in certain brain areas (Hirvonen et al., 2006).

Nevertheless, dopamine may not be the entire explanation of schizophrenia. The brain's release of dopamine is regulated largely by the neurotransmitter glutamate, and several lines of evidence suggest that people with schizophrenia have deficient glutamate activity in the prefrontal cortex (Lewis & Gonzalez-Burgos, 2006). Prolonged use of *phencyclidine* ("angel dust"), which inhibits glutamate receptors, produces both the positive and negative symptoms of schizophrenia (Olney & Farger, 1995). Drugs that stimulate certain glutamate synapses facilitate relief from the negative symptoms of schizophrenia, such as social withdrawal (Heresco-Levy & Javitt, 2004).

Side Effects and Alternative Drugs

Antipsychotic drugs produce unwelcome side effects, including **tardive dyskinesia** (TAHRD-eev DIS-ki-NEE-zhuh), *a condition characterized by tremors and involuntary movements* (Kiriakakis, Bhatia, Quinn, & Marsden, 1998). Presumably, tardive dyskinesia relates to the fact that antipsychotic drugs alter activity at dopamine synapses, some of which control movement. Researchers have sought new drugs that can combat schizophrenia without causing tardive dyskinesia.

Atypical antipsychotic drugs, such as risperidone and clozapine, *relieve schizophrenia without causing tardive dyskinesia.* These drugs produce moderate effects on specific types of dopamine synapses and additional effects on serotonin synapses. Atypical antipsychotic drugs relieve the negative symptoms of schizophrenia that most antipsychotic drugs fail to address (J. M. Davis, Chen, & Glick, 2003). Clozapine is regarded by most psychiatrists as the most effective drug for relieving the symptoms of schizophrenia (McEvoy et al., 2006). However, the atypical antipsychotic drugs have side effects of their own, and it is not clear that they improve overall quality of life significantly more than the older drugs (P. B. Jones et al., 2006).

 CONCEPT CHECK

27. Why is early diagnosis of schizophrenia important? (Check your answer on page 640.)

Family Matters

The intensity of any patient's symptoms varies from time to time. One hypothesis to explain the fluctuation is that patients react to variations in emotional stress, especially from their own family. Many young patients with schizophrenia live with their parents, and many parents grow understandably frustrated with an adult son or daughter who cannot hold a job, does not take care of even routine self-grooming, and seems unmotivated to change. Occasionally, a parent has an outburst of *hostile or critical comments,* known as **expressed emotion.** Many studies have found patients exposed to frequent criticism are likely to have frequent relapses of schizophrenic symptoms (Butzlaff & Hooley, 1998).

Most psychologists have assumed that the expressed emotion leads to the relapses. However, the evidence is correlational. Here is one more opportunity to remind you to beware of using correlational evidence to infer cause and effect: Perhaps the parents' high degree of criticism leads the patient to frequent relapses, or perhaps the patient's frequent relapses stimulate the parents to more criticism. One study examined both the parents' expressed emotion and the patient's behavior repeatedly over a year and a half. The amount of expressed emotion correlated better with the patient's *previous* levels of negative symptoms (social withdrawal and so forth) than with the patient's *subsequent* levels of those symptoms (King, 2000). These results suggest that a parent's expressed emotion is more a reaction to the patient's behavior than a cause of it.

In any case the families of people with schizophrenia need help, too. They need help for their own sake, as well as for making them more patient and more helpful to their son or daughter with schizophrenia. Research has confirmed that including the parents in the therapy program magnifies the benefits to the patients (Pitschel-Walz, Leucht, Bäuml, Kissling, & Engel, 2001).

IN CLOSING

The Elusiveness of Schizophrenia

Whereas anxiety disorders, substance abuse, and depression overlap somewhat in symptoms, causes, and genetics, schizophrenia stands apart. Most of us can imagine circumstances that would drive us to excess anxiety, depression, or addictive behaviors, but it is harder to imagine developing an apparent break from reality or losing interest in social contact.

As you have read about schizophrenia, you could easily become discouraged with how little we seem to know and how many major questions remain unanswered. An antidote to complete discouragement would be to read what the textbooks of 50 years ago had to say. At that time schizophrenia was blamed on bad parents, who gave their children confusing "come here, go away" messages or didn't show enough love. Those days, mercifully, have passed. We don't yet have all the answers that we seek, but at least we know what the answers are *not.* That progress is worth celebrating. ■

Summary

- *Symptoms of schizophrenia.* A diagnosis of schizophrenia applies if someone has deteriorated in everyday functioning and shows at least two of the following symptoms: hallucinations (mostly auditory), delusions, disorganized speech, disorganized behavior, and loss of normal emotional responses and social behaviors. (page 632)

- *Positive and negative symptoms.* Positive symptoms are behaviors that attract attention by their presence, such as hallucinations and delusions. Negative symptoms are behaviors that are noteworthy for their absence, such as impaired emotional expression. (page 632)
- *Thought disorder of schizophrenia.* The thought disorder of schizophrenia is characterized by loose associations, impaired use of abstract concepts, and vague, rambling speech that conveys little information. (page 633)
- *Types of schizophrenia.* Psychologists distinguish five types of schizophrenia: catatonic, disorganized, paranoid, undifferentiated, and residual. (page 634)
- *Genetic influences.* Much evidence indicates that it is possible to inherit a predisposition toward schizophrenia, although little is known about how the genes exert their influence. Researchers have not identified any gene with a major influence. (page 636)
- *Brain abnormalities.* Many people with schizophrenia show indications of mild brain abnormalities, especially in the prefrontal cortex. However, some of the damage may be due to alcohol abuse. (page 636)
- *Neurodevelopmental hypothesis.* Many researchers believe that schizophrenia originates with abnormal brain development before or around the time of birth, sometimes for genetic reasons but sometimes for other reasons, such as the mother's fever during pregnancy. (page 637)
- *Antipsychotic drugs.* Drugs that alleviate schizophrenia block dopamine synapses. Results are best if treatment begins before someone has suffered serious deterioration. (page 638)
- *Neurotransmitters.* The effectiveness of dopamine blockers in alleviating schizophrenia has suggested that the underlying problem might be excessive dopamine activity. An alternative hypothesis is that part of the problem relates to a deficiency of glutamate. (page 638)

Answers to Concept Checks

23. No, that would be dissociative identity disorder (multiple personality). (page 632)
24. Positive symptoms include hallucinations, delusions, and thought disorder. Negative symptoms include weak emotions, speech, and social contact. (page 632)
25. Whenever any of the special symptoms of catatonic, disorganized, or paranoid schizophrenia become less severe, the person is left with undifferentiated or residual schizophrenia. To shift between two of the other types, someone would have to lose the symptoms of one type and gain the symptoms of another. (page 635)
26. Perhaps schizophrenia leads to alcohol abuse, which in turn leads to brain abnormalities. (page 637)
27. Antipsychotic drugs are more helpful to people in the early stages of schizophrenia than to those who have deteriorated severely. However, psychiatrists need to make the early diagnosis cautiously because they do not want to administer drugs to people who do not need them. (page 638)

CHAPTER ENDING

Key Terms and Activities

Key Terms

You can check the page listed for a complete description of a term. You can also check the glossary/index at the end of the text for a definition of a given term, or you can download a list of all the terms and their definitions for any chapter at this website:

www.thomsonedu.com/ psychology/kalat

agoraphobia (page 602)
Alcoholics Anonymous (AA) (page 617)
alcoholism (page 615)

Antabuse (page 617)
antipsychotic drugs (page 638)
atypical antidepressants (page 626)
atypical antipsychotic drugs (page 639)
bipolar disorder (page 622)
bipolar I disorder (page 628)
bipolar II disorder (page 628)
catatonic schizophrenia (page 634)
compulsion (page 608)
delusion (page 633)
delusion of grandeur (page 633)
delusion of persecution (page 633)
delusion of reference (page 633)

dependence (or addiction) (page 612)
disorganized schizophrenia (page 634)
dopamine hypothesis of schizophrenia (page 638)
electroconvulsive therapy (ECT) (page 627)
explanatory style (page 624)
expressed emotion (page 639)
flooding (or implosion or intensive exposure therapy) (page 607)
generalized anxiety disorder (GAD) (page 601)

hallucinations (page 633)
harm reduction (page 618)
hyperventilation (page 602)
interpersonal therapy (page 625)
major depression (page 621)
mania (page 628)
methadone (page 618)
monoamine oxidase inhibitors
(MAOIs) (page 626)
negative symptoms (page 632)
neurodevelopmental hypothesis
(page 637)
obsession (page 607)
obsessive-compulsive disorder
(page 607)

panic disorder (PD) (page 601)
paranoid schizophrenia (page 635)
phobia (page 603)
physical dependence (page 613)
positive symptoms (page 632)
psychological dependence
(page 613)
residual schizophrenia (page 635)
schizophrenia (page 632)
season-of-birth effect (page 638)
seasonal affective disorder (SAD) (or
depression with a seasonal pattern) (page 622)

selective serotonin reuptake inhibitors (SSRIs) (page 626)
social phobia (page 602)
St. John's wort (page 627)
systematic desensitization (page 606)
tardive dyskinesia (page 639)
tricyclic drugs (page 626)
Type I (or Type A) alcoholism
(page 615)
Type II (or Type B) alcoholism
(page 615)
undifferentiated schizophrenia
(page 635)

 ## Suggestions for Further Reading

Charney, D. S., & Nestler, E. J. (2003). *Neurobiology of mental illness.* Oxford, England: Oxford University Press. An excellent reference source for more detail.

Jamison, K. R. (1997). *An unquiet mind.* New York: Random House. A psychiatrist describes her own lifelong battle with bipolar disorder.

 ## Web/Technology Resources

Student Companion Website

www.thomsonedu.com/psychology/kalat

Explore the Student Companion Website for Online Try-It-Yourself activities, practice quizzes, flashcards, and more! The companion site also has direct links to the following websites.

Psychological Disorders and More

www.psych.org/

The American Psychiatric Association offers facts about various disorders, drug therapies, how to choose a therapist, and much more.

National Clearinghouse for Alcohol and Drug Information

www.health.org/

Here is comprehensive information for those who want to overcome a drug problem.

Harbor of Refuge

www.Harbor-of-Refuge.org/

Postings by people with bipolar disorder for others with the same problem.

The Experience of Schizophrenia

http://www.chovil.com

This is the personal site of Ian Chovil, who began struggling with schizophrenia in late adolescence and suffered greatly until he began taking medication in 1990. He tells his own story in unsparing detail.

Walkers in Darkness

http://www.walkers.org/

This long-established and award-winning site is dedicated to helping people with schizophrenia, bipolar illness, and related mood disorders. Included are descriptions of each disorder, information on medication and therapy, links to a variety of resources, forums, chat rooms, and mailing lists.

 ## For Additional Study

Kalat Premium Website

http://www.thomsonedu.com

For Critical Thinking Videos and additional Online Try-It-Yourself activities, go to this site to enter or purchase your code for the Kalat Premium Website.

ThomsonNOW!

http://www.thomsonedu.com

Go to this site for the link to ThomsonNOW, your one-stop study shop. Take a Pretest for this chapter, and Thomson-NOW will generate a personalized Study Plan based on your test results. The Study Plan will identify the topics you need to review and direct you to online resources to help you master those topics. You can then take a Posttest to help you determine the concepts you have mastered and what you still need to work on.

Epilogue

Here we are at the end of the book. As I have been writing and revising, I have imagined you sitting there reading. I have imagined a student much like I was in college, reading about psychology for the first time and often growing excited about it. I remember periodically telling a friend or relative, "Guess what I just learned about psychology! Isn't this interesting?" (I still do the same today.) I also remember occasionally thinking, "Hmm. The book says such-and-so, but I'm not convinced. I wonder whether psychologists ever considered a different explanation. . . ." I started thinking about research I might do if I ever became a psychologist.

I hope that you have had similar experiences yourself. I hope you have occasionally become so excited about something you read that you thought about it and told other people about it. In fact I hope you told your roommate so much about psychology that you started to become mildly annoying. I also hope you have sometimes doubted a conclusion, imagining a research project that might test it or improve on it. Psychology is still a work in progress.

Now, as I picture you reaching the end of the course, I'm not sure how you will react. You might be thinking, "Wow, I sure have learned a lot!" Or you might be thinking, "Is that *all?*" Maybe you are reacting both ways: "Yes, I learned a lot. But it seems like there should be more. I still don't understand what conscious experience is all about, and I don't understand why I react the way I do sometimes. And this book—*wonderful as it is!*—hardly mentioned certain topics. Why do we laugh? How do we sense the passage of time? Why do people like to watch sports? Why are some people religious and others not?"

I have two good reasons for not answering all your questions. One is that this is an introductory text and it can't go on forever. If you want to learn more, you should take other psychology courses or do some additional reading. The other reason is that psychologists do not know all the answers.

Perhaps someday you will become a researcher yourself and add to the sum of our knowledge. If not, you can try to keep up to date on current developments in psychology by reading good books and magazine articles. One of my main goals has been to prepare you to continue learning about psychology.

Try to read critically: Is a conclusion based on good evidence? If you read about a survey, were the questions worded clearly? How reliable and valid were the measurements? Did the investigators obtain a representative or random sample? If someone draws a cause-and-effect conclusion, was the evidence based on experiments or only correlations? Even if the evidence looks solid, is the author's explanation the best one?

Above all, remember that any conclusion is tentative. Psychological researchers seldom use the word *prove;* their conclusions are almost always tentative and guarded. I once suggested to my editor, half seriously, that we should include in the index to this book the entry "*maybe*—see pages 1–643." We did not include such an entry, partly because I doubt anyone would have noticed the humor, and partly because our understanding of psychology is not really that bad. Still, be leery of anyone who seems a little too certain about a great new insight in psychology. The route from *maybe* to *definitely* is long and arduous.

References

Numbers in parentheses indicate the chapter in which a source is cited.

AbdelMalik, P., Husted, J., Chow, E. W. C., & Bassett, A. S. (2003). Childhood head injury and expression of schizophrenia in multiply affected families. *Archives of General Psychiatry, 60,* 231–236. (16)

Abercrombie, H. C., Kalin, N. H., Thurow, M. E., Rosenkranz, M. A., & Davidson, R. J. (2003). Cortisol variation in humans affects memory for emotionally laden and neutral information. *Behavioral Neuroscience, 117,* 505–516. (12)

Abramson, L. Y., Seligman, M. E. P., & Teasdale, J. D. (1978). Learned helplessness in humans: Critique and reformulation. *Journal of Abnormal Psychology, 87,* 49–74. (16)

Abrams, R. A., & Christ, S. E. (2003). Motion onset captures attention. *Psychological Science, 14,* 427–432. (8)

Abrams, R. L., Klinger, M. R., & Greenwald, A. G. (2002). Subliminal words activate semantic categories (not automated motor responses). *Psychonomic Bulletin and Review, 9,* 100–106. (4)

Ackerman, P. L., Beier, M. E., & Boyle, M. O. (2005). Working memory and intelligence: The same or different constructs? *Psychological Bulletin, 131,* 30–60. (9)

Ackil, J. K., Van Abbema, D. L., & Bauer, P. J. (2003). After the storm: Enduring differences in mother-child recollections of traumatic and nontraumatic events. *Journal of Experimental Child Psychology, 84,* 286–309. (7)

Adam, K. S. (1986). Early family influences on suicidal behavior. *Annals of the New York Academy of Sciences, 487,* 63–76. (16)

Adams, D. L., & Horton, J. C. (2002). Shadows cast by retinal blood vessels mapped in primary visual cortex. *Science, 298,* 572–576. (4)

Adams, J. S. (1963). Wage inequities, productivity, and work quality. *Industrial Relations, 3,* 9–16. (11)

Adams, R. B., & Kleck, R. E. (2003). Perceived gaze direction and the processing of facial displays of emotion. *Psychological Science, 14,* 644–647. (12)

Adams, R. B., & Kleck, R. E. (2005). Effects of direct and averted gaze on the perception of facially communicated emotion. *Emotion, 5,* 3–11. (12)

Adams, W., Kendell, R. E., Hare, E. H., & Munk-Jorgensen, P. (1993). Epidemiological evidence that maternal influenza contributes to the aetiology of schizophrenia: An analysis of Scottish, English, and Danish data. *British Journal of Psychiatry, 163,* 522–534. (16)

Adler, A. (1927). *Understanding human nature.* New York: Greenberg. (14)

Adler, A. (1964). Brief comments on reason, intelligence, and feeble-mindedness. In H. L. Ansbacher & R. R. Ansbacher (Eds.), *Superiority and social interest* (pp. 41–49). New York: Viking Press. (Original work published 1928) (14)

Adler, A. (1964). The structure of neurosis. In H. L. Ansbacher & R. R. Ansbacher (Eds.), *Superiority and social interest* (pp. 83–95). New York: Viking Press. (Original work published 1932) (14)

Adler, E., Hoon, M. A., Mueller, K. L., Chandrashekar, J., Ryba, N. J. P., & Zuker, C. S. (2000). A novel family of mammalian taste receptors. *Cell, 100,* 693–702. (4)

Adolph, K. E. (2000). Specificity of learning: Why infants fall over a veritable cliff. *Psychological Science, 11,* 290–295. (5)

Adolphs, R., Baron-Cohen, S., & Tranel, D. (2002). Impaired recognition of social emotions following amygdala damage. *Journal of Cognitive Neuroscience, 14,* 1264–1274. (12)

Adolphs, R., Denburg, N. L., & Tranel, D. (2001). The amygdala's role in long-term declarative memory for gist and detail. *Behavioral Neuroscience, 115,* 983–992. (12)

Adolphs, R., Russell, J. A., & Tranel, D. (1999). A role for the human amygdala in recognizing emotional arousal from unpleasant stimuli. *Psychological Science, 10,* 167–171. (3)

Adolphs, R., & Tranel, D. (1999). Preferences for visual stimuli following amygdala damage. *Journal of Cognitive Neuroscience, 11,* 610–616. (12)

Adolphs, R, Tranel, D., & Damasio, A. R. (1998). The human amygdala in social judgment. *Nature, 393,* 470–474. (12)

Aglioti, S., Smania, N., & Peru, A. (1999). Frames of reference for mapping tactile stimuli in brain-damaged patients. *Journal of Cognitive Neuroscience, 11,* 67–79. (10)

Ahn, W., Flanagan, E. H., Marsh, J. K., & Sanislow, C. A. (2006). Beliefs about essences and the reality of mental disorders. *Psychological Science, 17,* 759–766. (15)

Ainsworth, M. D. S. (1979). Attachment as related to mother-infant interaction. In J. S. Rosenblatt, R. A. Hinde, C. Beer, & M. Busnel (Eds.), *Advances in the study of behavior* (Vol. 9, pp. 1–51). New York: Academic Press. (5)

Ainsworth, M. D. S., Blehar, M., Waters, E., & Wall, S. (1978). *Patterns of attachment.* Hillsdale, NJ: Erlbaum. (5)

Alati, R., Al Mamun, A., Williams, G. M., O'Callaghan, M., Najman, J. M., & Bor, W. (2006). In utero alcohol exposure and prediction of alcohol disorders in early childhood. *Archives of General Psychiatry, 63,* 1009–1016. (16)

Albarracín, D., Gillette, J. C., Earl, A. N., Glasman, L. R., Durantini, M. R., & Ho, M. H. (2005). A test of major assumptions about behavior change: A comprehensive look at the effects of passive and active HIV-prevention interventions since the beginning of the epidemic. *Psychological Bulletin, 131,* 856–897. (13)

Albee, G. W. (1986). Toward a just society: Lessons from observations on the primary prevention of psychopathology. *American Psychologist, 41,* 891–898. (15)

Aleman, A., Kahn, R. S., & Selten, J.P. (2003). Sex differences in the risk of schizophrenia. *Archives of General Psychiatry, 60,* 565–571. (16)

Alexander, I. E. (1982). The Freud-Jung relationship—the other side of Oedipus and countertransference. *American Psychologist, 37,* 1009–1018. (14)

Alexander, K. W., Quas, J. A., Goodman, G. S., Ghetti, S., Edelstein, R. S., Redlich, A. D., et al. (2005). Traumatic impact predicts long-term memory for documented child sexual abuse. *Psychological Science, 16,* 33–40. (7)

Alicke, M. D., & Largo, E. (1995). The role of the self in the false consensus effect. *Journal of Experimental Social Psychology, 31,* 28–47. (13)

Alison, L., Bennell, C., & Mokros, A. (2002). The personality paradox in offender profiling: A theoretical review of the processes involved in deriving background characteristics from crime scene actions. *Psychology, Public Policy, and Law, 8,* 115–135. (14)

Alison, L., Smith, M. D., & Morgan, K. (2003). Interpreting the accuracy of offender profiles. *Psychology, Crime & Law, 9,* 185–195. (14)

Allen, N. B., & Badcock, P. B. T. (2003). The social risk hypothesis of depressed mood: Evolutionary, psychosocial, and neurobiological perspectives. *Psychological Bulletin, 129,* 887–913. (16)

Allik, J., & McCrae, R. R. (2004). Toward a geography of personality traits. *Journal of Cross-Cultural Psychology, 35,* 13–28. (14)

Allison, S. T., Mackie, D. M., Muller, M. M., & Worth, L. T. (1993). Sequential correspondence biases and perceptions of change: The Castro studies revisited. *Personality and Social Psychology Bulletin, 19,* 151–157. (13)

Alloy, L. B., Abramson, L. Y., Whitehouse, W. G., Hogan, M. E., Tashman, N. A., Steinberg, D. L., et al. (1999). Depressogenic cognitive styles: Predictive validity, information processing and personality characteristics, and developmental origins. *Behaviour Research and Therapy, 37,* 503–531. (16)

Allport, G. W. (1935). Attitudes. In C. Murchison (Ed.), *A handbook of social psychology* (pp. 798–844). Worcester, MA: Clark University Press. (13)

Allport, G. W. (1961). *Pattern and growth in personality.* New York: Holt, Rinehart & Winston. (14)

Allport, G. W., & Odbert, H. S. (1936). Trait-names: A psycholexical study. *Psychological Monographs, 47*(Whole No. 211). (14)

Alpert, J. L., Brown, L. S., & Courtois, C. A. (1998). Symptomatic clients and memories of childhood abuse. *Psychology, Public Policy, and Law, 4,* 941–995. (7)

Alroe, C. J., & Gunda, V. (1995). Self-amputation of the ear. *Australian and New Zealand Journal of Psychiatry, 29,* 508–512. (15)

Altmann, E. M., & Gray, W. D., (2002). Forgetting to remember: The functional relationship of decay and interference. *Psychological Science, 13,* 27–33. (7)

Alvarez, G. A., & Cavanagh, P. (2004). The capacity of visual short-term memory is set both by visual information load and by number of objects. *Psychological Science, 15,* 106–111. (7)

Amabile, T. M. (2001). Beyond talent. *American Psychologist, 56,* 333–336. (8)

Amanzio, M., Pollo, A., Maggi, G., & Benedetti, F. (2001). Response variability to analgesics: A role for non-specific activation of endogenous opioids. *Pain, 90,* 205–215. (4)

Amato, P. R., & Keith, B. (1991). Parental divorce and the well-being of children: A meta-analysis. *Psychological Bulletin, 110,* 26–46. (5)

Ambadar, Z., Schooler, J. W., & Cohn, J. F. (2005). Deciphering the enigmatic face. *Psychological Science, 16,* 403–410. (12)

Ambady, N., Shih, M., Kim, A., & Pittinsky, T. L. (2001). Stereotype susceptibility in children: Effects of identity activation on quantitative performance. *Psychological Science, 12,* 385–390. (9)

Amedi, A., Floel, A., Knecht, S., Zohary, E., & Cohen, L. G. (2004). Transcranial magnetic stimulation of the occipital pole interferes with verbal processing in blind subjects. *Nature Neuroscience, 7,* 1266–1270. (3)

Amelang, M., & Steinmayr, R. (2006). Is there a validity increment for tests of emotional intelligence in explaining the variance of performance criteria? *Intelligence, 34,* 459–468. (12)

American Medical Association. (1986). Council report: Scientific status of refreshing recollection by the use of hypnosis. *International Journal of Clinical and Experimental Hypnosis, 34,* 1–12. (10)

American Psychiatric Association. (1994). *Diagnostic and statistical manual of mental disorders* (4th ed.). Washington, DC: Author. (15, 16)

American Psychiatric Association. (2000). *Diagnostic and statistical manual of mental disorders* (4th ed., Text revision.). Washington, DC: Author. (15)

American Psychological Association. (1982). *Ethical principles in the conduct of research with human participants.* Washington, DC: Author. (2)

Amzica, F., & Steriade, M. (1996). Progressive cortical synchronization of pontogeniculo-occipital potentials during rapid eye movement sleep. *Neuroscience, 72,* 309–314. (10)

Anderson, A., & Phelps, E. A. (2000). Expression without recognition: Contributions of the human amygdala to emotional communication. *Psychological Science, 11,* 106–111. (12)

Anderson, A. K., & Phelps, E. A. (2002). Is the human amygdala critical for the subjective experience of emotion? Evidence of intact dispositional affect in patients with amygdala lesions. *Journal of Cognitive Neuroscience, 14,* 709–720. (12)

Anderson, C., Keltner, D., & John, O. P. (2003). Emotional convergence between people over time. *Journal of Personality and Social Psychology, 84,* 1054–1068. (13)

Anderson, C. A., & Bushman, B. J. (2001). Effects of violent video games on aggressive behavior, aggressive cognition, aggressive affect, physiological arousal, and prosocial behavior: A meta-analytic review of the scientific literature. *Psychological Science, 12,* 353–359. (2)

Anderson, C. D., Warner, J. L., & Spencer, C. C. (1984). Inflation bias in self-assessment examinations: Implications for valid employee selection. *Journal of Applied Psychology, 69,* 574–580. (14)

Anderson, S. W., Bechara, A., Damasio, H., Tranel, D., & Damasio, A. R. (1999). Impairment of social and moral behavior related to early damage in human prefrontal cortex. *Nature Neuroscience, 2,* 1032–1037. (3)

Andreano, J. M., & Cahill, L. (2006). Glucocorticoid release and memory consolidation in men and women. *Psychological Science, 17,* 466–470. (7)

Andreasen, N. C., Flaum, M., Swayze, V. W., II, Tyrrell, G., & Arndt, S. (1990). Positive and negative symptoms in schizophrenia. *Archives of General Psychiatry, 47,* 615–621. (16)

Andrew, D., & Craig, A. D. (2001). Spinothalamic lamina I neurons selectively sensitive to histamine: A central neural pathway for itch. *Nature Neuroscience, 4,* 72–77. (4)

Andrews, T. J., Halpern, S. D., & Purves, D. (1997). Correlated size variations in human visual cortex, lateral geniculate nucleus, and optic tract. *Journal of Neuroscience, 17,* 2859–2868. (4)

Anglin, D., Spears, K. L., & Hutson, H. R. (1997). Flunitrazepam and its involvement in date or acquaintance rape. *Academy of Emergency Medicine, 4,* 323–326. (5)

Anonymous. (1955). *Alcoholics anonymous* (2nd ed.). New York: Alcoholics Anonymous World Services. (16)

Antonio, A. L., Chang, M. J., Hakuta, K., Kenny, D. A., Levin, S., & Milem, J. F. (2004). Effects of racial diversity on complex thinking in college students. *Psychological Science, 15,* 507–510. (13)

APA Presidential Task Force on Evidence-Based Practice. (2006). Evidence-based practice in psychology. *American Psychologist, 61,* 271–285. (15)

Appelbaum, P. S. (1988). The new preventive detention: Psychiatry's problematic responsibility for the control of violence. *American Journal of Psychiatry, 145,* 779–785. (15)

Araneda, R. C., Kini, A. D., & Firestein, S. (2000). The molecular receptive range of an odorant receptor. *Nature Neuroscience, 3,* 1248–1255. (4)

Arboleda, C., & Holzman, P. S. (1985). Thought disorder in children at risk for psychosis. *Archives of General Psychiatry, 42,* 1004–1013. (16)

Archer, J. (2000). Sex differences in aggression between heterosexual partners: A meta-analytic review. *Psychological Bulletin, 126,* 651–680. (12)

Arden, R., & Plomin, R. (2006). Sex differences in variance of intelligence across childhood. *Personality and Individual Differences, 41,* 39–48. (9)

Ariely, D., & Wertenbroch, K. (2002). Procrastination, deadlines, and performance: Self-control by precommitment. *Psychological Science, 13,* 219–224. (11)

Arkes, H. R., & Ayton, P. (1999). The sunk cost and Concorde effects: Are humans less rational than lower animals? *Psychological Bulletin, 125,* 591–600. (8)

Arndt, S., Andreasen, N. C., Flaum, M., Miller, D., & Nopoulos, P. (1995). A longitudinal study of symptom dimensions in schizophrenia. *Archives of General Psychiatry, 52,* 352–360. (16)

Arnett, J. (1990). Contraceptive use, sensation seeking, and adolescent egocentrism. *Journal of Youth and Adolescence, 19,* 171–180. (5)

Arnett, J. J. (1999). Adolescent storm and stress reconsidered. *American Psychologist, 54,* 317–326. (5)

Arnett, J. J. (2000). Emerging adulthood: A theory of development from the late teens through the twenties. *American Psychologist, 55,* 469–480. (5)

Arnold, H. J., & House, R. J. (1980). Methodological and substantive extensions to the job characteristics model of motivation. *Organizational Behavior and Human Performance, 25,* 161–183. (11)

Aronow, E., Reznikoff, M., & Moreland, K. L. (1995). The Rorschach: Projective technique or psychometric test? *Journal of Personality Assessment, 64,* 213–228. (14)

Aronson, E. (1997). The theory of cognitive dissonance: The evolution and vicissitudes of an idea. In C. McGarty & S. A. Haslam (Eds.), *The message of social psychology* (pp. 20–35). Cambridge, MA: Blackwell. (13)

Aronson, E., & Carlsmith, J. M. (1963). Effect of the severity of threat on the devaluation of forbidden behavior. *Journal of Abnormal and Social Psychology, 66,* 584–588. (13)

Arvey, R. D., McCall, B. P., Bouchard, T. J., Jr., Taubman, P., & Cavanaugh, M. A. (1994). Genetic influences on job satisfaction and work values. *Personality and Individual Differences, 17,* 21–33. (11)

Asch, S. E. (1951). Effects of group pressure upon the modification and distortion of judgments. In H. Guetzkow (Ed.), *Groups, leadership, and men* (pp. 177–190). Pittsburgh, PA: Carnegie Press. (13)

Asch, S. E. (1955, November). Opinions and social pressure. *Scientific American, 193*(5), 31–35. (13)

Asch, S. E. (1956). Studies of independence and conformity: I. A minority of one against a unanimous majority. *Psychological Monographs, 70*(9, Whole No. 416). (13)

Ash, R. (1986, August). An anecdote submitted by Ron Ash. *The Industrial-Organizational Psychologist, 23*(4), 8. (6)

Atkinson, R. C., & Shiffrin, R. M. (1968). Human memory: A proposed system and its control. In K. W. Spence & J. T. Spence (Eds.), *The psychology of learning and motivation* (Vol. 2, pp. 89–105). New York: Academic Press. (7)

Au, T. K., Knightly, L. M., Jun, S.-A., & Oh, J. W. (2002). Overhearing a language during childhood. *Psychological Science, 13,* 238–243. (8)

Austin, D. W., & Richards, J. C. (2001). The catastrophic misinterpretation model of panic disorder. *Behaviour Research and Therapy, 39,* 1277–1291. (16)

Austin, J. T., & Vancouver, J. B. (1996). Goal constructs in psychology: Structure, process, and content. *Psychological Bulletin, 120,* 338–375. (11)

Averill, J. R. (1983). Studies on anger and aggression: Implications for theories of emotion. *American Psychologist, 38,* 1145–1160. (12)

Babkoff, H., Caspy, T., Mikulincer, M., & Sing, H. C. (1991). Monotonic and rhythmic influences: A challenge for sleep deprivation research. *Psychological Bulletin, 109,* 411–428. (10)

Baccus, J. R., Baldwin, M. W., & Packer, D. J. (2004). Increasing implicit self-esteem through classical conditioning. *Psychological Science, 15,* 498–502. (6)

Baddeley, A. D. (2001). Is working memory still working? *American Psychologist, 56,* 851–864. (7)

Baddeley, A. D., & Hitch, G. (1974). Working memory. In G. H. Bower (Ed.), *Psychology of learning and motivation* (Vol. 8, pp. 47–89). New York: Academic Press. (7)

Baddeley, A., & Hitch, G. J. (1994). Developments in the concept of working memory. *Neuropsychology, 8,* 485–493. (7)

Baer, J. S., Sampson, P. D., Barr, H. M., Connor, P. D., & Streissguth, A. P. (2003). A 21-year longitudinal analysis of the effects of prenatal alcohol exposure on young adult drinking. *Archives of General Psychiatry, 60,* 377–385. (16)

Bagby, R. M., Nicholson, R. A., Bacchiochi, J. R., Ryder, A. G., & Bury, A. S. (2002). The predictive capacity of the MMPI-2 and PAI validity scales and indexes to detect coached and uncoached feigning. *Journal of Personality Assessment, 78,* 69–86. (14)

Bagemihl, B. (1999). *Biological exuberance.* New York: St. Martin's Press. (11)

Bahrick, H. (1984). Semantic memory content in permastore: 50 years of memory for Spanish learned in school. *Journal of Experimental Psychology: General, 113,* 1–29. (7)

Bailey, D. S. (2004, February). Number of psychology PhDs declining. *Monitor on Psychology, 35,* 18–19. (1)

Bailey, J. M., & Pillard, R. C. (1991). A genetic study of male sexual orientation. *Archives of General Psychiatry, 48,* 1089–1096. (11)

Bailey, J. M., Pillard, R. C., Neale, M. C., & Agyei, Y. (1993) Heritable factors influence sexual orientation in women. *Archives of General Psychiatry, 50,* 217–223. (11)

Baillargeon, R. (1986). Representing the existence and the location of hidden objects: Object permanence in 6- and 8-month-old infants. *Cognition, 23,* 21–41. (5)

Baillargeon, R. (1987). Object permanence in 3½- and 4½-month-old infants. *Developmental Psychology, 23,* 655–664. (5)

Baird, J. C. (1982). The moon illusion: A reference theory. *Journal of Experimental Psychology: General, 111,* 304–315. (4)

Baker, T. B., Piper, M. E., McCarthy, D. E., Majeskie, M. R., & Fiore, M. C. (2004). Addiction motivation reformulated: An affective processing model of negative reinforcement. *Psychological Review, 111,* 33–51. (16)

Baker, T. B., & Tiffany, S. T. (1985). Morphine tolerance as habituation. *Psychological Bulletin, 92,* 78–108. (6)

Baker-Ward, L., Gordon, B. N., Ornstein, P. A., Larus, D. M., & Clubb, P. A. (1993). Young children's long-term retention of a pediatric examination. *Child Development, 64,* 1519–1533. (7)

Bakermans-Kranenburg, M. J., van IJzendoorn, M. H., & Juffer, F. (2003). Less is more: Meta-analyses of sensitivity and attachment interventions in early childhood. *Psychological Bulletin, 129,* 195–215. (5)

Baldessarini, R. J. (1984). Antipsychotic drugs. In T. B. Karasu (Ed.), *The psychiatric therapies: I. The somatic therapies* (pp. 119–170). Washington, DC: American Psychiatric Press. (16)

Baldessarini, R. J., & Tondo, L. (2000). Does lithium treatment still work? *Archives of General Psychiatry, 57,* 187–190. (16)

Baldessarini, R. J., Tondo, L., & Hennen, J. (2001). Treating the suicidal patient with bipolar disorder. *Annals of the New York Academy of Sciences, 932,* 24–38. (16)

Ballinger, B., & Yalom, I. (1995). Group therapy in practice. In B. Bongar & L. E. Beutler (Eds.), *Comprehensive textbook of psychotherapy: Theory and practice* (pp. 189–204). Oxford, England: Oxford University Press. (15)

Banaji, M. R., & Bhaskar, R. (2000). Implicit stereotypes and memory: The bounded rationality of social beliefs. In D. L. Schacter & E. Scarry (Eds.), *Memory, brain, and belief* (pp. 139–175). Cambridge, MA: Harvard University Press. (13)

Banaji, M. R., & Kihlstrom, J. F. (1996). The ordinary nature of alien abduction memories. *Psychological Inquiry, 7,* 132–135. (7)

Bandura, A. (1977). *Social learning theory.* Upper Saddle River, NJ: Prentice Hall. (6)

Bandura, A. (1986). *Social foundations of thought and action.* Upper Saddle River, NJ: Prentice Hall. (6)

Bandura, A. (2000). Exercise of human agency through collective efficacy. *Current Directions in Psychological Science, 9,* 75–78. (6)

Bandura, A., Barbaranelli, C., Caprara, G. V., & Pastorelli, C. (2001). Self-efficacy beliefs as shapers of children's aspirations and career trajectories. *Child Development, 72,* 187–206. (6)

Bandura, A., Ross, D., & Ross, S. A. (1963). Imitation of film-mediated aggressive models. *Journal of Abnormal and Social Psychology, 66,* 3–11. (6)

Baptista, L. F., & Petrinovich, L. (1984). Social interaction, sensitive phases and the song template hypothesis in the white-crowned sparrow. *Animal Behaviour, 32,* 172–181. (6)

Bardone, A. M., Vohs, K. D., Abramson, L. Y., Heatherton, T. F., & Joiner, T. E., Jr. (2000). The confluence of perfectionism, body dissatisfaction, and low self-esteem predicts bulimic symptoms: Clinical implications. *Behavior Therapy, 31,* 265–280. (11)

Bargh, J. A., Chen, M., & Burrows, L. (1996). The automaticity of social behavior: Direct effects of trait concept and stereotype activation on action. *Journal of Personality and Social Psychology, 71,* 230–244. (13)

Barnett, R. C., & Hyde, J. S. (2001). Women, men, work, and family. *American Psychologist, 56,* 781–796. (5)

Barnett, S. M., & Ceci, S. J. (2002). When and where do we apply what we learn? A taxonomy for far transfer. *Psychological Bulletin, 128,* 612–637. (3, 8)

Barnier, A. J., & McConkey, K. M. (1998). Posthypnotic responding away from the hypnotic setting. *Psychological Science, 9,* 256–262. (10)

Baron, A., & Galizio, M. (2005). Positive and negative reinforcement: Should the distinction be preserved? *Behavior Analyst, 28,* 85–98. (6)

Baron, A. S., & Banaji, M. R. (2006). The development of implicit attitudes. *Psychological Science, 17,* 53–58. (13)

Baron, J., & Norman, M. F. (1992). SATs, achievement tests, and high-school class rank as predictors of college performance. *Educational and Psychological Measurement, 52,* 1047–1055. (9)

Barrett, L. F. (2006). Are emotions natural kinds? *Perspectives on Psychological Science, 1,* 28–58. (12)

Barrett, L. F., Tugade, M. M., & Engle, R. W. (2004). Individual differences in working memory capacity and dual-process theories of the mind. *Psychological Bulletin, 130,* 553–573. (7)

Bartlett, F. C. (1932). *Remembering.* Cambridge, England: Cambridge University Press. (7)

Bartlett, M. Y., & DeSteno, D. (2006). Gratitude and prosocial behavior. *Psychological Science, 17,* 319–325. (13)

Bartoshuk, L. M. (1991). Taste, smell, and pleasure. In R. C. Bolles (Ed.), *The hedonics of taste* (pp. 5–28). Hillsdale, NJ: Erlbaum. (4)

Bartoshuk, L. M., Duffy, V. B., Lucchina, L. B., Prutkin, J., & Fast, K. (1998). PROP (6-n-propyl-thiouracil) supertasters and the saltiness of NaCl. *Annals of the New York Academy of Sciences, 855,* 793–796. (1)

Basabe, N., Paez, D., Valencia, J., Gonzalez, J. L., Rimé, B., & Diener, E. (2002). Cultural dimensions, socioeconomic development, climate, and emotional hedonic level. *Cognition and Emotion, 16,* 103–125. (12)

Batson, C. D., & Thompson, E. R. (2001). Why don't people act morally? Motivational considerations. *Current Directions in Psychological Science, 10,* 54–57. (13)

Bauer, P. J. (2005). Developments in declarative memory. *Psychological Science, 16,* 41–47. (7)

Bauer, P. J., Wenner, J. A., & Kroupina, M. G. (2002). Making the past present: Later verbal accessibility of early memories. *Journal of Cognition and Development, 3,* 21–47. (7)

Baumeister, R. F. (2000). Gender differences in erotic plasticity: The female sex drive as socially flexible and responsive. *Psychological Bulletin, 126,* 347–374. (11)

Baumeister, R. F., Campbell, J. D., Krueger, J. I., & Vohs, K. D. (2003). Does high self-esteem cause better performance, interpersonal success, happiness, or healthier lifestyles? *Psychological Science in the Public Interest, 4,* 1–44. (12, 14)

Baumeister, R. F., Smart, L., & Boden, J. M. (1996). Relation of threatened egotism to violence and aggression: The dark side of high self-esteem. *Psychological Review, 103,* 5–33. (12)

Baumrind, D. (1971). Current patterns of parental authority. *Developmental Psychology Monographs, 4*(1, Pt. 2). (5)

Baumrind, D., Larzelere, R. E., & Cowan, P. A. (2002). Ordinary physical punishment: Is it harmful? Comment on Gershoff (2002). *Psychological Bulletin, 128,* 580–589. (6)

Baxter, M. G., & Murray, E. A. (2002). The amygdala and reward. *Nature Reviews Neuroscience, 3,* 563–573. (3, 12)

Beauchamp, G. K., Cowart, B. J., Mennella, J. A., & Marsh, R. R. (1994). Infant salt taste: Developmental, methodological, and contextual factors. *Developmental Psychobiology, 27,* 353–365. (1)

Becht, M. C., & Vingerhoets, A. J. J. M. (2002). Crying and mood change: A cross-cultural study. *Cognition and Emotion, 16,* 87–101. (12)

Beck, A. T. (1973). *The diagnosis and management of depression.* Philadelphia: University of Pennsylvania Press. (16)

Beck, A. T. (1976). *Cognitive therapy and the emotional disorders.* New York: New American Library. (15)

Beck, A. T. (1987). Cognitive models of depression. *Journal of Cognitive Psychotherapy: An International Quarterly, 1,* 5–37. (16)

Beck, A. T. (1991). Cognitive therapy: A 30-year retrospective. *American Psychologist, 46,* 368–375. (16)

Beck, A. T., & Emery, G. (1985). *Anxiety disorders and phobias.* New York: Basic Books. (16)

Beck, A. T., & Steer, R. A. (1989). Clinical predictors of eventual suicide: A 5- to 10-year prospective study of suicide attempters. *Journal of Affective Disorders, 17,* 203–209. (16)

Beck, A. T., Steer, R. A., Beck, J. S., & Newman, C. F. (1993). Hopelessness, depression, suicidal ideation, and clinical diagnosis of depression. *Suicide and Life-Threatening Behavior, 23,* 139–145. (16)

Beck, A. T., Steer, R. A., & Brown, G. (1993). Dysfunctional attitudes and suicidal ideation in psychiatric outpatients. *Suicide and Life-Threatening Behavior, 23,* 11–20. (16)

Beck, K., & Wilson, C. (2000). Development of affective organizational commitment: A cross-sequential examination of change with tenure. *Journal of Vocational Behavior, 56,* 114–136. (11)

Becker, A. E., Burwell, R. A., Gilman, S. E., Herzog, D. B., & Hamburg, P. (2002). Eating behaviours and attitudes following prolonged exposure to television among ethnic Fijian adolescent girls. *British Journal of Psychiatry, 180,* 509–514. (11)

Becker, A. E., Burwell, R. A., Navara, K., & Gilman, S. E. (2003). Binge eating and binge eating disorder in a small-scale, indigenous society: The view from Fiji. *International Journal of Eating Disorders, 34,* 423–431. (11)

Becker, A. E., Franko, D. L., Speck, A., & Herzog, D. B. (2003). Ethnicity and differential access to care for eating disorder symptoms. *International Journal of Eating Disorders, 33,* 205–212. (11)

Becker, E. S., Strohbach, D., & Rinck, M. (1999). A specific attentional bias in suicide attempters. *Journal of Nervous and Mental Disease, 187,* 730–735. (14)

Becker, M. W., & Pashler, H. (2002). Volatile visual representations: Failing to detect changes in recently processed information. *Psychonomic Bulletin & Review, 9,* 744–750. (8)

Beckett, C., Maughan, B., Rutter, M., Castle, J., Colvert, E., Groothues, C., et al. (2006). Do the effects of early severe deprivation on cognition persist into early adolescence? Findings from the English and Romanian adoptees study. *Child Development, 77,* 696–711. (9)

Beeman, M. J., & Chiarello, C. (1998). Complementary right- and left-hemisphere language comprehension. *Current Directions in Psychological Science, 7*, 2–8. (3)

Beer, J. S., Knight, R. T., & D'Esposito, M. (2006). Controlling the integration of emotion and cognition. *Psychological Science, 17*, 448–453. (12)

Bègue, L., & Muller, D. (2006). Belief in a just world as moderator of hostile attributional bias. *British Journal of Social Psychology, 45*, 117–126. (14)

Bell, R., & Pliner, P. L. (2003). Time to eat: The relationship between the number of people eating and meal duration in three lunch settings. *Appetite, 41*, 215–218. (11)

Bellugi, U., Lichtenberger, L., Jones, W., Lai, Z., & St. George, M. (2000). I. The neurocognitive profile of Williams syndrome: A complex pattern of strengths and weaknesses. *Journal of Cognitive Neuroscience, 12*(Suppl.), 7–29. (8)

Bellugi, U., & St. George, M. (2000). Preface. *Journal of Cognitive Neuroscience, 12*(Suppl.), 1–6. (8)

Belmore, S. M. (1987). Determinants of attention during impression formation. *Journal of Experimental Psychology: Learning, Memory, and Cognition, 13*, 480–489. (13)

Belsky, J. (1996). Parent, infant, and social-contextual antecedents of father-son attachment security. *Developmental Psychology, 32*, 905–913. (5)

Bem, D. J., & Honorton, C. (1994). Does psi exist? Replicable evidence for an anomalous process of information transfer. *Psychological Bulletin, 115*, 4–18. (2)

Bem, S. L. (1974). The measurement of psychological androgyny. *Journal of Consulting and Clinical Psychology, 42*, 155–162. (5)

Benbow, C. P., Lubinski, D., Shea, D. L., & Efekhari-Sanjani, H. (2000). Sex differences in mathematical reasoning at age 13: Their status 20 years later. *Psychological Science, 11*, 474–480. (5)

Benes, F. M. (1995). Is there a neuroanatomic basis for schizophrenia? An old question revisited. *The Neuroscientist, 1*, 104–115. (16)

Benowitz, N. L. (1986). The human pharmacology of nicotine. *Research Advances in Alcohol and Drug Problems, 9*, 1–52. (16)

Benowitz, N. L., Jacob, P., III, Bernert, J. T., Wilson, W., Wang, L., Allen, F., et al. (2005). Carcinogen exposure during short-term switching from regular to "light" cigarettes. *Cancer Epidemiology, Biomarkers & Prevention, 14*, 1376–1383. (16)

Bensafi, M., Porter, J., Pouliot, S., Mainland, J., Johnson, B., Zelano, C., et al. (2003). Olfactomotor activity during imagery mimics that during perception. *Nature Neuroscience, 6*, 1142–1144. (4)

Benschop, R. J., Godaert, G. L. R., Geenen, R., Brosschot, J. F., DeSmet, M. B. M., Olff, M., et al. (1995). Relationships between cardiovascular and immunologic changes in an experimental stress model. *Psychological Medicine, 25*, 323–327. (12)

Benson, H. (1977). Systemic hypertension and the relaxation response. *New England Journal of Medicine, 296*, 1152–1156. (12)

Benson, H. (1985). Stress, health, and the relaxation response. In W. D. Gentry, H. Benson, & C. J. de Wolff (Eds.), *Behavioral medicine: Work, stress and health* (pp. 15–32). Dordrecht, The Netherlands: Martinus Nijhoff. (12)

Berdoy, M., Webster, J. P., & Macdonald, D. W. (2000). Fatal attraction in rats infected with *Toxoplasma gondii. Proceedings of the Royal Society of London, B, 267*, 1591–1594. (12)

Berenbaum, S. A. (1999). Effects of early androgens on sex-typed activities and interests in adolescents with congenital adrenal hyperplasia. *Hormones and Behavior, 35*, 102–110. (11)

Berenbaum, S. A., Duck, S. C., & Bryk, K. (2002). Behavioral effects of prenatal versus postnatal androgen excess in children with 21-hydroxylase-deficient congenital adrenal hyperplasia. *Journal of Clinical Endocrinology & Metabolism, 85*, 727–733. (11)

Berger, R. J., & Phillips, N. H. (1995). Energy conservation and sleep. *Behavioural Brain Research, 69*, 65–73. (10)

Berglas, S., & Jones, E. E. (1978). Drug choice as a self-handicapping strategy in response to noncontingent success. *Journal of Personality and Social Psychology, 36*, 405–417. (13)

Berkowitz, L. (1983). Aversively stimulated aggression: Some parallels and differences in research with animals and humans. *American Psychologist, 38*, 1135–1144. (12)

Berkowitz, L. (1989). Frustration-aggression hypothesis: Examination and reformulation. *Psychological Bulletin, 106*, 59–73. (12)

Berkowitz, L. (1990). On the formulation and regulation of anger and aggression: A cognitive neoassociationistic analysis. *American Psychologist, 45*, 494–503. (12)

Berlyne, D. E. (1981). Humanistic psychology as a protest movement. In J. R. Royce & L. P. Mos (Eds.), *Humanistic psychology: Concepts and criticisms* (pp. 261–293). New York: Plenum Press. (14)

Bernstein, D. M., Atance, C., Loftus, G. R., & Meltzoff, A. (2004). We saw it all along. *Psychological Science, 15*, 264–267. (7)

Bernstein, I. L. (1991). Aversion conditioning in response to cancer and cancer treatment. *Clinical Psychology Review, 11*, 185–191. (6)

Berntson, G. G., Cacioppo, J. T., & Quigley, K. S. (1993). Cardiac psychophysiology and autonomic space in humans: Empirical perspectives and conceptual implications. *Psychological Bulletin, 114*, 296–322. (12)

Berridge, K. C., & Robinson, T. E. (1995). The mind of an addicted brain: Neural sensitization of wanting versus liking. *Current Directions in Psychological Science, 4*, 71–76. (6)

Berridge, K. C., & Robinson, T. E. (1998). What is the role of dopamine in reward: Hedonic impact, reward learning, or incentive salience? *Brain Research Reviews, 28*, 309–369. (16)

Berry, J. W., Poortinga, Y. H., Segal, H., & Dasen, P. R. (1992). *Cross-cultural psychology.* Cambridge, England: Cambridge University Press. (15)

Berscheid, E. (1983). Emotion. In H. H. Kelley, E. Berscheid, A. Christensen, J. H. Harvey, T. L. Huston, G. Levinger, et al. (Eds.), *Close relationships* (pp. 110–168). New York: W. H. Freeman. (13)

Bertenthal, B. I., Longo, M. R., & Kosobud, A. (2006). Imitative response tendencies following observation of intransitive actions. *Journal of Experimental Psychology: Human Perception and Performance, 32*, 210–225. (6)

Bertolino, A., Blasi, G., Latorre, V., Rubino, V., Rampino, A., Sinibaldi, L., et al. (2006). Additive effects of genetic variation in dopamine regulating genes on working memory cortical activity in human brain. *Journal of Neuroscience, 26*, 3918–3922. (9)

Bickman, L. (1996). A continuum of care: More is not always better. *American Psychologist, 51*, 689–701. (15)

Billy, J. O. G., Tanfer, K., Grady, W. R., & Klepinger, D. H. (1993, March/April). The sexual behavior of men in the United States. *Family Planning Perspectives, 25*, 52–60. (11)

Binet, A., & Simon, T. (1905). Méthodes nouvelles pour le diagnostic du niveau intellectuel des anormaux [New methods for the measurement of the intellectual level of the abnormal]. *L'Année Psychologique, 11*, 191–244. (9)

Birch, S. A. J., & Bloom, P. (2003). Children are cursed: An asymmetric bias in mental-state attribution. *Psychological Science, 14*, 283–286. (5)

Birnbaum, M. H. (1999). Testing critical properties of decision making on the Internet. *Psychological Science, 10*, 399–407. (8)

Bishop, E. G., Cherny, S. S., Corley, R., Plomin, R., DeFries, J. C., & Hewitt, J. K. (2003). Development genetic analysis of general cognitive ability from 1 to 12 years in a sample of adoptees, biological siblings, and twins. *Intelligence, 31*, 31–49. (9)

Bjork, R. A., & VanHuele, M. (1992). Retrieval inhibition and related adaptive peculiarities of human memory. *Advances in Consumer Research, 19*, 155–160. (7)

Bjorklund, D. F., & Pellegrini, A. D. (2000). Child development and evolutionary psychology. *Child Development, 71*, 1687–1708. (5)

Bjorklund, D. F., & Shackelford, T. K. (1999). Differences in parental investment contribute to important differences between men and women. *Current Directions in Psychological Science, 8,* 86–92. (13)

Blackless, M., Charuvastra, A., Derryck, A., Fausto-Sterling, A., Lauzanne, K., & Lee, E. (2000). How sexually dimorphic are we? Review and synthesis. *American Journal of Human Biology, 12,* 151–166. (11)

Blackwell, A., & Bates, E. (1995). Inducing agrammatic profiles in normals: Evidence for the selective vulnerability of morphology under cognitive resource limitation. *Journal of Cognitive Neuroscience, 7,* 228–257. (8)

Blaine, J. D., Prien, R. F., & Levine, J. (1983). The role of antidepressants in the treatment of affective disorders. *American Journal of Psychotherapy, 37,* 502–520. (16)

Blair, R. J. R., Mitchell, D. G. V., Peschardt, K. S., Colledge, E., Leonard, R. A., Shine, J. H., et al. (2004). Reduced sensitivity to others' fearful expressions in psychopathic individuals. *Personality and Individual Differences, 37,* 1111–1122. (12)

Blake, R., & Logothetis, N. K. (2002). Visual competition. *Nature Reviews Neuroscience, 3,* 13–23. (10)

Blakemore, C., & Sutton, P. (1969). Size adaptation: A new aftereffect. *Science, 166,* 245–247. (4)

Blascovich, J., & Tomaka, J. (1991). Measures of self-esteem. In J. P. Robinson, R. R. Shaver, & L. S. Wrightsman (Eds.), *Measures of personality and social psychological attitudes* (Vol. 1, pp. 115–160). San Diego, CA: Academic Press. (14)

Blasi, G., Mattay, V. S., Bertolino, A., Elvevåg, B., Callicott, J. H., Das, S., et al. (2005). Effect of catechol-O-methyltransferase val[158]met genotype on attentional control. *Journal of Neuroscience, 25,* 5038–5045. (8)

Bless, H., Bohner, G., Schwarz, N., & Strack, F. (1990). Mood and persuasion: A cognitive response analysis. *Personality and Social Psychology Bulletin, 16,* 331–345. (12)

Bleuler, E. (1950). *Dementia praecox, or the group of schizophrenias* (J. Zinkin, Trans.). New York: International Universities Press. (Original work published 1911) (16)

Block, J. (1995). A contrarian view of the five-factor approach to personality description. *Psychological Bulletin, 117,* 187–215. (14)

Blount, J. D., Metcalfe, N. B., Birkhead, T. R., & Surai, P. F. (2003). Carotenoid modulation of immune function and sexual attractiveness in zebra finches. *Science, 300,* 125–127. (13)

Blum, D. (1994). *The monkey wars.* New York: Oxford University Press. (2)

Blum, G. S., & Barbour, J. S. (1979). Selective inattention to anxiety-linked stimuli. *Journal of Experimental Psychology: General, 108,* 182–224. (4)

Blumenthal, S. J., & Kupfer, D. J. (1986). Generalizable treatment strategies for suicidal behavior. *Annals of the New York Academy of Sciences, 487,* 327–340. (16)

Bogaert, A. F. (2003). The interaction of fraternal birth order and body size in male sexual orientation. *Behavioral Neuroscience, 117,* 381–384. (11)

Bogaert, A. F. (2006). Biological versus nonbiological older brothers and men's sexual orientation. *Proceedings of the National Academy of Sciences, USA, 103,* 10771–10774. (11)

Bogg, T., & Roberts, B. W. (2004). Conscientiousness and health-related behaviors: A meta-analysis of the leading behavioral contributors to mortality. *Psychological Bulletin, 130,* 887–919. (14)

Bohart, A. C. (2000). The client is the most important common factor: Clients' self-healing capacities and psychotherapy. *Journal of Psychotherapy Integration, 10,* 127–149. (15)

Bond, M. H. (1991). *Beyond the Chinese face.* New York: Oxford University Press. (15)

Bond, M. H. (2002). Reclaiming the individual from Hofstede's ecological analysis—A 20-year odyssey: Comment on Oyserman et al. (2002). *Psychological Bulletin, 128,* 73–77. (13)

Bond, R., & Smith, P. B. (1996). Culture and conformity: A meta-analysis of studies using Asch's (1952, 1956) line judgment task. *Psychological Bulletin, 119,* 111–137. (13)

Bonnie, R. J. (1997). Research with cognitively impaired subjects: Unfinished business in the regulation of human research. *Archives of General Psychiatry, 54,* 105–111. (2)

Bootzin, R. R., & Bailey, E. T. (2005). Understanding placebo, nocebo, and iatrogenic treatment effects. *Journal of Clinical Psychology, 61,* 871–880. (15)

Borch-Jacobsen, M. (1997, April 24). Sybil—The making of a disease: An interview with Dr. Herbert Spiegel. *New York Review of Books,* no. 7, 60–64. (15)

Borden, V. M. H., & Rajecki, D. W. (2000). First-year employment outcomes of psychology baccalaureates: Relatedness, preparedness, and prospects. *Teaching of Psychology, 27,* 164–168. (1)

Boring, E. G. (1930). A new ambiguous figure. *American Journal of Psychology, 42,* 444–445. (4)

Bornstein, M. H., Hahn, C.-S., Bell, C., Haynes, O. M., Slater, A., Golding, J., et al. (2006). Stability in cognition across early childhood. *Psychological Science, 17,* 151–158. (9)

Bouchard, T. J., Lykken, D. T., McGue, M., Segal, N. L., & Tellegen, A. (1990). Sources of psychological differences: The Minnesota study of twins reared apart. *Science, 250,* 223–228. (5)

Bouchard, T. J., Jr., & McGue, M. (1981). Familial studies of intelligence: A review. *Science, 212,* 1055–1059. (9)

Bouchard, T. J., Jr., & McGue, M. (2003). Genetic and environmental influences on human psychological differences. *Journal of Neurobiology, 54,* 4–45. (5, 14)

Boutla, M., Supalla, T., Newport, E. L., & Bavelier, D. (2004). Short-term memory span: Insights from sign language. *Nature Neuroscience, 7,* 997–1002. (7)

Bouton, M. E. (1994). Context, ambiguity, and classical conditioning. *Current Directions in Psychological Science, 3,* 49–53. (6)

Bouton, M. E., Mineka, S., & Barlow, D. H. (2001). A modern learning theory perspective on the etiology of panic disorder. *Psychological Review, 108,* 4–32. (16)

Bowers, K. S., Regehr, G., Balthazard, C., & Parker, K. (1990). Intuition in the context of discovery. *Cognitive Psychology, 22,* 72–110. (8)

Bowlby, J. (1973). *Attachment and loss: Vol. II. Separation.* New York: Basic Books. (5)

Bowmaker, J. K. (1998). Visual pigments and molecular genetics of color blindness. *News in Physiological Sciences, 13,* 63–69. (4)

Bowmaker, J. K., & Dartnall, H. J. A. (1980). Visual pigments of rods and cones in a human retina. *Journal of Physiology* (London), *298,* 501–511. (4)

Bracha, H. S. (2006). Human brain evolution and the "neuroevolutionary time-depth principle": Implications for the reclassification of fear-circuitry-related traits in *DSM-V* and for studying resilience to warzone-related posttraumatic stress disorder. *Progress in Neuro-Psychopharmacology & Biological Psychiatry, 30,* 827–853. (15, 16)

Bradbury, T. N., & Miller, G. A. (1985). Season of birth in schizophrenia: A review of evidence, methodology, and etiology. *Psychological Bulletin, 98,* 569–594. (16)

Braden, J. P., & Niebling, B. C. (2005). Using the joint test standards to evaluate the validity evidence for intelligence tests. In D. P. Flanagan & P. L. Harrison (Eds.), *Contemporary intellectual assessment* (pp. 615–630). New York: Guilford Press. (9)

Bradley, D. C., Troyk, P. R., Berg, J. A., Bak, M., Cogan, S., Erickson, R., et al. (2005). Visuotopic mapping through a multichannel stimulating implant in primate V1. *Journal of Neurophysiology, 93,* 1659–1670. (4)

Brainard, M. S., & Doupe, A. J. (2000). Auditory feedback in learning and maintenance of vocal behaviour. *Nature Reviews Neuroscience, 1,* 31–40. (6)

Brainerd, C. J., & Reyna, V. F. (2002). Fuzzy-trace theory and false memory. *Current Directions in Psychological Science, 11,* 164–169. (7)

Bray, G. A., Nielsen, S. J., & Popkin, B. M. (2004). Consumption of high-fructose corn syrup in beverages may play a role in the epidemic of obesity. *American Journal of Clinical Nutrition, 79,* 537–543. (11)

Brédart, S., Delchambre, M., & Laureys, S. (2006). One's own face is hard to ignore. *Quarterly Journal of Experimental Psychology, 59,* 46–52. (8)

Bregman, A. S. (1981). Asking the "what for" question in auditory perception. In M. Kubovy & J. R. Pomerantz (Eds.), *Perceptual organization* (pp. 99–118). Hillsdale, NJ: Erlbaum. (4)

Brennan, P. A., Grekin, E. R., & Mednick, S. A. (1999). Maternal smoking during pregnancy and adult male criminal outcomes. *Archives of General Psychiatry, 56,* 215–219. (12)

Brent, D. A. (2001). Firearms and suicide. *Annals of the New York Academy of Sciences, 932,* 225–239. (16)

Brereton, A. R. (2004). Dominance: Female chums or male hired guns. In M. Bekoff (Ed.), *Encyclopedia of animal behavior* (pp. 1–7). Westport, CT: Greenwood Press. (13)

Breslau, N., Dickens, W. T., Flynn, J. R., Peterson, E. L., & Lucia, V. C. (2006). Low birthweight and social disadvantage: Tracking their relationship with children's IQ during the period of school attendance. *Intelligence, 34,* 351–362. (9)

Brewin, C. R., & Beaton, A. (2002). Thought suppression, intelligence, and working memory capacity. *Behaviour Research and Therapy, 40,* 923–930. (7)

Broadbent, J., Muccino, K. J., & Cunningham, C. L. (2002). Ethanol-induced conditioned taste aversion in 15 inbred mouse strains. *Behavioral Neuroscience, 116,* 138–148. (6)

Brock, G., Laumann, E., Glasser, D. B., Nicolosi, A., Gingell, C., & King, R. for the GSSAB Investigator's Group. (2003). *Prevalence of sexual dysfunction among mature men and women in USA, Canada, Australia and New Zealand.* Poster presentation at American Urological Association, Chicago, IL, April 26–May 1, 2003. Retrieved from: http://www.pfizerglobalstudy.com/Posters/GSSAB%20AUA%202003_poster_FINAL.pdf. (11)

Brody, G. H., Murry, V. M., Kogan, S. M., Gerrard, M., Gibbons, F. X., Molgaaard, V., et al. (2006). The Strong African American Families Program: A cluster-randomized prevention trial of long-term effects and a mediational model. *Journal of Consulting and Clinical Psychology, 74,* 356–366. (5)

Brody, N. (2003). Construct validation of the Sternberg Triarchic Abilities Test: Comment and reanalysis. *Intelligence, 31,* 319–329. (9)

Brooks, R. (2000). Negative genetic correlation between male sexual attractiveness and survival. *Nature, 406,* 67–70. (13)

Brower, K. J., & Anglin, M. D. (1987). Adolescent cocaine use: Epidemiology, risk factors, and prevention. *Journal of Drug Education, 17,* 163–180. (3)

Brown, A. S. (2003). A review of the déjà vu experience. *Psychological Bulletin, 129,* 394–413. (10)

Brown, G. P., MacLeod, A. K., Tata, P., & Goddard, L. (2002). Worry and the simulation of future outcomes. *Anxiety, Stress and Coping, 15,* 1–17. (12)

Brown, G. W. (1989). Life events and measurement. In G. W. Brown & T. O. Harris (Eds.), *Life events and illness* (pp. 3–45). New York: Guilford Press. (12)

Brown, J. (1977). *Mind, brain, and consciousness.* New York: Academic Press. (8)

Brown, R., & McNeill, D. (1966). The "tip of the tongue." *Journal of Verbal Learning and Verbal Behavior, 5,* 325–337. (7)

Brown, S. M., Manuck, S. B., Flory, J. D., & Hariri, A. R. (2006). Neural basis of individual differences in impulsivity: Contributions of corticolimbic circuits for behavioral arousal and control. *Emotion, 6,* 239–245. (8)

Bruce, S. E., Machan, J. T., Dyck, I., & Keller, M. B. (2001). Infrequency of "pure" GAD: Impact of psychiatric comorbidity on clinical course. *Depression and Anxiety, 14,* 219–225. (16)

Bruck, M., Cavanagh, P., & Ceci, S. J. (1991). Fortysomething: Recognizing faces at one's 25th reunion. *Memory & Cognition, 19,* 221–228. (4)

Bruner, J. S., & Potter, M. C. (1964). Interference in visual recognition. *Science, 144,* 424–425. (8)

Brüning, J. C., Gautham, D., Burks, D. J., Gillette, J., Schubert, M., Orban, P. C., et al. (2000). Role of brain insulin receptor in control of body weight and reproduction. *Science, 289,* 2122–2125. (11)

Bryant, F. B., & Guilbault, R. L. (2002). "I knew it all along" eventually: The development of hindsight bias in the Clinton impeachment verdict. *Basic and Applied Social Psychology, 24,* 27–41. (7)

Brysbaert, M., Vitu, F., & Schroyens, W. (1996). The right visual field advantage and the optimal viewing position effect: On the relation between foveal and parafoveal word recognition. *Neuropsychology, 10,* 385–395. (8)

Buck, L., & Axel, R. (1991). A novel multigene family may encode odorant receptors: A molecular basis for odor recognition. *Cell, 65,* 175–187. (4)

Buehler, R., Griffin, D., & Ross, M. (1994). Exploring the "planning fallacy": Why people underestimate their task completion times. *Journal of Personality and Social Psychology, 67,* 366–381. (11)

Buka, S. L., Tsuang, M. T., Torrey, E. F., Klebanoff, M. A., Bernstein, D., & Yolken, R. H. (2001). Maternal infections and subsequent psychosis among offspring. *Archives of General Psychiatry, 58,* 1032–1037. (16)

Bulbena, A., Gago, J., Martin-Santos, R., Porta, M., Dasquens, J., & Berrios, G. E. (2004). Anxiety disorder & joint laxity: A definitive link. *Neurology, Psychiatry and Brain Research, 11,* 137–140. (16)

Burger, J. M. (1986). Increasing compliance by improving the deal: The that's-not-all technique. *Journal of Personality and Social Psychology, 51,* 277–283. (13)

Burgess, C. E., Lindblad, K., Sigransky, E., Yuan, Q.-P., Long, R. T., Breschel, T., et al. (1998). Large CAG/CTG repeats are associated with childhood-onset schizophrenia. *Molecular Psychiatry, 3,* 321–327. (16)

Burke, D. M., Locantore, J. K., Austin, A. A., & Chae, B. (2004). Cherry pit primes Brad Pitt. *Psychological Science, 15,* 164–170. (8)

Burke, K. C., Burke, J. D., Jr., Regier, D. A., & Rae, D. S. (1990). Age at onset of selected mental disorders in five community populations. *Archives of General Psychiatry, 47,* 511–518. (16)

Burns, B. D. (2004). The effects of speed on skilled chess performance. *Psychological Science, 15,* 442–447. (8)

Burns, M. O., & Seligman, M. E. P. (1989). Explanatory style across the life span: Evidence for stability over 52 years. *Journal of Personality and Social Psychology, 56,* 471–477. (16)

Burr, D. C., Morrone, M. C., & Ross, J. (1994). Selective suppression of the magnocellular visual pathway during saccadic eye movements. *Nature, 371,* 511–513. (8)

Burton, H., Snyder, A. Z., Conturo, T. E., Akbudak, E., Ollinger, J. M., & Raichle, M. E. (2002). Adaptive changes in early and late blind: A fMRI study of Braille reading. *Journal of Neurophysiology, 87,* 589–607. (3)

Burtsev, M., & Turchin, P. (2006). Evolution of cooperative strategies from first principles. *Nature, 440,* 1041–1044. (13)

Bushman, B. J., & Anderson, C. A. (2001). Media violence and the American public: Scientific facts versus media misinformation. *American Psychologist, 56,* 477–489. (2)

Buss, D. M. (2000). Desires in human mating. *Annals of the New York Academy of Sciences, 907,* 39–49. (13)

Buss, D. M., Larsen, R. J., Westen, D., & Semmelroth, J. (1992). Sex differences in jealousy: Evolution, physiology, and psychology. *Psychological Science, 3,* 251–255. (13)

Butcher, J. N., Graham, J. R., Williams, C. L., & Ben-Porath, Y. S. (1990). *Development and use of the MMPI-2 content scales.* Minneapolis: University of Minnesota Press. (14)

Butler, A. C., Chapman, J. E., Forman, E. M., & Beck, A. T. (2006). The empirical status of cognitive-behavioral therapy: A review of meta-analyses. *Clinical Psychology Review, 26,* 17–31. (16)

Butler, L. (2002). A list of published papers is no measure of value. *Nature, 419,* 877. (11)

Butzlaff, R. L., & Hooley, J. M. (1998). Expressed emotion and psychiatric relapse. *Archives of General Psychiatry, 55,* 547–552. (16)

Buunk, B. P., Angleitner, A., Oubaid, V., & Buss, D. M. (1996). Sex differences in jealousy in evolutionary and cultural perspective: Tests from the Netherlands, Germany, and the United States. *Psychological Science, 7,* 359–363. (13)

Byne, W., Tobet, S., Mattiace, L. A., Lasco, M. S., Kemether, E., Edgar, M. A., et al. (2001). The interstitial nuclei of the human anterior hypothalamus: An investigation of variation with sex, sexual orientation, and HIV status. *Hormones and Behavior, 40,* 86–92. (11)

Byrne, G. J. A., Raphael, B., & Arnold, E. (1999). Alcohol consumption and psychological distress in recently widowed older men. *Australian and New Zealand Journal of Psychiatry, 33,* 740–747. (12)

Cacioppo, J. T., Hawkley, L. C., & Berntson, G. G. (2003). The anatomy of loneliness. *Current Directions in Psychological Science, 12,* 71–74. (12)

Cadinu, M., Maass, A., Rosabianca, A., & Kiesner, J. (2005). Why do women underperform under stereotype threat? *Psychological Science, 16,* 572–578. (9)

Cahalan, D. (1978). Subcultural differences in drinking behavior in U.S. national surveys and selected European studies. In P. E. Nathan, G. A. Marlatt, & T. Løberg (Eds.), *Alcoholism: New directions in behavioral research and treatment* (pp. 235–253). New York: Plenum Press. (16)

Cahill, L., & McGaugh, J. L. (1998). Mechanisms of emotional arousal and lasting declarative memory. *Trends in Neurosciences, 21,* 294–299. (7)

Cahn, W., Hulshoff, H. E., Lems, E. B. T. E., van Haren, N. E. M., Schnack, H. G., van der Linden, J. A., et al. (2002). Brain volume changes in first-episode schizophrenia. *Archives of General Psychiatry, 59,* 1002–1010. (16)

Callaghan, T., Rochat, P., Lillard, A., Claux, M. L., Odden, H., Itakura, S., et al. (2005). Synchrony in the onset of mental-state reasoning. *Psychological Science, 16,* 378–384. (5)

Callicott, J. H., Straub, R. E., Pezawas, L., Egan, M. F., Mattay, V. S., Hariri, A. R., et al. (2005). Variation in DISC1 affects hippocampal structure and function and increases risk for schizophrenia. *Proceedings of the National Academy of Sciences, U.S.A, 102,* 8627–8632. (16)

Calvin, W. H., & Bickerton, D. (2000). *Lingua ex machina.* Cambridge, MA: MIT Press. (8)

Calvo, M. G., & Avero, P. (2002). Eye movement assessment of emotional processing in anxiety. *Emotion, 2,* 105–117. (12)

Cameron, P., & Cameron, K. (2002). What proportion of heterosexuals is ex-homosexual? *Psychological Reports, 91,* 1087–1097. (11)

Cameron, P., Proctor, K., Coburn, W., & Forde, N. (1985). Sexual orientation and sexually transmitted disease. *Nebraska Medical Journal, 70,* 292–299. (11)

Campbell, R. S., & Pennebaker, J. W. (2003). The secret life of pronouns: Flexibility in writing style and physical health. *Psychological Science, 14,* 60–65. (15)

Campbell, S. S., & Tobler, I. (1984). Animal sleep: A review of sleep duration across phylogeny. *Neuroscience & Biobehavioral Reviews, 8,* 269–300. (10)

Camperio-Ciani, A., Corna, F., & Capiluppi, C. (2004). Evidence for maternally inherited factors favouring male homosexuality and promoting female fecundity. *Proceedings of the Royal Society of London,* B, *271,* 2217–2221. (11)

Campion, M. A., & McClelland, C. L. (1991). Interdisciplinary examination of the costs and benefits of enlarged jobs: A job design quasi-experiment. *Journal of Applied Psychology, 76,* 186–198. (11)

Campion, M. A., & Thayer, P. W. (1985). Development and field evaluation of an interdisciplinary measure of job design. *Journal of Applied Psychology, 70,* 29–43. (11)

Campion, M. A., & Thayer, P. W. (1989). How do you design a job? *Personnel Journal, 68,* 43–46. (1)

Campos, J. J., Bertenthal, B. I., & Kermoian, R. (1992). Early experience and emotional development. *Psychological Science, 3,* 61–64. (5)

Camras, L. A., Chen, Y., Bakeman, R., Norris, K., & Cain, T. R. (2006). Culture, ethnicity and children's facial expressions: A study of European American, mainland Chinese, Chinese American, and adopted Chinese girls. *Emotion, 6,* 103–114. (12)

Canetto, S. S., & Sakinofsky, I. (1998). The gender paradox in suicide. *Suicide and Life-Threatening Behavior, 28,* 1–23. (16)

Cann, A. (2005). Predicting course grades: Accurate for others but biased for self. *Teaching of Psychology, 32,* 242–244. (7)

Cannon, W. B. (1929). Organization for physiological homeostasis. *Physiological Reviews, 9,* 399–431. (11)

Cardno, A. G., Marshall, E. J., Coid, B., Macdonald, A. M., Ribchester, T. R., Davies, N. J., et al. (1999). Heritability estimates for psychotic disorders. *Archives of General Psychiatry, 56,* 162–168. (16)

Carey, S. (1978). The child as word learner. In M. Halle, J. Bresnan, & G. A. Miller (Eds.), *Linguistic theory and psychological reality* (pp. 264–293). Cambridge, MA: MIT Press. (8)

Carlson, V. J., & Harwood, R. L. (2003). Attachment, culture, and the caregiving system: The cultural patterning of everyday experiences among Anglo and Puerto Rican mother-infant pairs. *Infant Mental Health Journal, 24,* 53–73. (5)

Carlsson, K., Petrovic, P., Skare, S., Petersson, K. M., & Ingvar, M. (2000). Tickling expectations: Neural processing in anticipation of a sensory stimulus. *Journal of Cognitive Neuroscience, 12,* 691–703. (4)

Carnagey, N. L., & Anderson, C. A. (2005). The effects of reward and punishment in violent videogames on aggressive affect, cognition, and behavior. *Psychological Science, 16,* 882–889. (2)

Carney, D. R., & Harrigan, J. A. (2003). It takes one to know one: Interpersonal sensitivity is related to accurate assessment of others' interpersonal sensitivity. *Emotion, 3,* 194–200. (12)

Carney, R. N., & Levin, J. R. (1998). Coming to terms with the keyword method in introductory psychology: A "neuromnemonic" example. *Teaching of Psychology, 25,* 132–134. (7)

Carpenter, P. A., Just, M. A., & Shell, P. (1990). What one intelligence test measures: A theoretical account of the processing in the Raven Progressive Matrices test. *Psychological Review, 97,* 404–431. (9)

Carroll, B. J. (1980). Implications of biological research for the diagnosis of depression. In J. Mendlewicz (Ed.), *New advances in the diagnosis and treatment of depressive illness* (pp. 85–107). Amsterdam: Excerpta Medica. (16)

Carroll, J. B. (1993). *Human cognitive abilities.* Cambridge, England: Cambridge University Press. (9)

Carroll, J. B. (2003). The higher-stratum structure of cognitive abilities: Current evidence supports *g* and about ten broad factors. In H. Nyborg (Ed.), *The scientific study of general intelligence: Tribute to Arthur R. Jensen* (pp. 5–21). Oxford, England: Elsevier. (9)

Carstensen, L. L., Mikels, J. A., & Mather, M. (2006). Aging and the intersection of cognition, motivation, and emotion. In J. E. Birren & K. W. Schaie (Eds.), *Handbook of the psychology of aging* (6th ed.) (pp. 343–362). Burlington, MA: Elsevier. (5)

Caspi, A., McClay, J., Moffitt, T. E., Mill, J., Martin, J., Craig, I. W., et al. (2002). Role of genotype in the cycle of violence in maltreated children. *Science, 297,* 851–854. (5, 12)

Caspi, A., Sugden, K., Moffit, T. E., Taylor, A., Craig, I. W., Harrington, H. L., et al. (2003). Influence of life stress on depression: Moderation by a polymorphism in the 5-HTT gene. *Science, 301,* 386–389. (14,16)

Cassia, V. M., Turati, C., & Simion, F. (2004). Can a nonspecific bias toward top-heavy patterns explain newborns' face preference? *Psychological Science, 15,* 379–383. (5)

Caterina, M. J., Rosen, T. A., Tominaga, M., Brake, A. J., & Julius, D. (1999). A capsaicin-receptor homologue with a high threshold for noxious heat. *Nature, 398,* 436–441. (4)

Cattell, R. B. (1965). *The scientific analysis of personality*. Chicago: Aldine. (14)

Cattell, R. B. (1987). *Intelligence: Its structure, growth and action*. Amsterdam: North-Holland. (9)

Ceci, S. J. (1995). False beliefs: Some developmental and clinical considerations. In D. L. Schacter (Ed.), *Memory distortion* (pp. 91–125). Cambridge, MA: Harvard University Press. (7)

Ceci, S. J., & Bruck, M. (1993). Suggestibility of the child witness: A historical review and synthesis. *Psychological Bulletin, 113*, 403–439. (7)

Cepeda, N. J., Pashler, H., Vul, E., Wixted, J. T., & Rohrer, D. (2006). Distributed practice in verbal recall tasks: A review and quantitative synthesis. *Psychological Bulletin, 132*, 354–380. (7)

Chabris, C. F. (1999). Prelude or requiem for the "Mozart effect"? *Nature, 400*, 826–827. (2)

Chamberlin, J. (1978). *On our own*. New York: Hawthorn. (15)

Chamberlin, J. (2000, February). Where are all these students coming from? *Monitor on Psychology, 31*(2), 32–34. (1)

Chambers, J. R., Baron, R. S., & Inman, M. L. (2006). Misperceptions in intergroup conflict. *Psychological Science, 17*, 38–45. (13)

Chambers, J. R., & Windschitl, P. D. (2004). Biases in social comparison judgments: The role of nonmotivated factors in above-average and comparative-optimism effects. *Psychological Bulletin, 130*, 813–838. (8)

Charles, S. T., Mather, M., & Carstensen, L. L. (2003). Aging and emotional memory: The forgettable nature of negative images for older adults. *Journal of Experimental Psychology: General, 132*, 310–324. (12)

Charlton, S. G. (1983). Differential conditionability: Reinforcing grooming in golden hamsters. *Animal Learning & Behavior, 11*, 27–34. (6)

Chase-Lansdale, P., Moffitt, R. A., Lohrman, B. J., Cherlin, A. J., Coley, R. L., Pittman, L. D., et al. (2003). Mothers' transitions from welfare to work and the well-being of preschoolers and adolescents. *Science, 299*, 1548–1552. (5)

Chaudhari, N., Landin, A. M., & Roper, S. D. (2000). A metabotropic glutamate receptor variant functions as a taste receptor. *Nature Neuroscience, 3*, 113–119. (4)

Cheetham, E. (1973). *The prophecies of Nostradamus*. New York: Putnam's. (2)

Chehab, F. F., Mounzih, K., Lu, R., & Lim, M. E. (1997). Early onset of reproductive function in normal female mice treated with leptin. *Science, 275*, 88–90. (11)

Chemelli, R. M., Willie, J. T., Sinton, C. M., Elmquist, J. K., Scammell, T., Lee, C., et al. (1999). Narcolepsy in orexin knockout mice: Molecular genetics of sleep regulation. *Cell, 98*, 437–451. (10)

Chen, D., & Haviland-Jones, J. (2000). Human olfactory communication of emotion. *Perceptual and Motor Skills, 91*, 771–781. (12)

Cheng, A. T. A. (1995). Mental illness and suicide. *Archives of General Psychiatry, 52*, 594–603. (16)

Cheng, C. (2005). Processes underlying gender-role flexibility: Do androgynous individuals know more or know how to cope? *Journal of Personality, 73*, 646–673. (5)

Cheryan, S., & Bodenhausen, G. V. (2000). When positive stereotypes threaten intellectual performance: The psychological hazards of "model minority" status. *Psychological Science, 11*, 399–402. (9)

Cheung, F. M., Leung, K., Fang, R. M., Song, W. Z., Zhang, J. X., & Zhang, J. P. (1996). Development of the Chinese Personality Assessment Inventory (CPAI). *Journal of Cross-Cultural Psychology, 27*, 181–199. (14)

Chivers, M. L., Rieger, G., Latty, E., & Bailey, J. M. (2004). A sex difference in the specificity of sexual arousal. *Psychological Science, 15*, 736–744. (11)

Choi, I., & Nisbett, R. E. (2000). Cultural psychology of surprise: Holistic theories and recognition of contradiction. *Journal of Personality and Social Psychology, 79*, 890–905. (13)

Chomsky, N. (1980). *Rules and representations*. New York: Columbia University Press. (8)

Christensen, A., & Jacobson, N. S. (1994). Who (or what) can do psychotherapy: The status and challenge of nonprofessional therapies. *Psychological Science, 5*, 8–14. (15)

Churchland, P. S. (1986). *Neurophilosophy*. Cambridge, MA: MIT Press. (10)

Cialdini, R. B. (1993). *Influence: The psychology of persuasion* (Rev. ed.). New York: Morrow. (6)

Cialdini, R. B. (2003). Crafting normative messages to protect the environment. *Current Directions in Psychological Science, 12*, 105–109. (13)

Cialdini, R. B., Vincent, J. E., Lewis, S. K., Catalan, J., Wheeler, D., & Darby, B. L. (1975). Reciprocal concessions procedure for inducing compliance: The door-in-the-face technique. *Journal of Personality and Social Psychology, 31*, 206–215. (13)

Ciarrochi, J., Hynes, K., & Crittenden, N. (2005). Can men do better if they try harder: Sex and motivational effects on emotional awareness. *Cognition and Emotion, 19*, 133–141. (12)

Cioffi, D. (1991). Beyond attentional strategies: A cognitive-perceptual model of somatic interpretation. *Psychological Bulletin, 109*, 25–41. (12)

Clancy, S. A. (2005). *Abducted: How people come to believe they were kidnapped by aliens*. Cambridge, MA: Harvard University Press. (16)

Clark, R., Anderson, N. B., Clark, V. R., & Williams, D. R. (1999). Racism as a stressor for African Americans. *American Psychologist, 54*, 805–816. (12)

Clarke, G. N., Hornbrook, M., Lynch, F., Polen, M., Gale, J., Beardslee, W., et al. (2001). A randomized trial of a group cognitive intervention for preventing depression in adolescent offspring of depressed patients. *Archives of General Psychiatry, 58*, 1127–1134. (15)

Clarkin, J. F., & Carpenter, D. (1995). Family therapy in historical perspective. In B. Bongar & L. E. Beutler (Eds.), *Comprehensive textbook of psychotherapy: Theory and practice* (pp. 205–227). Oxford, England: Oxford University Press. (15)

Clay, R. A. (2002, May). An indigenized psychology. *Monitor on Psychology, 33*(5), 58–59. (15)

Clearfield, M. W., & Nelson, N. M. (2006). Sex differences in mothers' speech and play behavior with 6-, 9-, and 14-month-old infants. *Sex Roles, 54*, 127–137. (5)

Clément, K., Vaisse, C., Lahlou, N., Cabrol, S., Pelloux, V., Cassuto, D., et al. (1998). A mutation in the human leptin receptor gene causes obesity and pituitary dysfunction. *Nature, 392*, 398–401. (11)

Clements, W. A., & Perner, J. (1994). Implicit understanding of belief. *Cognitive Development, 9*, 377–395. (5)

Clinicopathologic conference. (1967). *Johns Hopkins Medical Journal, 120*, 186–199. (12)

Coatsworth, J. D., Maldonado-Molina, M., Pantin, H., & Szapocznik, J. (2005). A person-centered and ecological investigation of acculturation strategies in Hispanic immigrant youth. *Journal of Community Psychology, 33*, 157–174. (5)

Cobos, P., Sánchez, M., García, C., Vera, M. N., & Vila, J. (2002). Revisiting the James versus Cannon debate on emotion: Startle and autonomic modulation in patients with spinal cord injuries. *Biological Psychology, 61*, 251–269. (12)

Cocodia, E. A., Kim, J. S., Shin, H.-S., Kim, J. W., Ee, J., Wee, M. S. W., et al. (2003). Evidence that rising population intelligence is impacting in formal education. *Personality and Individual Differences, 35*, 797–810. (9)

Cohen, B., Novick, D., & Rubinstein, M. (1996). Modulation of insulin activities by leptin. *Science, 274*, 1185–1188. (11)

Cohen, D. (2001). Cultural variation: Considerations and implications. *Psychological Bulletin, 127*, 451–471. (5)

Cohen, G. L. (2003). Party over policy: The dominating impact of group influence on political beliefs. *Journal of Personality and Social Psychology, 85*, 808–822. (13)

Cohen, J. D., Noll, D. C., & Schneider, W. (1993). Functional magnetic resonance imaging: Overview and methods for psychological research. *Behavior Research Methods, Instruments, & Computers, 25*, 101–113. (3)

Cohen, N. J., & Squire, L. R. (1980). Preserved learning and retention of pattern-analyzing skill in amnesia: Dissociation of knowing how and knowing that. *Science, 210,* 207–211. (7)

Cohen, S., Doyle, W. J., Turner, R., Alper, C. M., & Skoner, D. P. (2003). Sociability and susceptibility to the common cold. *Psychological Science, 14,* 389–395. (12)

Cohen, S., Frank, E., Doyle, W. J., Skoner, D. P., Rabin, B. S., & Swaltney, J. M., Jr. (1998). Types of stressors that increase susceptibility to the common cold in healthy adults. *Health Psychology, 17,* 214–223. (12)

Cohen, S., Lichtenstein, E., Prochaska, J. O., Rossi, J. S., Gritz, E. R., Carr, C. R., et al. (1989). Debunking myths about self-quitting: Evidence from 10 prospective studies of persons who attempt to quit smoking by themselves. *American Psychologist, 44,* 1355–1365. (16)

Coie, J. D., & Dodge, K. (1983). Continuities and change in children's social status: A five-year longitudinal study. *Merrill-Palmer Quarterly, 29,* 261–282. (5)

Colantuoni, C., Rada, P., McCarthy, J., Patten, C., Avena, N. M., Chadeayne, A., et al. (2002). Evidence that intermittent, excessive sugar intake causes endogenous opioid dependence. *Obesity Research, 10,* 478–488. (11)

Colantuoni, C., Schwenker, J., McCarthy, J., Rada, P., Ladenheim, B., Cadet, J. L., et al. (2001). Excessive sugar intake alters binding to dopamine and mu-opioid receptors in the brain. *NeuroReport, 12,* 3549–3552. (11)

Colcombe, S., & Kramer, A. F. (2003). Fitness effects on the cognitive function of older adults: A meta-analytic study. *Psychological Science, 14,* 125–130. (5)

Collins, A. M., & Loftus, E. F. (1975). A spreading-activation theory of semantic processing. *Psychological Review, 82,* 407–428. (8)

Collins, A. M., & Quillian, M. R. (1969). Retrieval time from semantic memory. *Journal of Verbal Learning and Verbal Behavior, 8,* 240–247. (8)

Collins, A. M., & Quillian, M. R. (1970). Does category size affect categorization time? *Journal of Verbal Learning and Verbal Behavior, 9,* 432–438. (8)

Collins, R. C. (2005). Sex on television and its impact on American youth: Background and results from the RAND television and adolescent sexuality study. *Child and Adolescent Psychiatric Clinics of North America, 14,* 371–385. (2)

Collins, W. A., Maccoby, E. E., Steinberg, L., Hetherington, E. M., & Bornstein, M. H. (2000). Contemporary research on parenting: The case for nature and nurture. *American Psychologist, 55,* 218–232. (5)

Colom, R., & García-López, O. (2003). Secular gains in fluid intelligence: Evidence from the Culture-Fair Intelligence Test. *Journal of Biosocial Science, 35,* 33–39. (9)

Colom, R., Juan-Espinosa, M., Abad, F., & Garciá, L. F. (2000). Negligible sex differences in general intelligence. *Intelligence, 28,* 57–68. (9)

Comings, D. E., & Amromin, G. D. (1974). Autosomal dominant insensitivity to pain with hyperplastic myelinopathy and autosomal dominant indifference to pain. *Neurology, 24,* 838–848. (4)

Conners, C. K., & Schulte, A. C. (2002). Learning disorders. In K. L. Davis, D. Charney, J. T. Coyle, & C. Nemeroff (Eds.), *Neuropsychopharmacology* (pp. 597–612). Philadelphia: Lippincott, Williams, & Wilkins. (9)

Connine, C. M., Blasko, D. G., & Hall, M. (1991). Effects of subsequent sentence context in auditory word recognition: Temporal and linguistic constraints. *Journal of Memory and Language, 30,* 234–250. (8)

Connor, T. J., & Leonard, B. E. (1998). Depression, stress and immunological activation: The role of cytokines in depressive disorders. *Life Sciences, 62,* 583–606. (12)

Constantinides, P. (1977). Ill at ease and sick at heart: Symbolic behavior in a Sudanese healing cult. In I. Wilson (Ed.), *Symbols and sentiments* (pp. 61–84). New York: Academic Press. (15)

Consumer Reports. (1995, November). Mental health: Does therapy help? *Consumer Reports,* pp. 734–739. (15)

Contrada, R. J., Ashmore, R. D., Gary, M. L., Coups, E., Egeth, J. D., Sewell, A., et al. (2000). Ethnicity-related sources of stress and their effects on well-being. *Current Directions in Psychological Science, 9,* 136–139. (12)

Coplan, J. D., Goetz, R., Klein, D. F., Papp, L. A., Fyer, A. J., Leibowitz, M. R., et al. (1998). Plasma cortisol concentrations preceding lactate-induced panic. *Archives of General Psychiatry, 55,* 130–136. (16)

Corkin, S. (1984). Lasting consequences of bilateral medial temporal lobectomy: Clinical course and experimental findings in H. M. *Seminars in Neurology, 4,* 249–259. (7)

Corkin, S. (2002). What's new with the amnesic patient H. M.? *Nature Reviews Neuroscience, 3,* 153–159. (7)

Cosmelli, D., David, O., Lachaux, J.-P., Martinerie, J., Garnero, L., Renault, B., et al. (2004). Waves of consciousness: Ongoing cortical patterns during binocular rivalry. *NeuroImage, 23,* 128–140. (10)

Cosmides, L. (1989). The logic of social exchange: Has natural selection shaped how humans reason? Studies with the Wason selection task. *Cognition, 31,* 187–276. (8)

Costa, P. T., Jr., McCrae, R. R., & Dye, D. A. (1991). Facet scales for agreeableness and conscientiousness: A revision of the NEO personality inventory. *Personality and Individual Differences, 12,* 887–898. (14)

Cotter, D., Mackay, D., Landau, S., Kerwin, R., & Everall, I. (2001). Reduced glial cell density and neuronal size in the anterior cingulate cortex in major depressive disorder. *Archives of General Psychiatry, 58,* 545–553. (16)

Coupland, N. J. (2001). Social phobia: Etiology, neurobiology, and treatment. *Journal of Clinical Psychiatry, 62*(Suppl. 1), 25–35. (16)

Courage, M. L., & Howe, M. L. (2002). From infant to child: The dynamics of cognitive change in the second year of life. *Psychological Bulletin, 128,* 250–277. (5)

Cowey, A. (2004). The 30th Sir Frederick Bartlett lecture: Fact, artefact, and myth about blindsight. *Quarterly Journal of Experimental Biology, 57A,* 577–609. (10)

Cox, B. J., McWilliams, L. A., Clara, I. P., & Stein, M. B. (2003). The structure of feared situations in a nationally representative sample. *Journal of Anxiety Disorders, 17,* 89–101. (16)

Cox, W. M., Fadardi, J. S., & Pothos, E. M. (2006). The addiction-Stroop test: Theoretical considerations and procedural recommendations. *Psychological Bulletin, 132,* 443–476. (14)

Craig, A. D., Bushnell, M. C., Zhang, E. T., & Blomqvist, A. (1994). A thalamic nucleus specific for pain and temperature sensation. *Nature, 372,* 770–773. (4)

Craig, S. B., & Gustafson, S. B. (1998). Perceived leader integrity scale: An instrument for assessing employee perceptions of leader integrity. *Leadership Quarterly, 9,* 127–145. (11)

Craik, F. I. M., & Lockhart, R. S. (1972). Levels of processing: A framework for memory research. *Journal of Verbal Learning and Verbal Behavior, 11,* 671–684. (7)

Cramer, P. (1996). *Storytelling, narrative, and the Thematic Apperception Test.* New York: Guilford Press. (14)

Cramer, P. (2003). Personality change in later adulthood is predicted by defense mechanism use in early adulthood. *Journal of Research in Personality, 37,* 76–104. (14)

Crandall, C. S., & Eshleman, A. (2003). A justification-suppression model of the expression and experience of prejudice. *Psychological Bulletin, 129,* 414–446. (14)

Creswell, J. D., Welch, W. T., Taylor, S. E., Sherman, D. K., Gruenwald, T. L., & Mann, T. (2005). Affirmation of personal values buffers neuroendocrine and psychological stress responses. *Psychological Science, 16,* 846–851. (14)

Crews, D. J., & Landers, D. M. (1987). A meta-analytic review of aerobic fitness and reactivity to psychosocial stressors. *Medicine & Science in Sports & Exercise, 19,* S114–S120. (12)

Crews, F. (1996). The verdict on Freud. *Psychological Science, 7,* 63–68. (14)

Crinion, J., Turner, R., Grogan, A., Hanakawa, T., Noppeney, U., Devlin, J. T., et al. (2006). Language control in the bilingual brain. *Science, 312,* 1537–1540. (8)

Critchley, H. D., Mathias, C. J., & Dolan, R. J. (2001). Neuroanatomical basis for first- and second-order representations of bodily states. *Nature Neuroscience, 4,* 207–212. (12)

Crocker, J., & Park, L. E. (2004). The costly pursuit of self-esteem. *Psychological Bulletin, 130,* 392–414. (14)

Crombez, G., Hermans, D., & Adriaensen, H. (2000). The emotional Stroop task and chronic pain: What is threatening for chronic pain sufferers? *European Journal of Pain* (London), *4,* 37–44. (14)

Crosby, F. J., Iyer, A., Clayton, S., & Downing, R. A. (2003). Affirmative action: Psychological data and the policy debates. *American Psychologist, 58,* 93–115. (13)

Cross, C. K., & Hirschfeld, R. M. A. (1986). Psychosocial factors and suicidal behavior. *Annals of the New York Academy of Sciences, 487,* 77–89. (16)

Crowe, R. R., Goedken, R., Samuelson, S., Wilson, R., Nelson, J., & Noyes, R., Jr. (2001). Genomewide survey of panic disorder. *American Journal of Medical Genetics, 105,* 105–109. (16)

Crowley, K., Callanen, M. A., Tenenbaum, H. R., & Allen, E. (2001). Parents explain more often to boys than to girls during shared scientific thinking. *Psychological Science, 12,* 258–261. (5)

Croyle, R. T., & Cooper, J. (1983). Dissonance arousal: Physiological evidence. *Journal of Personality and Social Psychology, 45,* 782–791. (13)

Crucian, G. P., Hughes, J. D., Barrett, A. M., Williamson, D. J. G., Bauer, R. M., Bowers, D., et al. (2000). Emotional and physiological responses to false feedback. *Cortex, 36,* 623–647. (12)

Crystal, S. R., Bowen, D. J., & Berstein, I. L. (1999). Morning sickness and salt intake, food cravings, and food aversions. *Physiology & Behavior, 67,* 181–187. (6)

Csikszentmihalyi, M. (1999). If we are so rich, why aren't we happy? *American Psychologist, 54,* 821–827. (12)

Culbertson, F. M. (1997). Depression and gender. *American Psychologist, 52,* 25–31. (16)

Cummings, N. A. (1979). Turning bread into stones: Our modern antimiracle. *American Psychologist, 34,* 1119–1129. (16)

Cunningham, E. J. A., & Russell, A. F. (2000). Egg investment is influenced by male attractiveness in the mallard. *Nature, 404,* 74–77. (13)

Cunningham, W. A., Preacher, K. J., & Banaji, M. R. (2001). Implicit attitude measures: Consistency, stability, and convergent validity. *Psychological Science, 12,* 163–170. (13)

Cutler, A., Demuth, K., & McQueen, J. M. (2002). Universality versus language-specificity in listening to running speech. *Psychological Science, 13,* 258–262. (8)

Cyranowski, J. M., Frank, E., Young, E., & Shear, K. (2000). Adolescent onset of the gender difference in lifetime rates of major depression. *Archives of General Psychiatry, 57,* 21–27. (16)

Czeisler, C. A., Johnson, M. P., Duffy, J. F., Brown, E. N., Ronda, J. M., & Kronauer, R. E. (1990). Exposure to bright light and darkness to treat physiologic maladaptation to night work. *New England Journal of Medicine, 322,* 1353–1359. (10)

Czeisler, C. A., Moore-Ede, M. C., & Coleman, R. M. (1982). Rotating shift work schedules that disrupt sleep are improved by applying circadian principles. *Science, 217,* 460–463. (10)

Dackis, C. A., Pottash, A. L. C., Annitto, W., & Gold, M. S. (1982). Persistence of urinary marijuana levels after supervised abstinence. *American Journal of Psychiatry, 139,* 1196–1198. (3)

Dadds, M. R., Bovbjerg, D. H., Redd, W. H., & Cutmore, T. R. H. (1997). Imagery in human classical conditioning. *Psychological Bulletin, 122,* 89–103. (6)

Dahlen, E. R., & Deffenbacher, J. L. (2001). Anger management. In W. J. Lyddon & J. V. Jones, Jr. (Eds.), *Empirically supported cognitive therapies* (pp. 163–181). New York: Springer. (12)

Daley, T. C., Whaley, S. E., Sigman, M. D., Espinosa, M. P., & Neumann, C. (2003). IQ on the rise: The Flynn effect in rural Kenyan children. *Psychological Science, 14,* 215–219. (9)

Dallenbach, K. M. (1951). A puzzle picture with a new principle of concealment. *American Journal of Psychology, 64,* 431–433. (4)

Dalman, C., Allebeck, P., Cullberg, J., Grunewald, C., & Köstler, M. (1999). Obstetric complications and the risk of schizophrenia. *Archives of General Psychiatry, 56,* 234–240. (16)

Damaser, E. C., Shor, R. E., & Orne, M. E. (1963). Physiological effects during hypnotically requested emotions. *Psychosomatic Medicine, 25,* 334–343. (10)

Damasio, A. R. (1994). *Descartes' error: Emotion, reason, and the human brain.* New York: G. P. Putnam's Sons. (12)

Damasio, A. (1999). *The feeling of what happens.* New York: Harcourt Brace. (12)

Damasio, H., Grabowski, T., Frank, R., Galaburda, A. M., & Damasio, A. R. (1994). The return of Phineas Gage: The skull of a famous patient yields clues about the brain. *Science, 264,* 1102–1105. (12)

Damron-Rodriguez, J. (1991). Commentary: Multicultural aspects of aging in the U.S.: Implications for health and human services. *Journal of Cross-Cultural Gerontology, 6,* 135–143. (5)

Daniel, M. H. (1997). Intelligence testing: Status and trends. *American Psychologist, 52,* 1038–1045. (9)

Dar, R., Rish, S., Hermish, H., Taub, M., & Fux, M. (2000). Realism of confidence in obsessive-compulsive checkers. *Journal of Abnormal Psychology, 109,* 673–678. (16)

Darst, C. R., & Cummings, M. E. (2006). Predator learning favours mimicry of a less-toxic model in poison frogs. *Nature, 440,* 208–211. (6)

Darwin, C. (1859). *On the origin of species by means of natural selection.* New York: D. Appleton. (1)

Darwin, C. (1871). *The descent of man.* New York: D. Appleton. (1)

Darwin, C. (1965). *The expression of emotions in man and animals.* Chicago: University of Chicago Press. (Original work published 1872) (12)

Das, J. P. (2002). A better look at intelligence. *Current Directions in Psychological Science, 11,* 28–33. (9)

Dasgupta, N., McGhee, D. E., Greenwald, A. G., & Banaji, M. R. (2000). Automatic preference for White Americans: Eliminating the familiarity explanation. *Journal of Experimental Social Psychology, 36,* 316–328. (13)

Davenport, D., & Foley, J. M. (1979). Fringe benefits of cataract surgery. *Science, 204,* 454–457. (4)

Davenport, J. L., & Potter, M. C. (2004). Scene consistency in object and background perception. *Psychological Science, 15,* 559–564. (8)

David, C. F., & Kistner, J. A. (2000). Do positive self-perceptions have a "dark side"? Examination of the link between perceptual bias and aggression. *Journal of Abnormal Child Psychology, 28,* 327–337. (12)

David, D., Brown, R., Pojoga, C., & David, A. (2000). Impact of posthypnotic amnesia and directed forgetting on implicit and explicit memory: New insights from a modified process dissociation procedure. *International Journal of Clinical and Experimental Hypnosis, 48,* 267–289. (10)

Davidson, D., Jergovic, D., Imami, Z., & Theodos, V. (1997). Monolingual and bilingual children's use of the mutual exclusivity constraint. *Journal of Child Language, 24,* 3–24. (8)

Davidson, R. J., Putnam, K. M., & Larson, C. L. (2000). Dysfunction in the neural circuitry of emotion regulation—A possible prelude to violence. *Science, 289,* 591–594. (12)

Davies, G., Welham, J., Chant, D., Torrey, E. F., & McGrath, J. (2003). A systematic review and meta-analysis of Northern Hemisphere season of birth studies in schizophrenia. *Schizophrenia Bulletin, 29,* 587–593. (16)

Davis, J. M., Chen, N., & Glick, I. D. (2003). A meta-analysis of the efficacy of second-generation antipsychotics. *Archives of General Psychiatry, 60,* 553–564. (16)

Davis, K. L., Stewart, D. G., Friedman, J. I., Buchsbaum, M., Harvey, P. D., Hof, P. R., et al. (2003). White matter changes in schizophrenia. *Archives of General Psychiatry, 60,* 443–456. (16)

Daw, J. (2002, October). Is PMDD real? *Monitor on Psychology, 33*(9), 58–60. (15)

Dawes, R. M. (1994). *House of cards: Psychology and psychotherapy.* New York: Free Press. (14, 15)

Dawson, D., & Reid, K. (1997). Fatigue, alcohol, and performance impairment. *Nature, 388,* 235. (16)

Day, R. H. (1972). Visual spatial illusions: A general explanation. *Science, 175,* 1335–1340. (4)

Day, S. (2005). Some demographic and sociocultural aspects of synesthesia. In L. C. Robertson & N. Sagiv (Eds.), *Synesthesis* (pp. 11–33). Oxford, England: Oxford University Press. (4)

Day, W. F., Jr., & Moore, J. (1995). On certain relations between contemporary philosophy and radical behaviorism. In J. T. Todd & E. K. Morris (Eds.), *Modern perspectives on B. F. Skinner and contemporary behaviorism* (pp. 75–84). Westport, CT: Greenwood Press. (6)

de Castro, J. M. (2000). Eating behavior: Lessons from the real world of humans. *Nutrition, 16,* 800–813. (1, 11)

De Corte, E. (2003). Transfer as the productive use of acquired knowledge, skills, and motivation. *Current Directions in Psychological Science, 12,* 142–146. (8)

de Groot, A. D. (1966). Perception and memory versus thought: Some old ideas and recent findings. In B. Kleinmuntz (Ed.), *Problem solving* (pp. 19–50). New York: Wiley. (8)

de Quervain, D. J.-F., & Papassotiropoulos, A. (2006). Identification of a genetic cluster influencing memory performance and hippocampal activity in humans. *Proceedings of the National Academy of Sciences, USA, 103,* 4270–4274. (9)

de Waal, F. B. M. (2000). Primates—A natural heritage of conflict resolution. *Science, 289,* 586–590. (12)

de Waal, F. B. M. (2002). Evolutionary psychology: The wheat and the chaff. *Current Directions in Psychological Science, 11,* 187–191. (1, 5)

de Wit, H., Crean, J., & Richards, J. B. (2000). Effects of *d*-amphetamine and ethanol on a measure of behavioral inhibition in humans. *Behavioral Neuroscience, 114,* 830–837. (8)

Deacon, S., & Arendt, J. (1996). Adapting to phase shifts: II. Effects of melatonin and conflicting light treatment. *Physiology & Behavior, 59,* 675–682. (10)

Deacon, T. W. (1997). *The symbolic species.* New York: Norton. (8)

Dean, K. E., & Malamuth, N. M. (1997). Characteristics of men who aggress sexually and of men who imagine aggressing: Risk and moderating variables. *Journal of Personality and Social Psychology, 72,* 449–455. (12)

Deary, I. J. (2002). *g* and cognitive elements of information processing: An agnostic view. In R. J. Sternberg & E. L. Grigorenko (Eds.), *The general intelligence factor: How general is it?* (pp. 151–181). Mahwah, NJ: Erlbaum. (9)

Deary, I. J., & Der, G. (2005). Reaction time explains IQ's association with death. *Psychological Science, 16,* 64–69. (9)

Deary, I. J., Strand, S., Smith, P., & Fernandes, C. (2007). Intelligence and educational achievement. *Intelligence, 35,* 13–21. (9)

Deary, I. J., Whalley, L. J., Lemmon, H., Crawford, J. R., & Starr, J. M. (2000). The stability of individual differences in mental ability from childhood to old age: Follow-up of the 1932 Scottish mental survey. *Intelligence, 28,* 49–55. (9)

DeCasper, A. J., & Fifer, W. P. (1980). Of human bonding: Newborns prefer their mothers' voices. *Science, 208,* 1174–1177. (5)

Deci, E. L. (1971). Effects of externally mediated rewards on intrinsic motivation. *Journal of Personality and Social Psychology, 18,* 105–115. (11)

Deese, J. (1959). On the prediction of occurrence of particular verbal intrusions in immediate recall. *Journal of Experimental Psychology, 58,* 17–22. (7)

DeFelipe, C., Herrero, J. F., O'Brien, J. A., Palmer, J. A., Doyle, C. A., Smith, A. J. H., et al. (1998). Altered nociception, analgesia and aggression in mice lacking the receptor for substance P. *Nature, 392,* 394–397. (4)

Degenhardt, L., Hall, W., & Lynskey, M. (2003). Testing hypotheses about the relationship between cannabis use and psychosis. *Drug and Alcohol Dependence, 71,* 37–48. (1)

Dehaene, S., & Changeux, J.-P. (2004). Neural mechanisms for access to consciousness. In M. S. Gazzaniga (Ed.), *The cognitive neurosciences* (3rd ed., pp. 1145–1157). Cambridge, MA: MIT Press. (10)

Dehaene, S., Naccache, L., Cohen, L., LeBihan, D., Mangin, J.-F., Poline, J. B., et al. (2001). Cerebral mechanisms of word masking and unconscious repetition priming. *Nature Neuroscience, 4,* 752–758. (10)

DeLoache, J. S. (1989). The development of representation in young children. *Advances in Child Development and Behavior, 22,* 1–39. (5)

DeLoache, J. S., Miller, K. F., & Rosengren, K. S. (1997). The credible shrinking room: Very young children's performance with symbolic and nonsymbolic relations. *Psychological Science, 8,* 308–313. (5)

Dement, W. (1960). The effect of dream deprivation. *Science, 131,* 1705–1707. (10)

Dement, W. C. (1972). *Some must watch while some must sleep.* Stanford, CA: Stanford Alumni Association. (10)

Dement, W., & Kleitman, N. (1957a). Cyclic variations in EEG during sleep and their relation to eye movements, body motility, and dreaming. *Electroencephalography and Clinical Neurophysiology, 9,* 673–690. (10)

Dement, W., & Kleitman, N. (1957b). The relation of eye movements during sleep to dream activity: An objective method for the study of dreaming. *Journal of Experimental Psychology, 53,* 339–346. (10)

Dement, W., & Wolpert, E. A. (1958). The relation of eye movements, body motility, and external stimuli to dream content. *Journal of Experimental Psychology, 55,* 543–553. (10)

DeNeve, K. M. (1999). Happy as an extraverted clam? The role of personality for subjective well-being. *Current Directions in Psychological Science, 8,* 141–144. (12)

DeNeve, K. M., & Cooper, H. (1998). The happy personality: A meta-analysis of 137 personality traits and subjective well-being. *Psychological Bulletin, 124,* 197–229. (12)

Dennett, D. C. (1991). *Consciousness explained.* Boston: Little, Brown. (1)

Dennett, D. C. (2003). *Freedom evolves.* New York: Viking Press. (1)

Dennis, P. M. (1998). Chills and thrills: Does radio harm our children? The controversy over program violence during the age of radio. *Journal of the History of the Behavioral Sciences, 34,* 33–50. (2)

Denrell, J. (2005). Why most people disapprove of me: Experience sampling in impression formation. *Psychological Review, 112,* 951–978. (13)

DePaolo, B. M., Lindsay, J. J., Malone, B. E., Muhlenbruck, L., Charlton, K., & Cooper, H. (2003). Cues to deception. *Psychological Bulletin, 129,* 74–118. (12)

deQuervain, D. J.-F., Roozendaal, B., Nitsch, R. M., McGaugh, J. L., & Hock, C. (2000). Acute cortisone administration impairs retrieval of long-term declarative memory in humans. *Nature Neuroscience, 3,* 313–314. (12)

Deshmukh, A., Rosenbloom, M. J., Pfefferbaum, A., & Sullivan, E. V. (2002). Clinical signs of cerebellar dysfunction in schizophrenia, alcoholism, and their comorbidity. *Schizophrenia Research, 57,* 281–291. (16)

DeSteno, D., Petty, R. E., Rucker, D. D., Wegener, D. T., & Braverman, J. (2004). Discrete emotions and persuasion: The role of emotion-induced expectancies. *Journal of Personality and Social Psychology, 86,* 43–56. (13)

Detterman, D. K. (1979). Detterman's laws of individual differences research. In R. J. Sternberg & D. K. Detterman (Eds.), *Human intelligence* (pp. 165–175). Norwood, NJ: Ablex. (9)

Deutsch, D., Henthorn, T., & Dolson, M. (2004). Absolute pitch, speech and tone language: Some experiments and a proposed framework. *Music Perception, 21,* 339–356. (4)

Deutsch, J. A., & Gonzalez, M. F. (1980). Gastric nutrient content signals satiety. *Be-*

havioral and Neural Biology, 30, 113–116. (11)

DeValois, R. L., & Jacobs, G. H. (1968). Primate color vision. *Science, 162,* 533–540. (4)

Devane, W. A., Hanuš, L., Breuer, A., Pertwee, R. G., Stevenson, L. A., Griffin, G., et al. (1992). Isolation and structure of a brain constituent that binds to the cannabinoid receptor. *Science, 258,* 1946–1949. (3)

Devlin, B., Daniels, M., & Roeder, K. (1997). The heritability of IQ. *Nature, 388,* 468–471. (9)

Devor, E. J., Abell, C. W., Hoffman, P. L., Tabakoff, B., & Cloninger, C. R. (1994). Platelet MAO activity in Type I and Type II alcoholism. *Annals of the New York Academy of Sciences, 708,* 119–128. (16)

Dewhurst, S. A., & Robinson, C. A. (2004). False memories in children. *Psychological Science, 15,* 782–786. (7)

Dewsbury, D. A. (1998). Celebrating E. L. Thorndike a century after *Animal Intelligence. American Psychologist, 53,* 1121–1124. (6)

Dewsbury, D. A. (2000a). Introduction: Snapshots of psychology circa 1900. *American Psychologist, 55,* 255–259. (1)

Dewsbury, D. A. (2000b). Issues in comparative psychology at the dawn of the 20th century. *American Psychologist, 55,* 750–753. (6)

Diamond, A., & Kirkham, N. (2005). Not quite as grown up as we like to think. *Psychological Science, 16,* 291–297. (5)

Diamond, L. M. (2003a). Was it a phase? Young women's relinquishment of lesbian/bisexual identities over a 5-year period. *Journal of Personality and Social Psychology, 84,* 352–364. (11)

Diamond, L. M. (2003b). What does sexual orientation orient? A biobehavioral model distinguishing romantic love and sexual desire. *Psychological Review, 110,* 173–192. (11)

Dick, F., Bates, E., Wulfeck, B., Utman, J. A., Dronkers, N., & Gernsbacher, M. A. (2001). Language deficits, localization, and grammar: Evidence for a distributive model of language breakdown in aphasic patients and neurologically intact individuals. *Psychological Review, 108,* 759–788. (3)

Dickens, W. T., & Flynn, J. R. (2001). Heritability estimates versus large environmental effects: The IQ paradox resolved. *Psychological Review, 108,* 346–369. (5, 9)

Dickens, W. T., & Flynn, J. R. (2006). Black Americans reduce the racial IQ gap. *Psychological Science, 17,* 913–920. (9)

Dickson, N., Paul, C., & Herbison, P. (2003). Same-sex attraction in a birth cohort: Prevalence and persistence in early adulthood. *Social Science & Medicine, 56,* 1607–1615. (11)

Diener, E. (2000). Subjective well-being. *American Psychologist, 55,* 34–43. (12)

Diener, E., & Diener, C. (1996). Most people are happy. *Psychological Science, 7,* 181–185. (12)

Diener, E., Lucas, R. E., & Scollon, C. N. (2006). Beyond the hedonic treadmill. *American Psychologist, 61,* 305–314. (12)

Diener, E., & Seligman, M. E. P. (2002). Very happy people. *Psychological Science, 13,* 81–84. (12)

Diener, E., & Seligman, M. E. P. (2004). Beyond money: Toward an economy of well-being. *Psychological Science in the Public Interest, 5,* 1–31. (12)

Diener, E., Suh, E. M., Lucas, R. E., & Smith, H. L. (1999). Subjective well-being: Three decades of progress. *Psychological Bulletin, 125,* 276–302. (12)

Dijksterhuis, A., & Bargh, J. A. (2001). The perception-behavior expressway: Automatic effects of social perception on social behavior. *Advances in Experimental Social Psychology, 33,* 1–40. (6)

Dijksterhuis, A., & Nordgren, L. F. (2006). A theory of unconscious thought. *Perspectives on Psychological Science, 1,* 95–109. (8)

DiLalla, D. L., Carey, G., Gottesman, I. I., & Bouchard, T. J., Jr. (1996). Heritability of MMPI personality indicators of psychopathology in twins reared apart. *Journal of Abnormal Psychology, 105,* 491–499. (5)

Dillard, J. P., & Anderson, J. W. (2004). The role of fear in persuasion. *Psychology & Marketing, 21,* 909–926. (13)

Dimberg, U., Thunberg, M., & Elmehed, K. (2000). Unconscious facial reactions to emotional facial expressions. *Psychological Science, 11,* 86–89. (4)

Dittmar, H., Halliwell, E., & Ive, S. (2006). Does Barbie make girls want to be thin? The effect of experimental exposure to images of dolls on the body image of 5- to 8-year-old girls. *Developmental Psychology, 42,* 283–292. (11)

Dixon, M. R., Benedict, H, & Larson, T. (2001). Functional analysis and treatment of inappropriate verbal behavior. *Journal of Applied Behavior Analysis, 34,* 363. (6)

Djordjevic, J., Zatorre, R. J., Petrides, M., & Jones-Gotman, M. (2004). The mind's nose: Effects of odor and visual imagery on odor detection. *Psychological Science, 15,* 143–148. (4)

Dobelle, W. H. (2000). Artificial vision for the blind by connecting a television camera to the visual cortex. *ASAIO Journal, 46,* 3–9. (4)

Dobrzecka, C., Szwejkowska, G., & Konorski, J. (1966). Qualitative versus directional cues in two forms of differentiation. *Science, 153,* 87–89. (6)

Doi, T. (1981). *The anatomy of dependence.* Tokyo: Kodansha International. (12)

Dole, V. P. (1980). Addictive behavior. *Scientific American, 243*(6), 138–154. (16)

Dollard, J., Miller, N. E., Doob, L. W., Mowrer, O. H., & Sears, R. R. (1939). *Frustration and aggression.* New Haven, CT: Yale University Press. (12)

Domhoff, G. W. (1996). *Finding meaning in dreams: A quantitative approach.* New York: Plenum Press. (10)

Domhoff, G. W. (1999). Drawing theoretical implications from descriptive empirical findings on dream content. *Dreaming, 9,* 201–210. (10)

Domhoff, G. W. (2001). A new neurocognitive theory of dreams. *Dreaming, 11,* 13–33. (10)

Domhoff, G. W. (2003). *The scientific study of dreams.* Washington, DC: American Psychological Association. (10)

Donnellan, M. B., Trzesniewski, K. H., Robins, R. W., Moffitt, T. E., & Caspi, A. (2005). Low self-esteem is related to aggression, antisocial behavior, and delinquency. *Psychological Science, 16,* 328–335. (12)

Donnerstein, E., & Malamuth, N. (1997). Pornography: Its consequences on the observer. In L. B. Schlesinger & E. Revitch (Eds.), *Sexual dynamics of antisocial behavior* (2nd ed., pp. 30–49). Springfield, IL: Charles C Thomas. (12)

Dovidio, J. F., & Gaertner, S. L. (1999). Reducing prejudice: Combating intergroup biases. *Current Directions in Psychological Science, 8,* 101–105. (13)

Dovidio, J. F., & Gaertner, S. L. (2000). Aversive racism and selection decisions: 1989 and 1999. *Psychological Science, 11,* 315–319. (13)

Dreger, A. D. (1998). *Hermaphrodites and the medical invention of sex.* Cambridge, MA: Harvard University Press. (11)

Drewnowski, A., Henderson, S. A., Shore, A. B., & Barratt-Fornell, A. (1998). Sensory responses to 6-n-propylthiouracil (PROP) or sucrose solutions and food preferences in young women. *Annals of the New York Academy of Sciences, 855,* 797–801. (1)

Driver, J., & Frith, C. (2000). Shifting baselines in attention research. *Nature Reviews Neuroscience, 1,* 147–148. (8)

Driver, J., & Mattingley, J. B. (1998). Parietal neglect and visual awareness. *Nature Neuroscience, 1,* 17–22. (10)

Duckworth, A. L., & Seligman, M. E. P. (2005). Self-discipline outdoes IQ in predicting academic performance of adolescents. *Psychological Science, 16,* 939–944. (9)

Ducommun, C. Y., Michel, C. M., Clarke, S., Adriani, M., Seeck, M., Landis, T., et al. (2004). Cortical motion deafness. *Neuron, 43,* 765–777. (3)

Duke, M., & Nowicki, S., Jr. (1979). *Abnormal psychology: Perspectives on being different.* Monterey, CA: Brooks/Cole. (16)

Duncan, J., Seitz, R. J., Kolodny, J., Bor, D., Herzog, H., Ahmed, A., et al. (2000). A neural basis for general intelligence. *Science, 289,* 457–460. (9)

Dunning, D., Heath, C., & Suls, J. M. (2005). Flawed self-assessment: Implications for health, education, and the workplace. *Psychological Science in the Public Interest, 5*, 69–106. (11)

Dunning, D., Johnson, K., Ehrlinger, J., & Kruger, J. (2003). Why people fail to recognize their own incompetence. *Current Directions in Psychological Science, 12*, 83–87. (7)

Durgin, F. H. (2000). The reverse Stroop effect. *Psychonomic Bulletin & Review, 7*, 121–125. (8)

Dywan, J., & Bowers, K. (1983). The use of hypnosis to enhance recall. *Science, 22*, 184–185. (10)

Eagly, A. H., & Crowley, M. (1986). Gender and helping behavior: A meta-analytic review of the social psychological literature. *Psychological Bulletin, 100*, 283–308. (5)

Eagly, A. H., Johannesen-Schmidt, M. C., & van Engen, M. L. (2003). Transformational, transactional, and laissez-faire leadership styles: A meta-analysis comparing women and men. *Psychological Bulletin, 129*, 569–591. (5)

Eagly, A. H., Kulesa, P., Chen, S., & Chaiken, S. (2001). Do attitudes affect memory? Tests of the congeniality hypothesis. *Current Directions in Psychological Science, 10*, 5–9. (13)

Eagly, A. H., & Warren, R. (1976). Intelligence, comprehension, and opinion change. *Journal of Personality, 44*, 226–242. (13)

Eagly, A. H., & Wood, W. (1999). The origins of sex differences in human behavior. *American Psychologist, 54*, 408–423. (13)

Eaker, E. D., Sullivan, L. M., Kelly-Hayes, M., D'Agostino, R. B., Sr., & Benjamin, E. J. (2004). Anger and hostility predict the development of atrial fibrillation in men in the Framingham Offspring Study. *Circulation, 109*, 1267–1271. (12)

Earnest, D. J., Liang, F.-Q., Ratcliff, M., & Cassone, V. M. (1999). Immortal time: Circadian clock properties of rat suprachiasmatic cell lines. *Science, 283*, 693–695. (10)

Eaton, J. (2001). Management communication: The threat of groupthink. *Corporate Communications, 6*, 183–192. (13)

Eaton, W. W., Anthony, J. C., Gallo, J., Cai, G., Tien, A., Romanoski, A., et al. (1997). Natural history of diagnostic interview schedule/*DSM-IV* major depression. *Archives of General Psychiatry, 54*, 993–999. (16)

Eaves, L. J., Martin, N. G., & Heath, A. C. (1990). Religious affiliation in twins and their parents: Testing a model of cultural inheritance. *Behavior Genetics, 20*, 1–22. (5)

Ebbinghaus, H. (1913). *Memory.* New York: Teachers College Press. (Original work published 1885) (7)

Eberhardt, J. L., Davies, P. G., Purdie-Vaughns, V. J., & Johnson, S. L. (2006). Looking deathworthy. *Psychological Science, 17*, 383–386. (13)

Ebling, R., & Levenson, R. W. (2003). Who are the marital experts? *Journal of Marriage and the Family, 65*, 130–142. (13)

Edelman, B. (1981). Binge eating in normal weight and overweight individuals. *Psychological Reports, 49*, 739–746. (11)

Educational Testing Service. (1994). *GRE 1994–95 guide.* Princeton, NJ: Author. (9)

Edwards, J., Jackson, H. J., & Pattison, P. E. (2002). Emotion recognition via facial expression and affective prosody in schizophrenia: A methodological review. *Clinical Psychology Review, 22*, 789–832. (12)

Edwards, K. (1998). The face of time: Temporal cues in facial expressions of emotion. *Psychological Science, 9*, 270–276. (12)

Eibl-Eibesfeldt, I. (1973). *Der vorprogrammierte Mensch* [The preprogrammed human]. Vienna: Verlag Fritz Molden. (12)

Eibl-Eibesfeldt, I. (1974). *Love and hate.* New York: Schocken Books. (12)

Eich, E. (1995). Searching for mood dependent memory. *Psychological Science, 6*, 67–75. (7)

Eich, E., & Macaulay, D. (2000). Are real moods required to reveal mood-congruent and mood-dependent memory? *Psychological Science, 11*, 244–248. (7)

Eichenbaum, H. (2002). *The cognitive neuroscience of memory.* New York: Oxford University Press. (7)

Eigsti, I.-M., Zayas, V., Mischel, W., Shoda, Y., Ayduk, O., Dadlani, M. B., et al. (2006). Predicting cognitive control from preschool to late adolescence and young adulthood. *Psychological Science, 17*, 478–484. (8)

Eimas, P. D., Siqueland, E. R., Jusczyk, P., & Vigorito, J. (1971). Speech perception in infants. *Science, 171*, 303–306. (5)

Eisenberger, N. I., Lieberman, M. D., & Williams, K. D. (2003). Does rejection hurt? An fMRI study of social exclusion. *Science, 302*, 290–292. (4)

Eisenberger, R., & Cameron, J. (1996). Detrimental effects of reward: Reality or myth? *American Psychologist, 51*, 1153–1166. (11)

Eisler, I., Dare, C., Hodes, M., Russell, G., Dodge, E., & LeGrange, D. (2000). Family therapy for adolescent anorexia nervosa: The results of a controlled comparison of two family interventions. *Journal of Child Psychology and Psychiatry and Allied Disciplines, 41*, 727–736. (15)

Ekman, P. (1992). Facial expressions of emotion: New findings, new questions. *Psychological Science, 3*, 34–38. (12)

Ekman, P. (1994). Strong evidence for universals in facial expressions: A reply to Russell's mistaken critique. *Psychological Science, 3*, 34–38. (12)

Ekman, P. (2001). *Telling lies* (3rd ed.). New York: Norton. (12)

Ekman, P., & Davidson, R. J. (1993). Voluntary smiling changes regional brain activity. *Psychological Science, 4*, 342–345. (12)

Ekman, P., & Friesen, W. V. (1984). *Unmasking the face* (2nd ed.). Palo Alto, CA: Consulting Psychologists Press. (12)

El-Islam, M. F. (1982). Rehabilitation of schizophrenics by the extended family. *Acta Psychiatrica Scandinavica, 65*, 112–119. (16)

El-Sheikh, M., Buckhalt, J. A., Mize, J., & Acebo, C. (2006). Marital conflict and disruption of children's sleep. *Child Development, 77*, 31–43. (5)

Eldridge, L. L., Engel, S. A., Zeineh, M. M., Bookheimer, S. Y., & Knowlton, B. J. (2005). A dissociation of encoding and retrieval processes in the human hippocampus. *Journal of Neuroscience, 25*, 3280–3286. (7)

Elia, J., Ambrosini, P. J., & Rapoport, J. L. (1999). Treatment of attention-deficit hyperactivity disorder. *New England Journal of Medicine, 340*, 780–788. (8)

Elicker, J., Englund, M., & Sroufe, L. A. (1992). Predicting peer competence and peer relationships in childhood from early parent-child relationships. In R. D. Parke & G. W. Ladd (Eds.), *Family-peer relationships* (pp. 77–106). Hillsdale, NJ: Erlbaum. (5)

Elkind, D. (1984). *All grown up and no place to go.* Reading, MA: Addison-Wesley. (5)

Elkins, G., Marcus, J., Bates, J., Rajab, M. H., & Cook, T. (2006). Intensive hypnotherapy for smoking cessation: A prospective study. *International Journal of Clinical and Experimental Hypnosis, 54*, 303–315. (10)

Ellenberger, H. F. (1972). The story of "Anna O": A critical review with new data. *Journal of the History of the Behavioral Sciences, 8*, 267–279. (14)

Elliott, C. (1997). Caring about risks: Are severely depressed patients competent to consent to research? *Archives of General Psychiatry, 54*, 113–116. (2)

Elliott, R., Sahakian, B. J., Matthews, K., Bannerjea, A., Rimmer, J., & Robbins, T. W. (1997). Effects of methylphenidate on spatial working memory and planning in healthy young adults. *Psychopharmacology, 131*, 196–206. (8)

Ellis, A. (1987). The impossibility of achieving consistently good mental health. *American Psychologist, 42*, 364–375. (15)

Ellis, A., & Harper, R. A. (1961). *A guide to rational living.* Upper Saddle River, NJ: Prentice Hall. (15)

Ellis, N. C., & Hennelley, R. A. (1980). A bilingual word-length effect: Implications for intelligence testing and the relative ease of mental calculation in Welsh and English. *British Journal of Psychology, 71*, 43–52. (7)

Ellwart, T., Rinck, M., & Becker, E. S. (2006). From fear to love: Individual differences in implicit spider associations. *Emotion, 6,* 18–27. (14)

Else-Quest, N. M., Hyde, J. S., Goldsmith, H. H., & Van Hulle, C. A. (2006). Gender differences in temperament: A meta-analysis. *Psychological Bulletin, 132,* 33–72. (5)

Emery, C. E., Jr. (1997, November/December). UFO survey yields conflicting conclusions. *Skeptical Inquirer, 21,* 9. (2)

Emmons, R. A., & McCullough, M. E. (2003). Counting blessings versus burdens: An experimental investigation of gratitude and subjective well-being in daily life. *Journal of Personality and Social Psychology, 84,* 377–389. (12)

Engel, S. A. (1999). Using neuroimaging to measure mental representations: Finding color-opponent neurons in visual cortex. *Current Directions in Psychological Science, 8,* 23–27. (4)

Engle, R. W., Tuholski, S. W., Laughlin, J. E., & Conway, A. R. A. (1999). Working memory, short-term memory, and general fluid intelligence: A latent-variable approach. *Journal of Experimental Psychology: General, 128,* 309–331. (7)

Engleberg, E., & Sjöberg, L. (2004). Emotional intelligence, affect intensity, and social adjustment. *Personality and Individual Differences, 37,* 533–542. (12)

Enns, J. T., & Rensink, R. A. (1990). Sensitivity to three-dimensional orientation in visual search. *Psychological Science, 1,* 323–326. (8)

Erel, O., & Burman, B. (1995). Interrelatedness of marital relations and parent-child relations: A meta-analytic review. *Psychological Bulletin, 118,* 108–132. (5)

Erev, I., Wallsten, T. S., & Budescu, D. V. (1994). Simultaneous over- and underconfidence: The role of error in judgment processes. *Psychological Review, 101,* 519–527. (8)

Ericsson, K. A., & Charness, N. (1994). Expert performance: Its structure and acquisition. *American Psychologist, 49,* 725–747. (8)

Ericsson, K. A., Chase, W. G., & Faloon, S. (1980). Acquisition of a memory skill. *Science, 208,* 1181–1182. (7)

Ericsson, K. A., Krampe, R. T., & Tesch-Römer, C. (1993). The role of deliberate practice in the acquisition of expert performance. *Psychological Review, 100,* 363–406. (8)

Erikson, E. H. (1963). *Childhood and society* (2nd ed.). New York: Norton. (5)

Eriksson, P. S., Perfilieva, E., Björk-Eriksson, T., Alborn, A.-M., Nordborg, C., Peterson, D. A., et al. (1998). Neurogenesis in the adult human hippocampus. *Nature Medicine, 4,* 1313–1317. (3)

Ernhart, C. B., Sokol, R. J., Martier, S., Moron, P., Nadler, D., Ager, J. W., & et al. (1987). Alcohol teratogenicity in the human: A detailed assessment of specificity, critical period, and threshold. *American Journal of Obstetrics and Gynecology, 156,* 33–39. (5)

Ernst, C., & Angst, J. (1983). *Birth order: Its influence on personality.* New York: Springer-Verlag. (5)

Esquivel, G., Schruers, K., Kuipers, H., & Griez, E. (2002). The effects of acute exercise and high lactate levels on 35% CO_2 challenge in healthy volunteers. *Acta Psychiatrica Scandinavica, 106,* 394–397. (16)

Esterson, A. (1993). *Seductive mirage.* Chicago: Open Court. (10, 14)

Esterson, A. (2001). The mythologizing of psychoanalytic history: Deception and self-deception in Freud's accounts of the seduction theory episode. *History of Psychology, 12,* 329–352. (14)

Etcoff, N. L., Ekman, P., Magee, J. J., & Frank, M. G. (2000). Lie detection and language comprehension. *Nature, 405,* 139. (3)

Evans, G. W., Bullinger, M., & Hygge, S. (1998). Chronic noise exposure and physiological response: A prospective study of children living under environmental stress. *Psychological Science, 9,* 75–77. (12)

Evans, J. S. B. T. (2002). Logic and human reasoning: An assessment of the deduction paradigm. *Psychological Bulletin, 128,* 978–996. (8)

Everson, C. A. (1995). Functional consequences of sustained sleep deprivation in the rat. *Behavioural Brain Research, 69,* 43–54. (10)

Exner, J. E., Jr. (1986). *The Rorschach: A comprehensive system* (2nd ed.). New York: Wiley. (14)

Eysenck, H. J. (1952). The effects of psychotherapy: An evaluation. *Journal of Consulting Psychology, 16,* 319–324. (15)

Eysenck, H. J. (1992). Four ways five factors are not basic. *Personality and Individual Differences, 13,* 667–673. (14)

Faedda, G. L., Tondo, L., Teicher, M. H., Baldessarini, R. J., Gelbard, H. A., & Floris, G. F. (1993). Seasonal mood disorders: patterns of seasonal recurrence in mania and depression. *Archives of General Psychiatry, 50,* 17–23. (16)

Fairburn, C. G., Welch, S. L., Doll, H. A., Davies, B. A., & O'Connor, M. E. (1997). Risk factors for bulimia nervosa. *Archives of General Psychiatry, 54,* 509–517. (11)

Faivre, R., Grégoire, A., Préault, M., Cézilly, F., & Sorci, G. (2003). Immune activation rapidly mirrored in a secondary sexual trait. *Science, 300,* 103. (13)

Fallon, A. E., & Rozin, P. (1985). Sex differences in perceptions of desirable body shape. *Journal of Abnormal Psychology, 94,* 102–105. (11)

Fanous, A. H., van den Oord, E. J., Riley, S. H., Aggen, S. H., Neale, M. C., O'Neill, F. A., et al. (2005). Relationship between a high-risk haplotype in the *DTNBP1* (dysbindin) gene and clinical features of schizophrenia. *American Journal of Psychiatry, 162,* 1824–1832. (16)

Fantz, R. L. (1963). Pattern vision in newborn infants. *Science, 140,* 296–297. (5)

Farah, M. J. (1992). Is an object an object an object? Cognitive and neuropsychological investigations of domain specificity in visual object recognition. *Current Directions in Psychological Science, 1,* 164–169. (4)

Faraone, S. V., & Biederman, J. (1998). Neurobiology of attention-deficit hyperactivity disorder. *Biological Psychiatry, 44,* 951–958. (3)

Farber, S. L. (1981). *Identical twins reared apart: A reanalysis.* New York: Basic Books. (9)

Farmer-Dougan, V. (1998). A disequilibrium analysis of incidental teaching. *Behavior Modification, 22,* 78–95. (6)

Farnè, A., Buxbaum. L. J., Ferraro, M., Frassinetti, F., Whyte, J., Veramonti, T., et al. (2006). Patterns of spontaneous recovery of neglect and associated disorders in acute right brain-damaged patients. *Journal of Neurology, Neurosurgery, and Psychiatry, 75,* 1401–1410. (10)

Farooqi, I. S., Keogh, J. M., Kamath, S., Jones, S., Gibson, W. T., Trussell, R., et al. (2001). Partial leptin deficiency and human adiposity. *Nature, 414,* 34–35. (11)

Fauerbach, J. A., Lawrence, J. W., Haythornthwaite, J. A., & Richter, L. (2002). Coping with the stress of a painful medical procedure. *Behaviour Research and Therapy, 40,* 1003–1015. (12)

Faust, M., Kravetz, S., & Babkoff, H. (1993). Hemispheric specialization or reading habits: Evidence from lexical decision research with Hebrew words and sentences. *Brain and Language, 44,* 254–263. (8)

Fawcett, J. (2001). Treating impulsivity and anxiety in the suicidal patient. *Annals of the New York Academy of Sciences, 932,* 94–102. (16)

Fawzy, F. I., Fawzy, N. W., Arndt, L. A., & Pasnau, R. O. (1995). Critical review of psychosocial interventions in cancer care. *Archives of General Psychiatry, 52,* 100–113. (12)

Fay, R. E., Turner, C. F., Klassen, A. D., & Gagnon, J. H. (1989). Prevalence and patterns of same-gender sexual contact among men. *Science, 243,* 338–348. (11)

Fazel, S., & Grann, M. (2006). The population impact of severe mental illness on violent crime. *American Journal of Psychiatry, 163,* 1397–1403. (15)

Feeney, D. M. (1987). Human rights and animal welfare. *American Psychologist, 42,* 593–599. (2)

Fehr, E., & Fischbacher, U. (2003). The nature of human altruism. *Nature, 425,* 785–791. (13)

Fehr, E., & Gächter, S. (2002). Altruistic punishment in humans. *Nature, 415,* 137–140. (13)

Feighner, J. P., Gardner, E. A., Johnston, J. A., Batey, S. R., Khayrallah, M. A., Ascher, J. A., et al. (1991). Double-blind comparison of buproprion and fluoxetine in depressed outpatients. *Journal of Clinical Psychiatry, 52,* 329–335. (16)

Feinberg, T. E., & Roane, D. M. (2003). Misidentification syndromes. In T. E. Feinberg & M. J. Farah (Eds.), *Behavioral neurology and neuropsychology* (pp. 373–381). New York: McGraw-Hill. (10).

Felitti, V. J., Anda, R. F., Nordenberg, D., Williamson, D. F., Spitz, A. M., Edwards, V., et al. (1998). Relationship of childhood abuse and household dysfunction to many of the leading causes of death in adults. *American Journal of Preventive Medicine, 14,* 245–258. (12)

Fendrich, R., Wessinger, C. M., & Gazzaniga, M. S. (1992). Residual vision in a scotoma: Implications for blindsight. *Science, 258,* 1489–1491. (10)

Fenn, K. M., Nusbaum, H. C., & Margoliash, D. (2003). Consolidation during sleep of perceptual learning of spoken language. *Nature, 425,* 614–616. (10)

Fenton, W. S., Hoch, J. S., Herrell, J. M., Mosher, L., & Dixon, L. (2002). Cost and cost-effectiveness of hospital vs. residential crisis care for patients who have serious mental illness. *Archives of General Psychiatry, 59,* 357–364. (15)

Fenton, W. S., Mosher, L. R., Herrell, J. M., & Blyler, C. R. (1998). Randomized trial of general hospital and residential alternative care for patients with severe and persistent mental illness. *American Journal of Psychiatry, 155,* 516–522. (15)

Ferguson, C. P., & Pigott, T. A. (2000). Anorexia and bulimia nervosa: Neurobiology and pharmacotherapy. *Behavior Therapy, 31,* 237–263. (11)

Fernald, D. (1984). *The Hans legacy: A story of science.* Hillsdale, NJ: Erlbaum. (2)

Fernandez, E., & Turk, D. C. (1992). Sensory and affective components of pain: Separation and synthesis. *Psychological Bulletin, 112,* 205–217. (4)

Fernández-Dols, J. M., & Ruiz-Belda, M. A. (1997). Spontaneous facial behavior during intense emotional episodes: Artistic truth and optical truth. In J. A. Russell & J. M. Fernández-Dols (Eds.), *The psychology of facial expression* (pp. 255–274). Cambridge, England: Cambridge University Press. (12)

Ferreira, F., Bailey, K. G. D., & Ferraro, V. (2002). Good-enough representations in language comprehension. *Current Directions in Psychological Science, 11,* 11–15. (8)

Festinger, L. (1957). *A theory of cognitive dissonance.* Stanford, CA: Stanford University Press. (13)

Festinger, L., & Carlsmith, J. M. (1959). Cognitive consequences of forced compliance.

Journal of Abnormal and Social Psychology, 58, 203–210. (13)

Fichter, M. M., & Quadflieg, N. (1997). Six-year course of bulimia nervosa. *International Journal of Eating Disorders, 22,* 361–384. (11)

Fiedler, K., Schmid, J., & Stahl, T. (2002). What is the current truth about polygraph lie detection? *Basic and Applied Social Psychology, 24,* 313–324. (12)

Fieve, R. R. (1975). *Moodswing.* New York: Morrow. (16)

Finch, J. F., & Cialdini, R. B. (1989). Another indirect tactic of (self-) image imagement: Boosting. *Personality and Social Psychology Bulletin, 15,* 222–232. (13)

Fincham, F. D. (2003). Marital conflict: Correlates, structure, and context. *Current Directions in Psychological Science, 12,* 23–27. (13)

Fine, I., Wade, A. R., Brewer, A. A., May, M. G., Goodman, D. F., Boynton, G. M., et al. (2003). Long-term deprivation affects visual perception and cortex. *Nature Neuroscience, 6,* 915–916. (3)

Fink, B., & Penton-Voak, I. (2002). Evolutionary psychology of facial attractiveness. *Current Directions in Psychological Science, 11,* 154–158. (13)

Fink, M. (2000). Electroshock revisited. *American Scientist, 88,* 162–167. (16)

Fisher, B. S., Daigle, L. E., Cullen, F. T., & Turner, M. G. (2003). Acknowledging sexual victimization as rape: Results from a national-level survey. *Justice Quarterly, 20,* 535–574. (12)

Fisher, S., & Greenberg, R. P. (1977). *The scientific credibility of Freud's theories and therapy.* New York: Basic Books. (14)

Fisher, S. E., Vargha-Khadem, F., Watkins, K. E., Monaco, A. P., & Pembrey, M. E. (1998). Localisation of a gene implicated in a severe speech and language disorder. *Nature Genetics, 18,* 168–170. (8)

Fiske, A. P. (2002). Using individualism and collectivism to compare cultures—A critique of the validity and measurement of the constructs: Comment on Oyserman et al. (2002). *Psychological Bulletin, 128,* 78–88. (13)

Fiske, S. T. (2002). What we know now about bias and intergroup conflict, the problem of the century. *Current Directions in Psychological Science, 11,* 123–128. (13)

Fiske, S. T., Harris, L. T., & Cuddy, A. J. C. (2004). Why ordinary people torture enemy prisoners. *Science, 306,* 1482–1483. (13)

Flack, W. F., Jr., Laird, J. D., & Cavallaro, L. A. (1999). Separate and combined effects of facial expressions and bodily postures on emotional feelings. *European Journal of Social Psychology, 29,* 203–217. (12)

Flatz, G. (1987). Genetics of lactose digestion in humans. *Advances in Human Genetics, 16,* 1–77. (5)

Flavell, J. (1986). The development of children's knowledge about the appearance-re-

ality distinction. *American Psychologist, 41,* 418–425. (5)

Fleeson, W., Malanos, A. B., & Achille, N. M. (2002). An intraindividual process approach to the relationship between extraversion and positive affect: Is acting extraverted as "good" as being extraverted? *Journal of Personality and Social Psychology, 83,* 1409–1422. (14)

Fletcher, R., & Voke, J. (1985). *Defective colour vision.* Bristol, England: Hilger. (4)

Fligstein, D., Barabasz, A., Barabasz, M., Trevisan, M. S., & Warner, D. (1998). Hypnosis enhances recall memory: A test of forced and non-forced conditions. *American Journal of Clinical Hypnosis, 40,* 297–305. (10)

Flor, H., Elbert, T., Knecht, S., Wienbruch, C., Pantev, C., Birbaumer, N., et al. (1995). Phantom-limb pain as a perceptual correlate of cortical reorganization following arm amputation. *Nature, 375,* 482–484. (4)

Flynn, J. R. (1984). The mean IQ of Americans: Massive gains 1932 to 1978. *Psychological Bulletin, 95,* 29–51. (9)

Flynn, J. R. (1998). IQ gains over time: Toward finding the causes. In U. Neisser (Ed.), *The rising curve* (pp. 25–66). Washington, DC: American Psychological Association. (9)

Flynn, J. R. (1999). Searching for justice: The discovery of IQ gains over time. *American Psychologist, 54,* 5–20. (9)

Fodor, J. (1998). When is a dog a DOG? *Nature, 396,* 325–327. (8)

Fogassi, L., Ferrari, P. F., Gesierich, B., Rozzi, S., Chersi, F., & Rizzolatti, G. (2005). Parietal lobe: From action understanding to intention understanding. *Science, 308,* 662–667. (6)

Foley, V. D. (1984). Family therapy. In R. J. Corini (Ed.), *Current psychotherapies* (3rd ed., pp. 447–490). Itasca, IL: Peacock. (15)

Folkman, S., & Moskowitz, J. T. (2000). Positive affect and the other side of coping. *American Psychologist, 55,* 647–654. (12)

Forer, B. R. (1949). The fallacy of personal validation: A classroom demonstration of gullibility. *Journal of Abnormal and Social Psychology, 44,* 118–123. (14)

Fotopoulou, A., Solms, S., & Turnbull, O. (2004). Wishful reality distortions in confabulation: A case report. *Neuropsychologia, 47,* 727–744. (7)

Foulkes, D. (1999). *Children's dreaming and the development of consciousness.* Cambridge, MA: Harvard University Press. (10)

Fox, C. R., & Rottenstreich, Y. (2003). Partition priming in judgment under uncertainty. *Psychological Science, 14,* 195–200. (8)

Fox, N., A., Nichols, K. E., Henderson, H. A., Rubin, K., Schmidt, L., Hamer, D., et al. (2005). Evidence for a gene–environment interaction in predicting behavioral inhibition in middle childhood. *Psychological Science, 16,* 921–926. (5)

Francis, L. J., Brown, L. B., Lester, D., & Philipchalk, R. (1998). Happiness as stable extraversion: A cross-cultural examination of the reliability and validity of the Oxford Happiness Inventory among students in the U.K., U.S.A., Australia, and Canada. *Personality and Individual Differences, 24,* 167–171. (14)

Francis, W. S. (1999). Cognitive integration of language and memory in bilinguals: Semantic representation. *Psychological Bulletin, 125,* 193–222. (8)

Frank, M. J., & Claus, E. D. (2006). Anatomy of a decision: Striato-orbitofrontal interactions in reinforcement learning, decision making, and reversal. *Psychological Review, 113,* 300–326. (3)

Frassinetti, F., Pavani, F., & Làdavas, E. (2002). Acoustical vision of neglected stimuli: Interaction among spatially converging audiovisual inputs in neglect patients. *Journal of Cognitive Neuroscience, 14,* 62–69. (10)

Fredrickson, B. L. (2001). The role of positive emotion in psychology: The broaden-and-build theory of positive emotions. *American Psychologist, 56,* 218–226. (12)

Fredrickson, B. L., & Losada, M. F. (2005). Positive affect and the complex dynamics of human flourishing. *American Psychologist, 60,* 678–686. (12)

Freedman, J. L., & Fraser, S. C. (1966). Compliance without pressure: The foot in the door technique. *Journal of Personality and Social Psychology, 4,* 195–202. (13)

French, A. R. (1988). The patterns of mammalian hibernation. *American Scientist, 76,* 568–575. (10)

French, S. E., Seidman, E., Allen, L., & Aber, J. L. (2006). The development of ethnic identity during adolescence. *Developmental Psychology, 42,* 1–10. (5)

Frensch, P. A., & Rünger, D. (2003). Implicit learning. *Current Directions in Psychological Science, 12,* 13–18. (7)

Freud, S. (1925). An autobiographical study. In J. Strachey, A. Freud, A. Strachey, & A. Tyson (Eds.), *The standard edition of the complete psychological works of Sigmund Freud* (Vol. 20, pp. 7–70). London: Hogarth Press and the Institute of Psycho-Analysis. (14)

Freud, S. (1925). *Three contributions to the theory of sex* (A. A. Brill, Trans.). New York: Nervous and Mental Disease Publishing. (Original work published 1905) (14)

Freud, S. (1935). *A general introduction to psychoanalysis* (Rev. ed.). New York: Liveright. (10)

Freud, S. (1955). *The interpretation of dreams* (J. Strachey, Trans.). New York: Basic Books. (Original work published 1900) (10)

Freud, S. (1961). *The future of an illusion* (J. Strachey, Trans.). New York: Norton. (Original work published 1927) (14)

Freud, S. (1963). *Dora: An analysis of a case of hysteria.* New York: Collier Books. (Original work published 1905) (14)

Fried, I., Katz, A., McCarthy, G., Sass, K. J., Williamson, P., Spencer, S. S., et al. (1991). Functional organization of human supplementary motor cortex studied by electrical stimulation. *Journal of Neuroscience, 11,* 3656–3666. (10)

Friedman, J. M. (2000). Obesity in the new millennium. *Nature, 404,* 632–634. (11)

Friedman, M., & Rosenman, R. H. (1974). *Type-A behavior and your heart.* New York: Knopf. (12)

Friedman, M. A., & Brownell, K. D. (1996). A comprehensive treatment manual for the management of obesity. In V. B. Van Hasselt & M. Hersen (Eds.), *Sourcebook of psychological treatment manuals for adult disorders* (pp. 375–422). New York: Plenum Press. (11)

Friedman, N. P., Miyake, A., Corley, R. P., Young, S. E., DeFries, J. C., & Hewitt, J. K. (2006). Not all executive functions are related to intelligence. *Psychological Science, 17,* 172–179. (9)

Frijda, N. H. (1988). The laws of emotion. *American Psychologist, 45,* 349–358. (12)

Fritz, C. O., Morris, P. E., Bjork, R. A., Gelman, R., & Wickens, T. D. (2000). When further learning fails: Stability and change following repeated presentation of text. *British Journal of Psychology, 91,* 493–511. (7)

Fritzsche, B. A., Young, B. R., & Hickson, K. C. (2003). Individual differences in academic procrastination tendency and writing success. *Personality and Individual Differences, 35,* 1549–1557. (11)

Fu, Q., Heath, A. C., Bucholz, K. K., Nelson, E., Goldberg, J., Lyons, M. J., et al. (2002). Shared genetic risk of major depression, alcohol dependence, and marijuana dependence. *Archives of General Psychiatry, 59,* 1125–1132. (16)

Fuligni, A. J. (1998). The adjustment of children from immigrant families. *Current Directions in Psychological Science, 7,* 99–103. (5)

Fuller, R. K., & Roth, H. P. (1979). Disulfiram for the treatment of alcoholism: An evaluation in 128 men. *Annals of Internal Medicine, 90,* 901–904. (16)

Fullerton, J., Cubin, M., Tiwari, H., Wang, C., Bomhra, A., Davidson, S., et al. (2003). Linkage analysis of extremely discordant and concordant sibling pairs identifies quantitative-trait loci that influence variation in the human personality trait neuroticism. *American Journal of Human Genetics, 72,* 879–890. (14)

Furnham, A. (2003). Belief in a just world: Research progress over the last decade. *Personality and Individual Differences, 34,* 795–817. (14)

Furnham, A., Hosoe, T., & Tang, T. L.-P. (2002). Male hubris and female humility? A crosscultural study of ratings of self, parental, and sibling multiple intelligence in America, Britain, and Japan. *Intelligence, 30,* 101–115. (14)

Furukawa, T. (1997). Cultural distance and its relationship to psychological adjustment of international exchange students. *Psychiatry and Clinical Neurosciences, 51,* 87–91. (1)

Gable, S. L., Reis, H. T., & Downey, G. (2003). He said, she said: A quasi-signal detection analysis of daily interactions between close relationship partners. *Psychological Science, 14,* 100–105. (13)

Gabrieli, J. D. E., Cohen, N. J., & Corkin, S. (1988). The impaired learning of semantic knowledge following bilateral medial temporal-lobe resection. *Brain and Cognition, 7,* 157–177. (7)

Gabrieli, J. D. E., Fleischman, D. A., Keane, M. M., Reminger, S. L., & Morrell, F. (1995). Double dissociation between memory systems underlying explicit and implicit memory in the human brain. *Psychological Science, 6,* 76–82. (7)

Gage, F. H. (2000). Mammalian neural stem cells. *Science, 287,* 1433–1438. (3)

Galef, B. G., Jr. (1998). Edward Thorndike: Revolutionary psychologist, ambiguous biologist. *American Psychologist, 53,* 1128–1134. (6)

Gallese, V., Fadiga, L., Fogassi, L., & Rizzolatti, G. (1996). Action recognition in the premotor cortex. *Brain, 119,* 593–609. (6)

Gallistel, C. R., & Gibbon, J. (2000). Time, rate, and conditioning. *Psychological Review, 107,* 289–344. (6)

Galton, F. (1978). *Hereditary genius.* New York: St. Martin's Press. (Original work published 1869) (1)

Gangestad, S. W. (2000). Human sexual selection, good genes, and special design. *Annals of the New York Academy of Sciences, 907,* 50–61. (13)

Gannon, N., & Ranzijn, R. (2005). Does emotional intelligence predict unique variance in life satisfaction beyond IQ and personality? *Personality and Individual Differences, 38,* 1353–1364. (12)

Garb, H. N., Florio, C. M., & Grove, W. M. (1998). The validity of the Rorschach and the Minnesota Multiphasic Personality Inventory: Results from meta-analyses. *Psychological Science, 9,* 402–404. (13)

Garb, H. N., Wood, J. N., Lilienfeld, S. O., & Nezworski, M. T. (2005). Roots of the Rorschach controversy. *Clinical Psychology Review, 25,* 97–118. (14)

Garcia, J. (1990). Learning without memory. *Journal of Cognitive Neuroscience, 2,* 287–305. (6)

Garcia, J., Ervin, F. R., & Koelling, R. A. (1966). Learning with prolonged delay of reinforcement. *Psychonomic Science, 5,* 121–122. (6)

Garcia, J., & Koelling, R. A. (1966). Relation of cue to consequence in avoidance learning. *Psychonomic Science, 4,* 123–124. (6)

Garcia Coll, C. T. (1990). Developmental outcome of minority infants: A process-oriented look into our beginnings. *Child Development, 61,* 270–289. (5)

Garcia-Palacios, A., Hoffman, H., Carlin, A., Furness, T. A., III, & Botella, C. (2002). Virtual reality in the treatment of spider phobia: A controlled study. *Behaviour Research and Therapy, 40,* 983–993. (16)

Gardner, H. (1985). *Frames of mind.* New York: Basic Books. (9)

Gardner, H. (1995). Why would anyone become an expert? *American Psychologist, 50,* 802–803. (8)

Gardner, H. (1999). *Intelligence reframed.* New York: Basic Books. (9)

Gardner, M. (1978). Mathematical games. *Scientific American, 239*(5), 22–32. (8)

Gardner, M. (1994). Notes of a fringe watcher: The tragedies of false memories. *Skeptical Inquirer, 18,* 464–470. (7)

Gardner, M., & Steinberg, L. (2005). Peer influence on risk taking, risk preference, and risky decision making in adolescence and adulthood: An experimental study. *Developmental Psychology, 41,* 625–635. (5)

Gardner, R. A., & Gardner, B. T. (1969). Teaching sign language to a chimpanzee. *Science, 165,* 664–672. (8)

Garlick, D. (2003). Integrating brain science research with intelligence research. *Current Directions in Psychological Science, 12,* 185–189. (9)

Garry, M., Sharman, S. J., Feldman, J., Marlatt, G. A., & Loftus, E. F. (2002). Examining memory for heterosexual college students' sexual experiences using an electronic mail diary. *Health Psychology, 21,* 629–634. (11)

Gaser, C., & Schlaug, G. (2003). Brain structures differ between musicians and non-musicians. *Journal of Neuroscience, 23,* 9240–9245. (8)

Gawin, F. H. (1991). Cocaine addiction: Psychology and neurophysiology. *Science, 251,* 1580–1586. (3)

Geary, D. C. (2000). Evolution and proximate expression of human paternal investment. *Psychological Bulletin, 126,* 55–77. (13)

Gegenfurtner, K. R. (2003). Cortical mechanisms of colour vision. *Nature Reviews Neuroscience, 4,* 563–572. (3)

Geier, A. B., Rozin, P., & Doros, G. (2006). Unit bias. *Psychological Science, 17,* 521–525. (11)

Gelman, R. (1982). Accessing one-to-one correspondence: Still another paper about conservation. *British Journal of Psychology, 73,* 209–220. (5)

Genoux, D., Haditsch, U., Knobloch, M., Michalon, A., Storm, D., & Mansuy, I. M. (2002). Protein phosphatase 1 is a molecular constraint on learning and memory. *Nature, 418,* 970–975. (7)

German, T. P., & Barrett, H. C. (2005). Functional fixedness in a technologically sparse

culture. *Psychological Science, 16,* 1–5. (8)

Gershoff, E. T. (2002). Corporal punishment by parents and associated child behaviors and experiences: A meta-analytic and theoretical review. *Psychological Bulletin, 128,* 539–579. (6)

Geschwind, N. (1979). Specializations of the human brain. In *Scientific American* (Ed.), *The brain: A Scientific American book.* San Francisco: W. H. Freeman. (8)

Gibson, J. J. (1968). What gives rise to the perception of movement? *Psychological Review, 75,* 335–346. (4)

Gick, M. L., & Holyoak, K. J. (1983). Schema induction and analogical transfer. *Cognitive Psychology, 15,* 1–38. (8)

Giebel, H. D. (1958). Visuelles Lernvermögen bei Einhufern [Visual learning capacity in hoofed animals]. *Zoologische Jahrbücher Abteilung für Allgemeine Zoologie, 67,* 487–520. (1)

Gigerenzer, G. (2004). Dread risk, September 11, and fatal traffic accidents. *Psychological Science, 15,* 286–287. (8)

Gilbertson, M. W., Shenton, M. E., Ciszewski, A., Kasai, K., Lasko, N. B., Orr, S. P., et al. (2002). Smaller hippocampal volume predicts pathological vulnerability to psychological trauma. *Nature Neuroscience, 5,* 1242–1247. (12)

Gilbreth, F. B. (1911). *Motion study.* London: Constable. (11)

Gilger, J. W., Geary, D. C., & Eisele, L. M. (1991). Reliability and validity of retrospective self-reports of the age of pubertal onset using twin, sibling, and college student data. *Adolescence, 26,* 41–53. (11)

Gilligan, C. (1977). In a different voice: Women's conceptions of self and morality. *Harvard Educational Review, 47,* 481–517. (13)

Gilligan, C. (1979). Woman's place in man's life cycle. *Harvard Educational Review, 49,* 431–446. (13)

Giros, B., Jaber, M., Jones, S. R., Wightman, R. M., & Caron, M. G. (1996). Hyperlocomotion and indifference to cocaine and amphetamine in mice lacking the dopamine transporter. *Nature, 379,* 606–612. (3)

Glantz, L. A., & Lewis, D. A. (1997). Reduction of synaptophysin immunoreactivity in the prefrontal cortex of subjects with schizophrenia. *Archives of General Psychiatry, 54,* 660–669. (16)

Glantz, L. A., & Lewis, D. A. (2000). Decreased dendritic spine density on prefrontal cortical pyramidal neurons in schizophrenia. *Archives of General Psychiatry, 57,* 65–73. (16)

Glasman, L. R., & Albarracín, D. (2006). Forming attitudes that predict future behavior: A meta-analysis of the attitude–behavior relation. *Psychological Bulletin, 132,* 778–822. (13)

Glass, D. C., Singer, J. E., & Pennebaker, J. W. (1977). Behavioral and physiological effects of uncontrollable environmental events. In D. Stokols (Ed.), *Perspectives on environment and behavior* (pp. 131–151). New York: Plenum Press. (12)

Glass, M. (2001). The role of cannabinoids in neurodegenerative diseases. *Progress in Neuro-Psychopharmacology & Biological Psychiatry, 25,* 743–765. (3)

Glick, P., & Fiske, S. T. (2001). Ambivalent sexism. *Advances in Experimental Social Psychology, 33,* 115–188. (13)

Goate, A., Chartier-Harlin, M. C., Mullan, M., Brown, J., Crawford, F., Fidani, L., et al. (1991). Segregation of a missense mutation in the amyloid precursor protein gene with familial Alzheimer's disease. *Nature, 349,* 704–706. (7)

Gold, P. E., Cahill, L., & Wenk, G. L. (2002). Gingko biloba: A cognitive enhancer? *Psychological Science in the Public Interest, 3,* 2–11. (7)

Goldberg, T. E., Egan, M. F., Gscheidle, T., Coppola, R., Weickert, T., Kolachana, B. S., et al. (2003). Executive subprocesses in working memory. *Archives of General Psychiatry, 60,* 889–896. (9)

Goldfried, M. R., & Wolfe, B. E. (1996). Psychotherapy practice and research: Repairing a strained alliance. *American Psychologist, 51,* 1007–1016. (15)

Goldin-Meadow, S., & Mylander, C. (1998). Spontaneous sign systems created by deaf children in two cultures. *Nature, 391,* 279–281. (8)

Goldstein, A. (1980). Thrills in response to music and other stimuli. *Physiological Psychology, 8,* 126–129. (4)

Goldstein, D. G., & Gigerenzer, G. (2002). Models of ecological rationality: The recognition heuristic. *Psychological Review, 109,* 75–90. (8)

Goldstein, E. B. (1989). *Sensation and perception* (3rd ed.). Belmont, CA: Wadsworth. (4)

Goldstein, E. B. (2007). *Sensation and perception* (7th ed.). Belmont, CA: Wadsworth. (4)

Golombok, S., Perry, B., Burston, A., Murray, C., Mooney-Somers, J., Stevens, M., et al. (2003). Children with lesbian parents: A community study. *Developmental Psychology, 39,* 20–33. (5)

Gomez, P., Zimmermann, P., Guttormsen-Schär, S., & Danuser, B. (2005). Respiratory responses associated with affective processing of film stimuli. *Biological Psychology, 68,* 223–235. (12)

Gonzaga, G. C., Turner, R. A., Keltner, D., Campos, B., & Altemus, M. (2006). Romantic love and sexual desire in close relationships. *Emotion, 6,* 163–179. (13)

Goodall, J. (1971). *In the shadow of man.* Boston: Houghton Mifflin. (2)

Goodman, G. S., Ghetti, S., Quas, J. A., Edelstein, R. S., Alexander, K. W., Redlich,

A. D., et al. (2003). A prospective study of memory for child sexual abuse: New findings relevant to the repressed-memory controversy. *Psychological Science, 14,* 113–118. (7)

Goodwin, C. J. (1991). Misportraying Pavlov's apparatus. *American Journal of Psychology, 104,* 135–141. (6)

Gordon, P. C., Hendrick, R., & Levine, W. H. (2002). Memory-load interference in syntactic processing. *Psychological Science, 13,* 425–430. (8)

Goren, H., Kurzban, R., & Rapoport, A. (2003). Social loafing vs. social enhancement: Public goods provisioning in real-time with irrevocable commitments. *Organizational Behavior and Human Decision Processes, 90,* 277–290. (13)

Gothe, J., Brandt, S. A., Irlbacher, K., Röricht, S., Sabel, B. A., & Meyer, B.-U. (2002). Changes in visual cortex excitability in blind subjects as demonstrated by transcranial magnetic stimulation. *Brain, 125,* 479–490. (3)

Gottesman, I. I. (1991). *Schizophrenia genesis.* New York: W. H. Freeman. (16)

Gottfredson, L. S. (2002a). *g:* Highly general and highly practical. In R. J. Sternberg & E. L. Grigorenko (Eds.), *The general intelligence factor: How general is it?* (pp. 331–380). Mahwah, NJ: Erlbaum. (9)

Gottfredson, L. S. (2002b). Where and why *g* matters: Not a mystery. *Human Performance, 15,* 25–46. (9)

Gottfredson, L. S. (2003). Dissecting practical intelligence theory: Its claims and evidence. *Intelligence, 31,* 343–397. (9)

Gottman, J. M., Coan, J., Carrere, S., & Swanson, C. (1998). Predicting marital happiness and stability from newlywed interactions. *Journal of Marriage and the Family, 60,* 5–22. (13)

Gottman, J. M., & Levenson, R. W. (2000). The timing of divorce: Predicting when a couple will divorce over a 14-year period. *Journal of Marriage and the Family, 62,* 737–745. (13)

Grabe, S., & Hyde, J. S. (2006). Ethnicity and body dissatisfaction among women in the United States: A meta-analysis. *Psychological Bulletin, 132,* 622–640. (11)

Graf, P., & Mandler, G. (1984). Activation makes words more accessible, but not necessarily more retrievable. *Journal of Verbal Learning and Verbal Behavior, 23,* 553–568. (7)

Gratacòs, M., Nadalm, M., Martín-Santos, R., Pujana, M. A., Gago, J., Peral, B., et al. (2001). A polymorphic genomic duplication on human chromosome 15 is a susceptibility factor for panic and phobic disorders. *Cell, 106,* 306–379. (16)

Gray, J. R., Chabris, C. F., & Braver, T. S. (2003). Neural mechanisms of general fluid intelligence. *Nature Neuroscience, 6,* 316–322. (9)

Graziadei, P. P. C., & deHan, R. S. (1973). Neuronal regeneration in the frog olfactory system. *Journal of Cell Biology, 59,* 525–530. (3)

Green, C. S., & Bavelier, D. (2003). Action video game modifies visual selective attention. *Nature, 423,* 534–537. (8)

Green, D. M., & Swets, J. A. (1966). *Signal detection theory and psychophysics.* New York: Wiley. (4)

Green, J. P., & Lynn, S. J. (2000). Hypnosis and suggestion-based approaches to smoking cessation: An examination of the evidence. *International Journal of Clinical and Experimental Hypnosis, 48,* 195–224. (10)

Green, J. P., & Lynn, S. J. (2005). Hypnosis versus relaxation: Accuracy and confidence in dating international news events. *Applied Cognitive Psychology, 19,* 679–691. (10)

Green, M. C., & Sabini, J. (2006). Gender, socioeconomic status, age, and jealousy: Emotional responses to infidelity in a national sample. *Emotion, 6,* 330–334. (13)

Greenberg, J., Martens, A., Jonas, E., Eisenstadt, D., Pyszczynski, T., & Solomon, S. (2003). Psychological defense in anticipation of anxiety. *Psychological Science, 14,* 516–519. (5)

Greene, J. D., Sommerville, R. B., Nystrom, L. E., Darley, J. M., & Cohen, J. D. (2001). An fMRI investigation of emotional engagement in moral judgment. *Science, 293,* 2105–2108. (12)

Greenhoot, A. F., Ornstein, P. A., Gordon, B. N., & Baker-Ward, L. (1999). Acting out the details of a pediatric check-up: The impact of interview condition and behavioral style on children's memory reports. *Child Development, 70,* 363–380. (7)

Greeno, C. G., & Wing, R. R. (1994). Stress-induced eating. *Psychological Bulletin, 115,* 444–464. (11)

Greenwald, A. G., & Banaji, M. R. (1995). Implicit social cognition: Attitudes, self-esteem, and stereotypes. *Psychological Review, 102,* 4–27. (13)

Greenwald, A. G., & Draine, S. C. (1997). Do subliminal stimuli enter the brain unnoticed? Tests with a new method. In J. D. Cohen & J. W. Schooler (Eds.), *Scientific approaches to consciousness* (pp. 83–108). Mahwah, NJ: Erlbaum. (4)

Greenwald, A. G., Nosek, B. A., & Banaji, M. R. (2003). Understanding and using the Implicit Association Test: I. An improved scoring algorithm. *Journal of Personality and Social Psychology, 85,* 197–216. (13)

Greenwald, A. G., Nosek, B. A., & Sriram, N. (2006). Consequential validity of the Implicit Association Test. *American Psychologist, 61,* 56–61. (13)

Greenwald, A. G., Spangenberg, E. R., Pratkanis, A. R., & Eskanazi, J. (1991). Double-blind tests of subliminal self-help audio tapes. *Psychological Science, 2,* 119–122. (4)

Greist, J. H., Jefferson, J. W., Kobak, K. A., Katzelnick, D. J., & Serlin, R. C. (1995). Efficacy and tolerability of serotonin transport inhibitors in obsessive-compulsive disorder. *Archives of General Psychiatry, 52,* 53–60. (16)

Griffin, D. R. (2001). *Animal minds.* Chicago: University of Chicago Press. (10)

Griffin, D., & Buehler, R. (2005). Biases and fallacies, memories and predictions: Comment on Roy, Christenfeld, & McKenzie (2005). *Psychological Bulletin, 131,* 757–760. (11)

Griffith, R. M., Miyagi, O., & Tago, A. (1958). The universality of typical dreams: Japanese vs. Americans. *American Anthropologist, 60,* 1173–1179. (10)

Grignon, S. (2005). Capgras syndrome in the modern era: Self misidentification on an ID picture. *Canadian Journal of Psychiatry, 50,* 74–75. (10)

Grillon, C., Morgan, C. A., III, Davis, M., & Southwick, S. M. (1998). Effects of darkness on acoustic startle in Vietnam veterans with PTSD. *American Journal of Psychiatry, 155,* 812–817. (12)

Grissmer, D. W., Williamson, S., Kirby, S. N., & Berends, M. (1998). Exploring the rapid rise in the Black achievement scores in the United States (1970–1990). In U. Neisser (Ed.), *The rising curve* (pp. 251–285). Washington, DC: American Psychological Association. (9)

Grønnerød, C. (2003). Temporal stability in the Rorschach method: A meta-analytic review. *Journal of Personality Assessment, 80,* 272–293. (14)

Gross, J. J. (2001). Emotion regulation in adulthood: Timing is everything. *Current Directions in Psychological Science, 10,* 214–219. (12)

Gross, J. J., Fredrickson, B. L., & Levenson, R. W. (1994). The psychophysiology of crying. *Psychophysiology, 31,* 460–468. (12)

Grossman, E. D., & Blake, R. (2001). Brain activity evoked by inverted and imagined biological motion. *Vision Research, 41,* 1475–1482. (4)

Grünbaum, A. (1986). Précis of *The foundations of psychoanalysis:* A philosophical critique. *Behavioral and Brain Sciences, 9,* 217–284. (14)

Grutzendler, J., Kasthuri, N., & Gan, W. B. (2002). Long-term dendritic spine stability in the adult cortex. *Nature, 420,* 812–816. (3)

Guilleminault, C., Heinzer, R., Mignot, E., & Black, J. (1998). Investigations into the neurologic basis of narcolepsy. *Neurology, 50*(Suppl. 1), S8–S15. (10)

Gunthert, K. C., Cohen, L. H., & Armeli, S. (1999). The role of neuroticism in daily stress and coping. *Journal of Personality and Social Psychology, 77,* 1087–1100. (14)

Gur, R. E., Cowell, P. E., Latshaw, A., Turetsky, B. I., Grossman, R. I., Arnold, S. E., et al. (2000). Reduced dorsal and orbital prefrontal gray matter volumes in schizophrenia. *Archives of General Psychiatry, 57,* 761–768. (16)

Gurling, H. M. D., Critchley, H., Datta, S. R., McQuillin, A., Blaveri, E., Thirumalai, S., et al. (2006). Genetic association and brain morphology studies and the chromosome 8p22 pericentriolar material 1 (*PCM1*) gene in susceptibility to schizophrenia. *Archives of General Psychiatry, 63,* 844–854. (16)

Gusella, J. F., & MacDonald, M. E. (2000). Molecular genetics: Unmasking polyglutamine triggers in neurodegenerative disease. *Nature Reviews Neuroscience, 1,* 109–115. (5)

Gustavson, C. R., Kelly, D. J., Sweeney, M., & Garcia, J. (1976). Prey-lithium aversions: I. Coyotes and wolves. *Behavioral Biology, 17,* 61–72. (6)

Gusterson, H. (1992, May/June). Coming of age in a weapons lab. *The Sciences, 32,* 16–22. (13)

Gynther, M. D. (1989). MMPI comparisons of Blacks and Whites: A review and commentary. *Journal of Clinical Psychology, 45,* 878–883. (14)

Haarmeier, T., Thier, P., Repnow, M., & Petersen, D. (1997). False perception of motion in a patient who cannot compensate for eye movements. *Nature, 389,* 849–852. (4)

Habermas, T., & Bluck, S. (2000). Getting a life: The emergence of the life story in adolescence. *Psychological Bulletin, 126,* 748–769. (5)

Hackman, J. R., & Lawler, E. E., III (1971). Employee reactions to job characteristics. *Journal of Applied Psychology, 55,* 259–286. (11)

Haeffel, G. J., Abramson, L. Y., Voelz, Z. R., Metalsky, G. I., Halberstadt, L., Dykman, B. M., et al. (2005). Negative cognitive styles, dysfunctional attitudes, and the remitted depression paradigm: A search for the elusive cognitive vulnerability to depression factor among remitted depressives. *Emotion, 5,* 343–348. (16)

Hafer, C. L., & Bègue, L. (2005). Experimental research on just-world theory: Problems, developments, and future challenges. *Psychological Bulletin, 131,* 128–167. (14)

Haggard, P., & Eimer, M. (1999). On the relation between brain potentials and the awareness of voluntary movements. *Experimental Brain Research, 126,* 128–133. (10)

Haggard, P., & Libet, B. (2001). Conscious intention and brain activity. *Journal of Consciousness Studies, 8,* 47–63. (10)

Haggarty, J. M., Cernovsky, Z., Husni, M., Minor, K., Kerman, P., & Merskey, H. (2002). Seasonal affective disorder in an arctic community. *Acta Psychiatrica Scandinavica, 105,* 378–384. (16)

Haidt, J. (2001). The emotional dog and its rational tail: A social intuitionist approach to moral judgment. *Psychological Review, 108,* 814–834. (12)

Hakkanen, H., & Laajasalo, T. (2006). Homicide crime scene behaviors in a Finnish sample of mentally ill offenders. *Homicide Studies, 10,* 33–54. (14)

Hakuta, K., Bialystok, E., & Wiley, E. (2003). Critical evidence: A test of the critical-period hypothesis for second-language acquisition. *Psychological Science, 14,* 31–38. (8)

Halberstadt, J., & Rhodes, G. (2000). The attractiveness of nonface averages: Implications for an evolutionary explanation of the attractiveness of average faces. *Psychological Science, 11,* 285–289. (13)

Hale, S., Myerson, J., Rhee, S. H., Weiss, C. S., & Abrams, R. A. (1996). Selective interference with the maintenance of location information in working memory. *Neuropsychology, 10,* 228–240. (7)

Hall, C. S., & Van de Castle, R. L. (1966). *The content analysis of dreams.* New York: Appleton-Century-Crofts. (10)

Hall, J. A., & Halberstadt, A. G. (1994). "Subordination" and sensitivity to nonverbal cues: A study of married working women. *Sex Roles, 31,* 149–165. (12)

Hall, J. A., & Matsumoto, D. (2004). Gender differences in judgments of multiple emotions from facial expressions. *Emotion, 4,* 201–206. (12)

Hall, L. J., & McGregor, J. A. (2000). A follow-up study of the peer relationships of children with disabilities in an inclusive school. *Journal of Special Education, 34,* 114–126. (9)

Halmi, K. A., Sunday, S. R., Strober, M., Kaplan, A., Woodside, D. B., Fichter, M., et al. (2000). Perfectionism in anorexia nervosa: Variation by clinical subtype, obsessionality, and pathological eating behavior. *American Journal of Psychiatry, 157,* 1799–1805. (11)

Halpern, S. D., Andrews, T. J., & Purves, D. (1999). Interindividual variation in human visual performance. *Journal of Cognitive Neuroscience, 11,* 521–534. (4)

Hama, Y. (2001). Shopping as a coping behavior for stress. *Japanese Psychological Research, 43,* 218–224. (12)

Hamann, S. B., & Squire, L. R. (1997). Intact perceptual memory in the absence of conscious memory. *Behavioral Neuroscience, 111,* 850–854. (7)

Hambrick, D. Z., & Engle, R. W. (2002). Effects of domain knowledge, working memory capacity, and age on cognitive performance: An investigation of the knowledge-is-power hypothesis. *Cognitive Psychology, 44,* 339–387. (7)

Hamby, S. L., & Koss, M. P., (2003). Shades of gray: A qualitative study of terms used in the measurement of sexual victimization. *Psychology of Women Quarterly, 27,* 243–255. (12)

Hamilton, S. P., Fyer, A. J., Durner, M., Heiman, G. A., Baisre de Leon, A., Hodge, S. E., et al. (2003). Further genetic evidence for a panic disorder syndrome mapping to chromosome 13q. *Proceedings of the National Academy of Sciences, USA, 100,* 2550–2555. (16)

Hamm, J. V. (2000). Do birds of a feather flock together? The variable bases for African American, Asian American, and European American adolescents' selection of similar friends. *Developmental Psychology, 36,* 209–219. (13)

Hammock, E. A. D., & Young, L. J. (2005). Microsatellite instability generates diversity in brain and sociobehavioral traits. *Science, 308,* 1630–1634. (5)

Haney, C., Banks, C., & Zimbardo, P. (1973). Interpersonal dynamics in a simulated prison. *International Journal of Criminology and Penology, 1,* 69–97. (13)

Hankin, B. L., & Abramson, L. Y. (2001). Development of gender differences in depression: An elaborated cognitive vulnerability-transactional stress theory. *Psychological Bulletin, 127,* 773–796. (16)

Hanoch, Y., Johnson, J. G., & Wilke, A. (2006). Domain specificity in experimental measures and participant recruitment. *Psychological Science, 17,* 300–304. (14)

Hanson, R. K. (2000). Will they do it again? Predicting sex-offense recidivism. *Current Directions in Psychological Science, 9,* 106–109. (12)

Harada, S., Agarwal, D. P. Goedde, H. W., Tagaki, S., & Ishikawa, B. (1982). Possible protective role against alcoholism for aldehyde dehydrogenase isozyme deficiency in Japan. *Lancet, ii,* 827. (16)

Hardy, J. L., Frederick, C. M., Kay, P., & Werner, J. S. (2005). Color naming, lens aging, and grue. *Psychological Science, 16,* 321–327. (4)

Harker, L. A., & Keltner, D. (2001). Expressions of positive emotion in women's college yearbook pictures and their relationship to personality and life outcomes across adulthood. *Journal of Personality and Social Psychology, 80,* 112–124. (12)

Harkins, S. G., & Jackson, J. M. (1985). The role of evaluation in eliminating social loafing. *Journal of Personality and Social Psychology, 11,* 457–465. (13)

Harley, B., & Wang, W. (1997). The critical period hypothesis: Where are we now? In A. M. B. deGroot & J. F. Knoll (Eds.), *Tutorials in bilingualism* (pp. 19–51). Mahwah, NJ: Erlbaum. (8)

Harlow, H. F., Harlow, M. K., & Meyer, D. R. (1950). Learning motivated by a manipulative drive. *Journal of Experimental Psychology, 40,* 228–234. (11)

Harper, L. V. (2005). Epigenetic inheritance and the intergenerational transfer of experience. *Psychological Bulletin, 131,* 340–360. (5)

Harris, B. (1979). What ever happened to Little Albert? *American Psychologist, 34,* 151–160. (16)

Harris, J. R. (1995). Where is the child's environment? A group socialization theory of development. *Psychological Review, 102,* 458–489. (5)

Harris, J. R. (1998). *The nurture assumption.* New York: Free Press. (5)

Harris, J. R. (2000). Context-specific learning, personality, and birth order. *Current Directions in Psychological Science, 9,* 174–177. (5)

Harris, R. J., Schoen, L. M., & Hensley, D. L. (1992). A cross-cultural study of story memory. *Journal of Cross-Cultural Psychology, 23,* 133–147. (7)

Harris, T. (1967). *I'm OK—You're OK.* New York: Avon. (14)

Harrison, Y., & Horne, J. A. (2000). The impact of sleep deprivation on decision making: A review. *Journal of Experimental Psychology: Applied, 6,* 236–249. (10)

Hartmann, S., & Zepf, S. (2003). Effectiveness of psychotherapy in Germany: A replication of the *Consumer Reports* study. *Psychotherapy Research, 13,* 235–242. (15)

Harvey, A. G., & Bryant, R. A. (2002). Acute stress disorder: A synthesis and critique. *Psychological Bulletin, 128,* 886–902. (12)

Hastie, R., Schkade, D. A., & Payne, J. W. (1999). Juror judgments in civil cases: Hindsight effects on judgments of liability for punitive damages. *Law & Human Behavior, 23,* 597–614. (7)

Hathaway, S. R., & McKinley, J. C. (1940). A multiphasic personality schedule (Minnesota): I. Construction of the schedule. *Journal of Psychology, 10,* 249–254. (14)

Haueisen, J., & Knösche, T. R. (2001). Involuntary motor activity in pianists evoked by music perception. *Journal of Cognitive Neuroscience, 13,* 786–792. (6)

Haukka, J., Suvisaari, J., & Lönnqvist, J. (2003). Fertility of patients with schizophrenia, their siblings, and the general population: A cohort study from 1950 to 1959 in Finland. *American Journal of Psychiatry, 160,* 460–463. (16)

Hauri, P. (1982). *The sleep disorders.* Kalamazoo, MI: Upjohn. (10)

Hays, R. B. (1985). A longitudinal study of friendship development. *Journal of Personality and Social Psychology, 48,* 909–924. (13)

Healy, D., Savage, M., Michael, P., Marris, M., Hirst, D., Carter, M., et al. (2001). Psychiatric bed utilization: 1896 and 1996 compared. *Psychological Medicine, 31,* 779–790. (16)

Healy, D., & Williams, J. M. G. (1988). Dysrhythmia, dysphoria, and depression: The interaction of learned helplessness and circadian dysrhythmia in the pathogenesis of depression. *Psychological Bulletin, 103,* 163–178. (16)

Heath, A. C., Neale, M. C., Kessler, R. C., Eaves, L. J., & Kendler, K. S. (1992). Evidence for genetic influences on personality from self-reports and informant ratings. *Journal of Personality and Social Psychology, 63,* 85–96. (5, 14)

Heatherton, T. G., & Baumeister, R. F. (1991). Binge eating as escape from self-awareness. *Psychological Bulletin, 110,* 86–108. (11)

Heaton, R. K., Gladsjo, J. A., Palmer, B. W., Kuck, J., Marcotte, T. D., & Jeste, D. V. (2001). Stability and course of neuropsychological deficits in schizophrenia. *Archives of General Psychiatry, 58,* 24–32. (16)

Heck, A., Collins, J., & Peterson, L. (2001). Decreasing children's risk taking on the playground. *Journal of Applied Behavior Analysis, 34,* 349–352. (6)

Hedges, L. V., & Nowell, A. (1995). Sex differences in mental test scores, variability, and numbers of high-scoring individuals. *Science, 269,* 41–45. (9)

Heider, F. (1958). *The psychology of interpersonal relations.* New York: Wiley. (13)

Heinrichs, R. W. (2005). The primacy of cognition in schizophrenia. *American Psychologist, 60,* 229–242. (16)

Heit, E. (1993). Modeling the effects of expectations on recognition memory. *Psychological Science, 4,* 244–251. (7)

Hejmadi, A., Davidson, R. J., & Rozin, P. (2000). Exploring Hindu Indian emotion expressions. *Psychological Science, 11,* 183–187. (12)

Hemmati, T., Mills, J. F., & Kroner, D. G. (2004). The validity of the Bar-On emotional intelligence quotient in an offender population. *Personality and Individual Differences, 37,* 695–706. (12)

Hempel, A., Hempel, E., Schönknecht, P., Stippich, C., & Schröder, J. (2003). Impairment in basal limbic function in schizophrenia during affect recognition. *Psychiatry Research: Neuroimaging, 122,* 115–124. (16)

Henderlong, J., & Lepper, M. R. (2002). The effects of praise on children's intrinsic motivation: A review and synthesis. *Psychological Bulletin, 128,* 774–795. (11)

Henderson, J. M., & Hollingworth, A. (2003b). Global transsaccadic change blindness during scene perception. *Psychological Science, 14,* 493–497. (8)

Hendin, H., Maltsberger, J. T., Lipschitz, A., Haas, A. P., & Kyle, J. (2001). Recognizing and responding to a suicide crisis. *Annals of the New York Academy of Sciences, 932,* 169–186. (16)

Hendrie, H. C. (2001). Exploration of environmental and genetic risk factors for Alzheimer's disease: The value of cross-cultural studies. *Current Directions in Psychological Science, 10,* 98–101. (7)

Henrich, J., McElreath, R., Barr, A., Ensminger, J., Barrett, C., Bolyanatz, A., et al. (2006). Costly punishment across human societies. *Science, 312,* 1767–1770. (13)

Herbert, A., Gerry, N. P., McQueen, M. B., Heid, I. M., Pfeufer, A., Illig, T., et al. (2006). A common genetic variant is associated with adult and childhood obesity. *Science, 312,* 279–283. (11)

Heresco-Levy, U., & Javitt, D. C. (2004). Comparative effects of glycine and D-cycloserine on persistent negative symptoms in schizophrenia: A retrospective analysis. *Schizophrenia Research, 66,* 89–96. (16)

Hergenhahn, B. R. (1992). *An introduction to the history of psychology* (2nd ed.). Belmont, CA: Wadsworth. (1)

Herkenham, M., Lynn, A. B., deCosta, B. R., & Richfield, E. K. (1991). Neuronal localization of cannabinoid receptors in the basal ganglia of the rat. *Brain Research, 547,* 267–274. (3)

Herkenham, M., Lynn, A. B., Little, M. D., Johnson, M. R., Melvin, L. S., deCosta, B. R., et al. (1990). Cannabinoid receptor localization in brain. *Proceedings of the National Academy of Sciences, USA, 87,* 1932–1936. (3)

Herman, C. P., Roth, D. A., & Polivy, J. (2003). Effects of the presence of others on food intake: A normative interpretation. *Psychological Bulletin, 129,* 873–886. (11)

Herman, J., Roffwarg, H., & Tauber, E. S. (1968). Color and other perceptual qualities of REM and NREM sleep. *Psychophysiology, 5,* 223. (10)

Hertenstein, M. J. (2002). Touch: Its communicative functions in infancy. *Human Development, 45,* 70–94. (5)

Hertwig, R., Barron, G., Weber, E. U., & Erev, I. (2004). Decisions from experience and the effect of rare events in risky choice. *Psychological Science, 15,* 534–539. (8)

Hess, T. M. (2005). Memory and aging in context. *Psychological Bulletin, 131,* 383–406. (5)

Hetherington, E. M. (1989). Coping with family transitions. Winners, losers, and survivors. *Child Development, 60,* 1–14. (5)

Hetherington, E. M., Bridges, M., & Insabella, G. M. (1998). What matters? What does not? *American Psychologist, 53,* 167–184. (5)

Hetherington, E. M., Stanley-Hagan, M., & Anderson, E. R. (1989). Marital transitions: A child's perspective. *American Psychologist, 44,* 303–312. (10)

Hettema, J. M., Neale, M. C., & Kendler, K. S. (2001). A review and meta-analysis of the genetic epidemiology of anxiety disorders. *American Journal of Psychiatry, 158,* 1568–1578. (16)

Hildreth, K., Sweeney, B., & Rovee-Collier, C. (2003). Differential memory-preserving effects of reminders at 6 months. *Journal of Experimental Child Psychology, 84,* 41–62. (5)

Hilgard, E. R. (1973). A neodissociation interpretation of pain reduction in hypnosis. *Psychological Review, 80,* 396–411. (10)

Hill, C. E., & Nakayama, E. Y. (2000). Client-centered therapy: Where has it been and where is it going? A comment on Hathaway (1948). *Journal of Clinical Psychology, 56,* 861–875. (15)

Hill, J. L., Waldfogel, J., Brooks-Gunn, J., & Han, W.-J. (2005). Maternal employment and child development: A fresh look using newer methods. *Developmental Psychology, 41,* 833–850. (5)

Hill, W. D., Blake, M., & Clark, J. E. (1998). Ball court design dates back 3,400 years. *Nature, 392,* 878–879. (11)

Hillis, A. E., Newhart, M., Heidler, J., Barker, P. B., Herskovits, E. H., & Degaonkar, M. (2005). Anatomy of spatial attention: Insights from perfusion imaging and hemispatial neglect in acute stroke. *Journal of Neuroscience, 25,* 3161–3167. (10)

Hilty, D. M., Brady, K. T., & Hales, R. E. (1999). A review of bipolar disorder among adults. *Psychiatric Services, 50,* 201–213. (16)

Hinson, J. M., Jameson, T. L., & Whitney, P. (2003). Impulsive decision making and working memory. *Journal of Experimental Psychology: Learning, Memory, and Cognition, 29,* 298–306. (7)

Hinton, G. (1979). Some demonstrations of the effects of structural descriptions in mental imagery. *Cognitive Science, 3,* 231–250. (8)

Hirvonen, J., van Erp, T. G. M., Huttunen, J., Aalto, S., Någren, K., Huttunen, M., et al. (2006). Brain dopamine D₁ receptors in twins discordant for schizophrenia. *American Journal of Psychiatry, 163,* 1747–1753. (16)

Hobson, C. J., & Delunas, L. (2001). National norms and life-event frequencies for the revised social readjustment rating scale. *International Journal of Stress Management, 8,* 299–314. (12)

Hobson, C. J., Kamen, J., Szostek, J., Neithercut, C. M., Tidemann, J. W., & Wojnarowicz, S. (1998). Stressful life events: A revision and update of the social readjustment rating scale. *International Journal of Stress Management, 5,* 1–23. (12)

Hobson, J. A. (2005). Sleep is of the brain, by the brain and for the brain. *Nature, 437,* 1254–1256. (10)

Hobson, J. A., & McCarley, R. W. (1977). The brain as a dream state generator: An activation-synthesis hypothesis of the dream process. *American Journal of Psychiatry, 134,* 1335–1348. (10)

Hodgins, S., Mednick, S. A., Brennan, P. A., Schulsinger, F., & Engberg, M. (1996). Mental disorder and crime. *Archives of General Psychiatry, 53,* 489–496. (12)

Hoebel, B. G., Rada, P. V., Mark, G. P., & Pothos, E. (1999). Neural systems for reinforcement and inhibition of behavior: Relevance to eating, addiction, and depression. In D. Kahneman, E. Diener, & N. Schwartz (Eds.), *Well-being: Foundations of hedonic psychology* (pp. 560–574). New York: Russell Sage Foundation. (11, 16)

Hoek, H. W., & van Hoeken, D. (2003). Review of the prevalence and incidence of eating disorders. *International Journal of Eating Disorders, 34,* 383–396. (11)

Hoffrage, U., Hertwig, R., & Gigerenzer, G. (2000). Hindsight bias: A by-product of knowledge updating? *Journal of Experimental Psychology: Learning, Memory, and Cognition, 26,* 566–581. (7)

Hogan, R. A., & Kirchner, J. H. (1967). Preliminary report of the extinction of learned fears via short-term implosive therapy. *Journal of Abnormal Psychology, 72,* 106–109. (16)

Holcombe, A. O., & Cavanagh, P. (2001). Early binding of feature pairs for visual perception. *Nature Neuroscience, 4,* 127–128. (3)

Holden, G. W., & Miller, P. C. (1999). Enduring and different: A meta-analysis of the similarity in parents' child rearing. *Psychological Bulletin, 125,* 223–254. (5)

Holland, R. W., Hendriks, M., & Aarts, H. (2005). Smells like clean spirit. *Psychological Science, 16,* 689–693. (8)

Hollingsworth, D. E., McAuliffe, S. P., & Knowlton, B. J. (2001). Temporal allocation of visual attention in adult attention deficit hyperactivity disorder. *Journal of Cognitive Neuroscience, 13,* 298–305. (8)

Hollister, J. M., Laing, P., & Mednick, S. A. (1996). Rhesus incompatibility as a risk factor for schizophrenia in male adults. *Archives of General Psychiatry, 53,* 19–24. (16)

Hollon, S. D., & Beck, A. T. (1979). Cognitive therapy of depression. In P. C. Kendall & S. D. Hollon (Eds.), *Cognitive-behavioral interventions* (pp. 153–203). New York: Academic Press. (15)

Hollon, S. D., Thase, M. E., & Markowitz, J. C. (2002). Treatment and prevention of depression. *Psychological Science in the Public Interest, 3,* 39–77. (16)

Holmes, D. S. (1978). Projection as a defense mechanism. *Psychological Bulletin, 85,* 677–688. (14)

Holmes, D. S. (1987). The influence of meditation versus rest on physiological arousal: A second examination. In M. A. West (Ed.), *The psychology of meditation* (pp. 81–103). Oxford, England: Clarendon Press. (10)

Holmes, D. S. (1990). The evidence for repression: An examination of sixty years of research. In J. L. Singer (Ed.), *Repression and dissociation* (pp. 85–102). New York: Wiley. (7, 14)

Holmes, T., & Rahe, R. (1967). The social readjustment rating scale. *Journal of Psychosomatic Research, 11,* 213–218. (12)

Holtzworth-Munroe, A. (2000). A typology of men who are violent toward their female partners: Making sense of the heterogeneity in husband violence. *Current Directions in Psychological Science, 9,* 140–143. (12)

Homa, D. (1983). An assessment of two extraordinary speed-readers. *Bulletin of the Psychonomic Society, 21,* 123–126. (8)

Hönekopp, J. (2006). Once more: Is beauty in the eye of the beholder? Relative contributions of private and shared taste to judgments of facial attractiveness. *Journal of Experimental Psychology: Human Perception and Performance, 32,* 199–209. (13)

Hong, Y., Morris, M. W., Chiu, C., & Benet-Martinez, V. (2000). Multicultural minds: A dynamic constructivist approach to culture and cognition. *American Psychologist, 55,* 709–720. (13)

Hoover, D. W., & Milich, R. (1994). Effects of sugar ingestion expectancies on mother-child interactions. *Journal of Abnormal Child Psychology, 22,* 501–515. (2)

Horn, J. L. (1968). Organization of abilities and the development of intelligence. *Psychological Review, 75,* 242–259. (9)

Horn, J. L., & Donaldson, G. (1976). On the myth of intellectual decline in adulthood. *American Psychologist, 31,* 701–719. (9)

Horne, J. A. (1988). *Why we sleep.* Oxford, England: Oxford University Press. (10)

Horne, J. A., Brass, C. G., & Pettitt, A. N. (1980). Circadian performance differences between morning and evening "types." *Ergonomics, 23,* 29–36. (10)

Horst, W. D., & Preskorn, S. H. (1998). Mechanisms of action and clinical characteristics of three atypical antidepressants: Venlafaxine, nefazodone, buproprion. *Journal of Affective Disorders, 51,* 237–254. (16)

Horvath, T. L. (2005). The hardship of obesity: A soft-wired hypothalamus. *Nature Neuroscience, 8,* 561–565. (11)

Houkes, I., Janssen, P. P. M., de Jonge, J., & Nijhuis, F. J. N. (2001). Work and individual determinants of intrinsic work motivation, emotional exhaustion, and turnover intention: A multi-sample analysis. *International Journal of Stress Management, 8,* 257–283. (11)

Houts, A. C., Berman, J. S., & Abramson, H. (1994). Effectiveness of psychological and pharmacological treatments for nocturnal enuresis. *Journal of Consulting and Clinical Psychology, 62,* 737–745. (15)

Howard, G. S. (2000). Adapting human lifestyles for the 21st century. *American Psychologist, 55,* 509–515. (1)

Howard, J. W., & Dawes, R. M. (1976). Linear prediction of marital happiness. *Personality and Social Psychology Bulletin, 2,* 478–480. (13)

Howard, K. I., Kopta, S. M., Krause, M. S., & Orlinsky, D. E. (1986). The dose-effect relationship in psychotherapy. *American Psychologist, 41,* 159–164. (15)

Howard, R. W. (1999). Preliminary real-world evidence that average human intelligence really is rising. *Intelligence, 27,* 235–250. (9)

Howe, C. Q., & Purves, D. (2005a). The Müller-Lyer illusion explained by the statistics of image-source relationships. *Proceedings of the National Academy of Sciences, USA, 102,* 1234–1239. (4)

Howe, C. Q., & Purves, D. (2005b). *Perceiving geometry.* New York: Springer. (4)

Howe, C. Q., Yang, Z., & Purves, D. (2005). The Poggendorff illusion explained by natural scene geometry. *Proceedings of the National Academy of Sciences, USA, 102,* 7707–7712. (4)

Howe, M. L., & Courage, M. L. (1993). On resolving the enigma of infantile amnesia. *Psychological Bulletin, 113,* 305–326. (7)

Howe, M. L., & Courage, M. L. (1997). The emergence and early development of autobiographical memory. *Psychological Review, 104,* 499–523. (7)

Hoyt, M. F., & Austad, C. S. (1992). Psychotherapy in a staff model health maintenance organization: Providing and assuring quality care in the future. *Psychotherapy, 29,* 119–129. (15)

Hrdy, S. B. (2000). The optimal number of fathers. *Annals of the New York Academy of Sciences, 907,* 75–96. (13)

Hróbjartsson, A., & Gøtzsche, P. C. (2001). Is the placebo powerless? *New England Journal of Medicine, 344,* 1594–1602. (4)

Hubbs-Tait, L., Nation, J. R., Krebs, N. F., & Bellinger, D. C. (2005). Neurotoxicants, micronutrients, and social environments: Individual and combined effects on children's development. *Psychological Science in the Public Interest, 6,* 57–121. (5)

Hubel, D. H., & Wiesel, T. N. (1968). Receptive fields and functional architecture of monkey striate cortex. *Journal of Physiology* (London), *195,* 215–243. (4)

Huber, R., Ghilardi, M. F., Massimini, M., & Tononi, G. (2004). Local sleep and learning. *Nature, 430,* 78–81. (10)

Hudson, J. I., Mangweth, B., Pope, H. G., Jr., De Col, C., Hausmann, A., Gutweniger, S., et al. (2003). Family study of affective spectrum disorder. *Archives of General Psychiatry, 60,* 170–177. (16)

Hudson, W. (1960). Pictorial depth perception in sub-cultural groups in Africa. *Journal of Social Psychology, 52,* 183–208. (4)

Huesmann, L. R., Moise-Titus, J., Podolski, C.-L., & Eron, L. D. (2003). Longitudinal relations between children's exposure to TV violence and their aggressive and violent behavior in young adulthood: 1977–1992. *Developmental Psychology, 39,* 201–221. (2)

Huff, D. (1954). *How to lie with statistics.* New York: Norton. (2)

Hugenberg, K., & Bodenhausen, G. V. (2003). Facing prejudice: Implicit prejudice and the perception of facial threat. *Psychological Science, 14,* 640–643. (13)

Hughes, J. C., & Cook, C. C. H. (1997). The efficacy of disulfiram: A review of outcome studies. *Addiction, 92,* 381–395. (16)

Hughes, J., Smith, T. W., Kosterlitz, H. W., Fothergill, L. A., Morgan, B. A., & Morris, H. R. (1975). Identification of two related pentapeptides from the brain with potent opiate antagonist activity. *Nature, 258,* 577–579. (3)

Hugoson, A., Ljungquist, B., & Breivik, T. (2002). The relationship of some negative events and psychological factors to periodontal disease in an adult Swedish population 50 to 80 years of age. *Journal of Clinical Periodontology, 29,* 247–253. (12)

Hull, C. L. (1932). The goal gradient hypothesis and maze learning. *Psychological Review, 39,* 25–43. (1)

Hull, C. L. (1943). *Principles of behavior: An introduction to behavior theory.* New York: D. Appleton. (11)

Hulshoff, H. E., Schnack, H. G., Mandl, R. C. W., van Haren, N. E. M., Koning, H., Collins, L., et al. (2001). Focal gray matter density changes in schizophrenia. *Archives of General Psychiatry, 58,* 1118–1125. (16)

Hultman, C. M., Öhman, A., Cnattingius, S., Wieselgren, I.-M., & Lindström, L. H. (1997). Prenatal and neonatal risk factors for schizophrenia. *British Journal of Psychiatry, 170,* 128–133. (16)

Hunter, J. E. (1997). Needed: A ban on the significance test. *Psychological Science, 8,* 3–7. (2)

Hur, Y.-M., Bouchard, T. J., Jr., & Eckert, E. (1998). Genetic and environmental influences on self-reported diet: A reared-apart twin study. *Physiology & Behavior, 64,* 629–636. (5)

Hur, Y.-M., Bouchard, T. J., Jr., & Lykken, D. T. (1998). Genetic and environmental influence on morningness–eveningness. *Personality and Individual Differences, 25,* 917–925. (5)

Hurovitz, C. S., Dunn, S., Domhoff, G. W., & Fiss, H. (1999). The dreams of blind men and women: A replication and extension of previous findings. *Dreaming, 9,* 183–193. (10)

Husain, M., & Rorden, C. (2003). Non-spatially lateralized mechanisms in hemispatial neglect. *Nature Reviews Neuroscience, 4,* 26–36. (10)

Huston, T. L., Niehuis, S., & Smith, S. E. (2001). The early marital roots of conjugal distress and divorce. *Current Directions in Psychological Science, 10,* 116–119. (13)

Hutcheson, D. M., Everitt, B. J., Robbins, T. W., & Dickinson, A. (2001). The role of withdrawal in heroin addiction: Enhances reward or promotes avoidance? *Nature Neuroscience, 4,* 943–947. (16)

Hyde, J. (2005). The gender similarities hypothesis. *American Psychologist, 60,* 581–592. (5)

Hyde, K. L., & Peretz, I. (2004). Brains that are out of tune but in time. *Psychological Science, 15,* 356–360. (4)

Iacono, W. G., & Patrick, C. J. (1999). Polygraph ("lie detector") testing: The state of the art. In A. K. Hess & I. B. Weiner (Eds.), *The handbook of forensic psychology* (pp. 440–473). New York: Wiley. (12)

Iggo, A., & Andres, K. H. (1982). Morphology of cutaneous receptors. *Annual Review of Neuroscience, 5,* 1–31. (4)

Ikonomidou, C., Bittigau, P., Ishimaru, M. J., Wozniak, D. F., Koch, C., Genz, K., et al. (2000). Ethanol-induced apoptotic neurodegeneration and fetal alcohol syndrome. *Science, 287,* 1056–1060. (5)

Ilies, R., & Judge, T. A. (2003). On the heritability of job satisfaction: The mediating role of personality. *Journal of Applied Psychology, 88,* 750–759. (11)

Imahori, T. T., & Cupach, W. R. (1994). A cross-cultural comparison of the interpretation and management of face: U.S. American and Japanese responses to embarrassing predicaments. *International Journal of Intercultural Relations, 18,* 193–219. (12)

Imhoff, M. C., & Baker-Ward, L. (1999). Preschoolers' suggestibility: Effects of developmentally appropriate language and interviewer supportiveness. *Journal of Applied Developmental Psychology, 20,* 407–429. (7)

Inhoff, A. W. (1989). Lexical access during eye fixations in sentence reading: Are word access codes used to integrate lexical information across interword fixations? *Journal of Memory and Language, 28,* 444–461. (8)

Inhoff, A. W., Radach, R., Eiter, B. M., & Juhasz, B. (2003). Distinct subsystems for the parafoveal processing of spatial and linguistic information during eye fixations in reading. *Quarterly Journal of Experimental Psychology, 56A,* 803–827. (8)

Inouye, S. T., & Kawamura, H. (1979). Persistence of circadian rhythmicity in a mammalian hypothalamic "island" containing the suprachiasmatic nucleus. *Proceedings of the National Academy of Sciences, USA, 76,* 5962–5966. (10)

Isaacowitz, D. M. (2006). Motivated gaze: The view from the gazer. *Current Directions in Psychological Science, 15,* 68–72. (12)

Isenberg, D. J. (1986). Group polarization: A critical review and meta-analysis. *Journal of Personality and Social Psychology, 50,* 1141–1151. (13)

Iverson, J. M., & Goldin-Meadow, S. (2005). Gesture paves the way for language development. *Psychological Science, 16,* 367–371. (8)

Ivry, R. B., & Diener, H. C. (1991). Impaired velocity perception in patients with lesions of the cerebellum. *Journal of Cognitive Neuroscience, 3,* 355–366. (3)

Iyengar, S. S., & Lepper, M. R. (2000). When choice is demotivating. *Journal of Personality and Social Psychology, 79,* 995–1006. (8)

Iyengar, S. S., Wells, R. E., & Schwartz, B. (2006). Doing better but feeling worse. *Psychological Science, 17,* 143–150. (8)

Izazola-Licea, J. A., Gortmaker, S. L., Tolbert, K., De Gruttola, V., & Mann, J. (2000). Prevalence of same-gender sexual behavior and HIV in a probability household survey of Mexican men. *Journal of Sex Research, 37,* 37–43. (11)

Jackson, D. C., Malmstadt, J. R., Larson, C. L., & Davidson, R. J. (2000). Suppression and enhancement of emotional responses to unpleasant pictures. *Psychophysiology, 37,* 515–522. (12)

Jacobs, B., Schall, M., & Scheibel, A. B. (1993). A quantitative dendritic analysis of Wernicke's area in humans: II. Gender, hemispheric, and environmental factors. *Journal of Comparative Neurology, 327,* 97–111. (8)

Jacobs, B. L. (1987). How hallucinogenic drugs work. *American Scientist, 75,* 386–392. (3)

Jacobs, K. M., Mark, G. P., & Scott, T. R. (1988). Taste responses in the nucleus tractus solitarius of sodium-deprived rats. *Journal of Physiology, 406,* 393–410. (1)

Jacobsen, F. M., Sack, D. A., Wehr, T. A., Rogers, S., & Rosenthal, N. E. (1987). Neuroendocrine 5-hydroxytryptophan in seasonal affective disorder. *Archives of General Psychiatry, 44,* 1086–1091. (16)

Jacobson, N. S., & Christensen, A. (1996). Studying the effectiveness of psychotherapy: How well can clinical trials do the job? *American Psychologist, 51,* 1031–1039. (15)

Jacobson, N. S., Dobson, K. S., Truax, P. A., Addis, M. E., Koerner, K., Gollan, J. K., et al. (1996). A component analysis of cognitive-behavior therapy for depression. *Journal of Consulting and Clinical Psychology, 64,* 295–304. (16)

Jacoby, L. L., & Rhodes, M. G. (2006). False remembering in the aged. *Current Directions in Psychological Science, 15,* 49–53. (7)

Jaffee, S., & Hyde, J. S. (2000). Gender differences in moral orientation: A meta-analysis. *Psychological Bulletin, 126,* 703–726. (10)

James, W. (1890). *The principles of psychology.* New York: Henry Holt. (1)

James, W. (1894). The physical basis of emotion. *Psychological Review, 1,* 516–529. (12)

James, W. (1904). Does "consciousness" exist? *Journal of Philosophy, Psychology, and Scientific Methods, 1,* 477–491. (10)

James, W. (1961). *Psychology: The briefer course.* New York: Harper. (Original work published 1892) (10)

Jancke, D., Chavane, F., Naaman, S., & Grinvald, A. (2004). Imaging cortical correlates of illusion in early visual cortex. *Nature, 428,* 423–426. (10)

Janis, I. L. (1972). *Victims of groupthink.* Boston: Houghton Mifflin. (13)

Janis, I. L. (1983). Stress inoculation in health care. In D. Meichenbaum & M. E. Jaremko (Eds.), *Stress reduction and prevention* (pp. 67–99). New York: Plenum Press. (12)

Janis, I. L. (1985). Sources of error in strategic decision making. In J. M. Pennings and associates (Eds.), *Organizational strategy and change* (pp. 157–197). San Francisco: Jossey-Bass. (13)

Janson, H., & Stattin, H. (2003). Prediction of adolescent and adult delinquency from childhood Rorschach ratings. *Journal of Personality Assessment, 81,* 51–63. (14)

Jaremko, M. E. (1983). Stress inoculation training for social anxiety, with emphasis on dating anxiety. In D. Meichenbaum & M. E. Jaremko (Eds.), *Stress reduction and prevention* (pp. 419–450). New York: Plenum Press. (12)

Jelicic, M., Bonke, B., Wolters, G., & Phaf, R. H. (1992). Implicit memory for words presented during anesthesia. *European Journal of Cognitive Psychology, 4,* 71–80. (7)

Jensen, A. R. (1980). *Bias in mental testing.* New York: Free Press. (9)

Jerome, L., & Segal, A. (2001). Benefit of long-term stimulants on driving in adults with ADHD. *Journal of Nervous and Mental Disease, 189,* 63–64. (8)

Ji, L-J., Nisbett, R. E., & Su, Y. (2001). Culture, change, and prediction. *Psychological Science, 12,* 450–456. (13)

Johns, M., Schmader, T., & Martens, A. (2005). Knowing is half the battle. *Psychological Science, 16,* 175–179. (9)

Johnson, J. G., Cohen, P., Brown, J., Smailes, E. M., & Bernstein, D. P. (1999). Childhood maltreatment increases risk for personality disorders during early adulthood. *Archives of General Psychiatry, 56,* 600–606. (15)

Johnson, J. G., Cohen, P., Smailes, E. M., Kasen, S., & Brook, J. S. (2002). Television viewing and aggressive behavior during adolescence and adulthood. *Science, 295,* 2468–2471. (2)

Johnson, M. K., Hashtroudi, S., & Lindsay, D. S. (1993). Source monitoring. *Psychological Bulletin, 114,* 3–28. (7)

Johnson, W., & Bouchard, T. J., Jr. (2005). The structure of human intelligence: It is verbal, perceptual, and image rotation (VPR), not fluid and crystallized. *Intelligence, 33,* 393–416. (9)

Johnson, W., & Bouchard, T. J., Jr. (2007). Sex differences in mental abilities: *g* masks the dimensions on which they lie. *Intelligence, 35,* 23–39. (9)

Johnson, W., Bouchard, T. J., Jr., Krueger, R. F., McGue, M., & Gottesman, I. I. (2004). Just one *g*: Consistent results from three test batteries. *Intelligence, 32,* 95–107. (9)

Johnston, J. C., & McClelland, J. L. (1974). Perception of letters in words: Seek not and ye shall find. *Science, 184,* 1192–1194. (8)

Johnston, J. J. (1975). Sticking with first responses on multiple-choice exams: For better or for worse? *Teaching of Psychology, 2,* 178–179. (8)

Johnstone, H. (1994, August 8). Prince of memory says victory was on the cards. *The Times* (London), p. 2. (7)

Joiner, T. E., Jr. (1999). The clustering and contagion of suicide. *Current Directions in Psychological Science, 8,* 89–92. (15)

Joiner, T. E., Jr., & Metalsky, G. I. (2001). Excessive reassurance seeking: Delineating a risk factor involved in the development of depressive symptoms. *Psychological Science, 12,* 371–378. (16)

Joint Committee on Standards for Educational and Psychological Testing of the American Educational Research Association, the American Psychological Association, and the National Council on Measurement in Education. (1999). *Standards for educational and psychological testing.* Washington, DC: American Educational Research Association. (9)

Jones, C. M., Braithwaite, V. A., & Healy, S. D. (2003). The evolution of sex differences in spatial ability. *Behavioral Neuroscience, 117,* 403–411. (5)

Jones, E. E., & Goethals, G. R. (1972). Order effects in impression formation: Attribution context and the nature of the entity. In E. Jones, D. Kanouse, H. Kelley, R. Nisbett, S. Valins, & B. Wiener (Eds.), *Attribution: Perceiving the causes of behavior* (pp. 27–46). Morristown, NJ: General Learning Press. (13)

Jones, E. E., & Harris, V. A. (1967). The attribution of attitudes. *Journal of Experimental Social Psychology, 13,* 1–24. (13)

Jones, E. E., & Nisbett, R. E. (1972). The actor and the observer: Divergent perception of the causes of behavior. In E. Jones, D. Kanouse, H. Kelley, R. Nisbett, S. Valins, & B. Wiener (Eds.), *Attribution: Perceiving the causes of behavior* (pp. 79–94). Morristown, NJ: General Learning Press. (13)

Jones, P. B., Barnes, T. R. E., Davies, L., Dunn, G., Lloyd, H., Hayhurst, K. P., et al. (2006). Randomized controlled trial of the effect on quality of life of second- vs. first-generation antipsychotic drugs in schizophrenia. *Archives of General Psychiatry, 63,* 1079–1087. (16)

Jones, S. S., Collins, K., & Hong, H. W. (1991). An audience effect on smile production in 10-month-old infants. *Psychological Science, 2,* 45–49. (12)

Joseph, R. (1988). Dual mental functioning in a split-brain patient. *Journal of Clinical Psychology, 44,* 770–779. (3)

Joseph, R. (2000). Fetal brain behavior and cognitive development. *Developmental Review, 20,* 81–98. (5)

Jouvet, M., Michel, F., & Courjon, J. (1959). Sur un stade d'activité électrique cérébrale rapide au cours du sommeil physiologique [On a state of rapid electrical cerebral activity during physiological sleep]. *Comptes Rendus des Séances de la Société de Biologie, 153,* 1024–1028. (10)

Judge, T. A., & Ilies, R. (2002). Relationship of personality to performance motivation: A meta-analytic review. *Journal of Applied Psychology, 87,* 797–807. (14)

Judge, T. A., & Laarsen, R. J. (2001). Dispositional affect and job satisfaction: A review and theoretical extension. *Organizational Behavior and Human Decision Processes, 86,* 67–98. (11)

Judge, T. A., Thoresen, C. J., Bono, J. E., & Patton, G. K. (2001). The job satisfaction–job performance relationship: A qualitative and quantitative review. *Psychological Bulletin, 127,* 376–407. (11)

Juhasz, B. J. (2005). Age-of-acquisition effects in word and picture identification. *Psychological Bulletin, 131,* 684–712. (7)

Jung, C. G. (1965). *Memories, dreams, reflections* (A. Jaffe, Ed.). New York: Random House. (14)

Junginger, J., & Frame, C. L. (1985). Self-report of the frequency and phenomenology of verbal hallucinations. *Journal of Nervous and Mental Disease, 173,* 149–155. (16)

Jusczyk, P. W. (2002). How infants adapt speech-processing capacities to native-language structure. *Current Directions in Psychological Science, 11,* 15–18. (5)

Juslin, P., Winman, A., & Olsson, H. (2000). Naive empiricism and dogmatism in confidence research: A critical examination of the hard–easy effect. *Psychological Review, 107,* 384–396. (8)

Just, M. A., & Carpenter, P. A. (1987). *The psychology of reading and language comprehension.* Boston: Allyn & Bacon. (8)

Just, M. A., Carpenter, P. A., Keller, T. A., Eddy, W. F., & Thulborn, K. R. (1996). Brain activation modulated by sentence comprehension. *Science, 274,* 114–116. (8)

Kagan, J., Reznick, J. S., & Snidman, N. (1988). Biological bases of childhood shyness. *Science, 240,* 167–171. (5)

Kagan, J., & Snidman, N. (1991). Infant predictors of inhibited and uninhibited profiles. *Psychological Science, 2,* 40–44. (5)

Kahn, A. S., Jackson, J., Kully, C., Badger, K., & Halvorsen, J. (2003). Calling it rape: Differences in experiences of women who do or do not label their sexual assault as rape. *Psychology of Women Quarterly, 27,* 233–242. (12)

Kahneman, D., Krueger, A. B., Schkade, D., Schwarz, N., & Stone, A. A. (2006). Would you be happier if you were richer? A focusing illusion. *Science, 312,* 1908–1910. (12)

Kahneman, D., & Tversky, A. (1973). On the psychology of prediction. *Psychological Review, 80,* 237–251. (8)

Kaiser, C. R., Vick, S. B., & Major, B. (2004). A prospective investigation of the relationship between just-world beliefs and the desire for revenge after September 11, 2001. *Psychological Science, 15,* 503–506. (14)

Kaiser, M. K., Jonides, J., & Alexander, J. (1986). Intuitive reasoning about abstract and familiar physics problems. *Memory & Cognition, 14,* 308–312. (8)

Kalick, S. M., Zebrowitz, L. A., Langlois, J. H., & Johnson, R. M. (1998). Does human facial attractiveness honestly advertise health? *Psychological Science, 9,* 8–13. (13)

Kalivas, P. W., Volkow, N., & Seamans, J. (2005). Unmanageable motivation in addiction: A pathology in prefrontal-accumbens glutamate transmission. *Neuron, 45,* 647–650. (16)

Kamin, L. J. (1969). Predictability, surprise, attention, and conditioning. In B. A. Campbell & R. M. Church (Eds.), *Punishment and aversive behavior* (pp. 279–296). New York: Appleton-Century-Crofts. (6)

Kaminer, Y. (2000). Contingency management reinforcement procedures for adolescent substance abuse. *Journal of the American Academy of Child & Adolescent Psychiatry, 39,* 1324–1326. (16)

Kanaya, T., Scullin, M. H., & Ceci, S. J. (2003). The Flynn effect and U.S. policies. *American Psychologist, 58,* 778–790. (9)

Kanazawa, S. (2004). General intelligence as a domain-specific adaptation. *Psychological Review, 111,* 512–523. (9)

Kane, M. J., & Engle, R. W. (2000). Working-memory capacity, proactive interference, and divided attention: Limits on long-term memory retrieval. *Journal of Experimental Psychology: Learning, Memory, and Cognition, 26,* 336–358. (7)

Kanizsa, G. (1979). *Organization in vision.* New York: Praeger. (4)

Kanner, A. D., Coyne, J. C., Schaefer, C., & Lazarus, R. S. (1981). Comparison of two modes of stress measurement: Daily hassles and uplifts versus major life events. *Journal of Behavioral Medicine, 4,* 1–39. (12)

Kanwisher, N. (2000). Domain specificity in face perception. *Nature Neuroscience, 3,* 759–763. (4)

Karlin, R. A. (1997). Illusory safeguards: Legitimizing distortion in recall with guidelines for forensic hypnosis—two case reports. *International Journal of Clinical and Experimental Hypnosis, 45,* 18–40. (10)

Karnath, H.-O., Ferber, S., & Himmelbach, M. (2001). Spatial awareness is a function of the temporal not the posterior parietal lobe. *Nature, 411,* 950–953. (10)

Karney, B. R., & Bradbury, T. N. (1995). The longitudinal course of marital quality and stability: A review of theory, method, and research. *Psychological Review, 118,* 3–34. (13)

Karno, M., Golding, J. M., Sorenson, S. B., & Burnam, A. (1988). The epidemiology of obsessive-compulsive disorder in five U.S. communities. *Archives of General Psychiatry, 45,* 1094–1099. (16)

Kasai, K., Shenton, M. E., Salisbury, D. F., Hirayasu, Y., Onitsuka, T., Spencer, M. H., et al. (2003). Progressive decrease of left Heschl gyrus and planum temporale gray matter volume in first-episode schizophrenia. *Archives of General Psychiatry, 60,* 766–775. (16)

Kasser, T., & Sharma, Y. S. (1999). Reproductive freedom, educational equality, and females' preference for resource-acquisition characteristics in mates. *Psychological Science, 10,* 374–377. (13)

Kasser, T., & Sheldon, K. M. (2000). Of wealth and death. Materialism, mortality salience, and consumption behavior. *Psychological Science, 11,* 348–351. (5)

Kassin, S. M., & Gudjonsson, G. H. (2004). The psychology of confessions: A review of the literature and issues. *Psychological Science in the Public Interest, 5,* 33–67. (13)

Katz, S., Lautenschlager, G. J., Blackburn, A. B., & Harris, F. H. (1990). Answering reading comprehension items without passages on the SAT. *Psychological Science, 1,* 122–127. (9)

Kaufman, A. S. (2001). WAIS–III IQs, Horn's theory, and generational changes from young adulthood to old age. *Intelligence, 29,* 131–167. (9)

Kaufman, L., & Rock, I. (1989). The moon illusion thirty years later. In M. Hershenson (Ed.), *The moon illusion* (pp. 193–234). Hillsdale, NJ: Erlbaum. (4)

Kawakami, K., Dovidio, J. F., & Dijksterhuis, A. (2003). Effect of social category priming on personal attitudes. *Psychological Science, 14,* 315–319. (13)

Kazdin, A. E. (1995). Methods of psychotherapy research. In B. Bongar & L. E. Beutler (Eds.), *Comprehensive textbook of psychotherapy: Theory and practice* (pp. 405–433). Oxford, England: Oxford University Press. (15)

Keel, P. K., & Klump, K. L. (2003). Are eating disorders culture-bound syndromes? Implications for conceptualizing their etiology. *Psychological Bulletin, 129,* 747–769. (11)

Keele, S. W., & Ivry, R. B. (1990). Does the cerebellum provide a common computation for diverse tasks? *Annals of the New York Academy of Sciences, 608,* 179–207. (3)

Keller, M. C., Fredrickson, B. L., Ybarra, O., Cote, S., Johnson, K., Mikels, J., et al. (2005). A warm heart and a clear head. *Psychological Science, 16,* 724–731. (2, 12)

Keller, M. C., Thiessen, D., & Young, R. K. (1996). Mate assortment in dating and married couples. *Personality and Individual Differences, 21,* 217–221. (13)

Kelley, H. H. (1967). Attribution theory in social psychology. In D. Levine (Ed.), *Nebraska Symposium on Motivation* (Vol. 15, pp. 192–238). Lincoln: University of Nebraska Press. (13)

Keltner, D., & Buswell, B. N. (1997). Embarrassment: Its distinct form and appeasement functions. *Psychological Bulletin, 122,* 250–270. (12)

Keltner, D., & Shiota, M. N. (2003). New displays and new emotions: A commentary on Rozin and Cohen (2003). *Emotion, 3,* 86–91. (12)

Kendler, K. S., Bulik, C. M., Silberg, J., Hettema, J. M., Myers, J., & Prescott, C. A. (2000). Childhood sexual abuse and adult psychiatric and substance abuse disorders in women. *Archives of General Psychiatry, 57,* 953–959. (16)

Kendler, K. S., Gallagher, T. J., Abelson, J. M., & Kessler, R. C. (1996). Lifetime prevalence, demographic risk factors, and diagnostic validity of nonaffective psychosis as assessed in a U.S. community sample. *Archives of General Psychiatry, 53,* 1022–1031. (16)

Kendler, K. S., Gardner, C. O., & Prescott, C. A. (1999). Clinical characteristics of major depression that predict risk of depression in relatives. *Archives of General Psychiatry, 56,* 322–327. (16)

Kendler, K. S., Gruenberg, A. M., & Tsuang, M. T. (1985). Subtype stability in schizophrenia. *American Journal of Psychiatry, 142,* 827–832. (16)

Kendler, K. S., Hettema, J. M., Butera, F., Gardner, C. O., & Prescott, C. A. (2003). Life event dimensions of loss, humiliation, entrapment, and danger in the prediction of onsets of major depression and generalized anxiety. *Archives of General Psychiatry, 60,* 789–796. (16)

Kendler, K. S., Karkowski, L. M., Neale, M. C., & Prescott, C. A. (2000). Illicit psychoactive substance use, heavy use, abuse, and dependence in a US population-based sample of male twins. *Archives of General Psychiatry, 57,* 261–269. (16)

Kendler, K. S., MacLean, C., Neale, M., Kessler, R., Heath, A., & Eaves, L. (1991). The genetic epidemiology of bulimia nervosa. *American Journal of Psychiatry, 148,* 1627–1637. (11)

Kendler, K. S., Myers, J., & Prescott, C. A. (2002). The etiology of phobias. *Archives of General Psychiatry, 59,* 242–248. (16)

Kendler, K. S., Myers, J., Prescott, C. A., & Neale, M. C. (2001). The genetic epidemiology of irrational fears and phobias in men. *Archives of General Psychiatry, 58,* 257–265. (16)

Kendler, K. S., Thornton, L. M., Gilman, S. E., & Kessler, R. C. (2000). Sexual orientation in a U.S. sample of twin and nontwin sibling pairs. *American Journal of Psychiatry, 157,* 1843–1846. (11)

Kendler, K. S., Walters, E. E., Neale, M. C., Kessler, R. C., Heath, A. C., & Eaves, L. J.

(1995). The structure of the genetic and environmental risk factors for six major psychiatric disorders in women. *Archives of General Psychiatry, 52,* 374–383. (16)

Kennett, S., Eimer, M., Spence, C., & Driver, J. (2001). Tactile-visual links in exogenous spatial attention under different postures: Convergent evidence from psychophysics and ERPs. *Journal of Cognitive Neuroscience, 13,* 462–478. (10)

Kensinger, E. A., & Corkin, S. (2003). Memory enhancement for emotional words: Are emotional words more vividly remembered than neutral words? *Memory & Cognition, 31,* 1169–1180. (7)

Keppel, G., & Underwood, B. J. (1962). Proactive inhibition in short-term retention of single items. *Journal of Verbal Learning and Verbal Behavior, 1,* 153–161. (7)

Kern, R. P., Libkuman, T. M., Otani, H., & Holmes, K. (2005). Emotional stimuli, divided attention, and memory. *Emotion, 5,* 408–417. (12)

Kerr, N. L., MacCoun, R. J., & Kramer, G. P. (1996). Bias in judgment: Comparing individuals and groups. *Psychological Review, 103,* 687–719. (13)

Kerr, R., & Booth, B. (1978). Specific and varied practice of motor skill. *Perceptual and Motor Skills, 46,* 395–401. (7)

Kessler, R. C., Berglund, P., Demler, O., Jin, R., & Walters, E. E. (2005). Lifetime prevalence and age-of-onset distributions of *DSM–IV* disorders in the National Comorbidity Survey Replication. *Archives of General Psychiatry, 62,* 593–602. (15)

Kessler, R. C., Borges, G., & Walters, E. E. (1999). Prevalence of and risk factors for lifetime suicide attempts in the national comorbidity survey. *Archives of General Psychiatry, 56,* 617–626. (16)

Kessler, R. C., Chiu, W. T., Demler, O., & Walters, E. E. (2005). Prevalence, severity, and comorbidity of 12-month *DSM–IV* disorders in the National Comorbidity Survey Replication. *Archives of General Psychiatry, 62,* 617–627. (15)

Kessler, R. C., Merikangas, K. R., Berglund, P., Eaton, W. W., Koretz, D. S., & Walters, E. E. (2003). Mild disorders should not be eliminated from the *DSM–V. Archives of General Psychiatry, 60,* 1117–1122. (15)

Kety, S. S., Wendler, P. H., Jacobsen, B., Ingraham, L. J., Jansson, L., Faber, B., et al. (1994). Mental illness in the biological and adoptive relatives of schizophrenic adoptees. *Archives of General Psychiatry, 51,* 442–455. (16)

Keysar, B., Barr, D. J., & Horton, W. S. (1998). The egocentric basis of language use: Insights from a processing approach. *Current Directions in Psychological Science, 7,* 46–50. (5)

Keysar, B., & Henly, A. S. (2002). Speakers' overestimation of their effectiveness. *Psychological Science, 13,* 207–212. (5)

Kim, H., Baydar, N., & Greek, A. (2003). Testing conditions influence the race gap in

cognition and achievement estimated by household survey data. *Journal of Applied Developmental Psychology, 23,* 567–582. (9)

Kim, J. E., & Moen, P. (2001). Is retirement good or bad for subjective well-being? *Current Directions in Psychological Science, 10,* 83–86. (5)

Kim, S. (1989). *Inversions.* San Francisco: W. H. Freeman. (4)

Kimble, G. A. (1961). *Hilgard and Marquis' conditioning and learning* (2nd ed.). New York: Appleton-Century-Crofts. (6)

Kimble, G. A. (1967). Attitudinal factors in classical conditioning. In G. A. Kimble (Ed.), *Foundations of conditioning and learning* (pp. 642–659). New York: Appleton-Century-Crofts. (1)

Kimble, G. A. (1993). A modest proposal for a minor revolution in the language of psychology. *Psychological Science, 4,* 253–255. (6)

Kimble, G. A., & Garmezy, N. (1968). *Principles of general psychology* (3rd ed.). New York: Ronald Press. (14)

King, M. L., Jr. (1964, November 13). Speech at Duke University, Durham, NC. (5)

King, S. (2000). Is expressed emotion cause or effect in the mothers of schizophrenic young adults? *Schizophrenia Research, 45,* 65–78. (16)

Kinsey, A. C., Pomeroy, W. B., & Martin, C. E. (1948). *Sexual behavior in the human male.* Philadelphia: Saunders. (11)

Kinsey, A. C., Pomeroy, W. B., Martin, C. E., & Gebhard, P. H. (1953). *Sexual behavior in the human female.* Philadelphia: Saunders. (11)

Kiriakakis, V., Bhatia, K. P., Quinn, N. P., & Marsden, C. D. (1998). The natural history of tardive dyskinesia: A long-term follow-up of 107 cases. *Brain, 121,* 2053–2066. (16)

Kirkpatrick, B., Buchanan, R. W., Ross, D. E., & Carpenter, W. T., Jr. (2001). A separate disease within the syndrome of schizophrenia. *Archives of General Psychiatry, 58,* 165–171. (16)

Kirsch, I., & Lynn, S. J. (1998). Dissociation theories of hypnosis. *Psychological Bulletin, 123,* 100–115. (10)

Kirsch, I., & Sapirstein, G. (1998). Listening to Prozac but hearing placebo: A meta-analysis of antidepressant medication. *Prevention and Treatment, 1,* article 2a. (16)

Kirsch, J., & Braffman, W. (2001). Imaginative suggestibility and hypnotizability. *Current Directions in Psychological Science, 10,* 57–61. (10)

Kitigawa, N., & Ichihara, S. (2002). Hearing visual motion in depth. *Nature, 416,* 172–174. (4)

Klein, D. F. (1993). False suffocation alarms, spontaneous panics, and related conditions. *Archives of General Psychiatry, 50,* 306–317. (16)

Kleinknecht, R. A. (1982). The origins and remission of fear in a group of tarantula enthusiasts. *Behaviour Research & Therapy, 20*, 437–443. (16)

Kleinmuntz, B., & Szucko, J. J. (1984). A field study of the fallibility of polygraphic lie detection. *Nature, 308*, 449–450. (12)

Kleitman, N. (1963). *Sleep and wakefulness* (Rev. and enlarged ed.). Chicago: University of Chicago Press. (10)

Kluger, M. J. (1991). Fever: Role of pyrogens and cryogens. *Physiological Reviews, 71*, 93–127. (12)

Klump, K. L., Miller, K. B., Keel, P. K., McGue, M., & Iacono, W. G. (2001). Genetic and environmental influences on anorexia nervosa syndromes in a population-based twin sample. *Psychological Medicine, 31*, 737–740. (11)

Kniffin, K. M., & Wilson, D. S. (2004). The effect of nonphysical traits on the perception of physical attractiveness. *Evolution and Human Behavior, 25*, 88–101. (13)

Knuttinen, M.-G., Power, J. M., Preston, A. R., & Disterhoft, J. F. (2001). Awareness in classical differential eyeblink conditioning in young and aging humans. *Behavioral Neuroscience, 115*, 747–757. (6)

Kocsis, R. N., Cooksey, R. W., & Irwin, H. J. (2002). Psychological profiling of sexual murders: An empirical model. *International Journal of Offender Therapy and Comparative Criminology, 46*, 532–554. (14)

Kocsis, R. N., Hayes, A. F., & Irwin, H. J. (2002). Investigative experience and accuracy in psychological profiling of a violent crime. *Journal of Interpersonal Violence, 17*, 811–823. (14)

Kocsis, R. N., Irwin, H. J., Hayes, A. F., & Nunn, R. (2000). Expertise in psychological profiling: A comparative assessment. *Journal of Interpersonal Violence, 15*, 311–331. (14)

Koepp, M. J., Gunn, R. N., Lawrence, A. D., Cunningham, V. J., Dagher, A., Jones, T., et al. (1998). Evidence for striatal dopamine release during a video game. *Nature, 393*, 266–268. (3, 16)

Kohlberg, L. (1969). Stage and sequence: The cognitive-developmental approach to socialization. In D. A. Goslin (Ed.), *Handbook of socialization theory and research* (pp. 347–480). Chicago: Rand McNally (13)

Kohlberg, L., & Hersh, R. H. (1977). Moral development: A review of the theory. *Theory into Practice, 16*, 53–59. (13)

Kolers, P. A., & von Grünau, M. (1976). Shape and color in apparent motion. *Vision Research, 16*, 329–335. (10)

Koob, G. F., & LeMoal, M. (1997). Drug abuse: Hedonic homeostatic dysregulation. *Science, 278*, 52–58. (16)

Koocher, G. P., Goodman, G. S., White, C. S., Friedrich, W. N., Sivan, A. B., & Reynolds, C. R. (1995). Psychological science and the use of anatomically detailed dolls in child sexual-abuse assessments. *Psychological Bulletin, 118*, 199–222. (7)

Kopelman, M. D. (2000). Focal retrograde amnesia and the attribution of causality: An exceptionally critical review. *Cognitive Neuropsychology, 17*, 585–621. (7)

Kopelman, P. G. (2000). Obesity as a medical problem. *Nature, 404*, 635–643. (11)

Koppenaal, R. J. (1963). Time changes in the strengths of A-B, A-C lists: Spontaneous recovery? *Journal of Verbal Learning and Verbal Behavior, 2*, 310–319. (7)

Koriat, A., Bjork, R. A., Sheffer, L., & Bar, S. K. (2004). Predicting one's own forgetting: The role of experience-based and theory-based processes. *Journal of Experimental Psychology: General, 133*, 643–656. (7)

Koss, M. P., & Butcher, J. N. (1986). Research on brief psychotherapy. In S. L. Garfield & A. E. Bergin (Eds.), *Handbook of psychotherapy and behavior change* (pp. 627–670). New York: Wiley. (15)

Kouider, S., & Dupoux, E. (2004). Partial awareness creates the "illusion" of subliminal semantic priming. *Psychological Science, 15*, 75–81. (4)

Kouider, S., & Dupoux, E. (2005). Subliminal speech priming. *Psychological Science, 16*, 617–625. (4)

Koyano, W. (1991). Japanese attitudes toward the elderly: A review of research findings. *Journal of Cross-Cultural Gerontology, 4*, 335–345. (5)

Kozel, F. A., Padgett, T. M., & George, M. S. (2004). A replication study of the neural correlates of deception. *Behavioral Neuroscience, 118*, 852–856. (12)

Kozel, N. J., & Adams, E. H. (1986). Epidemiology of drug abuse: An overview. *Science, 234*, 970–974. (3)

Kozlowski, L. T., Frecker, R. C., Khouw, V., & Pope, M. A. (1980). The misuse of "less hazardous" cigarettes and its detection: Hole blocking of ventilated filters. *American Journal of Public Health, 70*, 1202–1203. (16)

Kraemer, D. L., & Hastrup, J. L. (1988). Crying in adults: Self-control and autonomic correlates. *Journal of Social and Clinical Psychology, 6*, 53–68. (12)

Krähenbühl, S., & Blades, M. (2006). The effect of question repetition within interviews on young children's eyewitness recall. *Journal of Experimental Child Psychology, 94*, 57–67. (7)

Krantz, D. S., Sheps, D. S., Carney, R. M., & Natelson, B. H. (2000). Effects of mental stress in patients with coronary artery disease. *Journal of the American Medical Association, 283*, 1800–1802. (12)

Krebs, D. L. (2000). The evolution of moral dispositions in the human species. *Annals of the New York Academy of Sciences, 907*, 132–148. (13)

Krebs, D. L., & Denton, K. (2005). Toward a more pragmatic approach to morality: A critical evaluation of Kohlberg's model. *Psychological Review, 112*, 629–649. (13)

Kreitzer, A. C., & Regehr, W. G. (2001). Retrograde inhibition of presynaptic calcium influx by endogenous cannabinoids at excitatory synapses onto Purkinje cells. *Neuron, 29*, 717–727. (3)

Kreskin. (1991). *Secrets of The Amazing Kreskin.* Buffalo, NY: Prometheus. (2)

Kreutzer, M. W., & Holt, C. L. (2001). How do people process health information? Applications in an age of individualized communication. *Current Directions in Psychological Science, 10*, 206–209. (13)

Kripke, D. F. (1998). Light treatment for nonseasonal depression: Speed, efficacy, and combined treatment. *Journal of Affective Disorders, 49*, 109–117. (16)

Kripke, D. F., Garfinkel, L., Wingard, D. L., Klauber, M. R., & Marler, M. R. (2002). Mortality associated with sleep duration and insomnia. *Archives of General Psychiatry, 59*, 131–136. (2)

Kross, E., Ayduk, O., & Mischel, W. (2005). When asking "why" does not hurt. *Psychological Science, 16*, 709–715. (16)

Krueger, D. W. (1978). The differential diagnosis of proverb interpretation. In W. E. Fann, I. Karacan, A. D. Pokorny, & R. L. Williams (Eds.), *Phenomenology and treatment of schizophrenia* (pp. 193–201). New York: Spectrum. (16)

Krueger, R. F., Markon, K. E., & Bouchard, T. J., Jr. (2003). The extended genotype: The heritability of personality accounts for the heritability of recalled family environments in twins reared apart. *Journal of Personality, 71*, 809–833. (5)

Kruger, J., Wirtz, D., & Miller, D. T. (2005). Counterfactual thinking and the first instinct fallacy. *Journal of Personality and Social Psychology, 88*, 725–735. (8)

Krüger, S., Alda, M., Young, L. T., Goldapple, K., Parikh, S., & Mayberg, H. S. (2006). Risk and resilience markers in bipolar disorder: Brain responses to emotional challenge in bipolar patients and their healthy siblings. *American Journal of Psychiatry, 163*, 257–264. (16)

Krull, D. S., & Anderson, C. A. (1997). The process of explanation. *Current Directions in Psychological Science, 6*, 1–5. (13)

Krupa, D. J., Thompson, J. K., & Thompson, R. F. (1993). Localization of a memory trace in the mammalian brain. *Science, 260*, 989–991. (3)

Krupnick, J. L., Elkin, I., Collins, J., Simmens, S., Sotsky, S. M., Pilkonis, P. A., et al. (1994). Therapeutic alliance and clinical outcome in the NIMH Treatment of Depression Collaborative Research Program: Preliminary findings. *Psychotherapy, 31*, 28–35. (15)

Kübler-Ross, E. (1969). *On death and dying.* New York: Macmillan. (5)

Kuhl, P. K., Andruski, J. E., Chistovich, I. A., Chistovich, L. A., Kozhevnikova, E. V., Ryskina, V. L., et al. (1997). Cross-language analysis of phonetic units in language addressed to infants. *Science, 277*, 684–686. (8)

Kuhlmann, S., Piel, M., & Wolf, O. T. (2005). Impaired memory retrieval after psychosocial stress in healthy young men. *Journal of Neuroscience, 25,* 2977–2982. (12)

Kuhn, D. (2006) Do cognitive changes accompany developments in the adolescent brain? *Perspectives on Psychological Science, 1,* 59–67. (5)

Kuhn, D., & Lao, J. (1996). Effects of evidence on attitudes: Is polarization the norm? *Psychological Science, 7,* 115–120. (13)

Kumkale, G. T., & Abarracín, D. (2004). The sleeper effect in persuasion: A meta-analytic review. *Psychological Bulletin, 130,* 143–172. (13)

Kupfer, D. J., First, M. B., & Regier, D. A. (2002). *A research agenda for DSM–V.* Washington, DC: American Psychiatric Association. (15)

Kurihara, K., & Kashiwayanagi, M. (1998). Introductory remarks on umami taste. *Annals of the New York Academy of Sciences, 855,* 393–397. (4)

Kutchins, H., & Kirk, S. A. (1997). *Making us crazy.* New York: Free Press. (15)

La Grand, R., Mondloch, C. J., Maurer, D., & Brent, H. P. (2004). Impairment in holistic face processing following early visual displacement. *Psychological Science, 15,* 762–768. (4)

LaBar, K. S., & Phelps, E. A. (1998). Arousal-mediated memory consolidation: Role of the medial temporal lobe in humans. *Psychological Science, 9,* 490–493. (12)

Labouvie-Vief, G., Diehl, M., Tarnowski, A., & Shen, J. (2000). Age differences in adult personality: Findings from the United States and China. *Journal of Gerontology: Psychological Sciences, 55B,* P4–P17. (14)

Laburn, H. P. (1996). How does the fetus cope with thermal challenges? *News in Physiological Sciences, 11,* 96–100. (16)

Lachter, J., Forster, K. I., & Ruthruff, E. (2004). Forty-five years after Broadbent (1958): Still no identification without attention. *Psychological Review, 111,* 880–913. (8)

Lackner, J. R. (1993). Orientation and movement in unusual force environments. *Psychological Science, 4,* 134–142. (4)

Laeng, B., Svartdal, F., & Oelmann, H. (2004). Does color synesthesia pose a paradox for early-selection theories of attention? *Psychological Science, 15,* 277–281. (4)

Lai, C. S. L., Fisher, S. E., Hurst, J. A., Vargha-Khadem, F., & Monaco, A. P. (2001). A forkhead-domain gene is mutated in a severe speech and language disorder. *Nature, 413,* 519–523. (8)

Lake, R. I. E., Eaves, L. J., Maes, H. H. M., Heath, A. C., & Martin, N. G. (2000). Further evidence against the environmental transmission of individual differences in neuroticism from a collaborative study of 45,850 twins and relatives on two continents. *Behavior Genetics, 30,* 223–233. (5, 14)

Lalumière, M. L., Blanchard, R., & Zucker, K. J. (2000). Sexual orientation and handedness in men and women: A meta-analysis. *Psychological Bulletin, 126,* 575–592. (11)

LaLumiere, R. T., Buen, T.-V., & McGaugh, J. L. (2003). Post-training intra-basolateral amygdala infusions of norepinephrine enhance consolidation of memory for contextual fear conditioning. *Journal of Neuroscience, 23,* 6754–6758. (7)

Lamb, M. E., & Fauchier, A. (2001). The effects of question type on self-contradictions by children in the course of forensic interviews. *Applied Cognitive Psychology, 15,* 483–491. (7)

Lambie, J. A., & Marcel, A. J. (2002). Consciousness and the varieties of emotion experience: A theoretical framework. *Psychological Review, 109,* 219–259. (10)

Lamm, H., & Myers, D. G. (1978). Group-induced polarization of attitudes and behavior. *Advances in Experimental Social Psychology, 11,* 145–195. (13)

Land, E. H., Hubel, D. H., Livingstone, M. S., Perry, S. H., & Burns, M. M. (1983). Colour-generating interactions across the corpus callosum. *Nature, 303,* 616–618. (4)

Land, E. H., & McCann, J. J. (1971). Lightness and retinex theory. *Journal of the Optical Society of America, 61,* 1–11. (4)

Lande, S. D. (1982). Physiological and subjective measures of anxiety during flooding. *Behaviour Research and Therapy, 20,* 81–88. (16)

Lane, L. W., Groisman, M., & Ferreira, V. S. (2006). Don't talk about pink elephants! *Psychological Science, 17,* 273–277. (5)

Lang, A. J., Craske, M. G., Brown, M., & Ghaneian, A. (2001). Fear-related state dependent memory. *Cognition, 15,* 695–703. (7)

Lang, P. J. (1994). The varieties of emotional experience: A meditation on James-Lange theory. *Psychological Review, 101,* 211–221. (12)

Langer, E. J. (1975). The illusion of control. *Journal of Personality and Social Psychology, 32,* 311–328. (5)

Langlois, J. H., & Roggman, L. A. (1990). Attractive faces are only average. *Psychological Science, 1,* 115–121. (13)

Langlois, J. H., Roggman, L. A., & Musselman, L. (1994). What is average and what is not average about average faces? *Psychological Science, 5,* 214–220. (13)

Langworthy, R. A., & Jennings, J. W. (1972). Oddball, abstract olfactory learning in laboratory rats. *Psychological Record, 22,* 487–490. (1)

Larsen, R. J., Kasimatis, M., & Frey, K. (1992). Facilitating the furrowed brow—An unobtrusive test of the facial feedback hypothesis applied to unpleasant affect. *Cognition and Emotion, 6,* 321–338. (12)

Larsen, R. J., Mercer, K. A., & Balota, D. A. (2006). Lexical characteristics of words used in emotional Stroop experiments. *Emotion, 6,* 62–72. (14)

Larson, R. W. (2001). How U.S. children and adolescents spend time: What it does (and doesn't) tell us about their development. *Current Directions in Psychological Science, 10,* 160–164. (5)

Larson, S. J., & Siegel, S. (1998). Learning and tolerance to the ataxic effect of ethanol. *Pharmacology Biochemistry and Behavior, 61,* 131–142. (6)

Larzelere, R. E., Kuhn, B. R., & Johnson, B. (2004). The intervention selection bias: An underrecognized confound in intervention research. *Psychological Bulletin, 120,* 289–303. (2, 6)

Lashley, K. (1923). The behavioristic interpretation of consciousness. *Psychological Bulletin, 30,* 237–272, 329–353. (10)

Lashley, K. S. (1951). The problem of serial order in behavior. In L. A. Jeffress (Ed.), *Cerebral mechanisms in behavior* (pp. 112–146). New York: Wiley. (8)

Lassiter, G. D., Geers, A. L., Munhall, P. J., Ploutz-Snyder, R. J., & Breitenbecher, D. L. (2002). Illusory causation: Why it occurs. *Psychological Science, 13,* 299–305. (13)

Latané, B., & Darley, J. M. (1968). Group inhibition of bystander intervention in emergencies. *Journal of Personality and Social Psychology, 10,* 215–221. (13)

Latané, B., & Darley, J. M. (1969). Bystander "apathy." *American Scientist, 57,* 244–268. (13)

Latané, B., Williams, K., & Harkins, S. (1979). Many hands make light the work: The causes and consequences of social loafing. *Journal of Personality and Social Psychology, 37,* 823–832. (13)

Latner, J. D. (2003). Macronutrient effects on satiety and binge eating in bulimia nervosa and binge eating disorder. *Appetite, 40,* 309–311. (4)

Lau, H. C., Rogers, R. D., Haggard, P., & Passingham, R. E. (2004). Attention to intention. *Science, 303,* 1208–1210. (10)

Lau, H. C., Rogers, R. D., & Passingham, R. E. (2006). On measuring the perceived onsets of spontaneous actions. *Journal of Neuroscience, 26,* 7265–7271. (10)

Laugerette, F., Passilly-Degrace, P., Patris, B., Niot, I., Febbraio, M., Montmayeur, J.-P., et al. (2005). CD36 involvement in orosensory detection of dietary lipids, spontaneous fat preference, and digestive secretions. *Journal of Clinical Investigation, 115,* 3177–3184. (4)

Laumann, E. O. (1969). Friends of urban men: An assessment of accuracy in reporting their socio-economic attributes, mutual choice, and attitude development. *Sociometry, 32,* 54–69. (13)

Laumann, E. O., Gagnon, J. H., Michael, R. T., & Michaels, S. (1994). *The social organization of sexuality: Sexual practices in the United States.* Chicago: University of Chicago Press. (11)

Laumann, E. O., Nicolosi, A., Glasser, D. B., Paik, A., Buvat, J., Gingell, C., et al. for the GSSAB Investigators' Group. (2003). *Prevalence of sexual problems among men and women aged 40 to 80 years: Results of an international survey.* Paper presented at the second international consultation on erectile and sexual dysfunctions, Paris. Retrieved from http://www.pfizerglobalstudy.com/public/publications.asp. (11)

Laumann, E. O., Paik, A., Glassser, D. B., Kang, J.-H., Wang, T., Levinson, B., et al. (2006). A cross-national study of subjective sexual well-being among older women and men: Findings from the global study of sexual attitudes and behaviors. *Archives of Sexual Behavior, 35,* 145–161. (11)

Laursen, B., Coy, K. C., & Collins, W. A. (1998). Reconsidering changes in parent-child conflict across adolescence: A meta-analysis. *Child Development, 69,* 817–832. (5)

Lavin, J. H., Wittert, G., Sun, W. M., Horowitz, M., Morley, J. E., & Read, N. W. (1996). Appetite regulation by carbohydrate: Role of blood glucose and gastrointestinal hormones. *American Journal of Physiology, 271,* E209–E214. (11)

Laviolette, S. R., & van der Kooy, D. (2004). The neurobiology of nicotine addiction: Bridging the gap from molecules to behaviour. *Nature Reviews Neuroscience, 5,* 55–65. (16)

Lawlor, S., Richman, S., & Richman, C. L. (1997). The validity of using the SAT as a criterion for Black and White students' admission to college. *College Student Journal, 31,* 507–515. (9)

Laws, G., Byrne, A., & Buckley, S. (2000). Language and memory development in children with Down syndrome at mainstream schools and special schools: A comparison. *Educational Psychology, 20,* 447–457. (9)

Lazar-Meyn, H. A. (2004). Color naming: "Grue" in the Celtic languages of the British Isles. *Psychological Science, 15,* 288. (4)

Lazarus, R. S. (1977). Cognitive and coping processes in emotion. In A. Monat & R. S. Lazarus (Eds.), *Stress and coping* (pp. 145–158). New York: Columbia University Press. (12)

Lazarus, R. S., Averill, J. R., & Opton, E. M., Jr. (1970). Towards a cognitive theory of emotion. In M. B. Arnold (Ed.), *Feelings and emotions* (pp. 207–232). New York: Academic Press. (12)

Lê, A. D., Li, Z., Funk, D., Shram, M., Li, T. K., & Shaham, Y. (2006). Increased vulnerability to nicotine self-administration and relapse in alcohol-naïve offspring of rats selectively bred for high alcohol intake. *Journal of Neurosciece, 26,* 1872–1879. (16)

Lee, M. G., Hassani, O. K., & Jones, B. E. (2005). Discharge of identified orexin/hypocretin neurons across the sleep–waking cycle. *Journal of Neuroscience, 25,* 6716–6720. (10)

Lee, R. A., Su, J., & Yoshida, E. (2005). Coping with intergenerational family conflict among Asian American college students. *Journal of Counseling Psychology, 52,* 389–399. (5)

Lee, S.-H., Blake, R., & Heeger, D. J. (2005). Traveling waves of activity in primary visual cortex during binocular rivalry. *Nature Neuroscience, 8,* 22–23. (10)

Lee, Y. T., & Duenas, G. (1995). Stereotype accuracy in multicultural business. In Y. T. Lee, L. J. Jussim, & C. R. McCauley (Eds.), *Stereotype accuracy* (pp. 157–186). Washington, DC: American Psychological Association. (13)

Leff, J. (2002). The psychiatric revolution: Care in the community. *Nature Reviews Neuroscience, 3,* 821–824. (15)

Leff, J., Wig, N. N., Ghosh, A., Bedi, H., Menon, D. K., Kuipers, L., et al. (1987). Expressed emotion and schizophrenia in North India: III. Influence of relatives' expressed emotion on the course of schizophrenia in Changigarh. *British Journal of Psychiatry, 151,* 166–173. (16)

Legge, G. E., Ahn, S. J., Klitz, T. S., & Luebker, A. (1997). Psychophysics of reading: XVI. The visual span in normal and low vision. *Vision Research, 37,* 1999–2010. (8)

Leichsenring, F., & Leibing, E. (2003). The effectiveness of psychodynamic therapy and cognitive behavior therapy in the treatment of personality disorders: A meta-analysis. *American Journal of Psychiatry, 160,* 1223–1232. (15)

Leinders-Zufall, T., Lane, A. P., Puche, A. C., Ma, W., Novotny, M. V., Shipley, M. T., et al. (2000). Ultrasensitive pheromone detection by mammalian vomeronasal neurons. *Nature, 405,* 792–796. (4)

Lekeu, F., Wojtasik, V., Van der Linden, M., & Salmon, E. (2002). Training early Alzheimer patients to use a mobile phone. *Acta Neurologica Belgica, 102,* 114–121. (7)

LeMagnen, J. (1981). The metabolic basis of dual periodicity of feeding in rats. *Behavioral and Brain Sciences, 4,* 561–607. (11)

Lenneberg, E. H. (1967). *Biological foundations of language.* New York: Wiley. (8)

Lenneberg, E. H. (1969). On explaining language. *Science, 164,* 635–643. (8)

Lenzenweger, M. F., Johnson, M. D., & Willett, J. B. (2004). Individual growth curve analysis illuminates stability and change in personality disorder features. *Archives of General Psychiatry, 61,* 1015–1024. (15)

Leppämäki, S., Partonen, T., & Lönnqvist, J. (2002). Bright-light exposure combined with physical exercise elevates mood. *Journal of Affective Disorders, 72,* 139–144. (16)

Leppänen, J. M., & Hietanen, J. K. (2003). Affect and face perception: Odors modulate the recognition advantage of happy faces. *Emotion, 3,* 315–326. (12)

Lerner, M. J. (1980). *The belief in a just world: A fundamental delusion.* New York: Plenum Press. (14)

Lesko, A. C., & Corpus, J. H. (2006). Discounting the difficult: How high math-identified women respond to stereotype threat. *Sex Roles, 54,* 113–125. (9)

Lett, B. T., Grant, V. L., Koh, M. T., & Smith, J. F. (2001). Wheel running simultaneously produces conditioned taste aversion and conditioned place preference in rats. *Learning and Motivation, 32,* 129–136. (6)

Levav, J., & Fitzsimons, G. J. (2006). When questions change behavior. *Psychological Science, 17,* 207–213. (11)

LeVay, S. (1991). A difference in hypothalamic structure between heterosexual and homosexual men. *Science, 253,* 1034–1037. (11)

Levenson, R. W., Oyama, O. N., & Meek, P. S. (1987). Greater reinforcement from alcohol for those at risk: Parental risk, personality risk, and sex. *Journal of Abnormal Psychology, 96,* 242–253. (16)

Leventhal, H. (1970). Findings and theory in the study of fear communication. In L. Berkowitz (Ed.), *Advances in experimental social psychology* (Vol. 5, pp. 119–186). New York: Academic Press. (13)

Levine, J. A., Lanningham-Foster, L. M., McCrady, S. K., Krizan, A. C., Olson, L. R., Kane, P. H., et al. (2005). Interindividual variation in posture allocation: Possible role in human obesity. *Science, 307,* 584–586. (11)

Levine, L. J., & Pizarro, D. A. (2004). Emotion and memory research: A grumpy overview. *Social Cognition, 5,* 530–554. (12)

Levine, R. V. (1990). The pace of life. *American Scientist, 78,* 450–459. (12)

Levine, S. C., Vasilyeva, M., Lourenco, S. F., Newcombe, N. S., & Huttenlocher, J. (2005). Socioeconomic status modifies the sex difference in spatial skill. *Psychological Science, 16,* 841–845. (5)

Levinson, D. J. (1986). A conception of adult development. *American Psychologist, 41,* 3–13. (5)

Levy, D. A., Stark, C. E. L., & Squire, L. R. (2004). Intact conceptual priming in the absence of declarative memory. *Psychological Science, 15,* 680–686. (7)

Levy, J., Pashler, H., & Boer, E. (2006). Central interference in driving. *Psychological Science, 17,* 228–235. (8)

Levy, L. J., Astur, R. S., & Frick, K. M. (2005). Men and women differ in object memory but not performance of a virtual radial maze. *Behavioral Neuroscience, 119,* 853–862. (5)

Leweke, F. M., Gerth, C. W., Koethe, D., Klosterkötter, J., Ruslanova, I., Krivogorsky, B., et al. (2004). Antibodies to infectious agents in individuals with recent onset schizophrenia. *European Archives of Psychiatry and Clinical Neuroscience, 254,* 4–8. (16)

Lewis, D. A., & Gonzalez-Burgos, G. (2006). Pathophysiologically based treatment interventions in schizophrenia. *Nature Medicine, 12,* 1016–1022. (16)

Lewis, D. O., Moy, E., Jackson, L. D., Aaronson, R., Restifo, N., Serra, S., et al. (1985). Biopsychosocial characteristics of children who later murder: A prospective study. *American Journal of Psychiatry, 142,* 1161–1167. (12)

Lewis, M. (1995). Self-conscious emotions. *American Scientist, 83,* 68–78. (12)

Lewis, M., Sullivan, M. W., Stanger, C., & Weiss, M. (1991). Self development and self-conscious emotions. In S. Chess & M. E. Hertzig (Eds.), *Annual progress in child psychiatry and child development 1990* (pp. 34–51). New York: Brunner/Mazel. (5)

Libet, B., Gleason, C. A., Wright, E. W., & Pearl, D. K. (1983). Time of conscious intention to act in relation to onset of cerebral activities (readiness potential): The unconscious initiation of a freely voluntary act. *Brain, 106,* 623–642. (10)

Lickliter, R., & Bahrick, L. E. (2000). The development of infant intersensory perception: Advantages of a comparative convergent-operations approach. *Psychological Bulletin, 126,* 260–280. (3)

Lien, M.-C., Ruthruff, E., & Johnston, J. C. (2006). Attentional limitations in doing two tasks at once. *Current Directions in Psychological Science, 15,* 89–93. (8)

Lilie, J. K., & Rosenberg, R. P. (1990). Behavioral treatment of insomnia. *Progress in Behavior Modification, 25,* 152–177. (10)

Lilienfeld, S. O., Lynn, S. J., Kirsch, I., Chaves, J. F., Sarbin, T. R., Ganaway, G. K., et al. (1999). Dissociative identity disorder and the sociocognitive model: Recalling the lessons of the past. *Psychological Bulletin, 125,* 507–523. (15)

Lilienfeld, S. O., Wood, J. M., & Garb, H. N. (2000). The scientific status of projective tests. *Psychological Science in the Public Interest, 1,* 27–66. (14)

Lillberg, K., Verkasalo, P. K., Kaprio, J., Teppo, L., Helenius, H., & Koskenvuo, M. (2003). Stressful life events and risk of breast cancer in 10,808 women: A cohort study. *American Journal of Epidemiology, 157,* 415–423. (12)

Lin, L., Faraco, J., Li, R., Kadotani, H., Rogers, W., Lin, X., et al. (1999). The sleep disorder canine narcolepsy is caused by a mutation in the hypocretin (orexin) receptor 2 gene. *Cell, 98,* 365–376. (10)

Linday, L. A. (1994). Maternal reports of pregnancy, genital, and related fantasies in preschool and kindergarten children. *Journal of the American Academy of Child and Adolescent Psychiatry, 33,* 416–423. (14)

Lindberg, L., & Hjern, A. (2003). Risk factors for anorexia nervosa: A national cohort study. *International Journal of Eating Disorders, 34,* 397–408. (11)

Linde, K., Berner, M., Egger. M., & Mulrow, C. (2005). St John's wort for depression. *British Journal of Psychiatry, 186,* 99–107. (16)

Linden, W., Lenz, J. W., & Con, A. H. (2001). Individualized stress management for primary hypertension: A randomized trial. *Archives of Internal Medicine, 161,* 1071–1080. (12)

Lindsay, D. S., Hagen, L., Read, J. D., Wade, K. A., & Garry, M. (2004). True photographs and false memories. *Psychological Science, 15,* 149–154. (7)

Lindsay, D. S., & Read, J. D. (1994). Psychotherapy and memories of childhood sexual abuse: A cognitive perspective. *Applied Cognitive Psychology, 8,* 281–338. (7)

Lindsey, D. T., & Brown, A. M. (2002). Color naming and the phototoxic effects of sunlight on the eye. *Psychological Science, 13,* 506–512. (4)

Linhorst, D. M., & Dirks-Linhorst, P. A. (1999). A critical assessment of disposition options for mentally ill offenders. *Social Science Review, 73,* 65–81. (15)

Linn, R., & Gilligan, C. (1990). One action, two moral orientations—The tension between justice and care voices in Israeli selective conscientious objectors. *New Ideas in Psychology, 8,* 189–203. (13)

Lipkus, I. (1991). The construction and preliminary validation of a global Belief in a Just World scale and the exploratory analysis of the multidimensional Belief in a Just World scale. *Personality and Individual Differences, 12,* 1171–1178. (14)

Lippa, R. A. (2006). Is high sex drive associated with increased sexual attraction to both sexes? *Psychological Science, 17,* 46–52. (11)

Lipsey, M. W., & Wilson, D. B. (1993). The efficacy of psychological, educational, and behavioral treatment. *American Psychologist, 48,* 1181–1209. (15)

Lipton, P. (2005). Testing hypotheses: Prediction and prejudice. *Science, 307,* 219–221. (2)

Lisak, D., & Roth, S. (1988). Motivational factors in nonincarcerated sexually aggressive men. *Journal of Personality and Social Psychology, 55,* 795–802. (12)

Lisanby, S. H., Maddox, J. H., Prudic, J., Devanand, D. P., & Sackeim, H. A. (2000). The effects of electroconvulsive therapy on memory of autobiographical and public events. *Archives of General Psychiatry, 57,* 581–590. (16)

Liu, Q., Pu, L., & Poo, M. (2005). Repeated cocaine exposure *in vivo* facilitates LTP induction in midbrain dopamine neurons. *Nature, 437,* 1027–1031. (16)

Locke, E. A., & Latham, G. P. (2002). Building a practically useful theory of goal setting and task motivation. *American Psychologist, 57,* 705–717. (11)

Locke, J. L. (1994). Phases in the child's development of language. *American Scientist, 82,* 436–445. (8)

Loeb, J. (1973). *Forced movements, tropisms, and animal conduct.* New York: Dover. (Original work published 1918) (6)

Loehlin, J. C. (1992). *Genes and environment in personality development.* Newbury Park, CA: Sage. (5, 14)

Loehlin, J. C., Horn, J. M., & Willerman, L. (1989). Modeling IQ change: Evidence from the Texas adoption project. *Child Development, 60,* 993–1004. (9)

Loewenstein, G. (1987). Anticipation and the valuation of delayed consumption. *The Economic Journal, 97,* 666–684. (11)

Loewi, O. (1960). An autobiographic sketch. *Perspectives in Biology, 4,* 3–25. (3)

Loftus, E. F. (1975). Leading questions and the eyewitness report. *Cognitive Psychology, 7,* 560–572. (7)

Loftus, E. F. (1993). The reality of repressed memories. *American Psychologist, 48,* 518–537. (7)

Loftus, E. (2003). Our changeable memories: Legal and practical implications. *Nature Reviews Neuroscience, 4,* 231–234. (7)

Loftus, E. F., Feldman, J., & Dashiell, R. (1995). The reality of illusory memories. In D. L. Schacter (Ed.), *Memory distortion* (pp. 47–68). Cambridge, MA: Harvard University Press. (7)

Loftus, G. R. (1996). Psychology will be a much better science when we change the way we analyze data. *Current Directions in Psychological Science, 5,* 161–171. (2)

Logan, G. D. (2003). Executive control of thought and action: In search of the wild homunculus. *Current Directions in Psychological Science, 12,* 45–48. (7)

Long, G. M., & Toppine, T. C. (2004). Enduring interest in perceptual ambiguity: Alternating views of reversible figures. *Psychological Bulletin, 130,* 748–768. (4)

Longstreth, L. E. (1981). Revisiting Skeels' final study: A critique. *Developmental Psychology, 17,* 620–625. (9)

Lord, C. G., & Lepper, M. R. (1999). Attitude representation theory. *Advances in Experimental Social Psychology, 31,* 265–343. (13)

Lord, C. G., Ross, L., & Lepper, M. R. (1979). Biased assimilation and attitude polarization: The effects of prior theories on subsequently considered evidence. *Journal of Personality and Social Psychology, 37,* 2098–2109. (13)

Lorenz, K. (1950). The comparative method in studying innate behaviour patterns. *Symposia of the Society for Experimental Biology, 4,* 221–268. (11)

Lotto, R. B., & Purves, D. (2002). The empirical basis of color perception. *Consciousness and Cognition, 11,* 609–629. (4)

Lotze, M., Grodd, W., Birbaumer, N., Erb, M., Huse, E., & Flor, H. (1999). Does use of a myoelectric prosthesis prevent cortical reorganization and phantom limb pain? *Nature Neuroscience, 2,* 501–502. (4)

Lovallo, D., & Kahneman, D. (2000). Living with uncertainty: Attractiveness and resolution timing. *Journal of Behavioral Decision Making, 13,* 179–190. (11)

Lövdén, M. (2003). The episodic memory and inhibition accounts of age-related increases in false memory: A consistency check. *Journal of Memory and Language, 49,* 268–283. (7)

Low, K. S. D., Yoon, M. J., Roberts, B. W., & Rounds, J. (2005). The stability of vocational interests from early adolescence to middle adulthood: A quantitative review of longitudinal studies. *Psychological Bulletin, 131,* 713–737. (5)

Lowe, K. B., Kroeck, K. G., & Sivasubramaniam, N. (1996). Effectiveness correlates of transformational and transactional leadership: A meta-analytic review of the MLQ literature. *Leadership Quarterly, 7,* 385–425. (11)

Lucas, R. E. (2005). Time does not heal all wounds. *Psychological Science, 16,* 945–950. (12, 13)

Lucas, R. E., Clark, A. E., Georgellis, Y., & Diener, E. (2004). Unemployment alters the set point for life satisfaction. *Psychological Science, 15,* 8–13. (12)

Luciano, M., Wright, M. J., Smith, G. A., Geffen, G. M., Geffen, L. B., & Martin, N. G. (2001). Genetic covariance among measures of information processing speed, working memory, and IQ. *Behavior Genetics, 31,* 581–592. (9)

Lucio, E., Ampudia, A., Durán, C., León, I., & Butcher, J. N. (2001). Comparison of the Mexican and American norms of the MMPI–2. *Journal of Clinical Psychology, 57,* 1459–1468. (14)

Luck, S. J., & Vogel, E. K. (1997). The capacity of visual working memory for features and conjunctions. *Nature, 390,* 279–281. (7)

Lüer, G., Becker, D., Lass, U., Yunqiu, F., Guopeng, C., & Zhongming, W. (1998). Memory span in German and Chinese: Evidence for the phonological loop. *European Psychologist, 3,* 102–112. (7)

Luo, D., Thompson, L. A., & Detterman, D. K. (2003). The causal factor underlying the correlation between psychometric *g* and scholastic performance. *Intelligence, 31,* 67–83. (9)

Luthar, S. S., Cicchetti, D., & Becker, B. (2000). The construct of resilience: A critical evaluation and guidelines for future work. *Child Development, 71,* 543–562. (5)

Lyamin, O. I., Mukhametov, L. M., Siegel, J. M., Nazarenko, E. A., Polyakova, I. G., & Shpak, O. V. (2002). Unihemispheric slow wave sleep and the state of the eyes in a white whale. *Behavioural Brain Research, 129,* 125–129. (10)

Lyamin, O., Pryaslova, J., Lance, V., & Siegel, J. (2005). Continuous activity in cetaceans after birth. *Nature, 435,* 1177. (10)

Lykken, D. T. (1979). The detection of deception. *Psychological Bulletin, 86,* 47–53. (12)

Lykken, D. T., Bouchard, T. J., Jr., McGue, M., & Tellegen, A. (1993). Heritability of interests: A twin study. *Journal of Applied Psychology, 78,* 649–661. (5)

Lykken, D. T., McGue, M., Tellegen, A., & Bouchard, T. J. (1992). Emergenesis: Genetic traits that may not run in families. *American Psychologist, 47,* 1565– 1577. (5)

Lykken, D., & Tellegen, A. (1996). Happiness is a stochastic phenomenon. *Psychological Science, 7,* 186–189. (12)

Lymburner, J. A., & Roesch, R. (1999). The insanity defense: Five years of research (1993–1999). *International Journal of Law and Psychiatry, 22,* 213–240. (15)

Lynam, D. R. (1996). Early identification of chronic offenders: Who is the fledgling psychopath? *Psychological Bulletin, 120,* 209–234. (12)

Lynn, R. (1998). In support of the nutrition theory. In U. Neisser (Ed.), *The rising curve* (pp. 207–215). Washington, DC: American Psychological Association. (9)

Lyons, M. J., Eisen, S. A., Goldberg, J., True, W., Lin, N., Meyer, J. M., et al. (1998). A registry-based twin study of depression in men. *Archives of General Psychiatry, 55,* 468–472. (16)

Lyubomirsky, S., King, L., & Diener, E. (2005). The benefits of frequent positive affect: Does happiness lead to success? *Psychological Bulletin, 131,* 803–855. (12)

MacCallum, F., & Golombok, S. (2004). Children raised in fatherless families from infancy: A follow-up of children of lesbian and single heterosexual mothers at early adolescence. *Journal of Child Psychology and Psychiatry, 45,* 1407–1419. (5)

MacCoun, R. J. (1998). Toward a psychology of harm reduction. *American Psychologist, 53,* 1199–1208. (16)

MacCoun, R., & Reuter, P. (1997). Interpreting Dutch cannabis policy: Reasoning by analogy in the legalization debate. *Science, 278,* 47–52. (16)

Macey, P. M., Henderson, L. A., Macey, K. E., Alger, J., Frysinger, R. C., Woo, M. A., et al. (2002). Brain morphology associated with obstructive sleep apnea. *American Journal of Respiratory and Critical Care Medicine, 166,* 1382–1387. (10)

MacKay, D. G., & Ahmetzanov, M. V. (2005). Emotion, memory, and attention in the taboo Stroop paradigm. *Psychological Science, 16,* 25–32. (7)

Macmillan, M. (1997). *Freud evaluated.* Cambridge, MA: MIT Press. (14)

MacQuitty, J. (1996, August 1). Lily the stink loses its 33-year reputation by a nose. *The Times* (London), pp. 1–2. (11)

Madson, L. (2005). Demonstrating the importance of question wording on surveys. *Teaching of Psychology, 32,* 40–43. (2)

Magee, W. J., Eaton, W. W., Wittchen, H. -U., McGonagle, K. A., & Kessler, R. C. (1996). Agoraphobia, simple phobia, and social phobia in the National Comorbidity Survey. *Archives of General Psychiatry, 53,* 159–168. (16)

Maguire, E. A., Gadian, D. G., Johnsrude, I. S., Good, C. D., Ashburner, J., Frackowiak, R. S. J., et al. (2000). Navigation-related structural change in the hippocampi of taxi drivers. *Proceedings of the National Academy of Sciences, USA, 97,* 4398–4403. (3)

Maguire, E. A., Valentine, E. R., Wilding, J. M., & Kapur, N. (2003). Routes to remembering: The brains behind superior memory. *Nature Neuroscience, 6,* 90–95. (8, 9)

Mahowald, M. W., & Schenck, C. H. (2005). Insights from studying human sleep disorders. *Nature, 437,* 1279–1285. (10)

Maier, S. F., & Watkins, L. R. (1998). Cytokines for psychologists: Implications of bidirectional immune-to-brain communication for understanding behavior, mood, and cognition. *Psychological Review, 105,* 83–107. (12)

Major, B., Quinton, W. J., & McCoy, S. K. (2002). Antecedents and consequences of attributions to discrimination: Theoretical and empirical advances. *Advances in Experimental Social Psychology, 34,* 251–330. (13)

Maki, R. H. (1990). Memory for script actions: Effects of relevance and detail expectancy. *Memory & Cognition, 18,* 5–14. (7)

Malamed, F., & Zaidel, E. (1993). Language and task effects on lateralized word recognition. *Brain and Language, 45,* 70–85. (8)

Malamuth, N. M., & Brown, L. M. (1994). Sexually aggressive men's perceptions of women's communications: Testing three explanations. *Journal of Personality and Social Psychology, 67,* 699–712. (12)

Maldonado, R., Saiardi, A., Valverde, O., Samad, T. A., Roques, B. P., & Borrelli, E. (1997). Absence of opiate rewarding effects in mice lacking dopamine D2 receptors. *Nature, 388,* 586–589. (3)

Malmberg, A. B., Chen, C., Tonegawa, S., & Basbaum, A. I. (1997). Preserved acute pain and reduced neuropathic pain in mice lacking PKC. *Science, 278,* 179–283. (4)

Malmquist, C. P. (1986). Children who witness parental murder: Posttraumatic aspects. *Journal of the American Academy of Child Psychiatry, 25,* 320–325. (7)

Mandavilli, A. (2006). Look and learn. *Nature, 441,* 271–272. (3)

Mann, T., Nolen-Hoeksema, S., Huang, K., Burgard, D., Wright, A., & Hanson, K. (1997). Are two interventions worse than none? Joint primary and secondary prevention of eating disorders in college females. *Health Psychology, 16,* 215–225. (15)

Mannuzza, S., Klein, R. G., Bessler, A., Malloy, P., & LaPadula, M. (1998). Adult psychiatric status of hyperactive boys grown up. *American Journal of Psychiatry, 155,* 493–498. (8)

Manor, O., & Eisenbach, Z. (2003). Mortality after spousal loss: Are there socio-demographic differences? *Social Science & Medicine, 56,* 405–413. (12)

Mansky, P. A. (1978). Opiates: Human psychopharmacology. In L. L. Iversen, S. D. Iversen, & S. H. Snyder (Eds.), *Handbook of psychopharmacology: Vol. 12. Drugs of abuse* (pp. 95–185). New York: Plenum Press. (16)

Maquet, P., Laureys, S., Peigneux, P., Fuchs, S., Petiau, C., Phillips, C., et al. (2000). Experience-dependent changes in cerebral activation during human REM sleep. *Nature Neuroscience, 3,* 831–836. (10)

Maquet, P., Peters, J. M., Aerts, J., Delfiore, G., Degueldre, C., Luxen, A., et al. (1996). Functional neuroanatomy of human rapid-eye-movement sleep and dreaming. *Nature, 383,* 163–166. (10)

Marcia, J. E. (1980). Identity in adolescence. In J. Adelson (Ed.), *Handbook of adolescent psychology* (pp. 159–187). New York: Wiley. (10)

Marcus, G. F., Vijayan, S., Rao, S. B., & Vishton, P. M. (1999). Rule learning by seven-month-old infants. *Science, 283,* 77–80. (8)

Marder, S. R., Mebane, A., Chien, C., Winslade, W. J., Swann, E., & Van Putten, T. (1983). A comparison of patients who refuse and consent to neuroleptic treatment. *American Journal of Psychiatry, 140,* 470–472. (15)

Marian, V., & Neisser, U. (2000). Language-dependent recall of autobiographical memories. *Journal of Experimental Psychology: General, 129,* 361–368. (7)

Marin, R. H., Perez, M. F., Duero, D. G., & Ramirez, O. A. (1999). Preexposure to drug administration context blocks the development of tolerance to sedative effects of diazepam. *Pharmacology Biochemistry and Behavior, 64,* 473–477. (6)

Maris, R. W. (1997). Social suicide. *Suicide and Life-Threatening Behavior, 27,* 41–49. (16)

Markey, C. N., Markey, P. M., & Tinsley, B. J. (2003). Personality, puberty, and preadolescent girls' risky behaviors: Examining the predictive value of the five-factor model of personality. *Journal of Research in Personality, 37,* 405–419. (14)

Markey, P. M. (2000). Bystander intervention in computer-mediated intervention. *Computers in Human Behavior, 16,* 183–188. (13)

Marks, D., & Kammann, R. (1980). *The psychology of the psychic.* Buffalo, NY: Prometheus. (2, 14)

Marler, P. (1997). Three models of song learning: Evidence from behavior. *Journal of Neurobiology, 33,* 501–516. (6)

Marler, P., & Peters, S. (1981). Sparrows learn adult song and more from memory. *Science, 213,* 780–782. (6)

Marler, P., & Peters, S. (1982). Long-term storage of learned birdsongs prior to pro-

duction. *Animal Behaviour, 30,* 479–482. (6)

Marler, P., & Peters, S. (1987). A sensitive period for song acquisition in the song sparrow, *Melospiza melodia:* A case of age-limited learning. *Ethology, 76,* 89–100. (6)

Marler, P., & Peters, S. (1988). Sensitive periods for song acquisition from tape recordings and live tutors in the swamp sparrow, *Melospiza georgiana. Ethology, 77,* 76–84. (6)

Marlowe, F., & Wetsman, A. (2001). Preferred waist-to-hip ratio and ecology. *Personality and Individual Differences, 30,* 481–489. (13)

Marriott, F. H. C. (1976). Abnormal colour vision. In H. Davson (Ed.), *The eye* (2nd ed., pp. 533–547). New York: Academic Press. (4)

Marsh, A. A., Elfenbein, H. A., & Ambady, N. (2003). Nonverbal "accents": Cultural differences in facial expressions of emotion. *Psychological Science, 14,* 373–376. (12)

Marsh, H. W., & Byrne, B. M. (1991). Differentiated additive androgyny model: Relations between masculinity, femininity, and multiple dimensions of self-concept. *Journal of Personality and Social Psychology, 61,* 811–828. (5)

Marsh, H. W., & Craven, R. G. (2006). Reciprocal effects of self-concept and performance from a multidimensional perspective. *Perspectives on Psychological Science, 1,* 133–163. (14)

Marshall, J. C., & Halligan, P. W. (1995). Seeing the forest but only half the trees? *Nature, 373,* 521–523. (10)

Marshall, L., Helgadóttir, H., Mölle, M., & Born, J. (2006). Boosting slow oscillations during sleep potentiates memory. *Nature, 444,* 610–613. (10)

Martens, A., Johns, M., Greenberg, J., & Schimel, J. (2006). Combating stereotype threat: The effect of self-affirmation on women's intellectual performance. *Journal of Experimental Social Psychology, 42,* 236–243. (9)

Martin, D. J., & Lynn, S. J. (1996). The hypnotic simulation index: Successful discrimination of real versus simulating participants. *International Journal of Clinical and Experimental Hypnosis, 44,* 338–353. (10)

Martindale, C. (2001). Oscillations and analogies: Thomas Young, MD, FRS, genius. *American Psychologist, 56,* 342–345. (4, 8)

Martiny, K., Lunde, M., Undén, M., Dam, H., & Bech, P. (2005). Adjunctive bright light in non-seasonal major depression: Results from clinician-rated depression scales. *Acta Psychiatria Scaninavica, 112,* 117–125. (16)

Martorell, R. (1998). Nutrition and the worldwide rise in IQ scores. In U. Neisser (Ed.), *The rising curve* (pp. 183–206). Washington, DC: American Psychological Association. (9)

Martsh, C. T., & Miller, W. R. (1997). Extraversion predicts heavy drinking in college students. *Personality and Individual Differences, 23,* 153–155. (14)

Marx, J. (2003). Cellular warriors at the battle of the bulge. *Science, 299,* 846–849. (11)

Maslach, C. (2003). Job burnout: New directions in research and intervention. *Current Directions in Psychological Science, 12,* 189–192. (11)

Maslow, A. H. (1962). *Toward a psychology of being.* Princeton, NJ: Van Nostrand. (14)

Maslow, A. H. (1971). *The farther reaches of human nature.* New York: Viking Press. (14)

Mason, D. A., & Frick, P. J. (1994). The heritability of antisocial behavior: A meta-analysis of twin and adoption studies. *Journal of Psychopathology and Behavioral Assessment, 16,* 301–323. (5)

Massimini, M., Ferrarelli, F., Huber, R., Esser, S. K., Singh, H., & Tononi, G. (2005). Breakdown of cortical effective connectivity during sleep. *Science, 309,* 2228–2232. (10)

Masson, J. M. (1984). *The assault on truth.* New York: Farrar, Straus and Giroux. (14)

Masten, A. S., & Coatsworth, J. D. (1998). The development of competence in favorable and unfavorable environments. *American Psychologist, 53,* 205–220. (5)

Masters, W. H., & Johnson, V. E. (1966). *Human sexual response.* Boston: Little, Brown. (11)

Mathalon, D. H., Pfefferbaum, A., Lim, K. O., Rosenbloom, M. J., & Sullivan, E. V. (2003). Compounded brain volume deficits in schizophrenia-alcoholism comorbidity. *Archives of General Psychiatry, 60,* 245–252. (16)

Matheny, A. P., Jr. (1989). Children's behavioral inhibition over age and across situations: Genetic similarity for a trait to change. *Journal of Personality, 57,* 215–235. (5)

Mather, M., Canli, T., English, T., Whitfield, S., Wais, P., Ochsner, K., et al. (2004). Amygdala responses to emotionally valenced stimuli in older and younger adults. *Psychological Science, 15,* 259–263. (12)

Mathews, A., & Mackintosh, B. (2004). Take a closer look: Emotion modifies the boundary extension effect. *Emotion, 4,* 36–45. (12)

Matin, E., Clymer, A. B., & Matin, L. (1972). Metacontrast and saccadic suppression. *Science, 178,* 179–182. (8)

Maton, K. I., Kohout, J. L., Wicherski, M., Leary, G. E., & Vinokurov, A. (2006). Minority students of color and the psychology graduate pipeline. *American Psychologist, 61,* 117–131. (1)

Matsumoto, D. (1994). *People: Psychology from a cultural perspective.* Pacific Grove, CA: Brooks/Cole. (2)

Matsunami, H., Montmayeur, J.-P., & Buck, L. B. (2000). A family of candidate taste receptors in human and mouse. *Nature, 404,* 601–604. (4)

Mattson, S. N., Riley, E. P., Grambling, L., Delis, D. C., & Jones, K. L. (1998). Neuropsychological comparison of alcohol-exposed children with or without physical features of fetal alcohol syndrome. *Neuropsychology, 12,* 146–153. (5)

Matzel, L. D., Han, Y. R., Grossman, H., Karnik, M. S., Patel, D., Scott, N., et al. (2003). Individual differences in the expression of a "general" learning ability in mice. *Journal of Neuroscience, 23,* 6423–6433. (9)

Maunsell, E., Brisson, J., Mondor, M., Verreault, R., & Deschênes, L. (2001). Stressful life events and survival after breast cancer. *Psychosomatic Medicine, 63,* 306–315. (12)

May, C. P., Hasher, L., & Foong, N. (2005). Implicit memory, age, and time of day. *Psychological Science, 16,* 96–100. (10)

May, C. P., Hasher, L., & Stoltzfus, E. R. (1993). Optimal time of day and the magnitude of age differences in memory. *Psychological Science, 4,* 326–330. (10)

May, M. (1999, January/February). Speed demons. *The Sciences, 39*(1), 16–18. (8)

Mayberry, R. I., Lock, E., & Kazmi, H. (2002). Linguistic ability and early language exposure. *Nature, 415,* 1026–1029. (8)

Mayer, J. D. (2001). Emotion, intelligence, and emotional intelligence. In J. P. Forgas (Ed.), *Handbook of affect and social cognition* (pp. 410–431). Mahwah, NJ: Erlbaum. (12)

Mayer, J. D. (2005). A tale of two visions: Can a new view of personality help integrate psychology? *American Psychologist, 60,* 294–307. (14)

Mayer, J. D., Caruso, D. R., & Salovey, P. (2000). Emotional intelligence meets traditional standards for an intelligence. *Intelligence, 27,* 267–298. (12)

Mayer, J. D., & Salovey, P. (1995). Emotional intelligence and the construction and regulation of feelings. *Applied & Preventive Psychology, 4,* 197–208. (12)

Mayer, J. D., & Salovey, P. (1997). What is emotional intelligence? In P. Salovey & D. J. Sluyter (Eds.). *Emotional development and emotional intelligence* (pp. 3–34). New York: Basic Books. (12)

Mayer, J. D., Salovey, P., Caruso, D. R., & Sitarenios, G. (2001). Emotional intelligence as a standard intelligence. *Emotion, 1,* 232–242. (12)

Mazzoni, G., & Memon, A. (2003). Imagination can create false autobiographical memories. *Psychological Science, 14,* 186–188. (7)

McCall, V. W., Yates, B., Hendricks, S., Turner, K., & McNabb, B. (1989). Comparison between the Stanford-Binet: L-M and the Stanford-Binet: Fourth edition with a group of gifted children. *Contemporary Educational Psychology, 114,* 93–96. (9)

McCall, W. A. (1939). *Measurement.* New York: Macmillan. (9)

McCann, U. D., Lowe, K. A., & Ricaurte, G. A. (1997). Long-lasting effects of recreational drugs of abuse on the central nervous system. *The Neuroscientist, 3,* 399–411. (3)

McClelland, J. L. (1988). Connectionist models and psychological evidence. *Journal of Memory and Language, 27,* 107–123. (8)

McClelland, J. L., & Rumelhart, D. E. (1981). An interactive activation model of context effects in letter perception: Part 1. An account of basic findings. *Psychological Review, 88,* 375–407. (8)

McClintock, M. K. (1971). Menstrual synchrony and suppression. *Nature, 229,* 244–245. (4)

McClure, J. (1998). Discounting causes of behavior: Are two reasons better than one? *Journal of Personality and Social Psychology, 74,* 7–20. (13)

McCormick, M. C. (1985). The contribution of low birth weight to infant mortality and childhood morbidity. *New England Journal of Medicine, 312,* 82–90. (5)

McCornack, R. L. (1983). Bias in the validity of predicted college grades in four ethnic minority groups. *Educational & Psychological Measurement, 43,* 517–522. (9)

McCourt, K., Bouchard, T. J., Jr., Lykken, D. T., Tellegen, A., & Keyes, M. (1999). Authoritarianism revisited: Genetic and environmental influences examined in twins reared apart and together. *Personality and Individual Differences, 27,* 985–1014. (5)

McCrae, R. R. (1996). Social consequences of experiential openness. *Psychological Bulletin, 120,* 323–337. (14)

McCrae, R. R., & Costa, P. T., Jr. (1987). Validation of the five-factor model of personality across instruments and observers. *Journal of Personality and Social Psychology, 52,* 81–90. (14)

McCrae, R. R., & Costa, P. T., Jr. (1997). Personality trait structure as a human universal. *American Psychologist, 52,* 509–516. (13)

McCrae, R. R., Costa, P. T., Jr., Ostendorf, F., Angleitner, A., Hrebícková, M., Avia, M. D., et al. (2000). Nature over nurture: Temperament, personality, and life span development. *Journal of Personality and Social Psychology, 78,* 173–186. (14)

McCrae, R. R., & Terracciano, A. (2006). National character and personality. *Current Directions in Psychological Science, 15,* 156–161. (13)

McCrink, K., & Wynn, K. (2004). Large-number addition and subtraction by 9-month-old infants. *Psychological Science, 15,* 776–781. (5)

McDaniel, M. A., Maier, S. F., & Einstein, G. O. (2002). "Brain-specific" nutrients: A memory cure? *Psychological Science in the Public Interest, 3,* 12–38. (7)

McElheny, V. (2004). Three Nobelists ask: Are we ready for the next frontier? *Cerebrum, 5,* 69–81. (1)

McEvoy, J. P., Lieberman, J. A., Stroup, T. S., Davis, S. M., Meltzer, H. Y., & Rosenheck, R. A. (2006). Effectiveness of clozapine versus olanzapine, quetiapine, and risperidone in patients with chronic schizophrenia who did not respond to prior atypical antipsychotic treatment. *American Journal of Psychiatry, 163,* 600–610. (16)

McEwen, B. S. (2000). The neurobiology of stress: From serendipity to clinical relevance. *Brain Research, 886,* 172–189. (12)

McFarlane, A. C. (1997). The prevalence and longitudinal course of PTSD. *Annals of the New York Academy of Sciences, 821,* 10–23. (12)

McGeorge, P., Taylor, L., Della Sala, S., & Shanks, M. F. (2002). Word stem completion in young adults, elderly adults, and patients with Alzheimer's disease. *Archives of Clinical Neuropsychology, 17,* 389–398. (7)

McGorry, P. D., Yung, A. R., Phillips, L. J., Yuen, H. P., Francey, S., Cosgrave, E. M., et al. (2002). Randomized controlled trial of interventions designed to reduce the risk of progression to first-episode psychosis in a clinical sample with subthreshold symptoms. *Archives of General Psychiatry, 59,* 921–928. (15)

McGovern, P. E., Glusker, D. L., Exner, L. J., & Voigt, M. M. (1996). Neolithic resinated wine. *Nature, 381,* 480–481. (3)

McGrath, J. J., Féron, F. P., Burne, T. H. J., Mackay-Sim, A., & Eyles, D. W. (2003). The neurodevelopmental hypothesis of schizophrenia: A review of recent developments. *Annals of Medicine, 35,* 86–93. (16)

McGregor, D. M. (1960). *The human side of enterprise.* New York: McGraw-Hill. (11)

McGregor, I. S., Hargreaves, G. A., Apfelbach, R., & Hunt, G. E. (2004). Neural correlates of cat odor-induced anxiety in rats: Region-specific effects of the benzodiazepine midazolam. *Journal of Neuroscience, 24,* 4134–4144. (12)

McGue, M. (1999). The behavioral genetics of alcoholism. *Current Directions in Psychological Science, 8,* 109–115. (16)

McGue, M., & Bouchard, T. J., Jr. (1998). Genetic and environmental influences on human behavioral differences. *Annual Review of Neuroscience, 21,* 1–24. (9)

McGue, M., Elkins, I., Walden, B., & Iacono, W. G. (2005). Perceptions of the parent–adolescent relationship: A longitudinal investigation. *Developmental Psychology, 41,* 971–984. (5)

McGuffin, P., Rijsdijk, F., Andrew, M., Sham, P., Katz, R., & Cardno, A. (2003). The heritability of bipolar affective disorder and the genetic relationship to unipolar disorder. *Archives of General Psychiatry, 60,* 497–502. (16)

McGuire, S., & Clifford, J. (2000). Genetic and environmental contributions to loneliness in children. *Psychological Science, 11,* 487–491. (5)

McGuire, S., Clifford, J., Fink, J., Basho, S., & McDonnell, A. (2003). Children's reactions to the unfamiliar in middle childhood and adolescence: An observational twin/sibling study. *Personality and Individual Differences, 35,* 339–354. (5)

McGuire, W. J., & Papageorgis, D. (1961). The relative efficacy of various types of prior belief-defense in producing immunity against persuasion. *Journal of Abnormal and Social Psychology, 62,* 327–337. (13)

McGurk, H., Caplan, M., Hennessy, E., & Moss, P. (1993). Controversy, theory, and social context in contemporary day care research. *Journal of Child Psychology, 34,* 3–23. (5)

McGurk, H., & MacDonald, J. (1976). Hearing lips and seeing voices. *Nature, 264,* 746–748. (8)

McIntyre, R. S., Konarski, J. Z., Wilkins, K., Soczynska, J. K., & Kennedy, S. H. (2006). Obesity in bipolar disorder and major depressive disorder: Results from a national community health survey on mental health and well-being. *Canadian Journal of Psychiatry, 51,* 274–280. (11)

McKelvey, M. W., & McKenry, P. C. (2000). The psychosocial well-being of Black and White mothers following marital dissolution. *Psychology of Women Quarterly, 24,* 4–14. (5)

McMahon, F. J., Buervenich, S., Charney, D., Lipsky, R., Rush, A. J., Wilson, A. F., et al. (2006). Variation in the gene encoding serotonin 2A receptor is associated with outcome of antidepressant treatment. *American Journal of Human Genetics, 78,* 804–814. (16)

McMurtry, P. L., & Mershon, D. H. (1985). Auditory distance judgments in noise, with and without hearing protection. *Proceedings of the Human Factors Society* (Baltimore), pp. 811–813. (4)

McNally, R. J. (1990). Psychological approaches to panic disorder: A review. *Psychological Bulletin, 108,* 403–419. (16)

McNally, R. J. (2002). Anxiety sensitivity and panic disorder. *Biological Psychiatry, 52,* 938–946. (16)

McNally, R. J., Bryant, R. A., & Ehlers, A. (2003). Does early psychological intervention promote recovery from posttraumatic stress? *Psychological Science in the Public Interest, 4,* 45–77. (12)

McNamara, P., McLaren, D., Smith, D., Brown, A., & Stickgold, R. (2005). A "Jekyll and Hyde" within: Aggressive versus friendly interactions in REM and non-REM dreams. *Psychological Science, 16,* 130–136. (10)

Mechelli, A., Crinion, J. T., Noppeney, U., O'Doherty, J., Ashburner, J., Frackowiak, R. S., et al. (2004). Structural plasticity in the bilingual brain. *Nature, 431,* 757. (8)

"The medals and the damage done." (2004). *Nature, 430,* 604. (3)

Meddis, R., Pearson, A. J. D., & Langford, G. (1973). An extreme case of healthy insomnia. *EEG and Clinical Neurophysiology, 35,* 213–214. (10)

Medin, D. L., & Atran, S. (2004). The native mind: Biological categorization and reasoning in development and across cultures. *Psychological Review, 111,* 960–983. (2)

Mednick, S. C., Nakayama, K., Cantero, J. L., Atienza, M., Levin, A. A., Pathak, N., et al. (2002). The restorative effect of naps on perceptual deterioration. *Nature Neuroscience, 5,* 677–681. (10)

Medver, V. H., Madey, S. F., & Gilovich, T. (1995). When less is more: Counterfactual thinking and satisfaction among Olympic athletes. *Journal of Personality and Social Psychology, 69,* 603–610. (12)

Meeter, M., & Murre, J. M. J. (2004). Consolidation of long-term memory: Evidence and alternatives. *Psychological Bulletin, 130,* 843–857. (7)

Meichenbaum, D. (1985). *Stress inoculation training.* New York: Pergamon Press. (12)

Meichenbaum, D., & Cameron, R. (1983). Stress inoculation training. In D. Meichenbaum & M. E. Jaremko (Eds.), *Stress reduction and prevention* (pp. 115–154). New York: Plenum Press. (12)

Meichenbaum, D. H. (1995). Cognitive-behavioral therapy in historical perspective. In B. Bongar & L. E. Beutler (Eds.), *Comprehensive textbook of psychotherapy: Theory and practice* (pp. 140–158). Oxford, England: Oxford University Press. (15)

Meier, B. P., Robinson, M. D., & Wilkowski, B. M. (2006). Turning the other cheek. *Psychological Science, 17,* 136–142. (2)

Melis, A. P., Hare, B., & Tomasello, M. (2006). Chimpanzees recruit the best collaborators. *Science, 311,* 1297–1300. (13)

Mellers, B. A., Schwartz, A., Ho, K., & Ritov, I. (1997). Decision affect theory: Emotional reactions to the outcomes of risky options. *Psychological Science, 8,* 423–429. (8)

Mello, N. K., & Mendelson, J. H. (1978). Behavioral pharmacology of human alcohol, heroin and marihuana use. In J. Fishman (Ed.), *The bases of addiction* (pp. 133–158). Berlin, Germany: Dahlem Konferenzen. (16)

Meltzoff, A. N., & Moore, M. K. (1977). Imitation of facial and manual gestures by human neonates. *Science, 198,* 75–78. (6)

Meltzoff, A. N., & Moore, M. K. (1983). Newborn infants imitate adult facial gestures. *Child Development, 54,* 702–709. (6)

Melzack, R., & Wall, P. D. (1965). Pain mechanisms: A new theory. *Science, 150,* 971–979. (4)

Melzack, R., Weisz, A. Z., & Sprague, L. T. (1963). Stratagems for controlling pain: Contributions of auditory stimulation and suggestion. *Experimental Neurology, 8,* 239–247. (12)

Merckelbach, H, Dekkers, T., Wessel, I., & Roefs, A. (2003). Dissociative symptoms and amnesia in Dutch concentration camp survivors. *Comprehensive Psychiatry, 44,* 65–69. (7)

Mergen, M., Mergen, H., Ozata, M., Oner, R., & Oner, C. (2001). A novel melanocortin 4 receptor (MC4R) gene mutation associated with morbid obesity. *Journal of Clinical Endocrinology & Metabolism, 86,* 3448–3451. (11)

Mershon, D. H., Desaulniers, D. H., Kiefer, S. A., Amerson, T. L., Jr., & Mills, J. T. (1981). Perceived loudness and visually determined auditory distance. *Perception, 10,* 531–543. (4)

Mershon, D. H., & King, L. E. (1975). Intensity and reverberation as factors in the auditory perception of egocentric distance. *Perception & Psychophysics, 18,* 409–415. (4)

Mesmer, F. A. (1980). *Mesmerism: A translation of the original medical and scientific writings of F. A. Mesmer.* Los Altos, CA: Kaufmann. (5)

Messer, S. B., & Wampold, B. E. (2002). Let's face facts: Common factors are more portent than specific therapy ingredients. *Clinical Psychology: Science and Practice, 9,* 21–25. (16)

Messinger, D. S. (2002). Positive and negative: Infant facial expressions and emotions. *Current Directions in Psychological Science, 11,* 1–6. (12)

Metcalfe, J., & Wiebe, D. (1987). Intuition in insight and noninsight problem solving. *Memory & Cognition, 15,* 238–246. (8)

Meyer, G. J. (2002). Exploring possible ethnic differences and bias in the Rorschach Comprehensive System. *Journal of Personality Assessment, 78,* 104–129. (14)

Meyer, J. P., Becker, T. E., & Vandenberghe, C. (2004). Employee commitment and motivation: A conceptual analysis and integrative model. *Journal of Applied Psychology, 89,* 991–1007. (11)

Meyerowitz, B. E., Richardson, J., Hudson, S., & Leedham, B. (1998). Ethnicity and cancer outcomes: Behavioral and psychosocial considerations. *Psychological Bulletin, 123,* 47–70. (12)

Mezzanotte, W. S., Tangel, D. J., & White, D. P. (1992). Waking genioglossal electromyogram in sleep apnea patients versus normal controls (a neuromuscular compensatory mechanism). *Journal of Clinical Investigation, 89,* 1571–1579. (10)

Mikulincer, M., Shaver, P. R., & Pereg, D. (2003). Attachment theory and affect regulation: The dynamics, development, and cognitive consequences of attachment-related strategies. *Motivation and Emotion, 27,* 77–102. (5)

Milar, K. S. (2000). The first generation of women psychologists and the psychology of women. *American Psychologist, 55,* 616–619. (1)

Milgram, S. (1974). *Obedience to authority.* New York: Harper & Row. (13)

Milich, R., Wolraich, M., & Lindgren, S. (1986). Sugar and hyperactivity: A critical review of empirical findings. *Clinical Psychology Review, 6,* 493–513. (2)

Millar, J. K., Pickard, B. S., Mackie, S., James, R., Christie, S., Buchanan, S. R., et al. (2005). DISC1 and PDE4B are interacting genetic factors in schizophrenia that regulate cAMP signaling. *Science, 310,* 1187–1191. (16)

Miller, C. T., Dibble, E., & Hauser, M. D. (2001). Amodal completion of acoustic signals by a nonhuman primate. *Nature Neuroscience, 4,* 783–784. (4)

Miller, D. T., & Ross, M. (1975). Self-serving biases in the attribution of causality: Fact or fiction? *Psychological Bulletin, 82,* 213–225. (13)

Miller, G. A. (1956). The magical number seven, plus or minus two: Some limits on our capacity for processing information. *Psychological Review, 63,* 81–97. (7)

Miller, L. C., & Fishkin, S. A. (1997). On the dynamics of human bonding and reproductive success: Seeking windows on the adapted-for human–environmental interface. In J. A. Simpson & D. T. Kenrick (Eds.), *Evolutionary social psychology* (pp. 197–235). Mahwah, NJ: Erlbaum. (2)

Miller, R. J., Hennessy, R. T., & Leibowitz, H. W. (1973). The effect of hypnotic ablation of the background on the magnitude of the Ponzo perspective illusion. *International Journal of Clinical and Experimental Hypnosis, 21,* 180–191. (10)

Miller, S. M., Shoda, Y., & Hurley, K. (1996). Applying cognitive-social theory to health-protective behavior: Breast self-examination in cancer screening. *Psychological Bulletin, 119,* 70–94. (12)

Miller, W. R., & Brown, S. A. (1997). Why psychologists should treat alcohol and drug problems. *American Psychologist, 52,* 1269–1279. (16)

Milne, S. E., Orbell, S., & Sheeran, P. (2002). Combining motivational and volitional interventions to promote exercise participation: Protection motivation theory and implementation intentions. *British Journal of Health Psychology, 7,* 163–184. (11)

Milner, B. (1959). The memory defect in bilateral hippocampal lesions. *Psychiatric Research Reports, 11,* 43–52. (7)

Milton, J., & Wiseman, R. (1999). Does psi exist? Lack of replication of an anomalous process of information. *Psychological Bulletin, 125,* 387–391. (2)

Mineka, S. (1987). A primate model of phobic fears. In H. Eysenck & I. Martin (Eds.), *Theoretical foundations of behavior therapy* (pp. 81–111). New York: Plenum Press. (16)

Mineka, S., Davidson, M., Cook, M., & Keir, R. (1984). Observational conditioning of snake fear in rhesus monkeys. *Journal of Abnormal Psychology, 93,* 355–372. (16)

Mineka, S., & Zinbarg, R. (2006). A contemporary learning theory perspective on the etiology of anxiety disorders. *American Psychologist, 61,* 10–26. (16)

Mingroni, M. A. (2004). The secular rise in IA: Giving heterosis a closer look. *Intelligence, 32,* 65–83. (9)

Minto, C. L., Liao, L.-M., Woodhouse, C. R. J., Ransley, P. G., & Creighton, S. M. (2003). The effect of clitoral surgery on sexual outcome in individuals who have intersex conditions with ambiguous genitalia: A cross-sectional study. *Lancet, 361,* 1252–1257. (11)

Mischel, W. (1973). Toward a cognitive social learning reconceptualization of personality. *Psychological Review, 80,* 252–283. (14)

Mischel, W. (1981). Current issues and challenges in personality. In L. T. Benjamin, Jr. (Ed.), *The G. Stanley Hall Lecture Series* (Vol. 1, pp. 81–99). Washington, DC: American Psychological Association. (14)

Misrahi, M., Meduri, G., Pissard, S., Bouvattier, C., Beau, I., Loosfelt, H., et al. (1997). Comparison of immunocytochemical and molecular features with the phenotype in a case of incomplete male pseudohermaphroditism associated with a mutation of the luteinizing hormone receptor. *Journal of Clinical Endocrinology and Metabolism, 82,* 2159–2165. (11)

Mitte, K. (2005). Meta-analysis of cognitive-behavioral treatments for generalized anxiety disorder: A comparison with psychotherapy. *Psychological Bulletin, 131,* 785–795. (16)

Miyamoto, Y., Nisbett, R. E., & Masuda, T. (2006). Culture and the physical environment. *Psychological Science, 17,* 113–119. (13)

Mochizuki, T., Crocker, A., McCormack, S., Yanagisawa, M., Sakurai, T., & Scammell, T. E. (2004). Behavioral state instability in orexin knock-out mice. *Journal of Neuroscience, 24,* 6291–6300. (10)

Modell, S., Ising, M., Holsboer, F., & Lauer, C. J. (2005). The Munich vulnerability study on affective disorders: Premorbid polysomnographic profile of affected high-risk probands. *Biological Psychiatry, 58,* 694–699. (16)

Moffitt, T. E., Caspi, A., & Rutter, M. (2006). Measured gene–environment interactions in psychopathology. *Perspectives on Psychological Science, 1,* 5–27. (1, 5)

Mokros, A., & Alison, L. J. (2002). Is offender profiling possible? Testing the predicted homology of crime scene actions and background characteristics in a sample of rapists. *Legal and Criminological Psychology, 7,* 25–43. (14)

Moller, H. J. (1992). Attempted suicide: Efficacy of different aftercare strategies. *International Clinical Psychopharmacology, 6*(Suppl. 6), 58–59. (15)

Monahan, J. (1992). Mental disorder and violent behavior. *American Psychologist, 47,* 511–521. (15)

Monahan, J. (1993). Limiting therapist exposure to *Tarasoff* liability: Guidelines for risk containment. *American Psychologist, 48,* 242–250. (15)

Mondloch, C. J., Leis, A., & Maurer, D. (2006). Recognizing the face of Johnny, Suzy, and me: Insensitivity to the spacing among features at 4 years of age. *Child Development, 77,* 234–243. (5)

Money, J., & Ehrhardt, A. A. (1972). *Man and woman, boy and girl.* Baltimore: Johns Hopkins University Press. (11)

Monroe, S. M., & Harkness, K. L. (2005). Life stress, the "kindling" hypothesis, and the recurrence of depression: Considerations from a life stress perspective. *Psychological Review, 112,* 417–445. (16)

Montgomery, G., & Kirsch, I. (1996). Mechanisms of placebo pain reduction: An empirical investigation. *Psychological Science, 7,* 174–176. (4)

Monti-Bloch, L., Jennings-White, C., Dolberg, D. S., & Berliner, D. L. (1994). The human vomeronasal system. *Psychoneuroendocrinology, 19,* 673–686. (4)

Montoya, A. G., Sorrentino, R., Lucas, S. E., & Price, B. H. (2002). Long-term neuropsychiatric consequences of "ecstasy" (MDMA): A review. *Harvard Review of Psychiatry, 10,* 212–220. (3)

Moorcroft, W. (1993). *Sleep, dreaming, and sleep disorders: An introduction* (2nd ed.). Lanham, MD: University Press of America. (10)

Moorcroft, W. H. (2003). *Understanding sleep and dreaming.* New York: Kluwer. (5)

Moore, B. C. J. (1989). *An introduction to the psychology of hearing* (3rd ed.). London: Academic Press. (4)

Moore, J. (1995). Some historical and conceptual relations among logical positivism, behaviorism, and cognitive psychology. In J. T. Todd & E. K. Morris (Eds.), *Modern perspectives on B. F. Skinner and contemporary behaviorism* (pp. 51–74). Westport, CT: Greenwood Press. (6)

Moore, L. B., Goodwin, B., Jones, S. A., Wisely, G. B., Serabjit-Singh, C. J., Willson, T. M., et al. (2000). St. John's wort induces hepatic drug metabolism through activation of the pregnane X receptor. *Proceedings of the National Academy of Sciences, USA, 97,* 7500–7502. (16)

Morakinyo, O., & Peltzer, K. (2002). "Brain fag" symptoms in apprentices in Nigeria. *Psychopathology, 35,* 362–366. (15)

Morewedge, C. K., Gilbert, D. T., & Wilson, T. D. (2005). The least likely of times. *Psychological Science, 16,* 626–630. (8)

Morland, A. B., Lê, S., Carroll, E., Hoffmann, M. B., & Pambakian, A. (2004). The role of spared calcarine cortex and lateral occipital cortex in the responses of human hemianopes to visual motion. *Journal of Cognitive Neuroscience, 16,* 204–218. (10)

Morley, K. I., & Montgomery, G. W. (2001). The genetics of cognitive processes: Candidate genes in humans and animals. *Behavior Genetics, 31,* 511–531. (9)

Morris, G., & Baker-Ward, L. (in press). Fragile but real: Children's capacity to use newly acquired words to convey preverbal memories. *Child Development.*

Moscovitch, M. (1985). Memory from infancy to old age: Implications for theories of normal and pathological memory. *Annals of the New York Academy of Sciences, 444,* 78–96. (5)

Moscovitch, M. (1989). Confabulation and the frontal systems: Strategic versus associative retrieval in neuropsychological theories of memory. In H. L. Roediger, III, & F. I. M. Craik (Eds.), *Varieties of memory and consciousness: Essays in honour of Endel Tulving* (pp. 133–160). Hillsdale, NJ: Erlbaum. (7)

Moscovitch, M. (1992). Memory and working-with-memory: A component process model based on modules and central systems. *Journal of Cognitive Neuroscience, 4,* 257–267. (7)

Moskowitz, A. K. (2004). "Scared stiff": Catatonia as an evolutionary-based fear response. *Psychological Review, 111,* 984–1002. (16)

Moskowitz, B. A. (1978). The acquisition of language. *Scientific American, 239*(5), 92–108. (8)

Moss, E., Cyr, C., Bureau, J.-F., Tarabulsy, G. M., & Dubois-Comtois, K. (2005). Stability of attachment during the preschool period. *Developmental Psychology, 41,* 773–783. (5)

Moulin, C. J. A., Conway, M. A., Thompson, R. G., James, N., & Jones, R. W. (2005). Disordered memory awareness: Recollective confabulation in two cases of persistent déjà vecu. *Neuropsychologia, 43,* 1362–1378. (10)

Mroczek, D. K. (2004). Positive and negative affect at midlife. In O. G. Brim, C. D. Ryff, & R. C. Kessler (Eds.), *How healthy are we?* (pp. 205–226). Chicago: University of Chicago Press. (12)

Mroczek, D. K., & Spiro, A. (2005). Change in life satisfaction during adulthood: Findings from the veterans affairs normative aging study. *Journal of Personality and Social Psychology, 88,* 189–202. (12)

Müller, M. M., Malinowski, P., Gruber, T., & Hillyard, S. A. (2003). Sustained division of the attentional spotlight. *Nature, 424,* 309–312. (8)

Munakata, Y., McClelland, J. L., Johnson, M. H., & Siegler, R. S. (1997). Rethinking infant knowledge: Toward an adaptive process account of successes and failures in object permanence tasks. *Psychological Review, 104,* 686–713. (5)

Munhall, K. G., Jones, J. A., Callan, D. E., Kuratate, T., & Vatikiotis-Bateson, E. (2004). Visual prosody and speech intelligibility. *Psychological Science, 15,* 133–137. (8)

Munroe, R. (1955). *Schools of psychoanalytic thought.* New York: Dryden Press. (15)

Muraven, M., & Baumeister, R. F. (2000). Self-regulation and depletion of limited resources: Does self-control resemble a muscle? *Psychological Bulletin, 126,* 247–259. (12)

Murphy, G. L., & Medin, D. L. (1985). The role of theories in conceptual coherence. *Psychological Review, 92,* 289–316. (8)

Murphy, J. M., Laird, N. M., Monson, R. R., Sobol, A. M., & Leighton, A. H. (2000). A 40-year perspective on the prevalence of depression. *Archives of General Psychiatry, 57,* 209–215. (16)

Murray, H. A. (1943). *Thematic Apperception Test manual.* Cambridge, MA: Harvard University Press. (14)

Murray, J. P. (1998). Studying television violence. A research agenda for the 21st century. In J. K. Asamen & G. L. Berry (Eds.), *Research paradigms, television, and social behavior* (pp. 369–410). Thousand Oaks, CA: Sage. (2)

Musso, M., Moro, A., Glaucho, V., Rijntjes, M., Reichenbach, J., Büchel, C., et al. (2003). Broca's area and the language instinct. *Nature Neuroscience, 6,* 774–781. (8)

Myers, D. G. (2000). The funds, friends, and faith of happy people. *American Psychologist, 55,* 56–67. (12)

Nachson, I., & Zelig, A. (2003). Flashbulb and factual memories: The case of Rabin's assassination. *Applied Cognitive Psychology, 17,* 519–531. (7)

Nadig, A. S., & Sedivy, J. C. (2002). Evidence of perspective-taking constraints in children's on-line reference resolution. *Psychological Science, 13,* 329–336. (5)

Nagera, H. (1976). *Obsessional neuroses.* New York: Aronson. (16)

Nantais, K. M., & Schellenberg, E. G. (1999). The Mozart effect: An artifact of preference. *Psychological Science, 10,* 370–373. (2)

Nash, M. (1987). What, if anything, is regressed about hypnotic age regression? A review of the empirical literature. *Psychological Bulletin, 102,* 42–52. (10)

Nash, M. R., Johnson, L. S., & Tipton, R. D. (1979). Hypnotic age regression and the occurrence of transitional object relationships. *Journal of Abnormal Psychology, 88,* 547–555. (10)

National Institutes of Health. (2000). *The practical guide: Identification, evaluation, and treatment of overweight and obesity in adults* (NIH Publication No. 00-4084). Washington, DC: Author. (11)

Nebes, R. D. (1974). Hemispheric specialization in commissurotomized man. *Psychological Bulletin, 81,* 1–14. (3)

Nedjam, Z., Dalla Barba, G., & Pillon, B. (2000). Confabulation in a patient with fronto-temporal dementia and a patient with Alzheimer's disease. *Cortex, 36,* 561–577. (7)

Negy, C., Leal-Puente, L., Trainor, D. J., & Carlson, R. (1997). Mexican American adolescents' performance on the MMPIA. *Journal of Personality Assessment, 69,* 205–214. (14)

Neher, A. (1991). Maslow's theory of motivation: A critique. *Journal of Humanistic Psychology, 31,* 89–112. (14)

Neher, A. (1996). Jung's theory of archetypes: A critique. *Journal of Humanistic Psychology, 36,* 61–91. (14)

Neisser, U. (1997). Rising scores on intelligence tests. *American Scientist, 85,* 440–447. (9)

Nelson, D. L., & Goodmon, L. B. (2003). Disrupting attention: The need for retrieval cues in working memory theories. *Memory & Cognition, 31,* 65–76. (7)

Nelson, E. C., Heath, A. C., Madden, P. A. F., Cooper, L., Dinwiddie, S. H., Bucholz, K. K., et al. (2002). Association between self-reported childhood sexual abuse and adverse psychosocial outcomes: Results from a twin study. *Archives of General Psychiatry, 59,* 139–145. (16)

Nelson, K., & Fivush, R. (2004). The emergence of autobiographical memory: A social cultural developmental theory. *Psychological Review, 111,* 486–511. (7)

Nemeroff, C. B., Heim, C. M., Thase, M. E., Klein, D. N., Rush, A. J., Schatzberg, A. F., et al. (2003). Differential responses to psychotherapy versus pharmacotherapy in patients with chronic forms of major depression and childhood trauma. *Proceedings of the National Academy of Sciences, USA, 100,* 14293–14296. (16)

Nemeth, C. (1972). A critical analysis of research utilizing the prisoner's dilemma paradigm for the study of bargaining. In L. Berkowitz (Ed.), *Advances in experimental social psychology* (Vol. 6, pp. 203–234). New York: Academic Press. (13)

Nemeth, C. J. (1986). Differential contributions of majority and minority influence. *Psychological Review, 93,* 23–32. (13)

Nettelbeck, T., & Wilson, C. (2004). The Flynn effect: Smarter not faster. *Intelligence, 32,* 85–93. (9)

Newcombe, N. S., Sluzenski, J., & Huttenlocher, J. (2005). Preexisting knowledge versus on-line learning. *Psychological Science, 16,* 222–227. (5)

Newman, B. (1988, September 9). Dressing for dinner remains an issue in the naked city. *The Wall Street Journal,* p. 1. (13)

Newstead, S. E., & Makinen, S. (1997). Psychology teaching in Europe. *European Psychologist, 2,* 3–10. (1)

NICHD Early Child Care Research Network. (2006). Child-care effect sizes for the NICHD study of early child care and youth development. *American Psychologist, 61,* 99–116. (5)

Nicholls, M. E. R., Searle, D. A., & Bradshaw, J. L. (2004). Read my lips: Asymmetries in the visual expression and perception of speech revealed through the McGurk effect. *Psychological Science, 15,* 138–141. (8)

Nickerson, C., Schwarz, N., Diener, E., & Kahneman, D. (2003). Zeroing in on the dark side of the American Dream: A closer look at the negative consequences of the goal for financial success. *Psychological Science, 14,* 531–536. (12)

Nickerson, R. S., & Adams, M. J. (1979). Long-term memory for a common object. *Cognitive Psychology, 11,* 287–307. (7)

Nielsen, T. A., Zadra, A. L., Simard, V., Saucier, S., Stenstrom, P., Smith, C., et al. (2003). The typical dreams of Canadian university students. *Dreaming, 13,* 211–235. (10)

Nietzel, M.T., & Bernstein, D.A. (1987) *Introduction to clinical psychology.* Upper Saddle River, NJ: Prentice-Hall. (9)

Nieuwenstein, M. R., & Potter, M. C. (2006). Temporal limits of selection and memory encoding. *Psychological Science, 17,* 471–475. (8)

Niiya, Y., Ellsworth, P. C., & Yamaguchi, S. (2006). Amae in Japan and the United States: An exploration of a "culturally unique" emotion. *Emotion, 6,* 279–295. (12)

Nikles, C. D., II, Brecht, D. L., Klinger, E., & Bursell, A. L. (1998). The effects of current-concern and nonconcern-related waking suggestions on nocturnal dream content. *Journal of Personality and Social Psychology, 75,* 242–255. (10)

Nisbett, R. E., Caputo, C., Legant, P., & Marecek, J. (1973). Behavior as seen by the actor and as seen by the observer. *Journal of Personality and Social Psychology, 27,* 154–164. (13)

Nisbett, R. E., Peng, K., Choi, I., & Norenzayan, A. (2001). Culture and systems of thought: Holistic versus analytic cognition. *Psychological Review, 108,* 291–310. (13)

Noaghiul, S., & Hibbeln, J. R. (2003). Cross-national comparisons of seafood consumption and rates of bipolar disorders. *American Journal of Psychiatry, 160,* 2222–2227. (16)

Noel, J. G., Wann, D. L., & Branscombe, N. R. (1995). Peripheral ingroup membership status and public negativity toward outgroups. *Journal of Personality and Social Psychology, 68,* 127–137. (13)

Nolen-Hoeksema, S. (1990). *Sex differences in depression.* Stanford, CA: Stanford University Press. (16)

Nolen-Hoeksema, S. (1991). Responses to depression and their effects on the duration of depressive episodes. *Journal of Abnormal Psychology, 100,* 569–582. (16)

Nolen-Hoeksema, S., & Morrow, J. (1991). A prospective study of depression and post-traumatic stress symptoms after a natural disaster: The Loma Prieta earthquake. *Journal of Personality and Social Psychology, 61,* 115–121. (16)

Nopoulos, P. C., Giedd, J. N., Andreasen, N. C., & Rapoport, J. L. (1998). Frequency and severity of enlarged cavum septi pellucidi in childhood-onset schizophrenia. *American Journal of Psychiatry, 155,* 1074–1079. (16)

Norcross, J. C., Kohout, J. L., & Wicherski, M. (2005). Graduate study in psychology: 1971 to 2004. *American Psychologist, 60,* 959–975. (1)

Nordenström, A., Servin, A., Bohlin, G., Larson, A., & Wedell, A. (2002). Sex-typed toy play behavior correlates with the degree of prenatal androgen exposure assessed by CYP21 genotype in girls with congenital adrenal hyperplasia. *Journal of Clinical Endocrinology & Metabolism, 87,* 5119–5124. (11)

Norman, D. A. (1988). *The psychology of everyday things.* New York: Basic Books. (1)

Norman, R. A., Tataranni, P. A., Pratley, R., Thompson, D. B., Hanson, R. L., Prochazka, M., et al. (1998). Autosomal genomic scan for loci linked to obesity and energy metabolism in Pima Indians. *American Journal of Human Genetics, 62,* 659–668. (11)

North, R. A. (1992). Cellular actions of opiates and cocaine. *Annals of the New York Academy of Sciences, 654,* 1–6. (3)

Norton, A., Winner, E., Cronin, K., Overy, K., Lee, D. J., & Schlaug, G. (2005). Are there pre-existing neural, cognitive, or motoric markers for musical ability? *Brain and Cognition, 59,* 124–134. (3)

Nosek, B. A., & Banaji, M. R. (2001). The go/no-go association task. *Social Cognition, 19,* 625–664. (13)

Nosek, B. A., Banaji, M. R., & Greenwald, A. G. (2002). Harvesting implicit group attitudes and beliefs from a demonstration Web site. *Group Dynamics: Theory, Research, and Practice, 6,* 101–115. (13)

Nowak, M. A., & Sigmund, K. (2005). Evolution of indirect reciprocity. *Nature, 437,* 1291–1298. (13)

Nummenmaa, L., Hyönä, J., & Calvo, M. G. (2006). Eye movement assessment of selective attentional capture by emotional pictures. *Emotion, 6,* 257–268. (12)

Oberauer, K., Schulze, R., Wilhelm, O., & Süss, H.-M. (2005). Working memory and intelligence—Their correlation and their relation: Comment on Ackerman, Beier, and Boyle (2005). *Psychological Bulletin, 131,* 61–65. (9)

Oberauer, K., Süss, H.-M., Wilhelm, O., & Wittman, W. W. (2003). The multiple faces of working memory. *Intelligence, 31,* 167–193. (7)

O'Connor, T. G., Marvin, R. S., Rutter, M., Olrick, J. T., Britner, P. A., & the English and Romanian adoptees study team. (2003). Child-parent attachment following early institutional deprivation. *Development and Psychopathology, 15,* 19–38. (5)

O'Kane, G., Kensinger, E. A., & Corkin, S. (2004). Evidence for semantic learning in profound amnesia: An investigation with patient H. M. *Hippocampus, 14,* 417–425. (7)

Odell, S. M., & Commander, M. J. (2000). Risk factors for homelessness among people with psychotic disorders. *Social Psychiatry and Psychiatric Epidemiology, 35,* 396–401. (15)

O'Donohue, W., & Kitchener, R. F. (1999). Introduction: The behaviorisms. In W. O'Donohue & R. Kitchener (Eds.), *Handbook of behaviorism* (pp. 1–13). San Diego, CA: Academic Press. (6)

Ohaeri, J. U., Adeyinka, A. O., & Osuntokun, B. O. (1995). Computed tomographic density changes in schizophrenic and manic Nigerian subjects. *Behavioural Neurology, 8,* 31–37. (16)

Ohayon, M. M. (1997). Prevalence of *DSM–IV* diagnostic criteria of insomnia: Distinguishing insomnia related to mental disorders from sleep disorders. *Journal of Psychiatric Research, 31,* 333–346. (10)

Ohayon, M. M., & Partinen, M. (2002). Insomnia and global sleep dissatisfaction in Finland. *Journal of Sleep Research, 11,* 339–346. (10)

Öhman, A., Eriksson, A., & Olofsson, C. (1975). One-trial learning and superior resistance to extinction of autonomic responses conditioned to potentially phobic objects. *Journal of Comparative and Physiological Psychology, 88,* 619–627. (16)

Öhman, A., & Mineka, S. (2003). The malicious serpent: Snakes as a prototypical stimulus for an evolved module of fear. *Current Directions in Psychological Science, 12,* 5–9. (16)

Okasha, M., McCarron, P., McEwen, J., & Smith, G. D. (2001). Age at menarche: Secular trends and association with adult anthropometric measures. *Annals of Human Biology, 28,* 68–78. (5)

Olausson, H., Lamarre, Y., Backlund, H., Morin, C., Wallin, B. G., Starck, G., et al. (2002). Unmyelinated tactile afferents signal touch and project to insular cortex. *Nature Neuroscience, 5,* 900–904. (3)

Olney, J. W., & Farger, N. B. (1995). Glutamate receptor dysfunction and schizophrenia. *Archives of General Psychiatry, 52,* 998–1007. (16)

Olson, I. R., & Marshuetz, C. (2005). Facial attractiveness is appraised in a glance. *Emotion, 5,* 498–502. (13)

Olson, M. A., & Fazio, R. H. (2001). Implicit attitude formation through classical conditioning. *Psychological Science, 12,* 413–417. (6)

Olson, M. A., & Fazio, R. H. (2003). Relations between implicit measures of prejudice: What are we measuring? *Psychological Science, 14,* 636–639. (13)

Orne, M. T. (1951). The mechanisms of hypnotic age regression: An experimental study. *Journal of Abnormal and Social Psychology, 46,* 213–225. (10)

Orne, M. T. (1959). The nature of hypnosis: Artifact and essence. *Journal of Abnormal and Social Psychology, 58,* 277–299. (10)

Orne, M. T. (1969). Demand characteristics and the concept of quasi-controls. In R. Rosenthal & R. L. Rosnow (Eds.), *Artifact in behavioral research* (pp. 143–179). New York: Academic Press. (2)

Orne, M. T. (1979). On the simulating subject as a quasi-control group in hypnosis research: What, why, and how. In E. Fromm & R. E. Shor (Eds.), *Hypnosis: Developments in research and new perspectives* (2nd ed., pp. 519–565). New York: Aldine. (10)

Orne, M. T., & Evans, F. J. (1965). Social control in the psychological experiment: Antisocial behavior and hypnosis. *Journal of Personality and Social Psychology, 1,* 189–200. (10)

Orne, M. T., & Scheibe, K. E. (1964). The contribution of nondeprivation factors in the production of sensory deprivation effects: The psychology of the "panic button." *Journal of Abnormal and Social Psychology, 68,* 3–12. (2)

Ornstein, P. A., Ceci, S. J., & Loftus, E. F. (1998). Adult recollections of childhood abuse. *Psychology, Public Policy, and Law, 4,* 1025–1051. (7)

Ornstein, P. A., Merritt, K. A., Baker-Ward, L., Furtado, E., Gordon, B., & Principe, G. (1998). Children's knowledge, expectation, and long-term retention. *Applied Cognitive Psychology, 12,* 387–405. (7)

Ortony, A., & Turner, T. J. (1990). What's basic about basic emotions? *Psychological Review, 97,* 315–331. (12)

Ösby, U., Hammar, N., Brandt, L., Wicks, S., Thinsz, Z., Ekbom, A., et al. (2001). Time trends in first admissions for schizophrenia and paranoid psychosis in Stockholm county, Sweden. *Schizophrenia Research, 47,* 247–254. (16)

Osofsky, J. D. (1995). The effects of exposure to violence on young children. *American Psychologist, 50,* 782–788. (12)

Östling, S., & Skoog, J. (2002). Psychotic symptoms and paranoid ideation in a nondemented population-based sample of the very old. *Archives of General Psychiatry, 59,* 53–59. (16)

O'Toole, B. I. (1990). Intelligence and behaviour and motor vehicle accident mortality. *Accident Analysis and Prevention, 22,* 211–221. (9)

Ottati, V., & Lee, Y. T. (1995). Accuracy: A neglected component of stereotype research. In Y. T. Lee, L. J. Jussim, & C. R. McCauley (Eds.), *Stereotype accuracy* (pp. 29–59). Washington, DC: American Psychological Association. (13)

Otto, K., Boos, A., Dalbert, C., Schöps, D., & Hoyer, J. (2006). Posttraumatic symptoms, depression, and anxiety of flood victims: The impact of the belief in a just world. *Personality and Individual Differences, 40,* 1075–1084. (14)

Otto, R. K., & Heilbrun, K. (2002). The practice of forensic psychology. *American Psychologist, 57,* 5–18. (1)

Oyserman, D., Coon, H. M., & Kemmelmeier, M. (2002). Rethinking individualism and collectivism: Evaluation of theoretical assumptions and meta-analyses. *Psychological Bulletin, 128,* 3–72. (13)

Padgham, C. A. (1975). Colours experienced in dreams. *British Journal of Psychology, 66,* 25–28. (10)

Paladini, C. A., Fiorillo, C. D., Morikawa, H., & Williams, J. T. (2001). Amphetamine selectively blocks inhibitory glutamate transmission in dopamine neurons. *Nature Neuroscience, 4,* 275–281. (3)

Palinkas, L. A. (2003). The psychology of isolated and confined environments. *American Psychologist, 58,* 353–363. (10, 16)

Palmer, B. W., Heaton, R. K., Paulsen, J. S., Kuck, J., Braff, D., Harris, M. J., et al. (1997). Is it possible to be schizophrenic yet neuropsychologically normal? *Neuropsychology, 11,* 437–446. (16)

Panayiotou, G., Kokkinos, C. M., & Spanoudis, G. (2004). Searching for the "big five" in a Greek context: The NEO-FFI under the microscope. *Personality and Individual Differences, 36,* 1841–1854. (14)

Panikashvili, D., Simeonidou, C., Ben-Shabat, S., Hanuš, L. Breuer, A., Mechoulam, R., et al. (2001). An endogenous cannabinoid (2-AG) is neuroprotective after brain injury. *Nature, 413,* 527–531. (3)

Panksepp, J. (1998). Attention deficit hyperactivity disorders, psychostimulants, and intolerance of childhood playfulness: A tragedy in the making? *Current Directions in Psychological Science, 7,* 91–98. (8)

Papini, M. R. (2002). Pattern and process in the evolution of learning. *Psychological Review, 109,* 186–201. (1)

Paradis, M. (1990). Language lateralization in bilinguals: Enough already! *Brain and Language, 39,* 576–586. (8)

Parasuraman, R., Greenwood, P. M., Kumar, R., & Fossella, J. (2005). Beyond heritability: Neurotransmitter genes differentially modulate visuospatial attention and working memory. *Psychological Science, 16,* 200–207. (7)

Parish, A. R., & deWaal, F. B. M. (2000). The other "closest living relative." *Annals of the New York Academy of Sciences, 907,* 97–113. (13)

Parke, R. D., Berkowitz, L., Leyens, J. P., West, S. G., & Sebastian, R. J. (1977). Some effects of violent and nonviolent movies on the behavior of juvenile delinquents. In L. Berkowitz (Ed.), *Advances in experimental social psychology* (Vol. 10, pp. 135–172). New York: Academic Press. (2)

Parker, D. (1944). *The portable Dorothy Parker.* New York: Viking Press. (15)

Parker, E. S., Cahill, L., & McGaugh, J. L. (2006). A case of unusual autobiographical remembering. *Neurocase, 12,* 35–49. (7)

Parmeggiani, P. L. (1982). Regulation of physiological functions during sleep in mammals. *Experientia, 38,* 1405–1408. (10)

Parnas, J., Schulsinger, F., Schulsinger, H., Mednick, S. A., & Teasdale, T. W. (1982). Behavioral precursors of schizophrenia spectrum. *Archives of General Psychiatry, 39,* 658–664. (16)

Parrott, A. C. (1999). Does cigarette smoking cause stress? *American Psychologist, 54,* 817–820. (3)

Pascual-Leone, A., Wasserman, E. M., Sadato, N., & Hallett, M. (1995). The role of reading activity on the modulation of motor control outputs to the reading hand in Braille readers. *Annals of Neurology, 38,* 910–915. (8)

Pashler, H. (1994). Dual-task interference in simple tasks: Data and theory. *Psychological Bulletin, 116,* 220–244. (8)

Pashler, H., & Harris, C. R. (2001). Spontaneous allocation of visual attention: Dominant role of uniqueness. *Psychonomic Bulletin & Review, 8,* 747–752. (8)

Pasterski, V. L., Geffner, M. E., Brain, C., Hindmarsh, P., Brook, C., & Hines, M. (2005). Prenatal hormones and postnatal socialization by parents as determinants of male-typical toy play in girls with congenital adrenal hyperplasia. *Child Development, 76,* 264–278. (11)

Pate, J. L., & Rumbaugh, D. M. (1983). The language-like behavior of Lana chimpanzee: Is it merely discrimination and paired-associate learning? *Animal Learning & Behavior, 11,* 134–138. (8)

Patel, A. D. (2003). Language, music, syntax and the brain. *Nature Neuroscience, 6,* 674–681. (8)

Patterson, C. J. (1994). Lesbian and gay families. *Current Directions in Psychological Science, 3,* 62–64. (5)

Patterson, D. R. (2004). Treating pain with hypnosis. *Current Directions in Psychological Science, 13,* 252–255. (10)

Paulhus, D. L., Trapnell, P. D., & Chen, D. (1999). Birth order effects on personality and achievement within families. *Psychological Science, 10,* 482–488. (5)

Paunonen, S. V., & Jackson, D. N. (2000). What is beyond the big five? Plenty! *Journal of Personality, 68,* 821–835. (14)

Paunonen, S. V., Zeidner, M., Engvik, H. A., Oosterveld, P., & Maliphant, R. (2000). The nonverbal assessment of personality in five cultures. *Journal of Cross-Cultural Psychology, 31,* 220–239. (14)

Paus, T., Marrett, S., Worsley, K. J., & Evans, A. C. (1995). Extraretinal modulation of cerebral blood flow in the human visual cortex: Implications for saccadic suppression. *Journal of Neurophysiology, 74,* 2179–2183. (8)

Pavlidis, I., Eberhardt, N. I., & Levine, J. A. (2002). Seeing through the face of deception. *Nature, 415,* 35. (12)

Pavlov, I. P. (1960). *Conditioned reflexes.* New York: Dover. (Original work published 1927) (6)

Pavot, W., & Diener, E. (1993). Review of the satisfaction with life scale. *Psychological Assessment, 5,* 164–172. (12)

Pearce, J. M. (1994). Similarity and discrimination: A selective review and a connectionist model. *Psychological Review, 101,* 587–607. (6)

Pearl, P. L., Weiss, R. E., & Stein, M. A. (2001). Medical mimics. *Annals of the New York Academy of Sciences, 931,* 97–112. (8)

Pearlson, G. D., Petty, R. G., Ross, C. A., & Tien, A. Y. (1996). Schizophrenia—a disease of heteromodal association cortex. *Neuropsychopharmacology, 14,* 1–17. (16)

Peele, S. (1998, March/April). All wet. *The Sciences, 38*(2), 17–21. (16)

Peet, M. (2004). Nutrition and schizophrenia: Beyond omega-3 fatty acids. *Prostaglandins, Leukotrienes and Essential Fatty Acids, 70,* 417–422. (16)

Peigneux, P., Laureys, S., Fuchs, S., Collette, F., Perrin, F., Reggers, J., et al. (2004). Are spatial memories strengthened in the human hippocampus during slow wave sleep? *Neuron, 44,* 535–545. (10)

Penfield, W., & Rasmussen, T. (1950). *The cerebral cortex of man.* New York: Macmillan. (3)

Peng, K., & Nisbett, R. E. (1999). Culture dialectics, and reasoning about contradiction. *American Psychologist, 54,* 741–754. (13)

Pennebaker, J. W., & Seagal, J. D. (1999). Forming a story: The health benefits of narrative. *Journal of Clinical Psychology, 55,* 1243–1254. (15)

Pennisi, E. (2004). Bird in bush aids snake in grass. *Science, 303,* 951. (6)

Perez, E. A. (1995). Review of the preclinical pharmacology and comparative efficacy of 5-hydroxytryptamine-3 receptor antagonists for chemotherapy-induced emesis. *Journal of Clinical Oncology, 13,* 1036–1043. (3)

Perkins, A., Fitzgerald, J. A., & Moss, G. E. (1995). A comparison of LH secretion and brain estradiol receptors in heterosexual and homosexual rams and female sheep. *Hormones and Behavior, 29,* 31–41. (11)

Perry, D. G., & Bussey, K. (1979). The social learning theory of sex differences: Imitation is alive and well. *Journal of Personality and Social Psychology, 37,* 1699–1712. (14)

Person, C., Tracy, M., & Galea, S. (2006). Risk factors for depression after a disaster. *Journal of Nervous and Mental Disease, 194,* 659–666. (16)

Pert, C. B., & Snyder, S. H. (1973). The opiate receptor: Demonstration in nervous tissue. *Science, 179,* 1011–1014. (3, 4)

Peters, F., Nicolson, N. A., Berkhof, J., Delespaul, P., & deVries, M. (2003). Effects of daily events on mood states in major depressive disorder. *Journal of Abnormal Psychology, 112,* 203–211. (16)

Peterson, C., Bettes, B. A., & Seligman, M. E. P. (1985). Depressive symptoms and unprompted causal attributions: Content analysis. *Behaviour Research and Therapy, 23,* 379–382. (16)

Peterson, L. G., Peterson, M., O'Shanick, G. J., & Swann, A. (1985). Self-inflicted gunshot wounds: Lethality of method versus intent. *American Journal of Psychiatry, 142,* 228–231. (16)

Peterson, L. R., & Peterson, M. J. (1959). Short-term retention of individual verbal items. *Journal of Experimental Psychology, 58,* 193–198. (7)

Peterson, R. A. (2001). On the use of college students in social science research: Insights from a second-order meta-analysis. *Journal of Consumer Research, 28,* 450–461. (2)

Petitto, L. A., Holowka, S., Sergio, L. E., & Ostry, D. (2001). Language rhythms in baby hand movements. *Nature, 413,* 35–36. (8)

Petrill, S. A., Luo, D., Thompson, L. A., & Detterman, D. K. (1996). The independent prediction of general intelligence by elementary cognitive tasks: Genetic and environmental influences. *Behavior Genetics, 26,* 135–147. (9)

Petrill, S. A., Plomin, R., Berg, S., Johansson, B., Pedersen, N. L., Ahern, F., et al. (1998). The genetic and environmental relationship between general and specific cognitive abilities in twins age 80 and older. *Psychological Science, 9,* 183–189. (9)

Petty, R. E., & Cacioppo, J. T. (1977). Effects of forewarning of persuasive intent and involvement on cognitive responses and persuasion. *Personality and Social Psychology Bulletin, 5,* 173–176. (13)

Petty, R. E., & Cacioppo, J. T. (1981). *Attitudes and persuasion: Classic and contemporary approaches.* Dubuque, IA: William C. Brown. (13)

Petty, R. E., & Cacioppo, J. T. (1986). *Communication and persuasion: Central and peripheral routes to attitude change.* New York: Springer-Verlag. (13)

Pezze, M. A., Bast, T., & Feldon, J. (2003). Significance of dopamine transmission in the rat medial prefrontal cortex for conditioned fear. *Cerebral Cortex, 13,* 371–380. (6)

Pfungst, O. (1911). *Clever Hans.* New York: Holt. (2)

Phan, K. L., Wager, T., Taylor, S. F., & Liberzon, I. (2002). Functional neuroanatomy of emotion: A meta-analysis of emotion activation studies in PET and fMRI. *NeuroImage, 16,* 331–348. (12)

Phelps, E. A., Ling, S., & Carrasco, M. (2006). Emotion facilitates perception and potentiates the perceptual benefits of attention. *Psychological Science, 17,* 292–299. (12)

Phelps, E. A., O'Connor, K. J., Cunningham, W. A., Funayama, E. S., Gatenby, J. C., Gore, J. C., et al. (2000). Performance on indirect measures of race evaluation predicts amygdala activation. *Journal of Cognitive Neuroscience, 12,* 729–738. (13)

Phelps, M. E., & Mazziotta, J. C. (1985). Positron emission tomography: Human brain function and biochemistry. *Science, 228,* 799–809. (1, 3)

Philippot, P., Chapelle, G., & Blairy, S. (2002). Respiratory feedback in the generation of emotions. *Cognition and Emotion, 16,* 605–627. (12)

Phillips, P. E. M., Stuber, G. D., Heien, M. L. A. V., Wightman, R. M., & Carelli, R. M. (2003). Subsecond dopamine release promotes cocaine seeking. *Nature, 422,* 614–618. (16)

Phillips, R. G., & LeDoux, J. E. (1992). Differential contribution of amygdala and hippocampus to cued and contextual fear conditioning. *Behavioral Neuroscience, 106,* 274–285. (12)

Phillips, R. T., & Alcebo, A. M. (1986). The effects of divorce on Black children and adolescents. *American Journal of Social Psychology, 6,* 69–73. (5)

Piaget, J. (1954). *The construction of reality in the child* (M. Cook, Trans.). New York: Basic Books. (Original work published 1937) (5)

Pichot, P. (1984). Centenary of the birth of Hermann Rorschach. *Journal of Personality Assessment, 48,* 591–596. (14)

Pierri, J. N., Volk, C. L. E., Auh, S., Sampson, A., & Lewis, D. A. (2001). Decreased somal size of deep layer 3 pyramidal neurons in the prefrontal cortex of subjects with schizophrenia. *Archives of General Psychiatry, 58,* 466–473. (16)

Pigliucci, M. (2003, May/June). "Elementary, dear Watson." *Skeptical Inquirer, 27,* 18–19. (2)

Pind, J., Gunnarsdóttir, E. K., & Jóhannesson, H. S. (2003). Raven's standard progressive matrices: New school age norms and a study of the test's validity. *Personality and Individual Differences, 34,* 375–386. (9)

Pinel, J. P. J., Assanand, S., & Lehman, D. R. (2000). Hunger, eating, and ill health. *American Psychologist, 55,* 1105–1116. (11)

Pinker, S. (1994). *The language instinct.* New York: Morrow. (8)

Piolino, P., Desgranges, B., Benali, K., & Eustache, F. (2002). Episodic and semantic remote autobiographical memory in ageing. *Memory, 10,* 239–257. (7)

Pitschel-Walz, G., Leucht, S., Bäuml, J., Kissling, W., & Engel, R. R. (2001). The effect of family interventions on relapse and rehospitalization in schizophrenia—A meta-analysis. *Schizophrenia Bulletin, 27,* 73–92. (16)

Plaut, D. C., & Booth, J. R. (2000). Individual and developmental differences in semantic priming: Empirical and computational support for a single-mechanism account of lexical priming. *Psychological Review, 107,* 786–823. (8)

Ploghaus, A., Tracey, I., Gati, J. S., Clare, S., Menon, R. S., Matthews, P. M., et al. (1999). Dissociating pain from its anticipation in the human brain. *Science, 284,* 1979–1981. (4)

Plomin, R., Corley, R., DeFries, J. C., & Fulker, D. W. (1990). Individual differences in television viewing in early childhood: Nature as well as nurture. *Psychological Science, 1,* 371–377. (5)

Plomin, R., Fulker, D. W., Corley, R., & DeFries, J. C. (1997). Nature, nurture, and cognitive development from 1 to 16 years: A parent-offspring adoption study. *Psychological Science, 8,* 442–447. (9)

Plomin, R., Hill, L., Craig, I. W., McGuffin, P., Purcell, S., Sham, P., et al. (2001). A genome-wide scan of 1842 DNA markers for allelic associations with general cognitive ability: A five-stage design using DNA pooling and extreme selected groups. *Behavior Genetics, 31,* 497–509. (9)

Plomin, R., & Kovas, Y. (2005). Generalist genes and learning disabilities. *Psychological Bulletin, 131,* 592–617. (9)

Plous, S. (1993). *The psychology of judgment and decision making.* Philadelphia: Temple University Press. (8)

Plous, S. (1996). Attitudes toward the use of animals in psychological research and education. *American Psychologist, 51,* 1167–1180. (2)

Plutchik, R. (1982). A psychoevolutionary theory of emotions. *Social Science Information, 21,* 529–553. (12)

Plutchik, R., & Ax, A. F. (1967). A critique of "determinants of emotional state" by Schachter and Singer (1962). *Psychophysiology, 4,* 79–82. (12)

Polcin, D. L. (1997). The etiology and diagnosis of alcohol dependence: Differences in the professional literature. *Psychotherapy, 34,* 297–306. (16)

Polderman, T. J. C., Stins, J. F., Posthuma, D., Gosso, M. F., Verhulst, F. C., & Boomsma, D. I. (2006). The phenotypic and genotypic relation between working memory speed and capacity. *Intelligence, 34,* 549–560. (9)

Pole, N., Neylan, T. C., Best, S. R., Orr, S. P., & Marmar, C. R. (2003). Fear-potentiated startle and posttraumatic stress symptoms in urban police officers. *Journal of Traumatic Stress, 16,* 471–479. (12)

Polivy, J., & Herman, C. P. (1985). Dieting and binging: A causal analysis. *American Psychologist, 40,* 193–201. (11)

Polivy, J., & Herman, C. P. (2002). If at first you don't succeed. *American Psychologist, 57,* 677–689. (11)

Pollak, J. M. (1979). Obsessive-compulsive personality: A review. *Psychological Bulletin, 86,* 225–241. (16)

Polya, G. (1957). *How to solve it.* Garden City, NY: Doubleday Anchor. (8)

Pond, S. B., III, & Geyer, P. D. (1991). Differences in the relation between job satisfaction and perceived work alternatives among older and younger blue-collar workers. *Journal of Vocational Behavior, 39,* 251–262. (11)

Poole, D. A., & White, L. T. (1993). Two years later: Effect of question repetition and retention interval on the eyewitness testimony of children and adults. *Developmental Psychology, 29,* 844–853. (7)

Poole, D. A., & White, L. T. (1995). Tell me again and again: Stability and change in the repeated testimonies of children and adults. In M. S. Zaragoza, J. R. Graham, G. C. N. Hall, R. Hirschman, & Y. S. Ben-Porath (Eds.), *Memory and testimony in the child witness* (pp. 24–43). Thousand Oaks, CA: Sage. (7)

Pope, H. G., Jr., Gruber, A. J., Hudson, J. I., Huestis, M. A., & Yurgelun-Todd, D. (2001). Neuropsychological performance in long-term cannabis users. *Archives of General Psychiatry, 58,* 909–915. (3)

Pope, H. G., Jr., Hudson, J. I., Bodkin, J. A., & Oliva, P. (1998). Questionable validity of "dissociative amnesia" in trauma victims. *British Journal of Psychology, 172,* 210–215. (7)

Pope, K. S. (1996). Memory, abuse, and science: Questioning claims about the false memory syndrome epidemic. *American Psychologist, 51,* 957–974. (7)

Popper, K. (1986). Predicting overt behavior versus predicting hidden states. *Behavioral and Brain Sciences, 9,* 254–255. (14)

Porter, S., Birt, A. R., Yuille, J. C., & Lehman, D. R. (2000). Negotiating false memories: Interviewer and rememberer characteristics relate to memory distortion. *Psychological Science, 11,* 507–510. (7)

Posner, S. F., Baker, L., Heath, A., & Martin, N. G. (1996). Social contact, social attitudes, and twin similarity. *Behavior Genetics, 26,* 123–133. (5)

Post, R. M. (1992). Transduction of psychosocial stress into the neurobiology of recurrent affective disorder. *American Journal of Psychiatry, 149,* 999–1010. (16)

Posthuma, D., De Geus, E. J. C., Baaré, W. F. C., Pol, H. E. H., Kahn, R. S., & Boomsma, D. I. (2002). The association between brain volume and intelligence is of genetic origin. *Nature Neuroscience, 5,* 83–84. (9)

Poulin, F., Dishion, T. J., & Burraston, B. (2001). 3-year iatrogenic effects associated with aggregating high-risk adolescents in cognitive-behavioral preventive interventions. *Applied Developmental Science, 5,* 214–224. (15)

Povinelli, D. J., & deBlois, S. (1992). Young children's (Homo sapiens) understanding of knowledge formation in themselves and others. *Journal of Comparative Psychology, 106,* 228–238. (5)

Powell, R. A., & Boer, D. P. (1994). Did Freud mislead patients to confabulate memories of abuse? *Psychological Reports, 74,* 1283–1298. (14)

Pratkanis, A. R. (1992, Spring). The cargo-cult science of subliminal perception. *Skeptical Inquirer, 16,* 260–272. (4)

Pratkanis, A. R., Greenwald, A. G., Leippe, M. R., & Baumgardner, M. H. (1988). In search of reliable persuasion effects: III. The sleeper effect is dead. Long live the sleeper effect. *Journal of Personality and Social Psychology, 54,* 203–218. (14)

Premack, D. (1965). Reinforcement theory. In D. Levine (Ed.), *Nebraska Symposium on Motivation* (pp. 123–188). Lincoln: University of Nebraska Press. (6)

Principe, G. F., Kanaya, T., Ceci, S. J., & Singh, M. (2006). Believing is seeing. *Psychological Science, 17,* 243–248. (7)

Pronin, E., Gilovich, T., & Ross, L. (2004). Objectivity in the eye of the beholder: Divergent perceptions of bias in self versus others. *Psychological Review, 111,* 781–799. (13)

Provine, R. (2000). *Laughter.* New York: Viking Press. (2, 12)

Public Agenda. (2001). *Medical research: Red flags.* Retrieved February 8, 2007, from http://www.publicagenda.org/issues/major_proposals_detail.cfm?issue_type=medical_research&list=4. (2)

Purves, D., & Lotto, R. B. (2003). *Why we see what we do: An empirical theory of vision.* Sunderland, MA: Sinauer Associates. (4)

Purves, D., Williams, S. M., Nundy, S., & Lotto, R. B. (2004). Perceiving the intensity of light. *Psychological Review, 111,* 142–158. (4)

Putilov, A. A., Pinchasov, B. B., & Poljakova, E. Y. (2005). Antidepressant effects of mono- and combined non-drug treatments for seasonal and non-seasonal depression. *Biological Rhythm Research, 36,* 405–421. (16)

Pyszczynski, T., Greenberg, J., & Solomon, S. (2000). Proximal and distal defense: A new perspective on unconscious motivation. *Current Directions in Psychological Science, 9,* 156–160. (5)

Qin, P., & Mortensen, P. B. (2003). The impact of parental status on the risk of completed suicide. *Archives of General Psychiatry, 60,* 797–802. (16)

Quadrel, M. J., Fischhoff, B., & Davis, W. (1993). Adolescent (in)vulnerability. *American Psychologist, 48,* 102–116. (5)

Quattrocchi, M. R., & Schopp, R. F. (2005). Tarasaurus rex: A standard of care that could not adapt. *Psychology, Public Policy, and Law, 11,* 109–137. (15)

Quinn, P. C., & Bhatt, R. S. (2005). Learning perceptual organization in infancy. *Psychological Science, 16,* 511–515. (4)

Quraishi, S., & Frangou, S. (2002). Neuropsychology of bipolar disorder: A review. *Journal of Affective Disorders, 72,* 209–226. (16)

Rachlin, H., Siegel, E., & Cross, D. (1994). Lotteries and the time horizon. *Psychological Science, 5,* 390–393. (8)

Rachman, S. (1969). Treatment by prolonged exposure to high intensity stimulation. *Behaviour Research and Therapy, 7,* 295–302. (16)

Rachman, S. (2002). A cognitive theory of compulsive checking behavior. *Behaviour Research and Therapy, 40,* 625–639. (16)

Rachman, S. J., & Hodgson, R. J. (1980). *Obsessions and compulsions.* Upper Saddle River, NJ: Prentice Hall. (16)

Rahman, Q., Andersson, D., & Govier, E. (2005). A specific sexual orientation-related difference in navigation strategy. *Behavioral Neuroscience, 119,* 311–316. (5)

Raine, A., Lencz, T., Bihrle, S., LaCasse, L., & Colletti, P. (2000). Reduced prefrontal gray matter volume and reduced autonomic activity in antisocial personality disorder. *Archives of General Psychiatry, 57,* 119–127. (12)

Rainville, P., Duncan, G. H., Price, D. D., Carrier, B., & Bushnell, M. C. (1997). Pain affect encoded in human anterior cingulate but not somatosensory cortex. *Science, 277,* 968–971. (5)

Rainville, P., Hofbauer, R. K., Bushnell, M. C., Duncan, G. H., & Price, D. D. (2002). Hypnosis modulates activity in brain structures involved in the regulation of consciousness. *Journal of Cognitive Neuroscience, 14,* 887–901. (10)

Raison, C. L., Klein, H. M., & Steckler, M. (1999). The moon and madness reconsidered. *Journal of Affective Disorders, 53,* 99–106. (2)

Rakic, P. (2002). Neurogenesis in adult primate neocortex: An evaluation of the evidence. *Nature Reviews Neuroscience, 3,* 65–71. (3)

Ramachandran, V. S., & Blakeslee, S. (1998). *Phantoms in the brain.* New York: Morrow. (4)

Ramachandran, V. S., & Hirstein, W. (1998). The perception of phantom limbs: The D. O. Hebb lecture. *Brain, 121,* 1603–1630. (4)

Ramey, C. T., & Ramey, S. L. (1998). Early intervention and early experience. *American Psychologist, 33,* 109–120. (9)

Ramirez, J. M., Santisteban, C., Fujihara, T., & Van Goozen, S. (2002). Differences between experience of anger and readiness to angry action: A study of Japanese and Spanish students. *Aggressive Behavior, 28,* 429–438. (12)

Ramsey-Rennels, J. L., & Langlois, J. H. (2006). Infants' differential processing of female and male faces. *Current Directions in Psychological Science, 15,* 59–62. (5)

Ransley, J. K., Donnelly, J. K., Botham, H., Khara, T. N., Greenwood, D. C., & Cade, J. E. (2003). Use of supermarket receipts to estimate energy and fat content of food purchased by lean and overweight families. *Appetite, 41,* 141–148. (11)

Rapoport, S. I., & Bosetti, F. (2002). Do lithium and anticonvulsants target the brain arachidonic acid cascade in bipolar patients? *Archives of General Psychiatry, 59,* 592–596. (16)

Rattenborg, N. C., Amlaner, C. J., & Lima, S. L. (2000). Behavioral, neurophysiological and evolutionary perspectives on unihemispheric sleep. *Neuroscience and Biobehavioral Reviews, 24,* 817–842. (10)

Rattenborg, N. C., Mandt, B. H., Obermeyer, W. H., Winsauer, P. J., Huber, R., Wikelski, M., et al. (2004). Migratory sleeplessness in the white-crowned sparrow (*Zonotrichia leucophrys gambelii*). *PLOS Biology, 2,* 924–936. (3)

Rauscher, F. H., Shaw, G. L., & Ky, K. N. (1993). Music and spatial task performance. *Nature, 365,* 611. (2)

Raven, J. (2000). The Raven's Progressive Matrices: Change and stability over culture and time. *Cognitive Psychology, 41,* 1–48. (9)

Raymond, J. E. (2003). New objects, not new features, trigger the attentional blink. *Psychological Science, 14,* 54–59. (8)

Rayner, K. (1998). Eye movements in reading and information processing: 20 years of research. *Psychological Bulletin, 124,* 372–422. (8)

Rayner, K., Foorman, B. R., Perfetti, C. A., Pesetsky, D., & Seidenberg, M. S. (2001). How psychological science informs the teaching of reading. *Psychological Science in the Public Interest, 2,* 31–74. (8)

Raz, A., Kirsch, I., Pollard, J., & Nitkin-Kaner, Y. (2006). Suggestion reduces the Stroop effect. *Psychological Science, 17,* 91–95. (8)

Rechtschaffen, A., & Bergmann, B. M. (1995). Sleep deprivation in the rat by the disk-over-water method. *Behavioural Brain Research, 69,* 55–63. (5)

Redding, R. E. (2001). Sociopolitical diversity in psychology. *American Psychologist, 56,* 205–215. (5)

Redican, W. K. (1982). An evolutionary perspective on human facial displays. In P. Ekman (Ed.), *Emotion in the human face* (pp. 212–280). Cambridge, England: Cambridge University Press. (12)

Reed, J. M., & Squire, L. R. (1999). Impaired transverse patterning in human amnesia is a special case of impaired memory for two-choice discrimination tasks. *Behavioral Neuroscience, 113,* 3–9. (7)

Reed, T. E. (1985). Ethnic differences in alcohol use, abuse, and sensitivity: A review with genetic interpretation. *Social Biology, 32,* 195–209. (16)

Reicher, G. M. (1969). Perceptual recognition as a function of meaningfulness of stimulus material. *Journal of Experimental Psychology, 81,* 275–280. (8)

Reisenzein, R. (1983). The Schachter theory of emotions: Two decades later. *Psychological Bulletin, 94,* 239–264. (12)

Reneman, L., Lavalaye, J., Schmand, B., de Wolff, F. A., van den Brink, W., den Heeten, G. J., et al. (2001). Cortical serotonin transporter density and verbal memory in individuals who stopped using 3,4-methylenedioxymethamphetamine (MDMA or "ecstasy"). *Archives of General Psychiatry, 58,* 901–906. (3)

Rensink, R. A., O'Regan, J. K., & Clark, J. J. (1997). To see or not to see: The need for attention to perceive changes in scenes. *Psychological Science, 8,* 368–373. (8)

Rentfrow, P. J., & Gosling, S. D. (2006). Message in a ballad. *Psychological Science, 17,* 236–242. (14)

Repovš, G., & Baddeley, A. (2006). The multicomponent model of working memory: Explorations in experimental cognitive psychology. *Neuroscience, 139,* 5–21. (7)

Rescorla, R. A. (1968). Probability of shock in the presence and absence of CS in fear conditioning. *Journal of Comparative and Physiological Psychology, 66,* 1–5. (6)

Rescorla, R. A. (1988). Pavlovian conditioning: It's not what you think it is. *American Psychologist, 43,* 151–160. (6)

Restle, F. (1970). Moon illusion explained on the basis of relative size. *Science, 167,* 1092–1096. (4)

Reyna, V. F., & Farley, F. (2006). Risk and rationality in adolescent decision making: Implications for theory, practice, and public policy. *Psychological Science in the Public Interest, 7,* 1–44. (5)

Rhodes, G., Jeffery, L., Watson, T. L, Clifford, C. W. G., & Nakayama, K. (2003). Fitting the mind to the world: Face adaptation and attractiveness aftereffects. *Psychological Science, 14,* 558–566. (13)

Rhodes, G., Sumich, A., & Byatt, G. (1999). Are average facial configurations attractive only because of their symmetry? *Psychological Science, 10,* 52–58. (13)

Riccio, D. C. (1994). Memory: When less is more. *American Psychologist, 49,* 917–926. (7)

Riccio, D. C., Millin, P. M., & Gisquet- Verrier, P. (2003). Retrograde amnesia: Forgetting back. *Current Directions in Psychological Science, 12,* 41–44. (7)

Rice, M. E., & Cragg, S. J. (2004). Nicotine amplifies reward-related dopamine signals in striatum. *Nature Neuroscience, 7,* 583–584. (3)

Richard, C., Honoré, J., Bernati, T., & Rousseaux, M. (2004). Straight-ahead pointing correlates with long-line bisection in neglect patients. *Cortex, 40,* 75–83. (10)

Riddle, W. J. R., & Scott, A. I. F. (1995). Relapse after successful electroconvulsive therapy: The use and impact of continuation antidepressant drug treatment. *Human Psychopharmacology, 10,* 201–205. (16)

Rieger, G., Chivers, M. L., & Bailey, J. M. (2005). Sexual arousal patterns of bisexual men. *Psychological Science, 16,* 579–584. (11)

Rivas-Vazquez, R. A. (2001). Antidepressants as first-line agents in the current pharmacotherapy of anxiety disorders. *Professional Psychology: Research and Practice, 32,* 101–104. (16)

Ro, T., Shelton, D., Lee, O. L., & Chang, E. (2004). Extrageniculate mediation of unconscious vision in transcranial magnetic stimulation-induced blindsight. *Proceedings of the National Academy of Sciences, USA, 101,* 9933–9935. (10)

Roberts, B. W., & DelVecchio, W. F. (2000). The rank-order consistency of personality traits from childhood to old age: A quantitative review of longitudinal studies. *Psychological Bulletin, 126,* 3–25. (14)

Roberts, B. W., Walton, K. E., & Viechtbauer, W. (2006). Patterns of mean-level change in personality traits across the life course: A meta-analysis of longitudinal studies. *Psychological Bulletin, 132,* 1–25. (14)

Roberts, R. D., Zeidner, M., & Matthews, G. (2001). Does emotional intelligence meet traditional standards for an intelligence? Some new data and conclusions. *Emotion, 1,* 196–231. (12)

Roberts, S. B., Savage, J., Coward, W. A., Chew, B., & Lucas, A. (1988). Energy expenditure and intake in infants born to lean and overweight mothers. *New England Journal of Medicine, 318,* 461–466. (11)

Robertson, I. H. (2005, Winter). The deceptive world of subjective awareness. *Cerebrum, 7*(1), 74–83. (3)

Robertson, L. C. (2003). Binding, spatial attention and perceptual awareness. *Nature Reviews Neuroscience, 4,* 93–102. (3)

Robins, L. N., Helzer, J. E., Weissman, M. M., Orvaschel, H., Gruenberg, E., Burke, J. D., Jr., et al. (1984). Lifetime prevalence of specific psychiatric disorders in three sites. *Archives of General Psychiatry, 41,* 949–958. (15, 16)

Robins, R. W., Gosling, S. D., & Craik, K. H. (1999). An empirical analysis of trends in psychology. *American Psychologist, 54,* 117–128. (1)

Robinson, L. A., Berman, J. S., & Neimeyer, R. A. (1990). Psychotherapy for the treatment of depression: A comprehensive review of controlled outcome research. *Psychological Bulletin, 108,* 30–49. (16)

Robinson, R. J., & Keltner, D. (1996). Much ado about nothing? Revisionists and traditionalists choose an introductory English syllabus. *Psychological Science, 7,* 18–24. (13)

Robinson, T. E., & Berridge, K. C. (2000). The psychology and neurobiology of addiction: An incentive-sensitization view. *Addiction, 95*(Suppl. 2), S91–S117. (16)

Robinson, T. E., & Berridge, K. C. (2001). Incentive-sensitization and addiction. *Addiction, 96,* 103–114. (16)

Roca, C. A., Schmidt, P. J., & Rubinow, D. R. (1999). Gonadal steroids and affective illness. *Neuroscientist, 5,* 227–237. (16)

Rock, I., & Kaufman, L. (1962). The moon illusion, II. *Science, 136,* 1023–1031. (4)

Rodd, J., Gaskell, G., & Marslen-Wilson, W. (2002). Making sense of semantic ambiguity: Semantic competition in lexical access. *Journal of Memory and Language, 46,* 245–266. (8)

Rodgers, J. L. (2001). What causes birth order-intelligence patterns? *American Psychologist, 56,* 505–510. (5)

Rodgers, J. L., Cleveland, H. H., van den Oord, E., & Rowe, D. C. (2000). Resolving the debate over birth order, family size, and intelligence. *American Psychologist, 55,* 599–612. (5)

Rodgers, J. L., & Wänström, L. (in press). Identification of a Flynn effect in the NLSY: Moving from the center to the boundaries. *Intelligence.*

Rodin, J. (1986). Aging and health: Effects of the sense of control. *Science, 233,* 1271–1276. (5, 12)

Rodrigo, M. F., & Ato, M. (2002). Testing the group polarization hypothesis by using logit models. *European Journal of Social Psychology, 32,* 3–18. (13)

Roediger, H. L., III, & Karpicke, J. D. (2006). Test-enhanced learning. *Psychological Science, 17,* 249–255. (7)

Roediger, H. L., III, & McDermott, K. B. (1995). Creating false memories: Remembering words not presented in lists. *Journal of Experimental Psychology: Learning, Memory, and Cognition, 21,* 803–814. (7)

Roediger, H. L., III, & McDermott, K. B. (2000). Tricks of memory. *Current Directions in Psychological Science, 9,* 123–127. (7)

Roenneberg, T., Kuehnle, T., Pramstaller, P. P., Ricken, J., Havel, M., Guth, A., et al. (2004). A marker for the end of adolescence. *Current Biology, 14,* R1038–R1039. (10)

Rogers, C. R. (1951). *Client-centered therapy.* Boston: Houghton Mifflin. (15)

Rogers, C. R. (1961). *On becoming a person.* Boston: Houghton Mifflin. (14)

Rogers, C. R. (1980). *A way of being.* Boston: Houghton Mifflin. (14)

Rogers, T. B. (1995). *The psychological testing enterprise: An introduction.* Pacific Grove, CA: Brooks/Cole. (9)

Rogler, L. H. (2002). Historical generations and psychology. *American Psychologist, 57,* 1013–1023. (5)

Rohrbaugh, M., Shoham, V., Spungen, C., & Steinglass, P. (1995). Family systems therapy in practice: A systemic couples therapy for problem drinking. In B. Bongar & L. E. Beutler (Eds.), *Comprehensive textbook of psychotherapy: Theory and practice* (pp. 228–253). Oxford, England: Oxford University Press. (15)

Roisman, G. I., Collins, W. A., Sroufe, L. A., & Egeland, B. (2005). Predictors of young adults' representations of and behavior in their current romantic relationship: Prospective tests of the prototype hypothesis. *Attachment & Human Development, 7,* 105–121. (5)

Romero, A. J., & Roberts, R. E. (2003). Stress within a bicultural context for adolescents of Mexican descent. *Cultural Diversity and Ethnic Minority Psychology, 9,* 171–184. (5)

Ronen, T., & Rosenbaum, M. (2001). Helping children to help themselves: A case study

of enuresis and nail biting. *Research on Social Work Practice, 11,* 338–356. (6)

Rönkä, A., Oravala, S., & Pulkkinen, L. (2003). Turning points in adults' lives: The effects of gender and the amount of choice. *Journal of Adult Development, 10,* 203–215. (5)

Rosch, E. (1978). Principles of categorization. In E. Rosch & B. B. Lloyd (Eds.), *Cognition and categorization* (pp. 27–48). Hillsdale, NJ: Erlbaum. (8)

Rosch, E., & Mervis, C. B. (1975). Family resemblances: Studies in the internal structure of categories. *Cognitive Psychology, 7,* 573–605. (8)

Rose, J. E. (1996). Nicotine addiction and treatment. *Annual Review of Medicine, 47,* 493–507. (16)

Rose, J. E., Brugge, J. F., Anderson, D. J., & Hind, J. E. (1967). Phase-locked response to low-frequency tones in single auditory nerve fibers of the squirrel monkey. *Journal of Neurophysiology, 30,* 769–793. (4)

Rose, R. J., Viken, R. J., Dick, D. M., Bates, J. E., Pulkkinen, L., & Kaprio, J. (2003). It *does* take a village: Nonfamilial environments and children's behavior. *Psychological Science, 14,* 273–277. (10)

Roselli, C. E., Larkin, K., Resko, J. A., Stellflug, J. N., & Stormshak, F. (2004). The volume of a sexually dimorphic nucleus in the ovine medial preoptic area/anterior hypothalamus varies with sexual partner preference. *Endocrinology, 145,* 478–483. (11)

Rosen, V. M., & Engle, R. W. (1997). The role of working memory capacity in retrieval. *Journal of Experimental Psychology: General, 126,* 211–227. (7)

Rosenbaum, M. E. (1986). The repulsion hypothesis: on the nondevelopment of relationships. *Journal of Personality and Social Psychology, 51,* 1156–1166. (13)

Rosenbaum, R. S., Priselac, S., Köhler, S., Black, S. E., Gao, F., Nadel, L., et al. (2000). Remote spatial memory in an amnesic person with extensive bilateral hippocampal lesions. *Nature Neuroscience, 3,* 1044–1048. (7)

Ross, L. (1977). The intuitive psychologist and his shortcomings: Distortions in the attribution process. In L. Berkowitz (Ed.), *Advances in experimental social psychology* (Vol. 10, pp. 173–220). New York: Academic Press. (13)

Rosselli, M., & Ardila, A. (2003). The impact of culture and education on non-verbal neuropsychological measurements: A critical review. *Brain and Cognition, 52,* 326–333. (9)

Roth, B. L., Lopez, E., & Kroeze, W. K. (2000). The multiplicity of serotonin receptors: Uselessly diverse molecules or an embarrassment of riches? *The Neuroscientist, 6,* 252–262. (3)

Roth, W. T., Wilhelm, F. H., & Pettit, D. (2005). Are current theories of panic falsifiable? *Psychological Bulletin, 131,* 171–192. (16)

Rothbaum, B. O., Hodges, L. F., Kooper, R., Opdyke, D., Williford, J. S., & North, M. (1995). Effectiveness of computer-generated (virtual reality) graded exposure in the treatment of acrophobia. *American Journal of Psychiatry, 152,* 626–628. (16)

Rothbaum, F., Weisz, J., Pott, M., Miyake, K., & Morelli, G. (2000). Attachment and culture: Security in the United States and Japan. *American Psychologist, 55,* 1093–1104. (5)

Rotton, J., & Kelly, I. W. (1985). Much ado about the full moon: A meta-analysis of lunar-lunacy research. *Psychological Bulletin, 97,* 286–306. (2)

Routh, D. K. (2000). Clinical psychology training: A history of ideas and practices prior to 1946. *American Psychologist, 55,* 236–241. (1)

Rovee-Collier, C. (1997). Dissociations in infant memory: Rethinking the development of explicit and implicit memory. *Psychological Review, 104,* 467–498. (5)

Rovee-Collier, C. (1999). The development of infant memory. *Current Directions in Psychological Science, 8,* 80–85. (5)

Rowe, J. W., & Kahn, R. L. (1987). Human aging: Usual and successful. *Science, 237,* 143–149. (5)

Rowland, D. L., & Burnett, A. L. (2000). Pharmacotherapy in the treatment of male sexual dysfunction. *Journal of Sex Research, 37,* 226–243. (11)

Roy, M. M., Christenfeld, N. J. S., & McKenzie, C. R. M. (2005). Underestimating the duration of future events: Memory incorrectly used or memory bias? *Psychological Bulletin, 131,* 738–756. (11)

Royzman, E. B., & Sabini, J. (2001). Something it takes to be an emotion: The interesting case of disgust. *Journal for the Theory of Social Behavior, 31,* 29–59. (12)

Rozenblit, L., & Keil, F. (2002). The misunderstood limits of folk science: An illusion of explanatory depth. *Cognitive Science, 26,* 521–562. (8)

Rozin, P. (1996). Sociocultural influences on human food selection. In E. D. Capaldi (Ed.), *Why we eat what we eat* (pp. 233–263). Washington, DC: American Psychological Association. (1)

Rozin, P. (2001). Social psychology and science: Some lessons from Solomon Asch. *Personality and Social Psychology Review, 5,* 2–14. (13)

Rozin, P., & Cohen, A. B. (2003). High frequency of facial expressions corresponding to confusion, concentration, and worry in an analysis of naturally occurring facial expressions of Americans. *Emotion, 3,* 68–75. (12)

Rozin, P., & Fallon, A. E. (1987). A perspective on disgust. *Psychological Review, 94,* 23–41. (1)

Rozin, P., Fallon, A., & Augustoni-Ziskind, M. L. (1986). The child's conception of food: The development of categories of ac-

ceptable and rejected substances. *Journal of Nutrition Education, 18,* 75–81. (1)

Rozin, P., Fischler, C., Imada, S., Sarubin, A., & Wrzesniewski, A. (1999). Attitudes to food and the role of food in life in the U.S.A., Japan, Flemish Belgium and France: Possible implications for the diet-health debate. *Appetite, 33,* 163–180. (11)

Rozin, P., Kabnick, K., Pete, E., Fischler, C., & Shields, C. (2003). The ecology of eating: Smaller portion sizes in France than in the United States help explain the French paradox. *Psychological Science, 14,* 450–454. (11)

Rozin, P., & Kalat, J. W. (1971). Specific hungers and poison avoidance as adaptive specializations of learning. *Psychological Review, 78,* 459–486. (1, 6)

Rozin, P., Lowery, L., Imada, S., & Haidt, J. (1999). The CAD triad hypothesis: A mapping between three moral emotions (contempt, anger, disgust) and three moral codes (community, autonomy, divinity). *Journal of Personality and Social Psychology, 76,* 574–586. (12)

Rozin, P., Markwith, M., & Ross, B. (1990). The sympathetic magical law of similarity, nominal realism and neglect of negatives in response to negative labels. *Psychological Science, 1,* 383–384. (8)

Rozin, P., Markwith, M., & Stoess, C. (1997). Moralization and becoming a vegetarian: The transformation of preferences into values and the recruitment of disgust. *Psychological Science, 8,* 67–73. (1)

Rozin, P., Millman, L., & Nemeroff, C. (1986). Operation of the laws of sympathetic magic in disgust and other domains. *Journal of Personality and Social Psychology, 50,* 703–712. (1)

Rozin, P., & Pelchat, M. L. (1988). Memories of mammaries: Adaptations to weaning from milk. *Progress in Psychobiology and Physiological Psychology, 13,* 1–29. (5)

Rubenstein, R., & Newman, R. (1954). The living out of "future" experiences under hypnosis. *Science, 119,* 472–473. (10)

Rubia, K., Oosterlaan, J., Sergeant, J. A., Brandeis, D., & v. Leeuwen, T. (1998). Inhibitory dysfunction in hyperactive boys. *Behavioural Brain Research, 94,* 25–32. (8)

Ruch, J. (1984). *Psychology: The personal science.* Belmont, CA: Wadsworth. (5)

Rudman, L. A., & Borgida, E. (1995). The afterglow of construct accessibility: The behavioral consequences of priming men to view women as sexual objects. *Journal of Experimental Social Psychology, 31,* 493–517. (8)

Rudman, L. A., & Goodwin, S. A. (2004). Gender differences in automatic in-group bias: Why do women like women more than men like men? *Journal of Personality and Social Psychology, 87,* 494–509. (13)

Rumbaugh, D. M., & Washburn, D. A. (2003). *Intelligence of apes and other rational be-*

ings. New Haven, CT: Yale University Press. (6)

Rumelhart, D. E., & McClelland, J. L. (1982). An interactive activation model of context effects in letter perception: Part 2. The contextual enhancement effect and some tests and extensions of the model. *Psychological Review, 89,* 60–94. (8)

Rumelhart, D. E., McClelland, J. L., & the PDP Research Group. (1986). *Parallel distributed processing.* Cambridge, MA: MIT Press. (8)

Rusak, B. (1977). The role of the suprachiasmatic nuclei in the generation of circadian rhythms in the golden hamster, *Mesocricetus auratus. Journal of Comparative Physiology A, 118,* 145–164. (10)

Rush, A. J., Trivedi, M. H., Wisniewski, S. R., Stewart, J. W., Nierenberg, A. A., Thase, M. E., et al. (2006). Bupropion-SR, sertraline, or venlaxine-XR after failure of SSRIs for depression. *New England Journal of Medicine, 354,* 1231–1242. (16)

Rushton, J. P., & Bons, T. A. (2005). Mate choice and friendship in twins. *Psychological Science, 16,* 555–559. (13)

Russano, M. B., Meissner, C. A., Narchet, F. M., & Kassin, S. M. (2005). Investigating true and false confessions within a novel experimental paradigm. *Psychological Science, 16,* 481–486. (13)

Russell, J. A. (1980). A circumplex model of affect. *Journal of Personality and Social Psychology, 39,* 1161–1178. (12)

Russell, J. A. (1994). Is there universal recognition of emotion from facial expression? A review of the cross-cultural studies. *Psychological Bulletin, 115,* 102–141. (12)

Ruthruff, E., Pashler, H. E., & Hazeltine, E. (2003). Dual-task interference with equal task emphasis: Graded capacity sharing or central postponement? *Perception & Psychophysics, 65,* 801–816. (8)

Ruthruff, E., Pashler, H. E., & Klaassen, A. (2001). Processing bottlenecks in dual-task performance: Structural limitations or strategic postponement? *Psychonomic Bulletin and Review, 8,* 73–80. (8)

Rutledge, T., & Hogan, B. E. (2002). A quantitative review of prospective evidence linking psychological factors with hypertension development. *Psychosomatic Medicine, 64,* 758–766. (12)

Ryan, J. D., Althoff, R. R., Whitlow, S., & Cohen, N. J. (2000). Amnesia is a deficit in relational memory. *Psychological Science, 11,* 454–461. (7)

Ryan, L., Hatfield, C., & Hofstetter, M. (2002). Caffeine reduces time-of-day effects on memory performance in older adults. *Psychological Science, 13,* 68–71. (10)

Ryan, R. M., & Deci, E. L. (2000). Self-determination theory and the facilitation of intrinsic motivation, social development, and well-being. *American Psychologist, 55,* 68–78. (11)

Saarelainen, T., Hendolin, P., Lucas, G., Koponen, E., Sairanen, M., MacDonald, E., et al. (2003). Activation of the TrkB neurotrophin receptor is induced by antidepressant drugs and is required for antidepressant-induced behavioral effects. *Journal of Neuroscience, 23,* 349–357. (16)

Sabini, J., Siepmann, M., Stein, J., & Meyerowitz, M. (2000). Who is embarrassed by what? *Cognition and Emotion, 14,* 213–240. (12)

Sackeim, H. A., Prudic, J., Devanand, D. P., Nobler, M. S., Lisanby, S. H., Peyser, S., et al. (2000). A prospective, randomized, double-blind comparison of bilateral and right unilateral electroconvulsive therapy at different stimulus intensities. *Archives of General Psychiatry, 57,* 425–434. (16)

Sadato, N., Pascual-Leone, A., Grafman, J., Deiber, M.-P., Ibañez, V., & Hallett, M. (1998). Neural networks for Braille reading by the blind. *Brain, 121,* 1213–1229. (3)

Sadato, N., Pascual-Leone, A., Grafman, J., Ibañez, V., Deiber, M.-P., Dold, G., et al. (1996). Activation of the primary visual cortex by Braille reading in blind subjects. *Nature, 380,* 526–528. (3)

Saegert, S., Swap, W., & Zajonc, R. B. (1973). Exposure, context, and interpersonal attraction. *Journal of Personality and Social Psychology, 25,* 234–242. (13)

Safer, M. A., & Keuler, D. J. (2002). Individual differences in misremembering prepsychotherapy distress: Personality and memory distortion. *Emotion, 2,* 162–178. (15)

Saffran, J. R. (2003). Statistical language learning: Mechanisms and constraints. *Current Directions in Psychological Science, 12,* 110–114. (8)

Saffran, J. R., Aslin, R. N., & Newport, E. L. (1996). Statistical learning by 8-month-old infants. *Science, 274,* 1926–1928. (8)

Saleem, Q., Dash, D., Gandhi, C., Kishore, A., Benegal, V., Sherrin, T., et al. (2001). Association of CAG repeat loci on chromosome 22 with schizophrenia and bipolar disorder. *Molecular Psychiatry, 6,* 694–700. (16)

Salovey, P., & Birnbaum, D. (1989). Influence of mood on health-relevant cognitions. *Journal of Personality and Social Psychology, 57,* 539–551. (12)

Salthouse, T. A. (2006). Mental exercise and mental aging. *Perspectives on Psychological Science, 1,* 68–87. (8)

Samelson, F. (1980). J. B. Watson's Little Albert, Cyril Burt's twins, and the need for a critical science. *American Scientist, 35,* 619–625. (16)

Samuel, A. G. (2001). Knowing a word affects the fundamental perception of the sounds within it. *Psychological Science, 12,* 348–351. (8)

Sanchez, L. M., & Turner, S. M. (2003). Practicing psychology in the era of managed care. *American Psychologist, 58,* 116–129. (15)

Sandell, R., Blomberg, J., Lazar, A., Schubert, J., Carlsson, J., & Broberg, J. (1999). Wie die Zeit vergeht: Langzeitergebnisse von Psychoanalysen und analytischen Psychotherapien. [As time goes by: Long-term outcomes of psychoanalysis and long-term psychotherapy.] *Forum der Psychoanalyse, 15,* 327–347. (15)

Sanders, R. E., Gonzalez, D. J., Murphy, M. D., Pesta, B. J., & Bucur, B. (2002). Training content variability and the effectiveness of learning: An adult age assessment. *Aging, Neuropsychology, and Cognition, 9,* 157–174. (7)

Sandfort, T. G. M., de Graaf, R., Bijl, R. V., & Schnabel, P. (2001). Same-sex sexual behavior and psychiatric disorders. *Archives of General Psychiatry, 58,* 85–91. (11)

Sanna, L. J. (2000). Mental simulation, affect, and personality: A conceptual framework. *Current Directions in Psychological Science, 9,* 168–173. (12)

Sapolsky, R. M. (1998, March 30). Open season. *The New Yorker, 74*(6), 57–58, 71–72. (14)

Sapolsky, R. M., & Share, L. J. (2004). A pacific culture among wild baboons: Its emergence and transmission. *PLOS Biology, 2,* 534–541. (12)

Sapp, F., Lee, K., & Muir, D. (2000). Three-year-olds' difficulty with the appearance–reality distinction: Is it real or is it apparent? *Developmental Psychology, 36,* 547–560. (5)

Sartor, C. E., Jacob, T., & Bucholz, K. K. (2003). Drinking course in alcohol-dependent men from adolescence to midlife. *Journal of Studies on Alcohol, 64,* 712–719. (16)

Satterfield, J. M., & Seligman, M. E. P. (1994). Military aggression and risk predicted by explanatory style. *Psychological Science, 5,* 77–82. (16)

Saucier, D. M., Green, S. M., Leason, J., MacFadden, A., Bell, S., & Elias, L. J. (2002). Are sex differences in navigation caused by sexually dimorphic strategies or by differences in the ability to use the strategies? *Behavioral Neuroscience, 116,* 403–410. (5)

Savage-Rumbaugh, E. S. (1990). Language acquisition in a nonhuman species: Implications for the innateness debate. *Developmental Psychology, 23,* 599–620. (8)

Savage-Rumbaugh, E. S., Murphy, J., Sevcik, R. A., Brakke, K. E., Williams, S. L., & Rumbaugh, D. M. (1993). Language comprehension in ape and child. *Monographs of the Society for Research in Child Development, 58*(Serial no. 233). (8)

Savage-Rumbaugh, E. S., Sevcik, R. A., Brakke, K. E., & Rumbaugh, D. M. (1992). Symbols: Their communicative use, communication, and combination by bonobos *(Pan paniscus).* In L. P. Lipsitt & C. Rovee-Collier (Eds.), *Advances in infancy research* (Vol. 7, pp. 221–278). Norwood, NJ: Ablex. (8)

Saxe, L., & Ben-Shakhar, G. (1999). Admissibility of polygraph tests: The application of scientific standards post-Daubert. *Psychology, Public Policy, and Law, 5,* 203–223. (12)

Scarborough, E., & Furomoto, L. (1987). *Untold lives: The first generation of American women psychologists.* New York: Columbia University Press. (1)

Scarr, S. (1997). Rules of evidence: A larger context for the statistical debate. *Psychological Science, 8,* 16–17. (2)

Scarr, S. (1998). American child care today. *American Psychologist, 53,* 95–108. (5)

Schachter, D. L. (1987). Implicit memory: History and current status. *Journal of Experimental Psychology: Learning, Memory, and Cognition, 13,* 501–518. (7)

Schacter, D. L., Verfaellie, M., Anes, M. D., & Racine, C. (1998). When true recognition suppresses false recognition: Evidence from amnesic patients. *Journal of Cognitive Neuroscience, 10,* 668–679. (7)

Schachter, S. (1982). Recidivism and self-cure of smoking and obesity. *American Psychologist, 37,* 436–444. (11)

Schachter, S., & Singer, J. (1962). Cognitive, social, and physiological determinants of emotional state. *Psychological Review, 69,* 379–399. (12)

Schatzman, M. (1992, March 21). Freud: Who seduced whom? *New Scientist,* pp. 34–37. (14)

Schellenberg, E. G. (2004). Music lessons enhance IQ. *Psychological Science, 15,* 511–514. (9)

Schellenberg, E. G. (2006). Long-term positive associations between music lessons and IQ. *Journal of Educational Psychology, 98,* 457–468. (9)

Schellenberg, E. G., & Trehub, S. E. (2003). Good pitch memory is widespread. *Psychological Science, 14,* 262–266. (4)

Schenck, C. H., & Mahowald, M. W. (1996). Long-term, nightly benzodiazepine treatment of injurious parasomnias and other disorders of disrupted nocturnal sleep in 170 adults. *American Journal of Medicine, 100,* 333–337. (10)

Scherer, K. R. (1992). What does facial expression express? In K. T. Strongman (Ed.), *International review of studies on emotion* (Vol. 2, pp. 139–165). Chichester, England: Wiley. (12)

Schiffman, S. S., & Erickson, R. P. (1971). A psychophysical model for gustatory quality. *Physiology & Behavior, 7,* 617–633. (4)

Schkade, D. A., & Kahneman, D. (1998). Does living in California make people happy? *Psychological Science, 9,* 340–346. (12)

Schlesier-Stropp, B. (1984). Bulimia: A review of the literature. *Psychological Review, 95,* 247–257. (11)

Schlinger, H. D. (2003). The myth of intelligence. *Psychological Record, 53,* 15–32. (9)

Schmidt, F. L., & Hunter, J. E. (1981). Employment testing: Old theories and new research findings. *American Psychologist, 36,* 1128–1137. (9)

Schmidt, F. L., & Hunter, J. E. (1998). The validity and utility of selection methods in personnel psychology: Practical and theoretical implications of 85 years of research findings. *Psychological Bulletin, 124,* 262–274. (9)

Schmidt, R. A., & Bjork, R. A. (1992). New conceptualizations of practice: Common principles in three paradigms suggest new concepts for training. *Psychological Science, 3,* 207–217. (7)

Schmidt, S. R. (2002). Outstanding memories: The positive and negative effects of nudes on memory. *Journal of Experimental Psychology: Learning, Memory, and Cognition, 28,* 353–361. (7)

Schmitt, A. P., & Dorans, N. J. (1990). Differential item functioning for minority examinees on the SAT. *Journal of Educational Measurement, 27,* 67–81. (9)

Schmitt, D. P., and 118 members of the International Sexuality Description Project. (2003). Universal sex differences in the desire for sexual variety: Tests from 52 nations, 6 continents, and 13 islands. *Journal of Personality and Social Psychology, 85,* 85–104. (13)

Schmolck, H., Buffalo, E. A., & Squire, L. R. (2000). Memory distortions develop over time. *Psychological Science, 11,* 39–45. (7)

Schneider, P., Scherg, M., Dosch, G., Specht, H. J., Gutschalk, A., & Rupp, A. (2002). Morphology of Heschl's gyrus reflects enhanced activation in the auditory cortex of musicians. *Nature Neuroscience, 5,* 688–694. (8)

Schnider, A. (2003). Spontaneous confabulation and the adaptation of thought to ongoing reality. *Nature Reviews Neuroscience, 4,* 662–671. (7)

Schooler, C. (1972). Birth order effects: Not here, not now! *Psychological Bulletin, 78,* 161–175. (5)

Schooler, C. (1998). Environmental complexity and the Flynn effect. In U. Neisser (Ed.), *The rising curve* (pp. 67–79). Washington, DC: American Psychological Association. (9)

Schou, M. (1997). Forty years of lithium treatment. *Archives of General Psychiatry, 54,* 9–13. (16)

Schredl, M. (2000). Continuity between waking life and dreaming: Are all waking activities reflected equally often in dreams? *Perceptual and Motor Skills, 90,* 844–846. (10)

Schredl, M., Ciric, P., Bishop, A., Gölitz, E., & Buschtöns, D. (2003). Content analysis of German students' dreams: Comparison to American findings. *Dreaming, 13,* 237–243. (10)

Schriesheim, C. A., Castro, S. L., & Cogliser, C. C. (1999). Leader-member exchange (LMX) research: A comprehensive review of theory, measurement, and data-analytic practices. *Leadership Quarterly, 10,* 63–113. (11)

Schuckit, M. A., & Smith, T. L. (1997). Assessing the risk for alcoholism among sons of alcoholics. *Journal of Studies on Alcohol, 58,* 141–145. (16)

Schuckit, M. A., Smith, T. L., Kalmijn, J., Tsuang, J., Hesselbrock, V., Bucholz, K., et al. (2000). Response to alcohol in daughters of alcoholics: A pilot study and a comparison with sons of alcoholics. *Alcohol and Alcoholism, 35,* 242–248. (16)

Schulsinger, F., Knop, J., Goodwin, D. W., Teasdale, T. W., & Mikkelsen, U. (1986). A prospective study of young men at high risk for alcoholism. *Archives of General Psychiatry, 43,* 755–760. (16)

Schützwohl, A., & Borgstedt, K. (2005). The processing of affectively valenced stimuli: The role of surprise. *Cognition and Emotion, 19,* 583–600. (12)

Schwartz, B. (2004). *The paradox of choice.* New York: HarperCollins. (8)

Schwartz, B., Ward, A., Monterosso, J., Lyubomirsky, S., White, K., & Lehman, D. R. (2002). Maximizing versus satisficing: Happiness is a matter of choice. *Journal of Personality and Social Psychology, 83,* 1178–1197. (8)

Schwartz, C. E., Wright, C. I., Shin, L. M., Kagan, J., & Rauch, S. L. (2003). Inhibited and uninhibited infants "grown up": Adult amygdalar response to novelty. *Science, 300,* 1952–1953. (5)

Schwartz, M. B., & Brownell, K. D. (1995). Matching individuals to weight loss treatments: A survey of obesity experts. *Journal of Consulting and Clinical Psychology, 63,* 149–153. (11)

Schwarz, N., Strack, F., & Mai, H.-P. (1991). Assimilation and contrast effects in part–whole question sequences: A conversational logic analysis. *Public Opinion Quarterly, 55,* 3–23. (2)

Schwarzwald, J., Bizman, A., & Raz, M. (1983). The foot-in-the-door paradigm: Effects of second request size on donation probability and donor generosity. *Personality and Social Psychology Bulletin, 9,* 443–450. (13)

Scoboria, A., Mazzoni, G., Kirsch, I., & Milling, L. S. (2002). Immediate and persisting effects of misleading questions and hypnosis on memory reports. *Journal of Experimental Psychology: Applied, 8,* 26–32. (10)

Scott, D., Lambie, I., Henwood, D., & Lamb, R. (2003). Profiling stranger rapists: It's not so elementary, Doctor Watson. *American Journal of Forensic Psychology, 21,* 31–49. (14)

Scott, S. K., Young, A. W., Calder, A. J., Hellawell, D. J., Aggleton, J. P., & Johnson, M. (1997). Impaired auditory recognition of fear and anger following bilateral amygdala lesions. *Nature, 385,* 254–257. (12)

Scott, T. R., & Verhagen, J. V. (2000). Taste as a factor in the management of nutrition. *Nutrition, 16,* 874–885. (1)

Scovern, A. W., & Kilmann, P. R. (1980). Status of electroconvulsive therapy: Review of the outcome literature. *Psychological Bulletin, 87,* 260–303. (16)

Scripture, E. W. (1907). *Thinking, feeling, doing* (2nd ed.). New York: G. P. Putnam's Sons. (1)

Seamon, J. G., Lee, I. A., Toner, S. K., Wheeler, R. H., Goodkind, M. S., & Birch, A. D. (2002). Thinking of critical words during study is unnecessary for false memory in the Deese, Roediger, and McDermott procedure. *Psychological Science, 13,* 526–531. (7)

Sears, D. O., & Henry, P. J. (2003). The origins of symbolic racism. *Journal of Personality and Social Psychology, 85,* 259–275. (13)

Seeley, R. J., Kaplan, J. M., & Grill, H. J. (1995). Effect of occluding the pylorus on intraoral intake: A test of the gastric hypothesis of meal termination. *Physiology & Behavior, 58,* 245–249. (11)

Seeman, P., & Lee, T. (1975). Antipsychotic drugs: Direct correlation between clinical potency and presynaptic action on dopamine neurons. *Science, 188,* 1217–1219. (16)

Segal, N. L. (2000). Virtual twins: New findings on within-family environmental influences on intelligence. *Journal of Educational Psychology, 92,* 442–448. (9)

Segerstrom, S. C. (2001). Optimism and attentional bias for negative and positive symptoms. *Personality and Social Psychology Bulletin, 27,* 1334–1343. (14)

Seidenberg, M. S. (1997). Language acquisition and use: Learning and applying probabilistic constraints. *Science, 275,* 1599–1603. (8)

Seidman, L. J., Valera, E. M., & Makris, N. (2005). Structural brain imaging of attention-deficit/hyperactivity disorder. *Biological Psychiatry, 57,* 1263–1272. (8)

Sekuler, A. B., & Bennett, P. J. (2001). Generalized common fate: Grouping by common luminance changes. *Psychological Science, 12,* 437–444. (4)

Seligman, M. E. P. (1970). On the generality of the laws of learning. *Psychological Review, 77,* 406–418. (6)

Seligman, M. E. P. (1971). Phobias and preparedness. *Behavior Therapy, 2,* 307–320. (16)

Seligman, M. E. P. (1995). The effectiveness of psychotherapy: The *Consumer Reports* study. *American Psychologist, 50,* 965–974. (15)

Seligman, M. E. P., & Csikszentmihalyi, M. (2000). Positive psychology. *American Psychologist, 55,* 5–14. (12)

Seligman, M. E. P., Nolen-Hoeksema, S., Thornton, N., & Thornton, K. M. (1990). Explanatory style as a mechanism of disappointing athletic performance. *Psychological Science, 1,* 143–146. (16)

Seligman, M. E. P., Schulman, P., DeRubeis, R. J., & Hollon, S. D. (1999). The prevention of depression and anxiety. *Prevention and Treatment, 2,* article 8. (15)

Sellbom, M., & Ben-Porath, Y. S. (2005). Mapping the MMPI-2 restructured clinical scales onto normal personality traits: Evidence of construct validity. *Journal of Personality Assessment, 85,* 179–187. (14)

Selye, H. (1979). Stress, cancer, and the mind. In J. Taché, H. Selye, & S. B. Day (Eds.), *Cancer, stress, and death* (pp. 11–27). New York: Plenum Press. (12)

Semmler, C., Brewer, N., & Wells, G. L. (2004). Effects of postidentification feedback on eyewitness identification and nonidentification confidence. *Journal of Applied Psychology, 89,* 334–346. (7)

Senghas, A., & Coppola, M. (2001). Children creating language: How Nicaraguan sign language acquired a spatial grammar. *Psychological Science, 12,* 323–328. (8)

Senghas, A., Kita, S., & Özyürek, A. (2004). Children creating core properties of language: Evidence from an emerging sign language in Nicaragua. *Science, 305,* 1779–1782. (8)

Sensky, T., Turkington, D., Kingdon, D., Scott, J. L., Scott, J., Siddle, R., et al. (2000). A randomized controlled trial of cognitive-behavioral therapy for persistent symptoms in schizophrenia resistant to medication. *Archives of General Psychiatry, 57,* 165–172. (16)

Seo, M.-G., Barrett, L. F., & Bartunek, J. M. (2004). The role of affective experience in work motivation. *Academy of Management Review, 29,* 423–439. (11)

Sergent, C., & Dehaene, S. (2004). Is consciousness a gradual phenomenon? *Psychological Science, 15,* 720–728. (10)

Shadish, W. R., & Baldwin, S. A. (2005). Effects of behavioral marital therapy: A meta-analysis of randomized controlled trials. *Journal of Consulting and Clinical Psychology, 73,* 6–14. (13)

Shaffer, D., Fisher, P., Dulcan, M. K., Davies, M., Piacentini, J., Schwab-Stone, M. E., et al. (1996). The NIMH Diagnostic Interview Schedule of Children version 2.3 (DISC-2.3): Description, acceptability, prevalence rates, and performance in the MECA study. *Journal of the American Academy of Child and Adolescent Psychiatry, 35,* 865–877. (12)

Shafir, E. B., Smith, E. E., & Osherson, D. N. (1990). Typicality and reasoning fallacies. *Memory & Cognition, 18,* 229–239. (8)

Shafto, M., & MacKay, D. G. (2000). The Moses, mega-Moses, and Armstrong illusions: Integrating language comprehension and semantic memory. *Psychological Science, 11,* 372–378. (8)

Shahar, D. R., Schultz, R., Shahar, A., & Wing, R. R. (2001). The effect of widowhood on weight change, dietary intake, and eating behavior in the elderly population. *Journal of Aging and Health, 13,* 186–199. (12)

Shannon, D. A. (1955). *The Socialist Party of America.* New York: Macmillan. (13)

Shapiro, D. H., Jr., Schwartz, C. E., & Astin, J. A. (1996). Controlling ourselves, controlling our world. *American Psychologist, 51,* 1213–1230. (12)

Shapiro, D. L. (1985). Insanity and the assessment of criminal responsibility. In C. P. Ewing (Ed.), *Psychology, psychiatry, and the law: A clinical and forensic handbook* (pp. 67–94). Sarasota, FL: Professional Resource Exchange. (15)

Shapiro, K. L., Caldwell, J., & Sorensen, R. E. (1997). Personal names and the attentional blink: A visual "cocktail party" effect. *Journal of Experimental Psychology: Human Perception and Performance, 23,* 504–514. (8)

Sharot, T., Delgado, M. R., & Phelps, E. A. (2004). How emotion enhances the feeling of remembering. *Nature Neuroscience, 7,* 1376–1380. (7)

Shayer, M., Ginsburg, D., & Coe, R. (in press). Thirty years on—A large anti-Flynn effect? The Piagetian test *volume & heaviness* norms 1975–2003. *British Journal of Educational Psychology.* (9)

Shearn, D., Spellman, L., Straley, B., Meirick, J., & Stryker, K. (1999). Empathic blushing in friends and strangers. *Motivation and Emotion, 23,* 307–316. (12)

Sheese, B. E., & Graziano, W. G. (2005). Deciding to defect. *Psychological Science, 16,* 354–357. (2)

Sheldon, K., & Lyubomirsky, S. (2004). Achieving sustainable new happiness: Prospects, practices, and prescriptions. In P. A. Linley & S. Joseph (Eds.), *Positive psychology in practice* (pp. 127–145). Hoboken, NJ: Wiley. (12)

Sheldon, K. M., & Lyubomirsky, S. (2006). Achieving sustainable gains in happiness: Change your actions, not your circumstances. *Journal of Happiness Studies, 7,* 55–86. (12)

Shenkin, S. D., Starr, J. M., & Deary, I. J. (2004). Birth weight and cognitive ability in childhood: A systematic review. *Psychological Bulletin, 130,* 989–1013. (5)

Shepard, R. N. (1990). *Mind sights.* New York: W. H. Freeman. (4)

Shepard, R. N., & Metzler, J. N. (1971). Mental rotation of three-dimensional objects. *Science, 171,* 701–703. (8)

Sheppard, W. D., II, Staggers, F. J., Jr., & John, L. (1997). The effects of a stress management program in a high security government agency. *Anxiety, Stress, and Coping, 10,* 341–350. (12)

Shepperd, J. A. (1993). Productivity loss in performance groups: A motivation analysis. *Psychological Bulletin, 113,* 67–81. (13)

Shergill, S. S., Brammer, M. J., Williams, S. C. R., Murray, R. M., & McGuire, P. K. (2000). Mapping auditory hallucinations in schizophrenia using functional magnetic resonance imaging. *Archives of General Psychiatry, 57,* 1033–1038. (16)

Sherif, M. (1935). A study of some social factors in perception. *Archives of Psychology, 27,* 1–60. (13)

Sherif, M. (1966). *In common predicament.* Boston: Houghton Mifflin. (13)

Sherrod, D. R., Hage, J. N., Halpern, P. L., & Moore, B. S. (1977). Effects of personal causation and perceived control on responses to an aversive environment: The more control, the better. *Journal of Experimental Social Psychology, 13,* 14–27. (12)

Sherwood, G. G. (1981). Self-serving biases in person perception: A reexamination of projection as a mechanism of defense. *Psychological Bulletin, 90,* 445–459. (14)

Shih, M., Pittinsky, T. L., & Ambady, N. (1999). Stereotype susceptibility: Identity salience and shifts in quantitative performance. *Psychological Science, 10,* 80–83. (9)

Shih, M., & Sanchez, D. T. (2005). Perspectives and research on the positive and negative implications of having multiple racial identities. *Psychological Bulletin, 131,* 569–591. (5)

Shimaya, A. (1997). Perception of complex line drawings. *Journal of Experimental Psychology: Human Perception and Performance, 23,* 25–50. (4)

Shinskey, J. L., & Munakata, Y. (2005). Familiarity breeds searching. *Psychological Science, 16,* 595–600. (5)

Shogren, E. (1993, June 2). Survey finds 4 in 5 suffer sex harassment at school. *Los Angeles Times,* p. A10. (2)

Shweder, R., Mahapatra, M., & Miller, J. G. (1987). Culture and moral development. In J. Kagan & S. Lamb (Eds.), *The emergence of morality in young children* (pp. 1–83). Chicago: University of Chicago Press. (13)

Siegel, J. M. (2005). Clues to the functions of mammalian sleep. *Nature, 437,* 1264–1271. (10)

Siegel, S. (1977). Morphine tolerance as an associative process. *Journal of Experimental Psychology: Animal Behavior Processes, 3,* 1–13. (6)

Siegel, S. (1983). Classical conditioning, drug tolerance, and drug dependence. *Research Advances in Alcohol and Drug Problems, 7,* 207–246. (6)

Siegel, S. (1987). Alcohol and opiate dependence: Reevaluation of the Victorian perspective. *Research Advances in Alcohol and Drug Problems, 9,* 279–314. (16)

Siegler, R. S. (2000). Unconscious insights. *Current Directions in Psychological Science, 9,* 79–83. (8)

Sigman, M., & Whaley, S. E. (1998). The role of nutrition in the development of intelligence. In U. Neisser (Ed.), *The rising curve* (pp. 155–182). Washington, DC: American Psychological Association. (9)

Silberg, J. L., Parr, T., Neale, M. C., Rutter, M., Angold, A., & Eaves, L. J. (2003). Maternal smoking during pregnancy and risk to boys' conduct disturbance: An examination of the causal hypothesis. *Biological Psychiatry, 53,* 130–135. (16)

Silberg, J., Pickles, A., Rutter, M., Hewitt, J., Simonoff, E., Maes, H., et al. (1999). The influence of genetic factors and life stress on depression among adolescent girls. *Archives of General Psychiatry, 56,* 225–232. (16)

Silk, J. B., Brosnan, S. F., Vonk, J., Henrich, J., Povinelli, D. J., Richardson, A. S., et al. (2005). Chimpanzees are indifferent to the welfare of unrelated group members. *Nature, 437,* 1357–1359. (13)

Silver, E. (1995). Punishment or treatment? Comparing the lengths of confinement of successful and unsuccessful insanity defendants. *Law and Human Behavior, 19,* 375–388. (15)

Silverman, I., Choi, J., Mackewn, A., Fisher, M., Moro, J., & Olshansky, E. (2000). Evolved mechanisms underlying wayfinding: Further studies on the hunter-gatherer theory of spatial sex differences. *Evolution and Human Behavior, 21,* 201–213. (5)

Silverstein, L. B., & Auerbach, C. F. (1999). Deconstructing the essential father. *American Psychologist, 54,* 397–407. (5)

Simcock, G., & Hayne, H. (2002). Breaking the barrier? Children fail to translate their preverbal memories into language. *Psychological Science, 13,* 225–231. (7)

Simmons, E. J. (1949). *Leo Tolstoy.* London: Lehmann. (16)

Simner, J., & Ward, J. (2006). The taste of words on the tip of the tongue. *Nature, 444,* 438. (4)

Simons, D. J., & Levin, D. T. (2003). What makes change blindness interesting? *The Psychology of Learning and Motivation, 42,* 295–322. (8)

Simons, T., & Roberson, Q. (2003). Why managers should care about fairness: The effects of aggregate justice perceptions on organizational outcomes. *Journal of Applied Psychology, 88,* 432–443. (11)

Simpson, C. A., & Vuchinich, R. E. (2000). Reliability of a measure of temporal discounting. *Psychological Record, 50,* 3–16. (11)

Simpson, J. A., Oriña, M. M., & Ickes, W. (2003). When accuracy hurts, and when it helps: A test of the empathic accuracy model in marital interactions. *Journal of Personality and Social Psychology, 85,* 881–893. (13)

Singer, T., Seymour, B., O'Doherty, J., Kaube, H., Dolan, R. J., & Frith, C. D. (2004). Empathy for pain involves the affective but not sensory components of pain. *Science, 303,* 1157–1162. (4)

Singh, M., Hoffman, D. D., & Albert, M. K. (1999). Contour completion and relative depth: Petter's rule and support ratio. *Psychological Science, 10,* 423–428. (4)

Sirigu, A., Daprati, E., Ciancia, S., Giraux, P., Nighoghossian, N., Posda, A., et al. (2004). Altered awareness of voluntary action after damage to the parietal cortex. *Nature Neuroscience, 7,* 80–84. (10)

Sizemore, C. C., & Huber, R. J. (1988). The twenty-two faces of Eve. *Individual Psychology, 44,* 53–62. (15)

Sizemore, C. C., & Pittillo, E. S. (1977). *I'm Eve.* Garden City, NY: Doubleday. (15)

Skinner, B. F. (1938). *The behavior of organisms.* New York: D. Appleton-Century. (6)

Skinner, B. F. (1990). Can psychology be a science of mind? *American Psychologist, 45,* 1206–1210. (6)

Skinner, E. A., Edge, K., Altman, J., & Sherwood, H. (2003). Searching for the structure of coping: A review and critique of category systems for classifying ways of coping. *Psychological Bulletin, 129,* 216–269. (12)

Skoog, G., & Skoog, I. (1999). A 40-year follow-up of patients with obsessive-compulsive disorder. *Archives of General Psychiatry, 56,* 121–127. (16)

Skre, I., Onstad, S., Torgerson, S., Lygren, S., & Kringlen, E. (2000). The heritability of common phobic fear: A twin study of a clinical sample. *Journal of Anxiety Disorders, 14,* 549–562. (16)

Smith, D. M., Langa, K. M., Kabeto, M. U., & Ubel, P. A. (2005). Health, wealth, and happiness. *Psychological Science, 16,* 663–666. (12)

Smith, L. B., Jones, S. S., Landau, B., Gershkoff-Stowe, L., & Samuelson, L. (2002). Object name learning provides on-the-job training for attention. *Psychological Science, 13,* 13–19. (8)

Smith, L. D. (1995). Inquiry nearer the source: Bacon, Mach, and *The Behavior of Organisms.* In J. T. Todd & E. K. Morris (Eds.), *Modern perspectives on B. F. Skinner and contemporary behaviorism* (pp. 39–50). Westport, CT: Greenwood Press. (6)

Smith, M. L. (1988). Recall of spatial location by the amnesic patient H. M. *Brain and Cognition, 7,* 178–183. (7)

Smith, M. L., Glass, G. V., & Miller, T. I. (1980). *The benefits of psychotherapy.* Baltimore: Johns Hopkins University Press. (15)

Smith, M. W. (1974). Alfred Binet's remarkable questions: A cross-national and cross-temporal analysis of the cultural biases built into the Stanford-Binet intelligence scale and other Binet tests. *Genetic Psychology Monographs, 89,* 307–334. (9)

Smith, P., & Waterman, M. (2003). Processing bias for aggression words in forensic and nonforensic samples. *Cognition and Emotion, 17,* 681–701. (14)

Snyder, C. R. (2003). "Me conform? No way": Classroom demonstrations for sensitizing students to their conformity. *Teaching of Psychology, 30,* 59–61. (13)

Snyder, M., Tanke, E. D., & Bersheid, E. (1977). Social perception and interpersonal behavior: On the self-fulfilling nature of social stereotypes. *Journal of Personality and Social Psychology, 35,* 656–666. (13)

Society for Personality Assessment. (2005). The status of the Rorschach in clinical and forensic practice: An official statement by the Board of Trustees of the Society for Personality Assessment. *Journal of Personality Assessment, 85,* 219–237. (14)

Solanto, M. V., Abikoff, H., Sonuga-Barke, E., Schachar, R., Logan, G. D., Wigal, T., et al. (2001). The ecological validity of delay aversion and response inhibition as measures of impulsivity in AD/HD: A supplement to the NIMH multimodal treatment study of AD/HD. *Journal of Abnormal Child Psychology, 29,* 215–228. (8)

Solin, D. (1989). The systematic misrepresentation of bilingual-crossed aphasia data and its consequences. *Brain and Language, 36,* 92–116. (8)

Solms, M. (1997). *The neuropsychology of dreams.* Mahwah, NJ: Erlbaum. (10)

Solms, M. (2000). Dreaming and REM sleep are controlled by different brain mechanisms. *Behavioral and Brain Sciences, 23,* 843–850. (10)

Solomon, D. A., Keller, M. B., Leon, A. C., Mueller, T. I., Shea, T., Warshaw, M., et al. (1997). Recovery from major depression. *Archives of General Psychiatry, 54,* 1001–1006. (16)

Solomon, Z., Mikulincer, M., & Flum, H. (1988). Negative life events, coping responses, and combat-related psychopathology: A prospective study. *Journal of Abnormal Psychology, 97,* 302–307. (12)

Song, H., Stevens, C. F., & Gage, F. H. (2002). Neural stem cells from adult hippocampus develop essential properties of functional CNS neurons. *Nature Neuroscience, 5,* 438–445. (3)

Sonuga-Barke, E. J. S. (2004). Causal models of attention-deficit/hyperactivity disorder: From common simple deficits to multiple developmental pathways. *Biological Psychology, 57,* 1231–1238. (8)

Sorkin, R. D., Hays, C. J., & West, R. (2001). Signal-detection analysis of group decision making. *Psychological Review, 108,* 183–203. (13)

Sowell, E. R., Thompson, P. M., Holmes, C. J., Jernigan, T. L., & Toga, A. W. (1999). *In vivo* evidence for post-adolescent brain maturation in frontal and striatal regions. *Nature Neuroscience, 2,* 859–861. (16)

Spanos, N. P. (1987–1988). Past-life hypnotic regression: A critical view. *Skeptical Inquirer, 12,* 174–180. (10)

Spear, L. P. (2000). Neurobehavioral changes in adolescence. *Current Directions in Psychological Science, 9,* 111–114. (5)

Spearman, C. (1904). "General intelligence," objectively determined and measured. *American Journal of Psychology, 15,* 201–293. (9)

Speer, J. R. (1989). Detection of plastic explosives. *Science, 243,* 1651. (8)

Spelke, E. S. (2005). Sex differences in intrinsic aptitude for mathematics and science? *American Psychologist, 60,* 950–958. (5)

Spellman, B. (2005, March). Could reality shows become reality experiments? *APS Observer, 18*(3), 34–35. (2)

Spence, C., & Read, L. (2003). Speech shadowing while driving: On the difficulty of splitting attention between eye and ear. *Psychological Science, 14,* 251–256. (8)

Spence, J. T. (1984). Masculinity, femininity, and gender-related traits: A conceptual analysis and critique of current research. *Progress in Experimental Personality Research, 13,* 1–97. (5)

Sperling, G. (1960). The information available in brief visual presentations. *Psychological Monographs, 74*(11, Whole No. 498). (7)

Sperry, R. W. (1967). Split-brain approach to learning problems. In G. C. Quarton, T. Melnechuk, & F. O. Schmitt (Eds.), *The neurosciences: A study program* (pp. 714–722). New York: Rockefeller University Press. (3)

Spira, A., & Bajos, N. (1993). *Les comportements sexuels en France* [Sexual behaviors in France]. Paris: La documentation Française. (11)

Squire, L. R., Haist, F., & Shimamura, A. P. (1989). The neurology of memory: Quantitative assessment of retrograde amnesia in two groups of amnesic patients. *Journal of Neuroscience, 9,* 828–839. (7)

Staddon, J. (1993). *Behaviorism.* London: Duckworth. (6)

Staddon, J. E. R. (1999). Theoretical behaviorism. In W. O'Donohue & R. Kitchener (Eds.), *Handbook of behaviorism* (pp. 217–241). San Diego, CA: Academic Press. (6)

Stams, G.-J. J. M., Juffer, F., & van IJzendoorn, M. H. (2002). Maternal sensitivity, infant attachment, and temperament in early childhood predict adjustment in middle childhood: The case of adopted children and their biologically unrelated parents. *Developmental Psychology, 38,* 806–821. (5)

Stanton, M. D., & Shadish, W. R. (1997). Outcome, attrition, and family-couples treatment for drug abuse: A meta-analysis and review of the controlled, comparative studies. *Psychological Bulletin, 122,* 170–191. (16)

Starr, C., & Taggart, R. (1992). *Biology: The unity and diversity of life* (6th ed.). Belmont, CA: Wadsworth. (3)

Stayer, D. L., Drews, F. A., & Johnston, W. A. (2003). Cell phone-induced failures of visual attention during simulated driving. *Journal of Experimental Psychology: Applied, 9,* 23–32. (8)

Ste-Marie, D. M. (1999). Expert–novice differences in gymnastic judging: An information-processing perspective. *Applied Cognitive Psychology, 13,* 269–281. (8)

Steblay, N. M., & Bothwell, R. K. (1994). Evidence for hypnotically refreshed testimony. *Law and Human Behavior, 18,* 635–651. (10)

Steele, C. M., & Aronson, J. (1995). Stereotype threat and the intellectual test performance of African Americans. *Journal of Personality and Social Psychology, 69,* 797–811. (9)

Steele, C. M., Spencer, S. J., & Aronson, J. (2002). Contending with group image: The psychology of stereotype and social identity threat. *Advances in Experimental Social Psychology, 34,* 379–440. (13)

Steele, K. M., Bass, K. E., & Crook, M. D. (1999). The mystery of the Mozart effect: Failure to replicate. *Psychological Science, 10,* 366–369. (2)

Stegat, H. (1975). Die Verhaltenstherapie der Enuresis und Enkopresis [Behavior therapy for enuresis and encopresis]. *Zeitschrift für Kinder- und Jugend-psychiatrie, 3,* 149–173. (15)

Stein, M. B., Hanna, C., Koverola, C., Torchia, M., & McClarty, B. (1997). Structural brain changes in PTSD. *Annals of the New York Academy of Sciences, 821,* 76–82. (12)

Stein, M. B., Torgrud, L. J., & Walker, J. R. (2000). Social phobia symptoms, subtypes, and severity. *Archives of General Psychiatry, 57,* 1046–1052. (16)

Stella, N., Schweitzer, P., & Piomelli, D. (1997). A second endogenous cannabinoid that modulates long-term potentiation. *Nature, 382,* 677–678. (3)

Sternberg, K. J., Baradaran, L. P., Abbott, C. B., Lamb, M. E., & Guterman, E. (2006). Type of violence, age, and gender differences in the effects of family violence on children's behavior problems: A mega-analysis. *Developmental Review, 26,* 89–112. (5)

Sternberg, R. J. (1985). *Beyond IQ.* Cambridge, England: Cambridge University Press. (9)

Sternberg, R. J. (1997). The concept of intelligence and its role in lifelong learning and success. *American Psychologist, 52,* 1030–1037. (9)

Sternberg, R. J. (2002). Beyond g: The theory of successful intelligence. In R. J. Sternberg & E. L. Grigorenko (Eds.), *The general intelligence factor: How general is it?* (pp. 447–479). Mahwah, NJ: Erlbaum.(9)

Sternberg, R. J., Nokes, C., Geissler, P. W., Prince, R., Okatcha, F., Bundy, D. A., et al. (2001). The relationship between academic and practical intelligence: A case study in Kenya. *Intelligence, 29,* 401–418. (9)

Sternberg, R.J., & the Rainbow Project Collaborators. (2006). The rainbow project: Enhancing the SAT through assessments of analytical, practical, and creative skills. *Intelligence, 34,* 321–350. (9)

Stevens, S. S. (1961). To honor Fechner and repeal his law. *Science, 133,* 80–86. (1)

Stewart, A. J., & Ostrove, J. M. (1998). Women's personality in middle age. *American Psychologist, 53,* 1185–1194. (5)

Stewart, I. (1987). Are mathematicians logical? *Nature, 325,* 386–387. (9)

Stewart, J. W., Quitkin, F. M., McGrath, P. J., Amsterdam, J., Fava, M., Fawcett, J., et al. (1998). Use of pattern analysis to predict differential relapse of remitted patients with major depression during 1 year of treatment with fluoxetine or placebo. *Archives of General Psychiatry, 55,* 334–343. (16)

Stice, E. (2002). Risk and maintenance factors for eating pathology: A meta-analytic review. *Psychological Bulletin, 128,* 825–848. (11)

Stice, E., & Shaw, H. (2004). Eating disorder prevention programs: A meta-analytic review. *Psychological Bulletin, 130,* 206–227. (15)

Stice, E., Shaw, H., & Marti, C. N. (2006). A meta-analytic review of obesity prevention programs for children and adolescents: The skinny on interventions that work. *Psychological Bulletin, 132,* 667–691. (11)

Stickgold, R. (2005). Sleep-dependent memory consolidation. *Nature, 437,* 1272–1278. (10)

Stickgold, R., Malia, A., Maguire, D., Roddenberry, D., & O'Connor, M. (2000). Replaying the game: Hypnagogic images in normals and amnesics. *Science, 290,* 350–353. (7)

Stickgold, R., Whidbee, D., Schirmer, B., Patel, V., & Hobson, J. A. (2000). Visual discrimination task improvement: A multistep process occurring during sleep. *Journal of Cognitive Neuroscience, 12,* 246–254. (10)

Stiles, W. B., Shapiro, D. A., & Elliott, R. (1986). "Are all psychotherapies equivalent?" *American Psychologist, 41,* 165–180. (15)

Stipek, D. (1998). Differences between Americans and Chinese in the circumstances evoking pride, shame, and guilt. *Journal of Cross-Cultural Psychology, 29,* 616–629. (12)

Stompe, T., Ortwein-Swoboda, G., Ritter, K., Schanda, H., & Friedmann, A. (2002). Are we witnessing the disappearance of catatonic schizophrenia? *Comprehensive Psychiatry, 43,* 167–174. (16)

Stone, V. E., Nisenson, L., Eliassen, J. C., & Gazzaniga, M. S. (1996). Left hemisphere representations of emotional facial expressions. *Neuropsychologia, 34,* 23–29. (3)

Stoolmiller, M. (1999). Implications of the restricted range of family environments for estimates of heritability and nonshared environment in behavior-genetic adoption studies. *Psychological Bulletin, 125,* 392–409. (5)

Storbeck, J., & Clore, G. L. (2005). With sadness comes accuracy; with happiness, false memory. *Psychological Science, 16,* 785–791. (12)

Storms, M. D. (1973). Videotape and the attribution process: Reversing actors' and observers' points of view. *Journal of Personality and Social Psychology, 27,* 165–175. (13)

Strack, F., Martin, L. L., & Stepper, S. (1988). Inhibiting and facilitating conditions of the human smile: A nonobtrusive test of the facial feedback hypothesis. *Journal of Personality and Social Psychology, 54,* 768–777. (12)

Strange, D., Sutherland, R., & Garry, M. (2004). A photographic memory for false autobiographical events: The role of plausibility in children's false memories. *Australian Journal of Psychology, 56*(Suppl. S), 137. (7)

Strauch, I., & Lederbogen, S. (1999). The home dreams and waking fantasies of boys and girls between ages 9 and 15: A longitudinal study. *Dreaming, 9,* 153–161. (10)

Streissguth, A. P., Sampson, P. D., & Barr, H. M. (1989). Neurobehavioral dose-response effects of prenatal alcohol exposure in humans from infancy to adulthood. *Annals of the New York Academy of Sciences, 562,* 145–158. (5)

Struckman-Johnson, C., Struckman-Johnson, D., & Anderson, P. B. (2003). Tactics of sexual coercion: When men and women won't take no for an answer. *Journal of Sex Research, 40,* 76–86. (12)

Stuss, D. T., Alexander, M. P., Palumbo, C. L., Buckle, L., Sayer, L., & Pogue, J. (1994). Organizational strategies of patients with unilateral or bilateral frontal lobe injury in word list learning tasks. *Neuropsychology, 8,* 355–373. (7)

Sudzak, P. D., Glowa, J. R., Crawley, J. N., Schwartz, R. D., Skolnick, P., & Paul, S. M. (1986). A selective imidazobenzodiazepine antagonist of ethanol in the rat. *Science, 234,* 1243–1247. (3)

Sue, S. (1998). In search of cultural competence in psychotherapy and counseling. *American Psychologist, 53,* 440–448. (15)

Sujino, M., Masumoto, K., Yamaguchi, S., van der Horst, G. T. J., Okamura, H., & Inouye, S. T. (2003). Suprachiasmatic nucleus grafts restore circadian behavioral rhythms of genetically arrhythmic mice. *Current Biology, 13,* 664–668. (10)

Sullivan, E. V., Deshmukh, A., Desmond, J. E., Mathalon, D. H., Rosenbloom, M. J., Lim, K. O., et al. (2000). Contribution of alcohol abuse to cerebellar volume deficits in men with schizophrenia. *Archives of General Psychiatry, 57,* 894–902. (16)

Suls, J., Martin, R., & Wheeler, L. (2002). Social comparisons: Why, with whom, and with what effect? *Current Directions in Psychological Science, 11,* 159–163. (13)

Sundet, J. M., Barlaug, D. G., & Torjussen, T. M. (2004). The end of the Flynn effect? A study of secular trends in mean intelligence test scores of Norwegian conscripts during half a century. *Intelligence, 32,* 349–362. (9)

Süss, H. M., Oberauer, K., Wittman, W. W., Wilhelm, O., & Schulze, R. (2002). Working memory capacity explains reasoning ability—and a little bit more. *Intelligence, 30,* 261–288. (7)

Susser, E., Neugebauer, R., Hoek, H. W., Brown, A. S., Lin, S., Labovitz, D., et al. (1996). Schizophrenia after prenatal famine. *Archives of General Psychiatry, 53,* 25–31. (16)

Suvisaari, J. M., Haukka, J. K., Tanskanen, A. J., & Lönnqvist, J. K. (1999). Decline in the incidence of schizophrenia in Finnish cohorts born from 1954 to 1965. *Archives of General Psychiatry, 56,* 733–740. (16)

Swann, W. B., Jr., & Gill, M. J. (1997). Confidence and accuracy in person perception: Do we know what we think we know about our relationship partners? *Journal of Personality and Social Psychology, 73,* 747–757. (13)

Swanson, J. M., Flodman, P., Kennedy, J., Spence, M. A., Moyzis, R., Schuck, S., et al. (2000). Dopamine genes and ADHD. *Neuroscience and Biobehavioral Reviews, 24,* 21–25. (3)

Swanson, J. W., Swartz, M. S., Van Dorn, R. A., Elbogen, E. B., Wagner, H. R., Rosenheck, R. A. (2006). A national study of violent behavior in persons with schizophrenia. *Archives of General Psychiatry, 63,* 490–499. (15)

Sweetland, J. D., Reina, J. M., & Taffi, A. F. (2006). WISC–III verbal/performance discrepancies among a sample of gifted children. *Gifted Child Quarterly, 50,* 7–10. (9)

Swinkels, A., & Giuliano, T. A. (1995). The measurement and conceptualization of mood awareness: Monitoring and labeling one's mood states. *Personality and Social Psychology Bulletin, 21,* 934–949. (12)

Swinton, S. S. (1987). *The predictive validity of the restructured GRE with particular attention to older students* (GRE Board Professional Rep. No. 83-25P. ETS Research Rep. 87-22). Princeton, NJ: Educational Testing Service. (9)

Swoboda, H., Amering, M., Windhaber, J., & Katschnig, H. (2003). The long-term course of panic disorder—an 11 year follow-up. *Journal of Anxiety Disorders, 17,* 223–232. (16)

Symons, C. S., & Johnson, B. T. (1997). The self-reference effect in memory: A meta-analysis. *Psychological Bulletin, 121,* 371–394. (7)

Szasz, T. S. (1982). The psychiatric will. *American Psychologist, 37,* 762–770. (15)

Szechtman, H., & Woody, E. (2004). Obsessive-compulsive disorder as a disturbance of security motivation. *Psychological Review, 111,* 111–127. (16)

Szechtman, H., Woody, E., Bowers, K. S., & Nahmias, C. (1998). Where the imagined appears real: A positron emission tomography study of auditory hallucinations. *Proceedings of the National Academy of Sciences, USA, 95,* 1956–1960. (10)

Szymanski, H. V., Simon, J. C., & Gutterman, N. (1983). Recovery from schizophrenic psychosis. *American Journal of Psychiatry, 140,* 335–338. (16)

Takano, Y., & Osaka, E. (1999). An unsupported common view: Comparing Japan and the U.S. on individualism/collectivism. *Asian Journal of Social Psychology, 2,* 311–341. (13)

Takeuchi, A. H., & Hulse, S. H. (1993). Absolute pitch. *Psychological Bulletin, 113,* 345–361. (4)

Talarico, J. M., & Rubin, D. C. (2003). Confidence, not consistency, characterizes flashbulb memories. *Psychological Science, 14,* 455–461. (7)

Taller, A. M., Asher, D. M., Pomeroy, K. L., Eldadah, B. A., Godec, M. S., Falkai, P. G., et al. (1996). Search for viral nucleic acid sequences in brain tissues of patients with schizophrenia using nested polymerase chain reaction. *Archives of General Psychiatry, 53,* 32–40. (16)

Tanaka, J. W., Curran, T., & Sheinberg, D. L. (2005). The training and transfer of real-world perceptual expertise. *Psychological Science, 16,* 145–151. (8)

Tarr, M. J., & Gauthier, I. (2000). FFA: A flexible fusiform area for subordinate-level visual processing automatized by experience. *Nature Neuroscience, 3,* 764–769. (3)

Tassinary, L. G., & Hansen, K. A. (1998). A critical test of the waist-to-hip-ratio hypothesis of female physical attractiveness. *Psychological Science, 9,* 150–155. (13)

Tatler, B. W., Gilchrist, I. D., & Rusted, J. (2003). The time course of abstract visual representation. *Perception, 32,* 579–592. (8)

Taylor, C. B., Bryson, S., Luce, K. H., Cunning, D., Doyle, A. C., Abascal, L. B., et al. (2006). Prevention of eating disorders in at-risk college-age women. *Archives of General Psychiatry, 63,* 881–888. (15)

Taylor, S. E., Pham, L. B., Rivkin, I. D., & Armor, D. A. (1998). Harnessing the imagination: Mental simulation, self-regulation, and coping. *American Psychologist, 53,* 429–439. (12)

Taylor, S. E., Way, B. M., Welch, W. T., Hilmert, C. J., Lehman, B. J., & Eisenberger, N. I. (2006). Early family environment, current adversity, the serotonin transporter promoter polymorphism, and depressive symptomatology. *Biological Psychiatry, 60,* 671–676. (16)

Teasdale, T. W., & Owen, D. R. (2005). A long-term rise and recent decline in intelligence test performance: The Flynn effect in reverse. *Personality and Individual Differences, 39,* 837–843. (9)

Teesson, M., Ross, J., Darke, S., Lynskey, M., Ali, R., Ritter, A., et al. (2006). One year outcomes for heroin dependence: Findings from the Australian Treatment Outcome Study (ATOS). *Drug and Alcohol Dependence, 83,* 174–180. (16)

Teff, K. L., Elliott, S. S., Tschöp, M., Kieffer, T. J., Rader, D., Heiman, M., et al. (2004). Dietary fructose reduces circulating insulin and leptin, attenuates postprandial suppression of ghrelin, and increases triglycerides in women. *Journal of Clinical Endocrinology & Metabolism, 89,* 2963–2972. (11)

Teicher, M. H., Glod, C. A., Magnus, E., Harper, D., Benson, G., Krueger, K., et al. (1997). Circadian rest–activity disturbances in seasonal affective disorder. *Archives of General Psychiatry, 54,* 124–130. (16)

Terr, L. (1988). What happens to early memories of trauma? A study of twenty children under age five at the time of documented traumatic events. *Journal of the American Academy of Child and Adolescent Psychiatry, 27,* 96–104. (7)

Terrace, H. S., Petitto, L. A., Sanders, R. J., & Bever, T. G. (1979). Can an ape create a sentence? *Science, 206,* 891–902. (8)

Testa, M., Livingston, J. A., Vanzile-Tamsen, C., & Frone, M. R. (2003). The role of women's substance use in vulnerability to forcible and incapacitated rape. *Journal of Studies on Alcohol, 64,* 756–764. (12)

Tetlock, P. E. (1994, July 2). *Good judgment in world politics: Who gets what right, when and why?* Address presented at the sixth annual convention of the American Psychological Society. (8)

Tett, R. P., & Burnett, D. D. (2003). A personality trait-based interactionist model of job performance. *Journal of Applied Psychology, 88,* 500–517. (11)

Tett, R. P., & Palmer, C. A. (1997). The validity of handwriting elements in relation to self-report personality trait measures. *Personality and Individual Differences, 22,* 11–18. (14)

Thanickal, T. C., Moore, R. Y., Nienhuis, R., Ramanathan, L., Gulyani, S., Aldrich, M., et al. (2000). Reduced number of hypocretin neurons in human narcolepsy. *Neuron, 27,* 469–474. (10)

Thase, M. E., Haight, B. R., Richard, N., Rockett, C. B., Mitton, M., Modell, J. G., et al. (2005). Remission rates following antidepressant therapy with bupropion or selective serotonin reuptake inhibitors: A meta-analysis of original data from 7 randomized controlled trials. *Journal of Clinical Psychiatry, 66,* 974–981. (16)

Thase, M. E., Trivedi, M. H., & Rush, A. J. (1995). MAOIs in the contemporary treatment of depression. *Neuropsychopharmacology, 12,* 185–219. (16)

Theeuwes, J. (2004). No blindness for things that do not change. *Psychological Science, 15,* 65–70. (8)

Thieman, T. J. (1984). A classroom demonstration of encoding specificity. *Teaching of Psychology, 11,* 101–102. (7)

Thigpen, C., & Cleckley, H. (1957). *The three faces of Eve.* New York: McGraw-Hill. (15)

Tholin, S., Rasmussen, F., Tynelius, P., & Karlsson, J. (2005). Genetic and environmental influences on eating behavior: The Swedish young male twins study. *American Journal of Clinical Nutrition, 81,* 564–569. (11)

Thomas, A., & Chess, S. (1980). *The dynamics of psychological development.* New York: Brunner/Mazel. (5)

Thomas, A., Chess, S., & Birch, H. G. (1968). *Temperament and behavior disorders in children.* New York: New York University Press. (5)

Thompson, C. (2001, September). The know-it-all machine. *Lingua Franca, 11*(6), 26–35. (8)

Thompson, C. R., & Church, R. M. (1980). An explanation of the language of a chimpanzee. *Science, 208,* 313–314. (8)

Thompson, P. M., Hayashi, K. M., Simon, S. L., Geaga, J. A., Hong, M. S., Sui, Y., et al. (2004). Structural abnormalities in the brains of human subjects who use methamphetamine. *Journal of Neuroscience, 24,* 6028–6036. (3)

Thompson, W. F., Schellenberg, E. G., & Husain, G. (2001). Arousal, mood, and the Mozart effect. *Psychological Science, 12,* 248–251. (2)

Thoresen, C. J., Kaplan, S. A., Barsky, A. P., Warren, C. R., & de Chermont, K. (2003). The affective underpinnings of job perceptions and attitudes: A meta-analytic review and integration. *Psychological Bulletin, 129,* 914–945. (11)

Thorndike, E. L. (1918). The nature, purposes, and general methods of measurements of educational products. In E. J. Ashbaugh, W. A. Averill, L. P. Ayres, F. W. Ballou, E. Bryner, B. R. Buckingham, et al. (Eds.), *The seventeenth yearbook of the National Society for the Study of Education. Part II: The measurement of educational products* (pp. 16–24). Bloomington, IL: Public School Publishing Company. (9)

Thorndike, E. L. (1970). *Animal intelligence.* Darien, CT: Hafner. (Original work published 1911) (6)

Thornton, B. (1977). Toward a linear prediction model of marital happiness. *Personality and Social Psychology Bulletin, 3,* 674–676. (13)

Tiedens, L. Z., & Linton, S. (2001). Judgment under emotional certainty and uncertainty: The effects of specific emotions on information processing. *Journal of Personality and Social Psychology, 81,* 973–988. (12)

Timberlake, W., & Farmer-Dougan, V. A. (1991). Reinforcement in applied settings: Figuring out ahead of time what will work. *Psychological Bulletin, 110,* 379–391. (6)

Tinbergen, N. (1951). *The study of instinct.* Oxford, England: Oxford University Press. (3)

Titchener, E. B. (1910). *A textbook of psychology.* New York: Macmillan. (1)

Todd, J. J., Fougnie, D., & Marois, R. (2005). Visual short-term memory load suppresses temporo-parietal junction activity and induces inattentional blindness. *Psychological Science, 16,* 965–972. (8)

Todes, D. P. (1997). From the machine to the ghost within. *American Psychologist, 52,* 947–955. (6)

Toh, K. L., Jones, C. R., He, Y., Eide, E. J., Hinz, W. A., Virshup, D. M., et al. (2001). An hPer2 phosphorylation site mutation in familial advanced sleep phase syndrome. *Science, 291,* 1040–1043. (10)

Tolman, E. C. (1938). The determinants of behavior at a choice point. *Psychological Review, 45,* 1–41. (1)

Tolstoy, L. (1978). *Tolstoy's letters: Vol. I. 1828–1879.* New York: Charles Scribner's Sons. (Original works written 1828–1879) (5)

Tombaugh, C. W. (1980). *Out of the darkness, the planet Pluto.* Harrisburg, PA: Stackpole. (4)

Toomey, R., Lyons, M. J., Eisen, S. A., Xian, H., Chantarujikapong, S., Seidman, L. J., et al. (2003). A twin study of the neuropsychological consequences of stimulant abuse. *Archives of General Psychiatry, 60,* 303–310. (3)

Torgerson, S., Kringlen, E., & Cramer, V. (2001). The prevalence of personality disorders in a community sample. *Archives of General Psychiatry, 58,* 590–596. (15)

Torres, A. R., Prince, M. J., Bebbington, P. E., Bhugra, D., Brugha, T. S., Farrell, M., et al. (2006). Obsessive-compulsive disorder: Prevalence, comorbidity, impact, and help-seeking in the British national psychiatric morbidity survey of 2000. *American Journal of Psychiatry, 163,* 1978–1985. (16)

Torrey, E. F. (1986). Geographic variations in schizophrenia. In C. Shagass, R. C. Josiassen, W. H. Bridger, K. J. Weiss, D. Stoff, & G. M. Simpson (Eds.), *Biological psychiatry 1985* (pp. 1080–1082). New York: Elsevier. (16)

Torrey, E. F. (2002). Studies of individuals with schizophrenia never treated with antipsychotic medications: A review. *Schizophrenia Research, 58,* 101–115. (16)

Torrey, E. F., Bowler, A. E., & Clark, K. (1997). Urban birth and residence as risk factors for psychoses: An analysis of 1880 data. *Schizophrenia Research, 28,* 1–38. (16)

Torrey, E. F., & Miller, J. (2001). *The invisible plague: The rise of mental illness from 1750 to the present.* New Brunswick, NJ: Rutgers University Press. (15, 16)

Torrey, E. F., & Yolken, R. H. (2005). *Toxoplasma gondii* as a possible cause of schizophrenia. *Biological Psychiatry, 57,* 128S. (16)

Townshend, J. M., & Duka, T. (2003). Mixed emotions: Alcoholics' impairments in the recognition of specific emotional facial expressions. *Neuropsychologia, 41,* 773–782. (12)

Tracy, J. L., & Robins, R. W. (2004). Show your pride: Evidence for a discrete emotion expression. *Psychological Science, 15,* 194–197. (12)

Tracy, J. L., Robins, R. W., & Lagattuta, K. H. (2005). Can children recognize pride? *Emotion, 5,* 251–257. (12)

Trappey, C. (1996). A meta-analysis of consumer choice and subliminal advertising. *Psychology & Marketing, 13*(5), 517–530. (4)

Travis, F., & Wallace, R. K. (1999). Autonomic and EEG patterns during eyes-closed rest and transcendental meditation (TM) practice: The basis for a neural model of TM practice. *Consciousness and Cognition, 8,* 302–318. (10)

Treisman, A. (1999). Feature binding, attention and object perception. In G. W. Humphreys, J. Duncan, & A. Treisman (Eds.), *Attention, space and action* (pp. 91–111). Oxford, England: Oxford University Press. (3)

Treisman, A., & Souther, J. (1985). Search asymmetry: A diagnostic for preattentive processing of separable features. *Journal of Experimental Psychology: General, 114,* 285–310. (8)

Trevena, J. A., & Miller, J. (2002). Cortical movement preparation before and after a conscious decision to move. *Consciousness and Cognition, 11,* 162–190. (10)

Trick, L. M., Jaspers-Fayer, F., & Sethi, N. (2005). Multiple-object tracking in children: The "catch the spies" task. *Cognitive Development, 20,* 373–387. (8)

Trivedi, M. H., Fava, M., Wisniewski, S. R., Thase, M. E., Quitlein, F., Warden, D., et al. (2006). Medication augmentation after failure of SSRIs for depression. *New England Journal of Medicine, 354,* 1243–1252. (16)

Tronick, E. Z., Morelli, G. A., & Ivey, P. K. (1992). The Efe forager infant and toddler's pattern of social relationships: Multiple and simultaneous. *Developmental Psychology, 28,* 568–577. (5)

Trope, Y., & Liberman, N. (2003). Temporal construal. *Psychological Review, 110,* 403–421. (11)

Tropp, L. R., & Pettigrew, T. F. (2005). Relationships between intergroup contact and prejudice among minority and majority status groups. *Psychological Science, 16,* 951–957. (13)

True, W. R., Xian, H., Scherer, J. F., Madden, P. A. F., Bucholz, K. K., Heath, A. C., et al. (1999). Common genetic vulnerability for nicotine and alcohol dependence in men. *Archives of General Psychiatry, 56,* 655–661. (16)

Tsao, D. Y., Freiwald, W. A., Tootell, R. B. H., & Livingstone, M. S. (2006). A cortical region consisting entirely of face-selective cells. *Science, 311,* 670–674. (3)

Tschann, J. M., Johnston, J. R., Kline, M., & Wallerstein, J. S. (1990). Conflict, loss, change and parent-child relationships: Predicting children's adjustment during divorce. *Journal of Divorce, 13,* 1–22. (5)

Tu, G. C., & Israel, Y. (1995). Alcohol consumption by Orientals in North America is predicted largely by a single gene. *Behavior Genetics, 25,* 59–65. (6)

Tuerk, P. W. (2005). Research in the high-stakes era. *Psychological Science, 16,* 419–425. (9)

Tugade, M. M., & Fredrickson, B. L. (2004). Resilient individuals use positive emotions to bounce back from negative emotional experiences. *Journal of Personality and Social Psychology, 86,* 320–333. (12)

Tuiten, A., Van Honk, J., Koppeschaar, H., Bernaards, C., Thijssen, J., & Verbaten, R. (2000). Time course of effects of testosterone administration on sexual arousal in women. *Archives of General Psychiatry, 57,* 149–153. (11)

Tulving, E. (1989). Remembering and knowing the past. *American Scientist, 77,* 361–367. (7)

Tulving, E., & Thomson, D. M. (1973). Encoding specificity and retrieval processes in episodic memory. *Psychological Review, 80,* 352–373. (7)

Turkheimer, E., Haley, A., Waldron, M., D'Onofrio, B., & Gottesman, I. I. (2003). Socioeconomic status modifies heritability of IQ in young children. *Psychological Science, 14,* 623–628. (9)

Turner, C. F., Ku, L., Rogers, S. M., Lindberg, L. D., Pleck, J. H., & Sonenstein, F. L. (1998). Adolescent sexual behavior, drug use, and violence: Increased reporting with computer survey technology. *Science, 280,* 867–873. (11)

Turvey, B. E. (1999). *Criminal profiling.* San Diego, CA: Academic Press. (14)

Tversky, A., & Kahneman, D. (1981). The framing of decisions and the psychology of choice. *Science, 211,* 453–458. (8)

Tversky, A., & Kahneman, D. (1983). Extensional versus intuitive reasoning: The conjunctional fallacy in probability judgment. *Psychological Review, 90,* 293–315. (8)

Twenge, J. M. (2000). The age of anxiety? Birth cohort change in anxiety and neuroticism, 1952–1993. *Journal of Personality and Social Psychology, 79,* 1007–1021. (14)

Twenge, J. M. (2006). *Generation me.* New York: Free Press. (5)

Tyler, L. K., deMornay-Davies, P., Anokhina, R., Longworth, C., Randall, B., & Marslen-Wilson, W. D. (2002). Dissociations in processing past tense morphology: Neuropathology and behavioral studies. *Journal of Cognitive Neuroscience, 14,* 79–94. (8)

Uchino, B. N., Cacioppo, J. T., & Kiecolt-Glaser, J. K. (1996). The relationship between social support and physiological processes: A review with emphasis on underlying mechanisms and implications for health. *Psychological Bulletin, 119,* 488–531. (12)

Udolf, R. (1981). *Handbook of hypnosis for professionals.* New York: Van Nostrand Reinhold. (10)

Uhlhaas, P. J., Linden, D. E. J., Singer, W., Haenschel, C., Lindner, M., Maurer, K., et al. (2006). Dysfunctional long-range coordination of neural activity during Gestalt perception in schizophrenia. *Journal of Neuroscience, 26,* 8168–8175. (16)

Ulrich, R. E., Stachnik, T. J., & Stainton, N. R. (1963). Student acceptance of generalized personality interpretations. *Psychological Reports, 13,* 831–834. (14)

Ulrich, R. S. (1984). View through a window may influence recovery from surgery. *Science, 224,* 420–421. (4)

Urushihara, K., Stout, S. C., & Miller, R. R. (2004). The basic laws of conditioning differ for elemental cues and cues trained in compound. *Psychological Science, 15,* 268–271. (6)

Uttl, B. (2005). Measurement of individual differences. *Psychological Science, 16,* 460–467. (9)

Vaillant, G. E., & Milofsky, E. S. (1982). The etiology of alcoholism: A prospective viewpoint. *American Psychologist, 37,* 494–503. (16)

Vaishnavi, S., Calhoun, J., & Chatterjee, A. (2001). Binding personal and peripersonal space: Evidence from tactile extinction. *Journal of Cognitive Neuroscience, 13,* 181–189. (10)

van den Hout, M., & Kindt, M. (2003). Repeated checking causes memory distrust. *Behaviour Research and Therapy, 41,* 301–316. (16)

van der Pligt, J., de Vries, N. K., Manstead, A. S. R., & van Harreveld, F. (2000). The importance of being selective: Weighing the role of attribute importance in attitudinal judgment. *Advances in Experimental Social Psychology, 32,* 135–200. (13)

van der Pligt, J., & Eiser, J. R. (1983). Actors' and observers' attributions, self-serving bias, and positivity. *European Journal of Social Psychology, 13,* 95–104. (13)

van IJzendoorn, M. H., Juffer, F., & Poelhuis, C. W. K. (2005). Adoption and cognitive development: A meta-analytic comparison of adopted and nonadopted children's IQ and school performance. *Psychological Bulletin, 131,* 301–316. (9)

Vanman, E. J., Saltz, J. L., Nathan, L. R., & Warren, J. A. (2004). Racial discrimination by low-prejudiced Whites. *Psychological Science, 15,* 711–714. (13)

Vasterling, J., Duke, L. M., Brailey, K., Constans, J. I., Allain, A. N., & Sutker, P. B. (2002). Attention, learning, and memory performances and intellectual resources in Vietnam veterans: PTSD and no disorder comparisons. *Neuropsychology, 16,* 5–14. (9)

Velakoulis, D., Pantelis, C., McGorry, P. D., Dudgeon, P., Brewer, W., Cook, M., et al. (1999). Hippocampal volume in first-episode psychoses and chronic schizophrenia. *Archives of General Psychiatry, 56,* 133–140. (16)

Velluti, R. A. (1997). Interactions between sleep and sensory physiology. *Journal of Sleep Research, 6,* 61–77. (10)

Verplanken, B., & Faes, S. (1999). Good intentions, bad habits, and effects of forming implementation intentions on healthy eating. *European Journal of Social Psychology, 29,* 591–604. (11)

Verrey, F., & Beron, J. (1996). Activation and supply of channels and pumps by aldosterone. *News in Physiological Sciences, 11,* 126–133. (1)

Vgontzas, A. N., & Kales, A. (1999). Sleep and its disorders. *Annual Review of Medicine, 50,* 387–400. (10)

Viglione, D. J., & Taylor, N. (2003). Empirical support for interrater reliability of Rorschach Comprehensive System scoring. *Journal of Clinical Psychology, 59,* 111–121. (14)

Viken, R. J., Rose, R. J., Kaprio, J., & Koskenvuo, M. (1994). A developmental genetic analysis of adult personality: Extraversion and neuroticism from 18 to 59 years of age. *Journal of Personality and Social Psychology, 66,* 722–730. (5, 14)

Visser, B. A., Ashton, M. C., & Vernon, P. A. (2006). Beyond *g*: Putting multiple intelligences theory to the test. *Intelligence, 34,* 487–502. (9)

Visser, T. A. W., Bischof, W. F., & DiLollo, V. (1999). Attentional switching in spatial and nonspatial domains: Evidence from the attentional blink. *Psychological Bulletin, 125,* 458–469. (8)

Vitevitch, M. S. (2003). Change deafness: The inability to detect changes between two voices. *Journal of Experimental Psychology: Human Perception and Performance, 29,* 333–342. (8)

Vogel, E. K., McCollough, A. W., & Machizawa, M. G. (2005). Neural measures reveal individual differences in controlling access to working memory. *Nature, 438,* 500–503. (7)

Vokey, J. R., & Read, J. D. (1985). Subliminal messages: Between the devil and the media. *American Psychologist, 40,* 1231–1239. (4)

Volkow, N. D., Wang, G.-J., & Fowler, J. S. (1997). Imaging studies of cocaine in the human brain and studies of the cocaine addict. *Annals of the New York Academy of Sciences, 820,* 41–55. (3)

Volkow, N. D., Wang, G.-J., Fowler, J., Gatley, S. J., Logan, J., Ding, Y.-S., et al. (1998). Dopamine transporter occupancies in the human brain induced by therapeutic doses of oral methylphenidate. *American Journal of Psychiatry, 155,* 1325–1331. (3)

Volkow, N. D., Wang, G.-J., Telang, F., Fowler, J. S., Logan, J., Childress, A.-R., et al. (2006). Cocaine cues and dopamine in dorsal striatum: Mechanism of craving in cocaine addiction. *Journal of Neuroscience, 26,* 6583–6588. (16)

Vygotsky, L. S. (1978). *Mind in society.* Cambridge, MA: Harvard University Press. (5)

Wachtel, P. L. (2000). Psychotherapy in the twenty-first century. *American Journal of Psychotherapy, 54,* 441–450. (15)

Wade, K. A., Garry, M., Read, J. D., & Lindsay, D. S. (2002). A picture is worth a thousand lies: Using false photographs to create false childhood memories. *Psychonomic Bulletin and Review, 9,* 597–603. (7)

Waelti, P., Dickinson, A., & Schultz, W. (2001). Dopamine responses comply with basic assumptions of formal learning theory. *Nature, 412,* 43–48. (16)

Wagner, A. D., Desmond, J. E., Demb, J. B., Glover, G. H., & Gabrieli, J. D. E. (1997). Semantic repetition priming for verbal and pictorial knowledge: A functional MRI study of left inferior prefrontal cortex. *Journal of Cognitive Neuroscience, 9,* 714–726. (3)

Wagner, R. K. (1997). Intelligence, training, and employment. *American Psychologist, 52,* 1059–1069. (9)

Wagner, U., Gais, S., Haider, H., Verleger, R., & Born, J. (2004). Sleep inspires insight. *Nature, 427,* 352–355. (10)

Wagstaff, G. F., Brunas-Wagstaff, J., Cole, J., Knapton, L., Winterbottom, J., Crean, V., et al. (2004). Facilitating memory with hypnosis, focused meditation, and eye closure. *International Journal of Clinical and Experimental Hypnosis, 52,* 434–455. (10)

Wahlbeck, K., Forsén, T., Osmond, C., Barker, D. J. P., & Eriksson, J. G. (2001). Association of schizophrenia with low maternal body mass index, small size at birth, and thinness during childhood. *Archives of General Psychiatry, 58,* 48–52. (16)

Wainright, J. L., Russell, S. T., & Patterson, C. J. (2004). Psychosocial adjustment, school outcomes, and romantic relationships of adolescents with same-sex parents. *Child Development, 75,* 1886–1898. (5)

Wakschlag, L. S., Pickett, K. E., Kasza, K. E., & Loeber, R. (2006). Is prenatal smoking associated with a developmental pattern of conduct problems in young boys? *Journal of the American Academy of Child and Adolescent Psychiatry, 45,* 461–467. (5)

Wald, G. (1968). Molecular basis of visual excitation. *Science, 162,* 230–239. (4)

Wallace, C., Mullen, P. E., & Burgess, P. (2004). Criminal offending in schizophenia over a 25-year period marked by deinstitutionalization and increasing prevalence of comorbid substance abuse disorders. *American Journal of Psychiatry, 161,* 716–727. (15)

Waller, N. G., Kojetin, B. A., Bouchard, T. J., Jr., Lykken, D. T., & Tellegen, A. (1990). Genetic and environmental influences on religious interests, attitudes, and values: A study of twins reared apart and together. *Psychological Science, 1,* 138–142. (5)

Walsh, R., & Shapiro, S. L. (2006). The meeting of meditative disciplines and Western psychology. *American Psychologist, 61,* 227–239. (10)

Walster, E., Aronson, E., Abrahams, D., & Rottman, L. (1966). Importance of physical attractiveness in dating behavior. *Journal of Personality and Social Psychology, 4,* 508–516. (13)

Wampold, B. E., Mondin, G. W., Moody, M., Stich, F., Benson, K., & Ahn, H. (1997). A meta-analysis of outcome studies comparing bona fide psychotherapies: Empirically, "All must have prizes." *Psychological Bulletin, 122,* 203–215. (15)

Wandersman, A., & Florin, P. (2003). Community interventions and effective prevention. *American Psychologist, 58,* 441–448. (15)

Wang, P. S., Lane, M., Olfson, M., Pincus, H. A., Wells, K. B., & Kessler, R. C. (2005). Twelve-month use of mental health services in the United States. *Archives of General Psychiatry, 62,* 629–640. (15)

Wansink, B., & van Ittersum, K. (2003). Bottoms up! The influence of elongation on pouring and consumption volume. *Journal of Consumer Research, 30,* 455–463. (5)

Warneken, F., & Tomasello, M. (2006). Altruistic helping in human infants and young chimpanzees. *Science, 311,* 1301–1303. (13)

Warren, R. M. (1970). Perceptual restoration of missing speech sounds. *Science, 167,* 392–393. (4, 8)

Warren, R. M. (1999). *Auditory perception.* Cambridge, England: Cambridge University Press. (4)

Warwick, J., & Nettelbeck, T. (2004). Emotional intelligence is . . . ? *Personality and Individual Differences, 37,* 1091–1100. (12)

Washington, E. (2006). *Female socialization: How daughters affect their legislator fathers' voting on women's issues* (Working Paper No. 11924). Cambridge, MA: National Bureau of Economic Research. (2)

Wason, P. C. (1960). On the failure to eliminate hypotheses in a conceptual task. *Quarterly Journal of Experimental Psychology, 12,* 129–140. (8)

Waters, E., Merrick, S., Treboux, D., Crowell, J., & Albersheim, L. (2000). Attachment security in infancy and early adulthood: A twenty-year longitudinal study. *Child Development, 71,* 684–689. (5)

Watson, D., & Clark, L. A. (2006). Clinical diagnosis at the crossroads. *Clinical Psychology, 13,* 210–215. (15)

Watson, D., Suls, J., & Haig, J. (2002). Global self-esteem in relation to structural models of personality and affectivity. *Journal of Personality and Social Psychology, 83,* 185–197. (14)

Watson, D., Wiese, D., Vaidya, J., & Tellegen, A. (1999). The two general activation systems of affect: Structural findings, evolutionary considerations, and psychobiological evidence. *Journal of Personality and Social Psychology, 76,* 820–838. (12)

Watson, J. B. (1913). Psychology as the behaviorist views it. *Psychological Review, 20,* 158–177. (1)

Watson, J. B. (1919). *Psychology from the standpoint of a behaviorist.* Philadelphia: Lippincott. (1)

Watson, J. B. (1925). *Behaviorism.* New York: Norton. (1, 6)

Watson, J. B., & Rayner, R. (1920). Conditioned emotional reactions. *Journal of Experimental Psychology, 3,* 1–14. (16)

Watson, J. M., Balota, D. A., & Roediger, H. L., III (2003). Creating false memories with hybrid lists of semantic and phonological associates: Over-additive false memories produced by converging associative networks. *Journal of Memory and Language, 49,* 95–118. (7)

Waynforth, D., & Dunbar, R. I. M. (1995). Conditional mate choice strategies in humans: Evidence from "lonely hearts" advertisements. *Behaviour, 132,* 755– 779. (13)

Weeden, J., & Sabini, J. (2005). Physical attractiveness and health in Western societies: A review. *Psychological Bulletin, 131,* 635–653. (13)

Wegner, D. M. (2002). *The illusion of conscious will.* Cambridge, MA: MIT Press. (1)

Wegner, D. M., Schneider, D. J., Carter, S. R., III, & White, T. L. (1987). Paradoxical effects of thought suppression. *Journal of Personality and Social Psychology, 53,* 5–13. (16)

Wehr, T. A., Turner, E. H., Shimada, J. M., Lowe, C. H., Barker, C., & Leinbenluft, E. (1998). Treatment of a rapidly cycling bipolar patient by using extended bed rest and darkness to stabilize the timing and duration of sleep. *Biological Psychiatry, 43,* 822–828. (16)

Weinberger, D. R. (1987). Implications of normal brain development for the pathogenesis of schizophrenia. *Archives of General Psychiatry, 44,* 660–669. (16)

Weinberger, D. R. (1996). On the plausibility of "the neurodevelopmental hypothesis" of schizophrenia. *Neuropsychopharmacology, 14,* 1S–11S. (16)

Weinberger, D. R. (1999). Cell biology of the hippocampal formation in schizophrenia. *Biological Psychiatry, 45,* 395–402. (16)

Weiner, B. A., & Wettstein, R. M. (1993). *Legal issues in mental health care.* New York: Plenum Press. (15)

Weisberg, R. W. (1994). Genius and madness: A quasi-experimental test of the hypothesis that manic-depression increases creativity. *Psychological Science, 5,* 361–367. (16)

Weiser, M., Reichenberg, A., Rabinowitz, J., Kaplan, Z., Mark, M., Bodner, E., et al. (2001). Association between nonpsychotic psychiatric diagnoses in adolescent males and subsequent onset of schizophrenia. *Archives of General Psychiatry, 58,* 959–964. (16)

Weiskrantz, L., Warrington, E. K., Sanders, M. D., & Marshall, J. (1974). Visual capacity in the hemianopic field following a restricted occipital ablation. *Brain, 97,* 709–728. (10)

Weissman, M. M., Kidd, K. K., & Prusoff, B. A. (1982). Variability in rates of affective disorders in relatives of depressed and normal probands. *Archives of General Psychiatry, 39,* 1397–1403. (16)

Weissman, M. M., Leaf, P. J., & Bruce, M. L. (1987). Single parent women: A community study. *Social Psychiatry, 22,* 29–36. (5)

Weissman, M. M., Warner, V., Wickramaratne, P., Moreau, D., & Olfson, M. (1997). Offspring of depressed parents. *Archives of General Psychiatry, 54,* 932–940. (16)

Weisz, J. R., McCarty, C. A., & Valeri, S. M. (2006). Effects of psychotherapy for depression in children and adolescents: A meta-analysis. *Psychological Bulletin, 132,* 132–149. (16)

Weller, A., & Weller, L. (1997). Menstrual synchrony under optimal conditions: Bedouin families. *Journal of Comparative Psychology, 111,* 143–151. (4)

Wellings, K., Field, J., Johnson, A., & Wadsworth, J. (1994). *Sexual behavior in Britain: The national survey of sexual attitudes and lifestyles.* New York: Penguin. (11)

Wells, G. L., Malpass, R. S., Lindsay, R. C. L., Fisher, R. P., Turtle, J. W., & Fulero, S. M. (2000). From the lab to the police station. *American Psychologist, 55,* 581–598. (7)

Wells, G. L., Olson, E. A., & Charman, S. D. (2003). Distorted retrospective eyewitness reports as functions of feedback and delay. *Journal of Experimental Psychology: General, 9,* 42–52. (7)

Wender, P. H., Wolf, L. E., & Wasserstein, J. (2001). Adults with ADHD. *Annals of the New York Academy of Sciences, 931,* 1–16. (8)

Werker, J. F., & Tees, R. C. (2005). Speech perception as a window for understanding plasticity and commitment in language

systems of the brain. *Developmental Psychology, 46,* 233–251. (8)

Westerberg, C. E., & Marsolek, C. J. (2006). Do instructional warnings reduce false recognition? *Applied Cognitive Psychology, 20,* 97–114. (7)

Weston, D. (1998). The scientific legacy of Sigmund Freud: Toward a psychodynamically informed psychological science. *Psychological Bulletin, 124,* 333–371. (14)

Wethington, E., Kessler, R. C., & Pixley, J. E. (2004). Turning points in adulthood. In O. G. Brim, C. D. Ryff, & R. C. Kessler (Eds.), *How healthy are we?* (pp. 586–613). Chicago: University of Chicago Press. (5)

Whalen, P. J. (1998). Fear, vigilance, and ambiguity: Initial neuroimaging studies of the human amygdala. *Current Directions in Psychological Science, 7,* 177–188. (12)

Wheeler, D. D. (1970). Processes in word recognition. *Cognitive Psychology, 1,* 59–85. (8)

Wheeler, M. E., & Treisman, A. M. (2002). Binding in short-term visual memory. *Journal of Experimental Psychology: General, 131,* 48–64. (3)

Wicker, B., Keysers, C., Plailly, J., Royet, J.-P., Gallese, V., & Rizzolatti, G. (2003). Both of us disgusted in *my* insula: The common neural basis of seeing and feeling disgust. *Neuron, 40,* 655–664. (6)

Wicklund, R. A., & Brehm, J. W. (1976). *Perspectives on cognitive dissonance.* Hillsdale, NJ: Erlbaum. (13)

Wig, N. N., Menon, D. K., Bedi, H., Leff, J., Kuipers, L., Ghosh, A., et al. (1987). Expressed emotion and schizophrenia in North India: II. Distribution of expressed emotion components among relatives of schizophrenic patients in Aarhus and Chandigarh. *British Journal of Psychiatry, 151,* 160–165. (16)

Wildschut, T., Pinter, B., Vevea, J. L., Insko, C. A., & Schopler, J. (2003). Beyond the group mind: A quantitative review of the interindividual-intergroup discontinuity effect. *Psychological Bulletin, 129,* 698–722. (13)

Wilkins, L., & Richter, C. P. (1940). A great craving for salt by a child with corticoadrenal insufficiency. *Journal of the American Medical Association, 114,* 866–868. (1)

Williams, C. L., Barnett, A. M., & Meck, W. H. (1990). Organizational effects of early gonadal secretions on sexual differentiation in spatial memory. *Behavioral Neuroscience, 104,* 84–97. (5)

Williams, K. D., & Karau, S. J. (1991). Social loafing and social compensation: The effects of expectations of co-worker performance. *Journal of Personality and Social Psychology, 61,* 570–581. (13)

Williams, L. M. (1994). Recall of childhood trauma: A prospective study of women's memories of child sexual abuse. *Journal of*

Consulting and Clinical Psychology, 61, 1167–1176. (7)

Williams, L. M., Brown, K. J., Palmer, D., Liddell, B. J., Kemp, A. H., Olivieri, G., et al. (2006). The mellow years? Neural basis of improving emotional stability over age. *Journal of Neuroscience, 26,* 6422–6430. (12)

Williams, R. W., & Herrup, K. (1988). The control of neuron number. *Annual Review of Neuroscience, 11,* 423–453. (3)

Williams, W. M. (1998). Are we raising smarter children today? School- and home-related influences on IQ. In U. Neisser (Ed.), *The rising curve* (pp. 125–154). Washington, DC: American Psychological Association. (9)

Williamson, D. A., Ravussin, E., Wong, M.-L., Wagner, A., DiPaoli, A., Caglayan, S., et al. (2005). Microanalysis of eating behavior of three leptin deficient adults treated with leptin therapy. *Appetite, 45,* 75–80. (11)

Willis, J., & Todorov, A. (2006). First impressions: Making up your mind after a 100-ms exposure to a face. *Psychological Science, 17,* 592–598. (13)

Wilson, D. S., Near, D., & Miller, R. R. (1996). Machiavellianism: A synthesis of the evolutionary and psychological literatures. *Psychological Bulletin, 119,* 285–299. (13)

Wilson, J. R., & the editors of *Life.* (1964). *The mind.* New York: Time. (4)

Wilson, R. I., & Nicoll, R. A. (2001). Endogenous cannabinoids mediate retrograde signalling at hippocampal synapses. *Nature, 410,* 588–592. (3)

Wilson, R. I., & Nicoll, R. A. (2002). Endocannabinoid signaling in the brain. *Science, 296,* 678–682. (3)

Wilson, R. S. (1987). Risk and resilience in early mental development. In S. Chess & A. Thomas (Eds.), *Annual progress in child psychiatry and child development 1986* (pp. 69–85). New York: Brunner/Mazel. (5)

Winer, G. A., & Cottrell, J. E. (1996). Does anything leave the eye when we see? Extramission beliefs of children and adults. *Current Directions in Psychological Science, 5,* 137–142. (4)

Winer, G. A., Cottrell, J. E., Gregg, V., Fournier, J. S., & Bica, L. A. (2002). Fundamentally misunderstanding visual perception: Adults' belief in visual emissions. *American Psychologist, 57,* 417–424. (4)

Winerman, L. (2004, July/August). Criminal profiling: The reality behind the myth. *Monitor on Psychology, 35*(7), 66–69. (14)

Winkowski, D. E., & Knudsen, E. I. (2006). Top-down gain control of the auditory space map by gaze control circuitry in the barn owl. *Nature, 439,* 336–339. (10)

Winner, E. (1986, August). Where pelicans kiss seals. *Psychology Today,* 24–35. (5)

Winner, E. (2000a). Giftedness: Current theory and research. *Current Directions in Psychological Science, 9,* 153–156. (9)

Winner, E. (2000b). The origins and ends of giftedness. *American Psychologist, 55,* 159–169. (9)

Winocur, G., & Hasher, L. (1999). Aging and time-of-day effects on cognition in rats. *Behavioral Neuroscience, 113,* 991–997. (10)

Wirz-Justice, A. (1998). Beginning to see the light. *Archives of General Psychiatry, 55,* 861–862. (16)

Wirz-Justice, A., & Van den Hoofdakker, R. H. (1999). Sleep deprivation in depression: What do we know, where do we go? *Biological Psychiatry, 46,* 445–453. (16)

Witkiewitz, K., & Marlatt, G. A. (2004). Relapse prevention for alcohol and drug problems: That was Zen, this is Tao. *American Psychologist, 59,* 224–235. (16)

Wittchen, H.-U., Reed, V., & Kessler, R. C. (1998). The relationship of agoraphobia and panic in a community sample of adolescents and young adults. *Archives of General Psychiatry, 55,* 1017–1024. (16)

Wittchen, H.-U., Zhao, S., Kessler, R. C., & Eaton, W. W. (1994). *DSM–III-R* generalized anxiety disorder in the National Comorbidity Survey. *Archives of General Psychiatry, 51,* 355–364. (16)

Wolfe, J. M., Horowitz, T. S., & Kenner, N. M. (2005). Rare items often missed in visual searches. *Nature, 435,* 439–440. (4)

Wolkin, A., Rusinek, H., Vaid, G., Arena, L., Lafargue, T., Sanfilipo, M., et al. (1998). Structural magnetic resonance image averaging in schizophrenia. *American Journal of Psychiatry, 155,* 1064–1073. (16)

Wolman, B. B. (1989). *Dictionary of behavioral science* (2nd ed.). San Diego, CA: Academic Press. (9)

Wolpe, J. (1961). The systematic desensitization treatment of neuroses. *Journal of Nervous and Mental Disease, 132,* 189–203. (16)

Wolraich, M. L., Lindgren, S. D., Stumbo, P. J., Stegink, L. D., Appelbaum, M. I., & Kiritsy, M. C. (1994). Effects of diets high in sucrose or aspartame on the behavior and cognitive performance of children. *New England Journal of Medicine, 330,* 301–307. (2)

Wong, A. H. C., Smith, M., & Boon, H. S. (1998). Herbal remedies in psychiatric practice. *Archives of General Psychiatry, 55,* 1033–1044. (16)

Wong, R. Y., & Hong, Y. (2005). Dynamic influences of culture on cooperation in the prisoner's dilemma. *Psychological Science, 16,* 429–434. (13)

Wood, J. M., Nezworski, T., Lilienfeld, S. O., & Garb, H. N. (2003). *What's wrong with the Rorschach?* San Francisco: Jossey-Bass. (14)

Wood, W., & Eagly, A. H. (2002). A cross-cultural model of the behavior of women and men: Implications for the origins of sex differences. *Psychological Bulletin, 128,* 699–727. (2, 5)

Wood, W., Lundgren, S., Ouellette, J. A., Busceme, S., & Blackstone, T. (1994). Minority influence: A meta-analytic review of social influence processes. *Psychological Bulletin, 115,* 323–345. (13)

Wood, W., & Quinn, J. M. (2003). Forewarned and forearmed? Two meta-analytic syntheses of forewarnings of influence appeals. *Psychological Bulletin, 129,* 119–138. (13)

Woodhill, B. M., & Samuels, C. A. (2003). Positive and negative androgyny and their relationship with psychological health and well-being. *Sex Roles, 48,* 555–565. (5)

Wooding, S., Kim, U., Bamshad, M. J., Larsen, J., Jorde, L. B., & Drayna, D. (2004). Natural selection and molecular evolution in *PTC,* a bitter-taste receptor gene. *American Journal of Human Genetics, 74,* 637–646. (1)

Woodman, G. F., & Luck, S. J. (2003). Serial deployment of attention during visual search. *Journal of Experimental Psychology: Human Perception and Performance, 29,* 121–138. (8)

Woods, J. H., & Winger, G. (1997). Abuse liability of flunitrazepam. *Journal of Clinical Psychopharmacology, 17*(Suppl. 3), S1–S57. (3)

Woods, S. C. (1991). The eating paradox: How we tolerate food. *Psychological Review, 98,* 488–505. (11)

Woodson, J. C., & Gorski, R. A. (2000). Structural sex differences in the mammalian brain: Reconsidering the male/female dichotomy. In A. Matsumoto (Ed.), *Sexual differentiation of the brain* (pp. 229–255). Boca Raton, FL: CRC Press. (3, 11)

Woodworth, R. S. (1934). *Psychology* (3rd ed.). New York: Henry Holt. (1)

Worthington, E. L., Jr., Kurusu, T. A., McCullough, M. E., & Sandage, S. J. (1996). Empirical research on religion and psychotherapeutic processes and outcomes: A 10-year review and research prospectus. *Psychological Bulletin, 119,* 448–487. (15)

Woychyshyn, C. A., McElheran, W. G., & Romney, D. M. (1992). MMPI validity measures: A comparative study of original with alternative indices. *Journal of Personality Assessment, 58,* 138–148. (14)

Wright, I. C., Rabe-Hesketh, S., Woodruff, P. W. R., David, A. S., Murray, R. M., & Bullmore, E. T. (2000). Meta-analysis of regional brain volumes in schizophrenia. *American Journal of Psychiatry, 157,* 16–25. (16)

Wright, L. (1994). *Remembering Satan.* New York: Knopf. (7)

Wu, K. D., & Clark, L. A. (2003). Relations between personality traits and self-reports of daily behavior. *Journal of Research in Personality, 37,* 231–256. (14)

Wundt, W. (1902). *Outlines of psychology* (C. H. Judd, Trans.). New York: Gustav Sechert. (Original work published 1896) (1)

Wundt, W. (1961). Contributions to the theory of sensory perception. In T. Shipley (Ed.), *Classics in psychology* (pp. 51–78). New York: Philosophical Library. (Original work published 1862) (1, 10)

Wüst, S., Kasten, E., & Sabel, B. A. (2002). Blindsight after optic nerve injury indicates functionality of spared fibers. *Journal of Cognitive Neuroscience, 14,* 243–253. (10)

Xu, Y., Padiath, Q. S., Shapiro, R. E., Jones, C. R., Wu, S. C., Saigoh, N., et al. (2005). Functional consequences of a *CK1δ* mutation causing familial advanced sleep phase syndrome. *Nature, 434,* 640–644. (10)

Yarsh, T. L., Farb, D. H., Leeman, S. E., & Jessell, T. M. (1979). Intrathecal capsaicin depletes substance P in the rat spinal cord and produces prolonged thermal analgesia. *Science, 206,* 481–483. (4)

Yehuda, R. (1997). Sensitization of the hypothalamic-pituitary-adrenal axis in post-traumatic stress disorder. *Annals of the New York Academy of Sciences, 821,* 57–75. (12)

Young, A. M. J., Joseph, M. H., & Gray, J. A. (1993). Latent inhibition of conditioned dopamine release in rat nucleus accumbens. *Neuroscience, 54,* 5–9. (16)

Yu, D. W., & Shepard, G. H., Jr. (1998). Is beauty in the eye of the beholder? *Nature, 396,* 321–322. (13)

Zadra, A. L., Nielsen, T. A., & Donderi, D. C. (1998). Prevalence of auditory, olfactory, and gustatory experiences in home dreams. *Perceptual and Motor Skills, 87,* 819–826. (10)

Zahavi, A., & Zahavi, A. (1997). *The handicap principle.* New York: Oxford University Press. (13)

Zahn, T. P. Rapoport, J. L., & Thompson, C. L. (1980). Autonomic and behavioral effects of dextroamphetamine and placebo in normal and hyperactive prepubertal boys. *Journal of Abnormal Child Psychology, 8,* 145–160. (3, 8)

Zajonc, R. B. (1968). Attitudinal effects of mere exposure. *Journal of Personality and Social Psychology, 9*(Monograph Suppl. 2, Pt. 2). (13)

Zalsman, G., Huang, Y.-y., Oquendo, M. A., Burke, A. K., Hu, X.-z., Brent, D. A., et al. (2006). Association of a triallelic serotonin transporter gene promoter region (5-HT-TLPR) polymorphism with stressful life events and severity of depression. *American Journal of Psychiatry, 163,* 1588–1593. (16)

Zaragoza, M. S., Payment, K. E., Ackil, J. K., Drivdahl, S. B., & Beck, M. (2001). Interviewing witnesses: Forced confabulation and confirmatory feedback increase false memories. *Psychological Science, 12,* 473–477. (7)

Zehr, D. (2000). Portrayals of Wundt and Titchener in introductory psychology texts: A context analysis. *Teaching of Psychology, 27,* 122–126. (1)

Zeidner, M., Shani-Zinovich, I., Matthews, G., & Roberts, R. D. (2005). Assessing emotional intelligence in gifted and non-gifted high school students: Outcomes depend on the measure. *Intelligence, 33,* 369–391. (12)

Zepelin, H., & Rechtschaffen, A. (1974). Mammalian sleep, longevity, and energy metabolism. *Brain, Behavior, and Evolution, 10,* 425–470. (10)

Zhang, X., & Firestein, S. (2002). The olfactory receptor gene superfamily of the mouse. *Nature Neuroscience, 5,* 124–133. (4)

Zhong, C.-B., & Liljenquist, K. (2006). Washing away your sins: Threatened morality and physical cleansing. *Science, 313,* 1451–1452. (16)

Zihl, J., von Cramon, D., & Mai, N. (1983). Selective disturbance of movement vision after bilateral brain damage. *Brain, 106,* 313–340. (3)

Zillman, D., & Weaver, J. B., III (1999). Effects of prolonged exposure to gratuitous media violence on provoked and unprovoked hostile behavior. *Journal of Applied Social Psychology, 29,* 145–165. (2)

Zimmer-Gembeck, M. J., Siebenbruner, J., & Collins, W. A. (2004). A prospective study of intraindividual and peer influences on adolescents' heterosexual romantic and sexual behavior. *Archives of Sexual Behavior, 33,* 381–394. (5)

Zou, Z., & Buck, L. B. (2006). Combinatorial effects of odorant mixes in olfactory cortex. *Science, 311,* 1477–1481. (4)

Zucker, K. J., Bradley, S. J., Oliver, G., Blake, J., Fleming, S., & Hood, J. (1996). Psychosexual development of women with congenital adrenal hyperplasia. *Hormones and Behavior, 30,* 300–318. (11)

Zucker, R. A., & Gomberg, E. S. L. (1986). Etiology of alcoholism reconsidered. *American Psychologist, 41,* 783–793. (16)

Zullow, H. M., Oettingen, G., Peterson, C., & Seligman, M. E. P. (1988). Pessimistic explanatory style in the historical record. *American Psychologist, 43,* 673–682. (16)

Zuriff, G. E. (1995). Continuity over change within the experimental analysis of behavior. In J. T. Todd & E. K. Morris (Eds.), *Modern perspectives on B. F. Skinner and contemporary behaviorism* (pp. 171–178). Westport, CT: Greenwood Press. (6)

Name Index

Subject Index/Glossary

TO THE OWNER OF THIS BOOK:

I hope that you have found *Introduction to Psychology,* Eighth Edition, useful. So that this book can be improved in a future edition, would you take the time to complete this sheet and return it? Thank you.

School and address: _____

_____

Department: _____

Instructor's name: _____

1. What I like most about this book is: _____

_____

_____

2. What I like least about this book is: _____

_____

_____

3. My general reaction to this book is: _____

_____

_____

4. The name of the course in which I used this book is: _____

_____

5. Were all of the chapters of the book assigned for you to read? _____

   If not, which ones weren't? _____

6. In the space below, or on a separate sheet of paper, please write specific suggestions for improving this book and anything else you'd care to share about your experience in using this book.

_____

_____

_____

_____

_____

_____

_____

THOMSON

WADSWORTH

BUSINESS REPLY MAIL
FIRST-CLASS MAIL   PERMIT NO. 34   BELMONT CA

POSTAGE WILL BE PAID BY ADDRESSEE

Attn: Psychology Editor for Kalat,
Introduction to Psychology

Thomson Wadsworth

10 Davis Dr

Belmont CA 94002-9801

FOLD HERE

OPTIONAL:

Your name: _____ Date: _____

May we quote you, either in promotion for *Introduction to Psychology,* Eighth Edition, or in future publishing ventures?

Yes: _____ No: _____

Sincerely yours,

James W. Kalat

Let James Kalat take you beyond the book and connect psychology to your everyday life

Kalat's best-selling **Introduction to Psychology** blends fascinating content with interactive learning tools to reveal the study of psychology as a discipline that has relevance to your life in and out of the classroom. His compelling writing style blends with fun, hands-on Try It Yourself activities to give you an engaging learning experience that gets you involved with concepts. This proven approach will help you succeed in your course and open up a whole new world of understanding!

Study tools to enhance your learning experience

Kalat Premium Website*

Learn by doing! Available at the **Kalat Premium Website**, Kalat's **Critical Thinking Video Exercises** feature live-action video clips that show researchers studying things like addiction, neural networks, and virtual-reality therapy. Watch the videos to learn about areas in psychological research, and then answer accompanying questions to reinforce your understanding. The Kalat Premium Website also includes Try It Yourself activities, featuring bonus animations that allow you to explore even more topics from the text.

Book Companion Website

www.thomsonedu.com/psychology/kalat

This site features a wealth of learning tools, including hands-on **Try It Yourself activities** that offer short animations illustrating concepts like motion aftereffects, universal emotions, false memories, and hemisphere control. Also available on the **Book Companion Website** are flash cards, a glossary, self-scoring quizzes, web links, and more.

ThomsonNOW™ for Introduction to Psychology*

What do you need to know NOW? Take charge of your learning with **ThomsonNOW for Introduction to Psychology**, an interactive, web-based learning tool. **ThomsonNOW** helps you:

* Create a Personalized Study plan for each chapter of this text
* Understand key concepts in the course
* Better prepare for exams—and increase your chances of success

If your text came packaged with an access code, you can immediately start using **ThomsonNOW for Introduction to Psychology**. Take the diagnostic "What Do I Know?" pre-test to assess your current understanding. Based on your score, **ThomsonNOW** will build your unique and complete Personalized Study plan ("What Do I Need to Learn?"), directing you to specific text sections or interactive tutorials to study. Finally, the "What Have I Learned?" post-test enables you to check your progress in mastering the chapter concepts.

* Your instructor may have chosen to package the access card to **ThomsonNOW** and/or the **Premium Website** with your new text. In this case, you'll find the access card within this text. If your instructor did not order the free access card to be inserted in your text—or if you have a used copy of the text—you can still obtain an access code for a nominal fee. Just visit www.thomsonedu.com, where easy-to-follow instructions help you purchase your access code.

THOMSON
WADSWORTH

Visit Thomson Wadsworth at **www.thomsonedu.com**

ISBN-13: 978-0-495-10288-
ISBN-10: 0-495-10288-1

9 780495 102885